THE
AMERICAN
COLLEGE

by JOSEPH ADELSON · CHRISTIAN BAY
DAVID BEARDSLEE · HOWARD BECKER
CARL BEREITER · DONALD BROWN
JOHN BUSHNELL · ELIZABETH DOUVAN
JOSHUA FISHMAN · MERVIN FREEDMAN
BLANCHE GEER · PAUL HEIST
EVERETT HUGHES · CHRISTOPHER JENCKS
JOSEPH KATZ · CAROL KAYE
ROBERT KNAPP · T. R. McCONNELL
W. J. McKEACHIE · THEODORE NEWCOMB
DONALD O'DOWD · ANTHONY OSTROFF
FRANK PINNER · DAVID RIESMAN
NEVITT SANFORD · GEORGE STERN
CAMPBELL STEWART · JOHN SUMMERSKILL
HAROLD TAYLOR · HAROLD WEBSTER

edited by **NEVITT SANFORD**

Prepared for the
Society for the Psychological Study of Social Issues

Editorial Committee:
CHRISTIAN BAY · JOSEPHINE GLEASON
JOSEPH KATZ · ROBERT MacLEOD
HENRY MURRAY · THEODORE NEWCOMB
BREWSTER SMITH · CAMPBELL STEWART

JOHN WILEY & SONS, INC., NEW YORK · LONDON · SYDNEY

THE
AMERICAN
COLLEGE

A PSYCHOLOGICAL AND SOCIAL INTER-PRETATION OF THE HIGHER LEARNING

SEVENTH PRINTING, MAY, 1967

COPYRIGHT © 1962 **BY JOHN WILEY & SONS, INC.**

All Rights Reserved. This book or any part
thereof must not be reproduced in any form
without the written permission of the publisher.

LIBRARY CONGRESS CATALOG CARD NUMBER: 61-17362

PRINTED IN THE UNITED STATES OF AMERICA

Foreword

The explosion in knowledge that is radically reshaping our intellectual, political, industrial, cultural, and military environments has been stimulated largely by research initiated in the universities and colleges. Paradoxically, the colleges and universities have been relative laggards in applying scientific method to the understanding and evaluation of their own functioning. This paradox has inherent in it the dangerous possibility that our basic institutions of education and educational change are not preparing their students to live in and cope with the complex new environments which the universities themselves are helping to create.

Fundamentally, education should look to the future. It should prepare its students to live in a world of new possibilities and of new dangers. To do so, it must itself be able to change and develop rationally. A central thesis of this stimulating book is that scientific method, more than any other procedure known to man, provides the basis for intelligent change: for change based on systematic knowledge rather than on improvisation, hunch, or dogma.

This rich, comprehensive volume charts the way into relatively unexplored territory. The chart is sufficiently detailed to reveal the diverse, interesting terrain as well as the rich ore that has already been discovered in this area by systematic research. It contains more information about and more insightful discussion of the varied aspects of the American college than has been available hitherto. It is a splendid beginning; it highlights what needs to be done as well as what has been done.

The Society For The Psychological Study of Social Issues (SPSSI) is proud to have been able to sponsor this pioneering volume, which expresses and fulfills admirably SPSSI's central values: the setting of high standards of scholarship in the dissemination and application of social science knowledge to significant social issues. We are all indebted to Nevitt Sanford for his farsightedness in initiating this work and for his doggedness and imagination in bringing it to completion.

M. Brewster Smith, Robert B. MacLeod, Theodore M. Newcomb, Henry A. Murray, Christian Bay, Josephine Gleason, Campbell Stewart, and Joseph Katz—all of whom served on SPSSI's Editorial Committee for this book—are also to be thanked for a job well done.

MORTON DEUTSCH
President, Society For The
Psychological Study of
Social Issues

Acknowledgments

This book would not have been possible without help of various kinds from the administration, the faculty, the students, and the alumnae of Vassar College. The idea of the volume was conceived and its basic plan was worked out while the editor was Coordinator and several of the other authors—Donald Brown, John Bushnell, Mervin Freedman, and Harold Webster—were members of the staff of the Mary Conover Mellon Foundation at Vassar. It is to their association with this research organization that these contributors, and Carl Bereiter also, owe the opportunity to do their work for this project. Besides giving this very tangible support the College made an essential and unique contribution through allowing itself to be made an object of study. Ten of the chapters in this book have been based in considerable part upon, or inspired by, observations made at Vassar during the Mellon Foundation's research program, which began in 1952, and has been continuing since 1958 under the direction of Mervin Freedman. This program could not have been carried out without the courage, tolerance, curiosity, and practical help of the administration and the faculty of the College or without the faith and patient cooperation of large numbers of students and alumnae. The College administered funds that were obtained specifically to help bring this book to completion, and it made its facilities available for conferences of the editors and authors. Two members of the Editorial Committee, Josephine Gleason and Joseph Katz, were recruited from the ranks of the Vassar faculty, and a third, Campbell Stewart, was enlisted when he came to Vassar to teach in its Summer Institute. In addition to all these benefits the Vassar contingent among the editors and authors received from some of the faculty and administration of the College, from President Sarah Gibson Blanding most particularly, encouragement and moral support at times when these things were very much needed. Other educational and research institutions have aided our work and acknowledgment is made in the text, but the role of Vassar has been special. It is a happy circumstance that our volume appears in print during the celebration of Vassar's Centennial. The editors and authors take pleasure in expressing their heartfelt thanks to the College at the same time that they extend congratulations and best wishes for the next hundred years.

The editors and authors are also happy to express their gratitude to the Carnegie Corporation of New York for a grant that aided the preparation of the book. This grant made possible the completion of a comprehensive bibliography that was available to all the authors from the beginning of their work, and it also enabled the editors and authors to hold conferences that did much to promote the unity of the book.

During the last year of work on the book the editor was a Fellow at the Center for Advanced Study in the Behavioral Sciences, and his sojourn at this excellent place was largely supported by a special Fellowship of the National Institute of Mental Health.

The book is the result of a cooperative enterprise in which roles were not very sharply defined. More than half the editors were at the same time authors, and most of the authors, involved as they were with the project as a whole, did hard editorial work on chapters other than their own. Thus the makers of this book have had many occasions to thank each other; actually, at one stage, all the manuscripts included in their acknowledgments the names of authors of this book who had been particularly helpful, but we finally decided to eliminate these expressions of gratitude and instead to accent here the cooperative nature of the whole undertaking. In general, the author-as-editor helped the most with chapters that were closest to his fields of interest and expertness, but some authors gave critical readings to most of the contributions and all were ready to do whatever was asked of them. Apart from all this mutual aid the authors and the editor owe special thanks to those members of the Editorial Board who did not contribute writings of their own. These editors gave freely of their time and energy: attending the early planning sessions, responding to requests for advice on policy, giving critical readings to particular chapters. They are in no way to blame for the shortcomings of the book, but it owes much to their wisdom and care for any virtue that it may have.

The editor, as editor, owes a special debt of gratitude to all the members of the Editorial Committee. He leaned heavily on this Committee during all phases of the work. Often in need of help and not averse to asking for it, he placed the heaviest burden upon those who were closest to hand. Thus, when the work was centered at Vassar, Josephine Gleason and Joseph Katz were most often called upon;

when the editor moved back to the San Francisco Bay Area, Christian Bay, Joseph Katz (who was now in Berkeley), and Brewster Smith were constant sources of stimulation, advice, and tangible help. The other members of the Committee never failed to respond promptly to requests. The editor also received much help from the authors, who made many suggestions concerning the plan of the book as a whole and participated in difficult decisions affecting its production. Special mention should be made of Donald Brown and Mervin Freedman, colleagues both at Vassar and at the Center for Advanced Study in the Behavioral Sciences, who, always ready to be called upon, made the editor's problems their own and remained constant in their devotion to the project as a whole.

The editor as author probably owes a greater debt of gratitude to the other authors and to the Editorial Committee than does any other contributor. Taking advantage of his position, he was able to obtain for his manuscripts the critical attention of almost all the other authors and editors. He thanks them heartily and at the same time, and somewhat reluctantly, frees them from responsibility for the final version of the text.

The editor, as author and as editor, owes thanks also to colleagues and friends who read his and other chapters, and contributed valuable ideas and suggestions that affected the whole undertaking: Elizabeth Alfert, Frederick I. Carpenter, Richard Crutchfield, Alexander Meiklejohn, Robert Pace, Charles G. Sellers, Jr., Silvan Tomkins.

Thanks go also to the members in 1957–58 of the Council of the Society for the Psychological Study of Social Issues, who gave encouragement and general guidance when the idea of the book was first proposed to them, who responded to the first outline of the book with concrete suggestions concerning organization, content and possible contributors, and who continued as a source of encouragement.

Lillian Eisberg of the Mellon Foundation at Vassar gave valuable administrative aid, and Signe Best of Berkeley and Joan Warmbrunn of the Center for Advanced Study in the Behavioral Sciences typed or retyped, with patience and high competence, most of the manuscript. We are deeply grateful to them.

Finally, we wish to thank the authors and publishers who have given permission to quote from copyrighted publications. Specific acknowledgments are made in the text.

Nevitt Sanford
Stanford, California

September 1961

Contents

xi

part III
ACADEMIC PROCEDURES, 283

cepting, and resisting of models by students. IV. The many
sides of the good teacher. V. The antimodel and the disappointing model.

theoretical model. IV. Conclusion: a moratorium on prediction.

Introduction

Practice in higher education, as in politics, remains largely untouched by the facts and principles of science. What our colleges do, tends either to be governed by tradition or to be improvised in the face of diverse—usually unanticipated—pressures. In the literature of the field there is much partisan argument, and little evidence on the basis of which conflicting claims might be evaluated. Very little is known of what effects, if any, the experience of going to college has on students and less of what particular features of the college environment determine such effects as have been observed. The empirical studies that have been done in the past have been mainly of the *ad hoc* variety, separated from systematic theory and so local in their orientation as to make generalization impossible. This state of affairs has persisted despite the fact that during the past twenty-five or thirty years psychology and the newer social sciences have advanced rapidly, producing concepts and theories, methods of investigation and much factual knowledge, all of immediate relevance to problems of education.

In recent years, higher education has been the object of much new thought and research. An increasing number of specialists in the psychological and social sciences have joined forces with established educational researchers, and received the cooperation of some leading educators, in bringing to bear upon the processes of education in college the most recent findings and conceptions of their disciplines. The result has been that research in this field has been given a new impetus and some new directions, and some old problems are being perceived in fresh perspectives. Several large research projects have recently been completed, and others have been begun and are producing significant results. The present volume has as its major purpose the stocktaking that now seems called for. We, the authors, regard higher education—its policies and processes and the determinants of them—as a field of intellectual inquiry. We have undertaken here a mapping of this field; and we have sought to indicate for its areas what has been

1

done and what needs to be done. At the same time we have tried to construct a basis in theory for the interpretation of existing research and existing observations of the "case" variety, and for the analysis and criticism of current practices. It has been our hope not only that we might contribute to a better understanding of higher education but that, by encouraging more systematic study of what goes on in our colleges, we might also contribute to the general advancement of knowledge of social organizations and of personality development.

We have limited ourselves almost exclusively to the study of undergraduates and their college environments, and we have focused particular attention on what we believe is properly called liberal education. But we cannot say, at the start, what liberal education is. Certainly it is not vocational or preprofessional education, and it does not seek to inculcate any particular dogma. Presumably it does something of a more general nature for the individual, but what this something is or might be is a matter for study. In this volume we inquire what the liberal arts colleges do, and we repeatedly ask ourselves what they can do; we hope that in the end we shall have contributed to the continuing discussion of what they should do.

One does not need any fixed conceptions of educational goals in order to be convinced that American colleges are failing rather badly. They fail to achieve their own stated purposes; and they fail by other reasonable standards of accomplishment. This failure is rendered more poignant when one considers, as we have done, that the college experience might do—and that it does do in some cases—a great deal for the individual.

We are interested in helping to improve the work of the colleges, and we believe that to this end the best course at the present time lies through the detailed study of the processes of college education, rather than through the enthusiastic support of any particular philosophical position. What factors of structure and function make up a college and how are these inter-related? How do the particular policies and practices of institutions affect, if they do at all, the various activities and characteristics of students? Dependable knowledge of this kind is bound to lead to changes in current practice and, in our view, to greater clarity of thinking about ends.

It is assumed in the volume that any particular practice in a college depends on the organization and functioning of that institution as a whole, and that the operations of any college are constantly influenced by the society and the culture in which it exists. The present work begins on this note: it begins with a picture of the American college as a whole, a picture that conveys, we hope, the complexity and diversity of the institution and how it changes under the impact of forces in American society.

In our efforts to analyze this totality, we discuss first the student, attempting to summarize what is known and to indicate what might be known about the characteristics, susceptibilities, and potentialities of those who enter college. Next we turn to the student's environment, the influences arising within the college, which are chiefly the educational activities of teachers, that might be presumed to influence him. Then follow chapters on the behavior of students in college, on patterns of interaction between students and particular processes of the college, and, finally, on effects upon students of the college experience. The whole analysis is carried forward with the aid of theory; this pertains primarily to the nature and development of the individual personality and to the structure and functioning of social institutions such as colleges.

The field of our inquiries is in a relatively undeveloped state. In some areas it has been possible for an author of this volume to report and to summarize a large body of research, and to point out immediate implications for practice and for further investigation. In other areas the author has had to rely upon observation or clinical impression in pointing up problems for study or offering hypotheses for future testing.

The undeveloped state of the field accounts only in part, however, for the diversity among the contributions to this volume. We have wanted to show that the field is open to a variety of approaches, and that it may benefit at this time from being viewed in different perspectives. We have deliberately sought to bring into the great national symposium on higher education some people who, on this topic, have not been heard from before. Although there are some old hands among us, most of us have not until recently been identified with educational research or theory or policy making. All of us are or have been teachers of undergraduates, and all are researchers in fields that are clearly relevant to higher education; yet it did not occur to most of us until recently that we might make the processes of higher education an object of special study. Although different among ourselves in background, experience, and field of specialization, we all share the conviction that the processes of higher education can be studied, and that in studying them we are at the same time studying personality development and the functioning of social institutions, thus confronting some of the fundamental problems of our society. We may hope that other teachers and researchers, in specialties as varied as those represented here, will join us in the continuing undertaking.

Each of the chapters that follow was prepared specifically for this volume. We started with an overall scheme, and each author was asked to address himself to one of its constituent parts. Each was provided at the outset with a detailed outline of the book and, before he began writing, with drafts of Chapters 1 and 2. There were two conferences, one or the other of which was attended by each author and each editor, and in advance of which drafts of all papers were distributed among all concerned. Later drafts were also circulated, and comments exchanged. We hoped, by these measures, to achieve adequate wholeness. But not all parts of the scheme have been filled in. In some areas not enough material was available or could be produced in a reasonable amount of time; other areas had to be neglected because of the necessity of limiting the scope of our undertaking. As for the scheme itself, we have no doubt that it will in time be replaced by a better one.

The volume is addressed to all who are interested in the intellectual analysis of what goes on in our institutions of higher learning. We believe that this kind of intellectual activity should be an integral part of the teacher's work. Teaching, and influencing the young by other means, becomes more interesting and rewarding, and more effective, the more one knows about students—about their individual personality structures, their differences among themselves, their successive stages of development. And as colleges and universities become more and more like corporations, more bureaucratized, with more decisions by committees and less individual responsibility in high places, the individual who lives in them must, in order to maintain his humanity, be able to predict, or at least to explain, what happens. Members of these organizations who do not understand their machinery are destined to become cogs within it.

PART I

GENERAL

The aim of the three chapters in Part I is to present an out-look on the field of higher education as a whole, and thus to give a context in which the problems and processes treated in later chapters may be viewed. Sanford states in Chapter 1 some of the major issues in American higher education today, and in Chapter 2 he discusses the general conceptions that have guided the organization of this volume and which he believes to be fundamental to research in the field. Professor Riesman and Mr. Jencks then draw a picture of the American college as a social institution, emphasizing the extent to which the great differences among and complexities within our colleges depend upon forces in our larger society and culture.

Each of the chapters can be read independently of what precedes or follows it. And none of them undertakes to summarize, or to offer suggestions for interpreting, the content of later chapters. For a quick survey of what the volume contains the reader can do no better, probably, than to examine the table of contents and the notes that introduce the several Parts.

Chapter 1 is intended not only to state issues but also—let it be confessed—to evoke attitudes respecting them. Many people feel strongly about the matters discussed here, and it is hoped that the reader will do so too. It is hoped, indeed, that disagreement as well as agreement with the positions taken will generate emotional energy that will help sustain the reader during the fairly hard going that lies ahead. The accent at the beginning of the chapter is on the failure of the colleges to meet their commitments and on the lack of impetus to reform both on the part of the colleges and on the part of their constituents. It is argued that it is still possible for college faculties to bring about the needed reform and that they may find potent aids in

5

the knowledge and techniques of psychology and other social sciences. In order to serve this high purpose these sciences will no doubt have to be much more fully developed than they are at present; it is believed, however, not only that existing behavioral theory and research can improve our understanding of educational processes, but also that by way of this application we may help improve, at the same time, the theory and the techniques of research.

Chapter 2 attempts to outline the general scheme or frame of reference according to which the volume has been organized. This analytical scheme is intended to serve at the same time as a map of the field we propose to study, the field which we should like to see become the object of continuing investigation. The major conceptions here are that of the college as a complex organization, in varying degrees separated from the larger society with which it interacts; and of students, of great diversity and complexity as individuals, entering this organization to be developed in such a way that they will possess qualities or traits desired by those who support and those who operate the institution. This chapter, like the volume as a whole, begins with a discussion of objectives and proceeds to students, to educational activities, to more complex phenomena of college—student interaction, and finally to the immediate as well as the more lasting effects of college education.

In Chapter 3, Riesman and Jencks use an anthropological approach in which they compare colleges with each other and with other kinds of institutions, and the educational process with other kinds of processes. They are concerned with the similarities and differences among institutions "that are called 'colleges' in America," and with the range of variation in the particular features and in the overall patterns of these institutions. In comparing colleges and education with other kinds of institutions and processes they show how we may enlarge our understanding of higher education by viewing its characteristic structures and modes of functioning as instances of something more general.

In making their point that what happens in a college is continuously influenced by processes in the surrounding society and culture, the authors view the college in three different ways: first, as an institution *of* society, founded in order to perform functions desired by one or more interest groups; next, as a subculture that exists for its own sake *within* our society and culture—an environment that has geographic, political, and social features; and, finally, as a member of a population of colleges each of whose activities are constantly affected by what the others are doing. Once a college has been founded and set upon its course, it becomes interested in surviving; to maintain its "viability" in a world in which interest groups change in their purposes and power, the college must be prepared to redefine its mission, introduce activities that serve other interest groups besides the founding one, find ways of resisting or adapting to pressures from its political and social environments, and evolve in directions set by the leading institutions. In this light we can see that change in a college is usually in response to pressures from outside; but groups or individuals representing the administration, the faculty, or the students—groups who embody some of the outside influences—may help to determine the direction and the rate of change.

Riesman and Jencks use case studies or "vignettes" of three particular colleges in order to illustrate some of their major points; and they call attention to the need for this type of ethnographic study of modern organizations. We may emphasize here what it is that we may gain from such studies as these authors have made. In the study of organizations, as in the study of individual personalities, the intensive investigation of the single case remains the best means for revealing the wholeness of the system in action. The case studies presented in Chapter 3 permit us to see how particular components—objectives, curriculum, teaching methods, social organization, culture, and the final product—all participate in the character of the whole, and how the distinctive character of the whole consists in the pattern of interrelations among the components. Generalized knowledge of these inner dynamics and of their relations to outside forces will eventually form the core of a science of institutional functioning and the basis for planned change in particular institutions. More than this, such studies can help immediately to lift discussion of higher education to a higher level of realism and sophistication, and thus to make planning more effective. We have earlier called attention to public ignorance of what goes on in our colleges, and to the colleges' defensiveness in the face of widespread misunderstanding of their purposes and difficulties. The fog must be cut through, by an approach that has no interest but to tell the truth and thus to serve the interests of all concerned. The colleges that have been willing to expose themselves to this kind of study, Harvard (see Chapter 22) the University of Massachusetts, Boston College, and San Francisco State College, may now be added to a small but growing list of colleges, headed by Vassar, that have had the courage and the sense of responsibility to risk damage to themselves in the interest of activities that promised to aid higher education in general. Perhaps they have also had unusual foresight, for the "victims," as Riesman and Jencks call them, are likely to be the first to benefit from the operation. In the vignettes that we are offered the virtues of these institutions shine through, and there is a strong suggestion that by the time their weaknesses have been brought into the open and seen in their proper context, the forces that will overcome them have already been set in motion. Still, the approach taken in the present instance has its limitations, one of which has been pointed to by the authors; they have studied only relatively excellent institutions; it would be too much to subject the poorer ones to this kind of searching analysis, however enlightening the contrasts might be. Another limitation is that Riesman and Jencks have not studied an institution in crisis. The inner workings of institutions, like those of individual personalities, are best revealed when the whole system is under strain. There is still need for studies like those carried out at the University of California during its controversy over the loyalty oath (Stewart, 1950) (Sanford, 1953).

Riesman and Jencks refer to their approach as "impressionistic." It should be pointed out that it is so in a special sense, the sense that is intended when a clinical psychologist or a physician speaks of his "clinical impression." All observations or impressions depend in part upon the observer; the important thing, for the advancement of our knowledge, is that he be trained and guided by theory. The clinical impression, and the impressions set forth by Riesman and Jencks, are not so much descriptions of what is plainly manifest as they are insights into relationships that underlie surface events. The approach of the clinician, or his counterpart in social science, is to station himself in the middle of things, where a thousand events of human behavior and human interaction crowd in upon him and demand to be made sense of. His inclination as a scientist is to discover relationships among these events; he looks at them in different ways, using theoretical models, metaphors, and analogies as aids to understanding. And he is alert to the possibilities of generalization. If he can make an imaginative generalization that is broad in the sense that it brings into the same formula a diversity of events or processes, so much the better. There will always be a place for this kind of activity in science. For one thing, the impressions of which we are speaking, like the insights of the artist, are the stuff of which testable hypotheses are made. More than this, there is a durable place in science for the broad generalization that cannot be tested by methods available at any given time. Such generalizations serve as working hypotheses, and as orienting and stimulating ideas; their absence involves for the scientist the danger of becoming bogged in a narrow specialty, or even that of becoming the servant of his methods.

A final point. One could easily get the impression, not so much from the vignettes as from the main analysis of Riesman and Jencks, that a college is like a rudderless ship on a sea of impersonal social forces, and that the motives of people concerned with higher education are, typically, not very high, or high-minded. For example, a college is the "watch-dog of the upper middle class" rather than—as some of us might have supposed—the best arrangement that thoughtful men could contrive for educating our youth. Again, if a college changes its program the chances are that it is "copying" institutions of greater prestige rather than seeking the best way to do its work. The basis of this impression is the fact that we are offered here an analysis in dynamic terms, a study in the interplay of forces; the authors focus more upon the "institutional" than upon the "rational" aspects of higher education—to use a distinction that Dr. Bay makes in Chapter 28. Such an analysis, in bringing to light that which is commonly neglected, is bound to dwell more upon the relatively unpalatable than upon that which calls for congratulation. But this kind of socioanalysis, like psychoanalysis before it, is based on faith in the ultimate triumph of good sense. It assumes that it is precisely by calling attention to the lower, the irrational, the dysfunctional, the inappropriate, the antidevelopmental that we raise the level of rationality in human affairs. In any case the role of rationality in the evolution of the American college comes in for its due in Dr. Stewart's treatment in Chapter 26.

REFERENCES

Sanford, N. Individual and social change in a community under pressure: the oath controversy. *J. soc. Issues,* 1953, **9,** 25–42.
Stewart, George. *The year of the oath.* New York: Doubleday, 1950.

1 *Nevitt Sanford*

Higher Education as a Social Problem

DO OUR COLLEGES EDUCATE?

The trouble with students, the saying goes, is that they turn into alumni. Indeed, a close look at the college-educated people in the United States is enough to dispel any notion that our institutions of higher learning are doing a good job of liberal education. A professor in one of our great state universities arrived almost at the end of his career with the feeling that things had not gone too badly. Then he had occasion to work closely over a period of time with the organized alumni of his institution. He came quickly to the conclusion that these products of his and his colleagues' labors had no respect for learning, understood nothing of the conditions necessary to it, and were quite willing to sacrifice fundamental freedoms of the mind to the interests of expediency. Nothing happened later to rescue this retiring member of the faculty from his disillusionment.

The writer and one of his colleagues, in the course of their researches on the effects of college education, recently attended a reception in an upper-middle-class district of a large inland city. We had set ourselves the task of keeping in touch with a group of young women whom we had studied intensively during their four years at Vassar College. It is not that we aim to be present at each major event in the lives of these subjects, but now one of their number was announcing her engagement and, being in town, we were happy to attend her party.

The home was exactly as it had been described by our subject in her life-history interview—a huge, rambling house of about 1900,

10

located on a shady street and possessed of a vast garden with great trees bordering a swimming pool. The home was close enough to the center of town so that most of the other houses on the street had been converted into apartment dwellings. There were approximately 200 guests, representing the social, cultural, and artistic elite of the city. It was a gay party.

As we left, it was necessary to wait quite a while for a taxi, and our hostess—our research subject—undertook to fill us in a bit on life in her city. She explained that most of the people we had met were chronic party-goers, and she took the trouble to single out, among the departing guests, a number of notorious female alcoholics. It was explained that in this town there was nothing for educated people to do. There was a symphony concert one evening a week, but for the rest of the time people engaged in a round of parties, with heavy drinking the rule. With many of the women, the drinking started with three cocktails before lunch with the girls downtown. Then, about three o'clock, one of the group would say, "I have a wonderful idea—let's all go over to my house and have a drink"; this they did, and thus they whiled away the time until the husbands arrived to begin preparations for going out to dinner. Our subject's fiancé, who was from an eastern metropolis, was shocked. It was further explained that at the parties the talk usually focused on gossip and happenings inside the several organizations with which most of the men were identified. Undoubtedly the women of this social group, all of whom were college-educated, had had many occasions to complain about the lack of stimulation in this culturally-barren and sociologically depressed community. Depressed is the word. The center of the city revealed no signs of civic pride; there were shabby public buildings and a continuous snarl of traffic. In going any distance from the center of the city one passed through vast slums. The delinquency rate matched that of any of our large cities—and the college-educated people of the city were bored and could find nothing to do with themselves. Where is the capacity to go on learning and to go on demanding the kinds of esthetic and intellectual satisfactions that were enjoyed in college? Where is the sense of social responsibility that our colleges seek to encourage? In the case of the women, where is the sense of independence and self-confidence that would make it possible for them to assume leadership in a desperate situation? For that matter, where is the sensitivity and social awareness that would tell these women and men that the situation is desperate?

Of course it is not fair to blame all our social ills on the colleges, but it is fair to remind them and ourselves of the enormity of their problem, and to suggest that had they been able to achieve their stated purposes with, say, half of their students, the whole atmosphere of our inland city would have been different. (If the reader doubts the generality of the picture that has been drawn, let him ask himself and his friends *which* large inland city we are talking about. More than a dozen will be thought of right away.) And of course it must be noted that our informant, the young woman who was planning to be married, *had* been influenced by her college. She was able to see what was going on and to view the whole scene in perspective. She could give a compassionate sociological analysis, and reveal a set of values and a set of tastes according to which the scene about her could be properly evaluated. Unhappily, she was clearly an exception to the rule, and her development as a person was enough to make clear to her that she should leave this community—to live in a seaboard city with a husband who shared her outlook and interests. Her case makes it all the sadder to contemplate the great majority of her peers who will probably settle comfortably in localities such as her present one, and not even question the mode of life that has been described.

The gloom is not relieved by an examination of what goes on in one of our best colleges. Wedge and his associates (1958) in their study of student behavior at Yale described several "campus types." One was the "intellectual or scholarly type, consisting of persons whose interests are primarily intellectual and who are regarded somewhat askance by their fellow students." Other types were the athletes, the vocationally oriented, and those whose distinguishing features were social mobility and high business ambitions. And then there was "perhaps the largest group, an intermediate one composed of individuals who show good achievement without strong goals or drives but who are intellectually competent and who seem to be fairly well-rounded individuals without being deeply committed to anything."

If one supposed that the main business of a college was to nurture students who had intellectual or scholarly interests, he might well wonder how such students fared in an institution in which they were so sadly outnumbered. But they have not the worst of it. We may be reasonably certain that the great majority of the students belonging to Wedge's intellectual or scholarly type had professional aspirations and were benefiting from courses designed to prepare them for graduate school. There is good reason to believe that in the case of pre-professional work our better colleges are doing well—better than at any time in the past. The really serious question is what are our best colleges doing for the great mass of the uncommitted, the vocationally oriented, the anti-intellectual—those who are on the road to becoming "the alumni?"

These impressions of failure are well enough confirmed by objective studies of the impact of college. Probably the best known of these is the report of Jacob (1956) which assembles much evidence that colleges rarely succeed in bringing about important changes in attitudes or values and that the main effect of four years of college is to make students more like one another. The excitement generated by this report would have been even greater had it not been generally understood among educators that the main burden of the report was already taken for granted.

But the failures and shortcomings of the colleges seem to be not at all discouraging to the general public, or that large segment of it that supports the colleges. It is a remarkable fact that a culture that places relatively little value upon learning or the intellectual life, and has little understanding of, or sympathy for, what professors are trying to do, nevertheless regards college—the experience of college for young people—as one of the greatest goods, virtually as one of the necessities of life.

For the great mass of our middle-class high school students, "going to college" is a future event second in importance and glamour only to getting a job or to getting married and having children. If they fail to make the grade, or leave college to get married after a year or so, they are easy targets for an insurance salesman who has a policy that will make it easy "for the children to go to college." The case is much the same with the parents of these youngsters, particularly if these parents have, or aspire to, lower-middle-class status or above. They are willing to make painful sacrifices in order to pay the necessary fees, and their anxiety about acceptance is often greater than that of the youngsters most immediately involved.

It is clear that in the eyes of the general public, college offers important benefits quite apart from those described in the college catalogues. For one thing, it seems that increasing demands for college are a concomitant of our increasing affluence and our chronic state of overproduction. Since there is little need for young people in the world of production, a practical choice is to keep them in school for as long as possible, and college is the next step after high school. In an employers' market it is a simple matter to list "college degree" among the requirements of a job, and thus create the widespread conviction that "you have to go to college in order to get anywhere these days." College, of course, has long been a major channel through which one went up in the world economically; it has now become for the middle-class young person a necessary means for holding his own.

The social benefits of college seem to be regarded as highly as the economic ones, and to be inseparably inter-related with them. For the great middle class, college has become a social necessity, while for members of the lower classes it is a prime means for social advancement. Everyone has a chance to advance socially—or to maintain his existing high status—by attending one of the colleges of higher prestige. For example, if a young woman gets into one of the well-known Eastern colleges and then after a year or two returns to the state university, she will make a "better" sorority than would otherwise have been possible. In colleges one makes the friends and acquaintances and learns the modes of behavior that will be largely definitive with respect to social position and social opportunity for many years to come. Add to all this the fact that the colleges offer entertainment, glamour, excitement, and various kinds of wholesome and unwholesome fun.

Since they serve so many fundamental desires and needs of the people the colleges are subjected to little enlightened public criticism. It is a remarkable fact that the recent and continuing public discussion of education, occasioned by the sputniks, has left the colleges unscathed. There have been few suggestions that the colleges might improve or reform. Rather, the question has been how can they remain as they are in the face of social change and increasing demands for admission. The colleges have their own way of putting it: "how can we maintain quality?"—few ask the natural question "what quality?", or suggest that the problem is how to come closer to the realization of stated aims.

The official position of the colleges seems to be: "We must maintain quality by increasing faculty salaries, by getting money to ensure that increases in personnel and resources keep pace with any increases in enrollment, by raising the standards for admission. And of course we must reform the high schools." The structure and functioning of public high schools have been the objects of much scrutiny and discussion, with the promise of considerable benefit to all concerned. Why have the colleges been largely exempt from this kind of examination?

For one thing, it seems that the great majority of our articulate citizens value the nonacademic benefits their children derive from college and do not really want to see things changed. They can criticize the local high school because it may not be doing enough to get their sons and daughters into a good college. To get them into that college and, to a somewhat lesser degree, to keep them there is often an end in itself. Again, and perhaps more important, enlightened citizens have often been the victims of considerable bamboozlement. They do not know what goes on in the colleges, and have no ready means for finding out. Nor are there means for evaluating the effects of a college program. A man may be an influential critic of our foreign policy, of the conduct of the federal judiciary, or of the local city planning commission but when it comes to policy and practice in higher education he is silent. He likes to know what he is talking about; and besides, his real problem is how to find a good college for his daughter. He picks up some gossip and vague impressions from his friends, speculates wildly about how some imagined features of this or that college will bring out the various potentialities of his daughter, and supports her in her several applications. While he is in the position of having to wait upon the college's pleasure, he cannot bite the hand that might feed him. If he has to deal with a rejection of her application, his case is worse; he does not want to be a sorehead, and even if this were his inclination he would be silenced by the notion, effectively implanted by the college, that it's all his fault anyway— for not supplying her with the right genes or with the right solution of her oedipus complex.

But the chances are that the serious-minded daughter of this influential citizen will be admitted to one of those colleges which through careful public relations has been able to put across the notion that is is a highly intellectual place, but which is in fact just like all the others and still living on a reputation established thirty years ago. Having doubted that she was worthy of such a place the daughter reports her amazement that everybody is so friendly and helpful. The courses are "interesting." By the time she discovers that a set of academic prerequisites and distribution requirements do not add up to a stimulating intellectual life, she has found attachments and benefits which though different from those she had looked forward to are none the less real. Her reports home continue to be favorable, which is a great joy to her father who by now has invested so heavily in this venture that any other kind of report would be hard to take. So he recommends this college to his friends, and goes along with the idea that the colleges are doing a good job.

If the general public has little interest in improving the colleges, it must be said that many of the colleges themselves seem to have but little more. One might have supposed that the picture of Yale drawn by Wedge and his associates would have been greeted with expressions of dismay, or at least general dissatisfaction, on the part of the officials of that institution. But not so. The report goes on to say that the faculty and administration of the college devote much time to considering what might be the best means for the attainment of their educational objectives. "Despite periodic disagreement on particulars, however, most students and college officials would express the feeling that the solutions Yale has achieved to date are good ones and that even better ones will gradually emerge over the coming years."

To understand the attitudes of the colleges it is necessary to consider that they are in an important sense corporate enterprises. Much of their activity has to be devoted to surviving, expanding, maintaining a strong position relative to other institutions. To a very considerable extent this holds for state institutions as well as for private ones. Despite the fact that they appear to be riding high at the present time, operating as they do in a sellers' market, our colleges and universities are in fact very sensitive to the wants and needs of their constituents, and are prepared to stay within certain limits set by them. The ordinary private college or smaller state institution has a hard time rising above the level of value and taste that prevails in its immediate community. It often has to come to terms with the demands of large donors or the state legislature. We should expect a college in the inland city of the above example more to reflect than to influence the attitudes that prevail among the leading citizens.

With institutions that are well known throughout the country the situation is different, and more complicated. They are in competition for the status of leading intellectual center and they would further their cause by recruiting on a nationwide basis the brightest students and the most distinguished faculty members. The two go together. A distinguished faculty member is one who publishes, and typically he is more interested in research than in teaching, prefers graduate to undergraduate teaching, and has little patience with students who are not already devoted to scholarship. The constituents of these institutions go along with these arrangements—up to a point. However little they may value the intellectual life, the college of their choice must be a "good" one, by educational standards, in order for their sons and daughters to obtain the important "unintellectual" benefits to be had there. The excitement about "getting into college" today is greatest among people who are disposed by reason of background and financial solvency to think of the more distinguished places. But there is a limit to how far constituents will go in supporting a leading intellectual center. Obviously colleges like Yale could not exist if they went too far in the direction of excluding the sons and daughters of people who can afford the fees and support drives for funds and who feel with some justice that such institutions belong to them. These institutions are thus under some pressure to prevent their standards from going too high, too rapidly. But their main strategy is to silence their unhappy constituents. This is not too difficult, particularly if the colleges stick together, present a united front to the public, and discourage public discussion of their inner workings. This they tend to do instinctively. If the alumni, or the trustees, suggest that "the intellect isn't everything," they may be reminded that our institutions of higher learning do not exist to promote athletics or the acquisition of social skills, that not everybody has a right to go to college, that in a time of national crisis such as the present all good citizens should support the maximum development and utilization of our "human resources." The constituents do not know or cannot phrase the counter arguments, and there are few who will speak for them. The plain fact is that colleges like Yale do not do enough for their large majorities of uncommitted, or vocationally oriented, or unintellectual students. These students may not be the brightest in the world, but they are bright enough for most good purposes. Alumni and friends of these colleges have every right to ask that something be done for these young people besides preparing them for the scholarly or other professions. They have this right so long as they grant the same to people who cannot afford private colleges.

All this discussion is intended to underline the point that the American College, and American institutions of higher learning generally, are embedded in our culture and in our society. They are expressive of persistent trends, and persistent conflicts, in the American value system, and they have a diversity of important functions in society. This means that fundamental or widespread change in the colleges can come about only when there is a shift of emphasis in our general system of values or when there is a change in our general societal processes.

SOME OBSTACLES TO REFORM

Who, then, is to reform the colleges? And how is such reform to come about?

The notion that these institutions exist within a "surround" of cultural and social forces and necessarily reflect the prevalent trends is, from the point of view of social science, the beginning of wisdom. But it is not wisdom itself. There is another side to the picture that has been given thus far. The colleges are not quite, or nothing but, playthings of forces over which no one has any control. What saves them from this status is the element of rationality in our social processes; where we have knowledge of conditions and are free to use our intelligence we are able, within limits, to influence the course of events.

Our colleges and universities have the functions of supplying this knowledge and developing this intelligence. It would thus be a very sad state of affairs indeed if these institutions were completely overpowered by the forces they were designed to understand and to modify. Happily this condition has not been reached yet. Counterforces to the trends that have been described are readily to be observed, and we may expect these counterforces to increase in strength as the need for them grows more apparent. Things may well get better, after they have got worse.

Happily again, our professors and intellectuals are not without support, and not without sanction, in their efforts to supply the necessary criticism of our society and to raise the level of our culture. They are permitted these functions by our society—the same society that would utilize the colleges for keeping the youth out of trouble, showing them a good time, and offering them social advantages. This society not only arranges for the satisfaction of diverse lower-order wants and needs but it also pays its respects to ideals which have their roots in Western Civilization and in some of the American traditions. It expects the colleges and universities to look after these ideals, whatever else it may demand of these institutions and however many obstacles it may put in their way.

Linus in the comic strip "Peanuts" is, as every serious-minded undergraduate knows, addicted to his blanket, an unfailing source of comfort and gratification. But he wants to break himself of this habit, so he gives the blanket to Charlie Brown with the request that he hold on to it no matter what he—Linus—says or does. Then Linus immediately says he has changed his mind and that he must have the blanket back. Charlie says, dumbly, "Okay, here," and Linus screams, "You're weaker than I am."

Our society suffers from addiction to practicality, power, success, social adjustment, excitement, and the gratifications of popular culture, but in a sense it has asked of our colleges and universities "Get us out of this, no matter how much we may protest from time to time." The mandates of these institutions are from the people, but they come from the peoples' *better* selves, they were given at times when the people were thinking well or had found spokesmen who could express their higher aspirations. The colleges sometimes seem to forget this, and yield to impulsive demands for the return of the blanket. Or they may try to quiet the clamor arising out of desire and fear by undertaking to return the blanket for a little while, or by offering a piece of it. Faced with the necessity of existing as corporate enterprises they often have to calculate how much they can give the constituents of what they want right now without sacrificing too much of what they ought to want, or do want when fear and impulse are relatively quiet.

The crisis in higher education is chronic. The great problem today is not essentially different from what it has been for a long time. It is how to do better the things that the colleges were intended to do; how to realize more fully, despite pressures from without and divided councils within, the aim of developing the potentialities of each student.

I have accented the embeddedness of the colleges in society and in culture. The mutuality of the interactions of the college and the culture may now be stressed. Our colleges have the task of influencing the youth of the country, in directions set by the higher ideals of our culture. Granted that the public often seems to be of two minds about this directive, and contrives to put various difficulties in the way of its being carried out, the colleges still have a fighting chance to realize their objectives. They have in their hands for four years young persons who are or can be relatively isolated from the rest of society, and who are still open to influence by instruction and by example. If the colleges should achieve moderate success, if a substantial proportion of their students instead of a handful were influenced in the desired way, the level of our culture would be raised and, quite possibly, there would develop changes in our society itself. If our culture and our society are to be changed at all by the deliberate application of intelligence and foresight, no agency has a better chance of initiating change than our institutions of higher learning.

It is the college faculties who will have to take the major responsibility for the needed reform. The burden of carrying out educational policies rests mainly upon them, and, as professionals, they have the right to a major voice in the determination of these policies. There is no denying, however, that when there is a movement toward reform in a college it is the collective faculty who usually seem to be dragging their feet. There have been few fundamental innovations in higher education in the past twenty-five or thirty years, and in even fewer cases have innovations been initiated by college or university faculties. College presidents, students, trustees, foundations, large doners, influential citizens, and even state legislatures, have from time to time sought progressive change only to find themselves effectively blocked by faculties. The same, of course, holds for individuals or groups within the faculty who would like to undertake new departures.

What are the reasons for this state of affairs? For one thing, the typical faculty member is by training, by inclination, and by the requirements of his position, a specialist in an academic subject. He is devoted to the advancement of his specialty, by research and by teaching, and it is as a specialist that he expects to make his career. It is thus his natural inclination to see the problems of liberal education in a limited perspective. The college administration or the governing board—or the social scientist—may view the college from a distance as it were, attempting to gauge what progress is being made toward certain broad objectives; but the teacher, typically, is focused upon goals that are narrower, more immediate, and more personal. This characteristic of faculties led so sympathetic a critic as Beardsley Ruml (1959) to suggest that because each teacher is a special advocate "the liberal college faculty *as a body* (his italics) is not competent to make the judgments and evaluations required to design a curriculm in liberal education." One may be led to this conclusion either by observing faculty meetings, which are often futile rituals and sometimes mob scenes, or by examining existing curricula, which are best understood as uneasy compromises, or treaties intended to be broken. Ruml suggests that improvement will require a new instrument or mechanism for curriculum-making, one to be fashioned and used by the trustees or by the president. He may be right. But it is one of the main theses of the present volume that when we have sufficient knowledge of the processes of higher education and sufficient conviction about purpose, it will be possible to find and to apply the incentives necessary to induce faculties to do what they will know they ought to do.

Another barrier on the road to reform is the fact that college and university faculties, typically, have organized themselves in such a way as to make deliberate and concerted change of any kind exceedingly difficult. This state of affairs has its logic and its history. Although faculties have traditionally had the professional status necessary to free inquiry and instruction, they have always had to stand ready to defend themselves against unintellectual or anti-intellectual forces in the larger community. The struggles of American colleges and universities to withstand the demands of business, religious, or governmental groups are perennial. Even within the last decade faculties of some of our large state universities have by heroic efforts barely averted the loss of their professional status. Small wonder that the defensive stance of such faculties has not been altogether relaxed.

In order to resist pressures from outside, as well as to further their most immediate interests, faculties have fostered an ingroup spirit, built up traditions of faculty prerogatives, installed the machinery of campus democracy. These are the very things that now make change very difficult, even when the impulse to change arises largely from within the faculty itself. Measures contrived for one purpose tend to be put into service of other purposes as well, until they become autonomous. Interests become vested in different parts of the machinery itself, so that the machinery persists even after the connection with its original purpose has been lost.

Faculties sometimes go so far in protecting their professional status, or in using their professional status to satisfy their desires for security and the advancement of their own interests, that they neglect the legitimate needs and aspirations of the society that supports higher learning. Faculty-governed European universities, for example, have become extremely conservative institutions; it has sometimes required acts of parliament to bring about changes in the curriculum.

At the present time in America there seems to be an unhealthy alienation of the colleges and universities from the rest of society. But the situation is complicated and full of contradictions. Our institutions of higher learning do not lead in the way that they should; often they seem at once too aloof and too ready to adapt themselves to contemporary pressures. Although so firmly entrenched behind barriers against outside interference as to deprive themselves of needed flexibility, they none the less do not inspire confidence in their ability to resist a frontal assault. Their lines have been infiltrated by the enemy, and they do not have control over their own forces. It is not only that faculties must participate to some extent in their institution's appeals to its constituents, but also the value systems of individual teachers are by no means immune to the major contemporary trends of our culture. The trend toward disappearance of the campus individualist is a sign of a more general phenomenon; the college teacher who has become indistinguishable from other more or less successful men in appearance, dress, manner and mode of life is not very different in attitudes and values either. The public, no more respectful of learning or of professors than ever, are not in the least won over by these modern manifestations of the common touch.

But one of the main barriers to reform in the colleges is the lack of a scientific basis for educational practice. The profession of college teaching is constantly in the awkward position of having promised more than it can deliver. The public is told that the college experience will "liberate the mind," "build the capacity to make value judgments," "inculcate the attitudes and values of democracy," but little evidence is offered on the degree to which these changes are accomplished. There are rival claims for different policies and programs, but the public, and indeed the faculties themselves, have little basis for a reasonable choice among them. The reason, of course, is the lack of knowledge about what kinds of educational policies or practices have what effects with what kinds of students. More fundamental than this is the lack of a generally accepted theory of individual human development in accordance with which colleges may state hypotheses pertaining to the relations of ends and means.

In this last respect education suffers by comparison with psychotherapy, another applied art that seeks deliberately to change the person. Psychotherapy deals with processes at least as intangible as those involved in education, and it is at least as hard put to it to say what are its objectives. Yet its techniques and procedures are almost always derived from some theory in the terms of which the practitioner may hypothesize relationships between what he does and the effects that are achieved. Results of psychotherapy are often disappointing, but because there is a general rationale of the whole proceeding, failures may often be understood and made the basis for improvement in practice. Experimentation, and communication with colleagues, are integral with practice, and hence there is being developed a body of knowledge that will enable psychotherapy increasingly to achieve—even as it clarifies— its objectives.

One might hope that the profession of college teaching will develop in the same way. Colleges are in a position to bring about, and sometimes they do bring about, by means that are strictly educational, changes as profound as those commonly wrought by psychotherapy. The student entering college is in important respects like the patient or client whom the psychotherapist welcomes most heartily; both the student and the promising patient exhibit a "condition" that cries out for change, and both reveal a heartening potential for change. The condition of the student is likely to be characterized by such things as prejudice and narrowness of outlook, shallow and transitory interests, lack of creative phantasy and foresight, want of discipline in thinking, values derived automatically from childhood experiences or a contemporary parochial system and so adhered to rigidly. Unless he is educated, this condition will persist. But, as we know, it is possible for a student to become after four years of college or less, relatively broad in outlook and open to new experience, independent and disciplined in his thinking, deeply committed to some productive activity, possessed of convictions based on understanding of the world and on his own integration of personality. Such changes are profound, and profoundly significant; they are no less to be valued because they are theoretically within reach for every college student and need not be preceded by the kind of suffering that drives people to psychotherapy. The student, in a strong part of himself, wants to become an educated person, just as the promising patient wants to get well, but at the same time he would like this to happen to him without his having to give up the habits, the adaptations, the ways of looking at things that have served him well in the past. Thus it is that some of the striking and most important changes in college are those which occur after resistance to new learning has been overcome. Such changes do not just happen as a part of some inevitable growth processes; they happen rather because effort is exerted by someone and because this effort sometimes finds its mark. What makes the entering student promising despite his often distressing condition, is his relative pliability, and hence the possibility that among the diverse stimuli which the college environment affords there will be some which, for him, are crucial.

The present argument that the profession of teaching may profit in some ways from the example of psychotherapy should not suggest that the college environment ought to be conceived as a therapeutic community or that the individual teacher ought to learn the techniques of the psychotherapist. When I speak of profound changes of a desirable sort being brought about by education, I have in mind such means as the curriculum, teaching in the classroom, the social organization, and intellectual climate of the college. The techniques of the teacher and those of the psychotherapist are different in fundamental ways. More than this, psychotherapy is not a substitute for education; a person of college age who was psychoanalyzed for three or four years would still need to be educated in order to develop the desired qualities that have been mentioned. The point is that the basis for the profession of teaching must include systematic knowledge of what the entering student is like, particularly knowledge of his potential for learning and of his resistances to it, and knowledge of ways in which desired changes may be brought about. The instrument of change is not alone the individual teacher but the whole educational program, the whole college environment. How can the individual teacher, with a primary interest in his special academic subject, help to plan and then to assume a role within an overall program designed to achieve specified objectives? This is certainly one of the major dilemmas of higher education. The teacher, for the sake of his own humanity and—we have good reason to believe—for the sake of the goals of liberal education, must be free to advocate a point of view, to promote special interests, to win disciples. Here we are again confronting the old and so far unsolved problem of how to have maximum freedom within a planned society. All that can be said here is that teachers must take the major responsibility for planning so that freedom is allowed for, that in making and carrying out a plan they must have the professional identity of teachers of students rather than that of members of academic disciplines, and that social science may here be of considerable help. When the needed reform is carried out, the profession of college teaching will gain the amount of recognition that is required if the college is to have a real impact on its students and on society.

THE PROMISE OF A SCIENTIFIC APPROACH

Although wisdom and experience will always be fundamental, new knowledge of "how to do it," of how to induce desired changes in a variety of students, will have to come mainly from science. Different programs of education make different assumptions about the nature and processes of human development, and about the stage of development that characterizes the typical college freshman. These assumptions are subject to empirical investigation and testing. Policies and practices in the colleges, ranging all the way from the creation of a certain kind of "college climate" to particular educational devices such as small classes, the seminar method, an honors program, or a program of independent study, are based on hypotheses (however vaguely they may be stated) concerning how the introduction of certain kinds of stimuli will influence students in certain desired ways. Few such hypotheses have been satisfactorily tested. Sooner or later they will have to be tested, and this can only be done by the techniques of science. As scientific knowledge of development in college accumulates, new hypotheses will be conceived and put to the test.

But colleges may have knowledge of what to do in order to reach their objectives for students and still be ineffective because of difficulties in the functioning of the institutions themselves. Therefore the structure and functioning of colleges as institutions should also be the object of scientific study. In this area particularly there is need not only for scientific knowledge but for the scientific attitude. The field of higher education is so controversial, and there is often so much frustration for all concerned, that people find it difficult to deal with their problems without recrimination. The faculty blames the students, their families, the president, and the trustees; the president and trustees blame the faculty; the students blame their ill luck, or whomever is closest and at hand. The public, when it is interested, seems as likely to blame one of these groups as another, being consistent only in the use of a devil theory of explanation. A scientific approach to higher education can bring needed objectivity and appropriate attention to the interests of all concerned.

The sciences that promise the most for higher education today, and that are represented in this book, are the newer social sciences: social psychology, psychology of personality—including the contributions of psychoanalysis—sociology, and anthropology. In their applied aspects, all these sciences contribute to our understanding in general terms of how human behavior can be modified by means of human interaction, frequently, of course, verbal interaction. These sciences have been and still are subjected to many kinds of criticism, some of which will be discussed in the last Chapter (below pp. 1014–1016). It must suffice to say here that the present volume will testify, we hope, to the value of general psychological and social theory as a basis for and as a guide to research on educational processes.

In the past, most educational research has tended to be local and practical in its orientation. Psychological investigations have been designed under pressure to produce results of immediate usefulness, and hence they have tended to be too concrete and fragmentary, too specific to the particular situation in which they were carried out. Much the same criticism can be made of those expensive self-studies which colleges and universities have conducted in recent years. Quite apart from a natural inclination to put a good face upon things, these studies have focused upon the immediate concerns of particular institutions and have rarely produced results that could be seen to hold for other institutions. The basic terms of the studies have not been sufficiently abstract to permit the comparison of one institution with others, and hence, little has been added to our knowledge of the functioning of institutions in general. In short, the major shortcoming of educational research of the past is that it has not been sufficiently scientific in the best sense of this word.

Our mapping of the field will show that in some areas there is research of high quality, but that these areas are narrow in scope and relevance, and that the processes exposed there have not been related to processes in other areas. In some areas, of the highest importance for the educational enterprise, almost nothing has been done. (Some contributors to this volume devote themselves to pulling together large numbers of quantitative studies, evaluating, noting trends, and pointing to future prospects; other contributors have to rely upon anecdotal material and their own clinical or exploratory observations in thinking about what ought to be done and how one might proceed.)

An example of good research in a narrow field is the development of psychological tests for use in the selection of students by the colleges. The instruments that have been built up in this connection are as good as any of which psychology can boast. Yet, to show the constriction of this field of activity, one has only to note that whereas the instruments' purpose is to predict "success in college," there is little agreement about what this "success" is or how it is to be measured. Most psychological tests have been designed to predict grades, "the academic average," but few teachers regard the academic average by itself as a satisfactory criterion of educational outcome; and how grades relate to success in the eyes of the student, his parents, and other interested individuals or groups, or to success of various sorts in later life, are matters about which very little is known.

It is no accident that research on selection should have become highly developed as an isolated field. On the one hand, it is a field in which psychology itself is relatively highly developed, so that workers could lend their efforts to a practical undertaking without any threat to their professional pride. On the other hand, the colleges could see in selection research a possible means for improving their product that did not involve any extra effort on their part or any investigation into their own processes. Moreover, selection research is in keeping with the individualistic bias of traditional psychology which looks at human beings as units that can be studied independently of their social surroundings. Participation in this bias helps to maintain professional boundaries, both between the college and the psychologist, and between the psychologist and his fellow social scientists.

Nowadays some social scientists would regard it as poor practice to take any responsibility in connection with selection, without at the same time gaining permission to study the goals and procedures of the institution for which selection was being made. This is partly because selection cannot properly be conducted apart from its institutional context and partly because work on this problem offers an entering wedge by which the interested scientist may gain access to the structure and functioning of the institution itself. All organizations resist investigation by scientists of the newer disciplines. The colleges are no exception. Although they are corporate enterprises, and resemble in important respects the truly free enterprises of an earlier time, they have not fully accepted this self-conception, and have not developed a tradition of utilizing research departments and "staff officers" who supply information to serve managerial decisions. At the same time the new social sciences have been at a disadvantage relative to the older, most established disciplines. Since each academic department must guard its status, the social sciences could not be accorded the power which might go with the status of investigator of the whole academic enterprise. More than this, the colleges—though not the universities—have been largely in the hands of the humanities faculties. Many members of this group still have grave reservations about the social effects and indeed about the morality of social science, and participate in the criticisms referred to above.

Social scientists for their part have not been particularly interested in higher education as a field of research. In developmental psychology there has predominated until quite recently the view that the really interesting and important events take place relatively early in the individual life and that what happens after the age of 18 or thereabouts is largely the expression of personality dispositions that have already been well established. It is a striking fact that psychologists concerned with the study of the total adult personality in its historical aspects have not considered the college years to be of any particular importance. For example, in the several large-scale personality assessment projects that were carried out during and shortly after World War II it hardly occurred to the investigators to look to college experience for sources of major personality patterns. There was a strong tendency to suppose that crucially important determining events took place either very early—in childhood relations within the family—or relatively late—in the subject's responses to his more or less contemporary positions and roles. It is not possible in the present state of our knowledge to say that this view is altogether wrong. One who wishes to account for the personality structure of an adult may do well to attach more importance to social class, family background, experiences of early childhood, and the demands of adult life than to experiences in college. But there is accumulating evidence that changes of considerable profundity may take place during the college years. Efforts to conceptualize those changes have been at the center of much recent theoretical discussion, and personality development during the college years has become a lively field of research endeavor.

Why sociologists and anthropologists and other students of organizations have neglected the colleges and universities is another question.

No doubt they have had their hands full with other matters, or have preferred to work in situations where they were welcome or to which access was not too difficult. Perhaps, as in the history of science generally, there has been some inclination to postpone the investigation of that which was "closest to home." In any event, recent advances in the theory of organizations, and in the strategies and techniques of their study, hold considerable promise of increased understanding of our colleges and universities, and scientists of the relevant disciplines are becoming increasingly interested in investigating the "social structures" in which they work.

The major purpose of the present volume is to help put the resources of the newer social sciences into the service of liberal education. Although we summarize and evaluate much traditional educational research, we have given particular attention to concepts and theories that have been developed apart from higher education, and we have sought to make these the basis for a fresh look at higher education considered as a field of intellectual inquiry. Among the resources of the newer social sciences that enter largely into our considerations are facts and theories of personality organization and development, new knowledge of cognition and motivation, advances in the social psychology of small groups and of interpersonal relations, sociological theory pertaining to the structure and functioning of large organizations, anthropological insights and techniques as applied to contemporary cultures such as those found in colleges and universities. Utilizing concepts and theory from such sources as these, we have attempted to provide a tentative large-scale map of the field of higher education at the present time, a device that can be used to order present research data and intuitive knowledge and to guide future systematic inquiry.

It may be hoped that the work will not only further the development of a scientific approach to higher education but stand as a contribution to social science in general. This may seem a large order, but it will not appear unreasonable when it is considered that the two objectives are to be reached by following the same route. The activities that contribute to the one will also contribute to the other. Here the fundamental consideration is that the theoretical conceptions that are most relevant to the phenomena of development in college, that are necessary to an explanation of those phenomena, apply equally well to various other phenomena. The question of how students change under the impact of the college experience is an aspect of the broader question: What, in general, are the nature and conditions of personality change? This is a question of major concern not only to educators but also to a host of investigators and practitioners in fields as widely separated as experimental psychology and psychotherapy. Thus it is that some of the major contributions to our understanding of the effects of the college experience have been made, not by researchers on higher education, but by workers in quite different fields. By the same token, research on development in college may contribute directly not only to the solution of some practical problems of educators but also to our general knowledge of personality. It is being recognized by an increasing number of researchers in psychology that the college situation offers a particularly good opportunity for the study of personality change. Well and good. As these researchers pursue their special interests they will contribute to that body of fact and theory upon which practice in the colleges may eventually be based.

The same considerations hold for the study of the college as a social institution. The American college is in some respects a unique institution, but it is still an institution, and hence it functions according to laws that hold for institutions in general. We can learn about the workings of a college from studies of any other kind of large organization; and the social scientist interested in furthering our general knowledge of institutional functioning could do worse than to center his observations upon colleges.

The investigator of higher education may avoid parochialism and superficiality by adopting this simple rule: an educational problem is not worth investigating if it cannot be phrased in such terms, and attacked in such a way, as to yield results of interest to social scientists who are not concerned primarily with education. This would not be to neglect practical problems; it means merely that for science to be applied it must first of all be science. This should be taken in connection with the consideration that a practitioner in education cannot base his actions upon facts alone, however relevant to his problem these facts may be; he has to be guided also by values and by judgments of possibilities. The role of science in higher education is not to provide the answers to particular practical questions but to supply general knowledge of student development and institutional functioning which can aid in the solution of innumerable practical problems.

One might be tempted to speak of a "science of higher education," in order to accent the notion that the field may ultimately be constituted as a body of fact and theory, a discipline of sorts, in which individuals might become specialists. It is clear from the above, however, that the same science which applies to higher education applies to other fields of practice just as well. What needs to be further developed, as indicated above, is the profession of higher education, a profession that has its own sanctions, its own ethics, its own "know-how" as well as its scientific basis.

REFERENCES

Jacob, P. E. *Changing values in college.* New York: Harper Bros., 1957.
Ruml, B. *Memo to a college trustee.* New York: McGraw-Hill, 1959.
Wedge, B. M. (Ed.). *The psycho-social problems of college men.* New Haven: Yale University Press, 1958.

$\mathcal{2}$ _Nevitt Sanford_

Higher Education
as a Field of Study

Although concepts are defined and theories developed at various appropriate places throughout the book, it may be well to set down here some of the very general conceptions that have guided the organization of the volume; they may serve as a preliminary over-all view of the field.

We shall view a college or university as a complex organization of social structures and processes, in varying degrees separated from the larger society with which it interacts, into which students of great diversity and internal complexity enter, to be developed in such a way that they will possess qualities that are desired by those who support and those who operate the organization. The major activities of the college are carried forward in accordance with some theory, explicit or implicit, as to how the students are to be changed in the desired ways, and these activities are evaluated in terms of how much they contribute to the stated objectives. The major task of educational research is to test such theories, to discover and to demonstrate the processes by which students change in desired ways.

Three of the key elements in these processes are (a) the students entering college, each with his unique pattern of potentialities for, and resistance to, change; (b) the procedures by which the institution would develop the students; and (c) the objectives of the institution, stated in terms of the directions of change that are desired. We may discuss each of these conceptions in turn, beginning with objectives.

OBJECTIVES

It would be possible, of course, to study the educational procedures without mentioning objectives at all. One would simply inquire what effects, as described in suitable objective terms, result from the students' contact with the different features of the educational environment. Or, to put this in a different way, what qualities in entering students are modified, in what ways, by a given educational procedure. And one would not omit the effects of those aspects of the college environment that are not, in any formal sense of the word, educational. One comprehensive approach would be to compare leaving students with entering students, or the same students at the times of leaving and entering, taking into account all relevant qualities of the students, and attempting to account for changes by reference to events that intervened between entering and leaving. One would later attempt to demonstrate events-effects relationships by the use of experimental controls.

But this approach does not remove the study of education from the realm of value. Various kinds of effects of the college experience would be regarded as desirable, or as undesirable, by some of the people who had an interest in the matter; hence, there would be no essential difference between studying "events-effects" and studying *means-ends*. The scientist would thus do well to start with ends that large, or particularly significant, groups of people valued highly, and then ask himself how these ends might be achieved. This would be to place such science where it belongs—in the service of human aspirations. It would also be to assure the scientist that he was working on something significant, for, in the psychological and social sciences, things that matter a lot to people are usually just the things that have the ramifications, the connectedness with other things, that make for the greatest scientific interest.

I say *begin* with the study of means-ends relationships. Can we do this, while the professed objectives of higher education, particularly those of liberal education, are still so vague and controversial? One thing is clear, we cannot afford to wait until there is general agreement about the ends of education. This would be fatal. The thing to do is begin with *some* one objective, desired by some important group, and start investigating its conditions and correlates. The research activity would then be very likely to induce fresh thinking about that objective, aimed at its clarification. It might very well turn out that mere verbal agreement about the objective was not enough, that redefinition was necessary before any action could be taken; or that verbal statements were obscuring implicit or underlying "real" objectives. New knowledge might very well lead to the modification of the objective, or to the substitution of others for it.

Research into higher education, then, if it is directed to fundamental problems, soon becomes involved with questions of objectives. Not merely with how to achieve professed objectives, but with questions of what objectives are truly the best. The social scientist, as well as the social practitioner, has to be concerned with these questions because his activities have effects, and must therefore be viewed in a context of value.

Objectives can be studied. Although knowing and evaluating are different, we may none the less study objectives with attention particularly to their origins and consequences. It may be inquired who has what desires in what times and circumstances. This is not to deny the existence of universal values; it is to say, rather, that the search for the generally valid in educational objectives may be furthered through knowledge of their social and historical origins and development.

The objectives of American higher education, as Professor Stewart makes clear in Chapter 26, have their roots in the American ethos, and they show a tendency to change as the American situation changes.

It is characteristically American that our institutions of higher learning should be as diversified as they are. They differ in respect to all the features and dimensions that describe a particular college—in size, in the quality of students and of faculty, in standards, curriculum, departmental structure, methods of teaching, social organization, and climate of culture, and in various other ways. Most important, they differ in respect to what they try to do.

A basic feature of American higher education has been its decentralization; groups of people have always been free to start schools and colleges, in accordance with their needs and their ideas about the road to salvation. In consequence, it seems that virtually every objective that could reasonably be conceived of is somewhere represented, although diversity seems to be yielding somewhat in the face of the increasing organization of our society.

The variety and complexity of American educational goals are not so great that they defy classification. The anthropologists have provided us with one approach to the matter. Each nation seeks to introduce the young through education into its civilization, its society, and its culture. It undertakes to give to all some degree of competence in dealing with its civilization or the material environment, some useful basic knowledge of how to participate in its society, and some familiarity with and understanding of its culture. This is socialization or education for citizenship, in the broadest sense of these terms. Objectives of this kind are present in all educational systems, and are not altogether neglected in any educational institution.

At the same time education may be specialized with respect to each of the major areas of the environment. It may accent the acquisition of skills, or training for the successful manipulation of some particular aspect of the environment; it may be focused upon preparing the student for a particular social role; or it may give major attention to the inculcation of tastes, preferences, beliefs, and attitudes. In respect to this last the aim may be to bring about identification with a particular subculture, such as that of a national or a religious group, or it may be to bring about indoctrination in culture very broadly conceived. Where the aim is to introduce the student into the culture of Western Man, considered in its most inclusive terms, we have one conception of liberal education.

These kinds of specialized education are not, however, separated very sharply in current practice. A college that begins with the avowed object of training young people for vocations is very likely, as it prospers, to introduce more and more courses of a general or "cultural" nature. At the same time, it seems to be exceedingly difficult to keep vocationalism and professionalism out of the liberal arts colleges. Many graduates of such institutions say with respect to their college experience that they value most highly the particular skills acquired; and, as noted above, a great deal of the instruction in liberal arts colleges is clearly preprofessional, many teachers being interested in winning recruits for their own specialties. More than this, education that is frankly vocational or professional does not merely offer training for the work that lies ahead but it often inculcates at the same time an appropriate ideology or pattern of tastes, attitudes, and values. Finally, there is much evidence that in the United States today the kind of culture that is acquired in a liberal arts college is highly important to success in the more prestigeful professions, not so much because the culture prepares for the work to be done as because it makes possible the associations and styles of life that go with these professions.

Education that aims at the inculcation of skills and knowledge respecting the material, social, and cultural worlds may be distinguished from education that has as its aim the fullest possible development of the individual. The former begins by asking "what do people need to know?" if they are to live in our world and to ensure its perpetuation; its tendency is to instruct, to train, to mold individuals according to the requirements of our civilization, society, and culture and thus to make them alike in various respects; or, if the education is specialized with respect to one or another of these areas of our world, its tendency is to make individuals resemble others in the same area, and to be different from those in the other areas. The latter kind of education, instead of asking what the individual needs to know or be able to do, asks what qualities as a person he should have. It starts with assumptions about what the individual is, and with open-ended visions of what he can become, and it measures educational progress in terms of change in the personality, for example, from prejudice to broadmindedness, from indiscipline to discipline in thinking. Without denying the necessity of socialization or the values of being able to adapt to, and to aid the perpetuation of, our civilization, society, and culture, this kind of education assumes that the developed individual can do these things in his own unique way; it assumes that as he expands and becomes more complex as a person he becomes increasingly unlike other persons, only a part of himself—and that often a superficial part—being taken up with the requirements of life in the modern world. The developed individual, according to this view, is adequately adapted to his environment and able to utilize culture in the interests of his basic needs; more than this, he can criticize and help to improve society and, through creative activity, help to advance the civilization and to enlarge the culture. Commonly, the idea of the kind of environment to be constructed is one that will best promote the fullest development of each individual.

In education for individual development we have another conception of liberal education. The fundamental question here is: What is a fully developed individual and how is he to be recognized? Answers to this question are bound to be controversial, expressing as they do the ideals of different people in different times and places; and answers are bound to evolve as the world changes, so long as the imagination from which they spring is free. As indicated above, this does not prevent us from defining particular goals that are valued, finding ways of measuring progress toward them, and discovering the conditions of this progress.

Social scientists have for some time been concerned with the definition of goals of development. They have offered conceptions of the mature person, the mentally healthy person, the highly developed person, as well as the adjusted person. These conceptions in varying degrees embrace or overlap the commonly stated aims of our liberal arts colleges. But there is still a great deal of misunderstanding, and some genuine differences of opinion, between college teachers and social scientists.

Psychologists and psychologically oriented psychiatrists, as they have worked with college students and offered commentary upon college education, have sometimes put so much stress upon adjustment, health, well-being, and the like that they have led educators to exclaim, "This may all be very well but what has it to do with E D U C A - T I O N ? " The educators have suspected that these social scientists, while ostensibly helping to promote educational objectives, were actually introducing objectives of their own; and that the pursuit of these objectives might easily lead to a watering down of education. Some of the scientists, on the other hand, with plenty of support from parents and other citizens, have noted that many young people who had had a great deal of academic instruction, and freely displayed its effects, still showed much immaturity, weakness of character, psychopathology, and inappropriateness of values, and they have concluded, "Education may be all right, but obviously our young people need something in addition."

This implies a distinction between education on the one hand and other goals, such as maturity, mental health, high development on the other. It is possible to define these things in such a way as to maintain this distinction. One could say that education is the transmission of symbols; and that this definition holds for any kind of instruction that has as its sole object the inculcation of skills and knowledge respecting civilization, society, and culture. Education in this sense does not necessarily change the developmental status of the individual personality. The skills and knowledge acquired may remain peripheral in the sense that they never become integrated with the major or central processes of the person. Students may learn a great deal without changing their personalities in any important way. Much knowledge is quickly forgotten, and the person does not change from the forgetting any more than he changed from the learning. More than this, knowledge and knowledgeable modes of functioning may be quite persistent but at the same time superficial in the sense that they are not utilized in the interests of the person's inner needs. There are persons who can take the role of "intellectual" and carry on in their social relations with the use of symbols that could have been acquired only through contact with high culture, without this education being related in any functional way with those needs of the personality that determine the individual's attitudes and orientation with respect to values. Again, the individual may simply assimilate knowledge, sometimes vast amounts of it, to the organization of needs and purposes that he already has. A person might put great resources of academic learning into the service of his need to exhibit himself and to score points at the expense of the less well tutored. Or consider the case of ethnic prejudice. The difference between the uneducated anti-Semite and the educated one would be that the former might engage in overt actions against the Jews while the latter could invent clever remarks in parlor discussions, or perhaps write learned essays on why the Jews "get themselves into so much trouble." In short, the person who is educated in the narrow sense of this word has been given a set of terms in which to carry out his functions as a personality; if he is immature or psychopathic he may now display these characteristics in an educated way.

But to make the distinction with which we are concerned here it is not necessary to accent only that which education in the narrow sense does not do. Attention to its unique virtues may serve the same purpose. Graduate education, education in the European universities, and much instruction in our liberal arts colleges goes forward without attention to the student's development as a personality. Implicitly or explicitly, it is commonly assumed by educators in these settings, either that the student is already sufficiently developed, or that the level of his development does not matter. Failures testify to the fact that in individual cases neither of these assumptions is justified; none the less each of them offers a reasonable basis for proceeding. It may turn out that in the culture of today it is impossible to be both mentally healthy —or mature or highly developed—and highly educated, and that it is necessary at some point to choose between the two. In this circumstance educators would have every right to choose education.

There is merit in retaining our narrow definition of education. If we were able to measure educatedness in this sense, and then to measure such things as health or degree of development, we could study how these desiderata relate one to another. There is reason to believe that the relations are intimate and complicated. To consider some examples: first, although the mere acquisition of skills and knowledge does not change the organization of personality in any fundamental way it may nevertheless be of great service to the individual. It is a great advantage to be able to deal with one's problems at the level of symbols rather than at the level of overt action. The person who cannot read or find satisfaction in one or more of the diverse art forms is often reduced to action or sensation as the means for satisfying his needs and knowing that he is alive. This is the road to delinquency and the general primitivization of life. The educated person at least has easier access to the alternative of being neurotic.

Again, even when new skills and knowledge are ordered to the existing needs and purposes of the individual, their acquisition may change the personality in indirect ways. For example, the acquisition of a skill or the mastery of a body of information might raise the level of the individual's self-confidence, and thus enable him to venture into new situations and to have experiences that would develop his personality. Or a young person might encounter for the first time in the course of his professional training problems that tested his powers to the limit, and the finding of solutions might lead to involvement in an intellectual approach that spread from his specialty to various areas of his existence. And, more than this, commitment to an academic or professional specialty, with all that this implies for values, style of life, and association, may give to a young person much needed stability in his self-conception.

On the other hand, education may bring about changes in the personality that are not favorable from the developmental point of view, or it may act to prevent further development from occurring. Professional or vocational education often induces identification with the occupation in question, thus bringing about a state of affairs in which the individual's behavior tends to be determined by external factors rather than by his genuine needs; and when the individual's self-conception is largely dominated by his membership in an occupation, as is often the case in this country, his performances in social roles are likely to be restricted to those that would be consistent with that membership. Vocational choice that comes too early in the individual's life may induce a kind of premature closure of the personality, a kind of integration or "adjustment" that, being supported by external agencies, may effectively present further expansion and differentiation. No doubt any kind of specialized education courts the danger of restricting the individual's outlook by not permitting him variety of experience. These considerations hold not only for vocational and professional education; they hold as well for education in tastes, preferences, attitudes, and values that runs too far ahead of development in curiosity and in the critical spirit, so that the individual is left with a sense of knowing all the answers without having acquired the means for self-correction.

Viewing the matter from the other side, it appears that development in the personality is very likely to favor the processes of education. The stronger and better conceived the individual's motives, the more firmly they are based in inner needs and the better they are adapted to real possibilities, the more readily will the individual learn the facts and principles that he sets out to learn. The better his judgment, the greater his critical faculties, and the better integrated the diverse parts of himself, the more quickly will he assimilate knowledge and skills that can be shown to have relevance to his purposes. And of course when it comes to the performance of the tasks for which education in the narrow sense is supposed to prepare the individual, qualities of the developed individual often have an important, or even crucial, role to play.

Almost always, statements of the aims of the colleges will refer to qualities to be developed in the person. Sometimes there is a more or less explicit, and reasonable, theory of how the educational program will induce desired changes in the individual. And sometimes the educational theory is less explicit and less reasonable, as when it is supposed that the mere transmission of information will, somehow, lead to development. Even when the program of a college is heavily preprofessional, its defenders are likely to claim that it will have a generally liberating effect upon "those who are able to benefit from it."

Education in the narrow sense and education for development can rarely be distinguished solely on the basis of the names and descriptions of courses; these are likely to be much the same whether one kind of goal or the other is emphasized. Subjects may be taught with future professions in mind or with the object of giving information about Western Culture; where the object is individual development these same subjects will, for good reasons, be taught, though now they will be used as instruments for effecting changes in the individual's personality structure. The differences between the two major types of education may be expressed in the particular choice of material, in the manner of teaching, in the attitude of the teacher, and in the kind of response that is expected of the student.

To say just how the curriculum, or the various parts of it, may be utilized to induce developmental changes in the personality is probably the central problem of educational research. It is a problem at present poorly informed by psychological theory. This whole issue will be discussed in Chapter 11. Let it suffice to say here that the activity of using the curriculum for developmental purposes is best described as "intellectual"—and that this, indeed, is the best use of this term. Teachers who use the term in this sense do well to say, as they often do, that their concern is with the *intellect,* and it is not to be wondered at when they add that they will gladly leave "personality" to others. There is a semantical difficulty here, as we shall see in a moment. But the main reason, in the present view, why these teachers speak as they do is that they wish to stress their conviction that the highest development is to be brought about by what teachers consider to be educational means, by what goes on in the classroom and in the teacher-student relationship, rather than by extracurricular activities, psychological services, or the chance to "grow" willy-nilly in a pleasant environment. Since development through disciplined learning is likely to be difficult or even painful, and since college students are often resistant to such development, the educator is naturally opposed to anything that might appear to offer the students a chance to escape.

But it cannot be claimed that "the intellectual" is somehow disembodied, or separated from the rest of the personality. The basic fact is that a person is all of a piece. If teaching effects any changes in intellectual functioning these will ramify throughout the personality, just as processes already at work in the personality will help determine what happens in the classroom.

In a sense, therefore, changes in intellectual functioning beyond the mere acquisition of facts, such as might occur through learning within an academic discipline, are instrumental to other, more general developments in the person. At the same time there is evidence that certain kinds of developmental changes in the personality have to occur before the individual can be expected to exhibit a genuine love of learning or taste for intellectual activity. Where the educational aim is the development of the individual it is extremely difficult to separate means from ends, or to know what subgoals are necessary to the attainment of more ultimate goals.

It is clear that in the study of college education we have to deal with a diversity of inter-related goals and processes. As social scientists approaching this complex field we have to observe at the present time a wide pluralism in respect to accepted goals. It is one of our tasks to study these goals, discovering what we can about the means through which they may be reached and inquiring into their consequences for other goals. From one point of view the diversification of American education is a blessing; there is natural experimentation on a huge scale, the fruits of which may be harvested by sufficient attention to the effects of the various existing programs.

It has been said that the objectives of particular kinds of education may be viewed in different perspectives. This aspect of the problem becomes crucially important when we ask how successful is a college in the achievement of its objectives. To answer that question it is necessary to find some means of measuring "success." Since success is a highly ambiguous term it is necessary for purposes of measurement to take into account the definitions used by those doing the evaluating.

Success in college is usually measured in terms of grades in academic subjects—the academic average. This is the criterion of success that is almost always used by psychologists in their efforts to develop tests that will predict success in college. This is success from the point of view of the college. But it may not be success from the point of view of the student, or that of other interested people. For example, a girl goes to college with the objective, which she shares with her parents, of finding a husband in a higher social class than her own. If she accomplishes this she is a success from the point of view of herself, her parents, and her husband. Her performance in later life may well be such as to win her the approval of the larger society.

Success in this latter sense is not very highly valued by educators. There are other performances that *are* approved by educators but which, from a broader point of view, may not be marks of success in attaining educational objectives. For example, a mere conformity to a cultural outlook and facility with its symbols may be approved, being mistaken, perhaps, for a genuine internalization of intellectual values.

And then we must distinguish between success in college, as appraised at the time of finishing college, and success in later life. The two may or may not be positively associated. The distinction here is between immediate and ultimate success; it holds for different phases of the student's passage through college as well as for the college-later life relationship. The prediction of long-range success requires follow-up studies, and confrontation of the very difficult problem of determining that a later desired performance was due to the educational experience and not to events that had intervened since its occurrence.

Colleges are, of course, interested in turning out good products, that is to say, students who possess desired qualities. One way to accomplish this is to start with students who already possess these qualities, and take steps to ensure that these qualities are not lost, or overshadowed by undesirable qualities that might develop in college. Those who would predict success in college by means of tests or examinations administered prior to the student's entrance, must be clear in their minds whether they are predicting such a final state or predicting change or progress. The successful prediction of a final state tends to imply that the college experience itself has little effect one way or the other; there may be, however, a general movement up the scale of achievement. The prediction of change assumes either that the college is effective or that all young people develop with time in our culture. Success in prediction of this latter kind requires that the investigator take into account factors in the entering student as well as factors in the institution, and that he have some theory concerning the impact of each upon the other.

Educational objectives may further be distinguished according to whether they are minimal or maximal. When the concern is with selection for college it is one thing to choose students who are likely to graduate, quite another to identify students who show promise of extraordinary accomplishments in life. Minimal objectives such as graduating from college are relatively easy to define, agree upon, recognize and predict, whereas extraordinary performances, in the realm of creative work for example, are very difficult to study. Moreover, it seems that the kind of educational system designed to bring everybody up to a minimal level might be different from the kind of system designed to nurture or encourage, or merely to permit the flowering of, unusual talents.

THE ENTERING STUDENT

How a student turns out at the end of his college experience—the degree of his success from his own point of view, or that of the college—depends both on what he was like at the time of admission and upon the influences of college. Colleges attend to the former in their admissions policies and to the latter in their educational programs. Moreover, admissions policies and programs are always related in accordance with some kind of implicit or explicit educational theory. Students are supposed to be "ready for college," or so constituted that they can "benefit from our program," it being assumed that given qualities in students will be affected in desirable ways by given procedures.

Colleges for a long time have stressed *ability* and *preparation* and, to a less extent, *motivation* as the most important aspects of readiness for college. It is here that the mental testing movement in psychology and education has played a highly significant and influential role. It has been able to win wide acceptance for the view that all the relevant skills, aptitudes, and achievements present in students about to enter college can be adequately sampled by means of tests, and that these tests can then be used to indicate an individual's standing with respect to these characteristics. Mental testers have shared with teachers the assumption that with respect to these relevant features students will continue to be as they are, or rather that they will continue to move in the directions in which they are now headed, so that there is enough persistence or continuity of role dispositions to permit *prediction* of responses to educational influences. Experience has shown that abilities tend to be highly generalized, that is to say, that there are a relatively few general abilities that are basic to a wide range of expected academic performances. Thus it is that tests of verbal and mathematical ability have proved to be significantly predictive of average grades in college; and the addition of other more specialized tests does not improve prediction very much, either with respect to the academic average or with respect to the particular subjects for which the specialized tests were designed.

Because of their success in prediction, tests of verbal and mathematical ability have for some years been very widely used in American colleges and universities. As a result, much is known about the levels of these abilities that exist in students entering various institutions, and about the differences between young people who do and young people who do not go to college.

At the same time, the more or less unsuccessful search for other predictors, such as factors of motivation, has been going on for a long time and is continuing. There is a great deal of research, published or in progress, that attempts to relate performance in colleges—in general or in specific areas—to scores on specialized ability tests, to factors of personality, and to various kinds of factors in the student's background—his history and his situation.

This research has produced a great deal of information about the students who are entering our colleges. Diversity is here the striking fact. Diversity among institutions and diversity among students entering the same institution (Traxler, 1940; Fricke, 1958; McConnell and Heist, Chapter 5). This holds not only for abilities, but for a great variety of personality and social characteristics as well. Here it becomes necessary to deal with the whole problem of the *allocation* of students among the various institutions of higher learning. This has to be considered in respect to both its rational or planned aspects, and its irrational, or nonrational, aspects. Why does a given institution want the kind of students it does? How successful are the colleges in selecting or finding the students they want? Why does a given institution that has the prestige to attract able sudents, and can by means of tests take off the intellectual cream, get so many students that it does not want—for example, students who won't work? How well do school counselors, official and unofficial, direct students to colleges that are suitable for them? What actually happens—what kinds of students go where—as a result of the interplay of social factors?

Here the conception of a college existing within a matrix of social and cultural forces is highly relevant. Colleges, we know, have widely different standards of work and, accordingly, different levels of entrance requirements. Some colleges might be well designed for students of relatively low ability, and most of their students might actually be within this category, but such colleges almost never turn away students of high ability. On the contrary, they will seek such students, because what they are striving for is not so much to do something for average or below-average students, as to become more like those institutions that enjoy high prestige. Success in this sense, success in the eyes of the world, seems to depend mainly on the absolute value of the final product, rather than on how much change has been induced; and value of the product is believed to depend most heavily on the value of the entering material. Thus we should expect to find in colleges having relatively low standards a very wide range of ability in the students, and this not because of failures in selection, or because a wide range of ability was desired, but because of the social situation in which these institutions exist.

Colleges of high as well as those of low standards make various kinds of appeals to their constituencies, and students have a variety of reasons for going to college, for choosing a particular college, and for liking what they find there. Images of particular institutions, in different degrees at variance with what those institutions are actually like, become implanted in the mind of the public, sometimes because of, and sometimes despite, the efforts of college public relations departments. Colleges of very similar standards and similar programs may attract students who differ significantly in personality, and colleges offering radically different programs may attract students who are similar in ability and personality. To obtain the relevant facts about the allocation of students, on a nationwide basis, and to understand the processes determining allocation is clearly a task of enormous proportions.

If the nonrational processes that influence the selection of students by colleges, and the choice of colleges by students, can be understood and exposed, it may help to put the whole business of allocation on a sounder basis. But even when the nonrational has been eliminated, the task of choosing is difficult enough for both student and college. Students and their families and advisors have a hard time finding out what the colleges are really like. The colleges, assuming that they are clear about their objectives and know the kinds of students for whom their programs are best designed, and given the relatively efficient predictors that are available, have special problems that grow out of the present, and predicted, popularity of going to college. For example, as the colleges have more and more students to choose from, and as they continue to use selection devices that have proved successful in the past, the range of talent among those entering the colleges will be progressively narrowed. This means that the tests used in selecting for college will become increasingly ineffective as predictors of doing well, as opposed to doing less well, in college. Thus other tests will have to be found for distinguishing between those able students who can be expected to perform satisfactorily and those able students who are not such good bets. We may expect that much more attention will be given to personality factors other than ability, and to factors in the college situation itself, than has been the case in the past.

The discussion of the entering student has so far been centered on those factors of readiness—those "role dispositions" (Levinson, 1959)—that are considered to favor satisfactory performance, as measured in terms of grades, with respect to academic expectations. The qualities of entering students may be viewed in another way. Instead of asking what personality factors are associated with future high grades, we may ask what the attainment of high grades contributes to the development of personality, and how this contribution is made in the different types of entering students.

It has been pointed out that the academic average is not the only criterion of a student's success in college. Where our concern is with liberating education, all goals have to do with developments *in the student*, with the development of his personality. Suppose we were able to describe a developed personality, and to estimate some of its characteristic features, such as breadth of view, capacity for independent thinking, the existence of deep interests, an internal basis for value judgments, and so on. High grades might be to some extent indicative of high levels of development in respect to such qualities, but the relationship could not be expected to be anywhere near one to one. Thus it is that where development is the objective we cannot think of a student's success solely in terms of his ability to pass courses such as French; it would first be necessary to show that experience with French was actually associated with, let us say, greater breadth of view, as measured some time after the course in question was completed. Indeed if we had objective and independent measures of the different aspects of development, the whole curriculum could be evaluated in terms of how much its various parts contributed to stated objectives. For that matter, one could inquire whether colleges as now constituted are as favorable to development as other kinds of environment that might be conceived and constituted, or whether there ought not to be radical innovations in existing institutions. In selection by colleges, there would be less emphasis upon the prediction of good performances in academic subjects and more consideration of the kinds of potentials that might be fully realized under the influence of educational procedures. It would be found that different students presented different patterns of potential for, and resistance to, further development, and that for these different patterns different educational programs were called for. Colleges might then select the students whom they could help the most, rather than compete for the students who seemed most likely to help them.

In the perspective of a science of personality development the natural question is: What kind of changes in students *do* take place in college and why? To describe changes it would of course be necessary to have a clear picture of what the students were like at the beginning. Here we could not limit ourselves to factors that might be predictive of high levels of achievement, but would have to conceive of the student as a whole person in a stage of his development.

Actually, college officials have, implicitly at least, conceived of students in this way, and they have relied upon common sense and practical wisdom in judging how students would respond to different kinds of influences. These assumptions concern entering students in general. There is good reason for this. Although each student is a unique individual, he is *in some respects* like all other students, and an educational program has to be designed and carried out with most attention to what those who enter it have in common. Our whole plan of going to college—usually for four years—after four years of high school, is based on a conception of the common or typical status of the 17- or 18-year-old person. And insofar as our colleges are similar in their programs and arrangements, they are guided by common notions of what *the* late adolescent is like. Thus our general knowledge of personality development will properly include a number of tested generalizations about youth.

At the same time, however, students differ from one institution to another. Different institutions attract or select or develop different *types* of students. The general policies and practices of a given institution will have to be based on what all the students have in common, and if the policies and practices are appropriate they will take into account those common features that distinguish these students from those entering other institutions. Those teachers who deal with the student in face-to-face situations will become aware of each student's individuality—and we may hope that each is known well by some teacher—but it will almost always happen that actions affecting a student will not depend on what is unique in him but rather on what he is perceived to have in common with some others.

It follows, therefore, that our psychology and sociology of development in college will have to include significant and empirically demonstrated typologies of students. A type—a type of anything—is a set of qualities existing in specified amounts, the qualities being usually but not necessarily related in some way. We may assign individuals to type membership when we observe in them the specified qualities and amounts and relationships. But it should be noted that the student *is* not the type, and that it is not quite correct to say that the student *belongs* to the type either; the type is the set of related variables; it is exemplified in different degrees of completeness by different students. The type is characteristic of the student but it does not totally embrace him; nor will any two students express the type in exactly the same way.

A type need involve only one quality, if there are different specified amounts of it. Thus we may speak of bright and dull students as types. Bright, highly motivated students and bright, indifferent students are two more types. In students who are bright and highly motivated, we are likely to find that a number of other qualities are related to these two. In the literature of research in personality one may find descriptions of types that embrace many qualities, in complicated relationships. The difficulty with such broad and inclusive types, in practical work such as education, is that relatively few individuals may be assigned to them. To know that a student belongs to such a type would be to know him rather well; it might be to know much of his individuality; but, unhappily, in education there is not the diversity of practical actions to match the known diversity in types of personality. The question of how inclusive of psychological qualities the most useful types will be can be answered only through experience.

In his efforts to discover and to delineate types, the psychologist or social scientist cannot limit himself to the terms that educators have preferred. He must be guided instead by the concepts, theories, and methods of his science. There seems to be little danger, however, that types set forth by this approach will not be relevant to education or interesting to the educator. Any quality of personality is theoretically open to change; it may be changed in the direction of higher development, if its determinants are well enough known. The qualities of college students were best understood when viewed within a developmental frame of reference, that is to say, when they are viewed as expressions of phases or patterns of development. These phases and patterns are types, and when we assign an individual to a type we place him with respect to some developmental course. Seeing the individual from time to time we are able to note his progress or regression with respect to developmental goals, and knowing the conditions of change in his qualities we should know what, if anything, needed to be done.

This brings us back to the individual, who has been rather neglected in our consideration of students entering college. It is, of course, to be urged that everyone who has responsibility for the development of students should familiarize himself with the variety and complexity of personal structuring that is to be found in them. It is not that we can act differently toward each of them in an educational setting, but the more we know of them the better we may appreciate them. Students are most interesting, most to be appreciated, when they can be seen within a frame of reference that permits their comparison with other people and with developmental ideals. They are most interesting, in other words, when they exemplify or can be referred to something general.

ACADEMIC PROCEDURES

In the early days of educational research the college environment was considered to consist of the curriculum and the teachers. Different theories of education attached paramount importance to one or the other of these two components, and research undertook to evaluate their relative effectiveness. Today, the researcher in higher education, having been influenced by modern sociology, is inclined to see the college environment as something far more complex. In trying to deal with all the kinds of influence that are brought to bear upon students he will consider not only the policies and practices deliberately adopted by the faculty and administration but also a great variety of factors arising out of the general culture and social organization of the college community. At the same time he will be impressed by the fact that the environment of the developing student is not limited to the college itself; even in a highly organized and relatively isolated residential institution the students are still responsive to diverse aspects of the surrounding social and cultural matrix.

How to formulate this complexity? The idea of the college as a nonisolated system promises to be of some help. A system is a set of related components constituting a whole that is separated from other systems by a boundary of some kind. The system is nonisolated or open if it depends for its equilibrium upon transactions with other systems. The openness of the college system was accented above, in the discussion of its relations with its constituents and with the larger society. The inter-relatedness of the various components of the college becomes apparent as soon as we consider the problem of change in its functioning. It is well known to all who have attended faculty meetings that small changes, say in the curriculum or in the grading procedure, are exceedingly difficult to bring about by deliberation. This is because each function is so closely bound up with others that it could not change without their changing, and this would involve the interests of most members of the college community. When colleges do change, it is usually because of influences coming from outside. From this point of view the students, singly or in the aggregate, are parts of the system; they interact with the other components; and thus their college environment is to some extent of their own making.

This somewhat global view of the matter, however, does not spare us the necessity of conceptualizing, and if possible measuring, different features of the college system that effectively influence students. Here, once again, we may utilize the approach of modern sociology to the analysis of large organizations. According to this approach the college belongs to the general class of productive institutions, that is to say, those designed to produce effects that are important to society. As a productive institution the college falls into the category of institutions in which the "materials" that become the objects of technical activity are human individuals, and the effects achieved have the form of service to those individuals. The college is more special, but not unique, in that the performances of the service requires the cooperation of those who receive it, at least to the extent that they are willing to become members of the institution and to remain within it for a suitable period of time. In this way a college is like a hospital, a correctional institution, psychotherapy, or training programs of all kinds. In all of these the service consists in changes in the people who receive it.

Fundamental to the analysis of a productive institution is the distinction between its *formal* and its *informal organization*. Formal organization refers to all those arrangements that are made with a view to achieving stated objectives. It includes the recruitment of personnel, the assignment of tasks to individuals, and the ways in which technical activities are carried out. Informal organization grows out of the fact that the people who man a productive institution have the same kinds of personal dispositions, needs, habits, and anxieties as do people in general, and they are led by these psychological tendencies to enter into relationships, one with another, that need have nothing to do with prescribed activities.

In studying the formal organization of an institution we ask whether the arrangements are as effective as they might be. We ask such questions as whether the performance of a particular function contributes as it should to the overall effect, whether the performance is efficient, whether the function is sufficiently well integrated with the larger plan. Would a change in one function improve matters or would it endanger effective performance of other functions? We look for defects or shortcomings in the set-up as a whole. Perhaps different authorities in the institution have different and conflicting objectives, perhaps some individuals do not have a clear idea of what they are supposed to do, or perhaps they have assignments that are essentially contradictory. Necessary performances may be insufficiently rewarded, or beyond the competence of those to whom they have been assigned. Facilities may be inadequate. What is highly important, we ask whether the formal organization as a whole might not be having effects, desirable or undesirable, other than or in addition to those that were intended.

One might study informal organization in a productive institution in the same way that he would study social processes in any collectivity of people. He might, for example, be interested in friendship groups, or in the ways that prestige was conceived and sought. If, however, as is the case with the educational researcher, the major concern is with objectives, the informal organization will be studied with attention to the ways in which it helps or hampers in the attainment of stated objectives. It often happens in productive institutions that processes in the sphere of informal organization interfere directly with the planned activity. In the colleges this circumstance has been the source of much entertaining, though hardly constructive, literature. In a typical story some issue is debated as if all that was involved were purely rational considerations of how best to achieve some agreed objective, while everybody except those actually taking part understands that the conflict really has arisen out of the status aspirations of two groups of the faculty. Perhaps as often, however, it is the other way around, the informal organization contributes in unsuspected ways to the achievement of objectives—if not the stated objectives at least objectives that are equally to be desired. This was the notable discovery of the famous experiment at the Hawthorne Plant of the Western Electric Company (Roethlisberger and Dickson, 1939). The productivity of the workers in the bank-wiring room was found to depend not so much upon formal arrangements or the physical conditions of work as upon emotional factors operating in these employees as a group, factors expressed in their relations to each other and to the experimenter. Similarly in studying the colleges, when we encounter cases of extraordinary institutional accomplishments, or of dreary failure, we will do well to look to the informal organization for the sources of the crucial variations in morale. Colleges sometimes seem to achieve good effects with some students, despite, rather than because of, their formal arrangements. There might be an ill-conceived curriculum and a network of repressive requirements and regulations, and yet there may be groups of students whose members stimulate one another intellectually and succeed in reaching a high level of performance.

In attempting to describe the environment of the student, therefore, we must consider forces arising out of the informal as well as the formal organization of the college—and out of the inter-relations of the two. In the present volume, which is focused upon the student and his development, we view the college primarily as the setting in which this development occurs, or as an aggregate of influences upon development, rather than as an administrative unit, an economic problem, a particular kind of democracy, or a center for scholarly activity. When we discuss what is known about the general functioning of colleges and point to problems in this area it is with the object of increasing our understanding of the forces at work on students. We do not discuss some of the larger structures of the college, such as the faculty governance, faculty-administration relationships, or the work of the governing board, unless we can spell out how events in these areas get translated into stimuli that actually impinge on students, or unless activities in these areas can be understood as reactions to student behavior.

In a college the formal organization consists, most essentially, in all those policies and practices deliberately adopted with a view to the attainment of educational objectives—the curriculum, the departmental structure, the responsibilities of the faculty, methods of teaching, enrollment, attendance, examinations, grading, degrees, counseling, advising, planned extracurricular activities. Like those early educational researchers mentioned above, we give most attention to the curriculum and to teaching, including under teaching all the arrangements for the performance of this function. Perhaps unlike the early researchers, since we have the benefits of modern theory and of insights and knowledge that have accumulated over the years, we study the formal organization in its relations to the informal one.

Thus in considering a particular function, such as grading, we attempt to increase our understanding of the way in which it is performed, of why it is performed as it is, of its obvious and less obvious meanings for teachers, students, and parents, by examining its relations to social processess at work in the college community as a whole.

The things that the teacher is supposed to do in helping to carry out the formal educational program are *role-demands* (Levinson, 1959). Other role-demands arise out of the traditions, ideology, cultural climate, and social organization of the college. For example, there may be norms respecting amount of preparation for classes, or how much time is to be spent with students, that operate effectively among the faculty but which do not find any expression in official policy. When faculty committees plan ways to rearrange the educational program in the hope of increasing student productivity they typically come up with something that if carried out would create more work for all the faculty. In some settings the faculty actually undertake this added work, perhaps out of guilt feelings, perhaps out of a wish to believe that whatever they do is highly valuable to students. Probably more often, however, it is implicitly understood that each teacher will find ways to keep his effort on the same level as before. It is up to the new faculty member, as it is up to the new student, to learn how to distinguish between what is officially required and what is possible or necessary.

What the teacher actually does, as teacher, his *role-performance,* is of course largely determined by the role-demands. But role-performances are never completely in accordance with role-demands; indeed the discrepancy between the two may often be large. Intervening between the structurally given role-demands and the role-performance is the teacher's *conception* of the demands, which may conform in different degrees with what they actually are in a given situation. He can only do his duty as he sees it. Other determinants of the teacher's role-performance are the abilities, personality traits, physical and social characteristics that he brings to his task—his *role-dispositions,* the same notion that was used in the case of students. These may be in varying degrees suited to the role-demands. Still other determinants of role-performance arise out of the general social situation in which the teacher lives and works. In any particular college there will be among the faculty a common or typical conception of each role-demand, and common or typical ways of meeting these demands. These phenomena help to shape each teacher's conceptions and performances, but there are still important individual differences.

When we ask what the teacher is supposed to do and how he is supposed to do it, we immediately raise the further question: supposed by whom? It is a striking fact that college administrations and students, parents and other members of the larger society, and teachers themselves often have different conceptions of what the teacher's proper function is. In some institutions, for example, the students think that the teachers are supposed to teach while the administration thinks they are supposed to do research, serve on faculty committees, and render service to the larger community. Teachers may think of themselves as independent professionals while the governing board, and perhaps the students, see them as employees of the state or as if they were tutors or governesses in an aristocratic family. Teachers sometimes share this latter view of themselves. Social scientists may see the proper role of the teacher as that of intellectual leader of his time, but large segments of the general population see it as a channel through which information is passed, a role that is best filled by "those who can't *do.*"

How the role is perceived largely determines conceptions of the best preparation for it and of the kind of person who is best suited to fill it. One might easily conclude from the literature disseminated by the colleges, or from experience of life within them, that the official view is that the good teacher is "born" so and that he also has this role thrust upon him. All colleges are inclined to boast of their "good teaching," but the good teacher is not described, nor are we given any hint of how he got this way. Presumably he just *is,* "since he is one of ours." Preparation for teaching is, to be sure, stressed by accreditation agencies such as the association to which the college belongs, but the only attribute that is taken seriously is the possession of an advanced degree in a special field of scholarship. Every year hundreds of young men and women, fresh from several years of cloistered involvement with their Ph.D. theses, are suddenly thrust into the role of "good teacher." They may spend years in the academic world without hearing any discussion of teaching or without being given a chance to learn by precept or example how to perform or to improve their work. College teachers have enough professional identity to insist that no one else—not the administration or the trustees, not the students, not the public—can properly evaluate their work, but they have not, except in rare instances, developed a systematic basis for self-evaluation and self-improvement or for the indoctrination and instruction of newcomers to the profession. The explanation of this state of affairs would seem to lie not only in our lack of knowledge of the subtle and complex teacher-student interaction but also in the ways in which faculties perceive themselves. They tend to dislike the image of themselves as pedagogues; they tend to think of teaching as an artistic endeavor that does not lend itself to analytic evaluation; they are likely to feel more identified with a scientific or scholarly discipline than with the profession of teaching itself. These self-conceptions have their origins in the history of higher education and in the broad social situation in which the teacher lives and works.

The researcher's approach to the teacher's role is to ask what activities by teachers, in what settings and with respect to what kinds of students, are correlated with specified objectives. He assumes that in this way we can arrive eventually at clearer and more generally approved conceptions of what, in given circumstances, teachers *should* do. Whether teachers should be asked to lecture or to teach by the project method, for example, depends in the last analysis upon which of these role-demands, other things being equal, is the more closely associated with some suitable criterion of the student's success, and similarly for a wide variety of other teaching methods and arrangements, and for various features and phases of the teaching process.

The study of these matters occupies a central place in educational research. Here it is important to distinguish between activities that proceed directly from role-demands and those that express the teacher's characteristics and situation. What the planners assume in devising an educational program the investigator of teaching activities assumes as a matter of research strategy, that is, that all teachers carry out a given role-demand in essentially the same way or, more precisely, that for a given role-demand there is characteristic behavior and that this behavior characterizes all teachers who meet the role-demand. To speak of "authoritarian" or "permissive" teachers, for example, is to consider that there are ways of meeting role-demands which, though they are largely expressive of the individual personality or situation, may none the less be characteristic of the work of many teachers or of all teachers in some settings. It is possible to specify the actions which define such ways of doing things, and to embody them in role-demands.

The characteristics of individual teachers are important not only because they help determine the teacher's role-conceptions and role-performances but also because activities expressive of these characteristics may affect students directly. Relevant characteristics of teachers are ability, knowledge, attitudes, values, and other traits of personality, and such physical or social attributes as sex, age, training, experience, social class, and ethnic background. Very little is known about the influence of college teachers' characteristics upon students' learning and development. Although studies of this aspect of the educational process have often been carried out in elementary and high schools almost nothing has been done in the colleges. Here is a vast and significant area that awaits investigation.

It is activity proceeding from the characteristics of the individual teacher that largely makes up the teacher's art, and that gives rise to vague impressions of "good teaching"—the kind of thing that in academic circles is widely believed to be beyond the possibility of systematic analysis. We are faced here with a subtle and complex interaction of the teacher and the student. The latter, no less than the former, is likely to be uninformative about what goes on. (Of course, he has not often been asked.) Yet it is precisely here that much progress may be made toward supplying the basis for the teacher's self-improvement. The patterns of behavior that make up effective teaching can be understood and made explicit, so that all teachers will have a chance to learn how to perform as the best ones do.

One of the main reasons for delay in developing systematic knowledge of the teacher-student relationship is that such knowledge has had to wait upon the emergence of a serviceable psychology of personality development in students. The professional activities under discussion here have their effects not so much in the kind of learning that makes students able to pass examinations as in pervasive changes in personality. The teacher may be for the student a source of inspiration, a model of adult behavior, an object of unconscious "identification," an ally in his struggles with his parents, a realistically perceived "parent-figure" to be used in revising relationships with actual parents; the teacher may force a reorganization of the student's value system, induce self-insight respecting his childish or inappropriate tendencies, crucially strengthen his serious aspirations and his confidence in his intellectual abilities; or the teacher may be an object of dependent, submissive, or erotic phantasies; or he may finally convince the student that the intellectual life is not for him.

Such happenings may not be well understood at the present time, but they can be understood and made the basis for improved educational techniques. Understanding is largely a matter of conceptualizing and recognizing the readinesses for change in students and identifying the crucial stimuli in the teacher's behavior. In order to understand the processes of teacher-student interaction it is necessary to go as deeply into the personality functioning of teachers as into that of students. Although these matters are often intuitively familiar to the sensitive college teacher, they do not often find their way into the educational literature. How does the teacher use his authority to demand their best of students, without his slipping into authoritarianism, in which demands spring from his own needs rather than from a consideration of their interests? How does he maintain and present his essential convictions while at the same time encouraging students to differ with him? How does he convey his genuine concern for their welfare and his sense of involvement with their development without falling into a pattern of fraternization that endangers the values of respect? How can he utilize his tendencies to exhibitionism and omnipotence for purposes of effective teaching, without becoming merely an intertainer whom students applaud and forget? How can he enjoy his deserved popularity with his students without evoking the hostility of jealous colleagues? Does his tendency to be "hard-boiled" stimulate the students to greater effort or does it incite hostility and rebellion, and does his permissiveness encourage independence, or it is met with indifference or contempt? How does he deal with the feelings aroused in him by the passive, the provoking, the seductive, the sycophantic individuals among the students, and by those who come from a higher social class than he does? How does he manage a group effort by the students to force his conformity with their stereotype of a teacher, or his conformity with the collegewide norms of teacher conduct that students have found means of withstanding? And how does he deal with the depression that follows a bad day or a poor performance in class, or with the feeling, suddenly overwhelming in front of a class, that he has nothing to say and that even if he did the students would not be interested?

What the teacher actually does in circumstances such as those just mentioned depends on the individual characteristics that he brings to his job and upon various factors at work in his environment of the moment. We approach the explanation of his behavior—and of changes in *him* during the sojourn in a particular institution—in the same way that we approach explanation in the case of the student. We do not suppose that the effective teacher has been born that way, or even that his effectiveness has been mainly determined by events in his distant past. Rather we understand his performance as the result of interactions between personal characteristics and the contemporary environment, and we suppose that in different cases different weights should be given to factors of these two different kinds. There are some kinds of conditions, sometimes to be found in colleges, that make it impossible for the most gifted teacher to perform well. On the other hand it is possible to imagine arrangements under which a person with no particular talent for teaching, or even handicaps in this regard, might learn to take an entirely adequate part.

The environment of the teacher, like that of the student, includes social and cultural factors arising from outside the college as well as a complexity of forces from within the college system. Outside the college there is the general cultural climate of the day and the situation of the society—which determines the degree of mass pressure toward orthodoxy, toward certain kinds of accents in the curriculum (for example, on mathematics and science), toward conformity with popular conceptions of the teacher's role. Inside the college there are policies and practices with respect to employment and promotion, formal and informal role-demands having different degrees of explicitness, coherence, and flexibility, pressures to promote the interests of one's own department or subgroup and to meet the competition of other groups; there is a faculty society with its rules and regulations, its channels of communication, its arrangements whereby individuals may obtain status and respect, there is a faculty culture, with its values and ways, calling for adaptation; and there are physical arrangements for living, with their possibilities and limitations respecting comfort, social life, and relationships with people and objects outside the academic community.

Of all the pressures upon the college professor probably the greatest are those arising out of his poor economic situation. Current efforts to raise professors' salaries are in recognition of this fact. It must not be supposed, however, that it is possible to turn the colleges into happy and productive communities merely by raising faculty salaries. This act of simple justice would be but the first step toward reconstructing the professor's environment in the interests of better teaching.

STUDENT SOCIETY AND STUDENT CULTURE

In speaking of "society" and of "culture" we follow common sociological usage. *Society* is a constellation or structure of social roles, while *culture* is a pattern of values, beliefs, and prescribed ways of behaving. In college society as a whole the major roles are those of the faculty, the administration, and the students. At the same time there is always a variety of subsocieties to be observed. Although the members of these subsocieties usually belong exclusively to one or another of the three groups—faculty, administration, students—there may be some overlapping. For example, there may be faculty-student groups—committees, associations, interest groups—in which some roles may be taken either by teachers or by students. Experience in such groups might be of considerable educational advantage to students; they might in this way gain practice in adult roles and through seeing the faculty in fresh perspective begin to develop adult relationships with some of them. For most students, however, the most important subsociety is that to which only students belong. This society embraces formal structures, such as the student government and cocurricular activities, and various informal friendship or living or interest groups. Analysis may be directed either to the ways in which roles are organized in the interests of group goals or to the kinds of emotional satisfaction—support, friendship, prestige—that are afforded the individual. Student society may promote development through offering the individual opportunities to become familiar with a variety of social roles and by confronting him with situations to which he must learn to adapt himself. These roles and forms of adaptation may or may not be in accordance with official educational objectives.

In respect to culture, we may expect to find in the usual case an overall college culture, in which faculty, administration, and students participate, and a number of subcultures. The overall culture will embrace, to some extent at least, the avowed aims and educational philosophy of the college and its ideas and standards respecting levels, styles, and directions of work; and, not unrelated to these, there may be values, beliefs, and ways in the realms of religion, politics, economics, arts, and social relations. It is to be expected that each student, if he remains in the college for his allotted time, will assimilate this culture in some degree. For many individuals, however, a distinguishable subculture may be more important. Students may participate in a student-faculty subculture, for example, one centering about a particular major program or philosophical outlook, or they may be largely under the sway of a culture represented only by students.

Society and culture vary independently. Societies of different colleges, or subsocieties of the same college, may be essentially alike in their structure but yet very different in their values and beliefs. For example, of two liberal arts colleges organized in the traditional way, one might stand for preciousness in literature and the arts and extreme conservatism in respect to political and social questions, the other for stern Protestant virtues and political and social liberalism; of two fraternities having essentially the same social structure, one might go in for athletics and dating, the other for campus politics and the values of business. And similar cultures may be found in social organizations of different types. For example, an approach to contemporary life marked by studied disenchantment and sensation-seeking might be represented in an Eastern private college by a tightly cohering clique in one of the men's dormitories, while in a large state university the same approach might prevail in a loosely organized group of young men and women, some of whom were married to each other, who congregated upon occasion in one or another of the run-down rooming or apartment houses in the town.

Each society or subsociety must have culture—some shared values and beliefs—but individuals within these societies may have distinctive cultural outlooks without joining like-minded individuals in face-to-face groups. (But like-minded individuals who are different from the majority do tend to get together in the colleges, and this is one source of recognizable subcultures.)

Colleges aim, of course, to transmit culture, to bring about changes in the values and beliefs with which students arrive. But students do not change automatically as soon as new cultural stimuli are presented. A large factor of receptivity is involved, and this seems to be largely a matter of motivation. Some of the kinds of dispositions to which the individual teacher might appeal were indicated above; here it may be suggested that perhaps the strongest force behind the adolescent individual's acceptance of cultural or subcultural norms is his need to belong to some group or to feel that he is supported by other like-minded individuals. Thus it is that the kind of culture that the college student assimilates, given some choice, depends heavily upon the social organization of that college; there will be a strong tendency for him to take over values and beliefs from the group that has the strongest social appeal for him.

The faculty's opportunity to influence students would appear to depend on such factors as the faculty-student ratio and the amount of accent on teaching in the college; on the size of the institution or of that subdivision of the educational program in which the student is supposed to find an intellectual home; on the amount of official or traditional sanction for sports and other cocurricular activities. It may depend on the physical plant and facilities, with their capacity to suggest the level of dignity or quality of the educational enterprise; on the living arrangements for students—whether they are so far removed from the centers of academic activities as to encourage a sharp division between living, with one's friends, and studying; and on the amount of time students are on the campus.

The faculty's influence also depends, of course, on the general climate of student culture and on the structure of student society. These should be viewed against the background of the whole college community. Although student culture and society are important parts of each student's environment, already in existence at the time he arrives, they also have to be considered as responses—as ways in which students in the mass adapt themselves to the college situation. We have to inquire whether, and to what extent, a separate student society and a separate student culture are necessary; whether they are inevitable concomitants of the students' common age and role or results of failure in adult leadership or of particular ways in which the larger college community is organized. Student cultures may be largely understood in terms of collective responses to problems commonly encountered. But it appears that if students are to be educated, such problems must be put in their way, and the crucial question becomes whether the responses elicited are consistent with educational goals. Here, at least, students learn rapidly, and what they learn is expressed in changed attitudes and values. Are these attitudes and values desired ones, from the point of view of the educator? If the educator adopts the frame of reference being developed in this volume, he asks whether the collective responses are *developmental,* that is to say, whether or not they are on a higher level of complexity and integration than those that were previously characteristic of the individual student, and whether or not they are susceptible to further expansion and differentiation in the face of new challenges. Observation of some existing student cultures indicates that they may or may not be developmental, and that they may be so in some but not in other of these features. The whole problem calls for continuing analysis and investigation.

Educational programs are ordinarily constituted in *stages*. Different role-demands are imposed at different times, the expectation being that the student's responses to the earlier demands will leave him better able to meet and to benefit from the later ones. Thus it is that the environment of the freshman is different from that of the sophomore, and that of the student in the first two years of college different from that of the student in the last two years. At the same time, since much of the life of a college is organized around these stages of the educational program, role-demands arising out of the informal organization are brought to bear at times corresponding to the formal stages. In studying the behavior of students one may note that different patterns are common in different periods of the college course. Do these differences reflect *changes* of a more or less fundamental sort in the students, or are they to be ascribed to differences in the environment to which the students are responding? This difficult question is discussed later on. To raise it here is to suggest why it is that in the present volume the "stage" aspect of the college environment is treated in sections that are focused on the student's behavior and development.

There are various *general characteristics* of colleges that have not so far been considered: Type of education (technical, liberal, and so forth), level of training offered, type of control (public or private), type of student body (men, women, or both), religious affiliation, geographical position, size of city in which located. Since these characteristics are easily determined, and since colleges differ very markedly with respect to them, they have an important role in natural experimentation, referred to earlier.

Most colleges maintain a number of special services or functions that may become important parts of the student's environment. Counseling services, the general health service, the psychiatric service, the office of the chaplain, the vocational bureau, and research programs should be mentioned here. The activities of the people who perform these services or carry out these functions are too specialized to permit their systematic treatment in the present volume. Nevertheless it will be seen that reference to the special services is sometimes necessary to the explanation of student behavior or development, and that consideration of these services as subsystems in interaction with others is necessary to a complete account of the college as a nonisolated system.

An analysis of the student's environment would not be complete without attention to influences arising from outside the college. As we have seen, the accessibility of the outside environment to the student is a factor to be considered, and it has been suggested that, even in the most isolated residential college today, forces from outside are likely to be important. For one thing, the student's parents are still very much in the picture. Of course the student has already incorporated many parental influences into his personality, but these influences are usually still very much alive, and parental hopes, expectations, and values are continually brought to bear. Much the same can be said for the home community. The attitudes and values that the student has acquired, by virtue of his social class and cultural background, are re-enforced when he returns home or communicates with friends who remain there.

It is worth noting that the climate of opinion in the community in which the college is located may be an influence of some importance. If this community distrusts the college and looks upon it with hostility or contempt, this may serve to unify the college society. On the other hand, college officials may be highly sensitive to town opinion, and they may, in order to placate powerful outsiders, impose upon the students restrictions that are admittedly unreasonable, thus indicating to the students that they are being made victims of a certain hypocrisy.

The larger society seems particularly important in that its structure determines the kinds of future roles that students may anticipate. For example, where the society does not offer attractive roles for the highly educated woman, we cannot expect girls in college to exert themselves very much in order to obtain advanced education. As for the climate of culture that prevails in the society at large, we have seen that this has its impact upon college faculties; we should expect that students would be far more susceptible to it; they have just left the larger society and expect to return to it shortly, and, unlike the faculty, they are quite uncertain as to what they are going to do or be.

STUDENT PERFORMANCE IN RELATION TO EDUCATIONAL OBJECTIVES

In considering the responses of students to the college environment we make the distinction, fundamental in psychological theory, between *behavior* and *personality*. Behavior consists in observable acts, while we define personality as an inferred organization of processes within the individual. Behavior depends both upon personality and upon the environment of the moment, these two determinants being important in different degrees in different cases. When we observe similarity in the behavior of a group or population of people we consider it likely that all are being subjected to the same potent stimulus; when we observe differences among individuals in their responses to the same stimulus we suppose that factors of personality are largely determining the behavior. Consistency in an individual's behavior over time may be attributed either to factors in his personality or to the persistence of the same environmental condition. But observed consistency under varying conditions is the most reliable indicator of personality.

As suggested above, the distinction between behavior and personality is of crucial importance in any consideration of *change* in college. To determine whether observed changes are due to development in personality or to variations in the environment, or to both, the specialist in the psychology of personality brings to bear his most subtle instruments for diagnosis and measurement. It is unfortunate that in the present stage of our knowledge these instruments are often not adequate to the task.

In the study of student behavior one may focus on some aspect of the environment and ask what responses it commonly elicits, or one may note, in populations, common patterns or trends of behavior and ask what are the determining stimuli. The former approach was implied in the above discussion of the college environment, the latter in the consideration of student society and culture as response to the total situation of the student. The crucial question for education is what are the relations of present behavior and the future attainment of educational objectives, that is, the development in the student of desired qualities that will persist after college. One kind of relationship was considered above in our discussion of student society and culture. Common patterns of student behavior constitute a part of the individual student's environment; influences from this quarter may favor or hamper individual development, depending upon their quality and intensity. Another kind of relationship may be indicated here; the present behavior of the individual student may or may not favor the establishment of desired qualities in the personality.

The problem here may be stated in terms of role-demands, role-dispositions, role-performances, and educational objectives. Educational programs are designed on the assumption, which may be explicit or implicit, that if students do certain things in the right way and for a long enough time they will learn or develop in desired ways. In order to encourage appropriate performances, requirements and expectations are defined, and the attempt is made to recruit students who have the requisite abilities and inclinations. Sometimes things go according to plan, and sometimes not.

When educational objectives are not attained there are two major sources of failure. One is that the role-demands are ill-conceived, so that even though students perform in the expected way objectives are not reached, and the other is that the role-demands are appropriate but students do not perform in ways that are correlated with desired outcomes.

The difficulties in the way of knowing what educational procedures lead to given ends have been accented earlier in this chapter. In the present context it will suffice to point out that we may easily be deceived by appearances. Behavior that seems appropriate and attractive may not have the desired implications for the future. For example, students may meet the demands of a program of independent study by studying independently, but instead of developing independent habits of mind they may generate an extraordinary longing for authority and regime. To take it the other way around, rebelliousness or noisy complaining may be regarded by teachers or officials as a poor way to perform in the student's role, while actually such behavior may be positively associated with certain important objectives. It is possible that the same might be said for the lack of enthusiasm, even the cynicism, that seems to be so common on our campuses today. Probably a more clear-cut example of inappropriate role-demands is the case in which courses are too easy or too repetitive of what the student has experienced before so that he might do all that is asked of him without gaining anything. What is often true of particular courses may also be true of the whole college experience; the student's idea of a college to which he is suited is one whose role-demands he knows he can meet by remaining just as he is. Thus he might enjoy his association with kindred spirits without being challenged in such a way as to produce intellectual development.

Where role-demands are appropriate the student may fail in various ways to meet them, and for various reasons. He may simply not do what is expected, or he may do what is expected in such a limited way, or in such a half-hearted way, as to render the educational program virtually ineffective. The extent to which students may cut classes, neglect assignments, avoid contact with teachers and still remain in college often seems remarkable. Again, the student may perform with sufficient energy and enthusiasm but in the wrong way. He may rebel when he is expected to conform, or conform when he is expected to be independent. He may use his relationship with a teacher to further his tendency to be dependent when it was hoped that he would find in this teacher a model of adult responsibility.

In his efforts to explain such failures in role-performance the researcher looks for determining factors in the student's contemporary situation and in the personality structure that the student brings to the situation. Perhaps there is misunderstanding by the student of what is called for; perhaps the demands of one part of the educational program are in conflict with the demands of another part; very commonly, no doubt, the requirements of the formal program are in conflict with demands arising out of the informal organization of the student society, out of the student culture, or out of the environment that lies beyond the boundaries of the college. As for what the student brings—or does not bring—to the situation, there may be a lack of ability or of preparation, or there may be dispositions of personality that are peculiarly ill-suited to the academic requirements.

A majority of the students who enter our colleges meet the minimum requirement of remaining for the prescribed period, of four or two years. This means that they adapt themselves in some satisfactory way to the college environment as a whole, and attain at least minimum standards of academic performance and general behavior. Usually they like their college and leave with some regret and with a feeling of having accomplished something. But many—perhaps 40% on the average—of those who enter a given college withdraw from it prior to graduation. For the student this is often a painful experience, and it is always a significant one; the college is in no better position, for it has to face the fact of its failure, either in its selection or in its management of the student. For the private college the phenomenon of attrition is a continuing source of financial headache.

The problem has been the object of much discussion and more than a few investigations. Among the major circumstances of withdrawal, for example, we may distinguish between academic or other failures in the student and pressures from home, between transferring to another college and giving up higher education altogether; and we know that withdrawal is associated with a variety of factors in personality and background. The possibilities of predicting withdrawal on the basis of facts available at the time of the student's entry into college have been explored. The problem is highly complicated, owing mainly to the fact that successful predictions tend to be specific to the particular college, the particular circumstance of withdrawal, and the stage of the college career at which withdrawal takes place. It appears also that factors determining withdrawal are to be found in the student's college environment of the moment. Sometimes counseling will prevent a student's hasty or ill-considered withdrawal, and sometimes a college that is plagued by a high rate of attrition has to think of changing itself. But withdrawal is not considered a misfortune for the student or for the college every time it happens. Sometimes it is the best way to correct an obvious mistake or to induce a necessary facing of reality; sometimes students withdraw before graduation because they have already gained from their college all that could be expected. Leaving college, not to enter any other, may leave a student with a sense of unfinished business that will, in some cases, provide motivation for learning for the rest of his life.

Most liberal arts colleges require that their students enter a major program of study at the beginning of the junior year. This requirement is intended to make sure that the student acquires *depth* of knowledge in some field, breadth being taken care of by his earlier studies and by the usually accompanying minor program. The practice is closely tied in with the traditional way of organizing teaching and research, that is, dividing the labor among a number of specialized departments. Although depth is regarded as an essential feature of a liberal education, it is also generally considered that the student's work in his major may be the beginning of his training for a profession, scholarly or other, and the program of instruction is carried out with this possibility in mind.

For the student, choosing a major is usually a highly significant experience. Often it is the first time that he consciously commits himself to long-range goals after giving due consideration to reasonable alternatives. The choice usually has implications respecting his future vocation, and thus he approaches, perhaps for the first time, a socially defined identity that has an aspect of being irreversible. Choice of major is frequently expressive of deep-lying forces in the student's personality, but, on the other hand, it is sometimes derived from highly superficial considerations. In either case it may be regretted later.

The official expectation is that students will choose, or be guided into, major programs in accordance with their abilities, their enduring interests, and other factors bearing on the benefit they may receive from these programs. This expectation is often disappointed, however, by irrational or nonrational processes at work in the students, and by the fact that the departments, if they are not indifferent to the whole problem, sometimes compete for the ablest students without attention to what might be done for them.

The published research in this area has been directed mainly to showing that students in different major programs differ in various characteristics of personality and background. Little is known of the extent to which the major field attracts students who already possess the distinguishing characteristics of personality, or the extent to which such characteristics are developed through experience in the major program. The fundamental question, of course, is whether the dispositions that lead students to choose a given major field are also favorable to achievement in this field and to a desirable educational outcome.

Intensive studies of individuals indicate that choice of major is the outcome of an interaction of dispositions in the student and forces in his immediate environment such as pressures from his family, his friends, and the college departments. Such studies show that majors are chosen on different bases and in different ways, and they suggest that the basis and manner of choice are related to the student's fate in the major, and later on.

A third important aspect of performance in the role of student is academic achievement. Most of the research in this field has been concerned with the prediction of the general level of academic achievement from test scores or other indicators available prior to the student's admission to college. There is continuing effort by researchers to obtain a differentiated picture of achievement, to delineate different kinds of achievement—or lack of it—in different courses or fields, and to identify specific predictors of these achievement variables. The aim, of course, is to improve prediction, but there is the more fundamental question of how to improve achievement. The performance of the individual student is determined not only by the abilities and dispositions that are present when he enters college but also by a complexity of factors in the college environment. When the ways in which these latter influence the student are sufficiently well understood, it may become possible to modify them in such a way as to raise the student's level of performance. This is a field in which relatively little work has been done.

The way in which a student responds to one role-demand seems to be related to the ways in which he responds to others. If we should identify and measure, in a population of students, a number of characteristics or features (variables) pertaining to behavior in college, we should expect some of these variables to "go together," constituting patterns or types of response in the overall student role.

It is important to mention here also the distinction we have made between behavior and personality. Campus types are patterns of behavior, of response to campus role-demands. Although they undoubtedly depend to some extent upon personality we should expect them to change as the role-demands change or are withdrawn. The relations of campus types to patterns of personality constitute a special field of investigation. One would ask how personality types present at the beginning of college help to determine the campus types, and one would ask how a type of behavior in the student roles comes in time to influence the further development of personality. This way of looking at the college career as a whole may also be adopted when attention is restricted to some part or phase of that career. Thus there might be classroom types or dormitory types, types of freshmen and types of seniors.

INTERACTIONS OF STUDENTS AND EDUCATORS

Much of the life of a college community involves *interaction* of the faculty and administration on the one hand and the students on the other. The conception of students responding to an environment that has been largely made by the educators is, of course, central, but faculties and administrations react to what the students do and thus create new and often peculiarly important stimuli to student behavior —thus starting a fresh circle of interaction.

Let us consider an example. In a traditional college of high quality a majority of the faculty believe they note a serious decline in the general level of the students' effort and performance. As the phenomenon is discussed in formal and informal faculty meetings a sense of outrage builds up, and the general feeling is that there must be a tightening up all along the line. There are heavier work assignments, more frequent examinations, longer papers, more required reading, and classes are conducted in an atmosphere of increased grimness. Now, since for the individual student this discipline comes not from a particular teacher who knows him but from an impersonal "they," and since it is plain that with some of the faculty members narcissistic needs rather than devotion to intellectual aims are involved, the tightening up is generally perceived by the students as arbitrary punitiveness. The students generally, with a nice appreciation of the realities of their situation, but not necessarily with any conscious deliberation, do not rebel openly but respond rather with a kind of passive resistance. They do precisely what is required but no more; they invent and share among themselves numerous devices for judging the exact nature of the requirements and for carrying them out with a minimum of effort; they establish a kind of "norm" for amount of work and make life difficult for the individual who threatens to exceed it. Particularly do they look askance at any student who "gets too close" to any of the faculty, for this tends to break up the general strategy of doing what is required by the faculty without being influenced by them in any positive way. (On the other hand, a certain pretense of going along with faculty values may be allowed—may indeed become fairly general—if it appears that this will help to make life more comfortable.) Since this general pattern of response is very similar to that which upset the faculty in the first place, it is likely to be met with even stricter requirements. The vicious circle becomes increasingly taut. Now the students seek ways to hold the faculty strictly to *their* obligations and, if possible, to embarrass them by requesting more office appointments, expecting papers to be corrected on time, asking about books they suspect the instructor has not read, remaining silent and unresponsive in class. Some teachers do not go along with the majority; they seek to break what has become the common pattern, to "reach" the students. The students will have none of this. They have developed an effective system for handling their situation and they do not intend to be put off by any new or different methods of teaching or any appeals to their curiosity or creative impulses. They hold the deviating or innovating teacher to the pattern that has become common. They have the power to do this, for there are channels through which their complaints can reach the department chairman or the administration, and by now faculty morale has so deteriorated that the enterprising teacher has no assurance that his colleagues will back him up. Happily, the term now ends; the student leaders graduate, the faculty leaders take vacations, and there is a chance for a fresh start.

In episodes of this kind we may not only observe the mutual stimulation of faculty and students, but also we may note that patterns of response generated in one situation are carried over to others, there to give rise to fresh effects. A move of the faculty, initiated in the classroom, affects student-faculty relations in all situations; it also alters the students' ways of relating one to another; the students' reactions to the faculty's move, which may now be observed to have become generalized, not only result in counteractions affecting students, but in tensions within the body of the faculty and, quite possibly, disturbances in faculty-administration relations. It seems that there is sufficient connectedness among the subsystems of a college so that tensions set up in one of them tend to ramify throughout the whole college system. At the same time, in order to explain episodes of the kind just described, it would be necessary to have knowledge of the campus culture and role structure existing at the time of the faculty decision to tighten up; these would be of great importance in determining possibilities and setting limits of student responses, and of faculty counteraction.

Complicated, higher-order processes of the kind illustrated here seem, typically, to loom large in the life of a college community. It is from observation of these processes that one is able to make inferences concerning the general "atmosphere" or "climate" of a college, something that we should expect to leave its imprint on a student who remained there for four years.

THE EFFECTS OF COLLEGE EDUCATION

In confronting the crucial problem of change in individuals due to the college experience, and bearing in mind educational objectives, we have to consider the following possibilities.

a) Things may go according to plan. Examination of students at the beginning and at the end of their college careers may show that they have changed in desired ways and that these changes are due to educational procedures deliberately undertaken.

b) There may be no desired change. It is highly unlikely, of course, that there should be no change of any kind. Rather we should expect changes in directions other than desired ones; these might include the loss of desired qualities that the student once possessed, or the establishment of undesirable qualities. With respect to some important qualities, the student may hold his own; as suggested earlier, a graduate may stand high with respect to some standard of excellence without his having changed appreciably in college.

c) There may be changes in the right direction, but these may have nothing to do with the educational policies and practices of the college. Desired changes may be due to maturation; they may be of a kind such as we should expect to occur under any conditions in any population of college age; or desired changes may be due to incidental features of the college environment, for example, roommates or class associates, or the relative isolation in the company of peers, or the strain created by the requirement of getting a degree. To demonstrate that desired changes are due to educational activities deliberately undertaken, rather than to other influences, is a difficult but not impossible research undertaking.

d) There may be changes of a desired kind—due or not due to the educational program—that can be noted at the time of graduation, but the new state or condition of the individual is not sufficiently stable to serve him in later life. The changes may be unduly reversible under different conditions; on the other hand, the graduate may have attained to a condition that is *too* stable; it may be so fixed as to interfere with his further development—"the perennial college boy."

Thus it is that the study of the effects of college education must be directed both to the phenomena of change in college and to the problem of the lasting effects of the college experience. Such research should address itself to change in general, whether it be, from a given point of view, desirable or undesirable, and whether it be due to formal educational procedures or to other aspects of the college environment. It should inquire into the conditions and processes of change in diverse parts or features of the person, and of change in the way these parts or features are organized. And it should confront directly the problem of distinguishing between change in behavior and change in personality. When the concern is primarily with the latter, it is necessary to use valid instruments for diagnosing or measuring personality itself and to apply them at different stages of the college career, and at later times. The object of such a general approach to the problem of change is, of course, to enlarge our understanding and hence our control, to increase the effectiveness of current educational practices and to design new ones.

Quantitative studies of change in college have been fairly numerous. Most of these have compared groups of entering freshmen with groups of graduating seniors; some have examined the same students, with the same instruments, once at the beginning and again near the end of their college careers; in a few studies the same students have been examined at various intervals during the college course, throwing some light upon the timing of change.

Studies of the lasting effects of college, or of the different aspects of the college experience, have been relatively few. It seems that most attention has been given to the question of what factors in the college situation contribute most to the production of scientists and scholars, and to the question of what is the economic value of a college education or of education at particular colleges. Although the prestige of institutions has depended heavily upon how they fared in studies of these kinds, it is clear that such research has little bearing upon the aims of liberal education. Highly relevant but of little scientific value have been numerous surveys in which graduates have been asked to say what they derived from college or what college has meant to them. Then there have been large-scale statistical studies, usually concerned with other matters, in which college graduates and noncollege populations have been compared with respect to variables relevant to liberal education. There are a handful of studies in which subjects, something of whose college careers were known, have been followed up in later life.

Since the most fundamental questions in higher education can be answered only by considering the durable effects of different systems or different practices, one is forced to ask why this area of research has been so sadly neglected. Here it may be recalled that for the consumer of higher education its general value is not in question. Going to college is *the* road to membership in a profession, and to all the benefits of improved economic and social status. Whenever college graduates are asked in later life what they got out of college they have no difficulty in describing several kinds of important benefits, and also little hesitancy about registering complaints. But the discrepancy between the things that head their lists of benefits and the stated purposes of the colleges is usually glaring. As for the attitudes of college officials and of scientists, it may be added to what was said in Chapter 1 that for the scientist research in the present area is difficult and expensive, and that until quite recently it has not seemed particularly interesting.

There is evidence existing in the literature and in current studies that college does make a difference. Although the college experience seems typically to be incorporated within a life pattern the main lines of which have already been determined, the experience may none the less precipitate in many people crucial changes of direction. The fact that students of personality are more inclined than formerly to attach importance to the college years augurs well for future developments in this field.

CONCLUSION

The approach of the present chapter, primarily an analysis of the college into various component structures and processes that are later to be taken up in detail, may have tended to obscure a crucial conception—each college functions as a whole. But if this conception has been neglected here, it is sufficiently accented in this volume, and particularly in the following chapter by Professor Riesman and Mr. Jencks.

Of course we do not wish merely to breathe the word "whole" and mean by it something that could only be spoiled by analysis. Obviously a college is constituted of various components, and if one is not to content himself with a mere enumeration of these, if he supposes that they can be related in any way other than by addition, then he implies some kind of wholeness. The essential idea was at least hinted at before, the idea of the college as a system each of whose subsystems is related to the others and to the whole. This conception is fundamental to the problem of change in educational institutions. Or, one might state this the other way around; if one knows how an institution might change—what might initiate change and what would be its processes—then there is no question but that he has a good grasp of the functioning of that institution.

We have seen that the college itself may be viewed as a subsystem within the larger system of society. We may concentrate upon the inside structuring of the college without giving the fullest possible attention to the larger system in which it is imbedded, just as we may, for purposes of intensive study, abstract particular components of the whole college. But, as suggested above, when colleges change it is usually because of influences from outside. This means that where our concern is with the improvement of our colleges we must give attention to their interactions with the processes of society. This theme, which was accented in the beginning, in Chapter 1, is one to which we return in the end; it is the focus of concern in Part VIII of this volume.

REFERENCES

Fricke, B. G. Tests, students, standards and admissions officers. In A. E. Traxler (Ed.). *Long-range planning for education.* Washington, D.C.: American Council on Education, 1958.

Levinson, D. J. Role, personality, and social structure in the organizational setting. *J. abnorm. soc. Psychol.,* 1959, **58**, 170–180.

Traxler, A. E. What is a satisfactory IQ for admission to college? *School and Society,* 1940, **51**, 162–164.

Roethlisberger, F. J., and Dickson, W. J. *Management and the worker.* Cambridge, Mass.: Harvard University Press, 1939.

3

David Riesman and Christopher Jencks

The Viability
of the American College

O ur hope in this chapter is to give the reader a sense of the various kinds of institutions that are called "colleges" in America. Our method has been primarily anthropological. We have tried to look at colleges as complex wholes, describing in an impressionistic manner the different sorts of students, faculties, administrations, and publics that have practical and ideological stakes in the colleges, and that provide the faith, hope, charity, tuition, and taxes to allow colleges to grow more numerous in an era when other businesses grow somewhat less so. Both in this chapter and in our other contribution to this volume (Chapter 22) the limitations of our methods and materials cannot be too much emphasized. One of us (Riesman) has taught at Buffalo, Chicago, the University of Kansas City, Johns Hopkins, and Harvard; he has done research at Columbia and Yale, and is presently cooperating with Joseph Gusfield and Carol Kaye in a study of Monteith College of Wayne University and Michigan State University's new branch at Oakland. He took part in the

Note. For support of our work on this chapter, we are indebted to a grant from the Carnegie Corporation. Our approach has been greatly influenced by that of Everett C. Hughes (see the chapter by Hughes, Becker, and Geer in this volume). We are indebted for helpful criticisms to many friends and particularly the following: W. H. Cowley and his associate, J. B. Hefferlin, who allowed us to draw on their wide knowledge of the development of higher education; Bernard Berelson, Richard J. Storr, Wagner Thielens, Jr., Ralph M. Rust, Martin Trow, Burton R. Clark, Joseph Gusfield, Robert H. Knapp, David Gottlieb, Charles A. Bidwell, Jacob Getzels, Reece McGee, Adam Yarmolinsky.

Fund for the Republic's 1955 survey of the attitudes of social scientists at a sample of accredited institutions, visiting some 40 colleges and universities and studying interviews done at 130 more (Lazarsfeld and Thielens, 1958). He has also profited from the research on student culture carried out at the University of Kansas by Everett Hughes, Howard S. Becker, and Blanche Geer; and from analogous work at the Center for the Study of Higher Education in Berkeley. The other (Jencks) was a student at Harvard and a graduate student in the Harvard School of Education; he spent six months enrolled as a student of San Francisco State College, brief periods as an observer at Boston College and the University of Massachusetts, interspersed with visits to other New England institutions. Anyone familiar with the extensive work at, for example, Vassar or Kansas, will realize that such superficial experiences are no substitute for an anthropological field trip or a social-psychological survey, even when supplemented by informants, and by published materials such as histories, catalogues, and student newspapers. Although succeeding chapters in this volume deal with such discrete facets of a college as admissions, pedagogy, and alumni, we have hoped to place all these problems within a broader context, and thus have sought to make sense of activities that when taken in isolation sometimes appear bizarre or malignant.

THE COLLEGE AS AN INITIATION RITE

Whole libraries have been filled with books on higher education in America, and much can be learned from some of them. (See, e.g., Schmidt, 1957.) Many have been historical studies either of the single institution or of an educational tradition. Others have been quantitative appraisals of logistic problems in contemporary higher education. Our effort here is somewhat different: it is to compare colleges not only with each other, but with other institutions, such as factories or mental hospitals, and by a series of analogies to seek to relate what happens in college to other aspects of our national life. We risk the dangers, and invite the stimulation, of analogies and metaphors that may sometimes appear far fetched.

Looked at in terms of a theory of the labor force, one might describe colleges primarily as personnel offices, feeding properly certified employees into business and the professions. Some colleges supplement these general efforts by direct tie-ins between their education division and local schools, their engineering division and local industry, or their business division and local commerce. And most colleges inevitably participate in the informal network through which graduates of each college tend to recruit fellow alumni, or perhaps more correctly, alumni of their own fraternity or territory. Such enclaves may help explain why alumni of Harvard, Yale, and Princeton have incomes 30% higher than graduates of other colleges—or even the fact that half the trustees of major philanthropic foundations hold degrees from Harvard, Yale, or Princeton (Havemann and West, 1952).

But why, we may ask, should business and the professions depend upon colleges for employees, and why should scholars oblige by supplying them? During the 19th century, American higher education was not so heavily age-graded as it has become since, and college was not seen as a necessary prerequisite to the study of law or medicine. However, as the country has gotten richer, and the professions stronger, the latter have been able to postpone choosing their apprentices, compelling the colleges to provide a litmus for measuring both intellectual and social aptitudes. Quite arguably it is also true that the apprentice can be more readily turned into a respectable and responsible citizen, as well as a more discerning student of his specialty, if he has had the extra four years of collegiate education. But beyond such more or less rational considerations, the American college exists as a vast WPA project, which gives promising adolescents work to do while keeping them out of the job market, and also keeping several hundred thousand faculty members off the streets. Of course, such a comparison seems to ignore the great numbers of undergraduates who are actually in vocational programs, such as engineering, education, business administration, or nursing; however, many of the students in these apparently preprofessional programs are not actually committed to a career, but still shopping around. Several years ago, the *Saturday Evening Post* ran an article, "Are We Making a Playground out of Our Colleges?", which reflected the attitude many solid citizens had, during the Depression, to the WPA; such citizens failed to appreciate that it has become increasingly hard in our society to maintain a sense of worth without a degree; and that college does make possible (in Erik Erikson's term) a moratorium in which an individual has a culturally-justified pretext to spend four years growing up before committing himself to a career and a style of life. And as the WPA provided a good deal of valuable theatre and art, so the colleges provide cultural festivals for their communities, ranging from shows of contemporary music and art, or the many lecture series for adults, to the festivals for real and vicarious alumni provided by football.

To carry further the WPA analogy, it is difficult to say to what extent colleges, along with the rest of the educational system, train students to respond with a disciplined attitude toward work not of their own devising (and therefore provide employers and professional schools with a good yardstick for determining who will do well in highly organized and authoritarian settings), and to what extent colleges help inculcate a distaste for work precisely because of its frequently imposed and "alienated" quality. Certainly, quite apart from the technical skills acquired in college, the colleges do provide the locale for inculcating the social and personal skills on which employers put increasing emphasis, the more so since they themselves are increasingly college trained. For this purpose the curriculum is important only insofar as it spills over from the classroom to the dining hall, from the library to the fraternity, from the teacher-student to the administrator-student and student-student relationships. One major influence of most occupations on the attitudes of the worker is to encourage him to meet some people, and to prevent his meeting others. The same thing is true of a college. In this perspective it may be helpful to view the college as a human relocation project that removes a student from parents, community, and employment to submerge him in the "student culture" of his adolescent peers. In general, what a college does is to "nationalize" the student, taking him out of his ethnic, religious, geographic, and social parishes, and exposing him to a more cosmopolitan world in which the imagination is less restricted by preconception and ignorance. Even in the worst colleges, emancipation from the older generation can be stimulating. Many of the Negro colleges from which lunch-counter sit-ins were begun were institutions of low standards, which offered little to their students other than an opportunity to enter a sector of the "black bourgeoisie" sheltered behind the wall of segregation. And although the innovations of the younger generation in most contemporary colleges take less visible and less political forms than this, or the radicalism of the Thirties, it is too soon to say that the revolution of social and personal style that has emerged in the colleges since 1945 will have less significant effects on the shape of society.[1]

Ideally, of course, this emancipation from preconception and ignorance brings the student into an international, if still largely Western, Great Society which traces back to the Greeks. But such emancipation from national and historical prejudices is less common

[1] Yet, as the autonomous republic of the young extends its influence back into adolescence, it may be that colleges will lose this kind of importance, just as paperbacks, the mass media, and better teacher training have deprived many colleges of their monopoly on introducing adolescents to ideas, though adolescents so introduced generally continue into college.

than the partial escape from local parishes, into a regional, a national, or occupational one, for it depends upon the faculty and the curriculum, rather than on the students and the extracurriculum. In all but a handful of colleges, the student culture outweighs the efforts of the faculty to make direct contact with the students even when, as occasionally happens, these efforts are more than perfunctory.

All the above metaphors can perhaps be subsumed by the anthropological notion that college is an initiation rite for separating the upper-middle from the lower-middle class, and for changing the semiamorphous adolescent into a semi-identified adult. All studies of taste and opinion suggest that one of the great cultural cleavages in our society is between those who have been to college and those who have not. To go to college is to join what commencement orators call "the fellowship of educated men," and what Vance Packard more sceptically dubs "the diploma elite" (Packard, 1958). In part, this transformation is a matter of faith. People go to college expecting to become the upper-middle-class heroes and heroines who populate the American vision of the good life. When they graduate, they feel that they have "arrived," and they are changed by their very faith. Their new perception of themselves as responsible and respectable citizens is re-enforced by the fact that other people who have also "arrived" accept them as employees, husbands, wives, and friends, and expect them to play the role of the "educated" man. In this way some colleges may have a delayed effect, influencing students only after they have graduated, and must play the "college man's" role. Other colleges, catering to an upper-middle-class constituency, have no such impact on students who already reflect the collegiate values of their families.

By standing as the watchdogs of the upper-middle class, the colleges have greatly circumscribed the range of behavior common among the national elite. Indeed, a number of well-to-do young men, romantically convinced that the school of hard knocks produced greater diversity and excitement than going to college, drop out of college for a term or a year to hit the road or take on jobs, serve their term in the army, or seek the exotic or the difficult outside the country. Correspondingly, even the educated upper-middle class is far from homogeneous. Furthermore, precisely because college is now the gatekeeper to the upper-middle class, as well as a decisive influence on its styles of life, every minority group of any standing in America has an interest in preserving or creating colleges to suit its own particular needs. Hence we have some 1200 accredited (and over 200 not accredited) four-year colleges, each trying to initiate its students into the national diploma elite while also keeping them within the bounds of some narrow parochial tolerance. At the same time each enclave, whether geographic, ethnic, religious, occupational, or sexual has helped maintain the pluralism of even the upper social strata. Efforts to found a National University after the Revolution having failed, and an Establishment being only an Anglophile's dream, no uniform concept of what a college ought to be has prevailed in America. Nevertheless, minority interests, though in sum coloring and shaping the majority, are individually on the defensive. As American nationalism, the national economy, and the mass media reflect an increasing uniform color, colleges tend to copy one another in order to be sure of keeping their programs acceptable as certificates of respectability.

An additional complication is introduced by the fact that, while every college begins as the creation of a special minority interest group, its establishment makes it in some measure autonomous. In almost every case a college is first and foremost an economic enterprise, whose primary goal is survival. The trustees may, for example, be deeply committed to the education of Lutheran ministers, but they will not usually insist on this objective if the President tells them that their college will be bankrupt if it does not open its doors to other groups. Many colleges have in fact gone bankrupt, victims of the business cycle, of mismanagement (and very rarely, fraud), of sectarian competition, and of the characteristic American hopefulness that leads people to start small businesses over and over again, despite previous records of failure, temporarily subsidizing the community with their energies. In general, diversification brings stability to a college, as to other economic enterprises, and so the student body tends to become ever more heterogeneous. Each college gradually incorporates more of the tendencies generally found in the national upper-middle class, and thus becomes an agency for its further homogenization. Thus our hypothetical Lutheran seminary first admits local Lutherans who do not want a pulpit because the alternative is to send local churchgoers to a godless public college, while bankrupting the seminary. But once nonclergymen come, non-Lutherans apply for teaching jobs and are hired because no competent Lutherans apply. And so gradually the upper-middle class loses some of the puritanical ferocity that the old Lutheran preachers provided. At the same time, because this once-Lutheran college is available as a standing advertisement for attending college in its area, new social strata, previously not oriented toward higher education, tend to be drawn into the college-going group. Thus, although on the one hand the national academic disciplines and national student recruiting bring uniformity to higher education at one level, the very existence of such higher education brings into the upper-middle class diverse elements from depressed strata from which the elite were formerly more insulated. In an effort to encompass this diversity, we shall look at the occupations, religions, geographic regions, ethnic groups, sexes, social classes, age groups, political groups, and intellectual cliques that have a stake in higher education.

Occupational interest groups. In the Colonial Period some of the zeal that went into the founding and maintenance of the first American colleges came from the fear of educated immigrants that their children, born in less urbane surroundings than their European parents, might revert to barbarism. This fear evoked an effort to perpetuate the educated classes, which in most areas meant both the ministry and the class of gentlemen. The first American college, Harvard, taught Greek and Latin, which were not only the languages of clergymen, but also the symbols of the gentleman—indeed the aspiring clergyman needed these to be a gentleman if he was to command the respect of his parish. Grammar and rhetoric, philosophy and mathematics, were part of the formal curriculum; table manners and deportment, part of the informal. In Puritan New England during the Colonial Period, the scions of the merchant leisure class could not be sent for finishing to the Anglican colleges of Oxford and Cambridge, and even in the South distance was often such a problem that the Tidewater gentry had to settle for William and Mary. In all these institutions, the mixing of prospective clergymen with the sons of the rich and would-be rich tended to produce more worldly clerics—and to lead to the creation, temporarily, of newer, dissenting colleges of greater orthodoxy and less splendor, until these latter colleges in turn followed the primrose path.

This pattern of mixing occupational and social training persists down to the present day. Hundreds of colleges have been founded to provide some community with theologically orthodox leadership that could not be conveniently recruited from colleges elsewhere. As the theological and geographical schisms that generated the new college faded, the institution could no longer count on recruits and patronage from those who once thought its ideological specialization important; and so most such schools have expanded, sometimes to train men of several faiths, but more often to train nonministers who at least nominally hold to the college's beliefs. Such expansion has produced alumni of less religious commitment, who have in turn opened "their" college to new cadres of unbelievers or indifferents. Equally important, religious sects have tended to upgrade themselves socially, in part through these very colleges. As a result a pulpit that at first needed only a smattering of Biblical passion eventually demands a man with a liberal education who can converse with the now educated parishioners. Once the facilities for such instruction are provided, they can seldom be supported solely by future preachers. Yet even today there are nearly 500 theological schools, of which more than half are not part of a larger educational enterprise.

Even so, in the last century the need for ministers has inspired fewer new colleges than has the need for teachers. In the late 19th century, state normal schools spread across the country to provide teachers for the ever increasing primary school population. As the demand for secondary teachers caught up with the demand for elementary teachers, normal schools became teachers colleges, with liberal arts divisions. Conversely, liberal arts colleges added education units in order to cash in on the single biggest source of potential college students. Today the majority of teachers come from liberal arts rather than teachers colleges. With this distinction of purpose abolished the former teachers' college is likely to feel that it is distinguished only by low prestige and low standards, and will move with all possible speed to emulate the liberal arts college program. Furthermore, once a liberal arts curriculum is established, the teachers' college becomes suitable for the education of students headed for other careers, and resembles the liberal arts college even in its clientele.

In general, normal schools have changed faster than theological schools, because being under public control they could more easily find funds to redefine themselves, and being virtually without tuition, could more easily recruit new species of students from the armies of high school graduates to whom some kind of college training now seemed important. As a result, there are probably no more than 100 teachers' colleges left in the country, while another 200 colleges, which were formerly exclusively for teachers, today train students in the liberal arts, and sometimes also in professions other than education.

The growth of higher education in this era also created an unprecedented demand for college teachers. Scholars have generally found it easier to recruit within existing colleges than to found new ones for their own purposes. But the exceptions are interesting. When the academic profession emerged in America in the late 19th century under a heavy Germanic influence, several efforts were made to found universities, like Clark and Hopkins, that were "purely academic" (Storr, 1953). The German pattern, however, could not be transplanted unamended, partly because, as we have suggested, institutions devoted solely to graduate training and research had no ready source of recruits in a nation without a long intellectual tradition, and partly because even philanthropy could not keep universities solvent without tuition-paying undergraduates. More recently, the academicians have won foundation support for research institutes, miraculously cleansed of students. Yet scholars have often been unhappy in such an other-worldly setting, for without apprentices they have no excuse for those unproductive periods when no idea seems to flower. Lacking the attitude toward leisure that made it seem natural for All Souls College in Oxford to have no undergraduates when the endowment was sufficient, the research institutes have mainly been attached to universities and have employed their scholars only part-time, although such developments as the Stanford Research Institute, with its large contracts in science and the social sciences, may be closer to the more academic commercial laboratories such as Bell Telephone, General Electric, or RCA than it is to the Ford-financed Behavioral Sciences Center nearby.

The failure of the 19th-century universities has not, however, meant a complete rout for the academicians. Today there are perhaps three dozen universities that turn out almost all the doctorates in arts and sciences (Berelson, 1960). But none of these universities has seriously considered abolishing the B.A. degree, or eliminating undergraduates; some have merely neglected them; some (Columbia and Chicago) have set up semiautonomous undergraduate divisions; some (e.g., Harvard) have merged graduate and undergraduate instruction as much as possible.

As the academic profession itself, that is, college and university teachers, rise in power and prestige (cf. Lipset, 1960, Ch. X), the academic profession itself becomes a serious competitor with law, medicine, and engineering for talented students. College teachers are seldom professionalized as such, particularly so in the better institutions, but rather as members of a discipline who understandably prefer to send their favorite students into that discipline rather than into one of the other professions. Hence the graduate schools of law and medicine, and perhaps particularly those that insist on four years of college from their applicants, may increasingly have a hard time holding their own. Their problems may become similar to those of Clark and Hopkins, when, as wholly graduate universities, they lacked an undergraduate feeder college. As things are now, however, the major professional schools prefer to put off selection of their apprentices until they have had four years of college. This not only means that they are more mature, but it also means that they have had at least two years of a quasi-apprenticeship to some academic discipline. It is apparently easier to tell who will be a good medical student if one has some idea how he fared on the road to becoming a biochemist, just as it is easier to tell who will be a good lawyer if one has some idea how he did as an historian. Of course, the fact that such specialization provides useful predictive data is no guarantee that it provides useful pre-professional preparation. Two years of "majoring" may be just an extended medical aptitude test. Indeed, some professors of medicine urge this view, saying that they have to teach all the required scientific material over again in medical school anyway, and that the only point of undergraduate requirements is to allow the medical schools to reject misfits instead of having to flunk them out. On the other hand, there is much to be said for consecutive specialization in distinct fields. The lawyer who has learned something of the intricacies of economics or chemistry or philosophy may be both a better lawyer and a wiser man. Whether he would have been better off devoting the same time to a nonspecialist's reading of "Great Books" is an open question.

The preparation of school and college teachers was only one need that led to the creation of colleges. Some of the presently leading institutions have grown from the demand for trained engineers, ag-riculturalists, veterinarians, and technicians of every sort. Congress was moved in 1862 to pass the Morrill Act to provide for the training of such men and women in what were often called Colleges of Agri-culture and Mechanical Arts. In states that were relatively new these land-grant colleges often attracted an increasingly wide cross section of students not envisioned by their founders. This magnetism was enhanced in those states, such as Minnesota, Wisconsin, and Nebraska, that combined the technical college with the state university. In con-trast, such growth was retarded in states like Massachusetts, which had a tradition of private education and were long unable to see what legitimate functions a public institution might serve beyond those specified by Congress.

Like colleges for teachers, these vocational colleges were unable to retain a purely preprofessional program. Even before the Morrill Act, reformers like Francis Wayland at Brown had tried to replace the prevailing classical exercises by a curriculum (influenced by German examples) that seemed to him more adapted to a modern scientific and cosmopolitan age. Such hopes, and the analogous ones of Henry Tappan at Michigan, were defeated in part by the unwillingness of students and their parents to accept an education that was defined as socially inferior, and in part by the bitter rivalry of sectarian institu-tions (see Storr, 1953; also Riesman, 1959b). In general, under the Morrill Act the same pattern we have seen elsewhere has been repeated, if in less dramatic form, with the result that although the nation has 100 schools of agriculture and 200 schools of engineering, all but about 50 are under the aegis of a comprehensive college or university that lends the facilities and prestige of the "pure" liberal arts disciplines to technical programs.

So, too, the hostility of the liberal arts faculty toward preprofessional subjects has operated to prevent some economics departments from offering accounting, limited the clinical work in some psychology departments, and kept some departments of natural science from allotting as much space to engineering as the potential enrollment might justify. (Analogous fears or snobberies have been one element in keeping the performing arts out of many curricula—this in addition to uneasiness as to how to evaluate them in comparative and credit terms.)

Yet although all efforts at vocational training have been increasingly permeated by the liberal arts, and the vocations thereby elevated to more dignified positions, there are seemingly endless new occupations whose practitioners want colleges oriented in their direction. One recent area of rapid growth has been "business education," sometimes under the auspices of local magnates who want recruits, but more often sponsored by colleges which want to attract and retain local students to whom the liberal arts seem irrelevant and difficult. In many urban communities, a "Bus. Ad." program seems eminently practical, indeed a competitor in this respect with engineering to the first generation college student and his parents, as well as to the local business-class trustees, who may not themselves particularly want or need recruits, but who may feel that this is a way to keep "their" college soundly afloat. Yet often this enterprise turns out not to be practical at all. "Business" is not one but innumerable occupations, many of which are not easy to conceptualize for anticipatory training (cf. Merton, Reader, and Kendall, 1957); thus courses in business law often are more a laying on of hands to reassure students that they have learned something real than any introduction to the legal problems a businessman might confront. As a result, many undergraduate schools of business, despite the courses in marketing, production control, and so on, have in effect transformed themselves into second-rate departments of economics, with a smattering of social science and writing courses thrown in. Thus, their function has more often been to provide would-be businessmen with academic credentials than to provide them with any useful information. Unfortunately for the students, many personnel offices have discovered this, and increasingly prefer liberal arts graduates who are likely to be more sophisticated. One consequence of this development has been a greater interpenetration of business and academic values, at least in the upper reaches of large business enterprise. Like such graduate schools of business as Chicago, Harvard, and Carnegie Tech, some of the better liberal arts colleges have put scholarly men as gatekeepers on the road to economic success, so that the more ambitious and able students, if not deflected from business altogether, are prepared for business roles which will allow them to use their new-found intellectual powers. Although in the most selective colleges there seems to be an increasing tendency for students to avoid business careers altogether (cf. Riesman, [1959a]) most upper-middle-class college graduates consider business quite respectable and help to make it so as executives who are exposed to, and to some extent influenced by, such "academic" values as breadth of view, scepticism, and the ability to master complex chains of information.

The spread of the degree-hierarchy has encouraged many occupations requiring even less technical expertise than business to seek a certificate to set them off from mere high school graduates. For many this distinction has come from the two-year A.A. degree awarded by the junior colleges. But although these institutions were often founded to provide such terminal vocational programs, they have rarely been content to tie themselves to middle-level occupations. Today only one junior college student in three takes a vocational program, while the other two begin a transfer program that would, if completed, allow them to spend only two years away from home for the B.A. instead of four years. By encouraging the junior college to prepare them for further academic work, these transfer students have contributed to the diversification of junior colleges much as nonministers, nonteachers, and nonfarmers initially broadened more single-minded colleges.

The junior college has grown so fast in recent years, especially when known as the "community college," that it is now proper to speak of the junior college "movement" (Clark, 1960; Medsker, 1960). Many of the nation's junior colleges are supervised by local boards of education, some use the buildings of the local high schools, and most have recruited their faculties largely from secondary school teachers. Thus, the junior college may become, in its academic temper and its conciliation of local "needs" and powers, a near-automatic upward extension of high school to the 13th and 14th grades—an easy option for students who are not yet prepared to make the decision, or whose families cannot afford the sacrifices, that going away to college might entail. In this way, many students gain a higher education who would otherwise never encounter it, and the more academically alert and ambitious are encouraged to transfer after two years to a more substantial institution. Unfortunately, some students are also restrained from moving on by the established tendency of private institutions in the East to look askance at transfers, an attitude reflecting their high initial admission standards and remarkable ability to graduate nearly all they do admit. (More vacancies could be created by taking fewer freshmen.)

Some junior colleges have been tempted to retain gifted students by expanding their program, improvising a bachelor's degree that succeeds in holding students who would be better off elsewhere. If, on the other hand, the B.A. becomes established, the college is likely to neglect those seeking a technical degree in two years even though these may remain the great majority. But partly because the faculty without Ph.D.'s fears for its status and security if their institution upgrades itself, and partly because of a genuine commitment to general education for the many, most two-year colleges remain such. Academically ambitious faculty must either get out or be satisfied with the vicarious achievements of their protégés. In this they share a problem of the four-year college teacher who must watch his best students move on to graduate work elsewhere.

One further species of vocational training deserves mention, especially as it is in some ways quite distinct from the other patterns we have sketched. The authors know almost nothing about the specialized colleges of art, music, and design, such as Juilliard, Curtis, Pratt Institute, the Chicago Art Institute, or the Rhode Island School of Design. Some have followed the standard pattern of spicing their offerings with a heavy dose of general education and offering the B.A. But some apparently inspire a clarity of purpose and ambition that makes such paraphernalia seem unnecessary—something to be picked up on the side rather than made part of the educational machinery. These colleges can perhaps afford their indifference to the liberal arts partly because their recruits are often arty youngsters from culturally sophisticated and sometimes wealthy homes. Furthermore, many of the students see the arts and their future role as closely related to the general intellectual culture, and often in opposition to the "collegiate" values and "square" society that force other preprofessionals to acquire all the symbols of the standard B.A. More certain of their place on the intellectual and cultural map, they perhaps do not need course credits to establish it.

In addition to the institutions just mentioned, there are other variants that train students for specific occupations, instructing how to set up a broadcasting system for an underdeveloped country, or teaching ceramics, or indeed almost anything that one can find in the Yellow Pages of the phone directory. But here, too, occupational minorities come to college only partly to learn a trade. They also come unconsciously (or sometimes consciously) hoping to learn a social role and to become a certain kind of person, and this hope has allowed many colleges to use the degree as a lever for upgrading an occupation socially and intellectually. Technical curricula which could be mastered in two or three years now include "general education." This means not only that the program gains social eclat by taking four years and awarding the B.A., but also that entrants are entitled to think of themselves as professionals, and in addition to be at least casually familiar with "culture" and other marks of social sophistication. In part such shifts have been justified by vocational arguments. The liberal arts are supposed, for example, to teach engineers to communicate verbally with one another, and thus make them better engineers.

Another important consequence of "liberalizing" engineering is to help make this a possible career for upper-middle-class students, whose parents have been to college and who are therefore likely to regard a little culture as a *sine qua non* of any collegiate program. Such students have traditionally taken a liberal arts degree and then gone into law or medicine or business. But as the number of students from college-educated families grows, and as the prestige of the business world falls in the better colleges, new professions must be invented to supplement law and medicine as high status pursuits. By coming to terms with "culture," engineering and applied science, architecture and various forms of civil service, are attempting to fill this role, hoping to combine the economic rewards of business with the intellectual appeal of science, as medicine (and law, in another sense) have long done.[2]

One difficulty is that as technical colleges add liberal arts programs, the combination, although undoubtedly producing better employees and citizens, may keep out some of the traditional socially-mobile recruits who believe they can only afford a four-year meal ticket and have no time for "cultural bull." Furthermore, the seduction of the

[2] Not only do the more well-to-do and cosmopolitan students want to study engineering at a college that is not simply an "engineering college," but they also want to keep open the option to move into another specialty; this is one attraction that Yale or Stanford have for some prospective engineers and scientists, in competition with MIT or Cal Tech.

upper-middle-class student may be but a brief affair, for such students are likely to be sensitive to the intra-academic snobberies that make engineers less worthy than physicists and chemists. Under these circumstances the college that gets "too good," as Cal Tech and to some extent as MIT have done, may find itself turning out scientists instead of engineers. This is very satisfactory for the institutions, but by training its potential elite for another calling, it defeats the efforts of the engineering profession to upgrade itself. Similar problems arise in some schools of education, such as at Berkeley or Columbia's Teachers College, where graduates may become professors of education instead of "mere" school superintendents.

In similar fashion, a debate is under way within the business community and within educational circles concerning the advantages of liberal arts training as a basis even for technical industrial jobs. Increasingly, the men at the top insist that they prefer men initially trained in the liberal arts, in part because this has become a fashion, but in part also because of the awareness that the scientific revolution has outdated technical skills almost as fast as it has required them; hence many employers have discovered that their technicians must rapidly be replaced by younger men who know more recent developments, while older men must be given administrative positions that require the ability to organize one's fellows instead of the material environment. At the same time, at the lower levels of business that put specific job descriptions in the hands of campus recruiters, the demand often remains for the "tech" graduate. Many businesses have found it necessary to retrain these often gauche technicians when they are promoted to managerial posts—and even then they often find that men with a purely engineering background cope badly with many administrative problems whose intricacies apparently defy purely rationalistic analysis.

Thus, while some can proclaim the decline of the liberal arts, and note that two bachelor's degrees out of three are outside of the arts and sciences and that at least four in five are vocationally oriented, others can note that these officially preprofessional programs conceal much study that has no direct relevance to the students' future work and can be justified, if at all, only on intellectual grounds. Unfortunately, these courses taken as "general" education are likely to be as preprofessional as the student's own specialty, being aimed primarily at preparing specialists in another field. The engineer who optimistically enrolls in a literature course in order to broaden his mind will sometimes discover that literary criticism can be as narrowly technical and unintellectual as his courses in civil engineering, and he is likely to conclude from this that books are a waste of time, for he will usually not realize that the course is more or less unconsciously designed as a step toward membership in the profession of English.

The authors are backhandedly defending vocationalism here against merely narrow-minded snobbish criticism. In purely numerical terms, the liberal arts are better off in this country that at any time in the past. Thus it seems likely that if one examined the academic training of influential Americans in 1900 and 1960, today's elite would have spent far more time studying at least nominally liberal subjects. To be sure, many more would also have had vocational training, but it seems paradoxical to assume, as many humanists do, that "liberal" subjects are worse off when men study engineering than when they leave school after the eighth grade or after high school. It is true enough, as this section has shown, that hardly any American institutions can claim academic purity. The fact that colleges must serve many masters offends those who want institutions to serve a single clear-cut purpose and who perhaps correctly fear that what they most deeply care about cannot survive in pluralistic competition.

Religious interests. While occupational minorities have played an important part in encouraging new colleges, religious groups struggling to maintain orthodoxy have also been important. Originally this involved the "occupational" problem of getting theologically competent ministers to defend the faith, but usually the new colleges had the more general purpose of keeping the social elite of the faith within the bounds of orthodoxy. To exemplify from one small geographical area: Harvard was founded to help the Puritans escape Anglican Oxford and Cambridge, and Yale appeared in 1701 when a group of New Haven ministers, influenced in part by distrust of the liberal heresies that were coming to dominate Harvard, established a competing college to preserve the old social and religious order in Connecticut. Again, the Congregationalists who founded Amherst were in part moved by objections to the Unitarianism that shook Harvard in the early 19th century, and the Yankee Methodists who set up Boston University at the time of the Civil War felt that Harvard's classical curriculum and aristocratic values were destroying the ethos of pious dissent. The same era also saw the Jesuits establish Boston College, to help the new Boston-Irish community maintain its religious and social integrity in a Protestant society.

Today there are nearly 700 church-related colleges scattered across the country. About 400 (not including ones that have wholly left the fold) remain Protestant or Protestant-related, while nearly 300 are run by Roman Catholics. The Catholics, although late comers in the college-founding business, have now nearly caught up with the Protestants. Although theologically more uniform than the Protestants, competition and jealousy among the various Orders have resembled the rivalry among Protestant sects and have contributed in the same way to the multiplication of the Church's colleges. Contrary to what many think, there is no comprehensive plan for Catholic education in America, and many colleges have no better reason for existence than, let us say, the desire of Franciscan Fathers not to let the Jesuits capture all the talented local youngsters, or perhaps the conviction of the Dominican Sisters that the local Sacred Heart College is snobbish or intellectually radical.

Among the Protestant sects, only those with a completely rural base, such as the Amish and Hutterites, have been able to resist college altogether without losing their most ambitious and talented young. Other groups born into a tradition differing from the standard American brands have, if denominationally organized or bounded, ended up with the compromises of a college, and have gradually been "Americanized" both by their colleges and by other institutions until they are no longer "minority" groups. The smaller and more evangelical Protestant sects, such as the Seventh Day Adventists and Mennonites, have continuously faced the dilemma: either to try to keep their young people from attending worldly and hence corrupting colleges, or to found their own and see them in the course of time become more worldly. One by one, however, the quainter severities disintegrate, and the general American youth culture, led by disc jockeys in addition to community-minded clergymen, takes over. Middle-class values even infect the management and there is ample material for irony to be found in both Roman Catholic and Protestant intramural literature that in one breath attacks American "materialism" and in another boasts about the millions in new buildings and the tens of thousands in new students that will be forthcoming if current fund drives succeed—no doubt to the greater glory of the spirit.

The ties of the major Protestant denominations to "their" colleges have become increasingly attenuated, and subventions from the churches, although still of great importance, especially in the smaller institutions and in the South, seem less and less able to assure solvency. No less important, the merger of Americans into a kind of ecumenical Protestantism, impatient of sectarian distinctions, has lessened the monopolistic position of any given Methodist, Presbyterian, Baptist, or other college over a particular flock. Such monopolies survive only in the more other-worldly sects, such as the Adventists, whose tiny colleges barely stay afloat on the piety of their constituencies and the poverty of their faculties. The better established church-related colleges increasingly compete for the same students and endowments as the nonsectarian institutions, and can often be distinguished from the latter only by such archaisms as compulsory chapel, a few ministers on the Board of Trustees, and a tenuous connection with a mission college in the Middle East or Africa. Whatever the osmotic pressure of the Congregational tradition at Oberlin, the Episcopalian at Kenyon, the Quaker at Swarthmore or Bryn Mawr, these and similar colleges live today for all practical purposes in the secular world of the private institutions, seeking good students and faculty from everywhere and with every shade of belief and unbelief. In fact, publicity makes clear that Wesleyan is Methodist neither in management nor support. In a number of these liberal arts colleges, however, the surviving and tenuously religious tradition does have an impact in engendering or at least preserving among some of the students an interest in the public weal and even in public service (what would in an earlier day have been termed "Christian social action"), so that students from Oberlin, Swarthmore, and Wesleyan, for instance, often emerge with social and civic concerns linked to their academic ones.

Although comparable forces have been at work on Catholic education, the Catholic colleges will not necessarily become secularized, either *de facto* or *de jure*, as so many of the Protestant-founded ones have done and are doing. To be sure, if one resorts to analogies with Protestant developments one can discover in some Catholic institutions occasional "Jansenist" notes that remind one of the harsh asceticism and the fear of the gracious and worldly intellect that dominated some small, perhaps especially Southern, Calvinist colleges during the Jacksonian epoch and later. Moreover, the ethnic enclaves within Catholicism are not likely to resist general American patterns of commerce, intellect, and art. One can find a few small Catholic girls' colleges, run by teaching Sisters, that assure the parents of a safely hermetic, if not ascetically uncomfortable, education for their daughters. But such insulation within Catholic education against general American values seems rare. Catholic higher education (like Catholicism generally) copes with secularization by partial incorporation of it. Thus, the architecture of Catholic colleges, where they are not the converted mansions of the once-rich, is generally not ascetic but meant to be imposing—even though until very recently it has seldom been avant-garde and is about as tasteless and imitative as American collegiate architecture generally. The better girls' colleges seek to introduce their graduates to upper-middle-class "gracious living" and smile correspondingly on the arts, accepting these as part of the female stock in trade; a few of the best women's colleges (e.g., the College of New Rochelle, or Manhattanville) go further and sponsor an intellectuality that can be spirited and unparochial. And the best men's colleges and universities—many of them run by the Jesuits—foster an intellectual competence and assurance that, if not quite as cosmopolitan as many Catholics and non-Catholics would wish, still preserves the graduate from discomfiture at his first exposure to non-Catholic thought and experience.

Many problems of secularization, however, have been postponed rather than solved. Although of course some Catholic colleges and universities go back a long way in American history, most have been founded fairly recently to cope with the upwardly mobile children and grandchildren of Catholic immigrants; and they have perforce been founded in communities, mainly urban and suburban, where Protestant or secular colleges already existed. Hence, few Catholic colleges have thus far had to cope, as the Protestant ones did earlier, with students of different faiths who could not or would not go elsewhere for an education. Permanently, and as ethnicity dries up, it will be more difficult to maintain a "separate but equal" pattern on solely religious grounds. To be sure, another bulwark of orthodoxy only recently threatened has been the fact that many students came to a Catholic college as the first in their communities to seek higher education, and often looked forward to life in the same religiously homogeneous community. They were happy to attend a Church college as a sign of continuity between past and future. Moreover, many priests teaching in such colleges are themselves the sons of such families, for in America as in Quebec and elsewhere, the upper social strata have been chary of the clerical life, especially as it is not for them a channel of social mobility. Thus, priests and students, sharing an ethnic and familistic as well as a religious culture, have been able to share and support each other's sense of beleaguerment in America as a way of coming to manageable terms with the American scene.

However, as the appended vignette of Boston College may serve to illustrate, the story does not stop here. In recent years the teaching Orders have had to staff their colleges increasingly with laymen, particularly in the sciences, also drawing on non-Catholics; in many institutions the priests or nuns are now in a minority. Although clerical control of the institutions themselves remains intact (where they exist, Boards of Trustees, made up of prominent Catholics, have little au-

thority and are relied on primarily for fund-raising and public relations), the drive for academic respectability forces the abdication of
control over the "objective" subjects to the national academic disciplines, just as happened earlier in the Protestant-controlled colleges.
Few leading Catholic educators believe there is such a thing as "Catholic history," or "Catholic economics," let alone "Catholic physics";
to be sure, a Catholic economist may emphasize some of the less bourgeois and capitalistic teachings of the Papal encyclicals, just as a Catholic historian may try to counter Lutheran treatments of the Reformation. Leading Catholic laymen argue that Catholic students should
"get to know the Protestant viewpoint" by reading Protestant books,
if not by hearing Protestant teachers. Although in some dioceses (e.g.
St. Louis) Catholic students are under clerical pressure not to attend
secular institutions, a handful of Catholic educators (including the
Headmaster of Portsmouth Priory, an elite boys' boarding school) has
argued that a gifted Catholic student will do better attending a secular university, not only in terms of a more secure access to the main
streams of American intellectual life, but also in terms of finding his
own Catholicism strengthened there. For example, Newman Clubs in
secular colleges may offer a more realistic foretaste of the role of a
Catholic in America than do solid phalanxes of often complacent Catholics in Church colleges.

Suddenly, a whole new wave of upper-middle-class or would-be upper-middle-class Catholic students is attending college, and an enormous building and development program has been maintained by
Catholic educators and communities to keep up with the new requirements; and although some of the poorer students could be and sometimes are left to the equally expanding public institutions, an effort
has been made to find places within the Catholic fold for all who
could do the work. This movement has paralleled in some considerable measure the renewed interest in religion characteristic of postwar
America (cf. Herberg, 1955). Charter membership in the anti-Com-
munist club has helped speed acceptance of Catholics in some circles
where tolerance of other minorities is still slight. In this situation,
many Catholic colleges could offer a religious appeal not coupled with
serious social disadvantage. For most students, the demand for a reconciliation of Catholic ideology and secular thought is no more pressing than analogous problems for nominally Protestant and Jewish
students; for all three, discrepancies are handled by compartmentalization rather than by transformation.

But neither the best teachers nor the best students in the Catholic
universities are satisfied with such compromises. Even though they

can understand, they can also regret the relative paucity of Catholic contributions to scientific, scholarly, and intellectual life in the United States, and some may look longingly at the achievements of Catholic universities in Louvain or Milan, much as Protestant divines in the last century may have looked longingly to Augsburg or Basel or Edinburgh. As already implied, it is hard to sort out what is specifically Catholic in the dissatisfaction with Catholic achievement in American academic life from what is specific to the lower social strata from which many Catholics come. The upper-middle-class Catholic college graduate, when it comes to deciding where his own children shall attend college, may be torn between his feeling that most students and teachers at Catholic colleges are socially gauche and intellectually unsophisticated and his fear of disloyalty to his community if he seeks an "aristocratic" Catholicism of the European variety by sending his children to the leading secular colleges. (Of course, the state universities have the additional competitive advantage of low tuition.)

On the whole, what is striking here as elsewhere is the historical ability of the Church to expand and to hold within its orbits such conflicting departures and desires. The flood of newly college-conscious students who are attracted to or satisfied with the traditional type of Catholic college has not blotted out all attention to the small, self-conscious, intellectual minority who want these colleges to become more cosmopolitan. Yet the long-run future remains opaque. With the possible exception of the Mormons, who have brought to higher education the same enormous communal zeal as to other activities in the state of Utah, no religiously-oriented culture has so far managed to grapple with modern industrial society in the United States in a way that is satisfactory to the most sensitive and talented. The campuses where religious interests seem most intensely intellectual (as distinguished from devotional) are often the secular ones where Tillich and Niebuhr, Berdayev and Barth and Buber, Bernanos and Father D'Arcy, are read and discussed. On a Catholic campus the very presence of Churchly religion may somewhat minimize the search for personal insight that is characteristic of the religious concern among some Protestants and Catholics today. Many lukewarm-Protestants and lukewarm-Jews discover in secular colleges that their sect is a remarkable historical and intellectual achievement that can provide a frame of orientation, if not of devotion (cf. Fromm, 1950). On Catholic campuses too, the personal meaning of religion is brought home for some, while its social taken-for-grantedness is reinforced for most. Though so far as we know no satisfactory study exists, it would seem that the national scholarship and recruitment programs have done more to draw able Protestants away from Protestant-controlled colleges than to lure Catholics from the Catholic ones (see Knapp and Goodrich, 1952; Knapp and Greenbaum, 1953). Thus the Catholic colleges would seem to have a good deal of leeway to redefine their several missions. For the time being, we suspect, Jesuit practicality will continue to syncretize with American pragmatism, while Personalist, Integralist, and other variants, either dogmatic or profound, will remain small minority tendencies.

Geographic interest groups. We have seen that ethnic differences have been intertwined with religious ones in generating new colleges; so, too, geographic and religious interests have sometimes worked together. Thus, when the Connecticut ministers founded Yale, religion was only a symptom of a broader difference and of jealousy between Massachusetts and Connecticut, and when the Amherst divines revolted against Unitarianism a century later, they may have succeeded less because of their theological orthodoxy than because they represented the underprivileged western half of Massachusetts against the dominant Bostonians—a theme we return to in the appended vignette on the University of Massachusetts. One reason for the founding of colleges so quickly after the Indians were expelled from the western wilderness was the new states' desire to resist Eastern snobbery. Such resistance has never gone so far as to establish the prestige of locally relevant curricula such as those attempted by the founders of many land-grant colleges. But the local college has kept the American provinces from falling into the servile and impoverished condition of the European ones, by assuring that many able local youngsters can get a local education without being seduced by the great cosmopolitan centers. Most local institutions walk a fine line between being too local to help their alumni represent their parish on the national scene, and being too national to allow their alumni to remain satisfied with local life. The conflict is often acted out in dramatic battles over academic freedom.

In general, however, the provinces are becoming more cosmopolitan, and so are their colleges. In many Midwestern colleges the cadre of self-conscious intellectuals, usually said to come from "New York," is growing in both numbers and influence. (Many of these students are of course not from New York at all, and many who do go to the West or South from New York City are in flight from its provincialism.) We are developing a national market for college recruiting. Students are now solicited from all directions who would once automatically have attended either the nearest denominational institution, their parents' school, or the state university. And as this process robs the local institutions of their presumptive customers, they are in turn forced to expand their orbits of recruiting to compete regionally if not nationally. Just as many local brands of food have given way to the chain store brands, so students everywhere are gradually becoming conscious of the fact that they might apply to Cornell, to MIT, to Harvard, to Michigan, to Stanford, to Oberlin, or to Haverford. And even if large scholarship aid goes only to outstanding athletes and scholars, still the stir made by the recruitment of these individuals leaks over into the general college-bound population and helps to widen horizons of choice.

Ethnic interest groups. Among new colleges resulting from ethnic differences, the most noteworthy have been the hundred-odd institutions primarily for Negroes. But many newly-rich Jews, perhaps inspired by the wave of ethnic chauvinism attendant on the founding of Israel (or in a few cases, looking toward America as against Israel) have organized to found Brandeis and go after academic, social, and architectural distinction in a big way. Similarly, ethnic considerations play a role in the multiplication of church colleges, with French Canadians, for example, preferring Assumption College in Worcester to "Irish" Holy Cross or Boston College, or with Swedes supporting Gustavus Adolphus in Minnesota against neighboring Norwegian St. Olaf's.

Feminine interest groups. Although Oberlin admitted women in 1837, three years after its founding, and although the Universities of Iowa and Cornell also did so quite early, higher education for women continued, throughout the 19th century, to be regarded as debilitating to mind and body by many in both sexes. Today, women are the most numerous if not the most influential minority seeking higher education, constituting a third of the college population. The colleges founded for them in the 19th century in the already male-dominated East sought in general to provide them with the standard educational paraphernalia; Bryn Mawr, which went furthest in this direction, established standards higher than those of any men's college as an "answer" to discrimination. Some of the colleges founded in this spirit, like Radcliffe, have been virtually absorbed by the masculine models. Others, notably Mt. Holyoke, emphasize the sciences as well as the humanities in the hope that some girls will follow in their faculty's footsteps, rather than merely accept membership as walking delegates for culture in a suburban elite—matters touched on by Mervin Freedman in Chapter 25 (see also Riesman, 1956, 1960).

Only in the intellectually laggard institutions has the notion that women are the "opposite" sex led to an effort to create an equally "opposite" form of education. In some of the Southern women's colleges this has meant an emphasis on social skills and gracious living, and in the Catholic women's colleges, which constitute three-fourths of the nation's 200 feminine institutions, a similar emphasis on "learning to live together" is often evident. Sometimes, especially in coeducational colleges, the quest for distinctively feminine training produces programs in home economics (which can become a highly scientized and difficult kind of "women's engineering").

As the most obvious distinctions that once held women within narrow boundaries evaporate, so too the feminist counterattack of the "Seven Sister" colleges tends to disintegrate, and it is not easy to see what form the women's colleges, or "feminine" programs within the coeducational ones, can take in the future. One can imagine, with a declining work week and a lengthening life span, that women in college could prepare themselves for careers that might serve as insurance against widowhood and against having to marry (or to feel stuck with a bad marriage); these could also be pursued on a part-time basis subsequent to marriage and while the children are small, and on a more full-time basis later—at least if the alleged shortage of trained personnel eventually minimizes the prejudices against women employees in responsible posts. Women students who are clear about such long-run aims would help create a stimulating milieu in the colleges. At present, however, the most talented women college students hope to get married but see little way of linking their college work to their image of a future life. Caught between old and discarded goals and new and as yet undiscovered ones, it may be hard for the best women's colleges to maintain their present enviable standards of academic instruction, particularly as the ablest Ph.D.'s increasingly want to teach in the big universities and don't need to begin their careers as talented teachers of girls. Thus the long-run future of the separate women's colleges, especially outside the Catholic fold, or possibly even within it, appears as unpromising as that of the colleges set up initially for other disadvantaged groups.

Social class interest groups. Depressed social strata have also discovered in the colleges a useful instrument for legitimizing their position in society. Many American colleges are in touch with what is, in effect, a "backward country"—steeped in a rural tradition that has hardly been touched by the industrial revolution or the bourgeois cosmopolitanism that produced the Enlightenment. In many rural areas these colleges recruit directly from the farms. In the cities they recruit from second- and third-generation immigrants who came to urban America from an almost medieval peasant life and are now suddenly equipped with money and ambition to seek the symbols, if not the content, of higher education. In the countryside there have long been teachers' colleges in which, as Everett Hughes has pointed out, not only are there no broadly educated professors, but also no member of the faculty has, in his own schooling, encountered a broadly educated man. Similar phenomena are now visible in the cities, where the culturally backward groups that inundated the high schools after the First World War have been moving into the colleges since the Second World War. A generation ago most urban and sub-urban colleges were staffed with more or less standard versions of the Yankee college graduate. Today there are many institutions in which almost the whole faculty consists of first-generation collegians —young men in a hurry for social security and professional respectability. The old-style intellectuals are a minority, perhaps holed up in one of the humanities departments, or perhaps in the administration, when this is more than a sprawling civil service. In such settings tastelessness and laxity may not only feed on themselves but also renew themselves in the oncoming generation of teachers, and teachers of teachers. Of course some of the most cultivated men in America have been rebels from such depressed social strata. But such transitions were easier when students were self-consciously mobile and came to college hoping to change—as indeed they still do in England. Today assimilation may work the other way, and the more cultured faculty may find themselves gradually reduced to the level of their students. Thus many colleges can do little to alter the parochialisms of the culturally impoverished whom they equip with a diploma and other symbols of acceptability. Yet here again the pressures for academic stature in the faculty, and cultural savoir-faire in the students, gradually push the college toward a more sophisticated outlook, and gradually push the second and third college generations toward better institutions and higher standards.

Adult interest groups. Some colleges have actually begun as night schools for adults, and have gradually added daytime programs to produce a more stable economic picture, more efficient utilization of faculty and plant, and sometimes more responsive students. Other night schools have been marginal ventures, sometimes added by existing colleges to balance the budget and to keep the faculty in pocket money, or else established as hand-to-mouth experiments by dedicated men who hoped that higher learning might reach people as adults whom it failed to reach in adolescence. Adult education enrolls more than twice as many students as the regular colleges.

Political interest groups. It is worth noting that, although colleges have been founded to serve the special interests of occupational, religious, ethnic, geographic, sexual, social-class, and age groups, the relatively unideological cast of American politics has meant that no college has survived that was founded simply to turn out good Democrats, Republicans, or Progressives. Occasionally political movements capture a department or even a school within an existing institution, but the Universities of Wisconsin and of Minnesota are unusual in having once led as well as reflected the liberal political energies of their respective states.[3] And although, on the other side, many colleges have come under the wing of local conservative and reactionary groups, these have seldom founded colleges to perpetuate their creed but rather have used their power to monitor existing institutions with an eye to their preferred values. This seamy story of business control was once mordantly exposed by Upton Sinclair in *The Goose Step* and Thorstein Veblen in *The Higher Learning in America.* Today, scholars are in a much stronger position than when Sinclair, Veblen, Ross, and other muckrakers and academic critics sought to defend the classroom against the power of wealth. This is not because the American Association of University Professors (or even the American Historical Society, the American Sociological Association, or the American Chemical Society) is a strong union; regrettably, the procedure of the AAUP in investigating and blacklisting offending institutions can harass but seldom effectively counter the recalcitrant, and only a few college faculty members have joined real teachers' unions. But at least big business has become more civilized—some would say merely more subtle—and more hesitant to throw its weight around. At the same time, scholars have tended to become safer in the sense that they are less polemical, and the indirect impact on them of living in a climate shaped by American industrialism has been more effective than direct business pressure. In any event, arguments over capitalism as such have been caught up in the larger global issues

[3] The political impact of these state universities is not entirely dead even now. Thus, Senators Humphrey and E. McCarthy of Minnesota reflect the civic-minded and liberal climate of the state university, whereas a number of the Congressmen who banded together as a Liberal Study Project attended the University of Wisconsin.

of the Cold War (and in the South, the race war), and the principal pressures here have come not from businessmen but have been mobilized by demagogues like McCarthy, by church and veterans' groups, and by the press.

Philanthropic interests. Taken together, the interest groups we have described shape higher education in America. Few have been happy with the compromises they have had to make for the survival of a college, and still fewer have been pleased to discover that, having labored together, they bring forth progeny with a life of their own. This is what it means to speak of a college as an institution: that, once it is established, those nominally in charge become more interested in the college's survival than in the welfare and contentment of the interest groups that fathered it; and, metaphorically, a college gradually comes to have more respect for its "peer group" of other colleges than for the public that stands in *loco parentis*. When this happens, as we have indicated, the academic profession gradually comes to supplant its competitors as the dominant though never the sole voice in the operation of the college.

In theory this professionalization should be wholly praiseworthy, for if academicians were truly professional educators, they would presumably be able to serve competing interest groups better than these now serve themselves. Sometimes this actually happens. For example, we would argue that occupational interest groups that insist on a narrowly vocational curriculum continue to defeat not only the academicians who denounce them, but also their own self-interest. So, too, many youngsters who come to college simply to secure admission to the next higher social class do not understand the requirements of social mobility if they think that four years of unalleviated dedication to a mindless fun culture will suffice. And we might say the same for many other forms of special pleading, both local and national, that academicians feel they must resist.

The difficulty is that, although professional educators might in theory arbitrate the claims of competing groups and force them all to take a long rather than a short view of their interests, there is no such profession of higher education. The only aspect of college life that has been professionalized is research, and the professional scholars, as one occupational group among many, are often only trained as educators on the job and do not consider this their principal function. To be sure, there exist professionally committed teachers whose lives are dedicated to producing the right kind of alumni rather than to the equally important but different task of pushing back the frontiers of knowledge. But there are no graduate schools that offer an academic equivalent to the clinical years in medical school. There are no professional standards governing classroom activities, comparable to the standards governing research work. There is no effort at evaluation of teaching by outsiders, comparable to the evaluation of research. (The chapters by Katz and by Adelson [Chapters 9 and 10] indicate some of the subtleties that would be involved in such evaluation.) There are hardly any graduate schools that make a serious effort to induct graduate students into teaching, in contrast with throwing them as underpaid auxiliaries into large introductory classes to sink or swim, haze or be hazed (see Berelson, 1960). And of course if the situation in teaching is amateurish where it is not worse than that, the overall operation of colleges is frequently chaotic and improvised without being creative. Despite efforts, notably at the Harvard Business School, to give some minimum of training to college administrators after their selection, the administration of higher education has not been professionalized. This reflects partly the envy and resentment that college faculty members, along with other Americans, share against "bureaucrats," but this disdain has not prevented bureaucracy in the pejorative sense, but only professionalization. Of course, we are not implying here that what colleges need is streamlined administration in the clean desk or any other trivial sense; both Franklin D. Roosevelt and Robert Hutchins brought style to their administrations in important areas, even though they would have been dreadful lower-echelon civil servants in less important ones.

Furthermore, the colleges themselves, in their relations to their customers and each other, behave like small businesses before the entry of rationalization or union pressures. In national terms, there are hardly any policies for getting the right teachers and students to the right colleges, and then to the right classrooms. A few private and public commissions have made notable efforts to look ahead at the prospects for higher education, but most faculty members are unaware of their findings, and few colleges can be said to plan their future programs, let alone to support research on the development of the adolescent intellect in college—one reason why the creation of this volume was undertaken. In sum, it seems fair to say that the academic profession has superceded competing interest groups in the field of higher education without doing anything systematic to implement the legitimate aims of the latter. Thus, it is important and proper for scholars to argue that politicians have no business to investigate the political opinions of students, but this does not mean that the political naïvete and indifference of many students is no business of the scholar—indeed, one reason why the politicians have to be fought off is that the campuses most apt to encourage political responsibility are the "radical" ones. Similarly, the academicians rightly denounce vocationalism as short-sighted, but seldom take seriously the legitimate interest of the employer in getting graduates who enjoy work, know what they are good at, and are eager to find out what they do not yet know.

The academic interest groups, like many minorities, including that "minority" in all of us that was once a defenseless child, continue in their season of cultural power their defensive reactions built up in earlier periods. Academic men are more aware of their vulnerability (and McCarthy's heirs will continue to exploit this vulnerability while the Cold War lasts) than of their increasing power. If the academicians are to take over higher education from competing nonacademic groups, as seems likely to us, then they acquire an obligation to consider the colleges' impact, not only on the academic profession, but also on the world as a whole. Of course, professors and administrators appear to glory in that impact when asking for funds or support, stooping at times to link academic enterprises they favor to an alleged necessity of the Cold War. A gay or studious irresponsibility is to be preferred to that. It is even conceivable that parasitic colleges, harmful to their constituencies, could for a time nourish the life of the mind among some of the faculty, but students are of course the next generation of faculties, and willful ignorance of the consequence for them of the four college years creates in the long run, like other vested interests, a decay of the interest itself.

The hegemony of the academicians can, however, still be challenged. Philanthropic individuals and groups, some of them scholars, have periodically espoused an endowed experiment in this larger nonacademic species of education we portray. A number of small colleges have been founded or taken over by intellectuals in at least partial revolt against prevailing collegiate standards. Languishing old institutions, such as St. Johns or Antioch or Goddard, have sometimes been employed for this purpose. In other instances, a splinter college within a larger university has been created, as occurred in the fall of 1959 when Monteith College of Wayne University opened its doors (under a grant from the Fund for the Advancement of Education), and when Michigan State University set up a new semiautonomous liberal arts college at Oakland. But the most common pattern has been to start afresh, hoping to escape the rigidities and orthodoxies of traditional pedagogy, as at Reed, Emerson, Sarah Lawrence, Marlboro, the now defunct Black Mountain, or Bennington.

Hardly any of these institutions has been able to resist the demand that it provide a certain amount of academic paraphernalia, including the B.A., but many have avoided the more unfortunate concessions to departmentalism, graded competitiveness, and social orthodoxy. Today all these colleges increasingly take their faculty from the regular Ph.D. market and accept the regular standards of academic excellence, even though they still retain a sense of special mission and to some extent of independence. Conversely, the nonacademic intellectuals have increasing influence within "academic" colleges, as the creative arts win academic recognition and the more worldly disciplines flourish.

Academicians are not without power against such threats. Regional accrediting agencies have by no means eliminated the institutions that fail to provide academic minima, but almost all the 500 or more such institutions now in business have a marginal existence. A few of the more ambitious ones have banded together into an organization (CASC) that circulates ideas and seeks donations to keep them afloat, pending the attainment of accreditation. Occasionally, experimental and off-beat colleges such as Goddard and St. Johns have had an arduous time obtaining accreditation, with objections based on doubts about financial viability sometimes masking those based on frozen academic conventions. Only a few of the unaccredited institutions, however, are serious educational experiments with high intellectual standards, which lack only the money to buy academic prerequisites; many are simply diploma mills. As more and more students are interested in their acceptability to graduate schools, the unaccredited colleges have difficulty recruiting students; lacking students, they cannot get money; still, the durability of some of these institutions in the face of chronic crisis testifies to what to the outsider might appear to be misplaced zeal.

One of the writers, surveying the evolution of higher education five years ago in lectures at the University of Nebraska (Riesman, 1958a), concluded that while on the one hand the market pressures we have been discussing bring enormous activity and stir to the college scene and although colleges are therefore becoming more sophisticated and more academic (for much the same reasons that all America is becoming more cosmopolitan and metropolitan), on the other hand there is little effort to chart or even imagine programs of reform that might lead colleges away from the gathering American norm. Resistance to that norm, we would now add, is often merely nostalgic, juxtaposing the pastoral colonial college against a modern, impersonal university by the same mythology that peoples 19th-century farms and small towns with nascent Jeffersons and Lincolns. But this picture, whatever its period genuineness, is more often an excuse for laxity than a spur to innovation. The other traditional model that still seems alluring to many, is the European or British elite institution with its quasi-extraterritorial autonomy, though this too is a vanishing dream.

Yet there are instances where colleges have looked to the future, not the past, have developed and maintained a radically "un-American" subculture—and yet have survived. One of the most remarkable examples is Reed College, founded in 1911 with an exalted dedication to the highest academic and intellectual standards, and to the freest teaching and discussion. Operating with little endowment in the face of periodic financial crises, confronting a periodically hostile local public, lacking national support until very recently, and producing neither athletes nor Nobel prizewinners to earn publicity, it has still managed to attract an outstanding student body and to establish its viability as a fact of life. Enormous dedication is the price of liberty in such places, but conversely, liberty is likely to breed dedication, and new colleges with a unique platform have a greater chance of achieving distinction than those colleges that attempt to compete with established institutions on the latter's ground.

THE COLLEGE AS A SUBCULTURE

In describing college as an initiation rite, we have employed a variety of metaphors such as "personnel office," "WPA organization," and "relocation project." All involve comparisons with other American institutions. Yet a college is not only an institution, but also a subculture through which some students pass for a few years and to which faculty and administrators are likely to dedicate their adult lives. To the extent that a college is a subculture, with its own idiosyncratic customs and concerns, an anthropologist can study it in much the same way that he studies a primitive tribe or a modern community.

Although an increasingly preponderant majority of American anthropologists are attached to universities, only two have, to our knowledge, had an opportunity to look at their native academic tribe (Carl Withers, briefly, at Yale a dozen years ago; John Bushnell, recently, at Vassar). As is clear from the bibliography appended to the "Jacob Report," most investigations on campuses have been made by psychologists concerned with the impact of a particular course, or four-year sequence of courses, on the affective and cognitive development of individual students (Jacob, 1957 and see Barton 1959 and Riesman, 1958b). This is well enough but needs supplementing by anthropological field work that embraces not only the students, seen as individuals, but also the "student culture," the "faculty culture," and the other subgroups that make up the college.

Of course no college is immune to outside influence, because students have parents, and close to a quarter of American undergraduates are also married. Furthermore, most students have had jobs, and all have future occupations. Even among the faculty, aspirations and friendships often extend beyond academia, if only because no American is immune to messages from the mass media, and these are often at odds with the ideas and attitudes that the college culture purveys. Likewise the social scientist who attempts to study colleges as subcultures can escape neither his own background and his own experience in college nor "contamination" by the general American norms and their campus variants.

Geographic environment. Anthropologists have done much to explain the cultural patterns of their subjects by studying their relationship with the geographic, political, and social environment. So too, we may classify colleges by whether they are located in a city, a suburb, or in the country. In a society where there are hardly any hicks any more, and where the mass media have spread urban and suburban values to the remotest spot, location is no longer very important in itself. Rather, it makes itself felt by shaping the residential patterns of faculty and students, and in this way influences the intensity or thinness of their communication outside the classroom. It is no accident that some of the more experimental colleges have been located in the country, building an intense in-group spirit often in opposition to the hostile or indifferent "natives." Relative isolation probably helped Bennington, Black Mountain, Goddard, Antioch, and Marlboro to maintain a certain independence of current fashions in curricular organization. But Reed, Sarah Lawrence, and the University of Chicago under Hutchins, make clear that a strenuous and courageous independence can also be achieved in a suburban or metropolitan setting.

Most urban colleges lack the residential community that, with its Oxbridge and Colonial American image, is associated with high social prestige, and also with the "collegiate" impact of full-time residence. The "street-car colleges," as we have pointed out, are often as provincial as the rural colleges, and as much in touch with the "backward" part of our country. And like the two-year community colleges, few urban colleges represent a sharp break from high school, at least for the student who continues to live at home, frequently attends part-time, and thus fails to establish any firm identity as a college student. In a college that cannot channel leisure, students often fail even to make campus friendships or to maintain them after the term ends and the classroom no longer makes casual contact possible. But such places as the New York City Colleges, Temple, Wayne State, and Roosevelt present quite another model. These have been strongholds of political and cultural emancipation for students from Jewish, Italian, Negro, and other minorities in which parents have had little education. Widespread prosperity and the increasing democratization of the elite private universities have, however, now reduced the importance of these "radical" colleges. Bright boys from the Bronx High School of Science who in the Depression would have gone to CCNY now scatter to scholarship-granting colleges through the East and elsewhere.

Universities in the metropolitan areas take advantage of urban heterogeneity in order to attract a variety of publics to them; correspondingly, faculty members can find intellectual allies among the professional men, writers, artists, and communicators of the city. This may not only help preserve the faculty from narrow pedantry, but may also help raise the city's general intellectual level. Indeed, the symbiotic relation between a university and its community is one of the most interesting and least studied aspects of higher education. Why is it, for example, that Harvard has had far more impact on the educated public of Boston than Johns Hopkins on the educated public of Baltimore? Are we right in believing that Western Reserve has more weight in Cleveland than the not uninfluential University of Kansas City in the latter city? Are the specific qualities of Columbia and of New York University lost in the megalopolis of New York City? To sort out such questions, one would have to examine the university's influence on a variety of local groups, ranging from city planners to the dental association, and from union locals to elite clubs. In general, we can say that the large and well-established metropolitan residential universities, with the exception of Harvard, have tended to lose social prestige among their own local elite in the 20th century, even while they may have gained academic prestige in the country as a whole. Partly, this reflects the displacement of that elite by local poor boys, enough of whom do well on College Board exams to limit the access of the aristocracy. Partly, the universities have suffered from the general evacuation of the city by the well-to-do who prefer the suburbs, and the suburban or rural colleges that are the natural prelude to suburban existence. Thus boys from New York whose parents attended Columbia have been going to Princeton, Williams, Dartmouth, Stanford, etc. And Yale, though in a community of over 150,000 remains suburban in that sense. At times, colleges "born" in the central city have sought to recapture an old constituency or to find a new one by moving to the suburbs. Conversely, many colleges born in the suburbs have been unwittingly "moved" by urban growth to the city, and have likewise been forced to find new publics there. Neither location is likely to yield the combination of economical housing and adequate public schools that faculty look for in the community, and so in both cases the nine-to-five pattern develops. However, to some extent, a big and wealthy university may develop an "island of light" around itself, as Chicago and Columbia have sought to do through urban renewal.

Political environment. As we have suggested, any sizeable educational institution can be seen as a vast relocation project that upsets "normal" ecological expectations, disrupting typical patterns of taxation, land use, housing, and local business. These competitive strains and disruptions have been one source of the frequent political attacks on the colleges, combining economic complaints (usually, as in the charges about tax-exempt property, with little realistic basis) with ideological differences. The leadership in a small town will often coalesce in opposition to the liberals and other deviants at the college, usually in alliance with those faculty members who, through Rotary or sports or ideological ties, have become integrated into the business-minded community of Main Street. (A complex illustration is provided by the ousting of President George Stoddard and others at the University of Illinois after World War II by a combination of Champaigne-Urbana businessmen, their faculty allies, and the Republican-dominated State Board of Trustees.) On the other hand, the sort of small-town hegemony Veblen satirized is rare today, and both open Philistinism and open Veblenism are vanishing phenomena. The colleges that are the principal industry of the towns in which they are situated are often the dominant force in those towns. Some colleges in the smaller border-state communities have, for example, often provided the leadership for racial integration and tolerance. In some cases a good deal can depend on whether the students identify with their liberal professors, with the vocal local community, or remain indifferent. In a large and well-protected university the students may be a relatively minor audience for the faculty, but in a beleaguered college in a small town they can either provide decisive moral support, or else confirm the "deviant" faculty in its feelings of alienation and in its eagerness to get out. Yet even the big universities may be vulnerable, for they tend to employ scholars who, like the employees of other "national" organizations, regard local politics, history, and society as irrelevant, uninteresting, or even contemptible (see Chapter 27, p. 940 ff.). Such men, if not always their wives and children, are permanent strangers in their adopted homes, fleeing to New York or other cultural centers as often as poverty and overwork permit. To be sure, if they sought to influence local affairs, they might become even more vulnerable through arousing opposition, while if they allowed themselves to be cut to the local cloth, they would lose both local and national importance. Large national corporations now are beginning to try to train their local plant managers to take a safe but serious interest in local civic affairs, but the large universities that have been dropped by historical accident here and there on the American map, have not found any similar way to relate themselves at many levels to their local environment.

The environment of a college is, in a sense, a series of front organizations lying between the inner core of discipline-oriented faculty members and the outer rings of community-oriented alumni (and employers of alumni) (cf. Arendt, 1951). The trustees face both ways. In the wealthier private institutions, where to be a trustee is to face at once a great honor and a not inconsiderable task, the president and higher administration have an opportunity to educate the trustees as they are co-opted, and to use them as the first line of defense against outside attack as well as against insolvency. At best, these men are themselves well educated and sufficiently aristocratic not to bow to demagogic and quasi-populist pressures of the McCarthyite sort; their consciences may be mobilized to defend men they would not have in their homes or offices, and to educate students who may displace their own less scholarly children from Alma Mater's freshman class. At a slightly lower level of academic distinction, the trustees may provide an environment of "practicality" in which the president and many socially ambitious faculty members often become enmeshed, with the not infrequent result that principled stands for academic freedom may become attenuated more through jovial camaraderie than through actual bad faith. Liberal and outspoken faculty members quite generally see the trustees primarily in this minatory role, and feel that the trustees should raise money, build buildings, and then go away. Beardsley Ruml's (1959) interesting *Memo to a College Trustee* has therefore frightened or irritated many professors who fear (probably unnecessarily) that it may be a sign of trustee interference with teaching, premised on business values of efficiency and optimal use of "resources."

In the more provincial institutions the trustees are apt to be locally influential businessmen, bankers, and lawyers rather than nationally prominent ones, and pride in "their" colleges may not inhibit interference with its day-to-day affairs. Again, much depends on the strength (and longevity) of the president, and on whether the faculty itself can develop any counterpressures on him to balance the steady weight of community sentiment as filtered through the trustees. Some state universities, such as Wisconsin, Colorado, and Minnesota, have been outstanding in the defense of academic freedom, in the face of dependence on the legislature and the frequent inability of the board of regents (the elected or appointed public version of private trustees) to put up a united front on behalf of the institution. Conversely, there have been cases (as at the University of Illinois) where the regents have run for election on a plank opposed to academic freedom and, far from helping shield the university from aroused or alleged public opinion, have pierced its defenses from within. The proposals for a new college in the Connecticut Valley included selection of scholars as trustees, thus following the long-standing practice among many industrial corporations of inside membership or even control of the board of directors. If pursued, such a scheme might give American colleges the same kind of autonomy as Oxford and Cambridge Colleges where the Fellows are also the Trustees. In the long run, such cutting of ties to the business community would probably mean greater financial dependence on the federal government (as the government has had to step in in England through the University Grants Committee). There would seem to be something to be said for giving faculty members the experience of overall management that membership on a board of trustees might invite.

Like any other organization faced with multiple constituencies, the colleges have instituted public-relations departments in an effort to control or at least moderate the image they present to their public. Naturally enough, these departments also serve to remind faculty members of the tigers—or the customers—at the gates. Public relations activities are both the result and cause of the increasing awareness of all university personnel (including the students) that they may be watched, and that a "foolish" speech or donation may bring repercussions. Inevitably, the president of a university, like the president of a country or a corporation, becomes the chief public relations officer of the enterprise—an activity that, combined with fund-raising, takes him increasingly away from the more discipline-oriented phases of his work, just as it has taken the presidents of other corporations away from their industries into negotiations with Congress and other publics. As a result, the president, deans, and other ancillary non-teaching personnel often become scapegoats for faculty resentment and feelings of deprivation and insecurity.

In the graduate schools and elite colleges the faculty can look for protection to its own outside publics. The professional organizations of the various academic disciplines, the agencies that accredit colleges, and the general intellectual public all offer some support. In the weaker and less prestigeful institutions, as we have suggested earlier, the academic freedom arm (Committee "A") of the American Association of University Professors is more needed, and less able to help. In church-related colleges, the relevant Protestant ministry may be either a bulwark or a fifth column, depending on the denomination, the issue, and the history of previous incidents. Thus in the South the more liberal ministers have supported, and have been supported by, the colleges of the same denomination in tentative steps toward integration. On other issues, such as college humor magazine "pornography," the ministers may attack the college for its alleged secularism and backsliding, although even then the ministers may be less vindictive or zealous than their own flocks. As we have pointed out in describing Catholic higher education, the Catholic colleges are usually run by international orders (and very occasionally by a local diocese), but they are not wholly independent of local Church and business good will. In some Catholic institutions, issues that arise under the heading of "academic freedom" elsewhere are suppressed by the over-riding, if questionable, assumption that all good Catholics will agree, or at least should appear to agree in the face of outside and probably prejudiced inquiry. Where the issue gets too hot, as the race issue in the South has become, it cannot be contained in this way; thus the liberal prointegration policies of Loyola University in New Orleans have been, like the Archbishop himself, under unrelenting pressure from bigoted parishioners.

Social environment. Environmentalism in the study of colleges cannot, however, be confined to geography or politics. In a broader sense, what proves important is the range of publics from which the college recruits its faculty and student members, and this depends on the impressions of the college that are current in various academic and adolescent circles. The brand-name imagery of a college, like a car, is a complex thing, and little research has been done in this area.

Eugene Wilson of Amherst has, however, observantly described the kinds of inane questions evoked by the publicity college students receive (Wilson and Boucher, 1958), and here Douvan and Kaye in Chapter 4 point to some of the irrelevant factors that influence high school seniors in their college choices.

Much of this misunderstanding would occur whatever the colleges did. But as competitive free enterprises, individual colleges have not been willing or able to do much in the way of clarification. Their catalogues are seldom designed to help the high school student distinguish one institution from another, or tell what any of them are like (Fels, 1959). A few colleges have attempted to project usable information into the hands of applicants by such devices as supplying the high schools with College Board scores of entering freshmen (Bowles, 1960). But the majority of colleges have feared that this, or any other form of honesty, would be misunderstood or misused by the applicants. If the median Scholastic Aptitude Test score is high, the college fears this may scare away students with low scores but special aptitudes whom the college wants. If the median scores are low, the college fears freezing its mediocre image and thus obstructing its hope of getting better students. Indeed, most colleges resist consumer research not so much because they don't want people to know what they are now like as because they fear that their shortcomings, if generally recognized, will become fixed in the public mind, and hence be irremediable. Most secular colleges want to change faster than the "natural" evolution of their constituency would allow. The surplus of applicants in perhaps a hundred of the nation's colleges has helped these institutions to attract new constituents in keeping with their new images of themselves. All colleges seek such freedom even when, like Reed, their few applicants are mostly the "right" ones for the college, or when, like a few of the most sought after institutions, their admissions officers sometimes feel they could pick as well by lot as by free choice among the many highly qualified applicants. Graduates of evolving colleges often discover that their sons cannot gain admission and that "their" fraternities are now inhabited by liberals and semi-intellectuals who want to open the club to those Jews or Negroes who, by the newer liberal-intellectual college standard, may be the elite rather than the dregs.

Although college officials have been anxious to give themselves as much leeway as possible in picking their freshmen, they have shown very little consistency or planning in the formulae used for selection. These formulae compromise the pressures from alumni, faculty, parents, and high schools more often than they reflect any quasi-empirical determination of the optimal combination of students for mutual development and learning. Many admissions officers maintain considerable skepticism about psychological testing, as about sociological theories on the optimal balance of psychological types. They have sometimes found, for example, that when they fill the college "by the numbers" on College Board scores, the annual increases of ability recorded by these scores far outstrips anything the classroom teacher can detect. Reliance on these tests—and reliance on school recommendations or alumni interviewers, also—may eliminate some off-beat and creative students who make good scholars, and often make an important contribution during or after college (Getzels and Jackson, 1959). And of course reliance on such quizzes also may eliminate the sons of alumni, and thus not only constrict present financial support for bright students, but also eliminate the unscholarly students who in the next generation may have to subsidize the research of their more brilliant classmates. Some of these problems of the more selective colleges might be alleviated if tests could be developed to measure creative gifts that are not "purely academic." But there is a self-defeating quality in the very competitive climate that depends on tests, and McGeorge Bundy speaks in one of his papers of students who can even imitate creative thought, if that will get them an "A" (Bundy, 1959). And if the college itself validates its students only through grades, the result may be to engender feelings of inadequacy among those who do not do well by the going standards, while not providing a diverse and exciting student life even for those students who learn to win at the academic game. For reasons suggested in Chapter 1, the colleges where this kind of damage is done to the most talented and gifted are precisely among those where there is the greatest fear of social science and the greatest resistance to research that might discover these consequences and invite alternatives. Conceivably, these colleges may cling to haphazard admissions procedures, not because they think tests inaccurate but because they fear they might really work, leaving no defense against the creation of some brave new academic world.

These are problems of surfeit, based on the success of the brand-name and the attraction of students whom most colleges would be glad to have. Indeed the majority of institutions have no image whatever, other than the local coloration provided by one of the interest groups described in the preceding section. Many institutions, especially but not exclusively the newer ones, are seen by both high school and college students as essentially similar—just plain "college" (Clark, 1959). Students choose these imageless institutions because they are

convenient or because they offer some half-desired occupational training, or for other unformulated reasons. Yet such colleges, or at least
several hundred of them, are rapidly acquiring new constituencies,
often faster than they can handle them. There are deans whose most
difficult days stem from conflicts between the avant-garde students
from "New York" who run many provincial college newspapers, and
the fraternity boys, often from small towns, who still typically dominate student government. Faculty members find themselves in similar
positions, overflowing the traditional elite into the newer public
colleges. These, having grown up overnight, have no notorious academic image either positive or negative and provide a kind of ambiguous respectability while the faculty looks for a more congenial
community. Although these colleges may fear that consumer research
would scare away the talent they hope to attract and ruin their chances
of becoming something better, good college applicants are multiply-
ing so rapidly that many mediocre colleges will soon become much
better no matter what the public thinks. Perhaps the fear of consumer research is actually based on many colleges' desire to go on
fooling themselves (Caplow and McGee, 1958).

Much of what we have said so far would indicate that the relationships between colleges and their constituents are entirely irrational, based on imagery that the college manipulates or finds manipulated, without regard to reality. Often, this is true. But colleges do
provide communities with a variety of services or "products," and it
is by the quality of these that the college is known, at least partially
and occasionally.

The most obvious "product" of colleges is alumni. We have said
something above about the ways in which colleges are founded to
produce special religious, social, ethnic, and occupational types, and
how these specializations are gradually obscured as the college diver-
sifies its recruiting and its products. At least among the well-established
colleges, the alumni are probably the group who do most to determine
the brand-name image, and to keep it a generation out of date. These
"alumni-image" colleges tend to attract students familiar with the
world of college graduates, who can afford to want "culture" and
"liberal education"—partly because their vocational training will
come in graduate school or in a business that is likely to share their
values. Furthermore, the "alumni-image" colleges attract students who
want to become like these alumni—sophisticated and suave, and able
to converse, argue, and administer. This requires "collegiate" training, rather than a more technical program in business, engineering,
or some less liberal field.

At times the faculty in the better "alumni-image" colleges see their function as "training for leadership," through some American version of the Oxford "Greats" in which classics, political philosophy, and related humanities are geared to the recruitment, vocabulary, and cultural style of the prospective elite. Such a program can combine conservative and radical premises and consequences in paradoxical ways. Thus, professors who see themselves as handing on a cultural tradition that is classic, cosmopolitan, and in some sense "un-American" may place inspiration ahead of information in their teaching, and may try to convey a sense of historical perspective and detachment, or a style of poised responsibility, qualifying the future graduate to take charge of men and events—the style of a Roosevelt, an Acheson, a Harriman, or a Stimson. Such professors, typically in the better "Ivy" liberal arts colleges, fulfill themselves vicariously in their students' accomplishments in the great world, not in their own world of scholarship. In the women's colleges, such teachers transmit to their students a sense of civic responsibility, turning out future members of the League of Women Voters, the Board of the Museum of Modern Art, the PTA, and Volunteers for Stevenson.

In less happy outcomes, including many second-rate "Ivy" colleges, such training produces, not a sense of noblesse oblige but a comforting sense of the rightness of one's privileges. The unreflective conservatism of these students is barely ruffled by their professors, among whom the few radical ones may be regarded as entertaining, while the rest are to be got round as the price one has to pay for keeping up the fraternity's grade-point average. Although training for real leadership requires that the prospective leaders acquire a dedication to discovering the direction toward which they want to move men and shape events, what happens in most cases is that the future "leaders" are equipped to become "managers," with the unconscious cultural biases and fashionable flexibilities that will make them the prisoners of events and of stronger men.

The more serious and scholarly faculty members of most colleges are not happy about providing a patina of cosmopolitanism and a taste of literacy for "junior organization men" who will make more money than they, already have better cars, and who seem from the outside to lead untroubled happy-go-lucky lives. The result is a symbiosis in which the faculty proselytize for graduate school among the minority of politically, culturally, or intellectually alert and avid students, while subjecting the great majority of "stupid," "apathetic," and "anti-intellectual" students to only cursory screening—flunking out the most inept, and allowing the rest to coast through. Both the intellectuals and the indifferents are usually willing enough to accept the bargain, and it is a rare teacher who blames the curriculum rather than the students for majority apathy, or who seeks to proselytize for his values among the normally untouched. In most middle-level colleges there is the old eccentric professor who knows more football scores than most of the students, who "talks their language," and who ends up much like any "old boy" alumnus. But there are also men who have not allowed the gap between "we" and "they" to defeat their efforts to give the average student above-average ideas and values; a few such men can have an enormous impact (see Knapp and Goodrich, 1952).

But although the production of alumni dominates both the organization and imagery of the better institutions, there is a whole new echelon of colleges, especially among commuter colleges and community colleges, that produces not alumni, but simply education. This is true both literally and figuratively. In the literal sense, most of the students enrolled in these colleges never take a degree. Many are extension students, night students, and part-time freshmen and sophomores, seeking to "improve" themselves, or to accumulate course credits, rather than to become some new kind of person or acquire a new style of life. These colleges are often compared to supermarkets, and the analogy is apt in that it highlights not only the diversity of their offerings, but also the spirit in which they are taken.

When students come to a college to get its diploma, rather than to become its alumni, vocationalism thrives, both because most students are not going to graduate school and need certification for jobs, and because they are usually the first college generation, brought up in a psychology of scarcity, and unwilling to waste good time and money on "culture" and curiosity. They need a rationale for their college work, and this rationale usually comes from the pocketbook, rather than from seemingly vague theories about "broadening the mind." Such first-generation students are often as immune to the traditional "collegiate" round of football-fraternity-frivolity as to the intellectual claims of the academic world. In this, of course, the "diploma-image" college only emphasizes what has happened at all colleges in the last generation—a general toning down of adolescence, and breaking of the age-grade, so that as youth becomes more protracted and students enter work later, adolescence becomes more like adult life. This is manifested in the gradual substitution of unglamourous and proto-marital going steady for what Willard Waller a generation ago called "the rating-dating complex" (Waller, 1932, cf. Blood, 1956).

The job-orientation encouraged by such sophistication is often merely a veneer. Outside the scientized fields like engineering there are few students simple-minded enough to believe that their vocational courses are going to teach them the things they will need to know at once on their first job. They gulp eagerly for crumbs of "practical" information and "realistic" technique, but the majority in fields like education and business administration seem merely to want to accumulate enough credits to get a job. They count on learning the work after they are hired, and in this they are mostly correct. Such students only rarely respond to the introductory courses that are intended to broaden them, but the reason is not always that they are lazy, nor that they are Philistine (although many students of limited aims and limited backgrounds still are Philistine). Rather these students have answered the perennial question "What are you going to do when you grow up," and they are not prepared to involve themselves deeply in ideas that appear to be other people's business.

The production of alumni and course credits has been supplemented and sometimes supplanted by the production of collegiate imagery and romance. This has usually been dramatized to the public on the sports pages and has required the acquisition of at least one big-time athletic team. The disappointments referred to at the outset of Sanford's opening chapter are the outcomes of what we might term "romance-image" colleges. In many colleges, as he suggests, the romance image is kept alive in the present generation, despite the fact that an increasing number of students have some aspirations to "culture," and considerable reservations about mere muscularity or joviality; it is only when their reservoir of seriousness about college evaporates with disuse that they begin to view their freshman year as an academic requirement to be got out of the way so that they will be eligible for a fraternity. On the other hand, the romance imagery and the social and athletic distinction that goes with it have allowed colleges to attract students of considerable ability who come from such impoverished backgrounds that neither they nor their parents could imagine attending college for solely intellectual reasons; and some who come to a romance-image college to participate in the fun culture, stay to learn about the academic culture.

Only a few colleges have been able to predicate their publicity primarily on their intellectual productivity. In some urban colleges, this means producing lectures, little theatre, concerts, museums, extension courses, and television programs. More often, it means producing scholarly and scientific research that creeps into the consciousness of the high-brow and upper-middle brow public through the book review sections, the better monthly magazines, and the "little maga-

zines," and such other organs of diffusion as the education section of
Time. With such an appeal, the "idea-image" college can often afford to forego or at least de-emphasize athletics. Sometimes the alternative appeal is in the name of science, as at Cal Tech or MIT,
or to some extent Reed or Chicago. At other times the appeal is in
the name of a broadly humane culture, often romanticized with
real or imaginary bohemianism or radicalism, as at Reed, Chicago,
Columbia, Harvard, and to a lesser extent Swarthmore and Antioch.
Similar processes work in those women's colleges that do not themselves play football, but bill the football weekend as an integral part
of their social appeal. Here again the hegemony of entertainment can
be broken by a scholarly image such as surrounds Bryn Mawr, and to
an increasing extent Radcliffe, as well as the "radical"-experimental-
artistic colleges like Bennington and Sarah Lawrence.

Yet it would be deceptive to suggest that every college operates
with one or two of these "images" and shuns others; on the contrary,
what we said at the outset about the plurality of interests that go together to make up a college indicates that colleges are seldom willing
to beam their appeal at just a single constituency. Good luck and skillful public relations may even allow a college to attract not only students who want to become intellectuals and students who want to
stay adolescent, but also students who want to become great men
along with students who merely want a degree to get them into professional school or a job. Furthermore, for reasons explored by Sanford and others, students do not stay in one pile during the four
years of college, even though employers, friends, neighbors, spouses,
and the student himself might wish that they did. Other things being
equal, the larger the college, the greater the possibility of a shift of
identity.

The difference between the 750,000 students who enter college in
a year, and the 400,000 who graduate, like the difference between the
two-thirds of junior college students who plan to transfer and the one-
third who actually do so, might be taken as an index of American
optimism. Like the rate of small business failures, the differential is
highest in California. But even in the selective colleges, there is always a small group of intellectually well-equipped students who select
themselves out after having been selected in; frequently, they enter
the army, or work for a year, and then, confidence restored or illusions
about "life" dispelled, they re-enter and graduate. The combination
of careful admissions screening and students' faith in the B.A. as the
carte blanche to happiness has greatly reduced the attrition rate in
such selective colleges. But in the women's colleges, nearly half the

entering class may drop out before graduation. Some marry and finish their baccalaureate elsewhere; others work to support husbands through college. Some public colleges use their freshman year as the real basis of admission, and in many state universities less than half of those who begin the year finish it. Some of these dropouts certainly find other colleges that will allow them to earn a B.A. Others probably transfer to a junior college, and settle for the A.A. Still others may join the ranks of the academically fed up, raw material for the forces of anti-intellectualism and political reaction. Whether such people resent a college more if they flunk out than if they are refused admission we do not know. And their overall impact on the social environment is equally difficult to appraise. Furthermore, if the behavior of many alumni is any index, there are many degree holders who feel as bitter about their college as one would expect the rejects to feel (cf. Clark, 1960).

SOME EVOLUTIONARY APPROACHES

Although the environmental approach we have described takes account of the interaction of a college with its social and cultural environment, colleges also interact with one another, and determine each other's aspirations. Hence, just as the anthropologist may use a neo-evolutionary as well as an environmental or narrowly functional approach, so too the student of colleges can make tentative generalizations about the historical and cultural hierarchy among academic institutions. Obviously, he cannot seriously employ a 19th-century type scheme that would locate all colleges on a single evolutionary ladder from Colonial "savagery" through post-Civil War "barbarism," to the "civilization" of the present era. But neither can we be satisfied by the view that many anthropologists and historians would find more comfortable, namely that every college has its own unique culture and history, which will be violated by an attempt to fit it into a comparative or evolutionary framework. The mere fact that colleges themselves believe in evolution, and play follow-the-leader, makes an evolutionary perspective relevant. In a culture so "linear," metrical, and evaluative as America's it is understandable that academic institutions should seek to rank themselves along some scale, just as backward countries now tend to do. In both cases, of course, the scale is somewhat modified by the cultural relativism that allows that "low level" colleges also serve, and that "primitive" customs have their value. On a more *ad hoc* basis, the scale is relieved of some rigidity by the vagueness of evaluation that allows individuals to skew their perceptions and to rank their institutions higher than outsiders would. A college is a protean entity, and when one of the authors conducted a non-random survey of American college faculty, he found that half thought their institution ranked "in the top ten percent of American colleges." One explanation is that "the top ten percent" means 200 institutions, and no faculty member knows enough about that many places to be sure that his is not among them. Sheer multiplicity preserves many American illusions. In part, too, the high opinion many hold of their college rests on accepting the special aims of "their" college as particularly relevant criteria of success. When the criteria are nationally agreed upon, as they largely are in ranking one's department in the disciplinary hierarchy, the tendency to overestimate is reduced though not eliminated (cf. Caplow and McGee, 1958). Nevertheless, ranking is done largely by amorphous and unreliable stereotypes. One result is the brand-name phenomenon revealed by a study in Connecticut which shows that when two teachers colleges got legislative approval to change their names (e.g., from New Haven State Teachers College to Southern Connecticut State College), they had an easier time attracting both students and staff. (Those professors who find this merely laughable should ask themselves whether their own snobbery vis-à-vis "educationists" is not primarily responsible for the atmosphere in which such changes are necessary to bring about more substantive reforms.)

Economic hierarchies. The standards by which we habitually measure "lower" and "higher" stages in evolution are partly of economic origin. Like tribes that depend on hunting and gathering there are, as we have noted, at least 500 institutions without accreditation, struggling to survive without visible means of support, scrounging for private gifts or public appropriations while staving off creditors with promises, and gaining subsidies from an ill-paid faculty that lacks the connections to find jobs elsewhere, and from students in a similar fix. Some of these institutions are indirectly profitable to their founders, who are local boosters and merchants hoping to bring in trade and talent. But one can still discover colleges that are literally "proprietary," a source of handsome revenue to an entrepreneurial and not wholly scrupulous president, although in general, colleges seek a modus vivendi rather than profits. They hope to acquire accreditation and thus to gain one or preferably several staple crops of students who will introduce some stability in the economic struggle. Only a handful of universities have undergone what we might call the academic revolution, which introduces them to the affluent world of foundations, expense accounts, teaching assistants, offices, secretaries, and other luxury items. And even those are usually beset by optimism, and must make annual struggles to balance the income from tuition, taxes, and philanthropy against the outgo for buildings, professors, and the ever-rising costs for ancillary services such as landscaping, guidance, and administration.

Among the 600 public institutions, taxes are the most important source of revenue. Tuition, even for out-of-state residents, is quite nominal. These institutions also seek support for research from government agencies and foundations, but only a few, such as Berkeley, Minnesota, and Michigan, have produced alumni who are generous with buildings, professorships, and the like. Among the 1200 accredited private colleges, tax money may play a minor role, while tuition and philanthropy provide the main support. In practice, of course, the difference is less than appears, for legislatures in many ways resemble recalcitrant philanthropists; hence public institutions must cajole the reluctant lawmaker with the same coyness that private colleges exhibit in courting their alumni, or church-related colleges in trying to boost the subvention. Indeed one reason why most public colleges have in the past gotten little money from their alumni is that they organize these men's efforts to put pressure on the legislature rather than on one another, and are most successful in those states where the legislature is a kind of alumni association for the state university, containing a voting majority from the institution. A crucial difference between the public and private institutions is that the public institution knows a few hundred men it must court, whereas the private institution has thousands of potential benefactors and only a few dozen actual ones. In the legislature on the other hand, every vote counts for one, despite the tendency of crucial men, and the lobbyists around them, to make or break the annual budget. To be sure, each "constituent" of a college may help create a climate that stimulates others, more influential than he, to generosity or ill will—a situation not likely to alter as foundations and corporations increase their importance in meeting the deficits of higher education, despite the relatively small number of people on the giving end.

In general, colleges are increasingly divided into the "haves" and the "have nots." The "haves" attract able applicants and make these feel that attending college is a privilege that will in large measure be responsible for their future success. As a result, their alumni are likely to be both successful and nostalgic, and to be generous with Alma Mater, either as donors or legislators. Moreover, such alumni, as we indicated above in speaking of colleges as employment agencies, tend to gravitate to positions where they can ask mutual favors of one another on behalf of educational and other philanthropic goals. In this, as in all respects, the majority of "have not" colleges are caught, like backward countries, in a self-perpetuating poverty. Unable to attract gifted students and teachers in large numbers, they can seldom produce alumni or research that would bring solvency. Instead, they breed an atmosphere of mediocrity in which the talented minority feel alienated from "their" college. Nevertheless, since self-made men in America are often not ashamed of the fact, one or two graduates who do succeed in the world may come to the rescue of their Alma Mater, putting it, along with themselves, on the map. And one such strike gives hope to other struggling institutions, kept alive as part of the American Dream. Faced with analogous problems, many American high schools have consolidated, and most educators are convinced that this process will continue in the coming generation. However, despite possibilities of savings on overhead, libraries, laboratories and so on, very few colleges have taken this road out, even though the experience of the Claremont Colleges indicates what might be accomplished. There is of course no overarching authority to compel mergers and limit Balkanization by vested academic interests and institutional nationalism (often articulated in conflicts of temperament among leaders of various institutions).

Organizational hierarchies. But the evolutionary scale is more than a matter of economics in college as in other societies. It is also a matter of social organization. There are perhaps a dozen huge graduate universities, primarily concerned with research and the training of researchers, that play the same role in the academic world that the metropolises play in America. These universities shape, and are shaped by, the various academic disciplines, just as the metropolises shape, and are shaped by, the big corporations. Both universities and metropolises look largely to one another rather than to the provinces for examples of what can be done next. It is even tempting to make specific analogies between the private monoliths (Chicago, Columbia, Cornell, Harvard, Pennsylvania, and Stanford) and the older centers of commerce, or to compare the public superstates (Berkeley, Indiana, Michigan, Minnesota, Illinois, Texas, UCLA, Wisconsin) to newer industrial complexes. These institutions produce the most influential Ph.D.'s and most of the research (Berelson, 1960), and they have most of the "surplus" money that can be directed into experimentation and luxury.

Similiar only in name to these universities are about a hundred demi-universities both public and private, that produce many M.A.'s and an increasing but still small number of Ph.D.'s and are really indistinguishable from the perhaps 200 "complex colleges" that have a whole variety of preprofessional undergraduate programs to supplement their liberal arts divisions. Such institutions may, of course, have substantial numbers of graduate students (mostly terminal M.A.'s).

Often, an M.A. who is a good teacher is let go in favor of a Ph.D. who is an indifferent or vindictive one, because the doctorate looks better in the catalogue if not in the classroom. Furthermore, since the more ambitious institutions want not only Ph.D. holders but also professors who will become widely known beyond their classrooms, there has developed a kind of arms race, in which one or two showpiece departments are built up to do nationally-known work, subsidized where possible by "soft" foundation or government money. Such symbols often conceal the lack of supporting resources or "infrastructure" that might be usable to combat the problems the students or the local community face, as against the problems scheduled by the national disciplines. By the same token, the faculty acquired in this way comes from outside the community, remaining loyal to the discipline rather than to the institution; their readiness to pack up and move on to a better department may give leverage to the upgrading of their present institution, or may merely give them a temporarily privileged status at the expense of the less mobile faculty. The conflicts that ensue between itinerants and home-guarders bear some resemblance to the struggles in many middle-sized cities between the itinerant executives brought in by national corporations, and the traditional local elite.

Although many subsidiary and local markets remain for academic personnel as well as for students, markets delineated along the lines of the competing interest groups sketched in the first section of this chapter, it seems to us that more and more of the demi-universities and "complex colleges" want to become major universities, while still hanging on to a "most favored nation" position with respect to their original regional or ethnic or religious constituency (cf. Chapter 27).

In a few states, and notably in the states included in the Southern Regional Council, attempts have been made to limit and channel academic free enterprise in order to dissipate local resources somewhat less and to provide complementary rather than competing facilities in the less wealthy jurisdictions. Thus, as a hypothetical illustration, the University of Florida may be encouraged to push for a medical school but not a cyclotron, leaving the latter for Florida State or Georgia Tech. But trouble comes when a cyclotron becomes a symbol of eminence like atomic weapons in Britain and France, or like a steel plant in a "backward country" that would be better off with a textile or plastics plant ("better off," that is, economically if not psychically).

In order to attract scholars and enter the big league, an institution needs not only research money but also graduate students. Imported scholars want graduate students as research assistants and apprentice-colleagues. Graduate students grade, test, and instruct the undergraduates face-to-face, thus saving the professor's time and protecting him from having to confront often stultifying indifference to his academic interests. By working for nominal wages these teaching assistants also help to subsidize their professors, and the college can therefore keep a balanced budget while paying "decent" wages and giving relatively light teaching loads to the scholars at the top academic echelons. By acquiring its own graduate students a university may eventually save itself money in another way, for these students will come to regard the school as "their" university, and may not follow the pattern, set by professors trained elsewhere, of leaving whenever a better salary or department is offered (McGee, 1960).

The majority of American colleges are still too far from the world of scholarship and science to worry about such problems (just as the majority of towns are still too far from being wholly industrialized to worry about city planning). They are provincial and often unspecialized, with teachers handling a variety of subjects, and students usually taking a fairly limited repertoire of general courses, plus some preprofessional training. Very often, these colleges will resemble one-industry towns, relying on a single program in teacher training, for example, to carry the college both economically and otherwise. When such resources vanish, as sometimes happens in both colleges and towns, the college may fail unless enterprising leadership can quickly generate alternative sources of students, funds, and respect.

Small liberal arts colleges are scattered all over the country but are more heavily concentrated in the East and the old Northwest Territory. Some of the older and more eminent ones have no desire at all to become universities or even "complex colleges"; they should be compared rather to a "minor power" like Holland than to an underdeveloped country like Ghana. For certain specialized academic needs (library books, trained Ph.D.'s, periodic stimulation), they maintain traditional ties with large universities and urban centers, and approximate the cosmopolitan atmosphere of the latter. But as their academic models change, they too are under a certain relentless pressure to specialize. Some of these "exurbanite" academic communities have attempted to curb the pressures to become a university by curricular "zoning," as at Wesleyan, for example, where selected M.A. programs and a Center for Advanced Studies bring luminaries and specialized students to the campus for a short time without committing the College (in name, Wesleyan University) to primarily graduate training. Such schemes may work at highly selective colleges like Wesleyan, where faculty do not need graduate students to protect them from undergraduates, and can actually treat a large proportion of the undergraduates as apprentices and colleagues. In the women's colleges, the intellectual community is often kept alive (in a pattern first made explicit by President M. Carey Thomas at Bryn Mawr), by bringing in bright young instructors whose reputations are as yet unmade and who must therefore work for the small salaries that meagerly-endowed women's colleges can afford. But such a policy requires the prestige and wisdom to pick the unrecognized talents as well as the courage to face heavy turnover at the time these men publish their first or second book. In the small urban colleges, which hire men still working on the Ph.D., attrition is even earlier, for the degree boosts the better young faculty into another league.

More ambiguous has been the status of the university college, a kind of "uptown residential community" within the great academic metropolis, which tries to preserve the older ideals of individual intellectual development against the newer academic "industries" of the various disciplines and technologies. At times the liberal arts college seems all but lost in such universities, as the professional schools absorb more and more of the students' time, either by offering overtly preprofessional curricula to undergraduates, or else by professionalizing the traditionally liberal arts. The liberal arts have counterattacked by developing general education programs—a label that covers a gamut of bold and tired experiments, ranging from a textbook amalgam of the less intractable theories from various fields (a kind of academic *Reader's Digest*) to the most intellectually taxing and serious attempts to introduce cross-disciplinary perspectives, seeking to come to terms at once with research in the several disciplines and with student concerns that have not yet become departmentalized. In many institutions, such programs absorb the first two years of the student's time, while the last two are devoted to some major which, whatever the intellectual potential of the subject, is usually organized primarily for the benefit of students who will do graduate work in the same area. A few departments dedicated to teaching have resisted the temptation of making their undergraduate program a prelude and prerequisite to the Ph.D.—a pattern sometimes enforced by a partial separation of undergraduate and graduate faculties.

Efforts to cope with the competing pressures of specialization and of general education have sometimes, as in Hutchins' Chicago, taken the form of an attempt to shift the chronology of higher education. The program for Advanced Standing, worked out by a number of Eastern universities and outstanding secondary schools, offers one such direction. It takes for granted that, with the increased pressure to get into college, the better secondary schools can attempt a serious introduction to the world of ideas; and there is no doubt that the precocity of teen-agers has been rising, not only in such highly visible areas as dating behavior, but also in the attitude toward intellectual work. Moreover, paperbacks and educational television make "advanced" ideas available to ambitious teen-agers even where their high schools do not. A college like Harvard already accepts almost 10% of its students as sophomores under the program for Advanced Standing. And more and more high schools are seeking to enter a program that gives their better teachers the gratifying privilege of offering college-level courses. Those who have observed the programs' rapid rise in the last few years believe that in the better university colleges, the freshman year may increasingly be relegated to a remedial role for those brilliant students who are expected to profit from a good college but do not have the preparation to begin immediate specialization.

Another and contradictory trend is also visible, at least in some parts of the country. The development of the junior college as an upward extension of high school has meant that for many students college does not begin until the end of the 14th grade. And in many traditional colleges the first two years are increasingly devoted to general education, while professional training begins in the junior year and often continues to the M.A. rather than the B.A. Under these circumstances we may see the emergence of a "6-6-2-plus" curriculum, with "plus" standing for whatever terminal professional training the student is to get. For reasons that we hope are adumbrated in this chapter and elsewhere in this volume, changes of this sort can come with astonishing speed, in spite of all the institutional rigidities, once a few pace-setter institutions point the way.

Nevertheless, if we look at these organizational patterns as a whole, we are struck by the fact that, as in so many other areas of American life, rigidity is the price that we have paid for a certain elevation and reliability of standards. In the 19th century free enterprise was as luxuriant among academic institutions as among the railroads before the Interstate Commerce Act. The College Board and the regional accrediting agencies have reduced some of the wilder discrepancies, establishing an age-grade progression analogous to that of Europe (though with a different rhythm) and a certain modest caution with respect to terminology. Because these victories of rationality are incomplete, however, opposition is particularly great to experiments that look as if they would reintroduce an earlier chaos. Thus, the program for Advanced Standing has had to contend with the objections of many college teachers who cannot really believe that a secondary school teacher can do the job that they themselves are doing. And many parents and professors are likely to share the conviction that a 16-year-old boy is too young for college, at least emotionally, even though he may be more mature in every relevant way than boys in an earlier generation were at 18. Battling fear, condescension, and inertia as it must, innovation in academic organization progresses more slowly than innovation in merchandising or in military technology. The reader of college and university histories cannot help but be struck by the fact that embattled institutions stood firm against change —and yet eventually, as leading institutions broke the tacit pact, change occurred.

So far, the institutions most resistant to change have been the graduate schools, which, firmly in control of the disciplines, have in the larger institutions managed to maintain and even raise professional standards in the face of increasing demands for teachers and researchers. Jacques Barzun and others have commented on how long and hazardous is the course to a Ph.D. degree, particularly in the humanities and the social sciences. Meanwhile, as we have seen, the graduate school ethos reaches down into the better university colleges and liberal arts colleges, where faculty members want to make sure that their student ambassadors, when they enter graduate school, will have a well-furnished portfolio. (Many colleges are now in effect in the same position that many high schools have been in for some time, that is, of being cram schools for the next stage.) Martin Trow, however, has tellingly argued that the result of the maintenance of these traditional standards at the top of the academic profession leads to a break in the chain of continuity and influence, with many new and ill-equipped institutions, including former teachers colleges, bestowing the doctorate on barely literate and seriously uncultivated men for the lower academic echelons (Trow, 1959, see also Caplow and McGee, 1958; Berelson, 1960). Such teachers, Trow suggests, will represent to their students the vocation of teaching and will thus serve to perpetuate themselves and their constricted image of the life of the mind. Plainly, whether these several academic worlds can remain in contact with each other, or will lose touch entirely, will depend not only on the forms of academic organization and graduate training, but also on the general tendencies of our culture at once to mix people up and to stratify them.

Subcultural pressures. So far, we have primarily emphasized the evolutionary pressures stemming from the environment, although in the process something has been said about the campus cultures that may influence the rate and direction of change; we turn now more systematically to the latter.

We have already referred to the distinction between the institution-oriented and the discipline-oriented faculty member. If the professor is an alumnus of the college where he teaches, he may feel a special loyalty to it, which may engender parochialism but which may also produce a concern for the problems of "his" institution, instead of merely "his" department.

The administration is also likely to play a critical role in evolving the college toward university status (and thus toward the destruction of administrative initiative at the hands of a powerful and contemptuous group of scholars). College presidents are familiar with the social and economic advantages of the next upward stage of evolution and are committed, unlike many of the faculty, to their particular institution. Even when the president or dean hopes to move to a bigger college, he knows that his best maneuver is to make his present institution as prosperous as possible and thus to get a reputation as a builder.

At a lower level, however, the administration may become involved with the students, and with protecting or manipulating them. Deans in the big universities are likely to make knowledge of student life into their "discipline," and to use this as a foil for the contempt with which the faculty transfixes them. Where deans outrank professors, however, they do not need to rely on support from minority groups such as students. Such men, supported by institution-oriented faculty who hope to become deans, are likely to wield their power openly, manipulating faculty and simply coercing (rarely defending) students.

We have already touched on the role of graduate students in encouraging evolution, but in some ways undergraduates can be equally crucial. At the extreme, conservative students may act as informers against the more enlightened faculty and encourage them to get out, or even get them dropped, for deviations from the local political or racial line. More commonly, students band together more or less informally to make life difficult for the discipline-oriented faculty who are trying to "raise standards." In a big university these men are protected by the fact that there are fewer rate-busters among their colleagues, and more among the students, so that undergraduates cannot effectively boycott difficult courses, nor count on finding "guts." And the professor who offers demanding courses will almost always get a minimal enrollment of graduate students, proto-graduate students, and intellectuals, to whom long reading lists are not an anathema. Some university administrations even issue complaints to professors whose grade curves are inflated, and who are in effect undercutting their colleagues. In the smaller colleges, on the other hand, the lazy student may find support in the administration, which is reluctant to flunk out too many tuition-paying students, or, in the case of a state university, perhaps worried about the political repercussions of apparent faculty ruthlessness.

The students also determine the rate of evolution by forming various subcultures, which produce different kinds of alumni and different public images. Very little effort has been made to map these subcultures, or to channel students into the ones that seem most likely to encourage growth and productivity, rather than failure and departure. A few colleges, with Sarah Lawrence and Bennington in the vanguard, have elaborate and self-revealing admissions forms that make possible highly individuated initial guidance of students, assigning them to advisors (and roommates) in a genuine effort to create optimal matchings (Taylor, 1950, Murphy and Raushenbush, 1960). Others ask entering students in a very off-hand way to say what "types" they will and will not accept as roommates. Still others assign roommates and freshman advisors on a random basis, despite the often crucial nature of these decisions for the individual's career in college. In freshman orientation week such places ask neophytes to "buy" a variety of courses, sports, and extracurricular activities—a procedure often more like a country fair than a serious introduction to an intellectual or even social community (cf. Werner, 1958).

In some colleges choice of fraternities is also made at the beginning of freshman year, and although this has the advantage that freshmen are not entirely sorted out and combed over so that the fraternities make interesting mistakes and get some diversity, the freshmen are conversely forced into such mistakes, sometimes to their detriment as well as the fraternities'. These fraternities often function to encourage institutional evolution, however, by effectively embalming parental, alumni, and adolescent values within the college, and al-

lowing the faculty to move in its own direction without losing the
loyalty of the alumni and students who see the college and fraternity
as synonymous. On the other hand, the fraternities will usually obstruct evolution if it includes an effort to bring the students along,
and more than one scheme for educational reform, like Woodrow Wilson's at Princeton, has come to grief against this vested interest.

In our chapter on the Harvard House system (Chapter 22), we describe one set of critical choices which Harvard freshmen make
(namely, which houses to apply for) in virtual independence of the
formal organization of the College. In the larger institutions, such
decisions as whether to take athletics seriously, whether to join a fraternity, and what field to major in, are made on the basis of the networks of the peer culture. Despite the relative precocity of which we
have spoken, many students do not flounder productively—sometimes
because the ideology of independence makes them feel that they
ought to stand on their own feet and not consult anyone—and few
large colleges have done much to bridge the generational and occupational gaps that prevent faculty members from doing much to understand, much less influence, the choices students make during their
college years (cf. Perry, 1959). A few colleges, such as Yale, have tried
to make their advising systems more effective by mixing resident graduate students with freshmen. Yale has also, along with a few other
institutions, sought to provide students with ancillary psychiatric
guidance and to make advice from this quarter seem unthreatening
and "normal" (see Wedge, 1958; Farnsworth, 1957). Although in
part these efforts reflect sympathetic concern for the casualties attracted to or created by higher education, the psychiatric services can
also become a center for obtaining a fuller understanding of basic dissatisfaction with the overall pattern of college life—dislike for impersonality, suspicion of alienated learning, and a general concern with
the matters dealt with by Sanford in Chapter 1. Not all the evolution that occurs in the collegiate world needs to be blind.

But as Sanford is also well aware, evolution can, so to speak, be
overdirected, and at some colleges with extensive personnel services,
students may be well advised to avoid the guidance department. In
an effort to help students make only "right" choices of department or
occupation, it is possible simply to confirm existing tendencies both
in the students and in the institutions to which they are sent. Yet
it is only by allowing students to make apparently "wrong" choices
that a college can encourage them to change, becoming something
they are not, instead of confirming themselves as they are. Only a
few advisors have the gift of helping students discover their potential

rather than their visible abilities, encouraging them to try things at which they now look inept but may do well. Yet many students who have chosen a college for the wrong reasons profit immensely from their blunders, and many whom any judicious advisor would have told not to study physics, or enter the law, have been so changed by these experiences that they became immensely successful; and in some measure these recruits may have helped to change what law is, and what physics is, and hence recruitment to these fields in the future. Yet some of the enormous suffering that is the uncreative price of occasional anarchy might be alleviated if choices were less irrevocable.[4]

There is no doubt that, as Nevitt Sanford has suggested to us, we are extremely sensitive to the unnecessary suffering and misdirection of effort that colleges, like all other human institutions, can bring about. In *The Vanishing Adolescent,* a book written with a similar animus, Edgar Friedenberg describes the damage done to youngsters at a Midwestern high school, but he also portrays the way in which one of the students, whom he calls Stanley, was able to ride the school to his destination as if it were the Pennsylvania Railroad, relatively unaffected by such of its purposes as were not his (Friedenberg, 1959). In this chapter, however, where we have not dealt with individuals, we have left it to the reader's imagination to realize that it remains possible for some people to get an education in college in the sense of a liberal education relevant to their full development. There are students like Stanley in every college, who pursue their interests because they are talented enough and tough or pliable enough to do so. By the same token, whatever the deficiencies of higher education as an organized system, these scarcely excuse the lack of ingenuity of students and their readiness to assume that their own actions could not possibly make any difference (Riesman, 1960). Given the chaos and confusion of purposes, the cross-pressures from customers, the mixed motives of faculty members and administrators, the very idea that American colleges and universities form a hard and fast system needs

[4] Professor Robert Knapp at Wesleyan has described to us an admirable plan which allows students to receive fellowships for the year following their graduation from college in order to prepare to enter graduate school in a field different from their undergraduate major; there are hardly any fields in which one such intensive year of preparation will not suffice. If students could be guaranteed such a paid moratorium (as indeed they now are in a few fields which eagerly seek recruits), they might feel under somewhat less realistic pressure to choose majors in college with an eye to graduate school, or to stick with majors about which they have doubts. To be sure, no matter how speedily or comfortably the transition from one field to another can be bridged by practical steps such as this, many students will resist change in order to cling to a superficially clear identity.

demolition. One of the authors a few years ago sought to explain the organization of American higher education to a group of Russian youth leaders and student editors who refused to believe that anything could be so planless and lacking in central direction, if not from government then from some hidden elite. Nevertheless we must insist that there is no plan; there are only osmotic pressures that bear unevenly throughout the landscape, and models that are imitated at different levels of excellence and ambition. We have portrayed in this chapter some of the gaps that separate the ideals of higher education from the institutional practices, but the ideals have their own weight and an individual dedicated to them can exert enormous leverage if he wishes, and can still more easily avoid being influenced by the current pressures by creation of a niche or enclave for himself. Periods of reformation in higher education can always succeed periods of acquiescence.

COLLEGE ETHNOGRAPHY

We turn now to some specific illustrations of the processes we have discussed above, not with any conviction that we know enough about any college to make it illustrate all that we have said, nor even with the expectation that we can prove our arguments by discovering them in some specific college. Rather, we have felt that the study of colleges, like the study of other societies, needs a much greater body of ethnographic data than is now available. Many of our misunderstandings have been based simply on the absence of any body of relevant information against which to check our observations and surmises, and we suspect that our coauthors in this volume have had the same experience.

The fragmentary studies that follow present a problem not only in accuracy of reporting, but also in the justice of exposing particular institutions to the scrutiny of those who will read this chapter. The principal ethical problem we can see in naming colleges is that this may penalize in unintended ways those institutions that have given social scientists freedom to make investigations, while temporarily protecting those that have resisted inquiries. Moreover, luck will mean that some colleges are scrutinized, while their academic competitors escape sight unseen. All three of our victims, for example, are among the mythical "top tenth" of America's colleges, and it seems unfair to describe them without making abundantly clear how relatively excellent they are. Yet to make this emphatic enough for an intellectual audience would require a vignette of a truly bad college, and such an effort would be doubly unfair to the one college in a thousand chosen for comparison.

We have no certain answers to these doubts that must trouble all scholars who report on tribes that are literate, and who unlike children, prisoners, factory workers, and street gangs, have the power to make their objections felt. Since we strongly believe, along with the other authors of this volume, that more research should be done on institutions of higher learning, we hope that our work will be more a help than a hindrance. In order to protect the institutions as well as our own work, we have considered writing about composite colleges with fictitious names, similar to those pseudo-patients about whom psychiatrists write in case histories. But we have concluded that such a procedure could not long conceal actual settings from the interested gossip and guessing of the academic profession. More serious is the fact that the more we have learned about colleges, the more we have been struck by their uniqueness. True, colleges run to "types," and types ultimately converge on a national academic model. One might therefore lump together the Universities of Massachusetts and Connecticut, or Harvard and Yale, or Boston College and Fordham, or San Francisco State and San Diego. But on closer inspection these colleges appear to draw on quite different publics, and to have quite different flavors. Under what pseudonym is one to disguise an eminent university that combines high-power scholarship with ties to the aristocracy of a large American city? What composite can reconcile the different positions of the Boston and the New York Irish, or give Boston College the tone of Fordham without violating its unique pattern? What state has a system of higher education like California's or even a city with the same quality as San Francisco? Such difficulties have convinced us that the reader will do better if he is told what college we claim to be describing and is able to correct our biases from his own knowledge. Perhaps in this fashion social scientists will gradually develop a stock of reasonably accurate information, about specific institutions, that will make the study of colleges as sophisticated as the study of primitives.

Our commentary is controversial and this, we think, is probably as it should be. The effort to conceal value judgments behind laundered words and ambiguous tables seems to us unfortunate. We are writing about institutions many men, including ourselves, live by and for; institutions that could be better than they are for those who inhabit them. But for this very reason our analysis should be read with the skepticism one might accord an analysis of one political party by another, rather than being read with the faith one might accord an anthropologist talking about nonliterates.

The University of Massachusetts *

Our portrait of the University of Massachusetts is an impressionistic sketch and makes no pretensions to be a definitive report. The University is a cosmos of 6500 students and faculty, whose edges we have briefly explored through interviews and written materials.

CHANGING INTEREST GROUPS

Just as Harvard was founded by the Commonwealth to produce gentlemen and ministers, so the Massachusetts Agricultural College was founded 230 years later to produce farmers and agricultural scientists. We have already seen, however, that colleges when adeptly run have a good deal of power to redefine their mission. Thus Harvard College accumulated an enormous library for scholars, while widening its functions to include turning out men of many callings. Similarly, the Agricultural College, while serving the interests of the farmers for three quarters of a century, interpreted these in a large and spacious way so as to become by the late 19th century one of the leading land-grant institutions and a world-famous model of agricultural research, especially admired and influential in Japan. Even in the decade 1924–34, when its fame had been somewhat diminished by the still more expansive Midwestern institutions, Massachusetts continued to turn a larger proportion of its alumni into distinguished scientists than any other agricultural college in the country. Indeed, Knapp and Goodrich found that Massachusetts had outstripped every other institution in New England, far outranking not only colleges like Harvard, Yale, and Amherst, where the humanities were in the ascendant, but also MIT.[5]

* By Christopher Jencks and David Riesman. This vignette is indebted to an unpublished paper by Jo Anne Warren of Radcliffe College and to criticisms by her and by Henry Korson and Paul A. Gagnon of the University of Massachusetts; Edward Eddy, Jr., of the University of New Hampshire (now President of Chatham College); James H. Barnett of the University of Connecticut; and C. L. Barber of Amherst College. Needless to say, their criticism does not mean that they are in any way responsible for our conclusions.

[5] Only Clark University and Wesleyan, among New England institutions, ranked among the top fifty (Knapp and Goodrich, 1952).

In 1931, faced with declining local farms, "Old Aggie" changed its name to "Massachusetts State College." But it was not until 1947, faced with a still further declining livestock population, and a rapidly growing college population, that the Legislature finally "expropriated" the old Agricultural College and began to turn it into a multipurpose state university.[6] Today, although the College of Agriculture still gets more than its share of the money, it is no longer the center of the institution. Its influence is visible primarily to the historian, his eyes focused on the Morrill Act (and its successor legislation), who can see that the expansion of the University of Massachusetts has followed the "natural" pattern of evolution for an agricultural college. It is no surprise to him that one of the best known programs at the University is in food technology, teaching local youngsters to process food they no longer grow, nor is it coincidental that the University has a distinguished department of zoology. Likewise, the expansion into engineering is a natural one for an agricultural school, as the draftsmen of the Morrill Act long ago foresaw. And with such technical facilities available, the University soon found itself one of the state's leading producers of high-school science teachers. Even the existence of a first-rate program in psychology and a growing sociology department are not unrelated to the fact that the old agricultural school taught the sciences while not pushing the humanities.

Yet other programs have developed solely because Massachusetts' private institutions were not providing enough graduates in some fields. Thus, the University sends many of its women into elementary school teaching, and many men into business, not because these occupations emerged naturally from the agricultural college tradition, but because the twin genii of "student demand" and "public need" made such programs saleable to the Legislature. In urging such expansion the University seems, however, always to argue that the new program is necessary because of the failures of the private free-enterprise system. Few in New England seem ready to argue the "socialist" doctrine that public sponsorship is inherently more egalitarian, more efficient, and more in keeping with the public impact of the educa-

[6] It may possibly be an element in this development that Cornell provides a superior training in agriculture and related sciences for all the New England states, which can more than meet the need of Massachusetts for trained dairy men and county agents, while forestry can be studied at Yale and Syracuse. Possibly, public poverty in New England may force a kind of specialization of the state institutions —a process facilitated by the rational hopes and plans of the New England Board of Higher Education, which serves as an agency for collecting and exchanging information and ideas throughout the region.

tional system. The University of Massachusetts is a kind of educational New Deal, assuming only those residual functions that the private system cannot, or will not, fulfill. It is hard to find a single area in which the University has entered into a serious competition with the private system when that system was doing a job adequately, or to find a single proposal that has been approved by the Legislature solely to make the University of Massachusetts an academically outstanding institution of which the State might be proud. The contrast with California or Michigan is obvious.

Negative public assumptions about the role of the state university are of course rooted in the historical development of the private universities of New England in colonial times and in the 19th century; Massachusetts had no Thomas Jefferson to envision a state university that would be at once the possession of the elite and the pride of a broader public. At the same time, granted a general situation of underprivilege, the various New England state universities are not all underprivileged in the same way. For example, the University of Vermont resembles some of the Southern state universities in combining private and public aspects (until becoming wholly public very recently), and in being the largest and most visible educational enterprise in the whole State. It is also located in the largest city in the State, whereas all the other New England state universities are in small communities. The University of Connecticut has had to contend with less legislative antagonism than the University of Massachusetts, but appears to have translated the state's largesse into an enormous building program and a few eminent departments, rather than into a crusade on behalf of public education in Connecticut. Yale tends to supply and to influence the elite of Connecticut, and Harvard the professional, business, and even, in a few cases, the political leadership of Massachusetts. The state universities therefore do not focus the public imagination in the way that state universities do in the South and West. The University of Massachusetts has no medical school, no law school, and no business program suitable for training top-level corporation executives. These jobs are left to the institutions in the Boston metropolitan area.

To be sure, such situations are not entirely unknown in the rest of the country. Those land-grant colleges that were not established on the campus of their state universities have all suffered from their youth and their initially vocational character. Thus Kansas State still exists in the shadow of the University of Kansas, and Michigan State struggles to outvote, if not to outshine, the University of Michigan. But these disparities are disappearing, and in each of these states, unlike the situation in Massachusetts, the public institutions are the outstanding ones, and the conflict is carried on within the legislature and within the ambit of middle-class educational ideals. In contrast, when the University of Massachusetts seeks more than token support, it comes into tacit competition with Harvard as the "first" university of Massachusetts, with Boston University and Clark, or with the Catholic institutions, which would feel themselves threatened by a state-wide commitment to public secular education.

CURRENT "ECOLOGICAL" PRESSURES

We are suggesting here that, if the University of Massachusetts challenged aristocratic educational pretensions, whether represented by Harvard or by Amherst College, it might mobilize a good deal of support. But the difficulty is that in Massachusetts much of the resentment of Yankee dominance comes from Irish (and hence Catholic) sources, as readers of *The Last Hurrah* or *The Remarkable Kennedys* may remember. The Church is naturally reluctant to see the faithful taxed to support public education, since that leaves less money for the tuition and endowment of Catholic colleges. Perhaps even more important, the men who run the Catholic colleges need only look at the way the state university and the college system of a state like California competes with Santa Clara University or the (Catholic) University of San Francisco to anticipate that first-rate public education will attract young Catholics, especially those from still European home atmospheres who want to escape their families for the "freedom" of an American adolescent peer group. Hence, although 45% of the students at the University of Massachusetts are Catholic, their co-religionists in the State Legislature have not been very enthusiastic about supporting the University.

If the Catholics have been unenthusiastic about public education, the Yankee Protestants have not been much better. Almost all of New England's initially Protestant colleges have slipped into secular control, but they remain private, and with the notable exception of MIT and Clark, appear to continue to stand for the humanistic culture of 19th-century New England. Indeed, it has been largely because the older private colleges have done so little in science, technology, and the applied arts generally, that the public university has made as much headway as it has. But this very emphasis on technology has created a pattern in which the upper-middle-class student who wants some "culture" from his college faculty and fellow-students will gravitate to a more "Ivy" institution where the humanities are thought to thrive. The upper-middle-class student in California, if hostile to the presumptive conventionality of Stanford undergraduates, can choose Berkeley with confidence in its academic resources. A comparable student in Massachusetts can see no real alternative to the private colleges like Harvard even if he objects to their arrogance or complacency. Public education seems to him merely technical training rather than a real initiation.

Thus, both Catholics and Protestants are deeply committed to separate development, and are uninterested in efforts to provide a common meeting ground in a public institution. A more distinguished state university might not of course solve this problem. It might become identified with Yankee culture, to be avoided by all but a few Catholics as Harvard is now avoided. But a distinguished state university might also continue to look safer than Harvard both to Catholic students and to the parochial schools that can often influence the students' choice, just as the University of Massachusetts now seems "safe" to many. Such a university might thus provide Massachusetts Protestants and Catholics with a common basis for mutual understanding and open competition. The difficulty, we cannot help feeling, is that neither the Yankees nor the Irish really much want such a reconciliation, for they each claim a monopoly on virtue only slightly mitigated by American tolerance.

Less visible and probably less serious rifts in the middle-class support for the State University arise out of geographic schisms within seemingly tiny Massachusetts. The dominance of Harvard over the "second" state University is not only measured in the occupations for which it prepares but in the areas from which it recruits. The University of Massachusetts has been in some measure the University of Western Massachusetts. The reader will remember that a century and a half ago Amherst College was founded to bolster the western rural half of the state against urban Boston. Today, however, Amherst College has acquired a national constituency, and even with the assistance of nearby Smith, Mount Holyoke, and Williams, educates less than a hundred students from Western Massachusetts. Of course, Harvard and MIT have likewise lost their ties to Eastern Massachusetts, taking only a few hundred local students. The real rivals of the University of Massachusetts are Boston University (the local equivalent of NYU), Boston College, Tufts, and Northeastern, as well as many smaller colleges and specialized schools. A degree from any Massachusetts college, including the public University, will cost a Bostonian $4000 for some combination of room, board, and tuition. Hence, except among adventurous students who want to "get away from home," the State University has in the past commanded little support in Boston and its suburbs, and is still commonly thought of as a hick school. Lacking statewide support, and despite the cosmopolitanism of most of its newly recruited faculty, the University is still to some extent a provincial university, catering to the Connecticut Valley, and especially to those students, both Catholic and Protestant, to whom the risks of public education seem less than the risks of going far from home.

This intrastate provincialism is, however, fast fading. The Massachusetts Turnpike brings Boston within less than two hours of Amherst, so that the collapse of public transportation can be offset by the ever more numerous population of automobiles. More important, as the University of Massachusetts has risen in academic reputation, it has proved increasingly attractive to students from Boston who either cannot get into the private colleges they might have preferred, or who feel the atmosphere in those colleges alien or constricting. And, as more gifted students have attended the University of Massachusetts, they have reported to their friends that the University was not really a model farm for Berkshire lads, but a place where one could get a fine education in pleasant surroundings. As yet, this news has not spread beyond the state and, far from having to revise its present 5% quota for out-of-state students, the University's admissions standards are so high—higher indeed than many private liberal arts colleges—and its national reputation is so slight that only 3% of the students are from outside Massachusetts. Moreover, there are not many foreign students—and possibly less foreign contact than in the days when the Agricultural College was attracting visitors from all over. At present the narrow regionalism of the student body means on the one hand that gifted young people are seldom attracted into this state by its university, and on the other that some Massachusetts residents may not realize the advantages of leaving a state where the best jobs are often monopolized by the graduates of private colleges, where Catholic-Protestant prejudices seem more entrenched than elsewhere, and where the region—until the recent boom in electronics—has been periodically depressed economically.

THE RECRUITMENT OF STUDENTS

Like an enormous number of colleges and universities in the United States, the University of Massachusetts has a primarily lower-middle-class student body. These students belong to the first college-going generation in their families, and are likely to be in college partly because higher education vaguely appeals as a "good thing," and partly because the range of occupations they want to enter now requires a B.A. degree. A lower-middle-class college has to have high intellectual eminence (such as CCNY had in the thirties) to compensate for the absence of more sophisticated upper-middle-class and upper-class students who have a less vocational or immediate definition of the aims of education. This is important, of course, even in the narrowest vocational terms. The students who come to the University of Massachusetts do not quite realize that the middle-class jobs they want and can get will pay them only middle-class salaries. They know that in their first year out of college they can make as much money as their parents now make. They assume that as college graduates they will have opportunities for promotion and so it seems reasonable to aim at an income two or three times their parents' $5000 or $7500 a year. What they fail to realize is that although a Massachusetts degree is about as good as any other in certifying that one has certain technical skills, it is likely to be less helpful in getting promoted into the occupational-cultural elite, where technical skills count less than social and intellectual skills. Many leading colleges encourage the latter talents by providing a leaven of students whose parents have been to college, who can initiate lower-middle-class students into the mysteries of social mobility. Such students aim for top professions such as law, medicine, or research, and as a consequence the student culture, or at least some enclaves within it, provides an anticipatory socialization that in some measure rubs off on students with less lofty initial aims. Ironically, in the "diploma-image" colleges where vocationalism is rampant, it is often a very low order of vocationalism, and students have only the most limited sense of what callings might become available to them (we shall see that similar narrow horizons operate at San Francisco State College). In the state of Massachusetts almost all upper-middle-class students who could enlarge the career as well as the cultural horizons of their fellows are siphoned off into the elite private colleges and universities.

The students who remain are not inept. On the contrary, they are often brighter than students who will go further than they. But they lack a chance to associate with people who can exemplify the life-styles required by their economic hopes. There are, of course, at the University of Massachusetts some three hundred "activities" in which students can learn the rudiments of life in a bureaucratic world, and there are two dozen fraternities in which they learn a little bit of social polish. But lacking enlightened leadership, these potential agencies for socialization can easily degenerate into clubs, which confirm the students in their lower-middle-class outlook, and obstruct not only the acquisition of a "social" veneer, but also any tentative efforts by the student to move toward broader and more complex understanding.

At the same time, the University seems to appeal to many students precisely because it offers a diploma without apparent threat to their lower-middle-class values, other than the implicit threat involved in going away from home and parish. For students who feel (quite often mistakenly) that they would be socially out of place at Harvard or Amherst, Wellesley or Smith, the University of Massachusetts seems to offer an opportunity to move up in the world without having to become excessively worldly or sophisticated. When asked why they picked the University (and of course, in a brief visit, and chance contacts elsewhere, we could not ask many), some say they didn't get into their institution of first choice, but more often students say that they couldn't afford a private college. Quite frequently, however, this appears to be a rationalization, for such students usually confess that they did not apply for a scholarship or consider the possibility of a low-interest loan to help them through. Such students, we surmise, lack the self-confidence that would lead them to try to make it at "expensive" colleges; correspondingly, a university like Boston College, where students have to wear coats and ties, does not seem to them "their kind of college." No doubt, many of these self-deprecatory students fear that the private colleges are too difficult, even though the University of Massachusetts has high and steadily rising admissions standards in College Board terms. More important, we would guess, is the feeling that the social and the intellectual life at a private college would be over their heads.

STUDENT CULTURE AND FACULTY VALUES

We have been referring to a college that chiefly recruits students whose parents have not themselves attended college, as a "diploma-image" institution to which students come primarily to be certified.[7] Many students who are going into what might be thought of as first-generation vocations such as school teaching and engineering would

[7] Unpublished research by David Beardslee and Donald O'Dowd indicates that working-class children, when asked about their image of a college, refer to particular occupations, whereas middle-class children have a more generalized and less directly vocational image.

not be dissatisfied if the University of Massachusetts were to be defined in this way; and the engineers in particular are inclined to scoff at the extracurricular life and at what they regard as the laziness of many fellow students. But there are many at the University of Massachusetts, both among the faculty and the students, who would like to see it become an "alumni-image" institution to which students will aspire in the hope of becoming men of eminence in the professions and in public life. Given its late start as a university and the handicaps we have already recounted, the University has moved so fast and so far in the years since the Second World War as to give some ground for these ambitions. But to make such a transition is extraordinarily difficult, for it is very hard for even the best college to make distinguished citizens out of students who have undistinguished aspirations. Most colleges have had to go through an intermediate "romance-image" phase, during which students come expecting to change, although not in the way the faculty want them to change. Such students look on college, not as a place that will certify them for a specific job, but as a four-year "collegiate" moratorium of games, dates, and beer parties—interspersed with occasional bouts of "idle curiosity." Such men re-enforce in college the habits and outlook that will help them become rich and "successful," with sufficient social leverage as alumni to help "their" college to become rich and successful also. In other words, the social eclat of such alumni can help the college attract more intellectual students and a more academically eminent faculty.

Can the "romance-image" stage be skipped? Some urban universities, with the yeast of bright first-generation Jewish students, have managed to do so. The University of Massachusetts, however, exists in the rural atmosphere of Amherst, dependent for "culture" on concert series and foreign film series (as well as a recently established espresso bar). Neither faculty nor students can look to local professional and artistic cliques to enliven the academic perspective. A good deal of mutual stimulation results, however, from the existence of the three private colleges in the area, Smith, Mt. Holyoke, and Amherst. The University of Massachusetts' faculty and administration appear determined to establish the University's academic, while discouraging its "collegiate," reputation. For many years, the University has been known in some circles as a party school, whose fraternities were reputed among the hardest drinking in New England. But last year the Administration intervened to ban drinking on the campus, and such a rule, however ineffective, is likely to destroy the Bacchanalian image eventually. How long the "party school" label will persist is difficult to predict. In an upper-middle-class college where students often hear about what college is like from parents whose ideas are two decades out of date, the University could be thought of, for a generation, as a school with a great deal of drinking among the students. But lower-middle-class students hear about college primarily from older brothers or friends, whose prejudices are contemporary, and it may be that Massachusetts will be thought of, in a few years, as a school with a student body that is primarily sober.

The suppression of student drinking has been paralleled by continuing de-emphasis of football. Yet this may be a mixed blessing too. Beating Harvard a few years ago seems to have lifted student morale, and to have "put the University on the map" for large segments of the public that had not heard of the institution before. Such athletic triumphs may also have tightened ties with alumni, encouraging their help in the massive current building program. Furthermore, when MIT does not play football at all, Harvard plays it badly, and the state has no professional football team, there is some pressure on the University to provide autumn entertainment. (Whether this will be reduced when Boston gets its professional team, the Patriots, remains to be seen.) Yet such public "need" is more than offset by the academic "need" to keep unscholarly athletes from becoming student heroes, and to keep games from replacing ideas as a focus of student energy. Since the Administration knows that alumni solidarity is less important than legislative support, and that even state patriotism cannot make most nonalumni legislators care much whether victory goes to Massachusetts or Connecticut on the playing fields, athletes have trouble getting in, and little glory on arrival.

The desire to skip the "romance-image" phase is accentuated by the fact that Harvard and MIT have proved that a college does not need bread and circuses to survive. When Harvard played big-time football, some thought this the only way to prevent students from rioting, and to keep alumni gifts coming in. Today the faculty at Massachusetts knows better. Yet, like an underdeveloped country that tries to impose democracy without first acquiring the economic resources to create a bourgeoisie, Massachusetts may try to live by intellect alone before it has sufficient scholarly resources. Strikingly enough, some members of the faculty have raised money from alumni, as well as other patrons, to issue this last year the *Massachusetts Review*, a beautifully designed and well-edited literary "little magazine." Certainly, there is strong academic pressure from the Young Turks on the faculty to move toward the standard academic models. Such pressure may turn even legislative indifference to advantage, as when the inadequacy of the library helped impel the University to sponsor a cooperative arrangement with Smith, Mt. Holyoke, and Amherst, which boosted the number of books available from 47th among state universities to the third largest in New England. So, too, the resourceful Provost of the University became the energetic chairman of a joint committee of the four neighbor institutions to plan a new experimental college under a grant from the Fund for the Advancement of Education. Many in the faculty at the University who have come in since the Second World War feel themselves missionaries for the cause of public education in the state, and, despite frustrations, remain in the hope that better things will come. The most visible frustration is the hostility of many in the legislature to scholars and intellectuals, and more specifically to public education. Not only does Massachusetts make higher education accessible only to a tiny minority but also it insists on treating educators like middle-echelon civil servants and on running the University as if it were a prison or department of public works (not that these departments should be run that way either!), accountable for every action and penny.[8] One characteristic problem is that the budget does not provide for bringing men for an interview when they are being considered for teaching positions. This difficulty has been one reason for the heavy New England and Ivy League stamp on the newer faculty, as against the Big Ten flavor of the older generation of scientists, who could be hired more safely by professional references and recommendations. In any case, it is difficult to persuade men to migrate to Massachusetts to become assistant professors at $6000 a year, although some already trained in the East will remain there, so long as salary differentials remain small, held in place by the conventional New England feeling that the rest of the country is provincial and lacking in culture. How such regionalism will affect the faculty's long term definition of the University remains uncertain, however, for New Englanders may be more enthusiastic about making Massachusetts a Big Ten sort of institution than scholars who have themselves been trained in these institutions.

Yet despite such problems there is complete academic freedom, so that students can hear a professor explain that Communists do not have tails and that men once did, or that little boys loved their mothers when they were young but should feel free not to love them now. Furthermore, legislative niggardliness has brought undercover benefits, of

[8] A small group on the faculty has established a teachers' union (so far as we know, the only one in the state in an institution of higher learning), as if to respond to the state bureaucracy's implicit treatment of the faculty as petty civil servants. There is also, of course, an AAUP chapter.

which the most important is that by depriving the majority of higher education the Legislature has inadvertently made the public University highly selective and has thus fostered some of the attitudes useful in an elite. Perhaps because of selective admission most students seem to feel in some sense identified with the academic world, and side with it in its quarrels with the Legislature. Such solidarity may go so far as to convince the student faced with a dull professor that his boredom is the Legislature's fault rather than his instructor's, since no professor can be expected to be interesting on a low salary!

The embattled situation of the University has inevitably put the Administration in a position of leadership, in contrast to those more complacent and better endowed academic institutions in which a jealous faculty compels the abdication of leadership by the president and deans, and where department chairmanships rotate among presumptive equals. While President Mather pled the cause of public education before the Legislature, and before any audience that might conceivably listen, academic leadership was in the hands of the Provost. Numbers of department chairmen, however, holdovers from the prewar days, are men without scholarly reputations who confront a majority of younger colleagues who are far better trained and more scholarly. These chairmen must sometimes depend on their hierarchical rather than their personal authority, and they thus are ready to transmit any pressures or even suggestions from further up the chain of command. Unlike the situation at the University of Connecticut where the imperious builder-President has been all powerful, department chairmen at the University of Massachusetts have had considerable leeway, with some simply holding the fort and others hoping eventually to preside over a wider cosmos. For many of these, along with their younger constituents, the form of that cosmos is already given in plans for expanding graduate work, letting the teaching of nonhonors, lower division students gravitate to graduate students after the fashion of many of the major universities. However, there are emphatic voices in the faculty against traveling down this well-marked road, voices insisting that precisely such relatively unawakened students as are presently attending the University need the most gifted and dedicated teachers in their freshman and sophomore years if they are to become truly educated.

In this latter outlook, new and old strands mingle. There are for instance older scientists trained in Midwestern universities where bringing along bright students (such as they themselves had been) is taken for granted. In education and in business administration, a less cosmopolitan faculty with few metropolitan distractions can pay more attention to teaching (whereas the engineering faculty, as happens at many other institutions, is often distracted both from teaching and scholarship by consulting jobs). But some of the younger faculty in liberal arts do not want to sacrifice research to teaching but to stress both, stimulating the teacher by small classes and ample time for individual work with students, while encouraging research through frequent sabbaticals and easy access to funds.

We fear that those desiring the expansion of graduate work are likely to win out. Meanwhile it is our impression that the students most likely to be well taught, and to be interested in their work, are in the sciences. The students in the laboratories become apprentices. But the science students grouped around their teachers do not serve to create an intellectual and scientific culture on the campus as a whole; the split between what C. P. Snow speaks of as "the two cultures" is too strong for that. The bright students in the humanities get less support from the faculty and feel on the defensive; many are driven into a negative bohemian stance that often includes not doing any academic work whatsoever. In less rebellious students, solidarity may mean partial assimilation of the ideals of "well-roundedness" which characterize the dominant undergraduate culture. Whereas some engineers and chemists and the many mathematics majors seem able to work relentlessly without feeling guilty, looking only to their teachers and a few friends for social contact, the bright students we met in other fields seemed more suspicious of their own academic interests, and spoke to us contemptuously of "closet cases" who did nothing but study. Even bright students rarely staked their adequacy on intellectual skills and could admit that a book or teacher was "over their heads" (such a confession would be impossible for most Reed, Columbia, Chicago, or Antioch students). In general, the intellectual student at the University of Massachusetts seems uninvolved in his curriculum. He may find excitement in individual teachers, or in an enlightened group of friends such as those around the student newspaper, but our questions about profiting from reading in badly taught courses met only blank stares. In consequence, the potentially intellectual student who has not found inspiring teachers and friends is more hostile to the University than an equally disappointed Harvard student. The possibility that books might provide a range of vicarious experience transcending the limitations of the teacher or even the University does not mitigate his disillusion.

SOME GUESSES FOR THE FUTURE

Tied to the middle class rather than the elite, committed to technical rather than professional training, caught in a schism between Catholics and Protestants, and to a lesser extent between East and West, the University of Massachusetts is hardly in an enviable position. No other state of comparable wealth except New Jersey provides so few spaces for its local students. Yet many who have observed the University's trajectory since World War II believe it has a future, whatever the Legislature's inclination to keep the tax bill down and the eggheads in their place. In spite of the resignation of the President, his forces spent by seven years of campaigning, faculty members look forward to a brighter tomorrow, especially since (except in the sciences) their University has no relevant yesterday. All across the campus, new buildings rise to house the new students who have come with wartime and postwar fertility and with the spreading faith in higher education. New Ph.D.'s continue to be added to the staff, and, in many departments that have managed to maintain light teaching loads, scholarly "production" mounts. Those who worry about the quality of the students are also optimistic, foreseeing that the Legislature will continue to be unwilling to provide space for all applicants, and will therefore allow the admissions office to turn away two candidates out of three, and keep the University's average IQ among the highest in the country for a state university. As the veterans who got their college education in the late forties begin to send their children to college in the sixties, New England's nationally famous colleges will have to turn away more and more talented students who come from homes where they became familiar with books and ideas. The intellectual overflow is already being felt in Amherst.

Up to the present, the University of Massachusetts has not had to decide what its particular educational mission is, since it can continue to battle against the indifference of the public, and the undercover jealousy of private competitors. For some, it may be enough to bring public education to "backward" New England, while keeping an eye on the models of private academic respectability there. But others on the faculty are more ambitious or venturesome. An illustration is the plan for freshman orientation, which brings entering students in during the summer, small groups for a few days at a time, instead of exposing them in the fall to what might be called "disorientation week" when they are at the mercy of upperclassmen with activities, laundry, and other items to sell. Another illustration is the effort that the University of Massachusetts faculty and officials have put into the Four-College cooperative arrangements, not only in the library, but also in providing courses that no one of the institutions could alone arrange; thus, the University has taken the initiative in a program of studies in non-Western cultures, backed by the Ford Foundation. As a state university, charged with "residue" functions, the University of Massachusetts cannot shed its vocational aspects—nor should it seek to do so. What it can do, and what it is doing, is to add to these the emphasis on the liberal arts that traditionally accompanies a rise in social and academic standing. Whether this "liberalization" will be sufficient to create a student culture that is either scholarly or intellectual is less clear, both at the University of Massachusetts and in other colleges now emerging from a purely technical vocationalism.

Boston College *

If the foregoing vignette of the University of Massachusetts suffers from superficiality, this vignette of Boston College risks prejudice as well. For, although the authors are essentially sympathetic to the efforts of the former to raise the level of secular public education in New England, we have difficulty in grasping the mission of a church-controlled college, whether Catholic or Protestant. One possibility is to regard a church college merely as a secular college *manqué,* which could with due enlightenment and progress follow the well-worn path to secular academic grandeur. Perhaps another possibility is to regard the church college as a religious institution *manqué* that could, with due enlightenment and progress, express its religious outlook and ethic so searchingly as to challenge America's secular values and provide a genuine cultural choice for seemingly secular universities.

Of course, in our discussion of these issues and in our speculations on the future of Catholic colleges, we are aware of our position as outsiders, wanting in historical perspective and employing a secular

* By Christopher Jencks and David Riesman. We are indebted to the criticisms, of a draft of this vignette, of Leo J. Hines of Boston College; Frank M. Buckley of Assumption College; Thomas O'Dea of the University of Utah; Daniel J. Callahan and Paul Sigmund, Jr., of Harvard; George Z. F. Bereday of Teachers College; Peter New of the University of Missouri; and T. Scott Miyakawa of Boston University. Although some of their criticisms have been embodied in the text, there remain points of disagreement. In dealing with problems of ethnic succession and assimilation, as these affect higher education, we have been influenced by the work of Everett C. Hughes, Oscar Handlin, and their able students.

angle of vision and basis for comparison that may seem irrelevant if not offensive to the faithful.

Boston College is not merely a liberal arts school but a large complex institution. If the name "Boston University" had not been appropriated by the Methodists, the Jesuits would long since have re-labelled themselves. What we report here are simply impressions gained in the same rough-hewn way as with the University of Massachusetts, supplemented by brief visits to a few other Catholic colleges and by study of the interviews done at Catholic colleges and universities in the Fund for the Republic's survey of academic freedom (Lazarsfeld and Thielens, 1958).

As our foregoing analysis of religious interest groups indicates, we see American colleges as responding to a great diversity of pressures, and would not expect the explicitly denominational ones to remain aloof, tied only to other-worldly or spiritual goals. In this analysis of Boston College, too, we shall be concerned with the socio-economic context within which the College must exist, a context in which, as generally in the United States, ethnic issues cannot be separated from religious ones, or academic from theological ones.

THE ETHNIC HERITAGE

Perhaps the most important obstacle to fulfillment by Boston College of the hypothetical "Catholic" goals that we (and some Catholics) assign it is the still unliquidated legacy of the large Irish immigration to Boston that began in the 1840s. Whereas Catholic University, a Papal foundation, could early establish its importance as a graduate institution in a region where Catholics were among the earliest arrivals, Boston College was not founded until 1863 when a second generation in the Boston Irish community began to look for indigenous leadership to replace those priests from the old country who had initially tried to shield the immigrants from the brutal and disrupting pressures of the Yankee milieu. A few families, less impoverished than the rest, and often with some education in Ireland, wanted to send a talented son into the law or a Church vocation. Despite its still largely classical curriculum, Harvard was regarded as the enemy Yankee camp, and so Boston College was founded to provide a local alternative.

Most second-generation immigrants were too preoccupied with economic survival and building a parish to have energy or resources for higher learning. Yet such people often realized in middle age that the "American Way of Life" had eluded them, and they often concluded, or could be persuaded by a priest, that it could be secured for their children only through a heavier dose of education, including college. So, when the third generation began to come of age toward the end of the 19th century, the College began to play a really important role in the life of the community, and students who wanted to get out of the urban working class looked to it as a gateway to a richer and larger world.[9] Even for those who did not actually attend, the College became a symbol of what the Irish-American could accomplish in a hostile environment. Boston College, like other American colleges both Catholic and secular, had no real parallel in the old world, despite the fact that it initially adopted its curriculum and organization from European precedents.

For the gradually assimilating Irish-Americans of this era, Boston College offered an admirable compromise between the Yankee individualism of the old liberal arts colleges of New England and traditional Irish solidarity re-enforced by immigrant experience. The College provided intellectual discipline and prepared young men for professional life; at the same time it was Catholic rather than secular-Protestant; Irish rather than Yankee; and a commuter rather than a residential college. This last fact mattered to some families because in the parochial eyes of relatively uneducated parents and occasionally the diocesan priest, the intellectuality of the (sometimes French) Jesuits and the European heritage could seem suspiciously alien and cosmopolitan. Yet, so long as the student returned home every night, the family and the community could reassure themselves that he was not being changed beyond recognition, while in turn he could try to convince his family that the more emancipated ideas he was learning from the Jesuits were not heretical. Of course, family solidarity was not a prerequisite for every Catholic home, and other Boston students with more money and ambition enrolled in residential Holy Cross at Worcester. We need hardly add that, whatever the ethnic moorings, a dialectic between home and student operates at all colleges, differentially for commuters and for residents and for the first and second college-bound generations.

[9] The "third generation," crucial to theories of immigrant trajectories developed by Marcus Hansen and Oscar Handlin, is of course a social-psychological, not simply a genealogical, concept. Thus, the grandson of a man who arrived in 1845 might be more alien to America than the son of a man who arrived in 1880 because the latter's neighbors were more assimilated. So, too, immigrants, like native-born members of the working class, may in effect skip generations, by coming from families with a greater interest in education, or because of unusual qualities of personality or intellect, as these latter strike the American middle-class eye.

Inevitably many advantages of Boston College for the first college generation became more equivocal for the second generation. The sons of the College's alumni were more likely to be brought up in the suburbs than in South Boston. And in those suburbs where Catholics are a minority, the parochial schools have been less able to match the academic standards of their secular competitors than in Boston proper, and many of the more sophisticated and talented Catholics enrolled in public secondary schools. Once having tasted a world not restricted to Irish or even Catholic boundaries, many do not want to return. Attending Boston College threatened such a return, since it "typed" the alumnus as an Irish Catholic—at least if he stayed in Boston. Yet few of these students wanted to break radically with their background by choosing Harvard and typing themselves as Yankees, especially as the Yankees were not always very receptive to this new self-portrait. To avoid this dilemma many students simply went to school outside Boston, where such either/or distinctions were less common. Some picked secular colleges like the University of Massachusetts, while others picked Catholic colleges like Notre Dame or Georgetown. The latter bring social status within Catholic circles, whereas the former might help free the student from such circles. Still others, of course, did go to Boston College, in part because the College has evoked strong alumni loyalties and has provided a number of teachers in the better public schools, and in part because students want other things from their college career than a passport to polite society—although if other things are reasonably equal they may want that as well.

Of course these considerations are all mitigated by the fact that Boston College has never been purely Irish. Catholic universities, like Catholic parishes, have usually opposed in theory, if not in practice, the heresy of explicit ethnic control, even though some orders have had German or French roots just as some colleges have had Irish or French-Canadian personnel. Because Boston College has been the leading Catholic college in the Boston metropolitan area, Italians and East Europeans have usually aimed at it, whatever their personal or political animosities toward the Irish themselves. The fact that the full range of American Catholicism is not now mirrored at the College is more a comment on Boston than on the College; one does not expect to find many Puerto Rican or Mexican names in the New England college, nor many French names in the Eastern part of Massachusetts. But the College itself has encouraged all comers, even though it cannot single-handedly overcome the suspicions of various ethnic minorities for one another or for the Yankees (indeed one might raise the question whether any ecumenical ideal, either religious, American, or Communist, has been able to melt away ethnic nationalism within a single generation). There are Boston College alumni of Irish ancestry who regard an Italian name as not quite respectable, just as there are Yankee Harvard alumni who regret the replacement of "nice" Anglo-Saxons at their College by merely "bright" Jews. In both cases, however, the colleges, like the country of which they are a part, have worked in the long run to reduce the differences among these groups and the tensions built upon the differences.

Moreover, while moving to transcend its "Irish" label by greater ethnic heterogeneity, Boston College, through building dormitories, can now look to the whole country for students—again repeating a generic process. Attracted by whatever cultural magic still clings to Boston and by the interesting new academic programs Boston College has inaugurated, bright graduates of Jesuit high schools throughout the Northeast and Midwest are increasingly applying there. With a limited number of dormitory spaces available, admission standards for out-of-town boys are naturally higher than for commuters. And since only the comparatively well-off can afford to go away to college, or regard it as "necessary" (and since only a few brilliant students can get scholarships), the social standard of the residential students is higher than that of the commuters. In this fashion, the College appears to be developing two distinct constituencies: a national upper-middle-class group, who have consciously preferred it to other possibilities, and a local lower-middle-class group who have often not considered going elsewhere. It remains to be seen whether Boston College can maintain its hold on local Italians, Poles, and Irish who are taking their first steps out of the urban lower-middle class, while at the same time attracting and serving the sons of college-educated upper-middle-class Catholics from elsewhere. Rising admission standards may price the College out of the reach of the less talented and highly motivated students from limited home backgrounds (see Kahl, 1957), and the tendency of the most brilliant students to go where big scholarship money is offered may limit heterogeneity at the top. At the same time, however, the nearly universal tendency of intellectually and socially impoverished students to concentrate in the more directly vocational fields, like business and education, nursing and sometimes social work, will no doubt help Boston College to make its liberal arts program nationally attractive without having to turn away or flunk out too many local students. And if the Administration allows fraternities to spread from the Business College to the Liberal Arts College, this too may make it possible to maintain a heterogeneous constituency, by providing the social elite with "social security" against less sophisticated classmates. Devices of just this sort have allowed many state universities to maintain extraordinarily diverse patterns of recruitment, holding on to the state's leaders and the *jeunesse dorée* while also serving a wide range of less ambitious or less well-endowed youngsters. We are not suggesting that efforts to recruit and keep a socially and intellectually mixed constituency must be conscious or manipulative; rather such adaptive arrangements tend to grow through the uncoordinated free enterprise of individuals and groups among students, faculty, and administration. Limits to such expansion and diversity occur when boundaries cannot be crossed; thus Boston College is handicapped in attracting those Catholics who want to meet Protestants and Jews as well as other Catholics, just as the University of Massachusetts is handicapped by the limits put on its ability to recruit talented students from outside the state who would in turn provide a vigorous and challenging milieu for in-state young people.

OCCUPATIONAL SHIFTS

A second complication in the College's effort to realize distinctively Catholic aims has been the need to prepare students for jobs in the workaday world which pays ever less attention to religious differences. Originally, as we have seen, Boston College was concerned with creating an indigenous source of professional and religious leadership. Early alumni shied away from business ventures, perhaps reflecting less any distaste for business per se than the understandable belief that they would do better in professions rooted in their home communities than in commercial organizations dominated by Yankees (cf. West, 1953). With greater assimilation, the professions have lost much of their ethnic localism, and graduates of the College, like Catholics elsewhere, have increasingly found their way into large as well as small business; correspondingly, Boston College has begun to develop its graduate and undergraduate business programs. Recently the College has also sought to send students into the natural sciences, a career in which, as the Wesleyan studies show, graduates of Catholic colleges have played little part (Knapp and Goodrich, 1952; Knapp and Greenbaum, 1953). Nevertheless, the atmosphere of Boston College remains more oriented to the humanities than is the case with other colleges drawing on a similar socio-economic stratum. Today, although fewer alumni are taking holy orders, increasing numbers of alumni have been entering teaching, first in the schools, and now in the universities. The latter cadre may grow with the new Honors Program and the interest in the academic life this can evoke among gifted undergraduates. Boston College is one of the institutions which (as the University of Massachusetts did in the 1920s) manages to move some students from noncollege families into college teaching in a single generation.

CONFLICTING STANDARDS AND SUB-CULTURES

In addition to the Graduate School (which now stands about one hundredth in the country in number of doctorates produced but which until recently has been geared to M.A.'s, not Ph.D.'s) and the Business College, the College includes schools of Nursing and Education and graduate schools of Social Work, Law, and Business Administration. In all of these faculties, the Jesuits retain formal authority; and the fact that they live on the campus, while the lay faculty is scattered throughout the Boston area, enhances their influence, as at other Jesuit-controlled institutions. Until recently Jesuit policy has rotated the President every six years, strengthening the power of the entrenched faculty as against the itinerant Administration. This turnover is no longer required. But the needs of expansion and the desire to raise the scholarly reputation of the College have led the Administration to institute an up-or-out tenure system, with recommendations for promotion in the hands of faculty rather than of Administration. While the catalogue states: "On the Boston College faculty are 135 Jesuits, the largest community of priests at any Jesuit university or college in the world," the faculty contains four laymen for every priest, and as many laymen as priests even in the liberal arts; control of faculty employment is increasingly in the hands of the national disciplines rather than the Catholic Orders. Since the War, there has been an accelerating emphasis on research and publication and an increasing recruitment of Ph.D.'s from the leading secular graduate schools; and it is plain that many in the Administration and on the faculty are not satisfied to have the College remain a leader within the orbit of Catholic higher education but want to challenge the secular universities at their own game as well.

One handicap in this effort is that, like other Catholic colleges, Boston College has neither the support of the taxpayers nor many rich alumni. So long as the faculty were largely clerical, inability to pay first-rate salaries made little difference. But in order to recruit Ph.D.'s from the better secular graduate schools, as the College now seeks to do, faculty salaries will have to rise very fast in the next few years.

This in turn probably requires raising tuition well above its present level ($900) and losing touch with the traditional lower-middle-class constituency except for those brilliant students who can get scholarship aid. If salaries do not rise, the College, like most of its secular competitors, will probably have to fall back on the four teachers in five who now begin teaching with only an M.A. For, while there are a few Catholic scholars who find more sympathy for their special concerns in the Catholic rather than in the secular university, such scholars do not seem to be in the majority—especially when preferring a Catholic university means preferring a lower standard of living as well.

About these questions, including the implicit one as to whether there is anything distinctively Catholic about a "Catholic" college, we can only speculate. With the general renewal of religious energy in America, there has been an increased concern at Boston College with the implications of religion for humanistic scholarship. (This can be seen in *The Humanities,* the student-edited classical magazine which also reflects an interest in the Middle Ages.) Work in the social sciences, however, cannot so readily be anchored in tradition. Whereas Jesuits in Europe have studied such secular intellectual developments as psychoanalysis and Marxism and have made distinguished contributions to these fields as well as strengthening the Catholic intellectual and pastoral armory, many Jesuits at Boston College appear to believe that these domains are "covered" by Catholic humanism—a conviction encouraged by the history of conflicts between social scientists and Catholic theologians on such problems as population control, censorship, and the nature of religious experience. A Catholic variant of American concern for social problems, illustrated by Monsignor John A. Ryan of Catholic University or by the work of the Institute for Social Order in St. Louis University (also Jesuit), has its spokesmen in Boston College, but, as in the secular universities, this tradition has difficulty in connecting with the highly theoretical and "objective" concerns of most academic social science in this country. Indeed, the compartmentalization of the social sciences in America and the lack of contact among them on secular campuses only highlight the problems of bringing theological concerns to bear on them.

In the Protestant colleges when the Darwinian controversy arose, the "solution" arrived at was a de facto compartmentalization. In a few instances the clergyman president continued to give courses in moral philosophy while in others, nominally secular but actually Protestant, philosophers took up the burden. Meanwhile the professors of zoology and geology and later on sociology came to terms with the eventual secular state of their fields. So, too, it is our impression that the students at Boston College usually accept a divorce of religious and secular thought, just as they accept the divorce of history from sociology, or of literature from anthropology, as part of the inevitable academic order imposed by departments and courses—and perhaps by the very "Kantian" structure of knowledge itself. Students taught in theology class, for example, that their Church derives from certain supernatural historical events have no difficulty in accepting also the fact that in history classes supernatural explanations are disregarded by professors who have one eye on their own graduate training and the other eye on the graduate schools to which they hope their better pupils will go as testimonials to Boston College's academic integrity. Several students pointed quite cynically to instances when they had detected religious ideas "intruding" into secular thought, beyond the allotted beachhead of the courses in theology and philosophy. Others, more "fundamentalist" than their instructors, felt that lay and sometimes clerical faculty were sabotaging Catholicism by following some line of thought which appeared to ignore the Church's ideological commitments. Such students seem to expect a Catholic "line" on controversial subjects, even where none exists.[10]

But the majority of students, it is our impression, give such matters little thought. When prodded, they seem to support the idea that they should be protected from "error." No different from the equivalent students at a non-Catholic college, they are unwilling to argue with their teachers or textbooks. No doubt, the Catholic students of this sort have heard teachers or administrators say that Catholic higher education emphasizes "character" as well as "learning" (and, in fact, recruiters do speak of this); perhaps the students hope that their characters compensate for their lack of interest in learning for its own sake. Naturally, neither the Administration nor the faculty is satisfied with this, and the College is tentatively encouraging the evolution of a student culture in the hope of attracting more sophisticated students who can respond to scholarly professors.

Dissatisfied with the old "diploma-image" college whose recruits simply want a passport to white-collar existence, Boston College resembles a great many other universities in not being quite clear or secure as to the next step. Like other Catholic universities, it has had little enthusiasm for the "collegiate" or "romance-image" college. Al-

---

[10] Some years ago, at one of the Lutheran colleges of the Mid-west, one of the authors found a number of students, often children of small-town and rural ministers, who regarded the Department of Religion as the seat of subversion: some of its faculty had studied in Europe, and others were at home with the "heretical" views of theologians like Tillich and the Niebuhrs.

though the football team was once nationally famous and became a symbol of Boston Irish success, athletics have been de-emphasized in recent years despite characteristic alumni objections. Similarly, although fraternities have had a beginning in the Business College, they have not gotten anywhere in the Liberal Arts. As dormitories rise, it is plain that the Administration does not care to have them become the scene of the more traditional campus extracurricular obsessions; and Administration surveillance may be one reason why social activities seem not to have enlisted student initiative or imagination.

Likewise the Administration has been chary of coeducation, partly because in New England the "Ivy" single sex pattern has considerable inherited snob appeal and possibly also because coeducation might bring a good many girls and some boys not really interested in receiving a Jesuit education.[11]

Instead, as we have already indicated, the Administration is moving toward an "alumni-image" university, whose graduates attain scholarly and civic distinction. The Honors Program has helped channel creative energies into the intellectual world, where vivacious students find room for maneuver among like-minded fellow-students. But, although casual conversation suggests that some students share the preoccupations of writers for *Commonweal* or *America,* articulate undergraduate writers at Boston College appear to prefer sticking to the classic tradition rather than risking adult censure by debating the tensions of contemporary American Catholic thought. As compared with the University of Massachusetts, the style of Boston College strikes the visitor as less vocational and more academic; students have to work a good deal harder than in many non-Catholic colleges, and they learn to do assignments on time, memorize large amounts of material, and arrange this material suitably on frequent examinations. Creation of a large intellectual culture that goes beyond diligence is, however, held back in part by the fact that the College (which has an Evening College) remains a nine-to-five institution for all but the 1100 resident students and the clerical faculty and in part by the students' assumption that their personal concerns have no place in an academic institution.

At the same time, location in the Boston metropolitan area makes available many counterfoils to localism. By providing Ph.D.'s, visiting

[11] We might also speculate that the late-marrying Irish in Ireland have transmitted to their American descendants a cultural pattern of delaying contact with the opposite sex—a pattern only gradually breaking down under pressure from the all-American norm of early dating and mating.

speakers, libraries, and cultural events, Harvard, MIT, and the other neighboring institutions lend practical support to those at Boston College who regard the secular universities as a helpful if not wholly relevant yardstick. To others, including priests brought up to regard secular liberalism as the enemy, these universities, particularly Harvard, symbolize the dangers which current scholarly upgrading may bring. Such men are caught—or so it appears to the authors as outsiders—by the difficulty of delineating in terms that secularists can understand what specific kinds of syncretism between secular and Catholic learning the Catholic universities can achieve. However, such men may avoid the issue by supporting the College as an institution rather than supporting any intellectual ideal which it is supposed to embody, implicitly announcing "my college right or wrong." But upper-middle-class Catholic students concerned with meeting the challenges of secular thought, both in their own lives as Catholics and in their enlarging contacts with non-Catholics, may regard such men as dogmatic and paternalistic traditionalists to whom their parents might have responded but not they themselves.

The social and intellectual mobility of American life, and its industrial and technical and moral rationalism, create similar, if less immediately pressing, problems for all denominations, even in a period when ethnicity can still lend a sort of protective coloration to religion (Riesman, 1955). Boston College can continue to exist and even prosper by appealing to the vocational ambitions of the still-assimilating immigrant groups and to the social and intellectual ambitions of upper-middle-class Catholics in and out of the area. As we have seen in describing the University of Massachusetts, there is great and unfilled demand for higher education in the State; and Boston College profits from this, especially since it has, both within the Catholic community and in some quarters outside, greater eclat than the undervalued State University. As has already been indicated, Boston College may have the unwelcome choice of raising its tuition and losing the newer Catholic immigrants to the less costly public system (provided that this itself is permitted to expand) or else keeping tuition relatively low and losing the new Catholic scholars to the more affluent secular colleges—many of the less lushly endowed private colleges, whatever their original base of support, now are facing similar dilemmas.

On the whole, it seems to us that the future of Boston College is decidedly open. As we have implied throughout, its future is bound up with that of American Catholicism generally. Anti-Catholic prejudice appears to be declining, even in Boston.[12] Indeed, this very fact is one reason why thoughtful Catholics are so eager to build and strengthen their entire educational system, for as the Catholic population becomes generally upper-middle class, the "leakage" (of Catholics into the non-Catholic or indifferent world) can no longer be contained by Protestant pressure. (The rabbis and Jewish communal agencies face a similar problem with the decline of anti-Semitism although they have been able to fall back upon Israel.) But it is not easy to build a Catholic intellectual culture in countries such as America where the ablest Catholics in the sophisticated social strata seldom find their vocations in the Church. This difficulty is complicated by the Renaissance idea that an intellectual must be his own master in all ideological matters, and the corollary that, despite the counter-Reformation, Catholicism and intellectuality are somehow contradictory. The problem of developing an ideological base for Catholicism that can come to grips with intellectual and social developments in the last three centuries cannot be simply solved by appeals to dogmatism and by nostalgia for a simpler world, in spite of the fact that any "Catholic" approach to the problem must oppose many trends in today's secular life. Throughout its history the Church has frequently actually done both things, abandoning intransigence soon enough to avoid becoming anachronistic, and drawing from the wide gamut of Catholic thought over the centuries the justification for positions sufficiently progressive to help shape the future in line with Catholic ideals.

San Francisco State College *

Contrasts between Massachusetts and California have so long been a part of American folklore that undoubtedly they influenced our de-

[12] These lines were written before the 1960 election campaign with its revelation of large reservoirs of anti-Catholic bigotry throughout the country. However the authors still believe that anti-Catholic prejudice is receding, and interpret much anti-Kennedy animus as a last ditch desire to hold on to a royal family image of the presidency as part of the Protestant Establishment—an image enhanced by the monarchical nature of the Eisenhower regime.

* By Christopher Jencks and David Riesman. Like most community studies, this is a collective effort. Our work was assisted by Elizabeth Raspolic, who spent a nonresident term away from Bennington College helping our inquiries, and by numerous painstaking criticisms of several drafts of this vignette, some of which taught us as much as many weeks of "research." We are especially indebted to Dean Reginald Bell, and other members of the administration of San Francisco State College, who read several drafts of the vignette, and to S. I. Hayakawa and

cision to expand our parochial range by going to the opposite side of the country. For colleges in Massachusetts and California are nearly as different as the climate, geography, economics, and politics of the two states; indeed, many in California and a few in Massachusetts regard the contrast as historical and see the Massachusetts colleges as embodying a passing tradition whereas California heralds an emerging one. We knew that San Francisco State College had begun, not as a land-grant institution, but as a normal school, and that in the years since World War II, it had not only grown greatly as a liberal arts center, but also as a locale of energetic experiment—one that was open enough so that one of us (Jencks) could spend six months there as a part-time student in the Education Division, and as a part-time interviewer of students and faculty. Moreover, we knew that research on State was under way at the Center for the Study of Higher Education in Berkeley; and through the generous and discerning cooperation of Martin Trow and Burton Clark of the Center, we had access to extensive questionnaire materials comparing undergraduates at State with those at other institutions. This work at Berkeley, and Jencks' field experience, have in some small measure helped us to cope with the truly insurmountable difficulties of writing a reasonably accurate ethnography of a community of more than 10,000, including a full-time faculty of over 400. The reader, however, should keep in mind that, despite our own best efforts, and that of our critics at San Francisco State itself, our frame of reference, formed in the East and Midwest, may not be wholly appropriate to the college we are now discussing.

OCCUPATIONAL, SOCIAL AND GEOGRAPHIC PRESSURES

In very recent years, the scientific communities of MIT and Harvard have been among the factors in the development of a number of scientific companies in the Boston area engaged in research and development, primarily in electronics and related fields. But although these companies have absorbed some of New England's skilled labor force, their presence has not greatly increased the demand that public

Leo Young, of the San Francisco State College faculty, who did likewise. We are also indebted to Robert A. Nisbet, Herbert Maccoby, Ralph H. Turner, Nahum Medalia, Joseph Gusfield, Seymour Lipset, and Wilson Record for their commentary. Finally, we are indebted to the administration at San Francisco State, and especially to Merle Milfs, who not only allowed but also assisted our investigations.

institutions, such as the University of Massachusetts, increase their output of scientifically trained graduates. In California, however, the relation between occupational facilities and public education is closer and far more visible. Modern, highly technical industry, can follow its labor supply as earlier industries would have followed water power or basic minerals, and California's continuing investment in education has been one factor in providing the state with a larger supply of socially and technologically skilled employees than any other state possesses. To be sure, many Eastern-trained technicians want to live in California, and the aircraft and electronic companies in the southern part of the state have taken advantage of climate and scenery. The 30,-000 persons who graduate each year from California colleges have, however, along with the 400,000 new immigrants to the state, been an important factor in the spectacular increase of people and plants (the number of the former has doubled every generation for a century).

We do not, however, want to overstress the rationality of California's investment in education, rationality that is, in occupational and economic terms. California is the state in which a small aircraft company several years ago pioneered with a four-day week once a month to allow its employees to take even greater advantage of the leisure resources of Southern California, and the state whose public authorities commission surveys of the market for boating in order to see whether additional marinas should be provided at public expense. The existence of more tuition-free local colleges than in any other state, despite the presence of many old people afraid of inflation and resentful of tax expenditure, is as much a result of affluence as a cause of it, for California has gone further in developing all forms of leisure than most other states. The mere physical presence of a nearby college, socially and academically as well as geographically accessible, serves as a kind of automatic recruiting station for the collegiate way of life. In California, these local centers of simultaneous relaxation and advancement include the six branches of the state university, the spreading net of state colleges, now fifteen, and (at last count) some sixty-three junior colleges.

Since there is more money in California to pay whatever incidental expenses arise out of going to college (including the children's earnings foregone by parents), and since there are fewer people from peasant or proletarian backgrounds to whom education seems either irrelevant or dangerous, the ability to earn a degree is probably a better index of sheer diligence and ambition in California than in any other state. By the same token, employers find it easy to demand a college degree when they are in the market for skilled employees. Of the state's high school graduates, 45% go directly to college, compared to an average of 35% in other states. Beyond that, more than half the people who first entered the job market with high school diplomas eventually return to college for further study, either in hope of piercing the ceiling imposed on the "uneducated" or, at the very least, in order to confirm their convictions that a college degree is out of reach.[13]

California is second only to Utah in the democratization of education in this country. This does not necessarily mean that the public sector overshadows the private at all levels. There are states where the public systems have an even greater predominance, for instance Kansas, Washington, Colorado, or Wisconsin; California simply has more of everything; and the patterns and tendencies we shall describe for San Francisco State College may be indicative of prospects elsewhere. At the undergraduate level Berkeley's academic eminence offsets the social eclat (and rising academic distinction) of Stanford.[14] And although San Francisco State College overshadows the University of San Francisco (Jesuit), even for most Catholics, this is not true for all. Among the smaller institutions (Cal Tech, Mills, the Claremont Colleges) it is easier to find an idiosyncratic public that prefers private colleges to the state's best.

At many of the public urban colleges of this country such as San Francisco State, one finds a very different relation between academic and nonacademic work from that characteristic of the New England institutions we have sketched hitherto. Even in the land-grant orbit, the latter colleges were designed to train the unemployed for a workaday world about which they were largely ignorant.[15] At State (as San

[13] Accurate figures on the number of people returning to college are difficult to obtain. The enrollment of college freshmen in a given year averages about 80% of the previous year's high school graduates, but this figure is slightly inflated by the surplus of immigrant over emigrant college students in the state, and by the fact that some students spend more than one year as college freshmen. Furthermore, it is difficult to predict how many current high school graduates will return to college as adults, for it may be that with adolescent enrollments rising, there will be fewer late-starters in the future. All things considered, at least two high school graduates in three will get some college exposure.

[14] Although Stanford has more snob appeal than Berkeley outside the state (and in some parts of the state), "back East" has more than Stanford in the West; caught in the same squeeze as other private universities Stanford has increasingly had to look outside its own community for talent.

[15] Northeastern University in Boston is one of the few, along with Antioch and the University of Cincinnati, and Dearborn College of the University of Michigan, to make any systematic attempt to give students experience with jobs that might be relevant for future careers, or at least to capitalize on the experience of those students who are forced to work.

Francisco State College is often called) nearly a third of the students are working full-time while taking from one to five courses, while another third work part-time while going to school either part- or full-time. Furthermore, although even the well-to-do college youth today usually takes a summer job as camp counselor, waiter, or laborer, one freshman, two sophomores, and three seniors out of four at State have taken terms off for more regular employment. Men without job experience are almost unknown at State, and even girls are seldom innocent of work.[16] Certainly, we never heard anyone at State contrast undergraduate life to "real" life, or speak, as undergraduates in the East often do, of the the "outside" world. Indeed, we never even heard a student at State described as an "undergraduate," for the term implies a stylized collegiate age-grade, waiting to become "graduates," which is completely alien to the College. Many pupils at State are not even quite at ease when called "students," for subjectively their most important occupation is often not studying, but teaching, or accounting, or washing dishes.

Yet it would be a mistake to overemphasize the sophistication of these students about their careers. Nine out of ten freshmen say that they know what they want to do when they graduate, but many have very vague ideas and many others will change their minds when they find out what their intentions really lead to. That is why, although seven out of ten say that their main purpose in coming to college was to learn a skill, only five out of ten have decided what they are going to major in. Presumably the other two in ten must have rather unformed occupational plans, hoping to teach without knowing what they will teach, or hoping to go into business without having much idea what specific or even general activities will be expected of them. Many such students have a vocational attitude toward college because it has never occurred to them that one could have any other attitude. They know or assume that the kind of work they want to do, or perhaps the kind of life they want to lead, requires a B.A.

By the time they are sophomores, on-the-job experience and upperclassmen will have taught them that although certain components of an occupation can be learned in the classroom, many social and administrative aspects of work can only be learned on the job. At this point, some have the openness to accept the faculty's offer to give them

---

[16] Somewhat comparable data might be found at other urban institutions, e.g., the average student at Wayne State University takes eleven terms to complete an eight-term liberal arts degree—figures that might suggest the recession-proneness of Detroit as well as the greater fluidity of boundaries between college and non-college as one moves West.

a "general" education in lieu of technical training; others disbelieve the faculty, and keep looking for more and more technical courses in which they can get "practical" knowledge instead of "bull." As in any large institution, there are naturally faculty members who will take advantage of this quest, including some old-timers who entered State when it had fewer liberal arts ambitions. Nevertheless, when one studies questionnaire returns, what is surprising is the number of students who are converted to at least verbal acceptance of the ideals of liberal education. Admittedly, the majority pursue neither explicitly intellectual aims, nor sharply defined technical training, but stoically and unenthusiastically try to get through as quickly as possible. But considering the national obsession with employing B.A.'s, it is surprising how many students still think of education as an opportunity rather than an obstacle.

Even among those who never become interested in ideas, resistance rarely takes the form of an aggressive anti-intellectualism such as is common on many campuses. Intellectual problems are, however, diluted with nonintellectual considerations—something not unique at State —as when a prospective teacher asks, "What good will all this philosophy do me in the classroom?" It is easy for academicians to scorn the Philistinism of such a question, but it is less easy to see how a faculty can connect philosophy or other traditional academic disciplines with the students' present and prospective experience; we do not think the question of relevance can be automatically dismissed. Many State students seem to come to college without a preconceived prejudice against ideas or works of art. By the same token, the students have not come to the end of ideology because they were never at the beginning; faced with an idea, only a few students will pursue it with excitement, but neither will they reject or resent it. Rarely are they interested in brooding on their studies, but most are at least willing to assimilate the subject-matter put before them—especially if they are thinking of teaching it to school children in a few years. Intellectual indolence inevitably thrives among physically exhausted students who simply look blank if they are asked what they do with their leisure time. But lack of curiosity is also a cultural problem related to the narrow perspectives of insecure lower-middle-class students who are on their way up, but who are still a little afraid of heights. Naturally, the faculty who have come up as well without gaining a sense of the excitement possible in intellectual life either in their homes or in their college and postcollege work, may support the narrow outlook of the students by an equally narrow professional view of their own field. Faculty members are perhaps especially effective in doing this if they have "met a payroll" within their field. Thus, one obvious form of such professionalism is found among those instructors at State who have spent so long in the public schools coping with juveniles that they no longer see any point in the academicians' concern with intellectual consistency, precision, or elegance, and hence re-enforce the student in his eagerness to be practical and realistic.

The role of such teachers is certainly on the decline, even within the Education Division. For San Francisco State College has followed what we have described above as a typical career pattern for a state normal school. The College is trying simultaneously to raise the sights of prospective teachers and to expand rapidly into other occupational fields. Nevertheless, although emancipation from its past has been proceeding rapidly, teachers remain the occupational group most deeply committed to State.

Founded sixty years ago as San Francisco State Normal School, the College was California's fifth two-year training center for schoolmistresses. Soon, however, neither the program nor the students seemed adequate to a faculty and administration for whom higher education was often defined by graduate work at the University of California, Stanford, Southern California, the Big Ten, or more recently, Chicago, Teachers College at Columbia, and other Eastern schools. After World War I the faculty's academic aspirations combined with the public school teachers' social aspirations to persuade the legislature—already under pressure from constituents to provide "real" four-year local colleges—to upgrade the normal schools. State Normal became State Teachers: a four-year school granting the B.A. to those elementary school teachers who wanted the additional salary, kudos, and competence. By the Thirties, the required program was also extended from two to three years, and came to include some work in the liberal arts. These expanded offerings began to attract a few nonteachers who were neither among the academic elite qualified for the University, nor among the social elite who could afford a private college, but who still wanted a B.A. To mark the change, State Teachers became State College. At each point in this and later developments, the presence of some students who wanted more than the minimum provided the basis for a faculty beyond the minimum, and this in turn—in a legitimate form of academic check-kiting—provided the facilities that could then be used to lay claim to the next step up the ladder of academic aspiration.

A state college has quite a different relationship to the occupational world than has a teachers college. Up to the late Thirties, State had grown up with the teaching profession. Every effort to raise standards in the College had inevitably meant an effort to raise the standards of preparation and competence in the public schools. Indeed, the aspirations of the faculty had often been an important lever for upgrading the teaching profession and the schools, for it was only by doing this that professors in a teachers college could bring their institution closer to their own ideals. But when the Teachers College began in the Thirties to attract nonteachers, it began an entirely new means of evolution: the redefinition of the College to attract ever more impressive students and faculty from other walks of life. Able professors no longer had to struggle with the often unpromising future teacher. Instead, they could write such students off as hopeless, and direct their energies to more talented recruits to other occupations.[17] The abundance of students after 1945 encouraged this process, and the College was able to grow at an accelerating rate, beyond the need for the training of teachers. Indeed it had to do so, for once it recruited nonteachers it had to begin thinking of itself as an institution of higher education rather than as an arm of the public school enterprise, and consequently invidious comparisons with the University became inevitable. Yet we would guess that even the "neglected" teachers have actually profited from the growing cosmopolitanism of the College, for although they probably get less attention from the faculty than in the past, this faculty is certainly more talented.[18] Furthermore, it is almost certainly an advantage for future teachers to associate with fellow-students with wider experience and sympathy than the lower-middle-class girls looking for a respectable way to be cultured, useful, and safe, who dominated the old Teachers College.

The new State College did not really come into its own until after 1945, when the jockeying of a skillful and energetic president allowed it to exploit the unprecedented demand for education in a move toward real distinction. The University moved in the postwar years

[17] It is often an open question whether would-be businessmen, social workers, or civil servants are any brighter than would-be teachers. As other middle-level jobs have come to require B.A.'s, teaching has lost its monopoly on undergraduate mediocrity, and snobbery toward education now extends to business and other fields. Hence the current emphasis on "solid" liberal arts courses, and on "real education" instead of "mere training." Whether the prestige of the liberal arts depends on more than the superiority and snobbery of its students and teachers, and reflects inherently more enlightening subject matter, is not always asked.

[18] It could be argued that a more stimulating but also more theoretical college education will make prospective teachers dissatisfied with, or unequipped for, blackboard jungles and other depressing school conditions. But State is not yet pricing its teaching products out of the market, particularly the highly priced and on the whole well-protected (by credential minima) California market.

to set up other campuses, but these could not begin to create enough graduates with liberal arts degrees to meet California's needs. Nor was the University of California prepared to increase output by lowering its own admission standards. Unable to cope with shortages of college classrooms and college graduates, the University had to share responsibility for several kinds of training, including that of high school teachers. As the state colleges began to train secondary school teachers, they were forced to expand their subject-matter divisions further, and the improvement of these facilities attracted new cadres of liberal arts students, while at the same time encouraging undergraduates to abandon teaching careers for other interests. But of course such students in their turn wanted to be prepared for *some* career: if not teaching, then business, social work, creative arts, or more recently, nursing and engineering.[19]

To be sure, not all state colleges, pushed by energetic presidents, have sought upgrading to quasi-university status; some faculty members have feared the competition and pressures entering a new league would bring, whereas others have been satisfied with present prospects and capacities. But in those state colleges where the curriculum was broadened to absorb new occupations, it was also likely to be

---

[19] We cannot resist the suspicion that this gradual diversification of the old teachers colleges is one reason for the growing teacher shortage. There was a time when school teaching was a short-cut to respectability for those who could not manage four years away from home at the university but could devote two or three years to the local teachers college. Limited as it was, a teaching career offered such a student as much money, power, and prestige as he would be likely to earn in any other job to which he had access. Today other occupations such as corporate administration and engineering have discovered the advantages of having local "field representatives" in every community and, having won a place in the new state colleges they can easily offer the majority of students a richer life in terms of the conventional amenities. Nevertheless a small number of gifted young men are entering teaching, especially at the high school level, because they like it, feel the importance of the calling, and reject conventional definitions of success. Group averages show, however, that the majority of male recruits to teaching have lower aptitudes than those in engineering or the sciences. For the gifted and dedicated who want a career of service, work in technical missions abroad may soon compete heavily with teaching. The expansion of the state colleges, however, has so far opened relatively few alternatives for women, but if business and technology use any ingenuity in devising part-time employment for skilled wives, they may scuttle the schools even among this "minority." Today only a few people with very special talents can use them more effectively as teachers than in other careers, and the majority of male recruits are therefore the inept who cannot pass scientific courses and the ineffectual who cannot cope (or fear they cannot cope) with the adult world—and perhaps do not yet realize how hard it is to cope daily with the young.

lengthened to absorb still others. Having undertaken to train high
school teachers, the state colleges had to be given permission to offer
the year of graduate work that California requires of such employees.
Once graduate work was being offered, it was natural to complete
the picture by offering the Master's degree, first to school teachers and
then to junior college teachers and other specialists who were merely
going through the motions of getting certified in order to get an M.A.
in their field. Each step in this progression was resisted by the University of California, concerned that even California's educational
dollar could not be indefinitely stretched, and also fearful lest the
mushrooming of graduate programs across the Bay and elsewhere in
the State dilute its own effectiveness. Nevertheless, shortages of school
administrators and college faculty, especially in the junior colleges,
promised to undermine even the University of California's monopoly
on the doctorate in the coming decade, and the state's Master Plan
Survey Team has recommended that the state colleges be permitted
to offer this degree jointly with the University of California.[20] The
enormous expense to the State of duplicating graduate facilities led
to the decision of the Survey Team to recommend limiting the primarily graduate professions such as law, medicine, and much academic
research to the University of California (that is, in practice at present to Berkeley and UCLA), while giving the state colleges permission to grant Ph.D.'s jointly with the University. The present aims
of San Francisco State seem well represented by the message of President Dumke in introducing his 1960 Report:

> Realizing that state college faculty members come from the same man-
> power pools as the universities and have the same professional training and
> aspirations, we attempted, through our participation in the Master Plan ne-
> gotiations, to achieve for state college faculties recognition of their desire to
> do research to keep themselves professionally alive and to make their teach-
> ing more effective.
> We accept the fact that more emphasis will be placed in the state colleges
> on teaching than on research, but we recognize the necessity of the latter
> and the responsibility of every college and university to push at the frontiers
> of knowledge as well as to pass on the wisdom of the culture to succeeding
> generations . . .

As the foregoing historical sketch suggests, while the demand for
more trained graduates originates in the economy, it can develop independent momentum once it becomes entrenched in a college or
university. Thus, the state colleges now turn out so many B.A.'s that

[20] See *A Master Plan for Higher Education in California, 1960–1975.* Prepared for
the Liaison Committee of the State Board of Education and the Regents of the
University of California, Sacramento, Calif., Calif. State Dept. Education, 1960.

it is difficult for the economy to expand fast enough for all the new graduates to find the kind of jobs to which they feel entitled by reason of their diplomas. One result is that jobs that formerly could not demand a degree can now do so, often without comparable increases in salary, skill, or status. Similarly, jobs that were once open to B.A.'s gradually become restricted to M.A.'s, as may happen in school teaching if the unions have their way. This occupational inflation is often accompanied by devaluation of the academic currency, so that students know no more at the end of five years than they once knew at the end of four. In other cases, however, the effect is more constructive, and recruits to the newly professionalized jobs are actually more competent and more sophisticated, helping in their turn to produce a still greater demand for college graduates in the rest of the office or industry, and also in their outside leisure-time activities.

For this reason, it is impossible to conclude our discussion of occupational commitments without some general remarks about the overall pattern of social mobility in California. As already suggested, San Francisco State seems at first glance to be simply another instance of the standard type of "first generation" college, moving students from lower-middle to upper-middle class, from white-collar to professional jobs, from urban to suburban styles of life. But in California, as increasingly in the rest of the country, such neat patterns have become somewhat muddled. In a state where nearly everyone is socially mobile and over one-half eventually go to college, higher education may provide little real transition. Our hypothetical lower-middle-class State parent turns out to have an annual income of $6000 and in two cases out of three to live in suburbia already. Very often he has also absorbed many of the all-American collegiate values, and holds a job that requires as much talent and skill as any that his son will occupy. To be sure, many jobs are becoming more technically intricate, and such jobs are growing in numbers and proportion of the total labor force. Even so, however, the increasing number of diploma holders is met in part by a relabeling rather than a redesigning of jobs, so that many allegedly professional positions will demand not much more expertise or responsibility than the kind of white-collar work open to an earlier generation of high school graduates.[21]

[21] As a comparative background for the foregoing remarks, we have relied on Seymour M. Lipset and Reinhard Bendix, *Social Mobility in Industrial Society* (1959), in which the mobility of a sample of Oakland workers is described. This book calls attention to the subjective feelings that may accompany different trajectories, and that may make the son feel he has risen above his father's position even where this rise is partly the result of a shift in the entire labor force, and partly the result of the relabeling and relocation that an affluent society allows.

The parents of State students may not be proletarian, and may be earning incomes above the national average, yet it does not follow that they took college-going for granted in their progeny, many of whom landed in college because it was accessible and tuition-free, and because their classmates were going, and not because their homes prepared them for this journey.[22] Despite many cosmopolitan exceptions who come because they are attracted by specific programs, or because the city of San Francisco appeals to them, the majority of freshmen at State are an immense distance from the social and cultural attitudes of the highly educated among their own faculty. These freshmen come from homes in which neither books nor conversation (as opposed to talk) are available, and where the fund of general information seems depressingly low to teachers whose own undergraduate work began from a higher plateau.

And there is little in the still-underdeveloped student culture at State to warn the entering students that a more sophisticated outlook is expected of them; the freshmen may realize that they will have to study harder in college than in high school, but they are seldom aware of having to make a qualitative change in outlook. The democratization of education has meant the creation of colleges so uniformly lower-middle class in style that the very notion that college should mark a decisive change into the "diploma elite" may never enter, or may be dismissed as mere snobbery if it does. If they think about the matter at all, many students at State appear to assume that all they need to become upper-middle class is the right job, and that this job will become available once they have accumulated sufficient course credits. When these students discover that success in certain kinds of careers requires an upper-middle-class outlook and manner, of which the B.A. is merely the much abused symbol, they often abandon their ambitions and settle for less demanding careers that will require less in the way of social adaptation. Intellectuals like ourselves, who look with some distaste on what Lloyd Warner has called the "core culture" of the lower-middle class, may nevertheless take a certain wry satisfaction in the stubbornness with which many of these State students cling to their family values, preferring unadaptability to smoothness, innocence to sophistication.

Yet all this seems to be changing gradually. As at other urban col-

[22] We think that many Californians go to college who come from backgrounds like those described by Joseph Kahl (1953, page 188). Especially because so many of the California colleges are seen primarily as vocational training centers, attending them is not regarded as a betrayal of the father's own values but rather as a vicarious realization of the father's own aspirations.

leges, such as Wayne State and CCNY, some professors at San Francisco State look back nostalgically to the days when the College's convenient downtown location and the G.I. Bill attracted a more contentious and proletarian student body.[23] No one seems to know what has happened to these students. Professor Martin Trow suggests that in fact they are still present, but increasingly outnumbered by the nonproletarian ones. We have no solid evidence for the belief of some of the faculty that the species has vanished with postwar prosperity, or been scared off by the modern "middle-class" suburban campus of State, or that they are going instead to the Jesuit University of San Francisco in spite of having to pay tuition. Our own impression is somewhat similar: some "proletarians" are still at State; but as the College has grown, most of its additional students have come not from the urban working class, but from the suburban middle and lower-middle class. Today, State attracts several thousand students from homes where one or both parents have attended college, and these students, with their efforts to develop such "collegiate" appurtenances as fraternities and student government, are highly visible. To be sure, most students even today regard such nonvocational "activities" as silly and juvenile. In this view, and especially in antagonism to nationally affiliated fraternities, the students have support from many faculty members, both older ones who remember the Depression and younger ones with Ph.D.'s from the major universities. But much of the resistance of some of the students to fraternities is, unlike the faculty's, not ideological, and the gap remains at State, as at other city colleges, between the majority of the students of the 1950s who are vocationally oriented products of the welfare state and those faculty members who equate hard work with hard times and radical views.

THE EMERGING CONSTITUENCY

The University of California a few years ago started what is in effect a new experimental college in its branch at Riverside, which was designed as a small institution on the Oberlin model, emphasizing undergraduate rather than graduate work. So, too, the University branch to be built at La Jolla will be small and hopefully experimental. It seems in some ways easier to begin again in a new geo-

---

[23] Since the above lines were written, some State students took part in the riot provoked by the House Un-American Activities Committee in San Francisco in May, 1960, and SLATE has started a student political party there analogous to the one at Berkeley. There is also a small group of Socialists at State.

graphic spot, as Michigan State University has done in its new college at Oakland, and the University of Michigan may be able to do in its Flint and Dearborn branches. (Monteith College of Wayne State University is, as we shall see, unusual in being both geographically and administratively within Wayne.) However, San Francisco State College, although it has moved from the central city to a more suburban location (though within the city limits) must still respond to the pressures of its traditional constituency. It cannot abandon either the public schools or the lower-middle class, even though the ratio of would-be school teachers may continue to decline below the present 40%, and the ratio of college-educated parents may rise somewhat above 20%. It must continue also to depend on young women looking for a husband, young Italians becoming more "American," and adult "evening students" seeking promotion, relief from tedium, or both. Allowed as it is by the state budget to add a faculty member for every additional sixteen students, State is not likely to turn away recruits from the groups it has hitherto served.

Within the State of California, as within the nation as a whole, the processes of centralization and decentralization are both proceeding furiously, and it is difficult to say at any given moment which is the stronger. We have already indicated that the Berkeley campus of the University of California serves not only San Francisco but the whole state; and indeed, despite the immense growth of Stanford and of UCLA, Berkeley remains the academic and scientific center for the Western United States, and shares hegemony over the nation with the great centers of the East. (The Harvard émigré at Berkeley sometimes feels that the snobbery of the Bay area vis-à-vis the growing economic and cultural domination of the state by Los Angeles bears some resemblance to the snobbery of Bostonians vis-à-vis New Yorkers.) Even in the age of suburban shopping centers, the most sophisticated and affluent customers still seek out the department stores and the specialty stores of the metropolis, both because they can obtain a wider range of selection, and because they can get the most cosmopolitan and advanced designs—those that can only be marketed from a major center because they do not as yet appeal to the "middle majority" market. In this sense, Berkeley is still "the" University of San Francisco despite being half an hour away on the other side of the Bay.[24] Although there are many students at State who could meet the stiff entrance requirements of Berkeley (or the other half dozen

[24] In this respect there are similarities between the position of San Francisco State and the University of Massachusetts, for both of these institutions have higher standards and are harder to get into than many far better known state universities, and yet suffer by being in the shadow of still more eminent institutions.

branches of the University), and although some of these are attracted to State, as we have already said, by specific programs (as in the arts, or in education for handicapped children), many of those at State lack the time or money, energy or adventurousness that Berkeley connotes.

Meanwhile, as the network of state colleges grows (fifteen at present) and the junior college network likewise (over sixty at present), San Francisco State casts its own net steadily wider and seeks by the quality of its education as well as its specialized programs to attract a statewide clientele. Almost half the students still come from San Francisco, and only about 15% are from outside the Bay area.[25] Yet the fact that five students in six are from counties around the Bay hardly makes State parochial, for these counties encompass an area and population greater than Connecticut's. The fact that State can attract suburban students, competing not only with Berkeley but with other state colleges, indicates more than purely local appeal. Nevertheless, State has never drawn heavily from the southern end of the Bay, where students can more easily reach older and classier San Jose State, and the new state colleges in Alameda and Marin Counties will no doubt cut recruiting in these areas. Whether this will be a blessing or a curse remains to be seen. On the one hand, the College loses little in students who now prefer Alameda State only because it saves twenty minutes driving time and fifty cents in bridge tolls. On the other hand, the suburbs are, on the whole, likely to provide more responsive students than the city, especially as the better students in the city may be scared away by the outdated teachers college image, unknown in suburbia. Since, however, very few states are as generous as California in locating colleges within commuting distance of the great majority of the population, loss of nearby commuters could encourage a drive for less satisfied out-of-state students, who might be lured a thousand miles to San Francisco State almost as easily as a hundred or more miles to the nearest branch of their own state college system; and although many such out-of-state students are likely to think first of Berkeley, both tuition and admissions requirements for non-Californians are much higher there than at the State Colleges.[26]

[25] Statistics are distorted by the fact that more than one student in four maintains his own "home" in San Francisco. Even if students come from out of state, they will give their local address in order to avoid paying tuition. Hence less than 5% of the students admit to not being Californians, and of these nearly half are overseas students attracted by low admission standards and special programs for those who cannot speak English.

[26] Out-of-state tuition at the University of California is $250 per semester and at the state colleges $127.50 over and above other fees. Although this difference

In such out-of-state competition for students, San Francisco State would seem caught in a dilemma it shares with the other state colleges. The present division of labor in California between the State University and the state college system allows the state to save from five hundred to a thousand dollars per student by staffing its "retail" branch outlets with professors who are supposed merely to dispense ideas (instead of scholars who are supposed to invent or at least to categorize them). In certain fields such as the arts, or work with exceptional children, the University's patent on originality does not run; and in a few other fields, such as international relations, San Francisco State has successfully gained foundation support and developed its own research program. But it remains to be seen whether such areas of distinction can be generalized sufficiently to develop State as a real intellectual center for the West; undoubtedly, this is the aim of many leading spirits in the institution.

THE COMMUTER COLLEGE AS A COMMUNITY

When we turn from State's role in the local and national academic scene, and examine the College as a unique community, we find how much more difficult it is to use anthropological analogies for a commuter college than it is for a residential one. Although two new dormitories have just been opened to 800 students, hardly anyone lived on the campus when we were there, and the social organization resembled that of a factory, to which various people came for a limited number of hours each day. Or at least that is how it struck us in 1959 and 1960; since then, the situation has changed somewhat, with nearly 10% of the students residing on campus. Authorities at State believe that the new residence halls have already markedly influenced campus patterns (as it is pretty clear they have at Boston College). Still, the development of a full residential culture at State is a long way off.

Whereas students at a residential college often talk about "their" college with the same kind of romanticism most Americans reserve for their families, State students more often displayed the kind of cynicism typically saved for employers. These students did not identify with State, and they were usually involved only marginally in college

may not seem large compared to the cost of travel and subsistence, neither does the difference between the so-called low-priced and the so-called medium-priced cars seem very great, and yet the differential remains significant both as fact and symbol.

life.[27] They had not come to State in order to become its alumni, nor did they regard their "undergraduate years" as a stage of life through which they passed on their way to adulthood. Education did not appear to be an initiation rite, but merely a consumer good. Of course not every student had the same idea of what he was acquiring at the College, nor were all acquiring similar things. Perhaps one in five wanted an education in the traditional liberal arts sense, while another one in five seemed to want specific technical skills that would be useful on the job.[28] The great indifferent majority—those who, in a residential college, or more typical state university, would form the "collegiate" group—appeared to want simply sufficient course credits for the degree as a prerequisite for a job. Whereas the metabolic processes at a Big Ten institution operate through the student culture, turning even indifferent students into devout and potentially important alumni of "their" institution, San Francisco State presently escapes the mixed blessings of having such loyal products.

This reflects more than the lack of dormitories, and is not likely to have changed abruptly with the opening of two dormitories in the fall of 1960. Consciously or not, the educational planners in Sacramento have had an interest in preventing colleges from becoming tightly-knit and chauvinistic communities that would give rise to powerful alumni demands that "our" college be made as respectable and impressive as the biggest research center in the state. The continuing effort to use the Master Plan and other sophisticated compromises to prevent the Balkanization of California's higher education, and to assign relevant and hopefully not too competitive missions to the state's eighty institutions, can be successful only at the price of keeping the majority of the state colleges permanently "underdeveloped" as centers of research and graduate training, while allowing the University of California to play the role of benevolent mother-country. Such "underdevelopment" (by the almost universally accepted standards of scholarly industry), is in turn dependent on the ability to suppress institutional nationalism.

Indeed, higher education in California has many of the features that distinguish contemporary welfare capitalism. Although the so-called selective colleges of the East have made their recruiting process a mysterious and intimidating ritual, convincing the applicant that "making" the college of his choice is vital to his whole self-conception

[27] We draw here primarily on interviews Jencks did with 30 students.

[28] We draw here (as also in the discussion on page 162) on the study by Martin Trow and Burton Clark already referred to, although they are not responsible for our interpretation of their questionnaire data.

and his future, such anxieties are unusual in California despite the increasing selectivity of the State University and State College systems. For one thing, admission is based almost entirely on high school grades, and it follows that the student not only knows what he needs to do to get in, but can usually tell well in advance whether he has qualified. In consequence, there is no feeling for those who do get in of having been specially chosen by "their" college; for those who fail, there is no feeling of having been judged personally inadequate; and in addition—and characteristic of the second-chance quality of the West as a whole—there is always a second chance for transferring from a junior college if one can achieve an adequate academic record there.[29] In fact, the counselors at State encourage those who do not at first qualify to spend two years at a junior college and to reapply with the assurance that if grades are satisfactory, admission becomes automatic.[30] Under these conditions of recruitment and admission, San Francisco State cannot hope to exclude those who, although intelligent enough to make the grade, lack the intellectuality or sophistication that the faculty might find stimulating. By the same token it cannot offer special inducements to potential recruits who might serve as catalysts for an intellectual student culture that might draw in some of the faculty. Since State does have an increasingly intellectual faculty, the drive many of them have to do research is not likely to be mitigated by rapport with the large mass of students. There are at State zealous evangelists who are willing to seek recruits for intellectual values even among "ordinary" students, but the impersonality of the institution, which will increase with steadily rising enrollments (unless some scheme of internal decentralization is evolved, perhaps on the lines of Harvard's Dudley House), and the relative

[29] The unwillingness of the elite colleges in other states to accept more than a handful of transfers—which these colleges justify on the basis of their presently very low attrition rates—reduces the fluidity of the whole system and forces some junior colleges to extend their programs to four years because they cannot serve as sorting stations to send their most highly qualified and "redeemed" students on to finish their B.A.s at a major academic center.

[30] So far as we could discover, San Francisco State has no way of protecting itself against substandard junior colleges within the state system. The State University does inform the high schools—and state colleges could presumably do the same thing with the junior colleges—how much their graduate's grade-point average has fallen at college; this in effect tells every preparatory institution what its discount rate is, and serves as an implicit recommendation to raise standards. But the impersonality of the admissions machinery at the state colleges prevents its use for obstructionist purposes, whether good or bad, in particular cases.

lack of locales for solidarity between students and staff in a nonresidential college, all make such evangelism difficult.[31]

However, snobbish devotees of exclusiveness should not take too much comfort from the foregoing considerations. Overall in California, the chances of getting the right student doing the right academic job, and ultimately the right adult job, are probably much greater than in the Eastern "tribal" system, where selection for the elite colleges, and hence in a measure for elite professions, is largely a one-shot affair at "seventeen-plus." Systematic second chances in California mean that a student is not simply accepted in a college that will then certify him to graduate school, nor is he rejected to lose hope and settle for what he and his peers regard as a second-rate college and a second-rate career. Of California junior college students 65% are enrolled in a transfer program, and 20% do move on to a state college or the University—and there quite often do as well (or better) than those who started as freshmen. Conversely, the college "underachiever" is more often eliminated than in the East, for the faculty knows that he can continue his work at a junior college and is not being thrown out of heaven into an unknown limbo. Such patterns of mobility seem peculiarly appropriate to a state such as California to which many people have "transferred" after "flunking out" of a community in the East or Midwest. But of course after California, there is no place still farther West (Alaska hardly serves in this respect), and the state has not only an extraordinarily high rate of college attrition, but also San Francisco (the city, not the College) is known for its high incidence of alcoholism and suicide.

As already implied, if half the undergraduates move to a new college or job every year, the effect on the academic community is much the same as the effect on American residential communities of one family in three moving every year. With students always entering or withdrawing, no friendship is likely to last very long, and little commitment to the community itself can be expected. How-

---

[31] San Francisco State, like not a few other public colleges, has nearly doubled in enrollment between 1950 and 1960, with an even greater rise in numbers of full-time faculty. As a fighting battalion in the army can only assimilate a certain number of raw recruits from the replacement depot without losing its high morale and cohesiveness, so an educational institution also can only absorb a certain number of neophytes every year without a loss of traditions, and an attenuation of intellectual (or anti-intellectual) cohesiveness. But it is also true that traditions that are moribund can only be destroyed by extremely rapid growth that jars the control of entrenched yet indolent interests; and much that is vital at San Francisco State as well as what is problematical reflects the forced feeding of extremely rapid growth.

ever, more communal groups do spring up within the amorphousness of a large institution, and one observer describes the Creative Arts Division at State as resembling a small experimental liberal arts college with its own loyalties and pathos, providing coherent semi-diversity. This is so in spite of the fact that, taken as a total entity, very few rapidly expanding institutions can keep or create a sense of the faculty as a community, for even the more dedicated faculty have difficulty surrounding themselves with a sufficiently stable circle of colleagues and friends to allow the creation of a common way of life. Continual migration encourages students to take an impersonal view even of themselves, for they acquire no familiar identity in the eyes of others, and no comfortable style they can call their own. Instead, their lives consist of an endless series of first impressions made on new faculty and students. In dealing with the administration, for example, standardized and negotiable course credits, recorded on a transcript that from the College's viewpoint *is* the student, serve to mute complex questions about the quality of various intellectual experiences—in much the same way that the cash wage rate serves to mute analogous questions about the value and meaning of other kinds of work. The student can enroll in an "Introduction to American Literature" at the University, state college, or junior college. He will, of course, be introduced to rather different things in the three settings. The University course is designed for the top 11% of the state's high school graduates, while the state college course caters to 44% (now to become 33%) of all high school graduates, and the junior college is open to all comers. Yet in order to allow transferring from one institution to another the planners have decreed that all these courses are formally equivalent if satisfactory grades are achieved.

The student who resists the view that knowledge can be prepackaged may have a difficult time. If, for example, he figures out that the title of a course tells very little about the experience that awaits him in the classroom, he may try to select his courses by looking at the men who will dominate the classroom. But even a college like State, which encourages class discussion groups and espouses a philosophy of "student-centered" education, does not put out a catalogue that tells who will teach the various courses, much less making it easy for students to get the teachers of their choice. Still, a time schedule each semester does give the names of those teaching specific courses and sections, and thus permits a certain amount of shopping. A liberal arts college, which regards itself as turning out "educated men" and not specialists, can take pride in offering a "table d'hote" curriculum, treating virtually every course as the creation of its professor, and withdrawing it when a professor leaves or goes on leave. But many of the large state universities act as if they must provide an "a la carte" curriculum, meeting a variety of specialized needs as these turn up, and relying on large turnover or a conciliatory faculty to see to it that, if a course is to be taught, there is someone to teach it. This may be typical of state colleges in general, where the administration, rather than the professors, has the power. Perhaps because of criticism often leveled at educationists that they ignore subject matter (or perhaps despite this), the emphasis at State (and in California teacher certification) is precisely on subject matter rather than on the man himself. Although this may be a useful brake on some kinds of professorial vanity and egocentricity, it also contributes to State's impersonality.[32]

If it does not matter with whom one studies, then by analogy it also makes relatively little difference where one studies. The primary consideration is how long one sticks at it. This is especially true of work done prior to the terminal degree. If a student enrolls in a local junior college and then transfers at the end of his first two years to State, he will get the same degree as if he had done all his work at State. And if he then goes on to take an LL.B. at the University of California, then whether he took his B.A. at the University or at State may make little more difference to him than whether he went to one high school or another. The people and ideas he would meet at Berkeley as an undergraduate might make him a more successful lawyer than their equivalents at State, but such possibilities (hardly, we would say, certainties), which prey on the minds of many students at the University of Massachusetts, seems less salient in the California sunlight. And indeed we would guess that such possibilities are actually more remote in fluidly democratic California, where half the population has achieved success despite "graduating" from low status jobs and homes back East.

Taken together, the patterns of admission, residence, instruction, and transfer in California have largely dissipated the sense of community and the possibility of developing a common intellectual culture to influence incoming freshmen. Indeed, San Francisco State is in many respects a more mature, workaday institution than those "romance-image" colleges where freshmen are still singled out for special

[32] As the liberal arts colleges come more and more to see themselves as preparing students for graduate and professional schools, and as teaching falls increasingly into the hands of highly specialized men, it may well be that the state college model is the one that will spread to the private elite institutions as coverage supercedes charisma.

and invidious attention. Despite efforts we shall touch upon in a moment to develop fraternities and interest groupings, State is not a club or a series of clubs; and the students are not cut off from one world in the process of forcible assimilation to another. To the critic of mass culture and mass education, the result is merely deplorable, another proof that efforts to civilize the masses only aid in downgrading the elite. But this is what Veblen would have called a one-eyed view. State does not change its students as much as many on the faculty might hope, but neither does it turn out deracinated epigones who mistake a narrow band of intellectual appreciation for cultivation. In our vignettes of Boston College and the University of Massachusetts, we have mentioned the shadow that Harvard (and the Ivy League generally) casts on institutions where other models may be more appropriate. Coming from this background, we have the impression that Berkeley is slightly less a source of imitation and the focus of resentment for the state colleges, perhaps especially those like Sacramento and San Diego that are less geographically close. If we are correct in what is a difficult comparative judgment, the difference (which varies greatly among departments) may in part reflect the California psychology of abundance which suggests that there is enough prestige and distinction and money for everyone, although at the same time this very egalitarianism might be expected to give rise to what Freud called "narcissism with respect to minor differences."

In any event, whatever institutional inferiority complexes exist, California seems to manage some limitation on internecine jealousies and warfare by creating organs of central government and planning (such as the Master Plan Survey Team) and making strenuous efforts to assign missions to the different echelons of state educational enterprise.

THE COMMUNITY OF COLLEGES

Regional federations of colleges and universities, such as the Southern Regional Education Board, or the New England Board of Higher Education, have been able to curb the zest of educational free enterprisers only in the most peripheral way, as in the case of medical schools that are fearfully expensive, or schools of veterinary medicine for which there are few applicants. The State of California itself is bigger than many regions, and its education bill, comprising nearly half the total state budget, already approaches a billion dollars a year. Nevertheless, there is a somewhat better chance for secretaries of educational defense, such as Clark Kerr, to coordinate and rationalize the assignments of educational missions, than for Mr. McNamara or Sen. Symington to coordinate the rival armed services within a single Pentagon Master Plan. Yet the whole drift of our discussion in the foregoing pages has emphasized, perhaps even overemphasized, the power of institutional nationalism. Moreover, a reader of Bernard Berelson's *Graduate Education in the United States* (1960) would be justified in concluding that faculty and students in the leading graduate schools possess a nearly unidimensional standard for measuring the academic equivalents of power or gross national product in the competition among nations. The denominational college may exist somewhat outside this major orbit, so that a professor teaching at, say, the University of Redlands (Baptist) or the University of Santa Clara (Catholic), may vaguely realize that salaries twice his own are paid at Berkeley, but he also knows that his own institution's budget cannot possibly afford this, and he may feel committed to what he regards as his institution's special mission. But perhaps fewer teachers in the state colleges are likely to have a sense of special mission; thus, to bring culture and citizenship to students not of outstanding academic promise may require an ideology at once sterner and clearer than where the students are marked off, not by grade-point averages, but by religious or ethnic category. Moreover, the state colleges draw from the same tax-supported budget—though they are under a different administration—as the University of California. Indeed, many of them exist in the immediate locale of a branch of the University, and they cannot help but be aware that the size of the subsidy provided by the state varies with the talents of the students and the talents of the faculty thought necessary to teach them.

So too, in all the state colleges, construction of buildings is more austere than in the University system, and restrictions on esoteric courses and expensive research are tight. Still, the distinctions between State and Berkeley should not be exaggerated, especially below the very top. Except at the top, salaries are not markedly different and teaching loads not markedly heavier (twelve hours at State versus nine hours at the University), although far more professors at Berkeley than at State are able to reduce their loads still further through research appointments and leaves of absence. And although an effort in 1954 to allocate facilities set the size of libraries at one hundred volumes per student in the University, and thirty volumes per student at the state colleges, this in fact gives State a beautifully appointed library adequate for many nonesoteric needs. The great differences in amenities may be more resented because they are imposed by the state and not, or so it may seem, as the result of the free market. For the fact is that State, whatever its actual or felt subordination to Berkeley, now exists at a standard of living quite in line with the big state universities elsewhere.

The real burden of mass education falls, however, neither on the University nor on the state colleges (which taken together educate a more select minority than many Southern and Midwestern state universities), but on the junior colleges. These institutions are locally controlled and financed, with a generous subsidy from the state for those that conform to state regulations concerning their operation. Salaries are lower than in the state colleges, but higher than in the public schools, and similarly teaching loads are too heavy to leave much time for research, but not so heavy as in the high schools where teachers frequently do not even find time to read, or prepare classes other than cursorily. Since the majority of junior college teachers seem to be people who were initially headed for the schools rather than for college teaching, they are likely to see themselves as fortunate rather than deprived (Clark, 1960a).[33] Academic prerequisites such as leisure are beyond the ambitions of such instructors, and so too is the transformation of their institution into a "real" four-year college. The ambitious must either move on to a state college or follow the high school pattern of becoming administrators.

In other states, where the prestigeful state university has been separate from the land-grant college in the same state, the latter has been increasingly unwilling to stay in second place, but has followed the well-marked path of Michigan State University in competing for budgetary funds and in using friends made through serving the state to win the resources to go after national and international academic distinction. It remains to be seen whether the California state system can limit this sort of "socialist competition," and prevent the state colleges from mobilizing political pressures to lessen the distinctions that presently make the University of California cost 50 to 100% more per student than the state colleges. Conceivably the University of California could draw off from the state colleges their more ambitious or distinguished academic entrepreneurs, particularly so while they are still young; but at present there seems to be little such traffic, and no such intention. A more important possibility has already been suggested, namely to develop for the state college faculty a new ideology or sense of mission, one markedly at variance from that which dominates the graduate schools in which almost all these men are now trained. Something of this already exists at San Francisco

[33] See forthcoming studies of junior college faculty attitudes by Herbert Maccoby.

State, where the newer behavioral sciences have created a rationale for training unscholarly students. And this effort has been sufficiently dedicated and pervasive to give some parts of State something of the flair of an experimental college, although less dramatically so than still newer experiments such as Monteith College possess.

Indeed, the very size of San Francisco State, and the rapid growth of the faculty already referred to, have made it difficult to recruit professors on the basis of their competence to embark on new ways of teaching and motivating nonintellectuals. Paradoxically, the very label, "experimental," combined with the fact of being in San Francisco, has made the College attractive to people in other parts of the country who have only a vague idea of what is involved in educational innovation, and who have only a very limited desire to teach ill-prepared students—even if they are from San Francisco. Furthermore, in a faculty that has doubled in the last five years, it has been impossible to locate fifty or one hundred new teachers each year who care more for unearthing the gifts and aptitudes of nonscholars than for duplicating their own kind. Outside of the performing and creative arts, which have not as yet been quite domesticated as academic disciplines, experiments in education, in our observation, tend to attract some of the very best and some of the very worst in academic life: the dead-heads who couldn't make it within a discipline, and some of those who want to transcend their discipline, or carry it to the heathen. Unlike such small and relatively homogeneous experimental colleges as Sarah Lawrence, an institution like San Francisco State must therefore rely on the Ph.D. and scholarly recommendations to recruit new faculty, hoping at best to convert the recruits on arrival to an outlook that makes them willing to devote themselves to students previously defined as not first-rate and at worst to build a research team whose publications will bring more traditional sorts of academic eclat with which to paper over failures to reach "ordinary" students in the classroom.

For reasons already suggested, conversion remains more hope than reality. At San Francisco State, as elsewhere, the kind of teaching necessary to connect high culture with the mass culture from which the majority of students comes exists in only a few enclaves; and it is hard for this still uncodified style of teaching to spread among faculty who have usually spent more time in graduate school than at State. To be sure, a number of Ph.D.'s from leading institutions will prefer State because it seems to promise somewhat less pressure for research and the training of Ph.D. students. But for the more gifted and "disciplined" young faculty, their training will have imprinted on them an identification with continuing the academic profession in their own students. It would take an extraordinary combination of ingenuity and dedication to put before these Ph.D.'s a model for the state college that is not simply that of a lower-order Berkeley or UCLA. Failing this, such talented faculty members will naturally resent the inadequacies of their library and laboratories, the lack of time and money for research (which can only be obtained by going through channels within the institution), and the lack of a sufficient cadre of students who are potential Ph.D. candidates themselves. Even if many on the faculty are willing to accept the ideology that has filtered up from the public schools and down from the philosophers of education about "meeting the needs of the average student," they will lack specific and concrete illumination as to what these needs are (where they are not intellectual) or how to go about discovering and meeting them. We are sure that there exist at State instructors who share the preference for slow learners and onerous pedagogic challenges that can occasionally be found in school and junior college teachers; and that there are some, in the creative arts program and elsewhere, who reject the usual tests and academic standards as the basis for admission to the state colleges, as well as some who believe in education for citizenship, irrespective of academic aptitude. But those we ourselves encountered in our own naturally limited discussion were not opposed to the recent recommendations of the Master Plan Committee for raising standards of admission to the state colleges.

Efforts to emulate the scholarly distinction of the University have, then, been pervasive throughout the state college system. But evolution has proceeded at quite different rates in different economic and cultural settings within the state. The three most "mature" state colleges are San Jose, San Francisco, and San Diego, with Los Angeles and Long Beach rapidly overtaking them. Of the three, San Jose is the oldest, largest, and most socially respectable. Its demographic pattern hardly betrays its origin as a normal school, for only one student in four plans to be a teacher, and more than half of the students are male. (This latter achievement is partly accounted for by San Jose's scientific and technological programs, which feed local industry and create a public image of manliness.) San Francisco State attracts more would-be teachers and more women than San Jose. But the creation of an Engineering Division will probably do much to redress this balance, perhaps eventually giving males the numerical majority among freshmen which they already have among graduate students, and helping to shift the image of San Francisco State toward the university rather than the teachers college model. Certainly if the reputation of the faculty determines the quality of the students, San Francisco should have little difficulty overtaking San Jose. Not only does San Francisco have more Ph.D.'s (62% vs. 47% in 1955), but it also has a larger library, more graduate students, and more distinguished specialized programs, some of which have national reputations.

As already indicated, San Francisco State has managed to shift some competition with Berkeley and Stanford to its own ground by innovating programs outside of the traditional disciplines in such fields as the creative arts and semantics. And the strength in these fields has helped create a lively atmosphere in more conventional areas such as linguistics, international relations, and education. Moreover, as at the University of Massachusetts, State can capitalize on its sense of manifest destiny, for the prospect of growth makes everyone fairly sure of promotion,[34] and gives captains of intellect a sense of opportunity.

If competition from the University has held back the development of San Francisco State in the direction of becoming a full-fledged university, competition from the junior colleges has hastened State's evolution. The junior colleges offer freshmen and sophomores an apparently wider choice of courses than State, with its universally required general education program. State hopes to provide diversity after a general education foundation, but in doing this it risks driving potentially talented students into the junior colleges from which they may jump to the University. To avoid this, State must make students conscious that very often junior college is just two more years of high school. Of course both State and the University welcome junior college "competition" which decompresses bulging classrooms, as long as it draws off primarily the less gifted students. Neither did San Francisco State or Berkeley object seriously when a new state college was founded in Alameda County to service Oakland and its surrounding suburbs. But should Alameda try to provide research facilities that overlapped Berkeley's, or specialized curricula in creative arts or education for exceptional children that threatened San Francisco's monopoly of students in such fields, complaints about "unnecessary duplication" would almost certainly begin to reach Sacramento.[35]

---

[34] According to the President's 1960 Report, the Promotions Committee, a faculty body that includes two elected members, promoted 72 out of 115 candidates in the 1959–60 academic year.

[35] While the presence of junior colleges hastens evolution, their absence slows it even more dramatically. Humboldt State College serves sparsely populated Northern California as both state college and junior college, and this means that the intellectual level must be geared down for the more diverse student body, ac-

The effort to allocate resources and responsibilities in some reasonable overall pattern is embodied in a variety of regulations about what courses can be offered, what equipment purchased, and what degrees conferred in various kinds of institutions. Such regulations seem to exist only as a challenge to be gotten around by the ambitious and ingenious professors at the state colleges, despite the efforts of some administrators to keep the peace with Sacramento by keeping their faculty in line. When, for instance, a college wants to develop an engineering program, it begins by offering science courses for prospective teachers and recruiting scientists to teach them. Once the faculty is recruited, various technical programs can be developed to justify the purchase of appropriate equipment, and engineering courses can be offered under other names. At this point the legislature, beset by industrial pleas for more technicians, and by local parental complaints about the high cost of room and board away in Berkeley, can hardly resist the college's request for permission to give local engineering degrees. After all, as the college argues, no new faculty, equipment, or courses will be needed, and so it will not cost the taxpayers a penny.[36] On the other hand, the state colleges are caught by their own expansionist strategies if they seek to raise admission standards, for if they admitted fewer students (and no authority actually checks to see whether they live up to the agreement to admit only the top 44% of high school graduates), they would lose the faculty members to which they were entitled for every additional sixteen students (students are not flunked out before the fourth week of term for that is the date on which the budget is based). Hence, state college presidents are not likely to ask the legislators to raise admissions standards still higher, even though doing so might please many individual faculty members.

UTOPIAN VENTURES IN COMMUTER COLLEGES

It is very easy for scholars in private colleges, which are proud of not expanding in the face of increased demand, to dismiss California's educational politics as "empire building." Such a term of course obscures a mixture of motives and also the fact that the continuous opening of new intellectual frontiers in American higher ed-

counting for the lower scholastic aptitude and social sophistication of the student body there.

[36] In practice, of course, *some* additional investment is usually necessary even when the ground has been carefully laid in advance.

ucation depends on the kind of energy and enterprise that heads up in arguments over the California Master Plan. In an era when more people want education than can get it, there are very few Indians or Mexicans to suffer from the march of the state colleges' "manifest destiny." The real danger is that building such an empire distracts attention from serious disorders on the home front, just as building railroads and killing Indians did in 19th-century America. Efforts to reach untapped manpower pools and develop new and imaginative variants on the state college "mission" may similarly distract attention from the vast stretches of intellectual slum that still blight the undergraduate landscape in the state colleges. An *urban* slum has a certain romantic appeal, especially if it produces students of exotic backgrounds and radical dispositions, but a *suburban* slum of intellectually indolent and unresponsive students attracts only the heroically egalitarian or the idiosyncratically venturesome faculty—or the cynical and defeated.

For reasons implicit in our earlier discussion of "romance-image" colleges, some educators at State have thought that intellectual slum clearance should begin in efforts to fight social disorganization with such conventional "community centers" as the new dormitories. A related suggestion, that the local fraternities should be allowed to acquire national affiliations, has been voted down by the faculty. Football, which in many colleges provides at least an outward show of unity and community, has been deliberately de-emphasized, and few students feel any sense of identity with their team or the muscular protagonists of its weekend dramas. As an alternative, the College has supported the development of extracurricular activities tied to the departments or to other educational enterprises. Thus, the student newspaper carries course credits in the Language Arts Division, while the theatre is sponsored and directed by the Creative Arts Division. So, too, Student Government, which is intended to give the students a voice in the shaping of their life at State, becomes a device for communicating and legitimizing the plans of the Administration. As in so many universities, most students (if they think about the matter at all) regard student government as occupational therapy for "politicians" who enjoy parliamentary trivia. Many other interest clubs are creatures of their sponsoring department, and although this is better than nothing, it is not particularly encouraging to faculty members who dream of independent student activities as an incentive for intellectuality and creativity that transcends departments.

Taken together, all these devices for harnessing students' leisure life to the college community have been notably unsuccessful. Students look at the College as outsiders, and are too detached and cynical about it even to take seriously efforts to make them buy the yearbook as a record of "their" undergraduate years, or to attend dances that might deepen the bond of "classmate-ism." Whether the students would respond to encouragement given to fraternities or football as sources of pride and solidarity is doubtful, for many of them are not late adolescents, and they are protected from immersion in the more inane versions of the collegiate—already in retreat at many places elsewhere —by their job experience and an average age of 24.

Yet our observations at San Francisco State impress us with the fact that collegiate values are not the greatest threat to intellectuality— contrary to what many faculty members think. For students attracted to a "romance-image" college by its apparently graceful life of leisure are not afraid of intellectuality, but merely regard it as irrelevant, and their defenses against it are not deeply entrenched, although they have the support of the student culture. In contrast, students attracted by the prospect of a bigger pay check or a more respectable job to a "diploma-image" college like State tend to defend themselves against intellectuality because it represents a positive threat to their already formed identities and values: thus to many of these students General Education seems merely an irritating obstacle put between them and their vocations. And although students at State are not protected from ideas in any heavy-handed way by a tenacious student culture, being too much out on their own for that, they are still immured within the often more opaque walls put up by their occupational colleagues, their neighborhood chums, their families, and their political leaders. Hence, if State should move in the "collegiate" direction of, say, the Big Ten universities, this would surely not be the worst outcome for its present dilemmas.

This prospect, however, is far from the only possible trajectory, since universities, like "underdeveloped" countries, can skip stages that have been historically pursued by the older institutions. As we hope this account has made clear, San Francisco State is no longer, if it ever was, a homogeneous college, and its different departments and divisions are moving toward different models at quite uneven rates. As indicated by the faculty vote on fraternities, there is strong re- sistance at State against the "collegiate" culture, and such divisions as that of Creative Arts seek to provide a sense of belonging in a less adolescent (and expensive) fashion. In fact, as we have already indi- cated, it is the departments and divisions that carry the main burden of State's effort to upgrade its lower-middle-class student body, both in the classroom and in the departmental activities outside of class. It was our experience in encountering students to discover that they make friendships more easily on the basis of *doing* alike than *being* alike, so that "Are you in (e.g.) Education?" provided a more common conversational opener than the changeless weather, and the discovery that someone else was in a very disparate field often cut off further inquiry. Nevertheless, the students' concern with sharing a common skill is not obsessive. When asked in the Trow-Clark questionnaire what they had in common with their friends, more people answered "leisure activities" than anything else. This would seem to mean that they do not consider people real friends unless they see them off-campus, which is their "leisure" world. It is understandable, if hardly ideal, that the Dean should advise incoming students that, "The College is too big to provide a focus for your education. Your department will have to be your home." The difficulty is, of course, that efforts to civilize the young by involving them in stylized activities are less likely to take hold than efforts that bring them into rapport with civilized adults—a fact that slum workers with real delinquents have learned to their sorrow. The department is too easily seen merely as the antechamber to vocational life. Even students who lack any substantive idea as to what a business administrator should be like can avoid serious re-examination of their vocational goals and ideals by simply becoming good "business students." Moreover, after the first two years of General Education, their chances to meet other students are primarily bounded by the departments.

Yet it remains an open question for us whether the departmental and vocational identities are as settled and firm as they appear to be. To hear the faculty talk, an outsider would think that almost every State student was an engineer, busily digesting technical data and indifferent to anything that either minimized the importance of his narrowly defined treadmill or took time away from study. Our own impression is that when such engineers, really absorbed in their future professional roles, arrive at State in the next few years, they will be treated by most students as quite deviant for worrying so much about the future and so little about the present. Even at State where the role of a student is relatively undefined and therefore easy to learn, most students worry as much about getting along with their classmates as about their future employers. In part, no doubt, this is because, as Beardslee and O'Dowd point out in Chapter 18, they have no real idea what their future employers will want of them. If this is true, then perhaps if State and other commuter colleges could develop additional devices to supplement the departments, giving the role of "college student" a more exciting and demanding form, the college would be able to do more for its students.

As we have indicated, however, the efforts of State to make extra-curricular activities do this job have not worked very well. Nor, we would judge, have small classes usually bridged the gap between adult scholars (or pedants) and adolescent nonscholars. It is therefore worth looking briefly at two other experiments in commuter education, which have tried rather different schemes for civilizing the average high school graduate.

Michigan State University has established a new college in Oakland County outside Detroit, where a highly articulate and dedicated faculty, drawn from leading intellectual centers, is attempting to bring avant-garde academic life to the relatively unselected graduates of local high schools, 40% of whom are of working-class origin. All commute by car to the College, which has been established on a large exurban estate. The faculty is tenaciously proud of its high standards, which leave as many as two-fifths of the students to flunk some of the basic required courses; the students themselves work with the unquestioned diligence and obedience that is implicit in the lack of a protective student culture. The majority learn their lessons, but whether they learn to become intellectuals or to bring intellectual eagerness to their later life's work remains to be seen. If the intense and demanding program does take hold, the experiment will evidence the value of a sharp break between school and college and of insistence that students take on a new quasi-scholarly role. It would seem that the curriculum itself is not essentially different from that of many conventional and eminently academic colleges and smaller universities oriented to the liberal arts.[37]

A very different course has been taken by Monteith College, which unlike Michigan State at Oakland does not provide a total environment for its students, but takes them for half their time, while the other half is scattered among the different faculties at Wayne State University. The Monteith program is one of General Education, with the social sciences perhaps the most influential component. A determined effort is made to relate the students to the backgrounds from which they come. Meanwhile their vocational concerns are ameliorated by the fact that many of them are taking preprofessional courses elsewhere within Wayne. Monteith, which started at the same time as Michigan State at Oakland, holds its entering class to three hundred as against

[37] Michigan State University at Oakland is now in its second year; these remarks are based on discussions with administration and faculty members and a brief visit by one of us in November, 1960.

the five hundred expected at Oakland. Many of the faculty eagerly hope that a student culture will bring the students into a community different from their previous experience, in spite of the difficulties created by commuting and the many jobs students hold. Oakland, in contrast, seems more strictly academic, yet is dealing with students who have not had the mild advantages that come from living in Detroit and attending Detroit high schools as against those of such industrial suburbs as Pontiac and Rochester, Michigan.[38]

It is much too early to say what will be the impact of the radical departures, very different from the general run and different from each other, undertaken at Oakland and Monteith. Neither has followed the more characteristic state college and state university pattern of developing an honors program or honors college, to hold and help the most alert and capable students, and to attract and keep good faculty who like good students. Both Monteith and Oakland are more ambitious: they want in effect to turn all students, or at least all who can stay the course, into honor students. Realizing that many high school graduates have never before had the experience of a stimulating teacher, they have rejected the assumption that honors students will automatically reveal themselves by previous performance, or by becoming eager beavers when an honors system is open to them. Instead, by decentralization they have hoped to create a splinter culture within a big state university, and then to make this culture at once attractive to the untutored adolescent, and to the scholarly professor, and thus ultimately to breed alumni who, if they do not become scholars, as some hopefully will, may at least be intellectuals.

San Francisco State struggles with less adequate tools to awaken those students who now go through the motions of doing a job they do not care about and cannot do with grace and energy. It is clear from the work under way at the Center for the Study of Higher Education (Berkeley) that State, like most other colleges, does something to free the imagination from the bonds of social class, ethnic group, and nine-to-five job, as well as from the parochialisms of a particular community and family background. But how far such liberation is possible when General Education continues for only two years, to be followed by preprofessional training, and when the College cannot induct its students into any really new and distinctive style of life or offer an opportunity to participate in any community, academic or otherwise, we cannot

[38] This account of Monteith is based on several visits over the last several years and on research concerning Monteith students currently being conducted by Dr. Carol Kaye; see also the issue devoted to Monteith of the Wayne Alumni Magazine, *Graduate Comment*, vol. III, no. 5 (June, 1960).

say. Yet State, working with students of no more than average cultural background, social ambition, or intellectual equipment, and working with them only a few hours each day, seems to do as much as any other comparable college with whose efforts we have direct or vicarious experience.

REFERENCES

Arendt, Hannah. *The origins of totalitarianism.* New York: Harcourt Brace, 1951.

Barton, A. H. *College education: a methodological examination of "changing values in college."* New Haven: Hazen Foundation, 1959.

Berelson, B. *Graduate education in the United States.* New York: McGraw-Hill, 1960.

Blood, R. Uniformities and diversities in campus dating preferences. *J. of Marriage and Fam. Living.* Feb., 1956, **18**, 37–45.

Bowles, F. H. *Admission to college: a perspective for the 1960's.* College Entrance Examination Board, 57th Report of the President, 1960.

Bundy, McG. *An atmosphere to breathe.* (Pamphlet) New York: Woodrow Wilson Foundation, 1959.

Caplow, T., and McGee, R. J. *The academic marketplace.* New York: Basic Books, 1958.

Clark, B. R. *The influence of organization image on student selection.* (Mimeo.) Berkeley: Center for the Study of Higher Education, 1959.

Clark, B. R. The "cooling out" function in higher education. *Amer. Sociological Soc.,* 1960, **65**, 569–576.

Clark, B. R. *The open door college: a case study.* New York: McGraw-Hill, 1960a.

Farnsworth, D. L. *Mental health in college and university.* Cambridge: Harvard University Press, 1957.

Fels, W. The college describes itself. *Coll. Bd. Rev.,* Spring, 1959, 30–32.

Friedenberg, E. Z. *The vanishing adolescent.* Boston: Beacon Press, 1959.

Fromm, E. *Psychoanalysis and religion.* New Haven: Yale University Press, 1950.

Getzels, J. W., and Jackson, T. W. The highly intelligent and the highly creative adolescent: a summary of some research findings. C. W. Taylor (Ed.). *Research Conference on the Identification of Creative Scientific Talent.* Salt Lake City: University of Utah Press, 1959, 46–57.

Havemann, E., and West, Patricia Salter. *They went to college.* New York: Harcourt Brace, 1952.

Herberg, W. *Protestant, Catholic, Jew.* New York: Doubleday, 1955.

Jacob, P. *Changing values in college.* New York: Harper Bros., 1957.

Kahl, J. A. Educational and occupational aspirations of "common man" boys. *Harvard Educ. Rev.,* 1953, **23**, 186–203.

Kahl, J. A. *The American class structure.* New York: Rinehart, 1957.

Knapp, R. H., and Goodrich, H. B. *Origins of American scientists.* Chicago: University of Chicago Press, 1952.

Knapp, R. H., and Greenbaum, J. J. *The younger American scholar, his collegiate origins.* Chicago: University of Chicago Press, 1953.

Lazarsfeld, P. F., and Thielens, W., Jr. *The academic mind: social scientists in a time of crisis.* Glencoe, Illinois: The Free Press, 1958.

Lipset, S. M. *Political man: the social bases of politics*. Garden City, N.Y.: Double-day, 1960.

Lipset, S. M., and Bendix, R. *Social mobility in an industrial society*. Berkeley, Calif.: University of California Press, 1959.

McGee, R. The function of institutional inbreeding. *American J. of Sociology*, 1960, **65**, 483–489.

Medsker, L. L. *The junior college: progress and prospects*. New York: McGraw-Hill, 1960.

Merton, R. K., Reader, G. C., and Kendall, P. L. (Eds.). *The student physician*. Cambridge: Harvard University Press, 1957.

Murphy, Lois, and Raushenbusch, Esther (Eds.). *Achievement in the college years*. New York: Harper Bros., 1960.

Packard, V. *The status-seekers*. New York: David McKay, 1958.

Perry, W. Student's use and misuse of reading skills: a report to the faculty. *Harvard Educ. Rev.* Fall, 1959, 190–200.

Riesman, D. Some informal notes on American churches and sects. *Confluence*, 1955, 4, 127–159.

Riesman, D. *Some continuities and discontinuities in the education of women*. Bennington, Vermont: John Dewey Memorial Lecture, 1956.

Riesman, D. *Constraint and variety in American education*. New York: Double-day Anchor, 1958a.

Riesman, D. A review of the Jacob Report. *Amer. Sociological Rev.* 1958b, **23**, 732–739.

Riesman, D. The academic career: notes on recruitment and colleagueship. *Daedalus: J. of the American Academy of Arts and Sciences*, 1959a, 88(1), 147–169.

Riesman, D. Planning in higher education: some notes on patterns and problems. *Human Organization*. Spring, 1959, 18(1), 12–17.

Riesman, D. The uncommitted generation. *Encounter*, 1960, **15**, 25–30.

Ruml, B. *Memo to a college trustee*. New York: McGraw-Hill, 1959.

Schmidt, G. P. *The liberal arts college: a chapter in American cultural history*. New Brunswick: Rutgers University Press, 1957.

Storr, R. J. *The beginnings of graduate education in America*. Chicago: University of Chicago Press, 1953.

Taylor, H. *Essays in teaching*. New York: Harper Bros., 1950.

Trow, M. *Reflections on the recruitment for college teaching*. (Mimeo.) Berkeley: Center for the Study of Higher Education, 1959.

Waller, W. W. *The sociology of teaching*. New York: Wiley, 1932.

Wedge, B. M. (Ed.). *Psychosocial problems of college men*. New Haven: Yale University Press, 1958.

Werner, F. *Freshman orientation week*. Philadelphia: National Student Association, 1958.

West, Patricia Salter. Social mobility among college graduates. In Reinhard Bendix and Seymour Lipset (Eds.). *Class, status, and power*. Glencoe, Ill.: The Free Press, 1953.

Wilson, E., and Boucher, C. A. *College ahead!—a guide for high school students—and their parents*. New York: Harcourt, Brace, 1958. Ch. 5–7.

PART II

THE ENTERING STUDENT

Professor McConnell and Dr. Heist, in their chapter for this part, document, partly on the basis of their own work, the impressive diversity of American college students. It is shown that there are striking differences among institutions in respect to the students they attract or select and that students in a given institution differ widely, at the time of entrance, in respect to various educationally significant characteristics. This state of affairs is no doubt due in considerable part to the fact that colleges have different objectives and standards, in accordance with which they select their students with varying degrees of success. Dr. Douvan and Dr. Kaye point to another source of the diversity: students have different reasons for seeking higher education and for choosing a particular college. These motivations for college-going have their roots in the background, the social situation, the personality, and the developmental status of the individual student. Although the observations reported by Douvan and Kaye were made on high school students, there is good reason to believe that the dispositions described persist until after the student actually enters college and contribute to the diversity to which McConnell and Heist address themselves.

The Chapter of Douvan and Kaye may be regarded as a sketch for a social psychology of college-going. Although the authors give social and economic factors their due, the focus of attention is upon the psychological situation of the high school student who must decide what to do with himself. The authors utilize theory about the psychological state of the adolescent in selecting terms for describing differences between those who plan to go to college and those who do not, and for revealing some of the diversity in motivation among boys and girls who are college bound.

In their own research on the meaning of college to the teen-ager, which Douvan and Kaye report in some detail, differences in sex and in social class background loomed large. The authors document the point that for many young people of upper-middle and middle-class homes, going to college is taken for granted, while for those on the borderline of economic ease, college is likely to be seen as the royal road to improved economic and social status. Boys, more often than girls, conceive of college as a vocational preparation, while girls, more often than boys, think of college in terms of glamour and romance. Girls' college plans are rarely tied specifically to vocational goals. Boys who plan to go to college have established greater independence from their parents than have boys who do not plan to go. In girls, the need for autonomy is not as great as it is in boys, and girls who are college bound are no more independent of parents, or self-reliant, than are other girls. In their phantasies, however, girls who plan to go to college show more latent strivings for autonomy than do girls who do not plan to go. The most striking difference between girls who do and girls who do not plan to go to college is that the latter are more explicit in their desire to marry, and they have a more developed sense of their own sex role. The authors believe that in girls who are college bound the "college dream," with its accent on social-sexual glamour, transformation of the self, travel and the exotic, serves as a substitute for a more open interest in sexuality and marriage. Turning their attention to differences within the groups of boys and of girls who plan to go to college, Douvan and Kaye distinguish between the young person who has serious intellectual goals and the one who regards college primarily as a means for crossing class lines. They find that in practice the two groups are not easy to separate, and that the desire for social mobility does not imply values contradictory to the ideal of intellectual achievement.

Turning to the question of how adolescents choose the particular schools they enter, Douvan and Kaye consider the major criteria—geographic, academic quality, status-prestige, cost, and religion—by which colleges are judged and note the major sources of the information and the influences that affect the young person's decision. The practice of basing the choice upon inappropriate or transitory needs is widespread. Parental involvement in the process of deciding, although often very helpful to the adolescent, can easily interfere with a realistic choice, for the decision may touch one of their own needs or conflicts, for example, a neurotic investment in status. The authors show that the processes of deciding about going to college can be made more rational only through supplying high school students with much more accurate and relevant information than they are now offered, and through greatly increased understanding, on the part of all concerned, of the hopes, fears, and phantasies of the adolescent who is considering college.

The field of research surveyed by McConnell and Heist has a short history but has developed rapidly in recent years. During the last decade thousands of entering students in hundreds of colleges and universities have taken psychological tests, scales, inventories, and questionnaires, and thus contributed to the efforts of researchers to obtain objective measures of student characteristics. (It is safe to assume that in the years immediately ahead even more students will do their bit for psychological science. The Center for the Study of Higher Education at the University of California, Berkeley, and an increasing number of other researchers singly and in groups, will continue a line of investigation that has now been well laid out.) The result of all this activity is that we now have a great deal of quantitative data, obtained by means of instruments of known reliability and validity, not only on the abilities but also on the interests, attitudes and values, and various other characteristics of the students who are entering our colleges.

In the case of abilities, diversity among college students is very great indeed. When, for example, in a study carried out by the Center for the Study of Higher Education, 60,599 students in 200 representative institutions in the United States were tested by means of the American Council on Education Psychological Examination, it turned out that mean scores for institutions ranged from 37.5 to 142.2, the mean score for the total sample of students being 104.4. Clearly it is still true, as McConnell and Heist point out, that high school graduates of all levels of ability can gain admission to some college without going very far from home. Institutions are also differentially selective or attractive with respect to the interests of students. For example, students who attend colleges that are high in "productivity" of scientists and scholars are relatively high in intellectual interests as measured by the Strong Interest Blank, while students who attend less "productive" institutions are relatively high in pragmatic or applied orientation. In the realm of attitudes and values, differences among institutions may also be noted. But here uniformity is the striking thing. College freshmen the country over are rather overwhelmingly conservative in their political views and fundamentalist in religious outlook. It seems likely, however, that instruments that are more subtle than those in common use today will reveal differences in values as well as in abilities and interests. In recent years many striking and seemingly very important differences in other personality characteristics, both among institutions and among students in the same institution, have been found. For example, when two liberal arts colleges whose entering students were similar in level of ability were compared it was found that the freshmen in one institution were significantly less authoritarian in their thinking, more sophisticated socially, and less inhibited or constrained emotionally, more interested in matters of a theoretical and abstract nature, and more highly motivated for intellectual activity than were the freshmen in the other institution. Differences of these same kinds have been found among subgroups of students within the same institution.

In concluding, McConnell and Heist stress the relevance of characteristics present in the entering freshman to performance in college and to the achievement of educational goals. In pointing out the implications for policy of the reported findings, these authors raise questions about the desirability and the possibility of obtaining a better "fit" between the characteristics of the students and the educational programs of the colleges.

Sanford, in the concluding chapter of this section, undertakes to "place" the entering freshman within a developmental framework. Assuming that development is progressive and that it may eventuate in such desired states of the person as freedom of impulse, enlightenment of conscience, and differentiation of the ego, he asks what the freshman has accomplished and what major tasks still await him. The main argument is that the freshman is in a distinctive "stage" of development—one that might be called late adolescence. The maximum crisis of adolescence proper is over, and controlling mechanisms are again in the ascendancy. But these mechanisms, uncertain and unseasoned as they are, tend to operate in a rigid manner, thus forming a main basis for the authoritarianism that is a distinguishing characteristic of this stage. The freshman's stage is also distinguished by instability in respect to self-esteem. In his uncertainty, the freshman vacillates between overestimation and underestimation of himself, between overcompensatory self-forwarding maneuvers and withdrawal. He is highly susceptible to other people's appraisals, and overeager to commit himself to self-defining social roles.

On the assumption that knowledge of the freshman's developmental status will include understanding of what is required to change that status, Sanford offers a number of hypotheses concerning what the college might do in order to bring about desired developments in different areas of its students' personalities. In respecting freedom of impulse it is suggested, for example, that the development of scholarly interests may provide channels through which the individual can express his most primitive as well as his complex and socially fashioned needs. Again, conscience becomes more enlightened when old, automatically accepted values are challenged by competing ones, inducing conflict and hence a necessity for new perceptions and new thinking.

Sanford concludes with the argument that the major problem for the student is how to tolerate ambiguity and open-endedness in himself while he is preparing for adult roles, and that young people in college will be better able to meet this problem when there is a better definition and more social acceptance of the role of student.

The three papers do not cover the entire area that we have designated "the entering student." Lack of space has prevented us from including a presentation of available statistical information concerning the large number of biological and social factors that are known to be associated with college-going—factors such as sex, age, marital status, race, ethnic background, religion, locale, economic situation, status respecting military service, social class, values of parents, and subculture. Information of this kind is readily available, convenient summaries being offered by Havighurst (1960) and by Wise (1958). We have also had to omit any treatment of comparisons between the entering students of today and those of yesterday, and of tomorrow—any treatment of trends in college-going as related to social change. This subject has been discussed widely in recent years, perhaps nowhere more cogently than in the symposium organized by D. Brown (1960). Concerning psychological differences between today's students and those of the past very little is known. This seems to be due in part to the fact that, until recently, scientific interest in the matter has been slight, and in part to the fact that dependable information is very difficult to obtain. We do include a report of one of the few studies that bears on this problem; Freedman's study of college alumnae of different generations (Chapter 25) has permitted him to make some inferences concerning the characteristics of the young women who were entering our colleges at various times in the past.

In thus calling attention to some of the gaps in our section on the entering student we do not wish to imply that in the fields to which we *do* address ourselves everything is well in hand. Both Douvan and Kaye and McConnell and Heist call attention to how little work has been done in their fields, and these authors are clearly in the process of opening up a new field of research. It may be anticipated that students in many more kinds of institutions will be examined, and that as personality theory becomes elaborated and new measuring instruments are developed, more kinds of characteristics of the entering student will enter the picture.

REFERENCES

Brown, D. (Ed.). *Social changes and the college student.* Washington, D.C.: American Council on Education, 1960.

Havighurst, R. J. *American higher education in the 1960's.* Columbus, Ohio: Ohio State University Press, 1960.

Wise, W. M. *They come for the best of reasons: college students today.* Washington, D.C.: American Council on Education, 1958.

4 *Elizabeth Douvan and Carol Kaye*

Motivational Factors
in College Entrance

Within the limits set by intelligence, social class, and other objective factors that narrow or enlarge the adolescent's opportunity to choose to go to college, more allusive and subtle motivational variables play on the decision, producing surprises and creating slippage in predictions based strictly on more accessible and objective factors. This is the level of analysis we reach for when puzzles and paradoxes confront us: the gifted child of middle-class parents who wants to be a jazz saxaphonist and shows no interest in academic training, the boy of only middling-high intelligence who wins high grades and election to Phi Beta Kappa, the son of Italian immigrants who finishes medical school despite what seem insurmountable financial problems. Cases like these, the traditional delight of moralists and ideologists, are provocative to the psychologist as well. They demand explanation, it seems, on motivational grounds.

We have little systematic information about the decision to go to college. The current renaissance of research on the college student has not concentrated on determinants of college-going, and the older studies either focused on objective determinants like family income and residence or stirred motivational variables into one pot with these so that it is impossible to say anything very clear about the independent operation of either type of factor.

There are some exceptions to this general state of affairs. Havighurst (1957) has demonstrated the force of peer values in determining whether lower-class youths decide to go to college. Kahl's carefully designed study (1953) shows that in the lower-middle class, some subtle irritation of the parents, some dissatisfaction with their own lot, is the critical feature that distinguishes the family situation of boys who intend to go to college. In these families, the parents translate their personal dissatisfaction into a mobility quest as they communicate it to their sons. Equally able boys of the same class do not choose to go on to college, primarily because their parents, content with their lives and unable to value possible alternatives, do not support and encourage the choice.

The mobility theme also comes through in a four-year longitudinal study of high school students (Hill, 1954). The author concludes that "the most potent determinants of college proneness are in the cultural and educational traditions, ambitions, and hopes of the family. A history of college attendance in the family, friends in college or going, identification of college education as a means of improving one's lot —all are strong determiners of proneness." We do not know that family tradition and values respecting education are independent of family income; indeed, we doubt that they are. But the vision of college as a means to improve one's lot must be primarily a feature of lower-middle and lower-class youngsters, and so again mobility appears to be a factor of some importance beyond the operation of simple economics.

Apart from the desire for mobility, what motives impel adolescents toward college? What sources of influence, in addition to parents and peers, are important in this choice? In the present chapter we outline some of the varied psychological forces that may affect the decision to go to college. We consider what the image of college represents to youngsters in high school and to their parents, what adolescents seek in their departure for college. We devote some special attention to those who have strong intellectual motivation and those who hope to use college as a mobility channel. Finally, we look briefly at the processes by which particular schools are chosen, asking again what and who is likely to influence this choice.

WHAT DOES COLLEGE REPRESENT TO THE AMERICAN TEEN-AGER?

For many youngsters from upper- and upper-middle-class homes, the question of going or not going to college probably never arises. Continuing in school beyond high school involves no conscious decision; the child from his earliest years is taught that following high school comes college; so far as the family is concerned, this is all the child knows and all he needs to know. In this setting, a decision *not* to go to college is the major and highly individual one, and undoubtedly requires unusual and intense motivation and a deviant personal integration. Most middle-class parents see college serving several purposes; it is to provide the young person vocational preparation, a general intellectual broadening, and an opportunity to grow and develop for another four years, to grow in knowledge and skill, and also in emotional stability and autonomy. The children share many of these expectations, but their vision of college has additional dimensions, which are discussed later.

To young people of lower social status, the decision for college may be a more conscious and problematic one. On the borderline of economic ease one expects to find motivational factors most clearly distinguishing those who do and do not enter college. We have seen that for many of these less privileged youngsters, college represents the golden path to social mobility, the chance to increase their share of social and economic rewards.

Besides the images of college as a vocational training ground, an intellectual and emotional growth experience, and a mobility channel, at least two other concepts seem likely to enter adolescents' own picture of the college experience: a gay and glamourous social life, and release and relief from parental control. The departure for college often represents the adolescent's first experience in establishing and maintaining himself outside the immediate precinct of home. He will now govern his own life in dozens of details previously managed by his parents, and in some crucial areas as well. The prospect of being on his own must surely enter the adolescent's thought about college, either as the beginning of his adventure with adulthood—a grand prospect—or as a necessary beginning freighted with fear.

The glamour of college is so apparent that we need not concern ourselves long with it. A cursory survey of magazines and newspapers during late summer and early fall will reveal the glittering image of college life, and the importance it holds for our youth-oriented society. Fashion ads in the fall are devoted to campus fashions. Society sections —particularly in small and middle-sized city papers—contain long lists of who is entering or returning to which school. Pictorial sections and magazines present misty romantic pictures of life and love in the ivy cloisters. All of the nostalgia for the lost youth and the summer ending are captured in articles and pictures that tell of the youngsters now entering on the final path to adulthood. For those who have not yet reached college age, the experience is a montage of movie-like glamour: football games and formal balls, coke dates and convertibles. Of course, college students study, but this is an undertone that adds depth to the glamourous social and sexual phantasy.

On the basis of our research with adolescents, we speculated that the particular meaning of college emphasized in the thoughts and plans of any precollege adolescent would depend both on his sex and on social-class background. Social class, as we have indicated, would influence the conception of college as a mobility channel. And sex, we thought, would affect the degree of emphasis on vocational preparation, release from authority, and glamour in the youngster's anticipation of the college experience.

In a series of researches on adolescence, we have noted sex variation in the nature of the adolescent identity crisis, and in the areas of character development and authority relations (Douvan, 1957, 1957a). The identity issue for the boy is primarily an occupational-vocational question, while self-definition for the girl depends more directly on marriage. A number of differences follow from this distinction. The girl's identity centers more exclusively on her sex role—whose wife will I be, what kind of a family will we have; while the boy's self-definition forms about two nuclei; he will be a husband and father (his sex-role identity), but he will also and centrally be a worker. A related difference follows and has particular importance at adolescence: the occupational identity is by and large an issue of personal choice that can begin early and to which all of the resources of rational and thoughtful planning can be directed. The boy can begin to think and plan for this aspect of identity early, and can use this problem to focus and stabilize many of the unsettling aspects of the adolescent psychic situation. The sexual identity, so critical for feminine development, permits no such conscious and orderly effort. It is a mysterious and romantic issue, freighted with fiction, mystique, illusion. A girl may learn certain surface skills and activities of the feminine role, but she will be thought ungraceful and unfeminine if her efforts toward feminity are too clearly conscious. The real core of feminine settlement—living in intimacy with a beloved man—is a future prospect, for which there is no rehearsal. We find that boys and girls in adolescence have different approaches to the future: boys are actively planning and testing for future work identities, apparently sifting alternatives in an effort to find the role that will fit most comfortably their particular skills and interests, temperamental characteristics and needs. Girls, in contrast, are absorbed much more in phantasy, particularly phantasy about boys and popularity, marriage and love. They maintain a simultaneous focus on reality planning, apparently similar to boys. But this is an insubstantial, contradictory, and stereotyped set of gestures, a temporizing procedure that disguises the girls' major interest in marriage. In itself, the reality planning girls describe has little of the coherence and realism found in boys' thoughts of the future.

We expected that plans and concepts of college would show the imprint of these sex-specific orientations toward the future: boys would conceive college more often as a specific instrumental scheme for job preparation. Phantasies of glamour and sexual love should play a greater role in the young girl's anticipation of the college experience. We can support these hypotheses with data from two national studies of adolescents.[1] The suggestion that boys conceive college as a vocational preparation more often than girls, well withstands the empirical test. Boys often phrase college aspirations as vocational aspirations: they say that they plan to go to engineering school, forestry school, theological seminary, college and medical school or law school. Half of all boys' college plans are couched in specific vocational terms. Except for a few girls who say they plan to attend teachers' college, girls' college plans are not specifically tied to vocational goals.[2] In fact, many of the girls who intend to go to college have vocational aspirations that do not require college training, a discrepancy we virtually never find in the occupation-education plans of boys. For many girls, college obviously is an end in itself, only dimly conceived in an instrumental light. The enrichment from college may promise a better life, greater capacity to meet and realize pleasure from the challenges of adulthood, or a chance for social mobility, but specific vocational-instrumental functions of education occur only to a minority of adolescent girls.

The phantasy significance of college can be judged somewhat from these same findings. In an earlier paper (Douvan, 1959), one of us presented a typology of girls' motivations for college: traditional academic-intellectual motivation, desire for training in one of the femi-

---

[1] The studies were conducted at The University of Michigan's Survey Research Center and were sponsored by the Boy Scouts of America and the Girl Scouts of the U.S.A. Subjects were selected by a multistage probability sampling procedure (Bergsten, 1958), and represent the national population of children in school. Each student was interviewed at school by a member of the Center's field staff. Interviews, which followed a fixed schedule of questions, took from one to four hours. The sample consisted of 1045 boys and 1925 girls. For more detailed description of procedures and copies of the schedule, the reader may consult the basic reports (Douvan and Kaye, 1956; Douvan and Withey, 1955).

[2] Here and in later sections of the chapter, when we use data from the national studies of adolescents or the sample of freshman women, the differences we describe (e.g., between boys and girls, social class groups) have been tested by means of the Chi-square technique. All of the differences discussed are reliable differences between the groups: that is, they could have occurred by chance fewer than five times out of a hundred. For a description of sampling error measures used in our national studies, the reader may refer to the original reports (Douvan and Kaye, 1956; Douvan and Withey, 1955). Any standard psychological statistical text includes a description of the Chi-square test of significance. See, for example, McNemar's discussion (1949).

nine professions, and a third category designated "non-specific motives," which includes all girls who plan to attend college but have
vocational aspirations that do not require college training. The non-
specific category consists of girls who have only cursory interest in the
occupational world, are primarily interested in an active and glamourous social life and marriage in due time.

When we analyze boys' interviews, we do not find any comparable
category—boys who plan to attend college, but have occupational goals
for which this training is not necessary. When boys plan to go to college, they have either well-developed academic interests, or a specific
occupational goal for which they wish to prepare. The mode among
boys is not strong intellectual motivation, any more than it is among
girls, but boys take a practical-instrumental view of college much more
than girls do.[3]

Adults' conceptions of the function of college show a corresponding
division for boys and girls. When asked about the benefits of college
attendance, 90% of an adult sample list job benefits for boys, and
76% suggest such benefits for girls. Thirty-two percent think college will
make a girl a more desirable wife or help her find a husband; 3% think
of marital advantages in describing the functions college may serve for
the boy.[4]

Our data support our initial expectation about the component of
phantasy in boys' and girls' college plans. Girls have less specific vocational goals in mind; they reveal more phantasy than boys do in their
approach to this choice.

Girls' phantasies about college are not simple in content. The
dominant theme is a social-sexual one, but other themes—travel and
geographic mobility, transformation of the self, social mobility, and
a general sensuous longing for experience and the exotic—figure in
their thoughts as well.

The dream of college apparently serves as a substitute for more
direct preoccupation with marriage: girls who do *not* plan to go to
college are more explicit in their desire to marry, and have a more

---

[3] We make no claims for the accuracy of boys' ideas about jobs and job preparation, only for the fact that they show an active strain toward reality and the issue
of vocational preparation that girls' plans do not manifest. Undoubtedly many boys
choose fields on the basis of superficial impressions and transitory needs (see Chapter
17). One study of engineering students found that a major factor in failures and
dropouts was a gross misconception about the nature of engineering training (Hammond, 1959), and this may be equally true of other fields.

[4] These data are from a recent statewide survey conducted in Michigan by Withey,
McLeod and Swinehart (1959) of The University of Michigan's Survey Research
Center.

developed sense of their own sex role. They are more aware of and more frankly concerned with sexuality. The differences between those who do and do not plan to go to college hold up in each of the major social classes (Table 1), and at all age levels (Table 2) except for girls under fourteen years, where we find no differences in sexual reference or marriage intentions. Since we find nothing to indicate that girls who

Table 1. Relationship between Girls' College Aspirations and Direct References to Sex and Marriage, with Social Class Held Constant

	College Aspiration			
	Middle Class		Working Class	
Reference to Sex and Marriage	College	Noncollege	College	Noncollege
1. Decisions in next few years				
a. Relating to boys	2	1	2	2
b. Marriage, children	24	42	18	30
2. Plans for future				
a. Marriage mentioned	25	31	22	30
3. Sources of popularity with boys				
a. Sensitivity, consideration	27	31	20	27
4. Attitude toward dating				
a. Simple, positive response	47	50	44	52
5. Attitude toward steady dating				
a. General positive response	17	22	12	26
6. Conception of shameful act				
a. Reference to sexual misbehavior	10	15	10	27
7. Solution to problem of boy friend being attentive to another girl				
a. Try to win him back	2	5	5	3
b. Maintain relationship	57	59	63	61
8. Solution of conflict-loyalty to girl friend, chance for date				
a. Take date	8	19	12	20
9. Qualities admired in adult ideal				
a. Way handles feminine role	2	9	4	8
b. Good looking	3	11	2	15
10. Most wonderful thing				
a. Reference to marriage	17	26	2	20
11. Daydreams				
a. Marriage, husband, home	7	21	7	27
b. Doesn't daydream	11	17	8	22
Total N	(273)	(349)	(192)	(761)

Table 2. Relationship between Girls' College Aspirations and Direct
References to Sex and Marriage, with Age Held Constant

Reference to Sex and Marriage	Girls 14–16		Girls Over 16	
	College	Noncollege	College	Noncollege
1. Decisions in next four years				
a. Relating to boys	4	*	*	*
b. Marriage, children	27	35	34	44
2. Plans for future				
a. Marriage mentioned	22	37	34	44
3. Sources of popularity with boys				
a. Sensitivity, consideration	20	35	31	36
4. Attitude toward dating				
a. Simple, positive response	51	58	58	65
5. Attitude toward steady dating				
a. General positive response	12	24	19	26
6. Conception of shameful act				
a. Reference to sexual mis-behavior	58	66	60	68
7. Solution to problem of boy friend being attentive to another girl				
a. Try to win him back	2	7	2	5
b. Maintain relationship				
8. Solution of conflict-loyalty to girl friend, chance for date				
a. Take date	2	16	9	18
9. Qualities admired in adult ideal				
a. Way handles feminine role	2	10	3	9
b. Good looking	3	8	*	13
10. Most wonderful thing				
a. Reference to marriage	13	22	16	27
11. Daydreams				
a. Marriage, husband, home	15	21	22	41
b. Doesn't daydream	8	20	10	16
Total N	(276)	(546)	(85)	(171)

plan to go to college are late developers socially or sexually, we infer
that their sexual interests take some alternative form—and our guess
is that they inform the college dream.

This view of phantasy as an outlet for sexual impulses follows the
general psychoanalytic conception that impulses denied direct expression will seek some disguised mode of gratification in derivative forms
of behavior. We do not mean by this interpretation that the decision

to go to college is *merely* a converted wish for sexual experience. Far from it: no such wish can be counted on to maintain academic performance, fill out application forms, or effect any of the other realities that college-going contains. Our point is simply this: one cannot conceive the psychological system of an adolescent without including some notion of an intense sexuality. If direct evidence of the impulse does not appear in the youngster's preoccupations, one looks for derivative forms it may have assumed, and tests for its presence by predicting a higher incidence of the derivative behavior in those adolescents who give no direct expression to the impulse. This is essentially what we have done when we show that college and noncollege youngsters differ in their direct and expressed interest in adult sexuality. The theoretical point is, of course, still open to dissent, but until an alternative explanation accounts for the particular pattern of findings it predicted, we can regard the interpretation as having gained support from our data.

First semester freshman women at a major Midwestern university also give the romantic sexual theme. In answer to the question "What do you hope to get out of college?" 70% include in their objectives the happy encounter with *"the* man for me," or the desire to meet boys and have a lot of fun. But they also mention the desire for personal metamorphosis, a search for status and a different life style, the wish for unusual and exotic experience. These themes are to some extent class-bound. The upper-middle-class freshman most often looks at college as an end in itself; she wants an education and a lot of fun. She does not see college as a door to a new world, either in providing contacts and entree to a higher social class, or in facilitating a personal transformation and training that will make her more acceptable in high status circles. When upper-middle-class girls want to *use* college, in an instrumental sense, the object is either to meet a potential husband or to effect personal change and growth of a highly internal kind. In this last wish we note a strong individual quality: the girl who hopes to find a philosophy of life, a system of values, or a way of looking at reality that will increase and enrich her own existence, according to some internal criterion. She does not want to change in order to be more acceptable or to win a greater measure of economic and social return; rather she wants to change in order to realize and enrich her capacity for gratification.

Occasionally a girl will connect this desire for change to a future feminine role—for example, some girls want to gain wisdom and an enlarged system of values in order to teach their children to live happy lives. This interest in transmitting the fruits of personal change is never mentioned when the girl's interest in changing is inspired by a wish to achieve mobility or to make herself more appealing to others.

The lower-middle-class girl almost always considers college a means to some relatively clear goal: she wants to prepare for a job that will ensure security if she ever needs to work,[5] she wants to meet a lot of people with interests like her own, she hopes to meet a nice boy she can marry, or she hopes to realize a major self-change, one that will make her more attractive to others or more middle-class.

Two themes occur which are not clearly class bound: the desire to escape from home, and the wish for new and exciting experience. We postpone consideration of the first of these until we look at the concept of college as a release from control. The sensuous theme occurs in 15% of the answers of freshman girls. It is equally common in both social classes, though expressed in somewhat different forms. The lower-middle-class girl is likely to want "to do things and learn about things that I may never have a chance to do again"; the upper-middle-class girl more explicitly seeks the exotic: "I want to meet people from different countries and get to know them, find out what life is like in countries completely different from ours."

The frequency of this sensuous theme led to another analysis with the high school group. These younger girls evidence a marked interest in travel; it comes up in their judgments of potential occupations, in their daydreams, and in other connections. We suspected that this interest symbolized a general sensuous longing, and perhaps more specifically, a curiosity about the sexual mysteries. Girls who are anticipating a college experience very frequently give the travel response, while those who are not planning to go to college almost *never* indicate an interest in travel (Table 3). The difference is not attribut-

Table 3. Relationships between Girls' College Aspirations and References to Travel

Reference to Travel	College Aspiration	
	College	Noncollege
1. Reasons for choosing job aspiration: the chance to travel	23	7
2. Daydream about traveling	12	3
3. Most wonderful thing that could happen: reference to travel	15	1
Total N	(665)	(1236)

[5] A mildly morbid preoccupation with the premature death of their future husbands marks these answers.

able to social status. We interpret this finding in the following terms: college and travel are alternatives to a more open interest in sexuality. Girls who will complete their schooling with high school are closer to assuming an adult sex role in early marriages, and they have more developed conceptions of their sexual impulses and sex roles. Girls who will enter college, on the other hand, will delay direct realization and settlement of sexual identity, at least for a while. During the interim sexual energy is converted and gratified through a phantasy system that focuses on college, the glamour of college life, and a sublimation to general sensuous experience. They use sexual energy to enlarge their adolescent experience, while the noncollege group turns this energy more directly to marriage and the social search preliminary to direct sexual gratification.

The image of college as a means to freedom dictated our second analysis of the interview data. We knew that feminine character growth proceeds more slowly during adolescence than does that of boys. For the most part girls maintain a compliant-dependent relationship with their parents throughout adolescence; they show little of the dramatic thrust toward independence and internalization of values that characterizes the masculine staging of the period, and has often been seen as *the* central fact of adolescence.

We suspected, therefore, that the autonomy function of college would differ for boys and girls. For boys, the anticipation of departure from the parental home—which college represents at least in a partial sense—should be another step in the process of loosening ties of dependency and establishing independence. We thought that the decision to go to college would focus a good deal of the boy's interest in autonomy and signify progress in the growth of autonomy and internalization. The boy who is planning to depart would, in other words, be prepared for the step; he would show greater autonomy than the boy who has no such separation in view. For girls, on the other hand, we expected no clear relationship between college aspiration and autonomy. In most instances the college does not, in fact, promise the same autonomy to the girl that it permits the boy; for her it simply substitutes a new institutional set of rules for the guiding authority of the parents. Apart from this fact, we expected that the image of college might appeal strongly to girls' less conscious urge toward freedom and autonomy, but that they would not explicitly see and use the departure for college as a method of winning freedom. In conscious thoughts girls show little desire to be free of parental control; quite the contrary, they reveal a strong conscious identification with parental authority.

The few findings we have fit these speculations. Boys who plan to attend college have greater autonomy vis-à-vis their parents and are more self-reliant in issues involving values and personal controls—compared to boys who do not intend to go to college. The difference holds within the lower-middle and working-class groups,[6] and is particularly striking in working-class boys. Apparently in this group the decision to seek a college education signals intense motivation and a high degree of personal integration (Table 4).

Among girls we find no comparable differences. The college-bound are no more independent of parental control or self-reliant than other girls, nor do they reveal strong conscious annoyance with parental authority or active resistance against it.

Only when we move away from direct discussion of the girl's attitudes toward parental authority to phantasy do we find any interesting differences between girls who do and do not plan to go to college. We have discussed the travel theme that appears more often in interviews with the college group. We interpreted this in the context of curiosity for sensuous experience, but we also suspect that behind the urge to travel may lie a desire to escape, to be free and unfettered.

We have more direct evidence of latent desires for independence in girls' answers to two projective questions: one of these posed the dilemma of a girl who has a very good job away from home and is asked by her mother to come home because she (the mother) is lonely. Our subjects described what the girl would do and how she would feel in this situation. The other question read: "Jane wishes her parents were different—more like the parents of her friends. What does she have in mind?" In both cases, girls who intend to go to college reveal a stronger latent commitment to autonomy than other girls do. They do not, as often as other girls, think the girl should return to her lonely mother. They search more often for a solution that will help the mother without jeopardizing the girl's freedom, and they more often suggest outright rejection of the mother's plea. And in speculating on the sources of Jane's dissatisfaction with her parents, the college group suggest overprotectiveness and restrictiveness as the parents' objectionable traits more frequently than do girls who are not bound for college (Table 5). It seems that some muted chord of striving for independence *does* characterize girls who look forward to the departure for college. And, we would argue, the dream of college channels and expresses this reservoir of latent stirrings.

[6] In the upper-middle class we found only a handful of boys who do not expect to go to college. We were not able to test differences in this class, and we suspect that comparable differences might not occur because of the difficulty of the non-college choice for an upper-middle-class boy.

Table 4. Boys' College Aspirations in Relation to Selected Measures of Autonomy with Social Class Held Constant

Autonomy Measures **	Lower Middle Class		Working Class	
	College	Noncollege	College	Noncollege
1. Adult ideal				
a. An unrelated adult acquaintance	26	17	20	6
b. A family member	39	50	28	52
2. Concept of friendship				
a. Friendship can be as intimate as a family tie	44	33	54	37
3. Self-reliance on six issues of judgment				
a. Some indication of autonomy	23	16	23	7
4. Response to parental restriction				
a. Some indication of autonomy	33	26	27	15
5. Disagreements with parents				
a. Names some area of disagreement	67	54	59	32
6. Conditions for breaking a rule				
a. Internalized response	33	22	31	12
b. Noninternalized response	2	8	*	14
7. Reason for keeping a promise to parents				
a. Fear (noninternalized)	8	15	5	22
b. trust, responsibility	27	18	33	8
8. Reliance on adult authority				
a. high	33	47	38	56
Total N	(116)	(105)	(177)	(347)

In boys, therefore, college represents a next step in the gradual achievement of autonomy; in girls the plan to enter college does not indicate anything about the girl's actual autonomy or conscious drive toward independence, but may operate at a phantasy level to gratify latent desires for detachment and independence. We may speculate that the eventual fate of these phantasy wishes for independence—the nature of their integration with overt compliance—will depend upon the character of the educative process girls experience in college. For girls, the separation from home and parents may be necessary for the elaboration and testing of new wishes for independence. The sex difference in the development of autonomy reflects a cultural phrasing that nurtures and rewards dependency in girls, and permits a close, continuing mother-daughter tie during adolescence.

Table 5. Girls' College Aspirations in Relation to Projective Measures of Independence Striving

Indices of Latent Wishes for Independence	Middle Class		Working Class	
	College	Noncollege	College	Noncollege
1. Lonely mother				
a. Compromise suggestion	44	30	37	23
b. Would not return	15	7	21	9
2. Girl criticizes her parents for:				
a. Excessive restrictiveness	75	66	80	73
Total N	(273)	(349)	(192)	(761)

Our analysis so far has tended to obscure differences that exist within the population of boys—or girls—who expect to enter college.[7] But differences of orientation and motivation within each group are often found, and they are important. Two patterns are of special interest: the youngster who has serious intellectual goals which he expects to realize through college, and the one who sees college primarily as a mechanism for crossing class lines. The first is an unusual pattern, but it nonetheless serves as the ideal in this field. The mobility pattern is more common, and fits a strong traditional conception of the purpose of higher education. The number of young people using college as a means of mobility has increased since World War II, and it will probably continue to grow in the post-Sputnik era, with its emphasis on utilization of talent. Many people are concerned about the effect of the infiltration of the academic scene by children from lower-class

[7] We should also note that in a functional analysis of the kind we have done, which focuses on motives commonly held by average students, one tends to lose sight of the fact that there are young people whose commitments to college differ radically from the statistical average. Our analysis does not do justice, for example, to those adolescents who approach college with high academic motivation and an enriched system of values regarding education. We contend only that these unusual youngsters must prepare for and attend college in a cultural context set by their more average age-mates, and that this context follows the lines we have discussed. Intensive case analysis would be a more appropriate technique for understanding the motivation of unusual students or uncovering less developed motives and concerns among average youngsters.

homes. We can look at our mobility-oriented college candidates for clues about what they are likely to bring to the environment and atmosphere of American colleges.

In concrete analysis, we find that these two motivational types are not so easy to separate, for adolescents with intellectual-academic motivation are also often those who will use college to gain access to a higher social class. Aside from this and verbal facility, we found only a few variables on which they distinguish themselves from other college candidates. They are somewhat more conversant with phantasy, they have particularly close family relationships, and they are often from small rather than large families. Academically oriented girls are somewhat less feminine—according to traditional conceptions of the feminine role—than girls with less serious motives. Aside from these features, they look very like other adolescents who plan to attend college: in activity, social development, values and autonomy of values, and peer relationships.

One study of high scholarship students (Brown, Abeles, and Iscoe, 1954) found that they were characterized by a high activity level, decisiveness, and extreme willingness to conform to academic requirements, routine, and regulation. And findings from the Vassar study (Sanford, 1959) indicate that at least in one kind of scholarly girl, "close involvement with parents and early and persistent awkwardness in social relations with peers" are important background features. Close and problematic ties to the parents created for these girls certain strong emotional drives which were channeled into scholarly motives with support and encouragement from one or the other of the parents.

This, then, is the extent of our knowledge about the background and characteristics of the intellectual student. It is obviously not enough— for important questions remain unanswered; questions about the personality patterns that support highly focused academic motivation in adolescents, and the family and developmental backgrounds that stimulate it.

We have more adequate information about mobility as a motive for college attendance. The mobility group is large in our studies of adolescents and permits more intensive analysis. Our analysis focuses on the role of the college vis-à-vis students from lower-class backgrounds: must the college transform the values of these young people in order to tie them solidly to the goals of the education system? And if the college assumes this function of changing values, will it not necessarily do so at some cost to the more traditional pedagogic functions?

The argument hinges on the nature of the motives and values that mobile students bring with them to the college experience. We find —in contrast to the warnings of those who sense danger in the trend toward broadened selection of college candidates—that the desire for mobility does not imply values contradictory to the academic ideal. Among boys, in fact, mobility aspiration is accompanied by a seriousness of purpose, a willingness to postpone gratification, a highly developed internal morality, and values of individualism and individual competence. They approach college with a well-established desire to learn and do not, at least in this regard, need to be converted to the middle-class core values.

In girls the picture is more complex. Some mobile girls have serious academic or vocational interests in college; the mobile group hold such goals more often than the nonmobile upper-middle-class girls who plan to enter college. But the relationship between mobility aspiration and values is not nearly as clear in girls as in boys. We have attributed sex differences in the integration of mobility aspiration to the less realistic character of girls' mobility goals. When we isolate girls who conceive mobility as an individual achievement—who look at mobility as boys do—the desire for status ties into values and attitudes, as it does among the mobile boys. But for many girls the dream of mobility is just that—a vague conception linked to marriage, but without the kinds of instrumental ideas and values that accompany mobility aspiration when it is conceived as an individual achievement.

In our sample of freshman girls we were able to isolate a group of lower-middle-class girls who have relatively conscious mobility goals. When we compare them to the upper-middle-class group, we find again no evidence that they have difficulty adapting to the academic side of college life. Using five-week freshmen grades as an index, we find that they do just as well as the upper-middle-class girls.

We thought that the double adjustment of mobile girls, i.e., to academic demands and to the requirements of a high status environment, might place them under a strain. But data on social adjustment do not corroborate this expectation: mobile girls are just as satisfied as others with all aspects of campus social life; they are no more homesick than upper-middle-class girls; they are satisfied with housing, campus organizations, and their own dating opportunities. They have, in their brief period in college, taken part in just as many campus activities as higher status girls. They are unusual in only two respects: they hold part-time jobs more commonly than upper-middle-class girls do, and they do not think they will be active in campus affairs during their college years as often as do higher status girls. These are certainly not remarkable differences.

Our data, then, do not support the proposition that mobile students in general make special demands on the college or have serious problems of adjustment. However, these data are from students in a major residential university, and it may be that only unusually competent mobile youngsters have the sophistication and backing to seek admission to such a school.

We did find one group of mobile girls who may have serious difficulties in college adjustment. These are girls who, in addition to being mobile, hope to gain from college a major transformation in the self or self-concept. Compared to mobile girls who have a more established sense of self (or, at least, a less open and intense desire for change), they seem to have less personal competence and less energy for mastering the college environment. They do not differ significantly from other mobile girls in grade point average, but they are less likely to hold part-time jobs or scholarships, and they are less active in campus affairs.

These findings are fragmentary, but they suggest that the girl who hopes for both mobility and major self-change places too large a burden on the college experience, investing it with too large a component of phantasy. The girl who has a more established sense of self and hopes only to continue her development in college is more likely to reach her personal and social goals. She has apparently achieved the personal integration needed for social mobility before coming to college. In some cases, the shift in mobility itself may be well under way by the time the girl leaves high school.

Within the latter group—girls who have relatively stable self-concepts and look forward to college as a time for extending self-growth and finding intellectual and social gratification—we were able to distinguish two kinds of mobility orientation: girls who seek recognition through academic channels, and those who look to social ties as a central mechanism for reaching their mobility goals. Our limited data suggest that the hypothesis about the double nature of feminine mobility striving is worth more extensive exploration.

We divided the group on the basis of attitudes toward sorority affiliation. Those who do not plan to affiliate have higher grades and fewer extracurricular activities than do girls who intend to join sororities; they more often expect to complete the four-year college course, and say they would not leave college to get married. Girls who want to affiliate are currently more active in campus affairs and plan to be more active throughout the college years; they are less certain about finishing college and would more often leave school to marry.

Status motives can, we think, take two forms in girls who go to college: one type is represented by the girl who intends to achieve mobility before marriage by applying her talents to occupational goals, the other by the girl who plans to use college to gain access to high status social groups and to meet potential husbands.

Though both groups by definition are from families of lower-middle or lower-class status,[8] the socially oriented group includes more girls whose parents have had some college education. They are also more often from middle-sized cities, while the academically oriented girls come from farms or urban areas. This finding suggests a relationship between community size and access to mobility channels. The social life of high schools in middle-sized cities is often linked directly to the sorority-fraternity world of the college campus. The mobile adolescent in this setting may be trained during high school to look for mobility through this social channel. On the other hand, the ambitious youngster who is barred from such precollege social indoctrination—through the anonymity of the city school or the isolation of the rural one—will be more likely to see individual academic performance as the means to her status goals. The difference in parent education we have noted may re-enforce this difference in adolescents' awareness of mobility channels.

THE CHOICE OF SCHOOL

If we know little about the decision to go to college, we know even less about how adolescents choose the particular schools they enter. We are beginning—through the research program of the National Merit Scholarship organization (Holland, 1958, 1959)—to gain some understanding of the criteria students and their parents consciously use in judging and selecting schools. But other aspects of the problem —who influences the choice, where potential students get their information about and knowledge of schools, how unconscious motives may enter the choice—remain virtually untouched. At this point one must be content to outline various decisions implied in the choice, the forces and agents that may affect it, and the probable ranking or priority of these factors. The choice of a school is not a uniform process;

---

[8] We defined social status on the basis of father's occupation. Upper-middle-class status was assigned when the father held a professional position or a managerial position in a large or middle-sized company. Lower-middle class designates managerial jobs in small companies, traditional white-collar, sales, and clerical occupations, and skilled blue-collar jobs. Lower class indicates semi-skilled and unskilled blue-collar work.

a variety of types are required to describe this behavior. Before outlining the major variables that define and pattern the process of choosing a college, we shall look briefly at four cases for what they can tell us of the general process. The cases are very different one from the other, and they by no means cover all possible types. But they raise many of the critical questions to be probed in any study of the process of choosing.

Case A: An urban lower-middle-class boy who chooses a Catholic college for men in the city where he lives. The boy's parents, European immigrants, support the idea of college, although their attitude is strongly ambivalent. They want the boy to be Americanized and mobile, yet fear the rejection this plan may hold for them. The boy is attractive and has achieved some mobility already. His choice of college is determined mainly by limited financial resources and his mobility desires. Lack of money (and perhaps emotional features of the family situation) requires him to live at home. Of the two local schools, the Catholic men's college has greater prestige since it is a private school and attracts students from the whole country, while the public institution enrolls a more provincial group. This boy and his family are casual Catholics, and it happens that the upper-middle-class group of friends the boy has acquired in high school includes a number of Catholic boys who will enter the local Catholic college. Their decisions have had a strong influence on our subject's choice.

Case B: The brilliant only son of a wealthy businessman chooses a small Midwestern college with high academic standing. This boy won a National Merit Scholarship, and was accepted at all four of the schools to which he applied. His parents, highly sophisticated people, helped him with application procedures and arranged a trip so that he could visit each of the schools that interested him. Two of these were top Eastern private schools and two were good small private colleges in the Midwest. His parents would have preferred one of the Eastern schools, but did not actively put pressure on their son. The community of family friends expressed some surprise at the boy's choice, since in this social group it is generally assumed that a boy chooses a school outside the Ivy League only when he cannot get into the Ivy League. The boy himself seems quietly pleased with his choice and explains it on grounds of the school's excellent faculty and curriculum in the field of his major interest.

Case C: A middle-class girl from a small industrial city who chooses a Big Ten university. A peculiar family situation operated in this case, forcing the girl to rely on a friend for leadership in the choice of a school and, in some ways, subjecting her decision to the operation of forces irrelevant to her own talents and capabilities.

The girl's parents regard education highly, and fancy the mobility opportunities that college provides. They took some pains to see that their first two children entered distinguished schools. Their third child—our case—is the shy and awkward member of the family and has been consistently rejected by her parents. They have never encouraged her college plans, although she is a serious, conscientious student and has made a fine high school record.

Throughout her high school years, the girl has gained from one close and gratifying friendship much of the love and affection her parents deny her. Her friend is a warm, attractive, popular girl who might not have chosen this girl in friendship except for the fact that these two are the only middle-class members of their homeroom, in a school that serves mainly a working-class area. The girls, in any case, have come to be very close.

When the need to choose a college arose, the friend's parents urged their own daughter to select a major university in a neighboring state, an excellent choice for this outgoing, social girl. The shy friend decided on the same school, although her personality and serious academic interests would fit more happily in another setting. One cannot help but feel that her lack of social skill and assertiveness will interfere with her adjustment in the competitive social world of the Big Ten school. She made her choice on the basis of dependency, a dependency she was apparently not ready to yield. Yet, the choice itself seems destined to cause the separation she meant to avoid. Her friend will almost certainly enter one of the highly rated sororities on campus, while this girl is likely to be accepted by a less popular sorority if she is pledged at all. Girls sometimes manage to continue close friendships despite differences in affiliation, but this is not the common fate of pre-rush friendships at this school.

We do not necessarily predict maladjustment and misery for this girl. The school she has entered provides a range of environments broad enough for many kinds of adjustment, and this studious, shy girl may find a group to support her particular integration and provide her the opportunity for a successful and happy college experience. We do, however, think that there are schools in which the dominant values would support her and in which she would not have the individual burden of seeking and choosing a congenial subculture.

Case D: The average son of a college teacher chooses an obscure school of agriculture and mining in the far West. Factors critical in this case are the boy's lack of talent and his parents' need for status. The boy made a poor showing in high school, and could not enter the major university at which his father teaches or a school of comparable quality. He entertained the realistic notion of applying to a teachers' college in a nearby town, but this clearly threatened his parents. What to this point had been the relatively private skeleton of the son's lack of talent would automatically become public to their social circle if he entered this school. They suggested an alternative: a school of agriculture and mining in a distant state. This school, in fact on a par with the teachers' college academically, had distinct advantages for safeguarding the parents' somewhat neurotic investment in their own community status. "Going away to school" has some prestige in itself, apart from the quality of the school the child goes away to. More important, the exact status characteristics of a school—except for the very prestigeful ones—are likely to be less visible if the college is geographically distant rather than immediately at hand. So long as the school is not specifically titled with reference to its technical nature (which neither of the schools in question was), the "Northern College" of a distant state remains vague in status connotations, while everyone knows that the local Northern College is a mediocre teacher-training school with a new and fancy title. In our case, then, the choice accommodated the boy's relatively poor academic performance and also masked the parents' status face if it did not entirely save it.

A critical research lead emerges from these cases. Clearly, the appropriate first question to ask about the choice of schools is "What level or type of variable operates most decisively in this case?" Objective factors like social status must be examined because they condition the frame of reference within which the choice occurs; psychological factors can then be examined as determinants of choice. Within the class of motivational variables, one must still look to the issue of salience. To organize an analysis around any particular motivational variable without first determining the salience it holds in individual cases, will clearly lead to disappointment. So, for example, we might type our cases in terms of the criteria by which schools are judged; but this typology would not prove fruitful unless we first isolated the group for whom conscious school-related criteria play some determining part in the decision. The point our cases highlight is that there are youngsters in whom conscious judgment and deliberative criteria clearly determine the choice; there are others whose choices take their form slightly, if at all, from rational processes. In one the choice may depend on the influence of a friend or some other agent, as in our Case C. In another it may be a dramatic realization of some unconscious wish of the child or his parents.

The cases point to at least three kinds of psychological variables that are crucial for understanding the choice:

1. the criteria by which schools are judged and their relevance to the issue.
2. the individuals or agencies that influence the choice.
3. the nature of the parents' involvement in the process.

Criteria. These may be conceived as part of the conscious need-structure that the choice must satisfy, or as prior commitments of the adolescent and/or his family which define and restrict alternatives before specific schools are ever considered. Many of the criteria explicit in our cases correspond to those Holland reports for National Merit Scholarship finalists (1958). The major ones are:

a. Geographic criteria. The central distinction here is the local or national orientation. For many potential students, the decision to live at home—for either emotional or economic reasons—fixes the choice of school. Selection of a local junior college very likely proceeds from this commitment. Regional definitions of some kind—state boundaries or a day's drive from home—probably influence the decision of most youngsters by establishing an initial group of possible alternatives. About 15% of National Merit Scholarship finalists gave closeness to home as one of the reasons for their choice, and another 12% referred to the "desirable location" of the school chosen. A recent study reports that 72% of parents whose children plan to go to college think their choice will be a school within the home state (Withey, McLeod, and Swinehart, 1959). Of the parents who prefer a particular school 35% do so because the child will be able to live at home.

Students who are unconcerned about the geographic location of the school they choose are undoubtedly from more sophisticated, cosmopolitan families who can provide both information and financing necessary for the broad-based choice. Among our cases, only B chooses with no apparent regard for location: after considering alternatives. from all sections of the country, he settles on a school in his home region, but on grounds other than location.

b. Academic quality. In some minor degree this issue enters the decisions in all of the four cases. The boy, Case D, considers academic quality in its negative form: he must limit alternatives to schools with requirements modest enough to permit his acceptance. The question of quality affects A's choice within limits set by other criteria. Only B seems primarily directed by academic motives: he seeks the school most appropriately equipped to give him the kind of high quality training he wants, irrespective of location or prestige. Hammond (1959) finds that young men with strong scientific interests and aptitudes choose, more often than other National Merit Scholarship finalists, schools that have been outstanding producers of scientific talent in the past. Except in this group, Hammond thinks there is little indication that academic-intellectual criteria play a major role in the decisions of most students. His studies reveal that parents place more emphasis on academic quality than the adolescents do, and that academic criteria thus have more force in the choice than the students' own answers would indicate.

c. Status-prestige. We have seen that the parents in Case D lobbied energetically to ensure that their son's choice of school would not damage their status. Again only Case B seems unmoved by explicit status considerations although, assuredly, the school he attends has considerable prestige in informed circles. The fact that he did not choose one of the major Ivy League schools—to which he had access—reflects a degree of autonomy and relative freedom from status concerns.

Among National Merit Scholarship finalists, specific allusion to prestige as a basis for choosing a college was quite rare. On the other hand, a large group referred to their choice as a "good school," and we suspect that this cliché refers to the school's social prestige as much as to academic quality. Referring directly to status considerations is not easy, nor is it likely to be considered a socially acceptable response.

d. Cost. Low cost is not mentioned often by the National Merit Scholarship group, and indeed it is probably not as relevant to this group of potential scholarship students as it is to many others. But some general cost considerations probably influence most choices. One may not choose between two schools on the basis of cost, but one very likely considers only those schools that meet certain cost criteria.

e. Religion. One of our cases shows the operation of a religious criterion, though it is secondary to status considerations. The boy (Case A) is a practicing Catholic, and the more prestigeful of the schools to which he has access happens also to be a Catholic school. One suspects strongly that were the status positions of the two schools reversed, the religious issue would never have been raised and the boy would have chosen the nonreligious school. Religion unquestionably imposes itself more clearly than this in some cases: 8% of National Merit Scholarship finalists give religious affiliation as a reason for picking particular schools (Holland, 1958). For devout Catholic families and some of the more orthodox Protestant sects, it seems likely that only those schools maintained by the religious group are ever seriously considered.

Hammond reports a number of other criteria which do not make a major direct contribution to the choice in any of our cases. These include: (1) public or private support, (2) coed or like-sexed student body, (3) size, and (4) physical facilities.

And beyond these factors lies another group of more idiosyncratic ones which, however, can be very influential in particular cases—such things as the parents' feeling and loyalty toward their own school ties, and availability of scholarship aid, the recruitment programs of colleges and their alumnae groups.

Sources of influence and the role of the parents. Experienced counselors report with some agreement that choice of college as well as the decision to go is influenced in particular cases by any or all of the following classes of individuals:

a. Parents, b. teachers, c. counselors, d. unrelated adult acquaintances, e. peers, f. close friends, and g. older siblings and their contemporaries.

In most middle-class homes, parents play a major role in directing the choice of a school either explicitly or more subtly through the values and attitudes they build into the child and by setting certain limits—financial, geographic, religious, and others—on the selection. Having defined a relatively narrow area of choice, the parent can permit the child to exercise his choice with whatever advisers he may look to outside the family.

To enter directly into the youth's selection of a school, the parent must have some knowledge about various alternatives, or must at least know how to get the necessary information. When parents do not have this sophistication—as many lower class and uneducated parents do not—they must yield the major directing role to others in the youth's larger environment. The bright lower-class youth recruited for college by a teacher fits this pattern.

Our Case D raises an interesting issue about the parents' part in the choice of schools. The point to be noted is that to the extent that the decision touches a conflict or need of the parents, they will defend their role as guides in the choice. The motivation to take an active and responsible role was supplied in this case by a neurotic investment in status, but could equally well come from other needs or conflicts. The parent who assumes this responsibility sheerly out of a desire to help the child fulfill his own needs will be able to allow the child to use all sources of information and guidance; the parent in whom the choice promotes some deeper involvement will not. In any research approach to the problem of school selection, one needs an analysis of parents' motivation—of their conscious and unconscious stake in the selection —and the restriction this imposes on the young person's freedom to choose on the basis of relevant internal criteria.

Parental involvement is not the only force that can interfere with a realistic choice. The fact that this decision is often based on vague impressions of college reputations rather than on any more refined knowledge of schools and their offerings; [9] the fact that one adolescent chooses a school because his best friend—with different talents and needs—has picked it; these and other tangential forces lead to choices based on grounds other than realistic appraisal of the individual candidate and adequate knowledge of schools.

People often assume that the process of choosing should be dictated by and adapted to the special talents and needs of the individual adolescent. One may question the realism of this assumption: how many teen-agers have any realistic conception of their own talents,

[9] As colleges absorb a larger and larger proportion of the adolescent population, the range of talents and interests to which schools cater increases, and curricula tend to become specialized. This situation heightens the college candidate's need for accurate information about schools.

much less their own emotional needs? If such self-knowledge comes later, as a consequence of the college experience—and some research findings seem to indicate that this is so—then perhaps the specific choice of school is less important than college administrators like to think. So long as the school offers a varied curriculum and the student is able to make the grade, one school may serve quite as well as another to uncover and develop the child's potential. This may be true for many college candidates, yet even here the adolescent must settle on an appropriate *type* of school. And there are other candidates, undoubtedly, whose needs and interests are special enough so that they will *not* find a rewarding or fulfilling college experience unless they find the particular school that can uniquely serve them.

The dropout and exchange rates in American colleges suggest that something goes seriously awry in this choice process. Even discounting the large number of transfers that occur because of the move from junior college, the rates seem to reveal a widespread choice based on inappropriate or transitory needs. The shopping around that occurs *after* the adolescent is already in college must cause him a great deal of loss and unhappiness. One suspects, at least, that some of the grief might be prevented by more careful counseling of students at the time of the initial decision. One readily researchable question in this area is simply how stable (i.e., nontransferring) students and those who shift about differ in regard to the original selection of schools—in the use of various criteria, advisors, and so forth. An investigation of this kind could be done in a relatively short-term longitudinal research, or, at least for exploratory purposes, in a retrospective design. One thing is certain: we are badly in need of more accurate information on all aspects of this fateful process of deciding.

REFERENCES

Bergsten, Jane W. A nationwide sample of girls from school lists. *J. Exper. Educ.,* **26,** 1958, 197–208.

Brown, W. F., Abeles, N., and Iscoe, I. Motivational differences between high and low scholarship students. *J. Educ. Psychol.,* **45,** 1954, 215–223.

Douvan, Elizabeth. Character processes in adolescence. (Paper presented at American Psychological Association, August, 1957.)

Douvan, Elizabeth. Independence and identity in adolescents. *Children,* **4,** 1957a, 186–190.

Douvan, Elizabeth. Adolescent girls: their attitude toward education. In Opal D. David (Ed.), *The education of women.* Washington, D.C.: American Council on Education, 1959, 23–29.

Douvan, Elizabeth, and Kaye, Carol. *Adolescent girls.* Ann Arbor, Mich.: Survey Research Center, The University of Michigan, 1956.

Douvan, Elizabeth, and Withey, S. B. *A study of adolescent boys.* Ann Arbor, Mich.: Survey Research Center, The University of Michigan, 1955.

Hammond, M. Attitudinal changes of successful students in a college of engineering. *J. Counsel. Psychol.,* Spring, 1959, 69–71.

Havighurst, R. J., and Rodgers, R. R. The role of motivation in attendance at post-high school educational institutions. In Hollinshead, B. S., *Who should go to college?* New York: McGraw-Hill, 1957, 135–165.

Hill, G. E. College proneness, a guidance problem. *Person. Guid. J.,* 1954, 33, 70–73.

Holland, J. L. Student explanations of college choice and their relation to college popularity, college productivity, and sex differences. *College and Univ.,* 1958, 33, 3, 313–320.

Holland, J. L. Parental expectations and attitudes about colleges. *College and Univ.,* 1959, 34, 2, 164–170.

Kahl, J. A. Educational and occupational aspirations of "common man" boys. *Harv. Educ. Rev.,* 1953, 23, 186–203.

McNemar, Q. *Psychological statistics.* New York: Wiley, 1949, 186–215.

Sanford, N. Motivation of high achievers. In Opal D. David (Ed.), *The education of women,* Washington, D.C.: American Council on Education, 1959, 34–38.

Withey, S. B., McLeod, J. M., and Swinehart, J. W. *The public's picture of higher education in the State of Michigan.* Ann Arbor, Mich.: Survey Research Center, The University of Michigan, 1959.

5 *T. R. McConnell and Paul Heist*

The Diverse
College Student Population

A HISTORICAL PERSPECTIVE

The greatly increased curiosity about student *development*
during the last decade may be traced, not only to the widespread use of objective tests, invented earlier, but also to fairly recent
factors: the growth of the behavioral sciences, particularly anthropology, sociology, and psychology, and the cross-fertilization of these
disciplines; the expansion of student personnel programs, with emphasis on the emotional, social, and cultural factors that influence
academic achievement, and more recently, on a broader conception of
education as encompassing not only intellectual attainment, but also
emotional and social development as a desirable end in itself; advances
in the theory of personality development; and the sudden availability
both of large funds for research and the electronic computer. The im-
minent influx of students in colleges and universities and visions of the
still greater crowds to come have given impetus to searching consideration of educational values and objectives; to the educability of students
who vary widely in interests, motives, dispositions, and abilities; and
the possibility of attaining a better "fit" between students and institutions. The oft-asked question, "Who should go to college?" has now become "Who should go where and for what?"

Comprehensive studies of growth and development, and especially of
changes in values, attitudes, and fundamental aspects of personality
are strikingly few, and until the Vassar study there were almost no
efforts to determine the effect of the students' educational experiences

on such changes, or the relationship of such experiences to future behavior. As recently as 1959, a survey of institutional research in the
majority of colleges and universities in eleven Western states revealed
that only four colleges were conducting some sort of study of behavioral
changes (Sprague, 1959). Approximately 24% of all six hundred institutional studies uncovered dealt in some way with students, but only
seventeen investigations, or about 3%, included assessment of student
characteristics other than level of ability or degree of academic achievement, and the developmental studies were even fewer.

Knowledge about the student *at the time of entry,* beyond the widely
used academic aptitude scores and records of high school achievement,
seems to have been foreign to the interests of college administrators
and faculties. A few colleges and universities have made a practice of
administering one or two personality inventories to all incoming students (Black, 1956; Goodstein, 1954), but usually only with the idea of
utilizing scores for personal counseling. The collection of comprehensive information on interests, values, motives, attitudes, special aptitudes, and cultural backgrounds has remained a rarity; and, in schools
where such a variety of data was collected, it was seldom used in "fitting" the students to the educational program or in adapting the program to the clientele, or in dealing with the problems of individualizing instruction.

Early measurement of college students' behavior followed very closely
on the pioneering work in intelligence testing. Even before 1900,
Cattell administered a number of tests to a large sample at Columbia
University (Cattell, 1896); he was attempting, however, to measure differences in sensory perception, supposedly as a correlate of intelligence,
in contrast to the cognitive and attitudinal traits that have received the
most emphasis in the years since then. Three or four decades elapsed
before any investigations produced comparable data on the abilities or
aptitudes of groups of students enrolled within any single institution
or demonstrated differences in student characteristics among institutions. A few such studies, conducted near the end of the 1930s, will be
discussed in a later section. Because it is particularly related to recent
research and is one of the first large-scale investigations of diversity
among students and among institutions, the study by Learned and
Wood merits special attention here (Learned and Wood, 1938).

The results of this study furnished extensive data on the variations
in scholastic aptitude and achievement among forty-nine Pennsylvania
colleges. The general level of intellectual attainment, as indicated by
average scores on achievement tests in the principal academic fields,
proved to be strikingly different among the several colleges and uni-

versities. Scores on a test of mental ability presented a similar picture of diversity, not only among the student bodies of the institutions but also among groups of students majoring in various subjects. For example, the mean scores on a general culture test of sophomores in the liberal arts programs of thirty-five institutions ranged over two-and-a-half standard deviations. In the three colleges with the lowest mean scores on this test, no students scored above the mean of the highest college, and the student with the lowest score in the highest college did not approach the mean score in the other three.

Learned and Wood called particular attention to the consistency of the pattern of diversity among colleges at the sophomore *and* senior level. In interpreting the absence of any uniformity among colleges in the dominant pattern of senior scores, they commented:

> The (scores) tend at each college to cluster within certain limits. These limits may be characteristic of that college, and the institution's position on the scale may be duplicated from test to test, or it may fluctuate with successive tests given to different classes of students. So also the various curriculum groups within a college are themselves little institutions which either maintain fairly constant relations to one another in their (test score) indices or else shift about as their personnel changes; they tend, however, to maintain a more or less stable common center which fixes the position of the college as a whole.

Although Learned and Wood may not have been the first to point up the great differences in knowledge among students who had completed a certain level of education, they demonstrated statistically "that school status, as defined by time spent and courses passed in school or college, has (no) necessary relation to a definite body of ideas understood and available as a result of 'education'" (Learned and Wood, 1938, p. 4). Even more dramatically, in illustrating differences in achievement on common tests, they stated that over one-fourth of all college seniors made scores below the sophomore average, and that nearly 10% did less well than the average score of the high school seniors.

In the late 1930s a number of other researchers dealt with relatively large groups of students, more or less representative of either a class level or a college, but in almost every case these investigations involved a single institution. Two studies seem to stand out as most noteworthy for their historical contribution. The first, an exception to the intramural approach, was an investigation of student attitudes by Nelson. He obtained scores on samples of students in all four classes in eighteen colleges (Nelson, 1938), including four public universities and fourteen denominational liberal arts colleges. This study was unique both in its multi-institutional approach and in its follow-up of many of the same students after graduation. The second prominent study of that day, which set a pattern for research on students up to the present, was conducted by Newcomb at Bennington (1943). This was perhaps the most extensive and complete assessment of a single group of students over four college years conducted up to that time and for some years to come. It delineated for the first time an entire student culture that was distinct from most other college cultures. Both the Nelson and Newcomb investigations used attitudinal measures to determine change in students' basic values or philosophical perspectives.

Other studies reported near the end of the same decade (1930–40) described the student bodies of particular institutions and reported differences among some subgroups in these schools. These were essentially studies of specific attitudes and attitudinal complexes (e.g., attitudes toward religion or toward labor relations) and changes in such attitudes during college years. In instances where objective inventories were employed (Nelson, 1936; Newcomb, 1943; Arsenian, 1943), attitudes and values were measured in contrast to more general or basic personality traits (e.g., maturity, flexibility, introversion). Assessment of the latter for groups of students was apparently not attempted until some time later.

Except for the striking diversity among students and institutions revealed in the Learned-Wood report (1938), little evidence of the great variations in students' characteristics, even in aptitude and achievement, much less in attitudes, values, and dispositions, within or among institutions, has been accumulated. Furthermore, there has been little discussion of the implications of the meager data that are available on student diversity for college objectives, curricula, or instructional methods, or for the pattern of institutions that would seem to be necessary in a diversified, coordinated, statewide system of higher education. Not until very recently has much attention been given to the characteristics of the student body as determinants of the atmosphere of a college or of its educational effectiveness. Two important studies of differences among colleges and universities in the production of future scientists and scholars (Knapp and Goodrich, 1952; Knapp and Greenbaum, 1953) put more stress on the impact of the college than they did on the quality of students it attracted. But recent studies have shown that the product is a function of the "input" (Holland, 1957; McConnell and Heist, 1959), and so research has begun to turn to the interaction between student material and college environments (and/or subcultures) in explaining productivity and in charting the dynamics of student development.

The Center for the Study of Higher Education of the University of

California at Berkeley has conducted extensive studies of the composition of student bodies and of the differential selectivity of particular colleges and universities, as well as of groups of institutions. An underlying premise has been that in addition to measured ability, other student characteristics such as social and cultural background, personality traits or dispositions, attitudes, interests, and goals are important determinants of general institutional climate, of peer cultures and subcultures, and also of educational "product." Some of the findings on the characteristics of entering students are summarized below along with the results of other studies.

VARIATION IN SCHOLASTIC APTITUDE

A question of great interest in recent years is what proportion of high school graduates at various levels of ability should go to college. To many the question is two-edged: they are concerned both about too few going from the upper levels and too many from those of lesser ability. In a much quoted report (1954) Wolfle showed that only 53% of the top one-fifth of high school graduates entered college, but that 17% of the lowest one-fifth did so. A report by Educational Testing Service (White, 1954) indicated that in the Cleveland area 40% of the students with IQ's above 115 did *not* enter college immediately following graduation from high school. In another report published in the same year, Berdie indicated that 32% of the high school graduates above a score of 120 (the 70th percentile) on the ACE Psychological Examination (1947 edition) were not planning to go to college (Berdie, 1954). A more recent study conducted by Educational Testing Service (Stice, 1956) for the National Science Foundation showed that even among students in the top 10% in ability one-fifth had no expectation of entering college. Figures quoted by Havighurst (1960), showing the percentages of students who entered college in 1960, demonstrated that 34% of entering males and 23% of entering females came from the top two quartiles in ability but that 16% and 27% respectively from the same levels were *not* in college.

An extensive investigation of attendance patterns of high school seniors in the State of Minnesota presents the most complete analysis by ability levels (Corcoran and Keller, 1957). The data in this study were in the form of scores on the 1947 edition of the ACE Psychological Examination. They gave the following percentages of various groups scoring above the level of 100 on this test, which was the threshold for college entrance recommended by President Truman's Commission on

Higher Education: general population, 30%; high school graduates, 42%; and college entrants, 60%.[1] Of the high school seniors in that state 27% had scores of 110 or above, and 40% of these graduates went on to college. A score of 120 (a point above which 10% of the population in Minnesota fell) marked off approximately 15% of the high school seniors, but only one-fourth of this relatively superior group later attended college.

The statistics quoted in the Wolfle report (1954) help round out the picture. These data were obtained in a large-scale assessment program using the Army General Classification Test. By using conversion tables devised by the Center for the Study of Higher Education (Berkeley) the Wolfle mean scores have been translated to scores on the ACE Psychological Examination (1947 and 1952 editions) as follows:

| | Mean Scores | | |
Population (1951–52)	AGCT (Wolfle)	ACE	
		1947 ed.	1952 ed.
Total age group (17 years old)	100	62	70
High school graduates	110	85	88
College entrants	115	94	97

To the extent that these figures are accurate and allowing for a normal distribution, it can be seen that in the early 1950s the ability levels of a great many of the youth entering higher education fell below the threshold level (a score of 100 on the 1947 edition of the ACE) recommended by the President's Commission.

In order to estimate the selectivity of higher education as a whole, as well as of certain groups of institutions, and to discover the distribution of the ability of entering students among major types of colleges and universities, the Center for the Study of Higher Education drew a representative 11% sample (yielding 200 institutions) of the more than 1800 higher institutions in the United States. The sample was stratified by (1) region (Northeast, South, North Central and West); (2) form of control (public, private [nondenominational], Protestant and Roman Catholic); and (3) level of program offered (less than four years, bachelor's and/or the first professional degree, master's and/or the second professional degree, and doctor's and equivalent degrees).[2]

[1] The 1947 ACE score of 100 corresponds to a value of 104 for the 1952 edition, which is the edition used in the discussion of data reported by the Center for the Study of Higher Education, following in this section.

[2] The method of securing the sample is described in detail in a report in mimeographed form by J. G. Darley et al., which may be secured from the Center for the Study of Higher Education.

To determine its representativeness, the sample was checked against several factors that were not involved in the selection or classification of institutions. a) Each major classification and subclassification of the 200-school sample comprised 11% of all institutions in the particular subcategory. b) The 200-school sample included 11.3% (60,539) of the first-time students enrolled in the fall of 1952 (the year for which the ability data on college entrants was secured) in all the colleges and universities from which the sample was drawn. c) The institutions in the sample granted 11.6% of the doctor's degrees in the academic year 1955–56 (the year that most entering students in this study would normally have completed four years of college). d) The sample was composed of 145 coeducational institutions (73%, as compared with 75% in the parent population), 18 men's colleges (9% vs. 11% respectively) and 37 women's colleges (18% vs. 14%).

A preliminary inquiry had shown that the great majority of institutions had employed the American Council on Education Psychological Examination (ACE) in 1952 and the years immediately preceding or following. The staff had previously decided to collect scores on the incoming freshmen of 1952 since this would permit comparison of the data with those of other projects at the Center. Since the most frequently used form of the ACE was the 1952 edition, it was decided that this would be the reference point in arriving at a distribution of scholastic aptitude scores for the entire sample. In the relatively small number of schools in which tests other than the ACE had been used, conversions were made to ACE scores; for a somewhat larger number that had used other than the 1952 form of the ACE, conversions were made to equivalent 1952 scores. In every case raw scores were collected for all entering students. For a small number of institutions scores for the freshman class of 1952 were not available. To protect the randomness and representativeness of the sample, these institutions were retained and aptitude scores for the year nearest to 1952 were utilized.

Means and standard deviations based on the ACE total score (linguistic and quantitative sections combined) were computed for each of the 200 institutions. From these statistics means and standard deviations were computed for the total group and for all subgroups.

The data permit one to examine the degree of diversity in student ability from a number of approaches. The results summarized here will be limited to (a) diversity in ability in higher education in general, (b) diversity among and within institutions in the total sample, and (c) diversity within and among groups of institutions classified by form of control and by level of program offered or degree granted.

The mean ACE total score for the 60,539 students in the sample of

200 schools was 104.4 with a standard deviation of 27.1. Among the schools, the mean scores ranged from a low of 37.5 to a high of 142.2. This represents a dispersion of institutional means covering nearly four standard deviations in individual student scores of the entire sample. When converted to percentiles (ACE norms, Educational Testing Service, 1953) the two extreme mean scores were equivalent to the first and 92nd percentiles.

The range of institutional means differed somewhat from region to region, but diversity was prevalent everywhere. The distribution of school means in the South extended over three and one-quarter standard deviations and the distribution in the other three regions approximated two standard deviations. In the Northeast, where the mean of all colleges and universities combined was considerably higher than the means in the other three regions, the total gamut still accommodated an amazing variation in measured ability. The means for individual schools in this section ranged from 86.2 to 142.2. In a later follow-up study in the West, the state of California alone presented as astounding an example of diversity as one could find in any area. Here, the distribution of means encompassed a range of three standard deviations. With such diversification in states and regions, there seems to be little reason to doubt that high school graduates of all levels of ability can gain admission to some institution without going very far from home. In colleges at the extremes of the ability distribution, these students will live in very different intellectual worlds.

A number of colleges in 1952 attracted or selected freshmen nearly all of whose scores were above the national mean of all entering students; the reverse of this is also true in that the great majority in some schools scored below the national mean. On the basis of academic ability alone the composition of the student bodies on a great many campuses is highly unlike that in many others.

Of perhaps greater educational significance for individual campuses is the extent of diversity within single student bodies. Over 85% of the schools had an entering student body whose distribution of ACE test scores extended beyond three standard deviations of the distribution of all entering students in the total sample. And 35% of these schools had distributions extending over five standard deviations. If one considers only the colleges and universities with entering students whose scores spread over three standard deviations, it would be a conservative estimate that a great many faculty members were attempting to handle classes whose variation in IQ was more than 50 points.

Some readers will be interested in the scores of institutions grouped according to the three major categories. When all schools, of whatever level and form of control, in each of the four regions were combined the mean scores were as follows:

Northeast	116.5
North Central	105.4
West	100.7
South	94.9

Four-year colleges granting the B.A. or B.S. degree in the respective regions presented the same pattern of differences:

Northeast	112.5
North Central	105.0
West	103.2
South	92.0

When the schools were grouped by level, the means were distributed much as one might predict:

Level IV	(granting doctorates)	112.7
Level III	(granting masters)	106.3
Level II	(granting bachelors)	101.6
Level I	(two-year colleges)	93.8

The pattern of means by level, from high to low, in each geographical region was in line with those shown immediately above except in the West, where Level IV and II means were about the same. (However, the most selective university in the region did not happen to fall in the sample.)

When the institutions were classified by the four major forms of control, the private and Catholic institutions were at the top and the Protestant and public institutions at the bottom:

Private	113.2
Roman Catholic	111.7
Protestant	102.6
Public	100.9

This pattern held generally in each of the four geographical regions except for the private category. In the Northeast, South, and West the Catholic institutions were highest in each case by a margin of one or two points; in the North Central area the Protestant schools were slightly above the others. In the latter region the means were very much alike, and in the Northeast area the range was only about five points.

As one would expect, the variation within any one of the categories of institutions was more striking than the differences among the classifications. This can be readily illustrated with several distinctly different examples. In the North Central region, the four-year Protestant colleges in Level II (13 institutions in the sample) had a range of mean scores of approximately one standard deviation (27 points) based on individual scores of the entire sample. Twelve colleges of the same level and same form of control in the South had mean scores which spread over nearly two standard deviations. In the Northeast, six four-year Roman Catholic colleges had means ranging over one standard deviation. In the West, 10 junior colleges in the sample had mean scores extending over three-fourths of a standard deviation. Apparently, students who differ widely in ability could locate an institution in any area, of any type, or of any form of control in which they would find themselves among many intellectual peers.

To illustrate the relative internal heterogeneity of institutions in students' measured ability, a number of institutions were selected from Level II, in this case all four-year liberal arts colleges. These six, diagrammatically represented in Figure 5-1, are in the Northeast and North Central regions. They were originally selected to illustrate varying ranges of abilities *within* institutions, but they also very adequately demonstrate variation in institutional means (Heist, 1960). Only the two schools at the extremes, A and F, could be considered somewhat unique in intellectual composition. The other four could readily be matched in mean score by numerous other Level II and III institutions in these two regions.

A fairly high order of selectivity is indicated by the mean scores for institutions E and F at the far right of Figure 5-1. High selectivity is reflected also in the more limited range of scores in these two colleges and in the somewhat smaller standard deviations (approximately 19 points in both cases). Only a few students scored below the mean of college B, and none below the mean of college A, and the limits within which 84% or more of the students in schools E and F fell are entirely above the limits within which the same percentages of students were found in colleges A and B.

It is perhaps somewhat more surprising to find colleges, such as A or B, with means considerably below the national average but with somewhat limited variation in aptitude (standard deviations of 20 to 22 points). These student groups were definitely limited in an upward direction; only a very few students in college A exceeded the means of colleges E and F and none in college B reached or exceeded the means of E and F. In fact, only a small minority rose above the national mean. Colleges C and D were more typical of institutions at large, with means

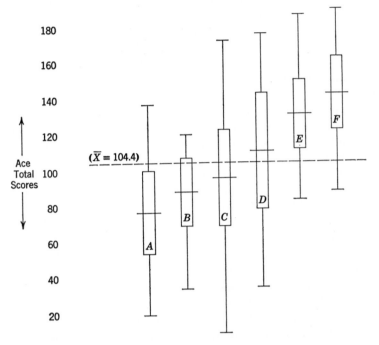

Figure 1. Distributions of American Council on Education Psychological Examination Scores (1952 edition) for six four-year liberal arts colleges. (The range of one standard deviation above and below the mean is represented by the areas enclosed by the rectangles. The mean scores are indicated by the solid lines running through the rectangles. The mean of the entire sample of entering students is represented by the dotted line across the chart.)

approximating the national student average and with greater heterogeneity of entering freshman classes. Institutions that were most heterogeneous tended to cluster around the mean of 104.4.

These findings raise many important questions, the answers to which are still to be found.

1. It has been suggested that each institution should select its students from a relatively narrow range of talent. Since only a small number of highly selective colleges are essentially homogeneous in student ability, how could such pairing of students and institutions, if desirable, be effected? Would such a distribution stimulate students of all levels of ability more nearly to measure up to their potentialities than would be the case in a diverse student body? Which is more important —to have a narrow range of ability among students, or to have in each

institution enough students of high ability to stimulate each other? What is the effect on his motivation when a student of high ability has to compete with other students equally capable, or nearly so, and has, perhaps, to adjust to getting C's when in high school he received mostly A's? Contrariwise, what is the effect on a student's motivation when he finds himself mentally far outclassed by most other students in his college?

2. Some institutions with student bodies possessing relatively low ability scores may enroll a few students of exceptional capacity. Should these students have been advised to enter a more selective institution, or should they be advised to transfer to another college? If it should be agreed that the appearance of a very few exceptional students in a student body of below average ability represents mismating of student and institution, how can this be avoided? Is the stimulus of a student of high ability—supposing that he performs reasonably well in an environment with low general demands—sufficiently valuable to ordinary students and to at least some faculty members to justify his retention in the institution with students of greatly inferior ability?

3. If an institution chooses to be highly selective in scholastic aptitude should it be equally selective on other grounds, such as social and cultural background, intellectual bent or disposition (for example, theoretical or applied orientation), attitudes, or values? More particularly, would a student whose interests and values are those that characterize engineering students do well at a college with many free-thinking liberals, even if his scholastic aptitude scores were adequate? Or, would an intellectually and socially unconventional student perform successfully at a college with students drawn almost entirely from a single, conservative religious denomination?

4. What kind of student "mix" with respect to a wide range of characteristics would be most productive for students with different *patterns* of interests, abilities, attitudes, values, emotional histories, and social backgrounds?

DIVERSITY IN "NONINTELLECTIVE" CHARACTERISTICS

The last two questions suggest that institutions are differentially selective or attractive, not only in students' academic ability, but also in their interests, values, attitudes, intellectual dispositions, and social backgrounds. Some examples of diversity among and within colleges and universities, on such "nonintellective" factors, will be given below.

Variation in students' vocational interests. The distribution of vocational interests and vocational interest patterns among individuals is conceivably a product of such influences as the interests of parents, the economic and cultural level of the home, sex and sex-role expectations, and previous social and intellectual experiences. Presumably mental ability also affects the number and intensity of interests, but there is only minimal evidence to indicate this (Strong, 1943). Support for the other determinants of interests is much more adequate (Bordin, 1943; Carter, 1941; Berdie, 1944; Tyler, 1951). With great variety in the determining factors, one might well expect the scores on measures of specific interests to be distributed normally in any group drawn at random in our society. Such normal distributions would not be expected in the scores of student bodies of collegiate institutions and much less likely in those of students in a particular major program (see Chapter 17). In fact, large proportions of students are found in certain curricular fields who exhibit similar and distinctive interests. Recent research by Weissman has again shown this clearly to be the case (1958). The interest patterns of the majority of students in business, for example, are very much alike, but they are also different from those of students in the theoretical sciences or in the humanities.

One wonders whether certain colleges and universities also draw or select groups of students with measured interests that are different from those of the general student population or of other institutions, such as has been shown to be the case for ability.

Weissman (1958), using a new method of profile analysis of the Strong Blank, showed that in "intellectual disposition" National Merit Scholarship winners could be arranged along an applied-theoretical continuum. With this approach to interest assessment he was able to differentiate among groups of students attending institutions that were more productive of scientists and scholars and those attending institutions which were less productive (according to the Knapp and Greenbaum indices) (1953). More students with a theoretical orientation and a preference for abstract thinking attended the schools that ranked high in productivity, whereas more students with a pragmatic and applied orientation went to less productive institutions. Undoubtedly a motivational factor served as a significant determinant in the choice of institution for many of these students of very high ability.

Darley and Hagenah (1955) found differences among the colleges within a university in the number of entering students with different "interest families" (on the Strong Vocational Interest Blank). The pattern of dominant interests differed widely between groups of students of equivalent ability, enrolled in the colleges of liberal arts and engineering. On the other hand, students with lower ability scores in the two-year General College program had interests rather similar to those of students of higher ability in four-year curricula in the liberal arts. Many students with interest patterns characteristic of people in subprofessional fields (such as those involving business detail and technical operations) were enrolled in divisions where the level of academic work was more intellectually demanding than their measured interests appeared to support.

The interest patterns reported by Darley and Hagenah (1955) also assist in giving some picture of the diversity of interests across the total student body of a single institution. The Strong scores of a sample of 1000 male students said to be representative of the freshmen entering the three undergraduate colleges of the University of Minnesota referred to above were classified into seven basic "interest families." [3] Each student's profile was not read for the specific pattern of scores but for the presence of a primary, secondary, or reject pattern, or none of the three patterns [4] in each of the seven interest families. The various patterns obtained for each individual in single interest families and combinations of patterns for one or more families (for example, primary in one and secondary in another interest family) were presented for this entire male sample. The result: tremendous diversity of interests among these individuals, accentuating the great heterogeneity of the student culture composed of these 1000 young men. The necessity for more diligent concern with individual differences in educational treatment is the implication to be drawn from every table in which the data were presented.

A broader perspective of the distribution of interests among a large group of college students, high ability men and women, was taken by Stewart (1958). He looked at the frequencies of primary, secondary, and reject patterns on the Strong Blank to see whether any differences existed among groups of students in the five major geographical regions. The most striking finding was the *similarity* of patterns for the high ability students across the different regions. Although no consistency in the differences that were observed was discernible, a few sufficiently

[3] The interest families are biological sciences, physical sciences, technical, social service, business detail, business contact, and verbal linguistic.

[4] "For an individual student, the *primary pattern* is the interest type within which he shows a preponderance (plurality or majority) of A and B+ scores on the specific occupational keys; the *secondary pattern* is the interest type within which he shows a preponderance of B+ and B scores; . . . . a reject interest pattern (is) recorded whenever the majority or plurality of the scores in any one family group lay to the left of the 'chance,' or shaded, area on the profile." (Darley and Hagenah, 1955, p. 76 and p. 79.)

large to merit consideration and explanation were found. Both the men and women from the Northeast and Southeast had fewer no-primary patterns than the men and women in the West. The women from the Northeast and the West had higher frequencies of secondary patterns in the biological sciences than did those in the Southeast. Women from the Northeast appeared to be the single most deviant group; none of them showed primary patterns in business detail and business contact but they had the highest number of verbal-linguistic patterns. Whatever the reasons for differences such as the latter one, the pattern of interests would undoubtedly be of motivational significance in academic pursuits.

The substance of the research on measured vocational interests, including the extensive findings of Strong (1943; 1955), suggests that this aspect of human behavior is a sufficiently potent differential to be regularly employed in analyzing the composition of student bodies (or subgroups on particular campuses) or in attempting to infer the variety and intensity of student motivation. The implication from several of the studies summarized above is that students who possess certain interests are more suited for some curricula than for others (as student personnel workers have long argued), and also that individuals' peculiar interests give them a greater "readiness" for some institutions rather than others.

Diversity in attitudes. How diverse are expressed attitudes at the time of entrance to college? Are there differences among institutions in students' attitudes, as well as in their interests and aptitudes? Are there identifiable subgroups in the more generally diverse attitudinal climate of a large, complex institution? To what extent do those who choose various academic majors differ in attitudes and opinions? Until fairly recently, very little research had been done on these questions. But the available evidence is adequate to justify further serious research, since the implications of the presently available data are of fundamental significance to higher education.

A study reported in 1938 may be considered a pioneering attempt in the attitudinal field. Nelson (1938) was mainly concerned with changes in attitudes over a number of years (see Chapters 24 and 25), but some of his findings reveal differences among students at a particular time. His study, which provided data on 3754 students in 18 institutions, both public and private and Protestant and Catholic, showed that in the late thirties the student bodies of *all* of these schools were essentially conservative, from mildly to highly so. In all colleges there were significant differences between the sexes; the women were the more conservative. Although Nelson unfortunately did not report the differences in attitudes among institutions, he did indicate that the differences between particular institutions exceeded the differences between types of institutions. He also found differences among groups of students coming from different regions. One of his most interesting findings had to do with the ranking of the 18 institutions on the obtained differences between the freshman and senior year (cross-sectional measurement), possibly suggesting the impact of the institutions as well as something about the extent of differences among the students who enrolled in them. A rank order of schools, based on differences between students of the first and last years, went from state universities and the more liberal denominations at the top to those that are generally characterized as more authoritarian and fundamentalistic.

In recent years, Coleman (1959; 1960) has been gathering information—opinions, preferences, attitudes—on a large sample of precollege adolescents to determine their major values, especially those concerned with academic achievement. He describes what appears to be the pervasive atmosphere of most high schools as one in which the existing pattern of rewards tends to inhibit learning and results in questionable goal orientations.[5] These are, of course, well learned by the majority of pupils in three and four years and are carried on to the college and university environments.

The Center for the Study of Higher Education has under way an investigation of the educational and intellectual development during the college years of a large sample of National Merit Scholarship winners and near winners, whose measured ability places them in the top 1% or 2% of all high school graduates. In their initial year in college they responded to a questionnaire that included attitudinal items on a variety of topics of cultural significance. A sampling of items on selected subjects will show that there was relatively little diversity in the attitudes of the students who had chosen certain academic majors. (The figures are included only for groups containing seventy-five or more students.) The percentages, shown in Table 1, are for combined-response categories. The possible five responses ran from "very definitely" to "definitely not" with "no opinion" in the middle position. The two categories at both the positive and the negative extremes have been combined (Yes and No) for tabular presentation here.

[5] In fairness to the comprehensiveness of Coleman's research to date, it should be added that he does analyze different secondary school environments to determine varying forms of behavioral reinforcement and attempts to examine how such environments, within the context of social theory, might be altered to gain other effects in students' values and goals.

Table 1. Percentage Responses on Selected Attitude Questions of a Sample of Male and Female National Merit Scholarship Students (Freshman Year—1956–57)

Questions	Major	Male			Female		
		Yes	No Opinion	No	Yes	No Opinion	No
1. Is it in the public interest to allow scientists to continue to explore whatever they wish without restraint?	Engineering	83	3	14			
	Physics	88	2	10			
	Mathematics	96	2	2			
	Other Natural Sciences	93	3	4			
	Humanities	89	1	10	74	11	15
	Natural Science and Mathematics				84	4	12
2. Is the best government the one which governs least?	Engineering	27	17	56			
	Physics	34	10	56			
	Mathematics	38	20	42			
	Other Natural Sciences	26	5	69			
	Humanities	23	8	68	21	8	71
	Natural Science and Mathematics				31	9	60
3. Should the government provide medical and dental care for citizens who cannot afford such services?	Engineering	56	15	29			
	Physics	59	7	34			
	Mathematics	55	26	19			
	Other Natural Sciences	54	15	31			
	Humanities	55	7	38	50	11	39
	Natural Science and Mathematics				51	7	42
4. Should American colleges place more emphasis on teaching religious values?	Engineering	35	20	45			
	Physics	30	17	53			
	Mathematics	33	16	51			
	Other Natural Sciences	37	12	51			
	Humanities	36	10	54	36	11	53
	Natural Science and Mathematics				44	8	48

A review of the percentages in Table 1 indicates rather consistent response patterns across the principal curricular groups. A majority of responses consistently seems to be in the liberal direction. The responses of the freshman women as a group were always a little more conservative than those of the men as a total group (figures not shown).

The men in engineering and the women in the humanities were somewhat less in favor of unrestricted scientific investigation than were the other groups. On the question of whether the best government is the one which governs least, more of the women in the humanities took a clear liberal position than did those in the natural sciences and mathematics. The men in both the humanities and the "other natural science" group responded more often than other male groups in the liberal direction. On the last two questions, the general agreement of response among the groups is the most impressive fact; however, some variation occurred among the males in the "no opinion" and negative response categories for the third question, and the two women's groups differed on the last one. On the whole, attitudes on items such as these seem ordinarily to be unrelated to choice of academic major, especially in the case of students of such exceptionally high ability. A question of major interest is the situation four years hence: will these students respond even more uniformly then but still in a predominantly liberal direction?

This large group of National Merit scholars was also queried somewhat indirectly about their attitudes toward education. Before their entry to college, they were asked to choose from a list of possible educational goals those they thought the ideal institution should emphasize. This resulted in some rather striking variation among the groups enrolled in institutions under different forms of control (McConnell, 1960). The percentages for only two of six goals, presented for the various groups in Table 2, illustrate the essentially different attitudes toward education on the part of many students. Half of these capable students in schools under public control indicated that they were pri-

Table 2. Percentages of Students in Institutions Representing Different Forms of Control Who Professed One of Six Educational Goals as Their Primary One (Results Shown for Only Two Goals)

Primary Educational Goals	Percentages in Types of Institutions			
	Public	Private	Catholic	Protestant
1. Vocational training	50	25	17	25
2. General education and appreciation of ideas	38	60	40	53

marily concerned with vocational training, whereas 25% or less of those in the other types of schools were so oriented. The percentages were reversed when students were asked if they were interested in intellectual matters above all others.

In a study conducted at Cornell University (Goldsen et al., 1960) the same list of educational goals as that employed with the National Merit scholars was included in questionnaires submitted to students in a number of colleges and universities. The results in this study also indicated considerable variation among institutions. For example, students at Wesleyan, Yale, Harvard, and Dartmouth most often checked "basic general education and appreciation of ideas" and least often stressed vocational training as their educational interests. On the other hand, men at the state universities checked vocational preparation much more frequently than those at the Ivy League colleges.

A major point to be made here is not that students whose vocational goals are primary should go to state universities rather than to private institutions, but that faculties in the public institutions that want to interest students in ideas will have a difficult challenge and a considerably different problem.

If one takes an overview of the responses to all attitudinal items for all institutions the major impression from the Cornell Study is one of considerable uniformity in the thinking of college students. For example, although there are definite manifestations (to infer from quoted percentages) of humanitarian and liberal attitudes, conservative thinking on the whole seems to be more typical. Although 95% of all students indicated a belief in God or in a Supreme Being and the great majority indicated "a need to believe in some sort of religious faith or philosophy," strong commitments to religion appear to have been generally lacking. The actual differences in percentages that were obtained among the colleges and universities on belief in God and a need for a religious faith can probably be related to several extramural determinants, such as the variations in level of ability of the incoming students, students' socio-economic backgrounds, and the predominant cultural patterns of the geographical area where the institution is located and from which it draws its students.

The responses of all students taken together may appear to contradict the report of the same research team to the effect that many Ivy League students differed from those in other groups of institutions in their basic educational orientation. Such is, however, not the case. Consistent differences among institutional groups across all the items, though seldom of great magnitude, do distinguish some institutions from others. One can gain some notion of the attitudinal atmosphere of a school by a "thread" of differences running through the various items. Through such an approach the eleven institutions can conceivably be grouped into several clusters. These subgroups are as follows: (1) Harvard, Yale, Dartmouth, and Wesleyan (Connecticut); (2) North Carolina and Texas; (3) UCLA, Michigan, and Wayne. Cornell and Fisk seem to be the most distinct; they do not readily fit into any of the three clusters. The major differences among these groups appear to be in the degree of general conservatism and in attitudes toward the general purpose of education. On religious attitudes the schools would fall in a somewhat different pattern. UCLA students now appear to be more like the Ivy League cluster, and Wesleyan and Cornell fit readily with Michigan and Wayne. Fisk falls in with North Carolina and Texas to make the most orthodox of the three groups. However, the extent and direction of these differences give no cues concerning the existence or size of subgroups on the campuses. The heterogeneity of religious attitudes within the student body on any one campus, or the existence of vocal minority groups, may give more color to the student culture than the beliefs of the majority.

It is to be noted that the eleven institutions are all prominent colleges and universities, although they may be noteworthy for somewhat different reasons. But, in the light of the diversity among the institutions, it is surprising that the differences in students' orientations are not greater. It would be difficult indeed for an observer to distinguish one student body from another as far as the expressed attitudes and beliefs of most students are concerned. The data strongly support Jacob's conclusion that a national "norm" of attitudes and values seems to prevail across the gamut of colleges and universities. The diversity that is discernible among institutions and groups of institutions seems to be obscured by the great similarity of students' thinking from campus to campus.

Variation in personality characteristics. The attributes of students presented in this section are termed *personality* characteristics not because they are essentially different from those of the earlier part of this chapter; most readers would probably agree that expressed aptitudes, interests, attitudes, and values can legitimately be viewed as aspects of personality. However, here the term is used to refer to a type of measured behavior that is complex and diverse in the personality structure. These characteristics are considered as more basic or fundamental in that they tend to influence much other psychological behavior. For example, the authoritarian syndrome may be expected to influence in significant degree much of a person's thinking, many of his more specific attitudes, and his relationships with other people. Consequently, differences of this type, whether characteristic of the individual student or of groups of students, may in numerous instances be as potent educational "determiners" as academic aptitude and previous academic achievement.

In describing college students it is appropriate to ask how college entrants compare with high school seniors in measured personality traits. Differences between students at these two levels will be illustrated from available data on the California Personality Inventory (CPI) (Gough, 1956), one of the most widely used instruments, and the Omnibus Personality Inventory (OPI) (Heist and Williams, 1957), an instrument assembled and constructed at the Center for the Study of Higher Education for research on student growth and development. These two inventories are more comprehensive than most others in the number of characteristics measured. Scores on the OPI are available for a sample of graduating seniors in one large California high school and for a sample composed of entering students on two of the University of California campuses. The comparisons on the CPI scales are made on the basis of the norms in the manual for high school and college groups drawn from large samples. These scores on the CPI cannot be taken as representative of high school seniors and college freshmen but as typical of high school and college students of various grade levels.

The chief differences on the CPI between students at the secondary and college level in the case of both sexes are on scales measuring: a) a composite of poise, sociability, sensitivity, extroversion, and confidence in human relations, b) responsibility, c) tolerance, d) achievement potential in an academic and intellectual sense, and e) flexibility. The college people are between .5 and 1.5 of a standard score higher on these scales.

Major differences on the OPI are essentially corroborative of the above, although the overlap in the characteristics supposedly measured may at first glance appear to be minimal. One dissimilarity is found in social introversion-extroversion. The social introversion scale from the Minnesota Multiphasic Personality Inventory, included in the OPI, results in scores that make the college student appear as the more introverted. This, however, may well indicate a need for independence and the strength or willingness to withdraw, rather than alienation, to judge by the results on some of the other scales. Beyond this, the differences between the seniors and freshmen show that the college students, including both sexes again, are: a) more socially mature, b) more responsible, c) less authoritarian and more tolerant, d) less impulsive, and e) more motivated or interested in an intellectual sense (supported by three scales measuring interest in ideas and reflective thought, complexity of outlook, and originality). On the scales mentioned the differences vary from .3 to 1.5 of a standard deviation.

When one considers the chief differences on both inventories he finds that the college student has attained a greater degree of maturity and more of an interest in academic and intellectual activities. It seems reasonable to conclude from the data on these fairly large samples, representing students across the nation in the first case and those within one state in the second, that the college students present a picture of greater readiness for education and for further personal development than do the high school seniors. One might say that the former are well along on a course of development that continued education should foster. More definitive data on the differences between high school and college students wait on longitudinal studies. Whether the greater maturity and educational readiness of college students is the result of age or selection cannot be decided from the data now available.

A good deal of information has recently become available that permits comparisons among student groups entering various institutions of higher education. The findings of selected recent studies that have revealed differences among student groups and subgroups, especially those existing at the time of admission, are summarized below.

In a significant contribution to research on students, Stern, Stein, Bloom (1956), and Stern and Cope (1956) categorized students into one of four major groups; three of these groups were found to be prominent, in varying proportions, on a number of campuses. These groups were called stereopaths (authoritarians), nonstereopaths (antiauthoritarians), rationals, and irrationals.[6] On a variety of other social and psychological measures they found numerous significant differences among these four "types." Some institutions had a predominance of authoritarians while others had a considerable supply of antiauthoritarians. Those classified as irrationals were found only in small numbers on campuses with a majority of authoritarians, but rationals seemed to be more randomly distributed among the different institutions. The extreme in differences between student bodies on two campuses was represented by one institution that enrolled about half authoritarians and half rationals and another whose enrollees were divided between antiauthoritarians and rationals. Whether or not the rationals in these two schools could have been exchanged is not known, but it would be safe to predict that the great majority of the authoritarians and the antiauthoritarians, if given the opportunity, would not

[6] For a further description of these groups see Chapter 21.

have reversed their schools. They seemed to be situated in locales that were congruent with their measured orientations.

Several projects at the Center for the Study of Higher Education at Berkeley have revealed that students who differ in motivation and personality have been distributed among colleges and universities in a nonrandom fashion. Two reports will be briefly drawn upon to illustrate differential attraction or selection of certain colleges and universities on other than academic ability. In one report on problems of selection (Heist and Webster, 1959) the entering students in two liberal arts colleges were compared on numerous personality variables. Their average academic ability scores placed both student groups at least a standard deviation above the national mean score of 104.4 on the ACE Psychological Examination, 1952 edition.[7] The freshman students in the college with the lower mean ability score presented a pattern of scores on most personality scales about two-thirds of a standard deviation above that of the entrants to the institution with the higher mean ability score. The former group's scores indicated more nonauthoritarian thinking, more social sophistication, less inhibition and emotional constraint, more interest in matters of a theoretical and abstract nature, and greater motivation for intellectual activity (reflected in significant differences on scales measuring interest in ideas and reflective thought, complexity of perception and response, and originality).

In line with the analysis of Stern et al., one would infer that the students in both institutions would be chiefly antiauthoritarians or rationals, with the freshmen in the college with the higher mean ability including a greater percentage of rationals.

Subgroups were identified on both campuses, largely according to criteria of social affiliation, general interests, and participation in college activities (Heist and Webster, 1959). Taking the institution with the higher ability level as an example, the smallest of the three subgroups appeared to be well described by Stern's characterization of the antiauthoritarians. A second group had many characteristics of the rationals; they were not authoritarians nor were they in any sense antiauthoritarians. A third group, falling between the other two on most personality measures, curiously enough possessed some of the identifying earmarks of both the antiauthoritarians *and* the rationals. The behavior of the "members "of the three subgroups was sufficiently potent to establish at least two prominent but somewhat diverse subcultures on this campus, with limited communication between them.

---

[7] The mean ACE score of the entering freshmen in the Center's representative national sample of institutions of higher learning.

Undoubtedly there is a difference in the general milieu and the educational atmosphere between colleges having but one dominant student culture and colleges composed of two or more identifiable subcultures.

Another project at the Berkeley Center dealt with students who were attracted to colleges and universities a large proportion of whose graduates later earned the doctorate (McConnell and Heist, 1959; Heist, McConnell, Matsler, and Williams, 1961). A group of students, male and female, entering the productive institutions (many of whose graduates later obtain the doctorate) were matched in ability with a group of individuals entering less productive schools. The larger population was composed of the National Merit Scholarship winners of 1956. On the basis of mean score differences on measured personality characteristics, the students who entered the institutions of greater productivity were more flexible in their thinking, more tolerant of ambiguity, more genuinely interested in learning, more theoretically inclined, and potentially more original and creative. Thus, the students that enter certain institutions are to be seen as a major consideration in scholastic achievement along with the impact of the institution as such.

May student bodies of average scholastic ability differ as much in personality characteristics as do those of much greater capacity? Utilizing data from an unpublished study at the Center for the Study of Higher Education, staff members compared entering classes in two colleges, situated within the same county, whose mean academic ability scores placed them both within two or three points of the national freshman mean. Only on two scales, one measuring interest in ideas and reflective thought and the other liberal vs. conservative attitudes, did these two freshman classes appear similar. On all other scales the scores would indicate that they were distinctly different. One of the institutions had many more students with theoretical and esthetic orientations, with more complex perceptions of the environment, and with considerably more manifest impulsivity in their routine behavior. Whether the personalities of the group with the higher scores on the tests measuring these characteristics make for greater intellectuality, or for greater ingenuity and creativity, is yet to be determined.

CONCLUSION

All too little is known statistically or experimentally about the relationship between the personality characteristics students bring to college and their academic achievement, either in the conventional sense of grades and persistence, or in the more subtle sense of independent, critical, and creative intellectual competence (which are seldom reflected in academic marks). Even less is known about the relationship between personality structure and the attainment of personal maturity and effectiveness. But the first step in making these studies is to *know* the entering student, to know him as an actual or potential scholar, to know him as a person and to see him against his background and against the college environment and its subcultures. While the research is being done, the unusually sensitive teacher will explore the relationships for himself and teach and counsel in the light of what he thinks he has discerned.

The assessment of such behavioral characteristics as attitudes, interests, aspirations, values, and dispositions is possible with increasing reliability and validity; it may be accomplished so simply that difficulty of test administration, or prohibitive costs, no longer are legitimate reasons for confining information about the new student to a narrow range of attributes such as scholastic aptitude test scores or high school grades. A minimal program of assessment, including academic aptitude and achievement, biographical information, social and cultural background, and a few relevant personality characteristics will provide a meaningful description of the student body as a whole, and of the student subgroups that are found on most compuses. By supplementing this body of data with measurement of beliefs, opinions, and attitudes a basis can be laid for analysis of changes in behavior that occur during college years and of the factors that impede or facilitate these changes.

One of the more fundamental problems in understanding student development during the college years is to determine what the student "mix" should be for optimal individual development. We have already asked, without offering an answer, what the composition of a student body should be in level and range of general scholastic aptitude for the most effective academic achievement of individuals of varying degrees of ability. We might also inquire about the most appropriate composition of a student body in social and cultural background: Will a student from a working-class home find himself so alienated from the dominant social groups in a college attended primarily by students from well-to-do families that he does poor or failing academic work? The answer is probably not a simple one. One student from a lower-class background may perform poorly in the classroom; another may compensate for social inferiority by devoting all his energies to study. What are the factors that are responsible for these differences in scholastic performance? Would the student who earned high grades but who had little social experience have been better off—from the criterion of full personal development—in a college where most of the students were comparable in social and cultural background, even if the institution's intellectual stimulus had been inferior?

There is growing interest in the significance of congruence between the student's characteristics and needs, on the one hand, and the nature and demands of the college environment on the other. An individual with strong authoritarian attitudes might make better grades in a college that condoned or rewarded conformity and dependency than in one that attempted to stimulate intellectual independence and which rewarded unconventional intellectual behavior. But should students and colleges be so paired?

One might also ask whether a student with a strong theoretical orientation should attend an engineering school where there is a decided bias of an applied and utilitarian nature. Or, one might inquire, would it be desirable for a student with the abilities, values, interests, and intellectual dispositions that are fundamental to research and scholarship to attend a medical school that stresses education for these careers and that attracts many students like himself, rather than to go to a school that is primarily oriented toward medical practice?

There is some evidence that the climate of colleges that produce many future scientists differs from that in colleges that are more noted for the undergraduate preparation of scholars in the humanities and the social sciences (Thistlethwaite, 1959; Pace, 1960). This leads one to ask again whether there should be a greater effort to fit the students to the college, or, whether in a complex institution (not necessarily a large one) to fit the student to the program or the program to the student. Before this question can be answered, however, the meaning of fitness in terms of optimal development will have to be investigated much more extensively than it has been heretofore.

It has been suggested that the distinction of a college depends less on what it does to students than on the students to whom it does it (Darley, 1956). A more fruitful hypothesis, however, would seem to be that the efficacy of a college is the product of the fortunate conjunction of student characteristics and expectations, *and* the demands, sanctions, and opportunities of the college environment and its subcultures. This is the hypothesis being explored by the Center for the Study of Higher Education at Berkeley in a five-year study of student development in eight institutions—Antioch, College of the Pacific, Reed, St. Olaf, San Francisco State College, Swarthmore, University of Portland, and the University of California at Berkeley.

REFERENCES

American Council on Education psychological examination for college freshmen, 1952 edition. (Norms bulletin.) Princeton, New Jersey: Educational Testing Service, 1953.

Arsenian, S. Change in evaluative attitudes during four years of college. *J. appl. Psychol.*, 1943, **27**, 338–349.

Berdie, R. F. Factors related to vocational interests. *Psychol. Bull.*, 1944, **41**, 137–157.

Berdie, R. F. *After high school—what?* Minneapolis: University of Minnesota Press, 1954.

Black, J. D. MMPI results for fifteen groups of female college students. In Dahlstrom, W. G. and Welsh, G. S. (Eds.), *Basic readings on the MMPI in psychology and medicine.* Minneapolis: University of Minnesota Press, 1956, 562–573.

Bordin, E. S. A theory of vocational interests as dynamic phenomena. *Educ. Psychol. Measmt.*, 1943, **3**, 49–65.

Carter, H. D., Taylor, K. V. F., and Canning, L. B. Vocational choices and interest test scores of high school students. *J. Psychol.*, 1941, **11**, 297–306.

Cattell, J. McKeen, and Farrand, L. Physical and mental measurements of the students of Columbia University. *Psychol. Rev.*, 1896, **3**(6), 618–648.

Coleman, J. S. Academic achievement and the structure of competition. *Harv. Educ. Rev.*, 1959, **29**, 330–351.

Coleman, J. S. The adolescent subculture and academic achievement. *Amer. J. Soc.*, 1960, **55**, 337–347.

Corcoran, Mary, and Keller, R. J. *College attendance of Minnesota high school seniors.* Minneapolis: University of Minnesota, Bureau of Institutional Research, 1957.

Darley, J. G. Diversification in American higher education. In NASPA, *Proceedings —38th Anniversary Conference of the National Association of Student Personnel Administrators.* Lawrence, Kansas: NASPA, 1956, 45–66.

Darley, J. G., and Hagenah, Theda. *Vocational interest measurement: theory and practice.* Minneapolis: University of Minnesota Press, 1955.

Goldsen, Rose K., et al. *What college students think.* Princeton, New Jersey: Van Nostrand Co., Inc., 1960.

Goodstein, L. D. Regional differences in MMPI responses among male college students. *J. cons. Psychol.*, 1954, **18**, 437–441.

Gough, H. G. *California psychological inventory—manual.* Palo Alto, California: Consulting Psychologists Press, Inc., 1956.

Havighurst, Robert J. *American higher education in the 1960s.* Columbus: Ohio State University Press, 1960.

Heist, P. Diversity in college student characteristics. *J. Educ. Soc.*, 1960, **33**, 279–291.

Heist, P., McConnell, T. R., Matsler, F., and Williams, Phoebe. Personality and scholarship. *Science*, 1961, **133**, 362–367.

Heist, P., and Webster, H. Differential characteristics of student bodies—implications for selection and study of undergraduates. In *Selection and Educational Differentiation.* Berkeley, California: Center for the Study of Higher Education, 1960, 91–106.

Heist, P., and Williams, Phoebe. Manual for the omnibus personality inventory. (Mimeo.) University of California, Berkeley: Center for the Study of Higher Educ., 1957.

Holland, J. L. Undergraduate origins of American scientists. *Science,* 1957, **126,** 433–437.

Jacob, P. E. *Changing values in college.* New York: Harper Bros., 1957.

Knapp, R. H., and Goodrich, H. B. *Origins of American scientists.* Chicago: University of Chicago Press, 1952.

Knapp, R. H., and Greenbaum, J. J. *The younger American scholar.* Chicago: University of Chicago Press, 1953.

Learned, W. S., and Wood, B. D. *The student and his knowledge.* A report to the Carnegie Foundation on the results of the high school and college exams. of 1928, 1930, and 1932. Bull. No. 29. New York: The Carnegie Foundation for the Advancement of Teaching, 1938.

McConnell, T. R. Problems of distributing students among institutions with varying characteristics. *North Central Association Quarterly,* 1961, **35,** 226–238.

McConnell, T. R., and Heist, P. Do students make the college? *Coll. Univer.,* 1959, 442–452.

Nelson, E. Radicalism-conservatism in student attitudes. *Psychol. Monogr.,* 1938, 50(4).

Newcomb, T. M. *Personality and social change.* New York: Dryden Press, 1943.

Pace, C. Robert. Five college environments. *Coll. Bd. Rev.,* 1960, **41,** 24–28.

Sprague, H. T. *Institutional Research in the West.* Boulder, Colorado: Western Interstate Commission for Higher Education, 1959.

Stern, G. G., and Cope, A. H. Differences in educability between stereopaths, non-stereopaths, and rationals. (Paper presented at the American Psychological Association convention in Chicago, September, 1956.)

Stern, G. G., Stein, M. I., and Bloom, B. S. *Methods in personality assessment.* Glencoe, Ill.: Free Press, 1956.

Stewart, L. H. Interest patterns of a group of high-ability, high-achieving students. *J. counsel. Psychol.,* 1959, 6(2).

Stice, G., Mollenkopf, Wm. G., and Torgerson, W. S. *Background factors and college-going plans among high-aptitude public high school seniors.* Princeton, New Jersey: Educational Testing Service, 1956.

Strong, E. K., Jr. *Vocational interests of men and women.* Palo Alto, Calif.: Stanford University Press, 1943.

Strong, E. K., Jr. *Vocational interests 18 years after college.* Minneapolis: University of Minnesota, 1955.

Thistlethwaite, D. L. College environments and the development of talent. *Science,* 1959, **130,** 71–76.

Tyler, Leona E. The relationship of interests of abilities and reputation among first grade children. *Educ. Psychol. Measmt.,* 1951, **11,** 255–264.

Weissman, M. P. An approach to the assessment of intellectual disposition among selected high ability students. Unpublished doctor's dissertation, University of California, 1958.

White, R. C. The potential and probable supply of college students. *Coll. Admissions* (ETS), 1954, **1,** 12–23.

Wolfle, D. *America's resources of specialized talent.* New York: Harper Bros., 1954.

6 *Nevitt Sanford*

Developmental Status
of the Entering Freshman

Let us consider the following description of the freshman entering Vassar College.

The typical freshman begins her college life with eagerness and confidence. She is proud to be a member of the college community and wants to live up to the honor of having been admitted. Knowing pretty well what the next few years hold for her, she is relatively untroubled by questions of what to do or be.

She is oriented primarily to the social group, and her very considerable social skill is freely displayed; she is friendly, cooperative, polite and—at least in her external aspect—poised. She participates comfortably and uncritically in the values of her family and home community, has high respect for our social institutions and, toward the powers that be, she is deferential and uncomplaining. . . .

In sum, the typical entering freshman is idealistic, sociable, well-organized and well-behaved. Small wonder that on the standardized personality tests, she scores as a pretty sound and healthy specimen. . . .

But this stable and happy freshman . . . is in for some eye-opening and disillusioning—and broadening and maturing—experience. By mid-way of her senior year, the chances are that she will feel rather confused, frustrated, anxious, and will look back on her Freshman year as a remote and happy time.

This was written after five years of observation of Vassar students, a part of the work of the Mary Conover Mellon Foundation. For present purposes it is not necessary to claim that the account is complete or scientifically impeccable, or even to raise the question of whether the picture given holds for students entering other colleges. The concern here is with an approach to the understanding of the kind of behavior exemplified.

In seeking to explain the behavior of the entering freshman we should take into account characteristics in respect to which he is a) like all other people or at least like personalities in contemporary American society, b) like all other people in his age range but different from older and younger people, c) like almost all other entering freshmen but different from people in the same age range who do not go to college, and d) like no other freshman, or at least like some but not others.

McConnell and Heist, in the preceding chapter, have focused upon d), that is, individual and group differences among students at the time of their entrance into college, while Douvan and Kaye, in Chapter 4, have given primary attention to c)—differences between young people who are college bound and those who are not—while taking note also of d) and, to some extent, b). The present chapter is focused mainly on b), characteristics that distinguish the freshman from people in other age groups; its main argument is that the college freshman is in a distinctive "stage of development" and that actions to promote his further development must be based in large part upon an understanding of this stage.

Before considering the distinctive characteristics of the freshman's age group, however, it will be well to note some important respects in which freshmen are like everybody else in American society. They are, first and foremost, persons with complex personalities, to be understood in the light of all we know about the functioning of personality in general. In Chapter 2 personality was referred to as an inferred organization of processes within the individual. What are the processes of personality and how are they organized? One approach to these questions that has proved useful in the past, and that may serve the purposes of this and other chapters in this book, conceives of the personality as comprising three major systems: a system of primitive impulses and feelings; a system of inhibiting or punishing forces that have been automatically taken over from the social environment—the primitive conscience; and a system that controls and adapts and integrates in accordance with the demands of reality—the ego. The inner life of the person consists largely in conflicts and alliances among these systems; and it is to patterns of their interaction that we may largely attribute observable traits of personality. Impulses are particularly likely to be in conflict with the demands of conscience, the internal moral authority; and the ego has the special task of finding, for impulses, modes of gratification that are acceptable to conscience and in keeping with the requirements of reality. Anxiety, doubt, guilt, or behavior that is restricted or peculiar, attend the ego's failures; satisfaction and joy attend its success. The college freshman is as much taken up with this task of the ego and—underneath his rather bland exterior—as susceptible to these feelings, as the rest of us.

Again, when we ask ourselves what might favor or induce further development of the freshman's personality we may refer to general principles that hold for him as well as for other people. We may look to such principles, for example, to explain why it is that the student entering Vassar, however well-organized and confident she may be as a freshman, is likely to feel confused and anxious by the time she is half through her senior year. This is because the system of attitudes, values, conceptions, and adaptive devices with which she entered college has had to give way in the face of challenges offered by her education, and by the prospect of life after college, while a new integration of the personality has not yet been achieved. The freshman develops when he is confronted with challenges that require new kinds of adaptive responses, and when he is freed from the necessity of maintaining unconscious defensive devices; these happenings result in the enlargement and further differentiation of the systems of the personality, and set the stage for integration on higher levels. But this does not distinguish the freshman from other people. Everybody has unconscious motives and mechanisms, and a repertory of coping devices that he hopes will be adequate to the challenges of life, and everybody can develop further when the necessary conditions are present. The point here is that when it comes to planning the freshman's education the characteristics that he has in common with other people may be just as important as those that distinguish him from others; and we can no better afford to neglect general human characteristics in our work with freshmen than we can in our dealings with any other group of people.

STATISTICAL DESCRIPTION OF THE COLLEGE FRESHMAN

We may begin to get a distinctive picture of the freshman by comparing him with other people in terms of *quantities* of general human characteristics. The freshman is resistant to change, but it stands to reason that he is *less* resistant to change than the adult—and *more* so than the child. The freshman's personality is differentiated—more than that of the child but less than that of the senior. And similarly with integration. If we had instruments for measuring general characteristics of this kind we could apply them to people of various ages and obtain curves of development, and then we could indicate by points on the curves where the average freshman stands in comparison with older and younger people.

Some curves based on average scores of people of different ages are available. For example, tests of various kinds of intellectual performance have been given to enough people of widely different ages so that we can say quite definitely that with respect to problem-solving ability, reasoning, and judgment the average 18-year-old is farther along than the child or adolescent but not so far along as the adult. But, as McConnell and Heist have pointed out in Chapter 5, it is rare that measures of interests, attitudes, values, or other aspects of personality have been obtained in large samples of college freshmen; it is even rarer that the same tests of these attributes have been given to freshmen and to younger and older people. Nevertheless, according to theory—and to common sense—there are numerous attributes of personality which we should expect to increase more or less directly with age. We may anticipate that despite serious technical difficulties there will, in time, be empirically drawn curves representing changes in various aspects of personality throughout the life cycle. Longitudinal studies are called for, as McConnell and Heist emphasize, but the work of Gough (1958) with his California Psychological Inventory and work with the Strong Interest Blank (Strong, 1943) show that much can be accomplished by massive cross-sectional testing programs. We know from Gough (1958), for example, that the college freshman stands somewhere between the high school freshman and the graduate student on tolerance, flexibility of thinking, and psychological-mindedness. And Strong was able to report some years ago that with respect to masculinity-femininity of interests people in the college freshman age range resemble adults more than they resemble the child at the beginning of puberty (Strong, 1943). For the years after the beginning of college a number of sound quantitative studies of change in personality characteristics are now available. Webster, Freedman, and Heist, in Chapter 24, and Freedman, in Chapter 25, report a number of such studies. It would greatly increase our understanding of change during these years if the curves representing the variations of personality characteristics with age in young adulthood could be hitched onto those which describe events during the much more intensively studied period of childhood to late adolescence.

THE FRESHMAN'S STAGE OF DEVELOPMENT

A set of distinctive average scores on personality tests, though valuable, is rather far from being a complete picture of the typical freshman's personality. Such a picture must include not only estimates of the various individual characteristics but also some representation of the dynamic relations among the major parts of the personality. These relations, above all, must be known by the educator who would change the freshman's personality. The question is, what processes of the personality are determining, and, also, how may these determining processes be affected by intervention from outside? To answer this double question we must utilize, as suggested above, a theory of the whole personality in its interactions with the environment. More than this, since personalities change in their structure over time, deliberate intervention at a particular time requires that account be taken of the particular structure existing at that time. Hence our interest in the freshman's "stage" of development.

The idea of a "stage" of development rests upon a conception of a *course* of development, that is to say, an order of events defining progress from lower to higher levels of development. A high level of development in personality is characterized chiefly by complexity and by wholeness. It is expressed in a high degree of *differentiation,* that is, a large number of different parts having different and specialized functions, and in a high degree of *integration,* that is, a state of affairs in which communication among parts is great enough so that the different parts may, without losing their essential identity, become organized into larger wholes in order to serve the larger purposes of the person. Using the terms introduced above to stand for the major systems of the personality, we may say that in the highly developed person there is a rich and varied impulse life, many different impulses having now found various modes of expression; conscience has been broadened and refined in the sense that it is sensitive to many different kinds of moral issues; and it is enlightened and individualized; it has been brought under the sway of the ego's processes and so operates in accord with the person's best thought and judgment; the ego's responsiveness to multitudinous aspects of the natural, social, and cultural environments is matched by the diversity of its inter-related sensibilities and adaptive capacities; although it judges events and controls action in accord with reality, it remains in close enough touch with impulses—the deeper sources of emotion and will—so that there is freedom of imagination and an enduring capacity to be fully alive. This highly developed structure has a fundamental stability which is expressed in consistency of behavior over time; it underlies the individual's sense of direction, his independence of thought and action, and his capacity to make and carry out commitments to others and to himself. But the structure is not fixed once and for all, nor is the consistency of behavior absolute; the highly developed individual is always open to new experience, and capable of further learning; his stability is fundamental in the sense that he can go on developing while remaining essentially himself.

Where does the freshman stand with respect to these objectives? If, as we may safely assume, he is far from having attained them, in what stage is he? And what are the conditions of his passing on to another stage that is marked by greater complexity and wholeness? Two conceptions are necessary to the explanation of progressive changes in the personality. One is the idea of *readiness,* the notion that certain kinds of response cannot be made unless certain states or conditions have been built up in the person; the other is that change in the personality is induced largely by stimuli arising either from the person's bodily functioning or from his social and cultural environment, and that the order of events in personality development depends on the order in which these stimuli are brought to bear. The condition of readiness is necessary to further development but it is not a sufficient cause of such development. The personality does not just unfold or mature according to a plan of nature. Whatever the stage of readiness in the personality, further development will not occur until stimuli arrive to upset the existing equilibrium and require fresh adaptation. What the state of readiness means most essentially is that the individual is now open to new kinds of stimuli and prepared to deal with them in an adaptive way.

But the picture is somewhat more complicated. As suggested above, when strains are too intense they do not lead to new adaptive responses but rather to a falling back upon primitive defensive stratagems. The child has often to deal with overwhelming strains, and it is common for him to meet them by repressing impulses or denying reality. Defensive devices of this kind, involving as they do unconscious processes, tend to persist, and to be utilized repeatedly in critical situations. It is a safe assumption that everyone who has passed childhood carries with him aftereffects of early struggles with overwhelming tension. This circumstance has to be taken into account when we consider the individual's readiness for further growth. For here the challenge-response formula is not directly applicable. That formulation was designed primarily to explain learning from experience. We cannot expect it to hold for cases in which the individual is prevented by unconscious processes from having the necessary experience, or for cases in which defensive mechanisms come so readily to the fore that new adaptive responses have no chance to be tried. These barriers to learning are readily observed among college students. For example, there is the girl who cannot learn economics because she cannot seriously entertain any ideas that might threaten her special relationship with her father; there is the boy who cannot work because he fears that any achievement by him would give away his desire to get the better of his father. No student is free of unconscious motives and complexes and unconscious mechanisms of defense, and many graduates are able to put the skills and knowledge acquired in college into the service of unconsciously determined and even socially destructive systems of beliefs and attitudes. It is clear, then, that development is to be promoted not only by (1) offering the individual challenges that require new responses but also by (2) making the unconscious conscious or, in other words, modifying unconscious structures and changing their relations to the conscious ego. This does not mean, however, that the application of strictly educational procedures has to wait until the students have had the benefits of psychotherapy. Far from it. Even with students who show marked "symptomatology" (excluding gross signs of psychosis) education may be devoted to expanding those parts of the student's personality that are not dominated by unconscious processes. As the consciously determined parts of the personality expand and develop, the unconsciously determined parts will shrink in relative importance. More than this, unconscious processes may become conscious under natural conditions in the normal course of events and, given sufficient knowledge of personality functioning, it may be possible to speed up this kind of developmental change. The ego is strengthened through learning from experience, and the greater

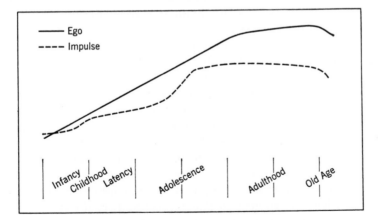

Figure 1. Development of the ego and of impulse according to dynamic theory of personality.

its strength the greater its capacity to assimilate unconscious impulses and ideas.

Several theoretical statements about the freshman's stage of development can be made on the basis of the curves shown in Figure 1, which have been drawn largely on the basis of the writings of Anna Freud (1946). But first it must be made clear that no stage of personality development is defined in terms of academic status—freshman or other—nor in terms of chronological age; such a stage is defined, rather, in terms of progress toward developmental goals—what has already transpired and what is now possible. The proposal here is that there is a stage of late adolescence that intervenes between adolescence proper and early adulthood. High school students and college sophomores as well as freshmen may be in this stage, and it may be that not all juniors and seniors have passed beyond it. But, partly because of age-linked factors and partly because of factors associated with going to college, the freshman seems more likely to be in this stage than do the other categories of older and younger people; certainly this stage is more characteristic of the freshman than is any other.

Returning to Figure 1, it may be noted that after adolescence the curves for both impulse and ego continue to rise, so that we may say of the freshman, or of the 17- or 18-year old, that he is more developed than the adolescent and less developed than the adult in respect to both impulse and ego. But what is striking, and particularly important, is the relation between these two; after adolescence there is a sharp increase in the ratio of ego to impulse. And this, in the present view, expresses a most important fact about the freshman's stage of development. The maximum crisis of adolescence is over, and controlling mechanisms are again in the ascendancy. But the controls developed for the purpose of inhibiting impulse are still unseasoned and uncertain; they are likely to operate in a rigid manner, that is, to be rather overdone, as if the danger of their giving way altogether were still very real. Thus the freshman tends to be like a convert to adulthood, an enthusiastic supporter and imitator of adult ways who knows what it is to backslide—which he sometimes does. The achievement of flexible control, an arrangement in which there is genuine freedom of impulses because there is little danger of their getting out of hand, still lies ahead; nevertheless impulses are now inhibited or contained with sufficient effectiveness so that the young person can turn his attention to other matters. He is now ready to concentrate upon his relations with the external world—to improve his understanding of that world and to find a place within it.

This picture of the freshman's psychological situation is essentially a picture of an authoritarian personality structure. Authoritarianism in personality is a particular pattern of relationships among impulse, conscience, and ego (Sanford, 1956b). It is a pattern in which strong impulses are directly opposed by an alert, rigid, and punitive conscience. The ego has to devote so much energy to restraining impulses that its other functions are not well performed; it has been able to integrate little of the primitive conscience with itself, so that the latter continues to function more or less as a foreign body. This state of affairs at the core of the personality is reflected at the surface in characteristic ways: in stereotyped thinking, intolerance of ambiguity, punitive morality, submissiveness toward the powerful and dominance toward the weak, conventionality, anti-intellectualism, hostility toward people perceived to be different from oneself. Jane Loevinger (1959) has recently stressed the point that authoritarianism is a stage of development through which we all go, and at which some of us become fixated. We may use this conception to elaborate our picture of the late adolescent. Authoritarianism, of a mild sort, is plainly manifest in the above sketch of the Vassar freshman—in the deference to authority, the dependence upon external support for her system of values, the neat organization of personality, and the good behavior. The freshman inhibits impulse by being morally strict with himself and others. He is ready to meet stiff requirements, to work hard, to conform with what he takes to be the prevailing standards of behavior—and he is inclined to be somewhat intolerant of those who do not. An element of perfectionism, of striving for purity of thought and action is characteristic of the freshman. He needs, and finds, moral heroes, and is likely to demand that they be perfect. He is rather unprepared for the discovery that his idols have feet of clay, or, at any rate, have some human weaknesses.

Closely related to this is the hatred of hypocrisy and of "phonies" so commonly found in the more sensitive freshman. Here is an expression of the authoritarian tendency to think in rigid categories, to demand that things be clear and uncomplicated—and what they appear to be. The freshman will have to learn to deal with shadings of good and bad, and with subtle mixtures of the worthy and the unworthy. He must learn, too, that he may cling to certain values without totally rejecting people who disagree with him; or, to put it in more general terms, he must gain some appreciation of the relativity of values without losing his capacity to become fully committed to a value position.

But this does not mean that the freshman has no right to expect

high standards in those who are in a position to influence his development. It would be a sad state of affairs indeed if the freshman had
already given up hope of finding nobility of character and greatness
of deed somewhere in the world. One of the hardest things about growing up in contemporary America is that at just the time when a young
person most needs models of private and public virtue he is likely
to become aware of corruption in high places, of organized immor-
ality in some of our major institutions, of the inconsistencies in our
economic system and in our sexual mores, and of meanness in people
close at hand whom he thought he could admire. If the young person
is not to remain in an authoritarian stage of development, and go
on naively to participate in and become blind to or even identified
with the prevalent moral shortcomings of our society, he must learn
to see things as they are, develop an articulate individual power of
judgment, and become able to criticize what he judges to be bad.
Now, however, he courts new danger: that he will reject the existing
order out of hand, and become totally alienated from the society
and value system represented by his parents and his community. If
this happens while the young person is still emotionally as well as economically dependent on his parents, and before he has had time to
develop a value system that is based on his own experience, we get
one type of modern "beatnik." For many freshmen, no doubt, the situation is saved or at least ameliorated by the fact that a young person's adult model does not need to be in actuality a model of perfection; he needs only to be capable of appearing to be that; he needs
only to be sufficiently free of gross imperfections or have enough admirable traits so that the young person can project onto him an image
of the ideal. But this mode of adaptation cannot persist indefinitely
in the absence of genuine worth in the world as the freshman comes
to know it. Thus it is that a society may become so disorganized and
demoralized that it is impossible for a young person to develop an internalized system of values. On the other hand, the same outcome may
be common in a purposeful and well-organized society, if its educational system is not calculated to carry the individual beyond the authoritarian stage of development.

Reference was made above to the young person who has not had
time to develop a value system based in his own experience. This is
the situation of the freshman. It is common to say, as do Douvan and
Kaye in Chapter 4, that his value system is not internalized. And this
is a defining feature of the authoritarian personality pattern. The
values of the entering freshman are supported, typically, by his family
and home community; he is dependent upon this support, but, at least

in the very beginning of the college career, the support is adequate enough so that the freshman is able to present a picture of organization and self-containment. But parental and community support now begins to be withdrawn, and values are challenged by other values represented in the college environment. The freshman's natural reaction is to seek other external supports for the values with which he arrived, or else to adopt different values that have powerful support in his new environment. This is a major basis for the freshman's susceptibility to influence by the student culture of the college. The dominant social group is an excellent substitute for an earlier moral authority. But be it remembered that the freshman is also highly susceptible to influence by the authoritative aspects of the faculty. If the social arrangements of the college are favorable, students are capable of taking over wholesale the values of the faculty—and of exchanging these values, even though they be liberal ones, for a different set once a different moral authority was brought to bear. Values acquired in this manner, whether from the faculty or through the influence of student culture, are not internalized but merely borrowed for the occasion. For values to become internalized they must be reflected on, and made the object of the individual's best efforts at judgment and decision-making; they must find their way into the personality structure through the activity of the conscious and developed ego rather than through automatic conditioning or unconscious mechanisms. One moves beyond the authoritarian position by developing a truly individual, enlightened conscience; and this, we have argued, is a major educational goal.

Closely related to the freshman's authoritarian propensities is his instability with respect to self-esteem. He does not know what he can do, how good he is, or just what to think of himself. Just as he looks to authority or the social group for guidance in the matter of moral values so does he look to external sources of definition and measurement of himself. These sources give conflicting testimony. On the one hand he is happy to remember his parents' faith in him, the accomplishments of high school and the plaudits received there, and, perhaps particularly, the fact that he was chosen for admission to his college. But, on the other hand, he suspects that he is now playing in a different league, and he knows that the major tests of life still await him. In his uncertainty he vacillates between overestimation and underestimation of himself. His inclination is to stick to patterns of behavior that have been rewarded in the past and to display such confidence as he can muster. When he encounters failures or near failures in his early contacts with academic problems or with his new peers, as he is bound to do, he is easily thrown into a state of self-doubt and anxiety, or even depression. This state will sometimes manifest itself in overcompensatory self-forwarding maneuvers, sometimes in withdrawal and self-punishment.

This vulnerability to other people's appraisals makes the average freshman highly susceptible to the influence of his fellow students; their approval or disapproval can make or break his self-confidence. In this situation it is often a good thing that he is given academic grades, and is told about the results of tests of ability and achievement. Bad news may be better than no news; better, that is, than uncertainty or than his gloomy imaginings. Freshmen flourish best not when they are given no grades, but when they are given searching and hard-hitting analyses of their performances—accompanied by intelligible and realistic pictures of what they can become.

One of the greatest dangers at the period of late adolescence is that the young person will commit himself prematurely to a social role, a role that helps to define him as all right in the eyes of the world but which is not in keeping with his genuine needs and talents. One of the easiest ways for a young man to define himself satisfactorily in the eyes of the world is to announce an intention of entering one of the prestigeful professions. Beardslee and O'Dowd have shown, as they report in Chapter 18, that college students—and faculties—readily arrange professions in a hierarchy of prestige and then tend to perceive those students who say they are preparing for a given profession in much the same way that they perceive people who are already in that profession. Douvan and Kaye have pointed out that young women entering college tend to accent romance and glamour, and the future role of wife and mother; but it is not uncommon to encounter freshman girls who have very clear-cut conceptions of their future places in the world of work. In girls, however, intentions to enter particular vocations are not usually very persistent; their main function often seems to be to facilitate satisfactory self-definitions and thus bolster self-respect during the early years of college.

Freshman girls who think in concrete terms of preparing for a job are likely to say that they want to be more than "just a wife." It is as if they were aware of the fundamental truth pointed to by Douvan and Kaye, that high school girls who do not expect to go to college are already leading lives that are largely dominated by sex roles. The girl who is entering college has, by virtue of her background and education, a more extensive life-space, and the prospects of a future life in which sexual and maternal roles will have a place within a broad context of other rewarding activities. Thus it is not difficult for her to inhibit the overt expression of sexual impulses. But she does have the problem of demonstrating her femininity in other ways. She asks herself how to be feminine though educated; or how to be feminine though committed to a program of activities that, apparently, have nothing to do with sex roles. Inexperienced as she is, she tends to restrict herself rather narrowly to culturally defined feminine activities and interests, and to be much concerned with the question of how she can keep up or increase her attractiveness to men. She still has to learn of the variety of things she might do, of the diversity of roles she might take, without endangering her capacity to carry out essential feminine functions.

The young man's doubts and fears, and hopes, about his masculinity are equally familiar phenomena. As a college freshman he has reached a place where the crucial tests cannot be postponed much longer. The chances are that he is still in doubt about the purely phallic aspects of his masculinity, and the task of integrating his phallic impulses with his feelings of tenderness in an intimate relationship with another person still lies ahead. Fears of homosexuality are likely to be very much in the picture, the more so if the young man now enters into a special kind of close and exclusive contact with members of his own sex. Since in the culture of the United States any display of feeling or of sensitivity among males is likely to be regarded as feminine, it is common to find on our campuses cults of masculinity in which young men display for the benefit of each other such power and potency as they possess or can imitate. Panty raids are but one example of a general phenomenon. In such situations genuine friendships among men, which require revelation of inner feelings, are difficult to form. The sensitive young man will most probably express his more human side in friendship with a young woman. This is a large determining factor in the early marriages so common on the campuses today. Such marriages solve for the time being many problems for the young man; but they do not promote genuine friendships with his fellows—which he may miss later on—nor a mature choice of spouse—which also may be regretted later.

The late adolescent must find adequate support for his self-esteem while he goes on with the long-range undertaking of finding himself and his place in the world. Or, to put this differently, he must somehow see to it that what he now does in the interest of his self-esteem, say, make a premature vocational commitment or cling to some pattern of behavior that is momentarily reassuring, does not interfere too much with his development as a person. Over the long pull he must, if he is to become highly developed, build up an internal basis for self-evaluation and learn to take satisfaction in accomplishments that are genuinely worthwhile, in the sense that they are in keeping with the best in our culture; he must evolve a self-conception that includes as much as possible of his real self, his abilities, inclinations, and underlying impulses, and is at the same time in sufficient accord with reality; the level of his aspirations must be adjusted to real possibilities but at the same time be high enough to enlist the best that is in him. These achievements are the work of the ego; or, more precisely, they become increasingly possible as the ego becomes increasingly expanded, differentiated, and integrated. For these things to happen the late adolescent must subject himself to testing, must *have* the experiences that he has been approaching with trepidation, must know failure and frustration. No doubt some reassurance from family, or peers, or friends is very helpful, and probably necessary. In the culture of today, with its accent on competition and success, everyone needs other people who can see worth in him as a person, worth that is not measured by his worldly success. But for the freshman in college, achievement is bound to be in the focus of attention, and he may be considered fortunate if he encounters teachers who can see his potential and encourage, through recognition and example, activities that are at once valuable in themselves and favorable to his further development. In general, as Erikson (1953) has pointed out, the college environment is, or could be, highly favorable to the stabilization of the young person's self-conception and self-esteem; here he is afforded a continuous opportunity to test himself in various spheres of activity without his failures being catastrophic and without his successes leading to premature commitments.

THE SITUATION OF THE ENTERING FRESHMAN

When we consider some of the common features of the freshman's situation—his absence from home, the academic requirements and expectations, the presence of a student society and culture to which he must adapt himself—it seems that we are justified in thinking of his entrance into college as bringing about a developmental crisis, in Erikson's sense of this term (Erikson, 1953). Certainly there are features of the freshman's environment that are challenging enough to induce development if they are mastered, but which at the same time may easily be so threatening or overpowering as to lead to fixation of present defensive stratagems or even to regression to earlier ones.

In considering the freshman's situation we have to reckon with considerable variability among the colleges, and we have to look below the surface of the particular environmental circumstances.

It would appear that, generally speaking, leaving home to go to college is in some ways highly favorable to the development of personality. The student is almost bound to encounter and to take seriously values and roles that are different from some that he has taken for granted; he is thus forced to make conscious choices and to take the first steps toward building a value system of his own. Again, when he is free of the expectations of family and community he is able to try new modes of behavior, stimulate new kinds of perceptions of himself by other people, and thus to expand his personality by trial and error along lines that in the long run will be in keeping with his fundamental inclinations. But before we conclude that the residential college is always to be preferred to the commuter college, other things being equal, we must consider that students of the former type of college do not necessarily leave home psychologically. They may still be geographically near home and see their parents often; or even if college and home are not close together the parents may still, through vigorous correspondence, retain their central place in the student's life space; or going to a particular college may have the essential meaning of remaining in the gravitational field of the family: it may have been the father's or the mother's college, there may be relatives or friends of the family or acquaintances from the home community there now, and they may effectively remind the freshman of his origins and of what is expected of him back home. Such circumstances may not only "cushion the shock" of leaving home; they may actually bar the student, throughout his college career, from ever having the experience of standing in principled opposition to his parents.

A truly effective community college, as Riesman and Jencks have pointed out in Chapter 3, may provide commuting students with both intellectual stimulation and social support to help them achieve independence of their parents. Whether or not it does so would seem to depend on such factors as the degree of contrast between the prevailing college values and those of the family, how much of a community and how attractive a community the college succeeds in being, and whether or not it is able to give the student a strong sense of membership within it.

Mervin Freedman, in his account of the freshman year at Vassar, shows that the impact of the first few weeks of college is very different for different girls, depending on variations in background and contemporary situation (Freedman, 1956). His "Group A" is composed of girls who have graduated from private schools that prepare for the Eastern private colleges, who have considerable prior acquaintance with the college—probably having visited it—and who, very likely, have friends or relatives who are or have been students of the college. College entrance makes few demands upon these students. They have been well enough prepared academically so that no great adjustments are now required, and their social life is very likely to be a continuation of what they are used to. Freedman writes, "If one important function of a college is to induce students to re-examine their established ways and accepted habits of thought, it appears that the difficulties in the way of carrying out this function with the present group of students are great." (Freedman, 1956, p. 18)

Freedman's "Group B" is composed of girls from public high schools, who are somewhat lower in social status than those of Group A and who have less familiarity with the college. For these students the academic life of the college does constitute a severe test; they are very likely to experience anxiety and feelings of incompetence but often, if they remain in college, they come to know the satisfactions of gradually attaining mastery of difficult subjects. Although, before coming to college, these girls worry much about the social fate that awaits them, it usually turns out that they are readily accepted by their fellow students; and although preoccupied with their academic difficulties they tend to be readily "absorbed into the main stream of student culture."

For students of "Group C" college is very much of a new experience. These girls come from geographic areas that do not ordinarily send many students to Eastern colleges; they may be of lower-middle-class origins and may attend college with the aid of scholarships; in many cases they belong to ethnic or religious minority groups. For students of this group academic demands are apt to be at least as great as they are for Group B. And at the same time girls of Group C have, by far, the most complicated problems of social adjustment. They are sufficiently different from the great majority of the students so that they cannot be automatically absorbed by the dominant student society and the prevailing student culture. They are likely to be aware of their differences from the other students in background and values and, hence, their entering into a new student society and culture is likely to entail a variety of conscious decisions and deliberate efforts. These students are in a situation where they are virtually forced to consider alternative values and modes of behavior; and their chances of evolving a system of values that is more complex than that with which they began college, and that is increasingly their own, would appear to be very good.[1]

It seems probable that Freedman's findings at Vassar can be generalized to other private women's colleges as well. On the other hand, things may well be rather different at other kinds of institutions, such as the large cosmopolitan universities, the private men's colleges, the state universities, or the community colleges.

Consider, for example, what is likely to be the case when students of Freedman's Group A find themselves at a place like the University of Chicago, where according to Stern (Stern, Chapter 21, and Stern, Stein, and Bloom, 1956) there is a high level of cultural sophistication, great diversity in the student body, and a maximum of freedom—both in respect to academic requirements and in respect to personal living. In these circumstances we should expect students of the Group A type, whose authoritarian tendencies appear to be marked, to experience considerable anxiety and eagerly to seek the association of students like themselves—if indeed they had not arranged for such association in advance. If such students fail to find support in any satisfactory peer group there is considerable likelihood that they will find the situation intolerable and leave college. This is in line with Stern's finding, reported in Chapter 21, that students who withdrew from the University of Chicago in the freshman year tended to be relatively high in authoritarianism.

Group C students might immediately feel more at home at Chicago than at Vassar, though with some differences having to do with the other kind of sex roles. Let us consider boys of a type corresponding to Freedman's Group A. If we assume that their private schools were among those that accent strictness and regimen, we should expect to find in this group the strongest tendency to hell-raising. The contrast between the authority of the school and the freedom of the college will often strike these boys as an open invitation to express their rebellious tendencies, to make fresh attempts to establish their independence and their male identity; but these boys are by no means ready to do without authority, and their efforts at outrageous behavior are unconsciously calculated to induce college officials to take a strong hand with them. When the officials oblige, as they often do, the boys are able to continue in their authoritarian ways, deferring to the officials, with an ever-ready "Sir," when they are present, while taking advantage of

[1] An account of the student culture at Vassar is given by Bushnell in Chapter 14; while in Chapter 13, Newcomb discusses in general terms the processes of the student's adaptation to the pressures of his peer groups.

their absence to undertake some new venture in "masculinity." An obvious difference between the boys and the girls of this group is that the latter rarely engage in behavior of which the police take notice, that is, impulsive group behavior of an aggressive or primitive nature. This is not only because both the boys and the girls wish to adhere to conventional sex roles; in addition, as Douvan (1957) has established, boys of this age are much more concerned than girls with establishing their independence, a task that is far from easy when there is an underlying tendency to authoritarianism in the personality. It is much easier for girls to submit to the authority of the college; their pride is not at stake, and they can wait to make their bid for independence. At colleges like Vassar it seems that the crisis of independence often comes at the time of graduation, when the young woman at last has the alternatives of really leaving home, by taking a job, doing graduate work, or making a somewhat unconventional marriage, or returning to the familiar surroundings and value-orientation of family and home community. But there is no doubt that the freshmen girls of Group A are like the boys of this group in their inclination to keep adults at a distance; this they accomplish by manifest politeness and a cool, often subtle, passive resistance to the faculty's efforts to educate them.

When boys of a type corresponding to Freedman's Group C go away from home to a much sought after college or university they usually expect to be changed; often they are consciously seeking a new system of values and a new personal identity. Typically, they have serious scholarly or professional interests, and have had the experience of being rather out of things socially. For such students there appears to be a wider range of alternatives than is the case with the boys discussed above. Boys of the Group C type are very open to influence by the faculty; when there is opportunity for moderate contact with faculty members, faculty values are readily taken over. If the boy already has a strong professional predilection he is readily picked off by one of the departments and prepared for membership in one of the scholarly or scientific professions. But these boys are also susceptible to influence by the student peer group; the fact that they have not been oriented to the social group before is no sign that they will not be happy to be taken in by a friendly and socially skillful group of their peers. Their very lack of social experience is a factor in their susceptibility. Such boys often give their parents and other well-wishers many anxious moments, as evidence mounts that they have gotten in with the wrong crowd. There may be considerable floundering and some near catastrophes before they find themselves in some style of life that embraces the aspirations with which they began college. Girls of Group C differ from the boys in at least one important respect: they can give up their professional ambitions quickly and altogether under the influence of their new-found college friends. It sometimes turns out that their academic motivations are based on a need for recognition, and with suitable recognition assured they are unable to find other reasons for seeking a career.

These examples suffice to show that in order to render a comprehensive account of the situation of the entering freshman we must specify for each type of institution the circumstances of academic work, social organization, and general culture that impinge upon students of varying personalities, backgrounds, and degrees of academic and social preparation. Analysis of this kind can show that for some students entering college is a critical event that initiates striking spurts in personality development. Other students are able, by their choice of college and by their academic and social preparation, so to reduce the strains of college entrance that no new patterns of adaptation are elicited. For still other students, the strains of the first few weeks of college are so great that there are set in motion maladaptive responses which may lead to leaving college in the freshman year (cf. Summerskill, Chapter 19).

THE COLLEGE AS A STIMULUS TO DEVELOPMENT

Adequate knowledge of the developmental status of the entering freshman will include understanding of what is required to change that status and, particularly, knowledge of what the college might do to bring about desired development in its students. The hypotheses offered below may suggest some directions for future investigation.

These hypotheses all have to do with ways in which the college might promote—or hamper—changes in the directions of the several major goals of development: freedom of impulse, enlightenment of conscience, and differentiation and integration of the ego. Impulse, conscience, and ego are intricately inter-related, as we have seen; a change in one will bring change in the others, and changes in the manifest characteristics of personality may usually be attributed to interactions of the three systems; nevertheless, for purposes of analysis, developmental trends in these systems may be considered separately.

Freeing of impulse. For the freeing of impulse the curriculum may be a most important instrument. In Chapter 2 the argument was advanced that the best way to free impulses is to develop the life of the imagination, and that this is best done by enabling the student to handle with ease the symbols of our culture. For example, the effective teaching of literature could reveal the student to himself, permitting him to bring into the open feelings and phantasies of which he was previously unaware. Again, the development of scholarly interests may provide channels through which the individual can express his most primitive as well as his complex and socially fashioned needs. All of these processes are described in detail in Chapter 11, where the curriculum is in the focus of attention.

It may be inserted here that when we speak of the joys of intellectual activity it is not implied that all intellectual excitement and aesthetic delight are rooted in the emotional needs of childhood. The general theory with which we are working allows for the emergence of complex cognitive and aesthetic needs that are not sustained by remnants of childish feelings and phantasies. But when we are talking about the freeing of impulse it seems well to keep constantly in mind the fact that the child is curious and filled with wonder, that these inclinations are often pretty well knocked out of him by the discipline and learning processes that are considered necessary to getting him into college, and that it is up to the college to try to restore to the fullest possible extent his natural inquisitive inclinations. One trouble with accenting the purely cognitive need—a concept that has good standing in psychology —is that this tends to support the primness, and grimness, that is so often permitted to pervade what is called "the intellectual life of the college." True enough, a great deal of intellectual activity is dominated by processes, such as discriminating, remembering, and organizing, that belong exclusively to the realm of the ego. But there is good reason to believe that in the highest forms of intellectual activity, those that contribute to culture, the naive curiosity of the child—and the child's capacity for entertaining the playful and the fantastic—have been brought back into the picture.

The liberalizing influences of college are not restricted to the imagination; the college may also show the way to freedom of impulse at the level of behavior. For one thing, unless he comes from an unusually sophisticated background, the freshman is likely to encounter at college norms of behavior that are more liberal than those he has relied upon before. He observes people doing things and saying things and adopting attitudes which he thought were proscribed. This is an aspect of that freedom of the college situation that was spoken of above; here is the sophistication, the liberality, about which he has perhaps been warned. The freshman's impulses incline him to do what the others are doing but, owing to his authoritarian personality structure, he finds it difficult to contemplate these things without anxiety. But the college usually affords safeguards—sometimes excessive ones, no doubt—against his going too far; and it provides an environment in which he may experiment with new forms of expression without the consequences of his mistakes being too serious. More important, the freshman may soon discover that the freer patterns of behavior and the more liberal norms are exhibited by people, faculty and older students, whom he can respect and admire. Thus encouraged, he may go on to observe that many patterns of behavior that he could not permit himself, or even dream of adopting, are not only harmless but intrinsic features of a productive adult life. Thus, if he is not defeated at the start by his anxieties and the revival of defensive mechanisms, he may go on to increase the range of his expressions of impulse.

Again, the freshman may be constrained in the expression of impulse not only by his moral code but by his ignorance—his ignorance, that is, of how deep and genuine feelings may be articulated or otherwise expressed. To give us tutelage in expression of our feelings is one of the major functions of literature and drama; but unless the freshman has been fortunate in his cultural background his conceptions of how to feel, how to be emotional, are likely to have been largely determined by the conventions of Hollywood movies and TV shows. As suggested above, his humanistic studies may now deepen his acquaintance with what is truly human. But he needs something more, and the college is in a position to offer it: that is, models of adult emotional behavior in people with whom he has day-to-day relationships. Older students, perhaps graduate students in particular, often contribute something to meeting this need. Much more is contributed when members of the faculty reveal themselves as human beings. They may do this in classroom or office, but these situations seem not as conducive to self-revelation as are more complex forms of social organization, such as faculty-student committees, in which faculty members take a variety of roles.

The impulse life of the freshman is restricted by the persistence of childish modes of expression. Robert White (1952), in his instructive discussion of personality growth after adolescence, lists among the "natural growth trends" a trend toward "freedom in personal relationships." This freedom amounts to ability to respond to people as individuals in their own right rather than as mere representatives of the important figures of one's childhood. White assumes, as would this writer, that the child conceives of his parents in simple and stereotyped ways and that his emotional relationships with them are in accord with his limited images of them. The whole pattern of conceptions and responses tends to persist, often because crucial elements in the pattern have been rendered unconscious. Thus it often happens that a student expects his teachers to be just like his images of his parents; and more, he reacts to teachers as if they *were* parents, his whole repertory of childhood tendencies now seeking expression. There is plenty of impulse, plenty of deep-going feeling and emotion, involved in these reactions to adults, but we can hardly speak of the impulses as being free. On the contrary, they are bound by the guilt and anxiety that accompany inappropriate past reactions and by the narrow view of what there is to be responded to. Freedom comes as one notices more about the other person, and achieves a greater range and flexibility of response. (As did Mark Twain when, as a young man, he noticed that his *father* had miraculously changed into a reasonably agreeable fellow.) Freedom in this sense means ability to be spontaneous, friendly, and egalitarian.

Favoring growth in the college situation are opportunities for new and varied friendships, and for relationships with faculty members which will show that they are not, after all, just like one's parents. Favorable also are opportunities for taking adult roles so that the student may learn something of what it means to be an adult. Usually, it seems, the college situation is sufficiently safe to encourage the individual to put out new feelers, and sufficiently permissive to permit a continual increase in the range of feelings.

But all may not be so favorable. For one thing, most social learning in college, especially during the first years, occurs under conditions of distraction; there is usually enough anxiety so that the tendency to fall back upon earlier responses is strong. Moreover, it is frequently possible for some students to find faculty members who will accept, and support by reciprocation, transferences of infantile patterns, whether these are dependent, submissive, or erotic. At the same time the student peer group may be quite productive of devices for keeping the faculty at a distance, forcing them always to behave like faculty—even to behave all alike—so that little is learned about adultness, either through observation or through forced variation of response. And to mention another important complex of peer group norms, there is likely to be pressure to accept patterns of dating behavior that practically guarantee that the object of one's interest will not be perceived and responded to as an individual in his or her own right.

In considering freedom of personal relationships in our work at Vassar (Sanford, Ed., 1956a), we distinguished between students who are primarily adult-oriented and students who are primarily peer-oriented, while admitting that there is a larger middle group who do not distinguish themselves on this dimension. If one is concerned about conformity, it is important to ask first: conformity with the demands of what group?

The best examples of classical lack of freedom are seen in the adult-oriented group. Here one may sometimes observe fairly clear-cut mother-transferences to older women teachers. A student involved in such a relationship will exhibit many signs of immaturity, including often a kind of compulsive devotion to duty that results in consistently good grades. Study of these cases will often show that the relationship is serving as a means for gaining freedom from a rather overwhelming actual mother. Powerful maternal influence, supported by a host of tendencies carried over from childhood, could hardly be opposed without a strong ally; and since the teacher usually represents more liberal values and a more flexible and enlightened conscience than does the accustomed mother-image, there is a good chance of educational gain from the relationship. The slower rate of growth on the part of the student who becomes involved in such relationships is by no means an indication that she will not eventually go as far developmentally as her more precocious sisters.

One might conclude from a first acquaintance with a typical peer-oriented student, on the other hand, that adults hardly ever entered into her world at all. Closer study, however, soon reveals that she manages them conceptually with one or the other of these stereotypes: they are either authorities, disciplinarians to be submitted to or subverted as the occasion requires, or else benevolent, easily exploited mamas and papas.

One of the main functions of peer culture, as suggested above, is to maintain this state of affairs; to avoid any real involvement with adults, such as would threaten to upset an internal organization and a view of the world which have served well enough in the past. One might ask then, when and how do these students ever achieve freedom in their relations with adults? One answer is that many never do. Other students do turn from the peer group by the time they are seniors; perhaps for some of these, membership in the group was necessary in order to show their ability to belong; having achieved mastery on this score, they in time exhausted the possibilities of peer cultures. For some, the development of a rewarding relationship with a student of the opposite sex is the basis for drifting away from the adolescent group.

It follows from the above conception of the peer group, however, that one way—perhaps the only way—in which peer-oriented students can attain freedom in personal relationships is for faculty members to enter importantly into their lives, stir them up, and produce situations that will expose the inappropriateness of old ways of reacting by revealing the differences between real adults and the stereotypes of adults that characterize the peer-oriented students.

Enlightenment of conscience. When conscience is individualized and enlightened the individual's moral standards and values are supported by his own knowledge, thought, and judgment; they are no longer mere remnants of the training of childhood, nor mere copies of what is espoused by figures of authority or by the immediately present social group. Standards and values are now the individual's own; they are based on his own experience, and may be espoused by his own motives. When conscience is enlightened there is no longer any great gap between what the individual wants to do and what he feels he ought to do.

Enlightenment of conscience does not necessarily bring any great change in the content of the values with which the student enters college. The developmental trend of which we are speaking has to do rather with change in the way values are arrived at, and in the relations of the value system to the rest of the personality. It does seem, however, that as conscience becomes enlightened values become more "humanized," in White's (1952) sense of this term. The humanizing of values involves movement from a literal belief in rules to an attitude of greater relativity; there is increase in the awareness of the human meaning of values, and in the inclination to see values in relation to their social purpose. These changes in the individual's system of values seem to be natural concomitants of movement from traditionally received values to a personally wrought system.

It is with respect to the enlightenment of individual conscience that differences between freshmen and seniors at Vassar have appeared to be most marked (Webster, 1956). Seniors are clearly more flexible and uncompulsive, more tolerant and impunitive, more rebellious and critical of authority, less orthodox in religious outlook, more rejecting of traditional feminine roles, more unconventional and nonconforming, more liberal in their views on interpersonal relationships.

What happens, we may suppose, is that old, automatically accepted values are challenged by competing values, inducing conflict and hence a necessity for new perceptions and new thinking. At the same time, wider experience of one's own impulses, and of empathic reactions to other people, confront the individual with new phenomena that must be taken into account.

But not all seniors differ from freshmen in the ways indicated above. We must seek some explanation of those cases that do not go along with the majority. Some students, as suggested above, do not succeed in extricating themselves from a peer culture that serves as a powerful support for a traditional value system. In other students, dependent relations with parents are maintained throughout the college years, owing to such factors as continued propinquity of influential parents.

Another possibility is that an authoritarian conscience may find re-enforcement in the college regime or in campus authority figures. The notion still persists among some college teachers that we may build character through discipline. The idea seems to be that if we pour on the work and make students toe the mark they will somehow internal-ize this strictness and become capable of governing themselves in the way we have governed them. Of course they do not; instead, their authoritarianism becomes more deeply entrenched. Late adolescents will genuinely accept discipline, that is, incorporate it in a way that can affect their characters, only when certain conditions are met. One such condition is that they must have clarified and adopted for them-selves the purpose in the name of which the hard work and sacrifice are demanded. The athletic coach can demand a great deal of his stu-dents because he and they share a social purpose that seems to them very important, and because he obviously demands as much of himself as he does of them. But these conditions can hardly be duplicated in the classroom, where students must try to shoulder others into the lower half of the grade distribution curve, and where it is hard to know just what the teacher is requiring of himself. The academic teacher may, of course, demand much of a student in the interests of a stand-ard that the student has set himself or in the name of an agreed con-ception of what the student can become. But this is possible only when student and teacher have developed a relationship, one in which the student admires the teacher and the teacher knows and cares about the student's progress. This condition is difficult to establish in the crowded colleges of today.

The problem can be even more complicated. Professional schools often deliberately set out to terrorize their students, and to put them through a long series of painful and humiliating disciplinary actions. Some such schools can be matched in this respect only by certain strict girls' boarding schools or some nurses' training programs. Presumably the discipline has some meaningful relationship to the goal that the student has set himself, that is, preparation for future practice. Yet it does not appear that the discipline is fully accepted. Instead, as Hughes, Becker, and Geer have shown in the case of a medical school (Chapter 15) students develop collective devices for resisting faculty influence and for setting their own rates of work; and when the students have become professionals they often seem to enjoy passing along to the next generation of students the kind of treatment to which they themselves were subjected. As with hazing in the social fraternities, the system affords excellent outlets for the sadistic impulses in the brothers, or teachers. This may be a main reason why the students cannot internalize the discipline; they can see that instead of serving their interests it serves the personality needs of the teachers. This kind of discipline is a defining characteristic of an authoritarian system; and we cannot expect such a system to stimulate other than authoritarian attitudes in those who are caught within it. It seems also that the failure of discipline in professional schools is intimately connected with the decline of idealism in these institutions (see Becker and Geer, 1958). What students might have accepted in the interests of the high ideals with which they began is seen as nothing more than an annoying hurdle when it is made instrumental to the private and worldly goals for which they so often settle. The most we can hope for when students are subjected to an impersonal and rigid system of discipline is that they will learn to see through it and to adapt to it in a realistic way; identification with it amounts to full-fledged authoritarianism.

Differentiation and integration of the ego. Development in the ego is intimately bound up with the freeing of impulse and with the enlightenment of conscience. As impulses find more forms of expression that are personally comfortable and socially acceptable the ego is under less necessity of maintaining defenses, and its energies may be devoted to other matters. And to take it the other way around, the more developed the ego the better able is the individual to admit his underlying impulses into his conscious self-conception. The situation is similar with ego and conscience. The more the ego is relieved of pressures from the primitive—goading or punitive—conscience the greater becomes its openness to experiences that can expand and differentiate it. And as the ego develops it becomes increasingly able to integrate conscience within itself, taking over functions that once were performed automatically in accordance with training of childhood.

There are other conditions and processes of ego development. Ego functions improve as they are performed with success in increasingly difficult situations. A major requirement is that tasks calling for a wide variety of ego performances be assigned the individual, but in situations that are not so difficult or anxiety-provoking that he is forced to make use of primitive defensive devices.

It follows that ego growth is hampered both by authoritarian or overprotective regimes and by permissive-chaotic ones. The former do not give the functions of the ego a chance for exercise; the latter, through too much stimulation of impulse with consequent anxiety, may put too heavy a strain upon the developing ego.

The academic work of the college, insofar as it induces the student to exercise his intellect, is well calculated to develop ego functions. The student is here required to make fine discriminations, to be objective, to judge, analyze, criticize. The role of the curriculum in the improvement of these activities is discussed in Chapter 11. And it was pointed out in Chapter 2 that the acquisition of skills and techniques gives the student confidence in his intellectual powers. This contributes directly to the strengthening of the ego. The role of knowledge per se in inducing personality change was minimized in Chapter 2. It must be pointed out, however, that insofar as knowledge of facts or understanding of relationships enables the individual to predict events, that is, to see things go according to his expectations, the ego is strengthened. It may be added that development of these functions is favored by encouragement, by expressions of faith in the student's serious abilities, by his being treated as a promising equal, and by his finding suitable models in the adult world. Development of these functions is hampered, on the other hand, by that type of teaching that seeks to overcome student lethargy by pouring on more and more routine work —and elicits resistance to learning in the form of routine competence to perform up to the letter of the law; by too great pressure to meet the demands of the nonacademic environment; by inadequacy in available adult models, and failure of enough adults to take the right kind of personal interest in the student as a potential serious scholar or responsible individual; and, of course, by embeddedness in a peer culture that regards serious involvement in academic work as eccentric if not disreputable.

Development of the ego not only involves increasingly differentiated perceptions of the world and the increasing refinement of one's responses to it, but it also involves increasing awareness of one's own processes. Here teaching has a crucial role to play. Effective teaching does not deliberately call a student's attention to his private motives or mechanisms; instead it undertakes to show the student something of the variety and complexity of the social world of which he is a part; it tries to show him the inner feelings and motives and mechanisms of people in general; it seeks to broaden self-awareness by inducing empathy with many kinds of people—real and fictional—and by confronting the student with some of the deficiencies of his old, automatically adopted values, so that he experiences conflict and is required to make decisions.

The nonacademic college environment may also provide important stimuli to development of the ego. The student is placed in many situations that require new responses. In the relative anonymity of the college society, he can be free of limiting expectations of the home community and can be himself in a variety of new social roles. That he may do so at a time when he must give serious consideration to possible future roles but is not yet required to commit himself fully to any one of them is one of the great advantages of the college situation.

So great are the benefits of confronting the student with new role-requirements—according to the present theory—that one is led to hope that each college will invent special devices for forcing the student to vary his habitual way of doing things. If the first few weeks of college constitute a kind of developmental crisis which can result in a spurt in development, then the college would be well advised to arrange for their students an educational program embracing a series of such crises. At the least students could be offered radically different kinds of tasks, in different kinds of social situations, during their four years of college. Even temporary shifts in the student's situation and role requirements might be highly beneficial. For example, it can be hypothesized that when students leave the campus to go to week-end conferences or workshops with students from other campuses, and are thus forced to abandon their usual role-behavior and to adapt to a new social situation, there is a general opening to new experience, and more academic learning occurs than during any comparable period of normal college routine.

The developments in the ego that have just been discussed all favor stabilization of self-esteem, a task with which the entering freshman is very much taken up, as we have seen. Success in the performance of ego functions produces justifiable pride; this encourages the student to continue striving for worthy objectives, thus putting self-esteem into the service of socially valuable activity; and it supplies a basis for the kind of objective self-appraisal that shows the student what he cannot do and how his level of aspiration may be adjusted to suit his abilities. Increasing self-awareness enables the student to include more of his inner needs within his self-conception; and increasing breadth of consciousness permits him to see himself in perspective, so that he is not too much moved by the successes or failures of the moment.

At the same time, stabilization of self-esteem makes possible further developments in the personality. It is only when the individual is relatively sure of himself, sure, that is, that he will not be possessed by rejected impulses or made to appear ridiculous or worthless in the eyes of the world, that he can throw himself into the most challenging and potentially enriching experiences of life. To get the most from experiences such as going abroad, getting married, entering into a vocation, and having children—and to perform well in the required roles —the individual must, in a sense, lose himself; that is, he must permit himself to be determined by or enveloped in the demands of the situation or role or task. It is this process that further expands and differentiates the personality. Losing oneself in this way means forgetting to be defensive; it means doing without external supports for self-esteem and surrendering the patterns of behavior that have had the sole function of giving reassurance. But this is possible only if there is an underlying stability in the self-conception. One cannot lose himself unless he is sure that he can change, and assimilate all kinds of new experiences, while continuing to be himself.

The problem for the student is how to wait; how to tolerate ambiguity and open-endedness in himself while he is preparing for adult roles. He is constantly tempted, as we have seen, to take short-cuts to maturity, neglecting the paths to full development by imitating adult behavior and prematurely defining himself in terms of future social roles. A major task of the college, therefore, is to help the student to wait. We do not know enough about development to speak with assurance about the optimum timing of events in the student's life. But it seems safe to say that the college may greatly improve its work by regarding the student as a person in transition. It might, for example, take a different view of "the junior year abroad" if it considered that many college juniors are still in an authoritarian stage of development, and that when people in this stage go abroad they tend to experience only what they have experienced before and to become confirmed in their pre-existing outlook. Again, the college might take a less approving view of student marriages if it considered that for many students marriage is more an attempt to establish a suitable self-conception than an expression of the natural inclinations of a well-formed personality.

It may be that in order to help the student to accept a postponement of various adult roles and, above all, adult commitments, the college must seek to make this waiting stage psychologically satisfactory to him. The college should not only guide its actions according to a developmental theory but also it should do more than it does now to make the concept of person-in-transition available to the student as a meaningful self-conception. The student needs to be able to think of himself as someone who will change—while participating fully in whatever it is that changes him; he needs to feel that it is all right for him to be uncertain about his future self and his future roles, as long as he is engaged in activities that are calculated to bring out his potential. In short, there needs to be a better definition and more social acceptance of the role of student, so that those who occupy this role may more comfortably and more profitably *be* what they are—developing persons. This, it must be granted, goes against a strong trend in American culture, which is to smudge the boundaries between developmental stages and permit younger people to define themselves as miniatures of older people—for example, social dancing at age 10, beer and a high-powered car at 16. Yet it seems that if we are to have an education that develops people we must somehow build into our culture the concepts of the developer and of stages of development.

The definition of a given stage, such as that roughly marked out by the college years, should include a clear statement about its termination. If we should succeed in creating a conception of the student's stage that was socially acceptable and personally satisfying to him, one might perhaps fear that some students would be happy to remain at that stage indefinitely. They have to face the realities of poststudent life eventually; whether or not they do so successfully would seem to depend not so much on how well they adapted themselves to the student's stage as on how much education occurred while they were in it.

REFERENCES

Becker, H., and Geer, Blanche. The fate of idealism in medical school. *American sociol. Rev.*, 1958, **23**, 50–56.

Douvan, Elizabeth. Character processes in adolescence. (Paper presented before the American Psychological Association, August, 1957.)

Erikson, E. H. Growth and crises of the "healthy personality." In C. Kluckhohn, H. A. Murray, and D. M. Schneider (Eds.), *Personality in nature, society and culture.* (2nd ed.) New York: Knopf, 1953.

Freedman, M. The passage through college. In N. Sanford (Ed.), Personality development during the college years. *J. soc. Issues*, 1956, **12**, 13–28.

Freud, Anna. *The ego and the mechanisms of defense.* New York: International Universities Press, 1946.

Gough, H. *Manual, California Psychological Inventory.* Palo Alto, Calif.: Consulting Psychologists Press, 1958.

Loevinger, Jane. A theory of test response. *Proceedings of the invitational conference on testing problems.* Princeton, N.J.: Educational Testing Service, 1959.

Sanford, N. (Ed.). Personality development during the college years. *J. soc. Issues*, 1956a, **12**, 1–71.

Sanford, N. The approach of the authoritarian personality. In J. L. McCary (Ed.), *Psychology of personality.* New York: Logos Press, 1956b.

Stern, G., Stein, M., and Bloom, B. *Methods in personality assessment.* Glencoe, Ill.: The Free Press, 1956.

Strong, E. K. *Vocational interests of men and women.* Stanford, Calif.: Stanford University Press, 1943.

Webster, H. Some quantitative results. In Sanford, N. (Ed.), Personality development during the college years. *J. soc. Issues*, 1956, **12**, 29–43.

White, R. W. *Lives in progress.* New York: Dryden Press, 1952.

PART III

ACADEMIC PROCEDURES

O ur section on the work of the teacher has been planned in accordance with the theory of social roles touched upon in Chapter 2 and elaborated in Chapter 28. First we take up the ways in which the role is defined: how people in other relevant roles and how teachers themselves conceive of the teacher's functions. Next, we treat the procedures and techniques that have been used in meeting the traditional requirements of the role. And then we consider how the teacher's motivations and personality interact with the role-expectations and with the developing personality of the student. Finally, we take up some of the social and economic circumstances that affect the teacher's performance of his functions.

There is progression in the section from more established knowledge toward newer and more speculative hypotheses and hunches. Also, there is a development in the section from established practices in teaching toward possibilities for the future. Thus the curriculum, which might be regarded as the essential "material" that the teacher uses in his work, is treated not at the beginning, in connection with procedures and techniques, but near the end. The concern of our chapter on the curriculum is not so much with the past as with the future, with what the curriculum might become after full account has been taken of modern theories of personality development.

Dr. Knapp poses a fundamental question. He believes, in company with many educators, that those major functions of professors that he distinguishes—research, information-giving, and character developing —ought to be combined in a "balanced and cohesive unity." But a main tendency in American education, he shows, has been toward a separation of these functions. The increasing emphasis on research has been accompanied by a decreasing accent on character development, while the research and informational functions have tended to grow apart. Today there is confusion and conflict. The public, the students, the educational administrators, and the professors themselves all have different ideas about what the professor actually does, and is like, and about what he ought to do. Forces at work in the colleges and universities and in society at large tend to pull the professor in different directions, making it increasingly difficult for any one man to perform according to the various role-expectations at the same time. How then is the ideal of a balanced and cohesive unity to be reached? As a detached observer Knapp judges it most likely that present trends toward fragmentation and specialization will be continued, but he does permit himself some hope for the eventual fusion of the "informational" and character-developing functions of the teacher. He bases this hope mainly in new conceptions of personality structure and of the educational process, which accent the mutual dependence of the "intellectual" and the "characterological." Also, he hopes that some gains may result from the increasing research attentiveness to the interpersonal relations of teacher and student as major determinants of learning in college.

Dr. McKeachie's survey of experiments on teaching suggests that the separation of the informational and character-developing functions may not have gone as far, and that the true picture of the future might not be quite as bleak, as Knapp fears. When during the past thirty years or more researchers have asked which activities of the teacher—what techniques and procedures—lead to the best results, they have typically used as criteria not merely the learning of course material, as measured by grades on examinations, but also desirable changes in attitudes and values. More than this, a major conclusion from numerous experiments on the conditions of learning is that particular arrangements or methods—for example, large or small classes or lecturing versus the discussion method—are not as important as are the various psychological factors operating in the teacher and in the student. It may well be largely because factors of this latter kind have not been adequately controlled that experiments on the procedures and techniques of teaching have often tended to be inconclusive.

But the work that McKeachie surveys has not been primarily concerned with individual differences among teachers and students. It has been directed rather to ways of carrying out the teaching function, and it has presupposed a general psychology of learning. However much might be known about personality factors in teachers and students, we would still need to know what procedures, methods, and techniques are best in given circumstances. Teachers and researchers have been asking questions about these matters for a long time, and the experimental work that has been done is extensive. Indeed, McKeachie's survey reminds one of Santayana's dictum that not to know history is to be condemned to repeating it. College teachers today who have just been introduced to educational research and would like to see some of it undertaken at their institutions are likely to think first of experiments on class size or on the optimal distribution of lectures and discussions. And it may be added that more than a few administrators and foundation men are, from their own point of view, interested in the "efficient utilization of teaching resources." There is much work on problems of this kind that does not need to be continued. It is true that many experiments, laboriously carried out, have by themselves yielded little, but McKeachie shows that when groups of experiments in a given area are considered together, and interpreted with insight and care, the addition to our knowledge is substantial. The point to be emphasized is that this kind of research should be carried out with full attention to the complexities and methodological pitfalls to which McKeachie has drawn our attention. Not the least of these is the consideration that any procedure or technique is carried out in a context of interpersonal relations, and that variables in the teacher, in the student, and in the interaction between the two are bound to influence the outcome.

Dr. Knapp's hopes should be considerably buoyed up by the work of Dr. Katz and Dr. Adelson. Both of these contributors have been guided by the kind of theory that Knapp recommends, and each focuses upon those psychological aspects of the teacher-student interaction that he believes most important to educational outcomes. Katz and Adelson both view the teacher and the student in the perspective of a dynamic theory of personality. The teacher brings to the educational enterprise a vast complexity of psychological dispositions, and it is the interaction of these with a like complexity of dispositions in the student that constitutes the heart of the teaching process. Katz and Adelson believe that this interaction can be analyzed and made the object of scientific study—that variables can be identified and estimated and the relationships among them can be gauged. The better we understand this whole process the more meaningful will teaching become, and the firmer will be the basis for its improvement. When teaching is viewed in this way the fusion of the informational and the character-developing functions becomes inevitable.

Katz delineates some of the general variables of personality that bear significantly on the teacher's work, and then he calls attention to a number of personality characteristics of the teacher that underlie the enormous variability in attitudes and behavior that may be observed in practice. He goes on to show that these characteristics of personality determine the kinds of goals that the teacher sets himself, the ways in which he views students, singly or in the aggregate, and the means by which he undertakes to reach his goals. Katz takes the position, moreover, that the teacher's modes of thought, his conception of knowledge, and his theory of how it is to be pursued are all integral with his functioning as a personality. Finally, Katz shows some of the ways in which the different personality dispositions of the students are affected by the varying aspects of the teacher's personality and behavior.

Adelson concentrates upon one type of teacher-student interaction —that in which the teacher serves as a model for the student. He finds that in order to approach this topic, it is necessary to develop a theory of "modeling," and to show something of the various ways in which students utilize the personality of the teacher in the maintenance or development of their own personalities. On the basis of the concepts and theory thus developed, Adelson goes on to distinguish several major types of teachers, pointing out in each case some typical reactions of students. Like Katz, Adelson is frankly relying upon his own observations and experiences, and both of these writers are offering hypotheses rather than tested propositions. They argue, however, that once their perspective has been adopted, there is every prospect that the phenomena with which they are concerned may be studied by increasingly improved objective methods.

The chapter by Katz and Sanford views the curriculum in the light of the kind of personality theory utilized here by Katz and by Adelson and touched upon in Chapter 6. This theory of personality is used first in an effort to formulate a theory of learning in college; it is then made the basis for a critical study of existing programs and content areas and, finally, consideration is given to the question of what kind of curriculum one would compose if he were guided by this theory of personality in setting goals for college education and in devising methods for reaching them.

Professor Ostroff's paper on economic pressure and the college professor takes up one aspect of a large subject: the situation of the teacher—the whole complex of circumstances in which he lives and that affects his performance of his functions. Contrary to some of the conceptions of the professor and his role that Knapp describes, the academic life is not well-suited for the faint-hearted, for those who cannot stand tension and frustration or give as good as they get. The academic world is psychologically dangerous—competitive, uncharitable, full of disappointments and other threats to the spirit. This is a fact that has been little understood. It has been necessary to rely upon professors themselves for accounts of their world, and when they have told the truth it has seemed that they were striving for dramatic effects, or expressing the kind of personal bitterness that comes through in some of the contemporary novels about college life. Things may be tough all over, as they used to say in the army, but it is the opinion of many men, including the writer, who have worked in other kinds of large organizations besides the academies, and been in close contact with business men and members of other professions, that the academic environment is peculiarly stressful. The large business or industrial corporation may be, by comparison, warmly nurturant, or even offer the kind of a "life in a crystal palace" that is described in a recent novel.

The shortcomings of professors are better known than the shortcomings of their environment. Indeed, the bad behavior of some professors has often been remarked and marveled at. Probably every student and graduate can recall a classroom sadist, and knowledge of the vindictiveness of professors toward their colleagues has spread from faculty wives to large sections of the wider community. This behavior is usually put down to the nature of the breed, academic man. This is wrong. Professors are not worse than other people; they simply live in a less tolerable situation. It is regrettable that limitations of space and time have prevented us from offering in this volume an attempt at analysis of this situation as a whole. Katz and Adelson do depict some of the hazards of the classroom, and Knapp spells out some of the major conflicts among the demands of the professor's role. A more complete account would deal with pressures arising outside the academy, in the culture and society of today, and with pressures arising from within the college or university: conflicts of interest between the professor and the other members of his department, between his department and other units of his institution, between his institution and others; the pressure to publish scholarly or scientific work, or if publication is not the only criterion of professional achievement, then a lack of clarity about how one's work is to be evaluated and rewarded; the demands that proceed from faculty responsibility for administrative and quasi-administrative work. In respect to the last, it is not just that time spent in committee meetings, department meetings, and faculty meetings is time taken away from more rewarding activities; it is, more, that there is often such ambiguity respecting policy, and such uncertainty about where power resides, that much precious and badly needed time seems to be wasted. In many, perhaps most, of our institutions of higher learning there is such confusion of the policy making and the administrative functions, or, better, such an erosion of the former function, with policy being made under the guise of administration, that the professor who would look after his interests is virtually forced to become a politician and take his place in the exhausting game of institutional intrigue.

But Ostroff, in focusing upon economic pressures, clearly has got hold of some forces that are central. He shows that the effects of economic deprivation ramify throughout the life of the young professor, and that economic pressure, through restricting freedom of choice, renders all the other pressures more potent. Ostroff was asked to give a picture of what it is like to live, as a teacher, on the typical academic salary. His is a study in phenomenology, a study of the psychological states caused by economic strains and of the relations of these states to others—and to behavior. Particularly does he show how the sense of economic deprivation affects the professor's scholarly work and his relations with his students. It was not Ostroff's task to estimate how often, or to say in what places and under what conditions, the phenomena described are to be found. He does not treat of professors who do not experience economic distress, either because they are well-off—possibly because of their families or possibly because they belong to that happy few, the "affluent professors," who can pad their income by means of their research grants and consultantships—or because their background or personality has rendered them relatively insensitive to such distress. And of course Ostroff does not take up the case of other middle-class people who are just as badly off as the teachers whose lot he describes. The picture that emerges invites sympathy for the young professor—and undoubtedly he would enjoy sympathy as much as the next man—but this is not the point. The point is that the professor has the task of instructing the youth and advancing our culture and he is hampered, in ways not heretofore made plain, in carrying out this task.

A word about some major omissions from this section. We have not been able to consider how people are recruited into the profession of college teaching, the subject of a recent excellent paper by Trow (1959). Nor have we been able to give due attention to the education of college teachers. This is a question to which very little research has been directed but which has been the subject of much searching discussion; for example, in a recent symposium of the American Council on Education (Axelrod, 1959). Perhaps a volume on the development of students in the college setting should not be expected to treat of the research functions of the professor. Yet, as Knapp shows, this function is often carried out at the expense of teaching, and the appropriately articulated combination of the two functions remains one of the burning issues in higher education. So here is a serious omission. An analysis of the activities that go on under the banner of research, and of the arrangements for these activities, would be just as complicated as the analysis of teaching in the following pages, and it undoubtedly would suggest just as great a need for reform.

REFERENCES

Axelrod, J. (Ed.). Graduate study for future college teachers. Washington, D.C.: American Council on Education, 1959.

Trow, M. *Reflections on the recruitment for college teaching.* (Mimeo.) Berkeley, Calif.: University of California, Center for the Study of Higher Education, 1959.

7 *Robert H. Knapp*

Changing Functions
of the College Professor

There are at the present time approximately a quarter of a million Americans engaged in college and university teaching. They constitute a professional class both of impressive numbers and of potentially immense influence upon the shaping of American civilization. Their number and influence is not likely to decline in future decades. On the contrary, recent estimates of the Federal Office of Education project that present numbers may well double in the next decade, although this is probably a generous estimate.

The rise of this profession in recent years has been sensationally rapid. A reasonable estimate of the total numbers engaged in college teaching at the turn of the century is approximately 20,000, and the total number of students in higher education at that time fell short of the present number of college teachers in the nation. Already in 1940 Charles Beard could observe that the college professors "represented a larger proportion of the population set aside for scholarly pursuits than had been the case since the dissolution of monasteries and convents" (Beard, 1942). In short, a vast and historically unique professional class has emerged in American society. It is the purpose of the present chapter to review some of the studies relating to the functions of this profession within our nation.

I should like to begin with some general considerations of the role of the college professor and with a discussion of his several basic functions as they exist and have existed for some decades. Then I shall consider historically some of the changes in the profession which have occurred in America. Third, I shall review some of the literature relating to the images of the college professor in America as he is viewed by the public and by students, as well as by himself. Next, after considering the literature which has sought to identify the qualities of the successful teacher, I shall evaluate some of the conflicts, contradictions, and frictions which beset this profession at the present time. Finally, I should like to offer some speculations concerning the future role of the American college professor.

THE FUNCTIONS OF THE COLLEGE PROFESSOR AND THE EVOLUTION OF HIS ROLE IN AMERICA

We might begin by drafting a catalogue of the functions that the American college professor has been historically called upon to perform. These would include the transmission of fact, the providing of good example in conduct, the reinterpretation of existing knowledge, the discovery of new knowledge, the indoctrination of the young in moral and, at times, also religious matters, the providing of personal counsel, and a variety of other functions. But when all these have been reviewed, it appears to me that they can be reduced to three focal functions, which I shall call the *research function,* the *informational function,* and the *character-developing function,* of which all others are aspects or combinations. Let us consider the first.

The college professor has taken upon himself, or been appointed to, the very general function of extending and coordinating human knowledge. In this sense he may be thought of as performing a sort of reconnaissance function. He must move intellectually into unexplored domains, obtain new information, and then return and report it with his interpretations, to the main host of society. In this function boldness, improvisation, astuteness, and even courage are all at a premium, precisely as they are in military reconnaissance. Just as a military reconnaissance party is licensed to forego many formalities and proprieties, so the professor in his intellectual reconnaissance has sometimes been granted the right to eccentric and unusual courses of thought and action. The first role of the professor, therefore, is, in the best sense, that of the scout, the outrider, whose function is the exploring of the frontiers of human knowledge. Let us designate this the *research function,* bearing in mind that this includes not merely scientific research in the narrow sense, but also humanistic scholarship and the reinterpretation of all kinds of accumulated learning.

The second function of the college professor is that of transmitting formalized knowledge concerning the nature of the world and of man. Here we can include such obvious disciplines as grammar, the sciences, and history. The college professor is expected to be, in some degree at least, a master of such subject material, and he is called upon to impart some of this mastery to the young. This, then, is the second major function of the college professor, and we shall call it the *informational function.*

The third function deals with the development of character and values. In the 19th century this function might properly have been called pastoral, since the relationship of professor to student had, in spirit if not in fact, a clearly religious tone. In many instances the professor was expected to indoctrinate his students with particular articles of religious belief, according to the prevailing conviction that this would foster their development as total persons. With the passage of time, indoctrination in the narrower sense gave way to a more general function of personal counseling and the inculcation of high moral standards. Lip service is still given to the proposition that the professor should be a builder of character as well as a transmitter of fact and knowledge. We shall call this third function the *character-developing function,* with the understanding that this defines the office of the professor as a guide and counselor of the total person of the student.

In summary then, the college professor in America has been asked to perform three quite disparate functions: first, the reconnaissance of the frontiers of human knowledge; second, the imparting of "information"; and third, the inculcation of values and the development of character. I submit at this juncture that although these functions have varied in emphasis in different times and circumstances, most of the paradoxes and most of the vicissitudes of the profession have resulted from the inherent difficulty in mixing these different performances. It is my thesis that the evolving role of the college professor in America has been characterized by a progressive decline of his character-developing function along with a strong tendency for the research and the informational functions to part company and form two separate callings.

The foundations of higher education began in this country with the establishment of Harvard in 1642. By the time of the American Revolution no less than eight universities had been established (Beard, 1934). All but one were the organs of church bodies. As such they developed a peculiar structure which has served as an abiding model, in many respects, for the subsequent development of higher education in America: administrative control was placed in a nonacademic supervisory body and the president, and the faculty occupied a subservient station. This pattern persisted even after denominational universities and colleges in America became secularized, and the peculiar institution of the college president and the administrative body of nonacademic trustees has become the almost universal pattern in both public and private institutions. Caplow and McGee (1958), in seeking to trace the origin of this pattern, have found it in the Italian and Scottish universities. These writers have noted that the role of the professor under this system is markedly different from that obtaining either in the German universities or in those of Oxford and Cambridge.

During the course of the 17th, 18th, and the first half of the 19th centuries the central focus of the American university remained relatively unchanged. As Riesman and Jencks have pointed out (Chapter 3), it was characterized by a clear commitment to the "classical" education in which heavy emphasis was placed upon Greek, Latin, history, theology, and other subjects particularly germane to preparation for the clerical calling. The professor in this phase of development was, by all modern standards, an intellectual generalist who might at once profess natural history, ethics, and theology while remaining a Latin or Greek scholar. Of the three basic functions of the professor that we have defined, we should note the very heavy emphasis placed upon his pastoral or character-developing function and the relative neglect of his reconnaissance, or research, function. The professor as a research scholar was as yet but dimly perceptible on the American scene.

But in the latter half of the 19th century several innovations that were of profound significance appeared. The first of these was the rise of state supported institutions, particularly in response to the provisions of the Morrill Act of 1862 (Riesman and Jencks, Chapter 3; Stewart, Chapter 26; Commager, 1951). This development can be designated as a sort of secularization process in which higher education now became deeply concerned with technology, science, and other practical affairs, while the older clerical and classical emphasis was largely superseded. This carried in its wake a host of institutional changes and trends of which the influence upon the role of the college professor was of marked significance.

A second change in the American university in the latter half of the 19th century, intimately related to the above, was the rise of the natural sciences (Knapp and Goodrich, 1953).

In earlier days it was not uncommon for the professor of theology to offer a course in natural history as a mere sideline to his central concern. But under the joint promptings of the growing secularization and technological demands, the several natural sciences came into their own. As this transpired, it was only natural for the German universities to serve both as models of organization and as sources of instruction in these disciplines (Stewart, Chapter 26). The "university" atmosphere came to replace the more intimate "college" atmosphere not only in the larger universities but in many small colleges as well. Thus, the rise of the natural sciences initiated a general change of climate that has profoundly conditioned the course of American higher education in the last six or seven decades. The role of the college professor, his image of himself, and the image he evoked in others necessarily responded to this trend.

A third trend of note, having its origins in the latter half of the 19th century, was initiated by Harvard but quickly spread to other institutions, universities as well as colleges. I refer to the overthrow of the relatively fixed classical curriculum and the emergence of the elective system (Stewart, Chapter 26; Beard, 1934). This, of course, went hand in hand with the rise of the natural sciences and the emergence of departmentalism; and it contributed to the proliferation of course offerings and to the specialization that will presently be discussed.

Thus there were set afoot in the closing decades of the 19th century a number of institutional trends that were to influence profoundly the ensuing development of American higher education and to shape and determine the peculiar profession of college teaching. It would, of course, be a grave error to assume that these trends were simultaneously manifest in all American institutions. Riesman in a recent book (Riesman, 1956) draws a telling image of the academic procession, a picture in which change is first initiated in a few select institutions, largely universities of distinguished reputation, while the patterns and fashions established there slowly seep down to the more obscure and smaller institutions (see also Chapter 3). At the turn of the century the head of the procession was already moving in new directions with enthusiasm and a sense of mission. It had formed a happy partnership on one hand with the growing industrial might and resources of the nation, and on the other hand, with the state and national government. It remained for the next six decades to see new patterns disseminated and further elaborated while the numbers of both students and college teachers increased dramatically. In considering this period of six decades during which the profession of college teaching became a major profession in American society, we should pause to note some specific trends.

First, there appears to have been a clear decline in what we earlier described as the character-developing function so vital to American colleges and universities during the period of close religious control. The causes of this were several, but in the main they represent merely the consequence of the diffuse secularization which gradually and progressively took hold of American higher education. With the rise of scientific and technological education and the emergence of the elective system, it was inevitable that the older emphasis upon the classical curriculum and the training of clergy should give way. The function of the college professor came increasingly to be that of imparting technical and compartmentalized information, not the supervision of character development. This latter function, at first neglected, was presently taken up by specialists in guidance, counseling, and psychiatry. The character-developing function of the college professor soon became the passive one of providing a good example in character and conduct rather than the active inculcation of morals, values, or even religious conviction. To be sure, this latter role still survives in some institutions, but in the main it has yielded to a general educational theory that the function of the professor in his relation to students is primarily to impart information. This trend was hastened by the policy of the Carnegie Foundation to grant the benefits of the Teachers Insurance and Annuity Program only to institutions without formal religious connections. Thus, to avail themselves of these benefits, a host of denominational American colleges in the second decade of the century severed their official connections with their parent religious body. For this reason, as well as others, clerical control of institutions, whether through presidents or trustees, gave way to secularism.

A second major trend has been the rise of professional societies and professional, as opposed to institutional, identification on the part of college teachers. Here again, the sciences have been in the vanguard, and it is among these disciplines that the greatest and also the earliest formalization of professional requirements were established. The net effect has been to pose a conflict of identification and loyalty among members of the teaching profession. On one hand, they see themselves as members of their particular academic discipline with its professional journals, annual meetings, employment centers, and committees. On the other hand, they are members of the faculty of an institution which pays their salaries and in other ways commands their loyalty and services. And, of course, loyalty to the discipline has undergone progressive elaboration, so that now most of the larger professional societies provide for divisions of scholarly specialization within them. This elaboration is a mere response to the growing numbers in, and complexity of, the various academic fields. But its effect is a fractionating one, producing an ever narrower and more intensive pattern of scholarship and direction of inquiry. It inevitably influences the professor's image of himself and that which others hold of him. No longer, as in the 19th century, is the professor seen as a sagacious and wise man whose opinion may be widely sought on all matters of concern. Instead, he is known by his discipline or that fraction of it that he has appropriated as his domain.

A third significant development since the turn of the century has been the rise of the doctrine of academic freedom. It is frequently assumed by younger members of the profession that in appealing to this principle they are invoking an ancient and honored tradition in American higher education. Such is clearly not the case. Prior to the First World War the idea had little currency, and surely little force. But beginning with the founding of the Association of American College Professors in 1915 and its Committee on Academic Freedom and Tenure (Bulletin of American Association of University Professors, 1954), the doctrine began to gain effective currency, and in a number of instances presumed violations of this academic right were reviewed by this body, and rectification of unwarranted dismissals obtained. In the latest and most publicized crisis in academic freedom, namely the oath controversy at the University of California, which began in 1949, the final legal decision in favor of the defendants will doubtless prove a significant precedent in the defense of this doctrine. The rise of the doctrine of academic freedom has done much to bolster a sense of security and dignity among college professors at a time when other forces have tried to restrict their freedom.

A fourth trend has been in the increased importance of research and publication as the marks of professional success and as the avenue to promotion and advancement. As Caplow and McGee (1958) clearly reveal, this is in many cases the sole criterion upon which employment in colleges and universities is granted or withheld. In consequence, there has developed, particularly among younger members of the profession, an almost obsessive concern with early and persistent publication. This concern, entirely realistic in terms of the present mores of the teaching profession, is supported by the entire pattern of doctorate training which is now the major pathway to admission into the profession of college teaching.

Fifth, and intimately related to the above, is the rise of the Ph.D. as the "union card" of the college professor. The Ph.D. was essentially a German importation from the latter half of the 19th century, and was initially of prime importance in the demonstration of advanced scholarly standing in the natural sciences. But presently it became the mark of respectability in all departments of learning, and college presidents vied with each other to obtain the greatest proportion of doctors on their faculties.

Although it is possible to obtain employment as a college professor without this degree at the present time, opportunities are largely limited to smaller and less prestigeful institutions, while promotions without this mark of distinction are surely made most difficult. Some numbers here will show the extent to which this symbol of scholarly excellence has become valued. In 1900 less than 400 Ph.D.'s were granted in American colleges and universities, while the count in 1959 is approximately 10,000. Moreover, in the latter year there were over 130 institutions granting this degree in the United States, while the present prospect is for a much larger number to be involved in this type of training in the next decade. The rising importance of the Ph.D., with its special emphasis upon scholarly attainment, must be viewed along with the rise of professionalism, research emphasis, and departmentalization, as further evidence of the marked and growing bureaucratization of the college teaching profession.

Another major trend that should certainly be noted, but which is more difficult to document or prove, is the decline of the college professor's influence in the management of affairs. A revealing index of this decline is the political allegiance of the college professor which has been, for a group of his education and class origins, far removed to the left of other professions. Thus, the clear propensity of college professors in the past several decades has been to ally themselves with the Democratic and not the Republican party, as Lazarsfeld and Thielens (1958) and others have shown. It is an interesting question also whether the current recruitment of college professors is not most often from homes of quite limited means, but with intellectual traditions. Gustad (1959) has shown that college professors, at least in the Southern sample studied, tend to come disproportionately from the homes of teachers and clergymen. Other evidence suggests that currently the college teaching profession is a favorite path of social ascent for individuals of humble backgrounds but high intellectual endowment. However this may be, it is at least a good hypothesis that there has been a kind of encystment, whether for ideological or economic reasons, that has progressively tended to alienate the college teaching profession from the managerial class in America (see Pinner, Chapter 27).

This trend is not without its counter currents, to be sure. Against this trend is the ever increasing degree to which industry has called upon the professional and learned talents of academic personnel, particularly in the sciences, in the execution of technical research and the providing of consultative services. Nor should we forget that the rise of American higher education to its present dimensions depended upon the exchange of clerical for industrial patronage, as Veblen has so well documented. On the other hand, the financial rewards of the teaching profession have been so meager (Ostroff, Chapter 12) that inexorably the college professor has commonly found himself barred from association with other groups of comparable education and cultural standards. Significant ideological differences have also conspired to increase the professor's isolation.

Next to be noted is the rise of impersonal bureaucratic structures within American institutions of higher education. Whereas six decades ago candidates for academic posts were commonly selected by presidents and became known to them through personal contacts, at the present time much of this function and a host of other administrative functions are taken over by an administrative bureaucracy of deans, associate deans, coordinators, provosts, and the like, who stand between the president and trustees on the one hand, and the teaching faculty on the other. The management of universities, and to a lesser extent of colleges, has become a highly professionalized and business-like affair. In many major institutions the functional grouping of the faculty has been reduced to the departmental level and this, in turn, has restricted identification with the institution as a whole and has narrowed the social and intellectual horizons of the professor.

It is a fair surmise that within the profession of college teaching there has been a fairly progressive decline in teaching enthusiasm, as Riesman (1956) has suggested. This is probably especially true in the more advanced, wealthy, and prestigeful institutions that appear at the head of Riesman's "academic procession." As Caplow and McGee (1958) point out, the main avenue to employment and promotion for the professor is through scholarly publications and research, and not through demonstrated proficiency in the teaching function. And, as we have noted earlier, the Ph.D. is now the prime educational requisite for entering the profession, and very few Ph.D. programs make any provision whatsoever for the development of teaching skills. Compared to the prestige and recognition, monetary as well as intangible, attaching to scholarly attainment, the few awards for distinguished teaching are pathetic. There are, to be sure, a few isolated examples of recognition for teaching effectiveness, such as the Orsted Medal in Physics, and it is also true that particular institutions may occasionally offer local awards for particularly effective teaching practices. But these are very small crumbs indeed compared to the over-whelming recognition given to publishing, research, and even administrative performance. It is probably all too true that many young college professors accept teaching as a painful chore, which they perform only to enable them to pursue their research and scholarly ambitions. The clear and marked decline of the character-developing function with the general secularization of American higher education we have already noted. Probably at the present time the informational function is competing for prestige at a severe disadvantage with the research function. This constitutes a truly grave threat to the effective operation of our higher educational system.

These, then, are some of the most important trends that have shaped the occupational status of the college professor in contemporary America. Let us now turn to a consideration of the characteristics and role-images that this profession has invoked among different groups.

IMAGES OF THE COLLEGE PROFESSOR

We can begin with the general public image of the college professor so far as it may be identified. The college professor has been, for example, a familiar figure in literature and more recently in radio and television. But apparently no formal analysis of his characteristics as so depicted has been undertaken. Still, even the most casual observer can identify some fairly typical models. There is, for example, the professor as the "mad scientist," a popular figure in science fiction and other kindred types of popular drama. Then there is the college professor as a fussy, absentminded but amiable bumbler, who serves a half-comic role in literature, cinema, and television. There is occasionally a depiction of the college professor, particularly in his older years, as a compassionate and sagacious counselor, but this seems to be a relatively rare model.

Of empirical studies of the public image of the college professor, perhaps the single most important one is that done by Claude Bowman more than twenty years ago. Bowman (1938) made a survey of a number of higher quality American periodicals from the turn of the century until 1938, searching in them for articles upon, and allusions to, the profession of college teaching. The stereotype personality of the college professor as it emerges in this study includes both favorable and unfavorable characteristics. Of the favorable characteristics, "idealism" is the most prominent, and thereafter a variety of desirable traits including "love of knowledge," "humanness," "unselfishness,"

"breadth," "dispassion," "practicality," "competence," and "charm."
Our author notes a peculiar absence of such attributes as "handsome-
ness," "eloquence," "brilliance," and "gayety." Of the unfavorable
attributes, the professor image is endowed with qualities of "dull-
ness," "social inadequacy," "unmanliness," "impracticality," "unwhole-
someness," etc. But, he is rarely charged with lack of moral integrity.
Bowman's study continues with an analysis of the professorial role
with respect to particular aspects of the academic life. These include
his economic position, his position with respect to academic freedom,
teaching and research, and political affairs. The array of assembled
quotations clearly supports the proposition that both among professors and among the public there has been a protracted recognition
of the financial vicissitudes of the calling. With respect to academic
freedom, the author notes, as we did earlier, that many of the con-
straints are derived from a heritage of the initial clerical control of
higher education, and he cites an impressive array of quotations both
supporting and denying this ideal privilege of the teaching profession.
Teaching and research come in for a persistent body of comment of
which the crux is whether research facilitates or inhibits the teaching
function. There is a persistent recognition of the danger that the prevailing emphasis upon research obscures the importance of effective
teaching, that "a teacher gets a position on a college faculty not because he can teach, but by demonstrating that he has been taught."
The teacher's role with respect to political affairs appears also to have
been a subject of considerable controversy, first as it related to academic freedom during the First World War, and second as the issue
emerged during the New Deal when professors in unusual numbers
were called upon to serve in high administrative office. With respect
to the nonacademic administrative control of American universities,
Bowman cites the German professor who introduced an American
professor to the Kaiser as "an 'Exchange Professor' since he comes
from a monarchy within a republic to a republic within a monarchy"
(Heller, 1927). In short, we have from this study an image of the college professor as a personality and an analysis of some of the areas
of his principal involvement that have been most fraught with controversy. Unfortunately, this study is already twenty years old, and
no attempt at the analysis of comparable contemporary materials appears to have been undertaken for similar purposes.

So far as can be determined, there have been no studies of the image
of the college professor held by administrators and trustees. We will,
to be sure, note below Kelly's (1929) study of the ideal attributes of
the college professor as returned by such groups, but here we must

pass on to the few studies involving student images of the college teaching profession.

One of the most recent and promising inquiries into images of different professions, including that of the college professor, is currently being carried out by Beardslee and O'Dowd (1959, and Chapter 18). Drawing upon the work of Cattell and of Osgood, they have devised a series of rating scales of a semiprojective character which permit the rating of different professions on a seven-point scale. Typical items of this scale include the following:

a. wealthy __:__:__:__:__:__:__ not well-to-do
b. conformist __:__:__:__:__:__:__ individualist
c. radical __:__:__:__:__:__:__ conservative
d. self-assertive __:__:__:__:__:__:__ submissive

This instrument has been administered to the entire faculty of a New England college as well as to a substantial probability sample of students at the same institution. Ratings were obtained on the images of some fifteen professions including doctors, lawyers, accountants, school teachers, social workers, scientists, and others.

Compared to other professions, the college professor is distinguished in the student image for the following qualities. He is rated highest of all the professions in such qualities as "intelligence," "thoughtfulness," "personal satisfaction," and "wisdom." He rates conspicuously high in such qualities as "playing chess," "interestingness," "having happy home life," and "colorfulness." Moreover, the college professor received the highest rating as the profession that the students would "like to be." The high prestige of the calling in this study confirms the results obtained elsewhere in several studies. On the other hand, the college professor receives relatively low ratings in such qualities as "wealth," "playing poker," "opportunity for advancement," "conservativeness," "absence of emotional problems," and "stability."

One comparison of particular interest is the difference between the image of the college professor and that of the scientist since there is a significant overlapping in these two callings. Here we find that the scientists are rated conspicuously higher than the professor on such qualities as "self-sufficiency," "cautiousness," "perseverance," and "opportunities for advancement," and lower on such qualities as "sociability," "attentiveness to people," "good taste," "having a pretty wife," "having a happy home," "interest in art," and "social popularity." It would appear, therefore, that there is actually a rather striking difference in the stereotype image evoked by these two designations. The scientist represents an intensification of the intellectual qualities of the college professor but a marked reduction in his social and personal attractiveness. Indeed, the scientist is placed the lowest of all professions for such qualities as "attractiveness to people" and "sociability." This would remind us that the common stereotype image of the college professor may be subject to marked qualifications, depending upon his field of knowledge.

Though we have dealt here only with the results obtained from the students of a single New England college, it should be noted that probability samples from other New England student populations reveal a remarkably similar image pattern. These include, among others, a women's college and a large state university, the latter drawing its students from a class and educational background quite different from those of the institution considered in the preceding report. The evidence thus far acquired in this study, therefore, indicates that there is, in the minds of students, a popular image of the college professor which differs sharply from that of other callings and which remains remarkably consistent in student samples from different institutions and from both sexes, at least within the region studied.

It is appropriate next to examine the stereotype that college professors have of themselves. Again Beardslee and O'Dowd have pertinent data on this from at least one institution. In this instance, cooperation was obtained from over 95% of the faculty. Compared with students at the same institution, the resulting picture of professorial qualities is generally quite similar. It may be noted, however, that college professors rate themselves higher on such qualities as "caution," "stability," "adaptability," "absence of emotional problems," and "calmness"; in short, the attributes associated with control. On the other hand, the faculty see themselves as less characterized by "self-assertiveness," "individualism," "realism," "confidence," "strength," and "popularity." They also ascribe to themselves lower social status than do students and feel they are less likely to have pretty wives. In short, the faculty appear less likely to ascribe colorful and assertive attitudes to themselves than do their students. This general trend has also been reported by Gustad (1959) with respect to the contemporary images of the public at large.

A further illuminating study of how professors view themselves is included in Lazarsfeld and Thielens, *The Academic Mind* (1958), although this study is largely confined to social scientists and is oriented with particular reference to the recent crisis in academic freedom. We find an essential confirmation of Gustad's (1959) conclusion that college professors have a poor opinion of the status of their occupation.

Furthermore, they present figures, based upon a limited sample, indicating that college professors feel themselves held in low esteem, particularly by businessmen, and then next by Congressmen, and to a lesser extent by trustees. For example, over half of the college professors felt that most businessmen would classify professors as of lesser significance and worth than the manager of a branch bank, an account executive of an advertising agency, or a lawyer. From these sources and from other evidence, it would appear likely that college professors view themselves as objects of disdain and even contempt in comparison with equally well-educated people in other callings.

CHARACTERISTICS OF SUPERIOR TEACHERS

Turning now to the question of the characteristics ascribed to successful and gifted teachers, we may divide the literature on this subject into three categories. First, there are idealized formulations of what the functions and qualifications of all college professors should be. These are abundant but of little worth for our purposes. The second category refers to studies endeavoring to obtain empirical data from different groups on what attributes are most admired or believed to be most effective in college teachers.

There are three studies of note which have sought to obtain ratings on the characteristics of ideal teachers. One of the earliest of these, reported by R. J. Clinton (1930), lists in descending order of importance some eighteen qualities that are attributed by students to the ideal college professor. Of these, the four most frequently mentioned—"interest in students," "fairness," "pleasing personality," and "humor"— all refer to social and moral qualities. "Mastery of subject" is then placed fifth, while such qualities as "keenness of intellect" and "wide range of information" rank very far down the list. A general survey of these results clearly indicates that students, in the main, are less impressed by intellectual command or creativity than by qualities associated with personal amiability and social skill.

Bousfield (1940) tested again, by a similar approach, the image of the ideal professor. The order of attributes appears to have shifted somewhat, in that "mastery of subject" now was placed second, with "organization of material" fourth, and "a clear exposition" in fifth place. Still "fairness" occupies the highest position, "interestingness of delivery" third, and "interest in students and helpfulness" seventh. Since both studies are based on relatively small numbers of cases and are confined to particular institutions, no very general conclusion can be drawn save probably the high importance attached by students to social and personal qualities of their professors.

A third study by Trabue (1950) attempts to summarize the attitudes of 419 presidents of liberal arts colleges concerning the ideal qualifications of faculty for instructing in the first and second years of college. This study has some very obvious methodological deficiencies but tends to emphasize again not intellectual distinction and attainment but rather social skills and organizational competency. Thus, "encouragement of individual thought," "emotional stability," "friendliness," "tolerance," and "sympathy with problems of college students" all are ranked in top position. Among these college presidents there is also a preference for the kind of instructor who identifies himself primarily as a college teacher rather than as a specialist in a subject. Among the fifteen desirable attributes listed, there was no allusion to high scholarly attainment. If this study may be taken at its face value, it would appear that the majority of college presidents tend to esteem the informational and character-developing functions of the college professor over his research functions, at least with reference to lower division courses.

We may now turn to several studies of a third category—studies having to do with the attributes of teachers of known or acknowledged distinction. One of the first of these is Kelly's study of "great teachers" based upon the participation of 187 church-affiliated colleges (Kelly, 1929). Here we find that the teachers rated as "great" were primarily characterized by interest in students—"sympathy," "helpfulness," "sincerity," "enthusiasm"—and similar qualities. "Knowledge and mastery of the subject matter" ranked third, while "breadth" and "industry" were respectively eleventh and twelfth. Again it would appear that the qualities esteemed in the college professor are only secondarily related to his intellectual distinction and primarily to his human and social qualities of personality.

Knapp and Goodrich (1952) in their study of the origins of the American scientists obtained a series of ratings on college teachers from their former students. These authors also devised ratings based upon interview material. Among those qualities correlating with high effectiveness of the teacher in motivating his own students to pursue his professional field were three general constellations derived from a factor analysis. Thus, in the field of biology, and less incisively in the field of chemistry, "masterfulness" (as exemplified by severe standards of grading, incisive leadership, and departmental entrepreneurship), "warmth" (as illustrated by the use of humor and other histrionic skills, and the maintenance of contact with former students), and third, "intellectual distinction" (as manifest in intellectual mastery of the field and scholarly production)—in that order—appeared to characterize highly effective science teachers.

Guthrie (1954) reported a fairly extensive survey of student and faculty ratings of the effectiveness of college teachers. This study indicated a substantial agreement in the ratings assigned by the two groups, though it would appear that the grounds for these ratings varied between the two groups, the faculty tending to rate scholarly attainments as more important and the students accenting specific personal and teaching qualities. It is to be noted that student ratings show a high degree of reliability, and that graduate students, as compared with undergraduates, were more influenced by intellectual and scholarly attainment. The most frequently mentioned negative attributes of college professors were "lack of warmth," "unfriendliness," and "a tendency toward sarcasm." Guthrie also noted that there was little evidence that the length of the teaching career correlated with the merit ranking of the teachers. It would appear that the size of classes was not a significant factor in such ratings, nor did students rate more highly teachers within the field of their own specialization. Finally, there appeared to be little relationship one way or the other between faculty ratings for teaching effectiveness and the research productivity of the professor in question.

A study by Bogardus (1946) sought to obtain ratings on former teachers from graduate students and alumni of thirty colleges and universities. Among this group the most esteemed qualities were "thoroughness of knowledge in the subject taught," "familiarity with recent developments in the field," "logical and forthright presentation," and "the stimulation of discussion." Beyond these qualities there are three personal attributes which were repeatedly mentioned. These include "fairness," "democratic attitude," and "enthusiasm and humor." Among the most frequently mentioned negative traits are "nervous mannerisms," "speech peculiarities," "poor grooming and posture," and "moralizing." It is probably to be expected that qualities of intellectual command should rank somewhat more highly with this group than with the general run of undergraduate students, since the respondents were for the most part graduate students intent upon scholarly careers.

Finally, a study by Maslow and Zimmerman (1956) involved the rating of college instructors at a large metropolitan college by both faculty and students. The teachers in question were rated for effectiveness "as a teacher," "as a personality," and for "creativeness." The authors were able to show a substantial agreement, exceeding slightly that reported by Guthrie, between student and faculty ratings of teachers for teaching effectiveness. Moreover, the ratings on the three variables all showed high positive correlations for both rating groups, with one possible exception. Maslow notes, as does Guthrie, that the estimate of teaching effectiveness is influenced in colleague rankings by "creativeness" while students tend to rate teaching more as a function of "good personality."

In terms of our earlier analysis of the three basic functions of the professorial calling, it would seem fair to conclude from the data surveyed that professors tend to esteem and respect themselves primarily on the basis of their research function. Students and administrators, however, especially in smaller institutions, tend to value most the informational and character-developing functions. On the other hand, it may well be that the public at large is probably inclined to attach great significance to what we have called the character-building function. Thus, different segments of the population, to whom the college professor must in some degree answer, apparently expect different kinds of performances.

I think it will be immediately apparent to the reader, however, that we have as yet very little solid research on the images evoked by the profession or on the supposed techniques and qualities of a good teacher. In most of the studies cited there is some obvious fault or limitation either of sampling or of instrument or analysis. Reported results in many instances derive from a particular class of respondents, e.g., graduate students, scientists, or administrators; we are dealing with noncomparable categories of judgment, which are used in different historical epochs. Other studies, such as that by Guthrie, are confined exclusively to one institution; still others, such as that by Knapp and Goodrich, to a single class of teachers. It is plain that despite the sophistication and skills that have developed in the social sciences for the evaluation of qualities and characteristics associated with different callings, that of the college professor, his image for different groups, the characteristics sought and esteemed, and the qualities associated with superior performance—all of these have been woefully neglected in educational research.

If the lack of adequate studies of the college professor is apparent, the need for them is equally evident. No one in the early 1960s can doubt that our society is changing at an ever increasing rate. And our educational system in particular is in all probability confronted with a turbulent and revolutionary period. The projected increase in the college-age population alone would fairly well ensure this. Add to this, however, the probable future increase in the proportion of college-age students attending college, the necessity of maintaining an educational performance that is satisfactory in comparison to that of other countries, the increase in adult education, the acceleration of advanced technology—all these factors contribute to the immense seriousness of the problem of higher education in our time. If these challenges of the future are to be met, they will, in the final analysis, be met by college professors. It clearly behooves us to study this profession more thoroughly and more extensively if clear and effective answers are to be found to the problems that confront us now and will confront us still more forcibly in the future.

CURRENT AND FUTURE STRESSES IN THE PROFESSORIAL VOCATION

It is now appropriate that we consider some of the current forces that produce conflict in the profession of college teaching, forces that introduce competing or even contradictory demands upon the time and performance of the college professor, and that are likely to shape his future role. We will attempt to enumerate these fairly simply.

1. First, there is the conflict between institutional loyalty and loyalty to the discipline. We have earlier noted the rise of professionalism and departmentalism as a salient and mounting force over the past five or six decades. This has now reached an acute phase and frequently imposes severe conflicts of interest and loyalty, especially in smaller and less prestigeful institutions where demands for teaching, administration, and extracurricular services compete directly with professional interests and research.

2. Second, and akin to the above, there is the basic conflict between the teaching and the scholarly or research function in most fields. As we have noted earlier, the second of these has become the royal pathway to prestige, honor, and advancement. Yet, despite this, many college professors are strongly attached to the teaching function both for the subjective satisfactions it brings and out of a larger sense of human service. And so these two functions may, and frequently do, contend for the time and energies of the professor.

3. A third source of conflict in the professorial role revolves about the peculiar conditions of academic employment. I refer to the protracted insecurity of the younger college teacher, who, after extended graduate study, then enters upon a period of contractual employment with its attendant uncertainties, until he eventually attains the security

of tenure. Thus the younger academic is frequently a highly unsettled individual, a sort of discontented intellectual nomad, who may teach briefly in several institutions before finally finding a relatively secure and permanent station.

4. Then there is the discrepancy between socio-economic standing and the educational level of the profession, especially in the earlier stages of the individual's career. This makes for a peculiar sort of role in society in which there is a strong tendency for academics to withdraw from the general middle-class population and establish a distinctive and relatively isolated subculture. This alienation from non-academic people of the same educational level is a source of role-conflict and sometimes personal distress.

5. Finally, there is the peculiar set of conflicts which arise out of the nature of administrative control of American higher education. The college teacher is rarely entrusted with the formulation of educational policy on the highest level. Instead, this function is assumed by presidents and boards of trustees, who themselves are frequently unfamiliar with the immediate and vital problems of education, as Ruml and Morrison (1959) have so convincingly noted. This has in many institutions resulted in diffuse resentment and feelings of humiliation among college faculties. In many instances it has raised the question of academic freedom and posed a sharp contrast between that ideal autonomy cherished by the professor and his actual subservience to administrative mandate.

Future changes in the role of the college professor in American society will no doubt bring about resolutions of one or more of the dilemmas we have reviewed. But, if present developments are continued, I cannot doubt that the pastoral, or character-developing, function which dominated the sectarian institutions of this country in the 18th and 19th centuries will be increasingly delegated to specialists. Bureaus of vocational and personal guidance seem likely to burgeon for yet a long while, and the professor will probably be called upon less and less to concern himself with the individual character development of his students. I further expect, unless present trends are reversed, that a segment of the profession of college teachers will separate themselves off by a sort of mitosis and constitute a class dedicated principally to the research or scholarly function and only incidentally to instruction. If this be so, then the insistent demands for "creative research" from college professors generally is likely to subside, especially if, as projected, the number of college professors will almost double in the next decade. For most college professors, if present trends continue, teaching will become their primary function. They will become increasingly devoted to the propagation of information, steadily more bureaucratized, and increasingly reconciled to the relinquishment of scholarly attainment.

Turning from future projections to things long past, it may be both edifying and amusing to note some parallels between the development of higher education in ancient Athens and modern America. As Athenian society moved from oligarchy to democracy, and as secularization grew ever apace, there arose the first prototypes of the college professor, the much belied Sophists of the 5th century. Protagoras, who commanded such a singular respect from Plato, was the first to take money for professing to make students wiser in knowledge and more virtuous of character. As a disciple of the pre-Socratic philosophers, he partook, too, in the vanguardism of that brilliant age of speculative thought. But characteristically he was pragmatic of temper, concerned with civic virtue and attainment, and a disciplined grammarian and literary critic. Though he, himself, was finally banished for atheism, the movement he initiated became the prime focus of higher secular education for the next century.

And it provided much of the intellectual ferment that gave rise to the brilliance of the age. Henry Jackson (1910), writing on Sophistry in ancient Athens, summarized its course as follows:

Lapse of time and change of circumstances brought with them not merely changes in the subjects taught but also changes in the popular estimate of Sophists and Sophistry. The first and most obvious sentiment which Sophistry evoked was an enthusiastic and admiring interest. The Sophist seemed to his admiring hearers to open new fields of intellectual activity and thereby to add a fresh zest to existence. But in proportion to the fascination which he exerted upon the young was the distrust which he inspired in their less pliable elders. Not only were they dismayed by the novelty of the sophistical teachings, but also they vaguely perceived that it was subversive of the authority of the parent over the child as well as the authority of the state over the citizen. Of the two conflicting sentiments, the favor of the young, gaining as years passed away, naturally prevailed; Sophistry ceased to be novel and attendance in the lecture rooms of the Sophist came to be thought not less necessary for the young than attendance in the elementary school for boys. The lively enthusiasm and the furious opposition which greeted Protagoras had now burned themselves out, and before long the Sophist was treated by the man of the world as a harmless, necessary pedagogue.

Certainly the rise of Sophism parallels closely the enthusiasm that attached to higher education in earlier decades of this century. And here, too, as in ancient Athens there have been conservative elements in our society who looked with deep dismay and distrust upon college professors and intellectuals in general. Thus far the parallels are indeed quite striking. But I should like to believe that there may be a happier fate in store for the future of college teaching than mere bureaucratized pedagogy.

Of course, ideally we should like to bring the functions of character-developing, information transmitting, and research back into a balanced and cohesive unity. But this ideal is likely to be attained only by rare individuals placed in very fortunate situations. I think it will probably prove most difficult to reunite the teaching and research functions. Governmental, industrial, and even institutional organizations within universities now threaten to remove serious research from the concern of the teaching professor. If this trend continues, it will seriously impair the recruitment and the intellectual development of high quality teachers. But the tendency to separation, already so clear in the physical and biological sciences, threatens to extend to the social sciences and perhaps eventually to the humanities. It will require planning, resourcefulness, and determination if these two functions are to be again creatively united, as they have been in earlier decades, in the role of the college professor.

On the other hand, I think there is a real possibility that the college professor in the future may bring once more effectively together the character-developing function and the function of transmitting facts and information. Their separation was in part fostered by the peculiar psychology that dominated American higher education from the turn of the century until quite recently. This was a psychology, formally enunciated by John Watson, that was peculiarly neglectful of the higher and more involved aspects of personality and learning. It tended to present man in general, and the educational process in particular, in a fractionated and depersonalized form. I believe that this tide of thought has spent itself and that the present body of insights concerning the nature of personality and of the educational process may restore the interpersonal relation of a teacher and a student to a focus of prime attention. It is now recognized that a kind of transference and reciprocal counter-transference may occur between teacher and student which immensely facilitate inner growth and development, both intellectual and characterological. It is now also quite widely recognized that intellectual and factual "input" may indeed have, under the proper conditions, significant influence upon the motivational and emotional fulfillment of the person.

The recombining of the informational and character-building functions will, of course, require thorough re-evaluation of certain current institutional practices. For example, however much institutions may protest to the contrary, most students see very little of their professors and then only in large classes. Conversely, under present conditions it is quite possible for a professor to teach in an American university and never know personally a single one of his undergraduate students. Partly, this is a consequence of the present fragmented and depersonalized pattern of higher education. But given the proper institutional setting, the wise and careful selection of both faculty and students, and a suitably organized program, and it is quite possible, I believe, to realize once again the effective fusion of the character-developing and informational functions.

REFERENCES

Beard, C. *The rise of American civilization.* New York: Macmillan, 1934, pp. 168 and 471.

Beard, C. *The American spirit.* New York: Macmillan, 1942, p. 335.

Beardslee, D. C., and O'Dowd, D. D. College student images of key occupations. (Paper read at American Psychological Association, Cincinnati, September, 1959.)

Bogardus, E. S. Behavior patterns of college teachers. *Sociology and social research,* 1946, **30,** 484–499.

Bousfield, W. A. Students' ratings of qualities considered desirable in college professors. *School and Society,* **51,** 1940, 253–256.

Bowman, Claude. *The college professor in America.* Philadelphia: University of Penna. dissertation, 1938.

Bulletin of American Assoc. of Univer. Professors, **40,** 1954, Report of Committee A for 1953, Academic freedom and tenure, pp. 62–79.

Caplow, T., and McGee, R. J. *The academic marketplace.* New York: Basic Books, 1958, p. 15.

Clinton, R. J. Qualities college students desire in college instructors. *School and Society,* **32,** 1930.

Commager, J. *Living ideas in America.* New York: Harper Bros., 1951, p. 582.

Gustad, J. W. They march to a different drummer: another look at college teachers. *Educ. Record.,* July, 1959.

Guthrie, E. R. *The Evaluation of teaching: a progress report.* Seattle: University of Washington Press, 1954.

Heller, O. The passing of the professor. *Scientific Monthly,* 1927, Vol. L.

Jackson, H. *Encyclopedia Britannica.* (11th ed.) 1910, **25,** p. 420.

Kelly, R. L. Great teachers. *Bulletin of Assoc. of Am. Colleges,* 1929, pp. 49–68.

Knapp, R. H., and Goodrich, H. B. *The collegiate origins of American Scientists.* Chicago: University of Chicago Press, 1952.

Lazarsfeld, P. P., and Thielens, W., Jr. *The academic mind.* Glencoe, Ill.: Free Press, 1958, p. 28.

Maslow, A. H., and Zimmerman, W. College teaching ability, scholarly activity and personality. *J. educ. Psych.,* **47,** 1956, 185–189.

Riesman, D. *Constraint and variety in American education.* University of Nebraska Press, 1956, Chapter 1 and p. 53.

Ruml, B., and Morrison, D. H. *Memo to a college trustee.* New York: McGraw-Hill, 1959.

Trabue, M. R. Characteristics of college instructors desired by liberal arts college presidents. *Bull. Assoc. of Am. Colleges,* 1950, 374–379.

8 *W. J. McKeachie*

Procedures and Techniques
of Teaching: A Survey
# of Experimental Studies

One of the hardest things for a college president to explain to a layman is his faculty's teaching load. When the layman learns that the college professor teaches only six to fifteen hours a week, he is aghast.

Most state university faculty members are familiar with the apocryphal story of the rural legislator who, while visiting the state university, asked a professor "What's your teaching load?" The professor answered, "Twelve hours." The legislator somewhat surprised but well-pleased said, "Well that's certainly a good day's work. I don't see how we could expect any more."

In explaining how his professors spend their time, the college president is well-prepared to argue the importance of scholarship, student advising, and the other activities of the professor. But despite the importance of these other duties the professor's primary role is that of teacher, and the hours he spends in the classroom are, for the average professor, the most important of the week. Teaching is the heart of higher education. The effectiveness of administrative organization or

Note. The author gratefully acknowledges the able assistance of Mrs. Virginia Lickey, in compiling the bibliography upon which this chapter is based. Portions of the literature survey were carried out in connection with projects supported by the Lilly Endowment, the Ford Fund for the Advancement of Education, and the U.S. Office of Education.

of curricular plans depends upon whether they facilitate good teaching.

The ultimate criteria of effective teaching are changes in students, in the direction of the goals of higher education. Thus research on college teaching begins with the consideration of institutional objectives and the goals of courses. Although it is not appropriate to discuss the goals of higher education here, it is important to note that attitudinal and emotional changes are usually listed, as in Chapter 2, along with more obvious cognitive goals of critical thinking and broad knowledge. Thus in evaluating the effectiveness of college instruction we need to consider not only the accumulation of knowledge but also the development of problem-solving skills and of desirable attitudes.

Seldom do we ask ourselves, "What do I contribute to the educational process?" We make assignments, lead discussions, reflect student comments, give and correct tests—all with the faith that they contribute to education. Is our faith justified? Is each activity important and worthwhile? Does it matter which methods we use? This chapter reviews the evidence bearing on these questions.

PRINCIPLES OF LEARNING RELEVANT TO METHODS OF TEACHING [1]

Let us first review briefly some principles of learning.

Motivation. We know that student learning and memory are closely tied to *motivation*. Students will learn what they want to learn and will have great difficulty in learning material in which they are not interested. Much as we would like to teach only students who are eager to learn, most of us have to recognize that not all students are deeply interested in everything we like to teach.

One of our primary problems, therefore, is motivating students. Usually the psychologist interested in learning stops with this point, but to be useful the principle of motivation needs to be accompanied by information about dependable motives of college students. We know, for example, that most of our students are taught by their parents to want to do well in school. Thus we can count on some motivation for achievement. We know, too, that most of our students want to be liked. This motive may work against us as well as for us. In some colleges students who want acceptance by their classmates may

---

[1] Portions of this section are based upon McKeachie, W. J., How Do Students Learn? in Cooper, R. (Ed.). *The two ends of the log.* Minneapolis: University of Minnesota, 1958, pp. 26–39.

avoid any conspicuous display of academic achievement. Many students suffer from real conflict between the need to get good grades and the need to be well-liked.

Many of our students have conflicting motives. One common conflict is between independence and dependence. This means that students are likely to resent the teacher who directs their activities too closely, but they also are likely to be anxious when given independence. As a result of this conflict some students disagree with the teacher not from any rational grounds but simply as a way of expressing emotions.

Many other important needs of students are discussed in other chapters. Our point here is simply that these provide the tools by which we get learning to take place, and as far as learning or retention is concerned, it does not seem to matter much which motives one uses—the important thing is that motivation exists and that conflicts do not become too serious.

Let us consider the case of our most important motivational device —grades. If a student is really interested in learning, grades represent an expert's appraisal of his success; if he is interested in getting into professional school, good grades are the key that will unlock graduate school doors; if he wants to play football, grades are necessary for maintaining eligibility. Most students are motivated to get passing grades, if only to remain in college.

Most professors are a little embarrassed by this state of affairs. We regard grades as one of the necessary evils of teaching. We try to discount grades in our discussion of the organization of the course, and try to arrive at grades in such a way that we can avoid trouble with disappointed students. But we frequently fail to use grades to bring about the sort of learning we desire.

Because grades are important to them, students will learn whatever is necessary to get the grades they desire. If we base our grades on memorization of details, students will memorize the text. If they believe our grades are based upon their ability to integrate and apply principles, they will attempt to do this.

A good deal of evidence has accumulated to suggest that negative and positive motives affect behavior differently. When negative motives predominate, students will work hard, but only if this is the only way to avoid undesirable consequences. The result frequently is that students do the least they can get away with.

Negative motives are not as effective outside the learning situation as are positive ones because fear is a more effective motivational device if the threatened danger is close than if it is distant. Thus the teacher who motivates his students by fear of bad grades or of reprimands needs to use frequent tests if his threats are to be effective.

The striking difference in behavior between the student motivated by fear and the student motivated by hope is illustrated in their behavior during examinations. A study by Atkinson and Litwin (1960) showed that male students who were high in anxiety about tests were among the first to complete the course examination and tended to do more poorly on the examination than in their work during the course. Students with positive motivation to succeed tended to stay in the examination room longer. This illustrates the tendency of the fearful person to avoid the situation that arouses his anxiety.

In sum, motivation is important in learning, and grades can be used as either positive or negative incentives.

Organization. A teacher's job is not done when he interests his class, for the amount they learn depends upon the amount he teaches, and this is not so simple as it may at first appear. It may well be that the *more* we teach the *less* our students learn! Several years ago several of our teaching fellows in psychology were arguing about how to teach about the nervous system. One group argued that since students would not remember all of the details, we might better omit them and teach only the basic essentials that we wanted everyone to learn. Another group argued that students would forget much of what they learned; "But," they said, "if they are going to forget a large percentage, we need to teach much more than we expect them to remember."

The combatants agreed that they would try their ideas in their own classes, and compare the results on the final exam questions covering the nervous system. The outcome was clear. The students whose instructor had omitted details were clearly superior to those whose instructor had given them the whole story. This result would not have surprised David Katz (1950), whose experiments demonstrated that, beyond a certain point, adding to the elements in an intellectual task causes "mental dazzle."

Fortunately, it is possible to teach more and have it remembered better. The magic formula is "organization." As Katona (1940) demonstrated experimentally, we can learn and remember much more when our learning fits into organization. Teaching that helps students find a framework within which to fit new facts is likely to be much more effective than teaching that simply communicates masses of material in which the student can see no organization. The ideal class would begin with a problem that was so meaningful that the students were always just a step ahead of the teacher in approaching a solution.

Variability and verbalization. Another group of objectives goes to the heart of the traditional intellectual objectives of education. How can we help students develop principles and concepts that they can apply much more broadly than to answer a problem requiring only a memorized answer? All teachers have been disheartened by having a student answer a routine problem perfectly and then fail to use the same knowledge in solving another problem where it is relevant. There have been a number of educational attempts to solve this problem. The theory of "learning by doing" was that if one learned something in the situation where the learning was to be used one would not have the added step of learning when to apply it. This makes sense psychologically, but the problem is that the number of situations in which one must use knowledge is infinite. Our whole civilization is based on the fact that man can use words to short-cut the long process of learning by trial and error. Direct experience may be useful at certain stages of learning. If we are to learn to apply a principle in new situations, we need to develop it from experiencing specific instances in *varying* contexts. Experiments have demonstrated that repetitive drill is much less effective than varying problems in developing principles that can be applied to new situations (e.g., Wolfle, 1935). *Verbalization* can help us identify the common elements in these situations and shorten the learning process.

Feedback, contiguity, and active learning. If we expect students to learn skills, they have to practice, but practice doesn't make perfect. Practice works if the learner *learns the results* of his practice, i.e., if he receives feedback.

Feedback is most effective when it is contiguous to the response being learned. One of the chief advantages of teaching machines is that the learner finds out quickly whether his response is right or wrong.

A number of experiments demonstrate that *active* learning is more efficient than passive learning. One reason for this may be the improved opportunities for feedback in active learning. Discussion techniques may help develop criticalness because students do the thinking and there is an opportunity to check their thinking against others. But one of the dangers of "student-centered" or "nondirective" discussions is that the *results* are not apparent. Students may make comments, express opinions, and participate actively, but this does not guarantee that their opinions are any more informed at the end of a semester than they were at the beginning. Of course not all feedback has to come from the instructor, but, in order to learn, students need to test out their ideas in a situation in which the results are immediate.

Nevertheless we need to go a step beyond the principle that students learn what they practice with knowledge of results. It is not always easy to get students to practice critical thinking in the classroom. After all, the student who remains quiet in class avoids the risks of disagreement, criticism, and embarrassment. To develop critical thinking, the student must want to think.

This brings us to another category of goals of education—developing interests, changing attitudes, creating motivation. If we want to develop an interest in thinking we have to make it satisfying. A smile, a nod of encouragement, an excited, "Good. Let's follow that idea through"—these are the tools that teachers use, not only to provide knowledge of results, but also to develop the motivation to continue intellectual activity.

To develop motivation we need to pose problems that are within the range of our students' abilities. Studies of the development of achievement motivation in children indicate that parents develop this motivation by encouraging the child to do well and setting standards that the child can achieve. For the purposes of motivating students for critical thinking and of developing the ability to think critically, experience in solving problems within the student's ken is essential. This by no means implies that the student should never experience failure or criticism, but it does mean that he should be faced with problems that will, more often than not, be soluble.

A common misconception is that a student's motives are fixed. We can teach students to enjoy learning for its own sake. Although we must make use of existing motives to create initial satisfactions in learning, we need not be limited by them.

METHODOLOGICAL CAUTIONS

Before turning to the evidence on the effectiveness of methods of teaching let us also review a few methodological points. Determining which of two teaching methods is more effective looks like a simple problem. Presumably all that is necessary is to teach something by one method and then to compare the results with those obtained by teaching the same thing by another method. This is essentially the research design of many of the studies that are widely quoted as showing the effectiveness of different methods. Unfortunately there are some hidden gimmicks that enthusiasts for one method or another are likely to overlook.

Suppose, for example, that a group of students are given an opportunity to take a class taught by some method quite unusual in their college. The very fact that the method is different gives it excitement.

Sometimes the reaction may be one of enthusiasm; other times it may be one of outraged hostility. The latter reaction seems to be particularly likely when students taught by a new method know that they are competing on examinations with students taught by traditional methods. In any case it is difficult to know how much of the improvement (or loss) in learning may be accounted for by the emotional reaction to a new method and how much we can expect when the new method is routine. This "Hawthorne effect" affects not only students but also professors. How many new curricula, new courses, or new teaching methods have flowered briefly but then faded as the innovators' enthusiasm waned or as new staff members replaced the originators? Unfortunately relatively few studies have made comparisons over a period longer than one semester. As we shall see later, students who have experienced a semester of instruction by a new method (except television) are generally more likely to choose a section taught by this method than are students without previous experience. This difference in motivation, as well as added skill in the requisites of "Studentmanship" in a new method, might result in greater advantages for a new method after two or more semesters of trial than after a single semester.

A second methodological problem is that of establishing a suitable control group. In some experiments a single instructor uses both teaching methods. Here the obvious problem is that it is difficult to determine how much the instructor's own personality and skills have influenced the outcome. We can't know whether or not other teachers would obtain similar results. The obvious remedy for this defect is to persuade several professors to use both methods, but the difficulties, and the cost in energy, of this control are tremendous.

Another problem in establishing controls is that the conditions of the experiment may introduce special factors that interfere with normal results. For example, the experiment may require extensive testing, the presence of observers in the class, or other interferences with normal classroom routine. A class in which a "live" professor is talking to television cameras is probably not a suitable comparison group for classes watching the lesson on television receivers.

A third problem is that of biased sampling. According to newspaper reports, studies of educational television have demonstrated that students taking the course at home learn as much as those on campus. The obvious problem is that people who sign up for a television course and come to campus to take the exam are probably somewhat different in motivation and background from typical college sophomores. As Greenhill points out (1959), efforts to equate such groups are rarely successful.

The criterion problem. The major problem in experimental comparisons of teaching methods is the criterion problem. It is illustrated by the recent experiment of Parsons, Ketcham, and Beach (1958). In order to determine the effectiveness of various methods, they took the brave step of setting up groups in which students did not come to classes at all. The results will probably be widely reported because they are so contrary to the layman's expectations. The groups who did not come to class did *best of all* on the final examination. The catch is that the examination was based entirely upon the textbook, and as the experimenters point out, their results with the other groups suggest that the more new ideas and points of view are introduced, the less likely students are to remember what the textbook says. This points to the problem of evaluation of effectiveness. If our goal is that students remember the textbook, a test on the textbook is appropriate, but we cannot conclude that a particular method is superior in achieving all goals, if we have measured only one.

For purposes of research, a high degree of student motivation for good grades may make it very difficult to evaluate the effectiveness of two teaching procedures. Because passing or excellent grades are so important to students, they may compensate for ineffective teaching by additional study in order to pass the course examination at the level to which they aspire. Thus the effects of ineffective procedures may be masked or even misinterpreted when course examinations are used as criterion measures. When significant differences in achievement are found in an experiment, the difference may simply reflect the degree to which students in differing classes were able to find out what the examination was to be and the degree to which it would determine their course grade.

The difficulty in arriving at an overall index of teaching effectiveness is complicated by the probability that a teacher who is effective in achieving one objective of a course is not necessarily effective in achieving others. Bendig (1955), for example, found a significant interaction between instructors and tests in an introductory psychology course. Some instructors' students did particularly well on certain tests during the course but not well on other tests. Cross (1958) and McKeachie (1959) found that instructors whose students did well on an objective test in psychology were ineffective when their students' achievement was measured on an essay test designed to measure understanding and integration of the materials. In studies of teaching it is thus important to specify objectives and to use measures of each objective. Measures of retention after the end of a course would often add to one's confidence in reported differences.

Because measures of achievement have been so insensitive to differences in teaching methods, most experimenters stress the favorable reactions of students to the new method they have introduced. Although the relationship between satisfaction and learning is low, we would generally prefer, assuming equal learning between two methods, to have students leave our classes with warm feelings about their experience. Moreover, we would expect this feeling to be related to interest in learning more. When we use student satisfaction as a criterion, however, we should be aware of the fact that it is highly influenced by the role-expectations students have of college teachers. Marked deviations from these expectations almost inevitably will be rated lower than more conventional teaching behavior. Laboratory studies of problem-solving groups reveal that authoritarian leaders are rated by group members as being more efficient than democratic leaders (Haythorn, 1956). This makes sense both in terms of our expectations for leaders and also because a leader who plays an active role is almost inevitably going to be more salient in his impression on a group than a leader whose behavior is more subtle. In evaluating the reactions of students, one therefore needs to be conscious of these role-expectancies and determine what is a proper base line against which to evaluate the reactions.

RESEARCH ON METHODS OF TEACHING

Lecturing. College teaching and lecturing have been so long associated that when one pictures a college professor in a classroom, he almost inevitably pictures him as lecturing. The popularity of the lecture probably derives from a conception of the instructor's primary goal as transmitting knowledge.

Since lectures typically provide few opportunities for students to respond, there is little opportunity for students to receive feedback except through periodic tests. Delay of feedback may not, however, be a major factor in acquiring knowledge if the learner is motivated and the material is not too difficult. We would, however, expect lack of feedback to be a greater handicap if the lecturer's goal were to develop concepts or to teach problem-solving skills. There is experimental evidence that when these are the goals active participation on the part of the learner is more effective than passive listening or observing. Consequently the passive role of the student in the lecture would be expected to be a handicap in achieving these objectives.

Lecture vs. discussion. The lecture has usually been compared in effectiveness with discussion. Since discussion offers the opportunity for a good deal of student activity and feedback, it could, according to theory, be more effective than lecture in developing concepts and skills in problem solving. Since, however, the rate of transmission of information is slow in discussion classes we would expect lecture classes to be superior in attaining these objectives.

Unfortunately, although there have been many studies of the lecture as compared to the discussion or other methods, few have used independent measures of outcomes in the different cases. The results of the experimentation are generally in line with our hypotheses but are certainly not conclusive. For example, using tests of information, several experimenters have found no significant differences or slight differences in favor of the lecture (Spence, 1928; Remmers, 1933; Husband, 1951; Ruja, 1954; Eglash, 1954). In one of the earliest comparisons of lecture and discussion, however, Bane (1925) found little difference between the methods on measures of immediate recall but a significant superiority for discussion on a measure of delayed recall. In all of these experiments, the information measured by the examination could be obtained from a textbook and in only one was a discussion group smaller than thirty-five students used.

When we turn to measures of more complex outcomes, the results are somewhat different. Hirschman (1952), using a measure of concept learning, compared the effectiveness of presenting material by dictation with that of presenting written materials followed by discussion and rereading. The reading-discussion method resulted in superior ability to identify examples of the concepts presented. Barnard (1942) compared the effectiveness of a lecture-demonstration teaching method with that of a problem-solving developmental discussion in a college science course. In this experiment the lecture-demonstration method proved superior on a test of specific information but the discussion method proved to be superior on measures of problem solving and scientific attitude. Other evidence favoring discussion was the experiment of Elliott (Beardslee, Birney, and McKeachie, 1952) who found that students in his discussion groups in elementary psychology became interested in electing more additional courses in psychology than did students in a large lecture course. Similarly, Casey and Weaver (1956) found no differences in knowledge of content but superiority in attitudes (as measured by the Minnesota Teacher Attitude Inventory) for small group discussions as compared to lectures. Thus the results point to the superiority of lectures for information learning and of discussion for achieving higher level objectives.

Many universities and large colleges use a method of distributing class meetings between lectures and discussions. Other studies, by Warren (1954), Becker et al. (1958), and Klapper (1958), indicate that in courses in which the instructors must not only give information but also develop concepts, the use of both lectures and discussions would seem to be a logical and popular choice.

The chief competitor of the lecturer is not the teaching machine, television, or film, but rather a much older invention—writing. If rate of transmission of knowledge is important, a good book is hard to beat. Not only can the reader control his own rate, but the motivated, skilled reader can traverse the printed page much more rapidly than even the fastest lecturer can deliver the material. Over a generation ago Greene (1928) conducted an experiment demonstrating that college students learned as much from reading a passage as from hearing the same material in a lecture.

Although printed materials have been almost as popular as television for a much longer time, lectures have survived. Even the advent of picture-book textbooks did not dislodge the lecturer. If we had stopped to think about this, we probably would not have been surprised that dozens of researches have not had much impact upon lecturers' attitudes toward television.

Perhaps the lecturer's arguments are rationalizations, for there is little research to support them. Nevertheless psychologists may have underestimated important factors in our usual analyses of the learning situation. Because we wish to maintain good experimental controls, rate and sequence of presentation are carefully controlled in most of our experiments. The materials used are meaningless to the learner. The results lead us to stress the importance of feedback to the learner. Lecturing, however, is largely devoted to communicating meaningful materials to somewhat motivated learners. Apparently such learning can take place with relatively infrequent checks on the progress of the learner. In fact, he can to some extent obtain feedback by himself. By our experimental controls we miss the important fact that when knowledge is presented by a teacher he is able to respond to feedback from the learners. This may be an important asset of the instructor. Although films and television present material at a relatively fixed rate, an instructor can go faster or slower when he gets cues of inattention, glares, or blank confusion from his class.

The reader too can pace himself, but the inexperienced student may not be able to separate the meat of a book from the fat. Even though lecturers are slower than books, a good lecturer may be able to give his students all they need from a book in much less time than it would take them to read it.

Textbooks, films, and teaching machines must be organized to fit average students if they are to be economically feasible. The lecturer can not only plan his lecture for his own class but he can also respond to feedback from his class as he delivers it. This responsiveness to cues from the class is probably the reason that material can be covered less rapidly in "live" classes than in television classes. Because the instructor responds to feedback, his presentation may appear to be unorganized. Yet one might hypothesize that this very responsiveness may make for greater effectiveness than that of a carefully organized, inflexible presentation.

Although there is little relevant evidence from research, we would thus expect live lecturing to be most effective in situations where there is considerable variation among groups in ability, relevant background, or motivation and where flexible adjustment to the group is thus important.

Most lecturers avow aims beyond transmission of information. College instructors often say that they provide the integration lacking in the text. Again one would expect that other means of communication could also provide integration. Probably what the instructor really does is to provide his own system of integration. Whether or not this is preferable to integration provided by textbooks, acceptance of the frame of reference of the instructor does at least make a difference in the grade received by the student. Runkel (1956) measured the structure of instructors' and students' attitudes in beginning college courses in psychology and zoology. He found that *agreement* with the instructor's position *did not* predict students' grades, but students whose attitudes were *colinear* with the instructor *did* earn higher grades. What we do not yet know is whether or not the instructor can communicate his structure to students who do not already have it.

Probably the most careful attempts to measure attitudinal and motivational outcomes have been those comparing live instruction with television instruction in the research programs at Penn State and Miami. In neither case does the live instructor seem to be very superior. Still if the students' tendency to identify with the instructor has anything to do with personal interaction with the instructor, it may be an ominous finding that students do not seek personal conferences with television instructors as much as with "live" instructors.

Methods of lecturing. Few experiments have compared the effectiveness of classroom lectures with other teaching methods in achieving attitude change, but if we turn from classroom experiments to other research dealing with change of attitudes, we find that there is a substantial and growing literature relevant to differing techniques of lecturing.

The research of Hovland and his associates (1953) indicates that such variables as credibility of the lecturer, order of presentation, presentation of one side vs. presenting both sides of an issue, and types of argument are important in determining the effects of a lecture. For example, the Hovland group found that a group of college students were more likely to change their opinions (at least temporarily) when they received a persuasive communication from a source they considered highly credible than when the same communication came from a less credible source. Although we assume that students perceive their instructors as credible sources, faculty rating scales including an item "knowledge of subject matter" have revealed that students do discriminate between professors on this dimension. Previously I have argued against inclusion of this item on the grounds that students are not competent judges of the instructor's knowledge. Regardless of the validity of the student ratings, however, they may be a good indication of the students' credence in the instructor's statements and thus of his effectiveness in bringing about attitude changes.

In presenting controversial points the lecturer often wonders whether he should present the evidence on both sides of the issue or simply present that favoring the position he accepts. Leaving aside the ethical problems involved in this decision, the results of Yale and Army research studies indicate the greater effectiveness of presenting both sides for (1) an intelligent audience, (2) those initially disagreeing with the lecturer's position, and (3) those who come into contact with the opposing arguments.

Research on organization of materials is also relevant to lecturing aimed at cognitive changes. In organizing a lecture the professor frequently is guided by the maxim—"Tell them what you're going to tell them. Tell them. Then tell them what you've told them." In a classroom experiment in a course in physics (Lahti, 1956), the instructor started with a statement of a principle and then illustrated and applied the principle. He compared this with a technique in which he developed principles by demonstration and analysis of application situations before the principle was stated. For students with poor backgrounds the results showed the latter (inductive) method to be superior to the former method on tests of ability to apply the principles. Katona (1940) found that learning by organization results both in superior retention and in superior application when compared to learning by rote memorization.

Size of lecture classes. The monumental studies of class size conducted at Minnesota in the 1920s indicated that large classes are actually superior to small classes. Fifty-nine well-controlled experiments were reported by Hudelson (1928). The experiments involved such widely varying subject matter as psychology, physics, accounting, and law. In forty-six of the experiments results favored the large classes. Although many of the differences were not statistically significant, the majority of significant differences favored large classes. In these experiments small classes tended to be 25 to 30 students, but they ranged from 12–60 in size while large classes ranged in size from 35–150. Extreme differences in size were no more favorable to small groups than were small differences. Although most of the criterion measures were tests of knowledge, some experiments also attempted to measure higher level intellectual changes with similar results.

More recent experiments are less favorable to large classes. Rohrer (1957) found no significant differences. In experiments by Macomber and Siegel (1957, 1960), the only statistically significant differences favored the smaller classes (particularly for high ability students) on achievement tests and on measures of change in misconceptions in psychology, on a case test of problem solving in a course in marketing, and on the measures of student attitudes toward all the courses. When retention of knowledge was measured one to two years after completion of the courses, large classes did not prove to be significantly inferior to small classes in any one course. In eight of the nine courses compared, however, differences favored the small class (Siegel, Adams, and Macomber, 1960).

At Grinnell students give instructors higher ratings in smaller classes (Lovell and Hainer, 1955); at Brooklyn (Riley, 1950) and Purdue (Remmers, 1927), there is no significant difference in ratings of small and large classes generally, although Remmers reports in a controlled experiment at Purdue (1933) that the students involved preferred a small recitation to a large lecture. The weight of the evidence seems to be toward small classes if one uses student or faculty satisfaction as criterion.

We have stressed the role of the lecturer as a communicator of information. Insofar as information is a one-way process, size of group should be limited only by the audibility of the lecturer's voice. In fact, as Hudelson suggests, a large class may have sufficient motivational value for an instructor to cause him to spend more time in preparation of his lectures resulting, we would hope, in better teaching and in greater student achievement. But if the effective lecture involves some interaction between instructor and students, the large class may be inferior even for lectures, for most lecturers report that fewer students raise questions or interpose comments in large classes than in small.

If there is less participation in large classes, some of the results of the Minnesota research may suggest that we hark back to the criterion problem mentioned earlier. Let us examine the evidence more closely. Were the achievement tests used biased against teaching that introduced varying points of view? If our tests place a premium upon exact recall of the materials presented by the teacher or textbook, the student who hears other points of view may be at a disadvantage.

To sum up; lectures of large size are not generally inferior to smaller lecture classes if one uses traditional achievement tests as a criterion. When other objectives are measured, large lectures are on somewhat shakier ground but are not consistently inferior. However both students and faculty members feel that teaching is more effective in small classes. Probably of more significance than class size per se is its relation to the teaching method used. For example, one would expect class size to be of minimal relevance in television teaching, of slight importance in lecturing, but of considerable significance in discussion teaching.

Discussion methods. We have anticipated our discussion of discussion methods in the previous review of research comparing the effectiveness of lecture and discussion. We implied there that discussion may be ill-adapted for communicating information because the rate of communication from instructor to student is slow. This implication, however, should hastily be countered by pointing out that not all information must come from the instructor and, in addition, not all information is eagerly received. When information encounters intellectual or emotional resistance, discussion methods may be necessary in order to bring the source of resistance to light so that it may be treated.

Moreover if we are trying to achieve application, critical thinking, or some of the higher level cognitive outcomes, it seems reasonable to assume that students should have an opportunity to practice application and critical thinking and to receive feedback on the results. Group discussion provides an opportunity to do this. Although teaching machines may also be programmed to provide prompt feedback, a group discussion permits presentation of a variety of problems enabling a number of people to gain experience in integrating facts, formulating hypotheses, amassing relevant evidence, and evaluating conclusions. In fact the prompt feedback provided by the teaching machine may actually be less effective than a method in which students are encouraged to discover solutions for themselves with less step-by-step guidance (Della-Piana, 1956). Since problem solving ordinarily requires information, we might expect discussion to be more effective for groups with more information than for those lacking in background. Some remote support for this hypothesis is provided by a study of the learning of children in visiting a museum. Melton, Feldman, and Mason (1936) found that lectures were more effective than discussions for children in grades 5, 6, and 7, but discussions were more effective for eighth graders.

In discussing the liabilities of lecturing, I mentioned that lectures usually place the learner in a passive role and that passive learning is less efficient than active. We would expect discussions to promote more active learning, and we have some relevant evidence. Bloom and his colleagues at Chicago used recordings of classes to stimulate students to recall their thoughts during class (1953). As predicted, it was found that discussion did stimulate more active thinking than did lecture classes. Unfortunately, no one has followed this up to see in what way active thinking relates to gains in knowledge or cognitive skills.

The idea that discussion methods should help overcome resistance to learning is difficult to verify. Essentially the argument is that some desired learning encounters emotional barriers that prevent it from affecting behavior. For example, a psychology student may learn that distributed practice is effective, but not change his study methods because his anxiety about grades is so great that he does not dare try anything different. In such circumstances experiments on attitude change suggest that the instructor must either bring about changes in underlying attitude and motivation or must change the individual's perception of the instrumental relationship between his belief and his motives. Psychotherapists believe that expressing one's attitude in a nonthreatening situation is one of the steps in the process of change. A group discussion may provide such opportunities for expression as well as give opportunities for other group members to point out other instrumental relationships. Also the presence of a group is a real advantage in bringing about changes in motivation and attitudes, as Lewin showed (1952).

Student-centered vs. instructor-centered teaching. The theories of client-centered counseling and of Lewinian group dynamics have led to an increased interest in discussion techniques. A wide variety of teaching methods are described by the labels "student-centered," "nondirective," "group-centered," or "democratic," discussion. They have in common the desire to break away from the traditional instructor-dominated classroom and to encourage greater student participation and responsibility. In Table 1, I have attempted to list some of the ways in which the student-centered method has been supposed to differ from the traditional "instructor-centered" class.

Table 1. Dimensions upon Which Student-Centered and Instructor-Centered Methods May Differ

Student-Centered	Instructor-Centered
Goals	
Determined by group (Faw, 1949)	Determined by instructor
Emphasis upon affective and attitudinal changes (Faw, 1949)	Emphasis upon intellectual changes
Attempts to develop group cohesiveness (Bovard, 1951)	No attempt to develop group cohesiveness
Classroom Activities	
Much student participation (Faw, 1949)	Much instructor participation
Student-student interaction (McKeachie, 1951)	Instructor-student interaction
Instructor accepts erroneous or irrelevant student contributions (Faw, 1949)	Instructor corrects, criticizes, or rejects erroneous or irrelevant student contributions (Faw, 1949)
Group decides upon own activities (McKeachie, 1951)	Instructor determines activities
Discussion of students' personal experiences encouraged (Faw, 1949)	Discussion kept on course materials
De-emphasis of test and grades (Asch, 1951)	Traditional use of tests and grades
Instructor interprets feelings and ideas of class member when it is necessary for class progress (Axelrod, 1955)	Instructor avoids interpretation of feelings
Reaction reports (Asch, 1951)	No reaction reports

From the standpoint of theory, student-centered teaching in its more extreme forms might be expected to have some serious weaknesses, at least in achieving lower-level cognitive goals. With the instructor's role as information giver reduced, his role as source of feedback virtually eliminated, his opportunity to provide organization and structure curtailed, it is apparent that a heavy burden falls upon the group member to carry out any of these functions that are necessary. We would expect that these functions could best be assumed by groups that not only have some background experience in the academic discipline involved but also have had experience in carrying out these functions in "democratic" groups.

Since student-centered teaching attempts to reduce dependence upon the instructor, it would be expected to diminish his influence as a prestige figure, and consequently the instructor's power to bring about attitudinal changes might be reduced. However, in terms of our earlier discussion this may be more than compensated for by increased freedom of expression and increased potency of group norms as sources of influence. Participation in discussion gives students an opportunity to gain recognition and praise which should, according to learning theory, strengthen motivation. Some support for this comes from Thistlethwaite's (1960) finding that National Merit Scholars check as one of the outstanding characteristics of the teachers who contributed most to their desire to learn, "allowing time for classroom discussion." Other characteristics mentioned included "modifying course content to meet students' needs and interests," "treating students as colleagues," and "taking a personal interest in students." In line with our earlier discussion of feedback, another trait mentioned was "providing evaluations reassuring the student of his creative or productive potentialities."

The advocates of student-centered or group-centered teaching also introduce another category of objectives, not usually considered in traditional classes. This is the goal of developing skills in group membership and leadership.

Since student-centered teachers often stress group cohesiveness, a possible explanation for the contradictory results in the experiments to follow may be found in the studies of group cohesiveness and productivity in industry (e.g., Seashore, 1954). These studies indicate that it is not safe to assume that a cohesive group will be a productive one. Cohesive groups are effective in maintaining group standards, but may set either high or low standards of productivity. Since cohesive groups feel less threatened by management than less cohesive groups, it may be difficult to change their standards. With this as an introduction let us review the experimental attempts to demonstrate the effectiveness of student-centered teaching.[2]

Faw (1949) studied a class of 102 students which met two hours a week to listen to lectures and two hours a week in discussion groups

[2] Much of the following material on student-centered discussion is based on Birney and McKeachie (1955) and is used with the permission of the American Psychological Association.

of 34. One of the discussion groups was taught by a student-centered method, one by an instructor-centered method, and one group alternated between the two methods. Scores on the objective course examination based on the textbook showed small but significant differences favoring the student-centered method.

In a very similar experiment Asch (1951), like Faw, taught all the groups involved in his experiment. Three sections of about 30 to 35 students were taught by an instructor-centered method, half lecture —half discussion. One section of 23 students was taught by a nondirective method, quite similar to that of Faw. There were, however, certain differences between Faw's and Asch's experiments. In Faw's experiment both student-centered and instructor-centered classes also spent two hours a week listening to lectures. Although Faw does not mention grading, one assumes that grades were determined by the instructor on the basis of the coursewide examination. In Asch's experiment, students in the student-centered class were allowed to determine their own grades.

Asch's results do not completely agree with Faw's. On the final examination in the course, students in the instructor-centered class scored significantly higher than members of the student-centered class, not only on the objective portion of the test, but also on an essay portion. Note, however, that the student-centered class was specifically told that this examination would in no way affect their grades in the course, and the two groups were thust probably not equivalent in motivation. As measured by the Bogardus Social Distance scale, attitude change in the two sections was not significantly different. As compared with the instructor-centered class, a greater percentage of members of the student-centered class improved in adjustment as measured by the Minnesota Multi-Phasic Inventory.

Following the model of Lewin, Lippitt, and White's (1939) study of authoritarian, democratic, and laissez faire group climates, the staff of the University of Michigan's general psychology course set up an experiment using three styles of teaching: recitation, discussion, and group tutorial (Guetzkow, Kelly, and McKeachie, 1954). As compared to discussion and tutorial methods, the more autocratic recitation method not only produced superior performance on the final examination, but also produced greater interest in psychology, as measured by the election of advanced courses in psychology. Furthermore, students liked the recitation method better than the other methods. The greater gains in knowledge produced by the recitation method fits in with the general principle that feedback aids learning, for students in the recitation sections had weekly or semiweekly quizzes.

McKeachie (1951) suggests that the popularity of this method is related to student anxiety about grades, which is most easily handled when students are in familiar, highly structured situations. Another factor in these results may be the inexperience of the instructors involved, most of whom had had less than a year of previous teaching experience.

Landsman (1950) experimented with a student-centered type of teaching as contrasted with a more direct type of democratic discussion organized around a syllabus. His experimental design involved eight classes in a course sequence of "Human Development," "Adjustment," and "Learning." Three instructors took part in the experiment, and each instructor used both methods. Outcome measures included a variety of personality measures and results showed no significant difference, between methods, on any of them.

Johnson and Smith (1953) also found no significant difference between small "democratic" and large lecture classes in achievement test scores. Bills (1952), Jenkins (1952), D. E. P. Smith (1954), Maloney (1956), Slomowitz (1955), Deignan (1955), and Krumboltz and Farquar (1957) also found no difference in achievement but most did find greater student satisfaction or motivation in classes taught by student-centered methods.

In an attempt to teach critical thinking, Lyle (1958) used a problem-oriented approach as compared with conventional lecture-discussion-text procedures. He apparently found that the conventional group was superior to the problem-oriented group in achievement. Gains in critical thinking were not greater in the problem-centered classes. When students were asked to write a question for the final examination, the conventional group wrote factual questions and the problem-centered group wrote thought questions.

Instead of attempting to control the instructor personality variable by forcing instructors to teach both instructor-centered and student-centered classes, Wispé (1951) selected instructors who were rated as naturally permissive or directive. He found no difference in final examination scores between students taught by different methods. Students preferred the directive method, and the poorer students gained more in directive classes.

As a counterpoint to Wispé's study with teachers using their preferred method we have Haigh and Schmidt's experiment (1956) in which students were given their choice of group-centered or instructor-centered teaching. The results showed no difference in the achievement of the two groups on a nongraded test.

One of the few studies supporting instructor-centered teaching is that of Burke (1956). In a freshman orientation course he found student performance in classes of 125 to be superior to that of students in 4 to 7 man cooperative groups. Moreover, this difference generalized to other courses. On the other hand Moore and Popham (1959) report that three student-centered interviews with students produced greater gains on the College Inventory of Academic Adjustment than did three content-centered interviews conducted outside of class in an educational psychology course.

Although scores on objective final examinations seem to be little affected by teaching method, there are, in addition to the changes in adjustment reported by Asch (1951), Faw (1949), Zelény (1940), and Moore and Popham (1959), other indications that student behavior outside the usual testing situation may be influenced in the direction of educational goals by student-centered teaching. The classes compared by Bovard (1951a and b) and McKeachie (1951) differed in the degree to which interaction between students was encouraged and in the degree to which the class made decisions about assignments, examinations, and other matters of classroom procedure. Like other experimenters, Bovard and McKeachie found that the groups did not differ in achievement as measured by the final examination. But two clinical psychologists evaluated recordings in the class discussions which followed the showing of the film, "The Feeling of Rejection." Both clinicians reported that the "group-centered" class showed much more insight and understanding of the problems of the girl in the film.

Patton (1955) believed that an important variable in group-centered classes was the students' acceptance of responsibility for learning. In his experiment, he compared traditional classes to two classes in which there were no examinations, no lectures, and no assigned readings. Students in the experimental classes decided what reading they would do, what class procedure would be used, what they would hand in, and how they would be graded. At the end of the course, these classes, as compared to the control group, (1) felt that the course was more valuable, (2) showed greater interest in psychology, and (3) tended to give more dynamic, motivational analyses of a problem of behavior.

But giving students power cannot work if students will not accept responsibility; so Patton also obtained individual measures of acceptance of responsibility within the experimental classes. As hypothesized, he found that the degree to which the student accepted responsibility was positively correlated with gain in psychological knowledge, gain in ability to apply psychology, rating of the value of the course, and interest in psychology.

Although the Pyramid Plan at Pennsylvania State University (Carpenter, 1959; Davage, 1958, 1959) included several departments, it may be represented by a description of the experiments in psychology. Each "Pyramid Group" of psychology majors consisted of six freshmen, six sophomores, two juniors, who were assistant leaders, and a senior who was group leader. The group leaders were trained by a faculty supervisor. One control group consisted of students who simply took pretest measures; another control group received comparable special attention by being given a special program of lectures, films, and demonstrations equal to the time spent in discussion by the Pyramid groups. The results on such measures as attitude toward psychology, knowledge of the field of psychology, scientific thinking, use of the library for scholarly reading, intellectual orientation, and resourcefulness in problem solving were significantly favorable to the Pyramid plan. Moreover a follow-up study showed that more of the Pyramid students continued as majors in psychology.

Gibb and Gibb (1952) have reported that students who were taught by their "participative-action" method were significantly superior to students taught by traditional lecture-discussion methods in role flexibility and self-insight. "The instructor, who played a constantly diminishing role in the decisions and activities of the groups gave training in role playing, group goal setting, problem centering, distributive leadership, evaluation of individual performance by intra-group ratings, process observing, and group selection, evaluation and revision of class activities." Gibb and Gibb also found that in nonclassroom groups the participative-action students were rated higher than other students in leadership, likableness, and group membership skills. DiVesta's results (1954a) tend to support this finding, and Anderson and Kell (1954) report that student-centered groups are characterized by positive attitudes toward themselves as participants.

Although McKeachie (1954a) reported significant changes in attitudes of students toward Negroes and toward the treatment of criminals, differences between leader-centered and group-centered classes were not significant. However, group decision did, as predicted, produce more accurate perception of the group norm and more conformity to the norm than lecture or discussion without decision. Wieder (1954) found that a nondirectively taught psychology class tended to produce more reduction in prejudice than conventional classes.

Student-centered teaching: conclusions. The results of the research on student-centered teaching methods are not impressive, but tend to support the theory with which our discussion began. We had suggested that student-centered methods might be ineffective in achieving lower-order cognitive objectives. There seem to be few instances of such a loss. Students apparently can get information from textbooks as well as from the instructor. The possible advantages of student-centered instruction in achieving the goal of application of concepts is supported by the experiments of Bovard, McKeachie, Patton, Carpenter, and Davage. The theory that student-centered teaching is effective in producing noncognitive changes is supported by the experiments of Popham and Moore, Faw, Asch, and Gibb and Gibb. Finally, the only experiment in which group membership skills were measured (Gibb and Gibb) did find the group-centered students to be superior.

Factors affecting effective discussion teaching

BUZZ SESSIONS. One of the popular techniques for achieving student participation in groups is the buzz session (McKeachie, 1956b). In this procedure classes are split into small subgroups for a brief discussion of a problem. Although many teachers feel that this technique is valuable as a change of pace or as a way of getting active thinking from students, little research has tested its effectiveness. Vinacke (1957) found that, as compared with performance on a pretest, students in two and three-man groups wrote more new ideas after a five-minute discussion than did students working alone. However, it is possible that similar changes could have been produced by a general discussion or a lecture.

LEADERSHIP. Laboratory and field studies of group processes may shed some light on factors that condition the effectiveness of groups and which thus may help account for the lack of effectiveness of many discussion classes. For example, one of the problems faced by the discussion leader is the student who dominates discussion or the clique who carry the ball. Research suggests that effectiveness of group problem solving depends upon the leader's ability to obtain a hearing for minority opinion (Maier and Solem, 1952).

Some student-centered teachers have assumed that all decisions should be made by the group. Hence the instructor should not determine objectives, make assignments, or give tests, but should ask the group to make these decisions. If the group does this, can the time lost from academic work in making decisions be compensated for by the increased motivation of the students? The general question of the areas in which the instructor should make decisions is one that different instructors have answered in different ways, and one well worth further discussion and research. One hunch based on research on business conferences is that the instructor should make most procedural decisions, leaving the class time for problems related to the content of the course (Heyns, 1952).

Even in discussion of course content, however, it appears that some direction by the instructor may be useful if the goals are the learning of relationships and the ability to apply this learning. In an experiment comparing groups given more vs. less instructor direction in discovering the basis of solutions of verbal problems, Craig (1956) found that the directed group not only learned faster but retained their learning better than the group given less help. This result is supported by Corman's research on guidance in problem solving (1957).

Studies of business conferences have also found that one of the most common causes of dissatisfaction is the member's failure to understand the purpose of the conference. When students have confusion about purposes of teaching procedures and this is coupled with the stress involved in getting a good grade, it is little wonder that the student with a high need for achieving success is frustrated and often aggressive in a democratic class. Bloom's studies of student thought processes in Chicago classes show that on the average 30% of the student's time in discussion classes is spent in thinking about himself and other people as compared with 18% of the time in lectures. With members of the group thus concerned about their own needs, it is no wonder that discussion groups are not always productive.

GRADING. Another important problem in conducting student-centered (or other) classes is that of grades. Not only does the instructor control the pleasantness or unpleasantness of a good many student hours, but because of his power to assign grades he can block or facilitate the achievement of many important goals. The importance of this aspect of the teacher's role is indicated by studies of supervision in industry. In one such study it was discovered that workers were most likely to ask a supervisor for help if the supervisor did not have responsibility for evaluating his subordinates (Ross, 1956). This implies that as long as students are anxious about the grades the instructor will assign, they are likely to avoid exposing their own ignorance.

The student's anxiety about grades is likely to be raised if his instructor's procedures make him uncertain about what he must do in order to attain a good grade. For many students democratic methods seem unorganized and ambiguous. In an ordinary course the student knows that he can pass by reading assignments and studying lecture notes, but in a student-centered class he is in a course where the instructor doesn't lecture, doesn't make assignments, and doesn't even say which student comments are right or wrong. The student often doesn't know what the instructor is trying to do.

Some instructors have thought that the grade problem might be licked by using a cooperative system of grading. Deutsch (1949) found no differences in learning between students in groups graded cooperatively and those graded competitively, although the cooperative groups worked together more smoothly. Following up Deutsch's work, Haines (1959) also found no significant achievement advantages for students working cooperatively vs. those working competitively for grades. But in an experiment in which a "teamwork" class using group incentives was compared with a lecture class, Smith (1955) did not find differences in satisfaction comparable to those of Haines and Deutsch.

Complicating the problem of grading is the probability that low grades produce different effects upon different students. Waterhouse and Child (1953) found that frustration produced deterioration in performance for subjects showing high interference tendencies as measured by a questionnaire but produced improved performance for those with low interference tendencies.

Considering the importance of grading for both students and instructors, it is regrettable that there is so little empirical research. How do students learn to evaluate themselves? How do they learn to set goals for themselves? Do differing grading procedures facilitate or block such learning? Can more educational substitutes for grades be devised? To these questions, we have no answers.

SIZE OF DISCUSSION GROUP. One of the earliest experimental studies on college teaching was that of Edmonson and Mulder (1924) on class size.

This study was conducted in an education course in which there were two sections—one of 45 students, the other of 109. Both sections were taught by the same instructor in order to control the possible effect of instructor differences, and both sections used the same text and had the same tests. The method of teaching used in each section was discussion. Forty-three students in each class were paired on the basis of intelligence and past experience. This pioneer study led to the conclusion that size of class is not a significant variable in effecting student learning as measured by usual course achievement tests, although students preferred the small class (if 45 can be considered a small discussion group!).

Like the size experiments reported in our consideration of the lecture, there seems to be little theoretical reason for the choice of the sizes represented in the experiment, and there is some doubt as to whether either size is optimal for discussions. Similar results are reported, however, by Hudelson using classes of 20 and 113, and by Brown (1932). In fact using special team procedures Brown produced slightly better achievement in groups of 60 than were obtained from discussion classes of 25.

Support for small classes however comes from the studies in the teaching of French conducted by Cheydleur (1945) at the University of Wisconsin between 1919 and 1943. With hundreds of classes ranging in size from 9 to 33, Cheydleur found a consistent superiority for the smaller classes. Mueller (1924) found similar results in an experiment comparing elementary psychology classes of 20 and 40 students. A study by Schellenberg (1959) suggests that even the smallest groups in these studies may be above optimal sizes. Working with discussion groups of 4, 6, 8, and 10 students he found higher satisfaction and higher instructor grading in the smaller groups. Although Schellenberg recognizes that grades are an unsatisfactory criterion since the instructor's judgment may shift from section to section, he refers to laboratory studies of group problem solving that point to optima in the area of 4–6 person groups.

From the standpoint of theory one might expect increasing size to have two effects. One of these would be to increase the resources of the group in member knowledge, different approaches to the problem, and ability to provide feedback. The second consequence of size, however, is likely to be a decreasing ability to exploit the total resources of the group because of the difficulty in obtaining contributions from everyone. Furthermore, with increasing size group members are likely to feel restraints against participation (Gibb, 1951). The consequence of increasing feelings of threat in larger groups is that group participation is increasingly dominated by a few people. In Princeton classes of 4 to 12 students, Stephan and Mishler (1952) report that increasing group size was related to increasing instructor dominance in participation. Thus group size becomes a much more relevant variable in classes taught by discussion than in those taught by lecture.

HOMOGENEOUS VS. HETEROGENEOUS GROUPING. One of the common criticisms of discussion classes is that class time is wasted either by discussion of problems, raised by the able students, that are beyond the ken of the other students or by problems, raised by poor students, that the other students feel are too elementary. One answer to such criticism is to use homogeneous groupings so that each student is discussing problems with other students of his own ability.

Recently concern about America's resources of high level talent has resulted in the proliferation of Honors Programs featuring such homogeneous classes for students with high academic aptitude and achievement. Although the logic of such programs is evident, there is little evidence that they are of educational value. In fact, one of the earliest college experiments on ability grouping showed no significant advantages for homogeneous grouping by intelligence and even a trend toward the opposite result in classes in psychology (Longstaff, 1932). Briggs (1947), on the other hand, found that special intensive seminars meeting less often than conventional classes produced greater achievement for superior students than did the conventional class. Unfortunately the seminar students volunteered and were selected by interview so that they were probably a group of higher motivation than were their controls.

Homogeneous grouping by personality proved to be ineffective in the experiment in group problem solving reported by Hoffman (1959). Comparing groups of four students who were similar in personality profiles to groups made up of dissimilar students, he found that the *heterogeneous* groups produced *superior* solutions. Hoffman accounts for this difference by suggesting that heterogeneous groups are likely to have a variety of alternatives proposed, and this permits inventive solutions.

On the other hand, in a study by Stern and Cope (Stern, Stein, and Bloom, 1956), groups of "authoritarian," "antiauthoritarian," and "rational" students in a citizenship course were segregated into homogeneous groups in which the instructor was unaware of the particular group that he was teaching. Authoritarian students in the experimental group achieved more than comparable authoritarians in conventional classes (see Chapter 21).

It is apparent that we need further analysis of what kinds of homogeneities or heterogeneities contribute to what objectives. If we omit from consideration general adjustment problems of segregated groups, the idea that one should be able to do a better job of teaching to a group of known homogeneous characteristics than to a heterogeneous group seems so reasonable that it is surprising to find little research support for it. It may be that the potential advantages of carefully planned grouping has not been realized simply because we have not yet learned optimal teaching procedures for such groups.

Laboratory teaching. The laboratory method is now so widely accepted as necessary for scientific education that it may seem heretical to ask whether laboratory experience is an effective way to achieve educational objectives. Fortunately there is evidence that laboratory instruction can be educational.

Laboratory teaching assumes that first-hand experience in observation and manipulation of the materials of a science is superior to other methods of developing understanding and appreciation. Laboratory training is also frequently used as a means of developing skills necessary for more advanced study or research.

From the standpoint of theory, the activity of the student, the sensory-motor nature of the experience, and the individualization of laboratory instruction should contribute positively to learning. But information cannot usually be obtained by direct experience as rapidly as from abstractions presented orally or by printing, and films or demonstrations may also short-cut some of the trial and error of the laboratory. Thus, one would not expect laboratory teaching to have an advantage over other teaching methods in amount of information learned. Rather we might expect the differences to be revealed in retention, in ability to apply learning, or in actual skill in observation or manipulation of materials. Unfortunately little research has attempted to tease out these special types of outcome, but studies by White (1945), Kruglak (1952), Balcziak (1953), Bainter (1955), Lahti (1956), and Burkhardt (1956) permit us to draw the general conclusion that the effectiveness of laboratory teaching depends upon the particular way in which the laboratory is taught.

Project methods and independent study. The recent interest in independent study as a means of utilizing faculty time more efficiently has brought to the fore a teaching method that has been used in some form for many years. If one of the goals of education is to help the student develop the ability to continue learning after his formal education is complete, it seems reasonable that he should have supervised experience in learning independently—experience in which the instructor helps the student learn how to formulate problems, find answers, and evaluate his progress himself. One might expect the values of independent study to be greatest for students of high ability and with a good deal of background in the area to be covered, since such students should be less likely to be overwhelmed by difficulties encountered.

Independent study programs frequently involve the execution of projects in which a student or group of students undertakes to gather and integrate data relative to some more-or-less important problem.

The results of research on the effectiveness of the project method are not encouraging. Experiments by Seashore (1928), Scheidemann (1929), Goldstein (1956), and Novak (1958), in which learning by "independent study" was compared with learning under the usual lecture-discussion-laboratory conditions failed to produce results that favored the project method.

Unfortunately, the measures of achievement used by the investigators are probably not sufficient measures of the purported objectives of project instruction. Presumably the real superiority of the project method should be revealed in measures of motivation and resourcefulness. Novak's experiment was laudable in its inclusion of a measure of scientific attitude, but neither conventional nor project classes made significant gains from the beginning to the end of the semester. Similarly, in a class in mental hygiene, Timmel (1955) found no difference in the effectiveness of the lecture and of the project methods in changing adjustment. One morsel of support comes from Thistlethwaite's (1960) finding that National Merit Scholars checked requirement of a term paper or laboratory project as one characteristic of their most stimulating course.

With the support of the Fund for Advancement of Education, a number of colleges have recently experimented with more elaborate programs of independent study. As with other comparisons of teaching methods, few differences have been found between achievement of students working independently and that of those taught in conventional classes. Moreover, the expected gains in independence have also often failed to materialize. Students taught by independent study do not always seem to develop greater ability or motivation for learning independently.

One of the most comprehensive research programs on independent study is that carried out by Antioch College (Churchill, 1957; Churchill and Baskin, 1958). The Antioch experiment has included courses in humanities, social science, and science, varying periods of independent study, and a serious attempt not only to measure cognitive and affective achievement but also to evaluate the effect of independent study upon "learning resourcefulness." In addition the Antioch staff, recognizing that not all students are ready to work independently, has planned programs of training for independent work.

The results of the experiments, however, do not point clearly to any conclusion. For example, in one experiment, independent small groups learned more subject matter in physics than students working independently as individuals. But in art, students working individually learned more than those in independent small groups. As in most experiments on teaching methods, the predominant results were "no significant difference." An exception to this may be found in various indices of student satisfaction in which several significant differences favor lecture-discussion over independent study and especially over independent small groups.

In an experiment carried out at Oberlin (McCollough and Van Atta, 1958), students in introductory science, psychology, and mathematics were required to work in small groups independently of the instructor. As in the Antioch experiment no significant differences in learning appeared either as measured by the usual achievement tests or as measured by a test of learning resourcefulness. Generally, Oberlin students seem not to have been unhappy about the independent study experience, although they indicated that they would have preferred several two-week periods of independent study to the single longer period.

Independent study experiments have varied greatly in the amount of assistance given students and in the patterning of instructional vs. independent periods. For example, merely excusing students from attending class is one method of stimulating independent study. The results of such a procedure are not uniform but suggest that classroom experience is not essential for learning. But the kinds of learning that take place out of class and in class may be different.

One of the first such studies was that of Jensen (1951). In this study four groups were compared, including one in which students were completely excused from class attendance. The results showed no difference in gains among the four groups, but those who had worked independently were more willing than other students to volunteer for further independent study. An experiment by Wakely, Marr, Plath, and Wilkins (1960) compared performance in a traditional four hours a week lecture class with that in a class meeting only once a week to clear up questions on the textbook. In this experiment the traditional classes proved to be superior. Similarly Paul (1932) found 55-minute class periods to be superior to 30-minute periods as measured by student achievement.

The results of studies in a course in child development by Parsons (1957), and Parsons, Ketcham, and Beach (1958) were more favorable to independent study. In the latter experiment four teaching methods were compared: a lecture, instructor-led discussions, autonomous groups that did not come to class, and individual independent study in which each student was sent home with the syllabus, returning for the final examination. In both the earlier and later experiments, students working independently made the best scores on the final examination, which measured retention of factual material in the textbook. There were no significant differences between groups on a measure of attitudes toward working with children.

In the 1958 experiment of these authors one group of students was made up of teachers commuting to campus for a Saturday class. The results for these students were quite different from those for resident students. In this case students in independent study performed significantly worse than other groups on the examination.

Automated techniques. The impending shortage of college teachers has sparked several hotly contested skirmishes about the virtues or vices of various techniques of teaching with devices substituting for a portion of the usual face-to-face interaction between instructors and students. Since some college faculty members are anxious about technological unemployment and resist innovations, research has often been used as a technique of infiltration rather than as a method of developing and testing educational theory.

TELEVISION.[3] The most glamourous of the newer technological aids to education is television. Before reviewing the research on teaching by television, let us consider two hypotheses that may help in analyzing the research results.

Television is not a method of instruction in the sense that discussion and lecture are methods of instruction. Rather it is a means of giving the student a clear view of the instructional situation. Therefore we would expect that (1) the relative effectiveness of teaching via television will vary depending upon the importance of being able to see clearly. For example, we would expect television to be effective when it is important for students to see demonstrations, visiting lecturers, or films, but to have little advantage when the communication is primarily verbal.

Television reduces the opportunity for students to communicate with teachers and for teachers to interact with students. We would thus expect that (2) the effectiveness of television will vary inversely with the importance of two-way communication not only for feedback to the student but also particularly for feedback to the teacher.

Research at Pennsylvania State University. Since 1954 Pennsylvania State University (Carpenter and Greenhill, 1955, 1958), with support from the Fund for the Advancement of Education, has been studying the effectiveness of courses taught for a full semester over closed circuit television. The results of this research may be used either to extoll or

---

[3] Some of this section was previously published in McKeachie, W. J., TV for college instruction. *Improving college and university teaching*, 1958, 84–89, and is used by permission of the publisher, Graduate School of Oregon State University, Corvallis, Oregon.

damn television. Essentially they indicate that there is little loss in student learning in courses taught by television as compared with courses taught conventionally. Students learned the information needed to pass examinations, and most did not object strongly to the televised classes although they preferred live instruction. Students in psychology were asked "How much they liked psychology" and "How much it contributed to their education as compared with other courses they were taking." On both counts ratings of the students in the television classes were lower than those of students who were in the same room as the instructor. The psychology students were also asked if they would like to take another semester course in psychology. About the same percentages signed up in all three types of classes, but when asked if they would prefer taking it in a large class or by television, a plurality preferred television. Although students at other colleges as well as Penn State, do not rebel at television, research findings are unusually consistent in reporting less favorable attitudes toward courses taught by television as compared with conventional classes (e.g., LePore and Wilson, 1958, Macomber and Siegel, 1960).

Factors Unimportant in the Use of Educational Television. The heading of this section would normally be "Factors Conditioning the Effectiveness of Educational Television," but the results of the research are indicated by the title chosen. The Penn State researchers investigated potentially important conditioners of television effectiveness. The results were consistently negative. For example, recognizing that instructor-student interaction is sometimes important in learning, they installed "two-way" microphone communication in the receiving rooms so that students in the receiving rooms could ask questions. (This technique has been used even more extensively at Iowa [Stuit et al., 1956] and at Case [Martin, 1957].) They found that this method of instruction was not superior to simple one-way communication, although students prefer two-way communication (Martin, Adams, and Baron, 1958). (Similar results were found in the Army's research on television instruction [Fritz, 1952].)

Another attempt to combine the value of interaction with that of television was an experiment in presenting a 35-minute television lesson followed by a discussion period of 15 minutes in each of the receiving rooms. Other students in the same course observed by means of television the 15-minute discussion conducted by the instructor with the eight students in the origination room. Still other students were allowed to leave or to study their notes. As with the other attempt to provide interaction, results showed no significant differences in test performance between students taught by each of these three methods.

A poll of students indicated that they preferred two hours of lecture per week followed by a full period of discussion to a short discussion each period.

Size of the viewing group is also not an important variable in television instruction. Neither do proctors in the viewing rooms contribute to student learning. Adapting a course for television by adding supplementary visual aids also proved to be no more effective than televised lecture-blackboard presentations. In fact both at Penn State and NYU (Adams et al., 1959) the "visual" productions tended to be *less* effective than "bare bones" television. This result should probably not startle us after having read the Parsons, Ketcham, and Beach results with independent study. Just as discussion and lecture apparently interfered with learning the textbook, so here visual materials may have distracted the students from the verbal content upon which the tests were based.

The Pennsylvania State research does provide some support for the idea that television's effectiveness is in giving the student a good view. In one experiment students who had three weeks of instruction were given their choice of whether to finish the course in television classrooms or in the originating room. Depending upon the course, one-third to two-thirds of the students chose television. The most interesting aspect of this finding was that these students were predominantly those who had been assigned seats toward the back of the lecture hall.

Research at Miami University. A second major project in closed-circuit instruction is that at Miami University (Macomber and Siegel, 1956, 1957, 1960). Miami's research is of particular interest because it compared closed circuit television both with large lecture classes and small semi-discussion classes, and because the Miami staff studied the possible differential effect of different types of instruction upon students of differing abilities and attitudes.

In Miami's first experiment, the primary measure of achievement was final examinations in each course, and the television classes were not inferior on this criterion. In fact, in "Human Biology" the television students scored higher than the conventional classes, although there were other factors that might have contributed to this difference. But in the second year of telecasting, live teaching produced greater achievement than did television in the second semester of the four courses, and in economics it proved to be superior in producing gains in critical thinking. Results of third-year experiments were less damning to television, although television classes in zoology proved inferior to conventional classes on a test of problem solving.

Since television is usually considered as a substitute for large classes, it is worth noting that large "live" classes did not consistently produce the inferior results of television in the cognitive outcomes, but did tend to be inferior to conventional classes in effecting changes in attitudes.

Other Experiments in College Teaching by Closed-Circuit Television. Among the largest and best-designed of other experiments on television teaching are those carried out at Purdue, Iowa, NYU, and San Francisco State. Although these experiments have already been cited where relevant in our discussion of the Penn State and Miami experiments, a few points remain. One of these relates to the teaching of English composition by television. Even though the Purdue experiment (Seibert, 1958) used television for only two of the three instructional periods per week and television students apparently had a good deal of practice in theme writing, television instruction proved to be significantly inferior to conventional instruction in several comparisons. The superiority of conventional teaching was most marked for the students of lower ability. NYU did not find similar differences in ability level but did find evidence of superiority of conventional methods as measured by theme writing. Similar differences favoring conventional instruction using objective tests of achievement were found during the first semester but reversed during the second semester.

Purdue also found television instruction to be inferior to conventional instruction in mechanical engineering (Seibert, 1958), military science (Kasten and Seibert, 1959), and, on some tests, in calculus (Seibert, 1958).

When a course demands the demonstration of small objects or parts, the use of television or film should be advantageous. In an experiment at Rensselaer Polytechnic (Throop, Assini, and Boguslavsky, 1958) in teaching a course called "Strength of Materials," television was not inferior to conventional methods in teaching instrumentation and specimen behavior, but was inferior in teaching theory and familiarity with machinery.

Student ability generally does not make a difference in the relative effectiveness of television. At Miami low-ability students in "Foundations of Human Behavior" and "Government" achieved more in conventional classes than in television classes. However, in physiology and zoology, low-ability students did better in television classes than in conventional classes. Although the best television instructors are liked by all types of students, the better students ordinarily dislike television and large classes more than do the poorer students. Attitudes toward television however do not greatly affect achievement. Students who dislike television achieve almost as much (or little?) as those who like it. One of the most interesting outcomes of the studies of student attitudes toward television instruction is that they tend to reflect those of the proctors in the viewing rooms.

Both in large lectures and in television sections, students complain of lack of contact with the instructor, but Miami students dislike television less than large lectures, while NYU students tend to prefer lectures. The attitudes toward television of both groups tended to become more negative during a second semester of television. (This seems to be true in several studies.) If they could have the same instructor, students would generally prefer a small section to television or a large class, but they would prefer television or a large class to a small class if they could be sure of an excellent instructor in the television or large class and had to take their chances in electing a small class. This is probably a pretty realistic alternative, although the student's choice may not always be wise, for in one of three experimental comparisons Miami graduate assistants proved to be inferior (as measured by student achievement) to regular staff members in one course and superior in another. Moreover, students taught by graduate assistants did more outside reading.

Uses of Television. From our hypothesis that television would be of most value in courses depending upon visual presentation of information we might expect it to be more effective in science and engineering courses than in social sciences and humanities courses. From our hypothesis that television would be of less value in classes where interaction between students and instructor is important, we might expect it to be relatively less effective in psychology, speech, and languages than in courses usually taught by lecture. Such comparisons are difficult to make, however. As we have seen, students learned as much by television as in conventional classes in chemistry at Penn State and this was also true at Purdue (Seibert and Honig, 1959), but in general psychology the television students both at Purdue and Penn State did more poorly than students in conventional classes. This evidence is in line with our assumption. Similarly, if we simply look at the direction of the differences about half the experiments in science classes favor television and half favor conventional instruction. In nonscience courses well over two-thirds of the differences favor conventional teaching.[4]

[4] The preceding comments have been primarily concerned with closed-circuit television instruction on campus. Although it is difficult to do adequately controlled studies of the educational effectiveness of broadcast television, it seems quite clear that students motivated enough to take a television course for credit at home learn

Insofar as student-instructor interaction is important for teaching a course, television would appear to be of little help. Television does not permit more students to talk, even with two-way audio connections. It is apparent that the student's opportunity to participate is an inverse function of the number of students in the class. If actual participation is important, larger classes should be less effective whether they are taught in one classroom or by television.

One experiment compared the effectiveness of teaching equal-size groups (Cutler, McKeachie, and McNeil, 1958) in face-to-face groups and by telephone. Both groups showed significant learning and attitude change and there was no significant difference in the two methods' effectiveness. Experiments using radio as a communication medium also report learning equal to that of face-to-face instruction. Thus if economy in instruction is desired, perhaps the expense of television cameras and receiving tubes is unnecessary. One of the few experiments comparing the effectiveness of radio and television, however, showed better learning and retention for television (Paul and Ogilvie, 1955).

Television can, however, have certain *advantages* in promoting interaction. On any large college campus one of the difficulties in education outside the classroom is that students have few common educational experiences. Since their common experiences tend to be social or athletic, these are likely to be the usual topics of conversation. Stephens College (1955) met this problem in a creative way by developing a required course—"Ideas and Living Today"—which consists of brief lectures viewed by students in small faculty-led discussion groups. The course has craftily been scheduled just before lunch so that discussions spill over into the dining halls.

It seems safe to conclude that television instruction is inferior to classroom lectures in communicating information, developing critical thinking, changing attitudes, and arousing interest in a subject but that this inferiority is probably not great. Although differences favoring conventional teaching appeared in about two-thirds of the studies reviewed, only a fifth of the differences were statistically significant. One's view of these results depends a good deal upon one's bias toward or against television. When compared with research comparing other instructional methods, the consistency of results favoring conventional instruction over television is unusual. However, when one weighs heavily the necessity for accommodation of higher education to large

well and have favorable attitudes toward television (LePore and Wilson, 1958; Dreher and Beatty, 1958; Evans, Roney, and McAdams, 1954).

numbers of students, the differences between television and conventional instruction seem small.

FILMS. The great mass of research on instructional films is relevant to our topic, even though most of it has not been concerned with college teaching. Although it would be impossible for us to summarize all of the relevant studies, certain principles have emerged. (For a more complete analysis, see Miller, 1957.)

1. Students can learn from films, and usually do learn at least as much as from a poor teacher (VanderMeer, 1950).

2. Such learning is not confined to details, but may include concepts and attitudes (Kishler, 1950; Mertens, 1951; Hoban and Van Ormer, 1950).

3. Repeating the film increases learning (McTavish, 1949).

4. Students learn how to learn from films; i.e., students with previous experience in learning from films learn more than those with no previous experience with instructional films (VanderMeer, 1951).

5. Presenting pictures is more effective than presenting words as stimuli in rote association tasks such as learning a foreign language (May and Lumsdaine, 1958; Kopstein and Roshal, 1954).

6. Participation increases learning (Hovland, Lumsdaine, and Sheffield, 1949).

Much of the preceding discussion of instructional television is also relevant to teaching by films. The chief differences seem to be in the greater mobility of movie cameras than of television cameras, the greater expense of producing a film than a television lesson (assuming that the television equipment is already available), and the presumed greater immediacy of "live" television. Unfortunately, we have very little evidence on the educational importance of immediacy. Intuitively it would seem that students would feel more involvement in watching a television professor on their own college's staff knowing that they are seeing him at the actual moment of performance than they would feel in watching a film made at some earlier time. Whether or not such differences in involvement do occur (and if they occur whether it makes any difference educationally) is still unknown.

TESTS AND TEACHING MACHINES. Although we usually think of tests in terms of their validity as measures of student achievement, it may be that their function as instruments for promoting learning is even more important. After dismal recitals of nonsignificant differences between differing teaching methods, it is refreshing to find positive results from variations in testing procedures.

In some of the earliest experiments in this area Jones (1923) found that immediate testing after a psychology lecture resulted in improved retention. The good effects of testing persisted or increased over an eight-week period.

Jones' results supporting the value of immediate feedback are supported by an experiment in a government class (Fitch et al., 1951) in which students having weekly noncredit quizzes made better scores on monthly tests than a nonquizzed control group. Similarly in a remedial English course at Purdue (Maize, 1954) students who wrote forty themes evaluated in class made greater improvement on a test of English usage than did a group that had workbook drill and wrote fourteen themes, individually corrected by the instructor. Similar results were reported earlier in the study of Guetzkow, Kelly, and McKeachie. May and Lumsdaine (1958) report that learning from film is also positively influenced by participation and feedback devices.

Tests provide knowledge of results, one of the major elements in learning, and we would expect that the more information contained in the knowledge feedback, the greater its value. In an experiment in the air force (Stone, 1955), performances benefited from return of multiple-choice tests with information about why the alternative chosen was wrong as well as why the correct alternative was right. This technique proved superior to four other techniques giving less complete knowledge of results ranging down to returning only a score on the total examination. Similar results were obtained by Bryan and Rigney (1956). In a related study McKeachie and Hiler (1954) found that students required to answer study questions performed better on test questions in the same area than did students not given the questions, and that the former also tended to do better than those whose answers were not required or graded. Thus the simple principle that knowledge of results facilitates learning is one of the few generalizations clearly supported by research on college teaching.

The bridge from tests to "automation" is found in the work of Pressey (1926, 1950) who has published the results of an extensive program of research with tests that students score for themselves by punching alternatives until they hit the correct one. Four types of studies were carried out, and Pressey concluded that:

. . . (a) the self-scoring characteristics represent a tremendous saving in time; (b) test taking is transformed into self-instruction by the immediate knowledge of mistakes; (c) supplemental use of the tests improves performance on regular objective tests; and (d) even more automatic self-scoring devices can be devised. This last conclusion proved to be prophetic for there is now a large number of models of "teaching machines."

The teaching machine is a device for presenting questions in predetermined sequences and providing immediate knowledge of results to an active learner. Teaching machines permit the learner to proceed at his own rate. The successive questions proceed in tiny steps from the simple to the complex. If a student makes a series of correct responses he may adjust the machine to skip some steps. If he fails items, they are repeated. The program of the lesson may include hints or other guidance. Thus teaching machines or workbooks have many theoretical advantages over lecturing or other conventional methods of instruction. Unfortunately, there has been little experimental work at the college level to determine the limits of their machines' usefulness. Among the studies supporting their use are those of Angell (1949), Little (1934), and Stephens (1953). Presently, a good deal of developmental work is going on, directed not only at the basic problem of devising appropriate sets of items but also at development of machines flexible enough to adjust to individual differences in the background and ability of the learners. As we pointed out earlier, one of the greatest advantages of the skilled teacher is his ability to utilize feedback in adapting his teaching to individual and group differences. Moreover, the instructor often provides feedback that not only tells the learner that he is wrong but also tells him how he went wrong. Experiments at the Systems Development Corporation (Coulson, 1959; Coulson and Silberman, 1959, 1960) suggest that teaching incorporating such human characteristics is more effective than the typical fixed-sequence machines. (In this experiment instead of using teaching machines to simulate human teachers, the experimenters used humans to simulate teaching machines!)

PRINTING. One substitute for the live teacher has been around for some time and unlike other technological aids has found wide acceptance by college faculties. Perhaps a few centuries of use will produce the same degree of acceptance of television and teaching machines. Despite the antiquity of printing as a technique device, there is relatively little research on its use. An early study is that of Greene (1928), who found that students learned as well from reading material as from listening to the same material read aloud. The better students, however, profited more from reading than from listening. Corey (1934) found better immediate recall for reading than for a lecture although the difference disappeared on a test later.

One of the newest developments in textbook construction is the "programmed textbook," an instructional book developed by utilizing the learning-in-small-steps sequence of the conventional teaching machines (Glaser and Homme, 1958). It seems entirely reasonable that books designed specifically to achieve specified objectives could be more effective than present textbooks. Unfortunately, we are probably better able to devise sequences optimal for cognitive learning than we are to devise sequences optimal for arousing and maintaining motivation. Information obtained by research on teaching-machine programs should be valuable to the textbook writer, but so far the art is not so well perfected that we can write textbooks on computers.

AUTOMATION: A SUMMARY. The research to date indicates that television, films, teaching machines, and books can be used to achieve educational objectives. Their usefulness varies depending upon the objective, the characteristics of the students, and the excellence of their materials. Research at present reveals no danger that these devices will eliminate the need for face-to-face contacts between professors and students.

STUDENT CHARACTERISTICS RELATED TO EFFECTIVE TEACHING

Our concern that opportunities for individualized instruction be protected is related to an awareness that differences between students are inadequately cared for by our usual teaching methods. Experienced teachers have felt for years that no single teaching method succeeds with all kinds of students. It is possible that one of the reasons for the host of experimental comparisons resulting in non-significant differences is simply that methods optimal for some students are detrimental to the achievement of others. When mean scores are compared, one method thus seems to be no different in its effect from any others.

We have already noted some analyses of teaching methods taking such individual differences into account. For example, Guetzkow, Kelly, and McKeachie found that students differing in intelligence or in preferences for teaching methods were not differently affected by three methods of teaching. Hudelson found similar results in his studies of class size. Macomber and Siegel's results are not in strong opposition to this, but they do reveal a tendency for high ability students to gain more in course related attitudes in small rather than large sections. They also report a small superiority in achievement in television or large classes for those who hold favorable attitudes toward the method used. However, other personality measures did not prove predictive of differential achievement in large and small classes. Ward's (1956) results also suggest that the ablest students benefit most from small groups. Calvin, Hoffman, and Harden (1957) found in three experiments that less intelligent students consistently did better in group problem-solving situations conducted in an authoritarian manner than in groups conducted in a permissive manner. The same difference did not occur for bright students. The experimenters suggest in a footnote that the inferior performance of dull students in permissive groups may be due to an inferior ability to adjust to a change from the usual methods of conducting groups. If this were true, we should expect brighter students to adjust more easily to new methods than less intelligent students. So far this has not been demonstrated although the trends reported seem to be in that direction. For example, in the Miami experiment students of high ability did as well in television classes as conventional classes despite the fact that these students had more negative attitudes toward television than did less able students.

The analysis of student characteristics in studies such as those above is laudable, but except for the last study the analysis of individual differences was largely peripheral to the main purpose of the studies and was undertaken with little theoretical basis for any hypothesis to guide the research analysis. As focus shifts to the characteristics of students, one would hope for research designs in which variations in the teaching method bear some theoretical relationship to important dimensions of individual differences or where the student characteristics studied are chosen because of their theoretical relationships to the teaching methods. For example, if we are going to investigate intelligence as a student characteristic affecting learning under different teaching methods, we need to develop a more specific theory about the conditions that are differentially effective in producing learning for students of high and low intelligence; and similarly for students who are independent or authoritarian or prone to anxiety, and for students of different sexes or value-orientations—to name a few characteristics that might influence response to different methods of teaching. Moreover, it may be presumed that the effects of variations in teaching methods not only interact with student characteristics but also with aspects of the college's culture. This problem is confronted by other contributors to this volume, particularly Brown (Chapter 16), Stern (Chapter 21), and Webster, Freedman and Heist (Chapter 24).

In summing up the studies on the interaction of personality characteristics and teaching methods as affecting student learning, it is safe to say that no major breakthrough has occurred. The results do appear promising, however. Fortunately, multivariate statistical techniques now permit precise analysis of the sort of complex interactions that appear to be involved in teaching. Although we have little data and in some studies no interaction is found (Guetzkow et al., 1954, Jenkins, 1952), it is probable that instructor characteristics and content characteristics also interact with teaching methods. For example in the Army studies of educational television some instructors proved to be more effective on television than face-to-face, while other instructors proved to be more effective in face-to-face teaching. Similarly the experiments of Russell (1951) indicate that some teachers are more effective with the abler students than with the less able ones while other instructors are more effective in teaching the poorer students. Such interactions pose exciting problems for investigation.

CONCLUSIONS: THE ROLE OF FACULTY ATTITUDES

What can we say about the work of the teacher? Clearly it is not possible to detail in a few summary statements the "best" methods of teaching. Nevertheless recent research suggests that decisions about teaching methods do have important consequences in terms of differential achievement of the differing objectives of a course, differential effects upon different types of students, and probable differential effects depending upon other factors such as the instructor, the course content, and the overall "climate" of the institution. To analyze such complexities would obviously be a task for a giant computor. In the absence of the data necessary for such an analysis, we must, as in other frontier areas, depend upon expert judgment. Most of the reports of research on teaching neglect to report the reactions of the faculty involved (except for television where reactions are generally negative). Yet, until we gain more confidence in our evaluation tools, we are almost forced to weigh faculty judgment heavily.

Faculty judgments of teaching methods, however, are extremely important even aside from their possible validity as expert judgments.

As was pointed out earlier, we seldom know how well a particular method was used in experimental studies of teaching methods, but it seems very likely that the effectiveness of a method depends upon the competence and enthusiasm of the teacher. If the teacher is important, his enjoyment of the method becomes a critical variable. Thistlethwaite (1960), finds that National Merit Scholars report that one of the critical variables influencing their choice of a field is the instructor's enthusiasm. It seems probable that such enthusiasm is unlikely to be communicated if the instructor finds teaching distasteful. Thus even though we found that a particular method when ideally used is superior to other methods, I would be dubious about urging its widespread adoption if teachers using it become bored or dissatisfied.

What are the satisfactions in teaching? Certainly one is the pleasure of seeing a student develop. Another is the pleasure of intellectual interchange with young people possessing questioning minds and fresh ideas. Perhaps a less laudable but none-the-less real satisfaction is that found in having disciples who respect and admire us. These satisfactions are difficult to secure without close sustained personal contact with students. If we are to know students well enough to see their progress, small classes are important, not only because they permit more individual interaction with students but also because they permit the instructor to use term papers, essay tests, and other evaluation methods that give him a greater understanding of what the student is thinking.

Moreover, if the satisfaction of observing student growth is important, we need to ensure opportunities for contacts between instructor and student over a period longer than a one-semester course. One of the advantages of the small college over the large university is that the student in a small college not only is more likely to come into contact with his instructor outside of the classroom but is also more likely to elect later courses from the same professor. In a community where professors know most of the students, professors are more likely to discuss students with other professors. In a large university the professor may teach a student one semester and never see him again. He is very unlikely to discuss the student with other professors because he does not know which colleagues know the student.[5]

Many professors conscientiously attend some student teas or other social functions to promote contacts between students and faculty. In the small colleges it is likely that the professor will meet at such functions some of the students he has taught, and will have an opportunity to use this contact to gain greater understanding of the students and perhaps even to stimulate their thinking. But the larger the college the less the statistical chance that he will meet students he knows at such functions; in fact, the larger the college the less the chance that he will ever meet again the student he meets at a tea. This means that even the professor who conscientiously devotes a portion of his time to such "informal" contacts with students is unlikely to have significant encounters. In short, any satisfaction received from observing and contributing to a student's growth must ordinarily come

[5] For further discussion of the size of the institution in relation to "intellectual community" see Jencks and Riesman (Chapter 22).

during the semester (or at most two semesters) that the student is enrolled in one's class. No matter how powerful one's impact, it is asking
a great deal to expect it to have great noticeable effects in sixteen
weeks.

Size of an educational institution has a very similar relationship to
the quality of education students receive from one another. The large
institution with a student body of heterogeneous background offers
students an opportunity to gain breadth, tolerance, and new perspectives from their contacts with one another. But large size is likely to
reduce educational values by reducing intellectual interchange between students. There is certainly no reason that a student at a large
college could not discuss with another student an interesting problem
raised by one of his professors. But he is probably more likely to do
so if he is living near another student who is also familiar with the
problem and concerned about it. In a large college the statistical
chances that another student in the same class will be in the same
living group are smaller than in a small college. Students in a large
college with many courses, and even many sections of the same course,
have few common intellectual experiences. Consequently it is difficult
for them to communicate about intellectual problems outside of class,
and the common concerns which become the basis of social communication are football, the student newspaper, dating, and the dormitory
food. With such barriers to interstudent education the professor misses
the good feeling one experiences when he finds that his teaching has
provided an intellectual stimulus reaching far beyond his classroom.[6]

Of course there are also satisfactions in teaching by television or in
a large class. One can gain a very satisfying sense of power from knowing that one is communicating one's ideas to a large number of students. The roar of laughter at a joke well told is music to a lecturer's
ear. The satisfaction of carrying through without interruption a well-
planned lesson is satisfying to the "Master Teacher" whose performance is televised.

Although these are valid satisfactions, they seem less directly related
to the goals of education than the satisfactions that are associated with
observing student development. What would a college be like if its
faculty were largely made up of teachers whose satisfactions were primarily those of a good performer?

As colleges increase in size in order to cope with a growing student
population, there is a natural tendency to routinize and automate educational processes, in the interest of increased efficiency. In industry,

[6] As a professor at a large university let me note that I don't consider our case
hopeless if we recognize what problems we need to solve!

assembly line methods have long been effective. Yet, in recent years, industry has found that workers are even more efficient if, instead of performing one specific, repetitive task, their jobs are enlarged enough to provide variety and interest. Although there is little likelihood that college administrators will intentionally insist upon uniform teaching methods, increasing class size indirectly limits the professor's choice of teaching methods, reducing his ability to select the methods best suited for his objectives and reducing his satisfaction in teaching.

Enjoyment of teaching is not only important for the enthusiasm that the professor communicates to his students but also in determining his interest in continued improvement. These important values are likely to be lost if teaching becomes so routinized and depersonalized that it is no longer fun. The motivated teacher is able to respond to feedback from his students in order to achieve better and better approximations to optimal solutions to the problems of teaching. As additional information from research accumulates, as better conceptualizations emerge, he should be able to do an even better job.

REFERENCES

Adams, J. C., Carpenter, C. R., and Smith, Dorothy R. (Ed.) *College teaching on television.* Washington: American Council on Education, 1959.

Anderson, R. P., and Kell, B. L. Student attitudes about participation in classroom groups. *J. educ. Res.,* 1954, **48,** 255–267.

Angell, G. W. Effect of immediate knowledge of quiz results on final examination scores in freshman chemistry. *J. educ. Res.,* 1949, **42,** 391–394.

Asch, M. J. Nondirective teaching in psychology. *Psychol. Monogr.,* 1951, **65,** No. 4 (Whole No. 321).

Atkinson, J. W., and Litwin, G. H. An experimental study of need-achievement and examination anxiety. *J. abnorm, soc. Psychol.,* 1960, **60,** 52–63.

Axelrod, J. Group dynamics, nondirective therapy, and college teaching. *J. higher Educ.,* 1955, **26,** 200–207.

Bainter, Monica E. A study of the outcomes of two types of laboratory techniques used in a course in general college physics for students planning to be teachers in the elementary grades. Unpublished doctoral dissertation. University of Wisconsin, 1955. (*Diss. Abstr.,* 1955, **15,** 2485–2486.)

Balcziak, L. W. The role of the laboratory and demonstration in college physical science in achieving the objectives of general education. Unpublished doctoral dissertation. University of Minn., 1953. (*Diss. Abstr.,* 1954, **14,** 502–503.)

Bane, C. L. The lecture vs. the class-discussion method of college teaching. *Sch. and Soc.,* 1925, **21,** 300–302.

Barnard, J. D. The lecture-demonstration versus the problem-solving method of teaching a college science course. *Science Educ.,* 1942, **26,** 121–132.

Beardslee, D., Birney, R., and McKeachie, W. Summary of conference on research in classroom processes. (Mimeo.) Unpublished manuscript, Department of Psychology, University of Michigan, 1952.

Becker, S. L., Murray, J. N., and Bechtoldt, H. P. *Teaching by the discussion method.* Iowa City: State University of Iowa, 1958.

Bendig, A. W. Ability and personality characteristics of introductory psychology instructors rated competent and empathic by their students. *J. educ. Res.*, 1955, 48, 705–709.

Bills, R. E. Investigation of student centered teaching. *J. educ. Res.*, 1952, 46, 313–319.

Birney, R., and McKeachie, W. The teaching of psychology: A survey of research since 1942. *Psychol. Bull.*, 1955, 52, 51–68.

Bloom, B. S. Thought processes in lectures and discussions. *J. gen. Educ.*, 1953, 7, 160–169.

Bovard, E. W., Jr. Group structure and perception. *J. abnorm. soc. Psychol.*, 1951a, 46, 398–405.

Bovard, E. W., Jr. The experimental production of interpersonal affect. *J. abnorm. soc. Psychol.*, 1951b, 46, 521–528.

Briggs, L. J. Intensive classes for superior students. *J. educ. Psychol.*, 1947, 38, 207–215.

Brown, A. E. The effectiveness of large classes at the college level: An experimental study involving the size variable and the size procedure variable. *University of Iowa Studies in Education*, 1932, 7, 3.

Bryan, G. L., and Rigney, J. W. An evaluation of a method for shipboard training in operations knowledge. Tech. Report 18, Electronics Personnel Res. Gp., University of South California, 1956.

Burke, H. R. An experimental study of teaching methods in college freshman orientation course. Unpublished doctoral dissertation, Boston University, 1955. (*Diss. Abstr.*, 1956, 16, 77–78.)

Burkhardt, Sara M. A study in concept learning in differential calculus. Unpublished doctoral dissertation, Columbia University, 1956.

Calvin, A. D., Hoffman, F. K., and Harden, E. L. The effect of intelligence and social atmosphere on group problem solving behavior. *J. soc. Psychol.*, 1957, 45, 61–74.

Carpenter, C. R. The Penn State Pyramid Plan: Interdependent student work study groupings for increasing motivation for academic development. (Paper read at 14th Natl. Conf. on higher Educ., Chicago, March, 1959.)

Carpenter, C. R. What are the most effective methods of improving instruction, with special reference to individual work programs? In G. K. Smith (Ed.), *Current Issues in higher Educ.* Washington: Assoc. for Higher Educ., 1959, pp. 187–196.

Carpenter, C. R., and Greenhill, L. P. An investigation of closed-circuit television for teaching university courses. *Instructional Television Res.*, Project No. 1, University Park: Pennsylvania State University, 1955.

Carpenter, C. R. and Greenhill, L. P. An investigation of closed-circuit television for teaching university courses. *Instructional Television Res.*, Project No. 2, University Park: Pennsylvania State University, 1958.

Casey, J. E., and Weaver, B. E. An evaluation of lecture method and small group method of teaching in terms of knowledge of content, teacher attitude, and social status. *J. Colo.-Wyo. Acad. Sci.*, 1956, 4(7), 54.

Cheydleur, F. D. Criteria of effective teaching in basic French courses. *Bull. of the Univer. of Wisc.* August, 1945.

Churchill, Ruth. Preliminary report on reading course study. (Mimeo.) Yellow Springs, Ohio: Antioch College, 1957.

Churchill, Ruth, and Baskin, S. Experiment on independent study. (Mimeo.) Yellow Springs, Ohio: Antioch College, 1958.

Corey, S. M. Learning from lectures vs. learning from reading. *J. educ. Psychol.* 1934, **25**, 459–470.

Corman, B. The effect of varying amounts and kinds of information as guidance in problem solving. *Psychol. Monogr.,* 1957, **71**, No. 2 (Whole No. 431).

Coulson, J. E. An experimental teaching machine for research at S.D.C. *Technical Memorandum,* TM-416, Santa Monica, Calif.: System Development Corp., 1959.

Coulson, J. E., and Silberman, H. F. Results of initial experiments in automated teaching. Report No. SP-73, Santa Monica, Calif.: System Development Corp., 1959.

Coulson, J. E., and Silberman, H. F. Effects of three variables in a teaching machine. *J. educ. Psychol.,* 1960, **51**, 135–143.

Craig, R. C. Directed vs. independent discovery of established relations. *J. educ. Psychol.,* 1956, **47**, 223–234.

Cross, D. An investigation of the relationships between students' expressions of satisfaction with certain aspects of the college classroom situation and their achievement on final examinations. Unpublished honors thesis, University of Michigan, 1958.

Cutler, R. L., McKeachie, W. J., and McNeil, E. B. Teaching psychology by telephone. *Amer. Psychologist,* 1958, **13**, 551–552.

Davage, R. H. The pyramid plan for the systematic involvement of university students in teaching-learning functions. Division of Academic Res. and Services, Pennsylvania State University, 1958.

Davage, R. H. Recent data on the pyramid project in psychology. Division of Academic Res. and Services, Pennsylvania State University, 1959.

Deignan, F. J. A comparison of the effectiveness of two group discussion methods. Unpublished doctoral dissertation, Boston University, 1955. (*Diss. Abstr.,* 1956, **16**, 1110–1111.)

Della-Piana, G. M. Two experimental feedback procedures: a comparison of their effects on the learning of concepts. Unpublished doctoral dissertation, University of Illinois, 1956. (*Diss. Abstr.,* 1956, **16**, 910–911.)

Deutsch, M. An experimental study of the effects of cooperation and competition upon group processes. *Human Rel.,* 1949, **2**, 199–232.

DiVesta, F. J. Instructor-centered and student-centered approaches in teaching a human relations course. *J. Appl. Psychol.,* 1954a, **38**, 329–335.

DiVesta, F. J. The effect of methods of presentation and examining conditions on student achievement in a correspondence course. *J. Appl. Psychol.,* 1954b, **38**, 253–255.

Dreher, R. E., and Beatty, W. H. An experimental study of college instruction using broadcast television. *Instructional Television Research,* Proj. No. I. San Francisco: San Francisco State College, 1958.

Edmonson, J. B., and Mulder, F. J. Size of class as a factor in university instruction. *J. educ. Res.,* 1924, **9**, 1–12.

Eglash, A. A group discussion method of teaching psychology. *J. educ. Psychol.,* 1954, **45**, 257–267.

Evans, R., Roney, H., and McAdams, W. An evaluation of the effectiveness of instruction and audience reaction to programming on an educational TV station. *Amer. Psychologist*, 1954, **9**, 361–362.

Faw, V. A. A psychotherapeutic method of teaching psychology. *Amer. Psychologist*, 1949, **4**, 104–109.

Fitch, M. L., Drucker, A. F., and Norton, J. A., Jr., Frequent testing as a motivating factor in large lecture classes. *J. educ. Psychol.*, 1951, **42**, 1–20.

Fritz, M. F. Survey of TV utilization in Army training. *Instr. Film Res. Rep.*, Special Devices Center Offices of Naval Res., SDC 530-01-0, Dec. 31, 1952.

Gibb, J. R. The effects of group size and of threat reduction upon creativity in a problem solving situation. (Abstract) *Amer. Psychologist*, 1951, **6**, 324.

Gibb, Lorraine M., and Gibb, J. R. The effects of the use of "participative action" groups in a course in general psychology. (Abstract) *Amer. Psychologist*, 1952, **7**, 247.

Glaser, R., and Homme, L. E. Relationships between the programmed textbook and teaching machine. (Paper read at Air Force Office of Scientific Res. and Univer. of Penn. Conf. on the Automatic Teaching of Verbal and Symbolic Skills. Dec., 1958.)

Goldstein, A. A controlled comparison of the project method with standard laboratory teaching in pharmacology. *J. med. Educ.*, 1956, **31**, 365–375.

Greene, E. B. Relative effectiveness of lecture and individual reading as methods of college teaching. *Genet. Psychol. Monogr.*, 1928, **4**, 457–563.

Greenhill, L. P. New directions for communication research. *Aud.-Vis. Comm. Rev.*, 1959, **7**, 245–253.

Guetzkow, H., Kelly, E. L., and McKeachie, W. J. An experimental comparison of recitation, discussion, and tutorial methods in college teaching. *J. educ. Psychol.* 1954, **45**, 193–209.

Haigh, G. V., and Schmidt, W. The learning of subject matter in teacher-centered and group-centered classes. *J. educ. Psychol.*, 1956, **47**, 295–301.

Haines, D. B. Cooperative vs. competitive discussion methods in teaching introductory psychology. Unpublished doctoral dissertation, University of Michigan, 1959.

Haythorn, W., Couch, A., Haefner, D., Langham, P., and Carter, L. The effects of varying combinations of authoritarian and equalitarian leaders and followers. *J. abnorm. soc. Psychol.*, 1956, **53**, 210–219.

Heyns, R. W. Conference leadership which stimulates teamwork. *Mich. Bus. Rev.*, 1952, **4**, 16–23.

Hirschman, C. S. An investigation of the small groups discussion classroom method on criteria of understanding, pleasantness, and self-confidence induced. Unpublished master's thesis, University of Pittsburgh, 1952.

Hoban, C. F., and Van Ormer, E. B. *Instructional Film Research*, 1918–1950. Tech. Rep. No. SDC 269-7-19. Special Devices Center, Dec. 1950.

Hoffman, L. R. Homogeneity of member personality and its effect on group problem solving. *J. abnorm. soc. Psychol.*, 1959, **58**, 27–32.

Hovland, C. I., Janis, I. L., and Kelley, H. H. *Communication and persuasion.* New Haven: Yale University Press, 1953.

Hovland, C. I., Lumsdaine, A. A., and Sheffield, F. D. *Experiments in mass communication.* Princeton: Princeton University Press, 1949.

Hudelson, E. *Class size at the college level.* Minneapolis: University of Minnesota Press, 1928.

Husband, R. W. A statistical comparison efficacy of large lecture vs. smaller recitation sections upon achievement in general psychology. *J. Psychol.*, 1951, **31**, 297–300.

Jenkins, R. L. The relative effectiveness of two methods of teaching written and spoken English. Unpublished doctoral dissertation, Michigan State University, 1952. (*Diss. Abstr.*, 1952, **12**, 268.)

Jensen, B. T. A comparison of student achievement under conditions of class attendance and non-attendance. *Coll. and Univer.*, 1951, **26**, 399–404.

Johnson, D. M., and Smith, H. C. Democratic leadership in the college classroom, *Psychol. Monogr.*, 1953, **67**, No. 11 (Whole No. 361).

Jones, H. E. Experimental studies of college teaching. *Arch. Psychol.*, **1923**, 10 (68), 5–70.

Kasten, D. F., and Seibert, W. F. A study of televised military science instruction. Purdue University, TVPR Report No. 9, 1959.

Katona, G. *Organizing and memorizing.* New York: Columbia University Press, 1940.

Katz, D. *Gestalt psychology.* New York: Ronald Press, 1950.

Kishler, J. P. The effects of prestige and identification factors on attitude restructuring and learning from sound films. Instructional Film Res. Rep. SDC 269-7-10. Spec. Devices Center, Office of Naval Res., March, 1950.

Klapper, Hope L. Closed circuit television as a medium of instruction at New York University. New York: New York University, 1958.

Kopstein, F. F., and Roshal, S. M. Learning foreign vocabulary from pictures vs. words. *Amer. Psychologist*, 1954, **9**, 407–408.

Kruglak, H. Experimental outcomes of laboratory instructions in elementary college physics. *Amer. J. Physics*, 1952, **20**, 136–141.

Krumboltz, J. D., and Farquar, W. W. The effect of three teaching methods on achievement and motivational outcomes in a how-to-study course. *Psychol. Monogr.*, 1957, **71**, No. 14 (Whole No. 443).

Lahti, A. M. The inductive-deductive method and the physical science laboratory. *J. exp. Educ.*, 1956, **24**, 149–163.

Landsman, T. An experimental study of a student-centered learning method. Unpublished doctoral dissertation, Syracuse University, 1950.

LePore, A. R., and Wilson, J. D. An experimental study of college instruction using broadcast television. *Instructional Television Res.* Proj. No. 2, San Francisco: San Francisco State College, 1958.

Lewin, K. Group decision and social change. In G. E. Swanson, T. M. Newcomb, and E. L. Hartley (Eds.) *Readings in social psychology.* (2nd ed.) New York: Holt, 1952, pp. 330–344.

Lewin, K., Lippitt, R., and White, R. K. Patterns of aggressive behavior in experimentally created social climates. *J. soc. Psychol.*, 1939, **10**, 271–299.

Lifson, N., Rempel, P., and Johnson, J. A. A comparison between lecture and conference methods of teaching psychology. *J. med. Educ.*, 1956, **31**, 376–382.

Little, J. K. Results of use of machines for testing and for drill upon learning in educational psychology. *J. exp. Educ.*, 1934, **3**, 45–49.

Longstaff, H. P. Analysis of some factors conditioning learning in general psychology. *J. appl. Psychol.*, 1932, **16**, 948, 131–166.

Lovell, G. D., and Haner, C. F. Forced choice applied to college faculty ratings. *Educ. psychol. Meas.*, 1955, **15**, 291–304.

Lyle, E. An exploration in the teaching of critical thinking in general psychology. *J. educ. Res.*, 1958, **52**, 129–133.

McCollough, Celeste, and Van Atta, E. L. Experimental evaluation of teaching programs utilizing a block of independent work. (Paper read at Symposium: Experimental studies in learning independently. Amer. Psychol. Assoc., Washington, Sept., 1958.)

McKeachie, W. J. Anxiety in the college classroom. *J. educ. Res.*, 1951, 45, 153–160.

McKeachie, W. J. Individual conformity to attitudes of classroom groups. *J. abnorm. soc. Psychol.*, 1954a, 49, 282–289.

McKeachie, W. J. Student-centered vs. instructor-centered instruction. *J. educ. Psychol.*, 1954b, 45, 143–150.

McKeachie, W. J. Group dynamics: implications from research instruction and for institutional programs. In G. K. Smith (Ed.), *Current issues in higher educ.* Washington: Ass. for Higher Educ., 1956a, pp. 175–181.

McKeachie, W. J. *Teaching tips.* Ann Arbor, Mich.: Wahr, 1956b.

McKeachie, W. J. How do students learn? In R. M. Cooper (Ed.), *The two ends of the log.* Minneapolis, Minn.: University of Minnesota Press, 1958a, pp. 26–35.

McKeachie, W. J. Motivating students' interest. In R. M. Cooper (Ed.), *The two ends of the log.* Minneapolis, Minn.: University of Minnesota Press, 1958b, pp. 36–39.

McKeachie, W. J. Appraising teaching effectiveness. In W. J. McKeachie (Ed.), *The appraisal of teaching in large universities.* Ann Arbor, Mich.: University of Michigan, 1959, pp. 32–36.

McKeachie, W. J., and Hiler, W. The problem oriented approach to teaching psychology. *J. educ. Psychol.*, 1954, 45, 224–232.

McKeachie, W. J., and Solomon, D. Student ratings of instructors: a validity study. *J. educ. Res.* 1958, 51, 379–382.

McTavish, C. L. Effect of repetitive film showings on learning. Instructional Film Research Report, SDC 269-7-12, Special Devices Center Office of Naval Research. Nov., 1949.

Macomber, F. G., and Siegel, L. Experimental study in instructional procedures. Progress Report No. 1. Oxford, Ohio: Miami University, 1956.

Macomber, F. G., and Siegel, L. A study of large group teaching procedures. *Educ. Res.*, 1957a, 38, 220–229.

Macomber, F. G., and Siegel, L. Experimental study in instructional procedures. Progress Report No. 2. Oxford, Ohio: Miami University, 1957b.

Macomber, F. G., and Siegel, L. Final report of the experimental study in instructional procedures. Oxford, Ohio: Miami University, 1960.

Maier, N. R. F., and Solem, A. R. The contribution of a discussion leader to the quality of group thinking. *Human Rel.*, 1952, 5, 277–288.

Maize, R. C. Two methods of teaching English composition to retarded college freshmen. *J. educ. Psychol.*, 1954, 45, 22–28.

Maloney, R. M. Group learning through group discussion: a group discussion implementation analysis. *J. soc. Psychol.*, 1956, 43, 3–9.

Martin, J. R. Two-way closed-circuit educational television, Research Report No. 941-1. Cleveland: Case Inst. Tech., 1957.

Martin, J. R. Two-way closed-circuit educational television, Research Report No. 948-2. Cleveland: Case Inst. Tech., 1957.

Martin, J. R., Adams, R. B., and Baron, M. R. Studies in educational closed-circuit television. Research Report No. 948-5. Cleveland: Case Inst. Tech. 1958.

May, M. A., and Lumsdaine, A. *Learning from films.* New Haven: Yale University Press, 1958.

Melton, A. W., Feldman, N. G., and Mason, C. N. *Experimental studies of the education of children in a museum school.* Washington: Publ. Amer. Assoc. Museums. No. 15, 1936, pp. 1–106.

Mertens, Marjorie S. The effects of mental hygiene films on self regarding attitudes. Instructional Film Res. Rep., SDC 269-7-22, Special Devices Center Office of Naval Res., July, 1951.

Miller, N. M. Scientific principles for maximum learning from motion pictures. *Audio-Visual Comm. Rev., Graphic Comm.,* 1957, 5, 61–113.

Moore, Mary R., and Popham, W. J. The role of extra-class student interviews in promoting student achievement. (Paper read at joint session of Amer. Ass. for the Advancement of Science and the Amer. Educ. Res. Ass., Chicago, Dec., 1959.)

Mueller, A. D. Class size as a factor in normal school instruction. *Education,* 1924, 45, 203–27.

Novak, J. D. An experimental comparison of a conventional and a project centered method of teaching a college general botany course. *J. exp. Educ.,* 1958, 26, 217–230.

Parsons, T. S. A comparison of instruction by kinescope, correspondence study, and customary classroom procedures. *J. educ. Psychol.,* 1957, 48, 27–40.

Parsons, T. S., Ketcham, W. A., and Beach, L. R. Effects of varying degrees of student interaction and student-teacher contact in college courses. (Paper read at Amer. Sociol. Soc., Seattle, Washington, August, 1958.)

Patton, J. A. A study of the effects of student acceptance of responsibility and motivation on course behavior. Unpublished doctoral dissertation, University of Mich., 1955.

Paul, J. B. The length of class periods. *Educ. Res.,* 1932, 13, 58–75.

Paul, J., and Ogilvie, J. C. Mass media and retention, *Explorations,* 1955, 4, 120–123.

Pressey, S. L. A simple apparatus which gives tests and scores—and teaches. *School and Society,* 1926, 23, 373–376.

Pressey, S. L. Development and appraisal of devices providing immediate automatic scoring of objective tests and concommitant self-instruction. *J. Psychol.,* 1950, 29, 417–447.

Remmers, H. H. Learning, effort, and attitudes as affected by three methods of instruction in elementary psychology. *Purdue University Studies in Higher Educ.,* 1933, 21.

Remmers, H. H., and Bradenburg, H. C. Experimental data on the Purdue rating scale for instructors. *Educ. Adm. Sup.,* 1927, 13, 519–527.

Riley, J. W., Ryan, B. F., and Lifshitz, Marcia. *The student looks at his teacher.* New Brunswick: Rutgers University Press, 1950.

Rohrer, J. H. Large and small sections in college classes. *J. higher Educ.,* 1957, 28, 275–279.

Ross, I. C. Role specialization in supervision. Unpublished doctoral dissertation, Columbia University, 1956. (*Diss. Abstr.,* 1957, 17, 2701–2702.)

Ruja, H. Outcomes of lecture and discussion procedures in three college courses. *J. exp. Educ.,* 1954, 22, 385–394.

Runkel, P. Cognitive similarity in facilitating communication. *Sociometry,* 1956, 19, 178–191.

Russell, H. E. Inter-relations of some indices of instructor effectiveness: an exploratory study. Unpublished doctoral dissertation, University of Pittsburgh, 1951.

Scheidemann, Norma V. An experiment in teaching psychology. *J. appl. Psychol.,* 1929, **13**, 188–191.

Schellenberg, J. A. Group size as a factor in success of academic discussion groups. *J. educ. Soc.,* 1959, **43**, 73–79.

Seashore, C. E. Elementary psychology: an outline of a course by the project method: *Aims and Progress Res.,* No. 153. Iowa City: University of Iowa Studies, 1928.

Seashore, S. E. Group cohesiveness in the industrial group. University of Mich. Survey Res. Center, Pub. No. 14, 1954.

Seibert, E. F. A brief report and evaluation of closed-circuit television instruction in the first semester calculus course. Purdue University: Audio Visual Center, 1957.

Seibert, E. F. An evaluation of televised instruction in college English composition. Purdue University: TVPR Report No. 5, 1958.

Seibert, E. F., and Honig, J. M. A brief study of televised laboratory instruction. Purdue University: TVPR Report No. 8, 1959.

Siegel, L., Adams, J. F., and Macomber, F. G. Retention of subject matter as a function of large group instructional procedures. *J. educ. Psychol.,* 1960, **51**, 9–13.

Slomowitz, M. A comparison of personality changes and content achievement gains occurring in two modes of instruction. Unpublished doctoral dissertation, New York University, 1955. (*Diss. Abstr.,* 1955, **15**, 1790.)

Smith, D. E. P. Applicational transfer and inhibition. *J. educ. Psychol.,* 1954, **45**, 169–174.

Smith, D. E. P., Wood, R. L., Downer, J. W., and Raygor, A. L. Reading improvement as a function of student personality and teaching method. *J. educ. Psychol.,* 1956, **47**, 47–58.

Smith, H. C. Team work in the college class. *J. educ. Psychol.,* 1955, **46**, 274–286.

Spence, R. B. Lecture and class discussion in teaching educational psychology. *J. educ. Psychol.,* 1928, **19**, 454–462.

Stephan, F. F., and Mishler, E. G. The distribution of participation in small groups: an experimental approximation. *Amer. sociol. Rev.,* 1952, **17**, 598–608.

Stephens, A. L. Certain special factors involved in the law of effect. *Abstracts of doctoral Dissertations* No 64, Ohio State University, 1953.

Stephens College. Courses to be taught over closed circuit TV. *Stephens College News Reporter,* 1955, **14**, No. 4.

Stern, C. G., Stein, M. I., and Bloom, B. S. *Methods in personality assessment.* Glencoe, Ill.: Free Press, 1956.

Stone, G. R. The training function of examinations: retest performance as a function of the amount and kind of critique information. Res. Rep. No. AFPTRC-TN-55-8, vi. USAF Pers. Train. Res. Cent., 1955.

Stuit, D. B., Harshbarger, H. C., Becker, S L., Bechtoldt, H. P., and Hall, A. E. *An experiment in teaching.* Iowa City: State University of Iowa, Department of Speech, 1956.

Thistlethwaite, D. L. College environments and the development of talent. *Science,* 1959, **130**, 71–76.

Thistlethwaite, D. L. College press and changes in study plans of talented students. Evanston, Ill.: Natl. Merit Scholarship Corp., 1960.

Throop, J. F., Assini, L. T., and Boguslavsky, G. W. The effectiveness of laboratory instruction in strength of materials by closed circuit television. Troy, N.Y.: Rensselaer Polytechnic Institute, 1958.

Timmel, G. B. A study of the relationship between method of teaching a college course in mental hygiene and change in student adjustment status. Unpublished doctoral dissertation, Cornell University, 1954. (*Diss. Abstr.*, 1955, **15**, 90.)

Tyler, R. W. The evaluation of teaching. In R. M. Cooper (Ed.) *The two ends of the log.* Minneapolis: University of Minnesota Press, 1958, pp. 164–176.

VanderMeer, A. W. Relative effectiveness of instruction by films exclusively, films plus study guides, and standard lecture methods. Instructional Film Res. Rep. SDC 269-7-13. Special Devices Center Office of Naval Res., July, 1950.

VanderMeer, A. W. Effect of film-viewing practice on learning from instructional films. Instructional Film Research Rep. SDC 269-7-20. Special Devices Center Office of Naval Res., Nov., 1951.

Vinacke, E. W. Some variables in buzz sessions. *J. soc. Psychol.*, 1957, **45**, 25–33.

Wakely, J. H., Marr, J. N., Plath, D. W., and Wilkins, D. M. Lecturing and test performance in introductory psychology. Paper read at Michigan Academy, Ann Arbor, Mich., March, 1960.

Ward, J. Group-study vs. lecture-demonstration method in physical science instruction for general education college students. *J. exp. Educ.*, 1956, **24**, 197–210.

Warren, R. A comparison of two plans of study in engineering physics. Unpublished doctoral dissertation. Purdue University, 1954. (*Diss. Abstr.*, 1954, **14**, 1648–1649.)

Waterhouse, I. K., and Child, I. L. Frustration and the quality of performance. *J. Persy.*, 1953, **21**, 298–311.

White, J. R. A comparison of the group-laboratory and the lecture-demonstration methods in engineering instruction. *J. eng. Educ.*, 1945, **36**, 50–54.

Wieder, G. S. Group procedures modifying attitudes of prejudice in the college classroom. *J. educ. Psychol.*, 1954, **24**, 332–344.

Wispé, L. G. Evaluative section teaching methods in the introductory course. *J. educ. Res.*, 1951, **45**, 161–186.

Wolfle, D. The relative efficiency of constant and varied stimulation during learning. *J. comp. Psychol.*, 1935, **19**, 5–27.

Wolfle, D. The first course in psychology. *Psychol. Bull.*, 1942, **39**, 685–712.

Zelény, L. D. Experimental appraisal of a group learning plan. *J. educ. Res.*, 1940, **34**, 37–42.

9

Joseph Katz

Personality and
Interpersonal Relations
in the College Classroom

I recently received a letter from a colleague who teaches at one of our most serious-minded colleges. He had just finished giving a course which he had offered several times before. This time he felt things had clicked, he was sure of his material, he thought he was getting his points across and he enjoyed himself. To his astonishment he found that only two students had enrolled in the course for the next year. He could not understand why. Now one might speculate as to the reasons. It is possible that scheduling was an important factor. My colleague's section had been shifted from the spring to the winter term, and a second section was to be given by another man in the spring. Perhaps other quite extraneous factors were at work. But it is

Note. This investigation was carried out during the tenure of a Special Research Fellowship from the National Institute of Mental Health of the United States Public Health Service. The ideas here presented have an empirical base in an interview study of university faculty carried on by the writer, Ruth Johnson, and Ving Ellis at the University of California in April and May of 1959. This research is now being continued by Ving Ellis and myself. Much of what I say is based on my experience and observations during almost 15 years of college teaching. I have not hesitated to present my ideas in a more comprehensive and conclusive fashion than my research and experience justify because we need ideas above all to have some significant hypotheses to test. Special acknowledgment is due to Professor Gail Kennedy and to Natalie Katz. This study has been carried on under the auspices of the Department of Psychological Medicine at the University of California and its director, Saxton Pope, provided both inspiration and encouragement.

also possible that the course was not chosen because of factors due to the instructor's or the students' attitudes, or both. There ought to be a way in which the instructor could assess what, if anything, had gone wrong. But he and thousands of others at the present time have no way. He will have to start another version of this course largely without benefit of learning from his past experience.

Let me cite another case. Many years ago I assisted a young professor in a course on Far Eastern culture. The professor had worked up the course in the summer before and prepared substantial lecture notes. He presented these notes to the class in what to me seemed a monotonous fashion, and I found missing both the spark of his material and the reflectiveness that his material invited. But in talking to the students I found that many liked the course, and the course guide published by the students that year bore out this impression further. Students particularly liked the clarity of presentation. The teacher was easy to follow and to take notes on. What did the course accomplish? Was it to the students a comfortable way of getting the outline of some exotic ideas, the illusion of understanding fostered by an intellectual Cook's tour? Or, on the contrary, were these strange ideas presented to them on a level close to their present intellectual state so that they could absorb them without either indigestion or hasty elimination. One does not know. The instructor of the course, if asked, would not have known and, in fact, might have been unconcerned about the question, thinking that his task was to present the material.

The fact is that in our colleges concern with the outcome of education tends to be regarded by many individual faculty members as a matter for the office of public relations, the front of college catalogues, and the oratory of commencement addresses. The lack of concern is so glaring that it cannot be explained as a simple matter of neglect or even as a result of the usual hesitation to engage in self-study. It rather suggests a deep-lying philosophy, one that is not articulate and hence needs some care in elucidation. The social scientist who has studied institutions is apt to think in terms of input-process-output models. But to many college teachers this model smacks of the mechanicalness of a commercial civilization to which they consider colleges a corrective or even an antithesis. The disagreement is deeper than the choice of metaphor and rests, I think, in the college teacher's conviction of the absolute worth of the subject matter he is teaching—a conviction not free from half-conscious doubts. The college teacher conceives of himself as offering knowledge of the world as he has grasped it. He sees any modification of the unvarnished presentation of the truth as concession and dilution which surely is to be kept to a minimum. The implicit model of the majority of college teachers seems to be one according to which they see themselves at their various stalls in the fair of knowledge, hopefully attracting the students who have interest and aptitude for the teacher's specialty. To each teacher his specialty has given a primary focus under which to organize his life and make it meaningful. He is little trained and often little disposed to see the college student, who is not a specialist, in the student's own perspective or to make the needed separation between the preservation and advancement of knowledge on the one side and education on the other.

Now in what is to follow it must be borne in mind that I in no way suggest that *all* teachers need in the same degree to become aware of what they are doing. The nature of college work is such that there always will be, or rather must be, room for individuals whose primary concern is to communicate what they know regardless of the consequences (*fiat veritas, pereat mundus*). But there also must be regard of the consequences. My notion is that the strategic people to help develop this regard are the college teachers themselves. This requires increased attention to the processes of teaching and learning. College teachers are highly professionalized in regard to the subject matter they teach. They are not at all professionalized as educators (and the very term "educator" has taken on the ill flavor of the pretenses of a retired military or businessman turned university president). College teachers do not know what the effects of their teaching are, and they have at this point no disciplined ways of learning and assessing what they are doing and how they might become more effective. The training of psychotherapists provides an instructive model. The aspiring psychotherapist, in addition to his theoretical training, passes through years of supervision wherein he discusses with experienced colleagues the minute details of his interaction with the patient. Not only are the patient's actions scrutinized, but the actions and reactions of the therapist as well. Only in this way does the therapist learn to assess what he is doing and develop more effective and appropriate techniques. One might say that teaching still resembles the level of medicine when practitioners had some universal remedy, say bloodletting, which they applied regardless of patient or disease. Some appropriate modification of the practice of supervision in psychotherapy, if applied to the training of college teachers, is likely to bring much benefit to college teaching in enabling teachers to recognize and deal with trouble spots and anxieties, and to make some discrimination as to which of their students they affect in what ways. Out of such practice the best research is likely to come also; for when there is some movement in the teacher's reaction to his classes and vice versa, the many facets of interaction are likely to emerge. Quite analogously some of our best knowledge of personality has been gained through analyzing the process of therapy, in which there is mobilization of the individual.

The following discussion will fall under four headings: (I) General and specific characteristics of the college teacher, (II) the classroom from the teacher's perspective, (III) the classroom and the teacher from the students' perspective, and (IV) the teacher and his subject matter.

GENERAL AND SPECIFIC CHARACTERISTICS OF THE COLLEGE TEACHER

The aim of this section is to attempt a sketch of a social psychology of teachers. As I have suggested, the description of teachers' characteristics is one thing, the possible need for college teachers to be aware of all of them is another. At the present time college teachers are not expected to have a disciplined awareness of their motivations and attitudes in teaching. Given the influence that college teachers have or *might* have on their students, some sensitiveness to human interactions may well come to be regarded part of the college teacher's job. But alternatives to increasing teachers' awareness need to be explored too, e.g., more attention to the placing of kinds of students with kinds of teachers.

Teachers as a group share some characteristics with the rest of society and they have some characteristics peculiar to themselves. But even the characteristics that a teacher may share with other men, e.g., a strong tendency to project his motives or feelings onto others, are worthy of special attention in considering the peculiar effects they may have in the classroom. In what follows, therefore, general and specific characteristics of teachers will be discussed.

An outstanding characteristic of teachers as a class is their ready acceptance of a subordinate status. While most groups in this country have by now organized themselves into effective, power-wielding associations and unions, teachers have remained unorganized and unrepresented, apart from the rather limited activities of the American Association of University Professors, or of a teachers' union here and there. The teachers' role on the campus has led the English philosopher Bertrand Russell to compare them to the educated Greek slaves who taught the imperial Romans. Teachers, in contrast to other people, never leave school and it is possible that an academic career has a special attraction for individuals with a strong inclination to depend on others. Sanford (1953) has shown how in a crisis situation dependency images (trustees seen as either good or bad parents) may tend to blur the realities of a situation. It is interesting to note that the current agitation for higher salaries comes largely from outside the college faculties and that faculties have only mildly supported it, even though griping about low pay is one of the staples of faculty conversation.

Another general characteristic of teachers is a sense of separateness from the rest of society.[1] One of the roots of this may have been early rewards, at home and in school, for exceptional intellectual performance, often in a peer culture in which this stamped the student as something of an outsider. College teachers tend to view students as belonging to an alien, even a hostile culture. One of our informants spoke of "the warfare between class and instructor." The definitions of the students' recalcitrance vary. Their resistance may be viewed in intellectual, social, political, or aesthetic terms. John Dewey has stated that one of the functions of the university is that of critic of the established order. But this critical function must be distinguished from the sense of social alienation that, in greater or lesser degree, seems to be a particular mark of faculty culture.

There is a third important distinction. The suggestion has been made that some college teachers are primarily economic men, others seekers of status or of power. It is clear that these and other motivations are found in all occupations. The difference is that although in many occupations these motivations are given explicit recognition or even considered needful, they tend to be regarded as incompatible with teaching. Intellectual ability, as any other, can be used in the service of economic, status, and manipulative goals; and novelists and other writers have at all times delighted in depicting these motivations at work on the college campus, however disguised by purported scientific or scholarly considerations (cf., most recently Barr [1958], Jarrell [1954], McCarthy [1952]). In a typology of teachers it is necessary to distinguish the *relative* degree to which nonteaching and/or nonacademic motivations compare with the teaching and/or academic ones. There is also a developmental consideration. The achievement of academic security (tenure or otherwise) seems to be a critical point for many academic persons. It is likely that for some this provides an opportunity for less restrained expression of their nonacademic motivations. There are other factors, some of which I will discuss when I come to the discussion of the process of becoming "deadwood."

The treatment that college teachers have received by their adminis-

[1] Compare Knapp, Chapter 7.

tration, by society at large, even by their students, has tended to confirm their sense of isolation from or even rejection by society. Yet the teachers' passivity in the face of this treatment suggests that they implicitly share some of this evaluation. Evidence for this is to be found, for instance, in the teachers' imitating the manner of the 9 A.M. to 5 P.M. working day of the businessman; in fact, going him one better in the frequent claim that theirs really is an 8 a.m. to 10 p.m. day. The seeking of committee work often may spring from a sense of uneasiness about leisure. Only some inner acceptance of belittling standards can explain why, for instance, it is not even questioned that two professors in one of our distinguished institutions should be herded into a narrow former coat closet for "office."

After these more general factors—dependency, isolation, latent motivations—we turn to some of the more specific factors defining the college teacher's role; in particular, those conditioned by his graduate school training. The orientation of graduate school training is almost exclusively toward the creation of research specialists. The Ph.D. is the highest degree attainable in any field, and it ostensibly certifies that a man has achieved expertness in his field, has made a significant original contribution, and is equipped and inclined to go on doing research for the rest of his life. In actuality many Ph.D.'s will fill roles different from that of creative researchers, but little provision is made for and little thought is given to this in graduate school training. This again is different in other professions. To become a Supreme Court Justice may well be the dream of every ambitious lawyer, but there is a sense of security and adequate role-fulfillment in less exalted positions. Similarly a general practitioner in medicine will not usually develop a sense of failure because he has made no contributions to medical literature. Not so with the college teacher. His ambitions are oriented to the outstanding men in his fields, the Deweys, Woodworths, Murrays, Mitchells, Webers. His own graduate school teachers will of course heavily influence the image of what he would like to become. But the graduate school teachers, too, are usually admiringly or even worshipfully oriented toward some fatherly specialty hero. Pressure to publish, for instance, does not emanate from administrators alone, but is well internalized.

The orientation toward creating research specialists has two consequences: (1) It often leads, particularly in the Ph.D. thesis, to an emphasis on the minutiae and triviae of the field; for the neophyte cannot yet be entrusted with the more important, and more lively, problems of the specialty heroes. This is the phenomenon of the Ph.D. octopus described by James (1911), Laski (1948), and others. (2) It leads to disorientation and frustration in the role that a majority of Ph.D.'s will assume. Some colleges of high quality and inner security, e.g., Amherst, make it possible for some of their faculty who are so inclined to give up the usual Ph.D. ambition and to turn fruitfully to undergraduate teaching. But for most college teachers, graduate school norms remain the predominant yardstick of achievement throughout their academic careers. Those who give up enter a kind of no man's land and many others hang on to a pretense of research without producing notable contributions in their field, meanwhile relegating their day-to-day functions as college teachers to a subsidiary role.

Under conditions prevailing in Europe, with its small and few universities or colleges, the ambition to become a creative scientist or scholar was indeed an adequate one for the university teacher. The much more diversified conditions and objectives of the American system of higher education have not given rise to a corresponding enlargement of role-images. Perhaps this is one aspect of the trained incapacity, and stifling of the imagination, that often goes with highly specialized training. What has been said about teachers applies to institutions as well. Institutional ideals often take very inadequate account of the kind of students they serve, the kind of faculty they can attract, and many other local limitations and possibilities. Instead, institutional ideals seem often to be determined by what might be called a Harvard complex (or depending on place or department, a Chicago, or Columbia complex). There seem to be institutional as well as personality fixations that interfere with adaptation or growth.

Let us turn now to the teacher's role in and attitudes to the classroom. The teacher arrives in the classroom unprepared. He is, of course, particularly in his earlier years of teaching, likely to have copious notes with him and they may be the product of long vigils. But he comes unprepared, not in his own knowledge, but for communication. The college teacher probably has never had even once the experience of systematically analyzing a single classroom hour in terms of the effectiveness of his job in communicating what he knows. Instead, the teacher has to rely on other devices: examinations, remarks by students, or faculty who report what students have said. Some teachers occasionally pass a questionnaire around. Above all, there is the presence of the class, quiet or restless, attentive or bored. But skill and orientation to evaluate class reaction, and to differentiate individuals and groups in the class, are lacking. Cues are likely to be filtered through the teacher's anxiety, vanity, obtuseness, or optimism, and hence often tend to be confirming of the original attitude. Teachers walking toward their classes frequently can be heard to say that they are unprepared, often after hours of preparation. This perhaps indicates an incipient sense of the communication factor involved.

Once in the classroom the teacher can conduct himself in a student-oriented, an objective-oriented, a self-oriented manner, or combinations of these. There are many variations under these three headings. Student-orientedness can describe the whole gamut from flattery and indulgence to realistic assessment of the students' needs, desires, and capacities. Under objective-orientedness fall a planned or prescribed amount of material, or having the student achieve a certain level of skill or mastery. Centering on objectives has a clearly defined place in professional training, where people are prepared for certain roles. In liberal arts subjects (or rather in the liberal arts way of treating subjects) objectives have a much less clearly circumscribed place. But the tendency often is to treat liberal arts subject matter as if it were a parcel of information needful for a future practitioner. Thirdly, the classroom serves as a reflection of the teacher's current or permanent interests, boredom, contempt, vanity, and a host of other motives or dispositions.

Teachers have varying images of their students. In the next section something will be said about the various ways in which teachers group their students according to ability and interest. Here I wish to emphasize other factors. A teacher may see himself more or less explicitly in the role of parent or in that of sibling in his relations with students. Depending in part on which variety of parental or sibling attitude he adopts he will have all sorts of different effects. If the attitude is one of sibling rivalry, then the classroom is likely to be a competitive arena, with the teacher trying to defeat the arguments of students and always to show his superiority. The very subject matter he teaches will appear under this light and, for particularly impressionable students, it may never lose the color of contentiousness again. It is possible to trace the heritage of some celebrated contentious teachers through the incessant polemics of a whole genealogy of students. (It is granted, of course, that students with a predisposition to antagonistic rivalry will be particularly attracted to this kind of "Socratic" teacher.) If the teacher's sibling attitude is a more cooperative one, he will try to establish a *Bruderbund* with his class. The outside world (outside the class) will then be seen as recalcitrant and the teacher will enter into a pact where everything, from the Dean's office to the social system, is viewed with suspicion. The teacher's very subject matter will take on some of the ideological qualities of articles of faith.

The developmental level of the teacher—the stage in which some of his major emotional needs had their origin—is equally important. Roughly speaking, there are "infantile," "adolescent," and adult college teachers. The adolescent type is particularly interesting because he is so close to the actual developmental level of his students. Anna Freud (1937) has given a vivid description of adolescent intellectuality: it is close to instinctual need and, with all its appearance of wisdom and sweep, is oriented less to the exploration of reality than to the verbalization of urge. The appeal of some very successful college teachers seems to be due precisely to their eternal adolescence—rebellious, sweeping, and given to the alternation of strong emotions. Other teachers tend to view their students as if they were infants, projecting onto their students and thereby fending off their own infantile strivings. The developmental stages of getting, retaining, and giving find many illustrations in daily classroom interactions between teachers and students. (Experiments with authoritarian and nonauthoritarian kinds of teaching, though conceived in situational terms, may well be taken to suggest the differential effects of teachers' personalities.)

College teachers vary much in what they consider the function of the classroom. Some consider the classroom a nuisance or inevitable evil designed to furnish the economic and institutional basis for making research possible. Others consider college teaching as a service, one that is socially desirable, but not on a par with more purely academic activities. Still others see in the classroom a chance to acquire disciples or find recruits for their specialty. To others, again, the classroom is a vehicle for social reform. Communicating what a teacher has found irresistible in his own field always plays a role, though it may be more or less overlaid with other factors. There are teaching situations in which concern for communication is at a minimum and self-centeredness is at a maximum. Thus, the classroom may provide the teacher with an opportunity to continue his own learning, with little regard for the effect on the students. Or it may provide an opportunity for the teacher to display his intellectual capacities or his powers of seductiveness. A teacher may use the classroom to satisfy his desires of being liked, or of being cruel, of manipulating people, or of preaching to them. Students of course are a particular variety of captive audience with only limited room for response or retaliation. The classroom, moreover, is an almost ideal place for compulsive reiterations. Teachers with notes and tricks twenty years old, unrevised and unreflected, are common on any campus. A teacher's focus may be outside of the classroom when he is guided in what he does in class by how it will affect his chances of staying in an institution or of being promoted in or out of it. In sum, although ostensibly talking to the students in front of him, a teacher's principal attention can be focused on himself, his administrative superiors, his local colleagues, his professional colleagues, his specialty heroes. The degrees to which this affects the task at hand vary considerably.

There are various ways in which a college teacher's attention is focused on the subject-matter of his course; at the extremes, apathy and resort to irrelevant pet topics may be marked. His conception of subject matter has many dimensions. He can stress results, or methods of arriving at them. He can focus on basic theory or concrete areas of specific facts, on problems at the borders of knowledge or well-established theory, on tangential aspects, on generally agreed upon theories, or heavily disputed ones. He can be historical or he can be summarizing, as in concentrating on a survey of leading ideas. A teacher, regardless of his field, may by intellectual temper be a generalist or a specialist. He may be empirical, speculative, abstract, given to pure theorizing, or oriented toward application. There are, moreover, many moods of presentation: Subject matter can be presented in an "as is" way, without being readied for student consumption. It can be adjusted to what are thought to be the capacities and interests of the student, including the "popularizations" that are a sure way of losing one's colleagues' respect. Some teachers wish to do more than to demonstrate. They wish to convince (propagandizing is an extreme) or they wish to draw morals (sermonizing). Teachers' attitudes may range from dedication, detachment, irony, belittlement, to negation in which jokes and other digressions have the center of the stage.

The process of becoming "deadwood." The foregoing remarks will have given some sense of the varieties of factors that go to make up the classroom situation. Any one of them may play a major role in determining the outcome of a series of classroom situations. None of them is likely to bring about strong positive or negative results when present in a mild degree. But it may be proposed that in specific classroom situations a cluster of a few specific factors has a decisive bearing on outcome. Further research will need to explore the dynamics of these factors in greater degree. But before this section is concluded, one phenomenon should be singled out for special discussion: the process of becoming "deadwood." I do not know a single discussion of it. Yet it is ubiquitous and seems one of the chief "cancers" of the teaching profession. Innumerable individuals are lost to themselves and to their students on account of it. Here is one of the strategic problems for research. In what follows a first brief analysis of the problem will be attempted.

Both observation and inference lead to the conclusion that the individual who later is to become "deadwood" often started as a bright and eager graduate student. It would be useful to find out whether there are not certain predispositions and how they could be recognized early. But it is clear that any predisposition meets a very supportive environment; hence the ubiquity of the phenomenon. Though the process has never been studied or discussed directly, papers by the anthropologist Sapir (1949) and the psychoanalyst Kubie (1953) bear on the problem. Both stress economic deprivation as an important factor. Sapir describes the gradual estrangement of the professor and his family from the finer things in life, including social isolation for want of the proper clothing on the wife's part. The professor's irony which at first charms his classes eventually turns sour when the deprivations have run their cumulative course. Similarly Kubie stresses that the young scientist, full of the joys and anticipations of the laboratory, hardly stops to consider the deprived life his salary will earn for his family. (Kubie's paper was written in the early Fifties. Since then some scientists, due to the opportunities for consultations, have begun to see lusher times.) Now economic deprivation obviously is an important factor. But the clue should be generalized and it should be asked what further frustrations condition the "deadwood" process.

Some of the factors already mentioned have an obvious bearing: frustration of status striving, disappointment about one's standing with one's professional peers, less creativity than the first rapture of graduate life seemed to promise. But perhaps most relevantly a chief determinant might be found in the very nature of the college teacher's work. It is obvious that much here invites stagnation. The students always are at the same age, between 17 and 21. They arrive in the professor's course with the same ignorance and naiveté as the class the year before and instead of going on where he had left off, he has to start again at the beginning. A professor will meet a student one year out of college and the student with some wonder will ask: "Are you still teaching such and such course?" From the student's point of view this is a most reasonable question; for he has gone on to other things, with or without using what he heard in the course. The professor is still there and will be there for the next decades.

Although there is a fairly rapid change of theory and lore in many acadamic fields, what can be taught to undergraduates remains more static. Neilson, who was president of Smith College and an Elizabethan scholar, decided to retire from teaching when he found his young graduate students "were more up-to-date on 'discoveries' and 'recent scholarship'" than he (Nicolson, 1946). But it is also quite conceivable that a man may give a course on Shakespeare for, say, forty years where it is not the aging of content, as against the manner, that makes it unacceptable. At the extreme are the teachers who have committed their courses to notebooks and thus are prepared for their annual recitals. Even this practice, though talked about unfavorably, is not considered unacceptable in our colleges.

The classroom then seems to offer insufficient challenge and stimulation to keep a teacher intellectually and emotionally alive. What is so frequently talked about as undergraduate apathy has its equivalent in the "deadwood" attitude that in differing degrees is shared by many college teachers. I see the "deadwood" process as a special case of demoralization due to the work conditions. This demoralization is due to such factors as highly insufficient clarity about what is achieved in the classroom and absence of any clear evaluation of what is being done. In the absence of sufficient concepts of outcome, almost anything seems to be acceptable and in the end nothing seems to make much difference, so evanescent a thing do college courses seem to be. The absence of supervision or assessment of teaching is presented, in the prevailing ideology, as a condition of freedom and independence in teaching. But it has an unrecognized side effect in that it deprives most if not all teachers of a firm sense of accomplishment, or a firm sense of mistakes to be learned from. Teaching, without assessment, leads almost necessarily to a cycle of repetition. Only detailed, sophisticated, continuing assessment can make teaching experience cumulative, instead of repetitive, and thus instruct the instructor. Students can hardly be expected to learn if their teachers have given up. When I speak of assessment I mean methodical examination by the teacher himself, with and without consultation. In the earlier phases of teaching, consultation should be part of regular procedure.

The following recommendations, apart from their possible pragmatic value, may help to describe the problem further. As already indicated, if conditions allow or stimulate the faculty to learn, teaching will improve too. One needed area of learning is about teaching itself. Besides greater attention to the classroom process, more work with individual students seems desirable. In many current discussions of the curriculum, individual tutorials tend to be viewed as a luxury that only schools with a very limited student body can afford. Yet working closely with individual students is essential for the college teacher's continuing education. At any institution, arrangements could be made so that every instructor might work intensively with one or two students whom he would accompany through the entire four-year period. He would then find out much about the student's background, interests, curricular, and extracurricular activities. He would get an individualized picture that would be very useful when he faced the semistrangers in his classroom. The changes in fashion and in the moods of college generations would then no longer be a puzzle to him. But most important of all, he would know much better where a piece of learning fitted into a student's life, successes, and failures.

Strange as it may sound to the outsider, institutional devices for keeping the learning process alive for faculty are extremely underdeveloped on most campuses. The prevailing note, often, is one of isolation. Teachers are separated not only from their professional colleagues nationally, but even from departmental colleagues locally. Probably only a minority of college departments spend as much time, in departmental meetings, in discussion of ideas as they do on administrative questions, evaluations of students for grades and degrees, or planning who will teach what course. Where people in a department are no longer sufficient to spark each other, such devices as regular seminars attended by invited colleagues from elsewhere, periodic brief or long residences of "visiting firemen" might be of some value in counteracting intellectual isolation. Another source of learning may be one's colleagues in the other departments. In this respect the American colleges, those that have no graduate school attached, are missing a unique opportunity. Graduate work tends to be highly departmentalized and specialized within departments. Interdepartmental and intradepartmental communication is often at a minimum. Here the college faculties, because of their much lesser specialization, have an intriguing opportunity for exploring the pooling of knowledge and methods from differing fields. Here indeed there is open to the college faculties an original research function, quite beside the effects of interdepartmental learning on teaching and teachers.

Finally, there are more external devices, beginning with the stipulation that no professor is to repeat the same course a great number of times. Teachers might frequently give courses in departments other than their own. The visiting and exchange system might be organized in a more purposive way, enabling teachers to become acquainted with a variety of institutions and colleagues. Caplow and McGee (1959) have demonstrated the great tendency toward inbreeding in the institutions they have studied. There often also is a sort of mutual tolerance of lethargy. A system of circulation in and between the campuses may work as well there as in the carp pond.

THE CLASSROOM FROM
THE TEACHER'S PERSPECTIVE

We are now in a position to turn more directly to the teaching situation itself and to discuss the classroom both from the teacher's and from the student's perspectives. I begin with the teacher's perspective. The preceding section has tried to indicate some of the teacher's general and specific characteristics. Thus the teacher arrives in the classroom with general attitudes of closeness or distance to other people, trust, fear, suspiciousness, domination, or submissiveness, and any combination and alternation of these and other traits. Like other citizens he may suffer from stage fright, not be able to lecture and hence have to rely on his own or his students' questions to keep the work going. (Some very respected teachers have been nearly unable to lecture.) He may mumble his words, shout, plead (love me!), intimidate, fake. Among his role-specific characteristics are those that determine whether his instruction will be geared to his students, to his subject matter, to his professional colleagues, or toward promotion. He may regard his students in a variety of ways, from something like an unpleasant nuisance in his scientific or scholarly career to the only raison d'être of his professional and personal *Existenz*.

One sort of question that has been subjected to much discussion is that of small vs. large classes, of lecture vs. discussion, and, more recently, of the aid that can be given by such impersonal devices as TV (see Chapter 8). In spite of the volume of the discussion, not much agreement has been reached—another indication of what happens in the absence of reasonably definite criteria of evaluation and hypothesis testing. There is not only the possibility that the decisive variables may be elsewhere, but also that much depends on how a particular variable is embedded in a specific context of other variables. Thus, at an institution in which the instructors are oriented toward ongoing research and where the student culture is supportive of intellectual values, lecturing is going to have a quite different effect from that had at an institution where the opposite is the case. (It is worth noting that on the comparatively rare occasions when college teachers seriously think of methods, they often will pull out some favorite panacea, e.g., smaller classes, a reading period, an honors program, more grades [such as minus and plus grades], less grades, no grades, more survey courses, fewer survey courses.) Thistlethwaite (1959) in a recent study, investigating the effectiveness of different colleges in stimulating their students to go on to graduate work, suggests that, among other things, a combination of informality and exacting standards is likely to produce future graduate students in science; while infrequent testing, a variety of courses with range of subject matter, and a high degree of energy and controversy in teaching are likely to produce future graduate students in the social sciences and humanities.

Clearer conceptions and measurements of results are the crucial desideratum. The common denominator at the present time is grades. But grades seem best to measure a student's grade-getting capacity, just as acquired wealth seems best to measure a person's wealth-getting capacity. A study of a group of creative research scientists, by the Institute of Personality Assessment and Research at Berkeley (MacKinnon, 1959), has found that "most earned no better than a C+ to B— average" in college, with apparently no higher grade performance in the subjects of their future specialty. There are indications, in a study by Donald Brown (1959) (see Chapter 16), that college teachers themselves put only limited value on grades and will, when asked to list outstanding students, nominate both some of those whom they gave A grades and some whom they did not. At the present time, college teachers rely for evaluation not only on examinations and papers, but also on the formal and informal responses of their students in and out of the classroom and on reports that come to them from colleagues and other "informants." Occasionally teachers make up questionnaires. This is more likely to be so when an instructor feels insecure, something that is often sensed by the students whose response then tends to be noble, thus somewhat invalidating the results. In such questionnaire sets one may find even highly laudatory comments about the professor, balanced by implicit signs of unease. In one course that a majority of students reported enjoying very much, a majority also felt that they lacked important prerequisites for following the course. There were several distinguishable subgroups, comprised of students with different majors, and the degree of satisfaction seemed to decrease with the distance of the student's from the professor's major field. The professor's experimental-mindedness in using no definite textbook found a not unrepresentative response in one student's advice that he publish his course as a text.

I suppose the first question to be asked about classroom interaction is who takes responsibility for what. A definition of the optimum might be: the teacher takes only as much responsibility as the students cannot take for themselves. But responsibility for what? In some courses syllabi and a fairly prescribed structure provide a statement of procedure and goals. Still, even in fairly rigid courses there is room

for discretion. Hence the common tendency of students to ask themselves: what does the instructor want, a question that often frustrates
them, in part because the instructor does not clearly know what he
wants. Nevertheless, orienting a course according to a syllabus or a
prescribed text is a way of relieving both teacher and class of responsibility.

Given the absence of clear-cut goals and of measures of progress
toward them, college teachers often tend to resort to magical thinking.
Some will assert that uncouth barbaric students benefit from mere
presence in a classroom. Apparently meager immediate results are
glossed over by reference to supposed long-range effects. The more
cynical among teachers will see the value of college less in the subject
matter of courses than in the discipline and self-denial learned incidental to obtaining a passing grade. Still more cynical ones see college
as a convenient episode before entering father's business or the like.

One look at the college curriculum, which embodies the history and
present state of every imaginable art and science, is enough to convince anyone that it is far beyond the capacity of a four-year program
addressed to 17 to 21 year olds, who seem by their very developmental
status barred from a proper appreciation of the material. Many serious
institutions handle themselves as if attainment of the curricular goal
could be actually expected of their students. A deliberate virtue can
even be made of talking "above the students' heads." At St. John's, for
instance, speakers invited to address the college are encouraged to
speak beyond the students' comprehension on the theory that by
presenting an elevated model of thinking they will provide an incentive to students and enable them to realize the distance that separates
them from more developed scholarship.

Responsibility is of course readily described in external terms: such
and such reading assignments, papers of this length due at such a date,
and so forth. But teachers are uneasy with mere compliance and every
teacher has known, with some despair, students who are letter-perfect
in their preparation and presentation of subject matter and who somehow seem to miss the spirit of the thing. Even then such students are
likely to be given an A or B, on the ground that, after all, they followed instructions.

There are subtler aspects to responsibility. One of our faculty informants felt, particularly with respect to favorite topics of his, that
he had to provide his students with the correct answer to their questions, including an appropriate and succinct bibliographical reference.
He objected to the idea of letting the students find these for themselves. He thought the answer was his responsibility. At the same time

he felt that eliciting the students' own views, as distinct from the arguments they presented in class discussion, was a form of prying. One wonders whether the teacher here is not over-reacting against a desire to convert his students, with the result that he overprotects them.

The issue of discipline is a related one. Power and learning are antithetical to each other. The use of power (grades, graduation), rather than internalization of discipline, characterizes college procedures to a high degree; and these evoke in their turn the students' resistance. In college one finds much less of the open defiance that creates disciplinary problems on lower educational levels. Some safety valves are, nevertheless, provided. Colleges have traditional days in which open rowdyism is permitted. Some of the more violent students end up in the hands of the police, and the college authorities are forced to resort to some embarrassed disciplining. (Even respectable women's college students are likely to be transformed into Bacchae on such days, and some wild scenes may be enacted on the streets of the town.) But in the classroom the teacher faces more subtle problems of discipline. The place of rowdyism is taken by more refined forms of inattention and defiance (such as sleeping, yawning, note writing, laughter, and reading the newspaper). Here students may defy their teacher subtly by closing their minds to his efforts.

Given the relative distance that separates teacher from students, the classroom is an ideal occasion for the development of images and myths. The myths that students develop about their teachers often are intensely florid, and worthy of systematic attention. Teachers in turn have to substitute images for clear perception when thinking of their students. In interviewing teachers one is struck by the undifferentiated or amorphous picture they have of their students. Even obvious groupings tend to be overlooked. An instructor in a natural science, for example, will disregard the groupings of engineering and chemistry majors in his class even though acknowledgment of this is crucial to the conduct of the class. Some teachers will make general social divisions of students into fraternity and nonfraternity people. It is common, however, for one type to be singled out: the outstanding student. "Outstanding" seems to mean responsive to the professor, at a level of performance acceptable to the professor. Responsive students of course are important to the professor, but the way they are singled out seems to emphasize the lack of responsiveness of the rest of the class and to leave response to accident and to the manipulativeness of some students.

A teacher's image is not only of what his students are but also of what he would like them to be or what he would like to make them, and of what he thinks they will be. Thus he may view them as future specialists in his field (even though the number of students in his class may be equal to that of all specialists in the country), as converts to his intellectual, social, or political vision, or as future Babbitts who will have no use for what he is giving them, or as future antagonists. A teacher at a woman's college once vividly expressed her disappointment. She thought she was raising a generation of independent women scholars, only to see her students return to the campus pushing baby carriages and absorbed in a life that seemed far removed from scholarship.

A particularly interesting question is what in the classroom causes a teacher to experience stress or anxiety. At the present time such anxiety, though quite pervasive, is virtually unacknowledged, and hence no channels are provided for its constructive handling. This is prominent among the factors that make teaching a very lonely profession. We have found that our faculty informants would express anxiety either in the form of worry over their adequacy in class or in the form of blaming their students for inadequacy. Anxiety, rather than analysis of the anxiety predominated. For example, one of our professors when asked to describe certain stress situations, mentioned his class getting mad when he criticized certain cherished beliefs. He found this upsetting. Yet is anger not a common reaction when a cherished conviction is challenged? If an emotion of this kind is recognized, it can be made a factor in the learning process.

It is a chastening experience for a professor to read through a dossier of interviews of students during their passage through college or to interview them several years after graduation. Even very modest expectations as to the number of references to the classroom are disappointed. Mention of teachers' personality characteristics, though rare too, is more frequent than reference to the contents of courses. One teacher's sarcasms or another teacher's quite incidental kindness will crop up here and there. It is not to be inferred from this that the influence of subject matter is a negligible one in American colleges. But the data are enough to give one pause. For they indicate that both in and after college students do not tend to talk readily or at any length about their classroom experience, about the great and exciting ideas to which they have been introduced in course after course. The records also indicate that the interviewer's picture is different from that of many a professor, whom some students in almost any course leave with the impression that he provided a turning point in their lives. The problem does not seem to be fundamentally different from the one the Lynds (1929; p. 211 ff.) posed in regard to the Middletown high school in the 1920s. They wondered why, in a culture in which going to school is so highly valued, the academic contents of education are considered the special province of grinds and freaks, and the athlete rather than the scholar is likely to be idolized.

Part of the answer lies of course in our popular culture, with its relative underdevelopment of a cultural middle class ("middle brows"). In line with this we have almost made the man of general culture a specialist and created a class of such "specialists" in the humanities teachers. Even they often strive to escape the onus of general culture by identifying themselves with some specialized part of their field, so that teachers of literature, for instance, turn into specialists in 17th-century science, linguistics, the press, Freud, and so forth. The distance of Americans from a liberal arts culture (exemplified by the proverbial Frenchman discoursing on Descartes during a three-hour business lunch) can be measured even in the recent popular concern with bettering our schools. It was sparked by and is oriented to the intention of keeping technologically ahead of Russia. Where men like Whyte (1956) call for more emphasis on the humanities, it turns out that the desire to broaden executive mentality is an important incentive. The American college curriculum, born out of and shaped by the needs of a small European intellectual and managerial-productive class, is in the custody of teachers who tend to identify with that European class, but it is presented to youngsters who grow up in an adolescent world in which there is much emphasis on jobs, cars, sports, and the fabulous intricacies of dating and other adolescent adventures. The adult society they grow into is perhaps even less supportive of the values held by their colleges.

THE CLASSROOM AND THE TEACHER FROM THE STUDENT'S PERSPECTIVE

This is the point to turn more directly to the student in his relationships to teacher and class. Like the teacher, the student arrives in the classroom insufficiently prepared. Typically, he arrives after having been shuffled through a rather soul-less and bureaucratic process of registration, one concerned with credit points, prerequisites, corequisites, grade point averages. He is herded into a frequently uncomfortable classroom, often assigned a seat, his attendance is checked, regular assignments are given, as well as frequent quizzes, tests, exams, and papers. His written work may be read not by his teacher but by arrogant or timid graduate students on whose desks there is always a groaning pile of unfinished blue or white books through which they plod agonizingly. Objective tests may be a further step in making learning impersonal. The whole process is recorded and presided over by the IBM machine which is increasingly taking the place of the registrar, who in the past was often a friendly human being to whom students could turn in the process of grade-getting. A revealing caricature of the whole process is presented in the campus story of the instructor who, Europe-bound, mailed his grade sheet to the registrar, complete and properly curved. Only it turned out that he had filled out the grade sheet of a class he had not taught, the form having been sent to him by mistake.

The students' individual evaluations of the entering teacher express a wide range of attitudes: from seeing the teacher as a representative of reality to seeing him as a representative of unreality, with the corresponding attitudes to his subject matter and his ways of presenting it. But gradually the individual students begin to become a group, and teachers may refer to the "personality" that classes assume. It would be useful to know more about how this comes about (which also would further enable teachers to have this process assume beneficial forms). It seems that some students function as opinion leaders, both in and after class; and, depending on how these leaders are viewed by the rest of the class, they can aid or hinder the class's openness to the teacher. College classes, like other human groups, seem to have their lieutenants. Some teacher's preferences for students considered "outsiders" by the bulk of the class may well contribute to having the teacher and his ideas stamped as outsiders. (The frequently discussed problem of whether to concentrate on the brighter or the laggard students, or the recently investigated problem of whether to mix or separate authoritarian from nonauthoritarian students, are related to the one here presented. (Chapter 21.)

The members of the class will have common concerns about a teacher, with obvious variation in intensity: How is he going to grade? Is he going to work the class hard or not? How is he going to present his material, and what learning effort is he going to call forth from his students? A student's evaluation of his teacher is continuous. An initial liking of the teacher's quality as an entertainer may give way to the realization that this goes on at the expense of learning. For some students a course, and its teacher, jell only when review is made before the final examination. In retrospect, even years after, a course may be seen as hollow, which at the time it was taken seemed subtle and profound, an illusion created by the teacher's verbal agility or his seemingly meaningful obscurity.

A word about "good teaching." "Good teacher" is a term liberally bandied around on campuses. But its operational referents are exceedingly varied. Sometimes it means not much more than a large enrollment, or favorable comments by students in the department chairman's or the the dean's office. I know of a department chairman who, under pressure, had to resort to a more "scientific" way of determining the "good" teachers in his department. He computed the percentage of students per instructor who, after their introductory courses, went on to intermediate courses in the department. But we need a much firmer definition of a "good teacher," a definition that would take into account both the student's grasp of subject matter and the disposition to further learning that he acquired as a result of the course. Such appraisal, moreover, should always be made with attention to the nature of the students considered.

One of the meanings of "good teacher" is that he is one who presents his subject matter in a clear and well-organized manner. While some students like this kind of teacher, others do not respond to him very well. They feel he is too close to their level, and too pat. They may prefer the teacher who seems confused and to whom they have difficulty catching on. (This will tend to be the reaction of students who wish to learn rather than merely to pass the course.) Thus it is not so much the teacher's preoccupation with research as its lack of vitality that tends to interfere with teaching. Part of the criterion of good teaching is the degree of challenge, of opportunity for growth it provides. A scientific study of teaching is likely, therefore, to increase the tolerance for varying teaching personalities rather than to restrict it, as is sometimes feared. The real task is to have each personality type express itself more effectively.

It is frequently held that a teacher's enthusiasm is a major, if not the major, factor in arousing the enthusiasm of his students. Even apparent exceptions seem to confirm this rule. Irwin Edman (1938; pp. 138 ff.) reports that he could keep himself awake in John Dewey's classes only by resorting to the device, unusual for him, of taking careful notes; it turned out that in this way he could catch the excitement of a creative mind in the process of developing novel ideas. A teacher's enthusiasm seems to be separable from subject matter and to affect students regardless of their disposition toward what is being taught. It is not uncommon for a student to remember a teacher well, but to be mistaken about the subject matter he taught.

That college students respond to enthusiasm is understandable. Being adolescents, they are likely to respond to passion, to passion no matter what it is. But the appeal may be as transitory as are so many adolescent affairs or it may have a more lasting effect upon development. Here is a further criterion of good teaching. It would also be intriguing to consider whether some students are steered into courses or graduate school subjects more in response to the vivid personality characteristics of a teacher than in response to the inherent appeal of subject matter or occupation. The teacher's enthusiasm is a many-edged thing.

"Transference" in the classroom. The student's reaction to the teacher's enthusiasm is only one facet of a more complex and underlying phenomenon: the transference and countertransference relationships between teacher and student. (I borrow the term "transference" from the clinic. It will need to be redefined for the classroom). Freud (1928) in a charming essay on his "Gymnasium" teachers has given a description of the parentlike significance of his teachers and the resulting effects they had on his learning and aspirations:

I do not know what aroused our attention more: the scientific subject matters we were presented with or the personalities of our teachers . . . With many of us the road to learning led only via the personalities of our teachers. Some of us remained stuck on this road and for a few of us—why should we not confess it?—the road was for this reason permanently blocked. We wooed our teachers or we turned away from them, imagined sympathies and antipathies on their part which probably did not exist. We studied their character and fashioned and misfashioned our own in reference to theirs . . . At bottom we loved them very much if they gave us any reason for that at all; I do not know whether all of our teachers observed this.

"Transference" is a phenomenon that many teachers (and students) would rather not have exist. It introduces a bothersome element into the supposedly dispassionate intercourse of minds. Yet it is a potent vehicle for learning, mislearning, and not learning. Resistance to the teacher needs as careful attention in college learning as does resistance to the therapist in psychotherapy. For resistance thwarts not only the teacher's educational endeavors, it often also thwarts the teacher himself in more personal ways, as was indicated in our discussion of "deadwood." A former Vassar student (Carrick, 1941; p. 139 ff.) in a somewhat self-conscious novel about her school experience, describes a conference with a female English professor who reduced the student to tears and impotence by impressing on her the insufficiency of her background for undertaking the critical study of a modern novel. The student is aware of the teacher's hostility. But the implications of this are not pursued further either by her or by her teacher. They need to be. For it is likely that having been frustrated by the teacher, the student will next try to frustrate her, or resort to some of the other devious ways invited by such situations. Plato, whom many consider the arch-representative of authoritarian education, was well aware of the resistance aroused by enforced learning (*Republic* 536–537). He suggested that education could accomplish its goal only if reason had an adequate emotional base (*Republic* 402). Reason then comes as a friend, not in the form of oversolicitousness, sermonizing, demanding, cajoling, sarcasm, impersonality, abstractedness in which it often comes in the classroom.

The college teacher is a special transference object for his students. He is an "in between" object, in between parents and the adult relations the student will establish in and after college. College itself, for large numbers of students, means living away from home for the first time and thus is transitional between adolescence and adulthood. (The absence of the college system on the European continent seems to have educational consequences worth a special study.) Teachers thus may become "associates" in the student's mind in his rebellion against his parents. As I have indicated, this is a role to which teachers often lend themselves readily, being frequently permanent rebels themselves. But teachers pay insufficient attention to the transitory nature of the student's rebelliousness. When the rebelliousness wanes, it is likely, therefore, to be replaced by renewed identification with the parent recently rebelled against. College teachers then are likely to throw up their hands in despair over students and alumni. All their efforts seem to have been wasted. Yet what they missed was the opportunity to help the student find secure identities other than the traditional ones, as he was seeking a new equilibrium.

Other students react to teachers more as if they were their parents. Then the brunt of rebelliousness against the parents will be experienced by the teachers too. In other students there is a prerebellious attachment or compliance. (See Chapter 6.) College teachers tend to take these very varied reactions at their face value; that is, they see them as "objective" responses to themselves and their subject-matter and then adopt "objective" ways of dealing with them.

How teachers miss the fact of transference is seen, for instance, in colleges whose constituencies tend to come from the upper social brackets. Some teachers at these institutions will complain about students reacting to them as if they were of menial status. Actually the student's view of the teacher is much more fundamentally influenced by the teacher's transference status than by his socio-economic one. The conceit that becomes a personality characteristic of many teachers is in fact a result of the teacher's coming to believe himself endowed with some of the qualities he is assigned in the phantasy of his students. This may increase his tendency to complain about being undeservingly treated; for the teacher may come to demand respect to the self woven out of his students' phantasies.

The intensity of the transference will of course vary much with the school and with individual students. Transference may be at a minimum where the classroom is regarded as a nuisance in the pursuit of socio-economic advancement or of fun, as with the girl attending a large university who exclaimed, "I love school, but I hate classes!" But wherever learning takes place, the transference reaction also has a certain intensity and calls forth all the variety of manipulative, erotic, compliant, defiant, passive, aggressive, and other reactions. These reactions both facilitate and interfere with learning. Moreover, they color the learner's intellectuality to a very significant degree. One wonders, for instance, whether the blandness, or even sterility, of some work exhibited in professional journals and meetings does not have a major root in the often very frustrating transference situations of graduate school life.

Teachers' relations to their classes vary all the way from pure monologue to fully developed and reciprocal communication. One of the most effective teachers I have ever witnessed was a colleague in a social science department. The notion of cultural variety and the limitedness of the mere American way had become one of the organizing focuses of her intellectual life. But while most teachers are restricted to talking about cultural relativity, this teacher was able to give a living demonstration of it. She held some of her classes in her own home, her children sitting around her and occupied with domestic and artistic tasks (sewing, carving, and the like). Her furniture, her family, herself, helped by her foreign origin, were a living embodiment of a culture different from standardized America. Students would sometimes stay for dinner or even sleep overnight. Their term papers were often covered with profuse "coworker" type comments. The personal attachments to their teacher that these students developed were intense, and she made an important intellectual and personal difference in their lives, even if they later went in quite different directions. Also, these students developed a unique empathy for cultural ways different from our own.

With this teacher the impact of personality was at a maximum, and I wonder how many teachers would be confident enought to expose themselves in the midst of their domesticity to their students. (The classroom, indeed, seems to afford to some teachers an opportunity to evade what they consider the unpleasant parts of their personalities.) In considering the impact of the teacher's personality one must remember that students tend to select the teachers they will let themselves be affected by. Nevertheless, the effect of personality, even on the otherwise often rather dull learning of languages, is cogently described by Nabokov (1959) in his novel *Pnin* when he refers to "those stupendous Russian ladies, scattered all over academic America, who, without having had any formal training at all, manage somehow, by dint of intuition, loquacity, and a kind of maternal bounce, to infuse a magic knowledge of their difficult and beautiful tongue into a group of innocent-eyed students in an atmosphere of Mother Volga songs, red caviar, and tea" (p. 9). Other teachers rely, often unwittingly, on an appeal to the student's sense of insufficiency. The spur to learning here is to have the student prove to the demanding parent that one is a good boy or a good girl. Still other teachers engage in a tacit agreement with their students that the classroom will provide occasion for indulgence in phantasy disguised under this or that "subject matter" and conditional upon the "reality" requirement of term papers and tests. To still other teachers classroom and subject matter are an exercise in duty, cold, clear, unsentimental, and subject to precise measurement. Some teachers tend to encourage their students, others to frustrate them or to encourage some students and to frustrate others. Some teachers thinks that almost nothing a student has to say on his own is worthwhile. Others think an empathic listening to what the student says is the only possible starting point of learning, with some teachers going as far as to fear to express almost any disagreement with their students. In all this it should be kept in mind that the teacher's need of students, though often unrecognized, is frequently intense. The students are sometimes the chief persons upon whom to direct his devotion or aggression or upon whom to project his dependence or inadequacy.

I have suggested that (1) transference takes place in the classroom, that it is (2) an important aid or obstacle in learning, that (3) personality development is influenced by it, and that (4) the very quality of intellectuality is further conditioned by it. In the light of this, academic subject matter can be recognized to assume many additional forms. It can be sentimental, pragmatic, polemical, censorious, ego-syntonic, ego-alien, subjective, objective, phantasy-oriented, reality-oriented, expressive, constrictive, collectinglike, abstract- schizoid, and so on. A psychology of knowledge discovers under the flag of "the pursuit of truth" this emotional variety of investigating, creating, and presenting subject matter. It is a corollary of my position not only that attitude is intimately related to intellectual creativity, but also that subject matter and attitude to subject matter subtly shade into each other.

It seems from what I have said here that we must add the study of transference to the traditional investigations of classroom interactions. That attention to transference would seem novel or inappropriate to most teachers testifies perhaps not so much to neglect of the task as to the difficulty of handling it. Yet it is implied in the very principle that liberal education is to develop the personality (though, of course, the belief that personality is mind still strongly persists in the actual practice of liberal education). College teachers who see attention to transference as an additional burden may well change their minds if they come to realize that here is their opportunity to turn, in their functions as teachers, from amateurs into professionals, and that their whole teaching existence may be transformed into an immeasurably more meaningful one.

Classroom types. Teachers, of course, do not do the only teaching on our college campuses or even the main part of it. The influence of the peer culture and the school's traditions and atmosphere has been referred to. Students teach themselves and each other, and this teaching, in and out of the classroom, is worthy of detailed study. Communication among students varies very much, from classrooms where students function as individual units to classrooms where much concerted action is possible. Isolation of particular students is often a marked phenomenon. There is the forever reappearing student who does not dare to speak up in class because he thinks that other students are much more knowledgeable than he. Such a student often weaves a composite portrait, comparing his individual reaction to the aggregate of a number of articulate students.

A most striking phenomenon is the underdevelopment of direct communication between class and teacher. Occasional student delegations may show up at some teachers' desks. These delegations may be the result of class discussion, or an individual student may take it upon himself to represent the presumed point of view of the class. But talking to the teacher is fraught with all sorts of hesitations: fear of offending him, of seeming to apple-polish, of seeming a teacher's pet to the class, of saying what the teacher knows anyway, and so forth. The establishment of more conscious and direct channels of communication, and creating the atmosphere for such communication, would seem to be beneficial for teachers and students alike. Teachers, as has been indicated, are sensitive to certain cues from their classes, but to others they are not sensitive, and they too rarely seek to create new ones. Even such simple observations as where a particular student chooses to sit on different class days (closer or more distant to the teacher, for instance) can be helpful. So can be a study of which students are absent when. Teachers tend to take absences as a reflection on their teaching. Actually it often tells more about the student than about the teacher.

It will be very desirable to develop a theory of classroom student types. Obviously the student's attitude in the classroom will be a function of his socio-economic background and of his personality, but this does not prevent the development of a typology specific to the environment of the classroom. (1) There is the student type mainly oriented toward passing the course. This type falls into two quite distinct subtypes: (a) the student who is indifferent to the course itself and regards it as a stepping stone to, or hurdle in the way of, other things and (b) the student who is compliant and conformist with the socio-psychological order (a course in philosophy and instructions in tennis and dates on Saturday may all be part of the glossy order of things that is recommended in *Mademoiselle* and *Time*).

(2) Type 2 is related to 1b, but distinguished by his greater involvement or tenacity in scholastic matters. This is the student who seeks to control knowledge. He will usually do well in his courses and cock his ear when something is mentioned he does not know (Goethe has described this student in the person of Wagner in *Faust*). He will often seem a well-motivated student, though he may be among the A students in Donald Brown's study who are *not* nominated by their professors as outstanding. (See Chapter 16.) For on closer inspection this student does not so much wish to know as he wishes to control. The type is one often found among academicians themselves: those who keep up with the journals and books, not so much because it feeds into their thinking as because it gives them a sense of control and command. (The one-up academician can say about a new contribution that it is rather like what X, Y, and Z have already done.)

(3) A third type is the curious student. Somewhere in the spectrum of this type falls the student whose curiosity is of a "sublimated" nature, i.e., curiosity that can address itself realistically to subject matter and the problems and questions from which subject matter springs.

Academic curiosity, by contrast, is often mixed: desire to know set against the desire not to know. This desire not to know is the academic manifestation of the general psychic tendency to limit awareness wherever it is painful. By tending to think of all academic research as directed to discovery, we have deprived ourselves of the opportunity of studying the ubiquitous instances of the desire not to know in academic work. The distinction here made is akin to the more familiar one between reason and rationalization, a device to assure not knowing. It is possible, for instance, that an overconcern with method, so common in the social sciences and philosophy, is a function of the desire not to know. In general, what may seem to be curiosity may well be the unconscious device of continually looking in the wrong place. "Research" can provide a respectable institutional flag for such not-looking.

Ruth Munroe (1942) made an interesting distinction between students who choose a subject matter to get away from themselves and those who seek to explore themselves by means of a subject matter. The same subject matter can serve either function; for example, biology may be viewed as a study of the bodily machine or it may be viewed as an opportunity for satisfying curiosity about one's own bodily functions. Munroe's distinction cuts across ours; for the degree of sublimation can vary in either the one or the other kind of students distinguished by her.

(4) In a fourth student type, related to 1b also, strong personal orientation to the teacher predominates. The student's attitude is similar to that of the devoted secretary. As we have indicated, transference is a major factor in learning. But here the personal element is so strong as to put relation to subject matter in the shadow, so that it does not become an object of interest in its own right.

The fact that the college student is an adolescent, or recently was one, means that his intellectuality, even his whole personality, has a transitional character. Parents seem to know this better than teachers. They are apt to think of college as a "phase" while teachers are likely to cry "betrayal" when yesterday's student shows up as alumnus. For example, when students show themselves very much concerned with prejudice and come to advocate the equality of everyone, it may mean some mighty intellectual liberation. But it may also mean a reorientation in regard to the "incest" problem, and the acceptance of the (often mythical and nonpresent) Negro may symbolically refer to John's accepting Jane. College teachers by seeing college as a phase could help the students to utilize their rebellions and gropings more effectively, so that the college phase would be more fully a stage in development and less of an episode. Teachers may unwittingly make college more episodic by an emphasis on the discrepancy between the school and the outside world.

While it lasts, much of college adolescence is a splendid phase. A colleague once referred to the renaissance life his students lead. "Renaissance" is an apt term for the unceasing activity, the sense of the infinite, and the oscillations between, and simultaneous embodiments of, asceticism and exuberance. Savonarola, Leonardo, and Cesare Borgia rolled into one. (Does it all need to peter out, as it often does, in row houses and organizational living?) As everybody knows, there tend to be active minorities among students who embody the "renaissance" type more purely. In the Thirties and Forties these tended to be liberals who had strong political convictions. In the Fifties, the beatniks, bohemians, and such seem to have taken their place, and the overtones are more strongly literary and artistic. Recently there has been a new upsurge of politico-social radicalism on some campuses. In each generation these minorities tend to be viewed as profligate and irresponsible. In fact, some of these students do some of the most responsible and creative thinking on our campuses. They often have a touch of madness. But *their* madness is all out in the open.

THE TEACHER AND HIS SUBJECT MATTER

A separate chapter (Chapter 11) will be devoted to the discussion of the curriculum. Hence attention needs to be called here only to the special role of the teacher in determining the nature of the subject matter presented in class. As every undergradute has found out, it is often difficult to get a clear idea of what a course is like from either its title or even its description in the college catalogue. The same course title may in different institutions or even in the same school denote a wide range of subject matter and manner of presentation. Thus, the same course title in philosophy may cover everything from mathematics to poetry. The course may be oriented toward method, toward content, history, the present, the general, the specific, theory, applications. (This variety of presentation is undoubtedly aided by the tendency of every academic field, particularly in the social sciences and humanities, to reduplicate within itself many segments of other fields.) A teacher, therefore, needs to be characterized not alone by his departmental affiliations or even his specialization within a department, but also by such further criteria as his orientation in regard to the following continua: method—content; general theory—special theory; hypotheses—facts; pure theory—applications; established theory—innovations; central problems—borderline problems; intradisciplinary problems—interdisciplinary problems.

It is worth noting, finally, that the presentation of subject matter in the classroom is influenced by the social, political, and economic structure of the college and its departments. The aims of each department to guard and enhance its status and to assure itself an adequate supply of students are factors in determining the nature of work requirements in the course, grading, content areas. Proliferation of course offerings is a case in point. As Gail Kennedy suggests, in a personal communication, the number of different courses in a given institution seems a function of the number of its teachers, as can be brought out by a comparison of college catalogues; every teacher must have his special course.

To conclude, the aim of this chapter has been to help establish the continuing study of the dynamics of teaching. The articulation of these dynamics is a prerequisite if teaching is to become a more purposive art and if academic attainment and human values are to be brought into greater accord with each other.

REFERENCES

Barr, S. *Purely academic, a novel.* New York: Simon and Schuster, 1958.

Brown, D. R. "Non-intellective factors and faculty nominations of ideal students." Report to the College Entrance Examination Board of a Pilot Study. Mellon Foundation, Vassar College, 1959.

Cantor, N. *The dynamics of learning.* Buffalo, N.Y.: Foster and Stewart, 1946.

Caplow, T., and McGee, R. J. *The academic marketplace.* New York: Basic Books, 1959.

Carrick, Gertrude. *Consider the daisies.* Philadelphia: J. B. Lippincott, 1941.

Edman, I. *Philosopher's holiday.* New York: Viking, 1938.

Ekstein, R., and Wallerstein, R. S. *The teaching and learning of psychotherapy.* New York: Basic Books, 1958.

Fleming, C. M. *Teaching: a psychological analysis.* London: Methuen, 1958.

Freud, Anna. *The ego and the mechanisms of defence.* London: Hogarth, 1937.

Freud, S. "Zur Psychologie des Gymnasiasten" (1914) in *Gesammelte Schriften.* Vienna: Internationaler Psychoanalytischer Verlag, 1928, 11, 287–290.

Highet, G. *The art of teaching.* New York: Knopf, 1950.

Jacob, P. E. *Changing values in college, an exploratory study of the impact of college teaching.* New York: Harper Bros., 1957.

James, W. "The Ph.D. octopus," in *Memories and studies.* New York: Longmans, Green, 1911, 329–347.

Jarrell, R. *Pictures from an institution, a comedy.* New York: Knopf, 1954.

Kubie, L. S. Some unsolved problems of the scientific career. *Amer. Scientist,* 1953, 41, 596–613 (1954), 42, 104–112.

Ladd, H. A., and Murphy, Lois B. *Emotional factors in learning.* New York: Columbia University Press, 1944.

Laski, H. J. American education, Chapter 8 in *The American democracy, a commentary and an interpretation.* New York: Viking, 1948.

Lynd, R. S., and Lynd, Helen M. *Middletown, a study in contemporary American culture*. New York: Harcourt, Brace, 1929.

McCarthy, Mary. *The groves of academe*. New York: Harcourt, Brace, 1952.

MacKinnon, D. W. Identifying and developing creativity, in *Selection and educational differentiation*. Field Service Center and Center for the Study of Higher Education, University of California, 1959, 75–89.

Munroe, Ruth L. *Teaching the individual*. New York: Columbia University Press, 1942.

Nabokov, V. *Pnin*. New York: Avon Publications, 1959.

Nicolson, Marjorie H. Neilson of Smith, *The Amer. Scholar*, 1946, 15, 539–549.

Roe, Anne. *The making of a scientist*. New York: Dodd, Mead, 1953.

Ruml, B. *Memo to a college trustee, a report on financial and structural problems of the liberal college*. New York: McGraw-Hill, 1959.

Sanford, N. Individual and social change in a community under stress. *J. of soc. Issues*, 1953, 9, 25–42.

Sapir, E. Psychiatric and cultural pitfalls in the business of getting a living. In *Selected Writings*. D. G. Mandelbaum. (Ed.) Berkeley, Calif.: University of California Press, 1949, 578–589.

Schwab, J. J. Eros and education: a discussion of one aspect of discussion, *The J. of gen'l. Educ.*, 1954, 8, 51–71.

Taylor, H. A. (Ed.) *Essays in teaching*. New York: Harper Bros., 1950.

Thistlethwaite, D. L. College environments and the development of talent, *Science*, 1959, 130 (3367), 71–76.

Whyte, W. H. *The organization man*. New York: Simon and Schuster, 1956.

Williams, G. *Some of my best friends are professors, a critical commentary on higher education*. New York: Abelard-Schuman, 1958.

Wilson, L. *The academic man, a study in the sociology of a profession*. London: Oxford University Press, 1942.

10 *Joseph Adelson*

The Teacher as a Model

BARRIERS TO UNDERSTANDING

There are any number of difficulties that beset us when we try to treat this topic. We find it hard to keep ourselves dispassionate; this theme—the teacher as model—is peculiarly likely to engage our capacities for self-deception. When we think of ourselves as we once were, as students, we tend to reconstruct ourselves at the feet of a great teacher—some great man, or perhaps only a kindly and devoted one—someone who infused in us whatever modest claim to merit we possess. Now this may indeed have happened to us; but I have come to believe that whether or not it has, we will rearrange the past to imagine that it has. There is something in us, something almost archetypal, which makes us feel that we achieved our maturity only by taking over the strength and wisdom of our teachers.

Then there is the other side to it, the teacher's perspective on himself as a model. I imagine that we vary greatly in the degree to which we recognize and accept this aspect of our career. For some of us, some few of us, to serve as a model is at the very heart of teaching: our self-esteem may demand it, and even more, the need to give meaning to our lives. We have here a *mystique* of the vocation; and its dangers to self-understanding are all too evident. When we so define ourselves, we end by overestimating our value: we collect testimonials to our influence; we mistake being tolerated for being liked, being liked for being admired, and being admired for being taken as a model. But this form of self-deception is, I would guess, fairly uncommon. The more usual reaction of the teacher nowadays is to deny or make light of his potential as a model. Perhaps we are, as Americans, too diffident about

396

exercising authority to perceive this part of the role easily. A model to youth—to so think of ourselves is to seem fatuous, narcissistic, even undemocratic. We permit ourselves the fancy only in our more elated or depressed moments, and even then, not too openly. The most we will allow is to see ourselves taken as a model not for what *we* are, but for what we represent—the self as a delegate from, let us say, the humanistic spirit or the scientific tradition. In defining ourselves so modestly, we may imagine that we are being matter-of-fact, down-to-earth, hard-headed; but I would argue that this view, which prefers to ignore or underestimate this side of teaching, is as fanciful, as mistily romantic as the earlier one.

These are some of the sentimental barriers to an understanding of the topic; there are substantive ones as well. One of these is that our knowledge of personality change in adolescence is still sketchy and uncertain; no doubt this problem will be considered elsewhere in this book and so I will not attempt to treat it here. Another and related difficulty is that we have no theory of modeling. Assume that the student does (or can) become in some degree like his teacher. How does it happen? Is it a learning process or does it go deeper than that? In any case, what do we mean by "becoming like?" The student does not become *exactly* like his teacher; he chooses and rejects, and what determines that? Does he take over the teacher's ego qualities? Does he set him up as an ego ideal? or does the teacher become a superego figure? And what is the teacher's part in all of this? How does his activity influence the process? It is rather startling to recognize how little we really know about these and other fundamental problems, the more so since theories of education require a theory of modeling; in fact, they often contain such a theory, implicit, unacknowledged, unexamined.

USES AND LIMITATIONS OF THE CONCEPT OF IDENTIFICATION

When I first began thinking about this paper I made the bland assumption—rather thoughtlessly, it now appears—that the intellectual demands of the topic would easily be met by the concept of identification. The student identifies with his teacher, and to the extent that he does, is changed. There is an elaborate literature on identification (so elaborate as to be ornate; there is a literature which categorizes the literature) and my task would simply involve applying our documented knowledge of the identification process to the specific problem at hand. A moment's reflection suggests how much more complicated the matter really is.

One trouble with the "identification" concept, as Nevitt Sanford pointed out several years ago (1955), is that it has become so fashionable, and thus so ubiquitously used, that it has lost the precision it once had. Not that it had much to begin with. It is an unusually docile and elastic concept, one that gives way easily to whatever stretching we want to impose on it. Since it seems to elucidate so many psychological phenomena, we have tended to stretch it to include more and more instances of behavior and experience. We find it used in discussions of hysteria and of depression, in descriptions of normal personality development, in the psychology of creativity, and so on, almost endlessly. Sanford suggests that there is not much similarity among the various appearances of the term "identification." The processes referred to are, presumably, vaguely analogous; but is that enough? Do we gain any deeper understanding through the total embrace of the identification concept? Are we not better served by a more limited use of the term?

The amorphousness of the identification concept is one problem; there is an even more serious one. When we review our experiences we are likely to come up with some dramatic examples of the effects of identification, cases where the student's life was changed, decisively, by the choice of model. These instances are likely to be highly persuasive, so much so that they may mislead us into feeling that identification is the critical process in personality change, that more moderate changes in the student simply involve a more moderate degree of identification. Let me illustrate what I mean through a pair of examples.

The first of these concerns what is probably the most striking example of character change I have ever seen. In college I had a friend who was an amiable, somewhat cynical, rather aimless sort of boy— pleasant enough, something of a buffoon in fact, and without much drive or conviction. He decided to go on to graduate school, not because he had received any inner call, but largely because many of his friends were doing so and because there seemed to be no viable alternative except to go to work. He made plans to study with a famous social psychologist, an ebullient, restless, imaginative man. When my friend arrived at the university he discovered that this professor had suddenly departed. There seemed to be nothing else to do than to study with another dominant figure in that department, a brilliant man, at his best willful and forceful, and at his usual worst, arbitrary and authoritarian to the point of being vicious. I next saw my friend a year later; he had become this man's disciple. This was surprising; what was unnerving was the change in manner and behavior that had taken place in him. He had been transformed from a rather affable, indolent boy, a kind of academic Good Soldier Schweik, to an academic tiger, disputatious, ill-tempered, mean-spirited, believing firmly that the world's salvation depended on its adopting his master's views on learning theory.

Now here is another instance, this time taken from psychotherapeutic work. The patient was a physicist whose career, after an extremely promising start, had petered out into haplessness. We soon learned that his career was from the beginning based on identifications: he chose physics largely because it was his older brother's field; he chose his specialty through an identification with an important teacher. For several years into his postdoctoral career things went fairly well for him. His research during this period, although decidedly his own, followed a path which had been pioneered by his teacher. Then suddenly he found it impossible to work. Two coinciding events seemed to play a part: he had exhausted the line of research begun in graduate school; and he had received a promotion in rank. Work was possible for him only so long as he defined himself as acolyte, apprentice, lieutenant. The change in rank, together with the need to find his own research interest, endangered the state of discipleship that was necessary for him to function intellectually.

Now what shall we make of these two accounts? We have in the first a rather plain example of "identification with the aggressor." My friend found himself in a situation which he took to involve the choice: "Identify or else," and more deeply, "Submit or be killed." He had taken this awesome, frightening teacher into himself and with a convert's zeal had transformed himself. The second case is rather more complex (I have given only part of the relevant information). Essentially, the patient found it necessary to contain a profound hatred of men in authority through fairly elaborate maneuvers; these involved splitting academic fathers into good and bad ones, pitting them against each other, and ending up as the favorite son, heir apparent and junior partner to the idealized teacher, after whom he modeled himself to the point of parody.

It would not be hard to find further examples in this vein. When you quiz people about their thoughts and experiences on the topic of modeling you find that almost everyone can contribute a bit of folklore. A dentist told me about one of his teachers at dental school: a pipe smoker, he had a golden palate plate made up for him, to reduce the chances of cancer. His two junior associates had taken up pipe smoking, had had plates made for themselves. When they met together at conference, all three would take out their plates, insert them, then light up their pipes—an unforgettable image. Almost all of us, I am sure, can chip in with similar anecdotes, where the disciples of an impressive teacher—the kind word is "dynamic"—took over his mannerisms, speech habits, tastes, interests, eccentricities, and what have you.

But this anecdotage, though seductive, is in the end deceiving. We remember these instances because they are vivid or amusing. Are they paradigmatic? Do they represent the extreme end of the continuum of modeling, the "far out" instances which display, in an exaggerated way, the normal processes of modeling? Or are they discontinuous, qualitatively different from the mundane forms of modeling? I would say the latter. This is not to minimize the importance of dramatic identification phenomena in the educational process; to the contrary. One can argue that we gain much in our understanding of teacher-student patterns if we take account of such phenomena. But first we will have to put identification in its place, so to speak, not permitting it to dominate our thinking.

This position is derived from Sanford's paper mentioned earlier. He argues very effectively that the identification processes we know from clinical work—mainly, introjection and identification with the aggressor—are defensive maneuvers designed to keep the personality intact and functioning in situations which threaten its integrity. The changes we see are brittle; they remain in effect only so long as the person is under duress; they then vanish. Genuine changes in personality are brought about not by unconscious defenses, but by processes, such as learning, where the ego's role is not entirely passive or regressive.

If we review our own experience with students, review them in totality as against singling out impressive exceptions—we are likely to find that what the student takes from the teacher is swiftly and silently synthesized into the existing personality. We may have here one criterion for appraising the quality of modeling: the ego's success in synthesizing the "introject." Whenever we see a radical alteration of the student's behavior, or when we see an "addition" to the ego repertoire which seems somehow alien to or disconnected from the totality of behavior (as in the student's adoption of the teacher's pet mannerisms)—we have some reason to be wary both of the genuineness and of the permanence of the "modeling." Under these circumstances we are probably right to suspect that the student is moved not by his best long-range interests, but by infantile or conflict-ridden feelings toward the teacher or the teaching situation—by anxiety, or ambivalence, or one of the many counterfeits of "love." We ought to be as mordantly skeptical of change in our students—especially when it seems too good to be true—as the psychotherapist is when he appraises the vicissitudes of behavior in his patient.

Up to this point I have followed Sanford's argument closely; but I have some disagreements with it. For one thing I think he gives too short shrift to the identification processes. They do have their uses. Granted that in the long run they tend to inhibit or distort the best development of the personality; yet that is sometimes a very long run indeed. Consider the two cases mentioned earlier. In my college friend we saw the emergence of initiative and purposefulness, of a sense of mission, that had been conspicuously absent before. The identification provided a momentum that carried him through graduate school and into a respectable, though lackluster, career. Something of the same was true of the physicist. To be sure, the identification failed him in the end; it depended on conditions that could not be met indefinitely. But we must remember that in this case we had a seriously flawed personality; the infantile attachment to his teacher did at least allow him to be launched into his career. I very much doubt that this would have happened otherwise. These are, of course, Pyrrhic victories. When the modeling is as deep and thoroughgoing as it was in these instances, the person is generally incapable of original or individual work. The master, now within, retains his influence beyond the point where he is needed. New ideas are likely to be subject to criticism by the internalized presence of the teacher; the result is a blight on thought outside of doctrine.

Identifications are useful in other and more benign ways. In adolescence especially they sometimes seem to provide the means through which needed restructurings or crystallizations of personality take place. In some cases the student can become himself only by first becoming someone else. He may find it difficult to acquire new and complex skills unless he protects himself psychically by borrowing, through identification, the teacher's power. Or he may use the identification as a mask, as a form of camouflage; while he pretends, to himself and to others, that he is being a certain someone, achieving this or that identity, he is actually accomplishing the inner changes which will allow him to achieve an identity closer to his own talents and dispositions. In all of these uses, the identification is shallow and temporary; it is used as a prop, a crutch, a smokescreen, or a shield; once it has served its purpose it is dissolved. The identification serves as the means of achieving a new and necessary identity.

IDENTITY AND THE SEEKING, ACCEPTING, AND RESISTING OF MODELS BY STUDENTS

What we have to do is to turn our attention from identification to identity (Erikson, 1950). If we are to comprehend the variations in the students' relations to their teachers as models, we shall have to do so by understanding often subtle and elusive differences in identity commitment. Consider that large group of students who are pleasant and polite enough, but carefully keep themselves remote from modeling. In most cases, I suppose we would find that they already feel themselves committed to life goals and styles to which the teacher cannot really contribute. But there are some interesting variations. For example, the student may actively resist the teacher's influence because the teacher is, in fact, too tempting as a potential model. We can see this quite clearly in some premed or prelaw students. The premed is often astute enough to recognize that he must manage a certain detachment from his physiology or biochemistry courses and teachers; to become too interested, or too involved, may divert him from the long-range goal of medicine. The student who may seem to us to be invulnerable to modeling may simply be waiting until it is safe to do so.[1]

In other cases the student who seems untouched and untouchable is in a state of limbo—in a "moratorium," to use Erikson's term—waiting for the proper time to commit himself. He does not feel ready to find a personal identity; he is, in fact, actively *not* looking for it, shielding himself from influence, keeping himself "loose" and unattached, committed, so to speak, to the bachelorhood of preidentity. He is not really waiting for the right model to come along; he is waiting for something to happen inside of him. Then he will make his move.

At the other extreme, we have those students who actively, even frenetically, shop around for models. Just as some students will spend the first weeks of a semester auditing different courses, so will some

[1] Sometimes it does not work out this way, especially so when the choice of vocation is more the parents' than the student's idea. In these instances, the choice of a new field (and of models within that field) becomes part of the adolescent rebellion. I remember a particularly striking example of this in a boy who had been carefully groomed by his parents for the ministry. He began taking psychology courses, presumably to help him in pastoral counseling, and found himself alternately fascinated and repelled by psychoanalytic theory. He could neither live with it nor without it. The ministry represented submission to the parents, to the superego, to "duty"; psychology meant rebellion, the id, and "pleasure."

(often the same ones) spend their college careers auditing different identities.[2]

In this group of model-seeking students, we again find revealing variations. The youngster may come to college with some idea of what he wants to become; what he is looking for is the external embodiment of a predetermined identity, some teacher who will personify an image of the self which the student has imagined. At a state university we see some intriguing examples: the young man from the provinces who has, out of his own resources, assisted only by his reading or by the mass media, imagined himself into the role of scholar, poet, painter. He needs only the living instance—in the form and presence of the teacher—to complete what the imagination has begun.

These variations in the identity-needs of students are also of some importance in influencing the teacher's qualities they are interested in acquiring. I was made acutely aware of this not long ago while interviewing some graduate students about to receive doctorates in the social sciences. I was interested, among other things, in the roles teachers had played in the choice of undergraduate major. One student I talked to told me at great length about a professor who had been, he said, of central importance to him. This man had been a real influence, he taught him much of what he knew; he had, in fact, been this man's undergraduate teaching assistant. What was his name, I asked. There was an embarrassed silence—he could not remember it. He could, however, remember his professor's research, accurately and in detail. We might consider this curious lapse of memory to be unconsciously motivated; but I think not altogether—it fit perfectly well with this young man's general lack of interest in his teachers as personalities. He struck most of his graduate instructors as unusually detached and independent, so much so as to affront some of them. He was brisk, brusque, businesslike. (He had, in fact, come from a business family, and it seemed to be a case where you might take the boy out of the business, but not the business out of the boy.) He looked to his teachers, one felt, more for what they knew and could teach him, for their skills, than for what they were as individuals.

Compare him with another young man, of the same age, training, and apparent ambitions. His manner was gentle and sensitive; he gave

[2] The student hungry for a model represents a particular trial and temptation to the teacher. For one thing, he is often a disappointment, promising more than he fulfills; he is frequently too ridden by ambivalence or too diffuse in identity really to take hold. For another, he appeals to the Pygmalion in all of us, and we have to be wary lest we overlook his needs in using him to fulfill our own.

the impression of being somewhat ineffectual. At the beginning of a professional career, he was still uncertain that he had made the right choice. This uncertainty and lack of conviction, the air of doubt and restlessness he conveyed, all of these suggested at least a mild case of identity diffusion (Erikson, 1950). As a boy he had been raised in a middle-class family and milieu which existed quite apart from the world of intellectual concerns. He was bright and received a scholarship to an Ivy League college. He was overwhelmed by what he discovered there—overwhelmed on a number of counts but most of all by the range and intensity of the intellectual life as it was felt there. While the young man I spoke of previously could not quite remember his teachers, this young man could remember little else. He dwelt on them lovingly, still filled with awe and childlike wonder at the flair and potency of his teachers. That was the trouble; he could not get over it. Perhaps we can put this down, ultimately, to the Oedipus complex. But the point that concerns us here is that he looked to his teachers not for what they could teach him visibly and tangibly, not for skills or techniques, but for what they could offer him as exemplars of an elusive and desired life-style.

This distinction—between skills and style—is of course a rough one; but it may help give us some sense of the differing modalities of the modeling process. Sometimes style—in the sense, now, of the professional identity—emerges or evolves out of the acquisition of skills. We may speak of a *progression* from skill to style. The student is changed gradually and by accretion; as he acquires skills, these become part of the ego repertoire, and finally, of the ego identity. The professional style—manner, attitude, and so on—is likely to be both role-syntonic and ego-syntonic.

At other times we see a *retreat* from skill acquisition to style acquisition. This may happen out of purely intrapsychic motives (e.g., the student mentioned above), but we may also find it occurring when the skills to be learned are in their nature difficult to master. In his despair or frustration the student may turn his interest from the achievement of craft to the premature absorption of the professional style or manner. We see this quite frequently in the teaching of psychotherapy. The skills here are complex and ephemeral. The student, feeling himself overwhelmed by the task, is tempted to retreat to the therapeutic *persona*. We sometimes find a kind of *ersatz* identity, the student in the guise of therapist, much given to a sonorous and sententious profundity of manner, or to overly brilliant formulations of psychodynamics. In most cases, I should say, these outbreaks of "modeling" are transient, and soon disappear. But when they persist, it may signal an end to learning; the "role" is a retreat from the oppressive demands of the apprenticeship.

Generally speaking, we have every reason to feel troubled when we observe the student to be overly eager to acquire the professional style at the expense of skill. In most cases he does so when he feels himself marginal or overwhelmed, either because of personal shortcomings or because the educational circumstances are such as to make him helpless or infantilized. We must recognize that some educational situations produce this effect in their very nature, and not because of the obtuseness or bad intentions of the educators. In some fields—especially the technical and "practical" ones—the student's performance can be judged objectively and unambiguously. The student has no trouble discovering how well he is doing; his competence and relative standing can be appraised by visible, concrete criteria of proficiency. In these circumstances he is not so dependent on the teacher's opinion, and gives his attention to the acquisition of skill. But in other fields the criteria of good performance are intrinsically ambiguous and depend upon a subjective assessment by the teacher; indeed, this is the case in any discipline at its higher levels, where good performance demands creative or synthetic capacities. Here the student cannot easily tell how well he is doing, nor can the teacher do more than measure him subjectively, or even intuitively. Furthermore, the teacher often cannot coach the student properly; he can say what the student is doing poorly, but not how to perform well. How do we tell someone to write a better poem, or for that matter, to think of a better research idea, or design a more interesting experiment, or write a more penetrating paper? The more demanding the work, the more ambiguous both the procedures and criteria of good performance, and the more the student is tempted to rely on hollow style modeling. He may take over the peripheral or irrelevant qualities of the teacher or of the professional role; or he may ape his teacher's mannerisms and tricks; in either case, he abandons his own resources to incorporate the teacher's, no matter how poorly they suit him.

THE MANY SIDES OF THE GOOD TEACHER

Discussions of the good teacher are likely to leave us more uplifted than enlightened. The descriptions we read generally amount to little more than an assemblage of virtues; we miss in them a sense of the complexity and ambiguity that we know to characterize the teacher's work. Here are some paradoxes to help us get going: a teacher may be a good teacher yet not serve as a model to any of his students; he may inspire his students and yet fail to influence them; he may influence them without inspiring them; he may be a model for them and yet not be an effective teacher; and so on. To say all of this is to make the point—an obvious one but generally overlooked in the more solemn and global discussions of the teacher—that charisma, competence, and influence do not necessarily go hand in hand. A great many college teachers, perhaps most of them, are "good" teachers—good in the sense that they are conscientious and devoted, that they are lucid, articulate, and fair-minded lecturers, and that more often than not they succeed in illuminating the subject matter. Their students learn from them, often learn very much; yet these teachers do not ultimately make much of a difference in their students' lives beyond the learning they impart. At another extreme we have those rare teachers who stir and enchant their students, and yet who may be spectacularly inept in teaching subject matter. I think now of a former colleague of mine, in some ways a truly great man, who is so ebullient, erratic, and distractible, so easily carried away by the rocketing course of his thought, that his students—even the bright ones—just sit there, benumbed, bewildered—and finally enthralled. They know themselves to be close to a presence, and are willing to suffer incoherence to join vicariously in that demonic enthusiasm.

What we must do, plainly, is to recognize the pluralism in teaching —the many styles of influence, the many modes of connection that bind student and teacher to each other. Teaching styles are so diverse that they can be categorized in a great many different ways. The grouping I want to try out was suggested by the yet unpublished work of Merrill Jackson, an anthropologist who has been doing a cross-cultural study of the healer's role. He has isolated five distinct modes of healing: shamanism, magic, religion, mysticism, and naturalism. Here is an abbreviated description of these types: the shaman heals through the use of personal power, using craft, charm, and cunning. The magician heals through his knowledge of arcane and complex rules, and his ability to follow ritual precisely; the priest claims no personal power, but achieves his healing capacity as an agent or vessel of an omnipotent authority; the mystic healer relies on insight, vision, and wisdom, through which he cures the sick soul; the naturalist (the present-day physician) is impersonal, empirical, task-oriented.

You may be struck, as I was, by the reflection that these separate modes of healing in some sense persist to this day. Although the present-day type of medicine is naturalistic (and in fact it is a common complaint that medical specialists are *too* impersonal, and do not give enough attention to the patient as a human being), we nevertheless find that the physician's relation to the patient is often patterned on an older style. Thus we have those physicians who follow the shamanistic mode, in that they implicitly define healing as a struggle between disease, on the one hand, and their own cunning and power, on the other; or those for whom medicine involves a ritualistic following of rules; or those who claim no personal charisma, but define themselves to the patient as humble servants of a Godhead, in this case modern medical science. This typology may be a useful one for treating other forms of interaction, such as those that obtain between teacher and student. For example, those teachers who define themselves primarily as experts in subject matter are roughly equivalent to naturalistic healers, in that the relationship to the client is in both cases impersonal and task-oriented. In any case, it is worth trying; I want to use Jackson's schema to consider in detail three types of teachers.

1. *The teacher as shaman.* Here the teacher's orientation is narcissistic. The public manner does not matter; this type of teacher is not necessarily vain or exhibitionistic; he may in fact appear to be withdrawn, diffident, even humble. Essentially, however, he keeps the audience's attention focused on himself. He invites us to observe the personality in its encounter with the subject matter. He stresses charm, skill, mana, in the self's entanglement with ideas. When this orientation is combined with unusual gifts, we have a *charismatic* teacher, one of those outstanding and memorable personalities who seem more than life-size. The charismatic teacher is marked by power, energy, and commitment: by power we mean sheer intellectual strength or uncommon perceptiveness and originality; by energy we mean an unusual force or vivacity of personality; and by commitment a deep absorption in the self and its work. Generally, all of these qualities are present to some degree: energy without power turns out to be mere flamboyance; power without energy or commitment is likely to be bloodless, arid, enervating.

This tells us only part of the story. In that group of teachers whom we term narcissistic, we find considerable variation in the degree of impact on the student. In some cases, the narcissistic teacher's impression on us is strong but transient; they move us, but the spell does not survive the moment. We admire them as we admire a great performer; in their presence we dream of doing as well ourselves. But when the occasion is past, we return to our mundane selves, out of the spell, unchanged, uninfluenced. In other instances, we may find the teacher's narcissism at the least distasteful and at times repelling.

Something in it warns us to keep our distance, to remain wary and uncommitted.

What makes the difference? I am not sure that we know, but I think we will understand it better when we know more about different forms of narcissism. There is a narcissism which makes a hidden plea to the audience; it cries out: "Look how wonderful I am! Admire me! Love me!" There is also a narcissism which is vindictive and vengeful; it says: "I love myself. Who needs you?" In either case the audience, or at least a good share of it, seems to sense the infantile source and quality of the teacher's narcissism, senses the petulance or anxiety which informs the teacher's manner, and keeps itself from becoming involved.[3]

There is another and rarer form of narcissism which affects us quite differently from these. It is directed neither toward nor against the audience; it is autonomous, internally fed, sustaining itself beyond the observer's response to it. The best description of its appeal remains Freud's:

> It seems very evident that one person's narcissism has a great attraction for those others who have renounced part of their own narcissism and are seeking after object-love; the charm of a child lies to a great extent in his narcissism, his self-sufficiency and inaccessibility, just as does the charm of certain animals which seem not to concern themselves about us, such as cats and the large beasts of prey . . . It is as if we envied them their power of retaining a blissful state of mind—an unassailable libido-position which we ourselves have since abandoned (Freud, 1934).

It is this form of narcissism—ingenuous, autonomous—which, when it is joined to other qualities, makes the teacher memorable. This orientation invites us to identification, to share in its bounty, to seek its protection and care, or to join its omnipotence. Yet teachers of this kind are most problematic. They tempt us into regressions. We may come to feel them to be too exalted to serve as models for us. Or we may feel defeated by them before we begin, thinking that anything we achieve will be only second-rate, that we can never grow up enough to equal them.

2. *The teacher as priest.* The priestly healer claims his power not through personal endowment, but through his office: he is the agent

[3] This is too bold a statement, for I have left out of this account a consideration of the great individual differences within the audience. People vary markedly in the degree to which they can tolerate or become attracted to narcissism of any kind. Narcissistic teachers of the exhibitionist type—the platform personalities—generally arouse controversy because their narcissism affects listeners so differently. They recruit a large audience of admirers, but also accumulate a body of students who despise them devoutly.

of an omnipotent authority. Do we have a parallel to this in teaching? I would say it is the teacher who stresses not his personal virtues, but his membership in a powerful or admirable collectivity, e.g., physics, psychoanalysis, classical scholarship. The narcissistic teacher to some degree stands apart from his discipline, and seems to say: "I am valuable to myself." The priestly teacher says: "I am valuable for what I belong to. I represent and personify a collective identity."

It is difficult to generalize about this mode of teaching, since the teacher's behavior toward the student varies so much with the nature of the collectivity. It is one thing when the collectivity is coterminous with a subject matter, and another when it is an enclosed or beleaguered sect within a discipline (e.g., the various "schools" within sociology and psychology). Collectivities differ in their openness, their degree of organization, their status vis-à-vis other groups. Some are easy to enter, whereas others are closed; some are loose and informal, bound by common interest and camaraderie; and others are stratified and formal; some are marginal in status, whereas others are secure, entrenched elites. Other differences involve the teacher's status in the collectivity: the undergraduate teacher may proselytize, seeking recruits among the promising students; the graduate-professional school teacher will first indoctrinate, then examine, and finally ordain the recruit.

To illustrate the teacher's activity in the priestly mode, I will refer to the more enclosed and differentiated collectivities. We generally find the following elements: *Continuity:* The collectivity defines itself along a temporal dimension. It has a version of the past and a vision of the future. In the past there were great ancestors whose qualities and trials established the collective identity. There is a program for the immediate future as well as a prophecy of the distant future. One of the teacher's tasks is to help the student absorb the sense of the collective past, and accept the common blueprint for the future. *Hierarchy:* Generally (though not always) the collectivity is stratified in prestige and authority. The teacher's personal authority depends in some part on his position on the ladder of authority. Although the teacher is superordinate to the student, he is in turn subordinate to more elevated figures. The student internalizes the group's system of hierarchy, and learns that he is beholden not only to his teacher but to other members of the hierarchy. One of the distinctive features of this mode of teaching is that both teacher and student may share a common model or group of models, either exalted contemporaries or great ancestors. *Election:* When the group is an elite, when membership in it is desirable and hard to achieve, we will generally find that emphasis is placed on discipline, the enduring of trials, and self-transformation. The educational process is in some degree an extended rite of passage; the teacher's role is to prepare the student for the trials he will endure, and to administer the tests which will initiate him. *Mission:* The collectivity often offers a utopian view of the future (especially when it is powerless and competitive), as well as a program for achieving dominance and instituting reforms. In these cases, the teacher's work is informed by missionary zeal; the student is expected to absorb the group's sense of mission, and in turn to recruit and socialize others once he himself has achieved office.

There is no question of the potency of the priestly mode of teaching. It achieves its effectiveness for a great many different reasons. Teacher and student are generally in a close relationship to each other. The student is encouraged to model his *activity* after the teacher's, very much as in those charming experiments on imprinting, where the baby duck follows the decoy. We also find a good deal of close coaching, both of behavior and ideology. In most cases the teaching is both positive and negative—that is, the student is trained not only to develop new behaviors, but is also required to eliminate competing or discordant responses. Generally the student is given an unambiguous ideal of character and behavior (he may be allowed, as part of the strategy of training, to feel uncertain whether he is meeting this ideal, but the ideal itself is usually clear-cut enough). In some instances the collectivity offers an encompassing doctrine, and the student is exhorted to reinterpret his experiences in the vocabulary of the doctrine; and when this is not the case, the training itself demands so complete a commitment of time and energy that the student's ideational world narrows to include only the collectivity and its concerns. The teacher customarily enjoys a great deal of power in relation to the student, which re-enforces the latter's dependency. The student's tie to the collectivity is further re-enforced by his close association with peers—rivals, fellow-aspirants, fellow-sufferers—who share his trials, sustain him in moments of doubt, restore his flagging spirits, and keep alive his competitive drive. Finally, this mode of teaching is effective because it offers to the student a stake in a collective, utopian purpose, and also in promising such tangible rewards as power, position, money, intellectual exclusiveness.

Less obviously, but quite as important, the collectivity makes its appeal to the student in helping him to resolve internal confusions. His participation allows a distinct identity choice; it supports that choice by collective approval; it reduces intellectual and moral ambiguity. A great many advantages also accrue to the collectivity; over the short run, at least, it is helped in achieving its aims by its capacity to recruit a cadre of devoted, disciplined believers. The history of my own field, psychology, has been decisively influenced by the ability of certain schools to select and organize students in the "priestly" framework, an ability which has very little to do with intellectual merit. But we also must recognize that this mode of education possesses some deadly disadvantages, both to the student and the group. The student purchases direction, force, and clarity, but does so by sacrificing some share of his own development; in some important ways he is no longer his own man. For the collectivity the danger is in a loss of flexibility and innovation. We have a perfect example in the history of the psychoanalytic movement. Through the 1930's it was, in its policies of recruitment and training, the most cosmopolitan of groups, a circumstance which produced an extraordinary boldness and vivacity of thought. Since its capture by American psychiatry it has developed a priestly mode of education, the result being a severe loss in intellectual scope and energy. It has now settled into its own Alexandrian age, repeating itself endlessly, living off its intellectual capital, affluent yet flatulent, an ironic example of the failure of success.

The dominance of this mode of teaching in the graduate and professional schools, although regrettable, is probably inevitable. It is more disturbing to note its steady encroachment in undergraduate education. For many college teachers the introductory courses have less value for themselves than as a net in which to trap the bright undergraduate, while the advanced courses increasingly serve only to screen and socialize students for what the faculty deems "the great good place"—namely, the graduate school. Furthermore, academic counseling at the freshman and sophomore level frequently produces a guerilla warfare between disciplines, each seeking to capture the promising talents for itself, and without too much regard for the student's needs and interests. If matters are not worse than they already are, it is not because the disciplines have any genuine concern for the undergraduate or for liberal ideals of education, but because the leviathans have managed to neutralize each other's demands. Even so, the pressure of required courses and prerequisites serves to force the student into premature career commitment, while the onerous demands on his time (especially in the laboratory sciences, but also and increasingly in other fields) keep him from trying anything else.

3. The teacher as mystic healer. The mystic healer finds the source of illness in the patient's personality. He rids his patient of disease by helping him to correct an inner flaw or to realize a hidden strength. The analogy here—perhaps it is a remote one—is to the teacher I will term *altruistic*. He concentrates neither on himself, nor the subject matter, nor the discipline, but on the student, saying: "I will help you become what you are." We may recall Michelangelo's approach to sculpture; looking at the raw block of marble, he tried to uncover the statue within it. So does the altruistic teacher regard his unformed student; this type of teacher keeps his own achievement and personality secondary; he works to help the student find what is best and most essential within himself.

At this point we are uncomfortably close to the rhetoric of the college brochure. This is what the colleges tell us they do; and yet we know how very rarely we find altruistic teaching. Why is it so rare? For one thing, it is a model-less approach to teaching; the teacher points neither to himself nor to some immediately visible figure, but chooses to work with his student's potential and toward an intrinsically abstract or remote ideal. For another, this mode of teaching demands great acumen, great sensitivity—the ability to vary one's attack according to the student and to the phase of teaching, now lenient, now stern, now encouraging, now critical.

But the reason that the altruistic mode is so rarely successful lies deeper than these. The mode is selfless; it demands that the teacher set aside, for the moment at least, his own desires and concerns, to devote himself, without hidden ambivalence, to the needs of another. In short, the teacher's altruism must be genuine; and altruism, as we know, is a fragile and unsteady trait, all too frequently reactive, born out of its opposite. If the teacher's selflessness is false, expedient, or mechanical, if it comes out of a failure in self-esteem, or if it gives way to an underlying envy—and in the nature of things, these are real and ever-present possibilities—then the teaching at best will not come off, and at the worst may end in damaging the student.

Some years ago I taught at an excellent progressive college which, quite unwittingly, induced some of its younger faculty to opt for a pseudo-altruistic mode of teaching. The college was committed to the ideal of student self-realization, and this was not, I should say, the usual pious cant, but a conscious, deliberate aim which showed itself in day-to-day planning and policy. In pursuit of this ideal, the college authorities stressed altruistic teaching; it was held that talent, productivity, and eminence were of only secondary importance in the hiring and firing of faculty, that teaching talent per se was primary. Here things went seriously awry; for a variety of reasons, the college managed to attract an astonishing proportion of charismatic teachers —either men of established reputation, or ambitious and talented young men on the way up, but in either case men of great vitality, self-confidence, and self-absorption. The presence of these teachers produced a star system: the students, quite naturally, adored them; and they gave the college its distinctive tone—febrile, impassioned.

When a young teacher was hired by the college it was quite natural for him to gravitate to the charismatic mode of teaching. But sometimes it did not work out for him—he did not have, or felt that he did not have, the necessary resources of talent, drive, and "personality." If he wanted to survive at the college, he had to (or so he believed) carve out a niche for himself, or even better, make himself indispensable. He had to find a new style, and he was likely to choose altruism, whether or not it really suited him. He played the role of the teacher who had given up his own ambitions to put himself at the service of youth. In some cases, I suspect, this role was chosen coolly and cynically, the teacher reasoning, quite correctly, that the college authorities would find it embarrassing to fire someone who was so true a believer in the college's ideology; in other cases, the teacher adopted this role gradually and without deliberation, waking up one morning, so to speak, to discover that this had been his métier all along.

Expedient altruism very rarely came off, either for the teacher or his students. The latter sometimes showed an uncanny, through largely unconscious, sensitivity in these matters—they could sense that the pseudo-altruist was somehow not quite kosher, not the real thing. They might deem him "nice," "friendly," and "very helpful," but they said so in a forced or lukewarm way which often concealed a polite disdain. The teacher's manner was often so artificial and oversolicitous that students were, I think, made uneasy by it, feeling that they did not really merit all that elaborate concern. This type of teacher tended to attract the marginal and unmotivated students, primarily because he was reputed to be soft. The more serious students continued to prefer the charismatic teacher, however difficult and demanding he might occasionally be; and this was so, I think, not only because of his greater gifts, but also because they would cleave only to someone who showed them that he loved himself.

Expedient altruism produced most of the time a kind of dead-level mediocrity in teaching; students were not much influenced, but neither were they damaged. It was a very different matter when this mode was chosen not as a survival technique but to perform some obscure personal restitution, when the teacher loved his students to avoid hating them, helped them to avoid harming them. As I suggested before, this equilibrium is ordinarily too delicate to sustain, and in fact I know of no examples where the students of the reactively altruistic teacher did not in some way suffer from a breakthrough of envy or sadism on the teacher's part. I remember one man, widely known to be lovable, who was warm and encouraging to his students and who would, when their backs were turned, write the most damning letters of recommendation for them. In another, more spectacular, instance a particularly sanctimonious advocate of good teaching was fired when his own major students petitioned the college to do so. It turned out that he had the habit of helping his students by being "sincerely frank" with them, expositing their "weak points" at great length and in excruciating detail, and so managing to wound and humiliate them deeply.

THE ANTIMODEL AND THE DISAPPOINTING MODEL

This last anecdote reminds us of what might otherwise escape our attention, that the teacher may sometimes serve as a negative or *antimodel*. Here student uses teacher as a lodestar, from which he sails away as rapidly as he can, seeming to say: Whatever he is, I will not be; whatever he is for, I will be against. Teachers who exercise this power of revulsion are, in their own way, charismatic types; indeed, the teacher who is charismatically positive for some will be negative for others. He breeds disciples or enemies; few remain unmoved. If we follow a student's development closely enough we generally discover both positive and negative models; the decision to be or become like someone goes hand in hand with a negative choice of identity and ideal.

An even more important topic on the negative side of modeling concerns the teacher whose value changes—the *disappointing* model. I would not have thought this to be so important—it does not come up in casual conversations on modeling; but close interviewing brings to light frequent mentions and examples of disappointments in the model.

Let me suggest why this may be so. It may be trite and facile to say so, but we are again led to the importance of the Oedipal motif, especially where we find a close relationship between teacher and student. These apprenticeships tend to be colored by the student's earlier tie to the father; they repeat or complete the Oedipal interaction. For most of us—and for some of us acutely—one outcome of the Oedipal situation was our coming to feel disappointed by the father. When we were very young, we thought him to be grand and omnipotent; then we learned better; and for some this was a galling discovery. In these cases the close tie to an esteemed teacher has the meaning of a second chance, an opportunity to relive and master that early disenchantment. The attempt to cure disappointment, however, generally leads to its repetition. The student must keep up the fiction of its teacher's perfection; any flaw, any failing in the teacher must be denied out of existence. It is too hard a position to maintain, and sooner or later the discovery of some defect in the now idealized teacher will send the student into a state of acute disappointment.

When the student uses his relation to the teacher in this (repetitive) way, he is especially vulnerable to any failure in the teacher's work or character. In the main, students are not so vulnerable; they learn to be realistic about their teachers, enough so that they are spared any strong sense of disappointment. Indeed, they manage it so well that we are likely to remain unaware that it *is* a problem, that even the "normal" student undergoes at some time some crisis, however minor, concerning the clay feet of an intellectual idol. I remember a poignant moment when talking to a young man who was telling me of his admiration for a brilliant teacher. After working for this man for some time, it dawned on him that the teacher was in some respects petty, petulant, and vain. At first, he told me, he had a hard time reconciling these traits with the man's great intellectual gifts; but then he was able to recognize that the two really had nothing to do with each other. What was poignant—painful in fact—was that the student told me this in a strained, bluff, overly hearty manner which spoke tellingly of the struggle it had been to accept it.

The student's response to disappointment depends not only on his susceptibility but also on the type of flaw he discovers in the teacher. It makes a difference whether or not the failing is *role-relevant*. It puts a greater strain on the student when the model's fault involves role-performance than when it is unrelated to how the teacher does his work. In the latter instance the student can more easily compartmentalize his image of the teacher.

Probably the most difficult type of failure for the student to accept is a moral one. By "moral" I do not mean, primarily, the teacher's living up to conventional standards in pleasure-seeking; rather I mean such qualities as integrity, fairness, ethical sensitivity, courage. The student is not overly demoralized to discover that his model's ego qualities are not quite what he thought or hoped they were, that his teacher is not as intelligent, penetrating, or perceptive as he first appeared to be. It is, in fact, part of the student's maturation that he learn to tolerate such facts, just as the child, in growing up, learns to give up his belief that the parents are omnicompetent. But a moral failure is not so easily accepted, and if it is serious enough in nature, is likely to be a disheartening or even a shattering experience. When we think of the teacher as a model, we think naturally of the teacher as an ego-ideal—an avatar of virtue—and take for granted, and thus ignore, the superego aspects. Yet some teachers influence us primarily because they embody the moral ideals of the role. Edward Tolman played this role for graduate students (and faculty too, I imagine) at Berkeley; many of us were not deeply influenced by him intellectually, but all of us were profoundly touched by his integrity and humility. For another example, Freud has told us how, many years later, he could still recall an incident of his student days when, arriving late to work, he was "overwhelmed by the terrible gaze of his (Brucke's) eyes." Most of us do our work in the silent presence of some such gaze, terrible or (nowadays) merely reproachful.

The teacher's life is as filled with moral tension and ambiguity as any other, but the moral dimension is most visibly operative in areas which do not affect the student—for example, departmental politics —consequently, moral issues do not ordinarily become problematic in the teacher-student relationship. But when they do, we become intensely aware of their tacit importance. I know of only one clear-cut occurrence of this kind: a group of students in one of the sciences discovered that their teacher—ordinarily full of pieties about the holy obligations of the scientist—was not entirely responsible in his handling of evidence; not outright fabrication, I should say, but cutting, fitting, and suppressing data to fit the needs of the study. Not all of the students were distraught by this discovery—here again vulnerability varies—but some were entirely demoralized, and in one case a student (who had been sitting on the fence) decided to give up research altogether and choose an applied career.[4]

Those of us who were at the University of California during the loyalty oath troubles had a unique opportunity to observe how the moral qualities of our teachers, ordinarily taken for granted and so overlooked, could assume overweening importance in a moment of moral crisis. It was an uncanny time for us: with one part of ourselves we lived in the routine of things, concerned with courses, prelims, dissertations; and all the while our inner, central attention was elsewhere, held in a fretful preoccupation with the morality play in which our teachers were involved. We wondered how things would turn out, of course, but beyond and deeper than that, the intimate,

[4] A fascinating account of the moral dimension in science is to be found in C. P. Snow's early novel, *The Search*.

compelling question was whether our models would behave honorably. They did not, not most of them, though for a time we kept ourselves from recognizing this, largely by allying ourselves psychically with the very few who acted heroically while ignoring the very many who did not. It taught us, on the one hand, that moral courage is possible, and on the other, that it is uncommon. All in all, it was a quick and unpleasant education. Perhaps it is just as well for all of us, teachers and students alike, that serious moral examinations occur so rarely.

REFERENCES

Erikson, E. H. *Childhood and society.* New York: Norton, 1950.
Freud, S. On narcissism. In *Collected papers,* Vol. IV. London: Hogarth, 1934.
Sanford, N. The dynamics of identification. *Psychol. Rev.,* 1955, **62,** 106–118.

11 *Joseph Katz and Nevitt Sanford*

The Curriculum in the Perspective of the Theory of Personality Development

Despite its central place in the program of the college, the curriculum rarely has been made the object of systematic investigation. There is, of course, a vast literature on the curriculum, but most of it has been concerned with descriptions of existing programs and with proposals for reform rather than with the demonstration of effects upon students. The great curricular revolutions that have taken place in the United States, such as Eliot's at Harvard (Stewart, Chapter 26), Erskine's at Columbia (Columbia, 1946), Meiklejohn's at Wisconsin (Meiklejohn, 1932) or Hutchins' at Chicago (Chicago, 1950), have not been accompanied by controlled observations that would permit comparison, in terms of effects, of one curriculum with another or give evidence that changes in students were due to the curriculum and not to other features of the college environment (see also Kennedy, 1955 and Taylor, 1950).

There have been some efforts to assess scientifically the effects of a particular kind of curriculum, for example, Dressel and Mayhew (1954), and there have been numerous studies of the effects of particular courses (Jacob, 1957, pp. 151–154). But when scientists have carried on investigations in the colleges they have tended to stress other aspects of the educational process—aspects such as methods of teaching, the student's sociological background and motivation, and the kinds of associations he forms with his peers. This has been due

418

not alone to the special interests of the investigators but also to the fact that the influence of the curriculum on students has appeared to be much less than the influence of other factors.

The paucity of studies may also be traced to the lack of theory that could serve as a guide for such studies. Owing to the hiatus that has existed between educational psychologists and social scientists on the one hand and those responsible for curriculum planning on the other, we have very little educational psychology that is applicable to the college years. Much practice in our schools and colleges looks as if it were based in a theory of the person that was current in the Twenties but which has been thoroughly outmoded. We refer to the theory of the person as an aggregate of specific habits. The theory of personality has taken giant strides since the Twenties, but this development seems not to have had much effect on practice in the colleges, nor has it led to much new thinking or new research on the core of the college program, that is, the curriculum.

PURSUIT OF KNOWLEDGE AND THE COLLEGE CURRICULUM

In adopting the perspective of the theory of personality we wish to suggest a new point of departure in the understanding of the curriculum. It seems to have been almost universally assumed by educators that the college curriculum, as presently constituted, defines the goals of achievement for the student and that the nature of the curriculum is to be largely determined by whatever is the present state of the "body of knowledge." This assumption usually implies (1) an identification of the "body of knowledge" with the curriculum of the graduate school—a very debatable identification—and (2) only very limited attention to the role of such knowledge in the development of the student. In regard to (2) it is usually assumed that the better the mental capacities of the student, the more he will assimilate of the "body of knowledge," and that the more he absorbs, the better for him.

To us this approach embodies an unduly abstract conception of the curriculum and of knowledge in general. Once the question is raised, what is the impact, or lack of impact of the curriculum on the student, the notion of the inviolability of the "body of knowledge" disappears. It turns out, moreover, that curricula, both past and present, embody a variety of unexamined and unavowed psychological assumptions. By making these assumptions explicit, it may be possible to narrow the distance that now separates the curriculum from the actual learning that students do.

A fresh look at the curriculum may well start with an analytic examination of the varying actual and potential functions of knowledge. For this purpose we distinguish two main functions of the pursuit of knowledge, the *practical* and the *imaginative* functions. In its practical function knowledge acts in the service of survival and successful mastery of the environment. In this attempt at mastery it confronts two worlds: the outer world, comprising both nature and human society, and the inner world of impulses. The attempt to understand these inner and outer forces has always characterized the pursuit of knowledge. It has not always taken a form, however, that would stand the approval of contemporary canons of scientific inquiry.

The other side of the intellectual pursuit has been an imaginative extension of the real world. "Poetry" originally meant "making," and intellect has served in the making of new worlds. This imaginative extension of reality has served two quite different purposes: (1) that of an enrichment of reality by lifting the person beyond sensuous and practical immediacy, and (2) that of a withdrawal from reality. The fundamental difference between the two purposes is that the second is served at the expense of the individual's vital and essential relations with reality, while the former is not.

There is no clear distinction between the practical and the imaginative dimensions of knowledge. For imagination is required in the tasks of mastering reality. The phantasies of the prophet or the plans of the architect—even when they seem to defy gravity—have often become tomorrow's reality. The imagination seems to be both a dependent and an independent entity in the make-up of human personality. In its dependent function it serves the purposes of mastery of reality. In its independent function it is close to being, and perhaps is, a primary need. One result of this is that it is nearly impossible for a human being to perform even the most prosaic task without some admixture of imagination.

In this light the evolution of science out of poetry and the other arts is not hard to understand. But there has been an increasing differentiation of function. Science is a part-function, recently so swollen up that it seems almost a whole culture of its own. Knowledge thus has come to be identified by many with conceptual manipulation. William James' and Bertrand Russell's distinction between knowledge by acquaintance and knowledge by description (Russell, 1912) began to call our attention again to the multidimensional meanings of knowledge. These meanings are illustrated in the full fleshly dimensions of the Biblical use of "know" or in contemporary researches on nonverbal communication.

The history of the term "theory" graphically underscores our point. The term has twice undergone very significant shifts in meaning, thus illustrating different part-functions of the pursuit of knowledge. Its meaning in Greek (*theoria*) is "looking at." The outcome of inquiry, that is theory, is not conception alone, but perception and conception combined. Knowledge in antiquity was seen as very much an aesthetic phenomenon and neither Greek language nor Greek philosophy ever arrived at clear distinctions between art and science. But in later antiquity we find the same word *theoria* used in a quite different sense, a sense indicated by its Latin and English translation "contemplation." *Theoria* becomes the contemplation of nonsensuous and other-worldly realms of existence. The latest shift is to the modern meaning of theory which is devoid of any aesthetic and religious implications and designates the conceptual and generalized outcome of methodologically approved procedures.

Varieties of curricula and the conceptual orientation of the modern university. It is obvious that such widely different conceptions of "theory" and knowledge give rise to quite different educational practices and institutions and that, moreover, they tend, in varying ways, to make the pursuit of knowledge and learning either curricular or extracurricular affairs. Many students get some of the knowledge most important to them, in science or in art, in an extracurricular way, outside the classroom. There have been throughout history various more or less informal groups that carried on the pursuit of knowledge outside the established schools. Ficino's "Academy" in Renaissance Florence and Freud's seminar in Imperial Vienna are two brilliant instances (Lewin, 1958). Important scientific innovations have frequently been achieved by individuals outside the institutional setup: examples are Darwin, Marx, and Mendel.

Plato, who himself founded something like the first university, has in his dialogues preserved and dramatized the nature of learning in the precurricular days. In these writings the reader encounters ideas in the context of vivid descriptions of the natural and social setting and of the interactions of different personalities with each other. Ideas are presented not just in their bare conceptual aspects, but with due regard to form and style. The spirit of the discussion is quite unlike that of hard academic work; it is one of play, sometimes hard play, and grace. Moreover, even when Plato gets to be most abstract, there is always an implication that what he says is relevant to the life of men in society.

Plato's Athenian young men, who moved with ease from the gymnasium to an encounter with Socrates in the market place, to an evening of drinking, flute play, and talk in the house of the tragic poet Agathon, had achieved an integration of learning which in the modern university is barely possible. It is worth remembering that "symposium" originally meant "drinking together." Our very word for school has undergone a significant reversal. In Greek *schole* means "leisure." We of the present time can hardly translate the term; for to us leisure and loafing are not too far apart. To us having leisure suggests *not* being busy, while in Greek "being busy" has to be expressed negatively. The Greek term for being busy is *"not* having leisure."

Other "curricular" practices have been described to us in many anthropological reports: learning taking place through the group's cooperative engagement in the practical and imaginative activities of the society and of the individuals within it. Older patterns of education on the farm in our own culture bear some similarity to this. It was the example of the comprehensiveness of rural education that gave John Dewey some main clues for his educational reforms (Schilpp, 1939). (Dewey, developing his ideas at the end of the 19th century, still gives special attention to the political and economic problems of society. Since then both economic prosperity and the absorption of Freud have pushed toward greater recognition of and emphasis on men's inner reality. This recognition is not inconsistent with Dewey's approach, but it represents an important shift in emphasis.)

The conceptual orientation of the modern university, then, presents only one of many possible choices for the pursuit and the organization of learning; and perhaps some of the peculiar limitations of the college are due to this orientation. The dominance of the conceptual symbol in the curriculum is of course not absolute. Some artistic activities, notably drama, have been finding their place in the college curriculum. But the place of the arts usually is a begrudged one. A student will be allowed to take a course in painting, for instance, if he is willing to take a certain number of credit points in art history. Analysis of art, rather than art itself, tends to be ground for admission to the curriculum. A notable exception to the dominance of conceptual symbols is the laboratory, which in spite of its manual-perceptual character has proved its indispensability to natural science theory. Even here, theory was the primary academic justification—though the technological utility of laboratory research may well have been the stronger determinant in forcing this curricular revision.

The admission of the laboratory meant that working with one's hands and the cultivation of the senses were thought deserving of some curricular recognition. A similar recognition for the domain of feelings still is largely lacking. Some models for teaching greater differentiation in one's own feelings and greater perceptiveness of the feelings of others already exist in the practices of psychotherapeutic training centers (Ekstein and Wallerstein, 1958). They provide a new answer to Plato's ancient query in the *Protagoras* whether "virtue," that is strength of character, is teachable.

Our universities, in spite of the seeming objectivity of their curricular orientation, seem in fact committed to one particular and quite subjectivistic position: the value premise of the dominance of the intellectualist; and this in turn is tied to an implicit personality theory which views personality as primarily intellectualist in nature. "Intellectualist" may be distinguished from "intellectual" if the former term is taken to denote an emphasis on the manipulation of conceptual symbols in more or less detachment from the needs of outer and inner reality. Making this distinction helps to clarify the claim of some recent defenders of the traditional view that they find no abundance of intellect on the campus. There is no abundance of intellectuality, but there is an abundance of intellectualism, and this may be one of the causes of intellectual apathy. Some students, of course, find that there are high rewards for conceptual agility as such. For in our society, as well as in others, examinations of increasing severity serve as an "objective" way of selecting people for positions of leadership and occupational superiority.

Structure of the contemporary liberal arts curriculum. In examining more closely the structure of the contemporary curriculum, we shall confine ourselves to the curriculum of the liberal arts college because this curriculum allows, at least theoretically, a greater range of possibilities than curricula that are tied to the demands, real or fancied, of particular occupations. The liberal curriculum serves at least three different purposes: (1) It is in some of its aspects avowedly preprofessional in nature, preparing the student for a career in the laboratory or in the law office. (2) It is preprofessional in a less avowed sense, too. Many college courses are in large measure designed as introductory to the professions or intellectual disciplines that the various departments represent. Sometimes the intent, whether recognized or not, is to win recruits or at least sympathizers for one's professional discipline (which also yields larger enrolments in advanced courses). Even where there is no such intent, instruction is so conducted that the structure and contents of the academic discipline, rather than the needs and capacities of the student, determine its nature. We might call this function "implicit preprofessional." (3) It is oriented to the development of the personality. This in our view is the prime meaning of liberal education.

Some college subjects such as literature, philosophy, psychology, that could be primarily oriented to personality development, often shift from the liberal aspect in the direction of the preprofessional and the implicit preprofessional. For instance, the history of the criticism pertaining to a piece of literature may or may not serve the purposes of a fuller appreciation of it, depending on whether or not the issues reflect special interests of the community of scholars or the evocative powers of the literary object. As indicated in Chapter 9, teachers address not only the students in front of them but also their professional colleagues or images of them.

THEORY OF PERSONALITY AND THE CURRICULUM

Our theory of personality and its development was introduced in Chapter 6. Here we must consider the question of what is the role of knowledge and of thinking in the functioning and in the development of the personality. And more particularly, how may the college curriculum be used to bring about greater freedom of impulse, enlightenment of conscience, and differentiation and integration in the ego? According to our theory, knowledge and thinking are in the service of needs. But the beginnings of cognitive functions are present from birth, and after some development has occurred, knowing and thinking may be motives in their own right. More than this, the particular needs that a person has will have come to depend upon what is known or thought.

One might say that a kind of thinking is present in the infant. If the gratification of one of his needs is delayed, there will be images of possible gratifying objects. After a bit of living, the infant or young child has a mind full of wish-fulfilling images or thoughts. This is his inner world, where generalization and a lack of differentiation are the rule. But the infant soon discovers that adequate gratification cannot be had by wish-fulfilling imagery. There is the necessity for discovering or producing actual objects. Hence knowledge and thought become, to some extent, oriented to reality. The person has to construe the world in order to act, and he acts according to what he believes or thinks. As the person develops, there is expansion of the domain of wish-fulfilling imagery, and at the same time his dealings with the external environment become more intelligent and efficient. There is an expanded store of usable memory images and increased powers of discrimination. With the development of language it becomes possible to deal with problems symbolically without having to try various overt actions. There is improved judgment, decision making, and increased skill in complex action. These reality-oriented functions become the basis for the construction of an ego system. This system, in Freud's words, "commends itself to the Id." In other words, the ego system is composed of needs which derive their energy from the impulse life but which achieve satisfaction through realistic action and thinking. For the ego to carry out its functions, to keep on commending itself to the id, it must have a reasonable degree of understanding of situations. Thus it is that the individual wants very much to know, to know what is really there, and not to be misguided by his hopes. He wants to understand, and to think straight. His self-respect comes to depend heavily upon these abilities.

At the same time, the person frequently finds himself in situations that he is unable to master through the use of his higher functions. Reality is sometimes too much for any of us, and it is often too much for the child.

This brings us to the question of how to describe, in the terms of our theory, the kinds of learning that occur in response to the college curriculum. It is our thesis that all the individual's knowledge is a part of his personality, and that all curricula either favor or hamper personality development regardless of whether they were designed with such development in mind. It was pointed out in Chapter 2, however, that much of the individual's knowledge is peripheral to the personality, in the sense that it is readily forgotten, and that much other knowledge remains superficial, in the sense that it does not become integrated with the individual's inner needs. Our major concern is with the kind of learning in college that can bring about a developmental change in the personality structure.

One thing that can and does happen, and that can be encouraged to happen more often, might be described as the expansion of the "primary process" (the process by which tension gives rise to wish-fulfilling images) or, one could say, the freeing of the imagination. Where this is our aim, the point to be stressed is that the teacher's best ally is not the student's conscience but his impulse life. The best way to manage impulses is to offer them outlets in phantasy, in dreams, in poetry, and in art; or, to put this the other way around, if we are interested in freeing the imagination, opening the individual to experience, encouraging creativity and spontaneity, we have no recourse but to free the individual's impulse life. A large part of education in schools, and perhaps even in colleges, is concerned to suppress the impulse life, while building up to the highest possible degree the controlling functions. Much of this is of course necessary, but one could put the major problem of college education in this way: how can one undo or set aside the restrictions upon the imagination that have been building for years? How can the student be shown that the world of literature and drama and art, and creativity in the sciences, offers the best means by which the impulses of childhood may now find gratification?

At the same time we must give attention to the possibility that knowledge of facts may be acquired now, without its being relevant to any central purpose of the person, and that it may be, as it were, stored, later to find a place in some fresh insight or in some creative achievement of the individual. Much of our college education is based on the assumption that this acquiring without change of structure may eventually serve the individual. We believe this happens, but we also believe that it is easy to overestimate the frequency with which it happens.

It may be doubted that such storing will occur unless the information has relevance to some need of the individual; but, happily, in people of college age the variety of needs that are in operation is very great. A need for mastery by itself may be enough to lead to the registration and retention of much factual knowledge. And then, college students have the possibility at least of achieving integration of personality, in which there is communication among the various subsystems or substructures of the person, so that knowledge acquired and stored, because of its relevance to one purpose, however superficial or temporary that purpose might have been, may now be utilized in the interest of some fresh purpose such as the solution of a new and vexing problem. Such knowledge, having been stored, may also make possible fresh insight into relationships existing in the world, once such relationships are presented to the student at times when he is suitably receptive.

THE CURRICULUM

Modes of presentation. In discussing the effects of curriculum in the light of our theory we need to distinguish between the mode of presentation and the content. Though mode of presentation is related to subject matter, quite different subjects may have similar modes of presentation. Thus, although it is not easy to present English as one does chemistry, it can be done if the teacher is determined enough.

Our argument is that some modes of presentation favor the development of personality while others have the opposite effect. We shall discuss some antidevelopmental modes first.

ANTIDEVELOPMENTAL MODES. Emphasis on *discipline* and hard work is a very common characteristic of the mode of presentation, although in practice there is a great deal of latitude. The amount of latitude has been reduced in recent years, however, and the emphasis on discipline increased since the advent of the sputniks, and with the unprecedented influx of large numbers of students. We saw in Chapter 6 that the late adolescent will accept discipline only under very special conditions that are hard to establish in the college of today. When discipline is given special accent it is likely to be perceived by the student as external to his own needs, and, if he does not rebel, his authoritarian disposition tends to be re-enforced. The grading system may be used as the stick to enforce externalized discipline, while concentration on collecting items of "knowledge" may serve to ensure that work is going on. Idleness is the arch-enemy of any compulsive system, and the students are kept so busy that on many campuses it is becoming harder to make an appointment with a student than with a professor.

A further chief characteristic of the mode of presentation is the teacher's *emphasis on the right answer*. The student gets the notion that there is only one or at best a very limited set of right answers to any one question, that the teacher is in possession of these answers, and that he expects the student to produce them. A class may have some of the superficial characteristics of open discussion and the teacher may be subjectively convinced that he is not intruding his own views, yet the students sense the push to conform to an external standard of correctness. This factor alone usually serves to make communication between students and teacher extremely difficult and discourages learning.

Impersonality is another antidevelopmental factor. In interviews with students we have found that students almost universally link their most significant educational experiences to teachers with whom they have had some personal relation in and out of the classroom. Even in classes of a hundred or more students, learning seems to be aided a great deal if the student can establish some sort of "personal" relationship with the professor. This is facilitated if the teacher's own personality is very vivid. If a student plans to enter the professor's field of specialization, anticipatory professionalization may well serve to make the relationship more personal even though the student remains a blur in the professor's visual field.

Abstractedness also tends to hamper development. Much attention has been paid to it and many teachers and programs have strenuously tried to tie subject matter to concrete events, particularly events anticipated in the future life situations of the students. The difficulty is that these life situations are in the future and that, moreover, they easily become stereotyped and idealized. The *present* life situation of the student tends to be ignored in favor of idealized conceptions of concreteness. This actual situation includes the very complex motivations of the student, often rather far removed from the motivations of the teacher or the intent of his subject matter (see Chapter 6). The tendency has been to deal with this discrepancy in disciplinary, punitive, or cynical fashions. None of these ways is likely to narrow the discrepancy or to combat abstractedness.

Excessive orientation to method and segmentation are two other antidevelopmental factors. *Orientation to method* becomes excessive when there is a concentration on details of method that is significantly out of line with the mastery of the content that the student has achieved at the time. Such emphasis on method is due both to the considerable sophistication that procedures have achieved in all fields of learning and to the purism of many teachers, particularly teachers who are at the same time researchers. But such emphasis is likely to leave the student at first frustrated and then either indifferent or intransigent.

Segmentation of presentation springs in part from the departmental organization of the curriculum. Teachers will occasionally report, with agreeable surprise, that a student has related something from another course. It seems that students tend, first, to segment information from the rest of their personality and then to segment departments of information from each other. As the information received is not adequately in touch with the spontaneous learning of the student, but is determined by external agencies, it seems to be preserved most easily if it is left in the compartmentalized form in which it has been received. It is pigeon-holed and "forgotten," to be drawn upon when the academic bell rings for it again. Students in courses conducted by two instructors, for example a professor and his assistant, need to sub-segment further so as to give the right segment to the appropriate instructor. Where students are not sure whether their papers will be read by one of their two instructors or by the other, they may become veritable virtuosi in writing in such a way as to appeal to both at once.

DEVELOPMENTAL MODES. The pursuit of *objectivity* is a major developmental factor. Conceptions and perceptions of reality that are undistorted by wishes and anxieties is one of the hardest things for the human organism to acquire. The emphasis on evidence that pervades much of our college teaching is an important antidote to distortion. Although the wish frequently is father to the thought, independence from the father, here as elsewhere, is a condition of mastering reality. Science has grown as it has succeeded in detaching the logical from the immediate pressures of wish and impulse. The psychoanalytic rediscovery of wish at first led to an emphasis on how logic can lead to an estrangement from reality, particularly inner reality. But a reverse influence also seems to be possible. *Intellectual mastery,* for example a college student's discovery of new competence in a subject hitherto unknown to him, may become a basis for revision of his self-image and of much of his inner and outer life. Furthermore, the symbolic widening of the possibilities of experience can be a chief stimulus to fresh experiences in the student's own life space. The pursuit of objectivity requires careful attention to the student's impulse and thought. Otherwise one sort of impetus will characterize the emotional part of the personality and another its intellectual part; this is the life story of many a liberal.

We have so far spoken of the pursuit of objectivity and logic as an individual experience. It can also be a social experience: learning *with and in view* of others. Our school set-up tends to make the curriculum competitive and many of the extracurricular activities cooperative. Under certain circumstances classroom learning can impress upon the student both the fundamental *otherness* of his fellow *and* the *communication* that is possible with him. We do not have in mind a superficial other-directedness, but rather that community that thrives best when its members have achieved their own distinctively separate identities. By contrast, present classrooms are characterized by a high degree of isolation of students from each other.

Learning to think by way of *hypotheses* is a further factor favoring development. Every hypothesis is the creative transformation of an ossified or at least a hardened conception or perception. Hypotheses begin in hunches and require freedom of association as a necessary condition. They imply willingness to have aliens touch each other, and willingness to suspend the taboos of segmentation and exclusion.

Some teachers might say that it is precisely the profusion of phantasy that needs to be disciplined. But the student productions such teachers have in mind here are best described not as the results of phantasy but of the more or less vacuous abstractions that have lost clear lines of relations to their impulsive promptings.

THE CURRICULUM: CONTENT AREAS

In discussing the psychological significance of subject matter we begin by considering curricula in their totality; then we give attention to the freshman curriculum, before turning to specific areas of content.

The curriculum as a whole. The Report of the Harvard Committee on General Education (Harvard, 1945) distinguishes (p. 181) five major approaches to general education: (1) distribution requirements, (2) comprehensive survey courses, (3) functional courses, (4) great books program, (5) individual guidance. It is our impression that these curricula make implicit assumptions concerning the developmental status of the students for whom they are designed, although they are not usually defended on this basis. One conception of the entering college student is that of a mature person whose value orientation has already been established. He is expected to make choices in accordance with his predilections and his conceptions of what he expects to do or be. It is assumed that he is already an independent person or, if he is not, that he will develop independence more rapidly if he is allowed or encouraged to do independent work. Where this conception of the entering student prevails, there is likely to be accent on free electives, and it is not to be wondered at if the student, in choosing courses, follows the path of least resistance or is guided by conventional considerations or by plans for a future vocation (see Chapter 17). The opposite conception is that the student is by no means ready to make such fundamental decisions, that far from permitting him to make choices in accord with the values that he already has, the college should be concerned with teaching him what are the values that he ought to consider. It is assumed that the student is, so far, in a relatively undeveloped state and that it is up to the college to guide his development in accordance with some conception of what people ought to become. Where this conception of the student prevails, required courses are the rule or, as in the extreme case of St. John's College, there is a full four-year program of required courses. The more common *distribution* type of curriculum, the type that seeks to achieve breadth of education through distribution requirements, and depth of education through a chosen area of concentration, seems to be something of a compromise. Perhaps this type of curriculum recognizes that we really do not know what are the most common developmental needs of entering students, and seeks to achieve the benefits of both of the former approaches.

The core curriculum is based on the assumption that the student is ready for core courses before there emerges readiness for independent or individualized work. Moreover, the required core curriculum often is defended on the basis that college freshmen, in order to develop intellectual interests and values, need the support of the social group, and this may best be achieved by ensuring that all members of the group have the same experiences, the same frustrations and gratifications, at the same time. So strong are the forces that distract students or that pull them away from the intellectual task ahead, that it seems that everything possible should be done in order to create an intellectual community.

It makes a difference whether or not the core curriculum and the community of experience are followed by arrangements for independent work. Students may easily become too attached to the group solidarity and the particular orientation to values that accompany their intellectual awakening. Particularly, a tradition-oriented core program might subtly influence the student in the direction of believing that authority resides in the great figures of the past, thus diminishing his sense of his own authority and giving him the idea that a gulf exists between the intellect and contemporary life. Of course, the impact of such a program could be expected to vary with the type of student. The student already so inclined might be strengthened in his tendency to retreat toward a fairly passive spectator role. Another student might acquire some distance from his immediate involvements and thereby gain needed perspective, without endangering his return to the present world.

Great difficulty is presented by the fact that different students mature at different rates (Murphy and Raushenbush, 1960, pp. 156–194). Within the same institution, at the same time, there are undoubtedly students who would benefit most from one type of curriculum and other students who would benefit most from a different type, and yet that institution offers and defends as universally good a single curriculum. A revolt against this practice has taken the form of individual education, as at Sarah Lawrence and Bennington Colleges. Everyone knows how difficult and expensive this kind of education is, and we believe that experience has shown that many students entering these colleges were not ready to take advantage of the opportunities for individualized programs (see Taylor, Chapter 23). We can only make a plea for further research, aimed at revealing what are the common development statuses of entering students, and showing how these entail different kinds and degrees of receptivity to curricula. And we would urge that in debates about types of curricula it be recognized that there is probably no one curriculum that is best for all students at all times, but curricula have to be devised with attention to multiple criteria.

The freshman curriculum. It is in the freshman year that the failures of today's curricula are most glaring. Freshmen arrive on the campus, typically, filled with enthusiasm, with eager anticipation of the intellectual experiences they are about to have. By the end of the year 10% have dropped out and a large proportion of the remainder are ready for what in the Eastern Colleges is known as the "sophomore slump." At Vassar it was found that the "sophomore slump" occurred in the spring of the freshman year (Freedman, 1956); at least this was a period of considerably reduced academic interest and effort, accompanying a dawning awareness that college was not coming up to advanced billing and that the exciting experiences would have to be postponed until one entered her major program. At Berkeley, no one has heard of a sophomore slump. Perhaps students enter with smaller expectations, or fewer illusions, than is the case in other liberal arts colleges; or perhaps the game of getting good grades or staying in college to graduate—whichever the aspiration—is played with the same coolness year in and year out. Listen to the talk on the campus:

I wanted to take 10-B this fall so I could get into 116 next year but the only section I could fit into my schedule was filled; so I'm going to take 7-A and get that out of the way. Did you know that you could substitute 24-C for 22-D and count it toward your natural science requirements? Freshmen can take it with permission of the instructor. That's where all the Phys. Ed. majors go.

We are speaking here of course of the common or traditional type of curriculum, drawn up with a minimum of attention to how students learn, but with a maximum of concern with how knowledge may be organized on paper—and of course with due concern for the rights and privileges of the departments. There are enough breadth or distribution requirements and enough prerequisites for courses that the student thinks he will want to take later so that for many students the whole freshman year is taken up with necessary evils, and for most there are no courses that can be regarded as ends in themselves.

The point is sometimes made that existing arrangements serve well to "weed out" inferior students. At some state universities indeed there is weeding out with a bulldozer. Nobody knows how many potential learners go out along with the unable and the indifferent; nor do we know to what extent remaining in college is a matter of gamesmanship or capacity to adapt oneself to conventional pressures.

Existing programs are easy to criticize. What is to be done? We suggest that where the foremost concern is with the development of personality the major aim of the freshman year should be to win the student to the intellectual enterprise; with full recognition of the fact that for many it is now or never, every effort should be made to capture the student's imagination, to give him a sense of what it means to become deeply involved in a discipline or subject, to learn things that make a difference in his life, to be a member of a community that is devoted to the pursuit of truth. Most essentially, the student must be shown that college education is a means for the expression of his impulse life, an opportunity for the gratification of his natural curiosity, and not merely a set of painful tests designed to make him more appreciative of his college degree.

There is one current approach to the freshman curriculum, already referred to briefly, that seems in keeping with the point of view expressed here. The entering student is allowed to indulge to the full any interest that he already has, the assumption being that if the interest is genuine he will soon be led into the study of various subjects that are related to it, and that if the interest is superficial, or if the object of interest is essentially insubstantial, it will be supplanted by others without loss in motivation. The trouble, of course, is that not many students have interests that are sufficiently developed so that they can serve as guides to protracted courses of study. (It is a common observation of the counselor of entering freshmen that students who arrive at college with a concrete proposal concerning a course of study leading to some vocational goal can easily be "talked out" of their plan; many have been under such pressure to say what they are going to do or to be that they have made superficial choices that were not in accord with their genuine needs or interests.) More than this, according to our theory of development, college freshmen are capable of enormous expansion and development in their interests, values, and modes of thought; we should be wary of proceedings that indulge their natural inclination to confirm themselves as they are.

Our main argument is that as educators we ought to ignore conceptions of what freshmen "ought to know," whether the concern be with their preparation for more advanced courses or with a suitable sampling of organized knowledge, and that we ought to concentrate instead on giving these students experiences that set in motion the developmental changes in which we are interested. Each course should be conceived as an end in itself; it should be designed with first attention to developmental objectives—and to the developmental status of the freshman (see Chapter 6). Subject matter has a crucial role to play, but the outcomes that we seek will have little to do with "how much is covered." There is irony in the fact that when we teach elementary courses we tend to look ahead to the advanced ones, asking ourselves what information is likely to be required, and supposing that we can impress the teachers of these advanced courses with how much our students know; but if we teach advanced courses we are likely to assume that very little has been learned in the elementary ones, and to make sure of "proper coverage" we proceed to teach what all the students have had before. The relations of college and high school courses, and of college and graduate courses, are much the same. For example, we have little notion of what is the best undergraduate preparation, in terms of courses, for graduate work in psychology. There is nothing to suggest that undergraduate psychology is best, and some psychologists are inclined to prefer students who have had little or no psychology but much literature, philosophy, mathematics, and biological science.

We are justified in looking far and wide, or close to home, and in making any kind of break with tradition, in our search for materials that will excite, involve, challenge, or win the commitment of freshmen. We might use what is now offered in an upper division anthropology course, a whole course devoted to a single English poet, the latest decision of the Supreme Court, an integrated course in 17th-century England, a course in economics taught as if this were the only exposure to this subject that the students would ever have. Or we might use another judicious selection from the liberal arts curriculum. In any of these cases we should, of course, have to present the material in ways that were suited to the freshman's stage of development. We might well choose more specific contents from areas such as those just mentioned, whatever we thought might reach into the student's life and provide genuine experience because it connected with experiences that he had already had or was having. We should in each case be guided by some hypothesis stating just how the content influenced development in people who had reached the freshman's level; so that we could learn from each experience and make more knowledgeable changes.

Certain aspects of psychology, sociology, and anthropology are very well calculated to involve students by offering them light on problems with which they are already preoccupied. When all else fails there might be resort to these "sure-fire" disciplines. Yet, consideration of the freshman's stage of development leaves us extremely reluctant to start them off with this very rich diet. We know far too little about the matter, but it does seem that the introduction of these subjects so early in the student's career might make it impossible for him to have certain kinds of experience to which he is entitled and which would be important for his overall development. For example, a student ought to have the experience, at least in one period of his development, of a passionate devotion to an overall religious or philosophical scheme which seems to him to explain everything. He will in time analyze such experiences, using the categories of psychology and social science—and come eventually, one might hope, to some truly useful scheme—such analysis will be far more educational if he has first had the experience himself than it will be if he has to utilize the reputed experience of others. Similarly for those course materials, chiefly literature and the arts, which may be used to educate—to refine and to help organize—the feelings or affective life. We should encourage students to *have* the feelings, to learn how to express them, before we offer categories with the use of which he may intellectualize about them.

Some specific content areas. In discussing the psychological functions of content, it must be kept in mind first that the official titles of college courses give only a very approximate idea of what particular teachers do in any particular course or section of a course. It seems, nevertheless, permissible to say that in literature courses there is more appeal to the impulse life than there is in, say, chemistry. (We assume at the same time that creative work in chemistry is impossible without sufficient openness to the primary process.) One might range subjects by their proximity to primary process materials; and in such a list one would proceed from subjects like English, to sociology, to physics. This is not an evaluative ranking, but simply an indication of proximity to direct appeal to impulse and feelings. Optimally, a student would broaden his impulse life by contact with subjects that are evocative of primary processes, he would turn analytic and become more aware of these processes by his contact with behavioral science and he would sharpen his reality testing by contact with natural science. As there is something of everything in every course, any particular student may give any of the variety of responses here noted to any type of course. Students' actual responses do not, of course, easily follow this pattern. A student may be attracted to a course because it is easy to get passing grades; or the very abstractness of a course may allow him easy transitions from the nonconcrete symbols of science or philosophy to personal phantasies of magic, omnipotence, and persecution.

The remoteness or proximity of the subject to the student's culture, time, and social class may be of important psychological significance. Distant subjects invite an imaginative trying out of different identities in relative safety. Proximate subjects, such as local government or housing, may strengthen a phantasy-impoverished acceptance of things as they are, or they may encourage a mature attempt to exercise one's powers in one's own life space. Curricular configurations in a student's program are in this regard more revealing than choice of any particular subject matter. A student interested both in the African Tiv and local housing trends is different from one interested both in ancient Greek history and Far Eastern literature.

In our consideration of how the study of particular subjects may favor or hamper development we limit ourselves to some examples. It is our belief that once the perspective of the theory of personality development has been adopted, a teacher of any subject may think of ways in which his material might be utilized in the interests of the student's development; and he may think of other ways in which that material is used, including ways that are antidevelopmental. In the discussion that follows we retain the current departmental divisions of subject matter, but this does not imply our acceptance of them. Our chief aim is to elucidate some of the psychological aspects of traditional academic subjects.

What impresses one most immediately about the array of fields of knowledge represented in the curriculum is their sheer bulk. Bulk looms particularly large in the humanities; and the social sciences are doing their best to catch up. One might guess that complete reading of all primary and secondary sources on the topic of, say, the 19th-century novel alone would in number of pages be greater than all reading in contemporary physics. This bulk is a consequence not only of the ever-increasing specialization of knowledge, but also of the conceptual omnivorousness of the present stage of our culture. The recent quiz shows highlighted the prestige in our popular culture of the man who knows the answers to every possible question, however trivial. Wide reading is a mark of distinction in academic culture as well. The sheer bulk of material can and easily does encourage a sort of indiscriminate collecting that is little connected to the inner and outer reality of the reader. In some fields the temptation to collect is greater than in others. An undergraduate will find himself easily encouraged in such collecting tendencies (be he a small or a big collector). Some people hoard ideas the way others hoard money, Dewey says in *Human Nature and Conduct* (1930).

Historical studies, for example, can serve such collecting tendencies easily. But all depends on the way in which history is handled. Take an undergraduate writing a paper on attitudes to the League of Nations between 1920 to 1926 as expressed in editorial opinions which he explores on his own in the bound copies of journals and newspapers in the library. Such an undergraduate not only may gain an excellent sense of the varieties of reasonableness and of approaches to social problems, but he also may gain the exciting sense of independent research, of discovery, and of disagreement with some authorities. The fact that the materials of history are readily available in the library is helpful in comparison to subject matters where the materials are less readily accessible.

The bulk of curricular subject matter makes selection a necessity and such selection is guided by conscious as well as by unconscious principles. Clearer conceptions of goals and how to achieve them are more urgently needed. Let us take the study of *foreign languages* as an example. In certain European systems of education the classical languages have the central place. Thus a "Gymnasium" graduate in Germany traditionally is one who is identified by having studied "Latin and Greek." In the American college foreign languages constitute one of five or six major segments of the curriculum. What are the goals in the teaching of foreign languages? No generally agreed upon answer exists to that question, and its very pursuit, when it occurs, is frequently lacking in vigor and extent. In what follows we attempt to state a variety of possible goals of language teaching in college, mentioning difficulties as we go along; and we are surely not exhausting the possibilities of goals.

(1) The most obvious goal is that of equipping the student with sufficient knowledge of the language so that he has access to the literature and the people of the foreign country. But this goal is only a paper goal and if the teaching of languages had to be evaluated in regard to it, only a very small percentage of all language teaching would meet it. (2) The study of a foreign language is to equip one with a sense of the structure of language, leading among other things to a better appreciation of one's native tongue. But when this is

said, it is left untested whether this goal is best, or even adequately, reached by present language teaching. Conceivably comparative linguistic courses might fulfill this function much better. (3) The study of a foreign language is a prime tool for acquainting the student with a foreign culture. It is also a prime device for making him hate French or Spanish, or for leaving him indifferent. To be frustrated in regard to the language of a culture, as students so often are, is hardly likely to contribute to international amity. (4) The study of foreign languages is antiethnocentric. But the experience of the German secondary school system alone, with its heavy emphasis on foreign languages, provides evidence that this need not be so. There may indeed be antiethnocentric uses to which the study of language can be put, but they do not reside in the teaching of foreign languages as such. In some students one can even note a re-enforcement of ethnocentrism by way of language learning. These are the students upon whom the foreign language courses have made an impact and who have become chauvinistic in the language and culture of their choice; in other words, their native chauvinism has remained intact, but has now become somewhat less accessible to insight because of the pseudo-cosmopolitan overlay. (5) The study of language can be viewed pragmatically in that it gives a skill usable for employment in business, government, research organizations, and the like. Russian seems currently to enjoy such a utilitarian vogue. But this goal eliminates language as a liberal subject.

There are three further pragmatic uses of language: (6) Some languages are required for entrance and exit requirements in college and for the obtaining of the Ph.D. degree, and in this context they are a well-known unfunctional hurdle. This use of language is of course nonliberal, too, and these requirements stem from the eternal logic, or illogic, of the university system, with little relation to the purposes of education. (7) The study of foreign language is good discipline for the mind. This is an almost frankly psychological goal, but it should be subjected to the legitimate psychological tests. Does the study of foreign languages instill discipline or obedience? Can one speak of discipline as desirable without regard to objectives that are meaningful to the student and that allow him a sufficient sense of accomplishment? (8) Some particular languages are considered to furnish a good basis for the learning of other languages. Thus Latin is recommended as a good base for learning modern romance languages. That may well be, but here our goals are becoming circular.

(9) The study of language can be viewed with certain leisure goals in mind. The most obvious one is the acquisition of a minimum of

knowledge, enough to ease foreign travel and conversation with foreigners in one's own country. Sometimes superficial knowledge of a language gives one a minimum of social savoir-faire, from reading a menu in a restaurant to establishing one's respectability by being able to recite in like company some detached lines of a classic. Such uses, although undoubtedly pleasant at times, again raise the question as to whether they are genuinely liberal.

The question may be raised whether college is the appropriate time or appropriate place for the learning of languages. In regard to time, we have some evidence that the optimal age for language learning comes much earlier than the college years. In regard to place, it might be asked whether the learning of language belongs in the college curriculum at all, or rather should be considered a prerequisite to it. Students might not be admitted to the foreign literature courses *until* they know the language. This would free foreign language teachers for the teaching they are interested in and prepared for. Teaching machines may soon free the language teacher from the elementary tasks anyway.

Our analysis of goals in foreign language teaching can be duplicated for every other subject in the curriculum. Discrepancy between professed goals and actual achievement is a general phenomenon and foreign languages, like mathematics, have the advantage of having the outcome more measurable, while in other fields memorization, cramming, and other devices make measurement more difficult.

After this discussion of goals we turn to considering some of the actual and potential effects of several academic subject matters on undergraduate learning.

Literature and the arts—drama, painting, music—may be considered first. These subjects offer one of the best means for freeing the impulse life. What we have in mind here is the possibility that through the guided study of literature the student may discover that impulses which he has found it necessary to inhibit can actually be expressed, sometimes symbolically and sometimes in other ways, if he knows enough about the world and about himself. We assume that literature is going to be taught in the right way—that is, that the teacher is going to require that the student understand the characters being studied before judging them. The student's natural inclination, of course, is to judge characters in literature, as well as elsewhere, according to the values that he brings with him to college. If his anxiety is so great that he cannot tolerate any change in these values, he will of course not be good in literature. But if he gets the point, if he discovers that anything can be done in the imagination and that everything that he has so far imagined has been done by somebody, and that those who did these things can be understood, then he is bound to admit into his scheme of things a broader range of human potentialities. These he can see as present in himself as well as in other people. The thing about literature, as we understand it, is not that it simply releases fundamental impulses to be expressed in their original fundamental form—this could hardly be called freedom; instead, it gives to the individual something of the very thing which made the creation of that literature possible in the first place, and that is the means for transforming the impulse life in such a way that it meets the requirements of reality and of conscience—but meets them just barely. If this kind of change in the individual is brought about through the study of literature, it will affect the individual's performance in all of his other courses, as indeed in his life generally. Thus change brought about by education in one discipline ramifies throughout the personality and affects ways of responding to any discipline.

Our point about literature and the arts may be emphasized by calling attention to the appeal of popular culture, that is to say the movies, television, comic books, and the like. These media afford means for conventionalizing the individual phantasy life. They put into socially acceptable form phantasy themes which are widespread among individuals in our society. It may be noted parenthetically that even the more extreme comic books do not offer phantasy themes that are more violent or perverse than are the phantasies which a child is capable of producing for himself. When he produces them for himself he has to deal alone with the anxiety occasioned by them. To know that other people have the same phantasy or that his own needs may be expressed in public ways, is probably a considerable relief to him. In the enjoyment of these kinds of popular culture it is easy to see that there is some gratification of impulses, the element of escape as we sometimes say, and there is also instruction in how to feel, how to express emotion, even instruction in what to feel on given occasions, and in how emotions may properly be expressed. The appeal of what we call good literature and art is in some fundamental respects the same, but with several important differences. As people develop, new needs are generated, and hence there is the possibility of more kinds of conflict among these needs. There is, as we have seen, more complexity of personality, and in these circumstances a person can derive benefit from literature and art only when what is presented is sufficiently subtle and complicated to match the development of the person. As a person becomes more differentiated he cannot identify himself with gross oversimplified emotional expressions, nor can he learn anything from childish material about how to express his adult feelings. Nevertheless, and perhaps more important, that which we value most highly in literature and the arts is typically in very close touch with the impulse life. It is far from being an accident that most of what is great in these areas comes at one time or another into conflict with the authorities and is subject to being banned; though we hasten to add that everything that is banned is not good. Consider, for example, the difference between a play by Eugene O'Neil and an ordinary television drama. The mark of the latter is always its conventionality. What is said and done and expressed is always in accordance with the prevailing mores. Although undoubtedly the impulse life finds some expression, the channels for expression have been sharply drawn by conventional morality, and the final product is more a triumph of the primitive conscience than a vehicle for the expression of impulse. The passion of the O'Neil play, on the other hand, is the real thing, that is, it is a true expression of the impulse life, but for this very reason the play must be good in the artistic sense in order for the mature or maturing person to enjoy it. Seen from this point of view, taste is not something that can be acquired from those who have it, or think they do, but it is that precise balance of the impulsive, on the one hand, and the realistic and socially conforming, on the other, that the individual requires in order to derive maximum satisfaction through his responses to literature and art.

We have spoken earlier about the necessity for challenging the cognitive structures—the conceptions of one's self and of the world, the ethical principles—with which the student enters college. These structures undoubtedly derive in the main from the family and the community, and many have been taken over automatically and have not been the object of the student's own thought and experience. It would seem that the study of *philosophy and religion and the history of ideas* is nicely calculated to provide the necessary challenge. One of the chief aims of philosophy is to instill a sense of the tentativeness of all conceptual formulations, of the possible flexibility of all conceptual devices, and of the possibilities of intertranslation among different conceptual systems. The study of religion affords a special opportunity of examining not alone the variety of conceptions but also the variety of beliefs that have been or are being held with great emotion, and thus to bring about understanding where the student might have felt strangeness or even repugnance before. It is to be recognized, of course, that the values and beliefs with which students leave college are, often, not very different from the values and beliefs with which they enter college. There is, however, the possibility that the values and beliefs are now held in a different way, that they have a firmer basis in the subject's own experience and thought, and hence a different relation to other processes of the personality. One might also expect that regardless of the content of one's values and beliefs at the moment, one has available to him the means for improving his decisions in this area as time goes on. (But we must remind ourselves that how the individual functions in this area depends on many potent factors that have nothing to do with the content of the curriculum.)

In approaching the areas of *mathematics and natural science,* we have to recognize that these subjects as they are often taught today, favor the maintenance of defensive structures, that they play into the hands of the conventional, the restricting, the suppressing functions of the personality. The study of these disciplines may very well support the aim of being a well-disciplined, well-controlled, well-behaved young lady or young man who grimly accepts the formulas, memorizes a mass of factual material, and hands in meticulous lab reports. But we know that things do not have to be this way, that it is possible to teach science in a way that conveys its spirit rather than its facts or its precise techniques, a way that introduces the student to its wayward aspects as well as to its discipline. Science, after all, is out to upset the existing order of things. It is essentially daring and unconventional. Its rules, its discipline, derive out of its own processes and needs, and have nothing to do with conventional morality. Many young people who choose science hope thereby to capitalize upon their prematurely organized consciences. When science is chosen in this way, and its discipline is used to support the suppressing and controlling functions of the personality, it is very difficult to see how instruction in these disciplines will later free the individual. Would it not be better to recruit for science those students who are passionate and curious and out to discover and to change the world, and then to undertake to teach them the necessary disciplines?

We hardly need to elaborate the point that if natural science is taught in the right way, or if the student discovers for himself what the subject is about, there is nothing that can be more instructive of how to think. Training in scientific thinking can make an enormous difference when it comes to dealing with practical problems or problems in human affairs as well. But it is obvious that our natural science teachers, given the vast array of facts and principles which they feel they must somehow cover, often neglect to assure themselves that the students have grasped the fundamental modes of scientific thought. It may very well be that for the time being, until training in the natural sciences has been reformed, psychology and social science might be the better instruments for teaching students how to think.

If taught in the right way, *mathematics,* offers one of the best means for training the intelligence. Mathematics, as Frank Pinner (Chapter 27) stresses, can exhibit the processes of thought and of feeling by which truth is discovered. The student may here learn that the maxims and theorems are not unalterable, that they do not have an objective existence but are creations of the human mind that aid the pursuit of truth. Pinner also points out that in mathematics one may learn of the close affinity between beauty and truth, how it is that an elegant solution or the demonstrated generality of a truth may be causes for joy. When one looks at the matter in this light it becomes very sad to contemplate how many young people are deprived of a great and inexhaustible source of joy by kinds of teaching that leave them either terrified of anything involving mathematics, or else fixed in the notion that mathematics involves nothing more than a set of devices for manipulating numbers.

CONCLUSION: CONDITIONS OF CURRICULAR REFORM

The college curriculum can be a uniquely potent instrument for the development of personality. Currently the curriculum fulfills its promise very inadequately because it does not incorporate a sophisticated attempt to make contact with the impulses and present situation of the student. The student is whatever he is: career oriented, rebellious, indifferent. One may decry any of these conditions. But the student is all that the curriculum has to work with. Undoubtedly the curricular task would be different if the entering freshman were an "ideal" student. There is no lack of intellectual vitality in students, but it is a vitality that is often systematically discouraged. The curriculum at present is too much allied with the mechanisms of social authority and of individual defensive control to make felt its full developmental potential.

We have indicated at the beginning that a redefinition of the curriculum is necessary in order to ensure its greater impact. Even now there is an implicit acknowledgement of the expendability of a great many curricular features. In most colleges, individual students select an enormous variety of different courses. This amounts to an acknowledgement that there are many ways of learning, and that any one of the present particular ways can be done without. The needed revision of the curriculum will, we believe, depend on at least the following four conditions: (1) A better articulation of the central features of differing curricular modes of presentation and content. (2) Continuing experimentation; curricular experiments hitherto have depended on a curricular philosophy; once a curriculum to fit the philosophy was found, the experiment was over. We need curricular science; that is, a continuing process of theoretically guided experimentation, and assessment of its results, so that a cumulative curricular reform can become built into the curriculum itself. (3) Self-examination of teachers. This could be done along the lines indicated in Chapter 9. (4) Recognition of the differing impact of the curriculum on differing students.

Adequate redefinitions of the curriculum will, therefore, have to wait for the future. But a beginning can always be made on the basis of past experience and present institutional patterns. The field is wide open to the exercise of imaginative and experimental skills.

REFERENCES

Columbia University. *A college program in action.* New York: Columbia University Press, 1946.

Dewey, John. *Human nature and conduct.* New York: Random House, The Modern Library, 1930.

Dressel, P. L., and Mayhew, L. *General education: explorations in evaluation; the final report.* Washington: American Council on Education, 1954.

Ekstein, R., and Wallerstein, R. S. *The teaching and learning of psychotherapy.* New York: Basic Books, 1958.

Freedman, M. The passage through college. In Nevitt Sanford (Ed.), Personality development during the college years. *J. soc. Issues,* 1956, **12,** 13–28.

Harvard University. *General education in a free society.* Cambridge, Mass.: Harvard University Press, 1945.

Jacob, P. *Changing values in college.* New York: Harper Bros., 1957.

Kennedy, G. (Ed.). *Education at Amherst: the new program.* New York: Harper Bros., 1955.

Lewin, B. D. Education or the quest for omniscience. *J. Amer. Psychoanal. Assoc.,* 1958, **6,** 389–412.

Meiklejohn, A. *The experimental college.* New York: Harper Bros., 1932.

Murphy, L., and Raushenbush, E. (Eds.). *Achievement in the college years.* New York: Harper Bros., 1960.

Russell, B. *The problems of philosophy.* New York: Holt, 1912.

Schilpp, P. A. (Ed.). *The philosophy of John Dewey.* Evanston, Ill.: Northwestern University, 1939.

Taylor, H. (Ed.). *Essays in teaching.* New York: Harper Bros., 1950.

University of Chicago. *The idea and practice of general education.* Chicago: University of Chicago Press, 1950.

12 *Anthony Ostroff*

Economic Pressure
and the Professor

The following essay was originally intended to be part of a
much larger study centering on what is called "academic pressure"—that is, on those professional and institutional pressures to
which the college teacher is subject, and which are reflected in his intense involvement in institutional politics, administrative and quasi-
administrative labor, and the desperate struggle for publication. Unfortunately, that larger study could not be completed in time for
inclusion here. One result is that the present essay, standing by itself,
fails to make clear two important points which would have been apparent in its originally intended context.

The more important of these two points, in terms of the intention
of this essay, is this: the most deplorable effect of the college professor's economic situation is that it denies him the option of refus-
ing to submit to those academic pressures which are most destructive
of his teaching function. He cannot choose to devote himself to teaching at the expense of producing a steady stream of "publishable research," and he cannot avoid participation in the vast bureaucracies
of committee routine and faculty politics. To refuse to join in any of
the nonteaching aspects of academic life means to forfeit hope of professional advancement—and the college teacher's sole hope for economic survival is to reach the top ranks of his profession.

All of this becomes particularly depressing when the intensity of
conflict between teaching and nonteaching activity is seen, and this
is not merely a matter of recognizing the direct usurpation of teaching time by professionally required but nonteaching activity; it is

also a matter of appreciating the subtle and pernicious effects of so-called "academic pressure" on the psychology of the individual professor. Indeed, it is here that the increasingly disruptive drama of academic life today is to be found. This is not to say that the psychological problems discussed in the present essay are trivial by comparison to the more intricate and devious problems created by academic pressure, but it is to suggest that their chief importance lies in the contribution they make to the total complex of problems arising from strictly academic pressure—that is, from pressure directly related to professional activity required of the college teacher today.

The second point to be made in this introduction is that what follows is chiefly concerned with *the college teacher in the humanities.* This may not always be kept sharply in focus in the essay itself. Many of the problems and pressures discussed are general in academic life, and it has sometimes seemed important to treat these in ways suggestive of their broadest relevance. However, the one constant frame of reference is the college teacher in the humanities.

I feel obliged to add that I powerfully suspect the problems delineated in this essay are more generally relevant to the whole spectrum of college faculty than most readers will be prepared to admit. For all the recent, dramatic improvement in the economic circumstances of some college and university professors in certain disciplines—especially the natural sciences—it seems doubtful that even the lot of the average college professor of physics or chemistry is very greatly improved over the average of the academic profession as a whole. The widely publicized availability of "fringe benefits"—consultantships, research grants, and the like—to supplement income in the natural and social sciences, would seem to a considerable extent misleading. One wonders how many of the total number of teachers in the "affluent" disciplines are privileged to enjoy these much-touted opportunities—and how many of *them* can use the opportunities to improve their circumstances for more than very brief terms.

However sceptical one may be of the extent of improvement in the economics of academic life in disciplines outside the humanities, there is no doubt that there has been some improvement generally. But within the disciplines of the humanities, which account for a majority of all college teachers, there has been no significant improvement for the past three or four decades. Real salaries have risen little, if at all; fringe benefits, practically speaking, are not available. Consultantships simply do not exist. Fellowship or research funds are meager, and individual opportunities for securing them are few indeed. If it is not consistently true throughout the academic profession, it is true that in the humanities professional income equals salary—and salaries are frightfully low. This fact, and some of its consequences, are the concern of what follows.

THE PROBLEM

Certainly the most discussed of all the problems faced by the professor is the economic problem. Whether or not teaching be a gentleman's profession, it has become very clear that one should not enter it without a gentleman's means. Too often, however, concern with academic salaries ends with the shocked recognition that our college teachers generally make a good deal less than almost everyone to whom they are compared, from milkmen in Manhattan to carpenters in California. The public cries that something must be done—and finds a grand topic for conversation in the relative salaries of the various professions and trades, and the time required to train for them. Attention seems rarely to arrive at what academic salaries actually mean in economic terms to the professor, let alone the special hardships the professor must suffer because of his low wages.

The fact is that in our present, prosperous national economy the academic profession as a whole belongs to the lower class, or, at best, the lower middle-class, economically speaking. In plain words, most teachers are poor. The Hollywood stereotype of the professor as a man in worn and tasteless clothes, driving a decrepit car from a home in need of repairs to give an address to the well-kept elders of the town is not inaccurate in the physical image it presents. It is only wrong in its suggestion that the professor, through some ivory-towered preoccupation with ideas, is indifferent to the things of this world. If he is ill-dressed, ill-housed, ill-transported, and otherwise ill, it is because he cannot afford good clothes, good housing, a good car, or even very elaborate medical attention.

Still and all, he stays alive. He is paid enough for clothing and shelter, even if not of the most elegant. There is no need for extreme anxiety over his economic plight. He will survive.

But there is some question as to whether he will survive as a teacher and scholar of much worth. The experience of poverty, though it may have some humanizing values, is, if continued long enough, destructive of the life of the mind; and the average member of the academic profession who lacks private means may today be assured of a long experience of poverty.

I use the word "poverty" advisedly. We are accustomed to thinking of it in melodramatic terms, as representing hunger, starvation, cold, helplessness, and of course where these circumstances exist they must make prior claim on our attention, whether we are genuinely concerned with the welfare of all mankind or merely interested in the spectacle of man. But there is a poverty of deprivation as well as one of destitution, and it can be a serious matter, which it is, in the case of the academic man. Of what does it—this "poverty of deprivation"— consist? It is difficult to describe. Like parenthood, it is something that has to be experienced to be understood. But perhaps a few figures may suggest some of its cold facts.

ACADEMIC SALARIES AND HOW TO LIVE ON THEM

In most of the published studies of the economics of the academic profession, the statistics given have to do with salaries of the various academic ranks and of the profession as a whole in relation to past salaries and real purchasing power, or in relation to what has happened to incomes in other occupations over the past decade or more. Indeed, some of these statistics are impressive. It is interesting to consider, for example, that in 1904 the top professor's salary in the U.S. was $7000—for which today's equivalent would be upward of $35,-000.[1] It is interesting to contemplate the fact that the percentage gain in real income from 1939 to 1957 was 79% for all forms of employment in the United States. By 1957, physicians had gained 93% over their 1939 real incomes—and over 400% in dollar income; dentists had gained 54%; lawyers, about 45%. During the same period the real income of the academic man actually *declined* 8.5%—from an income already inadequate in 1939. The average salaries of the learned professions of medicine (including dentistry) and the law, which only a few decades ago were more or less on a par with those of the academic profession, are now substantially more than double those of the academic profession.[2] And of course the income *possibilities* of other professions are so enormously greater than the very best offered by the academic profession that discretion forbids any specific comparisons.

[1] Beardsley Ruml, Pay and the professor, *Atlantic Monthly*, 199, April 1957. (Note: Ruml's figure for the 1957 equivalent to a 1904 salary of $7000 was $31,250. The 1960 equivalent would certainly be above $35,000.)

[2] Instructional salaries in 39 selected colleges and universities for the academic year 1957–58. (A study by the committee on the economic status of the profession of the A.A.U.P.—final report), *A.A.U.P. Bulletin*, March 1958, 44.

But although such figures as have just been quoted are interesting, even dramatic, their drama for most people seems to take place in a play of abstractions. What academic salaries actually mean with regard to the economic and social life of the college teacher and scholar is rarely signified by such figures, or even by the figures of actual salaries today. For example, what is told of a man's life when it is reported that his gross income is $5000 or $6000 a year? Not very much, no doubt, to most people who live on a larger income. So it is not much use to report that the average salary of the college and university instructor in the United States today is slightly under $5000 a year, or that the average salary for assistant professors is less than $6000. Nor is it very useful merely to report that these salaries account for most of the faculty below the age of forty—in other words, for most of those who, after an average of from three to five years of costly graduate study, have served from one to fifteen years in their institutions.

It may be helpful, however, to consider what such salaries may mean in terms of family budgets. The following examination, taken from the back pages of a 1957 issue of the house organ of a California Discount House,[3] is ". . . a specific example and we feel a fairly typical example of the economic situation, give or take a child or two, in which many . . . teachers find themselves." It is already out of date in terms of the continuing inflation (though not in terms of academic salaries), and it refers to a high school teacher with a Master's degree rather than to a college teacher with a Ph.D., but as it may thus err in reflecting a college teacher's budget today, it errs on the side of conservatism.

STATUS: Married Male teacher, age 30, 3 children, Master's Degree, in his 6th year of teaching.

SALARY: $5,050 per year BUT less income tax, retirement, medical insurance, yields TAKE-HOME PAY of $331 PER MONTH.

FIXED MONTHLY EXPENSES:

House payment (Purchase Price, $9,850)	$ 80.00
Gas, water, electricity, garbage	20.00
Telephone	4.50
Food for family of 5	125.00
Milk	12.00
Automobile (gas, oil, lubrication, repair) BUT NOT REPLACE-MENT	20.00
Payments for replacement or purchase of all household furnishings & furniture, tools, equipment, etc.	20.00

[3] A teacher's choice, *A.G.E.* (Associated Government Employees) *Reporter*, April, 1957.

FIXED MONTHLY EXPENSES (*continued*)
>   Insurance:
>   >   Reducing term mortgage on home
>   > $8,000 life on husband; $1,000 on wife
>   >   Automobile insurance
>   >   Total 35.00
>   Newspaper 2.00
>   Haircuts for husband (1 every 3 weeks, at $2 each) 3.00

               Total . . $321.50

TAKE-HOME PAY $331.00
MONTHLY EXPENSE 321.50

                                  $ 9.50

The problem is to BUDGET the remaining $9.50 to cover the following items:

1. Clothing for 5 people
2. Cleaning
3. Medicine and doctor office calls
4. Dental bills
5. Professional Growth
   a. Professional organizations' dues
   b. Books
   c. Periodicals
   d. Research travel
6. Car license and taxes
7. Books & magazines (non-professional), recordings, etc.
8. Family recreation
9. Family vacations
10. Christmas gifts, cards, etc.
11. Birthday gifts (children only)
12. Personal postage & stationery
13. Toiletries
14. Upkeep on home (paint, etc.)
15. Upkeep of lawn and landscaping (seed, fertilizer, plants, etc.)
16. Provision for children's education
17. Replacement of automobile
18. SAVINGS PROGRAM?? [4]

No doubt it is unnecessary to point out that most of the items listed under Fixed Monthly Expenses are almost grotesquely modest. (Housing, heating, telephone, and dairy bills, for example, are today substantially above those listed in the table, even at a minimum.) It does not seem unreasonable to assume that the $6000 a year man in

[4] *Ibid.* (Note: I have slightly revised item 5 above, substituting "research travel" for the original listing, which gave "Summer School & Extension Courses." This was done to bring the listing to conform to a college teacher's needs rather than to those of a high school teacher.)

1960 could do little better than the $5000 a year man represented in the above consideration. Nor does it seem necessary to point out that a gross income of *at least* an additional $1000 per year would be required for a viable salary in terms of the modest budget outlined.

From the budget as it stands, however, several things become perfectly obvious. The $5000 a year man in the academic profession (where, like it or not, members are usually docked a fair percentage of their gross income for retirement, medical insurance, etc.) simply cannot afford many of the necessities of his life. He cannot really afford out-patient medical treatment or dental care. Even personal grooming at its most minimal—and quite apart from his family's needs for clothes, toiletries, and the like—is a difficult expense to bear. One may wonder how he manages at all.

Well, how does he manage? If he has no private means, he rents house or apartment rather than owning his home, for he has little hope of saving money for a down payment for purchase. Thus he avoids some of the costs of upkeep of property which the home owner inevitably assumes—though he pays a price in such measure of economic and psychological security as the acquisition of real property might provide. (Needless to say, his house or apartment is likely to be a minimal facility if he is head of a family. He can't rent much of a place for what he can afford to pay.) He does almost all of his shopping at the cut-rate stores. He buys cheap clothes, guards them carefully, cuts down on cleaning bills the best he can. He encourages his wife to learn to press his suits for him, to cut his hair for him, and to inhibit sharply her own natural desires for service at the hairdresser's and beautician's, not to mention the women's apparel shop. His diet and his family's include an unusual amount of macaroni, beans, rice, and other cheap foods—casseroles will be coming out of his ears for years. If he lives in a state where it is possible to buy good horsemeat, he sometimes eats horsemeat instead of beef. He drinks cheap wine instead of good, and that is kept to a minimum. (Little or no liquor, of course.) He buys his furniture secondhand from Good Will or the Salvation Army. When he acquires them, his appliances are used, his automobile is secondhand; if he is fortunate enough to have friends or family to pass clothes on to him, he often wears used clothing. Most of the clothing and toys he acquires for his children are used when he gets them. And even then he goes into debt.

He feels obliged to provide reasonably good medical, optical, and dental care for himself and his family. He attempts to maintain the illusion of a normal home at least for his children, so Christmas and birthdays are observed (though he and his wife are likely to exchange only token gifts, if any at all, on these occasions). Once his children are beyond babyhood, he attempts to provide some sort of vacation, at least for them, if not for the whole family, and even though that is likely to be at a church or YMCA or community-sponsored camp, it means additional expense. Of course he has to replace the worn-out automobile, the broken bicycle, the torn winter coat. Probably, out of his rather more-intense-than-normal sense of community responsibility, he even gives a little something to charity each year. So he goes into debt. And he worries.

At the end of every month he is caught in the anxieties of not being able to pay all his bills—anxieties especially wretched for him whose sense of social and economic responsibility is especially keen (one notes in the tables of the bank and loan companies that the best credit risks —for *small* loans and financing—are teachers). Or he is caught up in the frantic business of trying to economize still further to make it until payday five days away. He may manage to keep his economic worries in the background of consciousness for most of each month, but the last few days of the month are likely to be times when all else is dominated by the search for ways *now* to meet the bills *now*. The especially bad months may lead to longer periods of desperate pre-occupation with schemes to solve the incessant financial problem. And always he is haunted by images of the disaster that could ruin him for months or even years—not the apocalyptic images of atomic war or earthquake or the melting of the polar icecaps which are the hobgoblins of epic minds, but images of social and natural disaster on a personal scale—another hike in the cost of living, an accident beyond the scope of his medical insurance, the sudden breakdown of the car, or explosion of the water heater, or hole in the seat of his pants. The smallest loss must be serious in the economy of his life.

This picture is not overdrawn. It will probably seem so to most people outside the academic profession, as well as to those many individuals within it who are privileged to possess other means of support in addition to their salaries—whether in the form of regular private income or in gifts such as automobiles or down payments on houses or other kinds of financial aid from families or friends. But the fact remains: the average salaries for the lower ranks of the academic profession do not provide even for the minimal level of economic existence the college teacher is required to maintain. At this moment there must be literally thousands of college and university teachers whose financial situations are similar to the general ones here suggested. Moreover, the condition of poverty here ascribed to the lower ranks of the profession is by no means confined to the lower ranks.

Only a minority of the entire working force of college and university faculty throughout the country makes over $7500 a year, including even those at the full professorship.[5] While in the junior grades, the academic man is likely to mortgage his future earnings for a number of the fifteen or so relatively "high" salary years he may hope to enjoy before retirement. Debts accumulated during the years as instructor and assistant professor may for some years usurp the increase of pay at the associate and full professorship. This, plus new tax differentials at the higher pay level, plus the usual attempt to raise his standard of living slightly—from horsemeat to beef, from an apartment to a house, or at least to private rooms for the children—may cause the average academician to continue suffering acute economic pressures well into his mature years in his profession, if not to the very end of his days.

CONSEQUENCES OF ECONOMIC DEPRIVATION FOR THE PROFESSOR'S RELATIONS WITH HIS JOB

What are the consequences of this economic predicament with regard to the relation of the professor to his job? For one thing, in the grim effort to draw abreast of his debts, he will probably be forced to spend his summer—that invaluable respite from the psychic drain of active teaching, that imperative calm for research and preparation to teach again—in teaching. At least, this will be true until he has reached a living wage in the senior ranks of his profession. And if he is not so fortunate as to get a summer teaching job, he will work as a bus driver, truck driver, factory hand, cannery worker, salesman, clerk, croupier [6]—whatever employment business and labor will let him have. During the academic year he will snatch at such jobs as his institution will allow him to take and as he can manage along with his regular teaching duties. He may legally take on extra teaching

[5] It should perhaps be pointed out that the figure for the college teacher in the humanities is probably considerably lower than this. Available salary studies of the academic profession cover the whole of the profession, or selected (and presumably representative) institutions within it. They do not, however, distinguish among various disciplines within the profession. There is no doubt that the humanities generally serve as low man on the economic totem pole of academia. At many institutions, salaries "above scale" must be paid to scientists, engineers, lawyers, medical doctors, and even certain social scientists, to hold such men against high-salary opportunities in business, industry, and private practice. Average and mean salaries for the profession as a whole reflect these relatively high salaries which are, for the most part, not available to the humanities professor.

[6] This is not mere rhetoric. I have known of college or university teachers working summers in all the occupations named—and some others as well.

chores in his university or college extension or adult education programs, he may accept speaking engagements before the Lions' Club or the Baptist Ladies Literary Group, and if he is good at disguise and can keep his mouth shut, and has a sympathetic chairman, and is otherwise lucky, he may get away with clerking for a distant hardware store or raising poultry for sale in his backyard.[7]

One direct result of this extraprofessional employment is, of course, its interference with professional activity. As needed time for class preparation, for research, for reflection, to say nothing of simple relaxation, goes into chores in which the academic man should not have to engage at all, he is left short of time for the best fulfillment of his professional obligations. This problem extends through all ranks of the academic profession, but it is especially serious for the younger members of the profession, who most desperately need time to work, not only to improve themselves by actual teaching and research experience, but also to prove themselves to their senior colleagues and qualify for professional advancement by specific scholarly accomplishment.

There are further consequences, however. More subtle, but at least equally destructive of his effective performance in his role as teacher, gentleman, and scholar, will be those psychological pressures the college faculty member suffers as a more or less direct result of his economic predicament. While struggling with his financial anxieties, while preoccupied with worries about feeding and clothing his family decently, educating his children, meeting the inevitable, unpredictable bills continually arising beyond the limits of his allowable indebtedness as well as his budget, he will not be able to give himself very fully to the jobs of research and teaching, which require nothing less than total concentration if they are to be done properly. As long as he remains truly dedicated to his job, any frustration of his ability and will to do it well will be especially painful to him. Indeed, as he finds himself doing less than the job he feels he should do, he may fall into feelings of insecurity and guilt which may still further inhibit him from fulfilling his academic role as he conceives it, and he may thus become involved in that vicious circle of personal insecurity which feeds and fattens on itself until some act of fate or fortune or will brings it to a stop.

But this disruptive pressure of financial anxiety on that peace of mind needed for good work is only the most obvious of the psychological pressures to which the professor's economic situation may con-

[7] *Ibid.*

tribute. There is also a problem of social insecurity which helps to undermine his morale.

The professor finds himself, in his secondhand life, in a difficult position in the community. He would hold up his head among his neighbors, but all those status symbols in terms of which he is likely to be judged seem to be arraigned against him. In all the public terms of his economic position (his clothing, automobile, furniture, ability to entertain, etc.), he is inferior to almost all those people with whom he would associate, except for colleagues. That this means he is necessarily looked upon by most of his community as a man who does not quite measure up is something of which he quickly becomes aware, and by which he may be considerably troubled. The problem is not merely one of social status in terms of the "right" possessions; it is also a problem of active social relations outside the academy.

As citizen and neighbor in a prosperous nation, if not as scholar and gentleman in whatever country of his mind, the professor would reciprocate dinner invitations; he would even offer his nonacademic friends the same fare they have offered him; he would now and then accept their suggestions that he accompany them to the theatre or opera; he would go with them to the week-end lake or skiing resort to which they so cordially urge him. His social ambition entirely out of hand, he would even reciprocate their gifts at Christmas time. That he can do none of these things, or, at best, can do them only very occasionally, and then only with considerable guilt at the insult to his already abused budget, pains him. He is likely to have an incorrigible sense of propriety in social matters—to say nothing of normal pride.

The college teacher may not care for the usual status symbols, per se, so much as his neighbors do, but he does care to live presentably in material terms, and he wishes to enjoy true equality with his neighbors. He wishes to participate normally in the social affairs of his community, not as a poor relation. However, even where he enjoys the affection of his nonacademic friends and neighbors, and a real— if somewhat curiously compartmentalized—measure of their respect, he finds that again and again in relations with them he is reminded of his precarious economic plight in humiliating ways, and there are usually unfortunate consequences.

An immediate and fairly common result of the academic man's insecurity in social relations outside the academy is that he tends increasingly to limit himself to association with members of his own profession. This is, of course, undesirable from the point of view of the whole society he serves. As an intellectual, simply as a man who thinks—if not also as one who is traditionally expected to possess not only a broad knowledge of human affairs but some wisdom in them, as well—the teacher and scholar is of great potential value as an active participant in the social and civic life of any free society. It is a shame when this value must be rendered endlessly potential—that is to say, inactive—by the academic man's withdrawal from the social life of his community at large.

His withdrawal is further undesirable in terms of his function as educator, if not also as scholar. Without doubt the teacher, ideally, should be in fairly intimate contact with the life of his society in all its aspects and on all its levels. Not only is this important with regard to the continual adjustment to reality of that criticism of life which it is his function to teach; it is important in terms of knowing how most effectively to teach. Insofar as he is not in contact with the thought, the values, the attitudes of milieus outside the academy, the professor risks failing to make contact with his students. His task may be to provide his students with new, larger, better frames of reference for experience than those they bring to college with them, but often he must first reach them within their own frames of reference, and to do so he must know what these are.

For all the importance of the above considerations, however, the most serious immediate consequence of the academic man's withdrawal from the general social life of the community may be (since such withdrawal is usually accompanied by commitment to the academy for social as well as for professional life) that it leads toward a kind of professional incest which often develops within the academy; that is, it is a helpful factor in the development of the academy as a closed system, socially, psychologically, and politically. The consequences of such development, in terms of institutional and professional pressures on the faculty member, may be great and highly destructive of those ideals of humanistic development which seem to characterize the highest aims of higher education—at least, as those are generally stated. (Problems of professional and institutional pressures, especially in relation to the structure of the college or university as a closed system in terms of the faculty member's position, are far too complex for discussion within the limits of this essay. They are mentioned here, however, because it is important to suggest that they are not to be divorced from the economic aspects of academic life.)

At the same time that the academic man may, for essentially economic reasons, suffer considerable frustration of his natural wish to participate normally in the social and civic life of his community, he also suffers another kind of frustration which may contribute psychic pressures capable of interfering with the best performance of his job. In his private life he is almost certain to be cheated in considerable measure of realizing those very values he had joined the academy to serve—not, perhaps, the intellectual values (although these would seem to be affected too), but certainly the aesthetic values, if one can separate truth and beauty, those two classical components of the good life. (And of course it is the good life in which the professor, in the humanities at least, seeks to instruct.)

To speak of beauty in the present context may seem an impertinence, especially when it remains as impossible to define as truth. But, as with truth, it can often be shown to our satisfaction where beauty lies: this is a beautiful suit of clothes; that is a beautiful house; here is beautiful music; there is a beautiful painting. And when one has spent one's life developing taste, it is usually easy to recognize the good, the beautiful, the true, when one comes upon them. These things, in their real forms, are imperative in their appeal to the man who can recognize them. But, ah, the cost of a well-wrought urn! [8]

To be sure, the professor can find his books in the library, paintings in the museum, gardens in the park, clothes, architecture, artifacts of fine design, on the streets. He is far from deprived of sight and experience of all that he necessarily admires. If his philosophy be true, he may fulfill his aesthetic needs well enough, with a little effort. He must be an imperfect idealist indeed to be made morbid by not being able to buy the book, the handsome table, the graceful chair, with which, all other things being equal, he would furnish his home. It is hard to take seriously his despair at sending his students to plays and concerts he cannot afford. He is already steeped in culture, and surely his mind, his memory, his imagination, if any good, will supply him in spirit with what he may miss in the flesh. Besides, eight years ago he traveled to Rome, and that should hold him for a while! But alas, it does not, except as a debt on which he is still paying.

What must be recognized is that although the academic man may, for the most part, be far less preoccupied with the material things of life than most other men, material things have their importance for him—and in some respects he must be interested in them in ways that may seem extravagant to a civilization mindful of those historical beginnings in which teachers and tutors were slaves.

What may to some people seem material luxuries may, to the teacher and scholar, be spiritual necessities. Although the professor will not

---

[8] The allusion is to John Donne's poem, "The Canonization," in which the following lines occur: "As well a well-wrought urn becomes/ The greatest ashes as half-acre tombs." (Ed.)

ask half-acre tombs of life, he may require well-wrought urns. Like all men he may sometimes dream of luxury, but unlike most men he must always require excellence—and to be deprived of it even in the most modest aspects of his private life is to be denied what he can scarcely help regarding as both his privilege and his right. There is small justice for him in working to create audiences for Shakespeare and being himself unable to afford attending productions of Shakespeare's plays. He cannot help but feel bitterly the irony that forbids him to support at least by subscription those intellectual and cultural journals to which he gives his allegiance and on the existence of which he may feel his own enterprise somewhat depends. He cannot avoid the humiliation of his own sensibility by the relative squalor in which he must live: the worn upholstery, the faded wallpaper, the ugly lamp, all in his home that is less than clean, less than well-wrought, must be an offense to his sensibility, shaped by training, if not by instinct, to value intelligence, grace, dignity, in the things of this world as well as in human action.

Moreover, in an important sense the personal or private aesthetic or spiritual needs of the professor suggested above are also professional needs. As he seeks to establish in his students habits of buying books, recordings, paintings, of supporting as well as appreciating the arts in all their forms, as he encourages them to commitment to the idea of beauty as well as morality, of grace as well as justice, of honor as well as honesty, he must feel an obligation to serve as a model of what he preaches. To be unable to do so, indeed, to have to contradict in the appearance of his life a good deal of what he professes, is to seem to betray himself in his role as mentor, as man of learning and the arts. The problem is, perhaps, a delicate one, but it may have indelicate consequences.

Both by his nature and by his professional sense of obligation to those ideals he serves, the professor must be given to espousal of the excellent. But because of his economic situation he must provide—in almost all the visible aspects of his private life—exemplification of the mediocre. The tension between the two may be very great. At best, the academic man must suffer a somewhat schizophrenic sense of himself, split between his aesthetic commitments on the one hand and his material realities on the other. At worst, he may fall into paranoia.

The professor is aware that as a model of what the life of the mind may lead to, he presents little to appeal to his students, most of whom know perfectly well that it is in the world *outside* the academy they are going to live *their* lives. Indeed, he knows that in the image he presents in his private life, which is often far from unknown to his students; he is a living comfort to the Philistinism he probably considers it his job to correct. Furthermore, he is aware that many, if not most, of his students regard him with a measure of condescension, however tempered by more congenial attitudes it may be. He is, after all, in terms of that image of the good life constructed by Hollywood and Madison Avenue, a failure. His students do not always forgive him this. What can they be expected to feel toward a man they are asked to treat as a superior but whose position in the "real world" outside the academy hardly commands respect?

As the professor is aware of the pity or disgust or contempt of his students, or at least of the logic that would produce such attitudes, he is likely to suffer a measure of despair. He feels he *must* command the respect of his students if he is to succeed as their teacher and mentor. To have some of the terms in which he will or will not command their respect be utterly out of his control (i.e., those aspects of his private life and relations to society which are determined by his economic situation) is a difficult thing to bear, at best. He may rise above the problem by his sheer brillance or devotion as a teacher, but the problem remains a problem, surmounted or not. Too often it may affect the professor adversely in his relationships with students.

For example, he may, in retaliation against his students' lack of respect for him (real or imagined), develop a contempt of his own for them. If he can view them as largely frivolous or witless, and generally unworthy of respect, he can comfortably discount any negative view they may take of him. Naturally, he will not consciously set about arranging his defenses, but arrange them he nevertheless may.

It is by no means uncommon for the college professor to develop rather strong negative attitudes toward his students, especially his undergraduates. (One may speculate that graduate students tend to escape such faculty attitudes in part because the faculty member sees them as apprentices to his own misery.) Fortunately, although almost every campus has its classroom tyrants, those teachers whose hostility toward their students is open and extreme are relatively few; but so are those teachers who feel no hostility at all. Most members of the academic profession are aware, on honest introspection, of a troublesome ambivalence in their feelings toward their students. Most *would* feel respect and even affection for their students, but at the same time they do feel these things they also feel resentment, envy, contempt, animosity. As such attitudes are general psychological defenses (rather than occasional functions of personal problems with particular students), they are bound to have their deleterious effect on teaching.

Certainly more than economic factors may contribute to the establishment of negative faculty attitudes toward students: sexual factors, factors of our general cultural situation of the moment, and factors of more or less purely institutional pressures, may also be extremely important. But there is no doubt that the economic factor *may* play a major role, if not as the main agent of conflict, as its necessary catalyst.

Again and again the professor must experience direct reminders of his economic inferiority not merely to his society in general, but to his students in particular. Again and again he must watch his students graduate into jobs far more remunerative than his own, and he must face them returning for visits after, in a few years, accomplishing a measure of material success he can never hope to equal. Again and again he must watch them, as students, soar off to their winter mountains or sunny islands, or summer lakes and luxuries, and witness them easing their difficult lot between vacations by balms of new clothes, convertibles, books, records, parties, and all the paraphernalia of upper-class student living perpetually before his eyes and beyond his means.

Although he will not often consider himself in direct competition with his students in any of these aspects, as he must nevertheless see many of his students as constant, ironic reminders of his own deprivation, he is almost bound to envy them sometimes. He may resist the change of his envy into resentment, by a supreme philosophical adjustment. He may even rejoice in the good luck of his more fortunate students, through some truly selfless interest in their happiness and acceptance of his own more difficult lot. But it is equally possible that he may resent them for having caused him envy, or to compensate for his guilt at feeling an envy he knows he should not feel, and the response can become habitual and generalized to include all students.

It is impossible here to discuss the forms of faculty resentment of students. The problem is clearly in the province of the psychologists. But it seems proper to suggest that various though the forms of negative faculty attitudes toward students may be, and wide though the range of their expression may be—from the most fawning and flattering behavior to the most savage kinds of classroom authoritarianism —they must almost invariably stand between the professor and the best performance of his job as teacher.

URGENCY OF THE ECONOMIC PROBLEM

Usually the plea for better salaries on the college and university levels of the teaching profession are made on two grounds. The first is the ground of expediency: we must pay better salaries if we are to continue to attract the necessary recruits to the academy to keep it staffed. The second is the ground of simple human decency: we should pay our professors more because—well, it's the right thing to do. Too often this second argument is sentimentally advanced; too often it smacks of charity and condescension. Sentimentality is a nice device for avoiding action, and it is a nice device for avoiding the facts. The facts do make the second argument a real one, but they also urgently present a third: greatly improved academic salaries are imperative if the academic profession is to function as it should.

In his present economic situation the professor finds himself, in his relation to the community, to his students, and to that complex of ideals he originally entered the academy to serve, trapped in conditions of frustration, humiliation, and irony, which are almost impossible to transcend and yet which must be transcended if he is to succeed in those ambitions of fine teaching and fine scholarship with which he began his career, and which conform to the nation's traditional and hopeful conception of his task. The personal insecurity, the inevitable sense of failure before family, neighbors, and even students, the helpless and frantic preoccupation with the most mundane concerns, which are all direct consequences of his poverty, obviously will make it difficult, at best, for the academic man to achieve that combination of command, detachment, and involvement, essential to effective teaching.

The urgency of the economic problem of the academic profession in terms of recruitment and retention of faculty has been much discussed in the past few years. There is no doubt that the problem is already severe or that it will become increasingly acute. On the one hand, the size of the demand for new recruits to the academic profession is without precedent, and it promises to grow enormously in the immediate future. On the other hand, the academy is now subject to competition for new personnel in ways it has never before had to face: we have never in the past had a situation in which so many forms of intellectual employment other than academic life were available as there are now; we have never had a situation in which much more lucrative employment was so generally available to men outside the academy as now; we have never had a situation in which men within the academy were so harassed and underpaid as at present. It would seem that unless the economic circumstances of the academic profession are rapidly and considerably improved, there will soon be critical problems in staffing our colleges to meet the national need for higher education, at least in the field of the humanities, if not in all areas.

But at least equally crucial are those psychological aspects of the economic problem—those little discussed side-effects of the economic disease in the academic profession which tend to cripple pride and self-respect, and to develop attitudes inconsistent with the proper function of college faculty.

Money is the sign of value in a capitalistic society. As the academic profession continues to see itself *un*valued, as it were, it may well recall Plato's complaint when he saw the Athenian democracy declining. "The young feel themselves on a level with the old. Teachers fear and flatter their students; students despise their teachers. Horses and asses have a way of marching along with all the rights and dignities of free-men."

It is too easy to imagine the college professor today, struggling to be the moral superman the world would evidently have him be—with fine philosophy accepting his second-class socio-economic status as a trivial price to pay for his academic career—wistfully reassuring himself, "I am neither a horse nor an ass . . ."

PART IV

STUDENT SOCIETY
AND STUDENT CULTURE

Having discussed educational procedures we turn now to another potent aspect of the student's environment—the
extracurricular social system in which he lives for four years. Recent
studies (Freedman, 1956; Suchman, 1958; Goldsen et al., 1960; Newcomb and Wilson, in press) including the studies reported in this part,
leave no doubt that what students learn in college is determined in
very large measure by their fellow students or, more precisely, by the
norms of behavior, attitudes, and values that prevail in the peer-
groups to which each student must belong. What are the groups that
make up campus society, what are their norms, and what are the means
by which conformity with these norms is induced? These are the
questions upon which the three chapters of this part are mainly focused.

But in approaching these questions we must at the same time look
at student groups in another perspective. As Dr. Newcomb makes
clear in Chapter 13, these groups and what they stand for are determined as much as they are determining. To a considerable extent, the
norms of these groups represent the collective responses of students,
who have certain dispositions in common, to the situation in which
they find themselves after entering college. Thus, student society and
student culture have to be regarded not only as aspects of the particular student's environment, but also as aspects of the behavior of students in general, as ways in which they adapt themselves to the situation of being young and in college. The present part, then, is a bridge
between Part III, which has dealt with what is clearly "environment" from the student's point of view, and Part V, which is con-

463

cerned with behavior in the role of student. It will be seen in Part V as well as in the present part, however, that the behavior of the individual student in college is closely connected with student culture, partly as response and partly as contribution to it.

The present part offers, first, a theoretical treatment of the formation and functioning of student groups, and then two concrete examples of student society and culture in particular institutions. Dr. Newcomb presents in Chapter 13 a contribution to the general social psychology of peer groups. Dr. Bushnell's report on Vassar students (Chapter 14) and Dr. Hughes, Dr. Becker, and Dr. Geer's report on student behavior in the University of Kansas Medical School (Chapter 15) are ethnographic studies; these authors, although offering some theoretical conceptions of their own, describe in some detail the content of the group norms that develop and are disseminated in these particular settings.

In Newcomb's theoretical framework, the conditions of peer-group formation are primarily precollege acquaintance, present propinquity, and similarity of the students' attitudes and interests. The main basis for the group's influence upon its members is to be found in the fact that because human beings need each other the group acquires power to reward conformity and to punish dissidence. The amount of peer-group influence is believed to vary with such conditions as the size and homogeneity of the group, its isolation from groups having divergent norms, and the importance the individual attaches to being accepted by his peers or to fulfilling his obligations as interpreted by them. Newcomb argues that peer-group influence and educational objectives are not necessarily antithetical, and he points to some conditions under which educational purposes may be served through the processes of peer groups.

Bushnell approaches the student culture at Vassar in just the way an anthropologist would approach the study of an American Indian tribe. We are offered a picture of life as it is lived by the student from day to day and from semester to semester. In the anthropological tradition, Bushnell has set about gathering a great many concrete facts to prepare the ground for generalizations about a particular culture and for instructive comparisons among a variety of cultures.

The details of student life at Vassar lend themselves well to treatment in theoretical terms. Thus we find in Bushnell's account examples of all the conditions which, according to Newcomb, are necessary to the formation of peer groups. We see here also why it is that the influence of the peer group is strong at Vassar: all the circumstances that in Newcomb's view favor such influences are clearly in evidence. But Bushnell is particularly interested in the *content* of the peer-group norms, in the whole configuration of attitudes, values, and ways of behaving that constitute the student culture. It is in the daily, weekly, and yearly rounds of the students that he finds the elements of this culture; and it is through close observation of student life that he is led to some of the sources of this culture and of its variations: in traditions that are maintained even though the circumstances that gave rise to them have changed, in the particular strains and possibilities of the college environment that call for collective response, in the situation of the middle- and upper-middle-class young woman in the society of today, and in the larger national culture, which the peer group interprets and transmits in a characteristic way.

In Bushnell's conceptual scheme there is in each American college a student culture and an academic (faculty and administration) culture; the two are in a "contact situation," in which the faculty has accepted the task of "acculturating" the "underdeveloped nation" of students, while the students, with a fairly realistic view of the prerequisites to a pleasant life on the campus, and of what is needed to achieve a secure life after graduation, are much taken up with socialization—"enculturation"—within their own group. In the terms of this scheme Bushnell describes some of the bases and forms of the students' resistance to acculturation, and he makes it clear that the faculty's task is a difficult one under the conditions that prevail at Vassar and in many of our colleges at the present time. Like Newcomb, however, he prefers to end on an optimistic note; he expresses the hope that increasing understanding of the social processes on the campus will lead to a reversal of existing trends.

The chapter by Hughes, Becker, and Geer represents the one instance in the present volume in which a graduate school, rather than the undergraduate college, has been made the object of study. There is a special reason for this inclusion. In the graduate school, and perhaps particularly in the professional school, as Hughes, Becker, and Geer point out, students begin with similar interests, attitudes, and goals; they are subjected to the same pressures—often intense ones— at the same time, and they work in close association with one another and in relative isolation from groups having different norms; hence, it seems, we find in such schools the clearest examples of the processes involved in the formation and functioning of student groups. We are reminded here of the fact that in Chapter 10 the best examples of students who adopt faculty members as models come from the graduate school. The implication to be drawn from this is not that in the graduate schools the influence of the faculty is strong relative to that of fellow students; it is rather that in graduate school the student is in a situation that leaves him peculiarly open to influence by his associates, both teachers and peers. He is now fully committed to a life goal—he is "playing for keeps"—and hence highly sensitive to whatever might appear to favor or hamper his progress; he is open to anxiety, disappointment, frustration; his "need for other human beings," to use Newcomb's phrase, is strong, and it is likely to find expression in deep-going relationships with his associates. A comparison of the student culture described by Hughes, Becker, and Geer with that described by Bushnell shows that processes that loom large in this medical school are present in less extreme degree in a college and, at the same time, that there are important differences between the two cultures studied. It was with considerable regret that the planners of this volume gave up their original intention of addressing themselves to higher education in general, rather than to education in the undergraduate liberal arts college alone. The larger undertaking would have forced our analysis onto a higher level of abstraction, and it is likely that our understanding of both graduate and undergraduate education would be deepened were we able to examine both, within the same general frame of reference. It will no doubt be agreed, however, that the scope of our inquiry is large enough as it is.

Hughes, Becker, and Geer conceptualize student culture much as Bushnell does: it is a system of definitions of the problems and situations with which students are confronted and a set of understandings and agreements concerning ways in which the problems might be solved and the situations mastered. Student culture in medical school, according to these authors, has two major functions: first, to provide modes of adaptation that make the pressures of the school tolerable and not too upsetting to the individual student, and, second, to provide support for patterns of behavior which, though they are in the interest of the students as they see it, may be at variance with what is desired by the faculty and administration. The authors describe, in a manner that is consistent with Newcomb's theory, the ways in which entering freshmen become a group and arrive at their common understanding of such matters as what medicine is, and how much work is necessary, and how to budget their time in order to pass examinations. Passing on to the clinical years, the authors show how the students, who have now arrived at an agreed conception of medical practice, decide as a group, what to study, how much work to devote to particular tasks, and what to demand of their instructors—all on the basis of what is considered useful to future practice. The problem for the medical educator, as Hughes, Becker, and Geer see it, is how to raise the level of suitably directed effort on the part of the students; and the solution, these authors suggest, lies in finding for the particular institution the right combination of types of students and of functions to be performed; this may involve inducing at least some students to create new images of themselves and of what they might become.

We have omitted from consideration in this part the most time-honored and widely used approach to what is sometimes called student culture; that is, the survey, in quantitative terms, of the beliefs, attitudes, and values of large populations of students. Katz and Allport (1931) were the pioneers of this approach, and findings of recent and continuing studies are readily available. To mention some prominent examples, there are the reports of the Cornell Values Study, among them Goldsen et al. (1960), Suchman (1958), Jacob (1957), and there are the contributions to the volume now being edited by Newcomb and Wilson (in press). Various chapters of this present volume report quantitative findings concerning the beliefs, attitudes, and values of students: we have seen in Part II something of the outlook of the freshman, and reports of what students of various categories think appear prominently in Chapters 17 (Bereiter and Freedman), 19 (Summerskill), 21 (Stern), 23 (Taylor), 24 (Webster, Freedman, and Heist), 25 (Freedman), and particularly in Chapter 17 in which Beardslee and O'Dowd describe their study of what students think about occupations. In planning the present part we were thinking of student culture not as the aggregate of beliefs, attitudes, and values that students, in general or by subgroup, express, and that have various sources; we were thinking rather of student culture as a system of "understandings and agreements," concerning the requirements of the student role, that is unique to each campus and to each campus subgroup; that may, in most places, be distinguished from the academic culture, and that is presumed to have its origins in conditions that exist on the particular campus. Studies guided by this conception do not lead to generalizations about what students think; we may hope, however, that such studies may lead to generalizations about the conditions and processes that produce particular patterns of culture, and about the ways in which student cultures influence individuals. General knowledge of this kind may eventually make it possible to modify student culture in ways that are favorable to educational objectives. The authors of all three of the chapters in this part address themselves to this problem; it is a prominent concern also of Pinner (Chapter 27), of Jencks and Riesman (Chapter 22) and, as we have seen, of Bay (Chapter 28).

REFERENCES

Freedman, M. The passage through college. In N. Sanford (Ed.), Personality development during the college years. *J. soc. Issues,* 1956, **12,** 13–28.

Goldsen, Rose, et al. *What college students think.* Princeton, N.J.: Van Nostrand, 1960.

Jacob, P. *Changing values in college.* New York: Harper Bros., 1957.

Katz, D., and Allport, F. H. *Students' attitudes.* Syracuse, N.Y.: The Craftsman Press, 1931.

Newcomb, T. M., and Wilson, E. K. (Eds.) *The study of college peer groups: Problems and prospects for research.* New York: Social Science Research Council, in press.

Suchman, E. A. The values of American college students. In A. E. Traxler (Ed.), *Long range planning for education.* Washington, D.C.: American Council on Education, 1958.

13 *Theodore M. Newcomb*

Student Peer-Group Influence

Students, like other people, are members of groups, and all groups (as distinguished from arbitrary categories) have power over their members. This paper deals, in necessarily oversimplified ways, with the nature, the sources, and the effects of such power, and also with the general problem of relationships between those effects and the presumed objects of college experience. I shall not for present purposes distinguish between formal groups (like a fraternity, or a freshman class) and informal ones (like a loosely defined set of students who, in a given dormitory in a given year, share a couple of classes and an interest in folk music). Nor shall I in any formal way attempt to define the term *peer group*, by which I shall mean simply any set of two or more students whose relationships to one another are such as to exert influence upon them as individuals.

THEORETICAL AND EMPIRICAL BASES

The theoretical argument for assuming that the effects of a student peer group *should* be rather considerable runs essentially as follows. People respond to a situation not necessarily as it "really" is but as they perceive it to be. And they perceive all but the simplest situations —especially human ones—not as they have been preordained, by their physiological make-up, to perceive them but as they have learned to do so. The matter of learning to perceive—of acquiring habits of per-

Note. Adapted from a chapter in *The study of college peer groups: Problems and prospects for research.* T. M. Newcomb and E. K. Wilson (Eds.) New York: Social Science Research Council, in press.

ceiving in one way things that might be perceived differently (and often are, especially by other people) is very complex indeed, but nearly all psychologists would agree that such habits are learned as a result of the successes and failures that follow from actions based upon "right" and "wrong" ways of perceiving situations. The notions of success and failure assume, of course, that individuals have motives— whether standard, universal, or idiosyncratic—in terms of which success and failure are experienced.

There are powerful reasons why groups have much to do with individuals' successes and failures, and thus with the kinds of perceptual habits that they acquire. This is true, first, because groups so often have it in their power to reward and to punish—as by applause or shame, or by the according or withholding of social status or of worldly goods. Group standards often seem arbitrary to members of other groups—and indeed they are and must be, in the literal sense, for in many areas of life it is the *fact* of consensuality, not its content, that matters. One needs to know, dependably and in advance, what kinds of behavior will and will not be rewarded. Such standards come to have the psychological impact of ineluctability, and are sometimes referred to as "social reality." Successes and failures are matters of group life, second, because human beings want and need each other. If we want and need other people, then their responses to us are potentially rewarding or punishing—regardless of whether our wants represent spontaneous affiliativeness or the calculated instrumental use of others. In either case, group members develop sets of consensual expectations about each other (e.g., husband, wife, and child all want and expect husbandlike, wifelike, and childlike behavior from the appropriate family members, as well as wanting and expecting certain similar, rather than differentiated, kinds of behavior from all).

For the purposes of the present argument, the outcomes of these two bases of group power over its individual members are the same: individual members develop attitudes toward each other—most commonly favorable ones,[1] and they develop consensual sets of expectations regarding each others' behavior and regarding important aspects of their common environment, by which their individual expectations of success and failure are guided. Such consensual expecta-

---

[1] The prevalence of favorable over unfavorable interpersonal attitudes, as outcomes of interaction, is by no means limited to voluntarily associating group members; witness the very common fact that most parents and children, the world around, have predominantly favorable attitudes toward one another, though they had nothing to do with choosing each other in the first place. Professor George Homans' observation (1950) that interaction and interpersonal attraction tend to increase together is, in general terms, a very dependable one.

tions about each other's behavior are known as *norms*. Baldly put, groups have power over their members because the same processes of interaction that result in members' feeling favorably toward each other also result, simultaneously, in their adopting norms that enable them to aim at success rather than failure.

The final step of the argument, of course, is that student peer groups, as a special case of a general phenomenon, are subject to the general rules. A plausible case can in fact be made for the assumption that most of the general rules should apply *a fortiori* to student groups. College students (particularly in this country, perhaps) meet each other with a ready-made consensuality compounded of needs for independence from parents in a setting where independence is relatively possible, and of strivings for adult status in a world that treats them half as children. These initial bases of consensus, together with the fact that students are inevitably thrown together in dining rooms, classes, and dormitories, inevitably result—and often rather quickly—in the joint processes according to which groups acquire influence over their members.[2]

The empirical grounds for concluding that substantial peer-group effects *in fact* occur in contemporary American colleges are not as solid as many of us would like to believe. Within the bounds of student peer-group studies, the following conclusions seem justified. (1) Under certain conditions there have been several demonstrations of marked changes in attitude, of consensual nature, during college or professional-school years. (Webster et al., Chapter 24, cf. Jacob, 1957; Newcomb, 1943; Sanford, 1956; Merton et al., 1957. (2) A much larger set of studies fails to show significant amounts of such changes (see, in particular, Jacob's review, 1957). Almost without exception, however, these studies have made no attempt to study differentiated peer groups. Their data have generally come from samples (more rarely, whole populations) of certain college classes, with no attention to group membership beyond the assumption that entire classes, or even entire student bodies, constitute membership groups. (3) Many and probably most of this larger body of studies have, quite understandably, concentrated upon the kinds of attitude changes that educators consider desirable.

In sum, I believe that the theoretical reasons for expecting important peer-groups effects within American colleges are very convincing, and that the expectations have been well supported when they

[2] More substantial bases for the general position outlined above may be found in Asch (1952), Cartwright and Zander (1960), Festinger et al. (1950), Gardner and Thompson (1956), Hare et al. (1955), Newcomb (1950), Schachter (1959), Sherif and Sherif (1956), Tagiuri and Petrullo (1958), Thibaut and Kelley (1959).

have been put to the proper tests. I shall later suggest certain conditions of peer-group influence that have emerged, or hypothetically would emerge, from such "proper tests."

A framework for the problem. It often happens, particularly in the world of human affairs, that the consequences of an event are best understood if viewed in the light of the circumstances of which that event itself is a consequence. The study of peer groups is a case in point: peer-group formation is an outcome of antecedent events; the nature of members' experiences, and thus the effects of those experiences, may be profoundly influenced by the circumstances attending the group's emergence. And so (in the language of contemporary social scientists) it is necessary to consider peer groups alternately as dependent and as independent phenomena.

More specifically, the nature of student peer-group experience is sure to be influenced by the various factors having to do with student selection, and these in turn are influenced by and (in time) also influence both the actual and the perceived nature of the college itself. In very direct ways, furthermore, various kinds of institutional arrangements—e.g., student living arrangements—influence peer-group formation. The schematic diagram (Figure 1) in which arrows indicate presumed directions of influence, will suggest the kinds of interaction effects which must be taken into account.

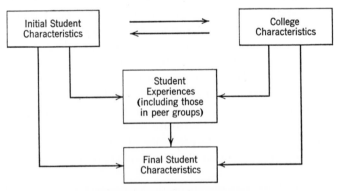

Schematic Diagram Illustrating Interdependent
Influences upon Final Student Characteristics

Figure 1. The diagram suggests the framework within which I shall examine some student peer-group phenomena. Within such a framework, at the heart of which are "student experiences" and in particular peer-group experiences, I shall look into the question of how peer-group membership arises and how it comes to have effects.

SOME CONDITIONS OF PEER-GROUP FORMATION

It is of course "natural" for people with common interests to associate with one another, and it is a truism that, in our own society
at least, not only early but also late adolescents (including most college students) seem to have strong needs for acceptance by age and
sex peers. The truism leaves unexplained, however, the entire matter
of selection. Even in very small colleges, not every one associates with
equal frequency or with equal intensity with all of his peers. There
are, moreover, wide differences among individuals; some are under-
involved and some overinvolved, in terms of local norms. Furthermore,
there are many possible bases for peer-group formation, ranging from
chance propinquity through more or less casual common interest to
shared concerns of great moment. And so, in order to gain our primary
objective of understanding the effects of peer-group experience, we
must examine such specific questions as why it is that particular peer
groups get formed in the first place. I am, of course, making the social
scientist's usual assumption that things happen in orderly rather
than in "uncaused" ways, and that, in any college community at any
given time, if certain conditions had been different the consequences
for peer-group formation would have been different.

The following discussion of conditions under which influencial peer
groups are likely to develop (like the subsequent discussion of their
effects) is necessarily a general one. Colleges in this country vary enormously, in almost every conceivable respect; moreover, peer groups
of the most diverse forms arise within all but the tiniest colleges. It
often happens, for example, that a total student body is an influential
group for many of its members; the stamp of the Bryn Mawr girl or
the Harvard man may be unmistakable—and quite consciously so, in
many instances. At the other extreme, a tiny clique—whose members
are bonded together, perhaps, by dissident values or beliefs—may be
an influence group par excellence; probably such groups are of more
importance in large than in very small colleges. In virtually all colleges, regardless of size and other characteristics, there are roommate
pairs or triads, interest and activity groups, and informal circles of
friends whose impact upon their members is often decisive. Associated
with such variations in the nature of peer groups are of course wide
differences among the kinds of motives that lead individuals to join
or remain in them, as well as differences in individual personality,
and differences in degree and kind of impact the groups have on their
various members. The rather general considerations noted below do

not apply with equal force, or in constant ways, to all these kinds of groups, but in one way or another I believe that the generalizations are none the less relevant.

In any case, there are three kinds of factors that may be considered of primary importance as independent variables, that is, as variables contributing to the formation of particular peer groups.

Precollege acquaintance. Particularly during early college experience, previous acquaintance—especially as established in secondary schools—may form the basis of college peer groups. One study of high school seniors' preferences among colleges (Coleman and Rossi, 1960) found that a small proportion of high school friends hoped to attend the same college. Neither this study nor any other known to me, however, provides much information as to the subsequent fate of precollege friendships.[3] It seems probable that many if not most of them are superseded by others developed in college with previously unknown persons. In the presumably rare cases where they do persist through a significant proportion of the college years, it seems more likely that they re-enforce existing attitudes and values of the individuals involved than that they mediate new ones acquired through college experience.

Propinquity. One cannot very well develop peer-group relationships with persons whom one has never met. Neither does one develop them with all of the persons whom one has met. But propinquity determines the probability of any two persons' meeting and, in particular, early propinquity in college—when most other individuals are relatively indistinguishable, since most of them are strangers—determines the probability of early meeting. This basic statement of statistical probabilities, together with a rather basic psychological consideration, has important consequences for peer-group formation. This consideration is that a currently known source of reward is not likely to be valued less than an alternative whose reward value is less certain (cf. G. Murphy, 1947, on "canalization"). Existing sources of reward enjoy a kind of squatter's right and peer-group acceptance is likely to be rewarding. This principle, the consequences of which are in a certain sense conservative, must of course compete with other and sometimes over-riding principles and therefore describes a probable rather than a required state of affairs. But the two kinds of probabilities, together, result in a considerably greater than chance frequency of

[3] Relevant findings will appear in my forthcoming report of a 20-year follow-up of students whose undergraduate attitudes were reported in *Personality and Social Change* (1943).

persisting peer-group relationships that originated in "chance" encounters facilitated by propinquity, as in dormitory residence or classroom attendance.

In view of the fact that marriage rates—even within a single city—vary directly with residential propinquity of marriage partners (cf. Bossard, 1932), we should scarcely expect that the formation of less intimate peer-group relationships would be immune to the same considerations, and the known facts support the expectation. Festinger et al. (1950), for example, have shown that in a housing project for married students the closest interpersonal relationships (in a statistical sense) developed not merely on the part of those whose apartment entrances faced the same court, but also, in particular, among those who used the same stairways and other facilities. A more recent investigation (Newcomb, 1961) shows that, even within a small, two-floor house accommodating only seventeen students, there were at first (but not following intimate acquaintance) significantly more close relationships among the eight men on one floor and among the nine men on the other than between men on the different floors. Roommates, whose proximity to each other was greatest of all, were particularly prone to develop close relationships.[4] (Cf. also Bushnell, Chapter 14, pp. 491, 504 f.)

The evidence concerning propinquity, and its attendant probability of interpersonal contact, has obvious implications for peer-group formation as related to the size of college populations. In small colleges, of course, where all students have frequent contacts with nearly all others, the student body as a whole is likely to have more important effects, as a peer group, than in larger institutions. But this does not mean that the totality of peer-group influence is likely to be greater in small than in large colleges. Other things equal, the more intimate kinds of interpersonal relationships that characterize smaller rather than larger groups have relatively great impact upon group members; and subgroup formation is quite as characteristic (if not more so) of very large populations as of smaller ones. At any rate the essential significance of the factor of propinquity is, I think, somewhat as follows. For any individual there are many others, potentially, with whom he might form significant relationships. Those with whom he does in fact develop them are limited by opportunities for contact and reciprocal

---

[4] The finding concerning same-floor and different-floor relationships holds even when roommates, whose relationships were generally close, were excluded from consideration. . . . It should be added that all of these 17 men were total strangers to each other on entering the house, and they had nothing at all to do with the choice of their own roommates.

exploration, which in turn are influenced by physical propinquity. And, other things equal, he is most apt to maintain close relationships with those with whom he first develops them (as determined in part by propinquity). Thus the proper generalization concerning college size is not that peer-group influence is more effective, but that it is of more diverse nature, in larger than in smaller colleges.

Insofar as we are interested in the study of formal peer groups (which are easier to identify than informal ones) it seems clear, from the available evidence, that they are likely to be found wherever local arrangements—of living, dining, studying, engaging in student activities—result in very frequent associations among a given group of students. Not all individuals whose associations with each other are frequent will necessarily be subject—and certainly not in equal degrees —to the effects of the norms that inevitably develop under such conditions, but a large proportion of those who are influenced by such norms can probably be thus discovered.

Similarity of attitudes and interests. Birds of a feather do flock together, and the kind of feathering that seems to be most essential for the human species is clearly marked by common interests. This truism both rests upon and illustrates some crucial principles concerning human interaction. People are most likely to interact—and thus, in terms of probabilities, to develop close relationships—when shared interest in some aspect of their common environment brings them together. The earlier principle (p. 474) that interaction tends to *create* consensual attitudes should not obscure the equally important one that interaction tends to *begin* on the basis of existing interests that are shared. The two principles, together, imply that interaction may lead to new (and often widening) kinds of shared interests. Also, of course, it may merely reinforce existing ones without leading to new ones. These matters are discussed in the following section.

Contiguity and common interests (or at least those assumed as common) together would seem to account for the beginning of most peer-group relationships. An initial basis may of course be provided by the common features of the shared environment, but the selective association that usually occurs within large groups, all of whose members have an environment in common, is likely to be based upon shared interests that are not inherent in the immediate situation— like preferred sports, hobbies, or tastes in music or sex partners. In my own study of the process of acquaintance on the part of small populations of college men, common interests in sports or college majors often served as a basis for early clique formation, but these did not necessarily persist; changes tended to occur with further opportunity to explore each others' interests. Closeness of interpersonal relationships after four months of acquaintance was in many (though not all) cases determined more by sharing of general values (religious, perhaps, or aesthetic) than by more specific interests held in common.

Common interests include common problems, of course, insofar as the latter are not too private to be communicable. The problems of the late adolescent in our society (see Chapter 6) may not be harder to bear than those of other ages, but many of them are such as to invite college students to share them with each other. The struggle for independence is apt to be one of these, and such a problem is more shareable with peers than with parents or teachers. In college, moreover, most students for the first time find themselves cut off from intimacies with adults; they probably see little of their parents, and their teachers neither invite intimacies nor welcome students into faculty society. Such a combination of circumstances is hardly calculated to aid the student in his search for identity—precisely at the time when he is least certain about it. Small wonder, then, that students tend to be thrown upon each other: their common problems together with their relative isolation from nonstudents make them ripe for peer-group formation. (For a special instance of peer-group formation in response to common problems, see Chapter 15.)

The common interests (including common problems) that are so essential to the formation of peer groups may or may not extend beyond those which students bring with them to college, or beyond those which they share with their contemporaries outside of college. If not, the consequences of membership in such groups may be quite unrelated, or even opposed, to the distinctive objectives of higher education, as educators commonly assume. I suppose no one really knows how generally it is true that peer-group effects are essentially irrelevant, in this sense, on the contemporary American scene. In the following section I shall discuss some of the conditions under which such irrelevant outcomes most probably occur.

Meanwhile, to pursue the question of how common interests contribute to the formation of student peer groups, it is well to remember that the interests of groups, like those of individuals, may change. There is a well-known principle in psychology according to which motives initially instrumental to the gratification of some other, overriding motive may take on a life of their own, independently of the goal to which it was at first subsidiary.[5] Means often become ends.

[5] Among various formulations of this principle, that of Professor G. W. Allport (1937) has perhaps been most influential; he uses the term "functional autonomy."

An analogous principle may be applied to groups. A group already characterized by consensuality of interests and attitudes, and by interpersonal attitudes that are favorable, may persist as a group on the basis of the latter set of attitudes even though the former set has become dissipated. A group that has acquired considerable interpersonal solidarity may prove to be autonomous, in this sense, but it does not follow that a subsequent basis of consensuality can be dispensed with entirely. If the originally common interests have disappeared, they tend to be replaced by others; if not, interpersonal solidarity is likely to decline, leaving nothing to hold the group together. The social-psychological fact seems to be that group continuity is fostered by high levels of consensuality of both of two kinds: favorable attitudes toward each other, and similar attitudes toward things of common importance—though most groups can tolerate less than a perfectly solid front.

In any case, the educator who despairs at the irrelevancies of student peer-group influences may take heart over the fact that yesterday's poisonous irrelevancy may, in the same group, become today's relevant meat. He may even anticipate that, as students reassort themselves, old groups giving way to new, some of the emerging groups will form around his favorite relevancies. He may, in fact, regard such possibilities as special challenges to his educational skills.

SOME CONDITIONS OF PEER-GROUP INFLUENCES

As I have already tried to show, it is students' attitudes—rather than their general skills, or specific capacities, or basic personality characteristics—that are most likely to be directly influenced by peer-group membership. Let me first indicate a little more clearly what I mean by attitude and then point to some conditions under which attitudinal effects are most likely to take place.

Attitudes, as social psychologists commonly use the term, refer to the ways in which an individual has learned to assess things with which he is more or less familiar. "Things" include any entity—cabbages or kings or concepts—that he recognizes and distinguishes from other entities. Assessment refers both to the attribution of qualities to the thing in question and to the evaluation of it in view of these qualities—evaluation, that is, in ways such as liking, fearing, approving, or their opposites. We generally think of attitudes as varying in intensity, or strength, in sign (favorable vs. unfavorable), and in generality (i.e., the inclusiveness of the entity to which they refer; one may have attitudes toward a specific man, toward men in general, or toward human beings in general). We often refer to highly generalized attitudes, especially toward nonconcrete entities, as values.

Insofar as groups have power over their members, I have argued, it is because two processes tend to occur together, as group members continue to interact. Members become more favorably disposed to each other, and they come to adopt as their own certain group-shared attitudes, or norms, and to feel that those norms are right and proper. Both of these consequences involve, in important ways, the yielding of power over oneself to others. But it is the second—which I have described as the sharing in group norms—that is of primary interest as an outcome of educational experience.

The import of these considerations seems to me to be as follows. Insofar as we are interested in what college experience does to students' attitudes we must, because of the nature of attitude formation and change, be interested in the groups to which students (wittingly or not) yield power over their own attitudes. Most attitudes—and particularly those in which educators are interested—are, as social psychologists like to say, anchored in group membership. This statement, let me hasten to add, in no way represents an advocacy of conformity, as opposed to personal independence and critical-mindedness. The latter, too, represents a kind of value orientation (highly prized by most social psychologists, incidentally) that, like most others, is nourished by group support, however narrowly selective. The assertion that, as a matter of empirical observation, values and other kinds of attitudes are nourished and even created through group membership, carries no implication that any given type or instance of the general phenomenon is to be applauded or decried.

Insofar as the proposition is correct, however, it is heavy with implications for educators: How can we direct peer-group influences in accordance with—rather than irrelevantly or in opposition to—our educational objectives? This question is really a double-headed one. It invites both scientific and "applied" replies—i.e., both statements of conditions under which the presumed effects are most likely to occur and prescriptions for creating those conditions. I shall touch only lightly on the latter.

At least four conditions that facilitate student peer groups' influence upon their members' attitudes appear to be well enough established to deserve mention. No one of them is an essential condition; perhaps any single one of the conditions, under exactly the right circumstances, might prove effective in the absence of all of the others. Most commonly, however, several or all of these conditions exist together when marked effects have been noted.

Size of groups. Perhaps the most obvious of these conditions has to do with group size. Membership in very large populations is not likely, of itself, to bring about the strong interpersonal attitudes that are so important an ingredient in peer-group effects upon attitudes. Small groups, in which such interpersonal relationships can be established, often mediate the attitudes for which a larger population (like "the college") stands, but membership in the latter without the former's mediation would probably not be very effective. From the point of view of formal arrangements which result in group formation, however, relatively large groups have the advantage of making it possible for individuals to be selective in their more intimate associations. From this point of view, the formal group should not be so large that most of its members cannot recognize one another, nor yet so small as to discourage the formation within it of spontaneously formed, congenial subgroups. The combination of strong interpersonal attitudes engendered by the latter, and the strength of support provided by the more inclusive group of which the subgroup is a representative, is often an effective one.[6]

Homogeneity. A second condition involves relative homogeneity of group members. Homogeneity of age, sex, social class, or religious affiliation contributes to effective peer-group influence primarily because of the homogeneity of attitudes that tends to go along with such similarities. The more readily observable forms of similarity without their attitudinal counterparts will hardly suffice for the formation of effective groups. The fact that existing homogeneity of attitudes is so important to group solidarity has, of course, implications of conservatism: if group solidarity depends upon the similarity of members' attitudes, its continuing solidarity is likely to be threatened by lessened similarity in those attitudes. But the same fact also provides the possibility of exactly the reverse. As the late Professor Kurt Lewin used to say, apropos of the effectiveness of "group decision" under certain conditions, "it is sometimes easier to change the attitudes of an entire group than of a single individual"—simply because group support

[6] Witness, for example, the colleges within Cambridge and Oxford Universities, the Houses at Harvard (see Chapter 22) and Yale, and several small colleges in which formal arrangements have resulted in groups of a few hundred that have proven capable of arousing effective group loyalties.

may be mobilized for change as well as against it. At any rate, if a group is not relatively homogeneous with regard to some existing attitudes of importance to its members, it will not have much power to change its members' attitudes.

Isolation. A third condition, relative isolation from groups having divergent group norms, is closely related to the second. Either the fact or the illusion of a membership homogeneous in attitudes may serve to strengthen the conviction that those attitudes are "right." It is communicative rather than physical isolation, however, that I have in mind. In a college community which I once studied from the point of view of freshman-to-senior attitude changes (1943), I found no students so untouched by the prevalent patterns of decreasing political conservatism as those, who, together with tiny groups of close friends, were so insulated from the majority of their fellows that they were quite unaware of the dominant trend that was so conspicuous to others . . . let me add, again, that to point to a condition of group effectiveness is not necessarily to approve of it. But whether one approves or not, there are many institutions of higher education, and many kinds of formal student groups within still more of them, whose policies of admission together with their selective drawing power result both in attitudinal homogeneity and communicative isolation. The effects of the combination are indubitably conservative, and also indubitably effective.

There is a particularly wry aspect of this condition of isolation from other groups in rendering peer groups effective. We faculty members who so often bemoan what we take to be the undesirable directions in which peer-group effects are expressed do a good deal to contribute to the insulation of students' isolation from ourselves. And then we wonder why student norms are not more thoroughly permeated with our own. (In the following section I shall have more to say on this point.)

Importance to individuals of attitudes that are group-supported. A final facilitating condition for peer-group effectiveness is also an obvious one—the importance to individual members of the group-supported attitudes. Other things being equal, the greater the importance to them of the attitudes for which the group stands the greater is the solidarity of the group, regardless of whether the sense of importance preceded or has been engendered by group membership. Again, the implications appear to be conservative, but again they are not necessarily so. It does not necessarily follow, from the fact that group members feel that something is very important, that existing attitudes (even consensual ones) toward it are immutable. It may follow, from the same fact, that its very importance requires accurate assessment of it, and group power may be mobilized toward recognizing new facts or widened perspectives from which changed attitudes follow. If so, the same group influence whch previously resisted change now comes to support it.

In sum, groups become more effective influencers of their members under some sets of conditions than under others. The effective combinations of conditions are not infrequently present in contemporary American colleges, whether or not by design of their educational architects. Very often, too, they are not met—and perhaps fortunately so. The educators' objective is not necessarily that of maximizing peergroup influence, but rather that of understanding how, when, and why it occurs in order that its effects may be consonant with his purposes.

PEER-GROUP INFLUENCE AND EDUCATIONAL OBJECTIVES

It is rather commonly assumed, among faculty members who are concerned about the problems to which this book is devoted, that the "quality of the college product" is more fully accounted for in terms of the characteristics that individual students bring to college with them than in any other single way. And a very considerable number of us assume that peer-group influence comes second in importance, leaving professorial tutelage in third-rank place. By assigning these relative weights we have no sense that we are necessarily denigrating our own roles as educators. It is possible that the characteristics of students, on entrance, are important not just because those characteristics (intelligence level, for example) remain relatively unchanged through college; perhaps, also—or even instead—initial characteristics are important because some of them make their possessors more likely to become different. In that case, professors may provide a necessary mechanism of change. And if, as seems to be the case, peer groups are also potent sources of change, then our task, as educators, may be stated as follows: How can we take advantage of students' potentialities for change, and of peer groups' power to induce change, in such ways that change will most probably occur in the directions of our educational objectives?

One of the considerations that we need to bear in mind in trying to answer this question is the fact of the diverse motivations that students have in subjecting themselves to peer-group influence. Some students, for example, have strong tendencies toward conformity, while some others seem to be compulsively deviant: both can find support from like-minded groups. Some need to be dependent upon authority, whereas independence is essential to some others; although the latter may seem to be immune to peer-group influence, the fact seems to be that they need it as much as the others, but tend to find it in smaller and more selective circles. For some, membership in high-prestige groups is the crucial thing; positions of "leadership" or dominance, or perhaps just prominence, is required by still others. Some students become group members because of the interests or attitudes for which the group seems to stand, while others appear quite willing to adopt the norms of any group that becomes important to them for other reasons. Many of these and other motives can be combined in the same person, as he finds different kinds of satisfactions in multiple and doubtless partially overlapping groups. The effects of peer-group membership will vary with such motives, and with the degree to which they find satisfaction through affiliation. But effects there will be, in any case, and whatever the motivations, or combinations thereof, there are comparatively few students in American colleges who are immune to peer-group influence.[7]

For the most part such motives are perfectly normal ones. Students need the experience of mutual exploration; of learning to take different kinds of roles in teams, clubs, house groups, etc.; of finding themselves through social experiences without benefit of adults. These kinds of learning are legitimate objectives of colleges, along with those of more intellectual and academic nature. For present purposes, however, there is a crucial distinction; the former objectives are reasonably well furthered, in most American colleges, by peer-group experiences; there are good reasons to doubt that this is true of academic-intellectual objectives.

Grounds for doubt on this score are not hard to find. As student bodies have become larger and less homogeneous in most American colleges, there has correspondingly arisen what might be referred to as a kind of academic anonymity. Most students develop friendships

[7] An occasional student does appear to be virtually immune to peer-group influence. There are genuine isolates. There are nonisolates who, while going through the forms of group membership, are inwardly untouched by it. And there are some whose important orientations are toward faculty members rather than toward other students. Such "types" probably represent rather special forms of personality dynamics. In extreme forms they are rare, and fall outside the topic of this paper.

with others whom they know as persons but not as students (in the literal sense). If peer groups of importance to their members include individuals who are sharing the excitement of academic-intellectual discovery, it is almost a matter of chance. It has become less and less probable, during recent decades, that individual students who know each other well, and who are important to each other outside the classroom, experience shared excitement in the same classroom. With exceptions which, though not rare, are far too infrequent, the domain of peer-group influence overlaps but little with the intellectual domain.

I believe that college faculty members, by and large, are nowadays no less capable of offering intellectual excitement than they used to be. But for the most part they now operate in social systems such that whatever excitement they offer tends not to be caught up, re-enforced, and multiplied by virtue of being shared outside the classroom. Time was when colleges were typically small, their student bodies relatively homogenous, and their general atmosphere communitylike. Most of the changes of the past few decades have tended to deprive large numbers of colleges of these characteristics. The result has been that peer-group influences are as potent as ever, but increasingly divorced from intellectual concerns. These developments have not been premeditated, of course; they have been "natural" adaptations to new conditions, and perhaps they have occurred so gradually that the divorcement has been almost unnoticeable. But there is no need to assume that new conditions cannot be adapted to in ways that retain the desirable aspects of the *ancien regime,* as well in ways that destroy them.

It is no accident, I think, that the more conspicuous exceptions to this general trend toward divorcement from intellectual concerns are colleges that remain small, relatively homogenous, and communitylike.[8] My point is not that the divorcement can be halted only in small colleges, but rather that small colleges can, almost without taking thought, provide the essential conditions for mobilizing peer-group influence around intellectual concerns, whereas if larger colleges are to provide them a good deal of thought will have to be taken. Students will in any case create their own peer groups, but the influence of the latter will not (even in small colleges) have much intellectual impact unless the conditions for sharing intellectual excitement are met.

One of the common student complaints, in larger colleges at least, is that "we never get a chance to meet the faculty." Most faculty mem-

[8] The reader may name his own examples. Mine, drawn primarily from my own experience, include Antioch, Bennington, Oberlin, Reed, St. John's, Swarthmore.

bers have some sense of guilt about this, and some of them go so far as to arrange an occasional tea for students. The assumption seems to be, on both sides, that there is some magic about "student-faculty contact." If magic there be, it is surely not intellectual magic. Let me cite one bit of evidence. An experiment was recently carried out at Antioch College, under the supervision of Professor E. K. Wilson (in press; Chapter 3). In eight different courses, including humanities, social science, and natural science, different groups of students were subjected to modes of instruction involving two or three different frequencies of student-teacher contact. Some groups had "continuous surveillance of the teacher," others only "sporadic contact," and in still others, students were "lone wolves studying—with the guidance of the syllabus—quite independently." Outcomes of these different procedures were evaluated in terms of various kinds of examinations, attitudinal responses, amount of "outside" reading, and in other ways. By none of these criteria were there any important differences, in any of the courses, among the different procedures. Other experiments —though none so comprehensive—in other colleges have yielded similar results. There is no research evidence, as of now, to indicate that intellectual outcomes vary—other things equal—with frequency of student-teacher contact.

The probable reasons for such "negative" findings seem to me pretty clear. Outcomes of studying are determined by intellectual capacity, motivation, work habits, *and* by prevailing norms about how seriously studies are to be taken. At Antioch (as would have been the case in other colleges, in varying degrees), students assigned to the various experimental groups were more or less alike in subscribing to the local norms and presumably, also, the groups did not differ much in capacity, motivation, and so forth. Teachers' influence, if it is to be effective, must be caught up in the norms of student groups, and the degree to which this occurs bears no necessary relationship to frequency of their direct contact with students. It can operate at a distance, mediated by some students so as to affect others. Indeed, if it cannot be made to operate in such manner the degree to which any but the smaller colleges can achieve their intellectual objectives seems to me very limited indeed.

Teachers' influence *can* operate at a distance—provided that colleges are willing to supply the necessary conditions. The major ones, I believe, all stem from the elementary principle that individuals who spend a good deal of time together—particularly if they do so without a sense of constraint—jointly create norms, concerning their common interests, by which each of them is influenced. Like all general principles of social interaction, this is true in a statistical rather than in an absolute sense; there are bound to be individual exceptions. The applications of this principle that seem most likely to be effective are as follows.

First, there are facilitating effects of having a formal membership group that is both moderate in size and that is characterized by relative homogeneity of interests that are relevant to the desired outcomes. The assumption here is not only that small and influential peer groups are most likely to develop within larger, formal groups, but also that certain norms of the former can also be supported by those of the latter. And (as Jencks and Riesman have suggested in Chapter 22) the formal group should be large enough to provide a range of selectivity based upon individual preferences for companionship, but not so large that it will be improbable that most individuals will at least recognize each other. The implication here is that larger colleges should be composed of smaller units—300 to 400 being a reasonable guess as to optimal size.

It is important, second, to take advantage of the fact that students' living arrangements provide the major single source of daily contact. Peer-group influence is almost certain to be enhanced—for better or for worse—if there is a considerable overlap between membership in formal college units and in living units. As with the application of any principle, there is a danger here of conflicting with another principle—in this case that of providing opportunity for the development of new interests. Hence complete or compulsory overlap between these two kinds of membership units is probably inadvisable. In large and heterogeneous colleges or universities, however—where the problem of mobilizing group influence toward intellectual objectives is probably most serious—opportunities for the development of new interests are plentifully available.

The third condition has to do with instruction and faculty contact. It calls, again, for overlap—both with formal college-unit and with living unit. In the typical large university it is hardly more than a chance occurrence if a set of students whose personal relationships are close find themselves simultaneously excited by the same lecture, the same book, or the same seminar, with resulting reverberations in their peer-group life, so that they re-enforce and sustain one another's excitement. Such outcomes are predictably more likely if arrangements concerning college (or subcollege) membership, living-group membership, and classroom experience are so dovetailed that groups of individuals who are important to one another come to share many interests, including intellectual ones.

Insofar as colleges are able to make curricular, residential, and other administrative arrangements that have such consequences, frequency of student-faculty contacts ceases to be a matter of concern. It is their *quality* that matters. Whether they be in the classroom or in the coffee-bar (preferably both, I think), we need only ask whether contacts result in students' discovery that ideas are worth further exploration with each other. If so, teachers' influence is likely to be strengthened and multiplied; if not, the consequence is too often that it is multiplied only by zero.

In pointing to kinds of educational arrangements that resemble those typically provided by many small colleges, especially some decades ago, I am neither pleading for a single, standard model nor calling upon time to turn backward. My intended implications are just the reverse. Many small, communitylike colleges, both of the past and of the present, have provided the basic conditions under which intellectual concerns have been caught up into the community life, but yesteryear's homogeneous communities can no longer provide today's pattern. Probably an outright majority of all students in American colleges and universities today are enrolled in institutions of more than 4000 students (cf. Commager, 1960). The educational advantages of the small, homogeneous community must nowadays be created and in diverse ways, in large heterogeneous institutions, and the required inventiveness is hardly beyond our capacities.[9] I suspect that more effort has been expended in applying social-science findings to factory management and to the organization of mental hospitals than to the achievement of intellectual objectives in our colleges.[10]

Student peer groups are here to stay, and so are colleges. I do not think that the one is about to become a cancerous growth within the body of the other; I prefer a different figure. I do think that, increasingly (in this country, at any rate) the social-psychological motors of student life are racing, disconnected from the wheels of intellectual development, and that the means of exploiting the power delivered by those motors are at our command.

[9] Cf. Jencks and Riesman (Chapter 22) and Pinner (Chapter 27) and Bay (Chapter 28) for fuller discussions of the community aspects of student-faculty relationships. Other stimulating treatments appear in Harris (1960) Part V, Meiklejohn (1932), Sanford (1958, 1960).

[10] On the research side, as distinguished from the administrative, there are several encouraging signs. Cf. Newcomb and Wilson (in press), for some descriptions, however incomplete, of contemporary research concerning college peer groups.

REFERENCES

Allport, G. W. *Personality: A psychological interpretation.* New York: Holt, Rinehart, and Winston, 1937.

Asch, S. E. *Social psychology.* New York: Prentice-Hall, 1952.

Bossard, J. H. S. 1932. Residential propinquity as a factor in marriage selection. *Amer. J. Sociology,* 1932, **38,** 219–224.

Cartwright, D., and Zander, A. *Group dynamics: research and theory.* (Rev. ed.) Evanston, Ill.: Row, Peterson, 1960.

Coleman, J. S., and Rossi, P. How high school seniors choose their colleges. Study in progress, National Opinion Research Center, University of Chicago, 1960.

Commager, H. S. Is ivy necessary? *Sat. Review of Lit.,* Sept. 17, 1960, pp. 69 ff.

Festinger, L., Back, K., Schachter, S., Kelley, H. H., and Thibaut, J. *Theory and experiment in social communication.* Ann Arbor: Institute for Social Research, University of Michigan, 1950.

Gardner, E. F., and Thompson, G. G. *Social relations and morale in small groups.* New York: Appleton-Century-Crofts, 1956.

Hare, A. P., Borgatta, E. F., and Bales, R. F. (Eds.). *Small groups: studies in social interaction.* New York: Knopf, 1955.

Harris, S. (Ed.). *The economics of higher education in the United States: the economic problems.* Cambridge, Mass.: Harvard University Press, 1960.

Homans, G. C. *The human group.* New York: Harcourt, Brace, 1950.

Jacob, P. E. *Changing values in college.* New York: Harper Bros., 1957.

Meiklejohn, A. *The experimental college.* New York: Harper Bros., 1932.

Merton, R. K., Reader, G., and Kendall, Patricia (Eds.). *The student physician: introductory studies in the sociology of medical education.* Cambridge, Mass.: Harvard University Press, 1957.

Murphy, G. *Personality: a biosocial approach to origins and structure.* New York: Harper Bros., 1947.

Newcomb, T. M. *Personality and Social Change.* New York: Dryden, 1943.

Newcomb, T. M. *Social Psychology.* New York: Dryden, 1950.

Newcomb, T. M. *The Acquaintance Process.* New York: Holt, Rinehart, and Winston, 1961.

Newcomb, T. M., and Wilson, E. K. (Eds.). *The study of college peer groups: problems and prospects for research.* New York: Social Science Research Council, in press.

Sanford, N. (Ed.). Personality development during the college years. *J. of soc. Issues,* 1956, **12** (4), 1–71.

Sanford, N. The professor looks at the student. In Russell Cooper (Ed.). *The two ends of the log.* Minneapolis, Minn.: University of Minnesota Press, 1958.

Sanford, N. Theories of higher education and the experimental college. In Seymour Harris (Ed.). *Higher education in the United States: the economic problems.* Cambridge, Mass.: Harvard University Press, 1960.

Schachter, S. *The psychology of affiliation.* Stanford: Stanford University Press, 1959.

Sherif, M., and Sherif, Carolyn W. *An outline of social psychology.* New York: Harper Bros., 1956.

Tagiuri, R., and Petrullo, L. (Eds.). *Person perception and interpersonal behavior.* Stanford: Stanford University Press, 1958.

Thibaut, J. S., and Kelley, H. H. *The social psychology of groups.* New York: Wiley, 1959.

14 *John H. Bushnell*

Student Culture at Vassar

The following summary of student life at Vassar College is based upon field data obtained through the anthropologist's customary combination of observation, participation, and utilization of informants. The writer served first as a teaching member of the faculty (1954–55) and subsequently as staff anthropologist with the Mary Conover Mellon Foundation at Vassar. The present report pertains generally to the period 1954–58, the years in which a sample of the class of 1958 was intensively interviewed, tested, and observed as a central feature of the Mellon study of the contemporary college student. The excellent rapport that developed with this pool of informants facilitated not only the collection of standard ethnographic data but also a probing in depth into the college experience. By the time these students were seniors, most of them would willingly and freely discuss most aspects of their lives—past, present, or future.

THE CAMPUS SETTING AND LIVING ARRANGEMENTS

Vassar is a century-old liberal arts college for women located in Poughkeepsie, 80 miles upriver from metropolitan New York. The campus lies inland from the Hudson on the eastern fringe of the urban community so that the city intervenes between Vassar and the river. The college has at its disposal an expanse of some 950 acres. In appearance and atmosphere Vassar is a typical old Eastern liberal

Note. A comprehensive and long-range study of the Vassar student, directed by Nevitt Sanford, has been financed by the Mary Conover Mellon Foundation for the Advancement of Education (cf. Sanford, 1956).

arts college. Architecture, both pleasing and disconcerting, is interspersed with well-tended lawns, venerable trees, formal flower gardens, an outdoor amphitheater, and two small lakes.

The college with its residence halls is, for its students, almost a self-contained community. "Main" with its administrative offices not only serves as the nerve center for the college but also houses the post office, bookstore, grocery store, and "Retreat" (a snack and coffee room). A commercial area with small stores, a movie house, and an occasional restaurant reaches one edge of the campus. Although the borders of the campus are marked off by wire or stone fences, there is always free access to the grounds by foot and bicycle. Students are not permitted (with some exceptions) to have cars at Vassar so that they do not normally range very widely off the campus except on weekends.

The student population. In recent years the student enrollment at Vassar has numbered approximately 1400. The freshman class in 1954 was composed of 421 students whose average age was just two weeks short of 18 years. Fifty-eight percent were admitted from private schools, 36% from public schools, while 6% had a mixed public-private high school background. Nearly half of the matriculants came from the Middle Atlantic states (35% from New York state) with the Central states and New England approximately tied for second place and accounting for 35%. All major areas of the United States were represented as well as 12 foreign countries. Of the freshmen 18% were receiving scholarship aid.

Since Vassar has been stereotyped nationally as a "rich girl's" college, it is of considerable importance that the character of the student body in this respect be clearly understood. There are the daughters of very wealthy families at one extreme and, at the other, girls who work part-time for spending money to supplement the scholarship aid they are receiving. The majority of parents have the financial ability to pay the annual $2500 tuition-residence fee and supplemental clothing and spending allowances. Upper-middle and lower-upper-class standing applies to the greater number of students (few Vassar girls in this decade voluntarily characterize themselves as "upper class," however).

Wealth differences play a surprisingly small role in student life on campus. The girls dress quite similarly with little or no ostentation. There are no sororities and no fees for membership in any campus organization. With all students living and eating in college housing and with bicycles the sole possibility in the line of student-owned transportation, neither incentives nor outlets to emphasize financial status come into play very often.

The Residence Hall. The Vassar student body is housed in eight houses and in the Main Building, which contains the seniors. The ground floor in the houses is largely taken up by a dining hall, a series of parlors, and one or more entryways. Centrally located, and usually within the immediate vicinity of the main entrance, is the desk and switchboard of the "white angel," an older woman (in white uniform) whose major duties are to relay verbal and written messages, route incoming calls to corridor phones, and serve as receptionist to visitors. Also on the first floor are the special apartments (usually two) of faculty members who are known as "house fellows" (see below).

The Vassar students live in single and double rooms with an occasional larger suite occupied by three, four, or more girls. Corridor groupings tend to be of considerable informal importance. More accurately, half a corridor may represent a close-knit group, either because friends have chosen to room close to each other or because spontaneous friendships have developed among girls who did not previously know each other.

Rooms and roommates are assigned by the college on the basis of student preferences insofar as possible. Before entrance, few freshmen express preferences; most hope to make new acquaintances and are content to let the college do the choosing. Beyond the freshman level, students select rooming companions and then ask for assignment to a particular set of rooms, usually on a corridor with friends.

For each student the college provides a bed, bureau, desk and chair, a closet, and a metal box with padlock for money and jewelry. A clean sheet and pillow case are issued each week (top sheets go to the bottom). Every year the first fall activity centers on transforming the room or rooms into comfortable quarters. When there are two or more rooms to work with, one will be set up as a living room. Rugs (often a cotton shag), a sofa, chairs (wrought iron canvas slings are much used), bedspread and curtains, bookcases, study lamps, and a phonograph will be purchased, brought from home, or picked up at a student furniture exchange. In general, a rather remarkable degree of livability is achieved.

Communal bathrooms with multiple facilities are located off the corridors. Morning use is staggered as different girls have their first class at different hours, and some students will elect to forego breakfast at 7:30 in favor of catching up on sleep lost through a late bed time.

Each house has its own dining hall complete with kitchen staff. Meals are served cafeteria style at designated hours with the dinner followed by coffee served in a first-floor parlor room. Bathrobes may be worn to breakfast (except in Main where members of the faculty or guests may be eating); skirts are required for the dinner hour. Menus are posted, and a girl who wants to pass over a given meal in the house can utilize the Retreat or one of the off-campus eating places. Certain culinary items gain a reputation for being unsatisfactory, e.g., "Pigs-in-blankets will clear out the campus!" Most students, however, are not given to complaining and accept the ups and downs in table fare as an inevitable concomitant of institutional life.

The girls in each hall elect officials who act as a governing body in conjunction with the two faculty members serving as House Fellows. This internal administrative unit is charged primarily with the regulation of student conduct and supervision of a work program known as "co-op" (cooperative work) whereby each student is expected to contribute what amounts to an hour a week to the physical functioning of the house.

The co-op jobs which each girl receives at intervals during the year are under the direction of a student Work Supervisor and consist of "Scrape"—scraping dishes in the kitchen for an hour at meal time, "Coffee Girl"—setting up and serving coffee during the after-dinner hour, "Corridor Sweep"—a daily sweeping of one's own corridor (considered to be the easiest of the co-op tasks), and "Message Center"—manning the local switchboard while the "White Angel" is absent at meal-time. Failure to appear for a co-op job results in "blacklist"—a penalty of additional work hours. An occasional complaint is voiced against "co-op" but, in general, the students regard the system as part of the expected routine at Vassar.

The "blacklist" penalty may also be incurred for failure to pass a weekly room inspection which is carried out on a specified day by a student elected from the house membership. Any reasonable effort toward neatness will suffice, i.e., bed made, ashtrays and wastebaskets emptied, stray clothes put away. The college provides cleaning equipment including vacuum cleaners. A student may gain a reprieve if her room is obviously not ready, and the inspector or student supervisor for the house is a friend, by promising to clean it up as soon as possible. Actually most Vassar girls make their beds every day and prefer a measure of orderliness to chaos. No onus devolves upon the students who fill the roles of supervisor and inspector.

ACADEMIC AND EXTRACURRICULAR ACTIVITIES [1]

The student at Vassar has no choice but to allot first priority to her studies. The college exhibits considerable pride in its academic standards and all matriculants, even those with a facility for learning quickly, soon find that the scholastic requirements demand a fair degree of consistent application and self-discipline. As a consequence, the daily and weekly need to meet assignments adequately with respite for other activities requires close attention to scheduling.

The formal pattern of the academic round—12 to 16 daytime class hours per week—adheres closely to that found elsewhere across the country. The assignments in terms of outside reading, projects, and papers or reports are, in general, quite extensive and the student with a penchant for procrastination is likely to find herself in serious difficulty.

Approximately 180 faculty members (of whom about 60% are women) teach in a departmental system. Vassar has tended to attract personnel who are primarily interested in teaching although professors who can carry forth research on their own initiative are highly valued.

As one would expect, the relationship of teacher and student is variable. As always, professors find some students more rewarding than others—and conversely. Most contact centers in and about the classroom and the scheduled conference. Here the student may aim for minimal interaction or for deep involvement. Occasionally, a student and teacher will develop a close working relationship based on their mutual interest in an area of study. For the student, this may represent the high point of her academic experience at Vassar.

There are, of course, other occasions for student-faculty contact. The Retreat provides an opportunity for conversations which may range over academic matters, world affairs, or the infinite foibles of humankind. Student-oriented campus activities may involve faculty in their planning and execution. Professors not infrequently invite students or perhaps a class to visit in their homes. These glimpses into the home life of the teacher, which may include a husband or wife and children, are sometimes salutary for the Vassar girl who finds it hard to visualize

---

[1] Since the formal structure of the college includes, from the student viewpoint, the administration as well as the faculty, both are discussed as components of the academic side of campus life.

her professor as an individual with interests in areas of life beyond the academic.

The House Fellow program, which is a fairly recent modification of the older Residents system, places faculty members (with their families, if any) in relatively close contact with Vassar students. Although House Fellows have kitchens in their apartments, they also have the dining hall facilities available to them and frequently eat with the students and/or join them in the parlors for the coffee hour following dinner. A Fellow will customarily invite the girls in the house to his (or her) apartment, a group at a time, for a social hour (usually tea). Different faculty people serving as House Fellows define the role with varying emphases.

The structure of the management side of Vassar College could be presented in the form of an organization chart plotting positions from president to custodian. Although the students are at least dimly aware of such a hierarchy, it is of little or no concern to them. Vassar girls are primarily involved with the small number of officers and personnel who impinge directly on their immediate lives.

The Department of the Dean and the Department of the Warden are the administrative offices most intimately intertwined with the day-to-day living of the Vassar students. The Dean and her associates, including the Recorder, are in charge of all academic matters and hence must advise on curriculum requirements, confer with the lagging student, schedule classes and examinations, pass upon leaves of absence, withdrawal, and so on. The Scholarship Office and the Vocational Bureau (part-time jobs, summer jobs, and postgraduate positions) are also in this department. The Warden is responsible for the social and extracurricular activities of the students including the often complicated issue of room assignments. The student who wishes to resolve a roommate problem, bring a car to college temporarily for a skiing weekend, or arrange a special activity for a campus club will confer with the Warden. In practice, the Dean and Warden work closely together in guiding the four-year destinies of the 1400 girls. Positions in these two departments have traditionally been filled by women, although recently a male faculty member has been appointed as the Assistant Dean with jurisdiction over freshmen.

The student body is much less involved with the General Manager, Comptroller, Director of Halls, the Public Relations Office, maintenance personnel and campus police. There are two exceptions to be noted here, however. Vassar girls do interact daily with kitchen employees and with the White Angel. The latter is rated on the basis of congeniality and her efficiency in getting incoming phone calls through to the correct party. Close rapport sometimes develops in the dining room where the cooks and their assistants meet the students of the house two or three times a day.

The extracurricular. The formal, organized student activities on the Vassar campus range from college government, which theoretically includes all students, through the "Big Five" major organizations, to the small special interest clubs. Every Vassar student, almost without exception, is involved at one time or another in one or several student organizations.

The Vassar College Government Association is a large, hierarchical structure encompassing the student body and segments of faculty and administration.[2] It has executive, legislative, and judicial branches, and is headed by elected student officers, such as President, Secretary, Chief Justice, Chairman of Freshmen Orientation, etc. There is a Senate, a Legislature, and a system of courts. Faculty and administration retain control of academic matters, the management of the physical plant, and jurisdiction in such areas as public relations and safety regulations while the students are responsible for the operation of clubs, house and class organizations, and the major, campuswide activities. Students and delegated faculty together formulate policy and rulings affecting the "co-op" system, student hours and leaves, scheduling of extracurricular events, and so forth.

Each class and each residence hall elects a slate of officers annually and promotes a series of traditional yearly events. The "Big Five" are the major organizations: (1) The Athletic Association which sponsors intramural athletics, "play days" (often with other colleges), awards yearly prizes, and includes a number of specific interest clubs (dance, riding, skiing, swimming, yachting, etc.); (2) The Community Religious Association which functions through a Council, education and worship committees (the latter assists the chaplain in arranging chapel services), an Intercultural Association, and affiliated denominational clubs (Christian Fellowship, Newman, Hillel, Canterbury, Christian Science); (3) The Political Association which sponsors week-end campus conferences and includes Young Republican and Young Democrat clubs; (4) The Week-End Activities Association which promotes social activities jointly with men's colleges; (5) Philaletheis, the dramatic association, which produces two or three major plays a year and assists the sophomore and junior classes in their annual musical productions.

A number of minor clubs usually related to departmental areas in

[2] This description pertains to 1954–58. The structure of the college government was extensively modified during the 1958–59 academic year.

the curriculum contribute to the diversity of the extracurricular opportunities. A weekly campus newspaper, the *Vassar Miscellany News,* is edited, managed, and published by students. The *Vassar Review* is a literary publication, and there are occasional issues of *Igitur,* a humor magazine. Interest in college government and in other formal student activities has declined in recent years, reaching a particularly low ebb in 1960.

There are, of course, a variety of events available to the student which are not subsumed in the formal extracurricular structure, such as lectures, concerts and recitals, art exhibitions, and weekend movies. The weekly calendar, published by the college, lists a steady succession of activities, and rarely does a weekend go by without one or more events being scheduled for interested students. A student center building with auditorium, club rooms, lounges, and campus publication offices is available for meetings, dances, dramatic productions, and so forth.

The variety of opportunities in the extracurricular realm allows the Vassar girl, if she so wishes, to fill her open time completely with participation in student organizations. As a deterrent to overextending one's extracurricular life (and also to limit the executive power which may be held by an individual student), the college has developed a "census" system which restricts the number of campus positions to which a Vassar girl may be elected or appointed.

There exists little or no formal pressure for a girl to involve herself in campus activities. It is only the highly marginal student, however, who foregoes this area entirely. A number of informal influences operate to channel a girl into the extracurricular—the contagion of peer enthusiasm, earlier interests carried over from high school days, a tradition in the student's family (particularly if the mother was an active Vassar girl), the fact that extracurricular participation is placed in the student's permanent college record.

Vassar matriculants are highly selected, primarily for scholastic achievement but also for their potential to contribute to campus life and, presumably, to community functioning in later years. Freshmen are frequently dismayed by the level of performance exhibited by peers in class work and the same general situation applies to leadership in campus organizations.

DAILY, WEEKLY AND YEARLY CYCLES OF STUDENT LIFE

Monday through Friday the events that start and stop by the clock hold the upper hand and generally work to structure the day for the Vassar student. The dining rooms are open at specific times, each girl has her class schedule (and seldom cuts—even the 8:30—except for the greater pressure of an unfinished term paper, an impending midterm examination or an early departure on Friday afternoon), the organized noncurricular events get under way at announced hours, and the residence halls close at a regular time in the late evening. These fixed points in the daily schedule do not constitute inexorable demands, however. No one, for example, has to get up for breakfast or take any other meal in the house. What is done with free daytime periods, the evening, or indeed the small hours in the room after midnight, is a personal choice subject only to the broader restrictions imposed by group living and campus standards for behavior.

The girls rely upon alarm clocks or a roommate who has arisen earlier to call them. Those who have an 8:30 or want breakfast are usually up by 7:30. The morning cafeteria hours are from 7:30 to 8:10 and the majority of students come down to breakfast, some in pajamas and bathrobe. The girls often eat with roommates or friends at the tables which seat six to eight, although a girl may come downstairs alone and sit with students she does not know well. Many of the girls subscribe to New York City morning newspapers which reach the house in time for breakfast and may be read over coffee.

While those with 8:30 classes (which are viewed as a rather grim and not wholly civilized undertaking by many faculty members as well as students) make their way across the campus by foot or bicycle, the others return to their rooms to dress, read the paper and perhaps tackle the crossword puzzle, work at studies, or prepare for a trip to the library. The 9:30 class hour prompts another exodus from the residence halls.

The 9:30 class is followed by a half-hour break which the vast majority utilize for a coffee break, an opportunity to check for mail, a chance to return to the hall, or an interlude for chit-chat with friends on the campus grounds. The center of Main building with Post Office and Retreat becomes choked with girls. The overflow from the Retreat traditionally fills the adjoining hallway with clusters of students sitting on the floor. The halls in this immediate area are lined with bulletin boards so that students find this hour an expedient moment to peruse the announcements and sign-up sheets for noncurricular activities. There may be an extended line obtaining free tickets for the next drama production at a table temporarily installed in the hall. The importance of mail, of coffee, of taking a break impart to this half hour in the morning a rather special and unique flavor or quality. In contrast, the other hours of the forenoon are usually given over to study and further classes.

Lunch is available between twelve and one. The girl who has "scrape" will finish her task around 1:15. Classes are in session until 5:45. On warm days in spring or fall, seminars or small classes may be held outside on one of the numerous campus lawns. The student with free time may elect to go off-campus to the bank or to neighborhood stores. Acquiring or maintaining a tan is avidly pursued by some students who may bring a reflector as well as their books to a sunny spot on the grass. With the need for frequent recourse to the library, Vassar students will devote afternoon hours to assignments and research in the stacks.

Dinner is served from 6:00 to 6:45 followed by a coffee hour in one or more of the house parlors. The student who has "coffee girl" duty pours demi-tasse size cups. Here again the girls often sit on the floor (carpeted in this instance, however) and talk is the main staple. Bridge is a popular pastime. There is frequently piano music rendered by one of the students. The House Fellow often takes this opportunity to interact informally with his (or her) charges.

At about seven o'clock the coffee hour dissolves, although an occasional bridge foursome plus kibitzers will persist until 7:30 or 8 o'clock. Some girls will stay in or about their rooms, while the activities of the major organizations or a concert, speech or rehearsal (drama, choir, etc.) will occupy the evening for other students. There are few boy-friends on campus unless it is a Friday or a week when the men's colleges are on vacation.

The library closes at 10:00, and students must be in their houses by 10:30 on week nights (11:30 on Friday) unless they have obtained "late permission," by the signature of the House Fellow on the appropriate slip which extends the hour of return to 11:30 P.M. (1:00 A.M. after Friday night). Beyond the stipulation that students are to be in the residence hall after a stated hour and are to observe quiet hours through the night, there are no directives to structure the night-time activities. The girl pursuing her studies is usually vulnerable to roommates wandering in and out and may find herself involved in a late evening talk-fest.

Bed-time is optional and reflects a combination of personal predilection and the modus vivendi of the roommate group. A few girls are in bed by 10:30 but 11 or 12 o'clock is the more general practice. The student with a paper to type may settle herself in one of the parlors. Within the locked building, which is now the responsibility of a night watchman, the girls are free to move about as they wish. Instances have been recorded in which girls have returned to the hall after hours to enter by a first-floor window or door with the connivance of friends inside, but this is an adventure which is seldom sought.

The weekly round. As a theoretical standard, the college expects that the student carrying a 15-point academic load will devote 45 hours per week to her studies. A "time survey" conducted by Vassar in 1955 showed that an average of 43½ hours went into a 15-point program.[3] The data were obtained through daily records kept by the students themselves (69% of the student body completed the three-week recording stint). In reporting on this survey, the administration recognized that there was "undoubtedly a tendency to exaggerate *academic hours*."

An analysis of daily activity reported verbally in the spring of 1956 by interviewed members of the Class of '58 revealed that approximately 6½ hours of the regular weekday were spent in academic and allied pursuits. The student who maintained this pace throughout the week would total 45½ work hours. However, for most students the pattern varies widely from a minimal or routine academic week to a sequence of days crammed with assignments and deadlines which occupy nearly every waking moment and cut deeply into the time span normally reserved for sleeping.

The prevailing attitude among students on the Vassar campus is that, as a general operating principle, the weekdays belong to the academic life and the weekends to the private, personal, or social sphere (there are no Saturday classes). If the student is planning an off-campus weekend, the wish to get an early start prompts a departure as soon as possible on Friday afternoon. Actually, the Vassar girl is probably more likely to stay at the college than to absent herself for the weekend, but this does not seem to impair the notion, common among students, that, ideally, the adequate Vassar student will be sufficiently "on top" of her studies by Friday afternoon so that these may remain

[3] The results of similar time surveys at Vassar College in earlier years suggest that contemporary students spend more hours on their studies and therefore presumably work harder than their predecessors. Academic work week for 15 points: 1925—36 hours; 1940—43 hours; 1955—43½ hours. (Vassar College, 1957.)

comfortably in a state of suspended animation until Monday morning.

Vassar girls may visit parents, boy friends, or a fellow student's home on a weekend. This may involve a trip to the suburban New York–New Jersey area, to New Haven, or perhaps Boston. Lacking a specific reason to go elsewhere, New York City with its myriad attractions is the usual destination.

On campus the weekend tends to a leisurely pace, even though special events are often scheduled. The library is closed Saturday evening and Sunday morning. Breakfast on Sunday is served half an hour later than usual. Free movies can be seen on Saturday night in one of the auditoriums.

Perhaps the most conspicuous feature of a weekend at Vassar is the number of young men visiting in the houses, strolling the campus with their Vassar dates or loading them into cars (often of the sports type) for a drive to one of the countryside restaurants in the Hudson Valley or nearby Connecticut.

Boy friends visiting Vassar can stay at nearby Alumnae House or off-campus. The girls may have men guests in their rooms during the afternoon and in the house parlors until 11:30 p.m. (1 a.m. on Friday or Saturday). The student must sign her visitor in and out on a special register. For the boy and girl who would prefer to be alone, the room with its roommates and the parlor with its traffic are far from idyllic. Considerate roommates may make an effort to isolate a serious couple for at least a brief period, but as a rule the group has priority and the boy friend is appended and, in a way, shared for the time being.

Sometimes the Vassar student takes her date to the library so that she (and sometimes he) can put time in on current studies. The athletic facilities of the college—tennis, golf, bowling, shuffle board, swimming, etc.—are available to the Vassar girl and her weekend date.

Although there are always young men at Vassar on the weekend (and now and again during the week), the frequent visitor will complain to his girl friend that they have exhausted the list of places to go and in view of the limited local choices, he would prefer that on the next occasion she visit him. The fact that boys get discouraged over the Poughkeepsie scene adds to a note of isolation which is already present and leads many Vassar students to wish occasionally that the college were in a more accessible and urban location.

The yearly round. Vassar follows the two-semester pattern which provides an annual double cycle of classes, mid-term examinations course papers, and final exams. The regular progression of the yearly round is interrupted by the customary vacation periods marking off waypoints usually welcomed by students and faculty alike.

The year is also stepped off by a series of traditional events, initiated by a convocation and terminated by the commencement exercises honoring the graduating seniors. Every freshman is instructed to bring a white dress to college so that she may be properly attired for the convocation exercises in the chapel which open the academic year. When freshmen, sophomores, and juniors have occupied assigned seats, the seniors march in, two by two, wearing their caps and gowns for the first time. A welcome by the President precedes the address by the convocation speaker. The ceremony holds its greatest meaning for the newly-arrived freshman, and for the seniors who now are to live together in Main and are formally grouped as a body in identifying academic dress.

The seniors put on caps and gowns for subsequent college assemblies although the formal marching entry is omitted. Since all students must appear to fill their allotted seats, some of the more blasé will "take something to do," i.e., read, study, or write a letter.

The sophomore and junior classes each produce an original musical, and the student dramatic association undertakes three major plays a year. The Experimental Theatre, drawing upon faculty, student, and extracampus talent, offers three or four professional-calibre productions.

Each residence hall conducts an annual week-end party of its own (sometimes two houses arrange a joint affair), featuring a cocktail party on Saturday afternoon and often a dance in Students Building in the evening. Drinking is quite restrained at these affairs, and the occasional heavy-drinking date who sometimes proves disruptive is rated as decidedly unsatisfactory by the girls. Class parties, which include the musicals noted above, also encompass a weekend. A jazz group may be brought in for the special event on Sunday afternoon. Weekend affairs of this kind offer an opportunity for the Vassar girl to invite a date to come to Poughkeepsie. Traditionally she expects to cover the expenses involved for meals and entertainment.

The Junior Prom is perhaps the most formalized social event of the year. The student committee in charge chooses "posts" from the freshman class—girls who participate by adding décor and marking off the route of the grand march which highlights the evening. To be selected as a "post" is considered a definite social honor. The Senior Prom is similar in formality to its Junior counterpart.

As noted earlier, there is a steady succession of campus events throughout the academic year, interrupted only by vacations and examination periods. Freshman Play Day, house teas, the week-end conference, a performance by the Corps de Ballet, the annual swimming show produced by the Swupper Club, the Athletic Association Banquet, notable visitors and speakers provide more opportunities for education and diversion than the average Vassar student can encompass. When college starts in the fall, the freshman is given a glimpse of this array through an open house held in Students Building where booths are manned by representatives of the campus organizations, and the newcomer's interest and participation are sought through explanation and enthusiasm. Seniors nearing the end of their undergraduate careers will often say that they wish they had taken in more of the concerts, speeches, and conferences which were passed up because of conflicting events or an immediate lack of interest in a more sober or serious campus offering.

The late spring is highlighted by Salve Night (pronounced "solway"), a ceremony which confers senior status to the junior class. Salve Night actually starts in the late afternoon with a college assembly which includes a transfer of symbols—a gavel to the incoming president of the College Government Association and a spade (the one used by Matthew Vassar to turn the first earth for Vassar Female College a century ago) to the Senior Class President—and a singing of the Salve marching song by seniors only, a prerogative of the graduating class. All others clap in rhythm. At a given point, however, next year's seniors pick up the song, changing, for example, "Salve 1957" to "Salve 1958," and at this moment the juniors have achieved senior standing. The ritual is followed by a picnic on the campus with beer permitted. The seniors then retire to Alumnae House for their own party while the juniors wander about the grounds singing and demanding recognition of their new status as seniors from lower classmen. The event occasions a good deal of hilarity and high spirits. An old fire bell perched atop Main Building is traditionally rung in mock defiance of college regulations.

Graduation exercises follow the customary pattern of U.S. colleges with baccalaureate service and commencement. Vassar's most famous trademark—the Daisy Chain—is a feature of this last day of the year. The long rope of flowers is carried by sophomores who have been selected by representatives of the graduating class not only on the basis of physical attractiveness but also on degree of involvement in campus life. If, as sometimes happens, a late spring has delayed the growing cycle in the Poughkeepsie area, daisies are flown in from California or Hawaii.

There are, of course, many other ingredients of student life which are a regular part of the annual cycle but not of a nature to be reflected in the college calendar. Bermuda shorts may give way to skirts and occasional slacks as winter closes in, and then reappear as spring breaks. Heat in the residence halls fades away after 10 p.m. on winter nights, forcing the issue of bedtime so that even the hardiest student finds 2 or 3 a.m. the ultimate limit. Parents come for visits occasionally during the year. Friendship groups will celebrate a birthday, sometimes with an off-campus party featuring cocktails and a cake. A shower for the recently-engaged student is a fairly frequent event, and occasionally a student marries during the academic year with her college friends invited as participants or guests. The late spring features going-away parties for girls who have decided not to return to Vassar the following fall. And each year the semesters are invariably marked by the pronounced build-up in tempo and tension that accompanies the deadlines for term papers and the onset of final examinations.

VALUES AND PROCESSES OF THE PEER GROUP

Vassar students spend most of their time with each other. The residence hall, by its very nature, contrives to place and keep its occupants in close association. The great majority of students seem to thrive on a diet of gregariousness, and the individual who seeks occasional respite from her fellows must make a deliberate effort to isolate herself.

The sustained tempo of interaction among Vassar students features an emphasis on being friendly, pleasant, and agreeable. Animosities do occur but critical remarks about peers are made in their absence and usually confined to one's own roommate or friendship group. Minor irritations are perhaps inevitable when living in close quarters. A dirty tub, the last students in the dining hall dallying over their food while the "scrape" girl waits and glares, the roommate who is lax in doing her share on room clean-up, the classmate who makes an obvious intellectual play for the professor's attention can create moments of resentment. The dominant desire on the part of most students, however, is to live along in a smooth and compatible manner—not without a measure of give and take but with a scrupulous avoidance of pushing differences or disagreements to the point of open hostility and disintegration of the interpersonal relationship.

Most important to the Vassar student, and hence crucial in her college career, is the immediate group of girls with whom she spends most of her time. The basic nucleus of a friendship unit usually is composed of roommates. Other girls may be appended to the room-mate group, and sometimes two or three roommate clusters may form an unusually large social entity. The concept of roommate is so bas-ically related to Vassar life that students who prefer singles but have chosen to room near each other will refer to a next-door friend as "my roommate."

It may be said that in a very real sense the roommate situation can "make or break" the Vassar girl with respect to both her academic and social life. Outright discord and conflict between two roommates is actually rather rare and largely confined to the freshman year when many students did not chose a roommate prior to matriculation either because they knew of no one else coming to Vassar from their own community or because they preferred to take a chance on developing new friendships rather than to depend on schoolmates who had also been accepted by the College. The occasional clashes between room-mates grow out of personality differences and associated living habits. As a rule in such instances, their separate sets of friends are also not sufficiently compatible. One roommate in such a situation will some-times try to resolve the problem by spending most of her time in the rooms of her friends, but she cannot avoid the necessity of using her own room for sleeping and finds herself definitely handicapped if she does not feel free to use her own quarters for study.

The college administration makes every effort to shift students who have severe roommate problems. The freshman often hesitates to complain, however, sometimes believing that the fault lies within her-self, and a semester or more may go by before a crisis forces the issue. Those who have been through this experience are prone to recall it as "the year (or semester) that I lost."

The sorting-out process with respect to roommates is largely taken care of at the end of the freshman year when students choose their companions for the following fall. There are some realignments in subsequent years either because an anticipated friendship wears thin or a girl decides to switch her allegiance to a group which differs rather markedly in attitude and interests. Most students, however, go through college within the framework of a friendship group carried over from high school days or developed in the first year on campus.

Not all social groupings derive from dormitory life, of course. Non-curricular activities such as drama, athletics, or serving on a campus newspaper staff provide a meeting ground for students with similar orientations. The classroom may bring compatible students together, although this medium is perhaps the least fruitful in producing new friendships. When firm alliances are made, they may be reflected in roommate choices for the succeeding year.

The room in the residence hall, the Vassar girl's "home away from home," fills and empties with the flow and ebb of roommates and friends. There is frequently a phonograph in the background playing classical music or sometimes "mood" music, show tunes, or folk songs. Much of the conversation derives from immediate activities and situations in the lives of the students and is as likely to center on fiancés or problems with parents as on academic matters or world issues. An international crisis or a national election arouses interest and concern but, by and large, it is the personal difficulties, the individual goals, and the on-going state of affairs with respect to campus life, both scholastic and extracurricular, that dominate the talk, and presumably much of the thought, of the Vassar student.

Women at college have their counterpart of the male "bull session," also frequently continued into the early hours of the morning, with the traditional dissection of large topics such as religion, sex, and politics. In the matter of religion, for example, the Vassar girl comes to know where her friends stand and how they feel, and any early efforts to challenge or proselytize are soon replaced by the peer-group emphasis on tolerance of differences and the academic ideal of regarding social phenomena from an objective diversity of viewpoints. Sex mores are discussed, but personal behavior, once again, is set against a philosophic background of "live and let live."

Perhaps the most striking aspect of the friendship group is the ever-present and reliable support which the members provide for one another. Although some students are beset with more problems than others, particularly if there are sharp differences with parents, a floundering in class work, or an upset in a serious boy-friend relationship, the course of the college career is never completely smooth for any Vassar girl. To think of a residential college as "monastic" or "sheltered" and therefore nonanxiety-producing and obviating the necessity for individual decisions is wholly misleading. Students at Vassar must variously contend with problems and situations which bear in on them from the academic side, from involvement in one or several of the noncurricular organizations, and from their continuing ties with persons and events beyond the campus. The strength of the immediate peer group is probably best demonstrated in those instances when a girl slumps into a severe and sometimes protracted depression. The loyalty and encouragement of roommates and other close friends is often the factor that enables the student to survive, that is, to stay on as a student while weathering a troublesome phase.

Attitudes held by the individual toward class work and higher education in general are, as a rule, highly congruent with those espoused by her friends. This close alignment of similar attitudes is reached by at least three different paths. First, there is the group of girls who transfer en masse, as it were, from the same school to the same college and carry with them a ready-made value system which is not usually subject to serious modification. Second, there is the freshman who arrives alone and on her own. For her the impact of the new group in which she finds herself may be a decisive factor which sharply colors the four years to follow. And third, since assignment of roommates for the freshman year often has an element of chance in it, there are students who realize, sooner or later, that their preferences are at odds with those of the majority of their associates and who consequently gravitate toward new friends and roommates.

Vassar students are quite aware of differing emphases (one might almost say contrasting life-styles) among campus subgroups. As might be expected, their own observations and categorizations bear a rough correspondence to classification by objective criteria (cf. Chapter 16). In student thinking there is a continuum ranging from the highly social to the highly intellectual girl. At one pole is the small minority of students who are intensely concentrated on their academic work to the detriment (from the majority viewpoint) of the other areas of their lives. These are known as the "super-intellectuals" or sometimes as "the science-major type." The socially-oriented are variously referred to as "good-time Charlies," "debutantes," or "Yale-weekend girls." They are charged by their critics with using Vassar as an address, taking "gut" majors, and going through the required academic motions in order to participate in the world of boy friends, weekends, and the latest recounting of who's engaged or pinned to whom. Needless to say, there is a high casualty rate in this group. As one senior put it when reviewing classmates in this category, "Most of them are gone but a few are limping through."

One small cadre of students stands out so sharply that it was mentioned almost without exception by every informant. These are the "bohemians" or "pseudo-intellectuals" who are stereotyped as sloppy nonconformists wearing black turtle-neck sweaters (or shirts with the tails hanging free), toreador pants, no lipstick, and hair uncombed or hanging long over one eye. Also known as the "intellectuals on probation," they are thought never to get their term papers in on time and always to look terrible because of a scorn for the ritual of sleeping. Commonly associated in student thought with the Drama Department, this "off-beat" type is actually rarely a serious drama student although she may play bit parts or work on the stage crew.

Campus leaders are viewed collectively as a particular brand of student—the ones "who like to run things," "the all-round doers," "the Joe-college people." Most Vassar girls, however, place themselves and the bulk of their peers in the middle range between the social and intellectual extremes and characterize themselves as the "normal group" which strikes a happy medium between seriousness and frivolity—"We get our studies done and have fun too." These are the bright, neat, sociable "B" and "C" level students (so goes the self-description) who are usually sufficiently organized and productive to carry off the peer-approved balance between the work week and the weekend.

It is important to note that getting good grades is not, in itself, held to be an undesirable achievement by any student group. Quite to the contrary, high marks are generally respected and the girl who makes Phi Beta Kappa, particularly if she does so in her junior year, is frequently accorded general admiration or, at a minimum, given credit for an academic performance beyond the reach of most of her peers. The one reservation voiced by most students is that scholastic excellence should not be the sole virtue. If there is an ideal Vassar girl, she is the one who receives consistently high grades without devoting her entire time to the endeavor. In fact, the emphasis on combining good marks with a reasonably full social life is so strong that some students who, in reality, have to work quite hard to maintain an impressive grade-point ratio will devote considerable effort to presenting an appearance of competency and freedom from academic harassment.

It is possible to speak also of other attitudes which cut across student groups on the Vassar campus. Although a professor may be asked to shift the date of his mid-semester examination to alleviate the pressure generated by a clustering of such tests in other courses, or there may be complaint voiced over an assignment of two term papers when one is the traditional expectation, the students always accept the academic requirements and demands of the faculty. A rebellious note is exceedingly rare and protest is largely confined to an occasional editorial or letter in the campus newspaper. With respect to national issues, organized protest action by Vassar students has been virtually nonexistent since the depression days of the Thirties. However, one recent local event may presage an impending break from the reputation American college students have acquired since World War II for self-centeredness and passive acceptance of the status quo. In March 1960 Vassar girls picketed a Poughkeepsie variety store in an expression of support for the Southern lunch-counter sit-ins.

With the possible exception of a few individualists in the "bohemian" category, the studentwide preference is for a life-style which stresses moderation, friendliness, cooperation, and a smoothly-moving

collegiate experience. The value placed on conflict-free, agreeable interpersonal relationships is reflected in the nearly-universal specification that "a sense of humor" in roommates, friends, or acquaintances
is one of the most important traits contributing to the continued success and stability of a given subgroup of peers. Acting on impulse or
losing control are felt to represent potentially dangerous kinds of behavior, and an avoidance of conflict with authority holds not only
with respect to the faculty but also in the area of social regulations.
The student who has been punished by a campus court for a serious
infraction of the rulebook neither hides the verdict nor takes pride
in a broken regulation.

There are a number of fundamental attitudes expressed by Vassar
students which have their original locus in the larger world beyond
the campus but continue to constitute important determinants of behavior within the framework of college life. Since the subject of
value configurations among students at Vassar has been discussed elsewhere (Bushnell, 1959, 1960; Freedman, 1956; Sanford, 1956), the present description is limited to a few brief highlights.

Jacob's summation of student characteristics for higher education
in the U.S. (Jacob, 1957, pp. 1–8; see also Goldsen, 1960) has considerable relevance for the Vassar population although his conclusions are
not fully applicable, particularly in the matter of kinds of changes occurring during the college years (see Chapter 28 of this volume). On
the basis of Jacob's description, the contemporary college student might
be epitomized as self-confident, self-satisfied, and self-centered. Very
broadly construed, these adjectives fit the Vassar girl, although there
are definitely times when her confidence is shaken by an academic
set-back or her self-satisfaction is plagued by insistent doubts as to
what will happen to her after graduation. Moreover, the self-centeredness is relative since it primarily excludes serious, personal involvement or concern with national or world issues but definitely includes
the immediate world of friends, relatives, hometown, and a future
milieu of husband, children, and community ties.

Attitudes in two areas seem to be of special significance for the Vassar student. The first constellation centers about the assumption and
belief that the existing social and economic order in this country will
prevail, perhaps with an occasional minor recession, for many years
to come. Although the students find it exceedingly difficult or impossible to project their lives twenty years into the future, successful
struggles with the imagination in this respect always take the form of
an older self immersed in a familiar, contemporary setting.

This image of stability carries with it several corollaries. Since the monolithic social order has jelled, there is little point to engaging in activities directed toward social reform. Moreover, Vassar students judge our society to be about as ideal as any, especially since they have now learned that a Utopia is an impossibility and are further convinced that the wrongs in our society will gradually right themselves with little or no direct intervention on the part of women college students.

The established system is viewed as providing on the one hand a framework within which to plan and predict a future life (especially so for a husband's career) and, on the other hand, as setting concrete limitations as to permissible life-styles and life-work ambitions. Vassar girls, by and large, do not expect to achieve fame, make an enduring contribution to society, pioneer any frontiers, or otherwise create ripples in the placid order of things. Future husbands should mark out and work directly toward a niche in the business or professional world which provides adequate remuneration and status, but a rise to the top is neither demanded nor expected.

The second important constellation of attitudes revolves about the Vassar student's concept of herself vis-à-vis the status and role of woman in modern United States society. In the past the basic decision for the young woman on campus may have hinged on the choice between marriage and career but today it is virtually impossible to find a Vassar student who views the two as incompatible. Not to marry is almost inconceivable and even the strongly career-oriented girl fully expects that someday she too will be a wife and mother. Not only is spinsterhood viewed as a personal tragedy but offspring are considered essential to the full life and the Vassar student believes that she would willingly adopt children, if it were necessary, to create a family. In short, her future identity is largely encompassed by the projected role of wife-mother. Since the validation of femininity and a full realization of the potential of womanhood is thought to reside almost exclusively in the realm of marriage and family, there is, perhaps inevitably, a corresponding diminution of interest and involvement in the intellectual, creative, and allied pursuits.

In describing the qualities to be found in an ideal husband, the majority of Vassar girls are quite explicit in their preference for the man who will assume the more important role, that is, handle his own career and make the majority of decisions affecting matters outside the home. Although most of them consider it desirable to maintain their own chastity before marriage, they usually believe, nevertheless, that a future husband who is sexually experienced is best qualified to introduce a bride into the intimacies of married life. Moreover, some contemporary Vassar students say that an occasional extramarital encounter on the part of an absentee husband need not be an alarming event, since it is assumed that the sexual needs of a husband cannot reasonably be thwarted for an extended period of time.

In the light of what has been reported, it is not surprising to discover that Vassar students view the suffragette movement and the whole issue of Women's Rights with indifference. That the female should attempt, in their thinking, to usurp the prerogatives of the male is a distasteful notion which would seriously disrupt their own projected role of helpmate and faithful complement to the man of the house. For these young women, the "togetherness" vogue is definitely an integral theme of future family life, with any opportunities for independent action attaching to an Ivy League degree being willingly passed over in favor of the anticipated rewards of close-knit companionship within the home that-is-to-be.

ACCULTURATION AND ENCULTURATION

A description of student life at Vassar College reaffirms the major general finding of earlier campus studies (cf. Chapter 13) which, broadly stated, holds that the role of the student peer group is of fundamental significance in determining the course of events in the college experience. Indeed, it would be strange if this campus did not reflect what appears to be a nearly universal phenomenon in United States colleges and universities. Given the fact of a distinct and viable student way of life, the immediate need is to move beyond a recognition of the pervasive influence of this student society to a consideration of how best to conceptualize and understand its relationship to the functioning of the entire college. Since students at Vassar and elsewhere exhibit a society and culture of their own, it is reasonable to accord the faculty in conjunction with the administration a similar standing which Sutherland (1949) has called "academic culture." This formulation recognizes that, in effect, two societies occupy the same territory and that cultural divergence and consequent conflict may bear importantly on the educational process. From an anthropological viewpoint the campus provides a culture-contact situation, and the possibility arises that a number of the processes which are activated when different cultures meet in the world at large may also be operating under our very noses in the academic world.

Whenever two societies are in contact the process known as *acculturation* is also under way, i.e., there is an interchange of cultural elements (language, ideas, artifacts), even in those instances where a strong antagonism exists. In most contact situations one of the two societies is stronger, larger, or more advanced in technology so that there tends to be a greater cultural flow from the dominant to the subordinate group. In the U.S. college, it is feasible to view faculty-administration as the donor society since this collectivity occupies an authoritative and presumably prestigeful position vis-à-vis the student body and, moreover, it is specifically oriented to the tasks of transmitting information and serving as a model for emulation, at least in the intellectual sphere. There is also a detectable counterflow from student to faculty and administration (at Vassar and probably all campuses) which is not without its repercussions in the dominant society. In the case of Vassar, the acculturative process is facilitated by an implicit agreement to maintain a friendly, stabilized relationship across an open cultural frontier—but with fraternization limited by tacit understanding on both sides.

The key factor in this matter of contact between intracampus cultures lies in the fact that the students, even though they constitute the "underdeveloped" population and are on the receiving end of most of the cross-cultural exchange, are nevertheless far from occupying a passive or subservient position since they have at their disposal the various techniques available to any society subject to acculturation pressures. For example, the kinds and amounts of cultural materials actually transmitted across the faculty-student frontier may be controlled by choosing only those elements or complexes that may be adapted comfortably to the student culture, while rejecting those aspects that might prove unsettling or disruptive. When the content is nonthreatening, there may be whole-hearted, even uncritical acceptance. A preference at Vassar for certain fields of study, such as art, history, or languages, would seem to be a reflection of this dynamic. But when diffused information is potentially disturbing or runs counter to peer-group values, contra-acculturative processes are activated which may take the form of surface compliance or superficial adaptation and a concomitant refusal to integrate or internalize the new offering.

The mechanism termed *syncretism*, that is, accepting a cultural item but utilizing it for a purpose not intended by the donor, is another technique open to the student who may, for instance, prefer to utilize course content mainly for small talk over cocktails. It should also be remarked that although Vassar students rarely, if ever, overtly reject faculty demands and, as has been noted, are likely to be agreeable, co-operative, and accepting of the status quo, they seldom seek out the faculty in what might be characterized as an attempt to speed up or intensify the acculturation process. The usual course of action is for students to keep the faculty at a distance and to rely on each other for counsel and support.

The ability of the student society to maintain control of the acculturation situation, even though the faculty has broad cultural sanction and direct institutional support for the pressures they bring to bear, would indicate a considerable unity, cohesion, and resiliency in the student culture. That this continues to be the case is due, in part, to the fact that student values and norms for behavior are passed down —with some modification—from one student generation to the next. The learning which takes place among students is, in terms of cultural dynamics, *enculturative* in nature. Enculturation, the acquisition of one's own culture, is at the college level a continuation of the socialization process formerly in the hands of the family and play group and now mediated by friendship units, campus organizations, etc. In contrast to the acculturation situation on the campus with its deliberate, highly-structured and often self-conscious learning environment of the classroom and conference, the inculcation of student culture takes place largely at a primary group level through a process that is more informal, less contrived, and more immediate in its rewards. Further, it is easier to come by, since much of the cultural content, e.g., the ground rules for peer behavior, the specialized symbols, the prevailing attitude-value system, can be absorbed effortlessly, almost by osmosis.

The viability of the student culture at Vassar derives also from the belief held by many girls that, in actuality, the donor culture of the professor is not the dominant, superior, or better of the two, and therefore the cultural offerings are of limited value. This feeling among students is fostered by their own sense of self-satisfaction, by the attitude that they know the direction in which they want to go and how to get there, and by the general conviction that they understand their own problems best. Vassar students are not, by and large, anti-academic. They place a definite value on familiarity with the intellectual approach and many are willing at least to sample what appear to be the rewards inherent in scholarly activity. Nevertheless, the students tend to regard themselves rather than their professors as located in the mainstream of contemporary civilization with the result that the teachers are assigned marginal status and are viewed as a group whose members are to be respected for their intellectual prowess but need not be permitted to intrude too far with their academic proselytizing which is seen as somewhat irrelevant to the larger scheme of things.

Briefly stated, the student society with its capacity for successful enculturation has a strong positive valence for its membership so that motivations for accepting externally-sponsored change, in this case acculturation via faculty and administration, are minimized. One might almost speak of the presence of a "rational nativism," to use Ralph Linton's (1943) term for describing the reaction of a dominated group which considers itself to be the superior society. Anthropologists, however, in examining cases of culture contact where the natives have successfully maintained a hard core of their own cultural values, have usually focused on dominated populations which stood more or less alone in their fight for ethnic survival. College students do not constitute a societal isolate set in the middle of a vast and notably different culture. In fact, their modus vivendi in a student culture such as Vassar's with its emphasis on moderation, collective harmony, and long-range security receives direct and continuing support and reenforcement from the prevailing value dictates of United States society-at-large.

The cultural influences and pressures that derive from the national society and play an integral role in student life also, of course, bear upon the behavior and attitudes of faculty and administration. A study of the total campus would explore the possibility that the younger generation of professors has also adopted a value system that places a premium upon finding one's niche as part of an overall strategy geared to the ideal of a predictable life trajectory.

It is far from clear at the present moment, of course, whether students or faculty-administration are more favored by emerging patterns in the national ethos. Two contrasting lines of development suggest themselves: a professoriate, isolated and ignored but faithfully preserving in a kind of monastic seclusion faintly echoing the Dark Ages, the academic ideals, traditions, and essence of Western civilization as contained in the liberal arts; or an ultimate blending and fusing of student and faculty cultures as both take most of their coloration from the larger social order. There is no need to assume, however, that existing trends are irreversible. The application of a schematic model is one approach to understanding and controlling the variables and dynamics of a given segment of the social order. Hopefully, the concept of two cultures on the campus with their potentials for conflict and congruence will facilitate the task of analyzing contemporary processes and perhaps predicting and directing future trends in our colleges and universities.

REFERENCES

Bushnell, John. What are the changing characteristics of the undergraduate and what do these changes mean for programs of general education? In *Current Issues in Higher Education*, Assoc. for Higher Education, Nat. Education Assoc., Washington, D.C., 1959, pp. 137–142.

Bushnell, John. Student values: a summary of research and future problems. In Marjorie Carpenter (Ed.), *The larger learning: teaching values to college students*. Dubuque: Wm. C. Brown Co., 1960, pp. 45–61.

Freedman, Mervin. The passage through college. In N. Sanford (Ed.), Personality development during the college years. *J. soc. Issues*, 1956, **12**, 13–28.

Goldsen, Ruth, et al. *What college students think*. Princeton, N.J.: Van Nostrand, 1960.

Jacob, Philip E. *Changing values in college: an exploratory study of the impact of college teaching*. New York, Harper Bros., 1957.

Linton, Ralph. Nativistic movements. *Amer. Anthropologist*, 1943, **45**, 230–240.

Sanford, Nevitt (Ed.) Personality development during the college years, *J. soc. Issues*, 1956, **12**(4).

Sanford, Nevitt. The students we teach today. In *Record*. National Assoc. for the Physical Education of College Women, Syracuse Univ., Syracuse, N.Y., 1956.

Sutherland, R. L. Some aspects of the culture of a campus. In E. G. Williamson (Ed.), *Trends in student personnel work*. Minneapolis: University of Minnesota Press, 1949.

Vassar College. *Results of time survey*. Poughkeepsie: Nov. 7, 1957, 4 pp.

15 Everett C. Hughes, Howard S. Becker, and Blanche Geer

Student Culture
and Academic Effort

For the past several years, we have been engaged in a study of a large state medical school. We have centered our attention, primarily, on the problem of academic effort: how hard do students work? What do they work at? What determines the level and direction of their effort?

We present here two aspects of our continuing attack on these problems. First we present very briefly a general consideration of the range of actual situations one may expect to encounter in studying American schools and of the concepts most appropriate for use in such studies; then, a brief sketch of what we found in the medical school.

LEVEL, DIRECTION, AND STYLE OF EFFORT [1]

The difference between an American and an Englishman is that the American pretends to work harder than he does, while the Englishman works harder than he pretends. Thus runs one version—whether true or not—of a joke on an ancient theme, that of the relation between appearance and reality. Any difference that may exist between some typical British student and some typical American student as to either the appearance or the reality of his academic effort is nothing compared to the differences among American students and American edu-

[1] Most of the first part of this chapter appeared as How colleges differ, *Planning college policy for the critical decade ahead.* New York: College Entrance Examination Board, 1958, pp. 16–22.

cational institutions. In the amount of effort put forth by teachers and students, in the quality of their product, in the direction of their efforts toward one kind of learning or another, our country may well exhibit a larger variety in educational institutions than does any other country.

They also differ from one another in what one might call rhythm and style of effort. David Daiches (1957) has written some observations concerning the rhythm of academic effort in Britain and America. In Britain he observes that youngsters put on the great push in secondary school, achieving quite remarkable knowledge of some subjects; in university, they take it easier, and perhaps do not make equivalent progress. The American youngster comes to college not very learned, and probably unaccustomed to hard work, but may enter into college work with such verve and lively curiosity that he may come out ahead of the English graduate in some respects. That is what we mean by rhythm of effort. At Oxford, one must preserve the appearance of doing little but enjoy the intellectual and other amenities of the place during term, while also giving the impression of doing naught but "swat" between terms. That is a matter of both rhythm and style, since everyone there knows he really must work hard to survive. A man who teaches in the most gentlemanly of our state universities reports, without bitterness, that the students cannot be made to work except for a mad burning of midnight oil during the last ten days of term; only out-of-state "odd-balls" start work at the opening of the term and do all of the assignments. It may be that these gentlemanly students accomplish more than those of another, much larger, and more folksy state university at which the students are kept so busy at little daily-assigned chores that they have no time to develop or pursue a program of study (not that most of them had thought of such a thing). In the effort to get some reasonable level of accomplishment and effort in his own course, each instructor had resorted to the device of assigning a quota of daily chores. The student gives each teacher his due, claiming in return the right not to be held responsible several months from now for debts for which he already has a receipt. The rhythm is one of small, slight pulsations of effort. At McGill University, the young ladies from the upper-middle and upper slopes of Westmount seemed to have as their goal a good, solid *Second-Class* achieved by competent, unstrained effort. *First-Class* would have indicated eager competitiveness worthy only of those "pros" who were working for prizes and graduate scholarships; *Third-Class* would have betrayed either slackness or lack of ability to take things in one's stride.

There is an analogy in industry. Groups of skilled workmen will nearly always set, by informal understandings, the proper level of production. If they hate the rate-buster, they also despise the man who has to strain to make "bogey." How unlike those young ladies are the pious hard-working students in a certain sectarian college, who lack goals and style altogether, having no one to give them a model of either; how unlike also is the moderately bright, frightfully earnest young man who is rewarded with a teaching assistantship by a professor grateful to have at least one promising "major," and stays on for a dreary second-class M.A.; then, as an instructor at his home university or one of its satellites, he becomes that drone of American education, the premature pundit teaching too many subjects, and who is driven by his wife, the administration, and the accrediting boards to get a Ph.D. by applying what are known as tests of significance (sic) to what are indeed *data,* since they were handed him by his academic master. The poor fellow may have life made even worse by having to teach at a certain college where the students simply say, "Everybody has a right to go to college, even though they don't want to work hard"; or at another, a state teachers college that has had its name changed by law to "state university," where the students will not answer any examination question based on a book not on the list of those issued free (as a perquisite for being part of the public school system of the state).

Anyone who looks at all the concerns that go by the name of college and university in this country will see their great variety as to administrative and financial situation, historical concept of function, sensitivity to community forces, actual or potential numbers and kinds of students, and other characteristics.* This variety is matched by one equally great in the amount, style, and directions of effort and accomplishment effectively expected of students by each other and by the people who teach them. Although we have a good many tests of the levels of accomplishment of students in various schools and colleges, we have less knowledge than we should have of the manner in which various levels of effort are set and maintained. From studies in industry we know that levels of production are set by many factors other than the wishes of management, ability of individuals to perform tasks at a certain rate, and by the formal rewards of wages, promotion, and security. It is safe to say, as did Max Weber about fifty years ago, that any group of workingmen possessed of any solidarity whatsoever, and with some common image of themselves and their situation, will not easily yield to any authority full control over the amount of work they do or over the strenuousness of the effort they put forth (Weber, 1924). They will wrestle with management when-

* *Editor's Note.* Compare Riesman and Jencks, Chapter 3.

ever a change is made in the conditions of their work and in the concept of normal effort. We have assumed that the individual goals of students are more compatible with those of the college than are the individual goals of workers with those of their employers, and that the main thing required to raise levels of accomplishment in the college is simply to raise standards required of individuals for entrance and graduation. We have not systematically studied the way in which students form their own cultures as we have studied the cultures of workers. By the term, student culture, we mean a whole body of conceptions and images of problems and situations and of proper and justifiable solutions of them arrived at by the students; in part passed along from one generation of students to another, in part apparently rediscovered—or at least re-enforced—by each succeeding generation as they pass through the same experiences. In the second part of this paper we shall discuss the student culture of the medical school in some detail. At this point, we need only note that the students in the school had a common goal—to become practicing physicians—and faced common problems: how to get through school without flunking out and how to prepare themselves to practice medicine. The resulting student culture is integral and homogeneous.

Ordinarily the students of a college or university will be less homogeneous as to goal and problems. That may make for a less distinctive and homogeneous student culture; it may be more difficult to discover just what it is in case of institutions with heterogeneous student bodies. But it does not mean that there is not a student culture, or that the understanding of it is not essential to the making and carrying out of educational policy.

A certain urban "underdog" college prides itself on providing education for those neglected by other institutions. Since the students work for a living many classes are held in the evening. The students, in spite of all the difficulties of their individual situations, have an exceedingly active collective life in the corridors and lounges. In their discussions, they—that is, some articulate group of them, at least—have come to the notion that since their education is so hard to come by, it is up to the professors to make it good, but good, and that allowance in assignments and in marking should be made for the fact that a student has to work long hours at some hard or tiresome task. It is not the attitude of passively accepting a hand-out from the professor, but of aggressively demanding it and of reserving the right to decide whether it is a good hand-out. These students work out their particular student-culture not so much in relation to a specific common goal (such as medicine), as in relation to a common set of difficulties in their immediate careers as students arising out of their life-situations. And note that their body of expectations includes some concerning what their professors owe them. When these students turn up in graduate school, as a good many of them do, they are at first resentful of the load of work given them and of what appears to them the indifferent attitude of the staff. Since, however, they are usually bright students and really eager, they often pick up the slack quickly. Their experience of life often makes them the good observers we prize in sociology and anthropology.

One solution offered for the problem of student cultures that are not what we would like is to pick the right young people to go to college, or, at any rate, to our own particular college. It should be pointed out that even in those cases where the college can and does pick its students from a national market, much of what is most prized is in the particular types of student culture achieved, and these emerge independently, for the most part, of the wishes of faculties. The issue is not presence or absence of a student culture, but its character. Most academic institutions, in any case, appear fated to offer several kinds of goods to several kinds of clients. And in colleges, as in hospitals for chronic ailments (which keep their patients around for a long time), the clients—or patients, as you wish—develop their own notions of what is wrong with them and of what to do with the medicines dispensed to them.

Although we all know it, it is well to remind ourselves of a certain great difference between the institutions called colleges and universities in this country and those of the same designations in Europe. There, these institutions provide for the later education of but a few young people in a very few lines of work. The great burden of vocational training is allocated to other institutions. In this country, a great and increasing part of vocational training is done in colleges and universities. The postponement of entry to work, in our era of automation, combined with the notion that he who does not yet work goes to school, and that college comes after high school, has brought about a huge increase in the number of things taught in American colleges, and in the number of vocational bachelor's degrees. The difference between this country and others is not that we or they do or don't support vocational training but that in this country a great and increasing part of the vocational training is done in the very institutions that also carry the burden of higher education. There is no way out of this, even if we wanted to find a way.

We all know that in many colleges and universities where the general level of aspiration and effort is miserably low, there are small nuclei of students of great intellectual verve. Such groups, in effect, create little subcultures all of their own, contrary in many respects to that of the prevailing mass student culture. We need to study such groups, so as to learn more of the circumstances in which they arise and disappear, and so as to learn how they may be planted, cultivated, and emulated. There are many experiments of this kind going on. We suspect that those experiments in quality will succeed best that make most use of knowledge of the propensities of groups of students for developing their own conceptions of their abilities, of setting their own group standards and goals. Encouragement of individual "rate-busting" will not succeed in more than a few cases (although all of us know of students who have wrung an education from an unwilling college). Nor will a general raising of minimum standards, or a purging of so-called extraneous matter, and unworthy material, create and increase the number of nuclei of students of superior effort and accomplishment. We would lay our bets on efforts to create or encourage groups of special quality within the bosom of the conglomerate institutions that go by the name of university or college.

American colleges and universities are, in a measure unknown in other countries, enterprises; it matters little whether they are private or public, they are still enterprises seeking formulas for survival or expansion in competition with others. A common formula for survival is retention of some measure of monopoly over an original function, while also entering into competition with other institutions for other functions and other kinds of students. Many of our colleges and universities are going concerns that have come to their present state through such processes and are still making adjustments of this kind to survive, consolidate their positions, or to expand. In each case, the students—usually several kinds of them—arrive with certain expectations and, in interaction with one another and with their faculties and with circumstances, gradually develop some culture of their own, including notions of how hard to work and what to work at. Our problem is to develop the means that will make it possible for experiments in excellence to be carried out in many of these weird and interesting going-concerns; we waste our energies if we limit ourselves to thinking about the one ideal kind of institution with the one ideal kind of student. The problem is to develop, in real institutions, combinations of functions and of kinds of students in which the number who will seek higher achievement will be made greater; this is, in turn and in part, a matter of getting some students—and their teachers—to create new images of themselves and their possibilities.

STUDENT CULTURE IN MEDICAL SCHOOL:
AN ILLUSTRATIVE CASE [2]

We turn now to a detailed consideration of one kind of student culture: the kind we found in an intensive examination of medical students. This is, clearly, an extreme type. One would not expect the students of any college to be so homogeneous in their goals, in their conceptions of the problems they face, or in the solutions they find to those problems. We have just begun a study of student culture in the undergraduate college of a medium-sized state university and hope that our findings there will enable us further to refine our present concepts and hypotheses.

Conditions for the development of subcultures. Subcultures (of which student cultures are one example) develop best where a number of people are faced with common problems and interact both intensively and extensively in the effort to find solutions for them, where people who face the same contingencies and exigencies in everyday life have an opportunity to deal with these communally (Sumner, 1907; Cohen, 1955). Medical school is an ideal hot-house for such a plant.

Medical students live with a number of pressing and chronic problems, the most important stemming from the fact that they are continuously presented with an enormous and, in any practical sense, unlimited amount of material to learn. Though students and faculty agree that the criterion for choosing what to learn should be relevance for medical practice, there is enough disagreement and uncertainty among the faculty as to what is relevant so that the student is never presented with a clear directive to guide him in his own studies. Students worry together over this problem, in one or another of its many transformations, during their four years of school.

Similarly, medical school provides extremely propitious conditions —intensive interaction and isolation from outside influences—for the

[2] This portion of the paper was originally read at the meetings of the American Sociological Society, August 28, 1957, Washington, D.C., and was later published in the *Harvard Educational Review*, Winter, 1958, 28, 70–80.

Our study of medical students was sponsored by Community Studies, Inc., of Kansas City, Missouri, and was further supported by grants from the Carnegie Corporation and the National Institutes of Health. Anselm Strauss has collaborated with us in both the field work and the preparation of the final report.

development of common solutions to these problems. Students usually spend eight or more hours in school every weekday, working and studying together in the labs and on the wards, and are likely to spend many evenings and weekends together in similar activity as well. Much of their work is carried on in groups of four to twelve students, and these are arranged so differently from course to course that the students come to know many of their fellows with the intimacy that arises from close, continuous association at work. The students are insulated from contact with other people, both by reason of their crowded schedules and because they find it difficult to talk with people who are not suffering under the same pressures as they are. Even those students who have friends or brothers only a year or two ahead of them in school report that they get little help with their immediate problems from these people. Each class of approximately one hundred students goes through school as a unit, meeting the problems they face together.

This intensive interaction in an isolated group produces a particularly meaningful and essential array of those understandings and agreements we call student culture. One set of understandings specifies goals and values, telling the students that they are in school to learn those things relevant to their prospective professional futures. In the school we studied, students came to believe that they were in school to acquire the knowledge and clinical experience one must have before he can assume the responsibility of the physician for the lives of his patients, a responsibility they intended and expected to have once they finished school. They based their interpretations of the worth of various school activities on the criterion of how well this function was served in each. Another set of understandings suggested modes of cooperation designed to meet examinations and other crises, and such recurrent problems as sharing loads of clinical work assigned to groups.

The student's interpretation of specific events and issues tends to be made in categories that are part of the student culture, because these events and issues are new and unfamiliar and do not fit easily into categories provided by his earlier experiences. These cultural understandings coerce his behavior though not, at least in medical school, by methods as crude as punishment by fellow-participants in the subculture (characteristic of subcultures in the underworld or industrial work groups). It is not that the student must abide by these informal and hardly conscious agreements, but rather that they constrain his thinking and perspective almost without his being aware of it (though an occasional student may be conscious of a degree of tension between what he might like to do and what the group norms specify as correct).

The academic years. Perhaps the most important factor in the development of student culture during the freshman year is the formation of a group in which all or nearly all members have opportunities for interaction with each other. When the freshmen arrive in medical school, although they come with the common intention of becoming physicians, they are not a group in any but the nominal sense that all are in the first year class. They begin to get to know some of their fellow students right away, but this takes place not in the class at large but within small groups. The small groups are of two types. First to form are friendship groups consisting of students similar in social status who have opportunities for leisure interaction because they live near or with each other. Fraternity members, for example, most of whom are unmarried, make friends in their own house, married students get to know other married students who live in the same neighborhood or trailer camp, and unmarried students who do not belong to a fraternity get together at the student center to eat and relax in their spare time. The second type of group forms in the anatomy laboratory. As the faculty assigns students in groups of four to a dissection tank, members of different friendship groups get to know each other under the intimate conditions that dissection of the same cadaver imposes. The intersection of work and friendship groups makes it possible for each student to learn the attitudes current in other groups toward student problems, and, at the same time, carry back to his own friends solutions he and his lab partners have tried out in the course of their work together.[3]

The spread of common understandings among the freshmen is also promoted by their isolation. Unlike most graduate students, all members of the medical school class are taught together. They spend an eight-to-five day in one building. Each morning and afternoon, lectures lasting as long as the instructors wish are followed immediately by laboratory periods. Review and preparation is done at night, usually at home (for there is little or no library work) or once again in the laboratory. On a schedule like this there is little opportunity for interaction with groups outside the class, nor do the students turn to the faculty with problems except about details of daily work. For as they begin to draw together and get a sense of themselves as a group, they think of the faculty as a group opposed to their own. To ask faculty advice is to break student ranks. Thus, the students come to an understanding among themselves of what the study of medicine is and how it should be accomplished. Their notions are derived from what the faculty says and does (which are sometimes quite different), from

[3] On intersecting groups, see Simmel (1955, pp. 149–150).

the future they envision for themselves as physicians, and from their past experience in getting through school and college.

The student concept of what medicine is develops first. They believe it is a great body of known facts, some of which will be imparted to them in the first year for eventual use when they become physicians. The idea that everything is important soon gets them into a dilemma, for there are more facts than they have time to learn. They are told this by the faculty, and prove it to themselves when, after studying four and five hours a night and on weekends as well, they have not mastered the material to their own satisfaction.

As they realize they can't learn everything, all but the most self-exacting students see that they must study only important things and let the rest go. But what is important? This question becomes the chief subject of discussion in student groups shortly before the first major examinations. Two points of view predominate. One group of students believes the most important facts are those they will use in medical practice. (Selection of these facts is a matter a student feels quite competent about even if he has only been in school a few weeks.) A second group of students, most of them fraternity members, takes into account the necessity of passing examinations to stay in school. On this basis, the important facts are those the faculty thinks important. Students who believe this develop various systems for finding out what the faculty wants them to know.

Although taking the examinations brings the issue of what to study to a head, it does not settle it. Rightly or wrongly, students consider some questions "impractical," unrelated, that is, to the practice of medicine. These questions lead students of the group that believes in studying things important for medical practice to begin thinking more about what the faculty thinks these are. In preparation for the next examinations these students pool their knowledge, make use of files of old tests, and consult members of the class who already study in this way. But the examinations also contain questions students consider "unfair"—points not emphasized in lectures or texts. Students who follow some system for learning what the faculty wants are unable to predict such questions. The faculty has not been "playing the game." As a result of their difficulties with the examinations, both groups of students begin to have doubts about the faculty. The practice-minded group wonders whether the faculty teaching first year subjects (most of whom are Ph.D.'s) knows much about practice. The system-minded group wonders whether the faculty is agreed about what is important; if not, perhaps it is impossible to predict what will show up on an examination. Both groups consider briefly whether the faculty is "out to get them." The significance of all this for the development of student culture is that in their bewilderment, students draw closer together and finally settle their problem in a way acceptable to all but a few.

They agreed that they ought to study the "basic medical facts." These are the only ones they have time for, as there is so much to learn. These are the facts important for practice, certain to be on examinations if the faculty is reasonable. To this central proposition the students add a number of other understandings which they apply to their daily activities.

1. Basic facts are most economically learned from textbooks. This means that lectures which do not follow the text are a waste of student time, and a faculty member who strays from the text is a poor lecturer who probably has some scientific axe to grind in connection with his own research which does not concern medical students. 2. Demonstrations and lab work which repeat classical experiments are a waste of time; the results are most easily learned in the text and students can't do them well enough to learn much anyway. 3. Theoretical material, concepts (except those which help to organize facts), and research findings not yet in clinical use are not facts and are not useful to medical students.

These understandings of the student culture can be summed up in the student phrase "give it to us straight," which has its counterpart in the derogatory faculty phrase "spoon feeding." A student will say that he does not want to be spoon fed, but points out that there is so much to learn he hasn't time to think or worry about "minutiae" (details) and "all that academic crud" (nonfactual material). Once they have decided the question of what and how to study, the students settle down to hard work. They are no longer worried about how to select the important things to read because "you just go by the black type." In the same way, they learn to get through their lab work by various short-cuts which are both approved by student culture and not penalized in examinations by the faculty. The following incident shows how such a short-cut became widely used in the class.

Each anatomy student is given a dissecting guide with explicit directions on what to do, in what order, and what to look for during the lab session. Reflection of skin is the first step in dissection of each part of the cadaver. The laboratory guide calls for great care in reflecting so as not to pull off the underlying layer of fat which adheres to the skin. Embedded in this subcutaneous fat are tough, threadlike fibers—the peripheral nerves. These are to be traced to their origins and identified. It is a slow, exasperating task; virtually impossible if reflecting is not cleanly done.

When the class began dissection of the lower leg, we noticed one group had taken off skin and fat together leaving the nerves undissected. A student at the tank said, "You see, it's easier this way. I think it saves a lot of time because you really can't get those nerves anyway." His partner agreed, saying, "It's much better to get the nerves from the book." Another student, speaking for himself and his tank partners, said, "We knew we couldn't do the nerves because they are all different on every body. It doesn't make any difference if you do the nerves or a lot of other things." By the third week of dissection, most groups observed were stripping off skin and fat together; identification of the peripheral nerves was omitted.

Collective behavior of this sort does not mean students do not work hard. They continue to work very hard on the things they think important. One reason for their neglect of peripheral nerves, for instance, is their haste to get to the next layer down which contains the larger structures, muscles and blood vessels, that every doctor must know about. It does mean that where the faculty fails to "give it to them straight" in accordance with student concepts of why they are in school and what and how they ought to study, various short-cuts are devised in more or less open defiance of faculty instructions, and students who have deviant interests outside the student culture keep them increasingly to themselves (see Becker and Geer, 1958).

The clinical years. During the last two years of medical school—the clinical years—the student's work consists largely of taking medical histories from and performing physical examinations on patients, in order that he may develop these skills and use the information so gained in learning how to diagnose and treat various diseases. Although he continues to be tested on his knowledge through formal examinations, he is told in various ways and believes that the crucial decisions about his future in school—whether he passes or fails, for example—are based largely on the faculty's evaluation of his clinical work. Furthermore, he believes that, having got this far, it is very unlikely that he will be flunked out of school; few such cases are known to have occurred.

The major problems requiring collective solution no longer lie in the realm of examinations. Rather, students focus their attention on how to deal with the continuous pressure of a heavy load of clinical work and how to get the most out of that work in terms of the future one envisions for himself in medicine. Student culture develops as a set of perspectives on and solutions for these problems.

The view that the function of medical school is, among other things, to train students to recognize and deal with diseases that are commonly run across in a general medical practice constitutes one such perspective, shared by almost all students, even those who do not contemplate becoming general practitioners themselves. This basic proposition itself derives in part from statements by the school's faculty and administration and in part from the inability of most students to visualize anything but general practice for themselves before they have had clinical contact with other medical specialties. Once formed, the proposition continues as a more or less unquestioned premise even after the students know more about specialized kinds of practices.

The students draw several more specific conclusions about their school work from this proposition, in the course of conversations and discussions of specific incidents. These specific items of student culture may be summarized as follows. 1. The patients whom it is really important to study thoroughly are those who have common diseases— whether simple or complicated—for which there are available treatments a general practitioner could utilize. 2. All those kinds of clinical work that they cannot imagine themselves doing in a general practice are regarded as a waste of time. 3. Courses in which they are not given practice in techniques they regard as important for the practitioner to know tend to be disliked. Matters of this kind are widely discussed among the students and have important consequences for the way they interpret their experience in school and distribute their effort and time among their many competing interests.

The following incident, one among many observed, provides a nice example of the way students collectively draw inferences from the basic proposition stated above and use these to guide their behavior in school.

In one of the third year courses students are required, at the end of the course, to turn in elaborate summaries of each case assigned to them during their time on the service. These summaries must include the important findings of their own examination, important laboratory findings, a discussion of all the possible causes for these findings, references to relevant literature, and a discussion of modes of possible treatment. They are long and require a great deal of time to prepare.

The students in one group we observed established an informal norm specifying the number of such summaries they would turn in, although they were definitely directed to turn in one on every patient they had been assigned. Over a period of several days preceding the date the summaries were due, the six students in this group discussed the matter at length and decided that they would all hand in no more than a certain number. Further, they agreed on the criteria for selecting those to be turned in, and on the premise that the real purpose for these summaries was to provide material for the faculty to quiz them on during oral exams, so that the actual number was unimportant (in spite of the definite order that all cases were to be so summarized).

The criteria for selection of cases discarded were those which it was agreed provided them with no knowledge they did not already have of treating common medical problems, or where the work involved in preparing the summary would not add to such knowledge. Thus, patients with fractures or simple infections, whose treatment was more or less standard and afforded the students no chance to participate were not summarized, and "crocks" were not summarized. ("Crocks" are patients who have no physical pathology, but only vague and untreatable psychosomatic complaints, thus patients from whom nothing can be learned that might prove of use in general medical practice.)

The decision that these criteria were the relevant ones was reached in a discussion between the students in the group and in discussions with students who had been through the course previously who confirmed this interpretation.

A similar set of attitudes has grown up around the routine laboratory work—blood counts and urinalyses—the students must do on incoming patients assigned to them. They greatly resent this work because, among other reasons, it wastes their time since they themselves will not do these procedures, they think, when they are in practice.

This general frame of mind, as we have said, coerces the students' thinking to a striking degree. The following excerpt from an interview, which also illustrates the way courses are judged with reference to the amount of training they provide for the exigencies of general practice, indicates this clearly.

I asked a third year student to compare his training in surgery at the University Hospital with that he had during the other half of the quarter at the Veterans Administration Hospital to which students are also sent. (This student had definite and realistic plans to specialize in internal medicine, having even made arrangements as to whom he would practice with and where; as an internist he would, of course, do no surgery at all.)

He said, "One thing about surgery over at the VA was that we really got to do quite a bit more. I mean, for example, they would let us sew up incisions over there, where you don't get to do that at the University. Another thing about surgery at the University is that they do a lot of very complicated operations. For example, they do a lot of heart surgery over there. Well, now, none of us are ever going to do any heart surgery. But every one of us will probably do some hernias and some appendectomies. And over at the VA you see a lot of these. So it is really a better experience for us in a lot of ways. We don't have the glamour of all that fancy surgery, but we do see the ordinary things that will be useful to us."

CONSEQUENCES OF STUDENT CULTURE

Student culture affects the larger social system in which it is embedded—the medical school—in two ways. On the one hand, it provides the basis for a modus vivendi between the students and their superiors, providing a perspective from which students can build consistent patterns of response enabling them to fit into the activities of the school and hospital. In this respect student culture is an accommodation on the part of the students to the facts of life of the school. On the other hand, student culture provides the students with the social support that allows them, in individual instances and as a group, independently to assess faculty statements and demands so that they can significantly reinterpret faculty emphasis and, in a meaningful sense, make what they will of their education. In this sense, student culture is a mechanism that creates the conditions for considerable deviance from formally stated institutional rules.

When students first enter school their emphasis on medical practice —their belief that they are in school to learn to save lives (Becker and Geer, 1958)—leads them to rebel against laboratory work, essentially nonmedical, and against the drudgery of studying for intensive academic examinations. Later, they must deal with the same problem of an overload of work in a clinical setting in which examinations are not so important although the possibility of being tested and found wanting is always present. The understandings and agreements that make up student culture, by solving these problems in one way or another, allow the students to fit into the system without being constantly so upset as to be unable to function. In this way, student culture is a mode of accommodation to what the students find expected of them in school.

At the same time student culture affects the level and direction of effort students expend while in school, by giving them a rationale for restricting the theoretically infinite amount of time and effort they might devote to their school work. More importantly, it provides them with sufficient collective support to allow them to direct their effort in quite different directions than those suggested by the faculty—considered as a unit or even considered with regard for the divisions of opinion within the faculty itself. Though members of a given department may feel that their course is really designed to put across such-and-such a brand of knowledge for this-and-that purpose, the students may remain relatively immune, drawing the strength to ignore the faculty's otherwise authoritative notions from the lore that makes up student culture. Student culture is thus the cornerstone of many faculty difficulties with students, one of the facts of life to which teachers must, in their turn, make some accommodation.

As we have said earlier, medical school represents an extreme case of the development and operation of student culture. We would not necessarily expect it to play so important a role in other educational institutions. But we do believe that it is likely to exist in such places and that it will likely be found to have at least the two functions we have discussed for the medical instance, that of providing a means of accommodation for the students to the difficulties of school life, and that of providing the basis for redirection of effort on the student's part, possibly in defiance of faculty standards and ideals.

REFERENCES

Becker, H. S., and Geer, B. The fate of idealism in medical school. *Amer. Sociol. Rev.*, 1958, 23, 50–56.
Cohen, A. K. *Delinquent boys: the culture of the gang.* Glencoe, Ill.: The Free Press, 1955.
Daiches, D. Education in democratic society. *Commentary,* 1957, 23, 336–343.
Simmel, G. *The web of group affiliations.* Translated by Reinhard Bendix. Glencoe, Ill.: The Free Press, 1955.
Sumner, W. G. *Folkways.* Boston: Ginn and Co., 1907.
Weber, M. Zur psychophysik der industriellen arbeit (1908–09). In *Gesammelte aufsaetze zur soziologie und sozialpolitik,* Tubingen, 1924, pp. 61–255.

PART V

STUDENT PERFORMANCE
IN RELATION
TO EDUCATIONAL
OBJECTIVES

The college sophomore is a familiar hero of psychological
literature. Intelligent, cheerful and, above all, available, he
has long been a favorite subject of experiments designed to establish
general truth about human behavior. But he has not often been investigated *as a student;* in other words, it is not often that psychologists
or other social scientists have studied his behavior as a response to
the demands of the role of student. As pointed out in Chapter 2, all
colleges require of students that they behave in ways considered necessary to the running of the institution and favorable to the student's
development, while other role-demands arise out of the informal organization of the college society. Each of the four chapters in this part
is addressed to an important formal role-demand: that the student
reach certain levels of achievement in his academic work (Brown,
Chapter 16), that he commit himself to some major field of study
(Bereiter and Freedman, Chapter 17), that he outgrow simple-minded
stereotypes about vocations and intelligently go about choosing and
preparing for a career that is suitable to his inclinations and talents
(Beardslee and O'Dowd, Chapter 18), and that he finish the course,
that is, that he remain in college for the prescribed two or four years
(Summerskill, Chapter 19).

All of these authors assume that behavior in the role of student

531

depends both upon role-dispositions, that is, the factors of ability, personality, and background that the student brings with him to college, and upon factors of the college environment. More precisely, the authors assert that the role-behavior is a result of the interaction of these two types of factor. In reviewing the literature in their several fields, however, these authors find that the tendency in the past has been to consider the determining factors in isolation; and that far more attention has been given to dispositional than to environmental factors. Understanding of the complex interacting processes underlying the student's performances in his role will improve with the production of more research that is directed by theory concerning the functioning of personality in its social setting. Some examples of this kind of research are offered in the chapters that follow.

Dr. Brown, in Chapter 16, argues that in order to study the determinants, or predictors, of achievement in college we must first have suitable criteria of achievement, and that these must be based in a conception of the goals of liberal education. In support of his argument he reports a study of his own in which the criterion of success in college was designation by faculty members as "the kind of student the college ought to produce." The relationships of this criterion to grades, and to various factors of personality and background, are shown to have theoretical significance and practical importance. We learn here of the kinds of personality and social functioning that appeal to a liberal arts faculty. To be nominated as "ideal" a student needs to be in the top half of her class, but she by no means needs to be a "straight A" person.

Brown then presents a survey of various studies in which factors other than ability have been found to be predictive of grades in college; he first considers studies that have focused upon factors of background and disposition, for example, ethnic background, type of school attended, and pattern of achievement developed before entering college, and then he reports some studies of a clinical nature that have stressed the impact of the college environment. Finally, Brown reviews several recent or on-going large-scale studies that have sought to bring personality, the college environment, and academic achievement into the same research design. He makes it plain that our problem is not so much how to predict achievement as how to promote it; and Brown, like McConnell and Heist in Chapter 5, concludes that different types of students will do well in different kinds of college environment.

When Dr. Bereiter and Dr. Freedman say "fields of study" they are thinking of something more than the traditional academic disciplines;

they have in mind a variety of ways in which the content and modes of intellectual activity might be analyzed. They would note kinds of questions asked, kinds of information and operations utilized, and styles of work, and they would study variations in these phenomena in relation to personality. First, however, Bereiter and Freedman review those studies, including their own, that have shown that people— undergraduates and professionals—in different disciplines differ in ability, in attitude, and in various other traits of personality. The authors then proceed with what might be called their differentiated approach to the problem of personality in relation to intellectual pursuits. We are shown that a given scholarly discipline embraces various areas of content and intellectual style and that it offers a variety of roles that an individual might take; and we are permitted to see that such different aspects of a discipline might have varying appeals to the individual; they may be perceived differently, evoke different attitudes, have different roles in the development of the individual personality. Experience in a discipline may change the individual; and in time the disciplines themselves may change. This last observation brings the authors to a consideration of fundamental questions of policy: should a scholarly or professional discipline recruit mainly or only people who are likely to be well-adjusted and successful, or does it need also people who are likely to be less happy with the present state of the field or profession and to press for changes? Should students be guided into a discipline on the basis that it will utilize and perpetuate characteristics that they already possess, or should they be advised to enter a field that promises further to broaden their development? Bereiter and Freedman conclude with recommendations concerning the directions and methodology of future research: they favor longitudinal studies as the means for expanding our knowledge of how students choose, and are later influenced by, the academic disciplines; and for a deeper understanding of the relations between personality and intellect they urge further analytical studies of the functions of intellectual processes.

One might suppose that when students choose their field of concentration they would do so mainly on the basis of a careful investigation and a considered judgment concerning how their studies might prepare them for the work they propose to do in the future. But apparently this is not the way things work out, in the typical case. Bereiter and Freedman show that motives for choosing a major are often irrational or superficial, if not entirely irrelevant.

This last general conclusion is supported by Dr. Beardslee and Dr. O'Dowd, who in Chapter 18, give evidence that most students, in their thinking about their vocations, are much less concerned about the work they will do than about the kind of life they will lead.

The focus of Beardslee and O'Dowd's study is upon the images that students have of different occupations. Using an instrument especially prepared for the purpose, and obtaining responses from students on four campuses, and from some faculty members, Beardslee and O'Dowd have been able to describe in some detail common beliefs about the people and the styles of life that are associated with most of the occupations entered by the college-educated. We learn also something of the student's level of vocational aspiration, the ways in which he modifies his goals, and the manner of his adaptation to the expectations that others have of him once he has made a tentative choice.

In their efforts to explain the behavior of students in the area of vocational planning, Beardslee and O'Dowd make reference to what the college expects of the student, to dispositions present in the student when he enters college, and to various factors in his contemporary environment.

It appears that in the first instance the student is the object of conflicting role-demands. On the one hand, there is in the liberal arts colleges some expectation that the student will delay his vocational choice in the interest of his general education, but on the other hand the student is well aware of the enormous social and economic implications of one's occupation in our society. In addition, his need for a suitable self-conception urges him to declare early what he is going to be or do. Thus college students are under considerable pressure to make early and definite vocational choices.

Different students, of course, approach the problem of career planning in different ways, and Beardslee and O'Dowd relate variations in thinking about occupations to such factors as sex, type of college being attended, class in college, and the influence of the college faculty. Having discovered that students have much the same stereotypes of occupations as do other educated people in our society and that little happens in college to change the student's thinking, Beardslee and O'Dowd come to a conclusion that aligns them with Douvan and Kaye (Chapter 4) and with Bereiter and Freedman: in choosing a vocation, as in choosing a college and a field of concentration, the young person's chances of making a happy choice—happy for him and for society— can be greatly increased by giving him fuller information about the realities of available alternatives, and also by reducing the insecurity and emotional stress that tend to dominate his thinking.

That the young person often does not make a happy choice of college is underscored in Dr. Summerskill's paper. Here it is pointed out that for the nation as a whole 60% of the students entering college drop out before finishing the prescribed course. Perhaps, in view of what McConnell and Heist have told us in Chapter 5, this should not surprise us. Colleges as well as students are very highly diversified, and at the present time procedures for fitting the student to the college are little better than hit or miss.

Dr. Summerskill makes it clear that attrition is a very serious economic and administrative problem for the college, and that dropping out of college often involves the student in an emotional crisis. For a number of students, however, leaving a college may be a blessing in disguise; it may be the only way of correcting a mistake that has been made, and it may be the occasion for the student's gaining a fresh perspective on himself and his situation.

It is a striking fact, pointed to by Dr. Summerskill, that despite much administrative concern and despite many studies of the problem, the rate of attrition has remained more or less constant over the years. No doubt considerable attrition is inevitable in the nature of things, but practical action still awaits understanding of the problem. Dr. Summerskill's survey of the literature makes it clear that the problem is complex: dropping out of college is associated with a great variety of interrelated actuarial, economic, sociological, and psychological factors. To make progress toward understanding, he concludes, we must bring all of these kinds of factors into a comprehensive theoretical scheme, a scheme that can guide basic research into the sociology and psychology of college students.

Achieving a satisfactory level of academic work, choosing a field of concentration, planning a career, finishing the course—these are not all the requirements of the student's role. Other requirements and expectations arise out of the college society and the college culture, particularly as these are expressed in its extracurricular life. More than this, requirements are different in different phases of the passage through college. Future research, aimed at providing a comprehensive account of the student's behavior in relation to educational objectives, will not only extend the work that the authors of this part have described, but it will go on to investigate performances in roles, such as roommate, athlete, campus leader, big brother—or sister—of the entering freshman. Such research might well relate performance in one role to performance in others and emerge with a scheme of student types; and its major orientation, of course, should be to the relations between behavior as student and the future attainment of educational objectives.

16 *Donald R. Brown*

Personality, College Environment, and Academic Productivity

It has become increasingly clear that education is not a disembodied process that can be applied to an individual much as a bright finish is sprayed on a new automobile at the proper point in its development. Rather it is a complex, dynamic, and poorly defined process likened by Sanford (Chapter 2) to psychotherapy which is continually going on as part of the total developmental history of the individual. The realization of the inter-relatedness of intellectual development with total development has led to an increased interest in the interaction of personal attributes and environmental characteristics, both of the larger community and of the college, to produce academic achievement.

The general aim of college selection has always been to predict academic performance although, of course, any given institution may strive for the ideal combination of high performance and other personal attributes, such as athletic prowess, white-Protestant background, or leadership qualities, which that institution desires in its student body. The basic requirement for the success of any study of prediction is the clear and operational statement of what is to be predicted, in technical parlance, the criteria. Specification of the criteria of academic success has not been a simple problem, since grades alone will satisfy few educators as the end all of academic achievement. Furthermore, since education as seen in its broader context includes personal as well as purely cognitive development, it is to be expected that

536

changes in both spheres must be included in the criteria to be predicted.

Inclusion of so-called "nonintellective" attributes complicates the mechanics of the prediction problem, but it also considerably increases the rewards to be reaped from a successful solution. (See Fishman, Chapter 20.) Consider, for example, the increased power the educator would have to maximize the intellectual potential of students if the contingent relationships of cognitive power, atmosphere for learning, social class values, and personal predispositions were understood sufficiently to allow bringing each of these attributes to bear on the educational development of the student.

Donald Thistlethwaite of the National Merit Scholarship Corporation has taken a similar tack in introducing the many studies directed at the above relationships by John Holland and himself.

The development of human resources may be thought of as involving three distinct, but interdependent, processes: the identification, motivation, and training of talented persons. They are interdependent since carrying out one successfully necessarily involves the other two. McClelland in the volume *Talent and Society* (McClelland, 1958) asks the somewhat embarrassing question, "Identification for what?" We all agree that identification of the gifted is desirable, but what do we propose to do with the potentially creative person after we have identified him? How should one manipulate the environment so as to maximize the contributions of talented persons? As long as we remain within the framework of a predictor-criterion model, we cannot hope to fulfill our responsibility to stimulate, enhance, and further the careers of promising young scientists, scholars, and artists (Thistlethwaite, 1959b, p. 1).

In recent years there has been an increasing interest in the approach suggested by Thistlethwaite and reviewed in the chapter by Fishman. Many factors serve to encourage this broader interest in selection research. Perhaps the most influential, on the one hand, are the pressures of numbers on admissions committees and the concern of college administrations with the attrition rate and, on the other hand, the new focus of academic psychologists and sociologists on problems of higher education. These scientists have been interested in many problems besides selection as such, as a survey of the chapter headings of this volume indicates.

The present chapter limits itself to describing a few studies in which personality and environmental factors appear to be relevant to academic achievement. The assumption underlying each of these studies has been described by Stern in Chapter 21 as the application of ecological principles to the study of students and of their environments as they exist for particular subgroups of students. These subdivisions or subcultures can be found not only between institutions, but often within institutions as well. In the latter case, evidence to be presented below indicates that students of differing personality and motivational types not only perform differently, but, from their descriptions of their college, evidently perceive themselves to be in differing environments.

The first task of research of the sort to be considered here would seem to be to define as clearly as possible the goals of liberal arts education in order to develop specific criteria for the prediction of their attainment. This is not an easy task. Indeed, in many discussions of the value of a liberal arts education, one is reminded of Mark Twain's farmer, who when asked if he believed in baptism replied, "Believe in it? Why, I've seen it done!" This kind of acceptance has brought higher education a long way, but it has also allowed educational resources to be channeled in a most pluralistic manner. Today the term "liberal arts" is used to cover a puzzling array of educational endeavors and goals with a consequent clouding of the selection problem both for the candidate and for the institution.

THE VASSAR STUDY OF FACULTY-NOMINATED IDEAL STUDENTS

Brown has attempted a study to specify the goals of a liberal arts faculty as part of a larger study of the total educational process at a women's liberal arts college (cf. Chapters 2, 6, 14, 17, 24, 25). The problem was to determine what qualities beyond grades were characteristic of students whom the faculty selected as ideal students. Longitudinal and cross sectional studies of personality development during the college years provided a rich source of data which was supplemented by the official records of the college. In designing the study, it was assumed that academic achievement and successful attainment of a liberal education was a broadening experience, inseparable from the total maturing of the personality.

The task, then, was one of clearly stating the criteria of academic goals that the faculty held, as indicated by their choices of ideal performers. Thus, the criteria of success in this study were not the classical intellective criteria such as grades and achievement scores. Rather it was believed that a need existed for more differentiated criteria which, based on theory, were associated with the successful attainment of a liberal arts education. It is obvious that a certain level of intellectual capacity is required, but above that minimal level there is found a wide range of actual college performance. The experience of many colleges that select students largely by scores on standardized aptitude and achievement tests indicates an increasing ability to predict, and thus avoid, failures; but, conversely, it also indicates a decreasing ability to predict the relative grade performance of those selected. Of course, the restricted range of talent involved in predictions at colleges with very high College Board cutting scores makes a high relationship impossible. It has been suggested, in fact, that faculty at such colleges are arbitrarily forcing the performance requirements up so that the traditional percentage of the class will do poorly. In other words, the faculty are subject to an adaptation phenomenon, and the bright, but relatively less bright, students are the victims.[1] Regardless of the artifacts of prediction that make it difficult, there is a practical need for more differentiated predictors that are related to intellectual capacity.

It was also believed that intellectual predictors alone did not throw light on the motivational problem, except insofar as the intellectual development at the time of testing is contingent on the proper motivational development, and that they are not causally related to growth and development. We have been struck by the fact—one that is often overlooked—that grades might be obtained in quite different ways. For example, in the one instance by a brilliant, independent, versatile, flexible thinker, and in another by a persistent, well-disciplined, well-organized, and obedient student with a good memory. Getzels (1960), indeed, questions the use of standard aptitude tests and grades themselves as measures of academic achievement, on the grounds that high scores on standard multiple choice tests and high grades both result more from a narrow and conformist interpretation of the test and/or demands of teachers than they do from creative and original behavior. In fact, creativity is penalized since the creative student is apt to give a highly original meaning to the question which in a machine scored test or in the presence of a "by the book" teacher will not be scored correctly or appreciated.

Furthermore, since the stated aims of most colleges go beyond imparting knowledge and developing skills to stimulating such quali-

---

[1] Spaulding (1960) reports correlations in the order of +.80 between achievement tests and freshman college grades when the grades have been adjusted for each college. She also finds that high school marks give the best prediction of college freshman grades when both predictor and criterion are adjusted for quality. The adjustment used by Spaulding for quality and the high correlation obtained would support the adaptation phenomena as an explanation.

ties as curiosity, responsibility, tolerance, flexibility, independence, and openness to new experience, grades were dismissed as an inadequate criterion.

The approach to setting the criterion for this study, then, was frankly exploratory. Although no claim of absolute validity for faculty judgments of individual students is made, it is argued that faculty judgments none the less have special relevance in an educational institution.

In order to provide as complete a specification of the criterion group as possible without prejudicing the judgment of the faculty, or making the task too difficult to get their cooperation, the following request was sent to all members of the faculty from the college admissions office:

Since, in our opinion, the best judges of successful college performance are the teaching faculty, we should like the teachers to nominate a group of superior students whose records will be studied. We would like to ask each of you to give us the names of any students in the class of '57 who, on the basis of advanced (Grade 3) work done with you, seem to belong to such a group. We are not attempting to define the criteria for selection, realizing there are different kinds of excellence among students whose development and achievement during their four years of college were such as to make their teachers think of each, "She is the kind of young woman we want at Vassar."

Obviously, if we were interested in grades alone we could select our group from available records. While we could expect most of the students nominated to have done generally superior work in college, it is possible that some have been outstanding in one field and would be overlooked if we relied on the credit ratio as the basis for selection.

Although we are not asking for any definition of general criteria for nominations, if possible we should like to know the basis for specific selections. Therefore, we would like you to indicate briefly, next to each student's name, why you think she should be included in this study.

If none of the members of 1957 who took advanced work with you seem to have been of the caliber that we are trying to identify, please return the nomination sheets with a statement to that effect.

This request resulted in the nomination of some 67 members of the Class of 1957 from a total of 310 (21.6%). Each name was accompanied by a statement, of varying detail, explaining the basis of nomination by a faculty member.

The nominated group was then classified by whether the nominee had achieved a four-year cumulative credit ratio of above or below 3 (3 corresponding to an A— average). Fifty-seven percent were above 3, and 43% below, the lowest being 2.4.

In order to determine what differentiated the various types of college achievement as seen by the faculty from the college grades received, all students in the class with credit ratios of 3 or above, but not nominated, were also included, as well as a random sample of non-nominees with credit ratios below 3. The former number 45 and the latter 41. There were no faculty statements on these people.

For cross-validational purposes a similar procedure was later followed with the Class of 1958, and 21.3% of the class was nominated with approximately the same proportions of above and below 3 credit ratios.

In addition to giving the names of "ideal" students, the faculty were asked to give the qualities of the nominees that led to their being nominated. These statements varied from a few descriptive adjectives to detailed statements of one or two pages. A content analysis of these data was performed using the following fifteen categories listed in order of the frequency with which they were mentioned.[2] The actual frequency is given as percentage after each category.

1. *Cognitive Intelligence:* brilliant, quick grasp of concepts, superior intellect, etc. 22.2%
2. *Directed Intellectual Curiosity:* wide range of interests, goes beyond assignments, alert, enthusiastic, directed orientation, etc. 17.7%
3. *General Likability:* pleasant, modest, cooperative, helpful, etc. 9.7%
4. *Growth During College:* shows high level of maturity as compared to freshman year, marked progress in work, etc. 7.8%
5. *Independence:* self-directed, works by self, etc. 6.6%
6. *Specific Skills:* writes well, talks well, good laboratory technique, etc. 5.4%
7. *Integration:* well-organized, retains and utilizes material from diverse sources, sees relationships within field, integrates subject with other fields, etc. 4.9%
8. *Penetration:* goes beneath surface, depth of understanding, etc. 4.8%
9. *Analytic:* shows critical judgment, etc. 4.8%
10. *Moral Responsibility:* good citizenship, leadership, etc. 4.8%
11. *Originality:* creative, etc. 3.7%
12. *Flexibility:* openmindedness, tolerance, respect for facts, profits from criticism, etc. 2.2%
13. *Promise for Future:* make a good scholar in the field, etc. 2.0%
14. *Aesthetic Appreciation:* sensitive to beauty, appreciates art, etc. 1.7%
15. *Intellectual Integrity:* honest, forthright, etc. 1.7%

[2] This content analysis was performed by Miss Susan Schonberg.

If one combines the total responses in categories 1 and 2 ("Cognitive Intelligence" and "Directed Intellectual Curiosity"), 40% of the total responses are accounted for by this almost pure intellectual factor. It is interesting, none the less, that such personality factors as "General Likability" and "Growth During College" are third and fourth in frequency followed by a general integrative-analytic factor which accounts for about 15%.

Thus, by their own statements, faculty see "ideal" students as having a high degree of intellectual power which is directed toward objects of intellectual interest in an independent manner and disciplined along integrative, penetrating, and analytic lines. It is important, however, that the cognitive-intellectual aspects of the student's development not be one-sided, so that qualities of friendliness, helpfulness, and cooperativeness are lost, or the moral qualities are slighted.

A student need not possess all of these qualities, of course, to be considered ideal. An unusual amount of originality or flexibility, or the possession of a highly developed skill relevant to college performance will often compensate for other lacks. Furthermore, the faculty is appreciative of marked growth in intellect or personality during college and interprets such growth in an honorific way. When one reads of the kinds of growth mentioned in the nominating statements, one is struck by the similarity to the kinds of normal developmental changes that psychologists believe to be desirable in late adolescence and early adulthood. Such trends as deepening and broadening of interests, the humanizing of values, the stabilizing of the ego functions, lessening of purely defensive mechanisms, etc., are frequently alluded to.

It appears, then, that the faculty admires high ability but prefers to find it housed in a well-integrated, developing, pleasant, purposeful young person. Nor are they overly influenced by performance as indicated by grades alone. The distribution of grades referred to above indicates that although a student must be in the top half of her class to be nominated, she need not be a "straight A" person. In some instances, students of Junior Phi Beta Kappa status were given negative nominations although these were not requested, suggesting that the grades achieved were by techniques of manipulation, overconformity, or brute effort without any saving grace or real intellectual interest.

These four criterion groups for the classes of 1957 and 1958 were then compared on the thirty-three quantified variables and the item analysis of the Vassar test battery. These data were available before the subjects were chosen for the study as a result of the ongoing Mellon Research Program (Sanford, 1956). All members of the two classes had taken the total Mellon Test Battery in both their freshman and senior years; this battery includes eighteen of the variables as test scores. Six of the variables are the freshman and senior year scores on three factors which had been found by Dr. Harold Webster (1957, and Chapter 24) to account for most of the variance in the Vassar scales.

In addition, nine measures from the college records were included. These were:

1. Type of high school—private or public
2. Number of schools attended
3. Admission group—rating given in the Vassar Admission Committee when the applicants are considered. Essentially, it amounts to a quartile rating with 1 as high.
4. College Entrance Examination Board Verbal Scholastic Aptitude
5. College Entrance Examination Board Mathematical Scholastic Aptitude
6. College Entrance Examination Board English Achievement
7. Sum of the two CEEB Achievements offered for admission
8. Rank in secondary school equated for size
9. Senior credit ratio

As was expected, the grade point ratio holds up as the most efficient predictor of faculty nominations. However, as indicated above, the nominees exhibited a wide range of grades, and from the descriptions provided by the faculty it is obvious that nonintellective factors played an important role in the nominee's being seen as ideal, and no doubt in achieving high grades as well. For example, during both the senior and freshman years, the general sequence of mean scores was almost invariably such that the nominated but below 3 credit ratio students had the most honorific scores. That is, they were seen as the most mature, confident, open to new experience, tolerant, able to suppress and tolerate impulse, showing much growth during college, being high on masculine interest, and low on the Berkeley-F-scale and ethnocentrism (Adorno et al., 1950).

The nominated above-3 credit ratio groups had the next highest scores on these variables, while the non-nominated high graded people and the non-nominated low graded people followed in that order.

A comparison of nominated and non-nominated above-3 students shows that a student who is nominated versus one who is not is apt to come from a public school, have a higher senior credit ratio, be low on maturity, confidence, and suppression, but high on dominance and self-confidence as a freshman, and show a decreasing degree of repression-suppression.

In contrast to these above-3 people, the below-3 students who were nominated show a somewhat different picture. In addition to higher grades than the non-nominated, we find again a high dominance and self-confidence but also a high impulse expression score; this implies that faculty members favor a certain amount of unrestraint and expressivity of impulse in students who are not able to achieve top grades in the system. Also, the nominated people are higher on impulse expression, lower on the authoritarianism and ethnocentrism scales, higher in social maturity, and have a factor pattern that indicates a personality more tactful about describing self and others, more perceptive, aware of strong impulses, more introceptive, less authoritarian, more realistic, and more mature than their non-nominated peers and for that matter than their nominated above-3 peers.

Comparing nominated groups with non-nominated groups with above and below-3 credit ratio people combined, we find that the teachers nominate people who have a good credit ratio, who are high on admission criteria but not necessarily top candidates, who have high social maturity, who show a moderate amount of impulse-expression, who are low on measures of repression and suppression, who achieve high developmental status as seniors, who are low on conformity and integration into the student peer culture, who have adequate self-confidence, who are mildly dominating, who tend toward masculine interests, and are low on authoritarian tendencies both personally and with respect to socio-political issues.

The descriptions arrived at by the use of personality scales taken independently of the selection of the nominees throws considerable light on the kinds of personality and social functioning that appeals to the faculty and could therefore be taken as a further specification of some of the implicit goals of a liberal arts education.

From a cross-validated item analysis of the total 677 item battery, it was clear that the nominated students differed from the non-nominated as freshman as well as in the senior year. For example, in the freshman year before college started, the nominated subjects gave self-descriptions showing less conventional social role-perceptions, more introception, more masculinity, more civic-minded interests, and a less hysterically repressive type of defensive structure. In the senior year the items remaining after cross-validation gave much re-enforcement to the denial of conventional social relations and of conventional women's role-prescriptions by these nominees. Also, there is a hypochondriacal trend running through the items which is probably more a reflection of frank admission of difficulties and lack of conventional suppression that actual exaggeration of symptoms or somaticizing. Other trends include a definite tolerance of ambiguity and acceptance of the theoretical and the abstract as worthwhile. The civic-minded and somewhat liberal type of orientation with an appreciation of the dignity of the individual reflects itself as well, although the personal orientation is often on the introverted and introspective sides. Combined with these social attitudes there is less dependence on supernatural, mystical events, and less false optimism, but this is not accompanied by cynicism or paranoid tendencies. Rather, there appears a sense of inner direction and tempered confidence and a strong sense of morality. In the realm of family relations there is a wish for greater freedom and a frank criticalness of parents, without strong guilt feelings but with social responsibility. There also is evident a sense of adventure, expressed in a morally responsible manner rather than as impulsive acting out.

The overall impression received from these self-descriptions, then, was quite favorable to nominees as against non-nominees. Whether these personal qualities are conducive to high performance or are a result of the confidence that comes from being admired by the faculty cannot be answered from Brown's study but it is not hard to see what the faculty found to their liking.

In addition to the implication that liberal arts faculty members respond to certain personality and motivational patterns in students, beyond strictly intellectual capacity, there is some suggestion in Brown's results that academic achievement is to some degree predetermined by patterns of achievement developed before college. Indeed, the work of McClelland (1953, 1958), Atkinson (1958), Strodtbeck (1958), McArthur (1960), and Rosen (1959) would place the origin of the achievement motive very early in childhood. There are a number of studies which bear on this implication. Many of these studies are longitudinal in their approach and rich in clinical detail. Of these, the studies of McArthur and Strodtbeck are discussed below, pp. 550–552.

THE VASSAR ALUMNAE STUDY

A study which, in a sense, provided the groundwork for the empirical work just described was one in which Brown (1956) obtained ratings on fifty alumnae 20 to 25 years out of a women's liberal arts college. These women were taking part in an intensive three-day personality assessment program similar to that described in the OSS report (1948). They were studied in five separate groups of ten subjects each. The part of the total research that concerns us for present purposes was the isolation of some of the lasting effects of college education and therefore:

> . . . It seemed reasonable to begin with the educational histories of the subjects as gotten from interviews and college records concentrating on the college years, noting the patterns of experience and performance that existed at that time and seeking relationships of these to background factors and to features of the contemporary lives of the subjects (Brown, 1956, p. 44).

The educational histories of the subjects were rated low, medium, or high on each of seven variables which were chosen in accordance with hypotheses concerning the major pressures arising in the college situation and the major kinds of response to them. These variables were:

1. *Social Orientation.* It is defined as the degree to which college was perceived by the subject as primarily a social experience.
2. *Degree of Orientation to Professional Role.* High ratings characterize those subjects who not only emphasize in their interviews the intellectual experience of college but who also saw college as a path to a career different from the usual accepted role of the woman of that day.
3. *Internalization of the Values and Ideology of the Faculty.* The degree to which the subject accepted or identified herself with the faculty's regard for the intellect, accent on social responsibility, and interest in social reform.
4. *Orientation toward Future Family Situation.* The degree of orientation during the college years toward the envisaged demands and gratifications of being a wife and mother. College was perceived as somehow enabling the subject to attain a fuller life in the future family pattern.
5. *Seeking New Identity.* The degree to which search for identity was brought to the foreground of the college career by discontinuity with previous life history and cultural values.
6. *Capacity.* Intellectual capacity as measured on the Terman Concept Mastery Test (Form B) taken during the assessment and on ratings by the assessment staff.
7. *College Performance.* Rated on the basis of rank in the subject's graduating class.

Analysis of the ratings resulted in the emergence of five syndromes that were remarkably consistent in their pattern of ratings on the seven variables. They are shown in Table 1.

These five patterns of college behavior were then compared on a wide variety of background, developmental, and current status factors, and such a remarkable consistency was found that it appears that the college experience is more determined than determining. Let me briefly present the patterns found.

Table 1. Ratings of High (H), Middle (M), or Low (L) on Seven Variables for Each of Five Patterns

Variables	Social and peer-group orientation	Over-achievers	Underachievers with family orientation	High achievers	Seekers of identity
Social orientation	H	M-H	M-L	L	L
Orientation to professional role	L	L	L-M	H	L-M
Internalization of faculty ideology and values	L	L-M	M-H	H	H-M
Orientation to future family	M	H	H	L	L
Seeking new identity	L	L	L	L-M	H
Capacity	L-M	L-M	M-H	H	L-M
College performance	L-M	H	L-M	H	L-M

Social Activity and Peer-Group Orientation. These subjects were characterized during their undergraduate careers by the amount of social activity and orientation to the peer group. They are ranked low on identity-seeking and internalization of faculty ideology and professional role, and low to medium on capacity and performance, but high on future family orientation. Here, then, is the student at college for a good time, not a notorious rebel and not primarily interested in the intellectual aspects of college, but enough interested in a college degree to get by. Typically, she entered college from some well-known private school where she had an undistinguished record academically but gave evidence of "all roundness, independence, poise, and spark" to quote the entrance files.

The fathers of the women were usually graduates of Ivy League colleges and were in law or business. These activities occupied most of their time so that the daughters saw them as busy and distant figures. The mothers were seen as poised, charming, active, and intelligent women of great energy. Often they were graduates of the subject's Alma Mater. The subjects tend to be strongly identified with their parents. Childhood is remembered only vaguely but in terms of stability and happiness.

Upon leaving college, they occupy themselves in Junior League activities until marriage; after marriage they devote themselves to suburban living, child rearing, and some soul-searching. The latter seems to have resulted in their now being liberal Protestants and left-of-center Republicans. At the time of the study these women were high on authoritarian scales, relative to the group, and were rated as lacking introspection, lacking capacity for further growth, and lacking complexity.[3] These women did not find college intellectually challenging nor did they gain high academic achievement.

The *overachievers*.[4] These are women whose college performance was much higher than their tested capacity would indicate it should have been. They are low on orientation to professional role, low to medium on internalization of faculty ideology and values, high on orientation to future family, and low on identity-seeking.

The explanation of overachievement seems to reside in the family history. The mothers of the subjects are college-educated women with very high social aspirations. The fathers are self-made business men who are greatly admired by the subjects. On the whole there is close conformity with strict parental demands. The family life is recalled only vaguely but said to be happy. At college these students worked hard and did well, but acquired little serious appreciation of the intellectual life; consequently their present lives tend to be devoid of intellectual pursuits or aspirations. The high college performance seems to be largely a matter of submission to authority, which paid off with academic rewards.

Since leaving college, these subjects have lived that type of conventional suburban existence so caricatured in much contemporary writing. Their lives have been routine upper-middle and lower-upper-class patterns with narrow scope and opportunity and very little deep meaning. As a consequence, these women show more signs of an approaching role crisis related to menopause and aging than do the other groups. Their social and political ideology is conservative and cautious. In religion they are traditionalist and Protestant. The picture would tend to support the often-heard complaint that grades can to some extent be achieved with only a reasonable capacity, little deep intellectual curiosity, and a good deal of "proper" behavior accompanied by some careful choice of content from the curriculum.

Underachievers with Future Family Orientation. These women are medium to high on capacity but medium to low on college performance. In spite of low performance, there is evidence of a good deal of intellectual growth during college. They are medium to low on social activities and medium to high on internalization of faculty ideology. The latter identification on their part appears to be related to one of three sources—either (a) they came from politically liberal families; (b) they reacted strongly to the depression of the Thirties while in college; or (c) their husbands, whom they began dating while in college, were liberal politically. In line with their main interest in

[3] Studies of current students, in progress at Vassar, show these women to be most similar to the group of students who drop out at the end of their sophomore year. In today's more competitive situation, the colleges are less tolerant of the socially-oriented student.

[4] The term "overachievers" in itself suggests a paradox. How can one achieve higher than he is capable of? One may be excused for using it only when it is defined, with the emphasis on the validity of grades as measures of either capacity or performance. The personality syndrome observed here as well as by Stern's Chicago studies (1956) suggests that this type of achievement is a spurious thing at best.

marriage and family, they were medium to low on professional role identification. However, many became active professionally just before and in the early years of marriage, particularly in areas of human welfare, such as social work or nursery school teaching, where the interest was more in the humanitarian aspects of the job rather than in ideas or professional status. Problems of self-identity did not bother these women in any serious manner during college.

These subjects came from more diverse social backgrounds than the other groups. They, in the 1920's, went to private but usually progressive and academically sound schools and chose their college on the basis of recommendations from school officials and friends. Scholarship aid was usually not needed.

The early family life is described by these subjects as happy and secure. Fathers are seen as having been competent, loving, lots of fun, and appear to have been in the family picture a good deal. Mothers were warm, sociable, happy, and accepting. They rate both parents positively, but identify more with the mother. They report more than the usual amount of freedom and independence in their relationships with parents, with little threat of deprivation for nonconformity.

In line with their intention and interest, they married soon after college. Their chosen spouse was a professional or business man of their own age, and the unions have resulted in three to six children born over a period of five to twenty years. In spite of the family obligations of these women, who are generally without servants, they are active in the community. Contrary to their earlier dedication to home and family, they are now looking forward to part-time employment.

Ideologically they tend to have conventional religious beliefs, but have arrived at them after a good deal of thought. They are low on authoritarianism, and they describe their political beliefs as moderate, with leanings toward the Democrats or "Independents."

High Achievers. This group is high on capacity now and at entrance to college. They performed very well at college, graduating at or near the top of their classes. They were low in social-peer group oriented activity while in college, but high in orientation toward professional role and in identification with faculty values. Future family orientation was low when these subjects were in college, and indeed, these women rarely marry and even more rarely have children when they do. Rather they attain advanced degrees and hold responsible professional positions. Although these women often have problems relating to their identity, they are usually able to achieve a satisfactory self-conception through their high capacity, strong interest, and actual achievements.

These women most often come from public schools—a fact not generally true of the sample in those days; furthermore, they were usually scholarship holders. Indeed, in this sample of fifty women, college performance is correlated significantly with years in public school, a fact which indicates that an economic selective factor, operating at that time, may have barred less brilliant high school girls from college. The families of these subjects were rarely socially or intellectually prominent, and the parents were usually not college-educated.

Presently, these women are oriented toward liberal political and social philosophies, tend to vote Democratic, to be interested and informed about politics, and agnostic in religious beliefs.

In their early life and adolescence, they have experienced conflicts arising from domineering and talented mothers, against whom there is considerable repressed hostility associated with strong guilt. As a group, their early lives tended not to be free of upsetting events, such as deaths, moves, economic crises, and the like, nor were their childhoods outstandingly happy. They rate their fathers more favorably, but accept the opinions of their mothers.

The intellectual development of this kind of woman may be described as early, intense, and continuing. They report an inclination toward intellectual activity dating from their earliest years, and consequently they are quite decided on an intellectual career before coming to college. Usually the college was chosen because of its academic prestige and because scholarship aid was available.

Identity Seeker. This is the final syndrome isolated in this study. The group comprises a miscellany of rather unhappy and confused people trying to break away from strong and domineering parental ties, or experiencing the need to make drastic adjustments to a social and economic situation at college that is very different from that at home. These women range in background from extreme upper-class Victorian upbringing to lower-middle-class, small-town girls. The identity-seeking process ranged from open defiance of home pressures to a maintenance of a weak conformity until conditions presented an opportunity for a break. On the whole, these women have been unable to arrive at stable lives except after prolonged therapy, or drastic change in the environment, or both. The families were either unstable and oppressive, or the sex-role conflict was so severe and sex identities so muddled that normal heterosexual relations were seriously impaired. These are the subjects who as students presumably could have profited most from currently existing therapeutic facilities on the campus. As it was, intellectual interests were largely forsaken because of the intensity of the personal struggle.

A later cluster analysis of clinical Q-sort ratings by Block and Baker (Brown, 1956) confirmed the existence of these syndromes, and comparable types were found in the current student studies at Vassar by Freedman (Freedman, 1956).

SOME SOCIAL AND CULTURAL DETERMINANTS OF ACHIEVEMENT

The Vassar alumnae study suggests that social variables, mediated through the individual student in the form of role-behavior toward and within the educational institution, often determine academic achievement. McArthur's (1960) observations of differences in academic performance at Harvard between boys prepared at public vs. private schools illustrates this effect directly. His sample of privately prepared students is limited to the traditional, well-established New England schools. Using a variety of clinical tests, McArthur finds a number of striking differences in the cognitive modes and social values of the two groups of boys; there is higher achievement and more orientation toward the sciences on the part of public school boys, more underachievement with orientation to the humanities and arts on the part of the privately prepared boys. In addition to the differences in social values that are related to academic and occupational goals, there are differences in "cognitive style." The private school sample tends to have a lot of creative impulsivity while the public school sample is more stimulus-bound and systematic in dealing with unstructured perceptual material. McArthur interprets these differences as being due to differing sets of values transmitted in the socialization process by families representing different subcultures of American society.

Strodtbeck (1958) has attempted to discover the roots of academic achievement in family interaction, and in values held by parents of Italian and Jewish ethnic origins. Although he worked with high school students rather than college students the findings are important and similar enough to observations at the college level that it would be well to consider them here. Strodtbeck's study is one of the very few well-executed investigations that relates achievement values in family interaction to academic achievement (see also Rosen, 1959).

Strodtbeck started with the theoretical relation between the value placed on achievement in a society and the major ideological institutions of that society, as proposed by Weber in his discussion of the Protestant ethic. He hypothesized that two subcultures that, as groups, had achieved differing degrees of status in American life would show value systems and family life patterns that differed, and that these differences would be consistent with the degree to which the subcultures held value systems similar to the Protestant ethic. A careful analysis of ethnographic evidence indicated that second generation Italian and Jewish families in the Northeastern United States would meet these requirements. That is, the Jewish tradition as reflected in this American subculture was closer to the Protestant ethic, which presumably was the underlying basis for the high level of achievement orientation. The two subcultures differed on the following five value orientations thought to be necessary for achievement in the United States, with the Jewish ethnic tradition being consistently more positive than the Italian in regard to each type of value in question.

1. A belief that the world is orderly and amenable to rational mastery; that, therefore, a person can and should make plans which will control his destiny.
2. A willingness to leave home to make one's way in life.
3. A preference for individual rather than collective work.

4. High belief in the perfectability of Man.
5. Great willingness to establish equalitarian power relationships in face to face interactions with children.

A questionnaire study of a large random sample of residents of New Haven, Connecticut, confirmed the ethnographic analysis. Then samples of twenty-four third generation Jewish boys and Italian boys were selected from the local high schools. They were stratified by socio-economic status and by overachievement or underachievement in school. The research team moved into each home for a two-hour (or longer) session with the boy and his parents during which the family was asked to resolve differences of opinion as expressed on a written questionnaire administered independently. In general, the value differences were borne out and, in addition, the relations of the power structure in the family to academic achievement was clarified as follows:

Both in the boys' reports of who was dominant at home and in the actual decision-winning in the homes we studied intensively, the Italians showed greater variations from equality of power than the Jews. While this finding is probably of less importance than those presented above, it nonetheless sharpens our curiosity about the effects of power balance on the son's achievement. Is it perhaps true that when relatively equalitarian relations exist in the home, the son can move to new loyalties for larger systems of relationships, such as those provided by college or a job, without an outright rupture of family controls? Is such an adjustment to new institutions outside the home harder the more the home has tended to be dominated by one parent or the other? Furthermore, what would be the cost to the son of such a rupture—both in performance and in motivation to continue on his own? One wonders, of course, whether the conflict would not be less, the frustration less, when the break came—and consequently the emotional and intellectual adjustment more efficient—if the son had come from a home where controls were already diffuse and equalitarian as they are in many situations in life? . . .

So we come back to one of the most persistent and important themes of this study: what have power and the adjustment of power to do with achievement? Let us review the steps of the argument briefly. We held that, to achieve on the American scene, one must adjust to a more or less impersonal bureaucratic system where power lies not with the individual but with the system, and is used to reward and punish according to the way individuals live up to impersonal specialized standards of performance. In addition, we argued that the family is also a "power system" and that the son's adjustment to it should generalize to his life outside . . .

Our data on this point are especially striking . . . we can feel justified in assuming that power balance in the family is of importance in giving a child ideas which will bear on his later success or failure. And, oddly enough, it is the power balance that is correlated with the ideas and not whether those same ideas are held by parents or not. (Strodtbeck, 1958, pp. 188–189.)

THE INTERACTION OF PERSONALITY AND COLLEGE ENVIRONMENT

It appears from such results as these that fairly stable personality structures exist at the time of the college experience and can be quite determining of that experience in the absence of other environmental pressures, arising from the college, strong enough to counteract the structures. We know, however, from the types of changes in attitudes reported by Brown and Bystryn (1956), Brown and Datta (1959), Lazure (1959), and Webster (1958) (see Chapter 24) that changes can and do take place as a function of college attendance. Even if one remains pessimistic as to the amount of change possible at the basic level of personality structure, it is logical to assume that no personality structure is unidimensionally related to any single form of future development, and that therefore differential experiences at college can, and do, effect important and lasting changes. Intensive clinical studies of alumnae and current students done by the Mellon Foundation at Vassar and by Wedge (1958) and his associates at Yale provide a rich source of often dramatic individual change, in the direction of greater intellectual growth and achievement, as a consequence of a favorable pairing of personality determinants and the environmental characteristics of a given college. Professors are fond of pointing to given students who, in their experience, have "caught fire in the junior year"; and the professors are usually happy to take some small share of the credit. Such observations are unfortunately often poorly controlled but, together with the evidence of attitudinal change referred to above, they provide some basis for the hope that college can and does make a difference.[5]

All of the above studies throw light on some of the personality determinants of academic achievement, but all are incomplete in a very essential manner. None was designed in a way that takes full account of the college environment. Descriptions of these environments and the dynamic interaction of personality structures with the culture found at various colleges (cf. Chapters 3, 14, and 15) constitutes an essential sort of data for both the prediction and the control of academic

[5] The Jacob's report (1957) on value change in college students takes a somewhat pessimistic view of the possibility of change. Jacob's study has, however, been criticized by Riesman (1958) and by Barton (1959) on methodological grounds and by Smith (1958) on definitional grounds. For a further comment on Jacob's report see the Jacob and the Fishman articles (1960) in the *Educational Record* symposium.

performance. Sanford (1959), drawing on the work of Freedman and Brown along with interviews of current students at Vassar, addresses himself to the motivation of high achievement among women students at a college such as Vassar. I shall quote Sanford directly since his conclusions stress both personality factors and general cultural and immediate college environmental factors in producing high achievement and therefore provide a good introduction to some remarks on the ecological approach of Thistlethwaite, Holland, Pace, and Stern.

. . . The observation that students largely educate each other, that the values and outlook of most students are profoundly influenced by those that prevail in the student society is not, of course, original with us. The same observation has been made from time to time concerning the British universities; and we know that those of our own colleges that have been able, largely through vigorous recruitment and selection, to create a campus society in which the highest prestige attaches to the highest scholarship, can count heavily upon social pressure to keep motivation at a high level.

. . . Criticizing student culture is like criticizing American culture generally. Some outsiders may not like the practicality, the empiricism, the ethical relativism, the egalitarianism, the accent on social skill, found in our student culture and in American culture generally, but there it is. Probably no one would call it all—or even mostly—bad, but the fact remains that ours is not primarily an egghead culture. And that is precisely the rub, when our concern is with motivation for serious intellectual work. We might as well face the fact that to be a serious scholar at the student level, or to be a genuine intellectual in our society, is to be exceptional. One may, if he is fortunate, belong to or find membership in an exceptional sub-culture; but usually he must be prepared to be an exception in the group in which he lives.

. . . In all four cases (of high achievers), one or the other of the parents was highly educated or placed high value upon scholarly attainments, and held high hopes and expectations for the daughter. In all four cases (cited in the original) there was early, close involvement with the parents and early and persistent awkwardness in social relations with peers. In all four cases, the drive toward academic achievement has more than one source; its determination is complex . . . in each case it seems that the early relations with the parents had a problematic aspect. Special tensions were generated and early emotional drives were channeled into the scholarship motive. Yet this channelization could hardly have occurred had not one or the other parent represented intellectual values.

. . . If we are interested in identifying high achievers early in their lives, we must remember that this is not just a matter of discovering factors that are correlated in populations with high achievements; it is also a matter of knowing and understanding the different contexts in which the same factor may operate with differing effects. Moreover, it won't do for us to suppose that the destiny of the high achiever is already determined before she arrives at college and that she will be "all right" in almost any kind of academic environment.

I believe our cases have presented some different kinds of educational problems. For example, they suffered, and profited, in different degrees from the experience of being in a kind of "outgroup" as far as the majority of their fellow students were concerned. Again, they were in different degrees frustrated, as they developed, by the relatively structured educational environment in which they lived, and reached a stage of readiness to move to a different environment at different times. (Sanford, 1959, pp. 36–38.)

Murphy and Raushenbush (1960) have also presented many stimulating and heuristic findings in a volume of collected studies carried on over a period of four years at Sarah Lawrence using a longitudinal approach with a single college class. The longitudinal approach, the intensive clinical analyses of the data, the use of faculty reports and ratings as criteria, and the focus on change during college make the Sarah Lawrence studies most valuable, even though one might have wished for a report with more quantitative data based on larger samples and standardized instruments, so that greater generalization would be possible.

Fortunately, a number of large-scale studies have begun to emerge in which comparative samples of many types of colleges and types of students are being studied with standard instruments. The intensive study of one group of students at one institution, such as at Sarah Lawrence, at Yale by Wedge et al. (1958), by Heath at Princeton (1958), and Sanford et al. at Vassar, to mention a few, are invaluable in explaining the relevant parameters and in giving a sense of the richness of the data, but ultimately the insights gained must be tested in a world which, as Egon Brunswik was fond of saying, is "ecologically representational and valid." Only then can one safely generalize beyond single institutions and particular samples of students.

At least three national studies which combine the fruits of intensive clinical studies with the rigors of psychometric instrumentation and representative sampling are now directed at the relations between motivational-personality factors, college environmental factors, and academic performance. Many other such studies are being carried out locally.

Some of the data from the work of the Center for the Study of Higher Education at the University of California is reported by McConnell and Heist in Chapter 5 and Webster et al. in Chapter 24. I should like here to report on two other studies focused on the interaction of student personality and college environment. The group of studies centered at Syracuse University in the work of Robert Pace and George Stern is reported in Chapter 21.

The great possibilities opened by the Pace-Stern scales for systematically studying the interaction of specific personality patterns with specific college environments are being exploited by the National Merit

Scholarship Corporation studies under the direction of John Holland and Donald Thistlethwaite. This group has the unique opportunity to gather data on thousands of top-performing high school students who each year compete for National Merit Scholarships. The research group has conceived their task very much in the tradition of the studies cited in this chapter. That is, rather than centering their interest only in predicting academic performance from their selection instrument—the National Merit Examination—they have intensively investigated a wide range of personal predispositions, societal influences, and college demands in order to determine how best to maximize the nation's intellectual talent.[6]

In order to fit these studies into their total research scheme and also to provide a framework for other researches described previously in this chapter, let us refer to Table 2, which has been presented by the National Merit Research team as a classificatory schema of the areas of knowledge which need to be developed and of the variables thought to influence intellectual achievement.

Table 2 distinguishes four major classes of intellectual determinants:

1. The conditions that produce the kinds of talent, interests, and motivations the student has when he is first identified by testing in the Junior year of high school by the National Merit Program.
2. The individual's intellectual and motivational qualities.
3. The educational environments to which the person is exposed.
4. Special activities of external agencies designed to foster intellectual development such as the National Merit Program.

In the words of the report:

If we look at research on creativity and achievement in this manner we see that studies of the identification, motivation, and training of the talented person are aimed at somewhat different kinds of knowledge. *Identification* studies are focused on the ADE axis of (the) Table . . . and aim to develop knowledge (1) of the antecedent conditions which produce different kinds of dispositions among talented persons and (2) of the relations between the person's dispositions (predictor's) at given stages of his educational career and the desired outcomes (criteria). Training studies are concerned with the CB relationships and aim to develop knowledge of (3) the types of college presses which stimulate student achievement and (4) the interaction of college presses and personal dispositions which determine achievement. *Motivation* studies (in this context) are concerned with methods of motivating the talented person to seek the kinds of educational experience which will help him to realize his potentialities. These studies are concerned with the DB relationship

[6] A summary of the studies since 1957 is presented in yearly *Technical Reports* issued by the National Merit Scholarship Corporation.

Table 2. A Model for Studying the Determinants of Intellectually
Talented Performance

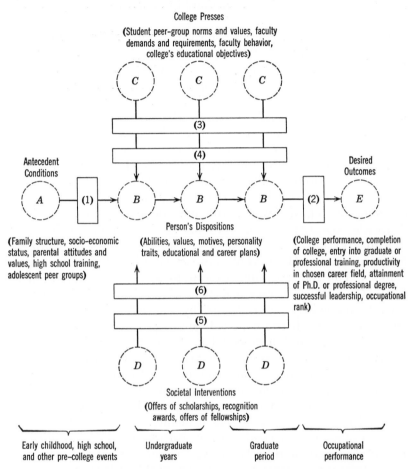

College Presses

(Student peer-group norms and values, faculty
demands and requirements, faculty behavior,
college's educational objectives)

(3)

(4)

Antecedent
Conditions

Desired
Outcomes

(1)

(2)

Person's Dispositions

(Family structure, socio-economic
status, parental attitudes and
values, high school training,
adolescent peer groups)

(Abilities, values, motives, personality
traits, educational and career plans)

(College performance, completion
of college, entry into graduate or
professional training, productivity
in chosen career field, attainment
of Ph.D. or professional degree,
successful leadership, occupational
rank)

(6)

(5)

Societal Interventions

(Offers of scholarships, recognition
awards, offers of fellowships)

Early childhood, high school,
and other pre-college events

Undergraduate
years

Graduate
period

Occupational
performance

(Reproduced from Technical Report No. 3, December 1959, Research and Studies, National Merit Scholarship Corporation.)

in (the) Table . . . , and are aimed at developing knowledge of (5) the effectiveness of special recognition and financial aid programs in motivating the gifted person to seek advanced training, and (6) the interactions of these activities with the attributes of the person in determining effects. (Nat. Merit Corp. Tech. Report, 1959, p. 4.)

The researches of Brown, McArthur, and Strodtbeck cited above, exemplify studies of antecedent conditions. Brown's study of ideal students relates to dispositions and the desired outcome while the work of Pace and Stern falls into the categories (3) and (4).

The studies of the National Merit group that we wish to refer to here are all by Donald Thistlethwaite (1959a, b, c) and belong in categories (3) and (4), that is, the relationship between student personality and college environment.

The latter studies follow out of the earlier work of Knapp and Goodrich (1952), and Knapp and Greenbaum (1953), which attempted to isolate and describe highly productive college environments, using the number of advanced graduate degrees and other scholarly rewards attained by a given institution's graduates as the criteria of productivity. Several methodological criticisms have been leveled at these well-known pioneering studies, chiefly the statistical bias in favor of the more homogeneous small college and the failure to correct for the talent of the entering classes at each institution, thereby making it hard to determine how much of the productivity as defined is due to a better entering class and how much is due to the college environment. Thistlethwaite, with data on over 9600 talented students who were tested by the National Merit program, was in a position to work out a Talent Supply Index for colleges in which sufficient numbers of Merit Scholars or Certificate of Merit winners were enrolled. This Index accounted for 40 to 50% of the variance in the Knapp-Greenbaum indexes and 15% of the Knapp-Goodrich measures. A productivity index, defined by Thistlethwaite as the discrepancy between a college's expected rate of producing Ph.D.'s (as predicted from its enrollment of talented students) and its actual rate of productivity, was computed for 511 colleges which enroll 70% of all freshmen. The correlation between the talent supply and the college productivity allowed the computation of the regression of one variable on the other and these prediction residuals gave an index of productivity independent of student quality.

The College Characteristics Index (Pace-Stern, 1958) was filled out by 916 National Merit Scholars and Certificate winners who were sophomores at 36 colleges. Later revisions of this scale were constructed so that items referring to faculty activities were placed in a separate scale to be answered in reference to faculty only.

About the formal structural features of institutions that are highly productive of Ph.D.'s after correction for Talent Supply, Thistlethwaite reports: [7]

    . . . type of student body is the characteristic most closely related to productivity. To be sure, the unproductivity of women's colleges and universities

---

[7] The reader is cautioned to bear in mind that the 36 colleges on which this and following characterizations of productive versus nonproductive institutions are made have been chosen because they recruited enough National Merit Scholars and Cer-

tends to depress the average for all non-coeducational institutions and so to make schools with coeducational student bodies look much more productive. However, in spite of their advantage in having an all-male clientele, men's colleges and universities are not significantly more productive in the arts, humanities, and social sciences than coeducational institutions. Thus, the high standing of coeducational schools suggests that a mixed student body may be favorable to the development of motivation to seek advanced degrees in these fields.

The only other characteristic related to both measures of productivity is the number of volumes in the institution's library. It is not surprising that schools with larger libraries tend to be more productive, since it is likely that superior faculties and resources will be found at such institutions.

The remaining correlations . . . suggest that natural science Ph.D.'s tend to come from a different set of baccalaureate institutions than do Ph.D.'s in the arts, humanities, and social sciences. NS (natural science) productivity is associated with large freshman enrollments, graduate programs offering the Ph.D., public support, and absence of religious affiliation.

These characteristics are typical of the state university, which, as we have already noted, tends to be outstandingly effective in stimulating achievement in the natural sciences.

It is more difficult to characterize institutions which are productive of Ph.D.'s in the arts, humanities and social sciences. They tend to be located in small cities and—contrary to expectation—to have relatively large numbers of students per faculty number. Student-faculty ratios are notoriously difficult to interpret: one would expect that the ratios for colleges would be smaller than those for universities; however, this is not the case for coeducational institutions in the present sample. No doubt, part of the difficulty arises from the practice of including the faculties of graduate and professional schools in the denominators of such ratios . . . (Thistlethwaite, 1959, p. 3).

The perceived characteristics of faculty as obtained from the College Characteristics Index items relevant to faculty behavior show that colleges that are high in natural science productivity have faculties that appear to approach students informally and with warmth: faculty are not embarrassed by open displays of emotion; they often refer to colleagues by their first names when talking to students; students do not describe them as practical and efficient in their interactions; students do not feel it necessary to use the title "professor" or "doctor" with them. Second, they emphasize high academic performance: their standards are seen as exacting, they see through the pretenses and bluffs of some students; they push students to perform at capacity; and they give meaningful exams. Third, they apply high standards to their colleagues: they emphasize basic research. Fourth, the faculty is not protective of the students but rather is understanding of mis-

tificate holders to permit statistical analysis. It is interesting to note that no college under an enrollment of 1000 was included by this criterion, although a number of colleges such as Reed, Bryn Mawr, and Haverford are known to be highly productive of Ph.D.'s.

takes in social and political spheres. Finally, they tend to be more nondirective in their teaching methods.

In contrast to the above, colleges that are more productive in the social sciences and humanities are characterized in students' perceptions as having excellent social science faculties, a flexible curriculum, and professors who teach in a controversial and very energetic manner.

Examination of the students' attitudes, interests, and peer-group norms as related to achievement support the notion that scientific and humanistic scholars thrive in different types of environments.[8] Student cultures characterized by humanism, breadth of interests, and reflectiveness are conducive to humanistic interests and achievement, while participation and aggression interfere with such achievement. Natural science achievement is typical of student cultures high in scientism and aggression and is inhibited by those that stress social conformity.

It is hoped that studies such as those reported by Stern (Chapter 21) and by Thistlethwaite will be expanded and refined, for such investigations seem capable of providing a significant increase in our understanding of the relation of personal predispositions to environmental factors in producing high academic achievement. Combined with more work focused on the socialization process itself, which will hopefully throw more light on the development of desire for intellectual achievement, we can look forward to the day when it will be possible to improve greatly the average attainment of college students.

After admitting that there is a paucity of data on academic achievement, what can be concluded from the sort of studies cited? First, that academic achievement is a function of more than intellective capacity. Motivational factors, arising from long standing predispositions in the individual, and current environmental demands are as important as capacity. The individual factors are mediated by the family and early social identity groups during socialization; and in turn, socialization is shaped by interpersonal family dynamics and broad social-ethnic ideologies relating individuals to the general scheme of life. Such factors as these predispose individuals to perceive and to react selectively to the educational experience. The educational experience, in turn, is mediated by a faculty working in a formal institutional structure that consists of several subcultures. Membership in and identification with

[8] Self-selection such that scientists and humanists both choose different schools and create differing environments at them, must be taken into account. Thistlethwaite (1960) has been working on this problem by studying the "holding power" of the differing fields for students expressing interests in specific areas of study before entering college.

any of these subcultures will color the nature of and the receptivity to the educational process and may interact with native capacity and individual predispositions in such a way as to determine the level of academic achievement broadly defined.

The problem of selection might better be thought of in terms of channeling the right students to the types of colleges that can maximize the potential of each type of student. It might be necessary, as suggested elsewhere in this volume, to create new types of environments if we want to be in a position to serve as many students as possible. With full appreciation of the individuality of each student, we must nonetheless look for the essential communalities that will allow educators to design the fewest possible types of institutional environments in order to foster the fullest intellectual development of the largest number of students. It is only with such knowledge of individual development and a clear statement of the goals to be achieved that education can become less haphazard than it is now.

REFERENCES

Adorno, T. W., Frenkel-Brunswik, E., Levinson, D., and Sanford, N. *The authoritarian personality.* New York: Harper Bros., 1950.

Atkinson, J. W. *Motives in fantasy, action, and society.* Princeton, N.J.: D. Van Nostrand: 1958.

Barton, A. H. *Studying the effects of college education.* New Haven: Edward W. Hazen Foundation, 1959.

Brown, D. R. Some educational patterns. *The J. of soc. Issues,* 1956, **12** (4), 44–60.

Brown, D. R. Non-intellective qualities and the perception of the ideal student by college faculty, *The J. of educ. Sociology,* **33** (6), 1960, 269–278.

Brown, D. R., and Bystryn, D. College environment, personality, and social ideology of three ethnic groups. *J. soc. Psychol.,* 1956, **44,** 279–288.

Brown, D. R., and Datta, Lois-ellin. Authoritarianism, verbal ability, and response set. *J. abnorm. soc. Psychol.,* 1959, **58** (1), 131–134.

Fishman, J. A. Why are the values of college students changing? *Educational Record,* **41** (4), Oct. 1960, 342–346.

Freedman, M. B. The passage through college, *J. of soc. Issues,* 1956, **12** (4), 13–28.

Getzels, J. W. Non-I.Q., intellectual and other factors in college admission: the coming crisis in the selection of students for college entrance. Washington, National Education Association, Feb. 1960, 21–28.

Heath, G. R., Jr. Personality and student development. In *New dimensions of learning in a free society.* Pittsburgh: University of Pittsburgh Press, 1958, 225–245.

Jacob, P. E. *Changing values in college.* New York: Harper Bros., 1957.

Jacob, P. E. Social change and student values, *Educational Record,* **41** (4), Oct. 1960, 338–342.

Knapp, R. H., and Goodrich, H. B. *Origins of American scientists.* Chicago, Ill.: University of Chicago Press, 1952.

Knapp, R. H., and Greenbaum, J. G. *The younger American scholar: his collegiate origins.* Chicago, Ill.: University of Chicago Press, 1953.

Lazure, M. C. An intercultural study of personality development in college women of the United States and French Canada. Unpublished master's thesis. Bryn Mawr College, April, 1959.

McArthur, C. Subculture and personality during the college years. *The J. of educ. Sociology*, 1960, **33**, 6.

McClelland, D., et al. *The achievement motive*. New York: Appleton-Century-Crofts, 1953.

McClelland, D., Baldwin, A. L., Bronfenbrenner, U., and Strodtbeck, F. L. *Talent and society*. Princeton, N.J.: D. Van Nostrand, 1958.

Murphy, Lois B., and Raushenbush, Esther. *Achievement in the college years*. New York: Harper Bros., 1960.

Murray, H. A. *Explorations in personality*. New York: Oxford University Press, 1938.

National Merit Scholarship Corporation. Tech. Report No. 3. Evanston: 1959.

Office of Strategic Services Assessment Staff. *Assessment of Men,* New York: Holt, Rinehart, and Winston, 1948.

Pace, R. C., and Stern, G. G. A criteria study of college environment. Syracuse: Syracuse University Research Institute, Psychol. Res. Center, 1958.

Riesman, D. The "Jacob Report." *Amer. sociol. Rev.*, 1958, **23**, 732–738.

Rosen, B. C. Race, ethnicity, and achievement. *Amer. sociol. Rev.*, 1959, **24** (1), 47–60.

Sanford, N. (Ed.) Personality development during college years, *J. of soc. Issues*, 1956, **12** (4).

Sanford, N. Motivation of high achievers. In Opal David. (Ed.), *The education of women*. Washington: American Council on Education, 1959, 34–38.

Smith, John E. *Value convictions and higher education*. New Haven: Edward W. Hazen Foundation, 1958.

Spaulding, G. The application of secondary school cumulative record data to the prediction of college success. Educational Records Bureau, July, 1960.

Stern, G. G., Stein, G., and Bloom, B. *Methods in personality assessment*. Glencoe, Ill.: The Free Press, 1956.

Stern, G. G. *Preliminary manual: activities index—college characteristics index*. Syracuse: Syracuse University Research Institute, Psychol. Res. Center, 1958.

Strodtbeck, F. L. Jewish and Italian immigration and subsequent status mobility. In D. McClelland, et al., *Talent and society*. Princeton, N.J.: Van Nostrand, 1958.

Thistlethwaite, D. L. College press and student achievement. *J. of educ. Psychol.*, 1959 (a), **50** (5), 183–191.

Thistlethwaite, D. L. The college environment as a determinant of research potentiality. Unpublished paper presented at the Third Conference on the Identification of Creative Scientific Talent, Alta, Utah, June 11–14, 1959(b).

Thistlethwaite, D. L. College environments and the development of talent. *Science*, 1959(c), **130**, 71–76.

Thistlethwaite, D. L. College press and changes in study plans of talented students. *J. of educ. Psychol.*, 1960, **51** (4), 222–234.

Webster, H. *Research Manual: V.C. Attitude Inventory and V.C. Figure Preference Test*, Poughkeepsie, N.Y., Mellon Foundation, 1957.

Webster, H. Changes in attitudes during college. *J. educ. Psychol.*, 1958, **49**, 109–117.

Wedge, B. M. (Ed.) *Psychosocial problems of college men*. New Haven: Yale University Press, 1958.

17 *Carl Bereiter and Mervin B. Freedman*

Fields of Study
and the People in Them

Educators are concerned with helping individuals find fields of study that are suitable for them and also with finding people who will benefit the fields of study they enter. Apart from its contributions in the area of ability measurement, psychology has not been of much help in this difficult enterprise. We do have, however, the beginnings of a factual description of the relations between personality characteristics and intellectual activities; some of the basic problems are becoming clearer, and we can see the way in which future research might most profitably proceed.

This chapter attempts a synthesis of the findings to date, with an emphasis on the clarification of issues and the drawing of implications for future research. We first consider the question of what are the personality characteristics that distinguish people in various fields of study. This rather simple question is embedded in a more basic question: what is it about the various fields that causes them to attract the people they do? We then turn to the problem of how a person's intellectual interests develop as a part of his total personality development; and this leads into the issue that we consider to have the broadest implications for higher education, the complex interaction that takes place as people are modified by the fields they enter and in turn modify the fields themselves.

Note. This study was supported in part by a cooperative research grant from the United States Office of Education. In the portions of the study concerning Vassar College students, use has been made of unpublished research by Harold Webster and Page Westcott.

TRAITS OF ABILITY AND ATTITUDE RELATED TO ACADEMIC FIELD OF SPECIALIZATION

College student curricular groups have been found to differ psychologically with respect to three main characteristics: intelligence, liberalism of attitudes, and psychological adjustment.[1] In each instance, the groups seem to be ordered in a systematic way. It is this systematic ordering that lends support to the hope that some basic understandings may come out of research in this area.

Differences in mental abilities. The kind of difference among groups of students in various major fields that has been most definitely established is the one that, as it now stands, has the least meaning. Several large-scale studies of the general intelligence of undergraduate students (Wolfle, 1954; Educational Testing Service, 1952; Learned and Wood, 1938) have produced remarkably consistent findings: the average intelligence test scores of major groups regularly fall into an order with the physical sciences, engineering, and mathematics at the top, followed by literature and the social sciences, with the applied fields, agriculture, business, home economics, and education at the bottom. An obvious explanation for this ordering is that it reflects the varying difficulty of the subjects as they are usually taught at the undergraduate level. The order has, in fact, been found to be substantially correlated with the reputations for difficulty that these fields enjoy among undergraduate students (Fosmire, 1956; 1959). It is for this reason that the average scores, though they may be of practical importance, have little theoretical significance. Any department could raise the average score of its students by raising entrance requirements or requiring a stiff course that would eliminate the dullards. It is one thing to keep out the less competent students and another thing to attract those of superior intelligence, however, and it is this issue that seems to have some basic relevance. Do some fields have more intrinsic appeal than others to students of superior intelligence?

To answer this question we must ask, not what proportion of the students in a given field are gifted, but rather what proportion of gifted students go into a particular field. Of the 911 gifted students whom Terman studied, 38% specialized in social sciences, 29% in

[1] We leave out a fourth way in which they differ, vocational interests, because it has been impossible to make anything of these differences other than that students are interested in the fields in which they major.

natural sciences and engineering, and 26% in humanities. There was a marked sex difference, however, with the men mainly choosing majors in one of the science areas and the women choosing social sciences or humanities (Terman and Oden, 1947).

More recent and extensive data from Wolfle (1954) permit us to estimate what proportion of the students within specified intelligence ranges are apportioned to different major fields. In trying to assess the attractiveness of different fields of study it seems best to ignore students of lower intelligence because they must, of necessity, be concentrated in the easier fields. Therefore in examining Wolfle's data we consider only the college graduates who rank in the upper 60% in general intelligence. These are students who would rank in the upper two-thirds of any group of the student body, so that it might be assumed, with a little generosity, that they could do passing work in any undergraduate field. In Figure 1 we compare the top 20% of college graduates with the next 40%, that is, with those ranking in the 41st to 80th percentiles on intelligence. If certain fields do have more attraction for highly intelligent students they should account for a larger portion of the higher group than they do of the lower.

What is most immediately striking in Figure 1 is the evenness of the apportionment of top talent to the various major fields. Fields, such

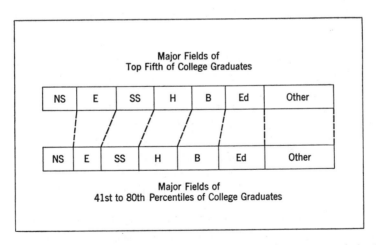

Figure 1. What fields attract the most intelligent students? Segments of the bar graphs indicate what portion of the most intelligent 20% and of the next highest 40% of college graduates majored in each of the following fields: NS—Natural Science, E—Engineering, SS—Social Science (incl. Psychology), H—Humanities and Fine Arts, B—Business and Commerce, Ed—Education. (Based on data from Wolfe [1954].)

as business and education, that look poor in terms of mean intelligence scores or overall distributions of scores come in for about the same share of the top students as do the more academic fields.

If, however, we lump engineering with natural science, as is often done, it is evident that this field does attract a large portion of the more intelligent students—over a quarter of them. Moreover, this field is seen to attract a relatively larger portion of the top group than of the lower group, whereas the reverse is true of business and education. Recent data fom Thistlethwaite (1959) on 1500 winners and near-winners of National Merit Scholarships generally corroborate these findings, although they reveal sex differences similar to those found earlier by Terman and Oden. After three years in college, 52% of these talented students were in the natural or biological sciences, 18% were in the social sciences, and 20% were in the arts and humanities. Broken down by sex, however, the respective percentages for men were 63%, 16%, and 12%, but for women they were 32%, 22%, and 35%. It therefore appears that any statement about the greater appeal of the natural sciences to students of high intelligence would need to carry the qualification, "for men."

There is, of course, nothing in data of this sort to prove that one field is intrinsically more appealing to the intellectually able than another. Any interpretation of the results shown in Figure 1 must take into account such extrinsic factors as prestige and remunerative-ness, as well as the intrinsic factor of difficulty, which is attenuated but not eliminated by our treatment of the data. The possibility of some fields being in a very general way more intellectually challenging than others is one that should not be summarily dismissed without further investigation, however.

The nature of the appeal of natural science will be considered later in a broader context. It may be pointed out here, however, that its appeal to superior intellects need not necessarily be of an exalted kind. It could, indeed, be of a purely negative sort, originating in the fact that natural science is one area in which the precocious youth can be effectively creative before he has acquired any great amount of emotional maturity and wisdom.

The data we have been discussing deal only with that ambiguous at-tribute measured by standard intelligence tests, which, it may be ob-jected, give a very limited if not prejudiced description of intelligence. These tests measure, in effect, a set of mental abilities that are so generally useful that they correlate substantially with performance in all academic fields. The question of the intrinsic intellectual appeal of different fields of study seems to imply such a global concept of intelligence that data from tests of general intelligence are relevant to this question. Their relevance to other questions, however, is much more limited.

With respect to the larger problem of the relations between academic disciplines and human personality, more specialized kinds of mental abilities need to be considered. A study by Fischelli and Welch (1947) illustrates an approach of this sort. They constructed a test of ability to recombine given ideas into different structures, for example, words into different sentences, pieces of furniture into different arrangements. They found that artists and art students did better on this test than did a control group of nonart students. The difference was largely accounted for by problems of an obvious artistic nature, however, and this finding points up a difficulty with which studies of this sort must contend: as one gets into more narrowly defined mental abilities, it becomes harder to measure them in a way that is not prejudiced in favor of special kinds of training.

Two related ways out of this difficulty are available. One is the use of factor-analytic techniques to develop tests of abilities that theoretically are basic to human intellectual organization but which are of a much more specialized type than the complex abilities measured by tests of general intelligence. Some 45 of these abilities are described by Guilford (1956). We may mention a few of these, the names being self-descriptive: eduction of perceptual relations, symbol manipulation, adaptive flexibility, and logical evaluation. Development of tests of this sort often depends on use of the second technique, which, however, can be used without any reference to factor theory. It is the development of mental tests that employ tasks of such an unusual sort that specialized training will not be directly applicable to them. A device originated by John (1957) called the "problem-solving and information apparatus" is a particularly ingenious example of this approach. It is an electronic game requiring the subject to solve problems in deductive logic by the use of information he himself asks of the machine. The device furnishes not only measures of the subject's efficiency in performing the tasks, but also measures of the kind of approach he takes. Natural science students were found to differ consistently from nonscience students in both respects.

There is every reason to suppose that studies applying tests of these sorts to students in different fields could rapidly get beyond the point of demonstrating the obvious. We should, for instance, be able to find out empirically whether the biological taxonomist has special aptitudes similar to his logical counterpart in the field of linguistics. And there are many comparisons whose outcomes it would be hard to foresee. In what fields do the various memory abilities flourish? Is adaptive flexibility more common in some fields than in others? Because, on the psychological end, these ability measures are tied to theories of the structure or functioning of higher mental processes, and because, on the philosophical end, the academic disciplines are tied to theories of logic and cognition, empirical data linking the two should be in little danger of remaining for long in the limbo where so many correlational data stay.

Differences in attitudes. During the past 30 years the attitudes of college students toward such public issues as war, Communism, labor unions, and religion have frequently been measured. With some consistency, students in certain fields of study have tended toward positions that are popularly regarded as liberal, and students in other fields have tended toward conservative positions (Boldt and Stroud, 1934; Carlson, 1934; Jones, 1938; Fay and Middleton, 1939; Bugelski and Lester, 1940; Newcomb, 1943; Hanchett, 1946; Drucker and Remmers, 1951; Stephenson, 1952; Lipsit, 1953; Noble and Noble, 1954; Pace, 1954; Stephenson, 1955; Lehmann and Ikenberry, 1959). The consistency is far from perfect, and the differences are so small that one investigator, Jacob (1957), was led to the conclusion that no differences exist.[2]

More often than not, however, students in social science come out as the most liberal of the groups in attitude studies. With much greater consistency, students in engineering and agriculture appear among the least liberal groups. Literature, arts, and natural science groups are usually found between these extremes, with the natural-science groups tending to be less liberal than the others. Students in education are difficult to pin down. Those in secondary education tend to reflect the attitudes of their prospective teaching fields, and those in elementary and physical education tend to be among the most conservative groups.

Small and irregular as these differences may be when compared to differences in intelligence, they are of considerable interest; for there is no obvious selective factor, such as the difficulty of the fields, to account for the differences. Liberalism is usually found to have a positive

---

[2] Jacob's point appears to be that no differences exist to the extent of one group being for something that another is against. When, however, all groups are against Communism, it is still possible for one group to be more strongly against it than another. Even Jacob's report on the Cornell data shows the social-science students usually differing from the others in the liberal direction (Goldsen, Rosenberg, Williams, and Suchman, 1960).

correlation with intelligence, but the ordering of groups on liberalism is clearly different from the ordering on general intelligence. Engineering is the most extreme case in point, regularly ranking among the first in intelligence and the last in liberalism.

The most conservative groups are all in applied rather than academic fields. One factor that may help to account for this conservatism is that these fields tend to draw students from lower social-class levels than do the academic fields (Wolfle, 1954). Looked at in another way, the attitudes of students in the applied fields differ from those of students in the academic majors in the same direction that the attitudes of the public as a whole differ from those of college students. It seems quite reasonable to suppose that students who seek higher education mainly for some special vocational preparation should tend to resemble people in the work-a-day world more than do academicians.

The differences among students in the liberal arts can similarly be given a common-sense explanation. Even if teachers in all liberal arts departments were equally liberal (studies show that they are not but that they are, at any rate, usually more liberal than their students) the amount of liberal teaching to which a student would be exposed could be expected to vary with the subject. A student entering a social science could expect a fairly strong dose of liberal teaching, one entering a literary field could expect somewhat less, and a student entering a natural science might expect the liberalism of his professors to show itself hardly at all. Thus it seems reasonable to suppose that the same kind of self-selection processes that are shown in Chapter 5 to result in attitude differences among students who choose different colleges may also operate intramurally to discourage conservative-minded students from entering fields where their beliefs will be directly challenged.

Whatever the reason, it does appear that some fields are relatively more attractive than others to liberal-minded people and some more attractive to conservative-minded people. If social attitudes exist in a vacuum, then these differences have little importance. But if social attitudes are but one manifestation of the way people view the world; if, as the authors of *The Authoritarian Personality* (Adorno, Frenkel-Brunswik, Levinson, and Sanford, 1950) assert, these attitudes provide an indication of how the individual's whole personality is shaped, then we have here an essential item of information in describing any field of study.

It happens that most attitude scales lend themselves to interpretation in terms of liberalism versus conservatism; but this is not the only dimension along which attitudes may differ, and it may not be the most meaningful one for studying college students. It tends to lump together those students who are serious liberals with those who have merely taken on the liberal coloring of the college community, and those who have strong conservative convictions with those who simply have no opinions on major issues and make conventional, childish responses to attitude items. We could therefore hypothesize a dimension which separates people with internalized social attitudes from those whose attitudes are largely external trappings, and which cuts vertically across the liberalism-conservatism axis.

Something like this may be accomplished by the Traditional Scale of Prince's Differential Values Inventory (Prince, 1957). This scale balances items upholding the values of hard work, individualism, strict morality, and deferred gratification against items favoring conformity to the peer group, enjoyment of life, sociability, and moral relativism. We would suggest that these items give a fair representation of the attitudes associated with Riesman's inner-directed and other-

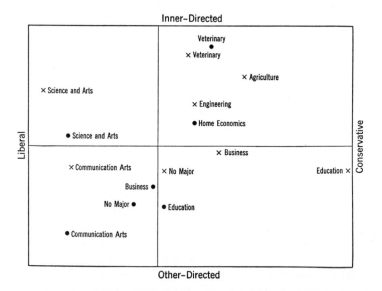

Figure 2. Location of Michigan State University curricular groups on two attitude dimensions (based on freshman test data from Lehman and Ikenberry [1959]). Crosses represent male students, dots represent female students. Liberalism is measured by Inventory of Beliefs, Inner- vs. Other-Directness by the Traditional scale of the Differential Values Inventory. The two axes represent mean scores for all freshmen (N = 2746). Distances from the two axes are in standardized units.

directed character types. In a study at Michigan State University by Lehmann and Ikenberry (1959) this scale was found to be uncorrelated with a measure of liberalism.

If our interpretation of the scales is correct, there seems to be a four-way split of major groups in attitudes, of the kind shown in Figure 2. In one corner are liberal, other-directed students, represented in the Michigan State study by those in communication arts; in another corner are liberal, inner-directed students, represented by those in the sciences and arts; then there are conservative, inner-directed students comprising those in the applied sciences; and finally the conservative, other-directed students, represented by education students and, to a lesser extent, by those in business and public service.

DIFFERENCES IN PERSONALITY RELATED TO ACADEMIC FIELD OF SPECIALIZATION

Familiar academic stereotypes assign quite different personalities to such figures as the art student, the engineering student, the business student, and the history student. Attempts to investigate these types by the use of mental tests have succeeded in establishing only that there exist what for the moment might be called differences in "adequacy of psychological adjustment."

Although the knowledge that one student group enjoys better "mental health" than another does not tell us much about what the groups are like, it does cause us to wonder what there might be about certain disciplines that would make them tend to attract students with less of what is often called mental health. As with attitudes, the differences among groups are not large and are not found with absolute consistency. The groups reporting the most fears, worries, conflicts, and the like are almost always in the literary or fine arts fields, however, and the applied majors, such as engineering, business, agriculture, education, regularly show the fewest of these psychological problems. In between, the natural-science students tend to show less disturbance than social-science students (Lough, 1947; Borg, 1952; Norman and Redlo, 1952; Clark, 1953; Hancock and Carter, 1954; Teevan, 1954; Sternberg, 1955).

This sequence—humanities, social science, natural science, applied science—suggests a sequence of increasingly concrete, down-to-earth content. Shall we hypothesize, then, that the more "neurotic" or complex and troubled people are drawn to intangibles or, conversely, that they are repelled by the mundane? There is evidence to support such a hypothesis. However, some other aspects of the sequence of major fields are worth attending to.

To a great many people, we suspect, the sequence would appear to run from the odd and effeminate on one end to the normal and acceptably masculine on the other. The man who elects to specialize in the arts or a social science thus runs counter to social expectations that may in some cases be fairly strong. By a not unreasonable generalization we can suppose that the men in the fields will represent a more deviant, nonconforming, and therefore, by definition, abnormal group. But in our study of the women at Vassar College, where the norm is quite the opposite, the humanities being the overwhelming choice and natural science majors being few, the order of the groups on tests of psychological adjustment is the same as that given above; and the differences are statistically significant.

To take another line of reasoning, it makes sense that a psychologically disturbed person should give some weight, in any major decisions he makes, to alternatives that promise some relief from his disturbance. It has been found, for instance, that students who elect courses in abnormal psychology tend to be more abnormal than those who elect other kinds of psychology courses (Wise, 1959). Fields that are concerned with human beings and their more human problems are certainly more directly relevant to an individual's own psychological problems. But this could well be a source of further disturbance rather than alleviation. It might make more "sense" for the neurotic person to seek refuge from his problems in a field where they would not be brought to his attention so often. We need not delve here into the psychological dynamics that might lead to one or the other course of action, except to note one point that bears directly on the data.

The evidence on psychological adjustment of college students is based largely on scores on the Minnesota Multiphasic Personality Inventory (MMPI) and a few other tests of the questionnaire type. Although these tests may have some power to unearth fairly deeply hidden disturbances, there is no denying that among reasonably normal subjects, like most students, those who are conscious of their difficulties will get worse scores than those who repress them. The small differences in scores between major groups could, therefore, reflect differences in degree of consciousness of disturbance rather than differences in amount of disturbance itself. If so, it would make sense that those people whose adjustment depends more on repression of symptoms should tend toward impersonal fields where their repressions are in less danger of being shaken.

In order for knowledge about people's pathologies to be relevant to what is known about their fields of study, we need to know the nature of their pathologies. The value of such information may be illustrated by comparing two Vassar College students who were interviewed by the staff of the Mellon Foundation. Both students showed relatively severe personality disturbances, and both of them were majoring in drama with the intention of becoming teachers of college drama or English, yet the relations between their personality disturbances and their choice of field of study were radically different.

Miss C. was a truly outstanding writer—of plays, poetry, novels, and short stories. In the eyes of many faculty members she was the best writer to appear in the student body at Vassar College in a good many years. But Miss C. was also quite an unstable personality, subject to periods of depression, apathy, and social withdrawal. In these periods her literary productivity suffered badly.

As one might anticipate, Miss C. was fully open to and appreciative of human feeling and thought of all kinds—in her own writing and in the works of others. The product of a broken home, the daughter of a father who had little to do with his wife and daughter except to indulge his sadism and make life difficult for them, she was keenly aware of life's tragedies and the complexities of human relationships. All in all it appeared that her writing was a kind of prop upon which her stability rested. Although interested in literary and dramatic criticism, teaching, and other aspects of the life of a college faculty member in the fields of drama and English, it is clear that her own creative writings were the focus of Miss C.'s activities as a student and her plans for her future teaching endeavors.

Miss R., on the other hand, possessed little creativity. She wrote only when required to in her courses and confined her dramatic activities to rather technical backstage enterprises. Mostly she liked to read and discuss plays and literature. In her evaluation and criticism of artistic work she tended to follow certain rather definite "party lines."

Miss R.'s chief academic interests in many ways were more in social relations than in the content of her studies. She was a member of a rather small group of students who held themselves aloof from and rather looked down upon the remainder of the student body. As a member of this group of students who were confidantes of some members of the literature and arts faculty Miss R. was privy to much of the gossip and talk that passed among the faculty. She knew the latest fads in literary criticism, was aware of what to like and dislike. In short, Miss R. was already rather an apprentice teacher.

Miss R. came from a home in which there was much strife between the parents, although they had not separated. Her relationship with her father was poor. It appeared that he had little use for women, at least for women who were so bold as to be interested in college and even postgraduate education. Her relationship with her mother contained some elements of essential warmth, but Miss R. really could not respect her submissive mother who had but a high school education and who had almost no intellectual or esthetic interests.

Miss R. seemed to be using various faculty members to establish more satisfactory relationships with adults than had characterized her experiences in her own family. Women faculty members became figures whom she could admire and provided models of behavior for her to emulate, unlike the situation with her mother. And male faculty who liked her were in a sense fathers who could appreciate and value intellectual activity in a woman. These substitute parental relationships and the identity of apprentice and future college teacher were the plaster that held Miss R. together. Her years in high school and her freshman and sophomore years of college as well had been ones of great strain and turmoil; but once she had become a member of what was for her a most congenial community and when she discovered a suitable role, that of student and teacher of literature, almost miraculously a great sense of order and stability was restored to her life.

Whether Miss R. or Miss C. will make the better English teacher appears to be an unanswerable question. The differences between them are so extreme as to defy such a simple evaluation. In terms of mastery of subject matter, Miss R. will probably appear sounder. Her need to fit securely into the role of English teacher will surely impel her to use her quite adequate intellectual resources in meeting all the scholarly requirements of that role. Miss C.'s scholarship, on the other hand, is more likely to be spotty, governed more by her highly individualized tastes than by traditional requirements. But whereas Miss C. will bring deep emotional sensitivity to her functions as scholar, critic, and teacher, Miss R. will bring only the language of feeling. Miss C. may be a stimulating and at times brilliant teacher, but in periods of depression and inner turmoil her teaching may also be confused or indifferent. Miss R.'s teaching, on the other hand, should be well organized, thorough, consistently up to standard, and only the latterday Miss C. in her classes may feel that anything is missing.

If one may generalize by casting these women into types, it is clear that the Miss C.'s and the Miss R.'s will tend to generate disciplines that, though they share the title English literature, are actually quite different and perhaps not even very compatible. A study of the personalities of people in a field like English that could distinguish not only degrees of psychological disturbance but also kinds of disturbance would be able to show whether such types do exist and would make it possible to examine how these types function and interact within the field.

Unfortunately the measuring instruments that have been used in past studies do not appear to be adequate for this purpose. Although the MMPI has scales for nine different kinds of pathological tendencies, the obtained results have not provided distinctions such as those made here between Miss C. and Miss R. Groups of students that are high on one scale tend to be high on all of them. An exception is the Masculinity-Femininity scale, essentially an interest test, which typically assigns high femininity scores to students in literature and the arts. The only other distinction that may have some validity is a tendency for students in psychology and sociology in the reported studies to have relatively high scores on the Psychopathic Deviate scale, a scale that measures hostility, rebellious attitudes toward authority, and disregard for convention.

The attitude and personality studies cited have compared groups on one measure at a time, leaving to speculation the relation of one difference to another. There is enough correlation among attitude and personality measures, however, so that worthwhile inferences may often be drawn by studying several measures and their interrelationships at the same time. A study of this kind carried out by the Mellon Foundation (Bereiter and Freedman, 1960) yielded results that suggest new bases for describing the differences among curricular groups.

In this study, the student groups in the various major fields were found to differ significantly on all seven of the Vassar Attitude-Inventory scales. It had previously been found that most of the variation among individuals on these scales could be accounted for by three composite measures, but it was discovered upon further analysis that the curriculum groups differed significantly on only two of these composites. It was therefore possible, by algebraic transformation of the scores, to isolate two factors that accounted for almost all the group differences and a third factor on which the groups were virtually indistinguishable.

The locations of various curricular groups with respect to the first two factors are shown in Figure 3. The vertical axis represents a factor we have identified as *unconventionality*. This is a factor that cuts across the distinction between attitudes and personality traits, for it involves not only unconventional (liberal) attitudes but also unconventionality in the conduct and style of one's life. Although there are discrepancies that may be attributed to the special characteristics of particular departments at Vassar, the tendency is clearly for students in literary fields to score higher on this factor than students in natural science and applied fields. The scores are consistent with prevalent Vassar stereotypes, which describe the high-scoring groups as more "off-beat" and "intellectual," the low-scoring groups as more conventional and conformist.

The horizontal axis represents a factor we have identified as *social confidence*. On this factor the overall distinction is between social-science groups, which tend toward the confident end of the scale and the natural-science and literary fields, which tend toward the less

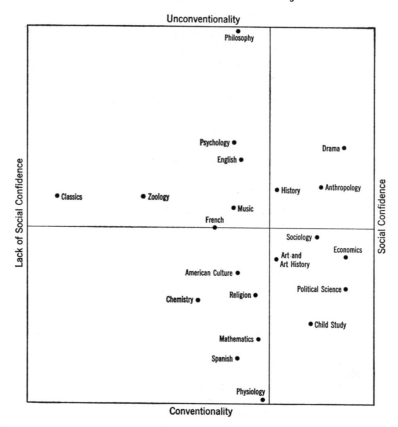

Figure 3. Location of Vassar College major groups on two attitude-personality dimensions. Based on freshman scores of classes of 1957, 1958, and 1959 (N = 739). The two axes represent grand means. Distances from the axes are in standardized units. A third dimension, *emotional stability*, on which the groups did not differ, is perpendicular to the two axes shown.

confident end. Again with reference to local stereotypes, the factor appears to distinguish groups reputed to be sociable and out-going from groups that have the reputation of being more "bookish" and socially withdrawn.

Now the third factor, on which the groups did not differ, could nevertheless be identified on the basis of the tests that made it up, and it appears to represent *emotional stability*, that is, control of impulses combined with a freedom from overt conflicts and worries. It was surprising to find that the factor that comes closest to representing what is popularly meant by mental health should be the factor on which the curricular groups do not differ. This seems to disagree with the findings of other studies reported in this section, but it is supported by the only other factor analytic study carried out in this area, the one by Sternberg (1955). Using men students at one of the New York municipal colleges, a group clearly quite different from students at Vassar, Sternberg analyzed measures of interests and the diagnostic scales of the MMPI. The factor that accounted for most of the individual differences on the MMPI turned out to be a factor on which the groups differed hardly at all. Furthermore, by applying our transformation techniques to Sternberg's other factors, some of which still suggested a substantial relation between college major and psychological adjustment, new factors were obtained that transferred almost all the remaining variance of the MMPI scales to a factor on which the groups did not differ.

What, then, is one to make of earlier studies that show curricular groups differing in mental health, and of the substantial body of findings relating vocational interests to psychological adjustment (Patterson, 1957)? It is necessary to realize that all three of the factors we have identified can be construed as facets of mental health. Unconventional people are likely to give unconventional responses to diagnostic test items and thus obtain scores indicating the presence of psychopathology. Similarly, socially withdrawn students are likely to give test responses that are scored as symptoms of psychological disturbance. Rather than consider these dimensions as indices of *adequacy* of psychological adjustment, however, it seems to us more reasonable to consider them as indices of *kind* of psychological adjustment. Thus among unconventional people one could expect to find some for whom unconventionality represented a healthy state of affairs and some for whom it was unhealthy, and similarly for conventional people, people who are socially outgoing, and people who are socially withdrawn.

Applied to differences among curricular groups, our results show curricular groups to differ in kind of psychological adjustment but not in adequacy. Earlier studies, which did not distinguish between these components, were obligated to interpret all differences in terms of adequacy of psychological adjustment, thus leading to what now appear to be misleading conclusions.

Of course, the two factors of unconventionality and social confidence do not begin to exhaust the possible personality differences that may distinguish curricular groups. Several studies have attempted, by means of projective tests and interviews, to get at more subtle differences.

Very suggestive results were obtained in a small scale study by

Teevan (1954) using the Blacky Pictures.[3] To discuss the findings in detail would require a prohibitively long digression into psycho analytic theory. Briefly, the study agreed with others in finding less evidence of psychological disturbance among students in the natural sciences than among those in social science and the humanities, but the latter groups showed different kinds of disturbances. The humanities majors showed a kind of disturbance that was called oral-erotic, a tendency to seek sensual gratification in oral, including verbal, activities. The social-science groups showed a constellation of aggressive and sadistic tendencies that, according to psychoanalytic theory, derive from disturbed relations with the mother. The finding about the humanities fits in with much psychoanalytic thinking about the nature of literary and artistic activity, such as, for instance, the theory of Bergler (1954). Corroboration of the finding about the social sciences has been afforded in studies by Roe (1953) and Nachmann (1957), in which social scientists reported more intense and disturbing child-hood relations with their mothers than were reported by other scientists.

Roe's intensive studies of scientists revealed other personality differences that may be sensibly related to people's fields of specialization. In responding to projective test stimuli, social scientists were more productive and showed less intellectual restraint than did natural scientists. Segal (1953) noted a similar difference between students of creative writing and students of accounting. Interesting differences were also found among subclassifications of the sciences. We cannot attempt to mention all of them, many of which invite speculation as to how they might be connected with differences among scientific disciplines. By way of illustration, however, we quote Roe's summary of the differences among different faculties in the biological sciences:

All biologists are more like other biologists than they are like physicists or social scientists. The anatomists are generally the least intellectually controlled; the physiologists seem to show more free anxiety and more concern with immediate personal problems than do the others. The botanists appear to be a generally rather well-adjusted group, and rather placid, with no particular deviant tendencies. The geneticists are a more colorful group than the others, with somewhat more emotional dominance, but this is of a sort different from that shown by the anatomists (Roe, 1956).

What is most impressive in Roe's findings, however, is the ubiquity of the contrast between a concern with people and a concern with

[3] In the Blacky Test (Blum, 1949) subjects are asked to tell stories based on pictures of dogs in various situations, the rationale for the test being that people will be less guarded and thus more revealing in their imaginative productions concerning infrahuman creatures than they would be if people were involved.

things. It appears in the scientists' recollections of childhood and adolescence and in their adult social lives. It also appears in their Rorschach test responses. The social scientists report many more human figures than do the natural scientists, who on the other hand report more abstract patterns. Evidence of a lack of close inter-personal relationships in the lives of natural scientists was also given in a projective test study by Clifford (1958); and evidence for the lesser sociability in childhood of natural scientists is provided in Terman's longitudinal data (Terman, 1954). There seems to be here a very clear-cut example of a difference in choice of fields of study reflecting a more basic and pervasive difference in way of life.

Personality measurement at the present time is at a stage of develop-ment where it is considerably easier to develop reliable measuring devices than it is to find out what they measure. As a result we have been able to speak confidently about the existence of personality dif-ferences between curricular groups but have had to remain vague about the nature of these differences.

The personality differences that have been noted in this chapter can all be grouped into two categories; which is not to say that there really are only two differences, but only that there is insufficient basis for further subdivision of categories. On the one hand are the differences related to signs of psychological disturbance, unconventionality, and awareness of psychological problems. These characteristics, which are hard to tell apart, all seem to have to do with the person's inner life —with his thoughts, emotions, and impulses and how he deals with them. The fact that choice of field of study is related to individual differences in this area thus indicates what we would of course expect, that a person's intellectual pursuits are integrated in some way with other aspects of his inner life.

The other category of relevant individual differences includes such things as differences in sociability, confidence in social situations, and interest in people. It clearly centers around the person's social life. Since choice of field of study is also related to individual differences in this area, we have a basis for supposing that the sort of intellectual activities a person pursues implies something about how he relates to other people, or vice-versa. The connection may be a very superficial one: some pursuits involve more contact with people than others, so that a person's choice of field may be influenced by how much he wants or doesn't want contact with other people. Or the connection may be more profound. It may be that there are basic ways of relating to things outside oneself that apply to one's relations to people as well as to impersonal objects and abstractions.

CHOICE OF MAJOR FIELD IN THE CONTEXT OF HUMAN DEVELOPMENT

The research we have been discussing is based on an essentially static view of human affairs. It is concerned with the way things are at a particular point in time. Carried to completion, this kind of research would provide us with detailed descriptions of various groups of people as they were at certain times and of the fields of study with which they were associated and, hopefully, one would be able to educe certain relationships between the two kinds of descriptions.

This static approach has a very desirable simplicity of conceptualization and technique, but, of course, it fails to contend with the state of flux that characterizes real situations. In order fully to understand observed relationships we shall probably have to consider people and fields of study as they develop over time.

Theorists concerned with vocations have found it useful to regard vocational choice as a process extending over a number of years rather than as a single act (Ginzberg, Ginsburg, Axelrad, and Herma, 1951; Super, 1953), and this approach is clearly applicable to choice of academic field of study. Two possibilities are suggested by this approach. One is that certain intellectual interests and the personality traits that are correlated with them can be traced to common sources. The other is that people who enter certain fields may not only have distinctive characteristics but also may have arrived at their choice of field by distinctive routes.

The studies of Roe have gone farthest in examining these possibilities. We alluded earlier to Roe's finding that social scientists, in contrast to natural scientists, reported intense and disturbing family relationships in childhood. This finding has led Roe to hypothesize that the same parent-child relationships that were the source of later personality disturbances were the source of a concern with human relations that led the individuals into careers in the social sciences (Roe, 1953). For the natural scientists, early family life seems to have been characterized by detached, unemotional, and vague relationships, so that the future natural scientists, Roe supposed, were led on the one hand to abandon efforts at intimate human involvement and on the other hand to turn their attention to the more approachable and comprehensible world of impersonal things.

Roe's natural and social scientists also had rather different educational histories. The natural scientists developed early interests in their fields and seem to have followed fairly straight courses toward their ultimate positions; the social scientists seem to have been lacking in any particular early commitment, to have gone off in various directions in college, often pursuing literary studies, finally coming to the social sciences as graduate students after having become disenchanted in some way or other with the fields in which they had previously been studying.

One cannot make too much out of this one finding, for there are many incidental factors, such as the stricter academic requirements for graduate study in natural science and the relative newness of the social sciences, that might account for it. But it does suggest an interesting way of elaborating studies of the differences between students in different curricula. As was true for Miss C. and Miss R., among the students majoring in a field like English we might be able to sort out groups who consciously viewed the business of majoring in this field in different ways. For some (for many girls, we suspect) it might be viewed as a temporal activity, something they do while they are in college. They stay in a certain dormitory, join certain clubs, and major in a certain subject—all of these chosen, perhaps, with some seriousness and with some eye to future benefits, but nevertheless as affairs of the moment. For others it might be a clear and orderly step in the direction of some future goal, even if the goal itself is something ambiguous like "being a good wife." In the case of Miss R. the goal was quite clear, that of a teacher of English in college. For others, like the social scientists Roe studied, it might be a kind of tree they sit in while they are looking around trying to get their bearings. And for some it reflects a deep involvement with literature and the content of the field. This was the situation with Miss C.

The differences here are more than just differences in attitude toward English as a field of study. They are differences in the role that studying English plays in the course of development of different individuals. We might reasonably expect that these subdivisions of English students would differ from each other psychologically, just as English students in the aggregate differ from students in other fields. Moreover, we might expect that goal-directed students in English would be something like goal-directed students in other fields, and that these similarities might sometimes cancel out the differences related to difference in field of specialization. The analysis of differences would therefore become a good deal more complex, but it might yield more valuable information.

A more objective facet of the developmental problem we are considering is whether the individual continues in the major field he first selects or whether he changes to another field. Only the crudest sort of comparisons of changers and nonchangers have been made, showing that changers do about as well academically as nonchangers (Fullmer, 1956) and that students change mainly because of poor performance or loss of interest in the original field (Brass, 1956). Much more could be done in this area, if account were taken of what fields students changed from and what fields they changed to.

Changes in personality may well produce changes in interests, but it is not to be expected that personality changes, even very pronounced ones, will necessarily lead to changes in field of study. People's paths through life are often not that reversible. One of the most striking instances of personality change observed by the Mellon Foundation staff illustrates this point clearly.

Miss B. entered college with the aim of majoring in chemistry and becoming a research worker in the field. She had been an outstanding student in high school, particularly in the physical sciences. The impression she made upon the research staff during her freshman and sophomore years was that of an extremely isolated person. An only child whose father had died early in her life she had been raised by her mother. Since her mother had had to work, Miss B. had from early childhood on been cared for by a series of housekeepers and baby-sitters. Although her relationship with her mother was free of overt strain or discord, no real intimacy between them seemed ever to have existed. Nor had Miss B. ever had any close friends. It is easy to see this student as fitting Roe's picture of the natural scientist—someone whose interest in impersonal things was fostered by the lack of satisfying human relationships.

Miss B. seemed to fit very well the classic picture of the schizoid personality, who glides through life without establishing any real emotional ties with other people but who does not manifest any noteworthy overt personality difficulty. It seemed to the research staff that her future was easy to predict. She would do well in her studies both undergraduate and graduate and would then go on to a research job in a laboratory. At no time, as a student or later, was she likely to establish a close relationship with anyone. The images came readily: a lonely figure working quietly and efficiently in a laboratory all day, then returning to her apartment for a cheerless dinner and a lonely evening—this going on uninterruptedly for some 40 years.

But things did not develop at all this way. Miss B. was assigned as a freshman to a roommate situation involving two other students. These two girls, being intelligent, sensitive, and warm-hearted, pretty much took it upon themselves to draw Miss B. "out of her shell;" and although it took some doing, they were very successful. By the end of her junior year, she was truly a changed person. There was a vivacity in her demeanor that had been almost totally absent in her freshman year, and she displayed social ease and poise that several years earlier one would never have expected her to possess. Both from her appearance and her interview reports it was obvious that her relationships with other girls had undergone profound changes in her college years. By graduation she was able to place a trust in other girls and in relationships with them in a way that had not been possible to her earlier. It is interesting to note, however, that as of the time of graduation her social isolation from men had not been altered. She had not had any dates during her college years.

Until her senior year Miss B. had stood rather firmly by her original vocational goal of research activities in a laboratory. In her senior year, however, she began to wonder whether she might not be happier and more productive if she went into teaching at the high school level. Her reasons for this change were expressed as follows. "Perhaps I'd like it better, if I were working more with people than I would be in a research lab." At the time of graduation she had not decided between these alternative plans.

Even if this student's original interest in physical science grew out of a lack of close interpersonal relationships, her later social development did not lead her away from physical science but rather toward a different role within this field. Much of the variety that one finds among the people within any field may well be due to this somewhat bewildering but highly encouraging fact that people go on developing after the die has seemingly been cast.

If people change in spite of their choice of field of study, they should also change because of it. That, after all, is what we expect of education. If intellectual disciplines have any of the potency they are supposed to have, we should expect them to influence how people develop. The individual who enters a field ought to change in some predictable direction—perhaps becoming more like the other people in the field, or perhaps, as may have been the case with Miss B., undergoing some more complex counterchange, as he reacts to the content of the field and to the other people in it.

Data on college students, among whom this sort of change ought to be most apparent, do not give a clear picture at all. This may in part reflect the technical difficulties in comparing changes in test scores (see Chapter 24, pp. 811–816). Jacob (1957) has summarized the research on attitude change, finding little evidence of differences in change among curricular groups. A few studies have shown a tendency for social science students to show greater gains in liberalism than other students (Boldt and Stroud, 1934; Bugelski and Lester, 1940; but compare Jones, 1938); however, this may indicate only a greater original disposition to accept liberal teachings, as we have suggested earlier.

Where mental abilities are concerned, the data are few, but a little clearer. Students who study mathematics seem to improve more than other students on measures of quantitative intelligence, and literature students improve more than others on verbal measures. There is evidence that social-science students, on the whole, do not gain as much as students in the arts and natural sciences (Shuey, 1948; Rogers,

1930; Louise, 1947; Learned and Wood, 1938). Students generally improve in verbal abilities regardless of what they study, but those who do not study mathematics in college sometimes decline in quantitative abilities (Rogers, 1930; Learned and Wood, 1938; Louise, 1947). Undoubtedly these findings reflect in part differences in training in specific skills, but they should not be brushed off as indicating no more than that. Quantitative intelligence scales are not mere measures of technical skills, any more than verbal comprehension tests are. To a large extent these scales measure ability to reason abstractly, so that the fact that large groups of students come out of college less capable in this respect than when they went in tells us something of psychological importance as well as giving us grounds for questioning the ideas of some people about what constitutes a liberal education.

Vassar College curricular groups, as we reported in the preceding section, differed significantly on all seven of the Vassar Attitude-Inventory scales. When changes from freshman to senior year were compared, however, the groups differed significantly in change on only one scale, the repression and suppression scale (see Chapter 24, p. 829). Scores for students as a whole show a tendency to increase a small amount on this scale over the four years, indicating evidently a slight tendency to be more guarded and evasive in answering test questions. History, english, and drama students have comparatively low freshman scores on the scale, but between freshman and senior year history students' scores increase. English students remain about the same, and drama students tend to diminish in evasiveness. Students in child study and in art and art history have comparatively high freshman scores, but the child study students score still higher as seniors, while the art and art history students show little change.

These differences can be interpreted in the light of the content of the fields, though such interpretations must be regarded as very tenuous without clearer evidence. It would appear that the study of English and drama tends to keep personal emotional problems in the foreground, whereas the study of history or art and art history tends to deflect attention to more impersonal matters. Child study, perhaps, furnishes already rather repressed students with more accurate cues as to what good "adjustment" should look like. It may well be, however, that child study and the other fields in which repression and supression scores increase do help the students who pursue them to resolve some of the problems they brought to college with them.

Considering the amount of change which the Attitude Inventory scales do reveal in Vassar students as a whole, as reported in Chapter 24, the present findings can only be taken to show precious little effect from major field of study. In contrast, the differences in change reported in Chapter 24 among National Merit Scholars in different fields indicate a substantial effect. One explanation for the discrepancy may be that in a relatively small, tightly-knit college like Vassar the effect of the total college experience greatly outweighs the influence of particular subjects or departments; whereas in larger institutions, where there may be considerable social and even geographical distance between departments, the school has less overall influence and the effect of particular departments and student subcultures is greater.

In considering individual development as it relates to fields of study we tend for the sake of simplicity to regard the fields themselves as "givens," as fixed entities to which the individual adapts. Actually fields develop too; and in many fields the rate of development is not slow compared to the rate of development of individuals, so that we have a problem there also, when an individual tries to adjust to a field that is not the same by the time he has finished adjusting. More to the point, however, is the fact that an individual does not adjust to a field per se but to the field as he perceives it and, most likely, only to selected portions of that. "Adjustment," in fact, is not a very good term in this context. The person who sets out to become a bricklayer may indeed have to adjust to the clearly defined role of the bricklayer, but the student who sets out to study Spanish literature or the scientist who tries to carve out a career for himself in the study of public opinion has much greater freedom. Within certain fairly wide limits he can define the field and the role he is to take in it to suit himself.

This point is obvious enough when we talk about individuals, but when we talk about groups of people, it is difficult to formulate the idea in a way that is not hopelessly confused. The terms "constraint" and "variety," which Riesman applied to a number of aspects of education (Riesman, 1956), can be used with a slightly different meaning to simplify our formulation here. Forces that tend to keep a field the way it is or to keep it developing in the way it is going, even at an accelerating rate, may be called constraining forces. Forces that tend to alter the nature or direction of development of a field we may call forces of variety.

The tendency of fields to attract people similar to those already in them will ordinarily be a constraining force, although in a changing society it may be a force for change. For instance, in a rapidly changing field like psychology it might be argued that the tendency of the field to go on attracting the same kinds of people produces novelty as much as it impedes change. Each new generation of "anachronistic" psychologists encounters a new discipline with which to be out of step, and their inclinations are as likely to lead them to form new movements as they are to lead them to sustain older ones. Thus in the Twenties the student who still saw psychology as a cultural science could resist the mechanistic tendencies of behaviorism by aligning himself with the newer *Gestalt* school rather than by reverting to Jamesian speculation; and the young psychologist of today who is still a pre-World War II experimentalist at heart and who has no taste for mathematical models may take up the study of teaching machines instead of sticking to his memory drums. Variety also arises from the tendency of fields to attract different kinds of people for different reasons and also from the fact that people often change in different ways in response to the same general situations. Opposed to these forces is a constraining force that is probably much stronger in some fields than in others, the tendency of a field to mold people into a likeness, to fit people out with a standard set of attitudes and styles of behavior.

Just as the selective and formative power that a field has over individuals is a major constraining force, so may we expect the powers of selection and redefinition that individuals have over the content of a field of study to be a major source of variety. Taking these factors into account, it ought to be possible to examine a field and arrive at some realistic estimate of its potentialities for change as against the likelihood that it will go on as it is. We should need to know what kinds of people it attracts as students and professionals and what sorts of changes it produces in them. We should want to know how susceptible its content is to redefinition, how resistant it is to the efforts of individuals to reformulate it in their private ways.

In the end this kind of information ought to have great value for people who have the wisdom to use it properly. One of the marks of professionalism is a concern over the future of one's field. Wisely exercised, this concern can lead to some stability and linearity of progress but also to variety and changes of direction, so that the future will not be merely an extrapolation from the past.

The relative weight given to these two objectives will, of course, vary from field to field and from time to time, but it appears to us that at the present time the forces for constraint are stronger than they ought to be. There is a clamor in most fields for greater selectivity in admitting students as well as staff. This emphasis is likely to result in making less room for the person who is deviant either in personal characteristics or in educational background.

An interesting example of the conflict that may exist between constraint and variety in various fields was furnished by one of the students interviewed by the Mellon Foundation research staff. Miss K. was majoring in one of the natural sciences; and as we have indicated earlier in this chapter, students in the natural sciences at Vassar College tend to be on the average somewhat more conventional than their fellow students.

Miss K. was, however, quite an exception. In originality of thought and outlook she resembled philosophy and English majors much more than she resembled her fellow students in the natural sciences. She was in fact very interested in philosophy, drama, and literature and took courses and read widely in these fields. Essentially she was less concerned with the more routine matters of knowledge and procedures in her field than she was with their wider theoretical and philosophical import. It might be said that her scientific interests were somewhat after the fashion of the theoretical physicists and mathematicians of recent years.

Now it happens that the faculty in the natural science departments who knew Miss K. did not have a high opinion of her as a student despite their ready acknowledgement of her considerable breadth of knowledge and interest. She was for them too disorganized, often too abstract, too unconcerned with the routines of basic textbook knowledge and laboratory procedures. The situation was very different in the case of her other teachers in philosophy, drama, and literature. They had the highest regard for her. These differences in evaluation of Miss K. emerged clearly in the ratings of the students in the Mellon Foundation's research sample that were made by the faculty. The ratings given Miss K. by the natural science faculty on such characteristics as creativity and originality, the extent to which the student being rated approaches the faculty member's notion of the ideal Vassar student, and general intellectual capacity were appreciably lower than the ratings made by faculty members in the arts and humanities.

Naturally the relatively low esteem in which Miss K. was held by her teachers in the natural sciences was not lost upon her. Her grades in her science courses were lower than those in her arts and humanities courses, and her relations with the science faculty were less cordial than those involving other faculty. Nevertheless she was unwilling to change her major. She was convinced that her views of what her chosen field should be like were right, even though they did not coincide with those of her teachers. And she was convinced that she would eventually make valuable contributions in her field. So Miss K. was intent upon continuing her studies after graduation, confident that in graduate school she would meet colleagues among students and faculty who shared her thoughts as to what her chosen discipline ought to be.

The somewhat negative attitude toward Miss K. on the part of her science teachers is understandable enough. To some extent she lacked the orderliness of approach, perhaps the discipline of thinking out of which much of science is fashioned. But it does appear that perhaps she possessed compensatory qualities that her teachers may have overlooked. She perhaps possessed a freshness of approach that can have a salutary effect on her field. Her qualities of mind and thought that are more characteristic of majors in the humanities than they are of students in the natural sciences may be the very avenues for discovery of new ways of looking at things in her field. At the very least, it would appear that she ought to have had a chance to try, that is, the opportunity to demonstrate at least to herself that she could or could not be a successful natural scientist. Not that attempts were made to bar her from continuing as a science major. Her grades were reasonably good. But all in all her experiences were such as to make a natural science major of her temperament and outlook think twice about remaining in the field.

In such fashion various disciplines tend to recruit adherents in their own image, thus cutting down upon potential sources of variety. We cannot with any authority speak for other fields, but in the newer social sciences there seems to be a premature need to define roles, to specify content, to establish standards—all of which serves to introduce an artificial hardness into the social scientists' materials, forcing him to chip away at clay, as if it were marble.

This same kind of desiccation seems also to have invaded a number of classrooms, particularly in applied fields where there is a desire to manufacture an intellectual discipline out of an amorphous body of techniques. Students themselves can be a strong force for narrowness, in their insistence on the removal of ambiguities and on intellectual respectability. Here the selection of students can be an important factor. We know that certain kinds of students have a much greater tolerance for ambiguity and are much more open to stimulation by complex and amorphous ideas than others.

Selection procedures, formal and informal, should not aim merely at attaining some single ideal of "quality." They ought to aim at acquiring a group of students among whom an atmosphere conducive to progress and intellectual adventure will prevail. In this context the "average" becomes a very meaningful concept. Small differences in mean scores can mean a great deal in terms of the proportion of students having certain characteristics and thus, by implication, in terms of the overall atmosphere of the group. By way of illustration, we can look at scores on two measures which previous research (Brown, 1959, and Chapter 16) had shown to be consistently related to faculty nominations of ideal students at Vassar College—verbal intelligence and social maturity (the reverse of authoritarianism). Students high on both scales presumably have superior capacity to learn and also superior readiness to accept new ideas and viewpoints. Approximately 30% of all Vassar students were above their class averages on both scales and 30% were below average on both. But in one large major group almost half the students were in the preferred category and only about 15% were in the nonpreferred category. In another large field the opposite was true. Only 15% were above average on both measures, and half were below average on both. One could expect considerable differences in the general level of class discussions and the climate of intellectual interaction in these two groups. Quite likely much greater differences would be found in schools having more heterogeneous student bodies.

A better understanding of the ways different personality traits relate to different kinds of intellectual pursuits would not only provide a sounder basis for selection of students but also for counseling the individual student in his choice of a field of study. Guiding the student toward a field that best fits his present characteristics tends to preserve the status quo both in the individual and in the field he enters. Ideally the student ought to pursue the curriculum that would produce in him the most beneficial growth, even if it meant taking a course in which he did badly and had a very trying time. But in the face of academic and social pressures to get good grades, the demands of employers that people study whatever it is they plan to work at, and the general "materialistic" view of education as preparation rather than as development, it is understandable that students, with the blessing of their counselors, play it safe.

Because students who "play it safe" in their educational decisions are likely to pass through college with fewer conspicuous troubles than others, the impression may grow among educators that this business of helping each student to find his most comfortable niche works pretty well. A closer look at students who by necessity or inclination do "play it safe," however, reveals that such a course can sometimes be educationally tragic.

Consider the case of Miss D. who majored in a natural science at Vassar College. She entered college with a natural science major in mind and with some practical notions for work after college, for example, working in a laboratory. She had little interest in literature and the humanities at the time of college entrance. She had not fared well in these courses in high school and had regarded them pretty much as requirements to be got out of the way.

It developed, however, that Miss D.'s freshman English course captured her fancy. Although her work in this course was just mediocre, her grade for the course being a C, she decided to take another course in English as a sophomore. She continued her natural science major, but the notion had entered her mind that perhaps majoring in English and literature might really be more interesting.

Miss D.'s experiences in her sophomore English class soon dispelled her thoughts about majoring in English, however. She found the work extremely difficult. The nuances of feeling contained in a poem or the motivations of characters described in a novel often escaped her, and she wrote slowly and with little style. Her papers hardly measured up to the standards of performance desired by her English teacher, and the comments on her papers reflected this. After she had turned in and had got back several papers with her teacher's comments, she began to dread new assignments. Moreover, she felt quite inferior to most of her fellow students in the class. They seemed to grasp things much more readily, and often their remarks in discussions reflected an awareness and insight that she thought she could hardly hope to possess.

Meanwhile Miss D.'s experience in her natural science courses was quite different. She did well in these courses with a minimum of effort. She felt a sense of control over the subject matter that eluded her in English. So at the end of her sophomore year she decided definitely to continue as a natural science major, and she took no additional literature courses. This decision was not made without some regrets. In her senior year she said: "I wish I could have continued in English. Something in me wanted to. Most of all I wish I could have taken a course in creative writing. But I know I wouldn't have been any good at it."

Superficially, Miss D.'s is the story of someone making a realistic adjustment to the facts of life. But from the point of view of the oft-repeated claim that college is a place where one's intellectual potentialities may find their fullest realization, her case is an academic atrocity story, one that is probably repeated many times in each collegiate generation. It must be noted that the emphasis in academic circles in recent years on excellence of performance, on specialization, and on early choice of major field can only tend to increase the incidence of such cases.

Miss D.'s experience is especially poignant because she had the desire for greater educational growth and was prevented by external forces from realizing it. The more typical case is that in which the principal resistance to educational growth comes from within the student himself—the case of the student who goes to college to attain certain practical ends and wants no one to meddle with his interests and values.

The underlying problem in this case, however, is the same as that with Miss D.: to what extent should higher education concentrate on strengthening whatever is strongest in the student (we might call this the process of "enhancement") and to what extent should it concentrate on developing those aspects of the student's personality that are underdeveloped (this could be called the process of "activation"). Both of these processes are legitimate aims of education. Both of them pertain to important aspects of personality development. But by failing to distinguish between them, educators have tended to emphasize almost exclusively the enhancement function of education and to leave the activation of students' latent potentialities almost entirely to chance.

We have been considering the relations between personality and intellectual pursuits only as they concern people's work in various fields. In the larger cultural arena where one field impinges on another and the work of various fields affects society as a whole, these relations are, if anything, more pertinent. Consider the much-discussed problem of the responsibility of the natural scientist for the uses to which his discoveries are put. Here it is often a matter of people in the humanities bringing their values to bear on physical scientists. It is of importance to note that humanists may be different kinds of people from physical scientists and may have rather fundamentally different values, but the issue is more complicated than that. As various findings reported in this chapter suggest, the typical physical scientist may have a way of relating to other people that is different from the ways of nonscientists, and moreover, this way of relating to people may be intimately tied up with his functioning as a scientist. It may not be merely his work that is specialized; he may be a specialized personality as well. Whether this is good or bad and whether or not something can or should be done about it, it is important to try to understand it.

CONCLUSION: SOME POSSIBLE NEXT STEPS

A good deal more research in these matters is needed, some of which need not be aimed at any particular theoretical solutions but merely at digging out information we can be fairly sure is there. Anyone interested in carrying out a comparative study of people in different fields of study will have no difficulty finding worthwhile psychological measures to apply. It does appear that perhaps certain tests have provided about all the information they can supply, namely, general intelligence tests, tests of liberalism of opinions, and tests of adequacy of psychological adjustment. More specialized tests of mental abilities, attitudes, and personality characteristics are available, and almost none of them have been used in this kind of study. In addition, all sorts of psychologically relevant biographical data could profitably be studied.

Future studies will do well not only to use a greater variety of measuring instruments but also to extract more information from the scores obtained. There has been a tendency for workers in this field to underanalyze their data. They have usually been content with comparing mean scores for various groups, but Wolfle's (1954) treatment of intelligence test data, discussed earlier in this chapter, demonstrates what can be gained by examining scores for upper and lower quartiles of students as well. Comparisons of attitude or personality test scores are often inconclusive because it is not known to what extent the observed differences may be due to differences in intelligence and socioeconomic status. Analysis of covariance techniques, which could control these factors statistically, have rarely been used.

Multivariate techniques, which are ideally suited to studies in this area, are still used by only a few researchers. Even a simple cross-tabulation of results would probably bring to light many interesting facets of the data. One of the earliest studies (Harris, 1934) is one of the few that have employed this valuable device. Here is an illustrative finding (because of the small number of subjects involved in this comparison it cannot be taken as anything more than illustrative): when subjects were classified according to major field, engineering and business majors scored lowest on esthetic interest; when subjects were classified according to religion, Jews scored highest. But cross-tabulation showed that Jews who were engineering students scored about as high as other Jews on esthetic interest, while Jews who were business majors scored about as low as other business majors. Other kinds of two-way classifications, such as major field and level of intelligence or major field and sex, are of such general interest that it would be well to employ them routinely.

In addition to survey studies, more complex studies need to be carried out. As we have already indicated, there is need for longitudinal studies to identify early determinants of choice of field, for studies measuring personality changes during college as a function of curriculum, and for studies of people who switch from one field to another. Some other likely possibilities are studies of people who have similar personality profiles but are in different fields, and conversely, people in the same field who have different personality profiles.

These studies are all of a strictly empirical sort. They should produce information of considerable intrinsic interest, but they will become theoretically relevant only in the light of later developments. To the person who is seriously interested in the theoretical possibilities of research in this area, however, a more direct approach is available. It would involve going above existing categorizations of fields of study and sorting out groups of individuals who seem, on quite abstract bases, to be functioning in similar ways intellectually—who seem to be using formally similar kinds of information and to be asking questions and carrying out operations to answer them that are also formally similar. When the groups are thus designated on a purely intellectual basis, abstracted from all the practical, material, and institutional distinctions that exist among fields, it would be most enlightening to see whether they could be differentiated in ways that have psychological meaning. Once such patterns had been identified, they could be used in carrying out much more refined examinations of people in different fields of study than those that have been reported here.

A positive step in this direction is reported in a study by Gough and Woodworth (1960), which may well serve as a standard of care and thoroughness for future studies along this line. They developed a set of items describing various "stylistic" aspects of research work; for example, "Likes to play his hunches in research work; is guided by his subjective impressions" and "Seeks out the help of others when he hits a trouble spot in his own research." They had each of forty-five research scientists sort these items according to how well they described his own *modus operandi*. They then used factor analysis to identify eight types of scientists distinguished by their research styles. Scientists representing each type were then given psychological ratings and tests so as to obtain fairly integrated descriptions of each stylistic type. This basic procedure could easily be extended to other kinds of intellectual activities and modified to answer different kinds of questions. Results of such work are almost sure to produce more significant bases for comparing groups.

Much still needs to be done at a less sophisticated level, however, and our last suggestion is addressed to people engaged in other kinds of psychological studies. We ask that they consider differences among fields of study as a worthwhile side issue. It usually requires little extra work to break scores or other information on college students down into major-field groups, and much useful information has been obtained in this way from studies principally concerned with some other kind of comparison.

REFERENCES

Adorno, T. W., Frenkel-Brunswik, E., Levinson, D. J., and Sanford, R. N. *The authoritarian personality.* New York: Harper Bros., 1950.

Bereiter, C., and Freedman, M. B. Personality differences among college curricular groups. *Am. Psychol.,* 1960, **15,** 435.

Bergler, E. *The writer and psychoanalysis.* (2nd ed.) New York: R. Brunner, 1954.

Blum, G. S. The Blacky Test. *Genetic Psychol. Monogr.,* 1949, **39,** 3–99.

Boldt, W. J., and Stroud, J. B. Changes in attitudes of college students. *J. educ. Psychol.,* 1934, **25,** 611–619.

Borg, W. R. Personality characteristics of a group of college art students. *J. educ. Psychol.,* 1952, **43,** 149–156.

Brass, R. V. An investigation of selected personal background factors and reasons related to students who change schools within Purdue University. Unpublished doctoral dissertation, Purdue University, 1956.

Brown, D. R. Non-intellective factors and faculty nominations of ideal students. Poughkeepsie, N.Y.: Vassar College, Mary Conover Mellon Foundation, 1959.

Bugelski, R., and Lester, Olive. Changes in attitudes of college students during their college course and after graduation. *J. soc. Psychol.*, 1940, **12.**

Carlson, H. B. Attitudes of undergraduate students. *J. soc. Psychol.*, 1934, **5**, 202–212.

Clark, J. H. The interpretation of MMPI profiles of college students: a comparison by college major subject. *J. clin. Psychol.*, 1953, **9**, 382–384.

Clifford, P. S. Emotional contacts with external world manifested by a selected group of highly creative chemists and mathematicians. *Percept. motor Skills*, 1958, **8**, (Monogr. suppl. No. 1) 3–26.

Drucker, A. J., and Remmers, H. H. Citizenship attitudes of graduate seniors at Purdue University, U.S. college graduates and high school pupils. *J. educ. Psychol.*, 1951, **42**, 231–235.

Educational Testing Service. *Annual report to the Board of Trustees, 1951–1952.* Princeton, New Jersey: Author, 1952.

Fay, P. J., and Middleton, W. C. Certain factors related to liberal and conservative attitudes of college students: sex, classification, fraternity membership, major subject. *J. educ. Psychol.*, 1939, **30**, 378–390.

Fischelli, V. R., and Welch, L. The ability of college art majors to recombine ideas in creative thinking. *J. appl. Psychol.*, 1947, **31**, 278–282.

Fosmire, F. R. Generality of some academic reputations. *Science*, 1956, **124**, 680–681.

Fosmire, F. R. The role of ego defense in academic reputations. *J. soc. Psychol.*, 1959, **49**, 21–45.

Fullmer, D. W. Success and perseverance of university students. *J. higher Educ.*, 1956, **27**, 445–447.

Ginzberg, E., Ginsburg, S. W., Axelrad, S., and Herma, J. I. *Occupational choice: an approach to a general theory.* New York: Columbia University Press, 1951.

Goldsen, Rose K., Rosenberg, M., Williams, R. M., Jr., and Suchman, E. A. *What college students think.* Princeton, N.J.: Van Nostrand, 1960.

Gough, H. G., and Woodworth, D. G. Stylistic variations among professional research scientists. *J. Psychol.*, 1960, **49**, 87–98.

Guilford, J. P. The structure of intellect. *Psychol. Bull.*, 1956, **53**, 267–293.

Hanchett, Gertrude. Attitude toward the British: Churchill and the war effort. *J. soc. Psychol.*, 1946, **23**, 143–162.

Hancock, J. W., and Carter, C. C. Student personality traits and curriculae of enrollment. *J. educ. Res.*, 1954, **48**, 225–227.

Harris, D. H. Group differences in values within a university. *J. abnorm. soc. Psychol.*, 1934, **29**, 95–102.

Jacob, P. E. *Changing values in college: an exploratory study of the impact of college teaching.* New York: Harper Bros., 1957.

John, E. R. Contributions to the study of the problem-solving process. *Psychol. Monographs*, 1957, **71**, No. 18 (Whole No. 447).

Jones, V. Attitudes of college students and the changes in such attitudes during four years in college. *J. educ. Psychol.*, 1938, **29**, 14–25, 114–134.

Learned, W. S., and Wood, B. D. *The student and his knowledge.* New York: Carnegie Foundation for the Advancement of Teaching, 1938, Bulletin No. 29.

Lehmann, I. J., and Ikenberry, S. O. *Critical thinking, attitudes, and values in higher education: a preliminary report.* East Lansing: Michigan State University, 1959.

Lipset, S. M. Opinion formation in a crisis situation. *Publ. Opin. Quart.*, 1953, **17**, 20–46.

Lough, Orpha M. Women students in liberal arts, nursing, and teacher training curricula and the MMPI. *J. appl. Psychol.*, 1947, **31**, 437–445.

Louise, Sister M. F. Mental growth and development at the college level. *J. educ. Psychol.*, 1947, **38**, 65–83.

Nachmann, Barbara. Childhood experiences and vocational choice: a study of lawyers, dentists, and social workers. Unpublished doctoral dissertation, University of Michigan, 1957. (*Dissert. Abstr.*, 1958, **18**, 2214.)

Newcomb, T. M. *Personality and social change: attitude formation in a student community.* New York: Dryden Press, 1943.

Noble, Lois A., and Noble, R. E. A study of the attitudes of college students toward civil rights. *J. soc. Psychol.*, 1954, **40**, 289–297.

Norman, R. D., and Redlo, Miriam. MMPI personality patterns for various college major groups. *J. appl. Psychol.*, 1952, **36**, 404–409.

Pace, C. R. University-wide studies in evaluation of general education at Syracuse University. In P. L. Dressel, *Evaluation in general education.* Dubuque, Iowa: W. C. Brown, 1954.

Patterson, C. H. Interest tests and the emotionally disturbed client. *Educ. psychol. Measmt*, 1957, **19**, 264–280.

Prince, R. A study of the relationship between individual values and administrative effectiveness in the school situation. Unpublished doctoral dissertation, University of Chicago, 1957.

Riesman, D. *Constraint and variety in American education.* Lincoln, Neb.: University of Nebraska Press, 1956.

Roe, Anne. A psychological study of eminent psychologists and anthropologists and a comparison with biological and physical scientists. *Psychol. Monogr.*, 1953, **67**, No. 2 (Whole No. 367).

Roe, Anne. *The psychology of occupations.* New York: Wiley, 1956.

Rogers, Agnes L. The growth of intelligence at the college level. *Sch. & Soc.*, 1930, **31**, 693–699.

Segal, S. J. The role of personality factors in vocational choice: a study of accountants and creative writers. Unpublished doctoral dissertation, University of Michigan, 1953. (*Dissert. Abstr.*, 1954, **14**, 714–715.)

Shuey, Audrey M. Improvement in scores on the American Council Psychological Examination from freshman to senior year. *J. educ. Psychol.*, 1948, **39**, 417–425.

Stephenson, C. M. The relation between the attitudes toward Negroes of white college students and the college or school in which they are registered. *J. soc. Psychol.*, 1952, **36**, 197–204.

Stephenson, C. M. The relation between the attitudes toward Negroes of seniors in a school of education and their major subject. *J. educ. Res.*, 1955, **49**, 113–121.

Sternberg, C. Personality trait patterns of college students majoring in different fields. *Psychol. Monogr.*, 1955, **69**, No. 18 (Whole No. 403).

Super, D. E. A theory of vocational development. *Amer. Psychologist*, 1953, **8**, 185–190.

Teevan, L. C. Personality correlates of undergraduate field of specialization. *J. consult. Psychol.*, 1954, **18**, 212–214.

Terman, L. M. Scientists and non-scientists in a group of 800 gifted men. *Psychol. Monogr.*, 1954, **68**, No. 7 (Whole No. 378).

Terman, L. M., and Oden, Melita H. *The gifted child grows up*. Stanford, Calif.:
    Stanford University Press, 1947.
Thistlethwaite, D. L. College press and changes in study plans of talented students.
    Mimeographed report, National Merit Scholarship Corporation, 1959.
Wise, L. M. Abnormal psychology as a selective factor: a confirmation and extension.
    J. educ. Psychol., 1959, **50**, 192–194.
Wolfle, D. *America's resources of specialized talent*. New York: Harper Bros., 1954.

18 *David C. Beardslee and Donald D. O'Dowd*

Students and the Occupational World

The relations of higher education and the occupational world have been greatly affected by rapid changes that have taken place in the American occupational structure and the organization of higher education during the first half of this century. This has been dramatically illustrated by the evolving recruitment patterns of business and industry. Many observers report that until the 1930s it was common for business firms to look with suspicion on the college graduate, preferring to hire and promote men with more limited educational achievements. It is now becoming difficult for a man without college training, regardless of his intellectual capacities, to rise in the structure of established business concerns. A large number of positions ranging from lower management and direct sales to the executive levels are accessible only on presentation of a degree bearing the proper seals and signatures. Similar changes have also taken place in the professions. It is unlikely that any future president will have read law in a law office, and engineers without college certification have all but disappeared. It is quite clear that college has become the gateway to professional and higher managerial status. This situation is exerting a powerful influence on the orientation of millions of young

Note. The research reported herein was performed pursuant to a contract with the United States Office of Education, Department of Health, Education and Welfare. Additional support for the research was provided by the Faculty Research Committee of Wesleyan University. We also wish to acknowledge our gratitude to Mrs. Beatrice M. Burford who has ably assisted us in the development of every phase of the Occupations Project.

people approaching college age. Their parents, teachers, guidance counselors, and the mass media are constantly impressing upon them that a college education is indispensable for achieving a respectable and satisfying status in American life.

In view of these trends, it is interesting to note that, with the exception of the writing on vocational guidance, the extensive literature about the academic process in liberal arts colleges and universities pays relatively little attention to the occupational outcomes of college training. When attention is given to this issue it is often in the form of a critical attack on the vocational emphasis of many academic programs. Surprisingly little has been written of the influence of career aspirations on the performance and activities of undergraduate college students in and out of the classroom. A wide range of research on the influence of courses and curricula on student knowledge and attitudes fails to take account of the motivating force of the vocational interests of male undergraduates in particular. One would think from reading these studies that most undergraduates have only the vaguest concerns about the career outcomes of their academic training. This may be partly explained by the fact that the liberal arts college teacher is not likely to be especially concerned with the career goals of his undergraduate students unless they show some inclination to follow his path. Rarely do liberal arts college faculty members see any need to develop for their students the importance of what they teach for the personal or career aspirations of the students.

In order to determine the degree of student concern with occupational alternatives open to them after college, the authors conducted interviews [1] with sixty-three Wesleyan University students. Since Wesleyan is strongly committed to a liberal arts curriculum and the pursuit of knowledge for its intrinsic and general value, it seemed that the discovery of extensive interest in occupations among such a population would be quite revealing. It was found without exception that in a nondirective interview students talked freely, at length, and with obvious emotional involvement about occupations that they had no intention of pursuing as well as about those in which they were personally interested. The students chose to talk primarily about the aspects of these occupations that may best be called their implications for a style of life. They commented spontaneously on how a lawyer, doctor, or engineer and his family live rather than on the character of his work. They described easily and naturally the community status associated with different occupational roles, the possessions and ac-

[1] E. Wayne Harbinger and Anthony LaCava, Wesleyan undergraduates, assisted in the execution of this study (Beardslee and O'Dowd, 1958).

tivities that follow from these roles; the personality and the quality of family relationships implied by each of several different jobs were regularly mentioned. In general, occupations were primarily seen as leading to different ways of life that varied considerably in attractiveness.

When in a subsequent study [2] a random sample of forty-nine Wesleyan undergraduates were asked about their occupational future, further surprising results were obtained. These students were asked what specific, day-to-day activities they would be doing in their chosen fields after graduation. Many students were unable to give any adequate description of anticipated occupational activities. Direct questions about daily work elicited such vague responses as, "I will deal with people," or, "I will help others," or perhaps, "I will answer the questions that people bring to me." Probing for more specific answers frequently was met by embarrassment and annoyance on the part of the respondents. The same students discussed at length the benefits that they expected to flow from their work in terms of life with their families, patterns of social relationships, and status in the community. For most students the working hours in their occupational future are far less real than the leisure hours. These students view the occupational world as the central means by which they will reach highly desirable goals. However, most of them are much more attentive to the ends than to the means while still within the protection of college walls. In summary, an occupation is, for most Wesleyan men, the means by which they will attain a given mode of living, and only secondarily a set of skills and responsibilities. These findings indicate that the occupational future with its rich, personal connotations is of great interest even to students in nonvocational training. This fact must certainly influence the attitudes with which they respond to their liberal arts education (cf. Douvan and Kaye, Chapter 4).

WHY OCCUPATIONS MATTER

The salience of the occupational world in the life of the student is a realistic response to the facts of modern social life. The importance of a person's specific occupational position appears to have increased in recent decades. Some of the reasons for this are implicit in current sociological analyses of American society. For example, as the rate of horizontal (i.e., geographical) mobility among the middle and upper socio-economic classes has increased, the need for nationally valid

[2] Thomas Schlesinger, a Wesleyan student, carried out this investigation.

status symbols has also increased. Whereas in the stable communities of an earlier era a person was automatically located in society on the basis of his life history and that of his family, it is not possible to evaluate the claims of the contemporary transient about his family history. Now it is a man's profession or managerial position that is used by others to locate him in the status system. Of course, the wealth that an individual controls correlates highly with occupational position. This is true both for those who have achieved status through the professions and those who have inherited wealth. The importance of occupation in status determination is vigorously evidenced by the importance given this characteristic in developing indices of socioeconomic position. Hollingshead and Redlich (1958) give the heaviest weight to occupation, among a series of objective indicators, in locating people by means of the Index of Social Position in the New Haven Community Study. Warner, Meeker, and Eells (1949) also assign considerable weight to occupation in the Index of Status Characteristics. Although occupation alone is not adequate for an exact placement of people in the status structure, it is the most readily available of the several objective indicators commonly utilized both by laymen and social scientists.

Additional evidence for the importance of occupations in the general public's placing of people is provided by the many studies in which diverse groups have ranked or rated a series of occupational titles for their "prestige" value or their "standing in society." Anne Roe (1956) reviewed the studies executed on this topic between 1925 and 1950. The correlations among the prestige rankings of occupations by different samples of people clearly indicate that occupation is a stable determinant of status location over a generation of studies. Correlations in the 90s were obtained when a number of pairs of rankings from different investigations were compared. It appears that many Americans participate in a system of beliefs and attitudes that makes it possible for them to place people reliably in relation to one another given only information about their occupations. Recent work by Inkeles and Rossi (1956) suggests that the prestige value of occupations is quite consistent within Western culture.

The importance of the occupational world is further enhanced for many college students by the fact that they must achieve the occupational status of their choice if they are to complete the promise of their education. For most upwardly mobile young people the route to success is through higher education to the prestige-bearing occupations. Data compiled by Lipset and Bendix (1959) indicate that even if they attended or graduated from high school only 28% of the sons of manual workers entered the job market in nonmanual jobs. On the other hand, 63% of manual workers' sons who attended or graduated from college obtained their first job in a nonmanual occupation. For the sons of manual workers, a nonmanual job usually represents an important upward step in status compared with their fathers' positions. The probability that the son of a manual worker will cross the line from manual to nonmanual occupational status in his first job is greatly increased by his entering college. The findings of Lipset and Bendix also are quite explicit in showing that the importance of a college education for the achievement of a high status initial job is greater for sons of lower-status families than for sons of higher-status families. There are several roads to success for the high-status youth but only one for the low-status youngster. But C. Wright Mills (1951) points out that, "In the white collar life and its patterns of success, the educational segment of the individual's career becomes a key to his entire occupational fate" (p. 266). Even those students who have virtually automatic access to desirable occupational roles are often as anxious about future status as their less favored fellows. For these seemingly fortunate young men the "prestige" university and the "prestige" fraternity or club set a high standard of professional and managerial attainment that can be reached only with effort and concentration. The promise of his educational opportunity must yet be fulfilled through the role the student assumes in the occupational world.

The general advantages of the college-educated are strikingly illustrated in the figures compiled by Havemann and West (1952). Although 84% of their sample of 9000 college graduates can be classified as either professionals or proprietors, managers, and executives, only 16% of the male noncollege graduates in the United States can be placed in these categories.[3]

Another way of demonstrating the relation of college education to occupational attainment is to seek out an elite group and study their educational background. Warner and Abegglen (1955) found that 57% of their sample of 8000 business leaders were college graduates while only 7% of the male population over 30 years of age at the time of the study were college graduates. They also report that the proportion of college graduates in leading business positions has grown much more rapidly than the proportion of college graduates in the general population.

When account is taken first, of the usefulness and ubiquity of occu-

[3] For further discussion of the findings of Havemann and West, see Freedman, Chapter 25.

pational role as a device for assigning people to a status; second, of the importance of occupational attainment as validating success in striving for upward mobility; and third, of the advantages associated with jobs achieved through college training, it is little wonder that students exhibit great concern about careers. This concern is noticeable not only at the level of responses to interviews, but also in phantasy life. Shaffer and Shoben (1956) find that, in several samples of graduates and undergraduates, the percentage reporting daydreams centered about vocational success is larger than the percentage reporting daydreams in a variety of other categories.

There is a second set of factors contributing to the importance of the occupational world in the lives of college students. The subjective side of the sociological picture that has been described centers about the importance of the choice of an occupation for a young person's perception of himself. Until he finds the place where he fits in the world of work, the young man often has not discovered the kind of person he is. Erikson (1956) states the problem in one brief sentence: "In general it is the inability to settle on an occupational identity which disturbs young people" (p. 218). For many students their college experience requires of them that they delay committing themselves in the sphere of our culture that is morally most worthwhile— the world of work. Also, of course, this delays their entry into the realm in which they will be acknowledged as persons with recognized achievements and potentials (cf. Chapter 6). Colleges offer future gains as justification for the delay, but they are rarely equipped to do more than provide youth with a temporary sense of identity. It is little wonder that students flock to "prestige" colleges and even to "prestige" majors in an effort to support their buffeted sense of self through the college years. Ginzberg and his associates (1951) contribute an interesting observation on the way in which college students manage their concerns about the occupational future.

> It is worth noting that the subject of occupational choice is seldom discussed even among close friends and almost never in a group. Yet freshmen are notorious for their "bull sessions." Apparently the subject is avoided because it is highly personal; relatively little help is to be gained from a generalized discussion. And, unlike discussions of sex or politics, there is small immediate gratification in conversations with others who also know very little about the subject. It is possible that discussion of a subject about which one is somewhat anxious will prove disturbing, not pleasant (pp. 103–104).

Observations at Wesleyan indicate that there is a great deal of general talk about careers and occupations among undergraduates, but it is not personalized conversation. That is, students in a group will talk at length about the merits and implications of going into law or engineering, but they avoid discussing their own plans and intentions. Rather, they volunteer their reactions and prejudices about the legal or engineering profession, not their own personal ambitions. If a student wishes to discuss his personal career interests, he will often share his sentiments with one close friend. These impressions do not contradict Ginzberg's findings, but they show that a fairly complex set of practices governs student behavior in the area of vocational planning.

Erikson (1956) points out that the alternative to the establishment of a sense of identity is the development of a sense of self-diffusion. This manifests itself in a purposelessness, an unwillingness to be productive, an inability to commit oneself to anyone or anything, most profoundly a sense of "don't get involved." Students frequently defend themselves against a sense of self-diffusion by devices that are of little value to the institution or to the preparation of the students for future activities. One common contemporary solution is the development of a "beatnik" pattern; another consists of shifting from one career goal to another in search of some sense of security. The students often envied by those who are unable to settle on an identity are the premedical students. These men have a goal reached by a series of graded steps that are visible to all from the very beginning of college. There is some evidence that on a national scale vocationally oriented students are more likely to succeed in college both from a psychiatric and an academic point of view (e.g., Iffert, 1957).

Among experts in the study of vocational choice the importance of a self-concept in orienting the young person to the occupational world has been given much attention. Super (1957) has suggested that locating a place in the world of work represents in part an attempt to implement one's concept of self as well as a means of refining and extending it. In Super's system the self-concept can be thought of as a series of hypotheses about the self, which are systematically tested and adjusted to the reality of an occupational role. Bordin (1943) proposed a similar theory of occupational choice in which beliefs about oneself are matched with stereotypes of the characteristics of various occupations in the process of selecting a career. Finally, Roe (1956) points to the fact that occupations are instrumental in the satisfaction of many physiological and psychological needs. They derive much of their importance from the vast range of satisfactions that are controlled by them.

These views are congruent with the formulation derived from Erikson. Basically, the occupation that a young person chooses to enter requires of him certain talents, traits, and attitudes. If he makes an early commitment then he will seek to develop those aspects of himself that match his conception of the properties appropriate to an ideal role model. In turn, he can derive from the field to which he aspires a sense of purpose, status, and future achievement which allows him to focus his efforts. The preprofessional undergraduate may at times be anxious about the adequacy of his striving— "Will he make it to medical school?"; but he should rarely manifest a loss of purpose and a sense of meaninglessness regarding his efforts. To borrow further from Erikson, there are students who have managed to establish their identity on grounds relatively independent of future occupational status. These fortunate young people are free to test a range of career alternatives for their goodness of fit in the hope of finding maximum play for the ego-strength already in their possession. This probably accounts for the academic and personal success of GI-Bill student veterans, which is reflected in the nostalgia for the late 1940s frequently expressed by faculty members.

Two important studies support the belief that occupation also plays an important role in the mental health of the individual. Investigations by Clark (1953) and by Frumkin (1955) show that the incidence of severe mental illness is closely related to the occupational status of adults. The higher the status of an occupational group, the lower the recorded rate of psychotic disorders. In both studies it was found that the correlation between prestige ranking of occupations and the incidence of psychosis in occupations had a higher negative value than the correlation between income level of occupations and the incidence of psychosis. Although not large, this difference is found in the two independent studies. It suggests that the esteem in which a career is held has a greater effect than its material rewards on the emotional stability of people identified with it. The more recent work of Hollingshead and Redlich (1958) supports these earlier findings.

These data do not establish a causal relation between occupational status and psychological integration. However, they certainly indicate that fruitful research remains to be done on this topic. Of particular importance in establishing links between occupational position, the integrity of a sense of identity, and emotional health are the findings of Myers and Roberts (1959). Their intensive study of a small group of schizophrenics and neurotics indicates the tremendous importance of college education and occupational attainment in the emotional stability of middle-class individuals. Their subjects were drawn from the Class III segment of the New Haven population. Class III, which constitutes 21% of the New Haven population, is largely made up of salaried administrative and clerical personnel, small business owners, semiprofessionals, technicians, supervisors, and highly skilled workers. This group overlaps with elements of the middle-middle and lower-middle classes of Warner's classification scheme. Myers and Roberts report that the schizophrenics they studied were characterized by very high aspirations for improvement in their social status. These patients tended to focus their hopes on academic success at the college level, preferably in a prestigeful university. For a portion of this group the first major psychic shock grew out of their inability to attend the college of their choice because of family financial limitations. Other critical frustrations were associated with the inability to complete work even at colleges that already represented for them a failure of status attainment, or the inability to translate their hard-earned education into a status-conferring occupational position. It is clear in the Myers and Roberts report that the dominant pattern of experience for Class III schizophrenics consisted of primary and secondary school success, followed by failure to attain aspirations in terms of type of college or college performance, and incomplete realization of personal goals in occupational success. At least in this limited but important segment of the population the inability to consolidate a sense of identity in which goals and possibilities were harmonized is the key to the understanding of emotional welfare. On other grounds it would seem reasonable to suppose that, in general, educational and occupational success plays its greatest role in identity formation for the people classified as Class III by Myers and Roberts. It is from this level that a substantial segment of the increasing college population is being drawn (cf. Wise, 1958). It is this group of students who must abandon some of the values, attitudes, and beliefs of their parents in order to fulfill the parents' aspirations for them. They must seek identification with such nebulous things as "liberal arts" and ultimately with an occupation, if they are to win through to an enduring and rewarding perception of themselves.

Most of what has been said so far applies primarily to the education and career development of men. The occupational structure presents special difficulties for women. The work of Sanford and his associates at Vassar (1956) has pointed to a crisis for women in the senior year which is similar to the sophomore difficulties of men. Liberal arts training leaves many women without an entry into the career world at a meaningful level, and it is also difficult for them to pursue a graduate program toward higher degrees. The terminal quality of women's liberal arts programs in particular leads to a crisis that can be resolved by marriage, but far less often by entry into the occupational world of men.

With respect to the career problems of college women, there are at least four issues that merit comment. First, according to the work of Douvan and Kaye (1957, and Chapter 4) only a small portion of the girls who strive for and presumably enter college are motivated to succeed in the academic aspect of college life. This means that from the outset their concerns in college are eccentric to the primary orientation of the curriculum. They frequently treat the curriculum as something to be endured rather than a source of potential fulfillment. Furthermore, this group of students is rarely motivated by career possibilities that would justify a modicum of rational planning of courses and vigorous academic effort. Second, the curricula of many colleges cater to these students and many of their more determined sisters by being either very narrow and specialized (institutional dietetics, adolescent women's physical education) or by providing a very broad and unfocused potpourri of the liberal arts. Most decidedly college training does not often equip them to enter the business or professional world either at graduation or after a family career. Indeed, it rarely gives them an opening into higher professional training at either time. Third, like men, women are immersed in a culture that rewards and values the person who is gainfully employed. The working person gains status, and income, both financial and psychic, for his direct participation in the economy. These rewards are frequently attained by the college-educated woman in a peripheral way. For example, she most easily finds her satisfaction in fields where she supports and often underwrites the male, such as secretarial work or nursing, or in volunteer work, which is not paid and is clearly valued by the sentimental side of community attitudes. In other words, women are not prepared for independent economic contribution outside the family although they are both sensitive to its rewards and fully capable of gaining them. The fourth point stems from the fact that a woman is largely dependent upon her husband for status and a style of life, at least in the child-raising phase of her development. The effect of this is to direct at least some women toward a desire to assert their capabilities at establishing and confirming the position of the family unit, contributing further to the sense of limitation derived from the factors mentioned earlier. In summary then, it is common for college women to orient themselves to the world of work through their future husbands. They usually prepare, if at all, for careers that will serve primarily to bridge the gap between college and marriage. When graduation approaches many find themselves ill-prepared to take a stable place in the occupational world. They are sensitive to its prestige and power structure, but they can enter this only peripherally or vicariously. They receive little support from their occupational opportunities in their search for identity. It may be that an identity formed around college values will be badly damaged by the fact that the self-concept must seek expression in a world for which the girl is poorly equipped.

The fact that students perceive occupations largely in terms of their implications for a style of life and a place in the community status system, and the importance of occupations in the formation of an identity, constitute pressures on the student to select an occupation early and to cling to it. This is certainly undesirable at the college level where many young men and women are being prepared for generalized roles requiring a maximum of self-confidence, flexibility, and originality (cf. Chapter 6). Ideally, a liberal arts education should provide a basis on which students whose personal integration is still weak can develop a sense of competence, mastery, and direction that will allow them to choose wisely and not prematurely among occupational alternatives. This process of forming character through higher education is just as vital for women as for men. Women graduates should feel free either to enter the occupational world immediately, or to undertake family responsibilities with the confident belief that they can claim a place at a later time in the occupational world because of their personal talents.

VOCATIONAL ASPIRATIONS OF FRESHMEN

What is known about the vocational aspirations of entering college students? First, it should be noted that virtually all studies of occupational preferences among high school and college students reveal an unrealistically high selection of professional careers. This is true whether youngsters indicate probable or possible occupations (e.g., Trow, 1941). The effect has been reported during a generation of research on this topic. A study by Cole (1956) of the idealized vocational aspirations of a national sample of high school seniors, who had scored sufficiently high on a standardized test to qualify for college, indicated 26% of the boys selected engineering and approximately 34% expressed a desire for other professional careers. Positions in the business world were chosen by only 16% of the sample. Although the data from college populations are somewhat limited, it appears that entering freshmen continue the excessive selection of the professions relative to other occupations. Iffert's (1957) national sample of advanced college students shows that when men who stated that they had been interested in engineering on entering college are combined with those who were aiming toward science, medicine, and law about 60% of the men are accounted for. In this study 20% of the men reported that they had begun college with an interest in business careers.

Additional observations on the occupational intentions of college freshmen were obtained, in the course of a study of the images of occupations held by college students, by asking freshmen men in three colleges to indicate their intended occupation. The colleges studied were Wesleyan University, a second small and highly selective Northeastern men's liberal arts college, and the College of Arts and Sciences of a state university in the Northeast. The data, then, are limited to students in the least vocationally oriented part of the academic setting. The percentages in Table 1 indicate the overwhelming proportion of the students aspiring to professional status as late as the second half of the freshman year in all three colleges. Data from two successive freshman classes at Wesleyan are presented to indicate the stability of the results. These data suggest that the arts and sciences are viewed by most freshmen as the road to professional status.[4] A look at the occupations of the fathers of these students, classified in the same categories in Table 1, reveals that for most students their occupational preferences represent a considerable rise above their fathers' occupational attainment (cf. Clark, 1960). Of particular interest is the attraction of students from managerial and entrepreneurial families, and at the state university from white and blue-collar families, into the professional and particularly the high-prestige professional careers. Further analysis of the data shows that the sons of executive-level business and industrial personnel select business careers more frequently than the sons of the lower groups of the business and industrial managers. It may be that the only young people with sufficient confidence to heed the protestations that liberally trained men are wanted in the business world are those who have a view from the top. Sons of professional men in these samples rarely select business careers; with very few exceptions they indicate a desire to remain in the professional sphere. A consistent 20% of the freshmen are undecided about their occupational future. Evidence from other studies would lead to the prediction

---

[4] It should be noted that the state university has a full complement of specialized undergraduate vocational colleges in business administration, engineering, etc.

Table 1. Vocational Preferences of Male College Freshmen and
the Occupational Attainments of Their Fathers

Occupational Status	Wesleyan University Class '61 (N = 77) [a]		Wesleyan University Class '62 (N = 227) [b]		Male Lib. Arts Coll. II Class of 1962 (N = 117) [a]		State Univ. Coll. of A&S Class of 1962 (N = 131) [a]	
	Sons %	Fathers %	Sons %	Fathers %	Sons %	Fathers %	Sons %	Fathers %
A. High-status professional (doctor, lawyer, college professor, etc.)	57	33	59	32	52	33	37	11
B. Lower-status professional (school teacher, pharmacist, librarian, etc.)	7	3	11	7	17	10	28	5
C. High managerial and entrepreneurial (executive positions)	18	12	3	13	8	21	3	6
D. Middle managerial and entrepreneurial (managers)	1	27	4	30	5	26	7	21
E. Lower managerial and small enterprise	—	12	—	7	—	3	—	16
F. White and blue-collar workers	—	4	—	6	—	6	—	40
G. Other, undecided, and no answer	17	9	24	5	18	1	25	1
Total	100	100	101	100	100	100	100	100

[a] Random samples from the freshman class.
[b] Exhaustive sample of the class.

that this group will contribute disproportionately to the dropouts in
the ensuing years (e.g., Iffert, 1957).

There are various pressures that influence this strong trend to professional affiliation. Some of these are implicit in earlier comments
on the prestige and reward system in which occupational labels play
a central role, and the importance of a clearly defined occupational
goal in providing the individual with a stable sense of identity. Another factor supporting this trend is found in the climate of opinion

in which students participate. The making, confirming, shifting, and testing of career choices, which inevitably take place in college, occur against a background of beliefs that students share about the attributes of various occupations and professions. Students bring with them to college fairly definite ideas about the occupational world, which they continually test and which influence the outcome of their deliberations about the future. Mead and Metraux (1957) have given a striking picture of the image of the scientist they encountered among high school students. It would seem reasonable to expect that similar images can be elicited from students for a variety of other fields of endeavor. In fact, the interviews reported earlier indicated that this is quite easily accomplished.

A STUDY OF STUDENTS' OCCUPATIONAL STEREOTYPES

The images or stereotypes of occupations that emerge in the talk of college students are not always very close to the "reality" represented by the descriptions of occupations in guidance literature. On the other hand, the images held by students often bear definite resemblance to the findings of occupational sociology and psychology. These stereotypes reveal a variety of connotations associated with occupations in terms of the personality characteristics, social location, and life-style implied by the fields. However, very little information is volunteered by students about the kind of day-to-day work that would be expected in an occupation. In other words, occupational stereotypes provide information on the very important questions of how an occupation places a person in the community, and what kind of person would commit himself to it. Of particular importance is the high degree of agreement among students about these nonwork features of a number of prominent fields of work.

One striking effect of a climate of opinion is to influence the perception by others of a person who carries the symbols that are the key to the opinion system. Studies by Haire (1955) and Triandis (1959) have demonstrated this effect in labor and management. This process works in two directions; not only may the individual apply a stereotype to others, but also he may mold his own behavior to conform with common expectations (e.g., Allport, 1954). In the case of occupational images, a person may be placed in the prestige hierarchy, and his personal and social attributes may be inferred, by reference to his occupation. A person can in turn recognize himself as suited for a field if he demonstrates or develops characteristics that qualify a person for membership in that field.

A partial test of the assumption that a person of college age is perceived in terms of the occupational role he selects was devised in the following way. A questionnaire [5] was distributed to 32 Wesleyan undergraduates in an introductory psychology course. The students were requested to rate a ". . . Wesleyan student who intends to go into business" and a ". . . Wesleyan student who intends to go into college teaching" on 35 two-ended, seven-point rating scales of the following form:

high social status ___:___:___:___:___:___:___ low social status

The mean scores on each scale for both categories of job-related students were then compared with the scores on the same scales attributed by a random sample of 154 Wesleyan freshmen and seniors to "business executive" and "college professor." In other words, one group of subjects rated the undergraduate planning to enter a field while a second group indicated their beliefs about the characteristics of people who are already participating in these two fields. Is it the case that an undergraduate who plans to be a college teacher is thought of in terms of the personal and social characteristics attributed to a person already active in the occupation? The images of the college professor and of the student intending to teach in college are remarkably similar. In statistical terms, comparison of the two images yields a correlation of $+.95$. High agreement is also found when the stereotype of the student planning to be a businessman is compared with the image of business executive ($r = +.88$). The magnitude of the agreement is highlighted by the fact that the images of the prebusinessman and the prospective college professor correlate with one another only $+.12$, and those of the business executive and the college professor only $+.07$.

This study provides evidence that once a person has indicated an occupational intention he is fitted by others into a system of beliefs about the personal, social, and emotional traits of participants in that occupational role. On first impression, he is expected to demonstrate appropriate behavior. There is little doubt that the student knows in general what is expected of him; and in time his actions are very likely to be influenced by the responses of others to their own stereotypes of what he should—if all is right with the world—be like. The climate

[5] E. Stanley Bowers, a Wesleyan undergraduate, conducted this study.

of opinion, then, not only governs what one believes of the people out there in the active world; it also affects how one student reacts to another student who is here and now in the throes of selecting his future personal attributes. It is not surprising that a certain amount of anxiety in college students is centered around occupational choice. Although students rarely discuss the details of the career world in personal terms, they are well informed about the career aims of their friends and acquaintances.

A certain amount of information has been gathered about occupational stereotypes from a variety of populations. These give a clue to the specific pressures that mold the behavior of college students selecting a place in the world. Remmers and Radler (1957) and Mead and Metraux (1957) have recently pointed to the unfavorable impressions high school students have of the scientist. On the other hand, Nunnally and Kittross (1958) have found that medical personnel engaged in mental health work are highly regarded by a sample of the general public. Studies by Grunes (1957), Walker (1958), and Davidson and Riesman (1959) indicate that stable and complex images of a number of occupations are held by high school and college students. These findings confirm the observations of Anderson (1934) and of Osgood and Stagner (1941) on the strength of occupational stereotypes among students of a generation ago.

A new study was designed in order to gain additional understanding of the images with which students operate in their approach to the career world. A major aim of this research was to determine rather precisely student perceptions of a number of high-level occupations in terms of the characteristics of the images, their degree of differentiation, and their stability when different categories of the college population are compared. This investigation was expected to shed light on the ideal personality dimensions to which students aspire, and reveal some of the reasons for the overselection of professional occupations by liberal arts students.

A research instrument was prepared drawing upon materials from several sources. A set of scales was selected on the basis of analyses of data derived from a series of exploratory studies conducted by the authors over a period of two years (Beardslee and O'Dowd, 1958). Particular emphasis was placed in these scales on assessing the style of life features of occupational stereotypes that emerged consistently in student essays and during interviews with students. Other scales were chosen from the work of Osgood, Suci, and Tannenbaum (1957) with the semantic differential, and still others were based on Cattell's (1957) analysis of personality ratings. These scales were organized into two forms of a questionnaire. In each form 15 occupational titles were rated on 34 scales. The questionnaires were so arranged that at the top of each page the name of the occupation appeared, followed by 34 two-ended, seven-point scales of the following form:

1.   wealthy __:__:__:__:__:__:__ not well-to-do
23.   optimistic __:__:__:__:__:__:__ pessimistic
26. indifferent to people __:__:__:__:__:__:__ attentive to people

The order of the scales was the same on every page of the questionnaire while the order of the occupations to be rated was varied randomly from one questionnaire to the next. The two forms of the questionnaire differed in that, although 21 scales were common to the two forms, 13 scales were different. One form contained the 21 common scales and 13 scales drawn from Osgood, while the second form contained 13 scales derived from Cattell in addition to the common scales. Two questionnaire forms were used in an effort to reduce the burden of the task for a given subject and yet provide a maximum amount of information. The scales employed on each form were of four general types. They were designed to determine the social position of an occupation (e.g., high social status—low social status), the life-style of a member of an occupational group (e.g., happy home life—unhappy home life), the personality associated with an occupation (e.g., excitable—calm), and the style of social participation implied by occupational membership (e.g., sociable—unsociable). The occupations to be rated were chosen to include the professional, business, and industrial occupational roles that are attained by a large percentage of male college graduates.

The instructions, adapted from Osgood, et al. (1957), asked the respondent to indicate how he felt about the occupations in terms of the scales. He was requested to work rapidly but accurately. Detailed illustrations of the procedure for using the scales were provided on the instruction page. At the end of the questionnaire the respondent was asked to indicate his major in college, his occupational intentions, the job held by his father, and other personal information.

Since it seemed quite desirable to discover to what extent college women share with men stereotypes about the occupational world, a special version of the questionnaire was prepared for use with college women. They were asked to rate the same occupations on the same scales. Their instructions, however, requested them to evaluate the occupations as they involve men in our society; that is, the women were asked to give their view of the male occupational world. The women were asked a rather complex series of questions about marital and occupational intentions at the end of the questionnaire. Otherwise, they responded to the same two forms of the questionnaire as did the men.

During the spring of 1958 the questionnaires were administered to a random sample of freshmen and seniors at Wesleyan University.[6] In the winter and spring of 1959 questionnaires were distributed at three other colleges: another small, highly selective men's liberal arts college, a highly selective women's liberal arts college, and a state university college of arts and sciences, all located in the Northeastern part of the country. Random samples of the freshmen and senior classes were questioned at each of these colleges. The

[6] E. Wayne Harbinger, a Wesleyan undergraduate, carried out this phase of the study.

samples ranged in size from 170 undergraduates at Wesleyan to 579 at the state university. The study was divided into 10 sampling units defined as freshmen and seniors, men and women at each college, with only the state university contributing both men and women. On only two of these ten subsamples did the percentage of completed questionnaires obtained from the samples fall below 90%.[7]

When the mean scale values for each occupation are calculated, very clear and definite profiles are obtained for each occupation. These can be organized to give a sense of what students believe about the kind of people and the mode of life to be found in each occupation. The following descriptive vignettes summarize the statistical profiles that emerge from the analysis. There was sufficient agreement among all the groups of respondents to make these portraits representative in a general way of the beliefs of the entire group questioned. Among the professional occupations the images of the doctor, lawyer, college professor, scientist, and engineer are presented. The school teacher is chosen to represent the lower-level professional jobs. The business executive is presented as a representative of the highest level of business occupation while the accountant is a member of a lower-status business field. Finally, the artist is included because of his many interesting attributes.

Doctor. The doctor is a culture hero for college students. He anchors the desirable end of a surprising number of scales. Indeed, the doctor's position on a scale, whether it be at an extreme end or in the middle, can be used as a reliable indicator of the ideal score on that scale. Medicine is rated by students as a calling that is richly rewarded by high social status, wealth, and success. The doctor is favored with high opportunity for advancement, and he derives great personal satisfaction from his work. Compared to men in most other occupations he can count on an unusually pretty wife and a very happy home life. The doctor is very much a realist. He approaches the world responsibly and with perseverance. He is outstandingly calm, confident, and self-sufficient; and his great stability, caution, and rationality are balanced by his adaptability. The doctor is seen as very much oriented to people. Although it appears that this attitude may be partially a professional concern, still he is thoughtful and unselfish; he gives of himself to others. The doctor's cheerfulness and optimism fit well with this unfailing orientation of other people. His high intelligence appears to be more a correlate of his strong, active, masterful qualities than a sign of the highest intellectual culture. There are no undesirable traits attributed to the doctor. All students recognize the remarkable personal and social attractiveness of the doctor's role.

Lawyer. The image of the lawyer has many characteristics that are also attributed to the doctor, but the doctor is usually rated more favorably on traits that they have in common. The lawyer possesses high social status, suc-

[7] A more complete description of the method and the findings of this research are contained in O'Dowd and Beardslee (1960).

cess, and wealth. He has considerable opportunity to advance in his job, and he is outstandingly powerful in public affairs. The lawyer is viewed as an outgoing, sociable person who likes to be with people and is at ease in the company of others. The lawyer shares with the doctor realistic, persevering, forceful, strong, and active qualities. He is a person who is effective in the world of objects, events, and people. These characteristics are qualified, however, by a high degree of hardness and self-assertiveness. There is more than a hint of a selfish, manipulative attitude in the lawyer that is wholly lacking in the doctor image.[8] The lawyer is perceived as having high intelligence and good taste. He rates a pretty wife, but his home life is not seen as particularly happy. The lawyer, like the doctor, is without negative properties, but on many more scales than the doctor he earns values that come in the middle of the distribution of means from the 15 occupations. The lawyer image combines most of the rewards promised by the medical profession and possesses many of the same desirable personal properties, while providing somewhat more scope for less service-oriented, less unselfish ambitions. Of particular prominence in the case of the lawyer is the stress placed on sociability and access to public power.

College Professor. Knapp (Chapter 7, p. 301 f.) has described some of the features of the image of the college professor. A dominant feature of the image is the great stress on intellectual competence accompanied by sensitivity to artistic or aesthetic experience. The professor is seen as an individualist with colorful, interesting, exciting qualities coupled with a degree of rashness, changeability, emotional difficulties, and lack of adaptability. It is quite likely that he is interesting because of his emotional, unpredictable nature. In spite of these characteristics and a high score on radicalism, he is granted considerable power in public affairs. Students rate the professor as very valuable, and they see his role as a source of great personal satisfaction. On the debit side, the professor is described as not well-to-do and lacking in opportunity for advancement. He does not equal the independent professionals in either social or worldly competence. Whereas the doctor and lawyer are stable and dependable, he is changeable and unpredictable. His intellectual qualities are the primary asset of the college professor. Probably the most striking impression emerging from this profile is its lack of masculinity. It is predominantly a volatile feminine picture with emphasis on intellect, sensitivity, and impulsiveness.[9]

Scientist. Two strong impressions are conveyed by this profile. First, the scientist is characterized by high intelligence dissociated from artistic concerns and sensitivities. This cool intelligence is linked with strong individualism in personal and political realms. Second, there is a clear lack of interest in people on the part of the scientist. He anchors the undesirable end of scale scores on sociability for all the occupations studied. A good deal of control is implied by the description of the scientist as self-sufficient, rational, persevering, and emotionally stable. He has power in public affairs, but he is rated only

[8] Whenever an occupation is said to differ from another on a specific trait this refers to a difference in mean scale value between the two occupations that is significant at the 5% level or less.

[9] A more detailed description of the image of the college professor is contained in O'Dowd and Beardslee, 1961a.

moderately responsible and quite radical. This suggests that uncertainty about the motives and trustworthiness of the scientist noted in younger people by other investigators lingers on in college students. The personal life of the scientist is thought to be quite shallow, his wife is not pretty, and his home life is not very happy. He is rewarded by great personal satisfaction, considerable success, and reasonable opportunity for advancement. He enjoys moderate wealth and social status. In summary, the scientist is a cool, controlled intellectual. He is competent in organizing the world of things, but disdainful of the world of people. Although more richly rewarded than the college professor, the scientist contrasts strikingly with him in aesthetic sensibilities and social skills. It should also be noted that the scientist is clearly a masculine figure in a desexualized way.[10]

Engineer. Engineering is a less colorful profession for liberal arts students when compared with the alternatives already mentioned. The image of the engineer is most easily understood when juxtaposed with that of the scientist, with whom the engineer has many features in common. The engineer is rated generally intelligent but not nearly so powerful in this regard as the scientist. On the other hand, although he is no social lion, he is considerably more socially adept than the scientist. The engineer is quite successful and reasonably wealthy, but he gains less satisfaction from his work than the scientist derives from pure research. Finally, the engineer is more conservative, and more likely to be a conformist than the scientist. Except for these important differences, the engineer is almost identical with the scientist.

School Teacher. In every classification of occupations according to social status the school teacher is located in the second or third tier among the professions. But school teaching accounts for the occupational preferences and choices of a substantial percentage of college graduates. The school-teacher image is dominated by the depressed economic state of the profession. The teacher scores conspicuously low in wealth, social status, and opportunity for advancement. He has little power in public affairs, and he cannot even command an attractive wife although he can count on a happy home life—just the opposite of the lawyer's situation. The teacher is considered intelligent, sensitive, and, like the professor, interested in art but to a lesser degree. Furthermore, he is attentive to people and unselfish in his relations with them. In this regard he has an orientation toward service somewhat like the doctor's. Finally, the teacher is seen as lacking in confidence and in hard, assertive properties. Once again the feminine component is high but now it is associated with a more nurturant, and at the same time dependent, quality. Unlike the professor, the teacher has a rather calm impulse life.[11]

Business Executive. The avoidance of business occupations by freshmen liberal arts students is at first glance surprising when the image is studied. The business executive is extremely high in social status, wealth, and success. He has power in public affairs, ample opportunity to advance himself, and even a very pretty wife. He is classified as very conservative, but when his conservatism is paired with his good taste, a picture of quiet elegance emerges.

---

[10] The image of the scientist is treated at greater length in Beardslee and O'Dowd, 1961.

[11] Additional discussion of the school teacher image appears in O'Dowd and Beardslee, 1961b.

He possesses the sociability earlier noted in the lawyer, accompanied by a confident, assertive, masculine manner. He is also rated strong and active, responsible and persevering. Thus far the sketch coincides with that of the highly favored lawyer. But the business executive lacks both the high intelligence and the hard, rational properties that make the lawyer a most formidable figure. The executive is even less service-oriented than the lawyer; he is in fact a selfish individual. Finally, the business executive is believed to possess a component of excitability and emotional instability, which probably relates to the popular belief about his tendency to suffer from peptic ulcers. The business executive has both weaknesses and personal problems that offset to some degree his wealth and status. It has also been pointed out that the road to this role is not so clear or so predictable for most college students as that which leads through the professional schools into the high-status occupations.

Accountant. This occupation represents a lower-status business activity, perhaps comparable in some ways to the status of school teaching among the professions. The image that surrounds the field is remarkably negative. If the doctor is the occupational hero, the accountant is the antihero of the occupational world. He is low in status, not well-to-do, and unsuccessful. He has little power in public affairs, not much opportunity for advancement, and his job is lowest of all the occupations studied in providing personal satisfaction. He is a conformist, with a minimum of social skills, limited intelligence, and inadequate personal and aesthetic sensibilities. He is rated as passive, weak, soft, shallow, cold, submissive, unsure of himself, and evasive in meeting life. His positive characteristics of caution, stability, conservatism, and calmness rest upon a shaky emotional interior. They probably refer most directly to his control of a limited area of occupational specialization. Students have a rather specific model in mind when they produce this wretched portrait. He is apparently something of a Victorian bookkeeper, chained to a desk and a ledger, from which he has no inclination to depart for traffic with the world or contact with man. Given this description there is some doubt as to whether, according to undergraduate liberal arts students, the accountant is alive.

Artist. This calling is for many young people either a positive or negative reference point in their thinking about career alternatives. On a number of scales the artist anchors the end opposite that marked by the doctor. The artist's notable sensitivity to matters of aesthetic importance is associated with a variety of traits reflecting violent emotions and impulsive expression. For example, he is intuitive, rash, changeable, excitable, attention-demanding, and at the same time, deep, interesting, and colorful. His outstanding individualism and radicalism accompany a group of traits indicating irresponsibility and unwillingness to contribute to society in a disciplined way. The artist is uninterested in people and evidently unsuccessful with them. His moods tend to be dark, depressed, and pessimistic. The only reward that he can expect for his work is a high sense of satisfaction. Neither wealth, nor status, nor any other marks of the rich, full life are associated with the artist. A blind labeling of the role might easily describe this profile as applicable to a teenager in the throes of adolescent problems.

The study (O'Dowd and Beardslee, 1960) from which these sketches are derived includes data on a series of business occupations that lie within the extremes set by the business executive and the accountant. These business occupations include industrial manager, office supervisor, personnel director, retail store manager, and sales manager. The other occupational role that is not reported on here is the social worker.

Comparisons among these profiles indicate that the frequency with which liberal arts men choose the independent and salaried professions is consonant with the quality of general stereotypes about these fields. Science seems to be in a rather weak competitive position among the high-status professions although it has advantages over business alternatives. The image of the business executive leads to some interesting inferences about the anxieties of the liberal arts student. The executive's lack of psychological strength, his tendency to conform, and his selfishness differentiate him from others equal to him in status. Other business occupations shade off toward the accountant with only industrial manager and personnel director possessing a balance of desirable characteristics. The business fields have little of the sharp definition that characterizes the profiles of professions.

The justification for drawing these rather broad portraits as representative of the images held by men and women in public and private colleges is found in the high agreement observed among the profiles produced by these different groups. For each occupation the profiles of mean scale values were correlated for all pairs of the ten sampling units of students. These correlations are so high (O'Dowd and Beardslee, 1960) that it is fair to say that for college students very general stereotypes exist for each of the 15 occupations studied. These images are produced with very little variation by independent samples of students.

This very high level of agreement on the shape of individual occupation profiles among different samples of students is accompanied by large differences between profiles of different occupations. Very large distinctions are made among the different occupations by all groups of students, and all of the groups are in substantial agreement on the form of the differentiations between occupations (O'Dowd and Beardslee, 1960).

FACULTY INFLUENCE ON STUDENT OCCUPATIONAL IMAGES

One more set of research results is relevant to the general concerns of this paper. Much has been written of late about the influence of faculty members on student values (e.g., Jacob, 1957; Eddy, 1959; Habein, 1959). To what extent do the images of careers that seem so important in the orientation of students to the occupational world respond to faculty beliefs? A study was designed that permitted a comparison of student and faculty images of occupations and provided an estimate at least of the degree to which changes occur in the direction of images held by faculty members.

A stratified random sample of 60% of the Wesleyan faculty was asked to fill out exactly the same questionnaire that was distributed to the students. A questionnaire was delivered to each faculty member with a careful statement of the aims of the project by one of the authors. Completed questionnaires were obtained from 97% of the 72 faculty members included in the sample.

When all differences between freshmen and faculty mean scores were correlated with the corresponding senior and faculty differences, a highly significant correlation (P < .001) of +.81 was found. Thus a difference in opinion between freshmen and the faculty predicts the existence of a similar difference between seniors and faculty. Evidence for a change in the direction of faculty beliefs is not obtained.

There are some occupations on which faculty and students differ greatly and some on which they are in basic agreement. In general, the faculty has much more negative views than the students of the three high-status occupations of lawyer, physician, and business executive. The other occupation of which the faculty possesses a much less favorable image than students is that of school teacher. In fact, the school teacher presents the largest difference between the two groups. The accountant, and the scientist, are occupational roles on which students and faculty are in substantial though not complete agreement. The artist is held in the same general regard by both groups, but the students rate him as somewhat more prosperous and intelligent than do the faculty, while the faculty is more inclined to find him less radical and impulsive. Knapp has pointed out in Chapter 7 that the college professor is seen in a less favorable light by faculty than by students. This difference is consistent with freshmen and seniors. The seniors continue to hold a picture of the college professor's life and personal qualities that is considerably more positive than the professor's own picture of his occupation, although there is a small shift in the negative direction for seniors. Apparently contact with the academic profession in the setting of a closely organized small college does not provide evidence to change in any notable way the beliefs of students about the college professor.

The extremely critical view of the school teacher on the part of faculty merits brief comment. The faculty, in contrast to the students, rates the teacher lower in worldly success, intellectual potency, sociability, and personal dynamism. The faculty still shares in the general stereotype, but they deviate from it rather systematically on these dimensions. Mainly the calm, cautious, stable properties of the image are agreed upon by the two groups.

The student view of the occupational world is remarkably stable. College faculty members, a group of people in a strategic position to affect these stereotypes, are in basic agreement with the students on the major outlines of the images. Where they are not in agreement there are few opportunities or facilities for the faculty's expression of their views on these matters. It is possible to conceive of the college professor as filling a vital role in questioning the beliefs that students acquire before entering college about the structure of the occupational world. There is little evidence that college faculty members are effective in advising students about career realities at the present time.

CHANGES IN CHOICE OF CAREER

The career orientations of men change during the four years of college under the impact of the differential demands of alternative academic programs, financial barriers to graduate training, changing interests, and other pressures. These changes suggest that many young men must alter their goals to more modest levels and that they must form an identity around different images and models. This is of necessity a painful but often maturing process for many of the most highly talented members of our society.

Iffert (1957), in his careful study of retention and withdrawal of college students presents figures on changes in academic fields of interest and concentration. The figures are based on retrospective reports, and the changes are stated in terms of the fields initially chosen. The data show that mathematics suffers the largest proportional loss, with chemistry and biology next. English and history also have a high degree of instability. Prelaw, with its unstructured undergraduate program, loses students to the business curriculum, but also recruits them, particularly from English and history. On the other hand, premedicine, with its specific undergraduate requirements and its promise of rich rewards, shows reasonable stability. Engineering has high retention, and it draws heavily from mathematics and the natural sciences, with small counterflow. Business administration has moderate retention, and it draws students from a number of other fields. On a national basis, at least, it appears that applied fields stressing under-graduate specialization are most likely both to retain students and to recruit from scholarly and scientific fields. For many of these students changes are made from preparation for occupations and professions that are mainly noted for their cultured intellectual component in the student images to fields that promise very comfortable living standards and high status. Not only do these data reflect a shift of interest more in keeping with visible job opportunities, but they also represent the acceptance of a different segment of the occupational world as compatible with the concept of self.

Rosenberg's (1957) study of occupational values provides further evidence of changes in occupational aims during college. Using a panel reinterview procedure, he gathered data on the changes in interest in a sizeable sample of Cornell students over a two-year period. These students were first questioned as freshmen and sophomores, then interviewed again as juniors and seniors.

Rosenberg's results are consistent with those of Iffert which were drawn from a much larger and more extensive sample. Of the original group of students intending to be engineers, 79% of those still at Cornell after an interval of two years remained interested in engineering. Of the students still in college after two years who were originally interested in business, medicine, or teaching, approximately half of each group maintained their initial intention. On the other hand, over this two-year period, business recruited a number of new students approximately equal to the original number who had signified an interest in business. Each of the other three fields recruited a number of new aspirants equal to approximately one-third of the number originally intending to enter them. In short, engineering is the occupational interest with the greatest power to hold students, and business gains an unusual percentage of new recruits.

A study by Sisson (1937) of Wesleyan undergraduates in the 1930s reported that 40.8% of two incoming freshman classes wished to enter medicine, law, or natural science careers. When one of these classes was polled two years later only 24.8% retained such professional aims. Business had increased as an occupational goal from 11.1% of the freshmen to 33.3% of the juniors. Teaching also shifted as a goal from 13.3% of the entering class to 19.7% of the juniors. This circulation system in a liberal arts college fits rather closely with the Iffert and Rosenberg results.

Comparison of freshmen and senior men at the two liberal arts colleges and the state university in the present study indicates that the percentage naming medicine, law, and teaching as career aims is constant. The dropouts from college are drawn proportionately from these fields, and people who shift from them to other fields are replaced. Science drops sharply in popularity at the two liberal arts colleges, but remains stable at the state university. Business shows a gain in percentage of students at all three institutions. Presumably business grows at the expense of the less frequently chosen fields like engineering as well as from science. The stability that appears in this recent sampling of men in arts and sciences suggests that there may be a tendency for students at the present time to adhere to a consistent level of occupational aspiration if they remain in college. The increasing demand for professional personnel and greater availability of funds to finance graduate study may each play a part in this system. It appears that the desirable images are being sought after with some persistence by contemporary college students.

To complete this overview of the flow of career choices in relation to the images of occupations it is necessary to comment on the distribution of college graduates in the occupational world. Havemann and West (1952) gathered information on the jobs held by recent college graduates—men and women under 30 at the time of their study. The people questioned were a sample of alumni from approximately 1100 colleges and universities, both liberal arts institutions and others. Super (1957) has used Havemann and West's data in summarizing the occupational activities of recent graduates. Men divide about equally between business and the professions, while working college-educated women are heavily concentrated in education. One explanation of the difference between these figures on occupational affiliation and the data on current goals of liberal arts students is a separation of function among the colleges, with the liberal arts group primarily serving as preprofessional institutions. These colleges, however, do not succeed in sending all their graduates to professional schools. For many of those who are left to the world of business this is clearly the second-best outcome of their college experience. It is surprising to discover evidence for a similar trend in a state university, but it is consistent with the evidence presented at the beginning of this chapter for the great importance of occupational achievement for contemporary students. Our data indicate that ideal achievement in the occupational world is the attainment of a high-status professional role.

The decision to enter business is often delayed by students until late in their senior year or after a postgraduate tour of military duty. Quite likely the acceptance of a business career can be faced only after considerable self-evaluation on the part of many liberal arts college men. In part this is due to the fact that one must proceed through the lowly regarded managerial ranks to achieve status in the world of business and industry. No comparable distinctions are perceived in medicine or law, teaching or science, where one graduates from professional school into the full glory of a professional role. Fortunately, it is possible for college graduates to enter business careers without extensive planning or preparation. Thereby, many students are provided a road to achievement and success despite their failure to plan and prepare for some well-defined occupational role.

CONCLUSION: OCCUPATIONAL ASPIRATIONS AND LEARNING

In a penetrating study of the values and beliefs of college students Gillespie and Allport (1955) write of the American student, "The best way to generalize his goals seems to be in terms of the search for a rich, full life" (pp. 13–14). They note further that the contemporary college student is not concerned with the political and social problems that surround him. Indeed, he is not even concerned with philosophical or religious issues. In a most profound sense he is involved with himself and his future.

One of the keys to this future is the occupational role that fulfills the promise of a college education. This place in the occupational system is not seen by most students as a chance to achieve great heights in work, but as an opportunity to find comfort, variety, interesting experiences, and pleasant acquaintances. For students, the occupation even specifies the personal qualities of its present and future members, providing a ready-made personality for those who cannot establish a secure identity from their own experience.

By studying the connotations of occupational roles it is possible to gain a picture of the values and symbols that characterize the thought and action of present-day students. Students are able to respond with interest and confidence to a wide variety of questions about the occupational world. They feel at ease giving judgments about many occupations with which they have had minimal contact. Their responses to names of occupations reveal a complex structure of beliefs organized about dimensions of personality, styles of life, and social relationships associated with the world of work. On the other hand, it has been noted that careful questioning of students about formal job characteristics shows a very limited grasp of the day-to-day demands of these same occupations even for those jobs to which a student aspires. The stability of these findings when different groups of students are compared suggests that this is a system of beliefs and attitudes of general importance. There are adequate grounds for believing that the stereotypes and belief systems that have been described in this chapter are shared among a large segment of the American college student population.

It is likely that the widespread agreement among students about the qualities of mind and personality associated with occupational roles limits the variety of human types any high-level field can attract. Attempts to encourage students to direct their talents toward fields for which they are especially suited should recognize the orientation of students to career alternatives. Recommendations of ways for promoting greater individual freedom in occupational choice and more efficient social utilization of abilities proceed in two directions.

First, it is desirable that occupations that can give adequate scope to talented people be presented on more equal terms. Leveling must take place in the cognitive currency that has been described in this study. Educators have a role to play in this re-education process along with representatives of the formal groups that concern themselves with maintaining the standards of the major occupations. It seems likely, however, that the results of such efforts will be limited since these images grow out of major cultural trends and receive constant re-enforcement from peers, parents, teachers, and mass media.

A second way in which this problem may be approached grows out of the recognition that the nature of the interest in the career world that students express reflects for many their lack of confidence in themselves (cf. Chapter 6). In general, by seeking to nurture in students personal attributes that will strengthen their claim to an independent identity, we may be able to lessen their dependence upon packaged occupational personalities and increase their ability to see themselves capable of creating a place in the occupational structure for their special combination of capacities. It is probable that self-confident youth would be responsive to the social and political problems that need dedicated attention in a way that is beyond the resources of insecure, self-centered young people.

A first responsibility of education is to see that the character of the educated individual is such that he can use the fruits of his academic experience. Accepting the concern of students with their own development and their place in the future, it may be possible to use this situation to engage their energies. There are aspects of their personalities to which students attach great importance. If their education is organized to develop their personal powers, they will grasp its relevance and gain a measure of freedom in the process. For example, it is becoming increasingly clear that in every field of endeavor requiring college training new skills and talents must constantly be acquired after formal education has been completed. An educational program that seeks to develop in students confidence in the face of new challenges and flexibility in the learning of new skills will both involve them and fit them for good performance in whatever they are called on to do.

REFERENCES

Allport, G. W. *The nature of prejudice.* Cambridge, Mass.: Addison-Wesley, 1954.

Anderson, W. A. Occupational attitudes of college men. *J. soc. Psychol.,* 1934, **5,** 435–465.

Beardslee, D. C., and O'Dowd, D. D. Images of occupations: Summary of research through August, 1958. Report No. 1: Occupations Project. Middletown, Conn.: Wesleyan University, 1958.

Beardslee, D. C., and O'Dowd, D. D. The college-student image of the scientist. *Science,* 1961, **133,** 997–1001.

Bordin, E. S. A theory of vocational interests as dynamic phenomena. *Educ. Psychol. Measurement,* 1943, **3,** 49–65.

Cattell, R. B. *Personality and motivation: structure and measurement.* Tarrytown, N.Y.: World Book Co., 1957.

Clark, B. R. *The open door college.* New York: McGraw-Hill, 1960.

Clark, R. E. Psychoses, income, and occupational prestige. In R. Bendix, and S. M. Lipset (Eds.), *Class, status, and power.* Glencoe, Ill.: The Free Press, 1953, pp. 333–340.

Cole, C. C. *Encouraging scientific talent.* New York: College Entrance Examining Board, 1956.

Davidson, Helen H., and Riesman, F. Personality characteristics attributed to several occupational groups. (Paper read at Eastern Psychol. Ass., Atlantic City, N.J., April, 1959.)

Douvan, Elizabeth, and Kaye, Carol. Adolescent girls. (Multilithed.) New York: Girl Scouts of U.S.A., 1957.

Eddy, E. E. *The college influence on student character.* Washington, D.C.: American Council on Education, 1959.

Erikson, E. H. Growth and crises of the healthy personality. In C. Kluckhohn, H. A. Murray, and D. M. Schneider (Eds.), *Personality in nature, society, and culture.* New York: Knopf, 1956, pp. 185–225.

Frumkin, R. M. Occupation and major mental disorders. In R. M. Rose (Ed.), *Mental health and mental disorder.* New York: Norton, 1955, pp. 136–160.

Gillespie, J. M., and Allport, G. W. *Youth's outlook on the future.* New York: Doubleday, 1955.

Ginzberg, E., Ginsburg, S. W., Axelrad, S., and Herma, J. L. *Occupational choice: an approach to a general theory.* New York: Columbia University Press, 1951.

Grunes, Willa F. Looking at occupations. *J. abnorm. soc. Psychol.,* 1957, **54,** 86–92.

Habein, Margaret L. (Ed.) *Spotlight on the college student.* Washington, D.C.: American Council on Education, 1959.

Haire, M. Role-perceptions in labor-management relations: an experimental approach. *Industr. and Labor Relat. Rev.,* 1955, **8,** 204–216.

Havemann, E., and West, Patricia S. *They went to college*. New York: Harcourt, Brace, 1952.

Hollingshead, A. B., and Redlich, F. C. *Social class and mental illness*. New York: Wiley, 1958.

Iffert, R. E. *Retention and withdrawal of college students*. Washington, D.C.: U.S. Dept. of Health, Education and Welfare—Office of Education, 1957.

Inkeles, A., and Rossi, P. H. National comparisons of occupational prestige. *Amer. J. Sociol.*, 1956, **61**, 329–339.

Jacob, P. E. *Changing values in college*. New York: Harper Bros., 1957.

Lipset, S. M., and Bendix, R. *Social mobility in industrial society*. Berkeley, Cal.: University of California Press, 1959.

Mead, Margaret, and Metraux, Rhoda. Image of the scientist among high-school students. *Science*, 1957, **126**, 384–390.

Mills, C. W. *White collar*. New York: Oxford, 1951.

Myers, J. K., and Roberts, B. H. *Family and class dynamics in mental illness*. New York: Wiley, 1959.

Nunnally, J., and Kittross, J. M. Public attitudes toward mental health professions. *Amer. Psychologist*, 1958, **13**, 589–594.

O'Dowd, D. D., and Beardslee, D. C. *College student images of a selected group of professions and occupations*. Final Report Cooperative Research Project No. 562, U.S. Office of Education. Middletown, Conn.: Wesleyan University, 1960.

O'Dowd, D. D., and Beardslee, D. C. Image of the college professor. *AAUP Bulletin*, 1961a, in press.

O'Dowd, D. D., and Beardslee, D. C. The student image of the school teacher. *Phi Delta Kappan*, 1961b, **42**, 250–254.

Osgood, C. E., and Stagner, R. Analysis of prestige frame of reference by a gradient technique. *J. appl. Psychol.*, 1941, **25**, 275–290.

Osgood, C. E., Suci, G. J., and Tannenbaum, P. H. *The measurement of meaning*. Urbana, Ill.: University of Illinois Press, 1957.

Remmers, H. H., and Radler, D. H. *The American teenager*. Indianapolis: Bobbs-Merrill, 1957.

Roe, Anne. *The psychology of occupations*. New York: Wiley, 1956.

Rosenberg, M. *Occupations and values*. Glencoe, Ill.: Free Press, 1957.

Sanford, N. (Ed.) Personality development during the college years. *J. soc. Issues*, 1956, **12** (4).

Shaffer, L. F., and Shoben, E. J., Jr. *The psychology of adjustment*. (2nd ed.) Boston: Houghton Mifflin, 1956.

Sisson, E. D. Vocational choices of college students. *School and Society*, 1937, **46**, 765–768.

Super, D. E. *The psychology of careers*. New York: Harper Bros., 1957.

Triandis, H. C. Differential perception of certain jobs and people by managers, clerks, and workers in industry. *J. appl. Psychol.*, 1959, **43**, 221–225.

Trow, W. D. Phantasy and vocational choice. *Occupations*, 1941, **20**, 89–93.

Walker, K. F. A study of occupational stereotypes. *J. appl. Psychol.*, 1958, **42**, 122–124.

Warner, W. L., and Abegglen, J. C. *Occupational mobility in American business and industry*. Minneapolis, Minn.: University of Minnesota Press, 1955.

Warner, W. L., Meeker, Marchia, and Eells, K. *Social class in America*. Chicago: Science Research Associates, Inc., 1949.

Wise, W. M. *They come for the best of reasons—college students today*. Washington, D.C.: American Council on Education, 1958.

19 *John Summerskill*

Dropouts from College

THE PROBLEM

Why do approximately half the students attending American colleges and universities leave before advancing their education to the point of an undergraduate degree? The extensive literature addressed to this question yields neither adequate nor conclusive answers. The dropout problem has been of continuing concern to educators and has been subject to perennial rediscovery in the research literature. Research on college student dropouts, college student attrition, has a history of at least 40 years.

In view of this long-standing concern, our knowledge of the attrition process is surprisingly meager. Scores of pertinent investigations have been conducted, including some thoughtful and well-designed studies at various colleges, and two major surveys have been undertaken by agencies of the federal government (Iffert, 1954; McNeeley, 1939). But the problem has apparently never captured the active interest of any substantial segment of the social science profession and there has been no concerted effort to pull together existing, fragmentary knowledge and deliver results of general value.

This chapter is a summary of existing findings on attrition culled from the research literature. These findings roughly sketch what is known and what is not known about dropouts from college. Obviously this one summarization cannot deal with all the facts or all the

Note. This work was sponsored by a grant from the Ford Foundation to the Department of Clinical and Preventive Medicine, Cornell University. This grant is gratefully acknowledged here.

questions pertaining to that dimension of complex human behavior here labeled attrition.

Previous research arose chiefly in institutional or administrative concerns, and only rarely has the process of attrition been analyzed in psychological or sociological terms.

The colleges' interest in attrition has at least three origins. First, there is a persistent underlying concept that the American college is organized as a training center rather than as an intellectual center. Colleges are supposed to qualify young people for entrance to careers in business or industry, science or technology, medicine or law, homemaking or community service. These are institutional objectives given strong support in our culture by students and parents, by corporations and professional schools, by state and federal governments. In this tradition, when students fail to make the grade, disappointment and hostility are frequently directed at the college, and the college with a high attrition rate is criticized for doing a poor job—regardless of the quality of its teaching and research. Consequently many educators and administrators are sensitive about the local attrition rate, and this has led to countless statistical analyses of the problem both within and between colleges.

Secondly, interest in student attrition has been stimulated by the marked increase in the size and complexity of colleges. Schools that became large colleges or universities, with far-flung educational activities and budgets running into millions of dollars, inevitably acquired full-time, highly organized, professional administrations. Charged with responsibility for the overall operations of these institutions and, in particular, with their financial operations, administrators have been necessarily concerned with efficiency. Hence, interest in attrition. As Sheeder (1939) stated: "The nature and extent of student losses constitute one measure of the efficiency of any educational institution." Throughout the literature on attrition one finds concern about educational efficiency, e.g., "for both students and colleges, these withdrawals mean a waste of time, of energy, and of money . . ." (Macintosh, 1948). One investigator even took the trouble to calculate that 144 students in academic difficulty absorbed approximately 1000 hours of special faculty committee time (Dressel, 1943)!

A third reason for the study of attrition is both less subtle and less talked about: dollars leave the income side of the budget when students leave the college. No matter what the nature and size of other income sources, most colleges depend heavily on student fees (or state appropriations on a per student basis) for unrestricted income with which to pay faculty salaries and certain operating expenses. When student attrition is high the college budget, typically under strain, may be unable to meet expenses, and, quite naturally, there is renewed concern at the college about student losses.

These administrative and economic concerns have generated research in kind, and much of the work to date consists of tabulation, statistical analysis, and actuarial study based on school records and related data. There have been a large number of investigations of attrition rate by type of college, size of graduating high school class, and age of entering student. There have also been many compilations of reasons for leaving as determined by official college records or brief questionnaires or "exit interviews." There has been continuous effort to determine the extent of correlation between "attrition" or "length of persistence" and high school grades, aptitude and achievement test scores, family financial status, and countless other variables.

It is one thing to recognize the economic and administrative consequences of attrition and quite another to see the process of attrition to be economic or administrative in and of itself. Yet this last has been the prevailing approach because most persons studying attrition have had institutional or official concerns—in the college admissions or registrar's office, in the department of education administration, in the educational offices of government. Research of this type has not been adequate to the development of better understanding of college student dropouts nor has it succeeded in substantially reducing high attrition rates.

RATES OF ATTRITION

The rate at which students drop from college has been carefully calculated for individual institutions and for nationwide samples. However, anyone interested in precise information on attrition rates should be aware of certain shortcomings in the data. First, colleges do not readily publish figures on students who have withdrawn or failed, and statistical surveys in this area are sometimes inadequate in their sampling procedures.

Secondly, "attrition rate" has been variously defined: for example, as the percentage of students lost to each of the separate academic divisions of a college; as the percentage of students lost to the college as a whole (disregarding transfers within the college); as the percentage of students lost to higher education as a whole. Furthermore, attrition rates have been computed on a graduated-in-four-years basis; on a graduated-in-four-years-or-still-enrolled basis; on a graduated-eventually basis. To ensure complexity, not to mention tedium, there is a jargon running through the literature with such terms as "holding power," "student mortality," "involuntary vs. voluntary withdrawal," "net vs. gross attrition," and so forth.

Fortunately, certain major studies give a fairly clear picture of how much attrition does take place in American colleges and universities. The first of these was supervised by McNeeley of the U.S. Department of Education and concerned dropouts and failures among 15,535 students who entered 25 universities in 1931 and 1932. In summary, these schools lost, on the average, 62.1% of these students in the succeeding four years. McNeeley established, however, that 17% were transfers to some other college or university, so the loss to higher education was 45.2% (McNeeley, 1937).

A similar survey was more recently sponsored by the Department of Health, Education, and Welfare, under the direction of Iffert, and this survey covered attrition among a sample of 12,667 students who entered 149 institutions of higher learning in 1950. The central findings indicate that these schools lost approximately half their students in the succeeding four years and graduated only 39.5% in four years. By extrapolation, Iffert arrives at a rough estimate of "59 per cent as the probable maximum percentage eventually graduating" (Iffert, 1957).

Both McNeeley and Iffert show that the attrition rate is somewhat higher at state-supported institutions than at private institutions; and it should be recognized in this connection that in certain states the institutions of higher education must, by law, accept all qualified high school graduates. Approximately half the total withdrawals occur before the sophomore year, according to Iffert and others, and this is undoubtedly due to the fact that the freshman year serves a screening function for many colleges.

The present writer reviewed 35 different studies that cited attrition rates for classes entering hundreds of varied colleges and universities from 1913 to the present. Median values were computed for the aggregate of these studies with results as follows: median loss in four years—50%; median percent graduated in four years—37%.

Apparently the attrition rate has not changed appreciably in the past forty years. Four studies conducted at different colleges in the 1920s showed a loss of 53% of entering students after four years. The equivalent figure for six other studies in the 1930s was 50%; for eight studies in the 1940s—49%; and for five studies in the 1950s—51%.

Variability in attrition rates among colleges is great, ranging from 12% to 82% in the 35 studies reviewed by the writer. The existence of this very considerable variability provides an interesting but un-exploited opportunity for comparative research in colleges selected for high and low attrition rates.

In summary, American colleges lose, on the average, approximately half their students in the four years after matriculation. Some 40% of college students graduate on schedule and, in addition, approximately 20% graduate at some college, some day. These have been the facts for several decades in American higher education.

FACTORS ASSOCIATED WITH DROPPING OUT OF COLLEGE

Biological and social.

Age at Matriculation. There have been a number of studies relating age at matriculation to subsequent success or failure at college. At three colleges attrition rates were similar for younger and older students (Gable, 1957; Suddarth, 1957; Thompson, 1953). Similarly, a follow-up study of "early admission" students at four universities produced no evidence that these students differed from their older classmates in rate of withdrawal or reasons for withdrawal (Farnsworth et al., 1955). On the other hand, investigations at other colleges have shown older students somewhat less likely to graduate (Cooper, 1928; Pope, 1931; Summerskill and Darling, 1955).

Results attributing a higher attrition rate to the older age group should be interpreted with care. Older students may have been delayed in entering college for personal or financial or other reasons that persist and contribute to withdrawal. In fact, Feder showed that a number of students who were delayed in matriculating had a higher withdrawal rate although their college grades were better than predicted (Feder, 1940).

The general conclusion to be drawn from the literature is that age per se does not affect attrition although older undergraduates may encounter more obstacles to graduation.

Sex. The most recent nationwide survey found attrition rates of 61% for college men and 59% for college women, a difference that is not significant according to Iffert (1957). Studies over the years at men's, women's, and coeducational colleges have either shown little sex difference in attrition rates (Cummings, 1949; Iffert, 1954; Johnson, 1954; Pattishall et al., 1957; Suddarth, 1957; Summerskill et al., 1955) or somewhat less attrition among women at certain colleges (Cuff, 1929; Hoffman, 1939; Wayne University, 1955).

The fact that men and women students withdraw at similar rates does not mean that they withdraw for similar reasons. The proportion of female high school graduates entering college is still less than 60% of the corresponding proportion of males (Bridgeman, 1959). College women are more highly selected and are characterized by better grades and less academic failure (Harris, 1940; Sheeder, 1939; Summerskill et al., 1955; Wayne University, 1955). There is evidence that the withdrawal rate for women equals that of men because more women withdraw for nonacademic reasons, primarily for marriage (Iffert, 1957).

Socio-economic Factors. College counseling experience suggests that a student's economic and social background affects his adjustment to the environment of a given college and is, therefore, a factor in attrition. Research findings on this hypothesis are equivocal.

Studies at two large universities did show more dropouts among students whose fathers were in skilled, semi-skilled, or service occupations (Suddarth, 1957; Summerskill et al., 1955). But in one of these studies the difference did not appear when controls were run on the students' high school performance (Suddarth, 1957). In the same vein, when a group of students with high college achievement was compared with a low achievement group, equated on scholastic aptitude and high school performance, there were no significant differences with reference to parental ages and nativity, home-language usage, parental occupation, and family income (Pearlman, 1952).

At the same time, the last mentioned study demonstrated that "overachievement" (cf. Brown, Chapter 16) is associated with the amount of the parents' education; it is more likely to be found when the students' fathers had studied beyond the baccalaureate level or the mothers had attended high school or beyond. Similarly, Farnsworth and his associates (1955) produced some evidence that the success of students admitted to college at an early age was closely related to the educational level of their parents. These authors, working in a clinical context, explain: if a student comes from a family where educational and intellectual matters are highly prized, and if the student is not blocked in his identification with his parents, he takes on these educational values.

These matters deserve close study. Colleges can be viewed as subcultures with numerous role-demands that they impose upon students who come from differing subcultures (cf. Chapters 2 and 3). To illustrate briefly, it is known that at a large Eastern university with high academic standards students with a Jewish heritage have a comparatively low rate of academic failure (Summerskill et al., 1955). The explanation may lie in home values upholding learning and cultural advancement, it may lie in stronger needs for professional and career success and attendant social and economic security, or it may lie in the fact of secondary school preparation in large cities with consequent advantages at a cosmopolitan, intellectually demanding university. A study directed toward an understanding of the valid reasons underlying this demonstrated relationship between religion and attrition would undoubtedly contribute to a better understanding of dropouts within this particular university subculture.

Open to much needed research is this question what are the relationships between socio-economic and other background characteristics of students and success or failure at colleges that have identifiable subcultural patterns?

Hometown Location and Size. According to previous research a student's hometown location and size may be factors in attrition. For example, higher attrition rates among students from rural homes than among students from cities or towns were uncovered in three earlier studies (Cuff, 1929; Strang, 1937; West, 1928). Also, one survey found that "out-of-state" students are likely to be underachievers (Feder, 1940) and another survey found that students from cities with populations over 100,000 are likely to be "overachievers" (Fredericksen et al., 1951).

These results have not always been confirmed. It is questionable whether location and size of home communities are in themselves variables that determine a student's chances of graduating from college. There are, however, differences between cities and towns with respect to quality and curriculum in secondary school education. Similarly, there are hometown differences with respect to cultural opportunity as indicated by the range and number of facilities and events for cultural enrichment. Students growing up in these differing environments enter colleges that also differ along these dimensions. Colleges are small or large in population and complexity, predominantly rural or predominantly urban in character, difficult or easy in their academic requirements, rich or meager in their cultural demands and opportunities.

Results to date indicate that a student's hometown is sometimes and somehow related to success or failure at college. The suggestion here is to look beneath the correlations involving variables of population and geographical location; to analyze the educational and cultural characteristics of given communities; to analyze the educational and cultural characteristics of given colleges; and to see to what extent attrition is a function of disparity between hometown and college environments in these educational and cultural terms.

Academic factors in attrition. Regardless of the student's age, sex, economic or hometown background, the central requirement for a college degree is the successful completion of courses offered and pre-scribed by the college. At the core of the social and emotional com-plexities of the college situation there is a job of work for which the student must have sufficient prior training and sufficient ability. Most colleges require applicants to have completed college preparatory studies; and the abilities of applicants are systematically evaluated in order to select those able to do the work. This section examines rela-tionships between academic background and ability, on the one hand, and college success or failure, on the other hand.

Secondary School Preparation. Secondary school grades are generally recognized as the best existing predictors of college grades. Many stu-dents drop from college with satisfactory grades, however, so the question remains: are grades in secondary school significantly related to college attrition?

The answer is yes. The writer found that in ten of eleven studies specifically concerned with this question college "dropouts" had lower average grades in secondary school than did graduates. It is difficult to give a meaningful figure describing the extent of this relationship because the studies varied with respect to schools, students, grading systems, and methods of statistical analysis. In some instances there were statistically significant differences in secondary school grades between college graduates and dropouts, and in other instances these differences were in the predicted direction but not statistically sig-nificant.

Nevertheless, it is possible substantially to reduce high attrition rates by simply raising college admissions requirements with respect to secondary school grades. Iffert found that the attrition rate for men attending twenty colleges and universities would have been reduced from 61.2% to 43.9% if admissions had been confined to the top fifth of high school graduating classes. He also concluded that: "The per-centages . . . seem to show that standing in high school graduating class was a much better indicator of the probability of graduation than standing in the placement tests" (Iffert, 1957).

Other aspects of secondary school preparation have also been ex-amined in relation to college attrition. For example, there is some evidence that students from larger high schools have significantly bet-ter chances of graduating from college (Suddarth, 1957; Thompson, 1953). Why? Because the larger high schools graduate students with better scholastic aptitude (Feder, 1940)? Because students from larger high schools tend to better "social development" ratings (Alexander and Woodruff, 1940)? What selective or educational forces within high schools produce students more likely to succeed at college? It is possible that attrition at college can be most effectively reduced by changes in educational policy and practice at the secondary school level.

Scholastic Aptitude. There have been at least 19 investigations of scholastic aptitude test scores in relation to subsequent attrition. Average scholastic aptitude scores were found to be lower for dropouts than for graduates in 16 of these investigations. The American Council on Education tests have received special attention, and in 12 of 13 studies there were aptitude differences (not always statistically significant) between college graduates and dropouts. Similar differences have been found with the College Entrance Examination Board tests, but results with the Ohio State Psychological Examination were equivocal in the studies reviewed by the writer.

Three studies also demonstrated that dropouts had significantly lower reading test scores (Freehill, 1954; Johnson, 1926; Pattishall and Banghart, 1957) and another study found results in the same direction (Hanks, 1954).

In summary, there is substantial evidence that colleges can reduce attrition by rejecting applicants whose scores on standardized tests of scholastic aptitude fall below the minimums set by the college. But this fact is not especially valuable to the many colleges now in a position to admit only students with the highest aptitude scores from an astonishingly large pool of applicants. Here there is need for better understanding and assessment of the capability of the student, beyond his measured intellectual potential, for grasping the content of college instruction. We need to know more about the capability of high school graduates for the job of scholarship with its demands on curiosity, initiative, and intellectual energy.

Research in this area has only scratched the surface, although some leads exist. For example, results at one college indicated that ratings by secondary school principals on the personality characteristics of students did not predict college success or failure, but ratings on students' intellectual and working characteristics did (Mercer, 1943). Another example: a study of student attitudes at a college showed that the more successful students held more favorable attitudes regarding their secondary school preparation (Weigand, 1951). Conversely, unsuccessful students at other colleges were found to be less satisfied with their high school preparation (Cooper, 1928) and with school in general, extending back in memory to elementary school experiences (Fredericksen and Schrader, 1951). Taken as a whole these data suggest that there are identifiable attitudes to school and to school work that affect chances of graduation from college in later years.

Rigorous research focused on the psychological content of the learning experience and the meaning of scholarship for the young people attending secondary school today would be exceedingly helpful. College teachers are familiar with the student who arrives at college with ample intellectual endowment but somehow lacks the inclination and the values required for scholarship. The psychology of the young student, the origins, meanings, and personal advantages that are found in attitudes favorable or unfavorable to scholarship—these matters are not well understood. Stated simply, what does it take to be a capable college student? Without sure answers to this question the schools and colleges have difficulty assisting young people in becoming scholars, and college admissions procedures are unable to identify accurately the young people who have this capability.

Academic Performance at College. Generations of students will testify that college grades are an important determinant of college dropouts. There have been at least 35 studies on college grades and attrition and it is clear that a significant relationship does exist. The results permit a number of statements describing this relationship:

1. In a series of 23 studies the percentage of academic failures among those who dropped out ranged from 3% to 78%, reflecting differences in the policies and standards of colleges and in the composition of student bodies.

2. The median value was 33%, i.e., one out of three dropouts occurred for academic reasons.

3. Academic failure was typically cited as the leading single cause of dropouts or as one of two or three leading causes—depending upon the college studied.

4. The relationship between grades and attrition appears to be continuous in that the probability of dropping out varies inversely with grade point averages throughout the whole distribution of grades at a given college.

5. Prediction of dropouts is better at the lower end of the grade scale, i.e., students with poor grades are highly likely to drop out while students with excellent grades may drop out.

6. Poor or failing grades at the beginning of a college career are highly predictive of dropouts. For example, samples of poor students at three different colleges had attrition rates of 78, 86, and 91% respectively (Dressel, 1943; Pope, 1931; Potthoff, 1931). Similarly, among 2118 students entering Purdue Unversity in 1952 very few who went on probation one or more times graduated (Suddarth, 1957).

Recognizing that up to one third of the college dropouts are due to poor grades and academic failure it is equally important to realize that the majority of students leave college for nonacademic reasons. Furthermore, among dropouts that college records ascribe to "academic failure" there are undoubtedly many cases in which the underlying problems are psychological, parental, social, or financial. For example, in one study of selected students 9 cases of "academic failure" were reclassified by psychiatrists as 4 cases of "inappropriate values," 2 cases of "immaturity," 2 cases of "psychiatric disorder," and 1 case of "realistic academic failure" (Farnsworth et al., 1955). In such cases "academic failure" may serve the student as a device for taking leave of school when the underlying problems are not solved on their own terms. In general, then, the attrition problems that predominate in the colleges involve the students' failure to meet the psychological, sociological, or economic demands rather than the strictly academic demands of the college environment.

It is still true, however, that tens of thousands of students leave college each year because they cannot make the grade academically and for no other known reason. Since the objectives of colleges are to educate and graduate the students they admit, academic failure must be viewed as a failure on the part of the institution as well as on the part of the individual student. When a student fails on purely academic grounds he testifies to inadequate admissions procedures or inadequate instruction. There is urgent need for further research on institutional practices that contribute to the current high rate of academic failure in colleges.

It is beyond the scope of this chapter to deal in detail with the vast literature on characteristics of students related to grade point averages and academic overachievement or underachievement. The literature suggests that good and poor students are differentiated with fair accuracy by patterns of work and study, i.e., time spent in study, time spent in class, library usage, methods of study, ability to keep up with work, reading speed and comprehension. Generally speaking, the work characteristics of students who fail academically are reasonably well known and understood. There is considerably less understanding of the individual motivational forces responsible for the emergence of effective or ineffective work patterns at college.

Motivation. The largest number of dropouts involve motivational forces—goals, interests, and satisfactions relative to college and other facets of the student's life. This is a difficult proposition to prove or develop because the motivational psychology of college students is still in a vague and crude state and there has been little critical experimentation. But in most existing studies of reasons for attrition the largest proportion of dropouts are typically attributed to "lack of interest in college," "lack of interest in studies," "marriage" or "marriage plans," "transfer," "entered military service," "accepted job," and so forth.

From existing data there is no way accurately to determine the percentage of dropouts for whom such motivational factors are of crucial importance. In one sample of 1450 "discontinued" students 48% of the men reported they lacked interest in studies, 45% enlisted in military service (Korean War time), 24% accepted full-time jobs, 11% had marriage plans. Among the women dropouts 49% reported marriage plans, 37% took full-time jobs, 33% lacked interest in studies, and 1% enlisted (Iffert, 1957). The percentage totals here, as in most similar studies, exceed 100, indicating that the individuals were classified more than once. This is due, in part, to a lack of distinction between reasons and outcomes, e.g., a dropout classified as dissatisfied with his studies is also classified as having entered military service. It is owing, in part, to multicausality which operates in the dropout process. A four year follow-up study of 300 students entering Cornell University found that there were, on the average, two-plus primary reasons for each dropout and two additional contributing reasons. The complexity of available data thus prohibits any concise statement about the percentage of dropouts attributable to motivational factors. It can be said that these are the factors which appear most frequently in the studies reviewed.

Lack of Motivation. One recurring description of dropouts runs as follows: The dropouts were . . . "in college because of various motives, which, however, did not include a desire to study. Most of them had momentum, were headed somewhither—but not toward those proximate goals which college courses present" (Woods and Chase, 1937). Another researcher writes in similar vein: "A group . . . primarily socially oriented . . . They have come to college to make a good marriage or to acquire a smattering of a liberal education for its usefulness in social situations, and they are quite resistive to real intellectual development . . . find academic demands of the college very onerous, and many are likely to withdraw at the end of the sophomore year" (Freedman, 1956). Likewise: "This lack of values for education associated with lack of motivation was also a frequent cause of academic failure" (Farnsworth et al., 1955).

Competent people who have studied attrition have concluded that lack of motivation with reference to college accounts for a substantial number of dropouts. The pertinent results differ, however, according to the research methods employed, and there is not clear and consistent support for the generally accepted conclusion. For example, Iffert found that "lack of interest" was one of the most important reasons reported by dropouts for discontinuing. On the other hand, the same investigator stated that "every effort in this study to find an association of sufficient magnitude . . . by comparing the ratings of reasons for going to college and the records of persistence has met with failure" (Iffert, 1957). In other words, attrition was associated with expressed attitudes toward the studies in which the dropouts had been engaged but was not associated with their reported reasons for undertaking these studies.

The trouble here is that we do not know what motivational forces are actually predictive of college success and we do not know how to accurately assess such motives in students. College teachers have fairly fixed conceptions of scholarly motivation and its importance but students—including excellent students—will report a wide variety of reasons for going to college, for example, to prepare for a particular vocation, to be independent, to meet interesting people, to satisfy parents, to get a good education, to gain security, to be of service, to make money, to become a better person, to see what it's like, to get away from home, to take advantage of a scholarship (cf. Chapter 4). In a sense, whether or not these various motives are scholarly is immaterial. It is important to examine all motives that are brought to the learning situation and to ask whether, in fact, they promote or deter scholarly accomplishment. This is a difficult research task because the student may have multiple reasons for going to college and these are not necessarily conscious or articulate in the 16-, or 17-, or 18-year old. Weigand concludes an intensive psychological study of 81 dropouts at the University of Maryland by suggesting an alternative approach, i.e., "future studies investigating motivational factors should emphasize the actual behavior of the individual" (Weigand, 1951).

Vocational motivation is more demonstrably related to attrition. Students with definite vocational choices are more likely to be overachievers at college (Alexander and Woodruff, 1940; Fredericksen and Schrader, 1951; Iffert, 1957; Rust and Ryan, 1952), but not at all colleges (Harris, 1940). Similarly, students with definite vocational choices are more likely to graduate from college (Iffert, 1957; Mercer, 1941; Weigand, 1951), although this, too, has not been a universal finding (Cooper, 1928; Thompson, 1953). It is noteworthy that the majority of students can report a "definite" or "probable" vocational choice early in their college careers. For many, these choices involve professional training and careers so that graduation from college is regarded as essential and is more likely to occur (Fredericksen and Schrader, 1951).

In any study of motivational factors in attrition it is most important to pay attention to institutional characteristics and values. To illustrate, a student with a definite vocational goal such as medicine or industrial management or agricultural sales has, in general, the best chance of academic success, according to the evidence reported above. Yet this same student can have considerable difficulty if he enters a college where the main concern is a liberal education and there is little support of essentially vocational aspirations. Indeed, contrary to the general evidence, one analysis of academic failure at certain universities states: "Although comparing favorably in intellectual level and college board scores with the successful students, many (failures) showed little value for learning per se and in particular for the liberal arts. They were more vocationally or, in anthropological terms, 'Doing,' oriented. They saw the value of a college education solely in terms of earning a living" (Farnsworth et al., 1955). The point here is that it is inadequate to ask whether a student has sufficient and appropriate motivation for college. The more meaningful question is: does the student have sufficient and appropriate motivation for a specified college with specified characteristics and objectives.

Finally, in conducting research in this area it is helpful to distinguish between motivation with respect to a college and motivation with respect to graduation from that college. Among students entering a given college there are those who explicitly have little or no intention of completing the degree requirements. Craven (1951) found, for example, that 62% of 611 withdrawals felt satisfied with their relatively brief careers at one university. In motivational studies of students who fail to graduate it would be advisable to exclude or treat separately those students who entered the college with intentions other than completion of degree requirements.

Change and Conflict in Motivation. To this point the discussion has assumed that there are some students with the motivation to do the work of a college and some students without such motivation. But motivation is not a static concept; and interests, needs, and goals shift and evolve in young men and women.

Attrition rates provide crude indices of the extent of the motivational change that takes place in the college population. Of the 60% of the college population that drops out more than one-third have demonstrated academic capability but leave college to pursue other interests and goals. In many studies the majority of dropouts state upon leaving their intention to complete their undergraduate education eventually. In fact, the majority do not.

If the proposition is true, that personality changes cause dropouts, it is not well understood. As Webster, Freedman, and Heist point out in Chapter 24, ". . . there is actually little agreement concerning either the relative importance of the various kinds of changes that can be observed, or how best to study them." Furthermore, existing knowledge of personality change in college students has not been systematically related to the process of attrition in known collegiate environments. Any discussion along these lines must be chiefly speculative.

The college counselor learns that there are two dimensions to the dropout problem that are not immediately apparent in the classroom. First, the student is still highly responsive to psychological and sociological forces originating outside the immediate college environment. Second, although colleges are principally concerned with cognitive and rational matters, students are human beings who act according to emotions, feelings, and desires.

Parents occupy key positions in the wider circle of influences upon the changing motivations of the college student. It is the writer's impression that in recent decades we, as parents, have been advised by PTA speakers, school counselors, and others, not to influence actively our children's motives with respect to college and career. Consequently it is not uncommon for a parent carefully to point out to the college counselor that the family conscientiously refrained from interference in these matters. But this is superficial, for the lives of many college students are influenced in important ways by feelings of dependency, ambition, fear, guilt, and rebellion, stemming from family aspirations, sanctions, or disapproval.

A college clinic or counseling office has countless examples of these psychological forces at work, but one must suffice here (cf. Chapter 4). A young man from a Midwestern high school decided, essentially on his own, to attend an Ivy League university for premedical study. This decision received backing and encouragement from the parents, who were of European and Jewish heritage, who had not attended college, and who had built a successful small business. The son worked reasonably hard at the university and later informed his parents that he had become interested in a possible career in teaching or research. This prompted the parents to visit the university where the father expressed concern that his son "wasn't getting anywhere." He was particularly disturbed that the boy had not made his mark in campus activities. The family's emotional support was subtly, progressively, and effectively withdrawn from this boy. Used to an overly protective and authoritarian relationship with his parents, the boy was now unable to act independently. He had quite strong feelings of resentment and guilt regarding his parents, he was unable to concentrate on his studies, and he gave up his new-found interests in research or teaching, leaving the university "to take a job." He did not return.

Change and conflict in the motivation that produces dropouts is not, of course, entirely rooted in family situations. Love relationships are established and mature during the college years and these may become more important to the individual than continuance of college studies. We have observed earlier in this chapter that marriage is a leading cause of dropouts among college women. Similarly, group and community relationships may become of such importance to the individual that they displace motivation for attending a particular college. Nearly all studies concerned with reasons-for-leaving report a minor percentage of students who left college to live in the home community, a smaller community, a less isolated community, or some other desired social environment.

Sometimes circumstances outside the college force the student to change his goals and plans regardless of positive motivation for college. The most obvious and frequent instance during the past 20 years has been the military service requirement, which in war time accounted for the largest percentage of dropouts. Although the number of students drafted from college now is small, the Selective Service requirement still influences some students to drop out in order to enter the armed forces, and it influences others to continue at college in order to remain exempt from military service.

There are other unavoidable, and often unexpected, environmental circumstances that cause dropouts. Among these are death or serious illness in the family, or a father losing his job or being transferred afar. Attrition studies show that these factors account for a relatively small number of dropouts.

The paucity of research on motivational change and conflict as it affects attrition has already been noted. There are, however, existing studies that should not be overlooked by anyone working in this area. A doctoral thesis by Craven (1951) contains a number of observations on family relationships and attrition; an investigation by Rust and Ryan (1955) that fails to relate students' reports on parental attitudes and interests to academic achievement in college; a doctoral thesis by Weigand (1951) that shows that discrepancy between students' desired occupations and their actual occupational and curricular choices are significantly related to academic failure. But the key questions remain unanswered. What are the motivational changes in college students that lead to success and satisfaction in academic activity? What are the motivational changes that cause students to leave college for success and satisfaction elsewhere? To what extent is it possible for students to reconcile and overcome differences between their personal goals and interests and those of the collegiate institution? To what extent is it possible for the college to accept and work with individual differences in student goals and interests?

Attrition owing to motivational causes has been widespread and essentially irreducible. The writer believes that a greatly expanded program of basic research in the psychology and sociology of college students is required to improve this situation.

Adjustment. To recapitulate, academic difficulty has been found in approximately one-third of college dropouts, and motivational difficulty has been ascribed to an even larger number.

The adjustment of college dropouts is still another question—how do these students get along, personally, emotionally, socially? Survey findings indicate that the dropouts who report feelings of dissatisfaction in the personal or social realm are in the minority. Iffert (1957) found that only 15% of 2580 discontinuees said that they were "lonesome and unhappy" and they gave this reason little importance in the decision to leave school. The writer reviewed eleven studies concerned with this type of student reaction and the percentage of dropouts with personal dissatisfaction was in the 4% to 17% range with a median value of 10%.

Clinical observation suggests that the percentage of dropouts with some degree of emotional difficulty is much higher. Farnsworth (1959) states: "No reliable statistics are available as to how many of those who leave college do so because of emotional conflicts. However, we have good reason to believe that in some institutions the proportion is considerably more than half." Among the psychological characteristics that have been attributed to unsuccessful students are immaturity (Farnsworth et al., 1955; Gilmore, 1951; Woods and Chase, 1937); rebellion and nonconformity (Farnsworth et al., 1955; Freedman, 1956; Woods and Chase, 1937); worry and anxiety (Freedman, 1956; Gilmore, 1951); social inadequacy (Freedman, 1956); nonadaptability (Weigand, 1951); lack of independence and responsibility (Grace, 1957) ; the more severe emotional difficulties including neurosis, character disorder, or psychosis (Darling, 1955; Farnsworth et al., 1955; Harrison, 1956); and others.

There is thus a discrepancy in results when one asks whether emotional maladjustment is an important factor in attrition. The dropouts themselves give relatively little weight to these variables, the clinicians considerably more. Considerations of both reliability and validity are involved in this discrepancy. One questions the accuracy of measurements of personal adjustment when questionnaires contain single items on these complex variables, when dropouts report in retrospect or when they are planning application to another college, and when routine college records are re-examined for evidence of emotional difficulty. Likewise, one questions the reliability of clinical observations that cannot be confirmed without controls involving randomly selected, successful students. Indeed, Fredericksen and Schrader (1951) found that 60% of a large sample of students drawn from several colleges reported that they felt worry and anxiety occasionally and 20% felt this way frequently, regardless of academic success or failure. And the validity problems here are perhaps most important. Clinicians are undoubtedly talking about quite different things when they evaluate "adjustment." The student who is seen as immature or rebellious or nonadaptable does not necessarily see himself in these terms.

Then what can be said about adjustment and attrition? First, 10 to 15% of dropouts report that personal adjustment problems are involved in their leaving school. Second, many clinicians believe that these problems are much more prevalent. Third, it is difficult to prove that the large dropout population is, in fact, different from the large graduate population with regard to the incidence of personal or social maladjustment at college.

Mercer (1941) draws the following conclusion from an attrition study that employed two independent ratings of advisors' records: ". . . . there have been no difficulties given as a reason for leaving college that have not been encountered by students in the high ranking and low ranking (graduating) groups."

Nor were significant differences found in controlled studies using the Bell Adjustment Inventory (Griffiths, 1945), the MMPI (Palubinskas, 1952), and a developmental scale (Webster, 1956). The Rorschach failed to differentiate between academic underachievers and overachievers in two studies (Pearlman, 1952; Ryan, 1951). On the other hand, there have been some reported correlations between attrition and test scores in studies employing the Bell (Fischer, 1943), certain MMPI scales (Grace, 1957), the Rorschach (Munroe, 1945) and ratings of social development (Alexander and Woodruff, 1940). Furthermore, there were an undue number of "problem diagnoses" among withdrawals from one class at Harvard (Monks and Heath, 1954) and there were a disproportionate number of "psychological complaints" in the medical records of one sample of withdrawals from Cornell University.

To summarize, certain instances of leaving college are clearly due to personal and social maladjustment at college but this is probably true for only a minor fraction of the total dropout population. Further understanding of emotional, personal, and social maladjustment in attrition awaits more precise definition of these concepts and more rigorous testing of their affects.

There have been several studies of attrition in relation to social adjustment measured in behavioral terms. For example, the recent governmental survey showed that: "Neither the type of activity nor the amount of time devoted to extra-curricular activities during the first registration period is related to length of attendance in college" (Iffert, 1957). The results of other studies confirm this conclusion or show some positive correlation between academic success at college and participation in extracurricular activities (Gable, 1957; Harris, 1940; Mercer, 1941). The research evidence does not support the common notion that dropouts are frequently caused by overparticipation in extracurricular activities. Similarly, fraternity or sorority membership is not generally a deterrent to graduation, for several studies (Iffert, 1957; Thompson, 1953; Vogt, 1929) indicate that: "Students who were members or pledges of fraternities or sororities had better persistence records and graduation rates in the institutions of first registration than non-members" (Iffert, 1957).

There has been sufficient research in this area to question some of the assumptions made in university circles concerning harmful affects of extracurricular and social activity upon academic progress. There has not been sufficient research to enable universities to reduce attrition by adopting extracurricular policy based on pertinent, demonstrated fact. In particular, there is a dearth of research on the co-educational aspects of extracurricular activity, the effects of differing sex ratios in campus enrollments, dating and marriage patterns, sexual problems and solutions, as these relate to attrition. These factors have prominence in the personal counseling of college dropouts and are of some institutional significance in view of recent coeducational arrangements for student dormitories, dining, and recreational facilities.

Illness and injury. Dropouts due to illness and injury have been recognized through four decades of attrition research. These constitute a relatively small but significant fraction of the total dropout population. In 18 studies reviewed, the percentage of dropouts citing medical reasons was, on the average, 8%. Similarly, Iffert found that 7% of male discontinuees and 10% of female discontinuees attributed "some importance" to medical factors (Iffert, 1957).

It is again necessary to point out that the attrition rate for any category of reasons, including medical, depends upon the particular collegiate environment. Data from Cornell University indicate that more than 90% of the student body seeks medical attention during the four-year college stay and 42% will be hospitalized at least briefly. Many withdrawals for medical reasons are prevented when proper medical care is available at the college. Thus, availability of medical care, and other factors, contribute to variability in the percentage of dropouts due to illness and injury and the range was 1% to 24% in the studies reviewed.

No evidence was uncovered that withdrawals, as a group, have more inherent physical disability than other students. The Cornell data show no differences between withdrawals, academic failures, and other students with reference to: significant deviations in medical histories; chronic disorders found in pre-entrance physical examinations; physique ratings by physicians; number of clinic visits at college (when length of college stay is controlled); incidence of most common medical complaints at college. In the same area, Lerner and Martin (1955) found that the attrition rate for women with physical handicaps entering Hunter College was lower than that for the college at large. Apparently medical factors are specific to a relatively small fraction of the students who drop out from college. Even within this group these factors may be overestimated when independent medical evidence is absent because student explanations of withdrawal on medical grounds find easy acceptance both at college and at home.

Fortunately, student deaths do not contribute materially to attrition. The yearly death rate in the full-time college population is estimated at approximately 1 per 1000. The majority of these tragedies are due to accidents, frequently involving motor vehicles.

Illness or death in the student's family is also responsible for a certain number of withdrawals from college. In fact, the percentage citing family medical factors was approximately the same as the percentage citing personal medical factors among the 2580 dropouts who responded to Iffert's (1957) questionnaire. Dropouts due to family medical crises may reflect a change in the student's financial status.

Finances. Financial difficulty is an important cause of college attrition. Pertinent evidence includes:

1. Personal financial difficulties were ranked third in importance as a reason for leaving college by the men and women surveyed by Iffert (1957).

2. In 16 of 21 studies reviewed by this writer finances were rated as one of the three most important factors in attrition.

3. The median annual income of parents of nongraduating students has been found to be significantly less than that of parents whose children graduate (Iffert, 1957).

The relationship between students' financial status and success or failure at college is complicated by several considerations:

1. The costs of attending college vary greatly from one institution to another, as do the colleges' resources in scholarships and loans.

2. Studies on the relationship between financial status and attrition require careful controls on academic ability because the good student frequently has more scholarship aid.

3. The importance of financial difficulty in attrition is overestimated if students find this reason more permissible than lack of motivation or lack of ability.

4. Self-support and part-time work are poor indicators of success or failure at college. Two reviews of the literature show no consistent relationships between self-support and college grades (Harris, 1940; Strang, 1937), four studies show no clear relationships between this variable and attrition (Cooper, 1928; Gable, 1957; Iffert, 1957; Strabel, 1935), and three studies suggest that self-support actually enhances chances of graduation (Mercer, 1943; Thompson, 1953; Weigand, 1951).

5. With the rapid increase in college tuition and expenses in recent years, particularly in private institutions, there has been a marked expansion of scholarship and loan funds. The federal government, many state governments, corporations, and alumni, have all contributed considerably more money for student financial aid. The college cost and financial aid situation is in a state of flux at this time.

For these reasons there is no meaningful statistic for the extent of attrition nationally due to student financial difficulty. Among the leading causes of dropouts financial problems rank next to motivational and study problems and are found in a substantial minority of the students who leave college before the undergraduate degree work is complete.

DIRECTIONS FOR FUTURE RESEARCH

This review of the literature on college dropouts points up the need for basic research with emphasis on student motivation in specified college environments. Certain questions should be carefully considered in the design and conduct of future research.

The student. What characteristics of students need further study? Demographic factors and scholastic aptitude and performance have been thoroughly investigated. But college students are growing, striving, feeling, thinking, aspiring individuals. In much prior research "the student is classified rather than understood"; future research might well "attempt insight into the frame of reference of the student himself" (Craven, 1951). As Feder (1950) notes: "The failure on the part of most colleges and universities to study clinically the causes of student mortality has denied to administrative officers and faculties valuable information in the area of serving constituent needs." We need to know more about what really motivates the successful college student, whether these motives be personal and essentially affective or academic and essentially rational.

The college. Sanford (1956) asks: "How can one discuss attrition without recognition of the goals of the institution, i.e., the qualities to be fostered in students, means of progress in these directions, and degrees of success?" In research concerned with the tabulation or immediate prediction of dropouts institutional variables have typically been taken for granted or treated as constants. The viewpoint and methodology of the cultural anthropologist are needed here to assess the forceful and changing demands of the college upon its students. These environmental pressures are both formal, e.g., the stated academic requirements of the institution, and informal, e.g., the opportunities for daily social contact, for casual association with faculty and advisors, and arrangements for housing and dining. Indeed, Craven (1951) found withdrawals from one university more concerned with these "inescapable realities of everyday life" than with the organized aspects of student life."

The attrition rate itself can be an environmental factor causing dropouts, for "the entire college atmosphere, both intellectual and social, is different on a campus where almost the entire student body will graduate from that on a campus where only a minority of the entering students will graduate" (Farnsworth et al., 1955). Rigorous research on these environmental determinants of attrition "might obtain evidence that the phenomenon had less to do with factors in the student than with a certain condition in the college itself, and this condition might immediately assume greater practical importance than withdrawal because it was now perceived as something that affected all the students" (Sanford, 1956).

Research procedures. What research procedures should be used in future investigations of attrition? Obviously procedures must be appropriate to the objectives of a particular study, but assumptions in future research should be carefully formulated in the light of what is now known and not known about the attrition process.

First, prior research does not permit the assumption that colleges have information on their dropouts and know the reasons for these dropouts. Both Macintosh (1948) and McNeeley (1939) found that many institutions possess no knowledge concerning a substantial percentage of dropouts and Craven (1951) had to abandon a canvass of advisors and instructors because of the high percentage of blank and incomplete returns. Until colleges develop more interest and better information with regard to dropouts, most researchers will have to devise procedures for collecting original data appropriate to their research aims.

Second, we can assume multicausality in attrition. Tabulations of reasons into neat, mutually exclusive categories (e.g., $X\%$ academic reasons $+ Y\%$ financial reasons $+ Z\%$ medical reasons $= 100\%$ of dropouts) simply do not cope with the realities of college dropouts and are of little value. It has been well established that the typical dropout is due to a "complex of causes" (Farnsworth, 1959; Fedor, 1950; Iffert, 1957; Pope, 1931). It is also helpful to distinguish between causes of primary and causes of secondary importance, and there is some possibility that a combination of causes has a cumulative effect that leads to withdrawal (Pope, 1931).

Third, we cannot assume that outcomes (e.g., jobs, marriage, military service) and causes of attrition are equivalent. As Mercer suggests, analysis in terms of outcomes may obscure the causes that exist in the college situation (Mercer, 1943). If the researcher automatically assumes that withdrawal from college must represent failure or maladjustment his research procedures will miss causal factors important in many dropouts. For example, some students withdraw because they have obtained the academic or personal satisfactions sought at college (Gable, 1957; West, 1928). For other students withdrawal may be a positive and satisfactory solution to problems of an academic, psychological, social, or financial nature. Sanford (1956) notes: ". . . increased knowledge of the withdrawal phenomenon might, quite conceivably, lead to the conclusion that the college should have more rather than fewer dropouts; perhaps too many students were remaining in the college after they reached a level of maturity such that further growth could only be stimulated elsewhere; or perhaps the admission of more students of the type who tended to drop out would be a means for changing the college in some desired way." In any event, research in attrition should clearly distinguish between outcomes and causes and should allow for the possibility that reasons for withdrawal can be positive and desirable from the viewpoint of the student or that of the institution.

Fourth, the reliability and validity of data on dropouts cannot be assumed. Tests of reliability and validity are infrequently encountered in this literature and these are necessary whenever the research objective is to predict success or failure at college in order to modify admissions and other institutional procedures.

Changing times. How will attrition be affected by the apparent intellectual and cultural renaissance among our young people? By the vast number of college applicants? By the growth in colleges and junior colleges? By the tremendous research burden that colleges have assumed in the national interest? By change and growing complexity within colleges as they struggle to meet these responsibilities?

Of course, no one knows the answers, but two things are clear. There is need for continuing re-examination of the facts about attrition that serve as the bases for current policy on admissions, instruction, grading, and counseling. There must be vigorous basic research on the business of going to college and learning, so that the colleges, always with limited resources, will know how to foster maximum intellectual development in the maximum number of students.

REFERENCES

Adams, B. S. Study of first year casualties in the Class of 1959 at Princeton University. Personal communication, November, 1956.
Alexander, H., and Woodruff, Ruth J. Determinants of college success. *J. higher Educ.,* 1940, 11, 479–484.
Allen, C. M. *Combating the dropout problem.* Chicago: Science Research Associates, 1956.
American Association University Professors. The selection, retention, and promotion of undergraduates. *Bull. A.A.U.P.,* 1926, 12, 373–481.
Andrew, D. C. A descriptive analysis of 248 non-high school graduates admitted to the University of Utah. *J. educ. Res.,* 1954, 47, 589–598.

Baker, H. B. The working student and his grades. *J. educ. Res.*, 1941, **35**, 28–35.

Bayley, R. E., Jr. Student retention and withdrawal at the University of Nebraska. Doctoral dissertation, University of Nebraska, in progress.

Berg, I. A., and Larsen, R. P. A comparative study of students entering college one or more semesters before graduation from high school. *J. educ., Res.*, 1939, **39**, 33–41.

Bertrand, J. R. Relation between high school average grade and academic achievement of agricultural students, Agricultural and Mechanical College of Texas. *Col. and Univ.*, 1955, **30**, 166–180.

Boyer, L. E., and Koken, J. E. Admissions tests as criteria for success in college. *J. educ. Res.*, 1956, **40**, 313–315.

Bragg, Emma W. A study of student withdrawal at "W. U." *J. educ. Psychol.*, 1956, **47**, 199–202.

Breen, L. C. The relations of reading ability to college mortality of certain entering freshmen at the University of Washington. Doctoral dissertation, University of Washington, 1954.

Bridgeman, D. S. Losses of intellectual talent from the education system prior to graduation from college. (Mimeo.) June, 1959.

Brown, R. W. Freshman casualties can be cut. *Col. & Univ. Bus.*, 1957, **22**, 26–27.

Byrns, R. K. Scholastic aptitude and freshman achievement. *Sch. & Soc.*, 1932, **35**, 713–718.

Coffey, W. The mortality and academic careers of two groups of college students. *Sch. & Soc.*, 1940, **52**, 269–271.

Cooper, L. B. A study in freshman elimination in one college. *Nation's Schools*, 1928, **2** (3), 25–29.

Corley, C. L. The incidence of certain factors relating to drop-outs from the 1948–52 class at University of Missouri. *Dissert. Abstracts*, 1954, **14**, 1972.

Courter, J. F. A study of student mortality in six Liberal Arts Colleges in Kansas. Unpublished Master's dissertation, Syracuse University, 1957.

Coyle, E. Longitudinal Mortality Study at Brooklyn College. (Mimeo.) Ten Phase Study, School of General Studies, Brooklyn College, February, 1957.

Craven, C. J. Why we withdrew. Unpublished doctoral dissertation, Syracuse University, 1951.

Crawford, A. B. Forecasting freshman achievement. *Sch. & Soc.*, 1930, **31**, 125–132.

Crawford, A. B., and Burnham, P. S. *Forecasting College Achievement.* New Haven: Yale University Press, 1946.

Cuff, Noel. Problem of elimination from college. *Sch. & Soc.*, 1929, **30**, 550–552.

Cummings, E. C. Causes of student withdrawals at DePauw University, *Sch. & Soc.*, 1949, **70**, 152–153.

Darling, C. D. One year's experience with psychosis. In Case Reports of the Cornell University Infirmary and Clinic. *Student Med.*, 1955, **3**, 102–109.

Detchen, Lily. Retention-transfer-marriage rates compared for four classes (1950–53). *Bull. Office of Evaluation Services,* Pennsylvania College for Women (Chatham College), 1952, No. 45.

Detchen, Lily. Who withdraws? Who transfers? Who remains? *Bull. Office of Evaluation Services,* Pennsylvania College for Women (Chatham College), 1955, No. 60.

Di Viesta, F., Woodruff, Asabel D., and Hertel, J. P. Motivation as a predictor of college success. *Educ. psychol. Meas.*, 1949, **9** (3).

Donahue, Wilma T., Coombs, C., and Travers, R. M. W. (Eds.) *Measurement of Student Adjustment & Achievement.* Ann Arbor: University of Michigan Press, 1949.

Douglas, H. R. Selecting good college risks. *Sch. & Soc.*, 1932, **35**, 140–147.

Dresher, R. H. Factors in voluntary drop-outs. *Pers. & guid. J.*, 1954, **32**, 287–289.

Dressel, P. C. Liberal arts students advised to withdraw. *J. higher Educ.*, 1943, **14**, 43–45.

Durflinger, G. W. The prediction of college success: a summary of recent findings. *J. Amer. Assn. Col. Reg.*, 1943, **19**, 68–78.

Dwyer, P. The correlation between age at entrance and success in college. *J. educ. Psychol.*, 1939, **30**, 251–264.

Dyer, H. S. Evidence on the validity of the Armed Forces Institute Tests of General Educational Development (college level). *Educ. psychol. Meas.*, 1945, **5**, 321–333

Eaton, M. T. A study of Indiana University withdrawals. *Bull. sch. Educ.*, Indiana University, 1942, No. 18.

Edgerton, H. A., and Toops, H. A. *Academic progress: a four-year follow-up study of the freshman entering Ohio State Univ. in 1923.* Ohio State Univ. Studs., Contributions in School Admin., Ohio State University Press, 1929, No. 1.

Edwards, T. W. A study of attrition rate of students at Southern Illinois University over a four-year period of time. Doctoral dissertation, Indiana University, 1954.

Eurich, A. Improvement in scholarship during the probationary period. *Sch. & Soc.*, 1932, **35**, 129–134.

Eurich, A. College failures. *Sch. & Soc.*, 1933a, **37**, 692–696.

Eurich, A. The photographic eye-movement records of successful and unsuccessful college students. *J. appl. Psychol.*, 1933b, **17**, 604–613.

Failing, Jean. A study of attrition among freshmen who entered the New York State College of Home Economics, Cornell University, 1938–1947. (Mimeo.) October, 1951.

Farnsworth, D. S. Academic success or failure in college students. *College board Rev.*, 1954, **24**, 3–7.

Farnsworth, D. S. Some non-academic causes of success and failure in college students. *College Admissions*, 1955, **2**, 72–78.

Farnsworth, D. S. We're wasting brainpower. *Natl. Educ. Assoc. J.*, March, 1959.

Farnsworth, D. S., Funkenstein, D., and Wedge, B. A study of the social and emotional adjustment of "early admission" college student. (Mimeo.) Report for the Fund Advancement of Education, 1955.

Faunce, L. D. A study of within-term male drop-outs at Michigan State College for the school years 1947–49. Ed. D. thesis, Michigan State College, 1952.

Feder, D. Factors which affect achievement and its prediction at the college level. *J. Amer. Assoc. Coll. Registrars*, 1940, **15**, 107–117.

Feder, D. Student personnel work—I. Student population. In *Encyclopedia of Educational Research* (Rev.). Walter S. Monroe (Ed.). New York: MacMillan Co., 1950.

Fischer, R. P. The role of frustration in academic underachievement: an experimental investigation. *J. Amer. Assoc. of Coll. Registrars*, 1943, **18**, 227–238.

Fredericksen, N., and Schrader, W. B. *Adjustment to College.* Princeton, N.J.: Educational Testing Service, 1951.

Freedman, N. B. The passage through college. *J. soc. Issues*, 1956, **12**, 13–28.

Freehill, M. F. The co-operative English test in academic counseling. *Col. & Univ.*, 1954, **29**, 244–252.

Freeman, F. S. Predicting academic survival. *J. educ. Res.*, 1931, **23**, 113–123.

Freeman, H. J., and Jones, L. Final report of the long time effect of counseling low percentile freshmen. *Sch. & Soc.*, 1933, **38**, 382–384.

Fund for the Advancement of Education. Evaluation Report No. 2, New York: 1957.

Gable, R. I. A study of the student drop-out problem at Miami University. *Dissert. Abstracts*, 1957, **17**, 61.

Gilmore, J. V. A new venture in the testing of motivation. *Col. Board Rev.*, 1951, 15.

Gilmore, J. V. Cross-validation of the Sentence Completion tests as a prediction of college achievement. Personal communication, November, 1956.

Goodrich, T. V. Flunking college freshmen. *Sch. Exec. Mag.*, 1931, **51**, 3–5.

Grace, H. A. Personality factors and college attrition. *Peabody J. Educ.*, 1957, **35**, 36–40.

Greene, F. D. Follow-up study of non-graduating women from the College of Education of Ohio State University. *Educ. admin. & Supervision*, 1943, **29**, 427–433.

Griffiths, G. R. The relationship between scholastic achievement and personality adjustment of men college students. *J. appl. Psych.*, 1945, **29**, 360–367.

Hale, L. B., et al. *From School to College.* New Haven, Conn.: Yale University Press, 1939.

Hanks, C. J. A comparative study of factors related to retention and withdrawal of freshmen students at the University of Arkansas. *Dissert. Abstracts*, 1954, **14**, 1171.

Hardaway, C. W. Study of enrollment and drop-out factors of freshmen on non-teaching curricula at Indiana State. *Teach. Coll. J.*, 1955, **27**, 30–34.

Harris, D. Factors affecting college grades: a review of the literature, 1930–37. *Psychol. Bull.*, 1940, **37**, 125–166.

Harrison, R. Leaving college because of emotional problems. *Student Med.*, 1956, **4**, 49–60.

Hilton, W. A., and Carpenter, W. W. Persistency of students. *J. higher Educ.*, 1943, **14**, 268–270.

Hoffman, W. S. Methods used to arrive at student mortality require careful analysis. *J. Amer. Assoc. Coll. Registrars*, 1939, **14**, 325–327.

Horler, Frances L. Factors related to withdrawal from the four year college of the University of Chicago. Doctoral dissert., University of Chicago, 1950.

Iffert, R. E. *What ought colleges and universities do about student morality?* Assoc. for Higher Education, Current issues in higher education, 1954, 170–180. Washington: National Education Assoc., 1954.

Iffert, R. E. *Drop-outs: Nature and causes; effects on student, family and society.* Assoc. for Higher Educ., Current issues in higher education, 1956, 94–102. Washington: National Education Assoc., 1956.

Iffert, R. E. *Retention and withdrawal of college students.* U.S. Dept. of Health, Education and Welfare, Bull., 1958, No. 1. Washington: U.S. Govt. Printing Office, 1957.

Johnson, G. B. A proposed technique for the analysis of drop-outs at a state college. *J. educ. Res.*, 1954, **47**, 381–387.

Johnson, J. B. Predicting success in college at time of entrance. *Sch. & Soc.*, 1926, **23**, 82–88.

Jones, E. S. Why students fail in college. *Assoc. Amer. Coll. Bull.*, 1953, **39**, 282–287.

Kelly, F. J. *Continuity of College Attendance,* U.S. Office of Educ., Bull. No. 24, 1937.

Kimball, Barbara. Relationship between non-intellective factors and scholastic achievement. Doctoral thesis. Harvard University, 1950.

Klein, A. J. Survey of land-grant colleges and universities. *U.S. Office Educ. Bull.*, No. 9, 1930.

Klogman, S. F. Test scores and graduation. *Occupations*, 1943, **21**, 389–390.

Knapp, A. B. Why they fail! *At Denison,* 1953, No. 14.

Knapp, A. B. A costly waste. *At Denison,* 1955, No. 15.

Koelsche, C. L. A study of the student drop-out problem at Indiana University. *Indiana Univ. Stud. Educ. Thesis Abstr. Ser.,* 1954, 5, 79–84.

Koelsche, C. L. A study of the student drop-out problem at Indiana Univ. *J. educ. Res.,* 1956, 49, 357–364.

Landskov, N. L. A survival study of three college of education classes, with implications for adjustment of admissions standards. Unpublished doctoral thesis, Coll. of Educ., University of Minnesota, 1946.

Landskov, N. L. Suggested student survival techniques tried out at the Univ. of Minnesota. *Coll. & Univ.,* 1948, 23, 234–241.

Langhorne, M. C. A university takes inventory. *J. Amer. Assoc. Coll. Registrars,* 1939, 15, 41–51.

Learned, W., and Langmuir, C. *Misplacement in College.* Thirty-third annual report of the Carnegie Foundation for The Advancement of Teaching. New York: Carnegie Foundation, 1938.

Lerner, Ruth S., and Martin, M. What happens to the college student with a physical handicap. *Pers. & Guidance J.,* 1955, 34, 80–85.

Lins, L. J., and Pitt, H. The "staying power" and rate of progress of Univ. of Wisconsin freshmen. *Coll. & Univ.,* 1953, 29, 86–99.

Long, L., and Perry, J. D. Mortality study of college students. *Sch. & Soc.,* 1953, 77, 103–105.

Lord, E. W. Student persistence in American colleges. Cited in *J. Amer. Assoc. Coll. Registrars,* 1939, 14, 325–327.

Luyten, B. Helene. Mortality of the student body of New York University, 1923–30. Doctoral thesis, New York University, 1933.

Macintosh, A. *Behind the Academic Curtain.* New York: Harper Bros., 1948.

McNeeley, J. H. *College student mortality.* U.S. Dept. of Interior Bull., No. 11, 1937.

McNeeley, J. H. College student mortality studies. *J. Amer. Assoc. Coll. Registrars,* 1939, 15, 119–124.

Malloy, J. P., Wysocki, B., and Graham, L. I. Predicting attrition-survival in first year engineering. *J. educ. Psychol.,* 1955, 46, 217–221.

Margulies, H. Rorschach responses of successful and unsuccessful students. *Arch. Psychol.,* 1942, 271, 61.

Mercer, Margaret. A study of student mortality in a home economics college. *J. educ. Res.,* 1941, 34, 531–537.

Mercer, Margaret. Personal factors in college adjustment. *J. educ. Res.,* 1943, 36, 561–568.

Miller, E. L. The success of freshmen in college. *North Central Assoc. Quart.,* 1927, 2, 140–145.

Minnesota University. Report of the Survey Commission VI: Student mortality. *Bull. Univ. Minn.,* 1924, 8, 27.

Minnesota University. Report of the Survey Commission VII: Student survival. *Bull. Univ. Minn.,* 1925, 4, 28.

Mitchell, F. T. Why freshmen leave college. *J. Higher Educ.,* 1942, 13, 95–100.

Monks, J., and Heath, C. A classification of academic, social and personal problems for use in a college student health department. *Student Med.,* 1954, 2, 44–62.

Moon, G. R. The student who drops out of college. *Sch. & Soc.,* 1928, 27, 576–578.

Mumma, R. The college record of students admitted on the basis of G.E.D. tests. *Coll. & Univ.,* 1950, 26, 79–86.

Munger, P. Factors related to persistence in college of students who ranked in lower third of their high school class. *J. couns. Psych.*, 1954, **1**, 132–136.

Munger, P. Student persistence in college. *Pers. & guidance J.*, 1956, **35**, 241–243.

Munger, P. Can we really predict who will graduate from college? *Coll. & Univ.*, 1957, **32**, 218–221.

Munger, P., and Goeckerman, R. W. Collegiate persistence of upper and lower third high school graduates. *J. couns. Psychol.*, 1955, **2**, 142–145.

Munroe, Ruth L. Prediction of the adjustment and academic performance of college students by a modification of the Rorschach method. *Appl. Psychol. Monog.*, No. 7, Stanford Univ., Palo Alto: Stanford University Press, 1945.

Nelson, Helen Y. Factors related to the extent of mortality among home economics students in certain colleges of Minnesota, Wisconsin, & Iowa, during 1943–50. *J. exp. Educ.*, 1953, **22**, 59–62.

Newson, N. W., and Sturm, M. W. Comparison of the college and high school marks of non-graduating college students. *J. Amer. Assoc. Coll. Registrars*, 1937, **12**, 217–221.

Palubinskas, Alice L. Personality changes in college women during four years of college experience. *Proc. Iowa Acad. Sci.*, 1952, **59**, 389—391.

Pattishall, E. G., Jr., and Banghart, F. W., Jr. A comparative analysis of school of education graduates and withdrawals. *Educ. Res. Bull. University of Virginia*, April, 1957.

Pearlman, S. An investigation of the problem of academic underachievement among intellectually superior college students. (Abstract) Doctoral thesis, New York University, 1952.

Phillips, W. S., and Osborne, R. T. A note on the relationship of the Kuder Preference Record scales to college marks, scholastic aptitude and other variables. *Educ. psychol. Meas.*, 1949, **9**, 331–337.

Philp, W. A. An investigation of undergraduate student withdrawals from the University of Mississippi. Doctoral dissertation, University of Mississippi, 1954.

Pope, Ruth V. *Factors affecting the elimination of women students.* Columbia University, Teachers College Series, No. 485, 1931.

Potthoff, E. F. Predicting the ultimate failure of college students on the basis of their first quarter's records. *Sch. & Soc.*, 1931, **33**, 203–204.

Powell, O. B. A study of freshmen drop-outs at Florida State Univ. during 1951. Master's thesis, *Personnel-O-Gram*, 1955, **9**, 14–15.

Pressey, L. C. A class of probation students. *J. higher Educ.*, 1932, **2**, 506–510.

Quarles, B. Student separations from college: an overview. *Assoc. Amer. Coll. Bull.*, 1949, **35**, 404–409.

Reeves, F. W., and Russell, J. D. *Admission and retention of university students.* Univ. of Chicago Survey Vol. 5. Chicago: University of Chicago Press, 1933.

Registrar, Temple University, Philadelphia, Pa. A study of students eliminated from Temple Univ. in June, 1938. (Abstract) *J. Amer. Assoc. Coll. Registrars*, 1939, **15**, 71–73.

Remmers, H. H. A diagnostic and remedial study of potentially and actually failing students at Purdue Univ. *Purdue Univ. Studs. in Higher Educ.*, 1928, **9**.

Roemer, J. Failures in higher institutions. *Proc. Assoc. Colls. & Secondary Schools of the Southern States*, 1925, 280–303; 1926, 188–207; 1927, 224–245; 1928, 214–248; 1929, 237–268; 1930, 226–265.

Roth, J. A. The study of academic success and failure. *Educ. res. Bull.*, 1956, **35**, 176–182.

Russell, J. W. A comparison of Michigan State College first term freshman drop-outs and non-drop-outs according to certain factors. Doctoral thesis, Michigan State College, 1952.

Rust, R. M. Average grades and estimated time spent in study. Memo to Course of Study Committee, Yale University, March, 1956.

Rust, R. M., and Ryan, F. J. Personality and academic achievement; a questionnaire approach. Paper read at the annual meeting of the APA, San Francisco, 1955.

Ryan, F. J. Personality differences between under and over-achievers in college. Doctoral thesis, Columbia University, 1951. Cf. *Micro. Abstrr.*, 1951, **11**, 967–968.

Sage, J. R. Freshman Mortality. *Proc. Amer. Assoc. Coll. Registrars*, 1927, 40–48.

Sanford, N. Personality development during the college years. *J. soc. Issues*, 1956, **12** (4).

Schrammel, H. E., and Wood, E. R. Success and failure of college students. *Kansas St. Teachers Coll. Studies in Educ.*, 1931.

Schwebel, M. Guidance for the withdrawing college student. *Occupations*, 1947, **25**, 381–382.

Segel, D. *Prediction of college success.* U.S. Off. Educ. Bull., No. 15, 1934.

Sheeder, F. I. Student losses in a liberal arts college. *J. Amer. Assoc. Coll. Registrars*, 1939, **15**, 34–40.

Sherman, R. B. College drop-outs: an overview. *J. educ. Sociol.*, 1956, **29**, 347–350.

Slater, J. M. Relationships between college persistence (attrition), father's occupation, and choice of curriculum. Doctoral dissertation, University of Illinois, 1956.

Slocum, W. L. *Academic Mortality at the State College of Washington.* State College of Washington, March, 1945.

Smith, H. P., and Waitt, R. E. A study of members of the Syracuse University Class of 1935 who did not graduate. Unpub. manuscript, Syracuse University, 1937.

Smith, Margaret R. A study of first year dropouts at Wayne State University (entering class of 1953). Wayne State University, Detroit, Mich., 1957.

Snitz, R. H. Study success, failure and causes of withdrawal of Indiana State Teachers College Students. Cited in Pope, Ruth, *Factors affecting the elimination of women students.* New York: Teachers College, Columbia University, 1931.

Snyder, L. M. Why do they leave? *J. higher Educ.*, 1940, **11**, 26–32.

Spencer, L. T. College achievement of private and public school entrants. *Sch. & Soc.*, 1927, **26**, 436–438.

Stalnaker, Elizabeth M. A four year study of the freshman class of 1935 at the West Virginia University. *J. educ. Res.*, 1942, **36**, 100–118.

Stalnaker, Elizabeth M. A four year study of the freshman class of 1935 at the West Virginia University. *J. educ. Res.*, 1945, **39**, 81–101.

Stalnaker, Elizabeth M., and Remmers, H. H. What kind of high schools contribute to college failures? *Purdue Univ. Stud. in Higher Educ.*, 1930, **14**.

Stewart, L. H., and Roberts, J. P. The relationship of Kuder profiles to remaining in a Teachers college and to occupational choice. *Educ. psychol. Meas.*, 1955, **15**, 416–421.

Strabel, E. What about warned students? *Sch. & Soc.*, 1935, **42**, 581–584.

Strang, Ruth. *Behavior and background of students in college and secondary school.* New York: Harper Bros., 1937.

Suddarth, Betty M. *Factors Influencing the Successful Graduation of Freshmen Who Enroll at Purdue University.* (Mimeo.) Progress Report No. 1, Nov., 1956; Progress Report No. 21, April, 1957. Purdue University.

Suddarth, Betty M. Factors influencing the graduation of freshmen who enroll at Purdue University. Unpub. report. June, 1957.

Summerskill, J. Factors associated with student attrition at Cornell University. Unpub. study, 1954.

Summerskill, J., and Darling, C. D. Sex differences in adjustment to college. *J. educ. Psychol.*, 1955a, **46**, 355–361.

Summerskill, J., and Darling, C. D. A progress report on The Student Stability Studies. *Stud. Med.*, 1955b, **3**, 85–91.

Tallman, R. W. A critical analysis of student persistence at the State University of Iowa. *Univ. Iowa Stud. Educ.*, 1927, **4**, No. 1.

Tenney, W. F. Drop-outs from the General Education Program at San Francisco State College, Sept. 1948 to Feb. 1949. Master's thesis, Stanford University, 1949.

Thompson, C. Mildred. Report of Officers. *Bull., Vassar Coll.*, 1928, **18**, 23.

Thompson, Martha. Admission information as predictors for graduation. Unpublished Master's thesis, Cornell University, 1953.

Travers, R. Significant research on the prediction of academic success. In *The Measurement of Student Adjustment and Achievement*, Ann Arbor: University of Michigan Press, 1949.

Truesdell, A. B. Accuracy of clinical judgments of attrition and survival of students in engineering training. *Proc. Iowa Acad. Sc.*, 1954, **61**, 442–445.

U.S. Office of Education. Factors related to application, registration and persistence in college: Cornell University. (Mimeo.) 1956–57, 1958.

Vogt, P. L. Why students fail. *Sch. & Soc.*, 1929, **30**, 847–848.

Walker, E. T. Student housing and success. *Sch. & Soc.*, 1935, **42**, 575–577.

Walters, J. E. *Individualizing Education*. New York: Wiley, 1935.

Warman, R. E. A study of applicants for readmission to college. *Pers. & guidance J.*, 1956, **34**, 553–558.

Wayne University. A profile of an entering class: Report by The Division of Admissions, Records, and Registration. (Mimeo.) August, 1955.

Webster, H. Personality development during the college years: some quantitative results. *J. soc. Issues*, 1956, **12**, 29–43.

Weigand, G. Motivational factors associated with success and failure of probational students. Doctoral thesis, University of Maryland, 1951.

Weintraub, Ruth, and Salley, Ruth. Graduation prospects of an entering freshman. *J. educ. Res.*, 1945, **39**, 116–126.

Wells, F. L. College survivals and non-survivals at marginal test levels: Cases LVII–LXXXIV. *J. genet. Psychol.*, 1950, **77**, 153–185.

Werner, O. H. *The Scholastic Persistence of 2,140 Unclassified Students in the University of Nebraska.* Publication No. 189, Contributions to Education No. 31, Univ. of Nebraska Printing Div., 1955.

West, R. M. Student mortality, student survival, and student accounting. In *Problems of College Education*. E. Hudelson (Ed.). Minneapolis: University of Minnesota Press, 1928.

Whitmer, C. A. A study of the scholastic progress of college probationers. *J. appl. Psychol.*, 1933, **17**, 39–49.

Wilcox, F. C. Comparative trends in the development of universities and colleges. Unpub. thesis. Stanford University, 1936.

Woods, A. H., and Chase, G. Forms of personality obstructive to progress in college. *J. soc. Psychol.*, 1937, **8**, 411–431.

PART VI

INTERACTIONS
OF STUDENTS
AND EDUCATORS

The chapters in this section are all addressed to the wholeness
of the college. In seeking explanations of observed phenomena or in studying the effects of particular processes the authors have
roamed freely over the vast area of student-college interaction, and
used, among others, all the major analytic categories that determined
the organization of this volume—the entering student, academic procedures, student society and student culture, performance in the role
of student, and educational effects. Thus, Dr. Fishman, in his treatment of the problem of selection, considers it in relation to philosophies of education, criteria of educational success, the developmental
goals and status of the student, and the contrasts between the college
environment and the high school environment. Dr. Stern is primarily
concerned with the question of how similar educational outcomes may
be achieved with students having markedly different personality structures, and in his consideration of "appropriate educational procedures" he ranges from particular kinds of techniques of classroom discussion to the atmosphere or major culture of the college as a whole.
Mr. Jencks and Professor Riesman evaluate Harvard's 30-year experiment with its residential houses and the implications of this experience for the task of creating an intellectual community; in doing so
they present a picture of Harvard that is comparable to the vignettes
offered in Chapter 3. Dr. Taylor, in the only chapter in this book that
attends closely to the role of administration in higher education, fo-

cuses upon the role of campus authority in the development of the individual student, and he shows that the kinds and degrees of power exercised by the administration and the faculty have effects in all areas of the student's life.

As in other parts of this book, chapters that treat of areas in which much research has been done or with problems that lend themselves to attack by highly developed quantitative methods come first (Fishman and Stern), while chapters dealing with frontier areas and relying mainly on participant observation or the case study come later (Jencks and Riesman, and Taylor).

Stern shows in Chapter 21 that students who score high on his scale for measuring "stereopathy-authoritarianism" behave in various characteristic ways in college and obtain lower grades than do students who score low on his scale. Fishman concludes from his review of studies that have sought to predict grades in college that the most successful predictors have been high school grades and a standardized measure of scholastic aptitude. When these two measures have been combined the average multiple correlation with freshman grades has been in the neighborhood of .55. Why, then, if one is interested in predicting grades in college—an "intellective criterion"—does he not supplement the "intellective predictors"—high school grades and aptitude—with a "nonintellective predictor" such as stereopathy-authoritarianism? It turns out that 168 investigators during the decade 1948 to 1958 had just this idea; and that the gain in multiple correlation obtained by adding a personality test score to one or both of the usual intellective predictors has usually been less than +.05!

It is through his consideration of the reasons for this state of affairs that Fishman is led to a critique of current research on selection, and to proposals for a new approach that uses new theoretical foundations. One of the main reasons why combining personality tests with high school grades and aptitude does not improve prediction of college grades, Fishman points out, is because such tests, although correlated with college grades, are also correlated with high school grades and aptitude; in other words, what the tests measure is so similar to what is already being measured by high school grades and aptitude that they add virtually nothing to the accuracy of prediction. High school grades, after all, are based on performance over a considerable period of time; they are a kind of "life story in capsule form," and frequently they are "indices of how closely the student's personality agrees with the model of the preferred personality of the middle-class academic world." Since college grades are often indices of this same preference, it is small wonder that high school grades are the best predictors of them. One might say that if high school students could be induced to remain as they are, and if colleges could be made to resemble high schools even more than they do now, then the predictive coefficients would be higher. Happily the correlation is only .55. Students *do* change during the school to college transition and colleges *are* different from high schools. Thus the best way to improve prediction of college performance is not so much by getting fuller and fuller pictures of the high school personality but by coming to grips with "contingency factors," the events that intervene between the taking of measures in high school and the outcome in which one is interested. This means utilizing theory concerning the development of students and concerning the ways in which factors in the college environment may be expected to influence performance. On the basis of such theory and, more specifically, on the basis of varying assumptions concerning the presence of, and interaction between, individual and institutional changes, Fishman proceeds to introduce a multivariate framework embracing nine different strategies for studies of selection and guidance. Fishman's theory calls for attention to the need for criteria of college performance in addition to grades or academic honors, but, believing as he does that intellective criteria will continue to dominate the American higher educational scene, he limits himself in this theoretical model to this latter type of criterion. But nonintellective factors enter into eight of the nine strategies; in five of these eight the nonintellective factors are contingency factors that moderate predictions of academic performance but cannot readily be incorporated into the predictions themselves. Struck by the importance of such factors Fishman is led to call for a moratorium on prediction of the usual sort, and he suggests, in their stead, studies of how college environments might be arranged "in order to make academic predictions based on individual potential and achievement come true."

Fishman's proposals, if carried out, would integrate studies of prediction with the kind of social-psychological investigation that has been accented throughout this volume. What in the logic of prediction are "contingency factors" are, in the frame of reference of those concerned with the development of students in college, the heart of the educational process. Several contributors to this volume, in addition to Fishman, have called for studies that might show how different educational procedures can lead to desirable outcomes in different types of students.

No one has come to closer grips with the problem than has Stern, in work reported in his chapter. His work, with Cope, on the modification of the academic performances of stereopathic-authoritarian students is one of the very few educational experiments that is based upon a dynamic theory of personality. Stern's measure of stereopathy-authoritarianism differentiates four types of students—"authoritarians," "antiauthoritarians," the "irrational," and the "rational." The fact that a student's type was predictive of grades, and of other performances such as withdrawal from college and ways of studying and learning, was not enough. The question was whether appropriate educational procedures could bring the authoritarian students' level of academic performance up to that of the "antiauthoritarian" and the "rational" students. The experiment showed that this can be done. A course in citizenship was divided into three sections, one composed exclusively of authoritarians, another of antiauthoritarians, and the third of rationals, all three sections being taught by the same instructor—who was unaware of the particular characteristics of the three classes. It turned out that the authoritarians not only did better academically than similar students in other classes to which they had been assigned at random, but also that the authoritarians of the experimental section did as well on the final common objective examination as the students in the other two experimental sections. Moreover, the authoritarians were the only group that showed academic gains.

Stern then goes on to consider, within a more general conceptual framework, relationships between types of student personalities and types of institutional environments. Here he introduces the Activities Index, for measuring dispositions of personality, and the College Characteristics Index for measuring the various kinds of pressures that are brought to bear upon students in colleges. It is shown that the systematic and quantitative descriptions of student bodies and of college environments that these instruments yield are readily confirmed by knowledgeable observers on the scene and are in keeping with what one who knew the major general characteristics of the college, e.g., public or private, denominational or secular, would expect. And since the terms of the descriptions are derived from personality theory, the way is opened to the investigation of numerous hypotheses concerning such important matters as how student bodies are composed, how colleges come to exert the pressures that they do, how images of colleges are built up in the minds of the public and what kinds of colleges exert the most influence upon the attitudes and values of students or are most productive of scholars.

When the reader has become familiar with Stern's scheme he will be able, as he reads the chapters of Jencks and Riesman and of Taylor, to ask himself how Harvard and Sarah Lawrence College might look when described in the terms of the scheme and how they might compare with the types of institutions that Stern exemplifies in detail. For in both of the concluding chapters of this part, we are told enough about the colleges under consideration to make such applications of the scheme possible. Indeed, if Stern has not already arranged with the authorities and students at Harvard to have his indices filled out by the students and masters at the various houses one might hope that he could do so. Jencks and Riesman show that the relations of the houses to the Harvard community are in important respects analogous to the relations of colleges to the larger American society. The recruiting activities of the houses and the criteria on which Harvard freshmen base their selections—particularly their use of stereotypes of the houses—are made the objects of special study by Jencks and Riesman, and their hypotheses concerning the processes of Harvard as microcosm can lead, through testing in other locations, to general truths about American higher education.

But the allocation of students to houses, according to myth and according to reality, is but one aspect of the workings of the Harvard experiment in residential education. We are given the whole story: Why the houses were, in 1929, considered necessary—in the light of developments in American education and American society at large —how the institution of the houses changed Harvard, what life in the houses is like, how the social life of the college relates to the academic life. Above all, we are offered an evaluation of this experiment in residential education. The basis for this evaluation is what the houses contribute to the intellectual development of the students—and here is meant intellectual as opposed, not just to the social, but to the academic with its emphasis on preprofessional education and grades and on work instead of leisure. By this standard the houses come off well. But not well enough. Jencks and Riesman want a true intellectual community, and in their consideration of its necessary conditions the Harvard House System appears as a good beginning.

The Harvard experiment and then the Sarah Lawrence experiment. It is noteworthy that Jencks and Riesman and Harold Taylor take it so much for granted that education is experimental that they do not trouble to state this proposition; they simply exemplify it in their work. Just as Jencks and Riesman size up the present situation at Harvard and propose new things to try, Taylor recounts things that have been tried at Sarah Lawrence during the years of its existence, evaluates the effects of these things and suggests what ought to be tried now.

Taylor's chapter is progressive education brought up to date.

Judging by his story the events at Sarah Lawrence seem to parallel those of other colleges that started with devotion to progressive ideals, including the ideal of a completely autonomous, self-governing student community. They went through a period of enthusiasm and high adventure, found success in the eyes of the world, relaxed, and then saw the old guard come in for their innings. Particularly striking in the Sarah Lawrence story is the role of the students; this is something that we know about in the present case because the officials of the college always made the activities of students an object of research. We are offered here the results of a comprehensive questionnaire that was filled out by Sarah Lawrence students in 1952. It is clear that at this time a great many of the students, perhaps a majority, were seeking some kind of escape from freedom; that is to say, they desired more structure in the curriculum, more adult supervision of social life, more participation by the faculty in matters that had been left to student government. Indeed, looking at the responses to the questionnaire one cannot escape the impression that a substantial number of Stern's stereopathic-authoritarian students had somehow found their way into the college—perhaps because its public image had changed radically since the Thirties. (Be it noted, however, that 31% of the respondents thought there should be more, rather than less, free discussion in the classrooms.) Taylor believes that the students of the Fifties were really different, in attitudes and values and personality needs, from those of the Thirties and Forties, and he is inclined to attribute this to the changing times. But he recognizes the legitimacy of some of the students' complaints about too much laissez faire, and we can imagine that he has had to listen to many people say "I told you so." Undoubtedly the students were not the only ones who favored change in the direction of a traditional college regimen.

But Taylor has no notion of returning to an authoritarian set-up; nor to the kind of all-out permissiveness or laissez faire that characterized some of the early progressive schools. The progressive way, in his view, lies through increased understanding of the complex interactions between the administration and faculty on the one hand and the developing personalities of the students on the other. If students are not to be permitted to escape from freedom, then the faculty cannot permit themselves to escape from authority; they have to stand for something, and they have to enter prominently into the lives of the students. They must realize that independence is not something that can be given to students, but rather something that they may ultimately achieve. Independence is based upon inner control. This is not to be attained, or consolidated, in college through authoritarian

discipline nor through permissiveness for which students are not prepared; it is to be attained through the experience of relationships with
adults who are willing to govern events in accordance with knowledge
of the student's developmental stage and in the interest of values that
the student may learn to appreciate.

It is a paradox, though an understandable one, that spokesmen for
institutions at the head of "the academic procession" are, of all educators, often the most articulate about the shortcomings of their institutions and most insistent about reform. Many educational researches
or studies of particular colleges or universities conclude that there
should be instituted something like the Harvard House System or
something like the Sarah Lawrence System—if only they were not so
expensive! Yet, when we are offered close looks at these systems, as we
are in Chapters 22 and 23, one of our strongest impressions is of how
much there is left to be desired. This is due in part, no doubt, to the
fact that institutions that are fundamentally confident of themselves
are not reluctant to reveal, or even to dwell upon, their mistakes and
shortcomings; but it is due more to the plain fact that it is very difficult
to change students in desired ways, very difficult, even, to know what
are the conditions and processes of developmental change. Nothing
in this volume is better calculated than Chapters 22 and 23 to drive
this point home. As we become increasingly familiar with the kinds of
complexities pointed out in these chapters, we gain a better appreciation of why it is so difficult to predict "success" in college, of why
Fishman urges that specialists in prediction concentrate on contingency factors, and of why Stern regards the College Characteristic
Index as but a first step toward the delineation of college environments. Educational research—if anyone needs to be reminded—has a
long way to go.

20 *Joshua A. Fishman*

Some Social-Psychological Theory for Selecting and Guiding College Students

THE SETTING OF CURRENT SELECTION AND GUIDANCE PROBLEMS

During most of the 19th century American colleges needed neither a philosophy of admission nor a procedure of selection. Secondary schools and colleges were really two phases of the same educational program. They served essentially identical clienteles. College preparatory secondary schools—and there were very few secondary schools of any other type—did not complain that their curricula were dominated by the colleges. Colleges did not complain that they could never be quite sure just what it was that applicants had studied in secondary school nor just what their grades implied with respect to level of proficiency. Parents and teachers responsible for guiding the young toward appropriate colleges did not complain that they were uninformed as to what the various colleges were like or what they wanted in an applicant. In fact, it was often a foregone conclusion as to which candidate would go to which college to study

Note. Sections of this paper were originally presented at the Conference on Selection and Educational Differentiation held at the University of California, Berkeley, May 25–27, 1959. I wish to express my gratitude to Natalie Rogoff, John French, Donald Thistlethwaite, and particularly Charles McArthur for their valuable criticisms of the earlier drafts from which I have profited so much in the preparation of this final version.

what, and the dropout, flunk-out and transfer rates were low indeed. Given this set of circumstances, problems of admission and selection were few and of a low order of intensity from the point of view of institutional or national well-being.

The above description is probably somewhat overidealized, but, like the story of the young George Washington and his cherry tree, it is instructive primarily in terms of its contrasts with what we know to be present-day reality. Today, American secondary schools and colleges frequently pursue quite separate, if not antithetical, educational programs. They may serve very different clienteles in terms of geographical origins and social compositions. Thus many colleges are faced by the need to select their freshman class from applicants coming from all over the country (and, in some cases, from all over the world), with widely varying family backgrounds and cultural traditions. What is more, these applicants arrive presenting credentials from secondary schools that vary widely in the content and in the quality of their curricular offerings, but that are as one in their objection to having anyone dictate to them in this respect. Faced by the problem of rendering commensurable all sorts of grades, courses, and curricula, American colleges have come to depend upon selection and guidance techniques that maximize descriptive impartiality and minimize proscriptive implications. With the development of the Army Alpha examinations, American psychometry had provided the reliable and objective mass measurements that have enabled the country's colleges to sort applicants without being overly burdened with matters of philosophy or theory. Thus, the problems and procedures of college admission and selection in our country bear a direct relationship to the peculiarly decentralized, unstandardized, and informally coordinated functioning of our secondary and higher education and to the developmental history of our educational institutions.

Even under "normal" conditions, the above situation would fully justify serious concern for the more rational management of admission and selection in American colleges. Even "normal" conditions would be sufficient to render the philosophical and the empirical problems in this area extremely complicated. However, the conditions surrounding college admission and selection today are currently far from normal. The explosion in college-going has brought about a geometric increase in the number of applicants without anything like a similar increase in college facilities. In addition, the growing precariousness of America's international position has focused the spotlight of inquiry and publicity on every aspect of higher education. As a result, those concerned with the philosophical and the empirical foundations of admission and selection are aware of more than the usual amount of public and professional pressure to introduce greater clarity and effectiveness into this field.

"Admissions" represents a theory of administrative action based upon knowledge of the interaction between a given college environment and various crucial characteristics of the applicant population. Selection and guidance represent the techniques and procedures through which this "philosophy" is implemented. Although logically these procedures should be derived from pre-existing theory, it is not unusual in the world of affairs for philosophy to be patched together out of the exigencies of organizational procedure. The pressures for improved selection have been so great that in the past quarter century no less than one thousand studies have been undertaken in order to validate and improve the techniques at hand. Since but little conceptual clarification has been advanced to accompany the growing display of statistics, test booklets, and data-processing machinery, my goal in this paper is to attempt some theoretical considerations—as well as some practical solutions—from the vantage point of social psychology. If social psychologists can be of any real help to measurement specialists, deans of admission, and directors of guidance, it may well be that, at the same time, the latter will be of some service to social psychology as well.

Current findings. A recent review of all of the college guidance and selection studies completed during the decade 1948 to 1958 (Fishman and Pasanella, 1960),[1] including both published and unpublished sources, has made me very much aware of what many must have long suspected, namely, that this research area is undoubtedly among those most intensively investigated in the entire field of educational research. There are certainly not many other topics that would yield 580 studies within a single decade, many of them translated into ongoing operations and routinized for use in educational institutions. Indeed, it would hardly seem to be too much of an exaggeration to say that nearly every investigator of higher education has done a study predict-

[1] In this work we not only had the benefit of the assistance and good offices of the College Entrance Examination Board, which I gratefully acknowledge here, but we also benefited by an opportunity to examine preliminary drafts of related reviews currently being conducted for the Board by Professors Irving Lorge and Paul Lazarsfeld, both of Columbia University. I wish to express my sincere thanks to both of them, although they are by no means responsible for the interpretations and conclusions at which I have arrived partially as a result of my familiarity with their work.

ing college achievement or adjustment. It also seems that every investigator has done only one such study.

What is the upshot of all of this research on college selection and guidance? Unfortunately, it can all be summarized rather briefly. The most usual predictors are high school grades and scores on a standardized measure of scholastic aptitude. The usual criterion is the freshman average. The average multiple correlation obtained when aiming the usual predictors at the usual criterion is approximately .55.[2] The gain in the multiple correlation upon adding a personality test score to one or both of the usual predictors, holding the criterion constant, is usually less than $+.05$.

THE ROLE OF NONINTELLECTIVE FACTORS

If the current state of affairs in college selection and guidance research is disturbing, it is not only because the magnitude of our predictions leaves so much to be desired. Rather, it is because so many are still doing exactly the same kinds of things that were being done two decades ago (Garrett, 1949) and even four decades ago (Jordan, 1920)—and getting exactly the same magnitude of results. This is particularly saddening in view of the growing number of studies employing personality tests, biographical inventories, and other so-called *nonintellective* predictors. Their number has grown to 168 during the decade under review. This is not only a large number in absolute terms. It also reveals an increase in the relative frequency of such studies in comparison with the immediately previous decade. My own hunch is that this trend will become even more accentuated in the decade ahead; in fact, that in this age of "popular psychology" such studies will quickly come to be considered as the "thing to do."

Superficially considered, the addition of a personality test to the usual prediction battery would seem to be a most promising approach. If applicants are so plentiful that all available seats can be filled even after raising admissions requirements in terms of high school average and college entrance test score—why not tack on a personality requirement as well? Furthermore, if the multiple correlation based on high school average plus scholastic aptitude test scores is no more than .55 there would certainly seem to be an awful lot of improvement in prediction that could be accomplished quite simply by the mere addi-

[2] For a simple statement of what multiple correlation is and how it is employed in college selection research, see Fishman, 1957.

tion of a personality test to the prediction battery. Unfortunately, this does not turn out to be the case, and for two very good reasons: on the one hand, there is not really as much room for improvement in prediction as, at first glance, there might appear to be, and, on the other hand, the personality predictors that have most readily come to mind correlate just as highly with the high school average (or with scholastic aptitude test scores) as they do with the freshman average in college itself. Bloom has recently provided us with the best illustration of the first proposition stated above. By utilizing a simple scaling method which counteracts the notorious differences in high school grading standards, he obtains an average multiple correlation of .75 between the usual predictors and the usual criteria (Bloom and Peters, 1959). Thus, when the unreliability of high school grades is corrected for, the amount of "unexplained variance" still available to be explained by current personality tests (whose reliability also leaves much to be desired) shrinks appreciably. Nevertheless, personality tests and other measures of nonintellective factors could still contribute something important, were it not for the second consideration, namely, that these instruments seem to be measuring something insufficiently dissimilar from whatever it is that our usual predictors are measuring. In order to overcome this last-mentioned difficulty some fresh theoretical insights seem to be needed. Since the number of studies of nonintellective factors is bound to increase under any circumstances, it would be highly desirable to provide some theoretical structuring for this domain before such studies come to be done in as completely routinized a fashion as that to which selection and guidance studies utilizing intellective factors have so largely succumbed in the last few decades.[3]

The distinction between "intellective" and "nonintellective" is

---

[3] It would probably be well to define my usage of the terms "intellective" and "nonintellective"—both denotatively and connotatively—as quickly as possible in order to avoid the misunderstandings which these terms invite. For my purposes the following "definitions" seem adequate:

Nonintellective predictors: personality and motivational tests and inventories, interest inventories, interviews and personal ratings, biographical information, and study-habits inventories.

Intellective predictors: aptitude and intelligence test scores, achievement test scores, high school rank or high school average.

Nonintellective criteria: overachievement and underachievement, extracurricular participation, "adjustment" and other personality or motivational ratings by self or others, postcollege success, postcollege interests and activities, and so forth.

Intellective criteria: first quarter grades, first semester grades, first year grades, grades beyond first year, academic honors, and so forth.

conceptually useful even though it is not always clear-cut. Intellective is being used here primarily to designate a concern with grades-in-course, or, more generally, with the measurement and evaluation of intellectual *products* or *levels*. I would not include in this rubric a concern with the intellective *processes,* i.e., with intellectuality as a value component or as a personality attribute. Perhaps this is a worthwhile distinction to make precisely because it forces us to recognize the nonintellective components in intellectual *interests* and in theoretical *dispositions*.

Predictor-criterion combinations. Nonintellective factors may enter into studies of selection and guidance either as predictors, or as criteria, or as both predictors and criteria. Although nine possible predictor-criterion combinations exist when an intellective, nonintellective typology is employed, only three of these combinations occur with any substantial frequency. As Table 1 reveals, the most popular com-

Table 1. Predictor-Criterion Combinations

Predictors	Criteria	Studies (S)		Colleges (C)	
		n	%	n	S/C
1. Intellective Only	Intellective Only	408	70	148	2.76
2. Intellective Only	Nonintellective Only	2	*	2	1.00
3. Intellective Only	Both	2	*	2	1.00
4. Nonintellective Only	Intellective Only	64	11	38	1.68
5. Nonintellective Only	Nonintellective Only	17	3	10	1.70
6. Nonintellective Only	Both	9	2	9	1.00
7. Both	Intellective Only	70	12	44	1.59
8. Both	Nonintellective Only	5	1	5	1.00
9. Both	Both	3	*	2	1.50
Totals		580	100%	**	**

* Less than 1%.
** Data is nonadditive.

bination by far is still the classical one in which intellective predictors only are aimed at intellective criteria (see combination #1). The two next most popular study designs are those that utilize both intellective *and* nonintellective predictors (combination #7) or nonintellective predictors *alone* (combination #4), with only intellective criteria being employed in each case. These three combinations (i.e., #1, #7, and #4) account for over 90% of all studies. The fact that the use

of intellective criteria is still the prevalent pattern for selection and
guidance studies, regardless of whether intellective, nonintellective, or
both intellective and nonintellective factors are employed as predictors, may well be considered regrettable. It implies that as with
most revolutions the introduction of nonintellective factors has really
not changed the "old order" of college selection and guidance as
much as superficial indices might suggest. Regrettable or not, this is a
fact of life that we must seek to understand, as well as one that we
must seek to cope with in our theoretical and empirical endeavors in
this area.

Difficulties with nonintellective criteria. Table 1 clearly reveals that
studies utilizing nonintellective criteria have been performed only
about a third as frequently as studies utilizing nonintellective predictors. Furthermore, it is evident that even the few colleges that have
departed from the ordinary and have undertaken nonintellective criterion studies have done far fewer such studies apiece than have those
colleges that have limited themselves to intellective criterion studies
alone. This is a puzzling state of affairs, particularly if we consider
that much of the uniquely American contribution to educational
philosophy and methodology has dealt with educational and societal
goals that would clearly be designated as other than narrowly or exclusively intellective according to our usage here.

Why have so few colleges done nonintellective *criterion* studies—
few even in comparison with the number of nonintellective *predictor*
studies—and why do those colleges doing such studies do so few of
them? The reasons are not hard to find and they have been pointed
out before, both by myself and by others (cf. Brown, Chapter 16).

If we should hazard to explain this phenomenon in psychological
terms we might say that the well-nigh exclusive accent upon intellective criteria represents a defensive clinging to the intellectual on the
part of academic people who are, after all, born intellectualizers. If
we want an administrative answer we could say that institutional arrangements themselves generate studies of this type. What aspiring
academician or administrator has not, at one time or another, found
himself face to face with the "obvious" data for a selection or guidance
study: high school records, College Board scores, and college grades.
One can quickly run off a study based on such data and then go on to
more challenging pursuits. Appealing as the "psychological" and the
"administrative" reasons may be, however they are really much too
superficial to serve as explanations of why intellective criteria remain
in undisputed ascendency in the field of college selection and guidance

study. It is not as if there were no interest in nonintellective criteria. Quite the contrary. Nonintellective criteria of the *college's* success as well as of the *graduate's* success are constantly being discussed by newsworthy public figures and educational administrators. Why then are there so few studies that utilize such criteria? To begin with, it is much more difficult to arrive at a consensus concerning nonintellective criteria, for there are few nonintellective goals of higher education that are accepted by both the academic community and by the public at large. Nothing as clearly indicates the difference which exists in America today between the public's view of higher education as a means of assuring material ends (whether through grades, "contacts," or "know-how") and the educator's view of higher education as a means of assuring certain nonmaterial ends (values, interests, *Weltanschauungen*) than our inability to resolve these two constellations of basically *nonintellective* criteria.

This is not the only problem surrounding nonintellective criteria. Among academicians as among the public at large, there is much doubt as to the very legitimacy of such criteria in conjunction with any immediate and day-by-day educational decisions and activities— and even some hostility against those who advocate such criteria. On the one hand, this is due to the fact that the tradition of uncontested intellective criteria commands very strong allegiance today. This was certainly true even before the appearance of Sputniks and Rickovers on our intellectual horizon. On the other hand, this is due to the fact that nonintellective criteria, when seriously developed, have implications not only for a philosophy of education but for a philosophy of life. Intellective criteria, in this sense, can be intermediate or "compromise" criteria, precisely because they approach being neutral with respect to ultimate questions. They do not attempt to answer the question "A college education for what?" Our national lack of concern for permanent philosophical and theoretical issues is the broader canvas against which the over-riding disinterest in nonintellective criteria in higher education may well be viewed.

A final problem attendant upon the use of nonintellective criteria is a more technical one. Even where such criteria can be agreed upon and even where the opposition to them in academic and in public circles can be overcome, the difficulties of getting good data relevant to these criteria are many and complex (cf. Brown, Chapter 16). The distinctions between predictors and criteria are likely to get fuzzy when we are faced by the obvious temptation to use a test of "social maturity" in both connections. These difficulties are further compounded by the fact that nonintellective criterion data typically become available late in the college career or even well after graduation. As a result, such data are both harder to obtain and harder to relate unambiguously to the college experience per se.

For the foreseeable future we seem to be involved in worldwide demands which are far more likely to lead to the diminution of nonintellective goals in elementary and secondary education than to favor greater accent upon these goals in higher education. This combination of technical difficulties, philosophical difficulties, and *Zeitgeist* antagonism is very likely to eliminate this direction (i.e., the utilization of nonintellective criteria) as a major avenue for selection and evaluation in American higher education—or so it seems to me. Most of our colleges are not in a position to withstand informed or uninformed accusations of being anti-intellectualistic. As college-going increasingly becomes a major public concern, colleges may become even less able to stand up to public and governmental pressures than ever before. Nevertheless, there is nothing that I should like to see more than a concerted research attack on the problems of developing, measuring, predicting, and securing acceptance for nonintellective criteria in higher education, for I am convinced that only in that context shall we be in a position to reap the real fruits of nonintellective predictors (Fishman, 1958).

Difficulties with nonintellective predictors. If nonintellective criteria of college success seem rather improbable for the near future, what can be said for the pattern which retains intellective criteria but which aims for a more frequent introduction of nonintellective predictors in conjunction with them? [4] In some ways, this appears to be a much more straightforward and empirical matter. We should soon be coming to the point where we can tell if there is any pay-off in this approach. As Table 1 reveals, this is the approach to nonintellective factors (see combinations 4 and 7) now most frequently followed. Although this approach has *rarely* produced anything startling in terms of the magnitude of multiple correlations or in terms of gains in prediction above and beyond what is obtainable through the use of intellective predictors alone, I am quite willing to say that at the empirical level the issue is still an open one. Perhaps all we need is

---

[4] I have in mind here only formal and objective nonintellective predictors— rather than such informal and subjective ones as principal's recommendation, letters of recommendation from friends, clergy, and alumni. Although regard for tradition and for public relations leads many colleges still to request such "data," these are rarely seriously employed. Their inadequacy as valid predictors has been demonstrated to all those seriously interested in such demonstrations.

the "better personality test" for which so many have been searching for so long.

On theoretical grounds, I tend to be pessimistic concerning the long-range value of most current approaches which seek to retain both the high school average (and/or a standard aptitude test) and a nonintellective predictor in the *same* predictive battery, with an intellective criterion to shoot at. The trouble with these approaches is not simply that they don't usually "pay off"—for even where they do we are at a loss, theoretically, to appreciate *why* they do. In addition, as college-going becomes an increasingly universal American experience, more and more information will become available concerning the high schools and the communities from which college applicants come. This information will permit those colleges that so desire continually to improve the high school average and/or the standard aptitude or achievement test scores as predictors of intellective college criteria. This "improvement" can come about by weighting the high school average and the test scores either in accord with the college perform-ance records of previous applicants from that high school (after the manner of Burnham at Yale [Burnham, 1959] or the National Regis-tration Office and Bloom in Chicago [Bloom and Peters, 1959]) or by weighting them in accord with community and school characteristics (as Schrader is doing at ETS) [5] or by weighting them in accord with social and cultural characteristics of the applicant's family and com-munity (after the manner of Wing at Tulane).[5] To the extent that this is done the role of many nonintellective predictors will be increasingly eroded (in conjunction with the intellective criteria that the high school average and the aptitude tests already predict so well).

The ubiquitous high school average. The most commonly employed selection methods, have their theoretical basis like much else in Ameri-can educational practice, in vague models of association and con-tiguity. The past is considered to be the best means available to us for understanding the future, and past performance the best predictor of future performance. I cannot undertake seriously to challenge this line of thought here, although I consider it inadequate in the same way that all half-truths are scientifically inadequate. I will content myself with indicating that it contains within itself many seeds of destruction (or at least curtailment) for most nonintellective predictors of intellective criteria. As things stand, the high school average, based as it is upon performance over an appreciable time period (and stand-ardized aptitude or achievement tests, intended as they are to equalize

[5] In studies currently in progress for the College Entrance Examination Board.

the marking scale across high schools) are *both* reflections of the consequences of nonintellective factors in the applicant and in his environment. When we refine our measures of high school performance (whether these measures be grade averages or test scores), we invariably do so by further increasing the degree to which they validly reflect stable nonintellective factors. Thus, test scores or high school averages differentially weighted (e.g., for the previous college performance records of the high school's graduates, for community size, and for the size of the applicant's graduating class) must correlate more appreciably with scores on many a nonintellective predictor than will high school averages or test scores that are not so weighted. It seems to me that this must be so because the corrected intellective predictors are being corrected for some of the very factors that many nonintellective predictors are seeking independently to predict.

It may be that the great expectations which many have had and still have for nonintellective predictors would be tempered somewhat if there were a somewhat different view of high school grades as predictors. High school grades reflect nonintellective factors to a much greater extent than has been commonly appreciated. They are very frequently indices of how closely the student's personality agrees with the model of the preferred personality of the middle-class academic world. High school grades (and scholastic aptitude test scores) are also indices of important social variables, a number of which have been revealed by the Elmtown studies (Hollingshead, 1949).[6] Since college grades are also indices of many of these very same personality and social preferences, it is scarcely surprising that high school grades should be the best predictors of college grades. What is more surprising, however, is that educators and even social scientists tend to regard this as intellective prediction solely or primarily. Perhaps it is indicative of the state of our social sciences that so many have been "talking social psychology" for so long without actually being aware of it.

Given the foreseeable future of personality measurement and given the foreseeable future of college admissions pressures, I am not entirely unhappy at this line of development as long as the "intellective" criterion maintains its undisputed lead. Perhaps the high school average and the standard aptitude test are not only the performance samples by which nonintellective factors in academic performance can *best* be tapped; perhaps they are also the performance samples by which such

---

[6] Also see: Stice, G., Mollenkopf, W. G., and Torgerson, W. S., 1956 and 1957; Rogoff, N., 1959; and McArthur, C., 1960.

factors are most *justifiably* tapped.[7] I do not propose to argue too strongly in favor of such a rough operational approach to nonintellective factors in college selection and guidance. At the moment I merely want to point out that such an approach is certainly still one of college admissions on a *multiple* basis rather than on the basis of intellective factors alone. A *mixed* predictor is still a *multiple* predictor. A mixed criterion is still a multiple criterion. High school grades are, in fact, a summary of a life story. It is easy to forget this and to dismiss them as a single intellective variable when, in reality, they reveal in capsule form a very complex life pattern. We must not permit the crudity and simplicity of our index to mask the subtlety and complexity of the real-life phenomena. Our experimental designs must of necessity simplify nature but we must not then reify our simplification. On the other hand, some of us may be overtaken by an intellectual drive to clarify and fragment the components that in combination constitute the index. To these individuals I would like to point out that we must distinguish between our compulsions conceptually to clarify the components in such mixtures and our hopes that such clarification will necessarily yield greater predictive accuracy. For the latter to occur, theoretical models on bases other than mere association and contiguity must first be developed. It is for the advisability and feasibility of such alternative models that I *do* want to argue.

Alternatives to personnel selection. I count myself as a believer in the importance of nonintellective factors. However, my own social and educational biases lead me to prefer to see them in the role of what Lazarsfeld has called *contingency* variables rather than in any other role.[8] The rising tide of college-going in American life must not

[7] The justice or desirability of selection for college on the basis of formal nonintellective predictors remains to be carefully pondered. The strongest arguments *against* such a policy are that (1) for a college to accept or reject an applicant on the basis of his nonintellective characteristics entails a surrender of a college's primary intellectual responsibilities, and (2) college may be particularly important to bright *maladjusted* students in making them useful to society. Both social and individual well-being might better be served by overlooking the queerness (or the adolescent rebelliousness) of the potential genius than by overlooking the intellectual limitations of even the most self-actualized personalities.

[8] The term contingency variable will be fully explained and illustrated in subsequent sections of this paper. At this point it may be sufficient to say that such variables are neither predictors nor criteria. They intrude themselves between predictors and criteria in ways that are not predictable in the individual case at a given point in our knowledge.

lead us—educators and social scientists—to an inflexible reliance upon personnel selection devices to accomplish all of our ends. Even industry, from which the personnel selection model has been borrowed, at times shows signs of awareness that it owes something to society other than an exclusive dedication to the maximization of profits. Similarly, American higher education owes something more to society than a continual pursuit of the "safest" cream discoverable at the secondary school level (cf. Chapter 2). Of course, given our great institutional and cultural diversity, it is certainly justifiable and desirable for some colleges to adopt this approach exclusively. An alternative approach also seems to have some merit, however—one which is based not only upon personnel selection but also upon deliberately changing individuals and educational environments to attain educational goals. Let me merely outline its broadest features here.

The need for new theoretical foundations. First of all, I believe that we suffer from a serious lack of a theory of personality factors that relates them to a theory of college behavior, generally, and to the academic learning processes more specifically. Of course, we also lack something even more fundamental, namely, a general theory of college prediction—analogous to the prediction of adjustment, or of marital success, or of voting behavior. It seems to me that our understanding of the relationship between nonintellective factors and intellective criteria will progress only as we locate the contextual *differences* (behavioral and environmental) between high school and college. Of course there are similarities between the two contexts, but behavior as it is governed by these similarities is already being predicted by our current "mixed" intellective predictors. If the differences between the two settings can be related primarily to factors of *individual* development, then there should be room for some effective individual nonintellective predictors. If the differences between the two settings are primarily related to "constant" *institutional* or environmental contrasts, then there should be room for some effective institutional nonintellective predictors. Finally, if the differences between the two settings are primarily related not to the individual per se and not to the institutional contrasts per se but to various *intrainstitutional* phenomena and to the individual's interaction with them, then the role of nonintellective factors might best be sought at some level other than that of the "predictor." I want to devote the rest of this chapter to giving some examples of just what I have in mind when I speak of such alternative models for the incorporation of nonintellective factors into selection and guidance studies. At this point I merely want to emphasize my strong conviction that nonintellective predictors of intellective criteria will finally become both important and comprehensive variables only if we realize that they require alternative theoretical models and empirical designs depending on the specific nature of the individual and of the institutional differences that are known or assumed to obtain between the high school and college settings in a given study context.

A PRELIMINARY THEORETICAL MODEL

In Table 2, I have attempted to summarize nine inter-related models or strategies for predicting criteria of performance in college.[9] Eight of these nine models (*cells 2 to 9*) deal with the utilization of one or another kind of nonintellective factor, although, as we shall presently see, I have assigned other labels to some of them so as to distinguish more readily between them. The two axes of Table 2 deal with the two components of school-to-college transition that I have thus far isolated for our consideration. One component deals with the environmental-institutional contrast between the student's high school and his college. I have dichotomized this component into instances in which the two environments are considered to be essentially the same, on the one hand, and into instances in which they are considered to be different, on the other hand. I have further dichotomized the instances of environmental difference into differences of two types, namely, constant differences and variable differences. These two types of high school-to-college environmental differences will be explained and compared in subsequent paragraphs. The second axis of Table 2 is concerned with a contrast between the individual as he is in high school and the individual as he is in college. This component is dichotomized into those instances in which the individual is assumed to remain essentially the same in the two settings and into those instances in which he is assumed to be different in the two settings. Two general types of individual change are then recognized. One type is labeled *developmental* change and the other *random* change. These two types of high school-to-college change in the individual will be discussed in sub-

[9] Let me once more emphasize my strong interest in the development of newer, nonintellective criteria in connection with which nonintellective predictors must ultimately be most rewarding (cf. Chapter 16). If I now proceed to dwell upon intellective criteria only, this is both because these are the criteria most commonly employed today and because I have concentrated upon nonintellective criteria in a previous publication (Fishman, 1958).

Table 2. Alternative Models for Predicting Intellective Criteria in the Context of School-to-College Transition

Individual Factors	Environmental Factors		
	High school and college environments are the *same*	High school and college environments are *different*	
		Constant environmental differences	*Variable* environmental differences
The individual remains the *same* in college as he was in high school	Intellective predictors only — **1**	Intellective and institutional predictors — **4**	Intellective predictors plus *institutional contingency moderators* — **7**
The individual is *different* in college from what he was in high school — *Developmental* change	Intellective and individual nonintellective predictors — **2**	Intellective and individual nonintellective and institutional predictors — **5**	Intellective and individual nonintellective predictors plus *institutional contingency moderators* — **8**
The individual is *different* in college from what he was in high school — *Random* change	Intellective predictors plus *individual contingency moderators* — **3**	Intellective and institutional predictors plus *individual contingency moderators* — **6**	Intellective predictors plus *individual and institutional contingency moderators* — **9**

sequent paragraphs. I do not doubt that there may be other components that might well be taken into account in theoretically structuring selection and guidance studies. I also do not doubt that even the components included in Table 2 lend themselves to more refined conceptual analysis than I have devoted to them. Nevertheless, I want to limit myself to a consideration of the components and categories shown, if only because their simplicity will enable me to cover my basic propositions more readily. If I may anticipate myself in this connection, I will say that I am certainly not about to recommend that every college undertake nine different types of selection and guidance studies. Selection problems are probably quite far from being sufficiently crucial at any institution to merit such extravagance. My real purpose is to point out that even given this simplified bifactor framework there are theoretically nine alternative approaches to improved selection and guidance studies and that, therefore, some thought should be given to choosing wisely among them.

Assuming no change in student or environment. Cell 1 deals with the prediction of academic criteria under those circumstances where neither the student nor the environment is assumed to change [10] in the process of school-to-college transition. Under such grossly simplified circumstances, intellective predictors alone should be entirely adequate to accomplish the desired selection or guidance. The addition of nonintellective predictors under such circumstances should be manifestly unrewarding in terms of predictive efficiency (although I have tried to make a case in a previous publication for more philosophical and less correlational guideposts for the selection of predictors [Fishman, 1958]). If neither the student nor the environment changes, then such additional predictors should correlate as highly with high school intellective performance as with college intellective performance and, therefore, add nothing to the magnitude of the resulting multiple correlation coefficient. This, indeed, is what has long been the most frequent outcome of the experimental introduction of nonintellective predictors into predictor batteries in which good intellective (i.e., "mixed" intellective) predictors are already present for the prediction of intellective criteria. Both the older reviews of the college-prediction literature as well as the still unpublished review by Irving Lorge agree in reporting a near-zero gain in the multiple correlations resulting from the addition of nonintellective predictors to the intellective predictor batteries.

[10] For the purposes of my argument, "no change" may be interpreted to include linear change at a regular rate whereas "change" may be taken to imply saltatory, irregular, or nonlinear change.

I think it is important to admit, at this point, that the "no change" model is patently an oversimplification of the conditions that usually characterize the school-to-college transition. If this is so, then it raises the interesting question of why studies that deliberately or inadvertently adopt this model seem to turn out as well as they do from the point of view of their predictive success. The answer may well be the one that we discussed earlier. The reason is not so much that intellect is the primary predictor of college grades as that the "intellective predictors" employed in such studies are much more than what we have usually claimed them to be. Because our usual intellective predictors tap so much of the variance contributed by self and social selection, most other measures of these factors simply replicate much of the information already contained in these apparently single, apparently simple and apparently intellectual predictors. Therefore, unless we go out of our way and consciously search for individual and institutional variables that are *not* reflected in the usual intellective predictors, there does not seem to be any theoretically sound reason why we should improve our predictions of college success by a mere "act of faith" such as the tacking on of nonintellective predictors merely because they are nonintellective.

For me, the usual disappointing findings with tacked-on nonintellective predictors have two implications. In the first place, the near-zero median gain in prediction implies that for many of the samples of individuals and for many of the institutional networks in reference to which they were studied, the experimental nonintellective variables selected were unrelated to any crucial aspects of change as a result of the school-to-college transition. On the other hand, the fact that there is also some range on either side of this near-zero median implies to me that there are valid instances in which nonintellective predictors can appreciably affect selection and guidance efforts in conjunction with intellective criteria. It is to a rapid consideration of such instances that I now turn.

Assuming change in the student. Cells 2 and 3 are also concerned with instances of assumed lack of change with respect to the high school-to-college *environmental* transition, but in both cases the individual is assumed to have changed. In *cell 2* the change in the individual is assumed to be of a general developmental variety. In a prediction study this would imply that there are individual nonintellective characteristics present, measurable, and minimally operative in the high school years (hence their low correlation with high school intellective measures) that subsequently become appreciably more operative during the college years. As a result of this predictable change in the individual's nonintellective make-up, the addition of such measures to the more common intellective predictors brings about an overall improvement in the magnitude of the multiple correlations obtained in some selection and guidance studies.

Developmental Change. What might be the nature of this developmental nonintellective change such that, were we to tap it, we could improve our predictions even where the institutional factors as such are considered as remaining invariant? We really do not know enough about personality development to say for sure, but some recent work in the area of personality theory definitely points to the conclusion that significant personality development does continue throughout the college years.

Most of our good ideas regarding the 18 to 28 age group are comparatively recent. The work of Erikson comes to mind, of course (Erikson, 1950). From the point of view of direct pertinence for studies that would be classifiable in *cell 2* of Table 2, some of the variables defined and measured by Nevitt Sanford and his colleagues (Sanford, 1956), such as social maturity and impulse expression, may turn out to be of value (cf. Chapters 24 and 25); so also may other variables, such as thinking introversion, complexity of outlook, originality, social introversion, theoretical orientation, and estheticism, now being defined and refined by T. R. McConnell and his associates,[11] and still others pioneered by Harrison Gough,[12] such as achievement under independence and responsibility. Whether or not this will actually prove to be the case will depend on whether these variables are really undergoing developmental change during the late high school and college periods and on whether their correlation with college performance is, therefore, greater than their correlation with high school performance. *If* both of these expectations prove to be justified, and if environmental change can be considered to be negligible (so as not to vitiate or counteract this individual change) then studies of the type envisioned in *cell 2* should be fruitful indeed within the limitations of errors of measurement and philosophical legitimacy.

Random Change in the Student. Cell 3 applies to an entirely differ-

[11] Although some indication of the scope of McConnell's work is contained in his 1957 paper (McConnell, 1957), most of the studies conducted by McConnell and his associates at the Center for the Study of Higher Education (Berkeley), employing these new measures, are as yet unpublished. Brief examples of several of McConnell's personality variables are given in McConnell and Heist (1959) as well as in Chapter 5.

[12] For a discussion and bibliography pertaining to these and other scales developed by Gough, see Gough (1958).

ent species of individual change. I have tentatively labeled this variety as "random change" because I consider it to be basically unpredictable. Given our current level of discourse, I consider such phenomena as protracted illness on the part of the student, deaths or other major dislocations in his immediate family, serious financial reverses (or, indeed, success) on the stock market, and other such "accidents" as unpredictable. Although they are likely to bring about rather dramatic changes in the individual, changes which must moderate our predictions of his academic success, such occurrences are of necessity contingency factors rather than factors that we can use in any preadmission selection or guidance studies. When a student comes under the impact of factors such as these, our counseling and guidance departments must extend their services to him in order to mitigate the disruptive influences of these factors. In this sense, counseling and guidance are attempting to salvage our predictions, to "make them come true," to enable the student to function in accord with his earlier potential and achievements. As I will point out in a later paragraph, I consider this to be one of the most important approaches available to colleges in the entire area of nonintellective factors.

Assuming institutional or environmental change. In turning our attention to *cell 4,* we enter the domain of environmental change and its implications for selection and guidance studies.[13] The new ingredient in *cell 4* is a type of nonintellective factor that I have labeled *"constant environmental differences."* [14] These are differences between high school and college which affect all (or whole groups of) students attending (or applying to) a given college. The auspices of a college may be one such difference (e.g., Catholic or other religious auspices for students coming from public high schools), the presence of one or both sexes on campus may be another, the geographic or rural-urban location of the college may be still others. Constant environmental differences may affect all students at any given college but they will affect many of them in different ways. Thus, the academic work of students coming to a Southern college from the Northeast may be affected differently than that of students coming from the Midwest. Similarly,

---

[13] My discussion of *cells 4 and 5* is particularly and directly indebted to Paul Lazarsfeld. In *cells 5, 6, 8, and 9,* I have related his ideas to my earlier thinking on individual change, thus producing a more complete multivariate classification system. Professor Lazarsfeld is, of course, entirely innocent of any conceptual errors on my part in either of these connections.

[14] Lazarsfeld has suggested the term "secondary environment" for this purpose. See Lazarsfeld (1959).

students coming to a small rurally located college from a large metropolitan high school may well be affected differently than students coming from a small prep school. Since at any one college self-selection and social-selection factors may result in one or another group of students being only inadequately represented within the student body, the effects of constant environmental differences may not be easily or reliably discernible. As a result, it may prove necessary to study such factors on an *interinstitutional* basis before their true relationships to academic performance are recognized. Nevertheless, on a theoretical level at least, it should prove possible to discover whatever the regularities that do exist and ultimately to feed them into our predictions of intellective criteria. We are dealing in this cell with differences or opposites in high school and college environments which are constant among students within subclasses defined on the basis of preadmission characteristics. Our goal is to predict, on the basis of such characteristics, the college performance of applicants whose college environments differ in particular ways from their high school environments. Such differences between high school and college might be ordered on a continuum which is monotonically related to the validity of the high school average as a predictor of college achievement. If this proves possible, then we could add an index of the degree of difference between high school and college to function as a moderator in our prediction battery. With little difference between the two environments the weight given to the high school average might be greater. With substantial difference the weight given to the high school average might be either zero, negative, or positive—depending on whether the difference was found to be nonfunctional, disruptive, or facilitative with respect to college achievement.[15] Since *cell 4* applies to those instances where no change in the individual is assumed to take place, we would merely add these *institutional* predictors or moderators to the standard intellective ones.

Random Environmental Change. Cell 7 deals with quite a different variety of environmental differences. I have dubbed these *"variable environmental differences"* [16] because some of them may impinge on one group of students whereas others may impinge on an entirely different group. Unlike the constant environmental differences, the variable environmental differences do not apply "across the board" to whole groups of students that can easily be recognized in advance or

[15] It is this individual-environment interaction that C. Robert Pace and George G. Stern may be getting at (albeit in purely psychological terms) via their Environment Index. See Pace and Stern (1958a and 1958b) and Chapter 21.

[16] Lazarsfeld has suggested the term "primary environment" for this purpose.

readily identified in terms of their preadmission characteristics. To the extent that this is so, the consequences of such factors are non-predictable in the individual case and must, therefore, remain as contingencies that moderate our predictions.

Under the rubric of variable environmental differences, belong such factors as peer-group relationships (i.e., student norms), student-faculty relationships, fraternity activities, other extracurricular activities, classroom atmospheres including varying teaching methods, and the socio-metric constellations and other social structures in which different students may become involved. Can we predict which student will become preoccupied with an on-campus jazz group? Can we tell in advance which one will wind up taking physics in a class also attended by two other students from his hometown? Will the social and athletic leader of his high school find the college competition too strong to enable him immediately to play a similar role on campus? To the extent that questions like these are not predictable at our current level of discourse, we have once more come upon a very crucial area of contingencies. If we cannot enter such factors into our prediction equations, we must expect that (a) they will tend to operate so as to upset our predictions in one direction or another, and that (b) we can identify and cope with them only by longitudinal or quasi-experimental studies of guidance, teaching, and counseling services on the *postadmission* scene. In some instances we may decide that the student should be led to a different course, to a different club, to a different self-concept. In others we may well decide that the college environment itself should be changed (e.g., by introducing changes in extracurricular activities, in administrative practices, in teaching techniques). Both types of actions are in the line of influencing *certain* predictions to come true while influencing others *not* to come true by helping students to function at their optimal level. Both types of actions constitute nothing more than attempts to bring about desired changes by educational means—i.e., by whatever means the college deliberately undertakes in order to reach its objectives. Attempts to change the student and attempts to change the college are both "obviously" called for once a college recognizes the multiplicity of factors that may moderate and invalidate its predictions of academic performance. It is good to keep in mind that the very core of the college experience and the very heart of a college's responsibilities revolve about those nonintellective factors (according to our restricted use in this paper) which must remain *contingencies* when considered from the point of view of prediction and selection. An appreciation of this fact should both humble us and strengthen us as scientists and as educators. It should also orient us more toward the type of action research in which the very failure of a system (a college) throws light on the nature of the system. It is precisely because *cell 7* is such an impenetrable no-man's land from the point of view of prediction and selection that we must appeal to counselors, teachers, and administrators to engage in basic studies of the educational process and of the ways in which social systems affect this process.

More complex interactions. I will not take the time to review *cells 5, 6, 8, and 9* of Table 2. Their contents are dictated by the headings of the rows and columns which intersect at their respective positions. Each of these four cells calls for more complex prediction and/or guidance studies than those that we have discussed above, although the constituents remain those with which we are familiar. Because of their greater complexity these cells probably come closer to recognizing the true interplay between various kinds of nonintellective predictors, as well as the actual relationship between all of these and intellective predictors, than we have been able to recognize in our discussion thus far. It is noteworthy that three of these four cells contain contingency moderators. Finally, before leaving Table 2, it must be admitted that a two-dimensional representation does not permit us to show the interactions that can undoubtedly occur among all of the factors (and their predictor or contingency measures). I have no doubt that many students undergo both developmental and random change during the years of their school-to-college transition. I also have no doubt but that many colleges represent both constant environmental differences and variable environmental differences in contrast with the high school settings from which their applicants and students come. These things being so, then the complex *interaction* between intellective predictors, individual nonintellective predictors, institutional predictors, individual contingency moderators, and institutional contingency moderators must all be recognized and investigated in our selection and guidance studies. When this is done, our handling of nonintellective factors will be vastly superior to present practice and their value to us will be correspondingly greater. We shall then be studying nonintellective factors in intellective performance in terms of a growing theory of individual-environment relationships. This would seem to me to be an appropriate context for studies in this area, an area that has so long been theoretically barren. It is precisely in this context of individual *and* environment, of predictors *plus* contingencies, that social scientists can make their greatest contributions to the study of nonintellective and intellective factors in American higher education.[17]

CONCLUSION: A MORATORIUM ON PREDICTION

It may even be that the social psychologist's greatest contribution will be that of persuading those who have been oriented to prediction to forget about prediction for a while. Psychologists learned early— perhaps too early—to do multiple correlation studies. The multiple regression design is a sophisticated one, perhaps too sophisticated for frequent utilization by social psychologists. Because he is familiar with cruder designs as well as with the crudest level of measurement— namely, measurement at the nominal level—the social psychologist is often likely to stress a level of refinement that involves going back to analyze variables that others have taken as givens immediately to be quantified. It may be of some help, for a while at least, to think of kinds of students, kinds of high school environments, and kinds of college environments. It may be of some help, for a while at least, to de-emphasize prediction per se and to consider how different kinds of students make different kinds of uses of different kinds of college environments. I am pretty confident that we shall get back to prediction ultimately. Our own research proclivities as well as larger social pressures will push us in that direction. Nevertheless, if we set prediction aside awhile in favor of some basic theory and research, we may ultimately return to it with greater understanding and flexibility than that which we now possess.

REFERENCES

Bloom, B. S., and Peters, F. R. The use of academic prediction scales for counselling and selecting college students. (Mimeo.) (Rev. Ed.) Chicago: University of Chicago, Office of the Examiner, 1959.
Burnham, P. S. The assessment of admissions criteria. *A.C.A.C. Journal,* 1959, 4, 1–9.
Erikson, E. H. *Childhood and society.* New York: Norton, 1950.

[17] There is no reason to assume that an overall theoretical framework like the one that I have here suggested could not also be applied to the problems of predicting nonintellective criteria. This task I must leave for another occasion. I also realize that my two-factor, nine-cell table is not in itself sufficiently complex to accommodate the multitude of variables that enter into college performance. Nevertheless, I do hope that it represents some progress from a position of no theory to one of some theory.

Fishman, J. A. The use of quantitative techniques to predict college success. *Admissions Information*, 1957, **1**, 49–61.

Fishman, J. A. Unsolved criterion problems in the selection of college students. *Harvard educ. Rev.*, 1958, **28**, 340–349.

Fishman, J. A. An introduction to the social psychology of school-to-college transition. *J. of educ. Soc.*, 1960, **33**, 249–251.

Fishman, J. A., and Pasanella, A. K. College admission-selection studies. Rev. Educ. Research, 1960, **30**, 298–310.

Garrett, H. F. A review and interpretation of investigations of factors related to scholastic success in colleges of arts and sciences and teachers colleges. *J. of exper. Educ.*, 1949, **18**, 91–138.

Gough, H. *Manual, California psychological inventory.* Palo Alto, Calif.: Consulting Psychologists Press, 1958.

Hollingshead, A. B. *Elmtown's youth.* New York: Wiley, 1949.

Jordan, A. M. Some results and correlations of Army Alpha tests. *School and Society*, 1920, **2**, 354–358.

Lazarsfeld, P. Progress report: on a project to map out the general area of nonintellectual factors in the prediction of college success. (Mimeo.) Committee on Research and Development, College Entrance Examination Board, New York, 1959.

McArthur, C. Subculture and personality during the college years. *J. of educ. Soc.*, 1960, **33**, 260–268.

McConnell, T. R. The diversity of American higher education, a research program. *Educational Record*, 1957, **38**, 300–315.

McConnell, T. R., and Heist, P. Do students make the college? *College and University*, Summer, 1959, 442–452.

Pace, C. R., and Stern, G. G. *Criterion study of college environments.* Syracuse University Research Institute, Psychological Research Center, 1958a.

Pace, C. R., and Stern, G. G. Approach to the measurement of psychological characteristics of college environment. *J. of educ. Psych.*, 1958b, **49**, 269–277.

Rogoff, N. American high schools at mid-century. (Mimeo.) New York, Bureau of Applied Social Research, 1959.

Sanford, N. (Ed.) Personality development during the college years. *J. of soc. Issues*, 1956, **12** (4).

Stice, G., Mollenkopf, W. G., and Torgerson, W. S. *Background factors and college-going plans among high aptitude public high school seniors.* Princeton: Educational Testing Service, 1956.

Stice, G., Mollenkopf, W. G., and Torgerson, W. S. *Background factors relating to college plans and college enrollment among public high school students.* Princeton: Educational Testing Service, 1957.

21 *George G. Stern*

Environments for Learning

The influence of the emotions and personality on learning is a distinctively contemporary interest in education. There are two positions from which to approach these nonintellectual (better called *less intellectualized*) factors in learning. One is to view the problem in terms of the individual learner—his motives, inhibitions, aspirations, and fears—for the ultimate purpose of counseling him to a more receptive state of educability. Student screening and placement test programs are closely related in philosophy to this approach. In both cases the objective is to maximize the learning potential of the learner, one by selection and the other by adaptation.

An alternative to this would be to study the learning situation for the purpose of maximizing the impact of the educational experience. One aspect of this problem lies in the formal structure of the methods of presentation, a topic which will not concern us here. The socio-psychological counterpart involves more evanescent factors associated with the emotional atmosphere surrounding the learning experience. The present paper is concerned with socio-psychological environments for learning in higher education, and their significance as an ecological setting for various types of students.

Lewin's (1939) classic comparison of democratic, autocratic, and laissez faire group atmospheres has had a lasting impact on educa-

Note. This is based on a composite of papers read before the American College Health Association, Philadelphia, Pa., May, 1959; the American Psychological Association, Cincinnati, Ohio, September, 1959; and the New York State Association of Deans and Guidance Personnel, New York, N.Y., November, 1959. Acknowledgment is hereby given to the editor of *Student Medicine* for permission to adapt and reprint portions of an article entitled "Congruence and Dissonance in the Ecology of College Students" appearing in the Spring, 1960 issue of that journal.

tional research and philosophy (cf. Chapter 8). Taken in conjunction with the "nondirective" innovations in psychotherapy then being introduced by Rogers (1942), the implications seemed inescapable: the key to maximal learning lay in establishing appropriately "democratic —nondirective—student-centered" classroom environments.

This continues to be the prevailing conclusion today, despite the absence of clearly supporting evidence. Most studies of classroom atmosphere have evaluated the effectiveness of different teaching procedures on either the acquisition of knowledge, improved social attitudes, or both. In a recent survey of seventeen such studies (Stern, 1960a), only one could be found which actually demonstrated that student-centered instruction resulted in greater mastery of the subject matter (Faw, 1949).

These studies suggest that the acquisition of knowledge is largely unaffected by the use of either directive or nondirective techniques in the classroom. The nondirective approach does appear to be more effective in obtaining favorable attitude changes, as measured by reductions in ethnocentric opinion and increases in insight into self and others. But these results may just as well be attributable to the fact that norms are more readily established in groups characterized by a high rate of intercommunication among the participants, a condition that is not necessarily limited to nondirective groups (McKeachie, 1954, 1958).

The evidence from student opinion regarding the relative merits of student-centered vs. instructor-centered techniques is even more ambiguous. The same studies are divided almost equally in claiming predominantly favorable, unfavorable, or mixed student reactions. If the samples of students in all of these studies were combined there would still be at least as many students who felt dissatisfied, frustrated, or anxious as a result of their nondirective experience as there were who considered it valuable. The nondirective technique is obviously controversial, whether viewed in terms of subjective opinion or evaluated on the basis of objective results.

GROUP ATMOSPHERE, STUDENT PERSONALITY, AND LEARNING

A study by Wispé (1951) was the first to suggest an explanation for the mixed student reactions. He found that student-centered groups were no more effective than subject-matter-centered groups in their performance on the final objective examination in an elementary psychology course. Furthermore, most students disliked the nondirective sections. However, students who placed a high value on personal independence not only preferred the student-centered classroom but were extremely critical of the subject-matter-centered sections. Conversely, students who expressed the strongest need for direction and organization were also most intense in their dislike for the permissive teaching techniques. Very similar results were obtained by Patton (1955) who found that students who rejected traditional sources of authority and were highly motivated toward personal achievement were most favorably disposed toward experimental classes run by the students themselves, and most able to handle the responsibilities involved.

If we can further assume that people work most effectively in situations that conform to their preferences (Wispé, 1951; Gross, 1959) then these studies also suggest a reason for the lack of definitive differences between directive and nondirective classes in facilitating the acquisition of subject matter knowledge. The maximal success of the learning process may well depend on the optimal combination of teaching technique and student need.

But no studies bear directly on this point. This is especially surprising since the essence of Lewin's approach was to stress the importance of both situational and personal variables as joint determinants of behavior. Indeed, an early report by Lewin, Lippit, and White (1939) called attention to the fact that an army officer's son was one of the few children who preferred the autocratic climate. No further elaboration was made of this point, but the suggested interdependence between group atmosphere and individual personality has been clearly established since then by Haythorn (1953, 1956) and Schutz (1955). Their investigations have shown very significant relationships between the characteristic performances of small groups and the essentially autocratic or equalitarian personality traits of the group members.

The authoritarian personality and general education. The implications of these relationships among situation, personality, and learning in higher education were investigated initially by Stern, Stein, and Bloom (1956). Their studies were based on a substantially modified version of the Inventory of Beliefs, a measure of "stereopathy-authoritarianism" (cf. Chapter 6) developed for the Americal Council on Education Cooperative Study of Evaluation in General Education (Dressel and Mayhew, 1954). Sixty items of this revision (Form T) are nativistic-fundamentalistic generalizations that are parallel to but not identical with items of the California scales (Adorno et al., 1950). The remaining forty items are reversals obtained by writing what might be called internationalistic-relativistic generalizations, rejected by authoritarians but acceptable to antiauthoritarians. An example of an authoritarian item would be:

"The many different kinds of children in school these days force teachers to make a lot of rules and regulations so that things will run smoothly."

A comparable antiauthoritarian reversal was:

"More playgrounds and fewer strict fathers would eliminate juvenile delinquency."

The intent of this scale was to facilitate the identification of a body of students whose personal needs and values might be expected to lead to conflict and the impairment of performance in a particular type of academic environment. Authoritarian personalities should tend to view general education programs as diffuse and lacking in specificity, and show poorer grades, more emotional disturbance, and a higher frequency of withdrawal from such a program than would nonauthoritarian subjects.

The reversed items were included in the scale for the purpose of differentiating the responses of *authoritarians* from three other groups. One of these consists of people who invert the content of the authoritarian ideology but are no less categorical in their beliefs: the *antiauthoritarians*. The remaining two groups are a little more difficult to abstract since their response patterns tend to be partially confounded with those of the authoritarian. The group which accepts either type of ideological generalization were called *irrationals*, while those who rejected both types were called *rationals*.[1]

In the initial studies (Stern et al., 1956) with this questionnaire institutions were found to vary considerably in the relative proportions with which each type of person was represented. The irrationals, for example, appeared in largest numbers among samples of high school and Southern college students. West Point cadets appeared to be equally divided between authoritarians and rationals, whereas samples of psychologists, theological students from liberal Protestant denominations, and Reed College students were just as predominantly

---

[1] Subjects are identified as authoritarian or antiauthoritarian by their appropriately selective acceptance and rejection of the two types of items contained in the inventory. Scoring for indiscriminate acceptance of both types of items yields an acquiescence dimension, at the acceptant end of which are those called ideological irrationals whereas those rejecting both kinds of generalizations were identified as rationals. This scoring procedure excludes acquiescent response set as a factor on the authoritarian continuum.

divided between antiauthoritarians and rationals. Representation among the four response types was seemingly nonrandom, the tendency being for either authoritarians or antiauthoritarians to predominate in a given institution. Rationals appeared as often in the company of authoritarians as they did with antiauthoritarians, but the more rarely observed irrationals were found only with authoritarians.

Extensive comparison of antiauthoritarians, authoritarians, and rationals at the University of Chicago revealed many statistically significant differences between them which can be summarized somewhat dramatically in three brief and overgeneralized sketches:

The *antiauthoritarian* undergraduate student at the University of Chicago tended to be a first-generation American, with no religious affiliation, the child of middle-European Jewish parents both of whom had received an extensive higher education. He was far above the University of Chicago average in intelligence, excelled in the social sciences and the humanities, and had selected a professional career for himself in one or the other of these areas. Although an outstanding student, with broad cultural and intellectual interests, the antiauthoritarian was likely to be regarded with mixed feelings by his instructors as a result of his challenging argumentative manner, marked independence, and social and intellectual impulsiveness. The stories these students made up to describe the contents of a series of especially contrived pictures [2] were readily identified by analysts unaware of the student's Inventory score on the basis of verbal facility, sensuality, psychological acuity, and strivings for personal independence that extended to identifications with other discriminated minorities.

The *authoritarian* undergraduate was almost the complete reverse of this pattern. His family had lived in this country for several generations, and were either Roman Catholic or else members of fundamentalist or evangelical Protestant denominations. Although not different in intelligence from the average University of Chicago student, the authoritarian did unusually poorly in the social sciences and the humanities, and strongly disliked both of these areas. His occupational choice lay in business, law, medicine, or engineering, and he saw higher education as having no other purpose than that of specific vocational preparation. His academic approach might be best characterized as somewhat obsessive-compulsive, stressing detailed organization and structure. A distinct minority group at Chicago, the authoritarians contributed most heavily to the withdrawal rate, complaining of the lack of professional courses and the looseness of a pedagogical approach that tolerated smoking in the classrooms, did not require attendance, and expected students to answer their own questions. The picture stories of the authoritarian students were readily distinguished in blind analysis in terms of a stilted and banal phraseology, submission to authority figures, rigid codification of personal relationships, and inhibition of sensuality.

The *rationals* cannot be so neatly typed. They came from diverse home backgrounds, had a variety of religious affiliations, and fell into no specific

[2] The Thematic Apperception Test (Murray, 1943).

occupational categories. They were brighter than the authoritarians, but not as bright as the antiauthoritarians, with a corresponding record of intermediate academic achievement. The only distinctive characteristic of the rationals appeared in their picture stories, which were identified blindly at a high level of statistical significance on the basis of their impersonal detachment and emphasis on intellectualization and abstraction.

The only thing known about the *irrationals* at the present time is that their appearance has been restricted to younger, less well-educated samples.

In an extension of these studies among students at Syracuse University, the entering class was found to differ in its composition from that of the University of Chicago. Both groups contained a very substantial number of rationals, but whereas 20% of the Chicago group were antiauthoritarians and less than 10% were authoritarians, the Syracuse population reversed these percentages. Despite the increased number of authoritarians and the lower intellectual capacity of the Syracuse freshmen, the same relationships were found to hold here as at Chicago. Differences in intelligence were considerable,[3] antiauthoritarians again being far above the group average, rationals somewhat higher, authoritarians identical with the ideologically unidentifiable students, and the irrationals below average. These differences seem largely attributable to verbal skills, but even when the effects of this contribution were controlled statistically, the groups continued to differ substantially [4] in their first year grade-point average.

Profiles of the authoritarians, rationals, and antiauthoritarians at Syracuse seem generally consistent with those at Chicago, but they also reveal intellectual and sociological differences between the Syracuse and Chicago student bodies. How fundamental are these differences? Are they limited to regional variations in the background of students recruited to these schools, or do they involve even more systematic differences that should restrain us from making generalizations about types as such?

Gladstein (1957) provided a partial answer to these questions in a study of 104 authoritarians, antiauthoritarians, and rationals drawn from both universities. He devised a multiple-choice Study Activities Questionnaire based on expected differences among these three types and administered it to 104 selected representatives of each type from the two schools. Analysis of actual high frequency responses revealed the following characteristics to be associated with each type:

The typical *authoritarian* student preferred studying alone, since working with others always meant a bull session in which nothing definite was ever

[3] Statistically significant beyond the .01 level.
[4] Statistically significant beyond the .01 level.

settled. He also preferred to study in the same place throughout the year, in a room that was neat and orderly and free from the distraction of the radio, television, or phonograph. He developed rigid time schedules for studying, reading, and review, and relied heavily on formal study aids, teacher suggestions on outlining and notetaking, and rote memorization of significant facts to get himself through. Difficult reading materials were particularly frustrating for him, and he dealt with this problem by going to the instructor or to better students for help. Theoretical discussions in class were another source of difficulty, and the authoritarian student most preferred a straightforward exposition by the instructor to any other classroom activity. He prepared for the final examination by reviewing classroom and reading notes and memorizing the main points. The only thing he liked about essays was getting them done. After the exam he compared his answers with those of other students and felt little need or ability to let himself go. The important thing about exams was to get a good grade, since his vocational aims depended on it.

The responses of the typical *antiauthoritarian* indicated that his place of study varied, as he alternated between satisfying his desire to be with people and isolating himself as a defense against this need. He enjoyed cooperative study because he liked other viewpoints, liked discussions, and because it gave him the opportunity to be with other people. He didn't care much where he studied as long as it was quiet. Readings challenged him and he sought out additional materials to improve his understanding. He liked it when the class discussed side issues and took notes of stimulating and challenging ideas that he intended to explain later. He prepared for the final examination by trying to arrive at some sense of the course as a totality, and liked essay assignments because they gave him a chance to work with ideas, to express himself, and to explore abstract concepts. He felt that an examination helped him to evaluate what he had learned, and this was more important than the grade, but after it was over he usually let himself go.

The typical *rational* usually studies alone and in the same place, for various reasons: for example, people are distracting, one accomplishes more alone, associating one place with work stimulates study. At times, however, he liked to study in groups because this was a way to get other viewpoints and to receive help. He followed a schedule during the term because he felt that this helped him to study and he was anxious to be prepared whenever he happened to be called on in class. Difficult readings frustrated him, but he liked to participate in the class discussions and liked discussing side issues. He preferred his own study aids to those of others, and rejected memorization as a useless activity for the kinds of courses and examinations he was taking. In reviewing for the final examination, however, he did try to memorize the main points made by the instructor and authors. The examination itself was both frightening and challenging, and he often cut class while preparing for it. He liked essays because he liked to work with ideas. Doing well on the test not only depended on a good preparation, he felt, but also on approaching each part and question in a rational, systematic fashion.

These summaries were obtained from the mean item responses made by each ideological type on the Study Activities Questionnaire. The differences in response among the authoritarian, antiauthoritarian, and rational students were considerable, regardless of the school they attended. There were no differences between the two schools, however, when the subgroups from each were combined and compared.

Gladstein's (1957) findings have particular significance since the Chicago students were not classified into ideological types on the basis of scores on the Inventory of Beliefs as were the Syracuse cases, but were identified by means of a series of nonideological scale items concerned with personality needs from an instrument known as the Activities Index which had previously been found to be equated with Inventory scores (Stern et al., 1956, 215–218). The consistency of student types between schools adds further confirmation, then, to the equivalence of the two measures. Many of the characteristics differentiating these student types were determined by voluntary verbal report alone, however. Ideological (Inventory of Beliefs), personality (Activities Index, Thematic Apperception Test), intelligence (ACE Psychological, Cooperative Reading Comprehension, ACE Test of Critical Thinking in the Social Sciences), educational achievement (course examinations), even study habits (Study Activities Questionnaire) differences were all obtained from responses to items on questionnaires and inventories. These various groups of students were evidently reared differently, and obviously have different viewpoints about a wide variety of things, but are they really recognizably different in their overt behavior? Do authoritarians prepare poorly in the humanities and social sciences for reasons associated with their authoritarianism? Is their lack of success in these areas a matter of ideology, personality, or something else? Perhaps all three groups of students look alike in the classroom, except for the general differences that hold between those who are doing well and those who are having academic difficulties.

The authoritarian personality in a special environment. Answers to some of these questions were attempted in a study by Stern and Cope in 1955. Three special classes were set up in the citizenship course taken by all liberal arts freshmen at Syracuse University. One of these sections was composed exclusively of authoritarians, the second of antiauthoritarians, and the third of rationals, as determined by scores on the Inventory of Beliefs which had been administered before registration to all incoming freshmen. All three sections were taught by the same instructor who had agreed to a special assignment of students but was otherwise unaware of the particular characteristics of the three classes.

The instructor met with each of these groups once a week throughout the semester, and maintained a diary of the events taking place during these meetings. By the end of the first week he commented spontaneously on his recognition of the three groups of students as types that he had encountered before. Other first impressions excerpted from the diary for the first two class meetings follow: [5]

Authoritarians: . . . lacking in curiosity or initiative . . . direct questioning required to get class discussion and there was much less interplay between the students . . . the only two students not reticent like the others proved to have gotten into class erroneously and have been removed . . . many of them are interested in religion.

Antiauthoritarians: . . . have a bargaining, critical attitude [although] not exactly hostile . . . many questions on details of course administration . . . continued attack [second session] on why we studied responsible thinking, why did I have certain articles in the text, why did I give them a pre-test on reading, and so on . . . students for and against labor unions in the class.

Rationals: These are obviously all the future campus leaders . . . . very responsive but friendly. There were some questions on the administration of the course but they were not pointed or sharp. In class discussion there was a terrific reaction. Most hands were up but the students were polite, amending rather than arguing with those who had spoken previously. The class was extremely pleasant, jolly and apparently enjoyed joking. . . . A note inviting a girl to go on a hot blind date to Princeton erroneously was mixed with the [class materials] . . . she practically clawed and scratched to recover [it].

The instructor's initial evaluation of the authoritarian section remains unchanged throughout the semester, although his understanding of the students continues to increase. But his reactions to the other two classes have been reversed by the third week, and these impressions persist from this point on:

Authoritarians: Very difficult to get discussion, although direct questions indicate they are well informed on the text . . . . a constant temptation to "lecture" rather than discuss . . . . split between those who despise the common man, . . . and those who are very democratic but feel repulsed, at their level of morality, in working for a better world.

Antiauthoritarians: This class is becoming my delight. They take nothing for granted, yet their criticism and controversy is friendly. . . . They sass the professor; the slightest disciplinary remark led [to a] retort that this would lead to frustrations.

Rationals: This group is going to seed, and it is probably my fault. They seem to have a sense of self-assurance and security, and a "we can't lose out" kind of confidence . . . . I cannot to date get anything but bland cooperation:

[5] The paragraph headings and all bracketed inserts here and in subsequent excerpts from the diary are my own, replacing the instructor's designations, and inserted here for the purpose of identifying these groups appropriately for the reader or clarifying a phrase. The only means available to the instructor for referring to the three classes was by the hour at which they met; at no time during the semester was he aware of the Inventory of Beliefs scores of these subjects or of any related data or classification.

creative, critical thought or self-criticism is hard to find here. Their quiz answers are often correct, but not creative.

Later in the semester the instructor summarized his impressions of these students in the following words.

Authoritarians: . . . this group finds reliance on God or some other firm power . . . removes the necessity of relying on others so much. . . . Their easiest adjustment is to bear their problems without relying on other persons in academic life. Theology is easier, often spoken to them in groups, rather than requiring personal reading or interviews.

Antiauthoritarians: . . . my easy first liking of this class for their intellectual independence made me overlook their haggling. . . . As a former U.S. Civil Service employee and Army personnel officer, I know now that these folks would make difficult soldiers, be security risks, refuse to accept a group decision on ethical grounds and choose the pressure group rather than being precinct committeemen. In a pressure group they would fight about how to run the world, I fear, while other people would run it . . . . professors and teachers—from Plato to now—may include more personalities like this than you might expect . . . . it is easier to propose and teach social reform to pliant students, than it is to run a creaking civilization. Our textbook in the first semester probably appeals to these personalities; it was written or edited by personalities [of the same type], so we get along with each other . . . . They can be personalities because they have balanced capabilities. [This group has the highest and least scattered scores in intelligence, aptitude, and reading]. My guess is that students of the same type with lower, or unbalanced scores don't get into college: their high school teachers slap them down.

Rationals: If you are one of these people you are much more likely to get political or economic power because you are then a common denominator personality. . . . On the other hand I'm not sure a group like this leads to political social progress. You have to mix some *domesticated,* progressive [antiauthoritarian] persons with them.[6] . . . The [rationals] are not as well balanced [in tests of intellectual capacities] and they don't have to be . . . . social adjustment to others can save the brilliant loafer and get him into the University, while the low scores of others [in this group] are offset by their social "cooperation" and steady work habits . . . . they have learned to lean on others, and trade their limited abilities for help from others.

What effect has this isolation of student personality types had on their achievement on the final common objective examination in this course? We know from previous work that the authoritarians do not like this type of course and usually do poorly in it. In the present case students with Inventory of Beliefs scores identifying them as authoritarians but whose assignment to other sections of this course was left to chance also did much more poorly than the rest of their classmates.[7] Not so the authoritarians in the experimental section,

[6] This is the same point made by Shils (1954, p. 48) in discussing the role of the authoritarian of the "left" on the American political scene.

[7] Statistically significant beyond the .001 level.

who did just as well as the antiauthoritarians and rationals in the other two experimental sections.

This result does not seem attributable to the general superiority of the instructor, outstanding as he was, since neither of the other two sections did any better than students of the same personality type randomly distributed among nonexperimental discussion groups. Nor was this improvement in performance for the authoritarians in the experimental class associated with any unique changes in ideology. Post-testing with the Inventory of Beliefs at the end of the semes·ter revealed statistically significant changes of the same magnitude for all authoritarians, whether in the experimental class or distri·buted among the nonexperimental sections, leaving them all at the level of the ideologically unidentifiable students at the beginning of the course. Neither the antiauthoritarians nor the rationals show any change in their respective Inventory scores. Apparently the citizen·ship course is effective in inducing a general change of attitude away from the extreme authoritarian position. But this change was reflected in the objective portions of the final examination only for those au·thoritarian students who had been isolated in their own discussion unit.

The diary provides a clue to experiences that may have been respon·sible for this outcome. The instructor emphasizes in many different ways that his primary objective was to stimulate the free exchange of ideas. His satisfaction with the antiauthoritarians stems from his perception of them as "dynamic, active, critical and willing to take on anything, including the instructor." His sense of failure with the ra·tionals he attributes to their apparent refusal to perform at the level of which he thinks them capable: "This class has a high potential in intelligence, but some kind of stimulant will have to be devised by the professor." The authoritarians, as has already been noted, were reti·cent from the beginning.

Throughout the semester, however, he continues to press for dis·cussion with the latter two sections. During the first month he con·tinually refers to the effort expended to get these sections to respond. Several techniques stand out: (a) continued pressure from him, in the form of direct questions, (b) a refusal on his part to lecture or to provide direct answers, (c) his encouragement and acceptance of any response from the students, and (d) his insistent adoption of ab·surdly extreme positions, e.g.

Week 3: Major discussions were about women in politics. I took the posi·tion initially that women were useless except for maternity purposes. I re·fused to call on any women, accepted and agreed with all male opinions and added to the slurs on the females until every girl in the class was ready to tear the plaster off the wall. From this impasse, we moved on . . .

Week 5: I took the position that voting was useless . . .

Week 7: I favored "slavery," i.e. putting the mob in any civilization into its place—"so you intelligent folks can operate a *good* democracy."

The slavery issue apparently marked the turning point. Prior to this time he says, in summary of their classroom responses, "The [authoritarians] had to be asked numerous leading questions. The [rationals] had several in class who would volunteer answers, if I would look around expectantly. It is generally true of the [antiauthoritarians] that I don't have to look around, you just have to arbitrate the urge to be heard." He describes slow gains during the first six weeks, but in the seventh he notes that a "discussion 'breakthrough' to a higher level of participation became evident in *all* classes. The foil that did it was to favor 'slavery.' " The effects were striking:

Authoritarians: This class gives evidence in more individual cases of willingness to fight back against the brutally dogmatic totalitarian rantings of the professor. I tried to seduce them to totalitarianism, and they indignantly, but politely, told me I was wrong. [The following session] the class was more relaxed . . . . they finally broke down and simply asked one interpretative question after another about the course . . . . [two students] came up after class to indicate that they wanted advice.

Rationals: This class too, including many previously silent, attacked my theories on slavery. The happiest thing appears to be that many of them now are apparently deciding that it is o.k. to disagree, verbally brawl with, and slap the prof in his place.

Antiauthoritarians: . . . . the period came to an end too quickly.

From this point on the discussions remained at a satisfactory level in all three sections. But this does not mean that they all turned into duplicates of one another. The diary goes on to record the ways in which each group otherwise remained consistent with itself, and the distinctive personal characteristics associated with their individual classroom performances. The significance of this study does not lie in the use of the discussion method as an educational panacea, but rather in the effect that the persistent application of particular discussion techniques had in helping a group of authoritarian students increase their knowledge in an area to which they are usually resistant.

For the antiauthoritarians the experiment described here was superfluous; they showed no gains, and succeeded mainly in demonstrating a competence they had already enjoyed prior to taking the course. The rationals also showed no gains, although their failure was not in their mastery of the course materials but in terms of a more personal objective set by the instructor himself. Viewed against general education objectives, the authoritarians were the only clearly deficient and dif-difficult group of students, and the only one to have been clearly responsive to the specialized techniques to which they had been exposed in their own isolated classroom environment.

STUDENT ECOLOGY

The literature on classroom atmosphere, summarized at the beginning of the chapter, provides an example of an ecological relationship between person and environment of particular interest to psychologists. We have in effect been engaged in the study of subcultural "strains" of men who show unique adaptations to what appears superficially to be a common environment. The studies cited strongly suggest that the selective student preferences and performances observed are related to differences in response which the same apparent environment elicits from each of several distinct subgroups of students. In the aggregate these effects tend to cancel out one another, but suitably segregated groups of students reveal them clearly. Stereopathic authoritarians, for example, are most critical of permissive teaching techniques (Wispé, 1951), and are least able to handle the responsibilities involved in such classrooms (Patton, 1955), have study habits which are ineffectual under nondirective conditions (Gladstein, 1957), and generally lead to either underachievement or withdrawal in these circumstances (Stern, Stein, and Bloom, 1956). But these same students may become overachievers when isolated in a special class (Jacob, 1957; Stern, 1960a). In certain institutional settings these students perform very poorly, but only in relation to a particular type of instruction that lacks congruence for them. They may perform very well indeed in an appropriately modified environment.

The same educational objectives may apparently thus be achieved by very different types of students if the environment is appropriately modified for each of them. But the study of personalities in relation to their environment requires more of a foundation than the special case of the authoritarian personality and its interaction with various classroom atmospheres. If our purpose is to develop a psychonomics of student life, we must study the relationship between types of student personality and types of institutional environments in a more general framework. There have been a number of steps in this direction (cf. McConnell and Heist, Chapter 5; Brown, Chapter 16; Knapp and Goodrich, 1952; Knapp and Greenbaum, 1953; Office of Scientific Personnel, 1955, 1956, 1958; Thistlethwaite, 1959a, 1959b; Heath,

1958; Riesman, 1958), ranging from primarily statistical appraisals of concentrations of characteristics of high excellence—such as Ph.D. production—to acutely observant descriptive reports of various types of programs. The project about to be described is another such attempt.

The measurement of need and press. The types of student personalities participating in the various studies of instructional climates discussed previously were identified on the basis of responses to some form of ideological inventory.[8] Although there is now very considerable evidence to suggest that ideological choice (at least insofar as authoritarianism is concerned) is related to more pervasive personality characteristics, socio-political values as such are only one of the many ways in which individuality among people can be discerned.

Personality Needs. Some years ago H. A. Murray (1938) proposed a system for classifying the organizational tendencies that appear to give unity and direction to personality. He called these tendencies *needs,* but the terms *drive* and *motive* have also been used to refer to the objectives which a person characteristically strives to achieve for himself. Whatever they be called, they stand for something we infer from a person's actions. The actions themselves may be quite diversified, and lend themselves individually to many different explanations in other contexts, but they are given a unified theme in the interpretation we place on them.

As an example of such a theme, consider the case of someone who likes to play practical jokes. By itself this preference might mean many things, but if we also learn that he likes to shock people by saying things that distress them, picks arguments with authority figures, and enjoys teasing people he thinks are conceited, we may begin to suspect that a strong tendency toward aggression and hostility underlies these otherwise discrete activities.

Because direct observation of behavior is typically impractical, the psychologist has turned to indirect sources from which to estimate characteristic behavior, making use of autobiographical data, interviews, projective tests, measures of physical and intellectual qualities, inventories of attitudes and values, and so forth. The simplest of such

[8] The Gladstein (1957) study, described earlier on pp. 696–697, is an exception. The selection of one of his two samples was based on student responses to a number of nonideological items which had been found to be correlated with ideological choices. These items were derived from the Activities Index. Webster, Sanford, and Freedman (1955) have obtained still other nonideological correlates of authoritarianism scales. An attempt is now being made by Stern, Sanford, Webster, Christie, and Lane to consolidate the various developments in this area and derive a single unified instrument.

indirect sources is the response a person gives when asked to indicate his preferences among verbal descriptions of various possible activities. Although the relationship between these choices and actual behavior is less than perfect, the procedure provides a useful approximation and has been the rationale for many widely used psychological instruments, including the Activities Index.

The Activities Index, which provides for the measurement of thirty needs, was developed initially for use in a series of psychological assessment studies conducted in the Examiner's Office at the University of Chicago in the early 1950's.[9] Its function in these studies was to provide a broad measure of personality for use in predicting student success in various types of academic programs (Stern, Stein, and Bloom, 1956). The current form, to be described more fully below, is based on items derived from analyses of subsequent adult and juvenile forms, and has been used effectively with persons from 13 to 63 years of age in various social and educational strata.

Environmental Press. The external counterpart of the personality *need* is called an environmental *press.* There are several meanings associated with this term. From a subjective point of view it has been used to describe the private world of the individual, the unique view each person has of the events around him (Murray, 1938). These idiosyncratic perceptions are best revealed through the use of ambiguous stimuli on which the individual must impose his own organization and meaning, as with the Rorschach (1942) ink blots or the provocative but undefined social situations depicted in the Thematic Apperception Test (Murray, 1943).

There is a level at which the person's private world merges with that of others like him: people who share a common ideology—whether terpretations of the events in which they participate, although these theological, political, or professional—also tend to share common inmay be quite different from those that might occur to a more detached observer (Stern et al., 1956). Both the private and the mutually shared press are of interest in their own right, but in the final analysis it is the inferences we make as observers which provide us with useful classifications of situational differences. It is the observer who can de-

[9] These studies were supported in part by the Human Resources Research Institute, United States Air Force, and the Social Science Research Committee of the University of Chicago. Benjamin S. Bloom, Morris I. Stein, Hugh Lane, Mary McCord Tyler, Sharon Goldberg, Paul Baer, James Sachs, Dorothy Whitman, and James Abegglen played an important role in the construction of the original Activities Index. It has since gone through several revisions, to which significant contributions were made by Charles Van Buskirk, Fred Carleton, Walter Stellwagen, John Scanlon, Louis DiAngelo, and many others.

scribe the situational climate, the permissible roles and relationships, and the sanctions, by his interpretations of the events to which the participant can only respond in terms of action and ideological evaluation.

The psychological observer of situations has the same need for indirect sources of information as does the observer of persons. The parallel source of indirect information about press comes from a participant's acknowledgment of characteristic events occurring in the environment. Thus, when we learn that there are regular drills for fire and civil defense at an institution, any of several interpretations might suggest themselves. But if we are also told that there are no contact sports, there are frequent and thorough medical examinations, and students are sent to the infirmary at the first sign of any kind of illness, we may feel justified in assuming that much pressure is being exerted here to get students to concern themselves about dangers to their physical well-being.[10]

Both needs and press are inferred from characteristic activities and events. Unlike needs, however, it is difficult to describe characteristic press in terms of activities that can be generalized to a wide variety of situations. The College Characteristics Index [11] is a measure of thirty kinds of press, analogous to the needs scales of the Activities Index, but restricted to the description of activities, policies, procedures, attitudes, and impressions that may characterize various types

[10] The participants themselves may consider the purpose of these activities to be of a different nature, or may fail to give them any formal recognition. This reflects the distinction between formal objectives, representing the stated purposes for which given institutional events are organized, and the informal objectives that are in fact served by institutionalized events regardless of the official interpretations. The distinction, which has been discussed more fully elsewhere (Stern et al., 1956), has a direct parallel in individual behavioral acts which may be interpreted differently by the observer than by the actor (who may also ignore or deny their significance).

[11] The initial development of the College Characteristics Index was greatly facilitated by grants from the College Entrance Examination Board, and the Carnegie Corporation. Support for the current research has been given by the United States Office of Education. But the most significant acknowledgment must be reserved for the thousands of students, and hundreds of teachers, who gave so generously of their time in marking responses to items in the various versions of the Activities Index and College Characteristics Index. It was developed in collaboration with C. Robert Pace, with the assistance of Anne McFee, Barnett Denton, Sally Donovan, Harriet Dorn, Dagny Henderson, and many others. Another version applicable to the high school setting has been prepared with the aid of John Dopyera, Vernon L. Woolston, James Lyons, and Eva K. Woolfolk, and used in an investigation of relationships between high school experiences and college expectations (Stern, 1961). Clifford Winters, Sidney Archer and Donald Meyer have similarly assisted in the adaptation of a form for use in extension programs and evening colleges.

Table 1. Miscellaneous Activities Index—College Characteristics Index Scale Characteristics

Scale	Forms AI-CCI, 1158 [1]							
	Mean		Standard Deviation		Reliability [2]		Item Index [3]	
	AI	CCI	AI	CCI	AI	CCI	AI	CCI
Abasement	4.07	2.99	1.88	1.93	.51	.67	.42	.51
Achievement	6.33	6.23	2.24	2.56	.73	.81	.60	.66
Adaptiveness	5.23	4.54	2.33	1.98	.64	.58	.58	.48
Affiliation-rejection	6.70	6.95	2.72	1.93	.81	.69	.66	.47
Aggression-blameavoidance	4.09	3.99	2.37	2.37	.69	.72	.59	.56
Change-sameness	5.34	6.41	2.33	2.02	.67	.44	.57	.47
Conjunctivity-disjunctivity	5.81	7.09	2.35	2.37	.70	.72	.58	.54
Counteraction-infavoidance	6.24	5.31	2.53	1.84	.66	.50	.57	.45
Deference	6.63	4.87	2.03	1.97	.56	.60	.50	.50
Dominance	6.04	4.50	2.51	2.12	.77	.57	.62	.49
Ego achievement	5.54	5.70	2.88	1.98	.80	.58	.70	.50
Emotionality-placidity	4.20	6.18	2.18	2.01	.64	.56	.53	.48
Energy-passivity	6.74	5.74	1.73	2.28	.40	.70	.41	.54
Exhibitionism-infavoidance	3.83	5.55	2.56	2.01	.75	.57	.65	.49
Fantasied achievement	3.34	4.72	2.06	1.74	.72	.40	.57	.43
Harmavoidance	4.93	5.66	2.40	2.11	.67	.70	.62	.51
Humanism	6.64	6.21	2.79	2.42	.83	.77	.65	.60
Impulsion-deliberation	5.61	5.62	2.06	1.86	.64	.50	.50	.45
Narcissism	4.61	4.98	2.37	2.31	.71	.74	.58	.58
Nurturance-rejection	6.50	5.78	2.38	2.19	.73	.70	.57	.54
Objectivity	8.90	7.40	1.43	2.14	.56	.70	.27	.51
Order	5.20	6.50	2.96	1.86	.82	.59	.74	.45
Play	5.00	5.26	2.40	2.33	.71	.75	.56	.58
Pragmatism	6.17	5.20	2.42	2.16	.74	.69	.59	.53
Reflectiveness	6.70	5.96	2.16	2.43	.68	.76	.54	.60
Scientism	5.34	6.14	3.18	2.48	.88	.77	.81	.58
Sentience	4.76	4.85	1.86	2.51	.53	.80	.43	.62
Sex-prudery	4.84	5.95	2.58	2.18	.78	.71	.64	.53
Succorance-autonomy	6.24	6.14	2.12	1.78	.67	.34	.52	.43
Understanding	6.98	6.55	2.34	2.21	.74	.75	.58	.54
MEAN	5.62	5.63	2.33	2.14	.69	.65	.57	.52

[1] Based on 1993 CCI, 1078 AI from undergraduates in 32 schools.
[2] Kuder-Richardson Formula 20.
[3] Average Ebel Item Discrimination Index per scale.

of undergraduate college settings. The current form has gone through three revisions, and has now been administered to well over 5000 students at nearly 100 colleges and universities.

Measurement Procedures. The Activities Index and the College Characteristics Index each consist of 300 items organized into 30 scales of 10 items each. The scales on each test parallel one another, one corresponding to *needs* manifestations of the variable in question, the other to *press* conditions associated with it. As an example, the *need* for *order* may be defined briefly as *a prevailing trend toward the organization of the immediate physical environment and a preoccupation with neatness, orderliness, arrangement, and meticulous attention to detail.* The magnitude of this need is inferred from the number of preferences a person indicates among such activities as "washing and polishing things like a car, silverware, or furniture," "keeping an accurate record of the money I spend," "arranging my clothes neatly before going to bed." The magnitude of the relevant *press* in a college environment is inferred from the number of respondents from the same institution who agree with such statements as: "in many classes students have an assigned seat," "professors usually take attendance in class," "student papers and reports must be neat," etc.

The thirty variables are listed alphabetically in Table 1, together with some fundamental data regarding the characteristics of the two instruments. It will be noted that the scale means on both instruments average only slightly above the arbitrary midpoint of 5.0, with standard deviations which indicate that a considerable number of respondents are to be found with extreme scores at either end of the ten-point range. The average scale reliability of .67 (Kuder-Richardson) is close to the practical maximum for scales of such short length, corresponding to a value of .92 if increased from ten to thirty items. It is also apparent from the high item discrimination indices that the scales are essentially homogeneous in content.

The scales on each instrument are systematically related to one another, forming a continuous circular order [12] which makes it pos-

---

[12] The structure is similar to that of a Guttman (1954) *quasi-circumplex.* It is particularly noticeable in the intercorrelation matrices which are characterized by a wide range of very high positive to very high negative values, distributed symmetrically around zero. The largest correlations are next to the main diagonal, becoming increasingly negative and then positive again in the corners of the matrix: adjacent clusters of scales are more related to one another than distant ones, and the end of the series reverts back to the beginning again. The data appear to provide an empirical demonstration of a law of order which Guttman postulated to exist between tests of the same degree of complexity but differing in the kind of

sible to plot scores in the form of profiles like those shown in Figure 1. The construction and interpretation of these profiles is available elsewhere (Stern, 1958); for our present purposes it will be sufficient to note that the circular portion of each profile involves a succession of interpersonal clusters of variables which range from depression and withdrawal at the lower left to increasing degrees of sociability toward the top. Variables at the upper right involve more outgoing and assertive behaviors, ending at the bottom right with scales which imply hostility, rebelliousness, and isolation. The rectangular grid at the bottom of the charts in Figure 1 incorporates variables involving intellectual activities which are statistically independent of those in the circle.

Figure 1 is based on Activities Index scores for three groups of college freshmen (23 in each) who were identified by means of their scores on the Inventory of Beliefs as antiauthoritarians, authoritarians, and rationals, as described in an earlier portion of this paper. The antiauthoritarians (nonstereopaths) would appear to be the most outgoing of the three groups, their Activities Index responses suggesting a higher degree of self-assertiveness, emotional spontaneity, and aggressiveness than either of the others. The authoritarians (stereopaths), conversely, appear to be more submissive and withdrawn, and distinctly reject intellectual activities as shown in the low scores on the scales in the grid at the bottom of the figure. The rationals seem to be a more socialized version of the antiauthoritarians in being socially outgoing but nonaggressive, and in having even broader, less specifically humanistic, intellectual interests.

VARIETIES OF CONSTRAINT IN HIGHER EDUCATION

A substantial body of information concerning these scales is now in existence, obtained from a number of studies performed over a period of years. The primary purpose of these studies has been to refine the tools for measuring needs and press characteristics: to study their strengths and weaknesses as measuring instruments, improve

ability they define. Such an order will have neither beginning nor end, but will be characterized by a continuous circular relationship between the variables involved. The precise relationships shown in Figure 1 were based on an early analysis of the Activities Index. Subsequent analyses, not yet complete, suggest that these basic relationships continue to hold for both instruments although not precisely as shown here (cf. Pace, 1960; Stern, 1961b).

them as much as possible, and learn more about how to work with them. Collectively, the studies have contributed to successive revisions of the scales and the techniques for utilizing them, and have also suggested the following points:

1. Descriptions of the behavior to be expected of individual students, psychiatric patients, and industrial personnel based solely on needs profiles appear to be recognized and confirmed by peers, psychiatrists, and administrators, as well as by subsequent

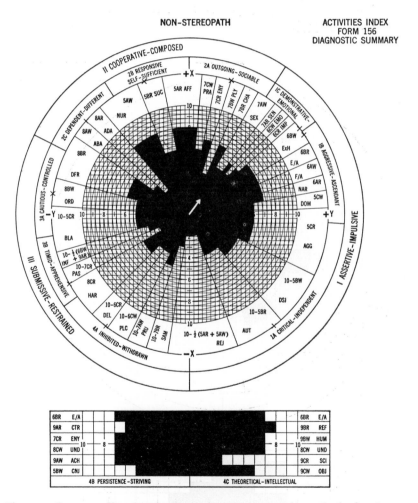

Figure 1. Group profiles of antiauthoritarian (nonstereopath), authoritarian (stereopath), and rational subjects ($n_1 = n_2 = n_3 = 23$). Stern, 1958.

behavior on the part of the subjects (Briggs, 1958; Chilman, 1959; Cole, 1958; Haring, Stern, and Cruickshank, 1958; Stern, 1958; Unpublished data).

2. Descriptions of college environments based solely on press profiles appear to be recognized and confirmed by academic participants and observers (Unpublished data).

3. People with similar needs profiles tend to be characterized by similar patterns of overt behavior (Briggs, 1958; Chilman, 1959; Gladstein, 1957; Haring, Stern, and Cruickshank, 1958; Scanlon, 1958; Stern, 1958, 1960a; Stern, Stein, and Bloom, 1956; Wassertheil, 1955).

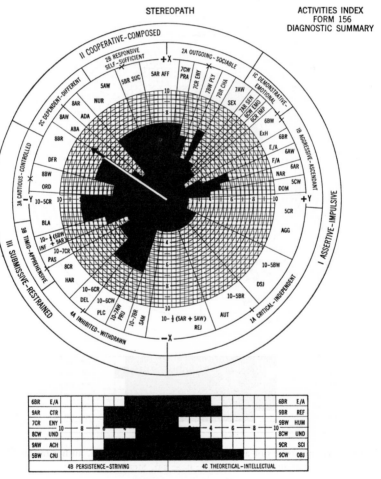

Figure 1 (continued).

4. Responses to needs scale items appear to be resistant to faking (Schultz, 1955), and

5. The social desirability of alternative responses to the needs scale items appears to be about the same for all items, none of them being considered important to accept or to reject by any substantial majority of subjects (Unpublished data).

6. Students or professionals in the same field have needs profiles that differ significantly from those of students or professionals in other fields (Siegelman, 1957; Stern, 1954, 1960b; Stern and Scanlon, 1958; Stern, Stein, and Bloom, 1956), and

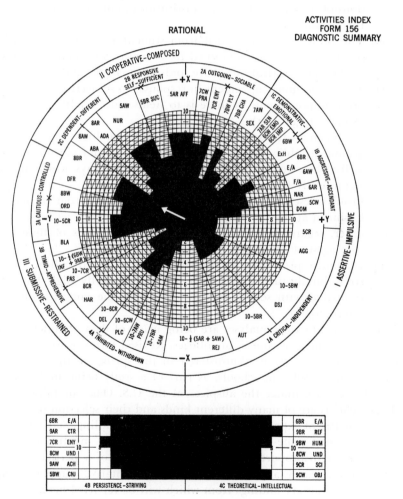

Figure 1 (continued).

7. Students with different backgrounds (public school vs. private) at the same institution have distinctive needs profiles, regardless of the field of study elected (Unpublished data).

8. Students from the same institution have press scale scores which are uncorrelated with their corresponding needs scale scores, the coefficients all falling between —.01 and +.06 (McFee, 1961). The student's description of the school is apparently not a function of the description he provides of himself.

9. The press profile obtained from small, highly-selected samples of National Merit Scholars and Finalists are highly consistent with those obtained from larger, more representative cross sections of students at the same institutions (Thistlethwaite, 1959a, 1959b), and

10. The press profiles obtained from student responses are highly consistent with those obtained from faculty and administration at the same institutions (Pace and Stern, 1958), and

11. There is as much agreement in responses to subjective or impressionistic press items as there is to items more readily verifiable (McFee, 1959, 1961).

12. Freshmen in the same college with different high school backgrounds (public school, private preparatory, and parochial) describe their respective high school press in ways which differ significantly from one another (Stern, 1961a).

13. Profiles describing the expected press obtained from incoming freshmen at the same college are highly consistent with one another, regardless of the high school backgrounds of these incoming students (Stern, 1961a).

14. Freshmen press profiles describing the expected college press stress intellectual activities at an unrealistically high level as compared with senior press profiles from the same institution (Stern, 1961a).

At the present time analyses are being made of data obtained from a national sample of American colleges. Revised forms of each instrument (Form 1158) were administered in the spring of 1959 to 5348 students at 62 different schools, as part of a study being undertaken with C. R. Pace under the auspices of the U.S. Office of Education. These schools are of many different kinds and their selection has been more a matter of expediency than of calculated sampling. Setting aside for the present some of the more unusual types of institutions, and reducing the disproportionate number of schools of a particular size or location, leaves a somewhat more representative sample of 32 schools, preliminary findings from which will be reported here.

The 32 schools are distributed among four general categories of institutions: 10 are *technical programs* (3 teacher-training, 3 business administration, 4 engineering); 7 are small *private liberal arts* colleges; 8 are small *denominational* colleges, of which 6 are Protestant and 2 Catholic; and 7 are large universities. The number of students participating at each of these schools ranges from 23 to 128, the average number being 62 per school, all of them upperclassmen.

This study ushers in a new phase of research with the Activities Index and the College Characteristics Index, the purpose being to show something of the variety among American colleges and their student bodies when measured in needs-press terms, and to lay the groundwork for exploring the significance of congruence or dissonance in the relationship between the characteristics of a student and the corresponding characteristics of his institutional environment.

There are several ways of treating Index data in order to show variation in need or press characteristics. The most detailed of these procedures would be based on a comparison of responses to the 600 items in the two instruments. An analysis of this sort adds further information of the following kind about these scales:

15. Of the 460 respondents from seven private liberal arts programs, 80% said it was *true* that "students are encouraged to criticize administrative policies and teaching practices," as compared with 92% of the 156 students from three business administration programs who said this was *false* at their colleges.[13]

The overabundance of detail characteristic of such an analysis can be reduced to some degree by restricting attention to the 60 scale means rather than the 600 items. Statistical comparisons of these means suggests:

16. Students enrolled in the same institution have needs scale scores significantly more alike than students at different institutions (Unpublished data).

17. Students describe their own institutions in terms of press scale scores that are significantly more alike than are the corresponding scale means among different institutions (Unpublished data).

18. Although the relationships between needs scores and press scores for the same students from a variety of institutions is not much higher than that obtained from samples located within the same institution, suggesting that perceptions of press are not projections of needs, there is a decided relationship between the mean

---

[13] A more detailed analysis of the differences in response between liberal arts and business administration students may be found in Stern (1960b).

needs scores and mean press scores at 43 institutions. The average level of specific needs among students at a given college tends to match the average level of the corresponding press at the same college (Stern, 1960b).

19. Students enrolled in different programs in a complex institution

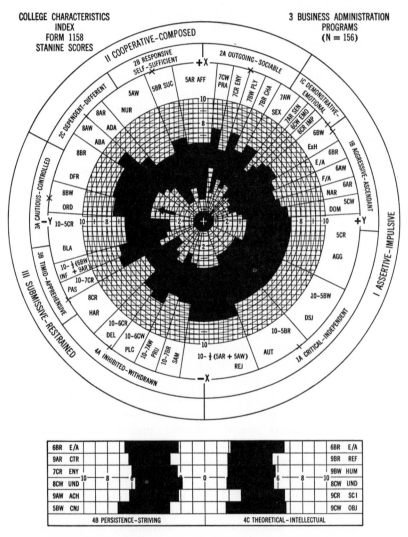

Figure 2. Stanine score press profiles obtained from 460 students at seven liberal arts colleges and 156 students in three business administration programs. Stern, 1960.

describe the press of the institution in significantly different ways (Stern, 1960b).

This type of comparison is even further facilitated by the organization of the scales into the profile format. Figure 2 provides a contrast, for example, between the average press profile of seven liberal arts colleges and that obtained from three business administration programs. Since the scores have been adjusted in these profiles so that the value of 5 on any scale corresponds to the average score for all

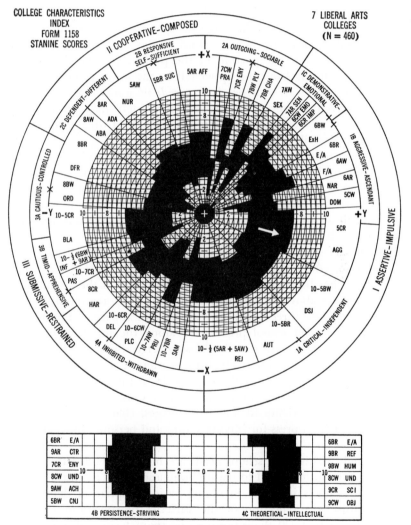

Figure 2 (continued).

32 schools, any deviation from a perfect circle at five units is easily read. It is reasonably clear from Figure 2 that the environments in these two types of college programs differ from other types of programs as well as from one another, particularly in those areas dealing with such manifestations of dependency as would be reflected in press for abasement, deference, and order (upper left quadrant of profile) and of intellectuality, notably in scores for understanding, reflectiveness, humanism, ego achievement, and objectivity in the grid at the bottom.

The grossest simplification of all can be made by reducing the profiles of Figures 1 or 2 to the three independent dimensions revealed by a second-order factor analysis. Two of these are accounted for in the axes of the circular portion of the profile: (1) one lies along a diagonal extending from the upper left to the lower right which can be identified in terms of *dependency needs vs. autonomy,* and (2) the other extends from the upper right to lower left and appears to involve *emotional expression vs. control.* The third dimension has already been described as an *intellectual* factor.

With the reduction of the data describing each academic environment and student body to these three dimensions, comparisons between schools in terms of either needs or press are greatly simplified, as is the description of correspondence between needs and press at the same institution. This procedure also makes available relatively powerful techniques of quantitative analysis.

The model shown in Figure 3 is based on data from all 62 schools available for study, reduced to points in three dimensions (the *intellectual* axis has been projected through the center of the circular profile, with scores above the population mean in the foreground). Several things about these three dimensions are at once apparent. The greatest differences between school press occur along the intellectual dimension. The 62 schools are distributed symmetrically across the middle of this axis. There is relatively little scatter on the remaining two dimensions: the majority of the schools lie in the upper left quarter of the circle, suggesting strong tendencies toward dependency and conformity. The private liberal arts colleges, characterized uniquely here by their high press for intellectuality and personal independence, are notable exceptions.

Although within each school needs are more diversified than press, the two distributions tend to parallel one another. The heavy weighting of all schools in scores involving various aspects of dependency relationships is a reflection of the varieties of constraint (to paraphrase Riesman, 1958) that appear to be characteristic of most of the

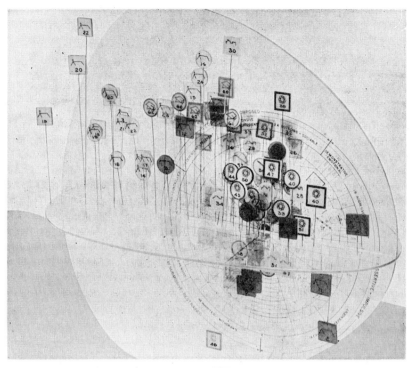

∧＼	PRIVATE LIBERAL ARTS COLLEGES
人	DENOMINATIONAL COLLEGES
⌐Γ⌐	UNIVERSITY AFFILIATED COLLEGES
▽	TEACHER - TRAINING PROGRAMS
＼	BUSINESS ADMINISTRATIVE PROGRAMS
✲	ENGINEERING PROGRAMS
○	AI MEAN RESULTANT
□	CCI MEAN RESULTANT

Figure 3. A three-dimensional model of mean A1 and CC1 responses from 5348 students at sixty-two institutions.

institutions and student bodies included in this sample. The denominational schools appear to be the most extreme in emphasis on conformity, although both the Protestant and Catholic institutions included in this analysis are scattered across the entire range of the intellectual dimension.

Inasmuch as this procedure represents the press of each school and the needs of its student body each as a cluster around a resultant point in a three-dimensional cube, we can measure distances between such points (and the scatter around them) and define and analyze formal relationships in the juxtaposition of needs and press with some degree of statistical precision. Table 2 summarizes data bearing on three such relationships. The first column lists the average distance between each student body and every other student body with respect to *needs,* providing a measure of student uniqueness. Two types of student bodies stand out in this connection: the business administration students who are least like the others due to their low intellectual strivings, and the university students who are more heterogeneous than any of the others.

Table 2. Mean Distance between AI and CCI Resultants for Thirty-Two Schools of Six General Types

Type	Number	Measure Uniqueness: (Increasing Distance)		Congruence of Students with Own Institution (Decreasing Distance: AI × CCI)
		Students (AI × AI)	Institution (CCI × CCI)	
Education	3	1.61	3.01	1.76
Business adm.	3	2.00	3.25	1.74
Engineering	4	1.47	2.89	1.47
Private lib. arts	7	1.64	3.68	2.55
Denominational	8	1.79	3.40	2.03
Univ.-affiliates	7	1.27	2.91	1.83
Combined types	32	1.61	3.26	1.89

The second column of Table 2 gives the average distance between each institutional press and every other institutional press: a measure of institutional uniqueness. The distances here are twice as great as those separating student bodies with respect to needs. The private liberal arts colleges emerge here as being the most distinctive, owing principally to their high intellectual press and strong nonconformist trends. These factors appear to be essentially congruent with the self-described characteristics of the liberal arts student bodies. The engineering and university-affiliated college programs are the least distinctive of all these various groups, being dispersed throughout all three dimensions.

The last column in the table lists the average distance between each student body and the press of their own institution (a measure of internal congruence). One type of school is distinguished from the others in presenting press that is most different from the needs of its students. This is the private liberal arts colleges which are not so much unlike their students as they are ahead of them, being characterized by a built-in strain toward high intellectual achievement and personal autonomy which is present in their students, but to a far lesser degree.

One more mode of analysis is available to us, based on the actual item responses to the AI and CCI. If we select the items that indicate a significantly high degree of consensus at the school, a somewhat clearer picture of the meaning of the spatial configuration begins to emerge. Two schools have been selected for this purpose, one of them an outstanding private liberal arts college for women (School 2 in the bottom right corner of Figure 3), and the other a well-known Catholic women's college (School 19 at the far left of Figure 3). Both have a high press toward intellectual achievement, but they diverge in opposite directions on the conformity dimension. By way of final contrast, we shall also look at School 30 (top center, Figure 3), a Southern State university known for its college spirit—in the terms of this three-dimensional space, an equal blend of conventionality and impulse expression!

The descriptions that follow are based exclusively on actual items from the AI and CCI, modified only by slight editing to make the passages flow more smoothly, and to reduce their length. The items employed are those on which 87% or more of the respondents have agreed.

School 2—a liberal arts college

Description. A well-known small private liberal arts college for women located in a small community in New England. A total of 36 AI's and 64 CCI's were obtained here from juniors and seniors. Although there are quite a few high consensus AI items, indicating a relatively homogenous student body, it is the extensive list of CCI items on which practically all of these students agreed which reveals the distinctive character of this school.

Student Needs

Intellectuality. These students all like work which requires intense intellectual effort. They are as interested in doing experiments in the natural sciences as they are in the works of painters and sculptors. They enjoy working for someone who will accept nothing less than the best that's in them, and are prepared to exert themselves to the utmost for something unusually important or enjoyable. They dislike superstitious practices.

Dependency Needs. These students like striving for precision and clarity in their speech and writing, but they reject other external restrictions on their conduct such as are implied in going to parties where all the activities are planned, shining their shoes or brushing their clothes every day, or working for someone who always tells them what to do and how to do it. Although they keep their hostilities toward others to themselves, they are intensely proud and don't like discussing their faults with others or having people laugh at them.

Impulse Expression. These girls like doing whatever they are in the mood to do, without much deliberation. They like to sketch and paint, and they sometimes like eating so much they can't take another bite. They have an especially strong negative reaction to phantasies of achievement, however, and uniformly reject a variety of common daydreams of success in love, finances, personal power, or self-control.

School Press

Intellectuality. The marked intellectual needs and aspirations of these girls are very strongly supported by the press at this school. They all agree that many of the professors are actively engaged in research, and that many students are actively pursuing careers in science. There are also especially strong facilities in the humanities, however, and the students express their interests in art, music, and the theater in many different ways. Long serious intellectual discussions are common here. There is also much concern with values, and the expression of strong personal convictions is not uncommon. No one needs to be afraid of expressing extreme or unpopular viewpoints at this school. It has an excellent reputation for academic freedom.

Most of the professors are dedicated scholars and thorough teachers. They put a lot of energy into their teaching. Most courses are a real intellectual challenge, requiring intensive study and preparation out of class. Tutorial and honors programs are available for qualified students. Professors and students both set high standards and work hard to achieve them, and the competition for grades is intense. If a student fails a course, however, he can usually substitute another one for it.

In class discussions, papers, and exams, the main emphasis is on breadth of understanding, perspective, and critical judgment, and a well-reasoned report can rate an A grade here even though its viewpoint is opposed to the professor's. The faculty members are liberal in interpreting regulations; they respect the students' motives, and treat violations with understanding and tolerance. Few students have special good luck charms or practices.

Dependency Needs. The intense rationality of this environment is further reflected in the thorough planning and organization that characterize most courses. However, students do not have assigned seats, and class attendance is neither taken nor required. An easy informality prevails between students and staff: faculty members, administrators, and counselors are always available and personally interested in the students, call them by their first names, and do not expect to be addressed as "professor" or "doctor." The students are treated with dignity and respect: they don't have to answer a lot of embarrassing questions when in need of help, tests are infrequent, grades are not posted publicly or reported to parents, written permission to leave campus overnight is not required, and freshmen don't have to take orders from upperclassmen. Students are encouraged to be independent and individualistic, and there is a high degree of respect for nonconformity and intellectual freedom: students are encouraged in many ways to criticize administrative policies and teaching practices. Religious worship does not stress service and obedience, and chapel services are not well attended. Although students will do things for which they know they may be criticized, they commonly share their problems and are rarely noisy or inattentive at concerts or lectures.

Impulse Expression. Courses stress the speculative or abstract, rather than the practical, and students are encouraged in their daydreams about varied or unusual careers. There is little interest or activity involving charities, community service, or concern with the underprivileged.

There are no social formalities or privileges here: there is no emphasis on tradition, proper social forms or manners, grooming, or various kinds of gracious living. On nice days many classes meet on the lawn. The students are serious and purposeful, spend much time at their studies, and local social activities are rare. Students frequently go away for football games or skiing weekends. There are no sororities.

Student rooms are likely to be decorated with art forms, and there is much interest here in all forms of esthetic experience on the part of students and staff. The students are impulsive and excitable, and student parties are colorful. Vivid and novel expressions in papers and reports are encouraged. Rough games and contact sports are an important part of intramural athletics. Channels for expressing student complaints are readily accessible, and when students do not like an administrative decision they really work to get it changed.

School 19—a denominational college

Description. School 19 is an outstanding Roman Catholic women's college located in a small Northwestern city. Thirty-two juniors and seniors contributed CCI's, 29 AI's. As in the case of the preceding school, there are a sufficiently large number of high consensus AI items to indicate some measure of homogeneity among the students matriculating here. Again, however, it is the extensive agreement in response to the CCI that reveals the distinctive character of this school.

Student Needs

Intellectuality. These girls are particularly interested in abstract intellectual games like chess, checkers, anagrams, scrabble, etc. They are also interested in understanding themselves and others better. They are curious about the arts, and about social problems, and would like to play an active part in community affairs. They set very high standards for themselves and work hard to achieve them, choosing difficult tasks to do and exerting themselves to the utmost in doing them. They particularly reject superstitious practices involving such things as black cats, good luck charms, and fortune tellers.

Dependency Needs. They not only like striving for precision and clarity in their speech and writing, but they also schedule time for work and play, organize their work carefully, and plan ahead. They make their beds and put things away everyday before leaving the house, and keep their personal possessions in perfect order. These girls like following directions, particularly from an older person who will give them guidance and advice from his own experience. They would like to direct other people's work, but they want others to offer their opinions when they have to make a decision. They don't like arguing with authority figures, and avoid expressing their hostilities openly. They like apologizing when they've done something wrong. Their general tendencies toward self-abnegation are also revealed in their finding satisfaction in suffering for a good cause or for someone they love, and in taking care of the young, the infirm, and the unhappy.

Impulse Expression. The girls here like being efficient and successful at practical things like typewriting, knitting, clothesmaking, etc. Although they like doing something crazy occasionally, like rearranging the furniture, they prefer routine and regularity. They dislike rough games and overeating, but they enjoy listening to the rain on the roof or the wind in the trees, and they like holding something very soft and warm against their skin. They don't care to go around with a crowd that spends most of its time playing around. A very strong trend toward impulse control is revealed in their rejection of emotional expression in any form, and in their avoidance of anything calling attention to themselves either overtly or in phantasy.

School Press

Intellectuality. The press at this college provides a fulfillment for the intellectual needs of these girls. The library is exceptionally well-equipped with journals, periodicals, and books in the natural and social sciences. A lecture by an outstanding scientist would be well attended, and many students spend most of their time in the laboratory. The broad social and historical setting of the material is discussed in many courses, and the students are very much interested in the analysis of art and music, and in literary criticism. Many students are concerned with developing their own personal and private system of values, and they also develop a strong sense of social and political responsibility, in part through involvement in the many student organizations active in campus and community affairs (although no faculty member plays any kind of significant role in politics).

"Alma Mater" is less important than "subject matter" here. Most of the professors are dedicated scholars and thorough teachers who put a lot of enthusiasm into their teaching and lectures. There is much student interest in formal discussions. Most courses are a real challenge and require intensive study and preparation: you can't bluff your way through. Students set high standards for themselves, and work hard for high grades on the finals. The exams are genuine measures of achievement, and the highest value is placed on understanding, perspective, critical judgment, careful reasoning, and clear logic, even if the conclusions are opposed to the professor's.

The faculty respect students' motives and are liberal in interpreting regulations. They welcome questions in class, are never moody or unpredictable, and the general atmosphere is a happy one. Few students have good luck charms.

Dependency Needs. The girls quickly learn what is done and not done on this campus. Their needs for order and organization are re-enforced in the classrooms where the course purposes are explained clearly, the presentation is well planned, assignments are clear and specific, there is a systematic schedule for studying and recreation, and attendance is taken. This orderliness extends to student papers which must be neat, and their rooms which must be tidy. The classrooms and buildings are also clean and tidy, and campus buildings are clearly marked by signs and directories. The students are conscientious about taking good care of school property.

Despite this emphasis on order, the relations between students and staff are warm: although counselors are practical and efficient, they and the faculty are always available and personally interested in the students, and call them by their first names. The faculty are especially patient, friendly, and helpful, although the student's personal privacy is recognized and there is no need to answer a lot of embarrassing questions when in need of help. Students are encouraged to be independent. Grades are not publicly posted and freshmen don't have to take orders from upperclassmen. However, tests are frequent and the professors regularly check up on the students to make sure that assignments are being carried out properly and on time.

Students are discouraged from criticizing administrative policies and teaching practices, but student complaints are given consideration. Student organizations are closely supervised, and their activities are planned carefully. Religious worship stresses service to God and obedience to His laws, and chapel services are well attended. Student publications never lampoon anyone, and the faculty are never joked about or criticized in student conversations or in any other way.

The school helps everyone to get acquainted, and everyone is friendly, considerate, and helpful. Students share their problems, and often do personal services for the faculty although there is no apple-polishing around here. Although students are careful to follow the rules and regulations, and are never noisy or inattentive, it is true that they occasionally plot some sort of escapade or rebellion.

Impulse Expression. The atmosphere is practical, emphasizing job security, personal adjustment, family happiness, and good citizenship. The girls are encouraged to be modest and practical in their goals. Education for leadership is strongly emphasized and students are expected to develop ideals and express them in action by means of service to the community.

There are no special groups or privileged students—everyone is treated alike. The girls take great pride in their personal appearance, and there are mirrors in the public rooms and halls. The students are serious and purposeful, spend much time at their studies, and local social activities are rare although there are sororities.

Student parties are colorful and lively, and most students enjoy such activities as dancing, skating, driving, and gymnastics. Rough games and contact sports are an important part of intramural athletics. It's easy to get a group together for games, singing, or going to the movies, and student gathering places are noisy. But sexy remarks, Bermuda shorts and pin-up pictures are uncommon, there are no paintings or statues of nudes on campus, and there is no informal dating during the week.

There are no rough initiations, no one drives sports cars, and drinking would not be tolerated. Students are careful to dress protectively against the weather, and are frequently reminded to take preventative measures against illness. Students generally show a good deal of caution and self-control in their behavior, and there are few expressions of strong feeling or disruptiveness.

Remarks. The most striking contrast between these two schools lies in the difference in control exercised over the students. The press at the denominational school stresses orderliness, planning, and deliberation, whereas the private school atmosphere encourages nonconformity and personal autonomy. Although intellectual achievement is of great significance at both schools, the underlying differences in the treatment of dependency needs at both places appear to pervade both the academic and extracurricular activities of the students.

The girls themselves are alike in being highly intellectual and serious minded. But here the similarity ends. Each group of students describe needs which are readily recognizable as personalized versions of the prevailing press. It is impossible to tell the extent to which this is a function of self-selection or of institutional impact, but an answer will be available when the needs of the freshmen at these schools are compared with those of the upperclassmen considered here. Whatever the findings, however, the girls at each of these schools should find it difficult to accept the conditions that prevail at the other. The private school girls would find the parochial school atmosphere stultifying and restrictive, and would no doubt shock faculty and administration with behavior which must seem disrespectful, brazen, and thoughtless under those conditions. Conversely, the parochial school girls are likely to find the private school atmosphere lacking in order, restraint, and consideration, as well as in being irreligious.

School 30—a state university.

Description. The press at both these schools may profitably be contrasted with that of School 30, a coeducational state university located in a small Southern city. This school has a full graduate program leading to the doctoral degree in several fields. Responses were obtained from 41 college upperclassmen from this institution.

At this school there are relatively few items concerned with *intellectuality* or *dependency needs*. The students agree that the libraries are good and the faculty is impartial. There is some emphasis on neatness, and the staff is addressed deferentially, but the students don't feel that the courses are well organized and they are rather critical of the faculty. The most important relationships appear to be between the students themselves, who borrow and share things, bring their problems to one another, help one another with their lessons, and prepare for examinations together.

This student togetherness is even more clearly delineated in the areas related to *impulse expression.*

Although the students all agree that the emphasis is on job security, personal adjustment, family happiness, and good citizenship, and that there are many really practical courses to this end in typing, report writing, human relations, etc., the major portion of the high consensus items deal with another aspect of the press. They all agree that there is much to do at this school besides going to classes and studying. Every year there are carnivals, parades, and other festive events on campus. There are many fraternities and sororities, and receptions, teas, and formal dances occur frequently. Students give much thought to dressing appropriately and interestingly for different occasions—classes, social events, sports, and other affairs. There is a lot of excitement and restlessness just before holidays, and students frequently go away for football games, skiing weekends, and similar activities. Most students really enjoy dancing.

There are frequent informal social gatherings and it's easy to get a group together for card games, singing, or going to the movies. Dormitory raids, water fights, and other student pranks are not uncommon. Students spend a lot of time together at the snack bars, taverns, and in one another's rooms. There is lots of informal dating during the week—at the library, snack bar, or movies, and there are several popular spots where a crowd of boys and girls can always be found. These student gathering places are typically active and noisy.

This atmosphere is clearly different from the two women's colleges. But which of these two groups of girls would find it more difficult to adapt themselves to this press? Perhaps it would be more precise, or more cynical, to ask which of the two would be likely to resist the temptations of this press the longest!

CONCLUSIONS: THE DESIGN OF EFFECTIVE ENVIRONMENTS FOR LEARNING

This analysis of relationships between student personality needs and the psychological press of college environments represents the first stage of a larger study of American colleges and their student bodies now in progress. The present data were based on a selected group of 32 schools, reflecting in equal degrees the characteristics of a small number of universities, denominational colleges, private liberal arts colleges, and technical schools, the latter including teacher preparatory, business administration, and engineering programs. Although the analysis reported here is incomplete, there is some tentative evidence to warrant the conclusion that the conceptual need-press schema (and the methodology now elaborated for it) is useful for the purpose of characterizing some of the important aspects of student ecology in American colleges.

The specific findings reported throughout this paper were primarily of relevance in establishing the general legitimacy of the procedures being developed here. A few speculative remarks may nevertheless be justified regarding the character of higher education as it emerges from these data.

What are the basic taxonomic classifications of American colleges suggested by needs-press analysis? The vast majority of institutions examined thus far are characterized by environments that emphasize some degree of conformity and constraint. This is not necessarily a matter of minding morals more assiduously than stimulating minds, for we have seen one instance in which a warm paternalism has been coupled with academic strength. Furthermore, there is some variety in the patterns of constraint, varying between tradition- and other-directed sources of social control. But the major source of diversity among these institutions lies in the level of their intellectual press: modesty in human relations appears to be more uniformly emphasized than modesty in intellectual aspirations.

There are at least two major exceptions to this pattern of short-term constraint, the first of which comprises the schools that have been known to exert considerable influence over their students in the long run. These are the small but elite private liberal arts colleges, which appear to be distinguished by their high level and breadth of the intellectual press and emphasis on personal freedom and informality. Variants within this class suggest two broad dimensions: (a) arts, science, or service, and (b) appreciation vs. creation. These characteristics seem likely to prove typical of most of the productive schools identified in the Knapp (1952, 1953) studies. A number of them have already been restudied from the present frame of reference by Thistlethwaite (1959a, 1959b).

The students tested thus far in any of these schools describe needs readily recognizable as personalized versions of the prevailing press. To what extent is this a function of student self-selection or of institutional impact? Are there specific sectors of institutional control which are more influential than others? What are the characteristics of institutions attracting students with particular sets of values or ideological characteristics? What are the characteristics of institutions which are most effective in changing student values? Is dissonance or stress in need-press relationship a motivating factor in student growth? Do students require some image of excellence just beyond their present level of aspiration? What happens as this gap widens? What happens when there is no gap, and when students feel superior to their academic environment?

We need to know more about the clarity of the image conveyed by particular schools, the factors associated with its development and change, and its relationship to the academic and extracurricular facilities offered by the school. Are the images of a college by those outside the campus (high school seniors and counselors, parents, the community) similar to those held by students and faculty? Are the expectations of freshmen characteristically confirmed or disappointed? Of what significance are different types of images: country club, ivory tower, sidewalk college, red cell, etc.? How long does it take to change the image of a college and what are the means by which this is accomplished?

The last question is perhaps most often raised at the third type of school revealed by the needs-press analysis. This is the group of schools which appear to be the remaining strongholds of the Fitzgerald tradition: fountains of knowledge where students gather to drink! These schools place a double emphasis on the practical virtues of their curricula: as a hard-headed virtue to their clientele (who are presumed to be anti-intellectual) and as a practical necessity to themselves (considering the qualities of the student body). And anyway, everyone does have fun! But you can't stoop to serve anyone, least of all youth, without exposing them to the temptation of kicking you where you're vulnerable. The students' own appraisals of these environments are unmistakable in meaning: they concede that they're just a bunch of Cheerful Charlies, playing together, helping one another with their lessons, and sharing one another's problems. But there is an undertone of necessity in this togetherness, because there are no other significant figures in their descriptions of these environments. The faculty are not only conspicuous by their absence from the press as the students perceive it, but there is also an undertone of criticism directed at the lack of course organization and the less than exciting teaching. These students do have an image of academic excellence, which they judge to be missing from their own institution. They are not alone in this. Their own faculty share the same secret ideal, and have arrived at the self-same judgment. Now if they could only get together . . .

But on what shall they get together? Is there any one ideal to which American education should be directed? Even if there were, we have already seen that different students require different treatments in order to arrive at the same end. One of the tasks ahead is to determine the consequences of practices now based on preference rather than purpose. An environment must be suited to the species; if it isn't, the organisms either die, or go elsewhere. But what *is* an optimal environment—one that satisfies, or one that stimulates? While it may be true that pearls come from aggravated oysters, you can only get milk from contented cows. Pearls and milk each have their uses, and people will continue to exercise their preferences for one or for the other, but it would be a pointless exercise of freedom to insist on milking oysters. The characteristics of the student and of the educational objectives must both be employed as guides in the design of maximally effective environments for learning.

REFERENCES

Adorno, T. W., Frenkel-Brunswik, E., Levinson, D. J., and Sanford, R. N. *The authoritarian personality*. New York: Harper Bros., 1950.

Briggs, D. A. The Stern Activities Index as a means of predicting social acceptability and improvement in reading skills. Unpublished doctoral dissertation, Syracuse University, 1958.

Chilman, C. S. A comparative study of measured personality needs and self-perceived problems of ninth and tenth grade students: half of the group possessing characteristics associated with early school leaving and the other half not possessing such characteristics. Unpublished doctoral dissertation, Syracuse University, 1959.

Cole, D. Some emotional factors in couples presenting a pattern of habitual abortion. Unpublished doctoral dissertation, Syracuse University, 1958.

Dressel, P. L., and Mayhew, L. B. *General education: explorations in evaluation.* Washington, D.C.: American Council on Education, 1954.

Faw, V. D. A psychotherapeutic method of teaching psychology. *Amer. Psychologist,* 1949, 4, 104–109.

Gladstein, G. A. The relationship between study behavior and personality for academically successful students. Unpublished doctoral dissertation, The University of Chicago, 1957.

Gross, L. Experimental study of validity of non-directive method of teaching. *J. Psychol.,* 1948, 26, 243–248.

Gross, N. The sociology of education. In R. K. Merton, L. Broom, and L. S. Cottrell, Jr. (Eds.), *Sociology today: problems and prospects.* New York: Basic Books, 1959, 128–152.

Guttman, L. A new approach to factor analysis: the radex. In P. F. Lazarsfeld (Ed.), *Mathematical thinking in the social sciences.* Glencoe, Ill.: Free Press, 1954, 258–348.

Haring, N. G., Stern, G. G., and Cruickshank, W. M. *Attitudes of educators toward exceptional children.* Syracuse: Syracuse University Press, 1958.

Heath, S. R., Jr. Personality and student development. In *New dimensions of learning in a free society.* Pittsburgh: University of Pittsburgh Press, 1958, 225–245.

Haythorn, W. The influence of individual members on the characteristics of small groups. *J. abnorm. soc. Psychol.,* 1953, 48, 276–284.

Haythorn, W., et al. The behavior of authoritarian and equalitarian personalities in groups. *Hum. Relat.,* 1956, 9, 57–74.

Jacob, P. E. *Changing values in college.* New York: Harper Bros., 1957.

Knapp, R. H., and Goodrich, H. B. *Origins of American scientists.* Chicago: University of Chicago Press, 1952.

Knapp, R. H., and Greenbaum, J. J. *The younger American scholar: his collegiate origins.* Chicago: University of Chicago Press, 1953.

Lewin, K., Lippitt, R., and White, R. Patterns of aggressive behavior in experimentally created "social climates." *J. soc. Psychol.*, 1939, **25**, 271–299.

McFee, A. The relation of selected factors to students' perception of a college environment. Unpublished Master's thesis, Syracuse Univ., 1959.

McFee, A. The relation of students' needs to their perception of a college environment. *J. Educ. Psychol.*, 1961, **52**, 25–29.

McKeachie, W. J. Individual conformity to attitudes of classroom groups. *J. abnorm. soc. Psychol.*, 1954, **49**, 282–289.

McKeachie, W. J. Students, groups, and teaching methods. *Amer. Psychologist*, 1958, **13**, 580–584.

Murray, H. A. *Explorations in personality.* New York: Oxford University Press, 1938.

Murray, H. A. *Thematic apperception test.* Cambridge, Mass.: Harvard University Press, 1943.

Office of Scientific Personnel. *The baccalaureate origins of science doctorates awarded in the United States, 1936–1950.* National Academy of Sciences—National Research Council, Publ. No. 382. Washington, D. C., 1955.

Office of Scientific Personnel. *The baccalaureate origins of doctorates in the Arts, Humanities, and Social Sciences awarded in the United States, 1936–1950.* National Academy of Sciences—National Research Council, Publ. No. 460. Washington, D.C., 1956.

Office of Scientific Personnel. *Doctorate production in United States universities.* National Academy of Sciences—National Research Council, Publ. No. 585. Washington, D.C., 1958.

Pace, C. R. Five college environments. *CEEB Review*, 1960, **41**, 24–28.

Pace, C. R., and Stern, G. G. An approach to the measurement of psychological characteristics of college environments. *J. Educ. Psychol.*, 1958, **49**, 269–277.

Patton, J. A. A study of the effects of student acceptance of responsibility and motivation on course behavior. Unpublished doctoral dissertation, University of Michigan, 1955.

Riesman, D. *Constraint and variety in American education.* New York: Doubleday, 1958.

Rogers, C. R. *Counseling and psychotherapy.* Boston: Houghton Mifflin, 1942.

Rorschach, H. *Psychodiagnostics.* New York: Grune & Stratton, 1942.

Scanlon, J. The Activities Index: an inquiry into validity. Unpublished doctoral dissertation, Syracuse University, 1958.

Schultz, D. Simulation by college students of prescribed patterns in the Activities Index. Unpublished Master's thesis, Syracuse University, 1955.

Schutz, W. C. What makes groups productive. *Hum. Relat.*, 1955, **8**, 429–465.

Shils, E. A. Authoritarianism: "Right" and "Left." In R. Christie and M. Jahoda (Eds.), *Studies in the Scope and Method of The Authoritarian Personality.* Glencoe, Ill.: Free Press, 1954, 24–49.

Siegelman, M. Distinctive personality patterns in three vocational groups as measured by the Stern Activities Index. Unpublished doctoral dissertation, University of Texas, 1957.

Stern, G. G. Assessing theological student personality structure. *J. Pastoral Care*, 1954, **18**, 76–83.

Stern, G. G. *Preliminary manual: Activities Index—College Characteristics Index.* Syracuse: Syracuse University Psychological Research Center, 1958.

Stern, G. G. Congruence and dissonance in the ecology of college students. *Student Medicine,* 1960a, **8,** 304—339.

Stern, G. G. Student values and their relationship to the college environment. In H. T. Sprague (Ed.), *Research on college students.* Boulder, Colo.: Western Interstate Commission for Higher Education, 1960b.

Stern, G. G. Continuity and contrast in the transition from high school to college. In N. F. Brown (Ed.), *Orientation to college learning—a reappraisal.* Washington, D.C.: American Council on Education, 1961a.

Stern, G. G. The measurement of psychological characteristics of students and learning environments. In S. J. Messick and J. Ross (Eds.), *Personality Measurement.* New York: Wiley, 1961b, in press.

Stern, G. G., and Scanlon, J. S. Pediatric lions and gynecological lambs. *J. Med. Educ.,* 1958, **33,** Part 2, 12–18.

Stern, G. G., Stein, M. I., and Bloom, B. S. *Methods in personality assessment.* Glencoe, Ill.: Free Press, 1956.

Thistlethwaite, D. L. College environments and the development of talent. *Science,* 1959a, **130,** 71–76.

Thistlethwaite, D. L. College press and student achievement. *J. Educ. Psychol.,* 1959b, **50,** 183–191.

Wassertheil, S. M. A study of the need patterns of negative and positive individuals. Unpublished Master's thesis, Syracuse University, 1955.

Webster, H., Sanford, R. N., and Freedman, M. A new instrument for studying authoritarianism in personality. *J. Psychol.,* 1955, **40,** 73–84.

Wispé, L. G. Evaluating section teaching methods in the introductory course. *J. educ. Res.,* 1951, **45,** 161–186.

22 *Christopher S. Jencks and David Riesman*

Patterns of Residential Education: A Case Study of Harvard

In the fall of 1930 Harvard opened the first two of seven "enriched" dormitories, and thereby inaugurated the experimental "Harvard House System." Twenty-nine years later, the University opened an eighth residential house, while soliciting money for two more. This decision to invest a substantial amount of new capital in dormitories gave public notice that the house experiment is now a "success," and that the administration believes money spent on these buildings will do as much to improve undergraduate education as money spent on faculty salaries, library books, and other essentials. Of course, not every decision to spend money on buildings rather than books reflects a serious evaluation of educational alternatives. In the case of the Harvard House system, however, it is widely believed that

Note. We are indebted to the Carnegie Corporation for a grant making possible these studies of higher education. We are also indebted to a number of the House Masters and tutors and other officials of Harvard College for their cooperation, and among them particularly to Leon Bramson, Charles Bidwell, John Bullitt, McGeorge Bundy, John Conway, John Finley, Kenneth Keniston, Delmar Leighton, Michael Maccoby, John Monro, David Owen, Eliot Perkins, William G. Perry, Jr., Lloyd and Susan Rudolph, Charles Taylor, and Dean Whitla; to a term paper by Edward Croman and a study of house stereotypes by Roger Brown of M.I.T.; also to Herbert Barry, David Braybrooke, James Davie, George Wilson Pierson, Ralph M. Rust of Yale; also to Harold Dodds, Richard Storr, and Adam Yarmolinsky. Needless to say none of these people is responsible for our analysis, and some disagree with essential points therein.

students and faculty members, associating in these residential units, can do much to educate each other in ways that are not encouraged by the formal curriculum; and we ourselves believe that the emphasis on the houses is not misplaced, given an academic setting where salaries and libraries are opulently adequate by general American (or foreign) norms.

It may represent a characteristic Harvard parochialism for us to think that the house experiment can have general relevance, not only in other large residential universities but also in small liberal arts colleges that do not seem to stand in need of similar subdivisions, and in commuter colleges which perform their educational task without residential trimmings. Still, on the one hand, Harvard's abundance offers a model; and, on the other hand, its experiment may throw light on the educational and miseducational potentialities of "student culture," even in the "emergent" institution.

Despite our hope for general implications implicit in Harvard's experience, we must begin by describing the unusual physical features of the Harvard arrangement. Unlike the fraternity houses which are often impressive (and architecturally appalling) monuments of alumni pride, the typical college dormitory suffers from the pinched quality characteristic of much of American education—even though it may appear luxurious to students from comparatively underprivileged homes. At an average cost of roughly $4000 per student, the typical student residence joins two students, two beds, two bureaus, two desks, two straight chairs, and 200 square feet of floor in an effort to produce enlightenment. This residential arrangement is economical, but it does not promote residential education, for it drives all but agoraphobic students out of their rooms—to fraternities, beer parlors, coffee shops, libraries, or occasionally to well-designed and inviting student unions or activity centers. At Harvard a more lavish standard has prevailed. The architects have estimated that it would cost $30,000 per student to duplicate the facilities which the houses originally provided for each resident. Every resident was given a private bedroom-study and, unless he had one of the many single rooms, shared a bathroom and living room (usually with a fireplace) with up to three roommates. From this sumptuous home each student had the opportunity to sally forth to such "community centers" as the pool room, the music room, the dark room, the ten to fifteen thousand volume house library, the "junior common room" (to be distinguished from the "senior common room" which in most houses was reserved for the faculty), and most important of all, the house dining halls, which served food (once with waiters, now cafeteria-style) to house members and guests for about five hours out of every day. In addition to these physical resources, every student also profited as much as he might from the presence of the master (who ran the house), the senior tutor (who has acted since 1952 as the local dean of students), and about a dozen resident tutors (usually graduate students, who coached students in their field of concentration). Each house also had a number of nonresident tutors (usually older married men, who sometimes conducted tutorial for house members and often joined them for conversation and free meals in the dining halls), and a dozen or more senior associates (leading faculty members from different fields who, with varying faithfulness, attend functions in their house).

All of this apparatus requires a prodigious initial investment. Furthermore, to maintain these facilities student rental fees must today be kept at about double the national norm, averaging $40 to $60 per student for each month of occupancy. Each student also today pays about $70 a month for meals. An institution that wanted to duplicate the physical plant of the house, and did not have a philanthropist to subsidize the operation, would have to charge more than twice the Harvard fees a year for room, board, and amortization. Yet the outsider would be foolish to write off the whole experiment as "impractical." Luxury was not the essential element. After 1945 all upperclassmen were required to live in a house and pay for their meals there, and students were forced to double up in many study-bedrooms. Rising costs also forced Harvard's architects to design the eighth house on more economical lines than its predecessors. Yet all our evidence suggests that despite these material cutbacks the houses are now making a more valuable contribution to undergraduate life than at any time in the past.

In discussing this contribution, we shall first consider the vacuum which the houses filled for Harvard in the Thirties. Second, we shall consider the impact of the houses on contemporary undergraduate life. Here we shall view the system not as an experiment but as part of the academic landscape, asking what effect this or any other residential pattern can have on education. Third, we shall look at the houses not as a unified "system" but as separate enclaves within the college, discussing the real and apparent differences among them. Here we shall have one eye on the analogous myths and disparities among the nation's several colleges, while with the other eye we probe the possibility and desirability of diversity and conflict within a college culture. Finally, we shall consider the relevance of the Harvard experiment to other colleges and universities, residential and otherwise. Here we shall focus primarily on our hope that more colleges might become intellectual communities, rather than aggregations of professional scholars and preprofessional nonscholars.

HARVARD PRIOR TO THE HOUSE PLAN

During President Eliot's 1869–1909 experiment in laissez faire, the 19th-century hostility between faculty and student was abated by the increasing indifference of both to education: the university focused its effort to increase productivity on the faculty, which was supposed to produce knowledge, while the faculty tended to regard the students as outsiders, or customers, who were allowed but never forced to buy their wares from Harvard, Inc. Much as the corner grocer has since been largely replaced by the supermarket, the prescribed curriculum was replaced by a catalogue full of different courses, chosen largely at random under the elective system. The college took even less interest in students' social behavior. Eliot's policies encouraged the creation of Harvard University, as distinct from the older Harvard College (see Morison, 1937).

Since the decline of Puritanism there had been little pretense that the college curriculum (e.g., Zumpft's *Latin Grammar*) was closely connected with the great ideas of the day, nor that it spoke to the perennial social and personal problems which the students would face. By the middle of the 19th century, when Henry Adams was yawning his way through Harvard, the very irrelevance of the curriculum was its *raison d'être*, for it certified matriculants as "gentlemen" (i.e., men with leisure to spend on trivia), and as "scholars" (i.e., men willing to suffer for their own advancement). After the Civil War, ambitious teachers turned to the European universities for an example, because there they saw men who were wrapped up in their work and who even managed to wrap some of their students up with them. Serious scholars, who had formerly preferred the greater leisure of the pulpit or a private income, began to find Harvard a comfortable "living." Conversely, the University acquired a commitment to academic research. The institution was no longer justified solely on the ground that it made students into better adults, but instead on the ground that it contributed to human knowledge. And as readers of *The Education* will remember, Henry Adams himself came to believe that only by making the students into academic apprentices could the faculty hope to prepare them for the complexities of adult life.

This conviction that every student could and should become something of a scholar led the faculty to accuse unresponsive students of "stupidity," or more recently "apathy," just as an earlier generation of pedagogues, who believed in the moral rather than the intellectual value of study, had accused the indifferent youth of "laziness" or "improvidence" when he ignored his tedious chores. The academicians' charge was made more plausible by the genuine stupidity and apathy of many students at 19th-century Harvard and a few even today. Yet the explanation appeared less relevant when one realized how few scholars in separate disciplines found it worthwhile to attend their colleagues' classes. These men were presumably not lacking in curiosity, or brains, or dedication, but still they found that developments in physics or economics were of no more personal interest or professional relevance than someone else's hobby of collecting match boxes or trading cards.

Sometimes this scholarly indifference to colleagues' lectures was justified by the belief that classes for undergraduates were too elementary for serious adult attention. But this argument was often belied both by the highly sophisticated and scholarly presentations of many lecturers, and by the fact that the majority of professors were in effect "undergraduates" in their colleagues' field. Even the argument that keeping up with research and one's own subdiscipline takes so much time that none is left for other fields rests to some degree on the assumption that disciplines develop autonomously from within, with minimum nourishment from a more general culture. Although the General Education program instituted at Harvard after the Second World War has aimed at forms of liaison among the disciplines and has attracted some of the ablest men on the faculty, the program has had to operate largely *ad hoc* and not as a center of intellectual effort. The more intellectually ambitious students sometimes feel that they are implicitly asked to bring order out of the chaos of autonomous professional disciplines.

In discussing this situation we have found it helpful to make a distinction between the *academic* and the *intellectual*. In our usage, an *academic* question is one raised by some lacuna or ambiguity in the data or interpretations of a worldwide discipline. In essence, it poses a professional problem, whose solution will advance "the field." In contrast, *intellectual* questions are of interest not just to people with an occupational interest in a particular set of ideas, but to intelligent men everywhere (including students), who find that life raises certain perennial problems to which they cannot help seeking solutions. Whereas *academic* inquiry is devoted to the liquidation of ignorance and the increase of knowledge, *intellectual* inquiry is dedicated to exposing foolishness and encouraging wisdom, or as it is now more usually called, intellectual maturity. In the University as President Eliot created it, laissez faire policies largely eliminated violent conflict between unstudious students and minatory instructors, allowing the faculty to regard the students as potential disciples rather than as eternal enemies. In the best cases, the scholars molded their researches around their intellectual questions, so that their work became relevant not only to the advance of their discipline but also to the concerns that sophisticated students and laymen possessed. Conversely, the enlivening of the disciplines through research made it possible for intellectual students to find stimulus and response therein, even when they had no vocational interests in the field. [Of course in some instances the students eventually found that their intellectual interests "belonged" in some university department and thus found themselves recruited to a scholarly career, although in general Harvard College has sent many more people into *Who's Who* than into scholarship (Knapp and Goodrich, 1950; Knapp and Greenbaum, 1952).] As a result of these possibilities, the distinction between the academic and the intellectual is a distinction not between what questions a man asks, nor between methods of getting answers, but between the motives which make the questions seem important. Such motives are, of course, always mixed, for men find their personal interests absorbed and redirected by their profession, just as the professions are continually reshaped by the kinds of personalities they recruit.

Despite occasions for creative symbiosis between intellectual curiosity and academic discipline, we think it fair to say that the majority of Harvard undergraduates down through the 1920s were not seriously committed to their academic work, and in many instances regarded the academic organization as a hostile and unmanageable system. Just as industrial workers were fleeing from their factories to urban and suburban ghettos, these students fled to a world of leisure which in this period organized itself around the social clubs, athletics, and other extracurricular attractions. There had been a time when the clubs were merely sociable, and elected anyone whom the members found congenial. But when, after 1865, the clubs became front organizations for society, screening and training young men for debutante parties and adults' clubs, such easy-going standards had to go. It was all very well to elect a jovial fellow of doubtful breeding as a four-year comrade-in-fun. But it was extraordinarily difficult to elect this same student when the decision meant a life-time commitment to seeing the man in Boston or New York clubs and—if the debutante parties served their purpose—perhaps seeing him as an in-law. Genealogy was further accentuated when alumni pressed "their" clubs to admit their sons, who now needed membership in a Harvard club to assure access to society in Boston and to some extent in New York. The clubs served these people as bastions of a bygone era, attempting to preserve cultural and ethnic homogeneity against "businesslike" academic or industrial organizations in which the only common denominator was in increasing measure likely to be occupational skill.

The clubs avoided complete desuetude both by permitting, even encouraging, students to do some academic work and by professionalizing social life in somewhat the same way that the curriculum professionalized intellectual life. Students were taught in the classroom that it was better to be ignorant than wrong, and better to write off gaps in their knowledge with "I don't know anything about that" than to risk looking ridiculous in the process of repairing ignorance (cf. Perry, 1959). Outside the classroom, students were taught to take the same attitude toward the social amenities, either classifying themselves as apprentices to society or else abandoning social ambition and seeking some other source of self-respect, as "grinds," "athletes," or "organizers." But for those who did become social apprentices the club system was in some ways as demanding and disciplined as the curriculum.

President Lowell (1909–1933) was determined to change this pattern. Even before World War I he led a growing minority in the college which sought to recreate some of the old intimacies of an earlier era by establishing a tutorial system at Harvard. When scholars became tutors, they often found that they had little in common with their students, but at times the gap was successfully bridged. Many professors shared their students' nonprofessional intellectual interests, and such mutual concerns were easier to explore in tutorial than in the officially academic classroom setting. Corresponding concessions came from students who acquired an interest in some academic discipline through close contact with a scholar. The college tutorial was usually interpreted as an extension of the course system rather than a substitute for it, and tutors were expected to help students meet their academic payrolls by writing a thesis and "covering" material for general exams rather than shaping tutorial to the students' interests as well as the faculty's prerequisites. Hence, like other reforms, tutorial in part succumbed to the very course structure it was intended to oppose. In the best cases it did succeed in establishing two-way communication between professors and students, especially when the latter presented themselves dramatically or imaginatively, or in those fortunate instances when a professor sought to take students along with him in his scholarly enterprises. With the growth of research and other extrainstitutional commitments, the faculty tended to turn tutorial over to younger men who were themselves coping with problems of "productivity" in their new fields and who found the world of student "inferiors" more of a temptation or distraction than a stimulus. The students on their part seldom sought to interest others or even themselves in their academic work and gave their tutors ample excuse for perfunctory performance. The students continued to escape, not only into their clubs, but into an increasingly professional round of extracurricular activities where exigent standards of performance—whether in writing, dramatics, or athletics—attracted rather than repelled recruits.

GENESIS OF THE HOUSES

Although many faculty members were not greatly dissatisfied with these compromises and passive treaties between their own interests and those of the students, a few notable academic reformers were. Early in the century, Woodrow Wilson proposed a scheme for the Princeton Quadrangles which would have drawn faculty and students together while short-circuiting the clubs. His scheme was defeated by opposition from students, alumni, and many faculty—and by its expense (McGeorge Bundy, 1959). In 1907, Professor A. Lawrence Lowell advocated an honors college at Harvard which would serve a similar purpose. He was likewise put off—first by the fact that President Eliot was opposed to such "interference" in undergraduate and faculty life, and later by the fact that money was not available. In 1926, the Harvard Student Council wrote a report advocating a similar system of residential "quadrangles" or "colleges." The report caught the eye of a Yale alumnus and Standard Oil magnate, Edward Harkness, who offered to bring the plan to fruition at Yale. Yale hesitated, and Harkness offered to do the job at Harvard. Lowell accepted instantly, Yale followed, and Harkness eventually provided money to house every Harvard and Yale upperclassman. (Actually, half the Harvard Houses were assembled from existing dormitories which Lowell had built with the hope of a house plan in mind.)

The houses, as Harvard called its dormitories, cannot be described as having had any single "purpose." They were supported (and opposed) by diverse segments of the Harvard community, many of whose arguments and aspirations were not only different but contradictory. Men who favored the houses could probably not have agreed on any statement of their aims or probable impact, even though they shared dissatisfaction with the status quo, and a general sense that "something should be done." If we take Lowell's original scheme for an honors college as an indicator of his motives a quarter-century later, we can say that he was driven by the same Puritanical quest for excellence that had animated both his Boston Brahmin ancestors and the Harvard tradition. But he believed excellence ought to be academic and intellectual, and his problem was how to offset the idolatrous claims of social and athletic pretenders. By building the houses he hoped to provide students with an academic alternative to the social clubs, and by making the houses both impressive and comfortable and, with some 300 students each, larger than a club, he hoped to seduce the socialites into meeting and then enjoying tutors and ideas. The houses were thus an attack on the parochialism of the young, vis-à-vis their elders, and of the aristocracy vis-à-vis the middle class.

Lowell's opponents feared that the houses would undermine the camaraderie of the clubs. But they could not, of course, appeal to the rhetoric of social excellence in the face of the College's officially academic purposes. Instead, they usually turned to another recent facet of the Harvard tradition, and argued that the houses would impinge on the freedom students had acquired under Eliot. They urged that students could not and should not be forced to associate with other students and teachers whom they preferred to avoid. Some among the faculty took a similar view, arguing that if thirteen million dollars were to be spent on education, the money should be spent on proven necessities like books, laboratories, or—if faculty-student contacts were the issue—improving the dismal classrooms. These objections were, however, of little avail, for Harkness did not offer the faculty a choice between a library or houses; and Lowell did not threaten the students with required participation in house life. Even the staunchest clubmen could say little about freedom when student residence was left voluntary.[1]

Like the suburbs and the clubs, the houses appealed to nostalgia. The very name was archaic. Harvard's first building had been called a house, although the nomenclature had soon been changed to "College." The architecture of the buildings was likewise reactionary, attempting to recreate Georgian splendors and rural greenswards rather than adopting the more "contemporary" and less expensive style. Each new house was topped by a tower, which provided symbolic unity presumably compensating for the personal diversity of the residents. Some of the proposed schemes for selecting these residents smacked

[1] Residence was, however, made compulsory in 1945, for all who did not live with parents or wife.

of nostalgia as well, seeking to create homogenized units much like the clubs. Nobody audibly proposed to select members according to income, but there were advocates of selection by fields of academic interest (ensuring that poets would meet no physicists, and so forth), of selection by geographic origins (ensuring that Bostonians would not be corrupted by contact with too many Midwesterners), or selection by academic proficiency (ensuring that Phi Beta Kappa students would not be forced to lunch with anyone indifferent to their abilities). To Harvard's credit, all these models were rejected, and instead the equally traditional English model of the college-within-a-college was adopted. There would be seven houses, each of which represented Harvard in microcosm, affording the students an opportunity that had not existed since the 18th century for intimacy with dissimilar students. Actually, of course, 18th-century Harvard was not so diverse as the proposed houses, although it was less homogeneous than any other American college of that time. A few students came from outside New England, many from outside the aristocracy, and most from outside the Congregational ministry.

The nostalgic element in the houses was nowhere clearer than in the appeal to the model of Oxford and Cambridge colleges. These institutions had survived almost intact from an earlier preacademic era, and had made little provision for the new disciplines and departments. Of course many dons were in fact scholars on the German model, and many neglected their responsibilities as teachers. But such "failures" were not emphasized in the Harvard image of the English college system. Like the image of Harvard's past, the image of "Oxbridge" was more a means to stimulate thinking about the future than an educational experiment to be realistically appraised. As with tutorial, the English example provided a contemporary version of Harvard's own past. Indeed, the intentions of the house system and of tutorial were in many ways similar, for the houses were supposed to do on the grand scale what tutorial had begun: restore communication between teachers and students.

Yet the houses were no more an attempt to revert to an earlier stage of academic evolution than the suburbs and the fraternities with their "manor-style" architecture were a "back to the soil" movement. Both the houses and tutorial attempted to further the academic revolution by extending it to the undergraduates, and in both cases the imagery out of the past and out of English tradition was only incidental. This commitment to academic excellence is nowhere clearer than in the pattern of recruiting teachers and students to the new communities.

The seven masters were, and still are, usually selected from the senior members of the History and English Departments, perhaps because such men were more willing to take a job which cut heavily into their time for research, and perhaps because more members of these departments had been Harvard undergraduates, and were therefore identified with the College, as against the University. But in general the masters, although not neglectful either of their symbolic or their actual roles in creating a residential community, continued to feel their prime loyalty to their departments, and managed somehow to find time for research as well as for attending to the affairs of the house.

In part they were able to do this because they have often been men of exceptional energy. Beyond that, although in some respects they resemble small college presidents, they are of course free of many of the financial, housekeeping, and public-relations obligations of a college president. And since 1952, they have been assisted by a senior tutor who has acted as the house's dean of students. Although some of these men have been dedicated researchers who have been torn between their scholarly concerns and their interest in students, there is at least a legend at Harvard that the senior tutorship is apt to be bestowed on someone whom the departments do not regard as quite promotable to tenure; indeed, many of the faculty consider the work of the senior tutor as a thankless task of spending half one's time with dilettantes and delinquents, or writing endless letters of recommendation to medical schools or Fulbright Committees. Even so, and granting that there is some truth behind the legend, the senior tutors must be men who are accessible to the conventional academic norms, for they would not be eligible had they not already climbed the first rung or two on the departmental ladder.

So, too, the choice of tutors has also been limited by departmental preselection. The houses have had to recruit their tutorial staff from the graduate students and faculty of the departments, and loss of departmental position has meant immediate elimination from the house community. Although distinguished work as a tutor might delay severance of a graduate student by earning a postdoctoral appointment as an instructor, unpublishable labor has rarely kept a man on more than a few years.

Among students, academic demands have been even more conspicuous, although somewhat less stringent. Every student was required to take four lecture-reading courses per year, in which he was asked to absorb as much knowledge as possible about academic questions of interest to his professors. Failure to pass these courses meant elimination from the College (and the house) and the houses could influence this process only in marginal cases. Furthermore, tutorial itself remained under departmental control, often with a departmentally prescribed curriculum, and always with departmental assignments of students to tutors. This meant that a student could only change the field of his tutorial by changing his departmental concentration, and departmental requirements made such switches difficult for many juniors and seniors.[2] Perhaps most important of all, house members were recruited as sophomores after a year's residence in the small dormitories and immense dining hall of Harvard Yard. This meant a year of undiluted initiation into academic values (partially modified in the last decade by the General Education program) transmitted through impersonally presented and competitively graded lecture-reading courses in which the student was spectator rather than participant. Lacking the support and visible alternative of a house (or a club, or a varsity team) most freshmen adapted to the demands of their professors insofar as they were able. This did not mean that freshmen were better students than seniors. It did mean that despite their distance from graduate schools, freshmen usually cared more about their grades than they would as upperclassmen, because for freshmen these grades provided almost the only visible measure of their success and personal worth, and were in addition the basis for admission into certain highly esteemed fields of concentration. It is difficult enough for a college to overcome the high school pattern of grade consciousness, connected as this is with the national passion for unilinear measurement (cf. Lee, 1959), when, as at Sarah Lawrence, one is dealing with a small group of young women, few of whom will go on to graduate work. It is still harder when the freshman year confirms the suspicion among hundreds of former high school valedictorians that only grades count.

With these scholastic limits on their selection of faculty and students, the houses have not transformed Harvard into a "postacademic" institution. The worlds of work and leisure have not been united. The houses have, however, given leisure a new focus, and have made it a worthy competitor for the workaday routine of the departmentalized curriculum. They have done something to break down parochialisms of all sorts, making today's Harvard undergraduate more cosmopolitan than his father. They have encouraged communication and often creative conflict between the aristocracy and the middle class, between the Northeast and the rest of the country, between natural sciences and humane studies, between upper classmen and graduate students,

[2] "Concentration" at Harvard is similar to "majoring" elsewhere, beginning in the sophomore year, and usually pre-empts about half a student's courses.

and to a much lesser extent between faculty and students. By doing all this the houses have perhaps done something to stem the further divorce of work and leisure, making the average student somewhat more receptive to the academic demands of the faculty. (Rising standards of admissions have, however, probably played a larger role in this transformation.) We turn in the next pages to an examination of this new world of leisure, in which the houses play such an important part.

THE HOUSES AS CENTERS OF LEISURE

If Harvard undergraduate life can be conceptualized into the social, the athletic, the intellectual, and the academic, and if the required academic efforts can then be described as the world of work, then social, athletic, and intellectual activities combine to form the world of leisure. Of course, the division is somewhat arbitrary. Some students "work" at football, or getting into a club, or getting on the *Crimson,* with the same joyless competitive spirit that so many bring to the curriculum. And a number enjoy the study of prescribed subjects as the majority enjoy sports, or conversation, or nonrequired reading. Nevertheless, similar exceptions could be found among industrial workers, and do not justify ignoring the general cultural gap between work and leisure.

Given this distinction, we have already suggested that the world of work is centered primarily on the departments rather than the houses. This is especially true of the natural sciences, in which the divorce between work and leisure is greatest, and distrust or contempt for the houses and their aristocratic or Anglophile pretensions is widespread. The scientific departments offer little tutorial (and command the resources to support their preference for giving able graduate students scholarships instead of tutorships). In turn, the graduate students in the social sciences ordinarily prefer the full and prestigeful subsidy of a fellowship or scholarship to the partial subsidy of a tutorial assignment. And this pattern is seldom combatted by the masters (only one of whom presently is himself a scientist), who often harbor a donnish reserve vis-à-vis the newer social sciences and the allegedly Philistine natural sciences (cf. Snow, 1959). In the social sciences and the humanities scholarships are less available and tutorial is more important. This tutoring is, at least in the sophomore and often the junior year, centered in the houses, and conducted by graduate students who can know undergraduates not only as potential apprentices but also as fellow house residents. Tutorial in these years is usually ungraded, and except in senior year is not usually oriented to the preparation of a preprofessional dissertation or a general departmental examination.[3] Yet for all of these reasons it usually lacks the formal and cumulative organization that many academic disciplines have proudly achieved, and is often frowned upon by work-oriented students. Since these latter students increasingly set the tone at Harvard (where half the students now graduate with honors), a free-wheeling intellectual bull session becomes, by definition, "mere" relaxation, and the feeling is strong that intellectual activity that is enjoyable cannot really be work, and thus cannot bridge the gap between work and leisure. In a few cases, however, tutorial does serve to bridge this gap and consequently also the gap between the intellectual and the academic; and these victories give life to the curriculum for students who might otherwise have floundered or become progressively alienated from learning.

Outside of tutorial there have been only a few hesitant efforts to mesh the houses with the curriculum. The houses have given a few professors office space, perhaps in the hope that their physical presence will make them more sympathetic to their neighboring students, or perhaps in the hope that some of their academic dedication will rub off on these students. Some large lecture courses have had small discussion sections organized in the houses (a pattern carried much further in the Yale Colleges), in the hope that these would engender academic interests among fellow students who were also fellow residents. Partly because neither the freshmen nor Radcliffe students have houses, and partly because administration is often as difficult as invention, such experiments have not spread. Tutors have occasionally experimented with noncredit evening courses and field trips, and with informal publishing ventures such as *The Adams House Journal of the Social Sciences*. Some houses have organized dining tables devoted to specialized fields, and all the houses sponsor occasional dinners for concentrators and faculty members in a particular department. With varying but at best limited success, the masters have endeavored to build up their "senior common rooms" as social centers for the faculty, but the center of academic gravity is still in the departments, and few would want it moved. It is perhaps symptomatic too that, although some students study in their house libraries, the majority prefer Lamont Library, available to all undergraduates, which in both

---

[3] Since these lines were first written, a ruling aimed at restoring the position of the tutorial vis-à-vis the regular courses required that tutorial be graded; many tutors felt that this effort to fight fire with fire endangered the freedom that in the best cases has given tutorial work and the relationship of tutor and tutee their special quality.

architecture and atmosphere resembles a modern office building. Despite the efforts to give every student a bedroom-study to himself, few like to "work at home" even if privacy is available.

Outside the world of work, the houses have been more influential, although their victory has been less than complete either on the athletic fields or in intellectual and even social activities. The houses are the basis of an extensive intramural athletic program, which is said to have made exercise more common than in the past. But although the amateur student "athletic secretaries" compete for talent with varsity coaches more successfully than amateur tutors compete with varsity lectures, the best athletes continue to play for the college-wide "big time." Yet the trend is away from such quasi-professional efforts, which take time from increasingly demanding academic work, and often endanger the student's chosen self-image as an intellectual or sophisticate. The quest for athletic excellence persists only in isolated enclaves, immune to both social and intellectual snobberies. Among the majority, the varsity athlete is likely to be patronized as a "jock," at least if he chooses his friends from his teams and thus types himself as an athlete. In contrast, the intramural player may be praised as an "all-round guy" at least if he can also boast achievements in academic or intellectual realms: Harvard recruits enough high school students from all over so that the ideal of "well-roundedness," though jeered at by many, is not wholly defunct. However, in bohemian or arty enclaves even the intramural athlete may be regarded as rather uncivilized, and ironically, the varsity athlete may be so incomprehensible as to be treated on occasion with respect—rather like a visiting television entertainer or a sports car driver who has perfected an art of no personal importance to the student and so can be given respect for his skill. All of these developments may be partly attributed to the increasingly lengthy shadow cast by the students' professional future. In this light the possibility of being physically "uncoordinated" ceases to terrify, whereas the possibility of being "stupid" appears damning. The antiathletic emphasis also represents a deliberate rebellion against high school values, with which probably a considerable majority of Harvard students were less than congenial. In such an atmosphere, athletics may be abandoned altogether, or else redesigned along lines relevant to the future. Students take up individual sports such as squash and tennis which can be continued into adult life, or intramural sports which will have their analogue in the office baseball party.

If the athletic balance is shifting toward the houses, and the varsity coaches find it increasingly difficult to attract the best players, the same cannot so confidently be said of the intellectual balance. As already indicated, the character of tutorial is largely academic, and the effort to set up other house-size intellectual and artistic organizations has met with uneven success. Several houses have active studio groups in painting and sculpture. And there has been a blossoming of theatre in the houses. But this effort is subject to collegewide standards of excellence, such as *Crimson* reviews, and one successful production usually leads to a more ambitious undertaking, thence to a search for more capable actors outside the house, and eventually to a drama group in which the amateur house spirit survives only in name. (Since the above was written, the Loeb Drama Center has opened on a collegewide basis, and house drama has suffered a sharp decline.) Similar problems have confronted musical organizations. These are somewhat less driven by the need to balance budgets but perhaps even more subject to professional standards of criticism. Houses have also spawned mimeographed newspapers and occasionally even literary magazines, but these are usually short-lived, and the newspapers have little of the intellectual orientation of the *Crimson*. Indeed, most have arisen because the *Crimson* neglects to cover "local" items and personalities which a few house members deem important.

Yet while the houses have not generated extracurricular activities to bring the intellect within their walls, they have gained leverage on the intellectuals in other ways. Although there are many intellectuals who come to Harvard and join activities because they want to define themselves as "more than grinds," there are others who feel that the "activities man" is as misdirected as the grind, and that intellectual endeavor must remain undirected. Thus although one might, for example, blame the decline of extracurricular activities partly on rising academic pressures, which make students feel they ought to "stop wasting time" before getting to the library where they would be "learning something," another explanation of the extracurricular apathy is that intellectuals can now meet one another in the house dining halls and no longer need a theatre or a newspaper for a clubhouse. The social anarchy of the houses thus provides an alternative to academic and creative activities as an outlet for highbrow energies. We are convinced that the houses have in this manner done much to restore the connection between intellectual and social life at Harvard, and this has perhaps been their most significant contribution to the College.

For all but the most reserved students, the choice of friends has enormous importance for behavior and growth, determining as it does what can be communicated and what remains inarticulate and therefore unrecognized. The primacy of friendship is officially recognized by the custom of assigning students to houses in groups, so that a student will be denied his choice of house rather than his choice of roommate. If Harvard had continued to develop into the commuter college which President Eliot (rather unintentionally) was allowing to grow, the basis of friendship would probably have become, as in many other commuter colleges, preprofessional interests of various sorts. Students would have met one another in classes, in their extracurricular activities, and in athletics. This would have meant meeting primarily people with whom they shared a skill—whether it be Greek grammar, journalism, or tennis. Instead, the houses have encouraged freer and easier interchange between students who could not possibly do anything together except talk. Extracurricular activities, sports, and some courses and seminars still provide avenues for meeting friends in today's College, but the most important social center is probably the house dining hall, in which most students eat most of the time since they are required to pay for all meals in order to live in the house. Although the dining halls are certainly dominated by Harvard reserve, meals evoke the students' developing ability to carry on an intellectual conversation more than any other situation in the College. Friends met elsewhere may, of course, become the kind of friends with whom one can explore personal and social ambiguities, but only dining-hall friendships are unscreened by the necessity of first finding a common activity. Only here, for example, can the gap between the scientists and the humanists be overcome, for few science concentrators can find the time for the demanding extracurricular activities and team sports which help others to transcend their departmental affiliation. Yet scientists eat, and in the house dining halls they may discover that they have something in common with the poets, the athletes, and the good-time Charlies whom they would otherwise be unlikely to meet in a large commuter college.

As important as the mixing of otherwise isolated student cliques is the mixing of the faculty with students in the dining halls. Since most resident tutors must be bachelors and since in America this means most are under thirty, the majority are graduate students. Their role is thus midway between that of the student and the professor, and they can act as a bridge between the two. Of course there are exceptions, such as the tutors who are less gifted than many students and protect themselves by making up in erudition what they lack in imagination, flexibility, and character. Such a man can sour a brilliant student on the academic world for years. Yet he may also serve a valuable function by eating with the students; for by giving them a closeup view of academic life, he may make the student's self-respect depend less on grades and comments administered by sometimes inept and often preoccupied judges. Even the unintellectual tutor may, moreover, run a kind of salon for bright students. Lively undergraduates sometimes gravitate to tables at which tutors are sitting hoping to discover one another rather than the tutor, and the tutor's presence may be a pretext for intellectuality despite his personal limitations. Even where this does not happen and the tutor's presence drops the conversational level, students may still appreciate, in what they regard as a very impersonal milieu, a well-meant effort to respond to them as individuals.

Of course not all tutors eat with the students. In part this is a matter of house policy, which varies considerably. One house has a rule that not more than two tutors can sit at a table, while the master of another discourages faculty congregations by sternly frowning upon them as he walks past. Other houses take a more fatalistic view and allow tutors to retreat to each other's company if they wish. And in the houses, as in universities generally, the "best" tutorial staff may serve the students least effectively, for high standards may encourage tutors to stimulate one another rather than their students. Despite these obstacles, the houses provide easier access to tutors and visiting senior faculty than the constrained atmosphere of hasty after-class discussions or faculty office hours.

Whatever the differences for individual students and houses, the overall system has facilitated a great change in the quality of mealtime conversation and hence the basis of friendships and acquaintances. This can be seen by comparison with dining patterns in other universities (where the student dining halls are often places one races through to get out again) and at other enclaves within Harvard, such as the Freshman Union or the Radcliffe dormitories. The house meals all appear leisurely to the visitor (the dining halls serve cafeteria-style, are open for two hours for each meal, and offer unlimited second helpings of food and coffee); all tables are small enough so that conversations can be restricted to two people (even the longer tables are narrow enough for this); and even the most allegedly gregarious house appears—we did not make an exact count—to have as many small clusters at meals as the most allegedly individualistic one.

In comparison Radcliffe meals are served at a set hour at large tables of eight or nine, at which only the most spirited can carry on a group conversation and only the most rude a tête-à-tête. Radcliffe lunch is served about a mile from classes in Harvard Yard. The rich eat elsewhere and the poor arrive having lost whatever train of thought their last class might have provoked. Meanwhile more than one noon-time class is, in effect, continued through the lunch hour for Harvard House residents, with teacher and students moving directly from classroom to lunchroom. Radcliffe supper, moreover, is not cafeteria-style; the students take turns waiting on table, and hence oblige each other by getting through as fast as possible. At both Harvard and Radcliffe, the general student culture frowns on snobbery and calculation, and encourages spontaneity; this makes it difficult for Radcliffe girls to plan a whole table ahead of time. In contrast, the Harvard students can come casually to meals and sit down where they happen to see friends or acquaintances, who may then linger on over a second cup of coffee if they can spare the time for talk.[4]

Often they can and do spare the time, in part as an assertion to themselves that, despite increasingly busy lives, they are still in some measure their own masters, and in part because the dining hall provides the kind of easy sociability which is lacking in other phases of Harvard's demanding preprofessional life. Yet it would be a mistake to assume that the dining halls are centers of real intimacy—intimacy being a relation which most undergraduates increasingly reserve for girls. All-male bull-sessions appear, from unsystematic observation, to be on the decline. Male conversation in the dining halls tends to intellectualize, and thus disguise, the problems of the "personality" in an artfully abstracted "impersonality." Women are allowed as dinner guests three nights each week, and this opportunity is increasingly made use of. Whether this will serve to render the conversational habits of diners less impersonal is difficult to say. Students who bring casual dates to the houses for dinner may introduce at their table a deliberate superficiality which has long characterized collective encounters between the sexes, but couples who eat together or with close friends frequently lapse into the easy intimacy which is today characteristic of those who are "going steady" (a phrase in disrepute at Harvard, but without an "aristocratic" equivalent).

The houses sometimes provide, then, especially through the dining halls, avenues to friendship between students of diverse skills who would otherwise seldom or never meet. These localized friendships have in large measure supplanted or transformed the older patterns of collegewide friendships with which the energetic and ambitious student of an earlier decade (and even some freshmen today) tried to ensure both his undergraduate and his alumni status. Today hardly

---

[4] By the same token, however, Harvard students often drift in to meals with their roommates, providing in this way a not wholly intended bodyguard against chance encounters—but to avoid the roommates and consciously seek out others would not be thought right.

anyone makes friends with an eye to "contacts" for later life, or even contacts for advancement within the University setting. Such bids for friendship are almost universally condemned as insincere, and those who make them are characterized as "politicians" (providing a commentary on one element in undergraduate apathy about or disgust with politics). Harvard's national image, moreover, attracts an ever greater number of students in more or less open rebellion against the market-place definitions of success. They prefer to dream of private utopias in which the good life assumes more familial forms. They practice what Professor Jacob calls "privatism" (Jacob, 1957) and are skeptical of the student who obviously seeks "public" acclaim or recognition at the Collegewide level. (Of course, despite these feelings, politicians are as necessary on the College as on the national scene. Students mostly want to be organized, however harsh their verdict on those who help out in this way. Contempt for those who administer charity or intramural athletics often means that these responsibilities fall to rejects, who are then further rejected for their activism, leading to an unwanted but irremediable decline of activity.)

In this atmosphere, the houses re-enforce the students' own desire to find friends in an unforced setting, uncontaminated by ambition, uncoerced by the "brotherhood" (which in a Freudian slip we first wrote as "botherhood") of the club or fraternity. The freshman, turned loose with a thousand others in the Harvard Yard and the freshman dining hall, often searches somewhat frantically for friends, selecting them from those met by chance through assignment to a dormitory entry (15 to 30 students), a section of a large lecture course, or a squad on the athletic field. The sophomore, new to a house that then seems very large (as large as Reed and Haverford, larger than Sarah Lawrence), may also flounder, not sure of how to establish himself or find his place either in or out of the curriculum. The houses seem to come into their own (as Professor John Finley, Master of Eliot House, has observed) in the junior and especially the senior year, when the student has the leisure and security to select his friends on a more personal basis and to take more chances in achieving deeper rather than superficial relations. These friends will largely be from within his own house which is large enough to satisfy his developing sense of self, and by this time familiar enough to seem protective and comfortable.

MYTHS AND REALITY IN HOUSE STEREOTYPES

To sum up the story thus far, it would seem that the houses have succeeded quite well in combatting the evils of undergraduate life at Harvard in the 1920s: they have weakened the pull of the clubs, the divorce of scholarship from the rest of life, and the withdrawal of the faculty into their research by day and their suburbs by night. (To be sure, other forces both in admissions policy and in national mood would have weakened, in any case, the snobbery of the clubs and the dilletantish approach to academic work.) Furthermore, the houses have made it easier for students to cope with the problems of the 1950s, such as the quest for casual but not superficial companionship and relaxed but not frivolous talk, and the wish to explore the self through intimate knowledge of others. The houses have even made a dent in the emergent problem of the 1960s, namely the divorce of the intellectual from the academic that only becomes manifest when intellectuals and academicians are no longer drawn together because both are small underesteemed minorities.

Naturally, if the houses take their problems from their environment, they cannot help reproducing in microcosm the situation of the American college at large. Just as a college recruits from and therefore depends upon society, so a house recruits from Harvard College. Some students go to college to avoid getting a job or taking responsibilities, while others seek to improve their occupational opportunities or to broaden their social horizons. Students' attitudes toward their houses are similarly mixed. Some find in house life an escape from the curriculum, while others join a house because this is the only way to remain a Harvard student. Likewise, however eccentric the staffs of colleges or houses may appear in individual cases, their roles are also defined partly by the larger society. Just as students and staff in a college are kept in line by pressure from parents, alumni, and the mass media, so too the students and staff of the houses are kept within the University's orbits of tolerance by the paternalism of the faculty and by the curriculum—the university equivalent of the mass media.

Nevertheless, both the houses and the colleges do manage to differ both from the larger society and from one another. Differential recruiting may encourage the development of cultural enclaves, which become still more dissimilar as their own traditions and patterns of socialization emerge. For example, though one can find at Harvard College virtually every social and intellectual type one can find at Yale College and vice versa, nevertheless subtle selective factors operate to divide those applying to the two colleges, thus helping to create somewhat different climates at each.[5] So too, although not all the Harvard Houses possess an equally distinct imagery in the eyes of students, all can be ticketed in some fashion. At Yale, such stereotyping got to the point where one of the residential colleges was thought to monopolize "white shoe" social prestige, while another was regarded as a ghetto; consequently, assignments are now made arbitrarily from a central office.[6] (Even so slight nuances of imagery persist.)

At Harvard, students list in March of their freshman year three houses (in order of preference) which they would like to enter. As we shall see, a quota system controls the extent to which the houses can choose those who choose them. In recent years, this has worked out so that about one student in three is denied his first choice, and one in ten is denied all his three choices, although it can happen—as it did in the spring rush of 1960—that a bunching of choices for a small number of houses forces larger numbers of students to accept unwanted assignments. But this two-way and chancy choice has not altered the freshman's assumption that the choice is largely up to him, and that it matters. The result, as Talcott Parsons has observed in commenting on romantic love in America (and as one might also observe when people buy cars and other big-ticket items), is that people develop pseudo-rational mythologies when they must justify choices among products whose differences are largely inscrutable (see Parsons, 1949).

It would have been interesting to conduct a survey on the imagery and salience of the various houses for different groups of Harvard students. But our own approach did not accomplish this; it did, however, include examination of the files of the *Crimson* (which every March devotes an issue to helping freshmen pick a house), conversations with all the masters and a number of senior tutors as well as other tutors, and with a nonrandom group of students in each house, as well as participant observations of freshmen tours during which each house solicits applications. We also consulted house alumni of earlier years, discovering the stability of "character" of some houses, the vari-

[5] An undergraduate honors thesis at Harvard explores differences in aptitudes, outlook, and self-image, of Phillips Andover seniors headed for Yale and those headed for Harvard (Blackmer, 1960).

[6] This curb on free enterprise is not possible within decentralized Oxford or Cambridge, much less among ultranationalistic American colleges, which compete for able students with little regard for one another or for students themselves.

ability of others. The houses have sometimes been crudely satirized as follows:

Adams: nonconformists and bohemians (e.g., musicians)

Dudley: unkempt "wonks" [7]

Dunster: Good-time Charlies and friendly amateur athletes

Eliot: aristocratic intellectuals and unfriendly socialites

Kirkland: Midwestern hustlers and organizers

Leverett: "the House nobody applies for"—non-entities [8]

Lowell: academic highbrows, grinds

Quincy: a new house, opened in the fall of 1959, the image of which is still amorphous

Winthrop: "jocks" (i.e., varsity athletes)

All of the stereotypes above represent the house as seen by outsiders, who use the typology to explain what their own house is not, rather than to explain what it is. Most students are, however, also outsiders toward themselves and "their" house, and are often willing to accept the same typology to describe their own house, for lack of any better way to structure such an amorphous group of 450 people. Yet some resist stereotyping their own house, especially if they feel out of sympathy with the "outsider's" characterization. Even those who accept the typology will often modify it to more congenial terms so that Dunster thinks of itself as friendly but not happy-go-lucky or Philistine; Adams sees itself as independent but not bohemian; and Eliot describes itself as reserved but not unfriendly.

Even among outsiders there will be some variations of emphasis, according to what aspects of his own house the speaker needs to clarify. Thus although Dunster men see Eliot as "aristocratic," in contrast to their own "democratic" ethos, Adams men pay little attention to this

[7] By the middle of the Fifties, the success of the houses had convinced many that the commuter was being educationally short-changed, and had led to the creation of Dudley House with such amenities as a cafeteria, a limited number of beds, and common rooms, as well as intramural athletics, social gatherings, dances, tutorial, and recently a master. Unfortunately for our inquiry, these commuters are not culturally comparable to the residents of other houses, and so cannot be used as a "control" to measure the impact of residential patterns. For many colleges, such nonresidential centers are the only workable equivalent to a house, but we have done little field work in this area, and cannot report fully on the extent to which this experiment has solved the problems of the "streetcar college," which Harvard is to these 450 odd students. Our generalizations about "the houses" therefore refer to the seven original houses, and occasionally to Quincy.

[8] Since this paper was written, a spectacular change has occurred in the image of Leverett, partly reflecting the determined efforts of a new master, and partly the acquisition of two twelve-story towers with attractive accommodations and handsome Charles River views.

"political" dimension, which is not so important in their own efforts at self-definition. Instead, they emphasize the alleged stuffed-shirtism, conformity, and affectation of Eliot's intellectual life, which highlights the quest for casualness and sincerity among the quasi-beat intellectuals who are one strand in the Adams product-mix.

Because these brand-names serve to define one's own house by exclusion, they cover a whole gamut of recognized undergraduate pigeonholes. Indeed, we suspect that some have been invented simply to give a locale to a well-known "type." When one speaks, for example of a "Winthrop House type" one both mutes and extends the meaning of "athlete" to fit the Harvard context better. In other cases, a house may provide a real symbol of something which has no verbal equivalent in the Harvard lexicon, so that, for example, although students (and faculty) know immediately what is meant by "an Eliot House type," paraphrase takes time and discussion, for the term indicates more than mere "breeding." Thus, the houses may give a journalistic sharpness to social typing, in the same way that "Brooklyn" or "Texas" or "Madison Avenue" do in common speech.

The impulse of the house resident to type the other houses rests primarily on a desire to say what he is not. In contrast, the stereotypes offered by freshmen have a somewhat less acid quality, for to them these images are possible future roles. Indeed, whereas the upperclassman will see Winthrop House as a home for athletes because he wishes a symbolic equivalent to the gymnasium, the freshman may be responsible for defining Kirkland as Midwestern—not so much because he needs a locale for Midwesterners as because he must have some idea of what Kirkland would be like to live in for the next three years. He knows that he will not be able to leave whatever house he chooses except by leaving the College (a rule rigidly held to in order to avoid the possible damage to a house and the endless jockeying that the possibility of transfer among houses might entail), and he correctly suspects that he will make most of his future friends in this house. Thus in choosing between houses he is choosing in some measure what he himself may become. Even if he thinks, as he usually does, that the brand-name imagery is bogus, he may cling to it in preference to a leap into the unknown. The need to make a choice thus both exaggerates and enforces the stereotypes.

Because there is little publicly available material about the different houses, their imagery is strikingly stable over time. Yet to say that imagery is conservative is not to say how it arises, and to say that the houses cover a rainbow of undergraduate stereotypes is not to say how a particular shade is assigned to a particular institution. Most house myths seem to sprout from the two most accessible symbols of the house: the master and the building.

The three houses that have retained their masters longest have the most clearly defined and generally agreed-upon brand names. It takes less than a year at Harvard to learn to speak of the aristocratic "Eliot House type," the scholarly "Lowell House type," or the gregarious "Dunster House type." The visibility of these images is re-enforced by the fact that whereas the other houses were assembled from comparatively inconspicuous pre-1933 dormitories, these three houses were built with Harkness money and are suitable monuments to his largesse. Their pastiche Georgian towers stand out against the skyline, and closed courtyards remind the pedestrian of these houses' existence by forcing him to detour around them. Differentiation is further enforced by the fact that these three house stereotypes are the most useful to the student seeking to localize such universal phenomena as middle-class sociability, upper-class restraint, and scholarly diligence. The images of Eliot and Lowell are also enforced by the aura of the expatriate poet, and the stern, energetically scholarly professor of government and president of Harvard.[9]

Beyond name and architecture, the master, like any college president, can do much to set the style of his institution, but the masters of the houses have seldom done this deliberately and there are many contradictions between what the master in fact is like and the reputation of his house. Only the Master of Eliot House comes close to embodying the popular idea of his house. He could hardly fail to mold the popular imagery, for he is the most eloquent spokesman for the house system, teaches a large freshman course in General Education, and is highly visible to almost every undergraduate. Furthermore, he believes that the function of the faculty is to testify to the intellectual life, and he does his best to do so. He is sympathetic to the idea that Harvard should train an educated elite, though not one selected solely from an earlier aristocracy.

The Master of Lowell House also has a distinctive personal style, illustrated by the fact that students dress for biweekly High Table. Lowell House, however, is known more for its excellent tutors than for its rituals, and it has attracted some very unritualistic "markhounds" for whom the many single rooms and the well-established tutorial staff are the principal attractions of the house. Likewise, Dunster

[9] Actually Eliot House is named for President Eliot, and Lowell House for the whole Lowell dynasty at Harvard (the same dynasty that built the early New England factories in Lowell, Mass.), but such facts make little difference so far as brand-name images are concerned.

House may owe its solidarity and camaraderie as much to the fact that it is further than any other from the Harvard Yard, where classes are held, as to the real or symbolic role of the Master, who is a reserved and distinguished public health expert. If anyone has symbolized the way of life associated with Dunster, it has been the Senior Tutor rather than the Master.

In addition to architecture and present company, historical differences, though long since forgotten by the student body, may have a shadowy influence on the houses. Thus, the first master of Eliot was a humanist, that of Lowell a mathematician.

In the 1950s, images of aristocracy, democracy, and intellect did not cover the gamut of developing undergraduate identities, even when supplemented by the outsiders' persistent equation of Winthrop with the playing fields. Coincident with the rise of coffee houses and the beat generation, there arose a "new" Adams House. Adams' dark-panelled dining room reputedly served the best food in the College, and it was the closest to classes. Thus the student who identified with no one and wanted a house that was merely a dormitory could easily rationalize his move to Adams. This tendency was further encouraged by the acquisition of a new master, who combined distinguished scholarship (in English) with personal unobtrusiveness and administrative laissez faire. As in other houses, the influence of the master was indirect, for no one could be farther from the rebellion of the beatnik. And as in the case of the other houses, architecture may have played a part in re-enforcing the image, for Adams has been the only house not entirely in the Georgian style. Its egregious city-hall Victorian is a remnant of the pre-1929 Gold Coast days, when its buildings were private apartments for the rich.

The desire of freshmen to find a house for every image and an image for every house is understandably always behind the march of events. Thus in the last several years Kirkland has gained an increasing vogue among musicians, but the fact has not yet been reflected in the fiction of house imagery. And the relative political quiescence of students in the last ten years deprived Leverett of its earlier recognition as the radical or political house, while the contemporary stirrings of students in the newest house, Quincy, has as yet made less of a dent in student consciousness than the built-in refrigerators and modern decor generally.

As in all caricatures, no matter how vicious, there is a grain of truth in each of the above stereotypes. The houses *are* different. At the same time, each house contains the whole gamut of subcultures which it attributes to others, although these may have different influences and visibility in the various house enclaves. Examining data from the Placement Office, the Committee on Educational Policy, and elsewhere, we found that the houses differed from year to year on such matters as athletic awards, Phi Beta Kappa elections, honors candidacies, and occupational choices. Eliot does well in crew, Winthrop in football. In one house two-thirds of all seniors are writing honors theses, in another house but half. Yet a new master like a new coach can build up a "team" in fairly short order, and there are substantial variations from year to year in these indices of house performance. The differences among the houses are less great and are far less consistent than the differences among colleges. Yet there are a number of students who come to feel that, either by their own choice, or by the accident of not being chosen, they got into the wrong house and feel ill at ease with its dominant culture. Nevertheless, the statistical data and our own observations suggest that there are socialites, athletes, and scholars in every house, along with musicians, actors, writers and premeds. Even in Winthrop House an athlete may feel marginal unless he can muster nonathletic skills and friends. Eliot, despite the distinctiveness of its image, has many non-Eliot "types," brought by their roommates, the luck of the draw, and idiosyncratic interests and attachments of all sorts. The evident social cruelties of an earlier day at Harvard are almost entirely a thing of the past, and in a Harvard-wide ethos valuing individuality and making a religion of tolerance, marginality is not punished and may even be valued. Thus the athletes, like other minorities, can usually find support in any house. For most students, it makes little difference whether the whole house accepts their style, so long as they can find a few friends who re-enforce their desire to act and feel in a certain way.

In order to ensure that every house will be all things to all people, the masters have established a system of social and academic quotas, aimed at making every house a microcosm of the College. Thus every house must select approximately the same number of "A" students (and "D" students) as every other. Analogously, every house must select approximately the same number of boys from the "select private" ("St. Grottlesex") schools. The Exeter-Andover group, the "unselect private schools" group, and the public school group must also be distributed with virtual evenness among the residential houses, although the commuter house does not benefit from these guarantees.[10]

[10] When it was pointed out to us that the order in which we listed these groups suggested a certain snobbery, since the public school group is larger than all the others combined, we realized that this residual bias had been incorporated by every informant. This is as close as Harvard can now come to the overt Colonial

There is also some overall control to prevent any one house from acquiring a monopoly on scientists, humanists, or social scientists, New Englanders, New Yorkers, Midwesterners, or Jews.

Yet such demographic screening has only a limited power to enforce similarity, because the variables measured are so crude. Several masters report, for example, that although they fill their quota of St. Grottlesex boys, they do not get anyone "typical" of that group. The St. Grottlesex boy who chooses "democratic" Dunster, for example, is very possibly trying to escape his background, his family, or his clique, and certainly not trying to live within them. Conversely, the public school boy who picks "genteel" Eliot is in all likelihood closer to the St. Grottlesex "type" than the genuine article who picked Dunster. Of course, similar self-selection prevents Harvard and other colleges from becoming as truly national and diversified in recruitment as they would like to be.

In principle, then, the statistical quota system allocates students according to their past background, whereas stereotypes allocate them to some extent according to their intended future trajectories. Yet there are probably more exceptions to this rule than illustrations. Since Harvard suites are priced by desirability, the cost of available rooms in any given year may vary from house to house, and some students will pick a house for economic reasons, or because it is supposed to have good food, squash courts, or ice-boxes. Yet such considerations may be rationalizations of ambiguous situations rather than decisive influences and many such "explanations" of house choice will not withstand critical scrutiny. The pattern is further complicated by those students who see the imagery atypically, usually because of chance contacts with the master, tutors, or students who actually compose the house.

Even those students who see the houses as we have claimed the majority see them, and are influenced by this imagery, may choose a house which represents them not as they are, but as they wish they were. Thus an intellectual may choose a "democratic" Dunster because he assumes that all Harvard students will be intellectuals, and hopes to find some who will be sociable as well. In this way he picks a house which he feels comes closest to compensating for the deficiencies of his freshman year. Students can also change in three years, and a student who comes, for example, to a "nonconformist" Adams to find a hotel, may discover that the house really offers him something more, and may take a renewed interest in college life. Perhaps

stratification which led the College to publish its class lists not in alphabetical order but in order of social eminence.

Adams has such a distinguished academic record because some of its recruits are freshmen underachievers, who later outgrow this alienation which brought them to Adams.

Since students are aware to a degree of the internal diversity of the houses and since they also see the choice of a house as not cutting them off from friends and even activities in other houses, there is of course far less soul-searching and heart-burning about the choice of a house than about the original choice of a college. But as with choice of college, second and third choices of a house are often insurance, and some students who do not make their first-choice house are disappointed at what seems to be a rebuff to their hope of becoming a certain type of person; most discover next fall that their self-portrait is about as viable in their assigned house as in the preferred one. Furthermore, once admitted to a house, myths that seemed important fade, and even the stereotypes of other houses may be attenuated by analogy.

The happy ending is not, however, universal. Occasionally a student is shunted into a house he did not want, and takes its inferiority for granted. Then there are other students who may be thought of as accident-prone with regard to rebuff in college: for example, a student who has gotten mediocre grades in his first term, and has come to fear that he cannot concentrate in the field in which he had hoped to specialize, may respond to rejection by the house he has himself selected as a further deflation of his sanguinity and self-confidence. Such feelings may be aggravated by the interview each applicant has with the master or tutors in his prospective house when he may, rightly or wrongly, feel he is not really wanted there—and indeed he may find himself assigned to a house in which he is pretty sure he is not wanted. Actual experience in the house may have a hard time penetrating the scar tissue of such interpretations.

Such mishaps might, of course, be reduced by several devices. Yale has tried randomized assignments, and competent statisticians might achieve a somewhat similar effect by revising the quota system. Thus, they might compute the extent to which the St. Grottlesex group overapply to Eliot. Taking this as evidence of an aristocratic image, they would reduce the St. Grottlesex quota, on the ground that Eliot will get its share of the upper classes from other schools. Analogously, they might analyze the extent to which Adams students are freshmen underachievers, and then reduce the quota of "A" and "B" students, on the ground that many "C" and "D" applicants to Adams are likely to be honors students by their senior year.

Such devices might do much to discourage competition among the masters for recruits, since every success would be penalized by a changed quota the following year. But probably the stereotypes would endure anyway. As we have indicated, some stereotyping persists even at Yale, where there is not even the stimulus of an apparently important choice, and myths can have little basis in reality. Furthermore, no statistical net can entirely eliminate real differences between institutions so long as students try to match their self-image to their house image. McGeorge Bundy has noted that the mark-hound can make noises like thinking, if that is what the system requires; so also the athlete can appear apathetic and the beatnik can play at being sociable, if that is what his chosen house appears to require for admission. Even college admissions officers have not successfully penetrated these façades, for how is one to measure in any largescale and systematic fashion the disillusion of the beat, or the togetherness of the chummy?

Quite different benefits might result from reversing the procedure, and allowing the houses to become more unlike one another. Under such circumstances, Lowell might become more like Columbia, Adams might move toward Reed, Dunster might become a local Oberlin, or Eliot might recreate Balliol—to illustrate the process with not quite comparable myths about colleges. Such diversification of student cultures would perhaps create more variety in standards of success and thus allow more students to retain their self-respect. Certainly the increasing hegemony of the single academic standard, embodied in grade averages, raises serious questions about the often traumatic consequences when a college admits 1200 brilliant students and then defines all but a handful as stupid or otherwise inferior.[11] If the houses could deviate more from one another, they could also deviate more from College norms, and thus might be able to mute the importance of academic indices of personal worth. Nevertheless, the University has shown no sign of encouraging the kind of nonacademic enclaves we are discussing, and perhaps this is for the best. When

[11] In part this is a matter of sheer size, in part a matter of changing admissions requirements. Thus Harvard's Phi Beta Kappa quota reflects neither the fact that the College now graduates a thousand students annually, nor the fact that the entering freshman is almost always chosen from the top 3% or so of his high school classmates (the SAT scores of the entering class of 1963 were: verbal 676, mathematical 691). Analogously, the *Harvard Law Review* is only slightly larger and more prestigeful than Yale's, despite the fact that it represents the cream of a school of 1500 instead of 300. On the other hand, the College Dean's List has grown with the times, and now includes 40% of the college. Likewise more honors degrees are now awarded, although not so many more as one might expect knowing that only the top half of the class of 1953 would have been admitted to the class of 1963.

students can appeal to Society, Culture, athletics, or friendship to offset their academic inadequacy, they are likely to use these values to create equally rigid nonacademic cultures, whose ideologies preclude even the possibility of scholarship. Truly pluralistic colleges are not created by formula.

For all of these reasons we certainly would not urge a return to the free enterprise system under which, in the early Thirties, Eliot House achieved a virtual monopoly on St. Grottlesex applicants. Since the best students will tend to excel in a number of fields, and the poorest to become apathetic in all, it is hard to see how, if free competition among the houses were allowed, one house could escape becoming the place for rejects who could not identify with any of the attractive images, whether social, academic, athletic, gregarious, or nonconformist. Although, as we have emphasized, Harvard culture has grown steadily more tolerant of deviance, it is still sufficiently American to want to rank people and houses.

The students, if actually forced (or allowed) to choose, might not themselves want a reality that conformed to their mythology of the houses. Many of them also share, though to a lesser extent than the faculty, the values of the University, and it follows that many who excel along lines not at present measured within the curriculum, such as sports or poetry or friendship, also do well in the academic forum. At present those who get into houses of their choice can often have the pleasures of feeling different without the risk of being confined to the company of those who are also different in just this respect; they can maintain a wide range of potential friends who share some but not all of their characteristics. Quite apart from the growth that can occur from freshman to senior year, many students are not sure enough of their identities to want to cut off access to other possibilities. Thus, the actual diversity within the houses that results from limiting self-selection along a few obvious boundaries means that students of whatever sort have a continuing chance for self-discovery. Even if, as increasingly happens, this discovery first comes with a girl, the house provides means for testing and confirming the new style or self-portrait. Certainly no experiment in strengthening house cultures should eliminate entirely the internal diversity which makes such development possible.

There is, however, little danger of homogenization. So long as the masters' visions of the ideal house are less diverse than the students of whom the houses are made, they will continue to protect one another by quota systems which ensure at least a few "good" students to each. Most masters look askance at the academically mediocre, the intellectually uncommunicative, and the socially gauche or irresponsible. Despite elevated admissions requirements, there seems to be an irreducible minimum of "mistakes" whom no master wants. Each will take a few of these students, for fear of otherwise getting them all—or at least having to meet regularly with other masters who got them. More generally no master wants to preside over a gymnasium, nor even to lead a colony of beatniks, and so all will band together to distribute these students into enclaves, where they can become a source of proud "well-roundedness" rather than embarrassment. On the other hand, although one or two masters might not be enthusiastic about a football captain or even a Student Council president (except insofar as these impressed outsiders and attracted more desirable recruits in the future), all want scholars who do well in courses, intellectuals who enliven the house, and students who can inoffensively organize other students, as well as stage designers, scenarists, sculptors, writers, and oboists (so long as all these bathe and shave). Each master may well suspect that if given the chance such people would congregate in a single house, and each master protects himself from privation by taking part in a system for distributing the wealth.

Despite all these considerations, we would still favor greater experimentation in house recruiting. By controlling the "mix" of various types of students, the masters could provide a laboratory for determining a more ideal freshman class. Yet it is not easy to conceive of the formula which will preserve marked differences without becoming invidious. On the one hand, free enterprise would lead to monopoly, while the present system of modified state capitalism tends inevitably to equate relative standing with gross similarities of recruitment. Perhaps novel modes of planning cannot emerge until one or more masters become willing to take the risks of seeking more idiosyncratic students within the limits of variability laid down by the quota system.

SOME UTOPIAN CONCLUSIONS

Measured by the utopian standards which have underlain this paper, the houses have not been a complete success. They have not reconciled work and leisure in the College, nor have they created a community in which ideas belong primarily to people rather than to the classroom or the library. But measured by more modest criteria, the houses have done more to preserve intellectual and humane qualities in the academic community than most educational ventures, and they suggest further experiments either at Harvard or elsewhere. Though the houses are unique institutions they suggest some of the problems and possibilities in that immensely complicated undertaking, the creation of an intellectual community.

Utopias are rarely of universal relevance. Those that are tend to become (in the broadest sense) religious. Certainly Harvard should make no such claim, nor has it since Cotton Mather's day. In all that we have said, for example, there has been a tension between the ideal of solidarity, friendship, and security, and the ideal of diversity, conflict, and adventure. Neither of these ideals can endure alone. Students must be stretched, but not to the breaking point. They must become involved in conflicts, but they must have enough security to believe that they may emerge victorious, for otherwise they become rigid with fright and learn nothing, or only by rote. Only in a university such as Harvard, where the presence of a graduate school, research, and academic departments guarantees the intellectual currency, can we afford to urge that the College should be made more sheltering and homelike. In small provincial colleges the houses and the utopias they suggest are irrelevant or even dangerous. These communities are likely to be so supportive and homogeneous that there is neither incentive nor room for original or imaginative thought. Harvard and other colleges which have been through the academic revolution can worry because their students and faculty get verbal indigestion from reading the massive "assignments" and often read for pleasure and curiosity only during vacation. But for most colleges such "postacademic" concerns are still over the horizon. The majority of colleges is still faced with students who don't read at all, and with faculty who suffer not from the esoteric malnutrition of journals but from the intellectual pellagra that comes of reading only textbooks and best-sellers.

Yet even in colleges where the students' intellectual potential will require another college generation to emerge, and where the academic revolution has not yet transformed the faculty into scholars, there are powerful national pressures which may make the houses relevant. The number of talented college applicants is growing faster than the number of spaces in the elite colleges, so that an increasing number of colleges is getting a share of the intelligent younger generation. A great deal depends, however, on how these students, often forced to attend second-choice colleges, react to the less prestigeful institutions they are made to discover. For although on the one hand the whole country is doubtless becoming more sophisticated, possessing many decentralized centers of light and learning, on the other hand, there are of course an enormous number of American colleges which are intellectually vacuous and where a bright but not exceptionally energetic student will have trouble finding an education on his own. This may be particularly the case as the competition for faculty among the leading institutions leaves the less privileged institutions, seeking accreditation or eager to retain it, with a mass of sadistic and otherwise incompetent teachers whose sole virtue is that they have managed to get a Ph.D. or want to obtain one locally (but cf. Berelson, 1960).

Let us add that one must be cautious about using such terms as "bright" or "intellectual" students in any absolute sense, although colleges, like other factorylike institutions, find it convenient to grade and label their products. Beyond a certain unascertained minimum of intelligence and energy, most students under optimal circumstances can discover that they might acquire intellectual interests that had never touched them in their families and secondary schools. At present, even the very "best" colleges are in this sense far from reaching all their students, or even the great majority, no matter how much work they get out of degree-hungry and honors-hungry undergraduates.

Most of the places that do come close to this ideal are small. In all these settings, even the urban ones, some kind of physical community would seem essential for the creation of an intense intellectual style. This does not necessarily mean the architectural splendor of a Harvard House. Although physically unified buildings, facing onto "their" courtyard or quadrangle, encourage their residents to identify with the community, we doubt that this is as important as many less expensive aspects of the physical and social architecture. It is proximity, not unity, which is essential. This means proximity not only of the bachelors who inhabit the Harvard Houses, but also of married students and professors, who at Harvard often live in the suburbs. Unless the academic relations of classroom and office are extended to the social and personal relations of dining room and living room, we doubt that the faculty can play an important role in shaping the community which educates the students. And although something can be done, as at Harvard, by providing free lunches for faculty who eat with the students, this is only a limited answer so long as home base is miles away.

It goes without saying that nostalgic and often snobbish values are often used to defend residential colleges as against commuter ones: there is no magic about living together, and ingenuity and imagination can overcome some of the disadvantages of a commuter college. Certainly, as the critics of "bedroom communities" constantly urge, the place where students and faculty sleep is less important than where they do their waking business. And, as the commuter center (Dudley House) at Harvard illustrates, much can be done when residental patterns are anarchic, and the community provides only limited curricular and extracurricular facilities. If the community also requires every member to contract for a certain number of meals as a condition of membership, it assures that every student and faculty member will have some opportunity to accept or reject his fellows. Sharing meals provides an opportunity for renewing and deepening casual acquaintances, which are likely to wither in a college which is only a collection of classrooms. Students are embarrassed at planning to meet people they hardly know, especially if sex does not legitimize such breaches in the ideology of casualness.

Such spontaneous meetings can also be broadened by providing coffee breaks between meals in the common rooms. "Morning coffee" gives even the busiest professor an excuse and opportunity to make nonbusiness acquaintances if he wants. As we have already implied, with such arrangements even a commuter college could create the human relationships required if scholars and students are to have a sense of intellectual identity which transcends their departments and courses, or to have the kind of intellectual curiosity which looks beyond advancing the discipline.[12]

Whatever the variations in living arrangements, we suspect that the size of the community is a critical factor in its shape. Unfortunately, we know no formula for determining optimal community size. In the first place, some individuals can cope with larger communities than others, and undergraduate transfers in both directions between "small" and "large" colleges indicate that students themselves often cannot always tell where they will prosper, or change, in the environments they need as they progress through college. In the second place, no community, intellectual or otherwise, encompasses the entire social life of the student, and optimal size will vary according to the alternative resources and diversions. A Harvard student invests only part of his energy in knowing and enjoying his fellow house members, for he has other interests as well. With such limited capital his house must remain relatively small or it will become a dormitory in which the student maintains a small clique of friends, while looking at the other residents from the defensive perspective of an outsider. In contrast to Harvard, a small liberal arts college can count

[12] At Monteith College, discussed supra pp. 189–190, a small Student Center in a run-down building has in fact provided some of these ties for a minority of the students.

on almost all a student's curricular and extracurricular activities to bring him into contact with other members of "his" community. Thus, unless the small college must compete with the student's home, job, or local community for his energy, it can perhaps afford to be larger than a house. Indeed, if a liberal arts college is to provide the special subcultures which make life endurable for many students, and make it interesting for the rest, it must be larger than a Harvard House, for unlike a house such colleges cannot count on a cosmopolitan university setting to counterbalance the parochialism and dogmas which thrive in all small communities.

The size of the community depends not only on the environment, but on the temperament of the recruits. If the students are slow to meet one another, as at Harvard, the community cannot contain as many as Harvard's 450 people and develop solidarity in three short years. In a somewhat more sociable community such as Yale, 400 students in a College might prove manageable, and conceivably the present 250 to 300 are not enough to support and nourish the diverse activities and attitudes for which the Yale admissions office provides the potential. Experience does show that the 20 to 40 members of a club are too few, and equally certainly, the 1250 members of the Harvard freshman class, or the 4500 members of the College (5700 when Radcliffe is added), are too many. One possible index of optimal size is that the residential unit should be small enough so that everyone can know everyone else's name. This allows the student to place every face, and saves him from fleeing the unknown—as an earlier generation fled the amorphous anonymity of Harvard College into the safe womb of a club. Students should know enough about everyone in a house so that they know which students they might want to know better, and in this context it is important to realize the danger of making a house even slightly too big. For, if a student feels he cannot know everyone, he reduces his effort to know even a majority— so that, for example, few Harvard freshmen know 400 classmates, although some sophomores may learn the names of all their fellow house members. But 400 is probably too large for the majority of students. The original size of the Harvard Houses was 250 to 300. Such numbers are more manageable for the majority, and might reduce the proportion of students who retreat to their own clique, even in the houses, without exploring the resources of their fellow residents.[13]

[13] Although there has been much talk of reducing the size of the Houses at Harvard to relieve "crowding," this seems not to be economically feasible, since it would spread the cost of maintaining a house over too few students. If the houses were reduced in size to their original 300, this would raise rents 30 to 40%. The

Yet once numbers are below the critical size at which the residents "massify" their image of one another into some defensive stereotype, further reduction of the population also means reducing the human resources available to the energetic student. In a house so small that everyone knows more than the name of every fellow student, privacy may become attenuated. Fraternity may replace community, with every brother so committed to the others that he fears antagonisms or the development of important "divisive" differences. This danger might, of course, be somewhat relieved by breaking the age-grading of the houses and importing freshmen and graduate students to give the community somewhat more internal diversity. Yet if more graduate students lived in the houses, tutors might be encouraged to retire to safety in academic cliques, thus negating the effort to broaden them through contact with nonacademicians. Still, the experiment would seem worth trying.

The question of size also depends upon how initially different the students are from one another. If, as at Oxford and Cambridge, there are yawning chasms between social classes, and between preprofessional students in various fields, the community must be quite small if it is to create the intimacy and mutual dependence which will bridge the gaps by driving students together at meals, on athletic teams, in extracurricular activities, or in social gatherings. If, on the other hand, as at a college like St. John's, everybody is studying the same thing, and if by the "accidents" of recruiting, the students are also socially homogeneous, then perhaps the college can be larger and still retain solidarity.

Another factor affecting size is the span of time the student has to identify with his community and meet his fellows. If a Harvard house were a four-year venture capitalizing on the enormous energy and adaptability of freshmen, it might be able to encompass more people than the three-year community. Similarly, a state university with high turnover might resort to even smaller units needed to retain solidarity. (However, in some state universities the glue of solidarity may need thinning rather than thickening, pending the victory of academic over collegiate values.)

As in all problems of social architecture, the problem of size de-

net impact on the cost of education would not be very great (perhaps raising the average college bills from about $2300 to about $2500) but most would prefer to use the additional $200 for more academic purposes. In future construction, however, the size might be smaller, although here difficulties arise owing to lack of space for expansion and to violent resistance from the city of Cambridge to the College's acquiring more land.

pends also on structure. Any intellectual community ought also to be an administrative community. Like the Harvard house, it should have its president and dean, and should do as much as possible to reduce to human scale the impersonal and often awkward and harried officialdom who otherwise may make the student in a large university feel like an outsider toward his own institution. The community should also administer its own recruiting process. This need not mean that, as in Oxford and Cambridge, the tutors elect one another and the master, nor that the master selects the students. Harvard's houses retain a notable sense of integrity and have a sense of self-perpetuation, despite the fact that the master is chosen by outsiders and has little power to retain either a tutor or student whom the University finds expendable. Each house has, however, the power of negative selection, and normally takes few students or tutors who repel the master.

But an educational community needs more than a political-administrative system to survive. It must also have its own culture and ideology, and for this it should be able to look to the faculty. At Harvard this is difficult. The house faculty consists largely of graduate students, only rarely supplemented by professors. To graduate students who are only in rare cases graduates of Harvard College, and to a faculty that often regards the houses as a refuge of outworn gentlemanly values, the houses naturally appear as alien, if entrenched, ground. No doubt, the fact that Harvard undergraduates are oft-times gifted, frequently the sons of the eminent or aristocratic, and on occasion both, gives Harvard College a drawing power even on that majority of the faculty which is oriented toward research and toward its graduate students. Nevertheless, as we have seen, this drawing power is distinctly uneven, and its very strength in the humanities, with their many Ivy League polemicists, helps give the scientists, and a few social scientists as well, the impression that the houses are not for them. By the same token, since perhaps 70% of the faculty remains unconnected with the houses, they largely forfeit their opportunity to reach the undepartmentalized among the students, who are sufficiently touched by Harvard to regard classrooms and scholarship as praiseworthy, but as objects of veneration to which they cannot possibly devote themselves in any life-long sense. If these students are to be brought into intimate affective contact with the curriculum, it might make sense for the faculty to follow the lead of the administration in decentralizing itself and moving a great deal more teaching to the houses than presently occurs there. Then, if courses, discussion groups, and tutorial were a part of the houses rather than the departments, the segregation of ideas into the classroom ghetto might be diminished and the contamination of dining halls, common rooms, and students' living rooms by serious thought might be increased. Lacking facilitating architectural arrangements, as Newcomb suggests in Chapter 13, students are discouraged from assimilating the ideas and attitudes they meet in the classroom by their inability to share and explore them immediately with friends.

Decentralizing the curriculum would also give both students and faculty some sense of manageable mutual responsibility. No faculty member, however conscientious, can do justice to 7500 "responsibilities" (4500 Harvard undergraduates, 1000 Radcliffe students, and 2000 graduate students). So he delivers lectures, and then waits in an office to which only the delinquent or the brash usually come. This does not mean that the other students have no intellectual problems or interests, but only that few can see what an office hour could add to a lecture hour. Many feel that they have nothing worth while to say that would justify taking up the time of a busy and often eminent professor. Moreover, they sense that the office atmosphere will be businesslike and constrained, and they feel the same reservations about taking intellectual troubles to academicians that they feel about taking personal troubles to psychiatrists. Under the present system, Harvard's 4500 undergraduates feel guilty about not meeting and exploiting their 500 distant and apparently unknowable professors, or the equal number of teaching assistants. If each house had only 50 professors, and as many teaching assistants, whom the student knew as part of "his" community, with special responsibility to him, students might find more usable opportunity to capitalize on faculty resources. So too the faculty could take more responsibility for 400 charges than for 4000. Certainly both groups would have a better chance to know one another as people, rather than as ambassadors from mutually fearful cultures.

There are of course several practical objections to such an alteration. The houses have no facilities for freshmen, for Radcliffe, nor for the married faculty who now commute from the suburbs. But such considerations would not necessarily affect other colleges, nor even future Harvard houses. Indeed, they might not even prove insuperable in existing buildings, for we have argued that these now contain too many students for all to recognize one another, and this would be a less serious problem if 100 residents were girls, or teaching fellows, or professors.

A more serious objection to decentralization is that the student would lose the intellectual resources of that nine-tenths of the faculty associated with houses other than his own. Insofar as the student knows what he wants, and knows how to get it from the faculty, this objection is valid. The Harvard catalogue is in a sense an immense menu, listing some 700 choice courses for undergraduates, and 500 for graduate students. Such a scheme works very well for a man who is on a preprofessional diet and has exacting requirements about what gives him indigestion. If a student is preparing to be a physicist, or a sociologist, or an art historian, his career is slowed down if he must postpone devouring the whole departmental offering until graduate school. But the student who is not apprenticed to a particular discipline cannot so easily tell which professors and courses he needs. His problem is not to get what he wants but to figure out what he wants. Under the present system he usually fills requirements and then wanders aimlessly, hoping to find a man who will speak to his particular intellectual dilemmas, and often winding up in the lecture hall of some pundit who has grown famous for addressing his parents' generation. If students had only to decide among the offerings of that tenth of the faculty associated with "their" house, they would be choosing among men whom they would very likely know at least casually after a year or two of residence, and about whom they would be able to gather considerable information from friends. This might give them a wider range of real choice than they now have, for students would confront partially known alternatives rather than choices based on the accident of opening the catalogue here instead of there, of having a class in one room rather than another in the previous hour, or of reading the *Crimson* writeup (*The Confidential Guide to Courses*) with its inevitable vagaries or irrelevance. And for the specialist who found the house offerings inadequate there would always be the graduate departmental program, in which many upperclassmen already enroll. Likewise, for the scholar who really thought he had something of general interest to say, there would always be the open lecture series—perhaps incorporated by some houses into their curricula if that seemed appropriate.

What we have sketched here as a residential utopia already exists in some measure in one or another of the houses. Thus, two of the houses have recently "affiliated" with Radcliffe dormitories, making possible joint tutorial in one case, and joint artistic and musical activities in another, and in both cases helping to break down the characteristic American dichotomy between the intellectual and the social. Indeed, we can say in general that, just as the suburbs have in many ways "corrupted" the industrial world, introducing both more humane and more sociable standards of achievement, so the houses have had something of the same effect on the curriculum at Harvard. Still, it is hard to say how much further this development would go if more of the curriculum were brought to the houses. Perhaps the houses would not change the academic offerings, but merely serve as retail distribution centers for them.

However, it seems conceivable that closer, more localized relations between students and faculty might influence the latter in the direction of somewhat less intense professional concern. This would not necessarily mean less specialization, but the specialization might revolve around concerns shared by students and teachers as well as concerns shared by teachers with other teachers. The postindustrial era into which our society is moving has found that productivity is not necessarily lowered by making the morale and well-being of the workers an additional "factor of production." Similarly, we think that a "postacademic" institution could introduce broad *intellectual* standards in addition to the older departmental criteria of *academic* achievement without risking superficiality or stagnation. To some extent this postacademic world already exists in various institutes, and a few free-wheeling industrial laboratories, and in some interdisciplinary research centers. So long as every teacher gets his degree in a graduate department and retains his affiliation with it, we doubt that there is any serious danger of watering down knowledge either in "applied" research or in "applied" teaching. Just as applied research should give the customer what he needs rather than what he wants, so the kind of teaching we have in mind would not be what one master scathingly brands the "baby knows best" approach to education. For one thing, the undergraduates are themselves less and less like babies, but increasingly precocious, demanding, and capable of responding to intellectual intensity. For another, as all we have said has made clear, the houses are never going to become the sole base for the Harvard faculty, with its ramified contacts in its own fields of scholarly endeavor and its increasing worldly connections in government, industry, and the mass media.

Despite all the guidelines which the houses suggest, the difficulties of creating an intellectual community are enormous. In the first place, students do not want to be patronized by their elders for their youth and inexperience, and they hasten into adulthood at breakneck speed. An intellectual community must attempt to resist such momentum and provide a moratorium in which the young may reconsider what they are about to become. For many, however, such shilly-shallying seems insufferable, and at Harvard nearly a quarter of the students withdraw for a year or two to discover "Life"; most of them later return to Harvard. Nor is the faculty ready to resist American activism. Academicians distrust the dilettante and the ruminative person. Professors try to justify their own curiosity by harnessing it to the "pushing back of the frontiers of knowledge," and they try to bring students to this professional level of research as rapidly as possible, often seeing little point in the play of ideas which has only subjective rather than publishable consequences. Like their students, professors want professional identities and would rather describe themselves as chemists or anthropologists or musicians than as mere professors, or—still worse—intellectuals.

Nor is there any model for the kinds of relationships which the intellectual community must encourage. Our resort to the negative phrase "postacademic" suggests the inchoate form of the communities which we hope—and believe—are gradually emerging in some sectors of the academic world. Yet our Utopia, nebulous as it is, is not likely to fire many imaginations. In many traditional fields and especially in many that have grown up interstitially (biophysics, psycholinguistics, political sociology), there has been ample excitement and enormous opportunity. The Cold War has dampened certain kinds of political exploration, while at the same time bringing support and justification to many fields of academic endeavor. In terms of educational ideas, the last dozen years have been a time of consolidation rather than advance in the major universities, with older experiments becoming partially assimilated and incorporated. Most educational debates have become so platitudinous and tired that intelligent professors yearn for the end of ideology and prefer not to debate such issues as general education, progressivism, or the relation between an intellectual and a residential community. In universities where men are harried by multitudinous demands and where real and relaxing intimacy sometimes seems difficult to find, to propose that men share not only friendship but also ideas may merely add one more "impossible" demand to their burdens. And in a world where togetherness based on superficial similarities makes rugged individualism nostalgically attractive, an appeal for solidarity on any basis seems untimely. Most of all, to a culture in which ideas are seen as either tools or possessions, the possibility of finding students and teachers who will use them as the basis for constructing a more livable community seems remote. Nevertheless we are convinced that closing the gap between the academic and the intellectual will become an increasing problem for higher education as the academic values spread throughout the university world. Simply as buildings, the Harvard Houses are of course not a practical model for the emulation of less affluent institutions. But as intellectual communities they could become such a model.

Since the Second World War, the great universities have made many changes designed to increase productivity, both among students and among staff. Increasingly careful selection of undergraduates has meant that growing numbers are digesting unprecedented amounts of printed matter. (Reading lists have become the tail-fins of the faculty). Students are making themselves at home in the academic atmosphere of libraries, laboratories, and seminars (but cf. Barzun 1959). Such achievements inspire envy among less selective or less cohesive institutions, but they provide inadequate ground for complacency among the successful. Just as Americans must eventually come to realize that a viable world order requires more than raising underdeveloped countries closer to the plateau of industrial affluence, so too educators can now begin to see that an adequate educational system demands more than the victory of university departments and academic professionalism over the collegiate fun culture. If the house experiment helps to illustrate some possibilities for and obstacles against radical "post-academic" reform, it will not only have helped Harvard overcome the social fissures of the Gold Coast era, but may also provide clues for an ideal of liberal education in large undergraduate colleges that would be more democratic, more intellectual, and more venturesome than anything now in sight.

REFERENCES

Barzun, J. *The House of Intellect*, N.Y.: Harper Bros., 1959.

Berelson, B. *Graduate education in the United States*, New York: McGraw-Hill, 1960.

Blackmer, A. *Andover to Harvard: a study of role transition*. Undergraduate honors thesis, Harvard College Library, 1960.

Bundy, M. *An atmosphere to breathe: Woodrow Wilson and the life of the American university college*. (Pamphlet) New York: Woodrow Wilson Foundation, 1959.

Jacob, P. *Changing values in college*, New York: Harper Bros., 1957.

Knapp, R. H., and Goodrich, H. B. *The collegiate origins of American scientists*, Chicago: University of Chicago Press, 1952.

Knapp, R. H., and Greenbaum, J. J. *The younger American scholar: his collegiate origins*, Chicago: University of Chicago Press, 1953.

Lee, D. *Freedom and culture*, Englewood Cliffs, N.J.: Prentice-Hall, 1959.

Morison, S. E. *Three centuries of Harvard*, Cambridge, Mass.: Harvard University Press, 1937.

Parsons, T. Age and sex in the social structure of the United States, *Essays in sociological theory*, Glencoe, Ill.: The Free Press, 1949.

Perry, W. T., Jr. Students' use and misuse of reading skills: a report to the faculty. *Harvard Educ. Rev.*, Fall, 1959, 190–200.

Snow, C. P. *The two cultures and the scientific revolution*, Cambridge, England: Cambridge University Press, 1959.

$\mathcal{23}$ *Harold Taylor*

Freedom and Authority on the Campus

The progressive or liberal view is that people become better when freed from authority, when they make their own choices and think for themselves, when they act out of personal judgment. The liberal and progressive movements of this century have called for the liberation of the individual from the authority of the state, the church, the family, from cultural and moral coercion. In the family, the father is not to be an authority but an older friend, or cochairman of a committee whose members are of various ages. In politics, government has only that authority granted to it by the electorate: it exists to carry out the wishes of the citizens, each of whom is his own authority and all of whom vote through their representatives to decide what the government should do on the basic issues. In religion, the clergy and the church exist not to decide ultimate spiritual questions and to hand down moral and theological doctrines, but to provide an institutional setting in which the church-affiliate can enjoy his own form of religious experience and find his way to his own ultimate truths and values. In the arts, neither the authority of the past nor of aesthetic convention are to determine what is honored and admired; the individual artist and his companion, the observer, create their own forms for expression and appreciation. The general theory which holds together these elements of the liberal position is the idea that the true human community is a group of individuals bound together by common interests, and an ethic of mutual respect.

Authority, in its proper function, is the set of general agreements which the members of the community are willing to abide by; these agreements change from time to time as circumstances change, as the community develops, and as a variety of individual experiences are shared in common and thus produce changes in community habits and customs. Within the liberal society, education therefore becomes the major instrument of social, political, and personal development. It is both an induction into the ethical and psychological attitudes of the liberal community and an instrument of social change.

When the ideas of progressive philosophy are translated into educational practice, the school and the college are organized as institutional models for a liberal society. The teacher is not an authority who tells his students what they should know, what they should think or what they should do. He is a friend who is helping students to become educated by the experiences which he is able to bring to them. He wishes no intellectual or personal authority over the minds and attitudes of his students, he does not direct their ideas toward established conclusions but acts in ways designed to help them to form their own judgments. Students in the progressive college may choose the courses they will study, take part in forming educational policy, form their own self-government for student and college affairs.

The principal of the progressive school or the chief administrative officer of the progressive college is not an administrator in charge of the faculty and students, but a chairman of the whole, serving at the will of the governing board, the faculty, and the students, a democratic leader who orchestrates the variety of interests, judgments, opinions, and decisions of all those connected with the educational institution, including students, faculty, parents, the board of control, members of the community, and the alumni, about whom there is usually information available through research studies. In schools and colleges, both of the conventional kind and those which are fairly advanced in progressive design, final authority for educational policy, although nominally in the hands of a governing body of trustees, is, in varying degrees, in the hands of the faculty. In progressive schools and colleges, what might be called semifinal authority for student affairs is in the hands of the students.

In a large sense, the problem of liberalism as a social philosophy and of liberals in the social movements of this century is to come to terms with the necessary instruments of power, to deal with the reality of power and its social use, and to come to new terms with the idea of authority. To put the matter broadly, the ultimate form of radical democracy in social organization or in education is either the anarchy of accepting no authority and thus deliberately cultivating the disorder of laissez faire, or it is a consensus resting upon the unanimous judgment of the community, thus enforcing a new, and in some ways, a more unpleasant kind of authority than that which the liberals have sought to overthrow.

The practical problems of government in radically democratic communities do not disappear simply because the concept of authority is rejected. They turn up in other ways, and there are many interesting questions which relate to the organization of educational institutions on the matter of what happens to education when it is administered democratically. One result is to be found in the conservatism and bureaucracy developed in faculty bodies. Another is in the orthodoxy of liberal values which may develop within the student community which then creates its own opposition in splinter groups of students who make a point of disengagement, noncommitment, and organized apathy.

However, it is with the educational use with students of the idea of freedom in relation to authority with which this chapter is concerned, the psychological and educational effects of certain methods derived from progressive theory. Some of the methods I shall discuss are based on a segment of theory which is outdated by a number of shifts in liberal culture and by the new situation of the contemporary student. If the progressive movement in education can be said to have been one of revolt and liberation during the first half of this century, the question now becomes, what do you do when the revolt has been successful and the liberation is real? The British Labor Party in a welfare state has the same problem.

THE SOCIAL STRUCTURE OF STUDENT LIFE

Between the two extremes of paternalism on the one hand and laissez faire on the other runs the life of most American colleges. Official attention is paid to the living conditions and the community life, but usually not with a clear or full conception of the educational effects of one or another part of the student's life in college. In the most familiar case, fraternities and sororities may set the intellectual and social tone for the whole institution, with the student body and the faculty organized as two separate parts of the institution, each with different functions and with few interests in common. In other cases, the social effects and relationships of the college environment may be the ultimately controlling influences and may provide almost the whole of the motivation of student effort. As John O'Hara describes the Princeton of 1915, the central character of *From the Terrace* finds himself as a freshman in one such environment.

Here at Princeton he was nobody, as all his classmates were nobody, most of them lonesome or homesick, nearly all of them being careful of the impression they were making, and all of them, admittedly or not, under self-induced pressure from the existence of the upper classes. It was lonesomeness as much as any other factor that brought freshmen together in friendships that might last weeks, might last out the year, or through the club invitations, through college, throughout life. . . . To be a nobody again, and in a place where he wanted not to be a nobody, made his first weeks at Princeton unhappy ones, and he was grateful for the routines of attending classes, eating meals, going to the movies. . . . It took three weeks for classes to become routine, in that on certain days of the week he automatically sent himself to the certain classes for those days. When he was thus settled in the classroom routine he at least became less alone of himself and part of the group, which was some improvement. He was thankful to be rooming alone. If you were going to be lonesome it was better to be lonesome by yourself than to have to pretend you were not.

A concern for the personal factors in the life of the student is a distinguishing characteristic of the progressive movement in education. It is sometimes assumed, for example, that loneliness of the kind expressed in O'Hara's description is to be prevented at all costs, and student groupings are arranged, student advisers are designated deliberately to counteract the strangeness and separateness of the new environment for the freshman. In order that the courses do not simply become a defense against loneliness or a routine and perfunctory set of duties to be performed, the campus society outside the classroom is linked with that inside, making an organic community life of intellectual, aesthetic, and social experience in place of the compartmental character of the conventional institution.

By the social structure is meant the total structure. This would include the size of the community, the number of students and faculty, whether or not faculty members and administration live on the campus, the close or distant relation between the faculty and the students, the number of students in a given dormitory, the location of the rooms in blocks or sections, the presence or absence of living rooms and common rooms in the dormitories, whether or not there is a student center, a common eating hall, the proximity or distance of the campus from a large city, the degree of freedom allowed to the students in making and administering college policy, the policy of the deans and counselors toward the students, the rules for student conduct, the way in which rooms are assigned, the number of Negro and white students, the proportion of non-Jewish to Jewish students, the geographic distribution of the student body, the number and kind of student organizations, the opportunities for student leadership, the attitude of the student newspaper to the college, whether or not there are resident-counselors in the dormitories, the number and character of planned social events, the opportunities for recreation and entertainment on the campus over weekends, and dozens of other factors.

Looked at in one way, the central question in building a social structure for a college campus is the question of how much responsibility and authority the college should take for the life of the student, and how much freedom should be left in his hands. In the history of American education, colleges have taken a great deal of responsibility and authority for students, with explicit rules which must be observed if the student is to remain in college, and with the authority of the dean and the president used to enforce college-made rules. In earlier years the college served in place of the family as the arbiter of conduct. This has been particularly true of the colleges for women, where rules have been strict and rigorously applied. In many women's colleges at the present time there are rules as to when students may leave the campus, how many weekends they may spend away from the college, and what they may or may not do, both academically and socially, when they are on the campus. Men's colleges have fewer rules.

Over the years, however, the concept of college authority administered by the dean to those in his charge has shifted away from the punitive toward permissive policies. Students sometimes have a part in forming policy, occasionally in administering it, and the dean and his staff act in the role of advisers and counselors who handle problems of discipline as part of the total educational process rather than as the enforcement of rules made by the college. It is assumed that learning to handle personal problems in a social context is one phase of the process of maturing in the young adult, and that in these matters the college should provide all the opportunities and help that it can.

THE EXPERIMENTAL APPROACH

Among the experimental colleges that grew out of the new movement in education during the 1920s and 1930s, a new concept of social structure and the relation of freedom to authority was developed. It rested on the idea that in planning a college, educators had an opportunity to build a community in which ideal conditions for individual fulfillment could be created. In doing so, it was assumed that whatever evils exist in undemocratic, competitive, acquisitive, materialistic, insecure, or authoritarian societies could be eliminated by planning, and a situation could be created in which the positive values of a democratic society would prevail, with optimum freedom for individuals and mutual respect among members of the community. The virtues of tolerance, understanding, generosity, and cooperation could then be taught as values implicit in the social structure.

As an experimental college, Sarah Lawrence has tried in a number of ways since its beginning thirty-two years ago to build such a community. The principle underlying Sarah Lawrence practice at the founding was that students should be liberated from all restrictions of college authority and should be given powers of self-government for which they took full responsibility. The students were asked to make the rules themselves through a system of representative government and to administer the rules through a student discipline committee without faculty control or supervision. The students were also responsible for making up their own social groups, both in forming student organizations and societies and in choosing friends with whom they wished to live in the dormitories. There were no sororities or honorary societies, and no prizes, awards, grades, or any special symbols of prestige were available except those won through the respect of others for service to the community. Any student group which wished to do so, whether political, social, or intellectual, could ask for a charter from the elected Student Council, and once chartered, could invite its own speakers and conduct its own programs, free of administrative or faculty supervision, in whatever way it wished, both on and off the campus.

Throughout the 1930s and 1940s, this degree of freedom was exciting, was vigorously used, and the student prerogatives were jealously guarded against any suggestion by the faculty or administration that they should be changed or modified. Students expressed their views strongly on most subjects, organized student meetings to take political action, kept their literary magazine, student newspaper, and student organizations almost completely to themselves, and seldom requested help from the faculty or administration in student affairs. The Student Council and the Student Discipline Committee made the rules and dealt with infractions; Council and committee members shared actively in making college policy through a Joint Committee of students and faculty, and through the Student Curriculum Committee.[1] Any efforts by the College to organize social events on the campus over weekends were discouraged by the students who wished to plan

---

[1] For example, in one instance, a group of students drew up the outline of a course which they believed should be offered, persuaded a faculty member to drop a course he was teaching and to agree to teach the new one, and received the approval of the faculty curriculum committee for the new offering.

their own weekends elsewhere. Many students felt that to spend weekends on the Sarah Lawrence campus would be an admission of social failure.

Beginning about 1950, however, the older assumptions on which the college system rested were shown to be in need of revision. It could no longer be assumed that liberation into freedom was the exhilarating experience that it had been for earlier generations of Sarah Lawrence students. Whereas in earlier years it had been possible to count on the strong motivation and initiative of students to conduct their own affairs, to form new organizations, to invent new projects either in social welfare or in intellectual fields, it now became clear that for many students, the responsibility for self-government was often a burden to bear rather than a right to be maintained. For others, the Sarah Lawrence system of community government was one to which they had already become accustomed in high school, and it lacked the degree of freshness as far as their experience as students was concerned. Many able students who would have been first-rate student officers refused to accept nomination in student elections. They felt they did not wish to take the time away from their college work. They also felt that they had had all the experience they could profitably absorb in the field of student affairs by their involvement in such matters in high school.

Nor was there a high degree of vitality in the concept of student freedom itself, since it was already theirs and it was not necessary to fight to keep it. Over the years from 1950 on, interest in political action declined to the point that even a student meeting on McCarthyism could not attract an audience which included the students who organized the meeting. Students tended to devote themselves to their own studies, to their own friends. They were apathetic about events or occasions planned for the whole college. They made less effort than before to identify themselves with the rest of the student body or with the College as an institution. They preferred to work within a smaller framework in which only the teachers with whom they studied and the small number of friends who meant most to them were significant parts of their college life.

Beginning about this same time, morale in the dormitories also showed evidence of decline. Infractions of student rules were more frequent than before and the mechanisms by which the students could correct the situation were little used. Some house presidents responsible for the conduct of individuals within their houses often failed to report glaring infractions; others who did report were punitive in their attitude and caused dissension in the houses when they exercised their authority. In general, instances of infringement of student rules went unchallenged. On the other hand, attempts on the part of the College administration to provide more guidance were opposed by the students.

In looking for the reasons behind the new attitudes, it was natural to assume, for example, that the lack of interest in political action and in independent thinking was due to the formidable pressures against political deviation which existed at that time in the country at large, and to special pressures then exerted against Sarah Lawrence College by patriotic groups and congressional committees. It was also natural to assume that the lack of interest in world affairs by student groups bore some relation to the helplessness which young people felt in the grip of the international situation caused by the Cold War. These pressures certainly played a part, but beneath this surface there were a number of other factors worthy of consideration. One of these was the possibility that to remove all instruments of college authority, and in their place put a system of complete self-determination, was not necessarily a liberating experience for the student, or one which enabled her to achieve her own freedom. Students who were given complete freedom to manage their own lives and to make their own decisions often did not wish to do so.

THE NEW GENERATION

On analysis, several other reasons could be found for the shift in student attitude. The 1950 generations of college students were born from 1935 to 1940. During their first six years they were living in a society recovering from a depression; they then entered the war years with a growing period of prosperity for their families, and a postwar period in which the world closed in more and more upon the United States, while the United States increased in prosperity and power. The combination of tension from the world situation and the growth in national prosperity produced an attitude of caution and conservatism in the country which was bound to be reflected in the attitude of families and of children to their lives.

At the same time, the growth of a new attitude to child-rearing meant that most parents in bringing up this generation have made a genuine effort to understand their children and not to impose parental authority in ways which might inhibit the young child. As a result, it is. extremely difficult for the child to rebel, since he is understood rather than repressed. This has its consequences in giving him nothing but feather pillows to fight, and in developing an attitude of self-understanding before there is a great deal of self to understand. We have all heard fifteen and sixteen-year-olds discussing with their parents and among themselves the correct way of handling sixteen-year-olds, including their own relation to the authority of their parents. If an effort is made by parents to assert an authority, it is usually rejected, since both parent and child know that there is little the parent can do about a refusal to accept authority. The parent is unlikely to threaten the sixteen-year-old with bodily harm, and threats to withhold money or special privileges very often produce more tensions and problems than they solve, since they set conditions which it then becomes almost impossible for the parent to meet when the showdown comes.

Most sixteen-year-olds are sufficiently sophisticated not only to know the limits of power possessed by their parents if it were to be put to the test, but are also prepared to live an independent emotional life by depriving the parents of a return of affection, by appearing a minimum amount of time at home, by surface conformity to demands, or by simply leaving home altogether. With the removal of the concept of parental authority, the balance of power in family life has shifted to the young. In a relationship at once informal, friendly, and mutually accepting, the parents become not objects of filial piety but adult friends with whom one may have a deep or fairly superficial relationship and who have certain obligations toward oneself. Having dropped the attitude of parental authority and with it the necessity of obedience to parents' wishes, parents now find themselves with a new set of consequences for which in many instances they have not been prepared. Having staked everything on a warm and affectionate relationship with the child, the parent cannot then resort to older methods of authority with its expectation of respect and obedience.

In this situation, the strongest force which parents exert for compliance with family wishes is usually to induce a feeling of guilt on the part of the child in causing distress to the parents whose requests are disregarded, a guilt which may from time to time have its own aggressive manifestations in a confused rebellion and a sense of frustration on the part of the child. A new syndrome thus emerges in which there is no longer a clear-cut authority-freedom issue for the adolescent, but instead there are ambivalent feelings of obligation, responsibility, and guilt. Whatever satisfaction there may be in open rebellion is stifled at the source. The adolescent is unable to rebel, since before overt rebellion occurs, his parents will no doubt demonstrate their "understanding" of his wish to rebel by assuring him that it is perfectly natural. The tension of opposites, so often a part in the healthy emotional situation of the adolescent disappears in a warm bath of parental affection. The parent therefore in fact has no control over the child; the child often has not yet had sufficient experience to exert control over himself.

This underlies and creates a new and different attitude on the part of college students to the authority of their parents. It also creates a different attitude on their part to the authority of their college. Such a shift in attitude has been foreshadowed by a change in the social structure of the high school and preparatory school. In place of the disciplinary methods of 25 years ago has come a philosophy of student responsibility, worked out in the early progressive schools and spreading from there to the rest of the school system. There is a great deal more structure than before in the social organization of the American high school, partly due to the fact that it has been asked to assume more and more duties which were formerly attached to the family— out-of-school play, entertainment, learning to play instruments, sports, and outings. Much more is arranged for the students, in many more areas, and students learn to move from one social group to another in regular ways. At the same time, students are given more responsibility for sharing in educational and social policy making. Added to this is the provision of entertainment by football games, television, radio, mass magazines, and community projects. The young person's attitude toward entertainment in general becomes that of a spectator and he no longer takes up with the same enthusiasm his opportunities for self-expression, either in student planning or in social affairs. Students in college seem to find it increasingly difficult to entertain themselves, having become accustomed to depend upon arranged entertainment in which their role is simply to participate in the arrangements already made.

SOME RESEARCH AT SARAH LAWRENCE

Some of these questions are subject to investigation and exploration on a college campus, particularly in an experimental college where research is an integral part of the change and development of the educational program. During the years from 1948 to 1952, a group of Sarah Lawrence faculty members under the chairmanship of Dr. Lois Murphy conducted a research project designed to discover something about the process of change and growth in college students.[2] The social life of the campus, the relationship of students to each other and to the college, their morale, their personal concerns, their attitude to the educational system as it was then operating were all part of the research interests of those who carried out the study. In connection with these interests, a questionnaire was constructed, pretested, administered, tabulated, and analyzed by Mrs. Mary Collins in collaboration with Mrs. Esther Raushenbush, then Dean of Sarah Lawrence, and with Dr. Marie Jahoda, who at that time had conducted a similar survey, with a similar questionnaire, of the Vassar student body. The results of the work were reported to the faculty and students, and formed the basis for some changes in educational procedures by faculty and student groups.

The answers to the questionnaire from 339 of the total student body of 390, were collected and analyzed in 1952, and the questionnaire was readministered in 1953 to determine its reliability and to discover whether there had been any significant changes in student attitudes over the year. The similarity in the results over the two years was quite striking, with a statistical correlation of .99 between the two sets of answers.

In what follows, I have taken from the results of this segment of the Sarah Lawrence research some of the material which might throw light on the question of how the concept of student freedom worked in practice.

My own experience in working with the students had led me to believe that during the early 1950s the transfer of responsibility to the students for running their own affairs was producing apathy rather than the creative results we had been accustomed to expect. If faculty members remained, on principle, aloof from working with the students in organizing student affairs, very little happened. Students were more often than not frustrated and discouraged. They said that they had few ideas of their own, and that even if they did, they would not know how to carry them out in the face of the apathy of other students. They spoke continually of the need for faculty guidance. By taking attitudes which, in educational terms, were intended to make the students independent of adult authority, we seemed in fact to have made them more dependent.

My information about these matters came from talking with members of the student committees, the Student Council, the presidents of student houses, and a variety of students whom I happened to know

[2] Some of the results of the research have been published under the title *Achievement in the college years* edited by Lois Murphy and Esther Raushenbush. Harper Bros., 1960.

fairly well. This kind of information can be misleading, partly because conversations about other people's morale may not be the best way to get information about it, and because student leaders may be more fully informed about each others' views than about those of the general student body. The research results were therefore useful in supplying a more objective account of what the students were doing with the freedom they had.

Student morale as a factor in learning. First I would like to comment on some aspects of student morale, since the factor of morale is related directly to the question of how students respond to the absence of institutional authority. Do they enjoy what they are doing? If you simply give them a free hand, do they have the personal resources and the maturity to make a satisfying life for themselves out of their own materials? The state of being free is certainly a state of mind and a state of feeling which reflects existing conditions. Although it is obviously not true to say that only in a free community can morale be high, it is true that to build a free community requires a high degree of morale on the part of those who are called upon to sustain it and make it work. It also requires a quality of mutual respect among the individuals in it, particularly if they are students, who, in the absence of regulation by the college administration, must answer to their peers.

One major assumption underlying the Sarah Lawrence program and curriculum is that learning in depth occurs only when the student moves with some degree of zest toward the material to be learned, has an intrinsic interest in the material itself and feels some degree of sympathy toward the aims of the course and of its teacher. The College's provision of freedom for the intellectual and personal life is intended not only as a means of teaching the students to be free and independent, but a means of inducing the positive attitudes which true learning must have for its consummation. The students choose the courses they wish to study, there are no examinations or competitive grades, there are no formalized subject-matter divisions and the subject matter within divisions is often informal and usually unconventional (in the freshman exploratory courses which each student takes, there is no prearranged subject matter), the work is for the most part independent study from the freshman year on, individual conferences with the teacher, seminars and discussions are used in place of the lecture; the classes, 95% of which in 1952 were from 6 to 15 in size, meet usually once each week, the rest of the time the student organizes her own work. This is not to say that the College assumes that students should study only those things which interest and stimulate them, but to say that the student must engage himself willingly in the tasks of learning before the discipline and rigor of learning can be realized in action.

The morale of the students, if this may be defined as a positive attitude and response to the expectations and ideas of the College, is thus an essential ingredient of education in Sarah Lawrence terms. This is an essential ingredient in anybody's terms, but in a relatively small community, in which individuals, both students and faculty, are closely inter-related, it matters a great deal more. The expectations of the students tend to be higher and any subsequent disappointments much greater; the Sarah Lawrence educational program will simply not work as it is designed to work unless the student community believes in it and works for it. So much depends on the contribution of the student to her own education that without that contribution on a fairly generous scale the College is unable to provide the quality of education it sets out to achieve.

Students themselves become quite sensitive to fluctuations of the mood of the College and the swings of attitude are fairly wide within each year and over a four-year period. The fall term, as is the case in most institutions, is usually the most productive and interesting time, with a low point reached in late February and early March, an upswing in April when the spring weather begins, and a mixture of confusion, haste, overwork, and gaiety as the college year ends in June. The questionnaire was therefore administered in January as a midpoint in the year when the experience of the fall term had been absorbed and the experience of Sarah Lawrence in the winter-time had tempered enthusiasms sufficiently without destroying them.

We asked the students to say whether or not they were happy at Sarah Lawrence, knowing that whatever that might mean to any one person it would at least give a full opportunity to those who disliked the free style of the college, or disliked it in general, to say so. Two-thirds of the students said that they were very happy, nearly all the rest said they were fairly happy, with 2% who said that they were not. Eighty-eight percent said that they would choose to come to Sarah Lawrence if they had it to do over again, and about half the students found life at the College better than they had anticipated, with 12% who found their experience at the College disappointing in one way or another.

We wanted to know as much as we could about the factors which contributed to low or high morale, and found that when asked to list their most satisfying experiences, the top of the list by a large margin had to do with the students' intellectual experience—a particular course, a teacher, or the satisfaction of working well with a teacher or in a course. Forty-three percent of the students mentioned this. A third of the students mentioned the satisfaction of general intellectual achievement, and specifically such satisfactions as learning to read well, to take in new ideas, the chance to work independently and in small classes. We had expected to find a fairly large number of answers which would put a high value on the amount of personal freedom granted to the students, and on the richness of the cultural life available on the campus. This did not turn out to be the case. Only 3% mentioned as of particular importance the amount of personal freedom granted; 7% mentioned activities outside their courses as being their most important experiences at the College. Since the degree of personal freedom is as great as is possible, consonant with the ordinary social proprieties, one can only conclude that the students, very shortly after their arrival at the College, take that freedom for granted. We were glad to see confirmed the fact that the center of the life of the Sarah Lawrence was where we thought it was, in the curriculum and not outside it. There is no formal division between the work inside the curriculum and the rest of the college program. Most of the "extracurricular" events are either directly or indirectly related to the work of the courses and either stem from them or feed back into them.

The dominant interest in the curriculum of courses was confirmed in another way when we sought to find the sources of any discontents which existed and found it mostly in the same place as the sources of satisfaction—in the work of the courses. In response to a question as to the least satisfying or frustrating experiences they had had at the College, 15% did not answer. Of the 85% who did, 22% listed as their major frustration, disappointment in a course or a teacher. Next in order (17%) were relationships with other students, roommate trouble, or dissatisfaction with residence life. Fourteen per cent mentioned disappointment or frustration about themselves—not living up to their own standards, not studying effectively, "not doing as well as I could," and about the same number, 13%, were dissatisfied with their relationships with faculty members. Fifteen per cent listed lack of friends and unsatisfactory social life, 8% complained of academic inadequacies in the Sarah Lawrence system, "the courses are too vague," etc.

We asked the students what they worried about when they were worried, by presenting a list of 48 "Worries" with the request to check "the ones which have been of some concern to you during the past year." The list was fairly comprehensive and was based on knowledge of the students; the items ranged from concern about money, conflict with the family, to not being popular. The results were compiled simply by ranking the worries as to the number of checks each received. The top three worries in both 1952 and 1953 were the following:

	1952 % of 339	1953 % of 324
Difficulties in concentration	48	44
Being depressed	45	37
Worry about family relations because the family is in difficulties (sickness, finances, emotional problems)	40	35

The next ten worries are:

1. Feeling inadequate	38	29
2. Not knowing what to think about yourself	36	29
3. Your relation to a friend in college	33	29
4. Conflict between you and your mother	30	29
5. Not knowing what to do with your life	30	29
6. Not wanting to work up to capacity	30	29
7. Being swamped with academic work	29	29
8. Worry about family relations because they want you to be more dependent than you actually are	29	29
9. Inability to read fast enough	29	29
10. Eating too much	29	29

There are nine worries which concern fewer than 10% of the students:

1. Not being popular on campus	8	4
2. Unfair reports	7	3
3. Homesickness	6	3
4. Not being an officer on campus	5	5
5. Political disagreement between you and the other girls	4	5
6. Concern over your family's social standing because of other students' snobbishness	4	3
7. Not being good looking	4	3
8. Political disagreement between you and your family	4	3
9. Lack of rules at college	1	3

Without comparable statistics on the responses of students on other campuses, it would not be possible to say whether the social organization of the Sarah Lawrence campus, which has tried to eliminate competition, social snobbery, or false prestige values has accomplished more in this direction than the conventional system. However, it is significant in a free system that only a very few students in the total number have worries connected with not being popular or not achieving student prestige. Nor does the lack of rules seem to be as important as we had been led to believe by student comment, since only 1% of the students mentioned this in their replies.

The role of the faculty. The normal concerns of the college student —difficulties in concentration, feelings of inadequacy, lack of self-identity, worries about personal relationships—seem not to have developed to extremes of anxiety through the openness of the Sarah Lawrence system. In any case, a college as an educational institution should be prepared to make constructive use of these concerns through the greater understanding students may gain of themselves and others by dealing with their anxieties directly. At Sarah Lawrence we have counted on a direct relationship between students and teachers to meet some of these needs. Each student has a faculty adviser, known as a don, with whom the student confers, usually once each week, and who is responsible for the general welfare of the student. The student goes to the don to work out a program of studies. The don's approval must be given to the program of three courses which his student wishes to take. After the freshman year, the student chooses her own don among the teachers she knows, and gains as much or as little advice as she wishes, although of course either party to the relationship can take initiative in making it more personal or less so. Other teachers with whom the students are working in their courses also give help and advice when asked, although again the initiative usually lies with the student.

We were therefore interested in knowing how this system was working, the degree to which students counted on the advice and help of faculty members, and to whom the students went with their personal concerns. The questionnaire asked the students to answer the question: "Some people, when they face a serious problem, feel like discussing it with someone; others do not. When you do discuss your problems, with whom do you tend to do so?"

Nearly four-fifths of the students list "a friend" as the person to whom they talk. Over half mention their mothers, about two-fifths mention their dons, almost as many mention a male friend or their fathers. Twenty-five per cent mention a member of the family, 22% a nonstudent female friend, 17% another faculty member who is not their don, 15% husband or fiance, and 8% say they consult a psychiatrist.

If we count the 17% of students who talk with a faculty member other than their don, along with the 40% who talk to their dons, there are well over half the students who turn to faculty members for guidance, about as many as turn to their mothers, with around 80% talking to other students, either instead of, or as well as to the family or their teachers. This confirms both the result of other studies and our own assumption that most of the talk about personal problems goes on between students, and tends to confirm the further assumption that the relationships among students in the residences are the greatest single factor in their general attitude toward the college and toward themselves.

We wished to know more about this, since the evidence, as I have pointed out earlier, seemed to be that in the early fifties the student self-government of residence life was not working very well. The residences at Sarah Lawrence are not uniform, and although a large proportion of the rooms are single, the houses vary in size from one large dormitory of sixty-four students (this has since been split in half after we saw the evidence of the effect a house this size has on the relationships within it) to small houses across the road from the main campus, each housing from seven to ten students.

One of the things we learned very soon, once the information of the questionnaire had been collected and tabulated, was that it was not possible to talk about residential life on the campus as a whole, or of "the sophomores" or the "freshmen," since the variations in attitude and morale were too great from house to house, and members of each of the four classes live in each of the houses. We therefore looked at the answers to the morale questions house by house. We found, for example, that the smallest house on the campus, one containing seven students, where presumably the relationships among the students would be most congenial and close-knit, produced evidence of the lowest morale. Seventy-one per cent of the students in this house checked as one of their worries, "Your relation to a friend in college"—a much higher percentage than any of the other houses—43% checked "Loneliness" as a worry and, 83% checked the question, "Have there ever been times outside the regular college hours (Monday to Friday, nine to four) when you wished there were an adult around to talk to?"

Over the whole student body, 42% of the responses showed the students wished to have adults on the campus during evenings and weekends. When this was pursued further by discussion with the students, it became clear that the students were against the idea of residential counselors or faculty members, and that their wish was for the presence of faculty members around the campus, at student meetings, or as informal visitors to the dormitories, but not as representatives of college authority. The student house presidents were in fact in the role of residential counselors, and it became clear through further analysis and discussion that the quality of life within a given residence depended most of all on the qualifications of the house president for holding office. Student suggestions about this problem resulted in marked changes in the nominations and election procedures, and changes in the methods by which student choices for residence in a given house were screened and allocated.

To me this was one of the most revealing parts of the study. The combination of the research results and direct statement from a variety of students showed that the big reasons for student apathy or frustration—the world situation, public pressures, McCarthy, and so on— were less important than the spirit and personal relationships of the students among themselves. When left to themselves they often imported into the College the attitudes of the society outside it and found no countervailing forces at work within the student community to serve as educational aids. When one saw that a group of thirty students who lived together could develop negative, nagging, and emotionally unhealthy attitudes simply by the internal relationships established by three or four of their number who were working out their problems at the expense of the rest, the need for more structure in the administration of residence life became obvious.

It also became obvious that in the selection of a student body to function in a free community, it was of first importance to consider the personal attributes of the applicants every bit as seriously as their academic qualifications. The College had always acted on that philosophy, but never until this study had it been proven to be of such importance. Intellectually ambitious students with a drive toward personal gratification could, if present in sufficient numbers in a given residence, produce sufficient tension and difficulty within their own environment to prevent the healthy development of the students around them and to block their own growth. To choose a student body with regard mainly to academic competence and achievement is unwise not only in the decision it implies to give the privilege of private education only to a particular kind of student, but unwise in the effect it has on the conditions for the development even of those most intellectually gifted. To put it simply, a variety of personality characteristics among the students selected for liberal education is to be sought at least equally with geographic, academic, and other conventional criteria. This is true not merely for experimental and progressive colleges, but for those which are at present moving quickly toward the establishment of what are called high academic standards, by which is usually meant a record of high grades in high school.

The sophomore slump. One trend we thought we observed during the 1952 study was the general phenomenon of the sophomore slump. The freshmen of 1952 showed a strong and positive response to all morale questions; the sophomores of that year had many more complaints, worries, dissatisfactions, and criticism.

But when the 1953 returns were in, they showed that the 1952 freshmen kept most of the positive attitudes when they became sophomores, and the 1952 sophomores were again out of line when they became 1953 juniors. We looked into this and discovered that the situation in the houses where the sophomores lived was the clue to their low morale, and that the class division was irrelevant. We also found that the larger the size of the house, the smaller the groupings of friendships. Most of the students throughout the campus found it easy to make friendships, an overall figure of 43% had three to five close friends, 34% had more than five close friends, with about two-thirds of the students reporting that they knew between two hundred and two hundred and fifty students by name, only 1% knowing less than fifty. When we looked at the answers to questions about the adjustment of the students to Sarah Lawrence when they first came, the most important factor in making it successful were the friendships in the residences. Of the students 78% mentioned this, followed by 56% who mentioned the opportunity to talk to their dons.

As far as our theory of student self-government was concerned, the fact that the student adviser (appointed by a student committee) was helpful to only one quarter of the students in their first adjustment to college, indicated that either the student advisers weren't very good at it, or that students preferred to get their own advice where they could informally through their friends.

The "social" life. In a sense, this was also true as far as the social events of the campus involved any formal planning by student committees. These events were in the hands of a Student Entertainment Committee, elected annually, whose responsibility was to arrange whatever social life of a formal kind there was to be, including weekend entertainment. The campus was usually deserted on weekends, and the committee found that when it went to the trouble of arranging a party or planning a concert, or in general making the weekend at the college an interesting and stimulating one, very few students stayed. We felt that it would be useful to find out what the students usually did with their weekends, and how they felt about the quality of the social life, apart from the daily life of the residence. There are 30 weekends in the college year. Thirty-four per cent of the students spent all of them or more than 20 away from the campus, usually at home or at a friend's home, 26% spent from 13 to 20 away, 28% from 7 to 12, and 11% from 2 to 6. In other words, nearly 60% of the student body was away for about 60% of the weekends.

Since they did this of their own volition, and had the means of planning events for themselves if they wished to stay, we asked whether they were satisfied with this arrangement. We found that 67% thought there was something wrong with the way weekends were arranged at the College, 37% said they would have stayed had there been some-thing interesting to do. The criticism of the College's social life most often heard was that it did not exist on weekends. Yet when given a full opportunity to make it exist, the students were unable to plan anything for themselves which they found interesting enough to en-gage in. After seeing the results of the 1952 study, the College itself took the initiative in planning such events as intercollegiate con-ferences, tennis tournaments, student concerts, student theater per-formances on weekends, and discovered that in answer to the same questions in 1953, only 45% of the students as against the previous 67% found the social life inadequate.

Although the students themselves were unable to solve this problem, we did discover something about the way in which the students spent the time they had for recreation, social life, and entertainment. We asked for responses to a list of eighteen different activities which we could assume to be normal for the students to engage in in their spare time, at home or on the campus. At the head of the list the students put "engage in bull sessions" (72%), followed by "listen to records" (71%), "go to concerts, plays, etc." (66%), read newspapers (65%), read unassigned books (64%), write letters (59%), listen to the radio (52%), do household chores (49%), go to the movies (45%). Only 19% indicated that they watched television.* Their favorite hobbies in terms of frequency of mention were, reading 35%, music 30%, sports 28%; 17% reported that they had no hobbies.

These preferences for private activities with small groups of friends meant to us that the regular attitude which college students are as-sumed to possess—the wish for incessant togetherness, to live the in-tercollegiate sporting life, to be "social"—did not exist in any degree on the Sarah Lawrence campus. Although the students missed the regulation college events and wished there were more of them, they found substitutes in activities which on the whole seem preferable to to the things which might have been substituted. They wished their social life to take place around common intellectual interests rather

---

* There were only two television sets on the campus at that time.

than on the basis of conventional dating practices. I would conclude that our students had the great advantage of possessing private interests and occasional periods of loneliness.

The practice of self-government. We asked some direct questions about student government and the use of student freedom in rule-making and rule-keeping. We found that nearly one quarter of the student body did not think that the student Council represented them, with an increase in the percentages from class to class, 22% of the freshmen to 31% of the seniors. More than half the freshmen said that they did not know what the Council did, the percentages declining from class to class to 23% of the seniors.

To the statements "The discipline system would work better if dons were more aware of the rule-breaking and did more about it," and "Quite a few girls get away with an awful lot which nobody knows about," nearly 40% of the sophomores, juniors, and seniors said yes to the first one, as did 29% of the freshmen, and 55 to 65% of the students agreed that quite a few girls get away with an awful lot. Of the students 45% replied yes to the question, "I have never reported another student for breaking rules; I would feel like a tattle-tale." I would conclude from this that there had been about as much rule-breaking as we thought there had been and that the students felt that the faculty should take more responsibility for the organization of the student community.

The student and the curriculum. Another phenomenon of the 1950s had been the amount of criticism by the students of the free curriculum and unconventional methods at Sarah Lawrence, a kind of criticism which had not seemed to exist at the college during the 1930s and 1940s. Students began to ask questions at student meetings about why Sarah Lawrence offered no lecture and survey courses in Western civilization of the kind in effect at other colleges, why there was not more systematic coverage of departmental subject matter, why there could not be a grading system so that students would know their status as compared with each other and with students at other colleges. Some students requested examinations so that they would be able to tell whether or not they could handle the examinations given at other institutions, whether they were "as good as" students in other places.

We therefore asked for student views of the Sarah Lawrence educational methods and found that approximately 85 to 90% of the students supported the discussion method, many of them with comments about how to avoid having bad ones; most often they called for more positive direction by the teacher, and said they quickly became tired of hearing each other unless the teacher's direction was fairly firm.

When we asked a series of five questions as to the method by which students felt they gained most from their classes, 59% answered, "When the teacher lectures about half the time, and the class discusses points raised by the teacher," 32% answered, "When the teacher does not lecture, but always keeps the class discussion to the point," 19% replied, "When the class raises points for discussion, and the teacher and the students discuss whatever comes up." Nine percent replied, "When the teacher lectures most of the time and answers questions."

We followed this with a question as to which of the following items the students would like to see more of, or less of, in the work of classes and conferences, (a) free discussion, (b) lectures, (c) direction on the part of teachers, (d) tests, and found that 63% wanted more direction, 2% wanted less, and 32% didn't answer. Thirty-four percent wanted more lectures, 18% less, 49% did not reply; 31% wanted more free discussion, 19% less, 51% did not reply. Eleven percent wanted more tests, 29% less, 60% did not reply.

The large number of those who did not reply is probably due to the fact that so much depends on who the teacher is who is doing the lecturing, leading the discussion, or giving the direction. The trend of the replies is certainly toward a wish for more direct instruction and less freedom, but the mixture, for example of the 31% of those who want more free discussion when there is already so much of it at the College, the 29% who want fewer tests when there are scarcely any, and 34% who want more lectures, confuses the results and confuses me. I conclude that the students would have liked to have more lectures from people who lecture well, more discussion led by those who are good at it and who keep it on the point. This is confirmed both by written-in comment in the questionnaire, and the fact that although 36% of the freshmen asked for more "free discussion," there were only 19% of the seniors who did so. But the most important reply for the purposes of my enquiry is that 52% of the freshmen ask for more direction as do 76% of the seniors. Freshmen speak of "need for more guidance," "I have never been offered such a wide range of possibilities and I was overcome," "The field was so broad that it made independent research very difficult," "I was just not able to work profitably as independently as the teacher expected me to," "I made too many false starts, and got little profit from any of them."

A few seniors were critical of the independent study projects of conference work and their comments mostly were to the effect that they needed more help from teachers in discovering how and where to find material, and in putting a problem in shape as a workable subject for study; that they needed more supervision of the projects themselves. Yet the main preference (47%) of the students in carrying out independent study projects was for readings assigned by the teacher accompanied by additional reading selected by the student, with 22% who preferred "mainly selecting one's own reading from a suggested list," and 40% "choosing a problem oneself and searching it out independently." Only 5% preferred assigned readings for conference projects, and 16% preferred to be given a problem and find their own readings.

Again, I would have thought from informal student comment that the students wished to have a greater amount of control by faculty members in giving assigned readings rather than leaving so much to individual choice by the student. They had complained often of never being finished with anything, that the faculty always expected students to go on finding more things and doing more work than was called for in the assignment, and I had found much sentiment for clear-cut, specific assignments which were over when a specific amount of work had been done. This did not prove to be the case. If we combine the students who wished to select their own subjects for independent study and work from a suggested reading list, with those who wished to select their own subject and work out their own readings, they account for around 70% of the freshmen, 66% of the sophomores, 52% of the juniors, and 70% of the seniors.

We found that in choosing the courses they wished to take that the first criterion of the students was a special interest in the subject (98% of them listed this) followed by the second most important factor, discussion with the don (76%), with a general interest in the subject and the reputation of the teacher as third and fourth ranking criteria for selection. In the middle range of importance came advice from other students, special needs, such as preparation for graduate school, and choice based on special talents of the student.

Social and political attitudes. One other fact about the student attitude of the 1950s has caused a good deal of public comment—their lack of involvement in social issues or political action. As I have already indicated, after a lively period in the 1930s and 1940s when the student body as a whole was politically aware and often took action as a whole college on political issues, the Sarah Lawrence students of the 1950s were relatively quiescent and uninvolved. This has been true of students on other campuses, and most people have put it down to the pressures toward standard political attitudes imposed on the country by the congressional investigations and the harassment of liberal intellectuals in the universities.

As I saw the effects on students at Sarah Lawrence and elsewhere, this was certainly an important factor. Any association with liberal causes marked the individual as one who might be suspect of Communist affiliation; in the case of men students, the men did not wish to risk losing an opportunity for a good job after college by liberal political action, and no other kind of political action was sufficiently interesting to attract them; in the case of women students, the virus of anxiety traveled from the men and from their own families as well as from the public sources which affected everyone else.

But perhaps more important than these immediate causes is the fact that students, both men and women, share the political attitudes of their mothers and fathers, and that most of the college-going population is from conservative middle-income homes where involvement with liberal causes is relatively rare, as is a vigorous political attitude to American life in general.

The irony in the Sarah Lawrence situation was that the College has always been looked upon as a place where radical thinking is encouraged and fostered and where the freedom of thought is said to create students who become political radicals, when in fact, the students are on the whole conservative in their politics, and, as our research showed, are not influenced in a given political direction by their Sarah Lawrence education. The study of political attitudes on the basis of the questionnaire was made during the height of the McCarthy time when the College was attacked over a period of two and a half years by a variety of organizations and individuals. The effect of the complete freedom of political action given to the Sarah Lawrence students was that they responded positively to the defense of academic freedom by the College, but did very little on their own initiative either in arranging meetings to discuss political issues or in taking specific action.

The students were asked in 1952 and again in 1953, "How would you describe your own political point of view to someone else?" The results appear in the following table.

Political points of view	% of 324 students
Republican; conservative Republican; liberal Republican; liberal conservative	23
Democrat; conservative Democrat; New Deal Democrat; Stevenson Democrat	14
Liberal (no party affiliation, word "liberal" used)	28
Independent (vote for the best man) "Left" of liberal	5
Can't say; changing opinions; no strong convictions	12
"I wouldn't say"	2
Miscellaneous *	5
No answer to question	11
Total %	100

* Included such answers as "I believe in fair judgment"; "I'm middle-of-the-road"; "I believe in social reform."

Since the questionnaire was administered in 1952, as well as in 1953, the opportunity presented itself to ask, one month before the nominating conventions for the 1952 Presidential election, "Whom would you like to see win the 1952 Presidential election?"

	% of 339 Students
Republican (Eisenhower, Taft)	50
Democrat (e.g., Stevenson, Kefauver)	19
Other (e.g., a "liberal," e.g., Wm. Douglas)	8
Don't know yet	23
Total %	100

The students were asked whether they and their parents held the same political views, and if not, were their parents more, or less liberal. The 97.3% responses were:

About the same	63%
More liberal	1.3%
Less liberal	33%
No answer	2.7%
Total %	100

Next the students were asked, "Since being at Sarah Lawrence, have you changed your political views? Yes or no, and if yes, describe the change.

Change in Political Opinion by Class

	Freshmen % of 94	Sophomores % of 81	Juniors % of 79	Seniors % of 70	Total % of 324
Yes	25	20	33	40	29
No	75	80	67	60	71
					100%

This question appeared on both the 1952 and 1953 questionnaire and with approximately the same results in each case; that is to say, there are no statistically significant differences between the two sets of responses.

Of primary interest are (a) the direction of the change in political opinions of the students who say they have changed since coming to Sarah Lawrence, and (b) a comparison of the opinions of the students who say they have changed, with the opinions of those who say they have not. A total of 94 students, or 29% of the total, say they have changed their political opinions. The following table shows the direction of political change as indicated by the responses.

Direction of Political Change	% of 94 (students who have changed)
Have developed some opinions; had none before	13
Became more thoughtful; more understanding; aware of issues; less gullible; aware of complexities	42
Became more liberal; less conservative	19
Became more conservative; less liberal	19
Became "less radical" (words used)	3
Miscellaneous	4
Total %	100

I was surprised to find the statistic of 19% who became more conservative and 19% who became more liberal, since I would have assumed that the free situation of the campus would have induced a larger degree of change in a liberal direction. I of course might claim as liberals the 42% of the students who felt that they had become more thoughtful and aware of issues, less gullible, and more understanding.

In summary, about one-fourth of the student body described itself as Republican, with half the student body hoping a Republican would win the 1952 Presidential election; one-third of the students described their views as liberal or independent; 14% Democratic; 12% say their opinions are changing ones and they have no strong convictions. The remaining students, 16%, either did not answer the question, or the descriptions they have given of their points of view could not be reduced to the categories in use. There are no differences between freshmen, sophomore, junior, and senior classes on the general trends of political points of view. There is, however, a trend toward forming political opinion of some kind after the freshman year, since fewer students after that time reported that they had no strong convictions or that their opinions were shifting. A few more students in the senior year, as compared to the freshman and sophomore years, said that they had changed their political opinions since coming to Sarah Lawrence. About one-third, 29% of the total student body, reported change in political opinion.

We can conclude that there is certainly no conformity of political attitude among the students on the Sarah Lawrence campus, nor is there any uniformity of change in the direction of political attitude. The majority of students, 71% of them, do not report change. Of the 29% who do report change, about half feel they have become more interested in political issues, but do not report moving in any given direction.

On the basis of these findings it is clear that in the first half of the 1950s, Sarah Lawrence students (and possibly students in other colleges in about the same proportion) are conservative, that they tend to accept their society as they find it, that their college education does not affect their political affiliation in any marked degree. It is not the function of a college to make an effort to change students' political affiliation. It is its function to teach students to become aware of social and political issues, to enable them to reach independent judgments on the merits of such issues, and to understand and participate as citizens in the functioning of the American system of government. We know enough about the way the Sarah Lawrence students conduct their own community affairs to say that the initiative in raising political and social issues was not coming from them, and that unless the issues were raised in the context of classroom and course discussions, or in student meetings sponsored jointly by faculty and students, it is unlikely that they would have been raised at all.

CONCLUSION: TRANSACTIONAL RELATIONSHIPS AND INTELLECTUAL GROWTH

The shift in attitude of Sarah Lawrence students toward their own freedom is certainly real, when the comparison is made between the early 1950s and the 1930s and 1940s. If students are given responsibility and authority for an autonomous student community, without a direct and working connection with the two other essential community components—the faculty and the administration—the system grinds to a stop and ceases to function as a true community.

However, in the light of these findings, the fundamental principle of progressive theory remains intact: true intellectual growth is an inner process which feeds upon environmental factors of all kinds. The effects of emotional, social, and physical factors in the environment are just as crucial as the progressives have always said they were. It is also true that the development of ethical and social values through college education remains an important area of achievement for experimental education. But the formation of student attitudes, if left completely to the natural developments of an autonomous student community will not necessarily produce positive results. The growth in ethical sensibility occurs as an effect of the total college atmosphere, but the seed of idealism is sown in the environment by teachers and educators who put it there; it is not magically produced by the student community through the operation of a free social system.

In fact, it is possible to argue on the basis of our results that it is fallacious to assume, as the older progressive theory held, that absence of institutional authority and the award of freedom to the young in a radically democratic system will develop an understanding of democracy. We have found that in many cases it tended to foster authoritarian attitudes. The fallacy lies in assuming that because students have student rights and an equality of status with all other members of the campus community, including faculty and adminstration, therefore the role of the student is of the same character (and "equal" in this sense) as the status and role of the faculty and administration. If this fallacy is acted upon in educational planning, students may insist upon a student right to make decisions on all questions, regardless of competence, experience, or knowledge, in disregard of the rights and judgment of the faculty and the administration. Or it may result in such an amount of continuous student bickering over legalisms and procedural questions that no student enjoys any part of the work of self-government.

To put it at its simplest (and most obvious), the role of the teacher *is* different from that of the student, and no amount of mutual friendliness between student and teacher will change that role. Attitudes throughout the student community grow in a negative or positive direction according to the way in which the teachers play a part in the free system of the total community. The teacher does not contribute to student freedom by withdrawal from a going relationship with the student subculture, nor by the older nondirective, permissive approach to students. On the other hand, the alternative to permissive attitudes is not a revival of institutional authority to control the students, any more than the answer to student requests for an examination system, grades, survey courses, and a conventional academic apparatus is to give it to them.

The alternative is to accept, without the edge of disapproval, the plain fact that the contemporary student is different from his predecessors and is at once more mature and less emotionally energetic than the more rebellious ones of the 1930s and 1940s. Granted the character of this generation, their educational need is for a greater understanding by the student leaders of the role *they* are now playing. That understanding will have to come, not only from their own ranks, but from their teachers. Since at Sarah Lawrence the center of gravity of the College as an institution lies in the work of the students in their courses, the most powerful motivation, positively as well as negatively, lies in the expectations of the faculty for certain attitudes on the part of the students. To separate the two communities on the grounds that students must be kept free from institutional authority except of their own making is to deprive the whole community of its chief source of motivation.

The faculty-student relationship must be conceived as transactional rather than mutually autonomous. The danger to be avoided on the one hand is a kind of orthodox liberal piety which by matiness and good fellowship smothers a community with so much tolerance and understanding that everyone becomes a neutered, polite, and conformist liberal. The danger on the other hand is that if there are no clear-cut aims, rules, and procedures with sanctions and authority of some kind against violations, there is endless discussion, ambiguity, confusion, and emotional fatigue from devoting too much energy to discussion and not enough to getting on with the program.

The changes in the Sarah Lawrence program over the past ten years reflect a recognition of these factors in student life. They have occurred in three areas.

1. In the administration of student affairs, the college psychiatrist and the Dean now maintain a closer relationship than before with the presidents of the houses, sometimes through meetings with them as a group for discussion of typical cases, or through consultations with individual presidents on general house problems. The student chairman of the House Presidents Council is much more active than before in regular consultation with the Dean, is better informed as to the affairs of each house, is closer to the other house presidents. This has tended to strengthen her authority. Student freedom remains unimpaired by any additional rules or supervision, although there is greater clarity in the relation of the student to her college. An Associate Dean has been appointed to work directly with students in their community life and with the faculty, particularly with the dons.

2. The college courses now include a greater variety of methods to give students an opportunity to learn where they stand in relation to the expectations of the College; although 90% of the instruction is carried on in classes averaging ten students in size, a group of larger classes, from twenty-five to forty in size has now been installed for all sophomores and juniors, with the lecture used for part of the instruction; tests are administered as requested or needed, although no grades are assigned; there are in some cases clearer *a priori* indications of course content, assignments are more often specific and less general than before; some deadlines for assignments are set to cover shorter periods of work; advice on suitable course programs for students is more precise: planning for careers is more specific in terms of appropriate subject matter; more information on career planning is now available through the appointment of a director of vocational planning with whom students may confer as they would with their dons.

3. The social and recreational life is more regularly organized through a student committee with representatives in each of the houses. The representatives are responsible for informing the committee about ideas, suggestions, and needs which emerge from discussions in the houses. Intercollegiate conferences have been organized to bring to the campus students from other colleges who share the intellectual interests of Sarah Lawrence students. A permanent Conference Committee of students plans the conferences for each year; a joint student-faculty committee meets weekly to plan public events and to bring to the attention of the student body, through meetings

with faculty speakers and others, current issues of political and social importance.

Coincident with these local changes both in the method and the attitude of Sarah Lawrence students has come a shift in the general attitude of students on campuses throughout the country. The members of the generation of the 1960s now assume that their responsibility is to make their own way, that their education is in their own hands, and that educational institutions exist to give the student an opportunity to work, not to push him into it, coax him into it, or to coerce him by threats of expulsion. The situation is open to anyone who wishes to take the time and the trouble to help the students of the 1960s toward their own fulfillment. They need all the freedom we can give them. But they need equally to learn by example whom and what they can respect.

PART VII

THE EFFECTS

OF COLLEGE EDUCATION

One might hope that having come so far, having seen so much of the student in the college environment, we might now be offered clear demonstrations of all kinds of desirable effects of college. It appears that this is not to be so. Dr. Webster, Dr. Freedman, and Dr. Heist in Chapter 24 and Dr. Freedman in Chapter 25 have no alternative but to begin with what in this volume has become a refrain: there has been too little research and there are great difficulties in the way of our finding out what we want most to know. Indeed, we are offered in these chapters empirical support for some rather strong statements made at the beginning of this book: that there is a remarkable discrepancy between the wide public acceptance of the value of college education and the paucity of demonstrated knowledge that it does some good, and that the claims of rival systems of education continue to be almost entirely without support in established fact.

Still, the picture is not entirely dark. Webster, Freedman, and Heist, in their discussion of the methodological problems involved in studying the development of students in college, show that the difficulties can be, indeed are being overcome; and Freedman shows in Chapter 25 that the even more difficult—and even more crucial—problem of appraising the lasting effects of college can be attacked effectively when energy and resources are sufficient. More than this, in Chapter 24 we are offered convincing evidence that students do change in some desired ways—at least in some colleges—and in Chapter 25 we are shown that at least some of these changes are lasting. The authors of both chapters are persuaded that the increasing use of good research procedures will not only demonstrate more kinds of effects of college than are now known but will so improve our understanding of college education as to make possible an increasing number of favorable outcomes.

Webster, Freedman, and Heist, after explaining the use of psychological tests in the study of changes in students, and after discussing the deficiencies of grades as measures of academic progress, consider the evidence of changes during college in skills and information, in mental ability, in attitudes and values, and in other personality characteristics.

There is no doubt that college students gain in skill and information but the authors conclude their discussion of the matter with the statement: "how much is retained is unknown." It remains for Freedman, in Chapter 25, to point up the paradox: increased skill and knowledge are widely supposed to be the major marks of the educated person and they are the easiest of all personal characteristics to measure, yet there does not seem to be a single study in which alumni have been compared with seniors in terms of achievement test scores. It is as if there were a conspiracy of silence on this point, as if educators well knew what interviews with young alumni in fact reveal—that very little of the content of college courses is retained three or four years after graduation. It seems that recognition of this fact would be bound to lead to de-emphasis upon the content of the college curriculum, or to the study of ways to increase retention, or to the generation of theory concerning how the teaching of certain contents in other ways may favor the development of desired characteristics in the person. So far, there does not seem to be much movement in any one of these directions.

Concerning mental abilities, Webster, Freedman, and Heist marshall evidence in support of a fact that has not been well understood: that ability itself—not mere achievement or knowledge—increases under some conditions during the college years. There is also evidence that the more able—the "brighter"—the youngster to begin with, the longer will his abilities continue to grow.

In the area of attitudes and values, recent studies, as well as those performed twenty-five years ago, show that between the freshman and the senior years in college there is, in general, change in the direction of greater liberalism and sophistication in political, social, and religious outlook. This is a more encouraging view than that taken by Jacob (1957); but, since the studies discussed report on average differences and not very large ones at that, and since it is by no means clear that observed changes were due to educational activities deliberately undertaken by the college, the authors see no occasion for general rejoicing.

More recent studies of college students have tended to stress, not attitudes and values themselves, but underlying, more generalized, dispositions of personality. Here the authors give particular attention to studies carried out by the Mellon Foundation at Vassar College, and they provide some support for the theory outlined in Chapter 6; for example, there is evidence that during the college years students in general move from an authoritarian position in the direction of greater freedom of impulse and greater complexity in the functioning of the ego.

Webster, Freedman, and Heist then pass on to the highly complex question of what kinds of colleges and what particular features of the college environments are responsible for different kinds of observed changes in students. There are some interesting studies in this area, but the overwhelming impression left by the authors' survey is of how little is known about these most crucial educational problems. But the authors are not discouraged. On the contrary, it is their view that a whole new area for research is just now being opened up. Indeed, many of their concrete suggestions for future research could hardly have been made were there not already more than a little activity in this field.

Freedman undertakes in Chapter 25 a task of large scope and complexity. Concerned with determining the possible lasting effects of college education he has to be prepared to give attention to any aspect of personality or behavior that may have been affected by experience in college; and since any change in any feature of the person, that occurs between college entrance and the time of assessment of alumni, could be due to any one of numerous inter-related features of the college environment, or to events intervening between graduation and assessment, his search for determinants is bound to range over a very broad area. It would be impossible to accomplish this task within the scope of a chapter—or of a book—were it not for two considerations: one is that studies of college alumni have been few enough in number so that a review of them is a reasonable undertaking, and the other is that Freedman has himself been involved enough with studies of Vassar graduates so that he is able to focus upon significant problems and leads for future research.

Freedman's review of studies of the sociological characteristics of college graduates provides ample confirmation for the assertion of Riesman and Jencks (Chapter 3) that college is the initiation rite for the middle class. It is not only in respect to income and occupation that college graduates, as compared with other citizens, are middle-class; this class status is also expressed in the greater stability of the lives of alumni, their conscientious voting behavior, their conservative political and economic outlook, their greater tolerance of political and social dissidents. When one examines trends over time in this area it seems that the economic benefits of college-going are decreasing, while gains in enlightenment with respect to political and social questions are increasing.

Given the evidence of Chapter 24 that seniors are more sophisticated and enlightened in their attitudes and values than are freshmen, we naturally raise the question of whether such gains are maintained —and for how long—after the graduate returns to the outside world of business and suburbia. On this point, Freedman assembles evidence that is at once encouraging and chilling. A number of sound studies, widely separated in time as well as in place, show that in general the changes achieved in college are sustained for at least three or four years afterward. There is some evidence that gains are maintained for very long periods of time, perhaps indefinitely—and this introduces the chilling note. Freedman's study of the attitudes and values of Vassar alumnae of various generations, going back to the class of 1904, leads him to the conclusion that the college years are not only crucially formative ones as far as attitudes and values are concerned but they offer what amounts to a "last chance" for enlightenment before entering the "thruway" of life. He bases this conclusion not only on evidence that attitudes and values persist for long times after college but also on the observation that differences among alumnae groups of different generations tend to correspond to differences in the climate of opinion that prevailed when these alumnae were in college. The challenge to educators is direct and formidable.

In dealing with the question of how well developmental changes in other aspects of personality are maintained after graduation Freedman has to rely almost entirely on the Vassar studies. The evidence is that, in general, gains in the direction of greater complexity of personality, made in college, are maintained three to four years after graduation. But change does not usually continue after college. Instead, what seems to occur mainly is a kind of stabilization. When groups of young alumnae were retested with the use of a variety of personality tests three or four years after graduation, the only really significant differences lay in the greater stability, freedom from anxiety, and general psychological well-being shown in the later testing. Interviews lent support to this finding. Taking this evidence in conjunction with evidence that personality change in college is much greater in the first two than in the last two years, Freedman is led to assume that there is a developmental phase, marked primarily by increasing stabilization of personality, that begins around the junior year in college and extends well into the alumnae years.

When one observes college graduates and notes that some have accomplished much and others little, that some are leading happy and effective lives while others have become burdens upon society, a question that naturally arises is what, if anything, in the college experience may have helped to bring about such differences. Research on this complicated question has usually produced inconclusive or even contradictory answers; for example, one study finds a relationship between grades in college and achievement in later life, while another study finds no such relationship. Freedman and his colleagues at least develop some new conceptual tools that may well open the way to better insights in this area. And they insist that performances in college must be seen in context, if their implications for the future are to be made clear. Thus, high grades earned by *Overachievers with Future Family Orientation* are one thing, and high grades earned by *High Achievers* quite something else as far as the future after college is concerned. And so for other educational *patterns* distinguished among Vassar students and alumnae (see also Brown, Chapter 16).

Probably Freedman's main argument is that in order to understand the lasting effects of college we have to see the place of college within the whole life cycle—or at least within a developmental course extending from childhood to adult life. This permits us to see that the college experience is utilized in different ways by different people, and that it has different functions in different lives. The proper study of the effects of college, then, is the study of lives; and such study must in the present stage of our knowledge rely mainly upon intensive interviews. Freedman concludes his chapter with a report on interview studies of Vassar alumnae. He organizes the discussion around some of the major problems or issues that confront educated women in our society, for example, marriage vs. career, achievement and identity, the problem of continued growth, and he shows that how these problems are met depends not alone upon college experience and antecedent events but also upon what happens during the years immediately after college—not least upon the kind of man the alumna marries.

Until a few years ago it would hardly have occurred to the psychologist or psychiatrist who wished to understand the development and characteristic functioning of a particular adult personality to look to the college years for important determining events. Attention would have been primarily focused on childhood experience, and then, next in order of importance, on the contemporary life situation. Probably the greatest significance of the two chapters that follow lies in their evidence that some important changes in the personality itself do take place during the college years and later. This means that students of personality development cannot any longer neglect these periods as they have in the past; they will have to study the college student and the young adult as a part of their regular work, and not merely when they give incidental attention to education. If they do, then traditional educational research, as it continues to find out more about what methods have what effects with what kinds of students, will now be supplemented and supported by new talents and new techniques.

24

Harold Webster, Mervin Freedman, and Paul Heist

Personality Changes
in College Students

Students change in many ways during college. Usually there are increases in the amounts of information possessed about various topics, and in degree of skill in performing certain tasks. There are changes in interests, which are often accompanied by changed attitudes toward the self and the world. And in some cases there are more fundamental personality changes, accompanied by the emergence of new values.

College students are available for study for a number of years, and it would seem a simple matter to record numerous systematic observations which could be used in the best scientific tradition to inform us about the lives of young persons and how they develop. This kind of research is, however, beset by numerous difficulties. There has been little agreement concerning either the importance of various kinds of postadolescent changes, or how best to study them. From our present perspective, it may well be that the obvious and easily measured changes are less important than more subtle ones.

Individual differences among college freshmen (Chapter 5) and differences among colleges (Chapter 21) are so large that we should not expect the same changes in all college students. Also, the absence of comparable control groups of noncollege subjects makes it difficult to distinguish change having its source in the college experience from other change due to other experiential or maturational influences. Analytical and statistical methods appropriate for attacking the problems that arise in intensive longitudinal studies are only partially developed; some difficulties that complicate the problem of designing instruments for measuring mental change will be described later.

Studies of college students will be more meaningful when the social function of the college is better understood, for personality development always takes place within social institutions that have aims or purposes. Psychoanalytic studies of development, for example, have emphasized phenomena that have meaning in relation to the family. College students are subjected to many extrafamilial influences, to which their reactions vary greatly, depending upon their earlier development. We need to learn more about the effects on students of differences and similarities between the home and the college cultures. Even more important, we need to know about the reciprocal influences which students might exert in order to modify these cultures.

College students are expected to adjust to the culture; change and development are acceptable only to the extent that they do not lead to "maladjustment," which is considered a problem for counselors and psychotherapists. The value of adjustment, in the sense that it entails minimizing the amount of effort or distress required of the individual in order to get along, has been increasingly questioned by social observers during the last decade. There has probably been too little criticism of conditions under which the individual is expected to conform.

Parents will probably continue, nevertheless, to hope that their children will have "no problems of adjustment" in going away to college. In America the college is regarded as an ally of the parents in the prolongation of adolescence, a time in life when there happens to be a maximum concern with—and perhaps in recent years a maximum respect for—cultural standards and values. In our affluent society college students now regard social issues or movements as irrelevant to more immediate problems; attaining adulthood is not viewed as a problem related to cultural change. Consequently a conservative attitude has prevailed.

Perhaps conservatism and the desire for stability of values has increased in reaction to the increased instability of world conditions. Wheelis (1958) and Snow (1959), among other writers, have described how it has become necessary, because of accelerating social changes, for educated persons everywhere to undergo basic value changes; for the first time in history this has become necessary for large numbers of persons during the span of a single generation. Yet there seems to be little thought given to this fact, even in our institutions of higher learning. Burkhardt (1959) has urged colleges to make radical changes in their educational programs in order to maintain integration of curricula under new and rapidly changing conditions. But resistance to change affects educators, too, who continue to seek stability in established standards and practices.

Traditionally, Americans have tended to deny the importance of individual differences. There has always been the danger that the ideal of equal opportunity for all would be misconstrued to mean that all persons are equal—on almost any characteristic. Recently the tendency to view college students as a homogeneous mass seems to have increased; just as it is supposed that, individually, they will remain basically unchanged during college, they are also viewed as practically indistinguishable, each from the other, in needs, aspirations, and development. Instructors who believe that students are all alike are of course in no position to help educate them individually. Conversely, students who see most adults, including parents and teachers, as personifications of a common set of stabilized cultural values are not likely to change much during college, or to see the need for change. The denial that important human differences exist also makes education more difficult, because it is intrinsic to the sciences and the arts that distinctions and changes be recognized and studied; and this is no less true of social science, which must focus increasingly upon group and individual differences and changes.

These introductory remarks merely suggest the complexities which must be faced today in studies of personality change in college students. Despite the difficulties that have been mentioned, however, it is possible to discuss in general terms some of the more obvious kinds of changes that have actually been observed in college students, and to pose some research problems. In the following section we shall first consider a more immediate research problem, however; one that has persisted partly because of cultural conservatism, or cultural lag.

THE USE OF MENTAL TESTS FOR STUDYING CHANGES IN STUDENTS

The modern social scientist knows that personality does not develop in a vacuum, and he is therefore interested in social, religious, and political beliefs or dispositions. Accordingly, he often needs to assess persons' attitudes toward parents, government, sex, deity, minority groups, and the like. But since these topics are often controversial, he may find himself in hot water. He may be attacked as unscientific or subversive (Nettler, 1959; Whyte, 1956) and it then becomes difficult for him to explain what he is trying to do without seeming unduly defensive. The study of personality is still, to use Pinner's expression, a "dissensual" discipline (Chapter 27).

Nevertheless, if we are really to "educate our publics," there seems to be no alternative to offering explanations. This is easier said than done, for much that might be explained is highly technical. For example, how does a personality test, or scale, work?

Any mental test is simply a device for arranging persons in order of the amount of some characteristic that, by inference, they possess. Scores for the responses to items that make up the test are added to give a total test score for each person. Consequently, the persons can be arranged in the order of their total scores, from low to high. Briefly, we say of any mental test, or scale, that it "orders persons." Different tests are constructed for the purpose of ordering persons, according to the amounts of different kinds of characteristics that they possess, for example, information, aptitudes, attitudes, and interests. In a single personality instrument, there may be a dozen or more scales, each of which orders the respondents on a different characteristic, or "trait."

How dependable is the inference concerning the relative amounts of characteristics that persons possess? There are two ways of checking it. First, the correctness, or precision, of any ordering obtained from a single administration of a test may be checked by statistical inference (Lord, 1955; Webster, 1960); if the test orders persons with relatively few errors (few departures from the true order), it is said to possess high *reliability*. Second, a particular order can be compared with other orders of the same persons on other characteristics that are of significance in psychology and education; it can be compared with orders resulting from different approaches to the same behavior, and the kind of *validity* which the test is said to possess will depend largely upon these "correlations with other variables."

A mental test is a measurement device that is useful for scientific purposes. The administration of a mental test is a scientific experiment, which is successful if the errors of measurement are sufficiently small, and if the characteristic measured is of importance in psychological theory. By analogy with physical science, administrations of test items are simply measurement trials, the sampling errors from which can be used to estimate the true differences among persons. If constants for human populations are also to be estimated, then, of course, persons, as well as items, must be sampled.

But the personality psychologist must obtain his data directly from persons. He is not in the position of a physicist or biologist who can closet himself in a laboratory, ignore social pressures, and emerge later with findings which make possible new weapons or vaccines. Personality tests are subject to public scrutiny and to the inexpert criticisms of academicians and laymen alike, who rarely understand the underlying principles.

Tests are substitutes for and, in some respects, improvements upon interviews. When there are large numbers of subjects it is seldom feasible to interview them intensively enough to learn very much about their basic personality characteristics. There has been a popular misconception that interview data are very helpful for predicting behavior, but in practice it has generally been found that test data are superior for this purpose. Interviews are indispensable for studying change in college students, but they serve rather different purposes and therefore cannot supplant test data. Interviews are especially superior to tests for basic research in which there is uncertainty about the exact questions to be asked.

It would be impractical to attempt to understand changes that occur in college students without relying heavily upon mental tests, including personality tests. Data obtained by other methods are less economical, less objective, less reliable, and less valid. But even the more precise tests order subjects imperfectly, and this seriously limits the usefulness of the test-retest difference scores which must be used for estimating the true change (Kelley, 1947; Lord, 1956, 1958; McNemar, 1958). It is impossible to measure change by means of test-retest difference scores unless the tests used have high reliability; otherwise the difference scores contain such a high proportion of random error that they are meaningless. An exact solution to the problem of *comparing* individuals or groups on amounts of change will probably have to await the development of new kinds of scales (Fagot, 1959; Siegel, 1956).

In addition to the criticism that personality tests are invalid or that they do not work at all, one sometimes hears the opposite complaint: they work too well, or they give too much power to the psychologist. Test data can be misused, of course, but so can any other kind of personal information, including interview data. It is always necessary to protect the privacy and best interests of the individuals who provide the information.

In summary, the use of mental tests, and especially personality tests, is viewed unsympathetically by large numbers of otherwise well-informed persons. This may be true because tests, unlike some measuring instruments, must be used in full view of, and with the cooperation of, the public. It is therefore mandatory, if research psychologists continue to use tests, that they demonstrate for others the scientific merits of testing. This will not be easy to do, partly because the explanations required pose difficult problems of communication. If we are to improve our understanding of the personality changes that take place during college, the evidence indicates that we have no alternative but to rely increasingly on test-retest data.

The following sections will be concerned with various personality changes that are important in college students, and that are currently studied by a variety of approaches, including mental testing.

CHANGES IN SKILLS, IN INFORMATION, AND IN MENTAL ABILITY

The change most generally expected of college students is the gradual acquisition of skills and information. Among all the kinds of change that occur, this one is most widely sanctioned as a legitimate educational goal, partly because it is thought to be essential for work to be undertaken later, but also because it is believed that it can be achieved individually by hard work. The value of individual effort that produces tangible results is acknowledged generally in our culture, and colleges have been eager to prove themselves by emphasizing the importance of their own tangible rewards, the most immediate of which are grades and diplomas.

The acquisition of skills and information is not only the most generally acceptable goal of education, but it has also been the easiest to measure by means of examinations. It has often been shown by means of achievement examinations that skills and information possessed by students increase during college. For example, in a study by Learned and Wood (1938) large samples of college students were tested for various kinds of academic achievement. Among a great deal of evidence of increases in skills and information was the finding that 85% of the sophomores tested in 1930 showed gains in achievement scores by 1932, the senior year. It is not known how much is retained after graduation.

The "grade-point-average" is regarded by many teachers—perhaps a large majority today—as an inadequate measure of educational growth. There are a number of reasons for this. First, most instructors directly delimit the meaning of assigned grades by informing students, usually early in courses, that grades will be based only upon specific kinds of material, usually assigned reading or problem-solving skills, the retention of which can easily be tested later. Second, in experiments where faculty are asked to identify students for whom the college has been most successful in its aims, those named are not always A-students

(Brown, 1959). Third, studies of college graduates, for example, Vassar alumnae (Freedman, see Chapter 25), reveal that grades achieved in college are usually obscurely related to functioning or performance after graduation. Fourth, college grades are only moderately related to identifiable antecedent variables (see Fishman, Chapter 20). Fifth, interviews show that the motives impelling students to achieve high grades are often indistinguishable from the desire simply to please and to obey parents, or similar authorities, who happen to value high grades. Sixth, students and teachers alike often suggest that high grades are only *formal* requirements—requirements for graduate school, prerequisites for later professional status, and the like—and it is inferred that grades cannot at the same time be measures of general educational status or development. Seventh, just as the achievement of high grades is insufficient evidence that education is taking place, failure to obtain high grades may not indicate that education has *not* taken place; at least this is found to be the case in studies of persons later identified as creative or highly productive (MacKinnon, 1959). Eighth, owing to the kind of curriculum that exists in most colleges, grades are insufficient as indicators of educational progress but are, nevertheless, necessary for that purpose; there have also been some educational experiments, however, in which grades were shown to be unnecessary. Ninth, it is now known that measures other than grades *are* related to personal growth and development (see below). Finally, nearly everyone knows a few students in whom the need to achieve high grades seems to interfere with the educational process.

Nevertheless, despite their obvious limitations, grades are not likely to be abolished. Indeed they are undoubtedly becoming more, rather than less, difficult to eliminate. Increasing numbers of young people are attending college, and grades based largely upon achievement examinations are a part of the traditional bureaucratic machinery for "processing" these students; also, emphasis on formal requirements for admission into the various occupational specialities, or into graduate school, is increasing rather than decreasing, and assigned grades are one of these requirements.

Acquisition and retention of skills and information require, of course, more than mere knowledge of the content of various fields, which is most readily measured by grades. Involved also are diverse kinds of intellectual functioning. Perusal of college catalogues shows that specified among the goals of education are enhancement of such qualities as independence of judgment, critical thinking, creativity, freedom from irrational prejudice, and the like. The extent to which grades reflect such characteristics is almost completely unknown.

A conspicuous exception to the dearth of research on this problem are the studies reported by Dressel and Mayhew (1954) and by Dressel (1958). These authors summarize and evaluate eleven years of investigation of programs of general education. The American Council on Education's Committee on Measurement and Evaluation had decided to attempt to evaluate the extent to which improvement in the ability to think critically and to communicate effectively took place among students enrolled in certain programs of general education. The following passage from Dressel and Mayhew's report illustrates the kinds of pioneering studies that were carried out and the complex nature of their design (p. 66).

After considering a number of objectives frequently claimed for general education courses in social science, the Intercollegiate Committee on Social Science Objectives selected critical thinking for its area of particular inquiry. The meaning of critical thinking in social science was specified in a list of abilities and was then exemplified by test situations and examples of student behavior. After the members of the committee were convinced of the validity of their conception of critical thinking in social science and had tried out on students various kinds of appraisal techniques, an objective-type test of Critical Thinking in Social Science was developed, revised, and printed in a final form. This test was administered to a great many entering freshmen at a number of participating colleges, and to these same students or to comparable groups at the end of the freshman year and at the end of the sophomore year. The changes in test scores over these time intervals were studied with a view to determining their magnitude and the factors associated with them. In general it was found that students gained in ability to think critically in social science over a period of a year, although the size of these gains varied widely, depending on the institutions that students attended. Attempts to teach critical thinking in social science by making minor changes in particular courses did not appear to result in greater growth than was found in courses not making overt attempts to teach this skill. Attempts to relate growth in critical thinking ability to course organization or to specific teachers suggested that both of these were highly important, although the research could not identify specific factors that seemed to be operative.

The problem of understanding the relationship between the process of acquiring knowledge, as measured by achievement tests, and the measured abilities and other personality characteristics of students is a complex one, the investigation of which has hardly begun.

Changes in mental ability. During childhood there are dramatic yearly increases in the ability to perform tasks that require reasoning, memory, judgment, and various kinds of perceptual and motor skills. From year to year these increments of ability become smaller for most of the tasks that are sampled by standard intelligence tests. As a result, it has been widely believed that by age 16 or 17 further increases in mental ability are negligible. This is an absurd oversimplification of a complex phenomenon of great importance, an oversimplification that persists despite growing evidence to the contrary (Pinneau and Jones, 1958).

There are large individual differences in the time of life at which a maximum, or ceiling, of measured mental ability is reached. Some individuals will fail to gain beyond age 18, but many will continue to gain after age 21 (Bayley, 1957). In a study by Bayley and Oden (1955) gifted adults were found to make substantial gains in reasoning ability even after age 30, and the obtained gains were substantially greater for the gifted subjects of either sex than for their spouses. A number of test-retest studies of growth in mental abilities (for example, Bayley, 1956, Figure 25) demonstrate that the more intelligent subjects at any particular age, in comparison with less intelligent persons of the same age, are not only increasing in measured ability at a faster rate, but also are further from their point of maximum ability (they are further both in time and in amount of ability). An immediate corollary is that at any given age, persons of higher ability in these samples could expect a greater total increase in ability in the future than could persons of lower ability. Of course, curves for single individuals sometimes show deviations from this, over the years, in the form of rather marked ups and downs; but usually even the individual curves show the same trend that is so striking for composite longitudinal data.

Many other observations agree with those just cited. For example, mental defectives usually reach their approximate maximum ability at an earlier age than do persons of average intelligence, just as the latter usually reach an approximate maximum earlier than gifted people. In general, the more complex an organism, or any growing organization, the longer will be the period required to reach maturity, or maximum development. This is true phylogenetically, for the period of dependence and great immaturity following birth lengthens as we move from species to species toward man. Terman and Oden (1947) reported that, in general, gifted persons are unlikely to become maximally productive until well after age 40.

Further increase in mental ability may therefore be anticipated for many students after they enter college; and marked increases in measured aptitude have been observed for some students (Florence, 1947; McConnell, 1934; Silvey, 1951). Even though the observed increases are striking, future improvement of intelligence tests will probably reveal even more ability change, both in kind and in degree. For college students are expected to perform tasks that require more ability, that is, more advanced reasoning, skill, judgment, and the like, than we are currently able to measure. For many tasks expected of college students, norms for younger persons *either do not or cannot exist.* For example, college students drive automobiles, solve integral equations, understand propaganda, and write poems. Concerning the simplest of these, automobile driving, data collected by insurance companies suggest that judgment in male drivers has not matured sufficiently before age 25 to entitle them to the ordinary premium rates. Both learning and mental ability are in a highly undeveloped state in college freshmen in comparison with older students. For example, abilities in philosophy, art, and mathematics are undoubtedly very poorly developed, even in "brilliant" college freshmen.

We could have written *especially* in brilliant freshmen. For we have noted that the higher the potential mental ability, or capacity, the less likely it is to have been approximated by the time of admission to college. And, therefore, the freshman student of superior ability will, more often than not, be *less mature, in terms of his own developing ability,* than will his less gifted friends. Superior students mature later than other students, and this should be taken into account in their education. The erroneous idea that gifted persons mature early has undoubtedly arisen because of comparisons of their behavior with that of others of the same age. Such comparisons provide evidence of superior performance by the gifted, but they cannot give information about the growth or maturing of ability within the individual. Records of the early precocity of geniuses may seem at first to contradict such a theory—until we also take into account their later functioning. The theory is certainly valid for such men as Beethoven, Freud, and Picasso, whose later productions reflect increased maturity.

Americans often deny that individual differences in ability are of much importance in education. It is commonly believed that any student's intellect can be trained by the simple expedient of giving him enough work to do. As a result the ablest freshmen enrolled at the "better" liberal arts colleges today are likely to say, in interviews, that they do not have time to think. And in the "more typical" liberal arts colleges they complain that a lot of sheer memorizing of minute details is required, and that the work is neither new nor challenging.

At the same time the student of low ability is not likely to be able to keep up in either of these kinds of institutions. There seems little doubt that any student can benefit from education beyond secondary school, *providing* he is not expected to compete directly with those who far exceed him in ability. We have interviewed students almost all of whose waking moments were spent memorizing material in order barely to remain in college. Even though such cases are not especially common, they are certainly no tribute to higher education today. Too often the only adults who might give the advice that would lead less capable students to choose less demanding academic programs are those who believe that individual differences in ability can somehow be ignored or minimized.

Even though the more intelligent freshman is likely to be less mature than others, he is well able, because of his high ability, to profit from great freedom in his studies; probably honors programs are to his advantage. Because the total change in his personality during college, including the increase in ability, is likely to be greater than average, however, it follows that he may be able to use even more adult guidance, tailored to his needs, than can those of less promise.

The recognition that students differ widely in intelligence, and also that they vary in their rates of mental growth during college, need not imply that more typical students will be either ignored or less well educated. Nor does it imply that constructive change will take us in the direction of creating an "intellectual elite." It is especially important to keep in mind that measures of ability can reflect only a part of personality functioning, and that, consequently, they will probably always be insufficient predictors of later intellectual performance (Fishman, Chapter 20; Heist and Webster, 1959). Increased interest in exceptional students, including the slow as well as the gifted, should help us to understand all kinds of students. Florence (1947, p. 81) has urged that "Individual faculty members must accept the responsibility of providing for varying rates of growth and different types of development," and Gregg (1957) has presented a number of ideas about the education of early and late-maturing students.

As we come to know more about the educational process it will be found that, owing to the complexity of personality, there are more and more students who are exceptional in some way. Study and appreciation of the diversity among students is more profitable than inventing reasons for ignoring their differences. The individual colleges could make a start at this by accepting more responsibility for understanding both differences in ability and differences in the rates at which abilities mature among their students.

CHANGES IN VALUES AND ATTITUDES

The functioning of personality is reflected by numerous observable characteristics, among the most important being interests, attitudes, and values. Attitudes toward the self, toward others, and toward institutions reveal to some extent the underlying motives (or needs) and values that are more central to personality, in the sense discussed by Sanford (see Chapter 6). When education produces important effects, it is likely to alter what is valued; in turn, changes in values influence attitudes and interests. In the actual developmental process the reverse also occurs, because new experience leads to modifications of interests and attitudes, and over a period of time the central values also become involved. In this process interests and attitudes tend to be interdependent; the diversification and deepening of interests, which is commonly observed in young adults, is often accompanied by modifications of attitudes, which in turn can lead to new or changed interests.

In the following presentation of research on changes in personality a brief historical treatment of earlier studies will be followed by a discussion of recent and contemporary investigations that have emphasized the importance of particular personality characteristics in the course of individual development. Next, some studies—all too few in number—that have related personality change to variations among and within college environments will be reviewed. Finally, there will be discussion of the general problems that have emerged.

It should be remembered that although attitudes and values are treated in the following discussion as if they were separable features of personality, they are in fact bound up with aptitudes, abilities, and other cognitive characteristics, some of which have been discussed earlier; but the relationships are often indirect or obscure (Heist and Webster, 1959; Mayhew, 1958). For example, it has often been found that authoritarian attitudes are negatively correlated with aptitude measures, but the interpretation of this fact has been subject to controversy. As another example, Kagan and his colleagues (1958) found that projective test data of children who showed large gains in intelligence over a few years differed in a number of ways from similar data for children who, over the same period, had shown decreasing IQ's. The observed differences are partly attributable to differences in motivation and attitude. In general, cognitive and motivational characteristics are interrelated within personality in very complex ways.

Early studies: cross-sectional and longitudinal. Although the earlier studies were often quite limited in scope, they provide a useful background for current investigations. Quite a few of the earlier studies compared concurrent (cohort) college classes on attitudes or values; but as Corey (1936) noted, it could not properly be assumed that the differences observed were identical to those that would have been obtained by retesting the same subjects as they proceeded through college. The sometimes exasperating technical difficulties inherent in the collection and analysis of longitudinal data should not serve as an excuse for avoiding longitudinal studies. On the other hand, chronological age is highly correlated with general development and easy to relate to secular social phenomena; therefore, age-level (as distinct from longitudinal) data may also be helpful for understanding human development, especially in relation to varying subcultures. For example, in a study carried out in the 1930s by Nelson (1938), which used data from eighteen institutions, it was found that differences between the four college classes were greatest in state universities and Quaker colleges, least for other denominational institutions. Freshmen were more homogeneous in attitudes than seniors, and, on the average, more conservative than upperclassmen. In some studies at Vassar College many freshmen-senior mean differences were of about the same magnitude whether cohort or longitudinal samples were used (Webster, 1956, 1958). Testing subjects of identical ages in different decades has also proved useful, for it reveals cultural trends in attitudes (Buck, 1936; Pressey, 1946).

Most of the earlier longitudinal investigations of changes in student values and attitudes revealed small but significant changes in one or a few kinds of attitudes. Usually investigators were limited to interpretation of test-retest scores on the Thurstone attitude scales (Thurstone and Chave, 1929), or on scales of the Allport-Vernon *Study of Values* (Allport and Vernon, 1931). Except for minor discrepancies, the differences observed would still be described today as changes in the direction of a *more liberal attitude on social issues and a more tolerant attitude toward persons.* Typical of careful longitudinal studies of the 1930s were those by Jones (1938) and by Farnsworth (1937).

Research reported after 1940 began to be more complex. Hunter (1942, p. 243) wrote, in a report on changes in attitudes of four successive classes of college women, that "no evaluation of educational outcomes is adequate without appraisal of attitudes and interests and other of the more subtle aspects of personality." He found that a number of changes, in the direction of increased liberalism, had taken place by the senior year. Seniors were more cautious than freshmen in indorsing extreme statements. Burgemeister (1940), in exploring the permanence of interests in Barnard women, administered an interest test, a values test, and several other instruments to 164 volunteer freshmen; subjects were interviewed after the first testing, and retesting took place at the end of the sophomore year. One of Burgemeister's conclusions was that students who minimized or avoided social participation and activities possessed deeper, or more permanent, intellectual interests.

Kuhlen (1941) administered the Pressey Interest-Attitude test (Pressey, Janney, and Kuhlen, 1939; Pressey, 1946) and other instruments to representative samples of students at Ohio State University, and later retested some of them in the senior year. Scale validity was sometimes checked against large numbers of anonymous ratings obtained from subjects' close acquaintances. Kuhlen concluded that interests had broadened during college, especially in the case of women, and that there had been a sloughing off of early "disapprovals." He asks a significant question, "Has there occurred an increased appreciation of human qualities?" From subsequent research the answer is very likely yes.

In a study by Arsenian (1943) before the war, conflicts over changes in religious attitudes were found to be extensive in men at Springfield College. A decline during college in the religious values mean score of the Allport-Vernon instrument was observed, the change being greater for students in some majors (health and physical education) than in others (social science majors). Arsenian noted that the change was away from formal, ritualistic, dogmatic belief to a more tolerant, humane, social belief. Three-fourths of the students thought that their attitudes on religion had changed during college, and upon further inquiry the others were also found to be aware of unresolved religious conflicts. In the study by Nelson (1938) freshmen were more favorably disposed toward religion than were older students; freshmen were more likely to indicate that they went to church and believed in God.

In sum, researches on attitudes and values carried out prior to the end of World War II showed that, in general, students in college changed in the direction of greater liberalism and sophistication in their political, social, and religious outlooks. There was also evidence of broadening interests during the college years.

Recent and contemporary studies. Undoubtedly the most prominent work in recent years on the topic of changes in attitudes and values during the college years has been Jacob's (1957) survey of recent and ongoing investigations. Jacob reports, pp. 1–3, that there is a profile of values which holds for 75 to 80% of all American college students. The current student generation are "gloriously contented" in their present activity and in their outlook toward the future. They are "unabashedly self-centered," aspiring above all to material gratifications for themselves and their families. Though conventionally middle-class they have an "easy tolerance of diversity" and are ready to live in a society without racial, ethnic, or income barriers. The traditional moral virtues, such as sincerity, honesty, and loyalty are highly valued, but there is little inclination to censor laxity, which students consider to be widespread. A need for religion is generally recognized, but students do not expect religious beliefs to govern daily decisions. Rather they expect that these decisions will be socially determined. The general tendency is to be "dutifully responsive toward government," but there is little inclination to contribute voluntarily to the public welfare or to seek an influential role in public affairs. "Students by and large set great stock in college in general and in their own college in particular," vocational preparation and skills and experience in social relations being regarded as the greatest benefits of college education. Jacob went on to report that there were few significant changes in values during the college years, and that among the few changes that could be noted the most striking were in the direction of greater conformity with the prevailing profile.

Jacob's book has been criticized from a number of different points of view. Riesman (1958) comments, for example, on the generally undifferentiated quality of Jacob's summaries. Studies that are on sound ground methodologically are not distinguished from those that are much less defensible; findings based on male students are treated as if they held for women as well, or vice versa. Riesman thinks that Jacob's view of students may be overly censorious. "Materialistic" is perhaps too strong a term to apply to individuals who are not seeking great wealth or power but instead wish to be left alone to live a family-centered life in one of our attractive suburbs. Riesman also notes that Jacob's emphasis on uniformity among college graduates probably tends to obscure the fact that colleges make some difference, for college graduates differ in important ways from the noncollege elements of the population, even though these differences may not be marked. Webster (1958) found, in agreement with a few previous studies, that students became more heterogeneous in attitudes during attendance at college, although the absence of a control group did not rule out the possibility that even more diversity might develop in some noncollege groups. The general effect of Jacob's work has been valuable, especially because, as Barton (1959) noted, it has served to highlight a number of very important research problems.

Actually, recent studies of particular attitudes and values have shown changes resembling those reported before 1945. Plant (1958b), for example, using the E scale—a measure of ethnic prejudice or ethnocentrism (Adorno et al., 1950)—compared students who withdrew voluntarily from San Jose State College with those who remained in school. The groups were initially matched on intelligence and ethnocentrism. Over a two-year period students who remained in college became significantly less ethnocentric in attitude, while those who withdrew did not. Apparently, education can diminish ethnocentric attitudes in students—if they decide to remain in college—an observation in agreement with that of Stern (Chapter 21). Subsequently, Plant (1958a) found college seniors to be considerably less ethnocentric than they had been as freshmen, a finding that agrees with results from the research at Vassar (Webster, 1956).

Religious crises, or disillusionments, with consequent value changes of the kind described by Arsenian before the war, are actually still fairly common in college students today. In most institutions freshmen are confronted for the first time with a wide range of professed religious beliefs and disbeliefs, and with a variety of seemingly disparate moral practices. They naturally compare the values of peers and faculty with those of parents, sometimes without much deliberation, but often with some misgivings. In a longitudinal study now being carried out at the Center for the Study of Higher Education, National Merit Scholarship winners attending a wide variety of colleges were asked about their need to believe in a religion, their opinion about the emphasis that should be placed on teaching religion in college, and how their religious attitudes had changed since entering college. Response alternatives possible for most of the questions ranged from definite agreement to definite disagreement. The first question was, "Do you personally feel that you need to believe in some sort of religious faith?" The proportions of affirmative responses for 395 men and 175 women, attending a wide variety of institutions, varied from year to year as follows:

	Men	Women
At time of entrance	88%	91%
By end of freshman year	70%	76%
By end of sophomore year	61%	74%
By end of junior year	51%	69%

Evidently the decrease in positive responses continues for the three years, but it appears to be leveling off in the case of the women. When the data for men in various major programs are examined, the trends are similar to that for the total group. There are exceptions, however; engineers change least, and humanities majors (who start with a larger proportion professing a need to believe) change most. A large change also occurs in the case of women studying in the humanities.

Responses to this and other questions about religion make it clear that there is a sizeable minority of these highly able students who change their religious attitudes during three years of college. There is a decreasing need for religious faith, especially among men, and a lessened belief that colleges should teach religious values. Changes appear to be related both to academic major and to the sex of the respondents.

Further findings from the study of National Merit Scholars may be of interest, because they are contemporary students who are quite homogeneous in ability; all groups have nearly the same high mean scholastic aptitude test scores. Results continue to support the general finding that students become more liberal during college. For example, data appear below for the question, "Should the government provide medical and dental care for citizens who cannot afford such services?"

	End of Freshman Year		End of Junior Year	
	Yes	No	Yes	No
Engineering—men	56%	29%	47%	42%
Mathematics—men	55%	19%	70%	11%
Humanities—men	57%	38%	77%	22%
Humanities—women	50%	39%	61%	26%

For the engineering students there was a significant shift from positive to negative, but for the mathematics and humanities majors the significant change is in the opposite direction. This shows that students of very similar ability may change attitudes in opposite directions during college, but whether this is due mostly to the kinds of students who enter the different programs, or mainly to variations in the influence of the different curricula, cannot be decided from these data.

When asked how they would vote if they were old enough, 30% of these able young persons checked "Republican," about 17% "Democrat," and about 50% "Independent." After two years the humanities majors reduced their Republican vote considerably—for men the change was mostly to Democratic, for women, to Independent. Many mathematics majors who previously had checked Republican also shifted to the Independent category.

In agreement with previous studies, some of these gifted students were therefore found to change their expressed attitudes during two years at college, and most change appeared to be in a liberal direction.

Humanities majors apparently changed the most, followed by male mathematics majors. The amount and direction of change is sometimes related to academic major, and the notion that educational experiences during the two years are contributing to the change cannot be ruled out.

Of course, it is hard to compare contemporary studies in the realm of political attitudes with studies carried out 25 or 30 years ago; times and issues change, and so do the words used to stand for particular positions and programs (see Freedman, Chapter 25). Yet it seems safe to conclude that today's students, like those of the Thirties and Forties, become more "liberal" in the sense of being more sophisticated and independent in their thinking, and placing greater value upon individual freedom and well-being. Liberalism in religion, and tolerance of ethnic differences, would appear to have much the same meaning today as in the recent past.

Perhaps the major feature of recent and contemporary studies, as distinguished from the earlier studies discussed above, is that they have been directed to more generalized tendencies in the personality, tendencies conceived as underlying and integrating particular attitudes and values. In an interesting study by Heath (1958, 1959), differential progress in college was reported for three types of students. Over 2000 interviews, plus many group discussions, were recorded in a longitudinal study of a representative sample of 36 men during their years at Princeton. The subjects were classified on an impulse-control dimension, and also according to their degree of involvement with work and with people. Students varied in impulse-control from moody, spontaneous "plungers" ($N = 8$), to the achievement-oriented "hustlers" ($N = 9$) and stable, noncommitted subjects ($N = 19$). It is interesting that the last group were relatively numerous; they showed more movement than the other groups during college, however, in the direction of genuine increased involvement with work and people. Heath observes that the three types responded best to different educational treatments.

At Vassar College, similar dimensions for measuring the expression of impulses and certain aspects of ego functioning and development (Webster, Sanford, and Freedman, 1957) were also devised in order to obtain optimum descriptions of women students. It may be significant that the independent utilization of these rather similar dimensions began in both studies during the subjects' second year in college. Heath's developmental involvement dimension may emphasize the gradual increase of ego control to a greater degree than do the Vassar measures which, in certain other ways, are similar to it.

In the research at Vassar College it was planned to emphasize such personality characteristics as intellectual functioning and achievement, authoritarianism (and its opposites), masculinity-femininity, and psychological health (Sanford, 1956a, 1958). It was possible to obtain measures of these characteristics—in some cases through carrying out a special program of test development. We will present some data obtained by using a number of scales, so brief descriptions of them are necessary.

Social Maturity. Low-scorers are authoritarian, compulsive, rigid, punitive, submissive to power, conventional, cynical, anti-intellectual, and emotionally suppressed. High-scorers are relatively free of these characteristics. The scale provided a measure of authoritarianism that was less ideological than the original F scale (Adorno et al., 1950; Webster, Sanford, and Freedman, 1955).

Impulse Expression. High-scorers, in contrast to low-scorers, have a greater readiness to express impulses, or to seek gratification of them in overt action or in conscious feeling and attitude. High-scorers are usually dominant, aggressive, autonomous, exhibitionistic, and express interests in sex, excitement, and change (Sanford, Webster, and Freedman, 1957).

Developmental Status. A scale made up of attitude items that distinguish younger from older students. In a sense such items reflect development from the freshman to the senior year—hence the name. High-scorers (seniors) in comparison with low-scorers (freshmen) are flexible and uncompulsive, impunitive toward persons but critical of the institutional authority of family, state, or religion; high-scorers are also intraceptive, nonconforming, free of cynicism, realistic, and mature in interests. Content from the two previous scales also appears in this scale.

Dominance and Confidence. High-scorers endorse items avowing social confidence, imperturbability, and ability to lead. In an assessment study of Vassar alumnae in the age range 40 to 45, low-scorers were found to be more troubled and less self-confident than high-scoring subjects.

Repression and Suppression. One kind of subject, in responding to items in a personality inventory, will tend, often quite unconsciously, to reject (answer "false" to) a disproportionately large number of statements which seem inexact, peculiar, or unconventional because he has a strong need to present himself in a "favorable" light; while another subject will do just the opposite, that is, he will endorse many such items, which collectively give an impression of imprudence, unconventionality, and lack of inhibition. The first subject is a high-scorer on Repression and Suppression, the second a low-scorer. The "realistic" place to score on this scale is therefore near the mean.

Social Integration. High-scorers are likely to be quite conventional and free of symptoms of social alienation; low-scorers usually feel that they are unhappy social isolates.

Masculine Role. High-scorers are usually active persons with interests and attitudes characteristic of men in our culture; low-scorers are, on the contrary, more passive, acquiescent, and conventionally feminine.

The data of Table 1 illustrate well some typical differences that distinguish older from younger college women. At the same time some rather striking institutional differences between two leading liberal arts colleges can be observed.[1] The freshmen from the two colleges are very different on some of these measures; for example, test ratios of 8.7, 5.6, and −3.1, for the differences on Developmental Status, Social Maturity and Repression and Suppression, respectively, are easily significant.

Obtained means for Bennington freshmen in Table 1 on Social Maturity, Developmental Status, and Impulse Expression are greater than the corresponding means for Vassar *seniors;* yet the means at Bennington increase over classes, so that senior means still exceed the corresponding Vassar senior means. In both schools the older students are more developed, more mature, and more free to express impulses than the younger students; yet the differences between colleges are also impressive. Seniors from the two colleges do not differ significantly on Dominance and Confidence; and Bennington seniors are the highest of any group on both Masculine Role and on Repression and Suppression. It seems reasonable, therefore, to infer that the other high scores of Bennington students are not achieved at the cost of either a decrease in prudence or a retrogression to a more conventional or passively feminine role.

The results in Table 1 support the view that differing public images attract different students to the two colleges, and that the differences persist despite developmental processes which lead students in both schools in the same direction—which is one of less conservatism, increased tolerance for individual differences, and more freedom to express impulses.

[1] The data for Bennington students were provided through the courtesy of Dr. Howard Smith, formerly of Bennington College, now with Rohrer, Hibler, and Replogle, Toronto, and President William C. Fels of Bennington College.

Table 1. Means and Standard Deviations of Bennington and Vassar Students on the Scales of the Vassar College Attitude Inventory

	Vassar freshmen	Bennington freshmen	Bennington sophomores	Benn. juniors	Benn. seniors	Vassar seniors
Social Maturity						
mean	82.13	94.08	97.88	98.48	104.86	92.99
s.d.	15.15	13.80	12.90	11.20	12.70	15.01
Developmental Status						
mean	23.57	36.26	39.57	41.60	41.64	34.70
s.d.	9.23	9.53	10.10	8.96	10.20	11.01
Impulse Expression						
mean	44.12	56.92	60.80	61.79	58.18	51.86
s.d.	15.57	18.80	17.80	16.30	14.40	16.79
Dominance and Confidence						
mean	53.86	53.28	50.49	55.98	57.14	54.70
s.d.	13.06	10.20	12.15	11.80	12.80	13.11
Social Integration						
mean	78.08	68.22	66.55	69.75	75.34	76.96
s.d.	14.39	15.80	17.30	15.80	14.00	13.74
Repression and Suppression						
mean	90.40	79.68	81.04	83.37	95.58	90.62
s.d.	22.67	22.90	21.90	23.70	22.30	20.85
Masculine Role						
mean	37.09	38.92	40.08	39.50	42.34	39.32
s.d.	6.87	7.83	6.14	6.73	7.07	7.09
Total N	321	50	51	49	50	197

Tables 2 and 3 contain data from an experiment in testing and from one replication, respectively, carried out at Vassar College as a part of the general research program. Despite the small size of these random samples, the trends are clear: test-retest difference scores are significant, and they increase in magnitude with time spent in college.[2] When plotted, using time as the abscissa, the gains usually form a convex

[2] Other Vassar scale scores are not included in Tables 2 and 3 because there was no theory which held that they should change during college. Except for small first-year differences on Repression and Suppression, and on Masculine Role, other changes observed were in fact negligible.

Table 2.

A comparison of test-retest norms for a random sample of each of three Vassar College freshman classes—each tested as freshmen during the first week of the college semester and with retesting taking place at the *end* of the freshman year for one group, the sophomore year for the second group, and the junior year for the third group. The scales include: 3 Vassar scales (IE: Impulse Expression, DS: Developmental Status, and SM: Social Maturity), Fx (Flexibility) from the California Personality Inventory, Pd (Psychopathic Deviate) from the Minnesota Multiphasic Personality Inventory, and F (Authoritarianism) and E (Ethnocentrism) from the Public Opinion Survey.

Scale		Freshmen 57–58 Retested as Freshmen N = 54		Freshmen 56–57 Retested as Sophomores N = 55		Freshmen 55–56 Retested as Juniors N = 53	
		$\bar{x}$	s.d.	$\bar{x}$	s.d.	$\bar{x}$	s.d.
IE	Test	42.33	11.51	44.20	14.14	42.98	11.60
	Retest	48.57	13.77	52.20	16.74	53.32	14.25
DS	Test	23.68	8.41	26.60	9.47	26.00	7.47
	Retest	29.81	10.48	34.51	9.25	36.34	8.44
SM	Test	84.22	14.75	84.27	14.75	85.26	10.83
	Retest	89.74	16.36	95.07	14.15	96.38	11.58
Fx	Test	12.37	3.97	12.07	3.90	11.72	2.96
	Retest	12.46	3.99	14.35	3.36	13.70	3.22
Pd	Test	16.96	3.76	15.58	4.23	14.87	2.93
	Retest	16.83	4.34	16.78	4.08	16.70	4.20
F	Test	118.31	19.59	104.27	24.25	109.56	18.48
	Retest	105.48	22.02	94.05	22.49	95.60	21.33
E	Test	58.33	18.83	49.64	16.21	48.62	14.11
	Retest	53.83	19.20	47.31	15.29	45.91	16.63

decelerating curve, showing that greater changes occur during the earlier part of college careers.

Included in the regular test batteries used at Vassar were the well-known Ethnocentrism, or E scale, and the F scale for measuring authoritarianism, or anti-democratic trends (Adorno et al. 1950). Without exception there were always large decreases in mean scores on these characteristics between the freshman and senior years. The personality syndrome now known as authoritarianism constitutes a

Table 3.

A replication of the experiment of Table 2. A comparison of test-retest scores for a random sample of each of three Vassar College freshman classes—each tested as freshmen during the first week of the college semester and with re-testing taking place at the *end* of the freshman year for one group, the sophomore year for the second group, and the junior year for the third group. The scales include: 3 Vassar scales (IE: Impulse Expression, DS: Developmental Status, and SM: Social Maturity), Fx (Flexibility) from the California Personality Inventory, Pd (Psychopathic Deviate) from the Minnesota Multiphasic Personality Inventory, and F (Authoritarianism) and E (Ethnocentrism) from the Public Opinion Survey.

Scale		Freshmen 58–59 Retested as Freshmen N = 62		Freshmen 57–58 Retested as Sophomores N = 59		Freshmen 56–57 Retested as Juniors N = 59	
		$\bar{x}$	s.d.	$\bar{x}$	s.d.	$\bar{x}$	s.d.
IE	Test	40.35	14.01	45.92	15.29	42.75	17.12
	Retest	45.65	17.99	53.86	18.85	50.17	15.61
DS	Test	24.76	9.97	25.32	9.03	25.37	8.44
	Retest	29.26	10.48	34.47	9.67	34.88	9.78
SM	Test	88.02	17.04	85.86	14.49	85.31	15.35
	Retest	93.11	16.32	94.41	14.44	94.27	16.62
Fx	Test	11.29	4.63	11.63	3.74	11.49	3.56
	Retest	12.27	4.27	13.76	3.72	12.64	3.64
Pd	Test	15.50	3.44	16.46	3.81	14.81	3.61
	Retest	15.60	3.46	17.27	4.87	16.42	4.27
F	Test	114.27	26.10	113.54	21.47	102.83	24.34
	Retest	104.85	24.10	97.46	21.87	94.21	24.18
E	Test	54.15	20.12	57.22	20.23	50.17	18.87
	Retest	52.34	18.27	50.68	18.95	44.10	16.95

particular failure of maturity about which there is available a large amount of convincing research of a quantitative type (Sanford, Chapter 6 and 1956b). Persons with high F scores have been described as anti-intellectual by a number of investigators. If it is true, as it appears to be, that many college freshmen are anti-intellectual, then the study of authoritarianism in college students should be of value in educational research. The fact that many high-scorers at Vassar were changeable, to the extent that *large* decreases occurred in their F scores during college, while others did not change at all, merits further study. It appears from interviews that in a few authoritarians the earlier fixations are so severe as to prevent a significant decrease in F scores during college.

Vassar students were also studied by means of the Minnesota Multiphasic Personality Inventory (Hathaway and McKinley, 1951), a test designed to measure the type and degree of psychopathology in the personality. A consistent trend is for seniors to be higher than freshmen on the following scales: Hypochondriasis, Depression, Hysteria, Psychopathic Deviate, Schizophrenia, and Mania. (The K, or Suppressor, Scale score does not differ significantly.) In short, seniors subscribed more frequently than freshmen to statements indicating psychological or physical disturbances and instability (Webster, 1956; Freedman, 1960b).

Three of the Vassar scales, Social Maturity, Impulse Expression, and Developmental Status, have also been administered at a variety of other women's colleges, for example, a Negro college in the South, a Catholic college in Canada, and an Eastern women's college that differed somewhat from Vassar, and in all cases the kinds of trends found were similar to those found at Vassar. There are impressive intercollege differences, but whatever the initial freshmen means may be, the students subsequently gain in scores during college.

The theoretical implication of the findings discussed above is that there are systematic personality changes going on, at least in college women, around the age of 17 or 18; and that the developmental changes during this period of late adolescence entail certain regularities in the way problems and conflicts are met and resolved. The Center for the Study of Higher Education at the University of California is currently studying these kinds of changes, plus changes on a number of new but related dimensions, for both men and women who attend several kinds of colleges and universities (Webster and Heist, 1959). The results should be of interest both to psychologists and to educators.

RESEARCH ON THE DETERMINATION OF PERSONALITY CHANGE IN COLLEGE

All the studies discussed above have had to do with the presence or absence—and with the amount—of change in particular characteristics of students during their college years. We turn now to a consideration of some of the conditions of change, as revealed by studies that have focused upon the effects of different kinds of college environments and different features of the educational process. Earlier chapters of this book have given attention to the effects of student society and culture, of the college climate as a whole, of different kinds of teaching and curricula, of different major programs. We shall not undertake to summarize all that has gone before; rather we shall bring together representative published researches that bear upon the determination of change in college, together with some interpretations.

The study of students at Bennington College by Newcomb (1943) was the first to relate expressed attitude change, in any systematic way, to both the initial values of students and to the social and academic values of the college as a community. Students as a group became less conservative during college, but maintained fairly well their relative positions within classes as conservatives or nonconservatives. Certain "response set" effects were noted, supporting Hunter's observation that seniors are likely to be more cautious or critical; for example, Bennington seniors were more likely to disagree with conservative statements than to agree with nonconservative statements. Attitude change was only weakly related to choice of major, but was strongly dependent upon community relationships. Active community participation and lack of conservatism were positively related; both were prestigeful and popular. Students known to be interested in public affairs were highly nonconservative, which may to some extent have been a function of the times. Since the students viewed the community as nonconservative, negativism toward the community was associated with conservatism, which is contrary to what can be observed in many communities. Newcomb believed that nonconservative social attitudes were developed at Bennington primarily by those who were both capable and desirous of cordial relations with community members.

Newcomb (1946) also showed that the process of acquiring and retaining information on a controversial matter is related to the process by which an attitude toward it is acquired, and that attitudes of others, that is, a local attitude climate, will be involved. It would be difficult to find a topic of greater relevance to education. Newcomb's work initiated a new trend in studies of college students; subsequently, it was essential not only to measure changes in students, but to study in more detail potential determinants of change that could be isolated, not only in the personalities of students, but in the social dynamics of the college community as well.

Newcomb has discussed in Chapter 13 the conditions of influence by student peer groups, and Bushnell (Chapter 14) and Hughes, Becker, and Geer (Chapter 15) have shown in concrete instances how attitudes and values are affected by membership in such groups. The Vassar research has so far not yielded findings on the relations between changes in scores on personality scales and different kinds of experiences in the student society, but concerning the impact of the student culture as a whole, Freedman (1956, p. 14) has written that it "is the prime educational force at work, for . . . . . assimilation into the student society is the foremost concern of most new students," and "academic aims and processes of the College are in large measure transmitted to incoming students or mediated for them by the predominant student culture."

There was a small but relatively distinct subculture at Vassar made up of students successfully undergoing psychotherapy (Nixon, 1960; Freedman, 1960b; Webster, 1956). These students differed consistently from their classmates in being more disturbed, but at the same time they were less authoritarian and more free to express impulses. These kinds of differences indicated that students entering psychotherapy were in general more like seniors than like freshmen, both in attitude and in the amount of personality disturbance experienced, and that experience in psychotherapy was favorable to educational development. In larger institutions, psychotherapy patients may not form as distinct a group.

A few other studies have emphasized the relationships between the student and the faculty subcultures. Hammond (1959) related survival in an engineering program to conformity of students to faculty expectations. For example, seniors showed less concern than freshmen with security in terms of money, but more concern with service to society and with personal status, which were also more acceptable values to the faculty.

Jervis and Congdon (1958) compared faculty rankings of nine educational objectives with those of students at the University of New Hampshire, and found there were marked discrepancies. For example, faculty ranked "intellectual growth" first in importance, while students placed it fourth; students put "vocational preparation" in first place. "Informal intellectual activity" with peers and "student-faculty relationships" were ranked last by students, while faculty preferred least "the degree" and "social growth." Another disconcerting finding was that senior goals, when compared with those of freshmen, failed to show any closer agreement with the faculty objectives.

As reported in Chapter 17, changes on various personality measures that take place between the freshman and the senior years at Vassar tend not to be associated with a course of study or a field of concentration. On the other hand, in the study of National Merit Scholarship winners described above there were interesting differences among the various major groups. For example, the tendency to value religion less the longer one stayed in college was greater among men in physics, mathematics, and the humanities than among men in other majors.

It may be that the different results are a function of the size and general organization of the institutions involved. At relatively small liberal arts colleges there may be a kind of pervasive college culture which somewhat uniformly affects all students, regardless of their field of study. This is not so likely to be the case, however, at larger institutions with separate schools in business administration, engineering, liberal arts, and the like. It seems reasonable to assume that each school within the institution would possess a somewhat different culture or intellectual climate that would affect students differently, at least in some ways. Results reported by Thistlethwaite (1959a) support this interpretation.

From Chapter 8 it can be seen that variations in teaching method often have resulted in only negligible differences in academic progress. Recent research suggests that some of the different methods may be more effective if allowances are made for differences in students' personality characteristics. For example, Graves (1958) reported differential achievement in some University of Michigan students, also known to differ on the dimensions of security-insecurity, introversion-extroversion, and some other measures. Stern and his colleagues (Chapter 21) have demonstrated differing rates of progress of authoritarians and nonauthoritarians under different educational programs, and Dressel and his colleagues (1958, pp. 163, 220, 232–241) have reported similar findings. Funkenstein, King, and Drolette (1957) were able to classify Harvard students according to their ability to master stress, as induced in experimental situations; the ability to master stress was related to ego functioning, measured in a number of ways, and therefore to certain kinds of college achievement or failure.

Earlier investigators sometimes expressed the view that changes in attitudes or values, or lack of such change, might be mostly a function of the particular college at which the study was conducted. McConnell and Heist (Chapter 5), Heist (1960), and Stern (Chapter 21) have described the great diversity which exists, on many characteristics, among entering freshmen; they have noted that colleges necessarily vary greatly, if only because of these large differences in the kinds of students they admit. Clark (1959) emphasized that the public image of the college is a powerful device for determining who will apply for admission. The social ideology of an institution, since it is a significant part of this image, may therefore lead to the admission of predominantly liberals or conservatives, changers or nonchangers, and so on. Jacob (1957) thought that significant changes in values, if any, would probably be confined to a few rather special liberal arts institutions possessing distinctive climates. From the above observations it would appear that both the distinctive climates and the students who change significantly might be due largely to the kinds of students admitted to colleges. The studies by Thistlethwaite (1959a, 1959b) also appear to support this view.

There have been a few studies of differences among colleges in respect to their power to induce change in the attitudes and values of their students. Brown and Bystryn (1956), for example, studied changes in authoritarianism in Catholic, Protestant, and Jewish students in three colleges: a Catholic liberal arts college for women, a nondenominational liberal arts college for women, and a large Eastern coeducational university. There were average decreases in authoritarianism at both the liberal arts colleges but not at the university. The differences in authoritarianism between freshmen and seniors were greatest for the Jewish minority group members attending the small nondenominational liberal arts college for women. The authors suggest that the Jewish minority group in the college for which the difference was greatest may have been especially challenged by the need to change, since most of them were not in fact minority group members in their precollege communities; they would therefore need to assimilate the social ideology represented by the college to a greater degree in the attempt to identify with a new in-group.

Lazure (1959) compared the kinds of changes observed in Vassar students with those observed in girls attending French-Canadian Catholic colleges. The differences seemed to depend mostly upon differences in the role-expectations for educated women in the two cultures. The Catholic Canadian role is rather clearly defined, and there are specific ideas about what constitutes acceptable or unacceptable behavior. Vassar's attempt to offer many choices of a way of life induces more conflict and arouses more inhibitory reactions; consequently, less personality disturbance is observed to develop among Canadian students.

Webster (1958) compared women students from three colleges— Vassar, Beirut College for Women, and a Southern Negro College— on the Developmental Scale described above. Although the freshman-senior difference was in the expected direction for each of the three samples, it was significant only for the Vassar sample. After considering variations in the test reliabilities for numerous groups, Webster concluded that the Arab students and the Southern Negro students would probably express "rebellious independence" (the general factor in the scale) somewhat differently than Vassar students.

The writers have interviewed students for several years at a number of different kinds of colleges. Very few entering freshmen at residential colleges are apathetic toward their new experiences, including their academic work. In fact, it is easy to be misled into believing that nearly all of them will, within a few years, develop and change in important and fundamental ways. For example, it is easy to imagine that many of these students will become scholars, articulate critics of the culture, and enlightened individualists who are more concerned with personal principles and social problems than with social acceptability or status. Of course, a few do appear to develop in this way. In speculating why the majority do *not* change as expected, it is necessary to turn for explanation, not only to the college situation and the educational experience it has provided, but also to the precollege histories of individual students.

We need not elaborate on the diversity of social background factors among entering students. Some are, of course, from families of greater wealth, or education, or status than others, and some have had more extensive experiences than others in living away from home. These kinds of factors may be very important, but for the most part they seem to be less fundamental, for purposes of understanding subsequent educational development, than certain psychological characteristics (which, however, are not independent of background). Research reveals that most new students are enthusiastic about college experience, but that very few have developed those psychological characteristics that will permit them the necessary freedom within the college culture, and within the larger culture, to become seriously committed to intellectual and esthetic problems. As a result, few will become interested in learning for its own sake. For example, few students have the kind of personal autonomy, or independence, or even, perhaps, the social alienation that permits them to defer for long their vocational or marital aims in the interest of following other pursuits. The majority of students soon forego experimentation with roles, and any questioning of basic values, in order to secure as soon as possible a relatively definite plan for the work of the future.

But this pervasive caution may be due in part to the absence of conflict during the precollege years. Freedman (1960b) reported that, contrary to generally accepted theory, there was little evidence that adolescence had been a time of strife or rebelliousness for the majority of Vassar students. In fact, the most common "crises" during the period of attendance at secondary school had been occasional worries about acceptance by peers. Other observers have also noted this fact about contemporary adolescents (Kuhlen, 1960; Stone and Church, 1957), and it may be that today, in contrast to earlier periods, certain developmental changes of adolescence are attenuated by deferment. For example, some of the disturbance that developed in Vassar students seemed quite "classically" adolescent, in that it was due to temporary failures of ego control over impulses.

The period of late adolescence, and of attendance at college, is normally marked by diversification and intensification of interests (Strong, 1943; Matteson, 1955). But interests of young persons are significantly influenced by experiences related to the interests. Dressel (1954) observed that the stability over time that has been observed for certain interest patterns may be largely due to lack of experience in activities about which interests are expressed. Matteson (1955; also see Dressel, 1958, p. 187) reported that levels and patterns of interests changed for college students as new experiences became available, and that the selection of educational objectives, for example, choice of major, was a "developmental process," observable in counseling.

Attitudes that distinguish seniors from freshmen also reflect the increased experience of the older students, and in one study of interview data (Webster, 1956) the attitudes of those freshmen who recalled the most conflict and instability in the home, and who had been more independent socially, were more like the attitudes of seniors. Huntington, Martin, and Fox (see Merton, 1957) have described how the development of medical students' attitudes is directly dependent upon experience. Lehmann and Ikenberry (1959), in a study of Michigan State University students, reported evidence that attitudes and values were affected differentially by different types of experience. On the other hand, attitudes are often *not* affected by changes in information, even though instructors may assume that they are (Mayhew, 1958). It seems from this research that a logical aim of education would consist in increasing the opportunities for diverse kinds of new experiences.

SOME SUGGESTIONS FOR FUTURE RESEARCH

Undoubtedly it is no surprise to the majority of educators that a great many students pass through college without experiencing significant changes in basic values, or without becoming much involved in problems that interest teachers. The vast enterprise that is American higher education today cherishes traditional cultural values, including vocational training, rewards for hard work, and social adjustment; these have prevailed, often to the exclusion of an interest in the intellectual and esthetic problems with which scientists and artists are preoccupied.

Nevertheless, even characteristics that are relatively stable and deeply embedded in personality are somewhat modified during college, and it is probably only a matter of time before we will know more about the way in which these changes are related ". . . to education, maturation, or just getting away from home . . ." (Mayhew, 1958, p. 230). Also, most educators believe that general education should attempt to provide conditions that favor the re-examination of attitudes and values, and the development of new ones. Dissenters from this viewpoint are mostly parents who want college to emphasize adjustment and the acquisition of skills, and students who view college mainly as a channel to higher income or status.

A number of recommendations can be made on the basis of the research that has been reviewed. In most of the studies it can be seen that three kinds of problems have been superimposed; these concern the changing social conditions, the diversity of personality characteristics of students, and the educational programs and climates of colleges.

Historians, political scientists, and other social scientists should combine forces to investigate the meaning of certain central concepts of development that vary in meaning with social conditions. For example, we need to know more about the liberalization that usually takes place in students during college, but that varies in meaning with variations in social climate. The same can be recommended for changes in religious values, which seem to occur universally, but which are at best poorly understood in varying cultural contexts. In addition to some of the studies reviewed in this chapter, there are a few others that seem pertinent to this problem, for example, the book by Riesman (1950) and a report by McClosky (1958).

The investigation of student characteristics in any intensive way has hardly begun. Educators and the general public must be kept informed about the value of mental testing in this kind of research. In particular, the interpretation of data on attitudes naturally raises serious questions in which verbal conventions and general ideologies are important, as well as the psychodynamics of persons. The centrality of ideologies in personality will require much more specialized research, in order to improve our understanding of attitudes and attitude changes.

New ways of conceptualizing interests, attitudes, and values should be explored (for example, see Weissman, 1958; and Dressel and Mayhew, 1954). Improved testing methods for measuring a large variety of personality characteristics, are needed. Measures already known to be important for understanding development, for example, Impulse Expression and Social Maturity, should be studied further, and the search for related measures should continue.

Comparisons should be made of students who show much developmental change with those who show little or no change during college. And these comparisons should be included in a variety of research designs which allow for variations in educational atmospheres.

Colleges should continue to experiment with their educational programs. Research indicates that the role of experience in personality change is crucial, and educational programs that vary in the opportunities provided for diverse kinds of experiences should be studied. Some effort should be made to involve faculty in research focused upon various kinds of evaluations of students, so that the limitations of particular methods, for example, the use of course grades, will be better appreciated. Relationships between faculty and students should be a topic for extensive research. In particular, it seems that differential teaching methods have often produced equivocal or insignificant results because personality differences among students and teachers have not been taken into account; here further research promises to bring some clarification.

Educational research should make full use of what is known in related disciplines, for example, psychiatric counseling and industrial psychology. Perhaps the educational process can be improved along lines suggested by some of the newer methods of psychotherapy, where maximum development is encouraged while dependence, or transference, is largely avoided (see Wedge, 1958, Chapter 14; Nixon, 1960; Farnsworth, 1957, p. 206). Industrial studies of *organizational behavior* have been sufficiently fruitful so that the principles that have emerged may also be of some value for understanding college subcultures (Argyris, 1957).

Finally, the challenge to educators and personality theorists alike is to continue the search for principles of development that apply for college students under varying social climates and conditions.

In this chapter we have discussed a number of kinds of changes that are important for understanding personality growth and development in college students. It is obvious that not enough is known about these changes, or about how they are inter-related within the personality. But the studies that have been reviewed suggest that research of this nature can produce much that is of scientific interest. At the same time there is every indication that continued research will increase our understanding of the educational process, to the advantage of higher education generally.

REFERENCES

Adorno, T. W., Frenkel-Brunswik, Else, Levinson, D. J., and Sanford, R. N. *The authoritarian personality.* New York: Harper Bros., 1950.

Allport, G. W., and Vernon, P. E. *A study of values.* Boston: Houghton, Mifflin, 1931.

Argyris, C. *Personality and organization: the conflict between system and the individual.* New York: Harper Bros., 1957.

Arsenian, S. Changes in evaluative attitudes during four years of college. *J. appl. Psychol.,* 1943, **27**, 338–349.

Barton, A. H. *Studying the effects of college education.* New Haven: Edward W. Hazen Foundation, 1959.

Bayley, Nancy. Individual patterns of development. *Child Development,* 1956, **27**, 45–75.

Bayley, Nancy. Data on the growth of intelligence between 16 and 21 years as measured by the Wechsler-Bellevue Scale. *J. genetic Psychol.,* 1957, **90**, 3–15.

Bayley, Nancy, and Oden, Melita H. The maintenance of intellectual ability in gifted adults. *J. Gerontol.,* 1955, **10**, 91–107.

Brown, D. R. Non-intellective factors and faculty nominations of ideal students. Rep. to the College Entrance Examination Board of a Pilot Study. Mellon Foundation, Vassar College, 1959.

Brown, D. R., and Bystryn, Denise. College environment, personality, and social ideology of three ethnic groups. *J. soc. Psychol.,* 1956, **44**, 279–288.

Buck, W. A Measurement of changes in attitudes and interests of university students over a 10-year period. *J. abnorm. soc. Psychol.,* 1936, **31**, 12–19.

Burgemeister, Bessie B. The permanence of interests of college women students. *Arch. Psychol.,* 1940, **36**, 1–59.

Burkhardt, F. *Science and humanities.* Founders Day Lecture, Antioch College. Yellow Springs, Ohio: The Antioch Press, 1959.

Clark, B. R. College image and student selection. In T. R. McConnell (Ed.), *Selection and Educational Differentiation,* Field Service Center and Center for the Study of Higher Education, University of California, Berkeley, 1959.

Corey, S. M. Attitude differences between college classes. *J. educ. Psychol.,* 1936, **27**, 321–330.

Dressel, P. L. Interests—stable or unstable? *J. educ. Res.,* 1954, **48**, 95–102.

Dressel, P. L. (Ed.) *Evaluation in the basic college.* New York: Harper Bros., 1958.

Dressel, P. L., and Mayhew, L. B. *General education: Explorations in evaluation.* American Council on Education, Washington, 1954.

Fagot, R. F. A model for ordered metric scaling by comparison of intervals. *Psychometrika,* 1959, **24**, 157–168.

Farnsworth, D. L. *Mental health in college and university.* Cambridge: Harvard University Press, 1957.

Farnsworth, P. R. Changes in attitude toward war during the college years. *J. soc. Psychol.*, 1937, **8**, 274–279.

Florence, Louise M. Mental growth and development at the college level. *J. educ. Psychol.*, 1947, **38**, 65–82.

Freedman, M. The passage through college. In Sanford, N. (Ed.), Personality development during the college years. *J. soc. Issues*, 1956, **12**, 13–28.

Freedman, M. *The impact of the college.* U.S. Department of Health, Education and Welfare, Office of Education, 1960a.

Freedman, M. Some observations on personality development in college women. *Student Medicine*, 1960b, **8**, 228–245.

Funkenstein, D. H., King, S. H., and Drolette, Margaret E. *Mastery of stress.* Cambridge: Harvard University Press, 1957.

Graves, W. A. Today's college students. *J. Nat., Educ. Ass.*, 1958, **47**, 498–500.

Gregg, A. *For future doctors.* Chicago: University of Chicago Press, 1957.

Hammond, Marjorie. Additudinal changes of successful students in a college of engineering. *J. counsel. Psychol.*, 1959, **6**, 69–71.

Hathaway, S. R., and McKinley, J. C. Manual for the Minnesota Multiphasic Personality Inventory (Rev. ed.) New York: Psychological Corp., 1951.

Heath, S. R., Jr. Personality and student development. In *New dimensions of learning in a free society.* Pittsburgh: University of Pittsburgh Press, 1958, pp. 225–245.

Heath, S. R., Jr. The reasonable adventurer and others—a two-factor model of ego functioning. *J. counsel. Psychol.*, 1959, **6**, 3–12.

Heist, P. Diversity in college student characteristics. In Fishman, J. A. (Ed.), The social psychology of school to college transition. *J. educ. Sociology*, 1960, **33**, 279–291.

Heist, P., and Webster, H. Implications for selection and study of undergraduates. In T. R. McConnell (Ed.), *Selection and Educational Differentiation,* Field Service Center and Center for the Study of Higher Education, University of California, Berkeley, 1959.

Hunter, E. C. Changes in general attitudes of women students during four years in college. *J. soc. Psychol.*, 1942, **16**, 243—257.

Jacob, P. E. *Changing values in college.* New York: Harper Bros., 1957.

Jervis, F. M., and Congdon, R. G. Student and faculty perceptions of educational values. *Amer. Psychologist*, 1958, **13**, 464–466.

Jones, V. A. Attitudes of college students and changes in such attitudes during four years in college. *J. educ. Psychol.*, 1938, **29**, 14–35.

Kagan, J., Sontag, L., Baker, C., and Nelson, Virginia. Personality and IQ change. *J. abnorm. soc. Psychol.*, 1958, **56**, 261–266.

Kelley, T. L. *Fundamentals of statistics.* Cambridge: Harvard University Press, 1947.

Kuhlen, R. Changes in attitudes of students and relations of test responses to judgments of associates. *Sch. Soc.*, 1941, **53**, 514–519.

Kuhlen, R. Adolescence. In C. Harris (Ed.), *Encyclopedia of educational research.* New York: Macmillan, 1960.

Lazure, Martha C. An intercultural study of personality development in college women of the United States and French Canada. Unpublished Master's thesis. Bryn Mawr College, April, 1959.

Learned, W. S., and Wood, B. D. The student and his knowledge: A rep. to the Carnegie Found. on the results of the high school and col. exams. of 1928, 1930 and 1932. Bull. No. 29. New York: The Carnegie Foundation for the Advancement of Teaching, 1938.

Lehmann, I. J., and Ikenberry, S. O. Critical thinking, attitudes and values in higher education. East Lansing: Michigan State University, 1959.

Lord, F. M. Further problems in the measurement of growth. *Educ. psychol. Measmt,* 1958, **18,** 437–451.

Lord, F. M. The measurement of growth. *Educ. psychol. Measmt,* 1956, **16,** 421–437.

Lord, F. M. Sampling fluctuations resulting from the sampling of test items. *Psychometrika,* 1955, **20,** 1–22.

MacKinnon, D. W. Identifying and developing creativity. In T. R. McConnell (Ed.), *Selection and Educational Differentiation,* Field Service Center and Center for the Study of Higher Education, University of California, Berkeley, 1959.

Matteson, R. W. Experience-interest changes in students. *J. counsel. Psychol.,* 1955, **2,** 113–121.

Mayhew, L. B. And in attitudes. In P. Dressel (Ed.), *Evaluation in the basic college.* New York: Harper Bros., 1958.

McClosky, H. Conservatism and personality. Minneapolis: Lab. for Res. in Soc. Relations, 1958.

McConnell, T. R. Change in scores on the psychological examination of the American Council on Education from the freshman to the senior year. *J. educ. Psychol.,* 1934, **25,** 66–69.

McNemar, Q. On growth measurement. *Educ. psychol. Measmt.,* 1958, **18,** 47–55.

Merton, R. K. (Ed.) *The student-physician: introductory studies in the sociology of medical education.* Cambridge: Harvard University Press, 1957.

Nelson, E. Radicalism-Conservatism in student attitudes. *Psychol. Monogr.,* 1938, **50,** 1–32.

Nettler, S. Test burning in Texas. *Amer. Psychologist,* 1959, **14,** 682–683.

Newcomb, T. M. *Personality and social change.* New York: Dryden, 1943.

Newcomb, T. M. The influence of attitude climate upon some determinants of information. *J. abnorm. soc. Psychol.,* 1946, **41,** 291–302.

Nixon, R. E. Approach to the dynamics of growth in adolescence. *Psychiatry,* 1961, **24,** 18–31.

Pinneau, S. R., and Jones, H. E. Development of mental abilities. *Rev. educ. Res.,* 1958, **28,** 392–400.

Plant, W. T. Changes in ethnocentrism during college. *J. educ. Psychol.,* 1958a, **49,** 112–165.

Plant, W. T. Changes in ethnocentrism associated with a two-year college experience. *J. genet. Psychol.,* 1958b, **92,** 189–197.

Pressey, S. L. Changes from 1923 to 1943 in the attitudes of public school and university students. *J. Psychol.,* 1946, **21,** 173–188.

Pressey, S. L., Janney, J. E., and Kuhlen, R. G. *Life: a psychological survey.* New York: Harper Bros., 1939.

Riesman, D. *The lonely crowd.* New Haven: Yale University Press, 1950.

Riesman, D. The "Jacob Report." *Amer. soc. Rev.,* 1958, **23,** 732–738.

Sanford, N. (Ed.) Personality development during the college years. *J. soc. Issues,* 1956a, **12,** No. 4.

Sanford, N. The approach of the authoritarian personality. In J. L. McCary (Ed.), *Psychology of personality.* New York: Logos Press, 1956b.

Sanford, N., Webster, H., and Freedman, M. Impulse expression as a variable of personality. *Psychol. Monogr.,* 1957, **72,** No. 11 (Whole No. 440).

Sanford, N. The professor looks at the student. In R. M. Cooper (Ed.), *The two ends of the log: learning and teaching in today's college.* Minneapolis: University of Minnesota Press, 1958.

Scheffé, H. Alternative models for the analysis of variance. *Ann. math. Statist.*, 1956, **27**, 251–271.

Siegel, S. A method for obtaining an ordered metric scale. *Psychometrika*, 1956, **21**, 207–216.

Silvey, H. M. Changes in test scores after two years in college. *Educ. psychol. Measmt*, 1951, **11**, 494–502.

Snow, C. P. *The two cultures and the scientific revolution.* The Rede Lecture. Cambridge: Cambridge University Press, 1959.

Stone, L. J., and Church, J. *Childhood and adolescence.* New York: Random House, 1957.

Strong, E. K. *Vocational interests of men and women.* Stanford, Calif.: Stanford University Press, 1943.

Terman, L. M., and Oden, M. H. *The gifted child grows up.* Stanford, Calif.: Stanford University Press, 1947.

Thistlethwaite, D. L. College environments and the development of talent. *Science,* 1959a, **130**, 71–76.

Thistlethwaite, D. L. College press and student achievement. *J. educ. Psychol.,* 1959b, **50**, 183–191.

Thurstone, L. L., and Chave, E. J. *The measurement of attitude.* Chicago: University of Chicago Press, 1929.

Webster, H. Some quantitative results. In Sanford, N. (Ed.), Personality development during the college years. *J. soc. Issues,* 1956, **12**, 29–43.

Webster, H. Changes in attitudes during college. *J. educ. Psychol.,* 1958, **49**, 109–117.

Webster, H. A generalization of Kuder-Richardson reliability formula 21. *Educ. psychol. Measmt,* 1960, **20**, 131–138.

Webster, H., and Heist, P. Construction of a multiple trait personality test for use with college populations. An interim res. rep. for the Soc. Sci. Res. Council Conf. on Personality Measures Relevant to Col. Purposes, January 26–28, 1959.

Webster, H., Sanford, N., and Freedman, M. A new instrument for studying authoritarianism in personality. *J. Psychol.,* 1955, **40**, 73–84.

Webster, H., Sanford, N., and Freedman, M. Research Manual for VC Attitude Inventory and VC Figure Preference Test. Vassar College, Mary Conover Mellon Foundation, 1957.

Wedge, B. M. (Ed.). *Psychosocial problems of college men.* New Haven: Yale University Press, 1958.

Weissman, M. P. An approach to the assessment of intellectual disposition among high-ability students. Unpublished doctoral dissertation, University of California, 1958.

Wheelis, A. *The quest for identity.* New York: Norton, 1958.

Whyte, W. H., Jr. *The organization man.* New York: Simon and Schuster, 1956.

25 *Mervin B. Freedman*

Studies of College Alumni

In the long run the best evaluation of the meaning of a college
education is likely to result from studies of alumni. What are
college graduates like—five, ten, twenty, and thirty years after graduation? How have they been influenced by college experiences? How do
college graduates differ from high school graduates? How do they differ
from individuals who have had but a year or two of college? What
differences exist among graduates of various kinds of colleges, for example, private vs. public, denominational vs. nonsectarian, large vs.
small, coeducational vs. schools of one sex? Knowledge of such matters
would, of course, be of great value in understanding what colleges
do to and for students and in formulating educational goals and procedures.

Unfortunately such studies are complex and not easily carried out.
For example, how do we separate postcollege from undergraduate experiences in accounting for the qualities of alumni? Social forces of
one decade may differ markedly from those of another and contribute
to differences among alumni that may be inaccurately attributed to the
influence of college experience. Again, how do we know that the qualities that distinguish college graduates from high school graduates may
not be primarily functions of the characteristics that lead high school
students to choose to go on to college in the first place? For example,

Note. The research reported in this chapter was supported in part by a contract with the United States Office of Education, Department of Health, Education,
and Welfare.

This chapter was completed while the writer was a Fellow at the Center for Advanced Study in the Behavioral Sciences, Stanford, California, and he wishes to take
the opportunity to express his gratitude for the ideal working conditions afforded
by the Center.

a study of Wolfle and Smith (1956) demonstrated that among high school graduates who do not go on to college as well as among those who do, rank in the graduating class and scores on intelligence tests are associated with income after graduation.

In the absence of systematic theory concerned with changes in the personality or behavior of adults, one is often at a loss as to just where to begin the study of college graduates. As we shall see, however, enough work has been done to give us some valuable suggestions about how experiences of the college years fit into the larger life patterns of individuals and how the meaning and implications of these experiences change with the times.

Relevant literature. There have been few studies in this important area. Most of the empirical ones center on various gross sociological factors, such as the income of college graduates, the age at which they marry, or the number of children they have. There are several studies, chiefly ones utilizing questionnaires, that assess such factors as the esthetic values of college graduates, their interests and opinions, and their attitudes toward various aspects of their college careers. Rare indeed are studies of the same people in college and again as alumni. There appears to be no study that evaluates the actual knowledge of alumni in various areas, something that might be assessed by achievement tests comparable to those given undergraduates. Considering the relative simplicity of the design of such studies, it seems surprising that none has been carried out.

Most of the prominent studies of alumni will be discussed below under appropriate topics. There are two books, however, which are quite extensive in coverage, and these will be described first.

"They Went to College," by C. Robert Pace (1941). Samples of the men and women who entered the University of Minnesota in 1924, 1925, 1928, and 1929 were surveyed by means of a 52-page questionnaire in 1937. About half of the subjects were graduates, the others having withdrawn prior to graduation. The questionnaire covered a wide variety of topics, such as work, income, family, recreation, and political opinions and activities.

The general findings are consistent with those of Jacob's more recent *Changing Values in College* (1957). The lives of alumni were pretty much centered in the "private" sphere, with the family, work, and recreation as the predominant interests. The alumni voted, and were interested in governmental policies, but tended to be rather passive politically. Intellectual and esthetic pursuits did not loom large in their lives, a fact which led Pace to suggest that "colleges may not be producing the cultural values they so frequently claim." The chief difference between graduates and the people who dropped out of college were in the vocational realm—the income of the graduates being somewhat higher and their reported job satisfaction somewhat greater. Otherwise, differences were inconsequential. Thus, for example, the level of reading matter was not appreciably higher for the graduates than for the "dropouts."

An interesting sidelight of Pace's study was the fact that "togetherness" in the home did not seem so prevalent in 1937 as it became a decade or so later. Thus Pace says, ". . . women were doing most of the work, and worrying most about the majority of the problems, around the home."

"They Went to College," by Ernest Havemann and Patricia Salter West (1952). This book reported on questionnaire returns from 9064 respondents representing 1037 colleges. The data were obtained in 1947. The study was designed originally to shed light on readers of *Time* magazine and was not intended to be a study of college-educated people as such. Since most *Time* readers are college educated, however, the data lent themselves readily to conversion to a study of the general state and activities of men and women who have attended college.

Data from this study will be utilized in various of the sections to follow, but a few of the more interesting results or observations that do not fit into any of the topics to be discussed later will be noted here. Satisfaction with a college experience in general was almost universal. Ninety-eight per cent of the respondents would choose to go to college again, were they reliving their lives, and 84% would choose the same college. This satisfaction did not hold, however, for the general type of curriculum or course pursued in college. In fact, this area was the focus of the greatest dissatisfaction with the college experience. In the matter of general versus more specific kinds of education, 44% were satisfied with what they had had, 35% wished they had had a more specific kind of training, and 21% wished they had had a more general educational experience. Graduates in the humanities were distinguished by their relatively low incomes, and the situation was "even worse for social science graduates." In the professions, those who had had a more general type of undergraduate education tended to be "the more active and interested citizens." The college graduates most dissatisfied with general education were those in business. Students with high grades were more likely to enter professions, and even to earn more money in a given profession, than were students with lower grades. Grades tended to be related to financial success in all fields except business. The degree of satisfaction with the college experience, though related to grades, was little related to type and extent of extracurricular activity. Alumni who had obtained higher grades as students were more content than others with their college, their major, and their extent of specialization.

CHARACTERISTICS OF COLLEGE ALUMNI

Sociological. In summarizing studies of the sociological characteristics of college alumni, the tentative nature of many findings must be borne in mind. Statistics pertaining to such matters as income or occupation are subject to much variation in accord with such factors as sex, age, race, religion, region, and size and type of college. Also, in most studies, the qualities of college graduates prior to or at the time of college entrance are incompletely assayed, if dealt with at all. Moreover, many conclusions and statistics vary with changing times and social conditions. Accordingly, it is likely that the 1960 census will lead to modification of a number of figures based on the 1950 or the 1940 census, or to re-interpretation of studies carried out in these decades.

Income. Most studies demonstrate a direct relationship between amount of schooling and amount of income. College graduates predominate in the higher paying occupations and earn more money job for job than people who have no college education or who have left college prior to graduation. As one would expect, when educational level and occupation are equated for the two sexes, the incomes of women are lower than those of men.

Working with the 1950 census figures (which are based on income in 1949) Glick and Miller (1956) reported the following mean annual incomes for men: for high school graduates, $4519; for men with one to three years of college, $5473; and for college graduates, $7907. The difference of $2434 between college graduation and college attendance was the largest increment between any two educational levels. Glick and Miller estimated that a man with a college degree earns some $100,000 more than a man who does not go on with his education beyond high school.

Bridgman (1960) pointed out that attention to the median rather than the mean quite drastically alters the census figures for 1949 income. Thus, the median rather than mean difference between college and high school graduates is about $58,000, a figure very different from $100,000. Bridgman fears that blanket statements about the economic value of college education may serve to obscure the importance of such factors as individual differences in ability, interest, and motivation.

In recent years Harris (1949, 1960) and West (1953) have discerned a decline in the purely economic rewards of a college education. As college education becomes accessible to more and more people, its particular value as an avenue to large financial gain diminishes. And as the incomes of groups with less education rise as a result of union activity and social legislation, the gap between college-educated people and others narrows. Allied to this tendency is an indication that the upward social mobility, which has been an important product or byproduct of American education, is somewhat on the decline—at least at the highest levels. Myrdal (1944) described education as the main prop to equality of opportunity in the 20th century. But West (1953) and Havemann and West (1952) have pointed out that as colleges become more accessible to individuals of lower socio-economic status, there is a diminution in the opportunities for entering the top occupational classes to which education has held the key.

Occupations. There is a direct relationship between years of schooling and kinds of occupations. Thus, except for Negroes, each increment of schooling is associated with a decline in representation in service or laboring activities. In recent years college education has become almost a sine qua non for placement in the top occupational strata. Exceptions, such as Harry Truman in the field of public affairs and Ernest Hemingway in the field of literature, were not nearly so rare in the 19th century or slightly earlier. The National Opinion Research Council (1947) reported that in 1947, although only 5% of the adult population of the United States held college degrees, over half considered that *some* college education was necessary for a young man "to get along well in the world" and 41% thought that a college *degree* was necessary.

Interests. A number of studies (Strong, 1931, 1943, 1951, 1955; Kelly, 1955) have been concerned with the relationship between interest scores obtained during the college years and those obtained from the same individuals after various intervals of time. This is one of the few areas in which longitudinal studies of college alumni have been carried out. Strong tested a number of freshman and senior classes at Stanford University between 1927 and 1949 with the Strong Vocational Interest Inventory and then retested these same individuals at later dates, the intervals between testings ranging up to 22 years. Strong reported that the test-retest correlations are "amazingly high" and concluded that "Interest scores may be as permanent as intelligence test scores. . . ."

Dressel (1954) has cautioned against too ready acceptance of the notion that interest patterns are highly stable and change but little. Correlations around .75 between tests and retests are high, to be sure, but they are nevertheless indicative of a fair amount of change since the original testing. It does appear evident, however, that there is a strong tendency for the interest patterns of college seniors to persist well into adulthood.

Marriage and Children.[1] The proportion of college graduates who marry, their age at marriage, and the number of children of such marriages have received much attention.

For the fifteen-year period between 1940 and the mid-1950s the proportion of the population that was married increased more than for any period in our history for which such data are available. In this period the increase in proportion of married people was greater for the better educated segments of our population than for those with less education. As Glick and Carter (1958) put it, "This positive relationship between educational level and increase in marriage . . . implies that more of the better-educated persons were forming families and that family formation was taking place at a younger age than before." They pointed out that by the autumn of 1956 one out of every four students in college was married. If older college students were omitted from consideration leaving only those of more typical college age, that is, 18–24, the figure dropped to about one in six, still a high proportion of married undergraduates.

College educated men and women tend to marry individuals of similar educational levels (Glick and Carter, 1958). Glick and Carter (1958), Havemann and West (1952), Shosteck (1953), and Lehman (1953) have reported that at all age levels the incidence of divorce is lower for college graduates than for people with less education.

College men have not differed much from other men in rate of marriage, although they tend to marry at a later age (Havemann and West, 1952; Bressler and Kephart, 1954; Grady, 1958). The marriage patterns of women college graduates are considerably more complex than those of males, however, and for this reason the literature on marriage and children of college educated individuals has tended to concentrate on the women.

Traditionally, smaller proportions of college women have married as compared to women with less education. Although it is still true that the rate of marriage of college women is lower than that of non-college women, the differences are considerably smaller than they

---

[1] The writer is indebted to Mrs. Sally Griffen, Vassar College, for aid with the library research on the subject of marriage and children of college alumni.

were for the decades prior to 1940 (Havemann and West, 1952; Bressler and Kephart, 1954; Newcomer, 1959). As in the case of college educated men, women college graduates tend to marry somewhat later than other women. The mean age of marriage of college women has been declining since 1940, however, just as it has in the case of less well educated segments of the population (McBride, 1958). Lehman (1953) demonstrated that this trend toward early marriage started quite abruptly with the war classes of 1941 to 45. Havemann and West (1952) showed that graduates of women's colleges tend to marry somewhat later than other women college graduates but that eventually the two marriage rates are equal.

Perhaps even more striking than the increased rate of marriage of women college graduates in recent decades is the higher incidence of marriage among women with advanced degrees, as McBride's (1958) study of Bryn Mawr alumnae indicated. Interview studies of Vassar College undergraduates carried out by the Mellon Foundation disclose that very few of the students planning on graduate work or careers believe that such activities will make them any less eligible for marriage. These attitudes contrast rather sharply with those of students of former generations. Studies of Vassar College alumnae of earlier periods indicate that choice of graduate schooling or a career was often made with a more of less conscious awareness that such activity reduced the likelihood of marriage.

Census figures over the years have revealed an inverse relationship between years of education and number of children. It is still the case that college-educated people are producing fewer children than are individuals who have had less education, although various studies (Population Reference Bureau, 1952; Lehman, 1953; Shosteck, 1953) have suggested that the fertility rate of college-educated men and women has been rising sharply since World War II. The 1960 census figures will undoubtedly reveal a substantial increase in the number of children born to college graduates.

Values, attitudes, and opinions. Attention to changes that take place during the undergraduate years (Chapter 24) raises many questions that can be answered only by consideration of the years after graduation. What is needed is a sufficient amount of empirical information to enable us to place the experiences of the college years within a larger theoretical or systematic framework. We need to know which of the changes that take place are relatively transient and which become relatively enduring parts of the character or the personality. Do the changes measured by questionnaires, tests, or interviews reflect only relatively isolated areas of verbal functioning, or do they influence large and important life patterns? Do the experiences or characteristics of alumni seem continuous or relatively discontinuous with the college years or portions thereof? Is it appropriate to think of the college years as a phase or period of individual development that comes to an end with graduation? Or does it appear that at least for some time after graduation the same sorts of progressions or regularities of development which characterize the college years are manifest?

Reasonably definitive answers to questions like these can be obtained only by studies of the same individuals during the college years and later. Studies of college alumni of different age levels are of value, but the imponderables of social change are likely to render results of such studies somewhat equivocal. Although most investigations of changes in values, attitudes, and opinions have stopped with graduation, a few longitudinal studies in this area have been carried beyond the college years. Indeed, this is just about the only area, aside from Strong's studies of the interests of college students (1931, 1943, 1951, 1955) and the Mellon Foundation studies of personality development to be described later, in which the same individuals have been studied as undergraduates and again as alumni.

Senior-alumni comparisons. The most comprehensive longitudinal study of political, social, and economic outlook is one carried out by Nelson (1954). In 1936 Nelson tested 3758 students at a variety of colleges, and in 1950 he repeated the testing with 901 of his original subjects. He discovered a postcollege trend toward "slightly more liberalism" over the 14 year test-retest period, but, for the most part, the results indicated that the original positions were maintained with a considerable degree of consistency. The differences in means for the various colleges between 1936 and 1950 were "significant but small and indicate persistence" of the original attitudes. The correlation for individuals in the test-retest sample was .57. "The differences between students in different institutions tended to persist, although time reduced the differences to some extent." The regional differences obtained in the first testing session (for example, the Southern colleges contained more conservative student bodies) tended to persist into the second testing.

In 1950 Nelson tested undergraduates at one of the colleges involved in the study and found them to be more liberal than their predecessors in 1936. He considers that this change between undergraduates at the different periods parallels the slight trend toward increased liberalism found among alumni, and he concludes that liberalism "does not seem to be a function of the age of individuals or of what they are taught in college." Rather it is "a product of the times."

Nelson is saying two very important things. First, that there is a considerable tendency for the attitudes or opinions of seniors to persist without substantial modification well into the adult years. And second, that although tendencies toward such persistence are strong, some change may take place in the alumni years as a function of general cultural or societal pressures.

The other longitudinal studies that are available support Nelson's first conclusion although, unfortunately, the intervals between the original testing and the retest are considerably shorter than in his study. Bugelski and Lester (1940), after discovering that seniors were more liberal in their political, social, and economic attitudes than were freshmen, carried their study one step further: they retested the same groups as alumni—in the case of two classes, after a period of three years, and in the case of a third, after the passage of two years. No significant senior-alumni differences were discovered. Parenthetically, it might be added that these authors contradict Nelson's view that liberalism is not a function of college teaching, since they observed differential senior-freshman differences that were associated with type of curriculum. Since the general cultural scene appears to be an important influential factor, we may note that the period in which Bugelski and Lester were at work was the middle and late 1930s.

In a study of attitudes and opinions expressed by alumnae of a women's college—a study carried out at about the same time as that of Bugelski and Lester—Newcomb (1943) obtained similar results. His subjects included not only alumnae who were actual graduates but also women who had left college after two or three years of attendance. The interval between the testing of undergraduates and the later retesting ranged from one to three years.

Newcomb discovered "no large differences" for any groups between the original testing and the retesting one, two, or three years later. If the original subjects had spent three or four years in college, their scores continued to change slightly in the liberal direction. This trend did not hold, however, for the group that had spent but two years in college. Their scores tended not to change. These findings led Newcomb to conclude that there is "no regression to the mean or to home and family standards" in the early postcollege years. But this conclusion held for groups one or two years out of college; not for those that had been out three years. In the case of the latter groups, there was a slight indication of a reversal of the freshman-senior tendency, leading Newcomb to postulate a trend toward reversion to the freshman position with greater lapses of time after leaving college. Thus, he hypothesized that, "those longest out of college and those who spent the least time in college are more like freshmen. Those most recently out and those who spent the most time in college are more like seniors."

The number of subjects comprising Newcomb's various groups was quite small; in most cases not large enough to meet the minimal requirements for dependable statistical manipulation. Also, Newcomb pointed out a possible source of bias. Not all alumnae and ex-students responded, and among the respondents was a significantly larger number of individuals with lower scores on conservatism than would be expected on the basis of chance. Inclusion of larger representation from high-scorers could conceivably have changed the results somewhat. Nevertheless, Newcomb's essential findings resemble those of Nelson and of Bugelski and Lester in indicating that the values, attitudes, and opinions with which one leaves college tend to persist.

The Mellon Foundation has studied in three different graduating classes samples of alumnae who had been tested as seniors. One class was retested after three years and the other two after four. The test batteries differed somewhat for the three classes, but each contained a number of scales relevant to the general area of values, attitudes, and opinions, chiefly the California F and E Scales (Adorno et al., 1950), the Vassar Social Maturity Scale (Webster, Sanford, and Freedman, 1955), and the Tolerance Scale of the California Psychological Inventory (Gough, 1957).

The samples of alumnae were obtained primarily by writing to women selected at random from the list of the graduating class. However, each alumnae sample contained returns for some fifteen to twenty women who were tested at alumnae reunions rather than by the mail procedure. Of course, not all of the alumnae included in the original samples returned their tests, completions amounting to some 60 to 70% of the original totals for each class. Comparisons of the means of the alumnae samples as seniors with those of the entire senior classes of which they form a part demonstrate that the responding groups are reasonably representative of the larger alumnae classes.

Results indicate that there are no clear trends in senior-alumnae differences for a three- or four-year period after graduation, and one may conclude that the results of the studies carried on by Nelson, by Bugelski and Lester, and by Newcomb in earlier decades are replicated by the Mellon Foundation studies. All these studies agree that there is no indication that the early years after graduation are ones in which large scale shifts in ideology or attitudes occur.

Utilizing the F and E Scales the writer (1959) made a study of alumnae of Vassar College for various decades going back as far as 1904. The classes involved were 1904, 1914, 1921 to 24, 1929 to 35, and 1940 to 43.

These alumnae were tested between 1955 and 1958 in two ways. In some cases the tests were administered at Vassar, when reunions or special studies made groups of alumnae available. Otherwise, the tests were sent by mail to alumnae selected at random from lists supplied by the alumnae office. In cases where results for one group or class were composed of data obtained in both fashions, there were no statistically significant differences between the two groups. At least as far as the F and E Scales are concerned, alumnae who attend class reunions do not differ from those who are not present at reunions but who respond to mail invitations to participate in a survey of opinion.

The alumnae involved in this study were members, although not necessarily active ones, of the Alumnae Association of Vassar College. Moreover, of course, in the case of the returns obtained by mail, our responses were limited to those of alumnae who were cooperative enough to return the questionnaire sent to them. Returns averaged 60 to 70% of the total number of questionnaires sent out. Accordingly, the extent to which our findings are representative of entire groups or classes of alumnae of the periods concerned is unknown. There is no apparent reason for thinking, however, that there may have been some systematic bias of sampling which would account for the differences between groups or classes of alumnae.

The results of this study showed substantial differences between some of the groups and classes. Thus, the Class of 1904 was significantly higher than the Class of 1914 on both the F and E Scales. Similarly, on the F Scale, the Classes of 1921 to 24 differed significantly from the Classes of 1929 to 35.

These results are in keeping with the findings reported above and suggest that the attitudes and values with which one leaves college have considerable permanence. We do not know, of course, what the original mean scores for these various groups would have been, had they been tested at the time of leaving college. The fact that the means of some adjacent groups differ significantly from one another tends to rule out chronological age or life experiences subsequent to graduation as cogent explanatory factors. Although on this basis one could account for differences between groups of women widely separated in age, such explanations do not appear adequate to explain the large differences between members of adjacent decades. On the basis of chronological age or life experiences subsequent to graduation one would not expect women averaging 74 years of age at the time of testing to differ appreciably from women who are 66 on the average, or women of 47 to differ from those who are 43.

What seems more likely is that the differences noted at the time of testing reflect differences which were present at the time of leaving college. Whether the differences which we surmise to have obtained at the time of graduation from college reflect the influences of events of the college years or earlier ones cannot, of course, be answered by these data alone. We know from Chapter 24 that considerable change in the kinds of sentiments that make up the *F* and *E* Scales is a common accompaniment or outcome of liberal education. It would seem reasonable to think that the scores of the groups of alumnae were higher as freshmen and that the scores obtained at the time of testing reflect lower senior scores. In any event, there appears to be substantial evidence that the various sentiments, values, attitudes, and opinions tapped by the *F* and *E* Scales have very likely persisted with little change from graduation well on into later life.

The above findings have considerable educational import. If the values, attitudes, and opinions with which one leaves college are likely to persist into later life with but little modification, the college years take on enormous importance. One cannot think of the college years as but one of a number of periods in life in which substantial modification takes place. For many students, apparently, changes in values, attitudes, and opinions or lack of such change end with graduation. As Chapter 24 makes clear, the origins of such changes during the college years are obscure. To a considerable extent, it may be that the changes that occur during this period are more a reflection of the cultural and societal forces that impinge upon the colleges and individual students than the effect of deliberate educational policy or program. But even if this be the case, it appears that the college years are ones characterized by a degree of openness to change that is not later duplicated. One is reminded of the remark of William James: "Outside of their own business, the ideas gained by men before they are twenty-five are practically the only ideas they shall have in their lives." (James, 1890, II, p. 411).

Thus far, we have emphasized the relative fixity of opinion and outlook after graduation. Yet, as has been mentioned, there is evidence that some change may take place. Hyman and Sheatsley (1953) pointed out that during "the McCarthy period," that is, around 1953, there was an increase among college-educated citizenry of restrictive sentiment with regard to the exercise of traditional American freedoms by Communist and other dissident groups. Gallup polls in that period showed that the proportions of college alumni who would deny various rights to individuals identified with Communist positions increased, even

Table 1. Percentages of Plus and Minus Responses for Economic Items for Six Groups of Vassar Alumnae

				Class(es)								
	'04		'14		'21–'24		'29–'35		'40–'43		'54	
					Number Tested							
	85		43		73		50		77		81	
Public Opinion Survey Items	+	−	+	−	+	−	+	−	+	−	+	−
1. It is up to the government to make sure that everyone has a secure job and a good standard of living.	29	71	23	77	15	85	28	72	08	92	17	83
2. The government should own and operate all public utilities (railroads, gas, electricity, etc.).	15	85	19	81	17	83	20	80	09	91	19	81
3. The only way to eliminate poverty is to make certain basic changes in our political and economic system.	46	54	40	60	41	59	32	68	37	63	38	62
4. In a new tax program it is essential not to reduce the income taxes on corporations and wealthy individuals.	29	71	31	69	25	75	24	76	26	74	29	71
5. In general, full economic security is bad; most men wouldn't work if they didn't need the money for eating and living.	66	34	60	40	58	42	47	53	52	48	45	55
6. There should be some upper limit, such as $25,000 per year, on how much any individual can earn.	21	79	12	88	15	85	15	85	05	95	02	98
7. Most of the present attempts to curb and limit unions would in the long run do more harm than good.	44	56	19	81	21	79	42	58	28	72	18	82

though college-educated people were more liberal than those with less education. Apparently, strong pressures, such as those exercised by the forces of public opinion in support of Senator McCarthy, can effect changes in beliefs and attitudes among college alumni.

Yet the studies of Vassar alumnae reported above suggest that such changes are not very frequent and often not great. Table 1 presents a number of items having to do with the general outlook on economic matters of the five classes and groups for which results on the F and E Scales were just reported, plus the Class of 1954, which was tested in 1958. The responses to these items indicate that the period of the New Deal during the 1930s, with the great economic changes which accompanied it, probably had little effect upon the outlook of Vassar alumnae. One might expect, for example, that the alumnae of the Classes of 1921 to 24, who were relatively young women when Franklin Roosevelt took office, would display some indication of having been influenced by the greatly changed economic climate of the 1930s as compared to the period of Presidents Harding, Coolidge, and Hoover. Yet, examination of their responses indicates that they are one of the more conservative alumnae groups. If they were influenced by Roosevelt and the New Deal era, the influence was apparently neither great nor very lasting.

These findings suggest that massive or profound social change may often be compounded out of slight shifts of attitude or belief among individuals. Probably many Vassar alumnae were influenced to some degree by Franklin Roosevelt and the New Deal. Many aspects of the welfare state, for example, our social security arrangements, are now pretty much taken for granted, although a generation ago they were regarded by many individuals as intolerable socialistic measures. It would appear that, in dynamic systems, slight initial differences can result in large differences in outcome.

Alumni and other citizens compared. In 1949 Pace (1949) wrote that since the President's Commission on Higher Education (1948) had stressed the importance of good citizenship as a goal of education, it was possible to appraise the outcome of our educational processes, at least in part, by taking inventory of the citizenship activities of college alumni. On the basis of analysis of responses to questions concerned with political activities, Pace reported that of the alumni figuring in the *Time Magazine* survey of 1947, fewer than one-third signed petitions, fewer than one-quarter sent telegrams or letters to office-holders, and fewer than one-fifth contributed money to political causes. Only about 20% of the alumni could be considered as truly active politically.

These findings were similar to those obtained by Pace in studies of University of Minnesota alumni carried out in 1937 (Pace, 1941). Although they are likely to be rather passive in political matters, college alumni do vote in national elections with greater frequency than other citizens. In the 1947 *Time* survey, 79% of the college graduates reported voting in national elections vs. a figure of 55% for the general population.

In actual political sentiment or party preference college-educated people definitely lean toward the Republican Party. In the 1947 *Time* survey, Republicans outnumbered Democrats by a margin of 3 to 2. Had there been exclusion of the South, where, of course, Republicans are relatively rare, the margin of Republicans over Democrats would have been even greater. Republicans were in the majority for all income levels indicating that preference for the Republican Party was not associated more with level of income than with education. However, age seems to play a part in party preference. There are fewer Republicans among the younger men. Also Havemann and West (1952) reported a tendency toward an increasing number of voters among the younger alumni who termed themselves "independents." There was some evidence that proclivity toward labeling oneself "independent" was associated with higher grades as an undergraduate. The "independents" were noted to favor very liberal positions on social and political questions.

As for the general social and economic views of college alumni as compared to the rest of the population, there is evidence that college-educated people are more conservative with respect to economic issues, but, as was mentioned earlier, they are more tolerant of radical ideas and unconventional people, less prejudiced toward minority groups and alien cultures, and more internationalist in outlook. On the basis of polls taken in 1954, Stouffer (1955) reported decreasing tolerance of the civil rights of dissident and minority political groups, as one descends in the educational hierarchy. The relationship was linear, with college graduates being the most tolerant, and it held for all age groups. Since the educational attainment of Americans increases yearly, Stouffer suggested that perhaps we may expect a more tolerant future population. Among college educated people beginning with age 40 there was a consistent tendency for the older age groups to be less tolerant than the younger, but there was little difference between college graduates in the 30 to 39 and the 21 to 29 age ranges. Whether the increase in intolerance of the older age groups was a function of increasing age or of differences that existed at the time of graduation from college cannot be answered by the data themselves. The studies reported above by Nelson, the Mellon Foundation, and others on the relative persistence of attitudes after graduation suggest that the latter may be the more likely explanation. Hyman and Sheatsley (1953) also envisioned long term trends in the American citizenry toward more tolerance in matters involving civil liberties as a result of increased educational attainment as well as "less authoritarian child rearing and school systems."

Levinson (Adorno et al., 1950) reported low but dependable relationships between intelligence and amount of education on the one hand and freedom from ethnocentrism on the other. Generally, college alumni display more liberal attitudes toward ethnic or religious minority groups, but the *Time* survey of 1947 indicated that this was particularly true of younger alumni. This survey also revealed that Southern alumni who moved North displayed less racial prejudice than those Southerners who remained in the South. Northerners who moved to the South did not display the converse, however, but remained steadfast in their liberal views of race relationships.

Table 1 indicates that Vassar College alumnae are extremely conservative in economic outlook; and although they may represent a somewhat more conservative group than college alumni at large, their sentiments reflect the general findings for college-educated people. College graduates distrust "welfare economics" and strong government. Generally they are on the side of business in conflicts with labor or in resistance to government regulation. Pace (1949) considered that some of the attitudes toward economic affairs displayed by college alumni bring into serious question the quality of teaching about such matters in our colleges. For example, he pointed out that a majority of alumni in the 1947 *Time* survey indicated a belief that government planning and socialist economic measures meant the end of liberty and freedom, despite the evidence to the contrary to be found in such countries as Great Britain or the Scandinavian states.

PERSONALITY DEVELOPMENT AFTER COLLEGE

Alumnae-senior comparisons, in terms of scores on the Vassar scales described in Chapter 24, are available for the Vassar classes of 1954 and 1955. The alumnae samples were obtained in the same fashion as that described in the preceding section, and both of them were retested four years after graduation. The only change that is significant in both classes comes on the Repression and Suppression (RS) Scale, the subjects obtaining higher scores as alumnae than they did as seniors. This finding may be interpreted to mean that the alumnae as compared to the seniors are more stable emotionally and more assured socially, less anxious and depressed, generally more confident and imperturbable.

Comparisons of alumnae (a representative sample) with senior scores on the Minnesota Multiphasic Personality Inventory (*MMPI*) (Hathaway and McKinley, 1951) are available for the class of 1955 tested again four years after graduation. The chief finding is that the alumnae are lower on all of the clinical scales. This indicates that the alumnae, as compared to their state as seniors, reveal less evidence of emotional difficulty, anxiety, or psychological unease and more evidence of physical and psychological well-being.

Senior and alumnae retests on the California Psychological Inventory (*CPI*) (Gough, 1957), an objective test of a wide variety of psychological and social characteristics, are available for 80 women in the class of 1956 who were retested in 1959. Comparison of the means of the alumnae sample as seniors with the total senior class indicates that the alumnae group compose a representative sample, inasmuch as the groups differ significantly on only one scale. The results of the *CPI* comparisons may be summed up by saying that the alumnae as compared to the seniors display increases in the following qualities: capability, cooperativeness, efficiency, resourcefulness, conscientiousness, patience, helpfulness, sympathy, calmness, deliberateness, spontaneity, and talkativeness.

In summary, studies of young alumnae show that they gain after graduation in feelings of stability, optimism, and contentment, as reflected in changes in the *RS* Scale, the *MMPI*, and the *CPI*; and that they remain unchanged three or four years after graduation in respect to the chief qualities that distinguish seniors from freshmen, for example, lessened authoritarianism and increased freedom of impulse expression and "rebellious independence."

A study carried out by Tate and Musick (1954) sheds some light on the generality of the findings involving Vassar students and alumnae. They tested 92 seniors at Virginia Polytechnic Institute in 1940, and retested eighty as alumni in 1947. The measures involved were a personal adjustment scale and the Bernreuter Personality Inventory (Bernreuter, 1933). The results resemble those obtained by the Mellon Foundation in its studies of recent alumnae of Vassar College. On the Bernreuter Personality Inventory the alumnae were lower on neuroticism and higher on extraversion and dominance. The repetition of the personal adjustment scale revealed fewer problems for the subjects as alumnae than as students. Apparently the turbulent years of the

Second World War did not prevent these students from making strides toward increased stability and "adjustment" in the years after graduation.

We have seen that the attitudes and opinions with which one leaves college are likely to persist relatively unchanged well on into middle and old age. One may ask if this is true also of the kinds of characteristics measured by the Vassar scales. It seems not unreasonable to hypothesize that the maturing and aging processes would be accompanied by a gradual reduction of scores on such scales as Developmental Status (*DS*) and Impulse Experience (*IE*) (see Chapter 24). There are data that bear upon this point. Fifty alumnae from the classes of 1929 to 1935 (a reasonably representative group of alumnae in their age range) were studied in 1954, when they were forty to forty-five years of age (Sanford, 1956; Brown, Chapter 16).

Comparison of scores for these alumnae with senior and freshman scores of the class of 1958 shows that on the *IE* Scale the alumnae resemble freshmen more than they do seniors and that on the *DS* and *SM* Scales they fall somewhere in between the freshmen and seniors. Lacking scores for these alumnae as seniors, we do not, of course, know whether their scores on these scales would have been higher, had they been tested as seniors. It is interesting to observe that the senior-alumnae comparisons on most of the other scales resemble very much the results obtained in the testing of the classes of 1954 and 1955 four years after graduation, except for the Dominance and Confidence Scale (*DC*) on which the alumnae are appreciably lower than seniors. The findings that the alumnae are fairly high on the Social Integration (*SI*) and Repression and Suppression (*RS*) Scales lends weight to the notion that the fairly low *DC* Scale score is not a function or accompaniment of increased feelings of anxiety, depression, or general psychological disorder, since the *DC* Scale is substantially correlated with the *SI* and *RS* Scales. Moreover, the *MMPI* profile of the alumnae of the classes of 1929 to 35 is almost identical with that of the alumnae of the class of 1955, retested in 1959. Perhaps, then, the low *DC* Scale score does not represent a drop from a hypothetical senior score but instead indicates a difference between younger women and those of earlier generations.

It was indicated in Chapter 24 that the bulk of the freshmen-senior change on the Vassar Scales has taken place by the end of the sophomore year. This finding plus those reported above for senior-young alumnae comparisons suggest that juniors and seniors should be regarded as belonging to a phase of development closer to that of the young alumnae than to that of freshmen and sophomores. Perhaps we should think of a developmental phase of late adolescence, beginning at some point in high school or prep school and terminating around the end of the sophomore year in college; followed by a *developmental phase of young adulthood* that begins around the junior year and carries over to a yet undetermined extent into the alumnae years. From this point of view, basic changes in qualities of character, outlook on life, and fundamental personality characteristics are consolidated by the end of the sophomore year, after the developmental phases of early and late adolescence in which rapid change has taken place; and for some time thereafter little change takes place in these characteristics, or at least, change is likely to be a more measured or gradual affair.

Further research is needed in order to clarify the meaning of the results involving the *RS* Scale and the *MMPI*. One tenable hypothesis is that the subsequent rise in *RS* Score and lowering of *MMPI* Scores among alumnae are an indication that the gains or changes of adolescence, painful or difficult to integrate into the personality at times, have now been consolidated. However, one may posit an alternative view of things: higher scores obtained on the *MMPI* by seniors as compared to freshmen, the increase of "neurotic" symptoms which takes place between freshman and senior years, should be regarded more properly as a kind of external phenomenon, a function of the considerable demands made by the faculty and administration of a school that maintains high standards of scholarship and academic performance. Considered from this point of view, the increased stability and well-being of alumnae as compared to seniors is primarily a product of the less rigorous lives of the former, the lessened intensity of demands made upon them.

In any event, the findings with regard to personality change between college entrance and three or four years after graduation suggest that there may be some basis for considering juniors and seniors to be in a developmental stage rather different from that of freshmen and sophomores. This may be an argument in favor of different kinds of curricula for the two groups of students. Because they are in a different stage of personality development, it seems very likely that upperclassmen will benefit from somewhat different kinds of experiences than will freshmen and sophomores.

RELATIONSHIPS BETWEEN EXPERIENCES OF THE COLLEGE YEARS AND EVENTS OF LATER LIFE

During the Second World War an accelerated program (graduation in three or fewer years) was available on an optional basis to undergraduates at Ohio State University. Pressey (1949) and Flesher and Pressey (1955) made studies of the status as alumnae of large numbers of women who were graduated in the accelerated program. On the basis of such characteristics as entrance tests, grades, and courses of study these women were matched against controls who matriculated in a nonaccelerated or regular program.

Ten years after graduation, on the average, the "accelerates" as compared to the controls had obtained a significantly higher number of advanced degrees; and a significantly larger number of the accelerates were working after having been married. A slightly higher percentage of the nonaccelerates were married, and a slightly higher percentage of the accelerates had been divorced; but these differences were small. Both groups participated to about the same degree in community activities. These studies led Flesher and Pressey to conclude that many students of ability can complete a four year program in less time with no unfortunate consequences.

It is disheartening to note the rarity of studies such as those of Pressey and of Flesher. Most experimental educational programs have been conducted with little or no regard for controlled measurement or evaluation of their effects. Accordingly, when such a program ends, there is usually no mechanism by which the experiences of the participants can be utilized in a systematic way to further the knowledge of educators and others involved in similar activities.

Pace (1954) reported on studies of alumni carried out in connection with a program of evaluation of general education at Syracuse University. A questionnaire was filled out by a "fairly representative group of 2,500 Syracuse graduates from the classes of '47, '42, '37, '32, '27, '17, and '07." This questionnaire contained a series of subtests designed "to measure the extent to which alumni engaged in various activities related to the broad fields of social science, humanities, and science." Another series of subtests was included to measure the extent to which the ideas of alumni about politics, art, literature, and science corresponded "to the concepts and points of view which are widely shared by experts in the various subjects."

Pace had the following to say about the results of this questionnaire study.

Graduates of Liberal Arts exhibit a more balanced picture of interest and attitudes than do graduates of the professional and technical schools. They are more active participants in a larger number of fields, and their few low scores on the various scales are not as low as the low scores of graduates of the professional and technical schools. It is possible, of course, that a similar pattern existed at the time these men and women entered the University. Whether the graduates were like this in the beginning or whether college was entirely responsible for making them this way is not the basic question. The simple descriptive fact is that these differences exist and that they correspond fairly well to the differences in academic emphasis between liberal and general education on the one hand, and professional and technical education on the other. We cannot say that the particular pattern of adult behavior was caused by the particular pattern of academic curriculum, but it has surely been influenced by it. *College does make a difference; and the particular kind of college education* also makes a difference. (Pace, 1954, p. 23)

As Chapter 17 indicates, the matter of the determinants of differences among seniors in different majors or among alumni of various kinds of colleges or courses of study is a complex issue requiring much empirical study. In some cases the differences that exist among seniors seem primarily to be functions of qualities already present in the students as freshmen rather than products of different courses of study. In other cases differences among upperclassmen seem to reflect the differential influences of courses and major fields.

In any event, Pace's studies of Syracuse alumni confirm the findings of the *Time* magazine survey of 1947. In that study it was noted that those alumni in the professions or in business who had had general rather than technical or preprofessional schooling as undergraduates were described as the more "active and interested citizens." This finding held true when graduates of the two kinds of undergraduate training within the same college were compared and also when graduates of Big Ten and Ivy League colleges were compared with alumni of technical schools. Although Ivy League and Big Ten alumni did not differ from one another in amount of political activity, they were both found to be more active than alumni of technical colleges. Pace (1949) considered that these results lent support to the view that specialized education should be preceded by some form of more general education.

The data from the 1947 *Time* survey were utilized by Plasse (1951) in studying the relationships between achievement in college and in later life. The college characteristics involved in the study were scholarship, leadership in campus organizations, self-support, and satisfaction with college life. These were compared with the following factors in postcollege life: home and family life, social activity (clubs and organizations), economic status, information (chiefly magazine reading), and civic participation.

Plasse found that over the entire range of subjects the relationships between the college and adult measures were largely insignificant. However, some significant relationships were obtained when groups high and low on various of the characteristics involved were compared, ignoring the individuals falling in the middle ranges. The college characteristic most broadly associated with the various indices of adult status was leadership in campus organizations. The group high on this quality as undergraduates displayed greater achievement as alumni than those who were low. Second among the college characteristics in degree of association with alumni achievement was the extent of reported satisfaction with the college years. Undergraduate scholarship was but little related to alumni achievement.

Bridgman (1930), however, has reported a study in which undergraduate grades were related to success in a career with the Bell Telephone System. Campus achievement—for example, leadership in various activities—was significantly related to later success as well, but scholarship was the best single index. The criterion of success in business utilized by him was salary weighted by years of service. Havemann and West (1952) reported that grades were related to financial success in all fields *except* business, and Bridgman's findings serve to point up the exceptions often involved in such generalizations.

Probably the most complex and yet systematic analysis of undergraduate characteristics and their relationships to activities subsequent to graduation was carried out by Brown (1956; Chapter 16). The subjects involved were the 50 Vassar College alumnae of the classes of 1929 to 35 mentioned earlier. On the basis of their retrospective accounts of what they were like as students, and on the basis of available college records, these women were rated on seven variables pertaining to behavior and experience in college. A coding procedure utilizing these variables produced five general educational patterns which tie together much otherwise diverse information and provide a much broadened context for evaluating undergraduate experiences and behavior.

The complexity of the matter of grades or academic performance is very clearly pointed up by this system. For example, the women in both the Social and Peer-Group Orientation and the Underachievers with Family-Orientation patterns of alumnae received approximately the same grades as undergraduates. Yet at the time of this study in 1954, there were rather clear intellectual differences between the two groups. It was evident that the women comprising the Social and Peer-Group Orientation category had developed little since their college years. Their interests were fairly narrow, their general intellectual and cultural development since graduation rather limited. The Underachievers with Family Orientation were quite different, however. It was evident that the processes of learning or broadening of outlook had not terminated or even slowed down markedly after college. Intellectually these women were alive and eager, their interests and activities spanning a very wide range. It seems apparent that the educative process of the college years held quite different meanings for the two groups. For the women labeled Social and Peer-Group Orientation, academic activities proper were probably regarded as relatively external obligations to be fulfilled. The Underachievers with Family Orientation were by no means hard working students as such, but their lives and activities subsequent to college conveyed the impression that the qualities of a liberally educated person had become an intrinsic part of their personality and general outlook.

A similar kind of phenomenon is revealed by comparison of the Overachievers and the High Achievers. The women in both of these groups received high grades as undergraduates; yet, the two groups differed considerably when they were studied in 1954. Like the women in the Social and Peer-Group Orientation pattern the Overachievers pretty much left the world of scholarship and intellect behind them after graduation. This was not the case with the High Achievers, whose intellectual growth continued after the college years, although perhaps in narrower ways than was characteristic of the Underachievers with Family Orientation.

The above discussion illustrates the value of studying educational patterns such as those devised by Brown. Events of the college years may be seen from the vantage point of years of perspective—in this case some 20 years after graduation. It becomes evident that apparently equivalent academic achievement or scholarship among various students may have very different meanings for these students and very different implications for the future. Clearly there is a great need for such enlargement of the context within which students and their achievements are viewed.

THE MELLON FOUNDATION INTERVIEW STUDIES OF VASSAR COLLEGE ALUMNAE

The quantitative studies reported in the previous section may now be supplemented by interview studies, which have greater flexibility and allow more opportunity for exploration.

In addition to the 50 Vassar College alumnae of the classes of 1929 to 35, the Mellon Foundation staff interviewed 40 alumnae of the classes of 1954, 1955, and 1956. Since these women were volunteers who responded to invitations to be studied and interviewed, they cannot be assumed to be representative of their fellow alumnae in each class. It is likely, however, that the great majority of patterns of life and modes of thought characteristic of Vassar College alumnae in general may be found among the subjects who were interviewed, al-though generalizations about the frequency with which these patterns may be met among the alumnae at large are dubious.

Most of the young alumnae were getting on very well. Whatever their state, whether married or single, whether in graduate or profes-sional school or at work, whether, if housewives, they worked outside the home or not, most of these young alumnae were distinguished by competence, flexibility, and efficiency; and most of them reported that they were at least reasonably satisfied with their lot in life. This pic-ture is in keeping with the test results, which revealed this group of alumnae to be more stable, optimistic, and content than they were as seniors.

Nowadays some 70% of an alumnae class are married by three or four years after graduation. An indication of the pressures toward mar-riage that exist among alumnae in the years immediately after gradua-tion was provided in the account given by one of the alumnae of her roommate group, consisting of six seniors. "Only one of us had plans for marrying after graduation, but all of us were married within four-teen months."

By and large the marriages of these young alumnae were distin-guished by their stability and general "conventionality." The hus-bands were working hard in their careers, and the women were hard at work helping their husbands in whatever ways they could, and in running the household or caring for the children. There were excep-tions to these generalizations, of course, and some of these will be presented later, but by and large the marriages as described seemed reasonably free of disaffection and tension. The rather commonly ac-cepted notion of the specter of Satan stalking our upper-middle-class suburbs in the form of alcoholism, adultery, loneliness, and feelings of lack of fulfillment of one sort or another did not seem at all appro-priate. Do such difficulties manifest themselves later in life? Or are these not really true of the lives of most of the women who attend col-leges like Vassar? Judging from the alumnae of the classes of 1929 to 35 who were studied in 1954 and extrapolating from the current lives of the younger alumnae, the latter seems to be the case.

The alumnae who were attending graduate or professional schools displayed a rather impressive picture of accomplishment. For the most part these students found the academic demands made upon them to be no greater than those to which they had been accustomed as under-graduates; in some cases the work was even a bit easier. Moreover, these women had learned that academic competition with men pre-sented no great difficulty.

The accomplishments of those students who had gone to work immediately or shortly after college were equally impressive. In many cases they started out in fairly unimportant positions, but in a reasonably short time, a year or two perhaps, they had worked into positions of some prominence and responsibility. Employers, it seems, are fairly quick to recognize intelligence, diligence, and good work habits.

In many cases it appears that these alumnae had enjoyed a sense of accomplishment after graduation, in additional schooling or at work, that they did not experience as undergraduates. To some extent this may have been a function of lessened competition. At Vassar College they were in a sense competing academically with many other intelligent and studious girls. After graduation, it is likely that the degree of competition was not nearly so keen. Many of the married alumnae reported a similar kind of experience as a consequence of participation in various community activities, for example, the League of Women Voters. For the most part they found themselves able to handle with dispatch the demands made upon them.

An interviewer cannot help wondering whether many of these alumnae would not have benefited by experiencing this sense of accomplishment during their undergraduate years rather than afterwards. Doubtless their lives before graduation would have been enriched thereby, perhaps contributing to greater achievement both during and after college. It does not appear that stern competition is the sole cause of this relative lack of a sense of accomplishment during the school years. To some extent it appears that academic procedures often re-enforce feelings of guilt instead of fostering feelings of competence and adequacy in students, perhaps particularly in college women who usually are anxious to please and to do the right thing. An assignment well done may not be a source of satisfaction to a student who is very much impressed by what she does not know and what she could have done better. Feelings of inadequacy rather than a sense of mastery may predominate at the expense of freedom and experimentation in the approach to academic work. No one wishes to range himself on the side of opposition to high standards, but one cannot help wondering whether the emphasis on excellence that is so powerful an influence in academic circles these days may not serve, at least in the case of many women college students, to re-enforce feelings of guilt and inadequacy rather than to stimulate outstanding performance or achievement. Perhaps increased recognition of achievement at intermediate levels and not solely at the highest levels of accomplishment would help to reconcile an emphasis on high standards with feelings of competence and mastery in a larger number of students.

The younger alumnae, as we have noted, were remarkably skillful, flexible, and adaptable in adjusting to the world as they found it. Few are attempting to remake the world or American life. Perhaps nowhere was this more evident than in their attitudes toward *the role of educated women in our society*—a role that is still ill-defined. The very weight of the body of literature on this problem attests to its prominence and importance. To cite just a few of the individuals who have written on this subject we may note literary figures, such as Simone de Beauvoir (1953), Sonya Rudikoff (1956), and Virginia Woolf (1935, 1938), and social scientists, such as Marie Jahoda and Joan Havel (1955), Florence Kluckhohn (1952), Mirra Komarovsky (1946, 1950, 1953), Margaret Mead (1949), Mabel Newcomer (1959), Riesman (1956), and Sanford (1958). These writers make it abundantly clear that American society is rather a long way from providing a means whereby an educated woman may combine with relatively little conflict or effort the role of wife and mother with that of professional or career woman. Combining the two is not easy, and the literature offers much evidence that many women have felt a sense of lack of fulfillment in devoting themselves exclusively to one or the other of these roles. There seems to be considerable unanimity of opinion among these authorities that this is one area in which American society is in need of substantial reform.

Yet, with a few exceptions to be noted later, one would hardly conclude on the basis of the interviews with the younger alumnae that a problem of this kind existed. These women were quite disposed to attune their lives to those of their husbands. The husband's career and the family unit took precedence over any ambitions or aspirations they themselves may have had. And these adjustments were made with a minimum of conflict or feeling of sacrifice. Certainly the manifest conflicts of the feminist era were a pretty dead issue among the young alumnae (Bushnell and Freedman, 1959).

In recent years much emphasis has been placed upon the *problem of the middle-aged educated woman*. With early marriages and labor-saving devices in the home, a housewife is likely to have some 20 or 30 years of relative freedom, after the children have reached an age of at least partial self-sufficiency. Considerable attention has been given to consideration of ways in which these years can be made personally rewarding and socially productive. Much has been written on this matter, and it forms a prominent part of conferences and discussions of the roles of educated women in our society.

The period of early middle-age has long been regarded by psychiatrists as rather a dangerous time in the lives of educated women. Apparently these physicians frequently have occasion to see such women enter into depressions or other kinds of emotional or psychological disorder some time around age 40 or 45. If psychiatrists are present during discussions of personality development during college and afterward, one of their first remarks is likely to be: "What about the middle-aged college women in mental hospitals?" The inference, of course, is that perhaps something could have been done during the college years to prevent such difficulty in later life.

The study of the 50 Vassar College alumnae of the classes of 1929 to 35 revealed a number of instances in which women who had previously appeared to be quite stable emotionally had experienced or were then experiencing some sort of personality difficulty. In such cases it seemed that these women had built their lives around various forms of external definition, that is, school and college, marriage, then children. These were the things that everyone did, and they kept one very busy, for a while. However, rather suddenly, when the youngest child entered adolescence, one was no longer very much needed—at least not in the physical or material way in which one had been needed previously. On this occasion many women found themselves thrown back upon their own resources for the first time in their lives. With no external guideposts to provide continuity and order, they were facing emotional or psychological difficulties that had been better dealt with at an earlier age.

Many of the younger alumnae, very busy as they were with jobs and families, seemed similar to what some of the older alumnae must have been like about 15 or 20 years earlier. The question arises, however, as to whether, in view of the attention and publicity given of late to the problems of educated women in middle age, the younger alumnae were giving much thought to their lives about 20 years hence.

Perhaps surprisingly, the matter of what life will be like in 15 or 20 years seemed to occupy but a small place in the thinking of most of the young alumnae. Of course, the situation was somewhat different for those alumnae with major professional or career commitments. These women were ready to remain in the home, when the children were small. They wished, however, to resume their careers, when their family commitments made this possible. On the other hand, the majority of alumnae who had no strong involvements outside of the home and family were but little concerned with the long-range future. They were very busy with their daily and monthly rounds of activities, and they gave the impression that they felt that the future would take care of itself.

It is interesting to observe that there was even less concern with the prospective activities of middle-age among the younger alumnae than undergraduates display. Probably as a result of the many discussions, conferences, books, and articles about the roles of educated women in our society, the undergraduates have been stimulated to think in long-range terms when considering the "after-life." Very likely the younger alumnae were just too busy to be concerned with making plans for 20 years hence.

Differences in educational patterns between younger and older alumnae. The 40 alumnae of the classes of 1954, 1955, and 1956 may be considered in terms of the five educational patterns described by Brown (1956; Chapter 16). This will provide an opportunity for comparison of student life in the mid-1950s with that in the period 1929–35.

What seems striking is the lack of clarity of the educational patterns of the younger as compared to the older alumnae. Although essentially the same patterns may be discerned among the younger alumnae, the boundaries separating one from another are somewhat blurred. For example, those who exhibit the Social and Peer-Group Orientation pattern were clearly better students as undergraduates than were their counterparts of a generation ago. Apparently it was once possible to "squeak through" Vassar College, living from one prom or social event to another and doing almost nothing academically. These days few students of such bent are admitted in the first place, and the few who are do not remain very long.

Also it seems that the Overachievers are less distinctive now. These were students of no marked intellectual or academic abilities who nevertheless obtained rather high grades by dint of diligence and docility. In rather narrow and uncreative fashion they labored at discerning what was wanted of them and then managed to perform these tasks to the satisfaction of their teachers. At the present time such unoriginal or dependent performance is likely to yield passing or moderately good grades but probably not very high ones. It appears that the patterns of Social and Peer-Group Orientation and Over-achievement blend now. What we have is an adequate student of no marked intellectual predisposition who engages in a reasonably active social life without going overboard on this score and who anticipates a fairly early marriage.

Similarly, the patterns of Underachievers with Family Orientation and the High Achievers blend at the present time. This is a consequence of two trends. On the one hand there is improved academic performance on the part of the Underachievers with Family Orientation. In fact, underachievement is not really characteristic of these students at the present time, the College being better able to stimulate such students academically. And on the other hand the High-Achievers are no longer distinguished, as they were around 1930, by a considerable likelihood of remaining single. A generation ago commitment on the part of a woman to the values of an intellectual life or to a profession or career carried with it a more or less explicit assumption that marriage might thereby be precluded. Nowadays, almost all Vassar students expect that they will marry.

The above discussion indicates that in many ways Vassar College is a more adequate institution "academically" than it was a generation ago. Fewer current students are preoccupied with social activities to the exclusion of intellectual interests, and a higher proportion of the gifted students are stimulated to achievement that accords with their abilities. To this extent, the blurring of the more distinctive patterns of a generation ago may be regarded as a step forward intellectually.

But this clouding of the boundaries of the educational patterns has an obverse side as well. No longer does there seem to be a group of students on the order of some of the High-Achievers of the classes of 1929 to 35, for whom the intellectual or academic life was all. Almost nonexistent today are students like those among the older alumnae who skipped lunch so that they could have more time to spend in the library, or those who went through four years of college without a date and hardly felt that they were missing anything, because their studies were so fascinating. The most dedicated of current students are likely to lead balanced lives and to have their share of recreation and social life. Just as the increasing homogeneity of our society has delimited ethnic and regional differences, so it may be observed that the current educational patterns within student society are less sharply distinguished.

Consistent with this trend a difference may be noted in the characteristics that enter into the pattern of Seekers of Identity. Among the older alumnae a Seeker of Identity was often a student for whom Vassar College was an experience very different from her prior life because of factors associated with social class. She may have come from a lower-middle class or perhaps even a lower-class background, and accordingly the upper-middle-class world of Vassar College presented, perhaps, a very different and in some cases trying experience. Or she may have had a rigorous upper-class upbringing somewhat after the fashion of Victorian England, thereby finding herself quite ill-equipped for the freedom and independence of student life at Vassar College. The lowering of class barriers in current American life is reflected in the younger alumnae who seem to belong to the Seekers of Identity pattern. These women are likely to be characterized as Seekers of Identity for reason of conflicts within the personality rather than because of discontinuities related to social class origins. Differences in surface characteristics and behavior among current Vassar College students tend to be relatively independent of social class origin. Not that social class differences are nonexistent. They are more subtle, however, than they were a generation ago.

Attitudes toward the college experience. Vassar College alumnae are in general much like the alumni described by Havemann and West (1952). They believe that college was a very valuable experience, and most of them would go to Vassar College again, could they relive their lives. A substantial number, however, would choose a different major were they again attending college. Unlike the alumni in Havemann and West's (1952) sample there is no disagreement about the matter of general vs. specialized education. Vassar College alumnae are almost unanimous in their belief that the best type of undergraduate education consists in liberal arts as opposed to a more specialized kind of training.

Interviews with the alumnae of the classes of 1929 to 1935 revealed that few of them, when queried about the academic aspects of their college years, referred to the content of their courses. What they remembered best were various faculty members—usually charismatic figures who had made a deep impression. These were faculty members who had somehow impinged upon the alumnae in a personal way; they had aroused emotional responses of one kind or another—sometimes pleasant, sometimes unpleasant. Some alumnae best remembered teachers who had been sources of inspiration. Some teachers were remembered because they had been kind, helpful, or sympathetic. Others were recalled because of powerful negative experiences involving sarcasm, rejection, and the like.

The members of the research staff assumed that the almost total lack of reference to the content of college courses in the recollections of the older alumnae was pretty much a function of the considerable passage of time since graduation—some 20 years. Rather surprisingly, however, it developed that the situation was very similar in the case of the younger alumnae. One of the interviewers of the younger alumnae [2] had the following to say about his interviews:

My interviewees referred little or not at all to the contents of the courses. Such references as there were, were to interpersonal factors, such as an in-

[2] Professor Joseph Katz of the Philosophy Department of Vassar College.

structor's sarcasms. Now offhand in an interview of the type we gave one might expect such references as: "Professor X's theory sounded plausible then, but I have since changed my mind." I mean the sort of statements that are quite common among graduate students. Reading my own interviews and those of the other interviewers has been a quite chastening experience for me as to the role of the classroom in a student's life in later years.

[Along these lines it is interesting to note that in Chapter 22 Jencks and Riesman refer as follows to a research carried out by Whitla of the Office of Tests of Harvard University.] In his study of the Class of '52, done five years after graduation, Dr. Whitla found that few graduates of moderate academic attainment recalled their tutors as important influences; more recalled famous professors.

Attitudes toward parents. White (1952) has remarked concerning the attitudes of young adult women to their parents: "She exhibits a trend quite common in the twenties, toward detachment and frank appraisal" (p. 287). The interviews with the younger alumnae seemed to reveal this same trend. By virtue of such experiences as increased independence—financial and otherwise—marriage, or their own motherhood, the majority of these women seemed to have settled into a position of increased understanding of their mothers.

Tying in this information with the testing and interviewing of Vassar College undergraduates, we see a long-term trend in attitudes toward their mothers somewhat as follows. Before college the students are quite submissive and respectful. College brings "rebellious independence," skepticism, perhaps some condemnation. In the early post-college years these tendencies toward either compliance or rebellion are replaced by more realistic evaluation and generally increased understanding.

Patterns of attitudes toward their fathers are generally similar. Students at Vassar, however, have somewhat less critical and independent attitudes toward their fathers than toward their mothers. And the post-college years seem characterized by somewhat less understanding of their fathers and less closeness with them. Perhaps this possible difference in attitudes to parents is a function of the fact that in general Vassar College students seem to be rather more strongly oriented to their mothers than to their fathers. To some extent, this may be a fairly common difference between students who go to women's colleges and those of comparable intellectual background and academic motivation who attend coeducational colleges.

Some important issues of the early postgraduate years as illustrated by individual alumnae of the classes of 1954, 1955, and 1956. There follow a number of brief discussions of kinds of development or ways of dealing with issues or problems that were displayed by some of the young alumnae who were interviewed by the Mellon Foundation research staff. Not in all cases but to some extent we shall focus upon sources of strain in these reports. In so doing we assume that these issues or problems are not confined to those alumnae who reveal them in manifest form but have some relevance for many if not a majority of the alumnae.

Marriage vs. Career. Although few people would deplore the demise of old-time feminism, in the sense of a woman's having to prove that she was as good as a man, some writers, Riesman (1956), for example, have pointed out that feminism was not without its "virtues." To some extent it provided an alternative to marriage, a way of life for a woman who was unsure as to whether she wanted to marry or at least was in no hurry to marry. Nowadays, as Riesman has pointed out, not marrying is regarded as more than perhaps a bit odd; it is considered to be almost the equivalent of a perversion of some kind.

Traces of the conflicts of feminism may be observed in current students and young alumnae. Thus, one of the alumnae of the Class of 1955, a graduate student at a prominent Eastern university, expressed herself as follows: "I wonder if each year spent in graduate school is not putting marriage that much behind. Perhaps by going on in school I am unconsciously putting chances of marriage behind. I would like to marry, but it seems to me that most men want to marry less educated women who feed their egos. I will not buy this kind of relationship." Like the career-oriented women of a generation or more ago, the young woman in question will not sacrifice or compromise her intellectual or professional activities in order to increase her opportunities for marriage.

Although this problem is rare among the young alumnae of Vassar College, Douvan and Kaye's report on the ambitions of high school girls (Chapter 4) and casual observation indicate that it may not be so rare among young women in technical colleges or in less cosmopolitan areas of the United States. On a recent visit to a small women's liberal arts college in the Midwest the writer was rather surprised to meet a number of students who were troubled because they wished to pursue careers after marriage (at least until children were born), while the men with whom they were involved objected to wives who worked.

It seems possible that we are dealing here with a conflict of generations. No doubt many of the mothers of present day Vassar girls were true feminists, whose styles of life are now regarded by their daughters as very much old hat. The mothers of girls in rural areas or of girls who want to go to technical colleges, on the other hand, were probably of a more traditional orientation and not often to be found among the nation's makers of opinion; accordingly, they left their daughters an open field in which to seek greater freedom for women.

More common than the determined feminist among our sample of young alumnae was the type of young woman who prepared for a career or actually entered a profession and then found herself pulling back, or compromising with the demands of the career, when it seemed that her chances of marriage were being too seriously threatened. An example is afforded by a graduate of the class of 1954 who gave up a good position in a research laboratory and the immediate prospect of a Ph.D. in chemistry in order to return to her home community and so improve, as she thought, her prospects of marriage.

Then there are young women who become aware of the problem of marriage vs. career only after they have married. So great are the pressures toward early marriage today that many college women seize their first opportunity, no matter how interesting their jobs or how bright their professional prospects. Some of them later experience a sense of self-betrayal. It turns out that they cared very much about "doing something on their own," as they put it, and now, with the nest becoming rapidly filled with babies, they wonder if they will ever get another chance to try their hands at demanding work outside the home. These are cases in which young people marry before achieving a sense of identity, in Erikson's (1959) sense of the term. This was a not uncommon occurrence among the young alumnae in our sample, and in some cases we were led to doubt that the marriage would survive.

The Problem of Achievement. It was our impression that in cases of dissatisfaction with marriage, or self-dissatisfaction in marriage, there was a special kind of achievement motivation or, more specifically, an unfulfilled need for achievement. The young women in whom this phenomenon was most clearly to be observed had not done well in college. Indeed, it seemed that one of the main reasons why they were unable to postpone marriage was because their college experience had left them without a sense of competence or adequacy. But marriage did not solve the problem; the need for achievement, unfulfilled in college, continued as a strong motive.

The young woman of our sample in whom this phenomenon was most marked had left college at the end of her sophomore year in order to marry. Although very happy with her family and general situation, she keenly regretted not having got her degree. As a consequence she had taken some courses at a local college after her marriage but could not continue after the birth of her second child. She hoped, however, to finish the work required for her degree as soon as possible. This young alumna was also extremely active in community affairs despite three children, a very active social life, and minimal domestic help, because she considered that such activity was an obligation that could not be evaded. Although her parents were by no means affluent, she believed that she had had many advantages, her two years at Vassar perhaps being the greatest of these. And these privileges imposed upon her an obligation to return something to society in the form of useful services to the community.

This young woman conveyed the impression of someone who had assumed the identity of a Vassar College alumna with all the demands of the role as she saw them. This identity was particularly strong, however, perhaps out of feelings of guilt engendered by failing to complete her undergraduate work. In any case, it appears that some lack of fulfillment in her undergraduate career persisted, demanding of her that she be a kind of ne plus ultra among Vassar College alumnae.

In contrast, there are young women in whose cases college seems to have offered too much in the way of satisfaction of achievement motives. There were among our sample of alumnae unusually able young women who had been brilliantly successful in college, receiving much recognition from faculty and fellow students alike, but who, four years after graduation, had been unable either to marry or to settle down to productive work. It was as if nothing in the "real" world could match the luster of the college years. Like the hero of Irwin Shaw's (1950) story, "The Eighty Yard Run," some of these women seemed fixed upon the adulation experienced in college and unwilling or unable to enter into activities that did not guarantee the same kind of success.

The Problem of Continued Growth. As indicated above, the majority of the young alumnae who were interviewed had married and were getting along quite well. They reported few difficulties or strains and their test scores showed that, as compared with their status as seniors, they were relatively stable emotionally and free of anxiety. There is one flaw in this picture, and that is the suggestion that personality growth may have stopped. We have interpreted the "upset" condition of seniors as a sign that development was occurring or about to occur, and, in Chapter 6, the situation of the freshman was considered as a "developmental crisis." What will induce further growth in the young married woman who spends virtually all of her time in blissful domesticity? The question was sharpened for us by the presence in our sample of young women in whom stability and contentment somehow seemed excessive.

For example, there was a graduate of the class of 1954 who had been married for four years and had two sons. She was married to a poultry farmer, and, as she put it, had "settled into a small town routine." When asked whether she felt any obligation to pursue activities outside of the home as a consequence of her education, she replied as follows: "No, I don't. I think the reason for this is that I am so seldom reminded—actively—that I've had the education. In other words I don't see the people, you know, who've had educations, who expect anything of me. Sometimes, though, it does pass through my mind. I wonder, if I am making use of it well enough, and then I think about it. I think my general attitude is that I've been broadened by my education; and right now there is really nothing concrete I can do, because I do feel so strongly that my place is in the home."

Again, there was a young woman of the same graduating class who came from a social register family and was living with her husband and daughter in an elegant apartment in New York City. She said she "couldn't be happier" and that "things were going along without a hitch." When asked what she thought college had contributed to her current life she replied as follows. "The different interests it opened—some things I wish I had more time for now. It made me much more curious, taught me how to study." And then she added, "I don't know how it affects my life at the moment."

Most Vassar graduates are happy to be consumed for the most part by the demands of home and family, at least for the time being. But often there is some sense of dissatisfaction, some concern that their education might be put to nobler use. The striking thing about the present two cases is the absence of such feelings. No one would begrudge these young women their contentment; and it must be granted that they are excellent wives and mothers; but it is difficult to accept their complacency. Given the present condition of our society and of the world it seems that we have the right to expect more of our most intelligent and best educated women than that they achieve stability and contribute to the population explosion. But this may not be the worst of it. Both of the young women just described were almost apolitical, and there was nothing to suggest that ideologically or intellectually they were more developed than they had been as college students. Clearly the college failed in these two cases to achieve the educational aim of generating a capacity for continued growth. Still, these women were quite young when interviewed, and it is possible that time may bring a depth and complexity of personality that we do not now see.

Contrasting with these two cases are those young women who during their first four or five years after college have rich and varied experiences and seem to gain as much developmentally as they did during the four years of college. An example of this pattern is afforded by a member of the class of 1956. Unlike most of her classmates, she had not experienced any real growth in independence from her parents during her college years. When she decided to marry out of the family religion, after being out of college for a year, much conflict with her parents developed. She considered that this discord had been basically a salutary thing in that it had led to increased understanding and mutual respect between her and her parents.

Not only had her religious views changed radically in the three years following graduation, but her political views had changed as well. In the course of moving about with her husband, a graduate student who had changed schools, and helping to support him, she had worked as a secretary, a retail sales clerk, a radio announcer, and an assistant in a nursery school. These experiences had taught her much about people and about other ways of life.

This young alumna had majored in sociology and had contemplated going on to graduate school and becoming a professional social worker. She was working and saving money toward this end during the first year after graduation, when she met her future husband and married. After marriage she became interested in writing, both poetry and prose, and she had had some commercial success in her writing ventures, having sold two short stories. At the time of the interview she was pregnant with her first child.

As compared to the two women discussed above, this subject's alumnae years have involved her in as much if not more new experience than did her undergraduate years. Much of this is the result of her marriage, the ideas of her husband to which she has been exposed—new ones for her—the people she has met through him, the different places in which they have lived together, the jobs she has had in helping to support the family, some of them being kinds of work she would not have undertaken voluntarily had not economic necessity forced them upon her. All this serves to illustrate the importance of the marriage or the husband in shaping the development of the alumnae. Since most of the married alumnae orient their lives to what is most helpful or useful to their husbands, the kinds of men they marry and the kinds of lives these men lead are often the chief determinant of what happens to young women in the alumnae years. We wonder, then, whether this young alumna would now be living a life as continuous with her college years and previous life as that of the two women just discussed, had she married a different sort of man. Or to what extent was her choice of a husband a motivated expression of a desire to change? Much additional research will be needed to answer complex questions like these.

We learn from the preceding chapter that considerable personality change takes place during the college years. Changes in mental ability and functioning, in attitudes and opinions, and in other qualities of personality—for example, authoritarianism and impulse expression—take place in this period.

We may conceive of seniors as being more developed, more complex than freshmen. They are less bland, more aware of themselves and their surroundings, more flexible, more open to new experience. At least this seems to be true of women who have attended women's liberal arts colleges. In this sense one is tempted to say that college seniors are now ready to be educated. The resistance to new experiences characteristic of so many freshmen has been dissolved—or at least inroads have been made into it.

One may ask what these qualities in seniors imply for the future. Do we see in alumnae some form of integration of the personality at a higher level of complexity than we find in seniors? Our test findings reveal no important changes in qualities of personality in the period three and four years after graduation, except that alumnae are more stable or less neurotic than they were as seniors. It may be, however, that this finding is a function of our testing of alumnae with scales and measures designed originally to illuminate changes during the college years. In some cases our interview studies reveal that much alteration in personality characteristics has occurred after graduation. Possibly tests developed expressly to tap changes in the years after college would reveal in systematic fashion modifications in qualities of personality that are not now apparent.

Perhaps what stands out more than anything else in the Mellon Foundation's studies of alumnae is the complexity of the relationships between events of the college years and later life. Generalizations about such things as the qualities of college alumni as compared to other people, or college graduates of different ages, or graduates of one kind of college as compared to those of another can be made fairly readily. But this is not the case when we attempt to relate experiences of the college years in some systematic way to occurrences thereafter. What we find here is considerable confusion. One student who is graduated with honors goes on to do well in graduate school. Her classmate, who also is graduated with honors, is a failure academically in graduate school. The Family-Oriented-Underachievers are most alert and alive intellectually twenty years after graduation. The Family-Oriented-Overachievers, the better students in a formal scholastic sense, have stagnated intellectually. And so for other educational patterns.

It is obvious that there is a pressing need for additional research on the relationships between experiences in the college years and personality characteristics in later life. Consideration of educational objectives involves more than asking what characteristics we wish to foster in students and how we go about doing this. In addition we must inquire about the persistence of these qualities after college. Ideally, college experience must be viewed from a developmental point of view that encompasses the whole life span.

REFERENCES

Adorno, T. W., Frenkel-Brunswik, Else, Levinson, D. J., and Sanford, R. N. *The authoritarian personality.* New York: Harper Bros., 1950.

Beauvoir, de, Simone. *The second sex.* New York: Knopf, 1953.

Bernreuter, R. G. Theory and construction of the personality inventory. *J. of soc. Psych.*, 1933, 4, 387–405.

Bressler, B., and Kephart, W. Marriage and family patterns of an academic group. *Mar. and fam. Liv.*, 1954, 16, 121–127.

Bridgman, D. S. Success in college and business. *The Personnel J.*, 1930, 9, 1–19.

Bridgman, D. S. Problems in estimating the monetary value of college education. In Harris, S. E. (Ed.). *Higher education in the United States.* Cambridge: Harvard University Press, 1960.

Brown, D. R. Some educational patterns. In Sanford, N. (Ed.), Personality development during the college years. *J. of soc. Iss.*, 1956, 12, 44–60.

Bugelski, R., and Lester, Olive. Changes in attitude in a group of college students during their college course and after graduation. *J. of soc. Psych.*, 1940, 12, 319–332.

Bushnell, J., and Freedman, M. Contemporary woman: the Vassar view. *Vassar College Chronicle*, May 2, 1959.

Dressel, P. L. Interests—stable or unstable? *J. of educ. Res.*, 1954, 48, 95–102.

Erikson, E. H. Identity and the life cycle. *Psych. Iss.*, 1959, 1, 1–171.

Flesher, Marie A., and Pressey, S. L. War-time accelerates ten years after. *J. of educ. Psych.*, 1955, 46, 228–238.

Freedman, M. B. A half century of Vassar opinion. *Vassar College Alumnae Magazine*, 1959, 44, 3–6.

Glick, P. C., and Carter, H. Marriage patterns and educational level. *Amer. Soc. Rev.*, 1958, 23, 294–300.

Glick, P. C., and Miller, H. P. Educational level and potential income. *Amer. soc. Rev.*, 1956, 21, 307–312.

Gough, H. G. *Manual for the California Psychological Inventory.* Palo Alto, California: Consulting Psychologists' Press, 1957.

Grady, L. A., Rev. Alumni—St. Peter's College. *Case Book—Education beyond the High School.* Washington, D.C.: United States Office of Education, 1958, 1 (29).

Harris, S. E. *The market place for college graduates.* Cambridge: Harvard University Press, 1949.

Harris, S. E. Introduction: some broad issues. In Harris, S. E. (Ed.), *Higher education in the United States.* Cambridge: Harvard University Press, 1960.

Hathaway, S. R., and McKinley, J. C. *Manual for the Minnesota Multiphasic Personality Inventory.* (Rev. ed.) New York: The Psychological Corporation, 1951.

Havemann, E., and West, Patricia S. *They went to college.* New York: Harcourt, Brace, 1952.

Hyman, H. H., and Sheatsley, P. B. Trends in public opinion on civil liberties. *J. of soc. Iss.*, 1953, 9, 6–16.

Jacob, P. E. *Changing values in college.* New York: Harper Bros., 1957.

Jahoda, Marie, and Havel, Joan. Psychological problems of women in different social roles. *Educ. Rec.*, 1955, 36, 325–335.

James, W. *The principles of psychology.* New York: Holt, 1890.

Kelly, E. L. Consistency of the adult personality. *Amer. Psychologist*, 1955, **10**, 659–681.

Kluckhohn, Florence. American women and American values. In Bryson, L. (Ed.). *Facing the future's risks.* New York: Harper Bros., 1952.

Komarovsky, Mirra. Cultural contradictions and sex roles. *Amer. J. of Soc.*, 1946, **51**, 184–189.

Komarovsky, Mirra. Functional analysis of sex roles. *Amer. Soc. Rev.*, 1950, **15**, 508–516.

Komarovsky, Mirra. *Women in the modern world: their education and their dilemmas.* Boston: Little, Brown, 1953.

Lehman, Ruth. The married home economics graduate. *Marr. and fam. Liv.*, 1953, **15**, 322–324.

McBride, Katherine. Alumnae—Bryn Mawr College. *Case book—education beyond the high school.* Washington, D.C.: United States Office of Education, 1958, **1** (28).

Mead, Margaret. *Male and female.* New York: W. Morrow, 1949.

Myrdal, G. *An American dilemma.* New York: Harper Bros., 1944.

National Opinion Research Council. *Report of the National Opinion Research Council.* Denver: National Opinion Research Council, 1947.

Nelson, E. N. P. Persistence of attitudes of college students fourteen years later. *Psychological Monographs*, 1954, **68** (Whole No. 373), 13 pp.

Newcomb, T. M. *Personality and social change.* New York: Dryden, 1943.

Newcomer, Mabel. *A century of higher education for American women.* New York: Harper Bros., 1959.

Pace, C. R. *They went to college.* Minneapolis: University of Minnesota Press, 1941.

Pace, C. R. What kind of citizens do college graduates become? *J. of gen. Educ.*, 1949, **3**, 197–202.

Pace, C. R. University-wide studies in evaluation of general education at Syracuse. In Dressel, P. L. (Ed.), *Evaluation in general education.* Dubuque, Iowa: William C. Brown, 1954.

Plasse, William B. Comparison of factors of achievement in college and adult life. Syracuse: Unpublished doctoral dissertation, Syracuse University, 1951.

Population Reference Bureau. The score of the colleges. *J. of Heredity*, 1952, **43**, 133–140.

President's Commission on Higher Education. *Higher education for American democracy.* New York: Harper Bros., 1948.

Pressey, S. L. *Acceleration: appraisals and basic problems.* Columbus: Ohio State University Press, 1949.

Riesman, D. Some continuities and discontinuities in the education of women. Bennington, Vermont: Third John Dewey Memorial Lecture, 1956.

Rudikoff, Sonya. Feminism reconsidered. *Hudson Review*, 1956, **9**, 178–198.

Sanford, N. (Ed.). Personality development during the college years. *J. of soc. Iss.*, 1956, **12**, No. 4.

Sanford, N. Changing sex roles, socialization, and education. In W. Henry (Ed.), *Human Development Bulletin,* University of Chicago, Human Development Student Organization, 1958, 58–75.

Shaw, I. The eighty yard run. In *Mixed company.* New York: Random House, 1950.

Shosteck, R. *Five thousand women college graduates report.* Washington, D.C.: B'nai Brith Vocational Service Bureau, 1953.

Stouffer, S. A. *Communism, conformity, and civil liberties: a cross-section of the nation speaks its mind.* Garden City, N.Y.: Doubleday, 1955.

Strong, E. K., Jr. *Change of interests with age.* Stanford: Stanford University Press, 1931.

Strong, E. K., Jr. *Vocational interests of men and women.* Stanford: Stanford University Press, 1943.

Strong, E. K., Jr. Permanence of interest scores over twenty-two years. *J. of Appl. Psych.,* 1951, **35,** 89–91.

Strong, E. K., Jr., *Vocational interests eighteen years after college.* Minneapolis: University of Minnesota Press, 1955.

Tate, Mildred, and Musick, Virginia. Adjustment problems of college students. *Soc. Forces,* 1954, **33,** 182–185.

Webster, H., Sanford, N., and Freedman, M. A new instrument for studying authoritarianism in personality. *J. of Psych.,* 1955, **40,** 73–84.

West, Patricia. Social mobility among college graduates. In Bendix, R., and Lipset, M. (Eds.), *Class, status, and power.* Glencoe, Illinois: Free Press, 1953.

White, R. W. *Lives in progress.* New York: Dryden, 1952.

Wolfle, D., and Smith, J. G. The occupational value of education for superior high-school graduates. *J. of higher Educ.,* 1956, **27,** 201–212.

Woolf, Virginia. *A room of one's own.* London: Hogarth, 1935.

Woolf, Virginia. *Three guineas.* New York: Harcourt, Brace, 1938.

PART VIII

HIGHER EDUCATION AND
THE SOCIAL CONTEXT

Although this volume is focused upon students and how they develop in the college setting, we have been unable to ignore the problem of institutional change. Findings reported in various chapters have led to suggestions about how educational processes might be improved, and a good number of the authors have been explicit in their support of educational experimentation. There is probably a wide agreement that institutional reforms, to be guided by such experimentation, are necessary if the profession of higher education is to advance in step with science and enlightenment.

But we have seen (Part I) that our colleges and universities are embedded in our culture and in our society, and that fundamental or widespread change in these institutions can come about only when there is a shift of emphasis in our general system of values or when there is a change in our general societal processes. At the same time, however, the direction of influence may be the other way; there is an *interaction* of the college or university on the one hand and the surrounding society and culture on the other.

In this part we return to the analysis of this interaction. We attack the fundamental question of how the college or university can carry out its essential tasks when the constituency on which the institution depends for its economic subsistence demands that it perform other functions and often opposes the very steps that are most necessary to the attainment of its major objectives. Professor Stewart's approach is historical. He shows that the relations of the university and society have not always been what they are in the United States today, that various patterns of interaction have existed in different times and places; and he shows that although many features of higher education have changed as society changed there has been a remarkable persistence, throughout hundreds of years, of ideas and ideals that have guided higher education in the Western World. Dr. Pinner and Dr. Bay address themselves to the contemporary American scene—and to the future. They introduce concepts and techniques of social analysis suited to elucidate some of the ways in which processes of our culture and society affect the functioning of our colleges, and some of their conclusions are drawn in terms of proposals for reform, within the college or outside. Pinner focuses upon the problems of the newer, fast-growing state universities in America, although his concepts and the processes he describes pertain to problems that recur in every college and university. Bay introduces concepts of a more general nature, concepts applicable to the functioning of any large organization in contemporary society. Stewart, viewing higher education in the perspective of 2500 years of history, makes it clear that the college and the university of today have evolved slowly, some features of them persisting virtually unchanged for several hundred years; but when he turns to happenings in America we are able to see that, during the past 100 years particularly, things speeded up considerably, and that the rate of change is accelerating. Pinner and Bay reveal themselves to be, in an important sense, products of the America that Stewart describes; they are very much aware of social change and they remind us more than once that it is later than we think. More than this, they do not conceive of inexorable historical processes to which we can only adapt ourselves; they believe that we can influence the course of events; they want us to make history.

At the first meeting of the editors of this volume someone asserted forcefully that we did not want to begin this study of the American college with a statement that Harvard College was founded in 1636. This provoked the answer that anyone who did not know this bit of history might be doomed to repeat it. (This was probably a Yale man, and a reader of Santayana!) What the committee of editors agreed was that the history of higher education should be integrated with the rest of the volume—not set forth in the beginning and then forgotten. It was agreed that we cannot completely understand our institutions of higher learning nor make reasonable predictions about their future without understanding their history; but it was also agreed that, as history is constantly being rewritten in the light of present knowledge, it would be a fine thing if we could introduce in this volume scientific facts and concepts and modes of analysis that would improve our understanding of the history of higher education.

Campbell Stewart's chapter is what the doctors ordered. On the one hand he gives us the facts, an account—necessarily highly compressed —of a continuity of events that began in Athens 2500 years ago, and on the other hand he interprets these events in the light of modern sociology.

In presenting the facts of history Stewart supplies background that for some—but by no means all—of the other authors is indispensable. As suggested above, we have been largely concerned with matters, such as the analysis of the behavior and personality development of students, that are essentially ahistorical. The "history" of personality testing is short, and the same may be said of the effort of social scientists to analyze the phenomena of student culture. But when we come to the policies and practices of the colleges, to the functions that the colleges perform for different segments of the society, and to the question of what we may expect in the future, the authors have been happy to make use of background that Stewart's chapter affords. Here it is plain that some of the factors at work in the current situation—in the college and in the larger society—are at work because of happenings in the past. And not least among these happenings has been the transmission of ideas and ideals, generated in antiquity, from one generation of scholars and teachers to another, down to the present. Thus, for example, one of the roles of the professor described by Knapp (Chapter 7), the character-developing role, is essentially the same as that practiced by the Sophists. Perhaps professors act according to the requirements of this role today for the same reason that the Sophists did, but Stewart shows that the educational ideas of these early teachers passed from Athens to Byzantium and from there to England by way of Spain and Ireland, and thence to the United States. Again, when Katz and Sanford (Chapter 11) discuss the system of free electives and mention Eliot of Harvard in this connection, they rely on Stewart to make it plain that this was not an idea that sprang in finished form from President Eliot's mind, that rather it was a system tried at Bologna 700 years ago, and again at Harvard in 1825. The contrast between the "socio-analysis" of Riesman and Jencks and the "rational" history of Stewart was pointed to in the introduction to Part I. The two approaches are plainly supplementary. In the analysis of the dynamic interaction of the American college and the American society attention has to be paid to the traditions, the intellectual heritage, that contribute heavily to the colleges' capacity to resist outside pressure. Obviously a complete account of the American college must trace the evolution of this heritage, and Stewart addresses himself to this task.

In other respects, the approaches of Stewart and of Riesman and

Jencks are similar rather than contrasting. Both approaches are in large part sociological. The university, Stewart says, has like any institution "answered to the pressure of the society that in a real sense it serves." The system of education of Sparta serves to illustrate his point as well as do the early land grant colleges of the United States. Just as we cannot understand the Athenian classical education without the concept of a stratified society, so we cannot understand the rise of vocationalism in American education without knowledge of the fusion of economic and political power in the United States in the last half of the 19th century. But institutions of higher education have not only adapted themselves to changes in society; they have fended off, and even overcome, pressures from outside. The faculty of the University of California during the loyalty oath controversy of 1949–51 (Sanford, 1953) could well have taken over more than they did of the strategies employed by the scholars of the medieval University of Paris. And powerful groups within society, when they have not been able to mould the universities to suit their purposes (it has usually taken an economic and social revolution to change a curriculum fundamentally) have been able to use the universities as they existed for purposes that were not intended by the founders of those institutions; for example, the "new" middle class in England could use the universities as a means for adding itself to the aristocracy. Thus, the history of higher education as Stewart recounts it is replete with examples of the interaction of the institution and the society. The episodes and the trends that are described lend themselves well to modern social analysis, and it becomes clear that the student of social processes will do well to direct his inquiries to historical events in the field of higher education. It is to be regretted that Stewart, Pinner, and Bay have not been able to supplement their contributions with a closely collaborative piece in which the concepts and theories of the latter two authors are brought directly to bear upon the events described by the former. We return to this point after noting what it is that Pinner and Bay undertake.

Pinner starts with the observation that as the state university develops, improving its faculty and becoming more like the leading universities of the nation, it becomes increasingly alienated from its local publics—the people of its town and surrounding countryside, its alumni and other benefactors, even its students and most of the older faculty members. The newer, more distinguished faculty members, who have been recruited from all parts of the nation and abroad, bring universalist values and a cosmopolitan outlook; these values and this outlook are not understood, and are even rejected, by the local publics, who nevertheless like the prestige associated with having a "great" university in their midst. Where once there was implicit understanding of a common purpose there are now many purposes. The break between the university and its local publics is clearly reflected in different conceptions of the kinds of knowledge that ought to be pursued and taught. Pinner here introduces his distinction between "consensual" and "dissensual" knowledge. "Consensual" refers to all those kinds of knowledge with respect to which the general public at a given time tends to have no reservations, either as to the competence of the scholars or as to the value of their work. "Dissensual" refers to those kinds of knowledge with respect to which the public has explicit or implicit doubts and which, accordingly, are less likely to be supported by the institutions of society. Indeed, the widespread public distrust of dissensual knowledge is at the core of the university's "public relations" problem. This is the kind of knowledge that the most distinguished and dedicated minds are eager to pursue, especially but not only in the social sciences and the humanities. It is the kind of knowledge that is needed but not wanted; it is needed because a changing world keeps enlarging its demands on the human mind, and it is not wanted because people with influence tend to like their comforts, including their comfortable habits of mind; and the challenges they do accept usually emanate from demands associated with their own positions of influence, not from the demands of the human experiment as a whole.

The university's conflicts with its publics are reflected also in divisions within its own ranks. Some professors and many administrators feel that the university owes "service" to its supporting taxpayers, largely on the clients' terms. Others insist, in the spirit of Socrates, that a university worth its salt must never give the public what it wants, only what it needs. And what it needs is to have its power of rationality and its levels of cultural attainment raised. Higher education is not for supplying skilled hands or clever administrators to the industry, to the state, or even to the universities themselves. Higher education is for teaching how to live responsibly and how to develop and enjoy a sense of beauty. Pinner stresses the importance of the development of aesthetic sensitivity in the students; he sees beauty as the unifying purpose of all knowledge and art. In order to advance toward its objectives the university must build within itself a community in which people share significant experiences that can transform them. To sustain itself and to carry out its functions this intellectual community must educate its publics. Its students should be its emissaries to its larger public.

Bay's contribution has been designed to meet a need that has been expressed from time to time in this volume. That is the need for theory, the means by which our knowledge may be made systematic. In Chapter 1 it was pointed out that educational research had so far failed to produce a substantial and theoretically coherent body of knowledge, and that the demands of practice had been one of the major reasons for this failure. There is irony in this, for, in the long run theory is the only dependable guide to useful practice. Anything that is undertaken with a view to producing desired results must begin with some notion, however crude, of what means—what instrumentalities and mechanisms—have what effects. As Bay points out, many human enterprises *begin* in a rational way; but, soon, interest becomes vested in the means themselves, often to the neglect of the original purposes and of continuing consideration of how they might best be achieved. The effort now is to rationalize what *is,* or what is being done; and the tendency here is to utilize theoretical notions that originated in science or in an attempt at science and that, though now outmoded as far as science is concerned, have found their way into our general culture. It is only by deliberate and recurrent, if not constant, attention to its theoretical underpinnings that practice can be prevented from degenerating into irrationality.

The kinds of theory that are needed for the study of higher education are theory of personality development and theory pertaining to the structure and functioning of institutions in their social settings. Theory of the former kind was introduced in Chapters 6 and 11; Bay now addresses himself to the latter. His social theory is not an alternative to personality theory but a supplement that accents developmental determinants in the social surroundings of the student, that is, in the college itself and in the larger society.

Bay focuses attention upon the goal of maximum intellectual development (rationality) and inquires how social factors in the college community and its larger environment favor, or hamper, the attainment of this goal. In his analysis of these social factors he begins with two highly abstract concepts: the concept of *institutions*—"persistent patterns of human interaction"—and the concept of *rationality*—"attempts to choose maximally effective means to promote given purposes." It is his major hypothesis that rationally determined programs for achieving human purposes become institutionalized and that, as they do, they become transformed in the direction of less rationality. It is this erosion of rationality that underlies the colleges' failure to achieve their highest purposes, and that must be a prime object of continuing study. In the analysis of the process of erosion Bay uses as his major tools the concepts of *social role* and *incentive*—concepts that lie on the borders between psychology and sociology. With the use of these concepts, and with the guidance of his major hypothesis, Bay proceeds with a consideration of some of the specific social factors and processes that, in college, appear to hinder or help the development of the intellect, and of rationality in the student and in society.

In suggesting above that Stewart, Pinner, and Bay might now, having made their contributions to this volume, join forces in further consideration of higher education in relation to social processes we were confronting the fact that the amount of integration achieved in this volume has its limits, and we were suggesting a direction that future work might take. Each of these authors wrote the bulk of his chapter without knowledge of what the others were doing, and none of them knew until this volume was in a very late stage of preparation that their three chapters would constitute Part VIII. We do not know whether Stewart, if he had his piece to do over again, would utilize the concepts of, say, "consensual" and "dissensual" disciplines or of "institutions" and "rationality." He has interpreted events in his own way, and, in doing so, he may have considered and rejected concepts very similar to these. And we do not know whether Pinner and Bay, were they concentrating upon, say, medieval Europe, would find their concepts as useful as they do in their analyses of situations and events in contemporary America. At any rate, it seems not unreasonable to hope that, in the future, the study of the history of higher education will utilize, increasingly, the concepts and analytic techniques of contemporary social science, just as the modern analysts of the college in society will see events against a background of historical development.

This last draws attention to a serious omission from our consideration of higher education in relation to the processes of society, and that is the comparative study of higher education. If educational systems are developed—rationally—to meet the needs of societies, and institutionalization is a truly general social process, then we should expect to find parallels between historical events in Western Europe and in the United States and happenings in some of the newer nations today; the stage of development of the latter might well correspond in significant respects to some stage that the former passed through at some earlier time. Knowledge derived from this kind of study might be an important aid to policymaking in the newer nations.

26 *Campbell Stewart*

The Place of Higher Education in a Changing Society

Hastings Rashdall, whose work, *The Universities of Europe in the Middle Ages,* is the best known on the subject, maintains that the university is a distinctly medieval institution and that it is entirely misleading to give the name to the schools of Athens, Rome, and Alexandria. He considers that the university such as we could recognize is characterized by features like a teaching corporation, courses of study, examinations, degrees, licenses to teach, and that these appear only in the 12th and 13th centuries. Although the Athenian teaching in law, rhetoric, and philosophy was of the highest order it was not organized into the forms of a permanent institution. The universities of Western Europe are the heirs of Paris and Bologna, not of Athens and Alexandria.

Yet, although this may be true in the strictly institutional sense, it is not true of the intellectual and educational tradition. Werner Jaeger says:

> The sophists have been described as the founders of educational science. They did indeed found pedagogy, and even today intellectual culture largely follows the path they marked out (Jaeger, 1936, Vol. I, p. 298).

And Marrou, another distinguished classical historian, says that in the history of education in antiquity we can trace the direct ancestry of our own educational tradition. He maintains that, in education above all, we are the heirs of the Graeco-Latins, particularly in the Renaissance of the 15th and 16th centuries, when there was a conscious and intentional return to the strict classical tradition, and a revival of interest in the Greek and Latin authors (Marrou, 1956, p.

354). We must look more closely at the higher education of Greece and Rome through roughly 1500 years, from 1000 B.C. to 500 A.D.

CLASSICAL EDUCATION

The aristocratic ideal. In understanding the tradition of classical Greek education, which came to its most developed form in and after the 4th century B.C., we must appreciate that the native culture arose out of an older, refined civilization, out of what we might now call a stratified society. There was an aristocracy of warriors and, as Marrou points out:

These Homeric heroes are not brutal old soldiers, prehistoric warriors. . . . In a sense they are already knights (Marrou, 1956, p. 5).

The younger warriors acted as squires and equerries, served at table and as cup-bearers, as a retinue in religious observances, as junior officers in war. Sport was a notable feature of Homeric society—wrestling, racing, javelin- and discus-throwing, archery, chariot racing. So, too, were music and dancing. All these features, and others, are present in Homer's epics which became one of the abiding influences in later Greek schooling. It was not primarily as literary masterpieces that his works were studied, but because they represented an ideal, a style of life and a composite appreciation of character. The ideal values in living are to be found in Achilles, a love of the short life of a warrior, bravery to endure death and the enigma of Elysium, courage and virtue in action, and the passion to be recognized for these qualities. Marrou, Burckhardt, Jaeger, and other classical scholars have all pointed to this desire to achieve the great deed which will dazzle and confound the hero's envious peers. Implicit in this ethic of pride and honor are the obverse motives of rivalry, jealousy, and hate. But the prevailing conviction in *The Iliad* and *The Odyssey* themselves of the significance of the heroic example is part of the explanation for the importance of these works in Greek education and life as a whole.

We can see two forms of development in the history of Sparta and Athens. Sparta is often thought to be the prototype of the totalitarian state, harsh, crude, with a people entirely submissive to the commands of the government. And at a later stage in its history this is certainly true, but not in the 7th and 8th centuries B.C. Sparta at this time was an excellent example of a conservative, aristocratic, and military city which well illustrates the chivalric ideal in Homeric thought. This aristocracy, so we learn from fragments of lyrical poetry and irrefutable archaeological evidence, made of Sparta in the 8th and 7th centuries a city noted for its interest in the arts and the principal center of Hellenic civilization. At the same time Sparta earned for itself a reputation as a great military power and its educational ideal was to train boys in the apprenticeship to war. But Sparta was a city-state and men were trained as soldiers dedicated to her service, not as warrior-knights seeking to perform the great deed. The chivalry of single-handed encounters to be found in the duels of the heroes was replaced by the clash of heavy infantry. The Homeric knight had served the king and the allegiance was personal. The Spartan officer served the state, the *polis;* regiments were bound together in common service as the instruments of the state. As Jaeger put it, the aim of Spartan education was to produce, not the individual hero, but an army of men ready to give their lives for their country. For more than two centuries the apprenticeship for war still allowed for the arts of music, poetry, and dancing in the religious festivals, and for high achievement in sport. But about 550 B.C. political events spoiled the bright promise. The aristocrats and the officers established their power, refused civic rights to new claimants from the lower orders, and prevented by police methods uprisings from any other sectors of the community. The military caste from the 5th century onward brought about the conditions and training that are usually thought to be characteristic of Sparta. Education was in the hands of the officers of the *polis* and their aim was to continue to train the Spartan infantrymen. The purposes of the whole enterprise were discipline and submission to authority, and to this end physical privation and if necessary stealing and lying were all included as part of the preparation. For the girls the training was to make them fit and ready mothers of Spartan men-children.

All of this is a pattern of such recent and painful familiarity that it need not be elaborated. Except to say that in the Spartan instance there really was no higher education in the specialized and advanced sense of the terms. And this in itself is important. Sparta represents the dead end of a debased Homeric ideal.

Athens and the beginnings of higher education. In Athens in the second half of the 6th century education lost its military characteristics. Military training had almost entirely disappeared and became part of the gymnastics and sports which young men undertook. Although this was formalized for the more aristocratic young Greeks into a kind of military apprenticeship in the 5th century (the *ephebia*), physical education became during that century a widespread pursuit. It is true that even 5th and 4th century Athens was a stratified society, but the strata were less exclusively military than in the old aristocratic tradition. Wealth enabled some citizens to provide tutors and coaches for their sons, a significant modification of the old ideal of warrior comradeship and the noble example, because many of these tutors and coaches were slaves. Schools began to appear and with them the era of the professional teachers with a group of pupils to teach in a special building.

What was taught? Physical education, music in the widest sense— poetry, song, playing the lyre or the pipe, and dancing. Although the old Athenian education was always athletic and artistic rather than literary and intellectual, by the end of the 6th century there were three main types of teachers—the gymnastics master, the music master, and the teacher of letters. At all times the moral values of loyalty, valor, and the appreciation and enjoyment of leisure were stressed in these activities. The guiding ideal of this old education was "a man both beautiful and good," developing the body as much as the character, not at all the Platonic stereotype we seem often to have in mind, the leisured and sophisticated intellectual interested in the philosophical ultimates. The critical redirection of the "new education" came in the 5th century with the work of the Sophists, and with them came the beginnings of what we now may look upon as higher education in Greece.

The Sophists and after. The most significant extension of the stereotyped man of fine physique, moral quality, and some accomplishment, characteristic of the late 6th century, was in the field of politics. The public exercise of political power, concern for the state's affairs, were relatively new in the 5th century and a group of teachers in the second half of the century offered to train anyone wishing to acquire these accomplishments. These Sophists, as we call them, were the immediate forerunners of Socrates, Isocrates, Plato, and Aristotle, as Plato's dialogue the *Protagoras* shows, for Protagoras was one of the Sophists. They were the first professional teachers, itinerants who were prepared to teach almost anything for money. They did not open schools but offered to tutor young men over three or four years for an all-in fee, and until the fashion caught on they had to mount a considerable personal publicity and there was some consequent charlatanism. Yet men such as Protagoras and Gorgias had an immense effect on the young men of their time. They were pragmatists who pointed to practical results as evidence of success. Solving problems here and now, producing practical solutions or plausible arguments was more to be desired than philosophizing, particularly philosophizing about truth or right or virtue—which was where Socrates and Plato joined their battle with the relativism of Protagoras, one of whose sayings "man is the measure of all things," sums up his humanism.

There are two consequences of the work of the Sophists which are of vital importance both for their own time and for higher education in succeeding ages. The first is the dialectical method and the conduct of argument which developed through Aristotle and others into the instrument of logic and was later formalized in the syllogistic structure of the official disputation of medieval times. The second result was that in presenting an argument on any subject, rules were not enough, ideas had to be created and clothed in words. So rhetoric as a study and a skill developed, and it was recognized that the good rhetorician, whether in parliament or the law courts or at a funeral or a festival, had to be a man of the widest culture—a polymath. We tend to think of Sophists as adroit and unprincipled word-jugglers, and this is, in part, true. But they extended the frontiers of knowledge and interest in ideas—for example in mathematics and in literary criticism and the problems of language. They widened the conceptions of what an educated man in Greece should know, and they began a way of thinking which continued for 2000 years in Western Europe (for good and ill) until the scientific revolution of the 15th and 16th centuries.

It is true that spoken rather than written language was the dominant interest of the Sophists, but the polymathy which they assumed and the intellectual virtuosity which went with it extended the horizons of the cultured young men whom they taught. Political prowess was part of the new educational ideal, but width of culture came to be desirable too. When Plato and Aristotle later condemned the man who sought to become "an expert," a technician, they were developing in their own quite different way a notion which the Sophists at their best had encouraged, the education of the whole man.

Socrates, Plato's great teacher, was a staunch opponent of the Sophists on many things. In the *Protagoras*, Socrates and Protagoras, the Sophist, discuss the great question "Can virtue be taught?" and the main differences in their points of view appear. These differences are of critical importance in the history of Western education for 2000 years. Socrates believed that the task of education was to discover the gifts of the pupils and help to develop them, but that right behavior could only be taught as the teacher detected the virtue, the idea and ideal of virtue, that the child carried with him from birth. Socrates was opposed to the opportunism and the pragmatic flair of the Sophists—he was an academic conservative who accepted an aristocratic tradition which concerned itself with ethics in education. The emphasis on character training in the English public school owes something to the Socratic as well as to the Christian tradition.

Further, Socrates was a metaphysician with an unshakeable belief in man, not as the measure of all things, but as the embodiment of a principle of Truth which was in the universe itself. Virtue cannot be implanted in a child; it is there already, but the teacher can enable it to flower and this was his first and last responsibility. Polymathy was not enough; the Sophists' emphasis on good teaching was not enough. In the end, to Socrates, education was concerned with wisdom and a religious view of man and the universe, not with the development of political and rhetorical acumen.

Plato opened his Academy in 387 B.C. and it had a continuous existence until 529 A.D. For over 900 years this kind of university had an influence in the Mediterranean world. But most of its influence in Western Europe has been through the writings of its founder, both as political theorist and philosopher. In the *Republic* he sought to sketch the ideal state based upon justice and ruled by wisdom. Here and in the *Politicus* and in the *Laws* (unfinished at the time of his death in 374) at various points he considers the education of his rulers. Plato was not a democrat—he was, like Socrates, faithful to the aristocratic outlook. Although it appears that the philosopher-kings of the *Republic* were not chosen for their birth, but rather for their worth as leaders of thought expert in political judgment, they were essentially an aristocratic group. Plato in the *Republic* was not concerned with the education of ordinary people, but of political leaders, and many such were produced from the Academy over the centuries. However, in doing this Plato emphasized the Socratic belief in truth and wisdom and in addition gave a new importance to knowledge and right reasoning as a means of coming to know the truth. The Socratic method enabled the teacher to ensure that a premium was placed on getting the pupil to find out the answers for himself and so the Academy was in a sense a center for higher education and something of a research school at the same time.

The Academy was to include gymnastics (in which dancing, athletics, and war games played their part), music in the old sense of the term, and the learning of reading and writing, the study of literature. Here we have come to a sharp break with the old classical education. In Books II, III, and X of the *Republic* Plato criticizes the poets for the debased versions they give of the gods. Homer, the pattern and exemplar of the classical period, came especially under Plato's censure and he was prepared to expurgate and rewrite Homer. Others in

Athens regarded such a proposal as altogether too extreme but the notion of control, censorship, and expurgation is one which constantly recurs throughout the history of higher education in Western Europe.

The other element in the preparatory education provided by the Academy was mathematics, which was regarded both as an instrument of direct social and intellectual value and as a means of selecting the most distinguished minds. These intellectuals proved themselves ready for the study of philosophy because they had shown that they could penetrate through the exercise of mere mathematical skills to understand the abstraction of number itself.

Literature, the understanding and enjoyment of the visual arts (not the practice of them), music, rhetoric, physical education, mathematics —these are the subjects, the curriculum (see also Capes, 1923). But they must be plotted on three other axes which give perspective and depth to this intellectual structure.

First, these studies were preparatory—they came after the preliminaries of learning which were placed between the ages of three and ten and they lasted from ten to eighteen. By that time those who were going to distinguish themselves with mathematical ideas had appeared, and before these few continued their intellectual novitiate they had to turn aside with all their contemporaries to the physical and military rigors of the *ephebia* for two or three years. According to the *Republic,* on their return to the life of the mind ten more years had to be spent with the sciences of geometry, arithmetic, astronomy, and acoustics. Only then at the age of thirty were these leaders ready to begin the long ascent to attain to the truth of reality through the study of philosophy. For twenty years they had to learn what philosophy had to teach them and how it was to be applied in the life of the city which they would both rule and serve. At the age of fifty they were ready to accept and exercise power because their minds and hearts were attuned to the Form and Idea of the Good.

If the study of language, the visual arts, music, rhetoric, physical education, and mathematics were preparatory to the more ultimate disciplines of science and the philosophy of dialectic, the second and third axes mentioned above became apparent. Very few stayed the full course and education at this high level was strictly selective. And, third, education was concerned ultimately with right action, right thinking, and the affirmation of the inner and permanent world of the true, the good and the beautiful. Education was concerned with wisdom, which detected, accepted, and worked out with deep satisfaction that virtue and justice were in the mind of man because they were *a priori* in the mind and purpose of his Creator.

In the educational development of Greece so far outlined the work done by the soldier, the cultivated citizen, the athlete, the artist, the politician, the rhetorician, the ruler, the nobleman, the philosopher, the intellectual opportunist, the professional teacher, the scientist, the mathematician, has been in some way represented. So, too, has been the Platonic educational ideal. I do not wish to make it appear that Plato carried this systematically into practice at the Academy or that his became the dominant view in the Athens of his time—Isocrates, for instance, was a most influential teacher of rhetoric whose down-to-earth humanism had a more immediate impact. In giving prominence to Plato I have intended to show how thinking about the purpose of education could suggest some of the content of the curriculum, and how a philosophic viewpoint of the greatest significance expressed itself in higher education in its original Greek context. Platonism has an elevated view of man and knowledge, it has a philosophy of life. This is an aristocratic, a selective view of higher education very different from that of the warrior—knights of the 8th and 7th centuries.

The Hellenistic ideal of paideia. During the 400 years of which we have been writing so far Greece was organized politically in small states. There was no national consciousness in any marked degree. Cities like Sparta, Athens, Phocis, Thebes were the centers of government and state capitals, and wars between them were not infrequent. The Peloponnesian War between Athens and Sparta lasted for twenty-seven years, ending at the battle of Aegospotami in 405. When we realize that Socrates was condemned to death in 399 for neglecting the gods of the state and corrupting the minds of young men, and that Plato, Aristotle, and Isocrates were teaching during the period of subjection to Sparta, we place the work of these men, known and valued throughout Western civilization, in its original perspective. Persia was the intermittent enemy of Greece as a whole, but the city-states had neither the will nor the means to unite against the common enemy. So the writings of the Athenians did not at that time spread far. But two men brought unwilling unity to Greece and formed the empire which enabled the Greek ideal of *paideia* to spread in what has come to be called the Hellenistic period.

Macedonia was a mountainous and neglected state north of the Greek mainland whose young king Philip defeated the armies of Thebes and Athens at Chaeronea in 338 and became the admitted master of Greece who would have led the new nation against the Persians. But Philip was assassinated in 336. Alexander, his son, was even more important in the history of Western Europe than his father.

In thirteen years he conquered Syria, Asia Minor, Persia, Egypt and marched over the Khyber Pass to India. Aristotle had been his boyhood tutor and Homer's heroes were his model. In his social, religious, and political agreements he showed an unusual degree of tolerance of those whom he conquered. He planned that his empire should cover the world and that he, as a wise, magnanimous, and cultured sovereign was to be given godlike honors, but he died when he was only 33 with many plans unrealized.

Philip and Alexander made possible the dispersion of Hellenistic ideas. The Greek language was introduced and Greek cities founded all over Asia, and Alexander sought to overcome any sense of racial superiority in any part of his vast possessions. The cities of Alexandria, Pergamum, Rhodes, and Antioch became centers for the greatest universities and libraries of their time and are symbols of the coming of cosmopolitan thought. The city states of Hellas lost their importance in the 4th and 3rd centuries and Greek language, philosophy, mathematics, literature, and art became the possession of a far wider public. Similarly, the conquered East offered riches in wealth and art forms and religious thinking and Greece itself experienced the influx of large groups of Greek-speaking aliens.

After the death of Alexander, however, his generals divided the empire and betrayed his master plan. Only when another power could reestablish an empire and a rule of law could the gains of the Hellenistic period be made secure and the diffusion of this distinctive culture be given settled conditions, and in the 1st century B.C. this power was Rome.

What were the chief characteristics of the Hellenistic *paideia* at this time? They are often summarized in the phrase "classical humanism," the notion of man as an autonomous personality, an individual who aimed at self-realization and self-fulfillment—as Plotinus said in early Christian times, man at his best is engaged in carving his own statue, moulding from the childish materials the matured form of the cultured human being. In his *Laws* Plato writes that individual culture was the most precious gift ever granted to man, and Hellenistic civilization considered that the man most to be envied was the man of taste, of intellect, and artistic sensibility. The powerful and well-organized Roman state was mesmerized and captivated by the mystique of *paideia* and provided the channels which carried the notions of classical humanism into the stream of Christian belief:

Classical humanism was able to lead to—and did in fact lead to—a higher kind of greatness, by putting itself at the service of a higher cause, to which the human person was in self-transcendence. . . . First, classical education put itself at the service of the State, the State of Rome in which the old city ideals burst forth again in civilization still Hellenistic; and then later, when the Empire became Christian, it put itself at the service of God (Marrou, 1956, p. 226).

Most of the authorities on the ancient world consider that one of Rome's historic functions was to complete the work begun by Alexander and establish the values of Hellenistic civilization in the Mediterranean, North Africa, and Western Europe so firmly that they survived the barbarian invasions which overthrew the Roman Empire itself. The study of rhetoric, of law, and of philosophy was the sum of Roman higher education in the first four centuries of the Christian era. There is a parallel to the Athenian *ephebia* in Roman colleges, but teaching based on language, spoken and written, is the mark of higher education. We find here an echo of Isocrates who claimed that rhetoric, the study of language and its uses, could teach a man not only to write well, but also to think clearly and to act, to discriminate feelings and to be a judge of persons.

Lest this introduction be thought to be of academic interest only, irrelevant to the university of later days, let Sir Richard Livingstone speak, writing in 1941:

Before they leave school, those who have not learnt Greek should be introduced to Greek thought in translation. . . . There seems to be a curious idea that Greek is not relevant to our world. Nothing could be more relevant: for Greek made modern civilization. . . . Greek literature *is* a view of life. Here as nowhere else in European Literature is a clear, unflurried vision of a rational human existence, which balances justly the claims of body, character and intellect, of material and spiritual civilization, of the individual and the State (Livingstone, 1941, pp. 122–123).

CLASSICAL AND WESTERN CHRISTIAN EDUCATION

One of the strange facts of history is that Christians in the Graeco-Roman world did not set up their own schools in the early centuries of the Christian era. They accepted the classical training given to non-Christian contemporaries in schools and added on the specifically religious education mainly in the home and through the Church. This was not the case in the countries of the Roman Empire beyond the influence of classical culture, where very often the Christian school was the main agency for education in the narrow sense and in addition for religious teaching and evangelism. It is likely that many of the valuations of classical humanism would seem self-evident to early Christians, although their conviction and dogma drew some sharp distinctions. For instance, they rejected polytheism, they could not accept happiness as the chief end of living, nor could they consider a civilized and cultivated urbanity the nearest an educated man could get to religion. Yet Christians operated within the educational system of the time and read the pagan authors, holding their noses, as it were, and relying on their Christian upbringing to expose the errors. After all, Christianity was a religion about man as part of God's creation and his unique relationship to God through the person, life, and death of Jesus Christ. It was not the miraculous birth of a new culture, though it reinterpreted the contemporary culture in terms of its own moral precepts, dogmatic system, and ecclesiastical forms as the first four centuries of the era passed.

St. Paul brings these matters to a focus in himself. He was a Jew of high birth, born in Tarsus and educated in Jerusalem at the feet of Gamaliel who taught him according to the law and the prophets of his forefathers. He spoke Greek and Latin as well as Hebrew. When the Roman captain in Jerusalem threatened to scourge him, Paul pointed out that he, a Jew, was a full Roman citizen. The captain had only come by his own Roman citizenship by his military service and by paying a sum of money—he was a first generation freeman. Paul, however, was born free, the son of a Roman citizen, yet a Pharisee and the son of a Pharisee. In him we have the *pax Romana* and the form of Hellenistic culture summed up. But also in Paul we have the conflict of the new Christian and the old humanist, a conflict which on a larger scale grows steadily during the first 400 years of the Christian era. If the believer has in the Bible the Word of God what need has he of other books? Even more, what need has he of pagan books? And in any case his task is to spread the gospel and to expose error for what it is. When in 362 A.D. Julian the Apostate forbade Christians to teach unless they were prepared to believe in the gods of Homer and Hesiod he brought to an end for a short while nearly four centuries of surprisingly amicable relationships in schools between Christians and non-Christians, and he gave the impetus to what might be called the Christian counteroffensive. Christians began to write their own text books, using the literary forms with which they had become so familiar in their own education. The Pentateuch was rewritten in the style of Homer and the New Testament became a series of Platonic dialogues. But this was short-lived and in the 5th century classical humanism prevailed once again in the curriculum of the schools, with religious teaching taking place outside the school in the teaching of the Church.

On the other hand, in the 4th, 5th, and 6th centuries the monastic school grew up, in which monks taught the Scriptures to boys in their care and the compromise between non-Christian classical humanism and Christian belief was over. Instead of classical stories, the Bible became the source of all reading and study, and from the 5th century onward the devotional works of the Church Fathers like Cyprian and Athanasius crept into the reading lists. After the fall of the Roman Empire, the secular school ceased to exist in the Western world and the monasteries and churches, where they survived, had to take up the burden of educating boys in the hope and expectation that many could be trained in the higher education necessary for the priesthood. In fact, these episcopal schools provided the main bridge from Roman and Hellenistic times to the medieval university, but they changed the kind of education available, because they were an instrument of a Church at first fighting for survival in a pagan world and then carrying the spiritual battle to the infidel in the mission of preaching and conversion.

Education still, as in classical times, began with the alphabet, but by the 7th century the texts to be read were no longer Homer or Plato or Vergil, but the Bible, the Divine Office, and later the patristic commentaries and homilies. The texts were not literature in the Greek or Roman sense. They were not the prototypes of a chivalric ideal as the Homeric text was. The Bible was the revealed Scripture, both the letter and the spirit, for the letter alone kills but the spirit gives life. The teacher was, likewise, a man of very different standing. Although the leading sophists and Socrates, Plato, Aristotle, Isocrates, and Quintilian were men highly regarded, the bulk of teachers in classical times were in low esteem. In early medieval times, however, the instructor was both teacher and spiritual mentor; he taught reading and writing so that his pupils might know more of God and his ways. Education had now become an instrument of the religious life and was no longer the prerogative of an aristocracy.

THE BYZANTINE STREAM IN EDUCATION

The Roman Empire in the west was over-run and Rome was plundered by Alaric in 410 A.D., but in 330 the Emperor Constantine had transferred the capital of the Empire to Byzantium, on the Black Sea, and here the continuity between the late Roman Empire and the early Byzantine Middle Ages was established and appears most clearly of all in the development of higher education.

I have tried to show the continuity between classical and Hellenistic, between Greek and Roman education and to indicate the discontinuity in the western Empire after the barbarian invasions of the 5th century. The rise of the Church and the decline of the secular school took place in a culture which had little respect for the written word and the fine arts. These are the Dark Ages, at the end of which Latin was the *lingua franca,* secular literature was no longer studied, and Greek was a dead language.

In Constantinople, as Byzantium was called after 330, the university maintained the Hellenistic classical tradition for over a thousand years. Despite vicissitudes it continued to teach music, physical education, mathematics, rhetoric, philosophy, law, medicine and to train an élite from which the state officials could be drawn. It steered clear of religious alignments and preserved the model of the convinced Christian who was also a man educated in the classics. In Eastern Christendom the secular school continued, while in Western Christendom the Dark Ages forced Christians to transform the culture itself and the material and forms of higher learning into a more or less coherent Christian civilization.

It is true that this is altogether too simple a picture which ignores on the one hand the ascetic and very influential monastic schools in Byzantium, which trained priests on Christian material, and on the other hand the influence of the Celtic Christian schools of Ireland, which, like Scotland, was not conquered by the Romans and did not have the Latin schools which appeared in England. St. Patrick and St. Columba brought the monastic tradition of Celtic Christendom to the north of Britain in the 6th century as St. Augustine sent by Pope Gregory brought Roman Christianity to the south of the country. But, admitting these qualifications in the large trends of history it is a fair generalization to sketch Byzantine education as I have.

Classical humanism died hard in Western Europe in the 400 to 500 years following the sack of Rome in 410, but by 1000 A.D. Western Europe was a continent in which Latin was the dominant language and the Bible the main literary source together with Christian commentaries and devotional works. The *trivium* in some form (grammar, rhetoric, and dialectic) was the basis of preparatory secular education. The *quadrivium* (music, arithmetic, geometry, astronomy) was the wider course of study for advanced students which was mentioned in Plato. But, as Rashdall says, "the heart and centre of the secular education of the time in northern Europe was the study of dialectic or logic." This is very different from the literary education of the Roman aristocrat or the training in rhetoric given by Isocrates to his students, for it is dominated by the syllogism and the formal distinctions of disputation. The resources of classical literature which were called upon were admittedly very fragmentary in the 11th and 12th centuries—they were mainly Latin translations of part of Aristotle's logic, one or two of Plato's dialogues in a Latin translation, and the letters of Cicero insofar as they were consonant with Christian belief. It was inevitable that a dialectical training in philosophy based on Aristotle and concerned with perennial problems like the nature and existence of Universals (whether objects exist separately or are an expression of essences or ideal forms) should turn its method on to the data and notions of theology. The chief substance of knowledge was the Scriptures, the commentaries made upon them, and the doctrines of the Church. The 11th and 12th centuries saw the birth and flowering of what we now call scholastic philosophy and the beginnings of the medieval university.

But if this is the thread of continuity from Greece, through Rome, and the Dark Ages of Western Europe to the medieval university, where does the thread from Byzantium interweave with it? Classical education and Christian belief were maintained in Constantinople and its possessions around the Mediterranean basin, but the empire was often under the threat of conquest, and in the 11th century Moslem Turks invaded the country. The Byzantine Church appealed to the Latin Church for help, even though many conflicts existed between the two. The history of the Crusades with their twin purposes of recovering the Holy Places in Asia Minor and of subduing the influence of Eastern Christendom, stretches confusedly over the 12th and early 13th centuries. One of the results of these Holy Wars was that Byzantine cultural achievements were made available to the West, and particularly the writings of Greek authors which had been preserved in Byzantine libraries for about 900 years, although Latin Christians destroyed great quantities of this material when they captured Constantinople after the scandalous diversion of the Fourth Crusade for this purpose. However, much remained and entered into 12th-century Western culture bringing about a renaissance of literary, linguistic, and philosophical learning. By the time Constantinople had been finally captured by the Turks in 1453 what amounted to its holding operation on behalf of Hellenistic culture for over 1000 years had been discharged and the continuity of Hellenism in Western Europe was assured.

There was another tributary to the medieval European university, linked with Byzantium. Mohammedan higher education had been in existence since the 9th century, and in its turn it had to harmonize Hellenistic ideas and Moslem theology. The translation of Greek works into Arabic was well established, and in Baghdad and Cairo a great deal of advanced study was undertaken in mathematics and science. Only in the 14th century, when Mohammedanism became much more orthodox and distrustful of secular knowledge, did Western European universities begin to establish an assured ascendancy. One of the great universities of Europe was to be found in the 9th and 10th century in Cordova in Moorish Spain, and to it Christians and Jews as well as Moslems went and there and at Toledo much of the translation of Greek authors was done. As Jewish scholars often did this work, many of the books were translated from Greek to Syrian, then to Hebrew or Arabic, and then to Latin. The Moslem contribution to the continuity of the classics and to the study of mathematics and science in Western Europe is crucial.

The Spanish scholar who has argued that the European Universities were the outcome of Islamic influence seems to us to be in error, but his argument may at least remind us that one of the greatest forces in the medieval university, Mohammedan learning, found a footing in the West in centres, especially Toledo, which were under royal and espiscopal influence, in Jewish and other circles in the south of France and, to some extent, in the royal court of Sicily. (Powicke & Emden, 1936, Vol I, Introduction, xxxix).

THE MEDIEVAL UNIVERSITY

The monasteries in Europe in the 10th and 11th centuries conserved knowledge, and by transcriptions added to it. The arts were deployed in the service of Christian worship as we can see in the illumination of manuscripts and in the development of music and architecture. In the 11th and 12th centuries the growth of so-called secular cathedrals added to the educational power of the Church. In 1179 the Third Lateran Council decreed that all cathedrals should have a master whose task was to teach clerks and poor scholars, and from this decree schools at the cathedrals developed. They were centered upon the persons of the teachers who had been given the approval of the bishop to teach within the cathedral precincts. The officer who later became responsible for approving the applications to teach within the precincts was called the Chancellor and the permission became a license. In the story of the development of the medieval university a principal theme is the connection with and the struggle against the Church, and the ambivalent regard for the Chancellor is a case in point. He was an officer of the bishop and capable of exerting the power of veto; sometimes he was venal and sometimes would refuse to license anyone he considered unorthodox.

In order to protect themselves against the manipulation of such power, the teachers or masters in such a great cathedral school as Notre Dame in Paris organized themselves into a self-protecting gild or *universitas*. They became adroit at playing both ends against the middle. The three main sources of pressure upon the gild of masters were the church, the secular power, and the townspeople. Again and again the masters of Paris scored off the local Chancellor and bishop by appealing directly to the Pope—as an example, in 1212 the Pope forbade the Chancellor to exact oaths of obedience from those he licensed, and be forbade payment for licenses and later on he forbade excommunication by Chancellors. He also insisted that if the masters wished a bachelor of arts to be recognized as a master, the Chancellor could not veto their recommendation.

As the masters were also clerics, they fought successfully for a university ecclesiastical court to try their own affairs, and this produced many clashes with the forces of law and order in the secular power and with the townspeople. An example is to be found in Paris between students, townspeople, and (as we should now say) police, in which many deaths took place. The scholars and masters of the University gave an ultimatum to the King, Philip II. They asked for protection against the police and against the townspeople, or else they would take the University elsewhere—and they got all they asked for. All arrested students were to be handed to an ecclesiastical authority, as they were actually or potentially clerics and not subject to civil law. Citizens and police had to respect the privilege of the scholars, and their goods could not be seized by secular officers in any civil action. By 1210 the *universitas* of masters had an organization with statutes, gild forms, and practices. They had the powerful support of the monarch and the Pope and relative immunity from retaliation by townspeople. In 1229 after another bloody brawl in which reprisals were taken on the students all members of the University resolved that "unless satisfactory reparation is made to the whole body of masters and students . . . . no-one shall be permitted to remain in the city or diocese of Paris to study, either for the purpose of teaching or being taught." If this form of evacuation took place, the document went on, on no account would the University return to Paris for at least six years. And the dispersion, the *cessatio* as it was called, took place and the scholars departed to Oxford, Cambridge (beguilingly invited by Henry III, the King of England), Toulouse, Bologna, Salerno.

Despite the arrogance, the violence, and the excesses of the students, Paris, in order to prosper, needed the University for its reputation (it was the undisputed queen in theology), and the Pope compelled the civil and ecclesiastical powers in Paris to concede liberties to the University in order to bring about its return. The University was granted the power to negotiate rents for lodgings, to arrange its own internal affairs in detail, and to go on strike until its demands were met in any dispute. All graduates of the University were on oath to obey its rules, and so if a *cessatio* took place all priests of the Church, all doctors and lawyers in Paris who had the University as *Alma Mater* were expected to join the strike. It was, and remained, a formidable weapon, and the University was established in Paris as virtual arbiter of its own destiny because Pope, Chancellor, King, and townspeople had been played off against one another with complete success. In the middle of the 15th century Pope Pius II and Louis XII broke two centuries of University dominance, but only when the King marched with an embattled army into the precincts of the University to break a threatened strike by force.

Paris had its gild of masters and was the pattern and exemplar of Oxford and Cambridge. Bologna, a free city in northern Italy, was the other originator of university ideas. Whereas Paris was supreme in theology and in constant conflict with Church and state, Bologna was pre-eminent in both civil and canon law. Whereas Paris developed logic and dialectic, Bologna maintained the long tradition of rhetoric which came from Isocrates in 4th-century Greece, through Quintilian in Rome in the 1st century of the Christian era. Paris had its *universitas* of masters, Bologna its *universitas* of students who appointed their own rector, hired and paid their teachers, and in large measure decided their courses. Other Italian universities grew up at Naples, Reggio, Padua, Siena, and elsewhere encouraged by these city-states to seek for the Papal Bull to give status and authority to their degree. In the course of three or four centuries the rule of the students was replaced by the control of the masters.

During the 300 years between the end of the 12th century and the end of the 15th century the medieval university took its distinctive shape. As I pointed out at the beginning of this essay, Rashdall claimed that the university as we know it is the heir of Paris and Bologna, not of Greece and Athens. Before we go farther we had better take stock.

Paris, Bologna, and Oxford are the progenitors of the universities of the Western world. They came into being through the conjunction of such factors as the growth of the cathedral school, the initiative of the city state, the welcoming charity of monasteries, the brilliance and reputation of teachers like Abélard and John of Salisbury, the interest of the Pope and the king. The *studium,* as it was called, started off as a local center, rather as Plato's Academy or Aristotle's Lyceum. As Paris, Bologna, and Oxford very soon drew scholars from all over Europe they became known as *studia generalia* and a master admitted to teach in one of these *studia* was recognized as qualified to teach in the others, or indeed in any other *studia* as they began to increase. The Papal Bull came to be the guarantee of recognition and approval, but this usually followed when the *studium* had established itself. For a *studium generale* to achieve this standing it had to possess a basic faculty of arts and in addition it had to have at least one of the higher faculties of medicine, law, or theology.

The gild of masters, the *universitas magistrorum,* represents an organization for self-protection and solidarity, and it has been suggested that this gild, like the *universitas scholarium,* was started by the foreigners in a strange city. Certainly, the students were divided into what were called Nations (four in Paris, two in Bologna, two in Oxford) and there is plenty of evidence of violence and enmity between the Nations although a united front was usually presented to police and townsfolk.

As time passed the term "university" came to cover both the institution, the *studium,* and the undergraduates and graduates in whatever *universitas* they were organized. The student entered the faculty of arts where he was required to study the *septivium* or seven liberal arts, the *trivium* of grammar, dialectic, and rhetoric, followed by the *quadrivium* of geometry, arithmetic, astronomy, and music. When he graduated as a bachelor he was granted the license to teach by the Chancellor. After a time he might be admitted by the gild of masters to their ranks. Here one of the most significant features of the university is to be found, the basis of its unique freedom which has lasted for 800 years to this day. Although the Church offered the license to teach, the masters examined and graduated the student and they elected him to their own number. This is the beginning of academic freedom, for no further formal examination was needed, and it is the origin of the practice at contemporary Oxford and Cambridge whereby the Bachelor of Arts need only wait for the required period of time, keeping his name in the university's records, before paying the fee required for his admission at a degree ceremony as Master of Arts. The degree of Doctor was offered as the highest academic honor in theology, law, and medicine after the presentation and defense of a thesis.

By 1500, therefore, the universities had an academic structure, a curriculum, an institutional dependence upon and independence of the Church and the state. Rashdall was right when he traced the organizational continuity of the modern university from the Middle Ages, and what came to be taught in the 15th-, 16th-, and 17th-century Renaissance, was in direct intellectual descent from Athens, Rome, Byzantium, Baghdad, and Cairo. Aristotle became the new authority in logic and dialectic in the 13th and 14th centuries through newly accessible translations and the massive achievement of St. Thomas Aquinas and Albertus Magnus.

In Chaucer's *Canterbury Tales* written toward the end of the 14th century we have in the Clerk of Oxenford a summary of the university man at his best at the end of the Middle Ages. This scholar had also been to the University of Padua in Italy and was wedded to logic. He wore threadbare clothes and was mounted on a skinny nag, being too unworldly to seek money and preferment. In any case, if he could ever get money he spent it on the works of Aristotle or for some cultural purpose. He was devout and humble, completely dedicated to learning and teaching.

Also in *The Canterbury Tales* we find the knight and his squire, the representatives of a quite different but equally powerful educational tradition of feudal times. Chivalry was the educational order for the aristocracy of the age and it sounds very like the apprenticeship which we read of earlier in the aristocratic ages of the development of Greece in 800 or 900 B.C. At that time the young men served and waited upon the older warriors, learning the arts of war and the virtues of loyalty and obedience.

Chaucer's Knight loved truth and honor, generosity and courtesy; he had fought for his Christian faith against the infidel all over the then known world and was both devout and wise. His squire had followed his lord as much as his years had allowed. He could sing, dance, and versify with grace and was an excellent horseman. He was brave and he was amorous, he attended his master everywhere and would defend his lady with his life.

The Clerk of Oxenford is the poor cleric, the devout, unworldly scholar, honest and magnanimous, humble and unselfish. The university and the Church have made him what he is. The knight and the squire are wealthy, modest, brave, and devout. They are noblemen by birth and by training in a noble household. They have spent no time at a university and their accomplishments are not in the *septivium*, but in gracious living, manly sports, good manners, responsible behavior, and Christian piety. They can administer their affairs and can write or tell a tale. But the chivalric tradition is not the university tradition, the knight is not the cleric.

Only later, in the Renaissance of humanism in literature, philosophy, and science, and of Protestant humanism in the Reformation, did the intellectual mould of the medieval university crack. Instead of the Nations of scholars in holy orders wandering over Europe from university to university, relying on Latin as the common language, living plainly but often boisterously, and enjoying freedom, patronage, and independence to an extraordinary degree, the pattern changes. The universities of the 16th and 17th centuries became more nationally organized and small colleges multiplied in Oxford and Cambridge and Paris. Pious founders endowed the colleges with land and money. They no longer traveled light, the *cessatio* became impossible, they became institutionalized. The end of the Middle Ages led on to the expansion of the Age of Discovery and the end of the feudal system to the rise of the merchant middle class. Taking a long leap in history to 16th-century England after the Reformation and the dissolution of the monasteries by Henry VIII and Edward VI in the second quarter of the century, we find that:

Hitherto the universities had been full of poor scholars, maintained by scholarships from the free schools. But the dissolution of these schools in the general appropriation of monastic resources, coupled with the subsequent rapid rise in the cost of living, led them to become dependent on the sons of the new Tudor bureaucracy. Well might Latimer complain to Henry's son, Edward VI, in 1549: "There be none now but great men's sons in colleges, and their fathers look not to have them preachers." (Armytage, 1955, p. 63.)

It would seem that the Clerk of Oxenford has been excluded and the knight's son, the squire, has taken his place.

THE PROTESTANT REFORMATION AND THE RENAISSANCE

From the 15th to the 17th centuries the universities changed in three main ways. First, in Protestant England the colleges of Oxford and Cambridge multiplied in the 16th and 17th centuries, founded with chaplains to ensure that the Anglican cause was presented and the lie given both to Rome and to Geneva. The link between the *studia generalia* of Paris, Bologna, and Oxford was broken because the Protestant universities of England had no common cause with the Catholic universities of the Continent. Secondly, laymen, men not in holy orders, entered the professions of the law and medicine in considerable numbers, and the merchants of Venice, Florence, Padua and the Hague and Amsterdam began the transformation of the economy of Western Europe. They had power and wealth and new and tempting jobs to offer. Thirdly, the Renaissance of learning began its long emancipation of the mind and spirit, bringing back the genuine study of Greek through the work of a scholar like Erasmus and reintroducing the humanistic spirit, which we have had reason to comment on many times as we have traced higher education from 9th century pre-Christian Greece through the five centuries of Roman *humanitas* (the Chair of Latin in the Scottish Universities is still called the Chair of Humanity). The outcome of Renaissance humanism was not only literary and artistic, it was also scientific. If we take England as the example for Protestant Europe, we can be wise after the enormous events of the time and sketch the broad outlines of the history of ideas from the beginning of the Protestant era in the middle of the 16th century to the beginning of the modern scientific era a century later.

The Aristotelian scientific system of medieval Europe received two severe shocks in 1544. First a Belgian anatomist, Andreas Vesalius, produced a book on the human body, *De Fabrica Humani Corporis*. It contained splendid drawings illustrating the structure of bones and muscles and the nervous system, and they were based on excellent and consistent dissection. The other revolutionary work was by Copernicus, *De Revolutionibus Orbium Coelestium*, which overthrew the Aristotelian theory of the fixed and unchanging universe, and offered instead the earth as a planet of the sun. The rest of the century contains many examples of the growing interest in medicine, mathematics, and geography. The volume of trade forced improvements in navigation and shipbuilding upon merchants and financiers and in economics itself insurance of goods began to become common and the penalties against usury were repealed.

In the 16th and 17th centuries we come on to the meeting ground of medieval cosmology of degree and order, "the chain of Being," and the probing forces of individual inquiry. In the medieval cosmology the dogmas of the Church were the data to which all thinkers had to bend their systems, and from such a situation scholasticism emerged. By the time of Bacon there was a change in temper and method. For the scholastics the important consideration might be the metaphysical status of things; for them, as Basil Willey remarks, there was little or no distinction between a "fact" and a theological or metaphysical "truth" (Willey, 1933, p. 14). Francis Bacon, however, states:

> Those, therefore, who determine not to conjecture and guess but to find out and know; not to invent fables and romances of worlds, but to look into and dissect the nature of this real world, must consult only things themselves (Bacon, Bohn ed., 1874, p. 16).

Bacon's serious purpose was to attack much of the superstition of the medieval tradition, rather than to strike at its metaphysical bases, to clear the accumulation of pseudo-science, astrology, magic:

> For the wit and mind of man, if it work upon matter, which is the contemplation of the creatures of God, worketh according to the stuff and is limited thereby, but if it work upon itself, as a spider worketh his web, then it is endless, and brings forth indeed cobwebs of learning, admirable for the fineness of thread and work, but of no substance or profit (Bacon, Everyman ed. 1915, p. 32).

This trend to empirical thought, this concern with things and processes, with forces and measurements, gathered strength in the 17th century. Harvey, Gilbert, Newton, Comenius, the Royal Society —these represent something of the rational and experimental tendencies. One of the great achievements of 16th- and 17th-century scientists was regaining for others their confidence in nature. However, there was also still for many people a dread of natural science, "black magic" or "forbidden knowledge" as we can see in Marlowe's Dr. Faustus, which was first performed in 1588. Probably not till the 18th century did this confidence become for Protestants what Chesterton has called "cosmic cosiness." Basil Willey says of Sir Thomas Browne whose *Religio Medici* was published in 1642:

> Perhaps no writer is more truly representative of the double-faced age in which he lived, an age half scientific and half magical, half sceptical and half credulous, looking back in one direction to Maundeville, and forward to Newton. . . . He had, in fact, what Mr. T. S. Eliot has called the "unified sensibility" of the "metaphysicals", which was the offspring . . . . . . of a scholastic training blended with the expansive curiosity of the Renaissance. . . . Many different worlds or countries of the mind then lay close together— the world of scholastic learning, the world of scientific experiment, the worlds of classical mythology and of biblical history, of fable and of fact, of theology and demonology, of sacred and profane love, of pagan and Christian morals, of activity and contemplation; and a cultivated man had freedom of them all. . . . . The distinctions were only beginning to be made which for later ages shut off poetry from science, metaphor from fact, fancy from judgment (Willey, 1933, pp. 41–2).

THE AMERICAN UNIVERSITIES

The Pilgrim Fathers landed at Cape Cod in Massachusetts in November, 1620, Protestant Dissenters from England and Holland, in many cases the alumni of Oxford or Cambridge before they became dissenters (for Oxford and Cambridge until 1871 had laws excluding those who did not support the Church of England). They knew well the religious and scientific controversies of the time, and their educational plans for grammar schools and universities show very clearly that they tried to transfer to America what they had become familiar with in England. So, when John Harvard's College was founded in 1636, it had in mind not only the traditions of learning which had been inherited in Western Europe from Greece, Rome, Palestine, and the Christian Church, but it had also to consider the needs of the new community seeking Christian freedom. In the Old World, Milton emphasized in his *Tractate on Education* in 1644 the connection between education and all public and private offices of peace and war. In the New World the connection was even more obvious. On the pillars of the gates of Harvard there is carved an extract from a pamphlet of 1643, *New England's First Fruits:*

> After God had carried us safe to *New England,* and we had builded our houses, provided necessaries for our livelihood, reared convenient places for God's worship and settled the Civil Government; one of the next things we longed for and looked after was to advance learning and perpetuate it to posterity dreading to leave an illiterate ministry to the Churches when our present ministers shall lie in the dust.[1]

By the side of the College was set up "a fair Grammar School" which prepared such as were "judged ripe in academical learning" for entry to the College. The learning of the students appeared in their public declamations in Latin and Greek and in logical and philosophical disputations, and their goodness appeared in "the savoury breathings of their spirits in their godly conversation." The course of study included logic, physics, ethics, politics, arithmetic, geometry and astronomy, Greek, Hebrew, Latin, rhetoric, and divinity. This kind of curriculum shows how little Harvard was affected by the scientific, technological, commercial, and political revolution which had been begun in Europe and of which the presence of the pioneers in New England was a striking consequence. Although they were nonconformists in religious terms, they were not so in educational terms.

The medieval university was closely knit to vocational preparation for teaching, the law, medicine, and the Church. Seventeenth-century Oxford and Cambridge were concerned with preparing clergy, but by then the lawyers had their own Inns of Court in London and the physicians their own College. Learning was reverting to the polite and amateur tradition of Athens. As Cowley has it:

> The Renaissance was a glorious age for Europe in general but not for the universities (Cowley, 1956, p. 196).

[1] The spelling has been modernized here.

The colonial period—1636 *to* 1789. It is no wonder that the liberal arts cause is tough and traditional and respectable to this day in the U.S.A. It is incomparably the oldest, and it has been the object of this essay so far to show that it is in direct line with European university tradition. It is true that the term "Liberal Arts" was not used until the end of last century, but the pedigree was and is there, and the intellectual respectability of the line has to be admitted. The United States is not likely to venerate anything simply because it is old, yet although there are many strong tributaries to the stream of American higher education coming from other sources which we shall have reason to examine, we must recognize at once that the liberal arts rose as a spring 2500 years ago and that as this spring broadened it has wound its way through nearly twenty centuries of the Christian era, sometimes shrinking to a narrow rivulet, fructifying very little, but only in the last 300 years and especially in the last 150 being joined by any other tributaries at all. While we do no service to learning by marching backward into the future with our eyes fixed on the past, we possess a false confidence if we ground our educational thinking only on what seems to be contemporary.

In the 17th and 18th centuries nine college institutions were founded: Harvard in Massachusetts; Yale in Connecticut; Brown in Rhode Island; Dartmouth in New Hampshire; Pennsylvania in Philadelphia (it adopted the name of the state in 1791); Princeton in New Jersey; Columbia in New York; Rutgers, the college founded by the Dutch Reformed Church for the Middle Colonies; and William and Mary, an Anglican or Episcopalian college for the Southern Colonies.

Oxford and Cambridge in the same period were interested in the arts and theology and less in law and medicine, as has been said earlier. All the American colleges prepared clergy, and the arts training was a necessary preliminary to theology. Law and medicine came to have an honored place in the universities, and at all times Harvard and other colleges sought to graduate men who were distinctive *tam doctrina quam moribus,* which might be freely translated in the words which my own college in England uses at present in its graduation ceremony, "satisfactory both in character and in learning." This is a formula which has been used, in Latin or English, for many centuries in English universities, and Harvard followed Oxford and Cambridge in this and in many other ways. Mathematics and speculative natural philosophy were studied during the 17th and 18th centuries but the classics and Hebrew were the pith and marrow of the curriculum, Latin in particular with Greek more subordinate. It was normal for an educated man of the time and it forms the basis of the liberal arts tradition in the United States, a literary provenance established in the oldest and most highly respected university institutions in America. Most of the fellows in the nine colleges were in orders, as they all had to be at Oxford and Cambridge, but unlike the English, the American tutors did not have to remain unmarried in order to retain their fellowships.

When Harvard was founded in 1636 the subjects studied were almost exactly the seven named by Martianus Capella at the beginning of the 5th century A.D. in *Marriage of Philology and Mercury* and reiterated by Boethius and Cassiodorus a century later. In many ways the content was quite different but the ways of dividing up knowledge for curricular purposes were much the same. The dialectic of the medieval university had been replaced by the linguistic and literary emphasis of the 17th century. In fact the early American colleges may be said to have taught the *trivium* (grammar, rhetoric, and logic) to their undergraduates. The *quadrivium* (geometry, arithmetic, music, and astronomy) was often reordered as the three philosophies of Aristotle and taught as advanced work. These three philosophies were advanced logic and a kind of psychology which together were called mental philosophy; politics, ethics, law, and some economics which were called moral philosophy; and physics and biology which were called natural philosophy.

The enduring bases of the liberal arts seem to be these. First, it is an education founded on language in one form or another, whether as classical literature or as rhetoric or dialectic. Second, Latin in particular, with Greek next and Hebrew and Syriac more rarely, were the favored languages—not, be it noted, the native spoken language. Third, liberal education in this sense appeared in England when the new middle classes, enriched by trade and commerce added themselves to the hereditary aristocracy, bringing new energy and ability with them as they in their turn learned to wear the coronet and the ermine with assurance and ease. The liberal education which their sons received at Oxford and Cambridge in the 17th, 18th, and 19th centuries was not intended to be vocationally useful or characterized by excellence of sheer scholarship. In a vague fashion it was intended to cultivate a quality of mind and to contribute to the habits of thinking of the gentleman, at least part of whose ancestry (and an enviable part) is to be found in the chivalry of Chaucer's "very parfit, gentyle knight." The company of other young gentlemen, sporting pursuits and various kinds of hell-raising went along with the Latin and Greek in Oxford and Cambridge to round out this liberal preparation. The gentleman's education corresponds to the aristocratic education of

5th-century Athens, appropriate to a free man and having nothing banausic, that is servile or fit for a serf, about it. Fourth, even the doctor, the lawyer, the clergyman, whose education might be expected to be vocational, had to take these liberalizing studies first and the specialized training later. A liberal education had to be, in the best sense of the term, useless. Politics, the law, medicine, finance, administration—these would all be learned from practical experience. Fifth, liberal education had to do with personal enrichment, hence the importance of the humanities, subjects such as literature, the arts, philosophy, religion, and history.

When the nine colleges were set up in America in the 17th and early 18th centuries they provided a liberal education with most of the qualities listed above. It is true that they were Puritan colleges and therefore on the whole better behaved than Oxford and Cambridge, and that they were more egalitarian. However, one of the sources of the strength of opinion in the U.S.A. for and against the liberal arts college, is that it is of European, minority, literary, aristocratic origin. Even though the sciences and social sciences have now modified the original structure, there are twenty-five centuries of life and thought behind it. To some this deserves respect and attention; to others it spells archaism and the need for change.

Independence and opportunity—1789 to 1862. In January 1776 Tom Paine wrote in his enormously successful pamphlet *Common Sense:*

I have heard it asserted by some, that as America has flourished under her former connections with Great Britain, the same connection is necessary towards her future happiness, and will always have the same effect. Nothing can be more fallacious. . . . I answer roundly that America would have flourished as much, and probably much more, had no European power taken any notice of her.

Paine told his readers that the time for debate was closed and the arbitrament of arms was all that remained. When in Congress on July 4th, 1776 the unanimous Declaration of the thirteen United States of America was signed, it began with classic dignity and restraint:

When in the course of human events, it becomes necessary for one people to dissolve the political bands which have connected them with another, and to assume among the powers of the earth, the separate and equal station to which the Laws of Nature and Nature's God entitle them, a decent respect to the opinions of mankind requires that they should declare the causes which impel them to the separation.
We hold these truths to be self-evident, that all men are created equal, that they are endowed by their Creator with certain unalienable rights, that among these are life, liberty and the pursuit of happiness.

The Constitution of 1787, drawn up "in order to form a more perfect union, establish justice, insure domestic tranquility," provided the machinery by which George Washington, as the first President, appointed two secretaries who summarized deep differences of view which existed then, and in large measure exist still. Alexander Hamilton, the Secretary of the Treasury wanted to make the new federal government a powerful agent of order and stability. To him communities divided themselves into the few, who were "rich and well-born" and sought order, and the many, the mass of the people who were "turbulent and changing." Public credit in the new United States would be built up by "the few." Hamilton championed an oligarchic control based on finance and aristocratic standing as a necessary beginning in the new republic. Thomas Jefferson was the Secretary of State, and he did not share Hamilton's fear of the masses. For Jefferson government was not primarily a means of preserving order and providing stability. As befitted one of the principal authors of the Declaration of Independence, he considered that the main function of government was to provide for the freedom and happiness of its citizens, to use the resources of understanding that the masses offered, and to respect the rights of the individual states.

After 150 years of colonial status and the upheaval of a revolution we find in these two men the conservative and the radical view of the present and the future as they faced gigantic problems of equilibrium, enthusiasm, inexperience, and internal conflict. Yet Hamilton and Jefferson were not strikingly different in political action. The rate of change was controlled and Jefferson's government had in it many products of the liberal arts tradition who served equalitarian ends more explicitly than Hamilton, but who respected the privileged position of the educated and responsible politician as the servant of the masses. Jeffersonians in 1800 were liberal aristocrats at heart.

When Andrew Jackson was elected President in 1828 the equalitarian pressure was of a quite different order. Political control moved out of the hands of the American aristocrat, a man of education, position, and wealth. Government was no longer a matter for professionals and gradualism was a principle that went by the board. Any man of normal intelligence was thought capable of holding any position in government and democracy required a rotation of office so that a political bureaucracy might be avoided. When a party won elections it had the right to sweep the board of existing officeholders and fill the places with its own nominees—to the people's choice belong the spoils. The frontier experiences of the expanding West and the industrial revolution taking place in the Northeast provided material for an active equalitarian policy or sentiment. Alexis de Tocqueville writing in 1840 says this:

> The men who live in democracies are too fluctuating for a certain number of them ever to succeed in laying down a code of good breeding and in forcing people to follow it. Every man therefore behaves after his own fashion, and there is always a certain incoherence moulded upon the feelings and notions of each individual, rather than upon an ideal model proposed for general imitation. This, however, is much more perceptible at the time when an aristocracy has just been overthrown than after it has been long destroyed . . . Men have lost the common law of manners, and they have not yet made up their minds to do without it (A. de Tocqueville, 1840, Vol. IV, p. 114).

However, he goes on to say, manners in a democratic people are frequently more sincere than in an aristocratic society. The ruggedness and the sincerity represent the ideal best of the Jacksonian era after the aristocracy of Washington and Jefferson, and at this point let us see how university education grew in this political context of the free, independent United States of America after 1789.

Just as Jefferson maintained a reasonable continuity with Hamilton, and Washington sought to preserve peace at all costs while stabilizing the new Republic, so in the liberal arts colleges the clientele and the curricula continued as in colonial days. Even in post-Jackson times the New England aristocrat continued, and the Ivy League came to be noticeable because there began to be other new colleges from which it differed. There are three factors that we must look at—college control; general and specialized education; the elective principle.

Perhaps the most important event in the whole story of college control was the Dartmouth College case. In 1769 George III granted a charter to the College, and in 1816 the State Legislature of New Hampshire ruled that the College be taken over and made into a state university. Many of the trustees fought this decision up to the Supreme Court and here a judgment was made of the greatest importance outside as well as inside the field of education. The Court ruled that a charter of this kind could not be violated by a state government. This protected private agreements in voluntary associations and in business, where corporations or companies could not be taken over. Furthermore it prevented the state or the federal government from organizing and controlling hitherto private concerns; it represents protection of a mixed economy and may be contrasted with what happened 25 years before in Paris and 100 years afterward in Moscow. Out of the chaos of French attempts at libertarianism Napoleon fashioned a rigid national educational system. The same kind of thing has happened in Russia. But the insistence upon honoring agreements in the Dartmouth College case ensured a certain proud continuity of the liberal arts tradition, imperceptibly tightening the bond with Oxford and Cambridge. It also put an end to the take-over bids of the state governments. In due time of course the state governments decided to set up their own universities.

In the meantime, however, private institutions had to be prodigiously private. Here we have one of the roots of the distrust of receiving state moneys in the present day and (until loyalty oath morality further clouded the matter) the double-dyed suspicion of federal grants. In fact, the Dartmouth College decision represents a vindication of Hamilton's "rich and well-born" which set back the emergence of a militantly equalitarian university or college system until the Land Grant Act of 1862. The formidable growth of colleges before the Civil War, reported by Tewksbury (he reports over 500 foundations of which just over 100 survived), was not of state colleges but mainly of private liberal arts colleges set up as the frontier pushed west (Tewksbury, 1932). They were very often religious foundations, controlled by a board of trustees on which the faculty was usually represented by the President alone. We are getting to the heart of the matter of college control when we try to answer the following leading questions. Are the students from a minority, aristocratic group? Is the college privately maintained, or does public money go into it? Is it concerned with the liberal arts primarily or only? What part do the alumni play in financing and/or governing the college? Such questions were not much considered in the early 1800s.

The second factor to be looked at in the period 1789 to 1862 is the relationship of general and specialized education. Although I have stressed the dominance of the liberal arts tradition, it would be a mistake to think that no attempts were made to introduce other subjects. Curtis shows in a recent study of Oxford and Cambridge 1558 to 1642 that the sciences, astronomy and mathematics were not entirely neglected there even then (Curtis, 1959, Chapter IX). Benjamin Franklin, the prototype of the American success story, introduced scientific and mathematical courses in his Philadelphia academy in the middle of the 18th century. In the 1820s in England the pressure of secularists, dissenters, medicals, and radicals brought about the foundation of University College in London, "that godless institution" followed in 1830 by King's College, its near neighbor and Anglican watchdog. In 1836 the University of London was commissioned by the association of these two colleges, and it was committed to a "liberal and enlarged curriculum" including classics, history, modern languages, mathematics, medicine and surgery, chemistry, and law. Thomas Jefferson had founded the University of Virginia in 1825 and was much interested in what happened in London, because University College was not un-like his own nonsectarian venture. The protective policy the Uni-versity of London pursued to other associated institutions in England opened up nonsectarian opportunities all over the country, while offering to them "external" degrees of the University of London in arts, science, and medicine. The University of London represented a counteroffensive to seven centuries of dominance by Oxford and Cam-bridge both in their affiliation with the established church and (our immediate concern at the moment) their severely limited acceptance of subjects other than the classics in their liberal arts form.

The 1820s represent a critical decade in the clash between general and specialist approaches to university education in America. Schools of medicine, law and theology began to open independently. In 1825 at the University of Virginia Jefferson established seven separate col-leges, which were really academic departments enjoying equal status and including subjects like mathematics, chemistry, and medicine. In 1826 law was added. In some universities a core of liberal arts studies was required and a combination of subjects ensured, but specialized studies followed. In Jefferson's university each "college" had its own curriculum and a student could choose to work in any one of the eight, taking courses elsewhere also if he had time without the require-ments of a prescribed liberal arts program. The Rensselaer Polytechnic Institute opened in 1824; the Sheffield Engineering School at Yale and the Lawrence Scientific School at Harvard were both established in 1847.

Ticknor, Everett, and Cogswell spent some years in Germany after 1815, and Ticknor wrote a tingling report to the Board of Overseers at Harvard in 1825 recommending freedom of choice and a wider range of studies for freshmen. Undoubtedly, the ideal of teaching and re-search which the University of Berlin exemplified from its foundation in 1809 had a most remarkable effect on British and American uni-versities in the 19th century, but in each country mainly on the new universities.[2] The increased range of subjects in the sciences and the social sciences led in one direction to expanded interpretations of the traditional liberal arts, and in another to the emphasis on research, one of the chief consequences of which was the later development of the graduate schools. Yet, although these in the 1820s are the powerful presages of change, to keep the picture balanced I should mention the classic exposition of the liberal arts case drawn up by the faculty of Yale in 1828 (Yale College, 1828).

[2] For a lively account of the effect on British Universities, see the early chapters of Ashby (1958).

Henry Tappan, who became President of the University of Michigan, wrote in 1851:

We inspire no general desire for higher education and fail to collect students because we promise and do not perform. Hence we fall into disrepute, and young men of ability continue to prepare themselves for active life without our aid. In connection with this, the commercial spirit of our country, and the many avenues of wealth that are opened up before enterprise create a distaste for study, and (are) deeply inimical to education. The manufacturers, the merchants, the gold-digger, will not pause in their career to gain intellectual accomplishments while gaining knowledge they are losing the opportunities to gain money. The political condition of the country, too, is such that a high education and a high order of talent do not generally form the same guarantees of success (quoted Kandel, 1959).

Michigan was the leading Western state university of the time in 1843 to 44, and of the fifty term courses offered 26 were in Latin and Greek and mathematics, 9 in natural sciences, 5 in intellectual science (that is logic, philosophy, and psychology), 3 in morals and religion, 3 in political science, and 4 in English. Until the applied sciences which the country most needed, i.e., agriculture and engineering, were taught in the universities their courses were far out of touch with a frontier society. The liberal arts was the minority study appropriate to an aristocracy, no matter what claims were made about its value as a general training of the mind.

In 1850 Francis Wayland, President of Brown University, wrote that studies should be offered by universities which answered the needs of the community and prepared students for their life careers. But the changes were slow to arrive in the fateful decade during which the South and the North came to ultimate crisis. Nevertheless the beginnings were there and the economic state of affairs in America and in Europe was such that the last forty years of the century provided the physical conditions in which both practical studies and pure scholarship surged forward on the tidal wave of specialist education. The liberal arts did not drown, but for the first time had to fight for their lives, or perhaps more appropriately, for their way of life and thought.

We have looked at the first two issues to be considered, the control of college affairs and general and specialized education. Now we turn briefly to the third, the elective principle during the period 1789 to 1862, linked as it is with the growth of specialist education.

One of the great virtues of the liberal arts courses was that they helped to create a common background of knowledge, attitudes, and skills in students which the establishment of specialist education tended to destroy. But the critics of the liberal arts indicated the narrow range of the common background, and adapting the German principles of *Lehrfreiheit*, the freedom of the professor to teach what he wants to, and *Lernfreiheit*, the liberty of choice of the student to learn what he wishes, and pointing to *Wissenschaft*, science and knowledge systematically pursued and prized for itself, many universities began to offer a wider range of subjects and to leave to the students the selection of courses. Harvard began to operate this principle in 1825, but against much opposition and the programs wavered for sixty years until Charles W. Eliot established in 1882 an elective system which lasted until 1910. There were (and are) many different forms of choosing courses, and the student was never really free to tailor his own course entirely, but Harvard tried to give as open a choice as possible, so much so that when Eliot's successor, A. L. Lowell, moved to apply required ranges of choice in 1910 he easily succeeded, and S. E. Morison, the Harvard historian, describes the liberty offered to the student by Eliot as the greatest crime of the century against American youth, depriving him of his classical heritage.

By 1860 many of the colleges of the East were offering a limited group choice to the student, and at Princeton, Yale, Pennsylvania, and elsewhere the beginnings of a group elective system were to be found. Incidentally, of course, this broke the dominance of the classics while offering to them a good chance for survival.

Only after 1862 did the American university begin to show its indigenous quality in half a century of fine confusion of aims and purpose in keeping with a declared faith in equalitarianism. Morison was right when he said that American youth no longer had a classical heritage, but this was due not only to the deficiencies of the colleges but to the fact that the aristocratic education of Greece and Rome, which had filtered through European stratified society, was not sufficient for a mobile, assertive, questing society like America in the last quarter of the century. What Jackson had promised in the 1820s and 1830s had been staved off by the universities in part at least by means of the prestige of the classics and in part by the inertia and conservative conviction of many academics and by the urgency of more important concerns like slavery and the westward expansion of the continent. Germany, on the other hand, could reform its universities and establish research and scholarship during the 19th century and yet maintain continuity with literary and classical traditions while establishing whole new realms of scientific discovery. Matthew Arnold in his 1868 report on German universities put it like this:

It is the function of the university to develop into science the knowledge a boy brings with him from the secondary school . . . Thus, in the university, the idea of sciences is primary, that of professions secondary (Arnold, 1892, p. 134).

In another place in the same report Arnold said that the German universities had both liberty and science, whereas the French universities had a ministerial control and the English universities had no science. Arnold suggested that both follow the lead of the Germans. The United States also saw what Germany was doing and began to follow, but its own politics swung many of the universities and colleges far away from the moorings of the European tradition after 1862.

Growth and development—1862 to 1920. The most significant fact about the period now to be considered is that the college may no longer be considered as an institution somewhat out of the main stream of American events, holding a traditional view, changing slowly, seeking models abroad. The violence of the 1860s brought America through the convulsions of the Civil War (and far too few Europeans realize that more than 600,000 Americans were killed during those four terrible years) to more intractable problems of assimilation than even in 1786. Many of the political and economic forms of modern America have their effective origin in the last thirty years of the century. The industrial North overcame the agrarian South and captured the government, both federal and state. Economic power gained political power to such a degree that they have been entangled in the United States ever since. The business goliaths are more remembered than the politicians—Carnegie in steel, Rockefeller in oil, Armour in meat packing, Pierpont Morgan in finance, and Hill, Stanford, Harriman, and Vanderbilt in railroads. The New England and the Southern aristocrats went into eclipse and gigantic industrial expansion made these thirty years the phenomenal age of enterprise.

To a European, being wise after the event, it appears that there are seven main things to comment on. First, since the earliest English settlement in 1607 at Jamestown, generations of Americans had moved the frontier westward for 250 years, along the Atlantic seaboard, to the Allegheny mountains, to the Mississippi, the Missouri, the Great Plains, the Rocky Mountains. And from the rich Atlantic farmlands to the oil of Texas and the gold strikes of California it was a fabulously rich continent. Second, the 1860s in Europe as in America gathered together technical inventions and improvements of all kinds and exploited them in road and rail transport, in chemical engineering, in communication, and in the uses of electricity. When many commentators on this period in America point to its stridently vulgar and debasing qualities they overlook the relentless, cut-throat imaginativeness of the robber barons. Third, investment capital gave to the financier a concentration of power across wide areas of the country. Fourth, the readiness of the national and state governments to erect tariffs, give land grants (it is thought that land the area of Texas was made over to the railroads), and protect monopolies, helped to establish this new power group. Fifth, the attraction this land of promise exercised on the marginal men of Europe's industrial revolution drew new nations to the United States. Sixth, the new ethic of the business civilization transformed the social order, and the secularization of affairs written into the Constitution out of respect for religious toleration took on a different cast. Seventh, the affluent capitalism combined with it an apparently paradoxical faith in democracy, the conviction that despite the enormous wealth and power in the hands of a few, all men were free and equal. Perhaps liberal, optimistic individualism more nearly describes the reality of the situation and the time. The expansive years led to the apparent conviction that equality was not an economic matter, but rather social, psychological, and cultural, an attitude of mind.

It is in this kind of context that we can see the beginnings of the truly indigenous American university. In 1862, in the early days of the Civil War, the Land Grant Act was passed, which effected by legislation a powerful change in higher education. There had been pressure on the federal government for almost a century to provide for advanced instruction suitable for farmers and "the industrial classes," and in 1862 was passed "An Act donating Public Lands to the several States and Territories which may provide Colleges for the Benefit of Agriculture and the Mechanic Arts." It was proposed that on this land each state should set up at least one college where "the leading object shall be, without excluding other scientific and classical studies . . . . to teach such branches of learning as are related to agriculture and the mechanic arts . . . . in order to promote the liberal and practical education of the industrial classes. . . ."

There were several main consequences of this and other similar acts. Where the European university in Arnold's words already quoted put the idea of science first and of profession second, the land grant colleges were plainly vocational. The training of the mind claimed for the liberal arts was simply not enough for a fluid society, and although these and the sciences were to be maintained, the new technical needs (and they later included commerce and business administration) were to be accommodated without any sense of inferiority. This is of the utmost significance in the later history of higher education in the United States. The new studies represent contemporary need and might be indefinitely expanded to the kind of particularized courses which Flexner, Hutchins and later Bestor, Barzun and others have castigated. The liberal arts were based on language, literature, and the habits of mind of 2000 years but the new subject matter was culled from the present and directed toward the future. For the liberal arts, history is part of the context of knowledge, and a mental continuity is a necessity for the cultured group which Coleridge called "the clerisy." For the modernist, history is, if not bunk, only about as help-ful as the chatter of a dotard. Tradition begins today and massive quantitative achievements in America could witness to the fact that Europe and the classical heritage had been outgrown.

A further consequence of the foundation of the land grant colleges was that the practical curriculum for the industrial classes was not introduced as a second-class course for the poor relations of academic life, or at least American equalitarian sentiment prevented this from becoming the case. This had two principal results: the first was to open up the possibility of college or university education to a far wider public (particularly after the Kalamazoo decision in 1874 when a court ruling permitted the support of a village high school from public funds) and so to run counter to the European principle of university education for a small minority, even bearing in mind the growth of civic universities in Europe in the latter half of the century. The second result was to start the mixed economy of American universities, not unlike the independent school—state school division in England. Were the private colleges and universities more solid, more scholarly, more aware of their esprit de corps, more traditional, more religious, more expensive than their secular state counterparts? Of course, the more pressing recent question is, can the private universities, whatever their distinctive features, continue to afford being private, research and running costs being what they are. Famous universities like Wisconsin, Minnesota, and Ohio State have grown up from land grant college beginnings, and they, in common with other state universities, have more solid financial backing for their development than private foundations.

Yet the development of land grant colleges into universities would not have taken place if they had stayed with the relatively low level vocational teaching with which they started. This could only be changed when enough schools with good standards of college pre-paratory work came into being, and that was only really possible at the state level after 1874, with the Kalamazoo (Michigan) judgment already mentioned. At the other end of the higher education spectrum the foundation of the graduate school deepened and extended the educational function of the universities. For our purposes one of the most important dates is 1876 when Johns Hopkins University opened its doors in Baltimore, a private secular university established under Daniel Coit Gilman, where teaching and investigation in arts, sciences, and medicine could go forward. It frankly emphasized its research function, and Gilman admitted undergraduates under duress and even tried to build up a separate research and graduate school staff. In varying ways at Harvard, at Cornell, in 1892 at the new University of Chicago, in 1893 at Stanford, and 1896 at Clark, the research function of university teachers was emphasized. This was in part a consequence of the fact that about 10,000 Americans took the German Ph.D. during the century before 1914 (Cowley, 1956, p. 222), and many brought back the conviction that research was the proper concern of universities and not only of learned societies and academies.

Kandel considers, as do others, that the graduate schools saved standards of scholarship at the best known American universities in face of the demand for practical and vocational training.

> A university in the sense in which I use the term—an institution consciously devoted to the pursuit of knowledge, the solution of problems, the critical appreciation of achievement, and the training of men at a really high level— a university in this sense we did not possess until the Johns Hopkins University modestly opened its portals in 1876 (Flexner, 1930, p. 42).

In 1900 the Association of American Universities was formed to strengthen the claims of graduate study and, as time passed, to fix standards and methods of assessment by which universities and colleges might qualify for membership.

The universities which supported the research function were, in the first place, private foundations, which had kept in touch with Europe. The land grant tradition was a native one related to a modest undergraduate level of practical and professional competence. It was the pragmatic, equalitarian expression of the American genius. A country as vigorous and untraditional as the United States was able to combine the two points of view, first by adopting the group elective system which ensured a certain spread of subjects, and second by going on in the 1880s and after to the "majoring" program, by which a concentration developed as the degree course progressed. By this means an undergraduate preparation for the first degree was taken by the mass, and the able minority revealed themselves and they could go on to research.

The liberal arts college became the most common undergraduate institution, or more precisely the college of arts and sciences, and a general program was offered from which choices were made. In the older and the most stringent institutions (usually private at first) the courses sprang from the traditional liberal arts subjects, which we have already discussed, and a spread of knowledge was required for the A.B. degree. Later grew up the "cafeteria system" which Flexner so ridiculed. In it several principles are involved. First, the elective choice for the student (and this operated in Bologna 700 years before as well as in contemporary Germany). Second, open-mindedness to new subject matter, characteristic of a fluid society. Third, the principle of adjusting the subject matter to the student, not vice versa. Fourth, the discovery of an American university style. Fifth, the "right" of each citizen who had passed through high school to a university education, if sought for. Sixth, the distrust of traditional intellectual requirements as the only adequate basis. Seventh, the refusal to elevate certain subjects as proper to a cultivated man.

From 1890 onward, then, we have features in American universities, some of which were direct descendants of earlier European loyalties, some of which were adapted from European experience of the 19th century, some of which were local products. But, most of all, it is the balance of tensions between these factors which made, and makes, what I have called the indigenous quality of American universities. For instance, the sheer *variety* was different from any European or Commonwealth practice. The consequence in education of a decentralized, loosely federal, uniquely capitalist, and democratic continent was a chaos of higher education standards from which a better coordinated nation is now trying to develop a plan and standards of comparison. The minority in Europe never lost its grasp on Oxford, Paris, and Berlin and no competitors following a different educational principle grew up. The minority in America was nearly swept away by egalitarian competitors, and even in survival had to modify its austerity. In American universities, besides the liberal arts and sciences and the traditional professional schools of law, medicine, and theology found in Europe since medieval times, there appeared schools of journalism, librarianship, business methods, nursing, and, later, practical arts, home economics, physiotherapy. In Europe few, if any, of these schools are to be found in universities but usually in separate institutions of subuniversity standard.

A further and related factor in the *omnium gatherum* of subjects studied in universities was the tremendous munificence of endowments. Carnegie, Rockefeller, Peabody, Vanderbilt, Stanford, and countless others gave support to education in general and higher education in particular during this period to an extent never before known anywhere and the scale of generosity of alumni was and is, to a European, staggering. Of course, from 1870 onward this was a very profitable investment for those who wanted engineers, agriculturists, and executives, and there was clearly a strong element of this in many benefactions. Such generosity helped to draw the lines of university development in some places. As an instance, George Washington University, in order to obtain a benefaction from John D. Rockefeller, in 1898 was willing to restore Baptist allegiances which had been discontinued in the 1870s (no money came in fact, so the University stayed nondenominational). Between 1862 and 1920 the private gifts of persons, and later of firms and cartels strengthened and developed the private sector of American higher education to an unprecedented degree. Although in many cases such support was given on the same side as the state in its land grant program (that is for specialist, relatively low level vocational training), equally the study of liberal arts and science was magnificently supported and so too were the graduate schools of arts and sciences.

The liberal arts colleges before the Civil War were almost entirely religious foundations with faculties which were largely clerical. Many private benefactors were religious men endowing what they hoped and intended to become religious communities. However, the total effect of the period 1862 to 1920, because of state universities, endowment conditions insisting on nonsectarian loyalties, the nature of the new research emphasis, the influence of the sciences, and the munificence of the research foundations, was the laicization and secularization of American higher education. Even in Baptist, Episcopalian, Quaker, and Methodist institutions conditions of entry became much less restrictive and boards of trustees were more nondenominational. Partly this was due to having to take students, in order to survive, from where you could find them. Presidents who in the early days had simply been the leading professor of the time being, combining administrative tasks with some teaching (Jefferson's University of Virginia tried for some years to operate without a president), became administrators wielding considerable powers. Each college and university had a board of governors or trustees, the powerful lay body on which the faculty had to fight to be represented other than by the president. This is a business-type organization, characteristic of the last quarter of the century. The president was a man of power and conviction, a combination of King Midas, St. Augustine, Alexander the Great, Machiavelli, and the boy next door. He usually would have been a scholar who moved into the role of chief administrator, policy maker,

and financier. The board of trustees in commercial terms represented
the shareholders, whether a private benefactor or the state, and acted
for them. Compare this with the medieval *universitas magistrorum,*
or the Oxford and Cambridge system of government of a college by
the fellows, an academic and equalitarian group. Even in the civic
universities in England where the council is a lay body, its powers, and
those of the principal or vice-chancellor, are much less than in many
instances in the United States.

The stereotyped product of the universities and colleges in this
period was no longer the religiously minded student prepared in the
liberal arts, but the informed specialist who had through the elective
system chosen as far as possible what he wanted.

Cowley quotes the proportion of the 18 to 21 age group in college
and university in 1870 as being 2.07% and in 1920 as being 8.14%.
Over this period the population of the age group had more than
doubled from about 3½ millions to about 7⅓ millions, and the student population had quadrupled, including in this increase the serious
beginnings of higher education for women in the United States
(Cowley, 1956, p. 230). We should add to this the stunning statistic
quoted by Dr. Gardiner in *The Pursuit of Excellence* (Gardiner, 1958)
showing that between 1870 and 1955 the population of the United States
increased by four times while its public high school population increased by *eighty* times. The period 1862 to 1920 was the era of the
mass migrations presenting enormous problems of assimilating quantity while at the same time identifying the indigenous American qualities in this new and different New World.

I have shown earlier that Hellenism permeated the Mediterranean
world and Western Europe. The period for this stretches from the
5th century B.C. to the 5th century A.D., appears to die for 500 years
and re-emerges in the medieval world to last for another 500 years and
longer. America had to identify itself between 1776 and 1862, to
exploit the bounty of the continent during the second 50 years of the
century, and teach a new population used to Europe what America
stood for in the years up to World War I. In other words, where we
think in terms of 20 centuries in relation to Hellenism, the United
States had 150 years for these tasks. Even allowing for the totally different scale of communications which helped to make this possible, it
is no wonder that, in this, the American universities ploughed their
own furrows in answer to professional and vocational demand, no
wonder that Veblen, Flexner, Foerster, and Hutchins flayed the universities for crudeness, superficiality, and philistinism. No wonder,
either, that Dewey claimed his following for instrumentalism as ap-

plied to education in general and universities in particular. Quantity of higher education there had to be, but the gyroscope of quality was at work too.[3]

In 1893 the National Education Committee reported on the standards in high school, and in 1899 the findings of a Committee on College Entrance Requirements led to the creation of the College Entrance Examination Board which has become increasingly important as the years have passed. The Association of American Universities established its own norms of assessment and provided expert and exacting panels of investigators who gauged the suitability of colleges and universities for membership in the Association. The Association of American Colleges followed suit, and independent bodies like the Carnegie Foundation for the Advancement of Teaching and the General Education Board also grew up as sectional prestige groups with regional and national coverage. Groups of experts undertook specific tasks of assessment following the American national custom of washing linen in public, whether clean or dirty. The United States Office (first called Bureau) of Education began its informational, investigatory, and advisory service early in the 20th century and a coordinating body on higher education called the American Council on Education was set up in 1918, partly to advise on the problem of the returning veterans.

It is in the latter part of the 1862 to 1920 period that the cult of the Ph.D. is strongest. As already mentioned, the pilgrimage to Germany was frequently made before 1914, and in 1918 all British universities (except Cambridge which followed later) instituted the Ph.D. in order to attract foreign students of good quality who were flocking to Germany, and, so Armytage tells us, *to America* (Armytage, 1955, p. 250). Although there is much irony and downright ferocity in Flexner and others about the Ph.D. in certain subjects and certain universities, it undoubtedly sifted wheat and chaff through a mesh of considerable selective value at that time.

Growth and development—1920. The reliance on Germany had ceased sharply with the outbreak of war in 1914, although it had been growing steadily less since the turn of the century. Cowley lists a number of differences which had become clear by 1920 between American higher education and its European counterpart (Cowley, 1956, pp. 96–98). First of all the general education college was and is the core of university structure in the United States, but in Europe a

[3] I have had particular guidance for the next paragraph from the essay by Kandel already cited.

much more specialized program of honors degree work is the prevailing pattern. General education has been completed for the most part in secondary schools. Yet the general education of the U.S.A. college student was severely criticized in 1938 by the Carnegie Foundation's report, *The Student and his Knowledge.* To the authors the elective system operated in higher education in Pennsylvania, to which the report referred, did not seem to provide a shared background of knowledge, and this lack of general culture was aggravated by the tendency to choose vocational and professional studies in which the uncultivated and particularized outlook of the teachers limited teaching to instruction in techniques and know-how. Similarly, at graduate level, the report claimed that specialization was destroying general education.

It is interesting to note that the honors degree program in England, particularly in the pure and applied sciences, was under fire at the same time and that after the war, in 1946, negotiations commenced leading to the foundation in 1950 of the University College of North Staffordshire, which now has a principal responsibility to ensure both general and special education in the humanities, the social sciences, and the sciences. It follows a pattern which would be readily recognized in the United States, though it is in some respects unique. So unique, in fact, that it is the only one of the 24 university institutions in Great Britain to do anything really serious about general education.

A close relation to the general-special education issue is the argument about standards which has its origin in the United States in the prodigal expansion of vocational studies within universities since 1862, especially in state universities. This is another American feature which differs from European practice, and its roots are not to be found simply in an administrative variance or in the conditions in America of industrial boom. They are to be found also in the way in which a university may be established and controlled. The long tradition of separation of state and university is at its most obvious in Great Britain where no university is private in the sense that Harvard or Stanford or Cornell is, but conversely no university is as directly governed by the state as Oregon, Ohio State, or California. The obstacles to founding a university or university college in Britain are great and a royal charter has to be obtained. In addition there are many means in the hands of the academics to control university policy and to regulate the speed of change. Recently the Labour Party has been advocating the setting up of a royal commission to review the position of universities and higher education in general. But even if sweeping changes were brought about, the strength of opinion is such that new courses considered for inclusion would only be accepted if they demanded a scholarly, coherent intellectual basis. They would have to have a pedigree and an impressive theoretical context. Standards lower than this would be accommodated in subuniversity institutions. Two examples will suffice. Technology has received a very cautious reception over the last thirty years. It is slowly finding its way into a university structure in which engineering has only recently become respectable. The other example is sociology. Cambridge is at present (1960) discussing whether sociology should be taught there. A "subject" has to prove itself before it is received into the university fold in England—this is the last stage in the climb to intellectual respectability, and it is the European university habit, a minority, inquisitorial tradition which I hope can now be seen in its context. It also exists in the United States, particularly in the liberal arts colleges and in the old established private universities and in state universities like California. But a number of American writers on higher education say that many practical courses appear in universities in answer to demand rather than as a result of examination of their scholarly bases which would not stand up to scrutiny. Yet, as Cowley points out, (Cowley, 1956, p. 90) the United States has about 50 structures comparable to the better universities of Europe, and that is not a small number.

The graduate schools are far more frequently patronized in the United States than are higher degree courses in Britain, though this is changing. All universities and colleges expect to conduct research as well as to teach undergraduates in Britain and in this they differ from the liberal arts college which is really not attached to a university, although many of these have a master's program and a few, like Bryn Mawr, Radcliffe, and Iowa State College (which has a program in the humanities as well as the applied sciences), a doctoral program too. The inter-relationships of universities, technical colleges, teachers' training colleges, and the like is much more flexible in the United States than in Europe. For instance, in Britain a bachelor's degree is only given by a university institution: a training college or a technical college can award only certificates or diplomas. Higher education has a history of stratification.

Since 1920 the percentage of the 18 to 21 age group at universities in the United States has more than doubled, and according to postwar trends and to the President's Commission on Higher Education for American Democracy it will double again in the 1960s. One of the agencies which has enabled such increased numbers to be managed is the junior college, a two-year institution appearing in some states and dealing mainly with students between 16 and 19. The state colleges have increased in number also, and many former teachers' training colleges have become liberal arts foundations. In fact, since 1920 the fluidity of educational structure both private and state-supported has been maintained. Inevitably problems of status and the clash of interests are commonplace. In California, a state adding each year about 700,000 to its population, there have been a series of committees advising on the growth and development of higher education and the relationships between private and publicly supported institutions, between the state university and the state colleges, between the state colleges and the junior colleges. Here we have an aspect of the problem of higher education taking on a new urgency—no longer is it a question of individual choice or ad hoc growth only, but a matter of planning involving the relationship between the university output and the estimated need of trained man power. The university degree, especially the doctorate, is an investment in the future in which, as Drucker has pointed out, there will be more people concerned with teaching at some level than with any other single form of earning a living.

GATHERING THE THREADS

Education has four elements in action and reaction—teachers, knowledge, students, institutions. According to the perspective of the investigator, one or other of the elements can seem to be dominant. In emphasizing scholarship and research, we concentrate on knowledge, and universities justify themselves in this context by their graduate schools and research institutes, by the work of investigators. This can and does produce magnificent and exciting discovery and on the possibility of innovation man's mental dignity largely depends. But as Caplow and McGee have shown in *The Academic Marketplace,* when this research function is looked at from the angle of the labyrinthine institution, then the pursuit of the argument wherever it leads, the vocation of the scholar, is seen to have become in the hands of teachers, the deans, the reverberating administration, keeping up with the intellectual Joneses, publish or perish.

Knowledge as research, whether rare new discovery or borrowed plumage tricked out in a way that will seem to be new, is only one interpretation. It is, however, likely to have especial power as an institutionalized version of the success story—onward and upward by the printed word. This is the myth which Logan Wilson (Wilson, 1942) and Caplow and McGee so brilliantly expose.

But there are many other interpretations of knowledge appropriate to the university. What should an undergraduate learn? Should there be a framework of knowledge which every intelligent person growing up in the present day should know something about? These are questions which have often been asked in the last forty years in the United States, and many answers have been essayed. One of the consequences of the rampant elective principle and the growth of unrelated courses was a concern with the coherence of education. Yet even in the liberal arts colleges many teachers have sympathy for the undergraduate course that leads on to the specialities of science or medicine or graduate studies in the arts and social sciences. This is certainly the dominant English pattern where so much of general education is left to the schools—and the uneasiness about this has mounted over the last twenty years.

Two principles of guidance operate in general education programs. The first is related to the ideal of a civilized and cultivated person, and in different ways the courses worked out in Amherst, Columbia, Chicago, Harvard, St. John's College, Sarah Lawrence, Scripps, Reed College and in England at the University College of North Staffordshire, have this principle to guide them. The courses have for the most part been planned by careful analysis of the main areas of knowledge and due weight has been given to history in all the schemes; the sense of continuity in the European and American traditions is strong and perspective is a principal watchword.

The second principle represents a continuation of the notions of adjustment characteristic of so many arguments about the curriculum at the high school level. Should knowledge be selected on the basis of the student's needs at present, and should the contemporary and the future take more of the time formerly given to the past? So courses in family living, the citizen and the state, science and the community, have been taught in various colleges.

The point of mentioning these general education topics is to relate them to the continuity of ideas developed earlier in this chapter, and to show that emphasis on knowledge in the university enterprise need not only lead to an overdeveloped concern for research.

The teacher is a person to whose role many novelists, psychologists, sociologists, and satirists have given thorough and exhaustive attention. Of late the university teacher has had his share, from Caplow and McGee to Mary McCarthy, Kingsley Amis, and Stringfellow Barr. In this present volume his problems and functions are looked at again (see Part III). Obviously the teacher is a man of many roles. We may see him in his family, as a competitor for promotion, as an academic politician, as a father-image, as a scholar, as a compensator for life's failures, as a midwife to the young intellect, as an authoritarian, as a wage earner, as a man or woman liable to all the tensions flesh is heir to.

So too with the student. In this chapter on the development of the university in the Western world, the students have been shadowy creatures in the large sweep of statements about Hellenistic values, medieval syntheses, liberal arts, European patterns, professional schools, research functions. Education is concerned with knowledge, teachers, students, and institutions. Knowledge, the power and achievement of the teacher, and the changing nature and purpose of the institution are in the foreground in this chapter. But what does the student, the undergraduate student, make out of this educational enterprise? How is his psychological economy as a learner entangled with the knowledge which is put before him? What does he take away as a possession from whatever sources, whether books, teachers, friends, or the social cachet? This volume goes to the student as a person with an experience and a system of values of his own. If the historical, economic, intellectual, and sociological scenery is set, it is so that the perpetual exchange of knowledge can be played through now and in the future. Is this scenery and is this theme understood by the student in any way that his teacher comprehends beyond the record of his academic performance and the part he played in college societies? This volume tries to bring the student's view of the university into the play.

Finally the institution of the university. Like any institution, it has answered to the pressure of the society that in a real sense it serves. Yet it has sought to mould ideas, government, standards, and curricula to its own patterns. The crux of the matter now may be presented as two questions which have to be answered both in terms of deliberate policy and declaration of aims, and by the outcome of an administrative momentum which cannot truly be called purpose. First, has the university in any distinctive sense a continuity? Second, how far is or can this be made explicit in the future inter-relationships of teachers, knowledge, students, and institutions?

REFERENCES

Armytage, W. H. G. *Civic universities*. London: Ernest Benn, Ltd., 1955.
Arnold, M. *Higher schools and universities in Germany*. London: Macmillan, 1892.
Ashby, E. *Technology and the academics*. London: Macmillan, 1958.
Bacon, F. *Advancement of learning*. Bohn Ed., 1874.
Bacon, F. *Advancement of learning*. Everyman Ed. Dent, 1915.
Capes, W. W. *University life in ancient Athens*. (Reprint) New York: G. E. Stechert, 1922.

Caplow, T., and McGee, R. J. *The academic marketplace*. New York: Basic Books, Inc., 1958.

Cowley, W. H. *An appraisal of American higher education*, Unpublished manuscript, 1956.

Curtis, M. H. *Oxford and Cambridge in transition*. Oxford: Oxford University Press, 1959.

Day, J., and Kingsley, J. L. Report on a course of liberal education. New Haven, Conn.: The Yale Corporation, 1828.

Flexner, A. *Universities, American, English, German*. New York: Oxford University Press, 1930.

Gardiner, J. Pursuit of excellence (Special Studies Project, Report V), Carnegie Corporation of New York, 1958.

Jaeger, W. *Paideia: the ideals of Greek culture*. 3 vols. Translated by G. Highet. London: Blackwell, 1936, 1944, 1945.

Kandel, I. L. *Yearbook of education 1959*. London: Evans Bros., 1959.

Livingstone, R. *The future of education*. Cambridge: Cambridge University Press, 1941.

Marrou, H. I. *A History of education in antiquity*. Translated by G. Lamb. New York: Sheed and Ward, 1956.

Powicke, F. M., and Emden, A. B. *Rashdall's medieval universities*. 3 vols. Oxford: Clarendon Press, 1936.

Tewksbury, D. G. *The founding of American colleges and universities before the Civil War*. New York: Bureau of Publications, Teachers College, Columbia University, 1932.

de Tocqueville, A. *Democracy in America*. 4 vols. London: Saunders and Ottey, 1840.

Willey, B. *The Seventeenth-century background*. London: Chatto and Windus, 1933.

Wilson, L. *The academic man*. New York: Oxford University Press, 1942.

Yale College. Report on a course of liberal education. 1828.

27 *Frank Pinner*

The Crisis of the
State Universities: Analysis
and Remedies

DISSENSUAL KNOWLEDGE AND THE UNIVERSITY'S PUBLICS

The careers of the newer American colleges and universities resemble those of religious denominations. In their early, sectarian state they appeal to special clienteles, often local or regional in character, recruited from narrow social layers, and largely agreed on fundamentals. But as they proceed toward churchly universality, they shed some of their former clienteles and aspire to new ones; they seek to enlarge their geographical domain by erasing its boundaries; and the undisputed verities of the past give way to a multiplicity of aims and convictions. Perhaps this is the growth pattern of all succesful institutions in a highly mobile society.

We who teach in the large new universities of America experience daily the strains and stresses of such transformations. These arise not merely from the growth in staffs and enrollments, the addition of teaching programs in areas previously neglected or deliberately omitted, and the development of physical facilities, but they also reflect many changes in policy. There is, for instance, the steady and insistent effort to stimulate "research," which administrators and professors alike regard as the open sesame to the world of universal scholarship. Many of the newer institutions, seemingly ashamed of their former provin-

940

cialism and bent upon escaping its remnants, eagerly embrace programs which will bring the faculty into closer contact with national and international affairs: government-sponsored or foundation-sponsored programs of technical assistance to underdeveloped nations typically are conducted by recently emerged large universities rather than those with older and more cosmopolitan traditions. Some will see such involvement with national policy as nothing more than a shift from local provincialism to that of the nation-state. At the very least, the province itself has become larger. And the enlargement of the university's geographical reference does imply some broadening of its intellectual scope.

This very urge toward universalism makes for ambiguities and tensions. Although reaching out toward far-flung horizons, the newly emerged university cannot and dare not forsake its familiar surroundings of town and countryside. It is bound to these by its own alumni and other benefactors, by its older faculty, by the origins and the expectations of its students, and by those of the surrounding community. In playing to two rather disparate publics, the local public of its immediate surroundings and the cosmopolitan audience of the republic of letters, it risks raising suspicions in both.

The alienation of the university from one or both of these publics tends to become a particularly acute problem for state universities. More than other institutions of higher learning, they depend on the good will of local people. Since public funds are the most important sources of their income, they must find ways to stimulate the generosity of lawmakers. They must not merely maintain good relations with legislators, but they must also nurse, within the state, their own social constituencies: groups of people who believe in the benefits of higher education and who are capable of exerting pressure toward its expansion.

Administrators of state universities, in appealing to the legislature and to supporters in town and country, tend to make two points: their university performs services important to the people of the state, and it is among the "greatest" or "most distinguished" in the country. The two arguments do not necessarily reflect congruent sets of facts: what is conceived to be "service" to the state is not likely to be closely related to the criteria of "distinction" in the academic world at large. Thus, the state legislator or the small town businessman may feel that the main services of a university are undergraduate training and acting as consultants for public and private bodies; but the current mood of the larger academic community bestows "distinction" upon schools with large programs of graduate—not necessarily undergraduate—instruction, and of "basic"—not immediately utilitarian—research.

The administrators of state universities must steer their course between these two positions. This is not to say that they are always articulately conscious of the issues. Whatever else they may think or do, they recognize at the outset that the building of a widely respected institution hinges upon the recruitment of faculties whose reputations rest on abilities or intellectual lineage. Their recruitment policies, accordingly, give much weight to academic titles and honors, and to the scholastic status of job candidates and the institutions from which they come. In thus "strengthening" their faculties they also diversify them. The new arrivals from the older, more established universities —whether young Ph.D.'s or men whose main contribution has already been made—regard with scorn the all-too-applied researches of their new local colleagues and the all-too-practical courses they teach. Thus the intrusion of universalist values is often the unintended result of the search for universal recognition. And to the extent that the state university is locally supported and committed, this intrusion brings about its alienation from its publics.

Administrators seem to look upon such developments with astonishment. In not too distant a past, they feel, the university's relations with its community and students were closer and more cordial. Since those happier days, the quality of the faculty has greatly improved. This larger and better faculty, they feel, should have more to give than the previous ones, and the university should therefore be more highly regarded by both students and the general public. It is not. Here lies the paradox.

I have tried to show—and will argue further—that the separation of the state university from its *local* publics has not occurred *in spite* of the improvement of its faculty, but *because* of it. Where once there was a community, there are now two or more separate groups. Where once there was implicit understanding of common purposes there are now many purposes.

Administrators are caught between their loyalty to the older members of the faculty and their esteem for the new men they have fought so hard to win. Unable to take sides they must, for they are human, rationalize their situation. They must make themselves the bearers of myths which might restore to the university the unity of a tribal society. One of these is the consoling belief that knowledge can be pursued in many ways and that each new set of facts is a building block destined to find its place in the structure of truth. I call this belief "consoling" because it so conveniently relieves its holders of the most arduous task facing academic administrators: to define criteria for encouraging some academic endeavors while discouraging others. I call it a "myth" because it yields no guide lines for policy.

Thus, the *dilemmas* of our state universities bring into sharp relief some basic problems in the growth and management of human knowledge. As teachers and researchers, we must become articulate about our grounds for preferring certain kinds of knowledge to others. For only thus can we expect university administrations to act with appropriate discrimination in allocating resources.

What criteria, then, can we propose? Which knowledge is it most urgent to pursue, to teach, to explore? In much of this essay I shall argue that the university must give preference to that knowledge which is least likely to be sponsored and supported by any other institution of society, that knowledge which only anxieties and fears prevent man from pursuing, that knowledge which is most needed because of these widespread apprehensions. I shall call it "dissensual" knowledge.

Dissensual disciplines and the pursuit of knowledge. I term "consensual" all those disciplines with respect to which the public at large tends to have no reservations, either as to the competence of the scholars and the truth of their findings or as to the values which inform their work. Correspondingly, I term "dissensual" all disciplines whose value or procedures are widely questioned among the public, either explicitly or implicitly.

Mathematics, the natural sciences, and such applied sciences as engineering or veterinary medicine are typically consensual disciplines. Philosophy, the social sciences, music, literature, and the fine arts are dissensual. Few people in the community will express doubts about the research findings and teachings of a chemist, nor will they ever question his motives and wonder about the values underlying his work. But the findings and teachings of philosophers and economists do not elicit similarly general confidence. The public tends to wonder about the worth of these scholars' work, it tends to look for hidden motives, and it easily discounts the teachings and even the data of dissensual disciplines either by directly opposing or by conveniently forgetting and ignoring them.

I do not believe that this has anything to do with the public's understanding of these disciplines. The man in the street knows no more about chemistry and the life work of chemists than he knows about economics and *its* practitioners. His reactions are not based on direct experience, but on the status the consensual disciplines have achieved in the community. And this status is the result, I would guess, of the publicity given to the benefits which the community is believed to have derived from the application of such disciplines.

If you wish to test whether or not a discipline is consensual you need only watch the reception which its latest findings receive in newspapers and magazines. If a physicist discovers a new particle of matter, this will be presented as another great advance in our understanding of nuclear structure. If a psychologist finds that certain symptoms are closely related to an oedipal attachment to the mother, this will be reported as an amusing oddity and serve as an illustration of the strange vagaries of the academic mind. In both cases, neither the newspaper man composing the copy nor his readers are usually in any position to evaluate the significance of the reported findings. Yet, the manner of presentation implies a considerable differential in the level of popular acceptance.

Nor does it seem to me that there is anything inherent in the nature of the two types of disciplines that would justify such discrimination. The logical deductions of a philosopher are just as secure, and the empirical findings of a sociologist often just as convincing, as are theories and findings of scholars in the consensual disciplines. It could be argued that disciplines in which aesthetic judgments play a role, e.g., music, are perhaps on less secure ground since these are "matters of taste." I doubt that this is so, but I know that this part of my argument is more difficult to sustain. (Personally, I am convinced that standards of beauty are as ascertainable as standards of truth in scientific endeavors. In either case, the exact formulation of such standards is by no means easy; and the fact that we have thus far made greater advances in formulating standards of truth than standards of beauty testifies to the direction of our interests more than to the feasibility of either task.)

There was a time, not very far in the past, when the medical man was looked upon with as much suspicion as is the psychotherapist today; and the findings of the early chemist (or alchemist) were held up to as much ridicule as those of social scientists today. Even in the recent past, advances in agriculture were made the butt of ridicule by farmers who saw agronomic innovations as a challenge to their accustomed way of life. To be sure, the disciplines which are now consensual have undergone a great expansion in knowledge and have gained much in precision and security of propositions. But much of this gain was made because the public came to perceive the utility of these disciplines and was willing to support them by the grant of money and status. Growth of knowledge and of public acceptance are closely inter-related, and neither of the two can for long proceed without the other.

There are, in all mainly dissensual fields, certain areas which the popular consensus judges legitimate. In political science, for instance, the description of formal governmental structure is largely consensual; so is the exposition of the political dogma which sanctifies our institutions—provided one does not go into too many details. In psychology, the physiological end of the discipline is consensual. I suspect that, conversely, there are dissensual enclaves in the chiefly consensual fields. In medicine, it is perhaps the area of psychosomatic afflictions; in organic chemistry, the inquiry into the "nature of life" by means of analyses of primitive organic substances exhibiting some sort of metabolism. In the remainder of this paper I will, for convenience, act as though all fields of knowledge are either entirely consensual or entirely dissensual. But let it be understood that the term "dissensual disciplines" is meant to cover fields of knowledge which are entirely dissensual as well as the dissensual areas of mainly consensual fields.

Much of the recent expansion of the newer state universities has taken place in the dissensual disciplines. The liberal arts, the social sciences, and education have seen great increases in the strength of their faculties and in student enrollments. Nor is this all. The frame of mind of the men who have recently joined our faculty tends to favor those areas of inquiry which are still largely dissensual.

There was, of course, teaching of the social sciences and of other dissensual disciplines before the recent large expansion. But this was, I suspect, rather innocuous in many of our institutions, and unlikely to raise suspicions. It would seem that teaching and research in these fields tended to emphasize the consensual segments of the disciplines. In schools that emphasized agriculture, the practical arts, or teacher education, the academic departments offering instruction in the humanities or in social science were not expected to turn out specialists; they were, rather, considered "service" departments charged with adding the gloss of a liberal education to the schools' technical training. Under these circumstances the dissensual disciplines had scant opportunities to affect the orientations of students.

But now the dissensual disciplines have become major fields of teaching and research. And the new men who have joined the faculties of growing state institutions are less likely than were their predecessors to compromise with community sentiment. They hold values and are led to findings which typically are not shared by the community. Economists know, for instance, that productivity is not necessarily a function of competition and that, indeed, productivity in our country has increased at an accelerated rate at the very time when insecurity in business and jobs was greatly reduced. No matter how well founded such findings of the economists might be, they do not really reach the public. Rather, at every public meeting of businessmen (and indeed, of many other groups), orators will sing the praises of business and job competition as the surest stimulants to productivity. Professor Galbraith, in his recent book, has dubbed such superannuated beliefs "conventional wisdom." Unaware of the questionable nature of such beliefs, the public expects the university professor to confirm them, rather than to challenge them. To cite another example, the public expects professors to uphold the belief that high voter turnout is the sign of a well functioning democratic system—this in spite of the fact that high turnout is often a sign of popular despair and has historically accompanied the rise of antidemocratic movements.

The implications are clear: the weaker the faculty, the less its concern for the inviolability of thought, the most likely it will be to make concessions to the conventional wisdom and to say the things which the community wishes to hear. Bring to the university people with better training, more deeply committed to their discipline, more enamored of the truth as they have come to know it—and the breach is bound to arise between the proponent of objective knowledge and the public committed to the conventional wisdom.

THE MAIN BASES OF CONFLICT

I shall now explore more fully three aspects of our experience as members of the faculty; in commenting upon them, I hope to lay bare some of the difficulties and tensions which create the gap between the university and its publics. There are, *first,* great divergencies in attitudes toward knowledge, particularly dissensual knowledge. *Secondly,* there are considerable differences in views as to the services which a university might and should perform, and as to the clienteles for whom they should be performed. *Thirdly,* and most broadly, we are set apart from our students, and they from us, by a disparity of backgrounds and life experiences which makes for altogether different expectations regarding the ends of learning.

Dissensus and conventionality. The intellectual is often portrayed as a rootless person. This characterization is oversimplified to the point of being false, and its intention is usually deprecative; yet it draws attention to the autonomy of creative thought, to its independence from the accidental bonds of birth, neighborhood, or community. A man may be a good neighbor and citizen, however these terms be interpreted, in most of his daily contacts; but as a scientist, a scholar, an artist, he must be able to step outside his communal environment. The love of a truth which transcends the concern of the neighborhood may thus reflect a somewhat limited love for the people next door.

Such commitment and love for truth are, of course, matters of degree. To some extent, every member of the dissensual disciplines shares in the conventional wisdom; for, no less than other people, he is a product of, and a participant in, his society. To divorce oneself from conventional beliefs requires intelligence and courage—the former being, probably, a function of the latter. It is for this reason that the best minds in each of the dissensual disciplines, the most intelligent and the most courageous, are most likely to believe in unaccepted truths. This is not to say that the best men in such disciplines are necessarily radical in their political and social convictions. Most of them are not. For radical beliefs of whatever shade are often just as highly conventionalized as are the beliefs of society at large. The difference between conservative and radical beliefs lies in the size and nature of the publics who hold them, not so much in their degrees of conventionality.

The resistance of the public to the proponent of nonconventional beliefs is automatic. It can be active or passive, and I have seen both types among my own students. Active resistance takes the form of overt rejection; the less acceptable teachings are discounted as being impractical, "long-haired," or heretical. Passive resistance takes the form of systematic, but unconscious, misunderstanding, selective perception, and gross distortion of the teacher's message. Active resistance is somewhat easier to deal with than passive, because it exists on the conscious level and is therefore a possible topic for debate. Unfortunately, it is comparatively rare. In the great majority of instances, resistance is passive, i.e., inarticulate, unrealized, amorphous. Passive resistance, at the same time, is most likely to result in the severance of all possible community ties between teacher and students: it makes communication impossible. Similar observations can, no doubt, be made about the relations between the able teacher of a dissensual discipline and the larger public of the university; but they are not so apparent and not so easily detected.

Resistance to unaccustomed knowledge and doctrine is, in general, not surprising; psychologists believe it to be a basic ingredient of most people's cognitive make-up. But when it occurs in *universities* as frequently and consistently as, in my judgment, it occurs in ours, we have reason to be perturbed. Our students do not expect to learn in the profound and the only meaningful sense of the word learning. They do not expect that their understandings of the world will change, that their beliefs will be altered, that old interests will be replaced by new ones, that on the day of their graduation they will be—as human beings—quite different from the freshmen who entered the university four years ago. They attend the university not as the truly religious person attends to worship, for the sake of an experience which will transform him; but rather as does the average Sunday churchgoer, for the sake of social conformity and from habit.

This, again, is not surprising. Our students have not been prepared to expect anything else, either by their high schools or by our own institutional advertising. To them, a gain in knowledge is similar to the gain in strength one can obtain at a health studio by exposing oneself to massages and performing exercises: one develops what one has and increases the size of one's muscles, but one does not emerge from the process with a different kind of body. Such treatment is, in fact, what we have been promising; this is what high school teachers, parents, and advisors have led our students to expect; and this is precisely the process in which the best among us participate with more or less articulate misgivings.

I doubt that an appreciable number of us do not like to teach, as is sometimes alleged now. Nor do I believe that many are opposed to rendering services to the community, speaking to interested groups and helping to solve problems. I should think that those among us who have something to say, the most fertile in ideas and richest in knowledge, would welcome any chance to say it. But academicians feel as artists do: they need to say the things that are closest to their hearts and minds, and they need to say them to appreciative audiences. Teaching becomes a chore if you come to feel that the truths most important to you will not be understood. Addressing the people in the community becomes a burden if you can talk only about matters in which you have little interest and dim belief. To be effective, any man must be able to give the things that are most genuinely his own: he will give them gladly and abundantly. I will concede that in certain endeavors, common in our society, insincerity pays off handsomely; but such pay-offs are the wages of intellectual prostitution rather than of personal effectiveness. Leaving aside what other people may do or think, I contend that academicians, like poets and artists, must above all be true to themselves.

The gap between the faculty and its publics thus stems from two mutually dependent sets of attitudes: the publics' distrust, and the faculty's frustration over the lack of an attentive audience. It all resolves itself into a mutual lack of appreciation. The publics have no respect for a faculty whose contributions are beyond their intellectual and—above all—their emotional ken. The faculty has no respect for audiences who do not seem prepared for the slightest effort of understanding (as distinguished from the effort of mental hoarding).

I have heard mathematicians and statisticians express despair over the manner in which they must retail their knowledge. To them, the elegance of a solution, the generality of a proof, even the explanatory power of a formulation in the world of facts, are supreme achievements and causes for exhilaration. This they cannot communicate to most of their audiences; for the bulk of their students are interested in little more than the computational devices whereby numbers can be manipulated. I expect that similar gaps exist in many a field, with resulting bewilderment on one side, and frustration on the other.

I should add, in case there is any doubt, that the gap does not arise from the differences in intellectual preparation and maturity which one ordinarily expects to find between students and teachers. All important ideas can be taught on many levels of complexity; and I have seen people of great profundity in their fields of knowledge genuinely excited by the task of teaching highly sophisticated ideas in a manner which will make them accessible to students with minimal preparation. The gap arises, rather, from a difference in *foci* of interest. The good academician focuses upon changes in the structure of knowledge, and he does so in both of his capacities, as a scholar and as a teacher. Our students and our wider publics are interested only in accretion.

Service. The university extends beyond the campus. In state universities this thought is common to the point of triteness. It is all too obvious that, financially and in other ways, the university depends upon the support of a larger public. It is also evident that this support is unlikely to be given unless people feel that they receive something in return. Beyond this, most of us feel a genuine obligation, divorced from any give and take, to be of service to society. None of this is in dispute.

Driven in part by necessity and in part by a sense of responsibility, the faculties of state institutions have always performed a variety of services off campus. A very large part of these services have been rather specific and have brought the university in contact with selected groups of people. This has tended to make the university as an institution dependent upon the support of narrowly defined clienteles. The political problems which can arise from such a policy are painfully obvious today: let one of these groups shrink in economic importance, let another lose some of its influence upon public affairs, and we are in the midst of a "public relations" crisis.

The improvement of our faculty has had its share in accentuating the crisis. The higher the qualifications of faculty members, the less they tended to esteem some of the services which had traditionally been performed for people on the outside. They thought that at least some of these activities did not require the knowledge and skill of scholars. Once more, they were faced with the unpleasant alternative of either having to give things they did not consider worth giving, or of resisting the demands that were made upon them.

These pressures and reluctances lead to a great deal of debate on our campuses; and the positions taken on one or the other side of the "service" issue distinguish most clearly between old-timers and new-comers on the faculty and in the administration. The traditional view is that a tax-supported institution is bound, both morally and politically, to "help" the "people" of the state. Extremists among the new-comers counter this by insisting on the total independence of the arts and sciences; they seem to feel that intellectual life can flourish only to the extent that it is divorced from the daily affairs of the community. Between these two alternatives, most people strike some sort of compromise.

I shall argue that the answer to this question depends entirely on the meanings one wishes to assign to the terms "service" and "people." But I must point out first that the two views just sketched do not realistically reflect any actual or possible state of affairs.

The service-oriented old-timers suggest that the "people" of the state expect the university to perform specific tasks; a proper analogy would be everyone's expectation that the post office will handle the mails. In actual fact, most such demands and expectations are generated by the university. This holds even for the agricultural extension programs—certainly the prototype of university sponsored service activities. The average county agent is not merely a counselor who waits in his office to be consulted by farmers faced with specific problems; most frequently, he is an active propagandist for agricultural progress. This holds with even greater force for other university "service" programs, whether in the field of traffic, municipal government, or assistance to school districts. At most, the citizenry has some general notions that a university should prove its usefulness. But the belief that there are constant pressures and demands emanating from the public and besetting the university administration belongs in the field of fiction. Perhaps it is a soothing rationalization whereby men prove to themselves that they are needed and appreciated.

The view held by some newcomers, which radically divorces scientific and artistic pursuits from everyday existence, ignores the realities of our involvement in the affairs of community, state, and nation. Our existence is anything but cloistered, and a modern university is anything but a monastery. We will be judged by others, and we will be allocated resources in the measure that such judgment is favorable. We cannot realistically set ourselves the task of escaping judgment; rather, we must see to it that it be based on acceptable criteria.

Among university administrators who think themselves enlightened and progressive, a compromise answer to the problem of service has gained great currency. We should perform those services, they say, which require academic expertise and which will contribute to the intellectual growth of students and teachers; but we should stay away from the bolts-and-nuts activities of the journeyman. In the social sciences, the proponents of this position have acquired a preference for "big" problems, national and even international in scope, and they shun the "man-hole counting" endeavors which have been the vogue of the past. Hence the interest in technical assistance programs, metropolitan surveys, and defense projects which, in addition to the magnitude of their problems, also involve large financial outlays and a measure of academic patronage.

It comes as something of a surprise to progressive administrators that even these programs, most of which clearly call for the employment of academic skills, meet with some opposition on the part of the faculty. Perhaps the mere circumstance that the initiative for undertaking large scale contract work lies with the administration rather than with the faculty raises apprehensions. There have been instances, no doubt, in which contracts were signed without sufficient evaluation of faculty capabilities, both as to the number of staff members available and as to their preparation for a given assignment. Some of the most professional faculty members believe at times that we have not reached a level of knowledge sufficient to tackle some of the more intricate international problems in a scientific manner. For this reason, and perhaps for others, technical assistance and similar programs rarely attract the most scholarly men among us.

Thus, even the most advanced service programs are suspect in the eyes of some professors. And those who have participated in such programs have been known to engage in much self-examination in order to ascertain whether, giving the best they had to give, they had actually been of service to anyone. Over and over, one is led back to the questions I sketched before: how to define service and how to reconcile service with other functions of the university.

The business of the university is the advancement of knowledge. We do not advance knowledge measurably by passing out nostrums for various types of malaise. We do not increase people's awareness of themselves and their ability to solve their problems by soothing their consciences and relieving them of responsibility for difficult decisions. We do not honestly serve the public by everlastingly showing our willingness to do their bidding. Above all, we are gravely at fault if we accept the public's own definition of its problems and try to solve these as they are presented to us. No responsible physician will blindly accept his patient's diagnosis, and no responsible garage mechanic will accede to a customer's erroneous demand for unneeded repairs. I am not so sure that we always avoid the mistake of accepting implicitly the public's definitions of problems.

What is service? We could define it as making the required response to consumer demands. Under this definition, we will have no difficulty in ascertaining whether or not we have been of service: we need only compare the contents of the demands and of our actions. Even if we wish to abstain from so narrow a definition, if we want to act more responsibly, it is usually quite possible to recognize an act of service, provided that our discipline or endeavor is consensual. The physician is expected to restore and maintain our health, and the garage mechanic to keep our car in running condition. Whenever they do this, they are of service. Although the definition of objectives by expert and clientele is frequently not too precise (just what is "health"?), it is sufficient for most practical purposes.

Neither of these two criteria of service applies to the pursuit of knowledge. Some types of knowledge may be consensually demanded because people have a fairly clear image of their social consequences; but it is scarcely possible to expect consensus about the search for knowledge, the effects of which cannot be anticipated. For this reason, intellectual work will always tend to be dissensual. Was the invention of Riemann spaces a service? I will not even refer to the use which an Einstein was able to make of Riemann's conceptualizations and to the consequent developments in physical science and technology. Riemann knew nothing of this, nor did his contemporaries. Yet who will say that the discovery of alternatives to Euclidian geometry were not a service, since few recognized it as such; whereas the development of model city ordinances—because clearly demanded—is a service? Riemann's conceptions have helped to increase vastly the range of human intelligence. To be sure, not everyone knows about them. But because of them the community can now count among its active members men whose understanding of mathematical and physical phenomena has been greatly increased. Is this not a service?

Shall we say, then, that service activities cannot involve creative innovation, whereas nonservice work should be creative? I doubt that many would want to maintain so paradoxical a position. I suspect, however, that a few consider the creation of new ideas a private hobby of professors which has very little relevance to practical affairs. If this position exists at all, I hope that it is indeed restricted to a very few people. Being clearly anti-intellectual, it hardly has a place in the university. Besides, the assertion is patently inconsistent with the facts of the nuclear age.

Shall we say, then, that services are always directed toward specific, somewhat narrowly circumscribed publics? Adoption of this view would place us in the strange position of excluding all educational services which benefit people at large. We would get rid of most of the programs of our radio and television stations, particularly the music programs. We would not invite the townspeople to attend public lectures, plays, and concerts on our campus. Clearly, this cannot be meant.

This lengthy exercise in definitions merely demonstrates a single point: that service, in intellectual affairs, is often hard, if not impossible, to define. Definitions which yield criteria whereby service activities can be most clearly recognized (e.g., response to demands, restriction to narrow publics) can, if adopted, easily lead us to offer only routine advice and help instead of innovations. And, we might end up documenting our high regard for our fellow citizens by giving them what we consider worthless, and keeping for our private edification what we consider worthwhile.

This, I am sure, has actually happened. Not through malice, not even through stupidity. It is bound to happen when one becomes preoccupied with the idea of public service. I doubt that the builders of medieval cathedrals had such preoccupations. They simply built the most beautiful structures that they knew how to build, in the service of God—which is as much as saying in the service of everyone and everything. As soon as you seek for tangible proof of your worth to the community, you are in grave danger of giving what brings almost immediate recognition; and since imagination is needed to perceive more remote but perhaps more important benefits, you tend to prefer the intellectual fast buck to the long-term investment of mental energies.

It is one thing to work for immediate credit, and it is another to think about the consequences of one's actions for community and mankind. If we wish to be responsible, we surely must do the latter. But all too often we will be alone in seeing the advantages which the community might derive from the successful completion of the tasks we set for ourselves. Where the territory is largely uncharted and its resources unknown, only a few people can make informed guesses about the possible yield of the still unexplored area. It is for us to make such guesses and to defend them in the face of uncertainty and incredulity. We will often be wrong. In such cases, we must be willing to admit that we have wasted our energies and those, perhaps, of other people in doing what, in our best judgment, we had expected to yield beneficial results. Whatever we do, no one can absolve us of the responsibility of making choices. Indeed, our responsibility to the community would be meaningless if we did not accept this burden.

Experience and the conditions of learning. In opening our doors to all who are able to learn we act in the equalitarian spirit of the American Frontier; but to the extent that we hand out knowledge in the form of "bagage intellectuel" (as French student argot puts it), we adhere to traditions of European university education. To be sure, we have made determined efforts to adjust methods of education to our special situation. But our measures have sometimes been superficial, and there still is much room for innovation.

Our students are the products of a mobile society: their very presence in our universities attests this. Yet as a rule they appear to be intellectually and emotionally more rigid than are students in less mobile societies. Oddly, the presence of barriers in the mind reflects the relative absence of barriers in society. Where education is still regarded as a privilege of gentlemen, students of plebeian lineage show a grasping and combative eagerness to acquire knowledge, refinement of taste, and new interpretations of human experience: to them, education is a step in the fight for social equality, and they enter it with a will to change. Such attitudes are still common in some of our Eastern universities where many of the students come from minority backgrounds. Our Midwestern students, although frequently from homes of moderate means and meager education, exhibit no such eagerness. They happily take it for granted, as does our society, that there are no social hurdles to learning. Our students, in entering the university, cannot feel that they are overcoming ancient restrictions and embarking upon a new way of life. For them education spells advancement rather than change, improvement rather than transition.

The fixedness of their viewpoints thus is a counterpart to our equalitarian ethos.

Yet we know such attitudes to be ill-adapted. Great transformations are under way in our society, and there are no signs of respite. We think it imperative that our students, once they leave the campus, be flexible enough in mind and personality to cope with unexpected and perhaps still inconceivable problems. A few simple precepts, such as those contained in conventional wisdom, can scarcely be of any help to the engineers of a still clouded future, however broadly or narrowly the term "engineer" might be construed.

We have thus two seemingly incompatible conditions of education: a changing world which calls for a leadership of insight and originality; and students who, in view of the relative ease with which they can cross social boundaries, are under no compulsion to play new roles and to cast off old habits of mind and heart.

Since our students come to us with improper orientations toward learning, it is for us to induce proper ones. Can these be generated by the methods of teaching which we have thus far employed? The present orientations of our students grow out of their life experiences in home and society; they are rather firmly established, and I doubt that either formal lectures or admonitions will modify them. But new and engrossing experiences might. And since most meaningful experiences are gained in intimate commerce with others, we are greatly in need of a strong academic community.

Once more, neither tradition nor the mottled sediment of the past serve us well. The methods of teaching and the forms of organization that we have inherited are not adapted to our task. Lectures and discussions are not conducted in the language of the community, the classroom is not a community center, and conversations between students and academic advisors are not likely to be meaningful. Nor were they meant to be. So long as higher education was a privilege, the academic community developed outside the lecture halls and embraced only a few professors and their favorite students who were likely to follow in their masters' footsteps. For most other students the university offered but one of many educational experiences; its main purpose was to provide them with a professional specialty. These students did not, for intellectual growth, depend upon an academic community; in their homes and in the circles of their friends, music, literature, and the discussion of the day's important issues were a steady fare. What the university had to offer could thus be understood in the context of a much larger and much more diversified experience on the outside.

Our students do not come to us with such preparation and capacity to form meaningful relationships outside the university. We know this, but we have not yet learned how to take it into account. Much of what we say in lectures relates to no experience of theirs and becomes, at best, intellectual baggage. At worst, it is not understood at all. Insight into foreign cultures is difficult to attain when the only culture you have ever known is that of a small town or a city neighborhood. Nor is it a simple matter to make clear to the student why we want him to gain such understanding; he may, of course, rehearse the current generalities about the shrinking size of the globe and the mutual dependence of all peoples on earth; but I doubt that such explanations, however honestly meant, reflect a serious concern of any sort. And so it happens that the teacher describing foreign cultures tries to awaken rational insight into the varieties of human experience, while the student considers his job well done when he has committed to memory a good portion of the facts mentioned in text and lecture. The teacher, having exhausted his pedagogical resources, wonders whether these young people can be taught. The gravity of his error matches the depth of his frustration.

We have for some time tried to cope with this difficulty in our universities. Many universities have programs of general education designed to give the student the background which was lacking at his arrival on campus. We bring to the campus great artists, lecturers, foreign films, and a variety of other "events." These efforts have usually fallen far short of expectations, and not for lack of good will or hard work. In our classes, we often find no difference between students who have been exposed to the general education course in our specialty and those who have not: even if the teaching in general courses were dismally poor (which by no means it is), this would hardly explain such minimal results. The number of students who attend concerts, theatrical performances, and discussion meetings is disturbingly small: even if these performances were consistently mediocre (which by no means they are) this would not explain such perennial truancy. Our students have no use for these things. Neither our own lack of talent nor theirs inhibits our students' understanding. We must accept it as a hard social fact that much of human thought and culture is, in the form in which we present it to them, unrelated to their experience and hence unintelligible.

We have our own share in the academic tragi-comedy of misunderstandings. American professors are, like their students, the creatures of a fluid social milieu. Since, in our world, status is achieved rather than ascribed, we feel forever impelled to prove to ourselves and to others that we deserve the trust and responsibility placed upon us.

Such proof is difficult, for we are producers of intangibles; and thus, status anxiety is our most frequent occupational disease.

Nor can we find comfort in aristocratic pride. Most of us do not issue from a nobility of rank or wealth, nor even from a patriciate of letters. We come from every social layer in every region of the United States and of the world. Even those among us who can point to generations of well-born ancestors are not prone to substitute vanity for exertion. All of us regard social equality as a fundamental tenet of the academic community; and we are sure that each man's academic worth should be measured by his intellectual contributions only. This is our ethic.

But convictions and personal feelings are often at variance. Intellectual worth is an uneasy standard, and many secretly yearn for a simpler definition of their status. Some of us, glimpsing antique images of academic gentility, affect a dignified aloofness; others react by a show of plebeian pride which tends to obliterate distinctions between the town and the gown. Few of us are content and willing to be who we are: part of the human multitude, and yet ennobled as bearers of the world's intellectual heritage.

Thus, we are both similar to our students and different from them. Like them, we are, most of us, recent arrivals; and like them, we came to the university because the hurdles were not too high. We are, perhaps, of more diverse and more mingled extractions than they are. But the main difference is this: *we have experienced change within ourselves, and they have not. We are not too sure of our position in the world; they are too sure of theirs.* Their status-striving has the determined push of careerism; our status anxiety is a gnawing worry lest we fail to live up to the expectations which we ourselves and others attach to our position.

Such feelings do not make for good teaching or learning. A snobbish professor alienates the student as he inculcates the unattainability of knowledge and good taste. His earthy colleague, by exhibiting an excess of common sense, affirms that there is not very much to be learned or communicated. The student, sharing the American public's ambiguous attitudes toward men of letters and sensing moreover his professor's disquiet, vacillates between formal subservience and excessive informality. This does not help the professor, who becomes even more defensive; and it does not help communication, which becomes even less articulate.

Clearly, our reactions do not help the student any more than they help us. They spell defensiveness, and unwillingness to reveal ourselves as we actually are, and ultimately a measure of self-deception.

While defensiveness inhibits the full utilization of our teaching skills, self-deception reduces our progress as scholars. The two go together and reflect the same self-defeating habits of mind.

I do not mention these things out of a morbid interest in self-dissection. Quite simply, they need to be known. We and our students are the materials with which the academic community must be built. We must know these materials well before we can decide what loads they will bear and how they can be joined together. University administrations, too, must know this. And the forms and rules of administration, like building regulations, must in some way take account of more than our place in the formal structure: they must also relate to our strengths and weaknesses and to the conditions under which we can be relied upon to stay together.

I fear that some of the rules currently in force in our universities do not perform this function well. They tend to separate students from faculty, both in the mind and in action. Universities are so organized that the faculty's responsibility for the students' welfare is limited to classroom and office. In all matters affecting the students' life outside the classroom, the faculty has nearly no voice and certainly no continuing share. It is a minor part of a complex administrative machinery which, in some way, enunciates and enforces norms for the campus community. This alone is enough to reduce our participation. Rightly or wrongly, we also tend to construe our segregation from the student community as a mark of administrative diffidence. Moreover, many of the norms currently enforced seem to be based upon assumptions about human behavior and upon value premises which often we do not share. Many of us do not believe that individual freedom and social responsibility are fostered by elaborate codes of personal conduct. We thus find ourselves in the uncomfortable position of having to give tacit consent to educational policies of which we do not approve. This makes many of us wonder about our role as educators—and given the typical status problems of professors, such self-interrogation does not contribute to the sense of security or the effectiveness of the profession.

Nor can this separation of educational powers increase the students' trust in their teachers. It conveys the impression that a professor may speak only of those things which are of no immediate relevance. As for students in the behavioral sciences, they will note that the doctrines underlying campus regulations often diverge from the theories and findings learned in class and textbook. Perhaps such findings should be considered untrustworthy; if so, we surely should not send out into the community students trained in these untrustworthy disciplines, to become teachers, clinicians, and experts in social organization. No more effective step could be taken to discredit the behavioral sciences in the minds of our students than to teach one thing in courses and another by way of community regulations. From this, students must come to believe that the knowledge of academicians has no relevance to the practical affairs of men. This does not help to commend the teacher to the student.

The manifold historical circumstances which have brought about the forms and practices of administration under which we live almost defy analysis. I would guess that many universities, in the rush of growing very large, took over mechanically from business and government such precepts of organization as seemed expedient. These may not always apply. The separation of powers may well have its place in government, but it can be a source of continuing trouble in education, where it often amounts to denial of responsibility. Whether or not such denial is intended, academic men are likely to infer that it is. Some of us will convert felt rejection into status anxiety, perhaps one of the most destructive among the social diseases which, because of its social etiology, is quite likely to take epidemic proportions.

Man's condition is neither fate nor of his own making: it is both. And in the fabric of our lives the strands of fate and freedom are so tightly intertwined as to be indistinguishable. Our students, brought up all too often with narrow conceptions, hesitate at the portals of broader understandings: their will is the outcome of their experience, yet it can also change their future experience. And so it is with our will and our experience. Having sped from station to station in life, and from altar to altar in spirit, many of us have been hurt in the passage; our fears are the memories of pain, but our pains can alert us to danger and drive us to rational decisions. All of us are heirs of venerable institutions both created by men of good will and adopted by them in fits of absentmindedness: we are in part the creatures of these institutions, but also, by our daily actions, their creators.

This is our condition. This is the condition of our universities. We cannot make ourselves over—nor our students, nor the institution— simply by hopeful wishing or grim determination. But, understanding our condition, we can deliberately try to create circumstances more conducive to new learning. And in each university we can set ourselves the long-range task of building a community devoted to the pursuit of excellence according to our standards of truth and beauty.

THE CRUCIAL TASKS OF THE UNIVERSITY

The case for the academic community. "We must educate the whole person"—the phrase is now hackneyed and almost meaningless. No doubt it signifies different things to different people. I suspect that, to many, it means that we should inculcate not only the ABC's but also polite manners and "good" attitudes. If this is the interpretation to be put upon the words, let us go back to the good old times when the schools restricted themselves to the ABC's and the more advanced fields of learning. Education and indoctrination are opposites.

To me education means openness to change. It means that we help the student to shed the conventional wisdom and enable him to make rational choices by the use of information, insight, and sensitivity. It means, first of all, that we generate the willingness to change. We communicate excitement about the worlds of knowledge and of the arts, so that our students will want to expose themselves to unaccustomed experiences. To the extent that they do, they will gain the respect of the faculty, and they will learn to appreciate their teachers. Education, thus, is the same thing as the creation of the academic community.

The existence of a community depends upon shared meaningful experiences. For education to take place, faculty and students on campus must be involved in activities important and rewarding to both. Coffee and doughnuts will not do; and no improvement is to be gained from switching to tea and petits fours. Half an hour's quiet conversation on a topic of real concern, if repeated over time, will do more than any number of monster receptions. Listening to music together, or making it together, or discussing the latest drama production, or politics, or religion, or the conceptual and ethical problems of the disciplines—these and many other humble acts of communication make up the academic communion for which we should strive.

For the teacher, education is forever an act of self-revelation. The good teacher does not simply attempt to fill minds with information as one fills barrels of wine; it is not a physical process. Rather, he exhibits himself as a demonstration case, showing his students how at least one member of his profession tackles a problem, how he feels about it, how he judges his own work, how he doubts and battles about its social value and the truth of his findings, how he is often tempted to cheat himself and others by saying more than can be responsibly asserted. Science, the humanities, and the arts are human and fallible activities and must be understood as such.

For the student, too, education is self-revelation. He must be able to expose himself to the teacher and to other students, so that he may be helped better to realize his own potential. All discussion that is not to some extent self-revelation is, in fact, anti-intellectual. The student of mathematics has not learned anything about his discipline unless he is able to exhibit the process whereby he arrives at a solution. The most elaborate repertoire of mathematical formulae and operating rules will never add up to the first beginnings of mathematics. In the dissensual disciplines, self-revelation is even more important; almost invariably, questions of value are mingled with questions of theory and fact, and if the student does not learn to be articulate about his values, if he takes them for granted, he has not begun to penetrate into his field of study. Self-revelation is the surest path to self-awareness; and without the latter, change is impossible and education an empty ritual.

Lest I be misunderstood, I wish to assert that I am vigorously opposed to planless self-expression. Education is not to be confused with free association, which has its place on the therapist's couch but not in classrooms, in laboratories, or even at the coffee tables of the nearby hamburger joint. Education is a public process, therapy is a private one. Science and the arts are public, personality is private. Public self-revelation in academic discussion is systematic exposition of one's own thoughts or feelings in a manner calculated to be understood by watchful and understanding fellow-students and teachers; hence it is as organized, as lucid, as straightforward as it can be made. For all its effort toward systematic statement, it need not be any less genuine: indeed, it is likely to be more genuine. The architect who designs a house must express himself in an organized fashion under severe restrictions; these are imposed upon him by the properties of building materials, by building regulations, by the prospective uses of the building, by the market for his ideas, and by the finances of his client; still, his buildings are the clearest revelation of himself. One would not think of writing his biography without presenting pictures of his buildings and discussions of his systematic writings on architecture; one would not present his mind only through casual conversations and anecdotes. Education in the sciences and arts is the public display of personal conscious and conscientious self-organization, as are the arts and sciences themselves.

There is an economy of feeling, as there is an economy of thought. Both are the result of successful processes of organization. Both are fit objects of human understanding. Both are present in every intellectual endeavor. Both must be exhibited in the process of education. I grant that the display of feelings is still infinitely more difficult than the display of thought; for we have failed thus far to develop languages for the expression of feeling that approach in precision the languages of the sciences; and our culture, with its orientation toward the tangible and its fundamental distrust of man's inner experience, has successfully prevented the development of such languages. But this should not deter us. At this point of human history, we need above all to train ourselves in the organized expression of feelings, so that we might better control ourselves.

The academic community must be an assembly of men and women humble enough and yet secure enough to exhibit to one another their doubts, their weaknesses, and at times their wretchedness. This is the price of knowledge and of truth. Set the teacher up on a pedestal and ascribe to him all the conventional virtues, and you will reduce his scope to that of a dog trainer. Limit the student's range of experience by imposing disciplines other than those emerging from the search for truth and understanding, and you will make him into a parrot. But foster understanding and the free but organized search for new forms of thinking and living, and you will be educating people.

Some will feel that such self-revelation might divert attention from the subject matter of instruction. I say it is necessarily part of this subject matter. If we neglect to reveal the processes of thought and feeling whereby we actually generate propositions, we will either perpetuate dogmatisms or substitute new for old ones.

Let us consider, as an example, the science of mathematics. In view of its abstractness and its elaborate logical structure, many people might feel that the teaching of mathematics cannot possibly be anything more than instruction in formal logical relations accompanied by drill in the manipulation of data. When so presented, mathematical rules will appear as though they were objective facts entirely untouched by human hands, and therefore invested with the special sanctity of unalterable truth. The student who thinks of mathematics in these terms has entirely missed the central point of the discipline.

From the very start, the student must be made aware that the axioms and theorems of mathematics are in principle no more unalterable than other kinds of human knowledge, for they are but the rules which men have adopted to control their thinking and increase their efficiency. In a sense they are arbitrary; yet they are far from unreasonable, because they have in fact made it possible for men to think with greater consistency and rigor and, in many instances, to formulate propositions which seem to describe observable events. The labor of mathematics thus consists chiefly in the invention and testing of rules which will produce the desired results: logical consistency, efficiency, and elegance. Good instructors, I am sure, will try to point this out.

But pointing out is not enough. The student who has never struggled with several alternative rules that might conceivably be adopted, or who has never observed anyone engaged with such difficult decisions, will never know what it "feels like" to be a worker in the field of mathematics.

Truth is forever the product of search. It is forever acquired and never possessed. The Euclidian axioms do not assert invariant facts within nature or beyond it; rather they are assumptions which, for centuries, have helped man in his search. The student who leaves the university without having understood the tentative, developmental nature of truth should never have come to the campus. But nothing about the nature of truth will ever be communicated by a cold intellectualism which divorces knowledge from human experience. If he is to learn about truth, the student must be present as his teacher struggles to obtain it, and as his own powers grow, he must begin to join the battle.

Teaching and research are not alternatives. Both are part of the same process of education, complementary activities in the academic community. It is of course possible to ask how much time should be allotted to the classroom and to the laboratory or desk; but in asking such a question we should be aware that the range of acceptable allocations is bounded by narrow limits—provided we care for the health of the academic community. Nor is the question important; for within the limits of tolerable allocations, there are likely to be variations owing to the nature of teaching and research in each field. There are also differences in individual working habits and inclinations which always have and always will control the distribution of each man's time. These are technicalities which will continue to be bitterly contested; but they will never greatly affect the academic community, so long as the allocations of time are not allowed to result in divorce between research and teaching.

There are those who will claim that students, and particularly our students, are not "ripe" for the experience of which I have written. The argument partakes conspicuously of the fallacy which Merton has called the "self-fulfilling prophecy." It is rather similar to the argument of racists who deny a good education to Negroes on the ground that they are mentally inferior; subsequently, having first denied the Negro the advantages accorded the white students, they find that Negroes are indeed inferior to whites in knowledge and intelligence. Let us not condemn our students before giving them a chance to learn.

I recognize that our students, being products of the training, indoctrination, and instruction to which we have allowed them to be exposed, are not particularly suited for education as I have tried to define it. I will go further. Not we alone have failed to prepare our students for participation in the academic community; the entire educational system from the first grade on has similarly failed. We thus find ourselves faced with a vast mass of students whose whole schooling experience appears to have made them quite resistant against our, and perhaps against any, attempts at their higher education.

This is why we do not have an academic community today. This is why students and teachers—those teachers who have the most to say—do not communicate with one another. This is why there is mutual lack of understanding, respect, confidence, and affection. This is why there is no common faith. This is why we are all lonely in the midst of a very large crowd.

Yet, I believe that the academic community can be built. But if we wish to build it, we should develop some notion of its plan and structure.

We must educate our public. And to the extent that we do, we will build the academic community beyond the campus. Our supporters then will not be clients, but genuine friends who, having come to understand some of our aims, will want to join with us in a common pursuit. These people may not belong to any particular group, nor are they likely to be, at first, the most highly placed men and women in their own communities. But I trust that they will be more committed to us and to the goals of education than are clienteles whose appetite for specific benefits must be continually fed.

We can educate our public. We can build the academic community beyond the campus. We can impart to groups in the community a sense of participation in the search for knowledge by introducing them, as best we can, to our real concerns as scholars. We can ask men and women in many walks of life to associate themselves with us in our research. There are many ways in which this can be done. The success of polio research is, in part, traceable to help which was given by millions of people everywhere. If we properly explain our intentions, people may perhaps be motivated to solicit and contribute funds. Beyond this, there are in the social sciences and (I suspect) such fields as agriculture and technology, many areas in which the actual participation of the public in experimentation and information gathering would be most profitable. Lack of imagination alone imposes limits upon the ways in which the academic community can be built beyond the campus.

The case for dissensual knowledge. I do not wish to argue here the relative merits of one set of disciplines over another. Clearly, my own preferences have led me into the social sciences. But I believe that all disciplines can be shaped and taught in such a way as to increase man's control over himself. I should like to think that the engineer of tomorrow will be modeled after the image of the architect: as the responsible architect, in designing a house, thinks of the life that people will lead in it, and of the effects which shape and color will have upon the texture of the community, so the engineer might well consider the consequences that his inventions and constructions will have for men. There is yet another way in which all disciplines can contribute to man's understanding and control of himself: if they are disciplines at all, they teach him how to think—some even teach him how to see and hear and feel . . .

In brief, it is the task of the university to advance dissensual knowledge in whatever field this may be. The connection between the dissensual character of knowledge and its likelihood of increasing human understanding and control is this: that knowledge in dissensual which appears to threaten in any way human institutions and accustomed behavior. Our lack of confidence in the fundamental rightness of our comfortable or even privileged ways causes us to be suspicious of any knowledge that could expose and challenge our position.

This rejection, I repeat, is by no means uniquely characteristic of the social sciences, humanities, and arts. The Copernican system was rejected at first not because it was thought to be scientifically inferior to the Ptolemaic system—indeed it was granted that the Copernican mathematics greatly facilitated the navigator's task of charting his course by reference to the stars. Copernicus' heliocentric system was rejected because it upset the topographical notions which at the time required that heaven should be "above" and hell "below." If there was no particular place in the world for heaven and hell, religion itself was thought to be in danger. To be sure, religious doctrines have changed. But few will argue that we are worse off for having lost the belief in the ancient cosmologies.

We have been celebrating the one hundredth anniversary of the appearance of *The Origin of the Species*. Darwin might have sneaked by the conventional wisdom with this book had he not written, twelve years later, *The Descent of Man*. Both books taken together were said to undermine godliness, morality, the very foundations of civilized life. In the debate that lasted for decades the logical and empirical foundations of Darwin's assertions were never at issue. Rejection was automatic, unthinking, informed by erroneous notions about the sacred and the profane.

The areas of human knowledge which are the exclusive domain of conventional wisdom and which are thus withdrawn from creative understanding have changed and shrunk over the centuries. In the days of Copernicus, virtually the entire experienced world, whether of stone, flesh, or mind, was still explained by means of assumptions which it was heretical to challenge. Any discipline inconsistent with these assumptions was dissensual. By the middle of the last century, the world of dead matter had become the uncontested domain of a now consensual science; but the sciences of life still were not entirely accepted, and parts of them, such as Darwin's theory of evolution, were dissensual.

In our day, the life sciences have become largely consensual; and the sciences which deal with man's thoughts, feelings, and actions have gained a foothold in the social consensus. Still, these sciences are far from consensual: few people will dare to prescribe household medicines for serious sickness instead of consulting a physician or to build a house without specific knowledge or expert advice; yet many still feel that no special knowledge is needed to deal with problem children; and our statesmen almost make a virtue of ignoring, of not even inquiring, what the social sciences have to offer.

The persistence of such popular attitudes is the surest way to disaster, for with our modern technology the price that humanity may have to pay for intellectual sloth and political irresponsibility may be its own destruction. Hence my conviction that the university, to discharge its responsibility toward the community, must encourage, nurture, defend, and spread those disciplines which are now dissensual. The university must educate the public while there is still time, rather than subject itself to the public's whims.

The case for aesthetic experience. The discussions of those concerned with higher education have turned in recent years upon the issue of "vocationalism" or "specialization" vs. "liberal education." There has been quite a resurgence in the camp of the proponents of "liberal education," so that the term itself has now been added to the book of magic formuli which we recite in moments of distress. Liberal arts colleges enjoy a quiet vogue and, significantly, several state universities have added independent "experimental" colleges in which teachers "experiment" with the old stand-bys: Aristotle, Saint Augustine, the calculus. The defenders of "liberal education," in spite of the ease with which they have been able to get their watchword accepted, assume the posture of pioneers and register ringing protests against "overspecialization" presumably fostered by the graduate schools and against "vocationalism" perpetrated by everyone else.

I am not at all clear what people ordinarily mean by the adjective "liberal" when used in conjunction with education; and it often seems to me that they talk about "liberal" education in the same manner in which one speaks of a "liberal" sprinkling of cheese on a dish of spaghetti: it means little more than "a lot of a good thing." Be that as it may, I take it that we all think of liberal education as that collection of facts, attitudes, and abilities without which we refuse to admit a person into the club of the truly educated.

Among those who currently agitate for more "liberal" education, there appear to be two major trends. The first of these is perhaps best represented by Robert Hutchins and the Great Books program; I shall call it the "scriptural" trend. The second trend, which I shall call "encyclopedic," is the appeal for the regeneration of Renaissance man.

The first position I have called "scriptural" because it apparently is an extension of certain religious doctrines, according to which all worthwhile ideas are to be found in some particular collection of writings; and in these ideas, all questions of current or future interest are implied; therefore, mastery of the basic writings ensures the fullness of an education.

The second, or "encyclopedic," position assumes that it is possible to bring together, in manageable compass, the fundamentals of the various branches of knowledge, which, when properly packaged and dispensed, will make the student into a "generalist." While the scriptural school believes in the existence of central ideas and principles, the encyclopedist thinks of knowledge as a collection of many ideas.

Neither of these two positions strikes me as very defensible. I see no particular reason for believing that all knowledge, past, present, and future, is conveniently enshrined in some set of writings, sacred or profane. I am unimpressed by the recurring efforts of my scripturally inclined brethren to demonstrate that Freud's basic ideas, for instance, were already present in Plato or Rousseau.

Also, I cannot see how, from the vast collection of facts, ideas, theories, and art products now available, one can draw a sample in any sense representative of the world's culture and learning. Our recorded heritage has so grown by both the passage of time and the geographical expansion of our dwelling space as to preclude the formulation of any criteria for culling from it the essential elements of a complete education for modern Renaissance man.

For my part, I tend to think that a decent education, call it "liberal," if you will, must rest upon a proper emphasis on certain characteristics common to *all* knowledge and art. And the most pervasive characteristic of all intellectual products, be they scientific theories, historical accounts, or works of art, is their beauty. I shall argue that our most determined efforts must be directed toward the stimulation and development of aesthetic sensitivity in *all* fields, irrespective of discipline, humanistic or scientific, professional or academic, "basic" or "applied."

Admittedly, this position is at odds with much official doctrine in higher education. There is a rather widespread belief that knowledge is pursued chiefly because of its usefulness either for improving man's material condition or for helping him adjust socially; and on these grounds, public education has been justified. To be sure, this kind of usefulness has legitimized intellectual activity in the eyes of politicians, businessmen, and the public in general; but I seriously doubt that usefulness is, as such, a significant motivation for serious research or intelligent study.

A good theory, one that is generally esteemed, is not merely true; it is also inspired. A good piece of history writing is not merely accurate as to its facts; it is also ingenious in its explanations. Whatever we do, whenever it is well done, it is in some measure a work of art.

Let us now consider the relation between liberal education and specialization. If we assume that liberal education consists in the study of some limited set of scriptures, then a high degree of specialization can easily cut into the time needed for scriptural scholarship. If we believe that liberal education consists in a liberal sprinkling of everything, specialization will, again, reduce the range of knowledge to which an individual can be exposed. If, however, we are willing to say that liberal education consists in the development of aesthetic sensitivity, then breadth of exposure certainly is not as important as are the intellectual habits of the student.

I can see no reason why a highly specialized person must be an intellectual dunce; and I seriously doubt that intellectual impoverishment should be charged to our research-mindedness. Stupidity is, after all, not such a recent phenomenon. During the worst periods of medieval scholasticism, and at many others thereafter, academics have managed pretty well to be arid and uninspired. It did not take modern specialization to achieve this end.

I would suggest, however, that any institution devoted to the assembly line production of intellectual wares, whether it be a medieval cloister or a modern university, is likely to end up delivering a considerable number of standardized minds unless something is done to prevent this. The common mark of such minds is that they are devoid of aesthetic sensitivity. We must, therefore, implant and nurture a feeling for beauty among ourselves and our students.

What is beauty? We do not know, of course. But let me suggest that the answer to this problem is today perhaps closer at hand than we often think. What makes a work of art beautiful is, quite clearly, a certain balance between adherence to convention and subtle departure from it. Similarly, an "elegant" thory combines in an artful arrangement habitual patterns of thought and unconventional departures from them. In a sense, art and science reflect man's most general and most disquieting experience: the everlasting alternation of the known and the novel. And this, perhaps, we call "beautiful."

Aesthetic experience thus yields a sense of balance and of rhythm. It teaches us to recognize established forms and patterns and thus to appreciate or reject the new and the unusual. Without it, human life would be either constant, senseless repetition or unceasing, chaotic change. Indeed, it may well be the rapidity of shifts in tastes and behavior standards in our society, our exposure to the unending parade of fads and fashions, that motivated some to return to the "solid" past through "liberal education."

I agree with the new advocates of the old ways that no civilization can afford innovation for its own sake. And we would commit a grave error were we to push dissensual knowledge without conserving a sense of past and present, of the value that may be in the old as well as the new, of the constructive impact of conventions when there is at the same time leeway and a chance to escape from them.

Our students must be prepared not only for the technical and economic pursuits that lie before them. They must also learn to enjoy themselves in a creative, satisfying manner. A one-sided intellectualism which develops only reasoning abilities would leave them without resources when away from the place of their paid employment. It would make them the unwilling passive consumers of mass-produced entertainment, each new form of which wears itself out soon after it gets started. None of us, I should think, can reconcile himself to a society in which intelligent people must be forever cynical about the sources of their enjoyment, the manufactured "stars" and the fabricated "stories," a society in which the very act of consumption is accompanied by feelings of nausea. Nor can we abide a society in which every style becomes cheapened into a fad, and every invention into a gimmick.

We shall be unable to achieve some stability in our world without producing young people who have a keen sense of beauty.

CONCLUSION: A NOTE ON ACADEMIC GOVERNMENT

Our universities do not govern themselves. Nor are they governed by any visible agency on the outside. In effect, they are not governed at all. Rather, they live by rules which have been devised by a variety of authorities and whose origins are often lost to memory. It is not likely that an academic community will come to exist so long as students, faculty, and administration feel that they are ruled by regulations not of their own making.

It is a paradox that we have been rather lax in directing the cultural life on the campus, while consenting to the continuance of rather strict controls over the students' personal conduct. Cheap entertainment, the foamy crests of the ocean of mass culture, are allowed to roll over our campuses and leave a sediment of slime and gravel. No dams are built to stem such tides. Yet, grave questions of public policy seem to be involved in such matters as the use of alcoholic beverages or the private relations between people of different sex.

It would seem that the opposite policy would be more in keeping with the purposes of an academic community. For if, as teachers and students, we took the responsibility for fostering good taste and human understanding, we might be less frequently faced with problems requiring the intervention of the policeman. I do not propose censorship of thought or styles. But I do think that we can distinguish the productions of the serious writer or artist from the wares of entertainment merchants and hacks. It is our responsibility as teachers to point out the differences and to guide our students toward the knowledge of genuine thought and beauty. I cannot agree that we should, in the name of democracy and freedom, maintain an attitude of benign tolerance toward any and all forms of thought or style that students may wish to espouse, often *because* they are uneducated; censorship and suppression is one thing, the absence of authoritative sanctions quite another. For the business of the university is the furtherance of truth in its two forms: verifiability and genuineness. And truth is not a matter to be subjected to a democratic vote; rather, it is determined by standards whose validity we accept and which, as intellectuals, we are determined to maintain.

Instead of sensible controls growing out of intellectual and educational concerns, we have regulations. Many of the norms which are thus enforced do not have the moral support of either faculty or students; and they are maintained by administrations only because their removal might conceivably offend some groups of people. This concern with public relations is a poor excuse for dispensing with genuine education. And the presumed division of labor between administration and faculty is a poor excuse for our leaving to others what is clearly an educational task.

The faculty must be given responsibility for *all* educational matters; for if our responsibility is restricted to the giving of lectures and of grades, we will be dispensers of information instead of teachers. Most of us consider our office as educational; to hold such an office without all of its responsibilities is to many of us frustrating, and to some humiliating.

Let us close our gates. For the academic community needs to be protected from the dictation of the multitude. Let us first of all be masters within our walls. Only then can we shift from a posture of defense to one of offense, which is our proper posture. For our mission is, after all, to see that the best of human achievements in the realms of truth and beauty come to conquer the world: not only to dominate the lives of our students inside our walls but ultimately those of the multitude outside as well.

28 *Christian Bay*

A Social Theory
of Intellectual Development

INSTITUTIONS AND RATIONALITY

All persistent patterns of human interaction, whether formally organized or not, will in this chapter be termed *institutions*. And all attempts, by one or more individuals, to choose maximally effective means to promote given purposes will be termed *rationality*. Any human behavior that is explicable neither in terms of conformity to institutions nor in terms of effort toward rationality will for present purposes be termed *incongruent* behavior, a category that includes purely impulsive or expressive behavior as well as idiosyncratic, autistic, and ego-defensive behavior.

In the study of any enduring social process, including any educational process, it may be fruitful to try to distinguish between its institutional and its rational determinants and components. It is a fundamental assumption in this chapter that any continuing process of human interaction is the outcome of conflicting pressures toward conformity and toward rationality, modified only slightly by incongruent individual behavior. This is not to imply that individual contributions to cooperative enterprises are slight; rather, it is claimed

Note. I want to thank two of my friends, Andrzej Malewski of Warsaw, Poland, and Sethard Fisher of San Andreas, California, for good advice during my work on this chapter. Also, I have benefited from the thinking of five students who discussed higher education with me for six weeks during a summer session course in Argumentative Discourse at the University of California in Berkeley: Miss Judith Crawford, Mr. Carl A. Flegal, Mrs. Anna Bow Lim, Mr. T. David McFarland, and Mr. Dirk A. Plummer.

that individual contributions attain great significance only to the extent that they are either highly expressive of traditions or are of considerable help in the solving of pressing problems.

A *problem* is any discrepancy between what is and what is desired, or between what may come to pass and what we might hope for. Some problems are posed by hazards, others by hopes. Survival raises one kind of problem; another kind is raised by the urge to adorn and improve human existence. Some problems are inherent in our human condition and press themselves upon us unless we individually are sheltered from them or can imagine that we are; other problems emerge with the formulation of purposes in the minds of human beings. Problems in the former category are concerned with the preservation or protection of what is valued, those in the latter category with progress or advancement toward what would be more valued.

All problems have this much in common: they stimulate efforts toward rationality. If there should be a total absence of problems in a community, people would live entirely according to traditional customs, and there would be no thinking and hardly any consciousness of being human. An aboriginal tribe may, theoretically speaking, survive for millennia without much social and cultural change if it is sheltered from enemies, fed by a bountiful nature, and prevented from expanding greatly in numbers. As soon as serious problems of preservation present themselves, however, a premium is placed on supplementing customs with rationality. And the basic trend over the many centuries of expanding civilization has been toward increasing stress on rationality and reduced emphasis on purely institutional patterns of behavior. The more serious and complex the problems, the more reason itself, and procedures to encourage the use of reason, become institutionalized; in the more advanced societies, new organizations are continually being created for purposes of solving problems. At this stage the distinction between problems of preservation and problems of progress has become blurred, since preservation in a changing world may well depend on comparable rates of progress in different societies. At any rate a written language, literature, political and legal institutions, and much else have developed, in the service of preservation and progress. And so have processes of higher education.

Even though human rationality and its organizational devices keep expanding, institutions do not become unimportant. In fact, rationality can displace institutional patterns only in given situations and for the moment; rational reforms either are abandoned soon or else they become institutionalized, and become transformed during this process. Institutions are the tissues of the enduring community. One might say that while reason proposes, institution disposes. Patterned regularities and predictability are the prerequisites of any interaction among individuals; neither a social order nor even a conscious self would be possible without the kind of stability of the social universe that enduring institutions provide. What characterizes a society that is oriented toward advanced rationality, then, is not a dearth of institutions but a capacity to place each institution—not all of them at once—under scrutiny to see if it works well. Adverse findings do not necessarily lead to a call for the abolition of the institution, but they suggest at the very least the value of research efforts to identify alternative ways of doing things, alternatives with a more favorable balance of advantages over disadvantages.

The system of science is the most advanced and complicated instrument of human rationality; and the system of higher education is the most advanced organization for the long-term improvement and expansion of human rationality and of science. Because our modern society has become so complex, and because its complexity continually appears to increase or even accelerate, we depend on increasingly complex and specialized sciences to help us tackle our problems. And we depend on a continually expanding and advancing educational system to provide not only the needed specialists of the general and applied sciences, but also the cultural perspectives and the constant reappraisals of purposes within which science can remain a means to human ends rather than become a soul-less end in itself.

The fact that striving or effort of any kind presupposes some kind of problem or difficulty is a fundamental principle of individual development as well as of social and cultural history. Within the personality this principle can be illustrated by the challenge-response model, as Sanford does in Chapter 6: any striving is seen as a consequence of tension or disequilibrium, and the implied goal of any striving is the reduction of the tension and the re-establishment of an equilibrium. This model serves to illustrate not only the cycles of elementary physiological drives such as hunger; at this level of abstraction the dynamics is presumably the same also for much more complicated strivings such as intellectual effort. When referring to the elementary drives toward the satisfaction of physiological requirements one may speak of a fundamental "rationality of the organism" (compare Krech and Crutchfield, 1948, pp. 168–173), since its survival depends on these strivings; and one may well adopt as a fundamental working hypothesis the proposition that all secondary or psychologically based strivings are analogously rational, too, in the limited sense of serving some immediate function for the personality.

Growth and maturation in the child can take place only when mere repetition no longer works well. The child's accustomed responses may become inadequate either owing to changes in his own developing physiology with the ensuing changes in the nature of his primary and secondary drives, or because his parents or peers come to expect more mature behavior as he grows older; both things keep happening, of course, in the life of every child. To the extent that he can cope with these problems and frustrations, he not only grows but matures; whenever they overwhelm him, neurotic developments ensue.

This last possibility makes it necessary to be explicit about three fundamentally different types of motivations for mental effort. Without problems, it has been implied, an individual could theoretically live wholly according to fixed habits, with little effort and indeed little consciousness required. However, every child faces problems of at least two kinds: how to be accepted by or win approval of parents or peers, and how to understand why they behave as they do and thus anticipate their future reactions. The former problem is resolved by palatable opinions; the latter by the development of beliefs that are realistic and that improve the child's capacity to understand and predict. For the adult, too, to hold and express a given opinion may serve primarily the purpose of facilitating his immediate social acceptance, or the purpose of cognitive enlightenment of his universe. Some opinions, however, may serve a third kind of purpose that may be called ego defensive: they serve to allow the individual a psychological escape from reminders of problems and past events with which he could not cope and which now persist unconsciously as sources of much anxiety.

Sarnoff and Katz have illustrated these three motivational bases of opinions with the example of anti-Negro prejudice (Sarnoff and Katz, 1954; Sarnoff, Katz, and McClintock, 1954).[1] For a young white person who grows up in the American Deep South, a belief that Negroes are racially inferior may in the first place serve the *rationality* function of explaining what could otherwise be a cognitive problem: how does it happen that Negroes everywhere seem to be in socially inferior positions? Alternately, or in addition, such a belief may serve the *social-acceptance* function in that it saves the person from getting into scrapes with parents or neighbors. Thirdly, the same belief may serve

[1] Similar psychological categories are developed and applied in Smith, Bruner, and White (1956). Some recent revisions and applications of the theory referred to in the text are found in the Summer, 1960, issue of *Public Opinion Quarterly*, which is edited by Daniel Katz; see especially Katz (1960).

the *ego-defense* function, too: a person who has experienced early over-powering humiliations may be neurotically anxious about his worth as a human being, and it may serve to reassure him somewhat if he can believe that he is superior to some racially, at least, if in no other way.

To understand the motivational basis of an opinion makes it possible to understand how it can be influenced. A rationality-motivated belief can presumably be influenced by new knowledge; a conformity-motivated belief can be influenced by statements issued by opinion leaders within the group to which the person belongs or aspires to belong; while a belief that serves ego-defense functions is a hardy perennial that may be subjected to change only in the course of psycho-analysis or some other sequence of fairly profound experience. It should be added that many of our beliefs and attitudes probably serve more than one of these kinds of motives; this circumstance sometimes means that we are pulled in opposite directions at the same time, and respond with neurotic impulses, indecisive acts, and vague language.

In a limited sense each type of motivation, or tension, is a rational basis for the appropriate opinion, in that the opinion does serve some immediate function for the personality. However, if a time perspective is added, the question of rationality comes in a different light. Ego-defensive opinions may for the moment help keep anxieties in check but are in the long run self-defeating in that they also help prevent the individual from seeing and grappling with the sources of his anxiety. Conforming opinions make for temporary external adjustment but keep the individual from gaining a broader understanding of himself and of society, an understanding that could help him anticipate his own future needs and society's changing requirements. Only what has been called rationality-motivated opinions indicate a type of response to problems that is constructive in terms of the individual's long-range needs, to say nothing of the fortunes of the society in which he has a stake as a citizen. The term *rational,* consequently, will from here on be used with reference to task-oriented efforts only, and never to self-oriented or ego-defense-oriented efforts.

Relatively simple traditional societies may require very little rational effort on the part of their members, as we have seen. Complex modern societies, on the other hand, require a great deal of rational intelligence of many of their members, and this is the ultimate reason for the existence of colleges and universities. It does not follow, unfortunately, that the colleges actually deliver the intellectual power they are assigned to produce. In fact, most of them fall far short of producing even a moderate proportion of graduates who have been educated to utilize their own minds effectively for meaningful purposes of their own choice.

Why is this so? One obvious explanation is that there are and have been divergent views on what higher education ought to accomplish. Another is that the practices of educators and administrators may not be appropriate to their purposes, particularly not during periods of rapid socio-economic change. Riesman and Jencks have shown in Chapter 3 that a college is likely to serve many nonintellectual functions and may have to look for much of its support on that basis. In Chapter 26 Stewart places the American college in a broader historical context, and makes it clear that the *universitas* has always been a political organization, whatever else it has been, which has depended on its own foreign and domestic policies to protect its corporate well-being as well as higher learning. And Pinner argues in Chapter 27 that the cultivation of intellectual excellence and of new knowledge with necessity brings about social conflict; for many of the comfortable insights cherished by men of habit or of vested interest are vulnerable indeed to the challenge of new ideas and insights.

The present chapter attempts to develop some general propositions to explain why universities generally fail to educate most of their students. Much of what will be said is presumably as applicable to the ancient universities of Bologna or of Paris as to Michigan State or any other modern American university; yet many circumstances have changed. The failure of the universities in our time is on a vaster scale, for the obvious reason, among others, that they have become so many and frequently so large. Our discussion will focus on the present and the future rather than the past; and we proceed on the bold assumption of our time that the university is duty bound to open its gates to all persons who can and who want to become educated, regardless of whether or not they can pay for what they get. "America needs all its brain power," is one familiar rationale for this; our preference is for another: "Individuals need to grow as much as they are capable of; this is what America is for."

Our theoretical point of departure is in a fundamental hypothesis that has been stated already: that all organizations, however rational in design, tend to become transformed as they endure and become institutionalized. But the dynamics of this process needs study, with particular reference to the college; and this kind of study needs some clarification of concepts. In the next section I shall attempt to define and discuss some key concepts in the study of what may be called the erosion of rationality in the processes of higher education. Utilizing these concepts, I shall in the third section assume that the main purpose of the college is to help develop rational, independent, intellectual individuals and then proceed to review various factors in the college community and in the larger society that seem to militate against the achievement of that purpose. In a fourth and final section I shall seek to account for the fact that some students nevertheless do become well educated, and to support the view that many more students—theoretically all—could, with incentives possible under different social circumstances, gain a fuller use of their rational faculties.

SOME KEY CONCEPTS

This chapter attempts a contribution to a *social theory* of *intellectual development*. This kind of theory is not an alternative to personality theory, but a supplement which emphasizes developmental determinants in the social surroundings of the individuals concerned; in this instance, of college students.

"Intellectual development," though of course a crucial concept, will nevertheless here be given a somewhat open-ended definition. The reference is to man's rational faculties, the extent to which the person becomes able to question conventional and habitual beliefs and develops a truly autonomous individual outlook on the basic issues of life and of society. "Intellectual" will mean roughly the same as "rational" in the sense developed in the foregoing; more precisely the reference of "intellectual" is to a rationality for the whole person and for his whole life-span. A person is an *intellectual,* one might say, to the extent that his mind produces and utilizes the insight—into himself, into others, into the nature of society—that is required for coping with and anticipating the problems of living a full life and of facing death with serenity. The long-range rationality associated with "intellectual" is also a broad-gauge rationality, moreover, in the sense that the intellectual recognizes his stake in an enlightened society and in enlightened citizenship on his own part. It is this propensity of the developed intellect that makes a rich and continuing supply of intellectuals not only an advantage but a necessity for a civilization if it is to survive in a complex and rapidly changing world.

The student's social surroundings should for present purposes of analysis be viewed as a variety of *social systems*. "System" here refers to "a set of related components constituting a whole that is separated from other systems by a boundary of some kind" (Chapter 2, p. 48). A social system is conceived as being composed, not of individuals, but "of the actions of individuals, the principal units of which are roles and the constellations of roles" (Parsons and Shils, 1953, p. 197). Like Chinese boxes, large social systems contain a succession of subsystems. And, what is more important, many social systems overlap, so that most individuals in a complex society belong to a variety of social systems. Sometimes overlapping systems are in harmony, but sometimes they are in conflict, and the man in the middle is torn. Both the persons and the social systems involved may change in response to the stress engendered by conflicting role expectations, but the amounts and directions of change, if any, may be difficult to predict.

The American society as a whole can be considered one large social system that can be analyzed in terms of an almost infinite variety of subsystems. Higher education in the United States, too, is one social system of which the many colleges and universities are the most obvious subsystems. Within each college, professors and students may for various purposes of analysis be said to form separate subsystems, crisscrossed for other purposes by other systems in which professors and students are united, for example along the lines of the various sciences or fields of study.

Every new rational venture, for example, a new college, or department, or type of course, creates a new social system. The difficulty of keeping a new venture rational should be apparent already from the fact that each individual who takes on a role in the new system continues at the same time to play many of his familiar roles in other systems, of which his habitual or deliberate kinds of behavior are component parts.

New social systems frequently are the result of deliberately planned human efforts; if so, they are *organizations* as well as social systems. A college, for example, is a deliberately established social system; it is an organization with explicit rules of procedure, including rules for determining who makes the important decisions, under what circumstances, utilizing what procedures, and guided by what criteria. By "organized"—a word used frequently also in the foregoing pages—is simply meant: deliberately arranged with some purposes in mind. Generally speaking, organizations are established in order to solve problems; that is, in order to expand the rational at the expense of the institutional components of social interaction.

However, as already stated as a fundamental hypothesis, no organization works entirely according to its rational design. Even the procedures for making decisions are invariably moulded in directions that deviate from those on the organizational chart. Partly, this may be because no planners, however well-informed and wise, are capable of making rules that fit all future situations. Partly, also, because social systems (like systems of ideas and other cultural systems) develop a momentum of their own, so far insufficiently explored by students of behavior; the merging and meshing of new institutions with old lead to unanticipated types of stresses and opportunities, which are influenced also by varying personalities of individuals in key roles at crucial moments. Partly, again, leadership groups in any social organization may be in a position to utilize their prerogatives of leadership to bolster their own power at the expense of other groups or potential groups within the organization. Every stable organization, to conclude, has presumably developed some informal compromise between deliberate plans with purposes in mind, unanticipated stresses and incentives, and general tendencies toward entrenchment of leadership, of privilege, and of institutional stability. This informal structure is often referred to as the "informal organization" in contrast to the deliberately planned "formal organization" (cf. Chapter 2, pp. 49 f.).

Most American colleges are stable formal organizations, within which a variety of informal organizations or social systems operate. It is always legitimate to ask to what extent the informal institutions tend to defeat the purposes which the organization should serve. But if we want to pursue this inquiry, we need to focus on what the college experience means to the student.

Individual human behavior is nearly always, it is safe to assume, a succession of compromises, often preconsciously or unconsciously developed, between what the person would most want to do and what the relevant social system seems to require of him. Yet the analysis of behavior is vastly more complicated than this statement would suggest, because the personality throughout its life cycle keeps adapting to and incorporating aspects of various social systems, while the systems in turn are molded and further developed by influential persons. Although it might, for most purposes, be sterile to discuss personal behavior apart from its social determinants, it would be equally fruitless, except for highly abstract and remote purposes, to discuss social processes apart from individual perspectives. Indeed, the most fruitful focus for inquiries into most social processes is probably in the area where personality theory and social theory overlap: the perspective of the individual who is confronted by a social system and induced to assume some kind of *role* in relating to other individuals and to the system.

The concept of role has for a number of years, even decades, been prominently displayed in the theory of the fundamental behavioral sciences—psychology, sociology, and social anthropology. "The world is a stage"; so plausible is the concept of role, that it has been widely used in entertaining as well as in serious literature, in fiction as well as nonfiction, in articulate discussions as well as in the vernacular. Since the concept needed no justification, neither has it by and large received, in the behavioral sciences, the amount of attention commensurate with its general explanatory assignments. In consequence, the more specific explanatory uses of the role concept have been few; as Neiman and Hughes observed in 1951, relatively few testable hypotheses had employed it (1951, p. 149; cf. Sarbin, 1954, p. 255).

One reason for the limited practical use of the role concept until recently has surely been the insidious ambiguity of the term. As Levinson has pointed out in a recent paper (1959), even some of the most articulate and careful theorists of modern sociology have tended to overburden the term "role" with at least three operationally quite separate meanings: organizational role-demands; personal role-definitions; and actual role-behavior, or personal tendencies to act in relation to given roles. "Role-demand" is, as Levinson points out, a sociological concept, in the sense that the term usually refers to supposed requirements of the organization or social system; "role-definition" and "role-behavior," on the other hand, are both psychological concepts, respectively referring to the individual's cognitive and his behavioral response to the situation in which he finds himself. One of Levinson's conclusions is that "personal role-definition . . . becomes a linking concept between personality and social structure. It can be seen as a reflection of those aspects of a given personality that are activated and sustained in a given structural-ecological environment" (1959, p. 179).

A most extensive survey of concepts of role is found in *Explorations in Role Analysis* by Gross, Mason, and McEachern (1958), a book that also has contributed the most sophisticated and fruitful empirical study, so far as I know, of the expectations and behavior connected to a given role. (Another discerning study is contributed by Gouldner, 1957–58.) The role chosen for study by Gross et al. was that of school superintendent in the Commonwealth of Massachusetts, a role that carries a considerable amount of prestige and power, and whose incumbents tend to be highly articulate and self-confident persons. The authors chose to restrict their definition of "role" to *"a set of evaluative standards applied to an incumbent of a particular position"* (authors' italics). Perhaps the most important accomplishment of that study is the demonstration of how widely the degrees of agreement may differ, both among role incumbents and among members of the boards which hire the school superintendents and presumably determine their roles, with respect to the various aspects of their roles.

Quite apart from what Gross et al. have contributed of insights into the exigencies of being a school superintendent in Massachusetts, they have helped to sensitize the reader to the crying need for more precise terms and a more specific clarification of contexts in the analysis of social roles. Their work also raises the question in this reader's mind, however, of whether "role-expectation" is fully adequate as *the* key concept in the analysis of how individuals behave in social systems. Both this term and Levinson's "personal role-definition," while they no doubt are well suited to refer to essential variables in rational as well as institutional behavior, may well need to be supplemented by a term referring to more dynamic (and less purely perceptual-cognitive) variables in individual motivation. Also, in role theory and in most discussions of role concepts, including those just referred to, there seems to be too much of an assumption that the task of the individual is indeed to play his role; whether this implication is normative (saying in effect that this is the proper behavior, from society's or from the investigator's point of view) or merely descriptive (asserting that this is what people by and large do), it is an unfortunate one, in my judgment, because the individual's scope for challenging conventional expectations and for creative redefinitions of his role is either discounted or unduly de-emphasized. Different persons approach the same kinds of roles with very different degrees of independence, "willingness to play the game," loyalty to the various reference groups, personal involvement in objectives, and so on; moreover, the same person's attitude to his role may undergo considerable changes during a given time interval, and such changes may be due primarily to factors in his own private life or personality development, and not necessarily be responsive mainly to changes in the social environments of his role.

For a supplementary concept conducive to connect "role-expectation" and "role-definition" with the whole range of motives that account for the individual's attitude to a given role I shall here use the term *incentive*. This latter term shall refer to the relative prospects of motive satisfaction by way of a given role or a given effort, as these prospects are seen from the individual's point of view at a given time, when compared to roles or efforts which he sees as available alternatives. All the variables and components of measurement developed in the study of role-expectations by Gross et al. must be taken into account in the operational analysis of incentives, too; but in addition, we must develop variables such as the apparent instrumentality of role-conformance to larger aims, degrees of cultural integration or alienation, perhaps general optimism or pessimism, activism or passivism, and so on. The strength of a given incentive, generally speaking, depends in part on the relative strength of the relevant motive, in part on the degree to which the individual thinks or feels it can be satisfied in this way rather than by other means, and in part on the apparent probability that this approach will be successful by less expenditure of effort or incurring of risk than would be involved in alternate efforts or roles. Needless to say, incentives can be established by way of conscious deliberation, by way of preconscious "hunches," or by way of unconscious anxieties or wishes; most often, perhaps, elements from all three realms contribute to the total incentive situation from which a person acts.

If individual behavior normally is a succession of compromises between what the person would most want to do and what appears socially expected of him, then it may be said that an analysis of the relevant roles and incentives is the most hopeful approach toward clarifying the terms of those compromises.

Incentives are in a sense embedded in the social system, where they correspond to motives in the individual; as the individual perceives the various elements in his situation, those elements that he values or disvalues, and thinks or feels that he can do something about, are for him incentives. In a stable social system, institutions provide whatever incentives are minimally required, at least to keep enough persons motivated to behave properly in terms of the system's various role-requirements. In an organization deliberately established and charged with the task of solving given problems, incentives are artificially stimulated by way of rewards and punishments calculated to activate appropriate motives for persons in given roles or in all roles. The fact that no organization ever keeps functioning entirely in terms of its rational design and initial purposes can probably best be accounted for, generally speaking, in terms of the difficulty of designing a self-perpetuating system of over-riding incentives; that is, of incentives prone to keep activating motives that remain stronger than all possibly less appropriate (and relevant, that is, dysfunctional) motives combined, in all persons influentially involved in the organization.

It would be rash to assume that American colleges have in fact been established for men for whom the promotion of higher learning was the only or even the main purpose. Chapter 3 above ought to dispel any such notion and to impress on the reader the variety of social purposes that a college may serve. Among these purposes it may well happen that the task of intellectual development gets lost; we shall see in the next section what some of the odds may be, and on what social circumstances they may depend. But let me first define what, for the purposes of this inquiry, are the principal types of incentives: the social, the academic, and the intellectual incentives.

By *social incentives* is meant the relative attractiveness of prospects of social acceptance, of being admitted to membership in desired groups, and of being respected, liked, admired, or loved by relevant persons. Every human being appears to desire some kind of social acceptance, though there are great variations in the apparent intensity of this need and still greater variations in the categories of persons from whom acceptance is desired. Some persons appear to want everyone's approval, while others are satisfied by the approval, real or imagined, of very few. Perhaps it can be generalized that the better the individual is able to control his anxieties—be they unconscious, preconscious, or conscious—the less dependent he is on being approved by many. One application of this rule is that the more meaningful relationships a person can establish with a few (and this presumably depends in large part on his capacity to control his anxieties), the less dependent he is on social acceptance by greater numbers, and the more open he is to the development of other kinds of incentives. By "meaningful" relationships is here meant relationships between independent persons capable of forming other attachments as well,—not including the symbiotic type of relationship described by Erich Fromm (1950, p. 138 and pp. 149–154; and 1959, pp. 30–36).

Our concern with social incentives will have reference to the college community, and that means in particular, as we shall see, a concern with the student's incentives to seek acceptance among his peers.

By *academic incentives* is meant the value the student attaches to making a good academic record, in terms of conscientious fulfillment of course requirements and, above all, the achievement of good grades. This is something very different from *intellectual incentives;* the latter term here refers to the satisfaction the student perceives in the striving to broaden his understanding and sharpen his power of reflection.[2] Combinations are of course frequent, but this makes it not less but more important to distinguish the two concepts.

Purely intellectual incentives are tuned only to the development of the individual's intellectual development, or the growth of his rationality in tackling all of the problems of living, the problems of preser-

[2] I am indebted to Christopher Jencks and David Riesman for having suggested this distinction. (See above, Chapter 22, p. 735).

vation that are pressed on him as well as the problems of progress that he and other intellectuals formulate. Purely academic incentives, on the other hand, are directed only toward solving the problems of preservation or of holding his own in relation to the immediate academic challenge; academic advancement in many disciplines requires only the development of skills, not the broadening of the mind or the use of the mind toward formulating a meaning for the individual's existence. It is possible to become academically proficient and yet remain a child or an adolescent in the intellectual sense of lacking coherence of and independence of judgment on the basic issues of human existence.

Perhaps this conceptual distinction can be clarified by anticipating a proposition to be discussed in the next section: while one student's social anxieties may be of such nature that any development of intellectual incentives is barred by the predominance of his social incentives, another student's type of social anxieties may lead him to develop narrowly academic incentives to the exclusion of all others. The first type of student is concerned only with immediate acceptance, the other only with future acceptance in the larger society; both are barred from intellectual development by their social anxieties.

There are no doubt other types of incentives, too, of importance to various types of student. For one thing, I have made no allowance for students whose anxieties are not so much social as they are ego defensive; such students may be obsessed with desires for power, notoriety, defiance, conquests among the opposite sex, punishment, or much else. College teaching and college curricula are not designed to help in the mastery of severe neuroses, however; this task must be left to counselors and psychiatrists. My inquiry in this chapter assumes that most freshman students arrive in college with a certain amount of ego control and task-orientation, so that they are not barred from learning by personal circumstances beyond the reach of most professors.

Social anxieties can be almost equally constricting, however; but *they* can presumably be remedied by appropriate processes in the college, including proper teaching. And it seems important to ask why the college so often fails in giving its students the intellectual competence and mastery that would help them conquer their social anxieties and become task-oriented individuals. The urgency of this problem is underscored by the vast intellectual waste that this considerable degree of failure entails, in my judgment. Let me now turn, then, to a discussion of some probable social determinants, in the college community and in its larger environment, of intellectual development or its prevention in college students.

SOME SOCIAL DETERMINANTS OF STUDENT INCENTIVES

I have assumed that the university exists to promote the intellectual development of its students. Although there are many motives under the sun, a reading of almost any university or liberal arts college catalogue will confirm the impression that this is among the purposes most prominently claimed. It is on this or some very similar basis that students are invited to enter the hallowed grounds. And the students for their part, although they look forward to going to college with a variety of hopeful expectations, tend to stress as the most important one that they will get "a basic general education and appreciation of ideas." At any rate, this goal formulation has come out ahead of alternate goals, such as learning how to get along with people or acquiring skills applicable to one's career, in studies of attitudes and opinions of students from a broad variety of universities and liberal arts colleges in recent years (Goldsen et al., 1960, pp. 5–13 and 208). I do not know of any corresponding survey of what administrators and professors hope to achieve by their own efforts in the colleges.

It is open to doubt, of course, how much depth of intention is connected with the various goal formulations for higher education that one encounters, on either side of the ivied fence. College catalogues as well as young people's minds may thrive on clichés, as can happen to professors' minds, too. Yet clichés are not without consequences of their own, even though their primary function may be to hide more complex realities. One thing that distinguishes attempts at scientific inquiry from good common sense inquiry is a determination to try to unravel both these consequences and the underlying complexities, and by the use of appropriately abstract concepts try to make sense of what is discovered.

There is unquestionably a demand in our culture that at least some of the clichés of intellectual development as a main purpose must be approved by those who undertake to transform the money of taxpayers or private donors into organizations in the service of higher learning. And these clichés stimulate a variety of responses; for one thing, they are extensively communicated to students. Yet I am sure we can go much further than this, and assume that a great many administrators and professors, perhaps the great majority of both, sincerely and energetically try to determine what it takes to stimulate intellectual development in their students and to do what they can to provide whatever they believe it will take. The aim of the present inquiry is to contribute toward a fuller sociological understanding of circumstances that tend to defeat the labor of the many able and devoted educators; no sociological inquiry is needed to explain why those who fail to try are unlikely to succeed.

The sociologist's point of departure should be the concept of social system and the general empirical knowledge of social systems. As we have seen, the general dynamics of social systems characterize new organizations as well as the more traditional or institutional social systems; as new organizations, too, become institutionalized, their rational purposes may become dimmer, or even tend to evaporate within a pleasant mist of airy clichés. Colleges and universities, however intellectual in task-orientation and however rational in design, provide roles and careers for individuals who are rarely fully task-oriented and never fully rational in their choice of purposes. For one thing, even those teachers who are enthusiastically devoted to the cause of higher learning are likely to be interested also in their own and their families' social and economic welfare, and most of us also exhibit from time to time such human frailties as desires for comfort, or prestige, or personal influence or power.

While the ideal liberal arts college organizes the various staff roles according to an overall plan that seeks to promote a maximum intellectual development in a maximum proportion of the students, all the staff roles from the president's to the humblest teaching assistant's inevitably become reinterpreted in terms of the overall incentive situation of each person involved. The visibility of the various kinds of incentives may vary and, to some extent, so may the awareness people have of their own motivating incentives. Some relevant incentives are fairly obvious even without explicit recognition in print and may be widely recognized in the college community, especially if the people involved have power. Other incentives, important determinants of behavior though they may be, are more subtle and may be recognized only by acute observers or investigators. What needs to be stressed is that every college, ideal in design or not, soon becomes an institutionalized social system in which a fairly stable system of compromises is established. This latter system, with varying degrees of success, reconciles educational ideals with the variety of incentives and motives of the persons who occupy the significant roles inside and outside the college. (Some outside influences are discussed below, pp. 994–998.)

What practical conclusion should be drawn from these general observations? At least this one, that he who prepares plans for a new college should seek to emulate the intellectual techniques of the chess-player, even though he has hundreds of "opponents" instead of only one: He should so far as possible anticipate what incentives are likely to emerge in connection with each role, academic and nonacademic, of every person on the staff, given the kind of person who at a given salary is likely to occupy each kind of position; and he should deliberately seek to manipulate the design of the various roles, with their inter-relating obligations and rewards, so as to minimize sources of friction and to maximize the conditions for positive contributions to the purposes of the proposed college. Also, it may be concluded that those who head existing colleges should encourage experiments with separate subcolleges within the college, to provide new experience and new insights into how the discrepancies between ideals and performance can be reduced in the larger setting and in colleges generally.

I shall return to the idea of experimental colleges. First, however, an attempt will be made to analyze what happens now, as most colleges and universities operate at the present time. In succession, and without any claim to exhaustiveness, I shall review some of the social circumstances that appear to stimulate the principal categories of student incentives,—social, academic, and intellectual.

Each student who enters college is motivated by a variety of *social* incentives; the immediately obvious reference group, or group in which he aspires to be accepted, is normally that of his peers, or that of a section, at least, of the student community. Because all students on each campus will have many interests in common, a social system of all students will develop, along with a *student culture* influenced by and in turn contributing to the various norms and expectations that make up the variety of student subcultures. The norm-orientations embedded in the student culture and subcultures will also be influenced by various deliberate organizational enterprises, including a central student government as well as the various athletic, political, and social organizations that solicit memberships among all students. Also, there are other organizations seeking to recruit minorities only, including academic discipline-oriented associations as well as living groups such as fraternities, sororities, and student housing cooperatives (the latter usually recruit among all students, but can of course accept only limited numbers). By "student culture" is meant the profusion of beliefs and attitudes that emerges and endures for a while with an impact on the social system of all students; analogously, we speak of "subcultures" whose impact is limited to subsystems.

Is it inevitable that the student culture becomes rather antagonistic to the faculty culture or to the purposes of the administration? Conflicting interests always tend to create antagonisms; for example, workers and employers tend to develop mutual antagonism unless class differences are either alleviated or explained away. The role of the student is rather different from that of the worker, however; if the university is compared to an industrial corporation, the student's role is in important respects more similar to that of a stockholder: the university works for him, to provide benefits for him. He works, too, but supposedly for himself rather than for the university. The student is both the raw material and the end product of the university. Or, more precisely, the end product is a certain amount of change, either in the student's personality or in his social equipment, or both; the end product is either an unspecified amount of change in the student's intellectual habits and powers, or a specified number of course credits and an academic degree to his name, or both.

Depending on which of these types of end product is emphasized by each student, his orientation to the faculty will be primarily contractual or primarily collaborative. To the extent that the faculty is disposed to reward intellectual efforts more than mechanical efforts of memorizing, the intellectually bent students will tend to feel associated with professors in a joint enterprise while the more narrowly grade-oriented may become confused and antagonistic. If the professor, on the other hand, rewards primarily efficiency in memorization, the grade-seekers will tend to see him as a reasonable man with whom they have to bargain, while the intellectually bent will see him at best as an obstacle to be overcome in their own learning process, and at worst as a representative of an educational system toward which they feel alienated.

For the average entering student, then, his new social role as a student must appear a very complex one. There are, first of all, the role-expectations developed by his peers in the student culture; in the vast majority of the colleges these norms are primarily nonintellectual as well as nonacademic, and sometimes anti-intellectual though rarely anti-academic. One reason for this nonintellectualism may be that students with social skills almost inevitably acquire more influence on the shaping of peer-group culture than do those with intellectual skills, who by and large participate less persistently in social activities or at any rate tend to strive less hard for student leadership (at least when it comes to purely social leadership or leadership in organizations without independence and political influence). Since most entering students are at a developmental stage where social acceptance is very important to them, they will tend to model themselves after the social leaders, not the studious types. Furthermore, those who become social leaders will tend to be recruited in part from those with a self-assurance and relative lack of concern for academic achievement associated with an upper-class or wealthy upper-middle-class family background, and in part from the star athletes. In many colleges the system of fraternities and sororities serves to magnify even further the dominating influence of the less intellectually bent students in the continuous development of the student culture; very frequently these socially prominent nonintellectuals dominate as a matter of course the formal organs of student governments as well.

And from the point of view of university administrators the nonintellectual nature of this kind of student leadership, both formal and informal, has a considerable advantage, particularly from a public relations point of view: these students are never politically radical and rarely even relatively liberal; in fact, they tend to be externally submissive to symbols of authority and obedient to the deans as they are to their own fathers; they feel they have a head start and expect to remain in the upper strata in an unequal society by their ability to get along with and be accepted by influential people, not by intellectual effort. Occasionally, however, the leadership of the socially prominent nonintellectuals over the formal organs of student government will be challenged by more intellectual and more liberal students, particularly if the college has a considerable number of graduate students, who do tend to be more liberal than the undergraduates. The college administrators are in such situations likely to side with the nonintellectuals, as the more liberal students may be embarrassing campus critics and also tend to engage in wider political activities that may offend conservative legislators or donors to whom the college looks for financial support. Thus it happened on a large campus not long ago that the administration chose to separate the graduate students, the most mature part of the student body, from the general association of students, following the election of liberals to student leadership, as if to make sure that the less intellectual and more pliable students next time would recapture the positions of organizational leadership that had traditionally been theirs.

It goes without saying that a college administration cannot hope to create an even moderately intellectual college community unless it is prepared to guarantee complete freedom of political discussion and association within its walls. If a desire to placate outside interests leads the administration to discourage the expression of certain ideas, however misguided or even harmful these ideas may seem, then it is itself acting in a profoundly anti-intellectual manner, and is in a singularly weak position to encourage professors and students to apply their powers of rationality to the utmost in realms other than the political. The circumstance that most colleges today seem to practice a less than complete freedom of political controversy no doubt contributes significantly to the substantial degree of cynicism many students express concerning matters political *and* intellectual. In this way more often than not a gulf has come to separate intellectual faculty members from the "practical-minded" majority of their students, who have no use for idealism or indeed for any ideas whose practical utility for their own anticipated careers is dubious. These students are in college to earn the necessary grades with whatever minimum effort this will take; the reference group to which they look for recognition and approval remains during four years the student community or parts of it, not the faculty, except insofar as individual faculty members must be related to in order to provide grades.

The desire for reasonably good grades does provide certain kinds of powerful incentives, of course, which compete with and at times overshadow the purely social peer group-oriented incentives. And the college does have the power to strengthen these *academic* incentives by increasing course requirements or by instituting tougher grading policies. Also, the college can, aided by parents, impress on the students that they live in a competitive society and that success depends on diligent effort all the way, from now on.

Everyone must agree that efforts to do well on assignments benefit most students more than would the absence of all efforts of the mind. Yet it is regrettable, from an intellectual point of view, that grades receive as much emphasis as they do; they constitute by long odds the most plausible and widely accepted measuring rod for college performance, in nearly all colleges. The hunt for grades can be as much of an obstacle to intellectual growth as the striving for social popularity; both strivings are similar in that they aim at social acceptance instead of individual excellence of the mind. The social status seeker strives for acceptance in the student community, while the academic striver seeks acceptance later in the larger community by acquiring the grades and the skills that seem to be in demand; neither is primarily concerned with the broadening of his mind or the development of his rational powers in the service of his full range of needs as a human being or in the service of his society's genuine needs.

If academic incentives in this narrow sense tend to overshadow intellectual incentives for most students, this is in large measure because the system of teaching so frequently is tuned to the desires of the academic strivers rather than to those of the intellectuals in the class. This is so for many reasons. One is that academically oriented instructions are easier to communicate to students, who usually want to know specifically what is expected of them in each course; it is hard to be specific about how to meditate and become wiser. Another is that the proliferation of courses and the fragmentation of the student's time and the process by which he is given a daily spoonfeeding of reading assignments and lectures, all militate against opportunities for quiet reflection. Still another circumstance is the fact that the teacher's time is fragmented, too, by the variety of courses he teaches and by the extent to which he feels pressured to publish at frequent intervals; it is easier to throw the narrowly academic course requirements at one's students than it is to try to develop the frame of mind for embarking on a joint intellectual adventure. Also, the teacher has to give grades and it is far simpler to assess narrowly academic achievement than to evaluate intellectual effort or reflective achievement. In fact, sometimes owing to the sheer size of classes it may be a necessity to give objective exams that control only the ability to memorize data, and even when this is not a necessity it may be mighty convenient to the busy instructor. To make matters worse, many instructors determine grades quantitatively on the basis of a "curve" system, with predetermined proportions of good and poor grades. This further depersonalizes the grading process and also serves notice that students are in class together not so much for a joint intellectual enterprise as for a period of competition in memorizing, to be ended by that all-important contest, the final exam. This approach to learning may be appropriate in courses where the acquisition of skills or data is clearly the only purpose, but it should not be tolerated in any course that deals with problems of human or social significance.

A further circumstance that strengthens the academic at the expense of the intellectual incentives is the tendency for many teachers in uninspiring environments to lose whatever intellectual interests they may once have had, so that for them, too, the classroom experience may tend to become a primarily social experience with students, regulated only by the essential academic duties of teaching performance that are stipulated in the college employment contract. The problem of "deadwooditis" is not limited to second-rate colleges, of course (cf. above, Chapter 9, pp. 374 f.). And among the younger teachers, less susceptible to this disease, the desire for financial security through academic tenure may well forestall the development of a strong interest in teaching. In the better colleges and universities they are given to understand that their promotion prospects depend almost entirely on the quantity or quality of their published research and other academic works. Most young professors are in effect told to publish or perish, and they by and large choose to publish at the expense of time and effort invested in teaching, in preference to becoming first-rate teachers who will perish for lack of published output, or at any rate will be relegated to less prestigeful and lower paying colleges. Tenure is normally granted only when the instructor is too old to take a renewed interest in his students and to improve his teaching. Moreover, the race to publish tends to be a life-long one, with both future pay-hikes and academic prestige, and sometimes even one's self-esteem, dependent on—as one college faculty employment form is alleged to have phrased the question —one's "current rate of publication."

Another circumstance of pervasive significance is that the horizons of most schools of education appear to have been limited by the far greater ease with which research can be done on academic as compared to intellectual achievement. The large literature on prediction of college achievement has invariably focused on narrowly academic achievement as the dependent variable (see above, Chapter 20). So has the vast literature on experiments in teaching techniques and classroom arrangements (see above, Chapter 8). The reason that much of this literature is so uninspiring is perhaps a feeling one gets that what is studied is not particularly important. In fact, this whole situation reminds one of the story of the man who was searching for his lost watch under the street lamp since it was light there, though he had lost it in the shadow nearby; we study grades because they are easy to measure, although the crucial task of the educator, most of us would agree under closer questioning, is to develop the minds of the students rather than equip them with masses of facts and the kinds of skills that make for good grades in the majority of college courses.

One of the crucial needs, I believe, if academic incentives are to allow more room for intellectual incentives, too, in the role perspective of the average college student, is a greater research inventiveness in the study of educational processes. It is obviously easier to count A's and B's than to make estimates of intellectual alertness and vigor; but this is not a good reason for continuing to count A's and B's to the exclusion of more meaningful inquiries. It is difficult but far from impossible to develop a variety of indices of such variables as reflectiveness, intellectual curiosity, depth of intention in interpersonal and

political attitudes, universalism of moral judgment, psychological insight, and so on; qualities which in an intellectual college community
would be promoted in preference to agility in memorizing.[3]

Even if most instructors had the incentives and the ability to make
most courses stimulating, both the social pressures of the student community and the academic pressure toward competing for grades are,
as we have seen, likely to discourage a concentration on intellectual
pursuits in most students. Days or even weekends devoted to reflection,
serious extracurricular readings, or participation in nonrequired task-
oriented discussion groups are either unknown or are rare events in
the lives of most students. Such activities are indulged in by a few,
however, who are undaunted by or whose energies are not exhausted
by demands for social acceptance and for grades. But those few appear
to be primarily those who plan a life-long pursuit of learning inside
the ivied walls, not those who aim at nonacademic careers.

And this brings us to a third source of pressures that militate against
allowing intellectual incentives much scope in the educational experience in most colleges. I refer to the nature of the larger society of
which the college is a small part, and in particular to the tenuous relationship in the larger society between intellectual quality and social
mobility. What matters as one determinant of student incentives is
the perceptions most students have concerning the instrumental value
of their various kinds of efforts in college toward facilitating the performance of the roles they anticipate in their future careers. This is
an area of inquiry where much more research is needed, but the following proposition may nevertheless be ventured: those students who
believe that their future career prospects will depend heavily on skill
in dealing with people, or influential people, are likely to be found
exerting less academic effort as well as less intellectual effort than are
those who believe that academic or intellectual effort is highly instrumental to their long-range purposes.

To what extent and in what ways may *intellectual* effort seem *useful*
for the long-range career purposes of most students? To a very limited
extent, I suspect. From the perspective of certain academic career
anticipations intellectual incentives are likely to become prevailing in

[3] The extensive researches sponsored by the Mary Conover Mellon Foundation at
Vassar College have incorporated promising innovations in this area. Some of these
approaches toward the measurement of new variables are discussed above in Chapters 24 and 25. Publications reporting more extensively on the Vassar research are
forthcoming; a preliminary report is found in Sanford, 1956.

a fair proportion among the hopefuls: in literature and the humanities, in liberal theology and philosophy, in art and music and psychology, and to a lesser extent in some of the other social sciences and in the more fundamental among the natural sciences. In these fields the more alert students may at some stage discover the enormous gains in understanding and motivation that can be won by way of cultivating broad extracurricular interests and habits of speculation about deeper meanings and deeper connections; in a word, by developing a zest for "useless" enterprises in reflection. In most other fields there are few if any incentives for the average student to exert his mind for any purposes other than mastering the isolated fragments of human knowledge to which he is exposed. His mind becomes tailored to the anticipated needs of the type of job to which he aspires, not to the needs of his own person and to the fuller individuality that he might have developed.

It is probable that women students in most fields are in a somewhat better position than men students, on the average, to focus on intellectual incentives at the expense of the academic in their student role. They are not equally widely doomed to full-time participation in the kind of fierce competition for income and status that many male students anticipate; quite realistically, young women more often may come to believe that efforts toward a fuller understanding of men and of themselves may be highly useful; also, the anticipated role of wife and mother leaves more room for relaxed reflection than does the anticipated role of a socially up-and-coming young man in a business world. (On the other hand, the prettier coeds suffer the risk of not developing any capacity for effort of any kind; if they are placed on a pedestal of admiration too early they may be content to remain there, and spend a decade or two in shallow narcissism, until their mainly external attractiveness wanes.) Yet there are powerful incentives against the development and especially the display of intellectual excellence in women, as it is widely believed that the vast majority of young men would not marry women of superior intellect or intelligence (cf. Goldsen et al., p. 89; and for an intellectual woman's point of view on the ensuing dilemma, see Mannes, 1960).

The generalization may be ventured that a relatively low esteem for the intellect and for intellectual excellence prevails in contemporary American society; while "ability" in all jobs is admired, a display of articulate reflectiveness is widely considered "high brow," or something peculiar to a special breed of impractical people who are not to be imitated. The somewhat derisive term "egghead" tells more than volumes of analysis could about the orientation of the contemporary mass culture toward the more reflective and sophisticated minds. This general orientation is nobody's fault in particular if it indeed is a fault; the "mass" was not better but worse educated in earlier times, although what passes for mass opinion is taken more seriously today. This is so in part because the mythology and ideology of democracy require it, but also and more importantly because it is profitable to exploit most people's lack of discriminatory powers. In a commercially oriented "mass culture," phony and effortless ideas and other products easily hold their own when competing against more genuine and more carefully developed ideas and products; when the mass of judges are uninstructed, they will tend to favor not the best but the best advertised, most of the time. As Riesman has put it, the way to a fortune is no longer the proverbial invention of a better mousetrap—a genuine service, after all—but the placing of the same old mousetrap in a new wrapping (1954, p. 104). Because the schools and colleges by and large have done such a poor job, and this is not entirely the fault of the educators, most people in our modern society are not, so it appears, equipped to distinguish between the genuine and the phony, between excellence of character or mind and the superficial appearance of excellence of character or mind. From the vantage point of many a student hoping for future success in this kind of society, to develop skill in "selling his personality" may appear far more important than to develop any personality worth selling, or indeed worth having, in terms of his own long-range personal needs. A manipulative congeniality may appear more useful to the student than a contemplative genius, if he has acquired or held on to the conventionally supported goals of a suburban ranch home and the like. Students with this attitude to learning, whether they are conscious of the attitude or not, may acquire no more profit from college than a verbal glibness and the shallow smugness of half-learning; by a trained incapacity to serious reflection, they may become genuine bores and be doomed to bored lives.

Yet, such people may in terms of their careers become eminently "practical men" and become affluent and in the conventional sense of the term highly successful, and become models for succeeding generations of students. Not only for their own sons and nephews, who sometimes keenly perceive the personal costs that conventional success may require, but even more for people who rely on the mass media for their conceptions of success. Most of the mass media display the glories of economic success in second place only to the forbidden glories of sex. Not only do they convey the view that practical smartness and maybe a little luck is what it takes to succeed (and the explanatory function of the reference to luck is to account for failure and personal ruin as being nobody's fault, least of all the economic system's). The mass media frequently go much further, and urge that what the nation needs, too, even and indeed especially in the positions of highest leadership, is practical men, not men of intellectual excellence. Witness, for one example among numerous similar occurrences, a newspaper column by George Dixon who came to the defense of one candidate for the Presidency in 1960 who had been said to read few serious books; Mr. Dixon scornfully asks, "Since when has bookishness been a requisite for President (sic) of the United States?" And he concludes: "I don't think I would feel too easy about a President of the United States who prepared himself for the job by reading books, or even taking a correspondence course. I feel he should have some practical experience" (*San Francisco Examiner*, June 27, 1960).

It is possible that these cruder varieties of anti-intellectualism are on their way out. There is still a long way to go before candidates running for national office in this country would be likely even to *be* intellectuals, and longer still until candidates with intellectual erudition would want to emphasize this type of background—or even a habit of serious reading—as a qualification for important office.[4] But it does seem that more people are becoming aware of the need for better education and for less waste of intellectual resources, if American civilization is to hold its own in competition with other social systems in which ideas and their power have been taken more seriously for some time.

Another reason to anticipate a moderate reduction of anti-intellectualism in this country, including its college student population, is the apparently growing concern for liberal education and some of the liberal arts values among influential leaders of America's business world. Some large corporations even have made a practice of assigning a number of their junior and senior executives to participate in occasional liberal arts workshops. Whyte reports an increasing interest in people with liberal arts backgrounds for executive jobs in some of the corporations, though so far it seemed that it was the higher-ups rather than the actual recruiting agents who were so inclined; however, a significant trend may be in the making (Whyte, 1957, pp. 111–120). David Riesman has pointed out an increasing trend toward what he calls "conspicuous production," which may well come to include a greater attention to the "useless" adornments of the mind. More im-

[4] When a professor of my acquaintance recently decided to become a candidate for national office, he was strongly and convincingly advised against stressing his qualifications as an educator or a professor.

portant, or at any rate more certainly, the business leaders as well as the population generally are becoming better educated and more literate, and competitiveness is becoming reduced as oligopolies and gentlemen's agreements on prices and marketing policies are established; more people of influence than before have some time and ability to think of their lives as something separate from their jobs, and I suspect that business leaders will become more and more prone to pay attention to admonitions such as John Ciardi's: "an ulcer, gentlemen, is an unwritten poem" (1960).[5]

It would be beyond the scope of this chapter to pursue an inquiry into the probable determinants of and the long range prospects for anti-intellectualism in the American society as a whole. Let it only be observed that every failure of rationality in a social system, as in a personality, surely is a symptom of insecurity; if those who rule the social order become more confident about the legitimacy and the strength of their positions and programs, or if they are replaced with people with more confidence in the future, a climate of greater hospitality to new ideas and to intellectual activity is likely to come about. The colleges could perform better, by and large, than they do now if a time comes when bold new ideas are communicated freely and intellectual excellence of all kinds is in heavy demand.

The interdependence of the colleges and the larger social system is both close and complex. If most of those college graduates who are now influential in government and business are disposed to tolerate or even support a considerable amount of anti-intellectualism, it is evident that these people never became intellectuals themselves; social or academic anxieties and incentives have dominated their college years, and they never developed their full powers of rationality. They probably never experienced as a personal matter the challenge of new ideas about man and society, for lack of intimacy with good books or with good intellectuals among faculty or students. This is a failure of the college first of all, whose crucial function, I have assumed, is to produce graduates capable of creative rationality in the service of their own needs and in the service of their society's stake in survival in a rapidly changing universe.

It seems clear enough that political changes could bring about a

---

[5] F. Scott Fletcher, President of the Fund for Adult Education, argues in the Introduction to the same book that executives need "big" minds and that "the best way to cultivate the requisite 'bigness' of mind is through the liberal arts studies . . . which, at their highest levels, assist them to develop the capacity successfully to deal with these abstract ideas that illuminate and allow them more wisely to control the world in which they live."

better college. Let us instead ask: given substantially the present political and economic system, what can be done most effectively to improve the American college? The principal answer is, I believe, in the small experimental college within the larger college. We cannot build the intellectual university community, much less the intellectual society, all at once; as Pinner concludes in the previous chapter, the builders of intellect and the men at the frontiers of new knowledge must first of all achieve protection against the consensus and the power of the multitude. Once academic freedom has been vindicated, to the extent that dissensual ideas compete freely for the minds of scholars and students, it is time to establish smaller enclaves within the larger college, in which new ideas and indeed all great issues can become the objects of vigorous cooperative inquiry. Ideas must become truly important to a few professors and students before they can excite most members of a college community; and a good beginning is made if we by way of organizational experimentation can learn how to create small groups within the college in which a vigorous exchange of intellectual stimuli is pursued.

Much of the discussion by Jencks and Riesman in Chapter 22, especially in their concluding section (pp. 762–773), bears on this issue; a number of conclusions are drawn from the achievements as well as the failures of the Harvard experience with undergraduate houses of residence. Nevitt Sanford has in a discussion elsewhere (1960) addressed himself more directly to this issue, and I shall list some of the ground rules he proposes for the establishment of experimental colleges; his proposals overlap widely with those of Jencks and Riesman: Only a limited number of students, maybe around a hundred, should be admitted to this organization; they should live together, have their meals together, and have all or most of their courses together; also, faculty members should share many of their meals. It is of vital importance that the learning processes and other social processes in the experimental college be studied carefully, and compared to what is achieved elsewhere in the larger college. For this reason, no attempt should be made to recruit outstanding freshmen to the experimental college; on the contrary, this student body should be as comparable as possible to the whole body of entering freshmen. If research comes to establish persuasively that far better results are achieved inside than outside the experimental college, then it is important that it should be easy to establish additional ones without substantial costs; consequently, the teacher-student ratio should be the same as in the college generally, and this also goes for the amount of time each teacher is expected to spend with his students. Since in the experimental college the teachers will be expected to be available frequently on an informal basis, the number of formal teaching hours must be cut, while efforts must be made to teach students how to study effectively by themselves and in small work-groups, and report to the professors in tutorial conferences.

What are the prospects that a rationally designed experimental college can remain maximally task-oriented, or as impervious as possible to the processes of institutional decay of purpose? I have been assuming that everything practically possible will be done to reduce the social and narrowly academic incentives of students in the new setting, for example by avoiding competitive grading and by encouraging practices of student-faculty as well as student-student cooperation in intellectual inquiry. What I am asking now is how it may be possible to discourage dysfunctional incentives also on the part of the faculty and the administration in the experimental college. Here, too, it would seem vital to establish roles of relative security; for one thing, only persons who like to teach, and who have tenure or are unworried about achieving tenure, should be employed in this context. There should be a regular turnover of faculty members, each of whom should serve for at least two and at most four years. The director, too, should be exchanged at intervals, to reduce incentives to empire-building; but he must be expected to stay long enough to allow an impact of his particular contribution to become discernible. To maximize the prospects for enduring rationality, the whole experimental college should be started all over again, as it were, though utilizing accumulated experience and existing facilities, every few years.

This is not the occasion for pursuing in greater detail the characteristics of the proposed experimental ventures. I have wished to say only enough here to make it clear that piecemeal innovations are possible within the present system of higher education, innovations which conceivably may lead to wider changes of educational processes even in the absence of any previous improvement of the intellectual climate of the larger social system. For the rest, I have tried in this section to contribute to explaining why the current turnout of truly educated minds from the colleges as they function today is so distressingly low.

THE ENDURING INTELLECT

For all that has been said about social circumstances inside and outside the college which at the present time appear to forestall intellectual learning and development, the fact remains that some students nevertheless do develop into full-grown intellectuals. At least so it appears, though if speaking strictly one should never assert that any man or woman is full-grown in the sense that he or she has become all of which he or she is capable. Potentialities are difficult to assess with exactitude, and it is conceivable that even a Socrates or a Gandhi might have been capable of living even more wisely and nobly than he did. Every mature and advanced intellectual mind might for all we know have been even more mature and advanced had his family or his college or his society given him a better chance to grow toward the fullest size, intellectually speaking, of which he was capable. And conversely, instead of saying of some young people that they are unable to learn, we should in all humility say that the sum total of the circumstances they have been up against, capped by a type of educational experience that we did not know how to tailor to their needs, has barred them from the use of faculties which are likely to remain undiscovered.

To account for the apparent successes as well as the far more frequent failures we need propositions on drives or pressures in both directions. I have in the previous section described social circumstances that seem destined to divert the developing student from intellectual incentives; it remains to be explained why some students not only refuse to be so diverted but go after intellectual stimuli and soak them in like sponges, and later report that the intellectual challenges in their college have transformed their lives.

Harry Stack Sullivan frequently spoke of a basic tendency toward health, both mental and physical: man has somewhere in himself a will to recuperate; the organism is not indifferent to the alternatives of illness or health. Educators need a similar assumption: there is embedded in every man and woman a will to grow, mentally as well as physically; the personality is not indifferent to the alternatives of unfolding or stymieing the rational faculties. The intellect is like a fragile plant. It requires the right kind of surroundings and nourishment, of soil and air and water; within the limits set by the surrounding social circumstances, the intellect will grow to whatever stature each individual is capable of achieving.

The social limits to intellectual growth appear primarily as anxieties from the individual's perspective; in addition, there is the kind of limit that is imposed by keeping information or knowledge or stimulation away from the individual. By virtue of the fact that the colleges in the Western democracies give students physical access to almost all varieties of books, the failure of most students to take advantage of this opportunity of broadening their rationality must be explained primarily in terms of the limits set by their various kinds of anxiety. Some anxieties, I have argued, are deeply rooted and subconscious; they drive the individual to acquire and hold on to beliefs and attitudes that serve ego-defense needs. These anxieties usually revolve around fundamentals such as guilt and shame and doubts about one's own worth as a human being, and they frequently emanate from experiences of having felt rejected by one's parents during infancy or early childhood. Other anxieties are preconscious or conscious and revolve around one's social relationships; some take the shape of worries about being accepted in the appropriate peer groups or by the appropriate reference groups, while others are concerned with the unknown future and are manifested as worries about adequate performance or rewards in future social roles. All varieties of personal and social anxiety presumably have one thing in common: while they may or may not stimulate mental effort, they invariably forestall a fully rational, fully task-oriented approach to the problems of the individual's life and of his society.

The beliefs we develop serve functions that are either ego defensive, social, or explanatory, as we have observed. And it is not a matter of chance to what extent an individual acquires beliefs that serve one or another of these functions. It depends on the nature and strength of the various anxieties in the individual's life: he is doomed to have his central beliefs serve ego-defensive functions at the expense of other functions until the ego anxieties become manageable; at the next step, he is doomed to concentrate on socially instrumental beliefs until his social or career anxieties are at bay; only from then on, or with what mental energies he has to spare, can he concentrate on the task of making sense of his life and his world and pursue intrinsically rewarding challenges to his mind at his leisure. As Rokeach observes toward the end of his important book, *The Open and Closed Mind* (1960, pp. 400–401):

> The beautiful thing about a belief system is that it seems to be constructed to serve both (purposes) at once; to understand the world insofar as possible, and to defend against it insofar as necessary. We do not agree with those who hold that people selectively distort their cognitive functioning so that they will see, remember, and think only what they want to. Instead, we hold to the view that people will do so only to the extent that they have to, and no more. For we are all motivated by the desire, which is sometimes strong and sometimes weak, to see reality as it actually is, even if it hurts.

The intellect endures as potential capital in every new human being. But few, unfortunately, get to see reality as it actually is, except in brief and fleeting fragments; our anxieties keep our gaze focused on the ground immediately or in a straight line ahead of us most of the time, and we fail to study the wider horizons, even though the wider vision might have eased our walk and certainly would have helped us decide more independently where to go. Like rats in the psychologist's maze, most of us are driven through our social labyrinths by our needs and anxieties; physically we walk erect but mentally we are too unsure of ourselves and our steps to stand upright and gain an overview of society and a perspective on life. Higher education exists, I assume, to give us this opportunity, both for our sake as individuals and for society's sake, on the assumption that a fuller view of reality produces a more responsible and a wiser, more foresightful citizenry. Students will take advantage of this opportunity to the extent that they can, as implied in Rokeach's argument; but the social odds against any spectacular unfolding of the fragile intellect are large, given the present type of college community and our present social order.

John Dewey's contributions toward a better understanding of educational processes are difficult to exaggerate; of particular importance in this context is his insistence that the child's impulse life must not only be tolerated in school but must be encouraged and utilized as a main motivational basis for his learning process. The child should not go to school to be asked questions by awe-inspiring teachers; on the contrary, the child should go to school to give vent to his natural curiosity and direct questions of his own to a friendly, permissive teacher in a relaxed atmosphere, and the only awe that belongs in the classroom concerns the infinite richness of nature and of potentialities in every human mind. Yet what Dewey and his successors took insufficiently into account is that while the removal of authoritarian teaching patterns eliminated some real obstacles to learning, other social anxieties tended to take the place of those that were removed; worries about social acceptance in a more democratic classroom may give the intellect no more of a chance than is given by worries about how to pacify an authoritarian teacher. Indeed, in moderate amounts the latter worry produces academic incentives, at least, which I have termed preferable to purely social incentives in that they activate some kind of mental effort rather than none at all.

Schools and universities are the products of their social order—of the politics and economics of the larger society—not only in the fairly obvious sense that they are expected to function in the service of general social needs as those are defined by those who rule the general social order. The incentives toward or against intellectual development in every school and university depend to a large extent on the types of anxieties that are most prominently institutionalized in each social order.

Perhaps it may be a helpful frame of reference to see every human life as a sort of handicap run toward the liberation of the full rational faculties. Few are able to come anywhere near the goal, for a combination of reasons: first, unloving parents may divert the individual into a life-long process of proving himself worthwhile; second, a precarious self-esteem may lead him to a constant quest for social approval and popularity, and the school and college become mainly an arena for developing social skills; third, the worries induced by a competitive society may make the individual acutely conscious of the hazards of an uncertain future, and the school and college experience is marked by a frantic striving for the improvement of his future prospects by hard work on assignments and striving for good grades; fourth, if his career ambitions become disappointed and the individual "goes down in the world," socially speaking (or if it so appears to him), then his social anxieties and the need to rationalize or to hate may occupy the front of his consciousness for the rest of his life; or, fifth, if his ambitions become gratified the chances are that he will come to see his own identity in terms of his role, in the sense that his vision will be limited by his status: he will reflect *as* a lawyer, doctor, man of wealth, executive, labor leader, or what have you; also, in many cases, *as* a professor.

Genuine curiosity belongs to the child, and to the child in man. In most lives the capacity to be curious keeps declining; every time a young person is induced to accept an answer for ego-defense reasons or on the ground that a belief is socially expected, his capacity to be curious is cut. On the other hand, every time a person is permitted to make an intellectual discovery on his own, to see a new connection, or make sense of a new idea, for example, his curiosity is nourished and expanded. This is how it happens that intellectual development tends to become either stymied at an early age or self-generating in a lifelong process. It becomes stymied in college or earlier if the student remains a prisoner of his immediate or anticipatory social anxieties; a person who has no intellectual curiosity at twenty is unlikely to develop it later, though there are exceptions to this rule. The intellect becomes liberated in college or earlier to the extent that the student has been helped to achieve a fair degree of mastery of his personal and social anxieties, and has developed the courage to define for himself what kind of life *he* wants to live. The chances are that he will want, if he in a real sense is able to choose for himself, a life of long-term humanitarian solidarity with his fellow men, in preference to a psychologically lonelier life in quest of more narrowly self-centered short-term goals.

REFERENCES

Ciardi, J. An ulcer, gentlemen, is an unwritten poem. In Goldwin, R. A., and Nelson, C. A. (Eds.), *Toward the liberally educated executive*. New York: Mentor Books, 1957.

Fromm, E. *The fear of freedom*. London: Routledge and Kegan Paul, 1942.

Fromm, E. *The sane society*. New York: Rinehart, 1955.

Goldsen, Rose K., Rosenberg, M., Williams, R. M., Jr., and Suchman, E. A. *What college students think*. Princeton: Van Nostrand, 1960.

Gouldner, A. W. Cosmopolitans and locals: toward an analysis of latent social roles. *Admin. Sci. Quart.*, 1957-58, **2**, 281–306, 444–480.

Gross, N., Mason, W. S., and McEachern, A. W. *Explorations in role analysis*. New York: Wiley, 1958.

Katz, D. The functional approach to the study of attitudes. *Public Opinion Quart.*, 1960, **24**, 163–204.

Krech, D., and Crutchfield, R. S. *Theory and problems of social psychology*. New York: McGraw-Hill, 1948.

Levinson, D. J. Role, personality, and social structure in the organizational setting. *J. of abnorm. and soc. Psych.*, 1959, **58**, 170–180.

Mannes, Marya. "Female intelligence: who wants it?" in *New York Times Magazine*, January 3, 1960.

Neiman, L. J., and Hughes, J. W. The problem of the concept of role—A re-survey of the literature. *Soc. Forces*, 1951, **30**, 141–149.

Parsons, T., and Shils, E. A. *Toward a general theory of action*. Cambridge, Mass.: Harvard University Press, 1953.

Riesman, D. *Individualism reconsidered*. Glencoe, Ill.: The Free Press, 1954.

Rokeach, M. *The open and closed mind*. New York: Basic Books, 1960.

Sanford, N. (Ed.). Personality development during the college years, *J. of soc. Issues*, 1956, **12**(4).

Sanford, N. Theories of higher education and the experimental college. In Harris, S. E. (Ed.), *Higher education in the United States: the economic problems*. Cambridge, Mass.: Harvard University Press, 1960.

Sarbin, T. R. Role Theory. In Lindzey, G. (Ed.). *Handbook of social psychology*, Vol. I. Cambridge, Mass.: Addison-Wesley, 1954.

Sarnoff, I., and Katz, D. The motivational bases of attitude change. *J. of abnorm. and soc. Psych.*, 1954, **49**, 115–124.

Sarnoff, I., Katz, D., and McClintock, C. Attitude-change procedures and motivating patterns. In Katz, D., Cartwright, D., Eldersveld, S., and Lee, A. McC. (Eds.), *Public opinion and propaganda: a book of readings*. New York: Dryden Press, 1954.

Smith, M. B., Bruner, J. S., and White, R. W. *Opinions and personality*. New York: Wiley, 1956.

Whyte, W. H., Jr. *The organization man*. New York: Simon and Schuster, 1956.

EPILOGUE

EPILOGUE

29 *Nevitt Sanford*

Research and Policy
in Higher Education

This volume has shown, we may hope, that higher education is a field of inquiry, one that has scope, structure, and content and that can enlist the best efforts of the scientist and the scholar. In many areas of this field there are substantial research findings and numerous hypotheses that invite investigation. Yet our main impression as we come to the end is of how much remains to be done. We are far from having produced a body of systematic knowledge that would be satisfying to the scientist. And the social problem of higher education remains. It should now be plain to all that our colleges are not doing what they might to realize their potential or even to achieve minimal objectives. It should be plain, indeed, that our colleges, with the cooperation—both deliberate and unwitting—of major forces in our society and through ill-designed social organization and poorly motivated teachers, actually deprive thousands of students of the opportunity to find themselves and to educate themselves. The colleges will change only when more knowledge of what they do and of what they might do has been produced and made available to educators. Our best hope for this volume is that it will help to provide a vision of what is possible. Our work is a beginning, a beginning of what we hope will be an expanding and deepening inquiry. This inquiry can produce a basis in knowledge for an educational practice that will enable more of our young people to become what they are capable of becoming.

SOME DIRECTIONS FOR FUTURE RESEARCH

What directions ought inquiry now to take? In the first place, there should be an increased effort to develop theory—theory of personality development and theory pertaining to the structure and functioning of institutions in their social setting. From time to time in this volume the authors have called attention to the need of such theory. They have been prompted both by a sense of what might be achieved when modern theories are utilized and by an appreciation of what might result from a continued lack of theory: research on higher education will continue to increase, and unless theoretical work keeps pace with empirical observation we shall court the danger of being overwhelmed by a mass of disconnected facts.

Several of the authors who have been concerned with students have called specifically for theory pertaining to development in late adolescence. It has been the lack of such theory and, more particularly, the lack of research inspired by such theory, that accounts for the largest barren area in the field that we have sought to map. This is the area having to do with the determination of developmental change in college. The barrenness was exposed most clearly in Chapter 24 (Webster, Freedman, and Heist). Here we were offered considerable evidence of changes in personality during the four years of college, but when it came to the question of what makes such changes occur there was very little to report. There are, of course, some tentative findings pertaining to the relations between measured change and certain factors in the college environment, and we have from time to time offered various hypotheses concerning the effects of different aspects of the college experience, but it seems fair to say that we have so far prepared the way for studies of the dynamics of change rather than come to grips with the fundamental problems. Since it is precisely knowledge of what determines change that will ultimately be of most value to the educator, we seem to have here a clear direction for future research.

How is the necessary theory to be produced? Not just by sitting and thinking and not, it would appear, by making generalizations from observations of children and adults and supposing that these hold for late adolescents. The investigator who is interested in theory must observe young people in all their variety, in college and outside college, and strive to produce general propositions about what he observes. And since the propositions that are needed pertain to development, that is to say, to progressive change during relatively long periods of time, the theory-maker must be prepared for an enduring inquiry. The need is for long-term exploratory studies of development in college—and after. The investigator need not start from scratch, however. Many tentative formulations already exist; for example, many have been introduced from time to time in this volume, particularly in Chapters 6, 10, 11, 14, and 20. These need to be further developed, tied together, confirmed, or challenged. The investigator may start with the objective of answering some specific questions, or of testing some particular hypothesis, but he must have the freedom and the inclination to go wherever his curiosity, and his search for the more general proposition, lead him.

Suppose our theory-maker has done his work, and we now have a proposition concerning the conditions of some kind of developmental change in late adolescence. And suppose he agrees that these conditions are embodied in a given educational procedure, say a particular curriculum, a particular pattern of teacher-student relationships, or a peer society of a given composition. A confirmation of this proposition can be achieved only by carrying out an experimental design. Indeed a fairly comprehensive set of experimental controls would be required to see whether the change in question was due to the conditions stated rather than to others. It is possible, of course, to lend considerable plausibility to hypotheses by means of careful prediction or postdiction studies of certain aspects of college as it naturally functions. We may find a college in which there is an educational procedure that meets the conditions stated in the proposition, and we may with suitable attention to controls compare this procedure to those found in other colleges. But sooner or later it will be necessary to initiate large-scale experiments in education; experiments in which whole colleges, or whole educational programs within colleges, are set up in accordance with stated hypotheses concerning the conditions and processes of change in specified kinds of students.

In long-term investigations of the kind just outlined, hypothesis-testing and hypothesis-making may go hand in hand. We may be glad that this is so, for in the present state of our knowledge time and talent would be wasted if investigators who had stationed themselves to carry out an educational experiment did not take the opportunity to observe students in various aspects of their lives and on this basis seek new hunches. If investigations in the colleges are not to be long-term—and for impelling practical reasons it seems likely that most will not be—it is particularly important that the research be guided by theory of personality development and that, if possible, it be designed to test some explicitly derived hypothesis. For example, if it is proposed to study some foreign students in this country, or some American students abroad—some members of the Peace Corps, perhaps—the researcher might be well advised to state his problem in terms of the theory of acculturation and enculturation (Bushnell, Chapter 14). He certainly would also do well to inquire into the stage of development of the students who are going abroad. He should, indeed, do more; he should make specific predictions concerning what will be the forms of adaptation of students who are in particular stages of development; and the research should check the accuracy of the predictions. In other words the research should be calculated to add to our general knowledge of personality development.

When we consider the structure and functioning of educational institutions, the situation is somewhat different from that which exists in the case of studies of students. Here the need for theory is also apparent, but what is more striking is the paucity of empirical studies. In the field of student behavior and development we have hundreds of local and ad hoc studies, many of doubtful significance; in the social sphere there are few studies of any kind. The most glaring need is for empirical work that relates to the theory that is now available. Riesman and Jencks (Chapter 3) have shown how anthropological concepts can help make sense of the vast complexity of the college-in-society, but these authors recognize that their ethnographic studies are only the beginning of what is needed. Pinner (Chapter 27) and Bay (Chapter 28) have introduced social theory of great suggestiveness, but the application of their concepts and propositions to masses of concrete material remains for the future. The field of student society and student culture (Part IV) is more developed. Here is a lively field of inquiry in which theory and observation have been tied together, and we may expect this field to expand rapidly in the immediate future.

Our greatest lack, in this social sphere, is of knowledge of the inner workings of colleges considered as large organizations. We may see the dimensions of this lack by considering the matter first in practical terms. Newcomb, Jencks and Riesman, and Bay have urged the importance of attempting to establish "intellectual communities" and have argued that the most hopeful approach is by way of "experimental colleges." How are these to be established? How do colleges innovate? It is not only that the introduction of such programs as have been proposed would change the colleges in which they were introduced; the colleges would have to change *before* the programs could be started. How can a college be changed deliberately? Some years ago when a new Institute of Personality Assessment and Research was being set up at Berkeley (a change in the University, requiring official decision), with support from the Rockefeller Foundation, Dr. Alan Gregg's advice to the innovators was that it was first necessary to locate the "citadels of power." Well and good. But anyone who has undertaken to initiate change in a college or university knows that there are citadels within citadels, that power is distributed in complex fashion, and that whereas it takes a great deal of it to push through an innovation it does not seem to take much to prevent one. We are raising here the question of institutional dynamics, the question of which subsystems can influence events in others, and which are open to influence from outside the total system. The need is for studies as concrete and detailed as "The Masters" or "The Groves of Academe" but which are carried forward in terms that permit generalization from one college or university to others, and from academic institutions to other types of large organizations. The concepts of institution, roles, and incentives, discussed by Bay (Chapter 28), should prove useful in such studies.

SOCIAL SCIENCE IN MODERN SOCIETY

The kinds of research that appear to be most needed—intensive, theoretically-oriented, long-term studies of students and intensive, probably also long-term, studies of the inner workings of educational institutions—will require close involvement of the researcher with the processes of the college or university. Just as the typical Navajo family is now said to comprise a father, a mother, two children, and a Harvard anthropologist, so the time may come when the typical college will be made up of the faculty, the administration, the students, and the social researchers! This prospect, and the fact that the argument in much of this book extols its desirability, makes it pertinent to consider some of the criticisms most widely advanced against the newer social sciences and in particular against their application in educational and other traditionally humanistic contexts.[1] Such criticisms were alluded to but not discussed in Chapter 1. We shall deal with them briefly and rather summarily, and in the same process address some concluding remarks to what we take to be the proper status and functions of these sciences in modern society and particularly within the realm of our inquiry. These remarks will bear not only on what kinds of research are needed, but also on its organization and on the strategies social scientists ought to employ to carry out their research and to see that their findings are not ignored. Since answers to these

[1] For a further discussion of these criticisms see the author's paper (Sanford, 1957).

questions depend on a general philosophy of research in educational institutions we may consider first the role of the newer social sciences in society and, more particularly, their role in the improvement of higher education.

The major functions of social science, we believe, are *research, consultation,* and *reform* or initiation of changes by means of special understanding and special techniques.

The *research* function seems to be as well understood and legitimized as one could realistically hope for within a largely dissensual (Pinner, Chapter 27) realm of inquiry. Few people would care to argue that it is bad to have more knowledge about people and their relations to one another. Few, we may hope, would argue that those with responsibility in higher education are worse off for having at their disposal the reservoir of knowledge to which this volume contributes, or that increased knowledge does not mean increased opportunity to seek objectives more effectively. So long as the social scientist limits himself to discovering and reporting not-too-disturbing facts, and so long as he does not interfere too much with other people's activities, he does not encounter much serious opposition. Unless the nature of his reports generates suspicion in some quarters that he is a wild-eyed radical in a scientist's clothing, it will generally be assumed that adequate control of the researcher's work is assured by his membership in a scientific profession.

The *consultant,* as this role is understood and sanctioned, contributes knowledge of relevant facts but does not participate, or have any voice, in policy making. He may go so far as to suggest that for achieving a given end certain particular methods might be more effective than others, or, with respect to a particular action that is being considered, he may call attention to probable consequences. But with respect to the ends themselves he is supposedly neutral or at least sufficiently detached so that his judgments of means-end relations are not biased. Consulting is not as well defined as is research, but it may be said to have a fair amount of sanction in our society.

When the social scientist is acting in the role of *reformer* or initiator of change, he himself is concerned about objectives, and, obviously, he is guided by values of his own. It is this role, naturally, that is most in need of clarification; and it is this role that seems to stimulate the most vociferous antagonism to social science.

The critics of social science may be divided into two groups: first, those whose objections arise from the fact that their interests are believed by them to be damaged or endangered or not properly served, and, second, the "ideological" objectors who believe that the whole approach of social science is wrong—undemocratic or immoral. The first group, the "interested" objectors, would not mind using social science if they could and if they believed it would serve their ends, while those who object on ideological grounds would not, if they could help it, use social science for their own ends—even if they believed it could be helpful.

We may pass over what might in a psychological sense be called "resistance" to social science, that is, objections based on unconscious motives or other irrational processes. Suffice it here to call attention to the phenomenon of emotional resistance to the type of understanding that science seeks to bring to social structures and processes. It seems that the same kind of defensiveness that used to be aroused by questions about class membership and social mobility is now aroused by inquiries into the individual's position, role, or status within his class or social group. The techniques of social science should include means for coping with resistance; anyway, this is not the major source of the difficulties that the new social sciences encounter when they seek to expand their activities into new fields. The concern here is with intellectual or principled criticisms of social science. These, it seems, can be reduced to two: that social science is immoral in the sense that it violates human individuality, and that it is undemocratic.

The ultimate objectives of social science, that is, truth and freedom, have not often been called into question. But these objectives are pretty general; and critics have questioned intervening or instrumental objectives, and asked whether the ultimate ends have been pursued properly and consistently.

When social scientists have named particular goals that men ought to seek, or spoken of what men themselves ought to become, and then have pointed out the means to these ends, they have been accused of such things as conformism or totalitarianism. On the other hand, when they have refused to speak about the "positive" or the "integrative" and have confined themselves to the analysis and explication of men's behavior, they have been charged with being soul-less creatures bent upon destroying the image of man.

To deal first with the last kind of charge, it is difficult to see what can be gained by denying any facts about man. He does exhibit machinelike and animal-like proclivities; rather than refuse to acknowledge these aspects of his nature, man might base his claim to be something more than an animal or a robot on his ability and indeed his yearning to recognize and to overcome such tendencies. And the systematic study of such tendencies is demonstrably helpful in that endeavor. The critics sometimes write as if they believed we could not possibly *like* man once we really got to know him; or as if, once his illusions about himself were shattered, he would go to pieces. The stubborn fact is that there is no use in trying to recapture the pre-Copernican or pre-Darwinian conceptions of man. We know too much about him. The only thing now is to know more, particularly about what man has to put up with and what he has to overcome; the more knowledge we accumulate, the more articulate and the more effective man's compassion for man is likely to become.

When social scientists, perhaps in response to such criticism as that just considered, have tried to explicate some positive goals for man as an explicit basis for empirical efforts to clarify means-end relationships, they have really got into trouble. For example, they have tried to define the characteristics of mental health, or maturity, or good functioning. Not only has this led to the accusation of totalitarianism; but actually, things have worked out as if the accusation were justified; that is, so great is the need of many people for positive guidance, that they have adopted the new objectives mechanically, and begun behaving as if they were healthy or mature—to the detriment of their individuality and essential humanity.

It is because of a widely shared concern for freedom that social scientists concentrate so heavily on the restraints upon freedom: both those within the individual—like unconscious impulses and mechanisms and the workings of conditioning—and those in the social situation. And it is on the basis of this same concern that many social scientists are wary about enunciating definite positive goals for men and thus inviting automatic conformity. The values of truth and freedom command many others; and it is because of their adherence to these values that when it comes to most social, political, and moral issues, most social scientists turn up on the side of the angels.

Yet, as indicated above, these values are sufficiently general so that when the social scientist works with other people on some particular problem, there is plenty of room for conflict about subsidiary ends. Thus it is that any individual, group, or institution that enters into a working arrangement with the social scientist will sooner or later have to work out with him an adequate clarification of goals.

The means of the social scientist, that is, his special knowledge and techniques, are, of course, the basis of such power as he has: they comprise most essentially his specialty, his "mystery," and they are usually the aspects of his work that are least understood by people who are not social scientists. It is precisely at this point that the principled criticisms are most forcibly directed. The major criticism seems to take one of two forms: (a) that the social scientist "manipulates" people, that is to say, gets them to do things without their full consent, by taking them as if they were unaware, and appealing to something lower than their fully conscious selves; and (b) that the social scientist does not respect the uniqueness of each individual personality, but instead, by treating people as if they were nothing more than units in a mass, or by concentrating on particular functions or mechanisms which are then lifted out of their living context and treated as averages for a group, he contributes to the construction of a false image of man and makes it harder for people to be unique.

The methods of social science do not in their nature *require* any manipulation of people or any damage to their uniqueness. Where the concern is with the individual, as in psychotherapy, the social scientist as therapist has as a major aim the preservation, and the development, of the individual's autonomy. When the social scientist works in an institution with a view to bringing about desirable changes, his methods do not necessarily entail any manipulation of people or any assaults upon their individuality. There are circumstances in which he has to be particularly careful to avoid this, as, for example, when he comes to the communication of results of research on the functioning of that institution. Here the social scientist follows the simple rule that scientific knowledge belongs to everybody. He does not, of course, tell everything he thinks he knows as soon as he thinks he knows it; and since considerable time ordinarily elapses between the preliminary gathering of data and the production of demonstrably valid results, people may get the impression that someone is holding out on them. Actually, there is no justification and no necessity for withholding research findings from those most likely to be concerned with them. There is no denying that the truth may be painful to some people, for a time, but the maintenance of our humanity does not require that for the sake of avoiding temporary pain we foster illusions about ourselves or our situation.

With respect to the value of the unique individual personality it may be pointed out that it is impossible to take any planned action affecting groups of people without taking into account their similarities as well as their differences; and that it is impossible to take any planned action with respect to any individual without some conception of his generally human tendencies and modes of functioning.

Some of the principled critics, aware of these truths, have thought that they would avoid any semblance of "manipulating" people by taking no action at all. But this is impossible, unless one virtually withdraws from the human race. In any human relationship, apparent inaction is simply an action of a particular sort, often one with very considerable consequences.

Other philosophic critics speak and act as if they believed they were doing all right, with respect to the integrity of the individual personality, so long as they did not know what they were doing; as long as they did nothing deliberately, as it were, and were aware of nothing but good intentions. They should not, of course, be permitted to get away with this. Actually, even the most vigorous exponents of uniqueness do not, themselves, in their relationships with people, behave in ways so singular that they defy study and prediction; when, for example, they move into administrative roles, as they sometimes do, their stratagems resemble very closely those of most other administrators.

In the last analysis, the only way to avoid bad actions with respect to people is to know what will be the consequences of particular actions—in particular individuals or in people in general; and since people can be reached only through their modes of response these are precisely the data with which the social scientist must work.

The final general criticism is that social science tends toward undemocratic results in the sense that it, in effect, puts more power in the hands of those who already have the most. The case of the "efficiency expert" is still remembered; or there may be a reference to a paternalistic industry using social science techniques to keep the workers happy and submissive. In the same category belong the protests against the wide use of social science techniques for the manipulation of people or the "engineering of consent"—in advertising, public relations, political campaigns, and the like.

This line of criticism has truth and justice on its side—but social science itself is not its proper object. The criticism is properly directed, rather, to our society, or to certain large and important trends within it. If science is freely to pursue the truth it cannot be put off by considerations of what use a particular society at a particular time chooses to make of scientific knowledge. The truth that today is used to exploit people may tomorrow be the means for setting them free. The scientist must assume, as must every good citizen, that the more knowledge we have and the greater the people's access to it, the more democratic can public decisions be.

The social scientist may hope to escape the present line of criticism only so long as he adheres strictly to the role of researcher, or to that of consultant, and does not participate in or lend himself to the undemocratic uses of his science. His task is not easy, for in practice his several functions are not readily segregated. In the case of consulting, it is a rare social scientist who would care to claim complete detachment with respect to the ends being sought by his client. For example, it is extremely doubtful that a White Citizen's Council could find a social scientist to help with its work even if it should want one, while the Supreme Court of the United States and the NAACP have made very considerable use of consultants in social science.

In the case of research it must be borne in mind that social institutions, like individual human subjects, are very likely to change as a result of being studied; hence the social scientist must try to ensure that such changes are in accordance with considerations of welfare.

In answering the critics of social science our concern is not that these sciences will be hampered in their efforts. They will be able to take care of themselves, in any struggle with the humanistic disciplines. Our real concern is that the humanistic critics of social science will give aid and comfort to the real enemies of contemporary man, which are anti-intellectualism and despair. In the confused, mechanized, dangerous, and often opaque world of today our task as human beings is to understand ourselves and our situation as fully as possible. To be ourselves, we must think well, while accepting the guidance of our humane feelings. To alter our situation, we must use all the knowledge and intelligence that can be found. Social science has no monopoly on these objectives, nor, in seeking them, any inclination to go it alone. It should, indeed, expect to find natural allies in its humanistic critics. Wrong-headed as they often are, their hearts are usually in the right place. If only they would look about them, address themselves to contemporary social phenomena, and permit themselves more systematic thinking. Instead of offering poetical commentary on practical problems, they ought to help the social scientists to arrange things so that more people can become poets.

RESEARCH AND PRACTICE IN HIGHER EDUCATION

The proposition that research has consequences requires further examination. It is not merely that the results of research may be applied in such a way as to alter the course of events; it is that the research activity itself has social effects. There has been a growing realization in scientific work of various kinds that the observation of events is itself a determinant of the events being observed. In social psychological work there has been increasing attention to the observer as a factor in the determination of the processes under study. When social research is carried out in real life situations the effects of the research activities themselves can be plainly observed. When, for example, students are interviewed intensively during their four years of college, being asked searching questions about their past experiences and their current attitudes, feelings, and intentions, these students become more aware of themselves, see themselves in different perspectives, entertain ideas that would not otherwise have entered into their scheme of things. The same kind of thing happens when the social scientist observes students in the mass and then reports to them his observations and interpretations. People cannot read about and discuss their own culture in this way and go on behaving as they did before; there is a changed perspective and a changed attitude; there is greater awareness and hence greater freedom of choice. If students change, faculty attitudes toward them change—a new process is set in motion. If individuals and social institutions change as a result of being studied, then clearly the value-orientations of the social scientist are bound up with his most characteristic scientific activities.

Faced with this situation the social scientist may take one or the other of two main courses. He may conduct his work in such a way as to affect his subjects minimally, as in a laboratory experiment or in a survey of opinions. This has been the usual approach of psychology and social science, and its success has been such as to ensure its continuation. The trouble is, the investigator often does not know whether his subjects have been affected or not, and there is always the suspicion that if they were not affected then the processes being investigated were not very important. The other course for the investigator is to assume that change will occur and that the observer is an agent of change. This requires that he make sure that the change is valuable or at least not harmful and that he himself is treated as a variable in the experimental design.

It is this latter course that seems most appropriate and promising for the kinds of educational research that have been said to be most needed. We may consider this way of proceeding first in connection with inquiries aimed to produce understanding of what *is* and then in connection with investigations designed to find out how things might be done better.

When during the course of the research under the Mellon Program at Vassar College it was first proposed that a sample of students be interviewed intensively by the research team there were objections from quite a few members of the faculty. It was argued that this kind of interviewing would amount to counseling—something that ought to be carried on only by members of the faculty—and that the selection of a sample of students for this special activity would have a disturbing influence not only upon them but also upon the student community as a whole. These objections were appropriate and reasonable. It could not be claimed that the interviewing would make no difference, to the subjects or to the community. But it could be claimed that the long-range objectives of the researchers were in keeping with those of a liberal arts college and that the kinds of influence that the research would exert would not be fundamentally different in its direction from that exerted by an effective liberal arts program. It was only when the faculty members became convinced of this that they came to support the research program.

College students are being studied by means of personality tests and interviews at a great many colleges and universities today. This activity is usually defended on the ground that it does not harm the students—who cheerfully volunteer in the interests of "science"—and that it will produce information useful to educators. It would be a sad thing if faculty members did not rise to question this activity and to focus particularly upon the underlying objectives and value-orientations of the researchers. And it would be even sadder if the researchers had not looked to their own more ultimate objectives, or were not prepared to defend the claim that their means were at the same time ends; that is, that the research activity itself favored development in students by giving them new kinds of experience and by involving them in continuous inquiry.

In 1961 it seems that colleges by and large welcome the study of their students by psychologists and social scientists. This is very good; it clearly embodies the promise that our fund of knowledge about student development in college will soon be vastly expanded. Yet at the same time we cannot avoid certain apprehensions in this matter. It may be that college faculties have become convinced not only that this research will not harm the students but also that it involves no serious threat to the college's time-honored way of doing things. We might ask if the social scientist might not be well advised to direct some of his attention to something more "dissentual," say the way in which the curriculum is made, or the contributions of the several departments to the achievement of certain liberal educational aims. This brings us back to the need for studies of the inner workings of colleges. And here as well as in the case of long-term studies of students the approach of "action research" seems to have the most to recommend it.

A model of this approach has been provided by Freud's psychoanalytic method of investigation and treatment. The essence of this method is the contractual arrangement according to which both therapist and patient become investigators, and both objects of careful observation and study; in which the therapist can ask the patient to face the truth because he, the therapist, is willing to try his best to face it in himself; in which investigation and treatment are inseparable aspects of the same humanistic enterprise. This method may be the best model for all those human relationships in which an expert in the psychological and social sciences undertakes in a face-to-face relationship a scientific approach to the problems of persons or groups.

The crucial feature of this kind of scientific approach to organizations, which has in many respects been pioneered by the Tavistock Institute in London (Jacques, 1951; Sofer, 1961), is an advance contractual arrangement that guarantees the investigator the right to study the organization in *all* its parts and functions. He cannot understand a part-function without seeing it in its relations to the whole. And if he accepts the assignment of aiding the performance of a single function, for example, selection of personnel, without looking into anything else, he may very likely lend support to the organization's irrational, if not ultimately self-destructive, defenses. What Freud said about analytic patients holds here almost as well. "If there is a house in the city where the police are forbidden to go, we may be sure that all the local thieves and scoundrels will congregate there." If the social scientist accepts the assignment of consultation in the interests of a particular subgroup, he is likely to be denied access to just those subgroups that could provide data explaining the most irrational and dysfunctional processes.

It is because of the nature of colleges that the social scientist may go a long way just by discovering and communicating the truth. All colleges have implicit and untenable assumptions, all produce some effects that are undesirable and unanticipated; all, we may safely say, are potentially capable of some further release of their creative energies. In their nature all colleges are resistant to change and, since their members suspect that research is an instrument for inducing change, so are the colleges resistant to research into their essential structure and functioning. Resistance to research, after a research team has entered the organization, is best understood as an aspect of the structure's adaptation to the intruding body. The host prefers changing the intruder to changing itself; at the least it persists in trying to find out what it is up against. Resistance is an expression of the organization's underlying dynamics. To understand it is to understand some of the organization's basic processes, and to interpret it, or even to wait it out while remaining on the scene, is to become an important factor in the determination of the organizational processes.

It is because of the inevitability of resistance, and its crucial place in the investigative-reforming process, that negotiation in advance of actually entering the organization is so important. Resistance can best be met from a previously prepared position. Indeed, the concessions needed to gain the opportunity to inquire into the more sensitive aspects of the organization whose "life" is to be studied can probably be secured during the honeymoon period at the latest. Advance negotiation is the best safeguard against being forced into the disastrous roles of authority, or man-Friday, or that of kindly ineffectuality, from which it is impossible later to extricate ourselves. If the social scientist chooses to begin by presenting himself as harmless or agreeable, hoping to win his way later by helpful performances, he is likely to be disappointed.

The approach involves for the social scientist a major dilemma. Organizations are concerned with finding effective means for achieving their objectives. An educational institution, for example, has to have an educational philosophy and policy and is responsible for its effects upon the lives of its students and for other social consequences of its existence. Science may appropriately concern itself with the demonstration of educational ends-means relationships, using the method of hypothesis-testing. Now if we are to proceed scientifically we have to have precise definitions of objectives, and means for measuring attainments. But no matter how liberal the objectives might be, they are bound to sound dogmatic, and be susceptible to mechanical and rigid implementation. This poses a threat to the basic purpose of an institution of higher learning: to create and maintain conditions under which teachers are free to teach as they please. College and university faculties fear, and with some justification, that social science, or psychiatry, or psychology, or, more likely, outside agencies in society, are going to declare certain objectives and acquire the power to efficiently organize everybody in such a way as to attain them. This is where the present approach has its most important role to play. Its major task would be to discover and point to whatever was being overlooked in the situation. Its way of maintaining liberality with respect to means would be to concentrate upon specific means-ends relationships, in particular after particular: "if we do this, it must be because we believe such and such, but this other is what in fact happens; or, we definitely do not want consequence A, but our activity B seems to be favoring this consequence, so let us try something that is more conducive to avoiding A."

The inter-relatedness of research and action is particularly clear in the case of educational experimentation. Experimentation here means not merely innovation but the designing of new programs in accordance with hypotheses, and the use of experimental controls to determine the effects of the programs. Experiments of this kind have been proposed by several authors of this volume and by educators from time to time in the past. Sometimes they have actually been undertaken, as at Montieth College (see Chapter 22). But, as we have seen, proposals, or practices, of this kind usually encounter opposition from college faculties and administrators. The objections—if we leave aside practical administrative ones and those that grow out of defeatism and obscurantism—seem to be mainly of two types: (a) it is not possible to perform a truly scientific experiment in education because it is not possible to establish and to maintain the necessary controls and (b) if a proper experiment is carried out it may harm the subjects.

The Hawthorne experiments (Roethlisberger and Dickson, 1939) in which workers in an experimental group at the Western Electric Company increased their output under various objective conditions, presumably because they were stimulated by being in an experiment and wished the investigation to "succeed," are well known among nonscientists in the academic world; and there is irony in the fact that an extraordinary achievement of social science is now used against it. Proposals of educational experiments often meet with the response: "The experiment is bound to succeed because it is something new and because the experimenters want it to succeed. Effects would be due to these factors as well as to the new conditions that you propose to establish, so what could you conclude?" One answer, which follows from the general argument being advanced here, is: "We could conclude that more experimental programs ought to be set up."

The problems of research design involved in educational experimentation of this kind are serious; but they are not too serious. It would not take too much ingenuity to arrange things in such a way that sound knowledge could be derived from the carrying out of new programs. If students are affected by the knowledge that they are taking part in an experiment, then there would be a control group of students who also felt that they were taking part in an experiment. If experimental programs tend to attract the ablest students and teachers, then arrangements would be made in advance for the equal distribution of talent among experimental and control groups. And so for other "variables" that seemed likely to affect final outcomes.

The objection that experimentation might harm students has more far-reaching implications. Research has consequences; and it must be admitted that passage through an experimental program—say, an experimental college within a college or university—might indeed have some temporarily upsetting or painful effects on the student, such as being regarded as special or queer or being disadvantaged to some extent upon entry into graduate school or the job market. One answer to this is that any educational program might have harmful effects, and that many of them commonly do. It might be said that in the present state of our knowledge all education is experimental, in the sense that it is guided by some kind of theory, however implicit, and that the effects of particular policies and practices are largely unknown. But the main point is that where education is concerned social science and social practice cannot really be separated. It is unfortunate that educators and foundation men who promote educational experimentation do not usually mean "experimental" in any strict sense of the word, but rather innovation, that might stimulate educational thinking; there is a pulling back from the "scientific experiment." Here, it seems, science is being thought of only in its operational aspect rather than in its attitudinal aspect.[2] The word "science" makes people think of guinea pigs and men in white and Martin Arrowsmith's dilemma, rather than of a great humanistic enterprise that can help to free those who practice it as well as those upon whom it is practiced. It is inconceivable that anyone would start an experimental college, or any other kind of educational experiment, in order to demonstrate by harming students that certain things are indeed harmful to students. And it may be hoped that no one will feel the need to do this in order to show himself or others that he deserved the name of scientist. A person can demonstrate that certain existing practices are harmful, without thinking up new tortures. Since the main object of science, when education is its field of endeavor, is to develop students as individuals, it could hardly begin by doing something that might be irreparably damaging to that development. This is not to say that the end never justifies the means, but it is to say that in social science means are also ends or are inseparable from them, and that when students volunteer, with their eyes open, for studies of themselves or for experimental colleges they are already doing what

[2] In the training of scientists in this country it seems clear that the accent has for some time been upon the method rather than upon the attitude. Indeed the image of the man who is dominated by the spirit of science, a man who is thoughtful, serious, eccentric, and quite possibly wise in some matters, seems a bit old-fashioned if not actually quaint. The modern scientist is likely to strike the observer as practical, efficient, administrative and, of course, well-heeled. A resurrection of the earlier image would be desirable. Quite possibly this would occur if we spent as much time instructing our students, and ourselves, in the attitudinal aspects of science as we spend on teaching methods.

the advancement of knowledge will permit them and others to do more often; that is, participating as free individuals in activities that can broaden experience and enrich the personality.

Experimental education programs would not, of course, be run by social scientists; such a program would be initiated and carried out by educators who believed this was the best way to do things, but who could be convinced by experience that it was not. The role of the scientist would be to assist in the formulation of the guiding hypotheses, helping to ensure that they were in keeping with existing social scientific knowledge, and to carry out the testing or checking up that is necessary if knowledge gained from educational experimentation is to become cumulative.

Although no educational experiments will be undertaken *just* to find out something, there is no doubt that social science needs this kind of activity in order to further its aim of producing systematic knowledge that can guide practice. Cartwright (1958) has pointed to "a set of functions that are typically missing in current efforts to go from basic knowledge to social practice" (p. 16). He suggests that these functions are something like what has been called "engineering" in the physical sciences. "If the experience of natural science and engineering is any guide, a long period of developmental research—of pilot runs, evaluation, and redesign—is required before a dependable product can be attained" (p. 17). "Product" here means a changed form of human behavior, or a new technique of social management. In higher education the need is for precisely this kind of developmental activity. Probably it would be a mistake to try and go from such basic knowledge as we now have to wholesale or radical experiments, which can be costly and will not necessarily be very instructive. Instead, there should be limited and theoretically carefully prepared experiments, designed and carried out in such a way that they could contribute cumulatively to our knowledge. Such experiments need cost but little; and they can serve as a tonic for the whole institution in which they are carried out. They can stand as a constant threat to institutionalized and vested interests that have become dysfunctional in terms of major objectives. What is learned from one experiment can help in the planning of the next; and the next should be continuously in the offing —to prevent what was once experimental from becoming the traditional or the tried and true. Thus, continuing experimentation can help colleges better to reach their objectives both by its presence and by the new knowledge it can produce.

Experimentation in the present sense of the word need not begin as such, or even have the name. Innovations can be turned into experiments simply by making arrangements for the careful specification of what is done and for comparing the effects of the new proceeding with those of the old, or with those of proceedings at other places. With increasing enrollments and rising costs, colleges are bound to innovate. It is quite possible that some of the educational procedures introduced, because of the force of circumstances, will be better than those they replaced. In any case there is no reason why we cannot take advantage of innovations to add to our systematic knowledge of education.

THE ORGANIZATION AND SUPPORT OF RESEARCH

We come now to the question of how to ensure that needed research is carried out. How is the necessary effort to be organized and supported?

One form of organization, surely the best for some important purposes, is *no organization*. The lone, unorganized investigator will always have a crucial role to play. He is the main generator of ideas and initiator of new departures; and thus one may say that the most essential research activity has already been carried out by the time research teams are composed, plans for large scale studies are laid, and committees are formed to judge the merits of proposals. But it seems clear that long-term studies of student development and of the functioning of colleges require the organized efforts of groups of workers.

The College Research Department has been proposed (Sanford, 1956) as one agency for organizing the necessary research effort. The establishment of such a department could ensure that theoretically-oriented, long-term studies of student development were carried out and that investigators remained on the scene long enough to become familiar with the functioning of the college and to learn something of the conditions of institutional change. The department would be free to address itself to scientific questions, free or relatively free of demands from its host institution for information relevant to its immediate problems. It would not hesitate, however, if it saw fit, to tackle problems of practical importance, for it would be guided by the above conception of the relations between research and practice. The research department should be set up independently of any other department of the college or university and its staff members should devote themselves solely to their research, for it could not identify itself with any specific policy or action and it would have to have equal re-

gard for the interests of all departments, groups, subgroups, and individuals of its host institution.

As an agency for the study of students the College Research Department is without question a workable arrangement. It already
exists in modified forms in some of our leading institutions. But when
it comes to the study of things that powerful groups within the college
do not want studied, e.g., institutionalized practices that have become
dysfunctional, it may be doubted that a department within the college
or university is the most effective arrangement at the present time.
Social science as here conceived is not fully enough accepted. Particularly would the kind of clinical-analytic approach described above
be hard on both the research staff and other members of the college
community. Here the well-established or well-supported outside research organization recommends itself. It is well known that outsiders
can broach subjects, raise questions, and look into matters that members of a community find it wise or necessary to avoid. And if an investigator should undertake to "deal" with resistance to change or to
research he would probably find it important that he have some dependable outside group membership. Outside research organizations
can also, of course, carry on long-term investigation of students, as
some are now doing. But the College Research Department remains
an ideal. We may hope that research groups that now exist in colleges
or universities will go as far as they can toward making these institutions aware of all their processes including, of course, the processes
within these research groups. These groups would thus contribute
toward the ultimate objective of making inquiry into its own functioning a regular feature of the college's activities.

The problem of financial support for long-term research in colleges
and universities deserves some consideration. In many of the areas of
research that have been exemplified in this volume the investigator
who applies for funds may expect to encounter no more than the
usual difficulties. Some lines of investigation are of such immediate
and obvious relevance to the problems of our colleges that support
may be expected from agencies that ordinarily finance educational research. In other areas the investigator can state his problem in the
terms that are current in his discipline (for example, the psychologist
or the sociologist might propose to study attitude change, or processes
in small groups, in a college setting) and go to the usual sources of
support for "pure" or "basic" research. But in the case of long-term,
theoretically-oriented, exploratory studies of the kind that have been
called for here difficulties in finding support may become acute. Such
studies are expensive; and so is the maintenance of a College Research

Department or outside research organization that could carry out such studies. It is not unreasonable for those who have the responsibility for public, or more or less public, funds to ask for evidence that the research will contribute to social practice. But such evidence can be produced only by doing the research for which funds are needed. Although we are calling for research that is carried forward in the "field," in the real-life situation of the student and the educator, we are insisting that the research be scientific, that is, that it be guided by theory and that problems be stated in scientific terms rather than in the conventional terms of everyday practice. This means that those who control the funds have to be asked to believe that social practice, including the particular practice that they are interested in at the moment, stands to gain the most from the development of a general body of social science knowledge. It has to be admitted that a study of the kind we are advocating might not yield the particular set of useful facts that its supporters hoped for; but it can be confidently urged that such a study is very likely to yield something that its supporters will find valuable. It is the systematic study that has always contributed the most to practice in the long run—while expensive ad hoc studies, for example the "self-studies" of the colleges, have been forgotten almost as quickly by practitioners as by scientists. An additional argument was put earlier: the *doing* of research in an educational institution yields immediate benefits, quite apart from its contribution to knowledge.

To approach an agency that supports pure research with plans for a long-range exploratory study is to encounter even harder sledding. The allocation of funds for pure research is appropriately carried out with the advice and consent of the scientists themselves. And the committee of scientists has seemed to be a suitable arrangement for sorting out applications for funds. But several forces appear to have conspired to make it extremely difficult to arrange support for exploratory studies and even for researches inspired by a new idea. For one thing, the question of how to get committees to function creatively or unconventionally, particularly in the realm of ideas, remains one of the unsolved problems of social science. Again, social scientists are not used to handling large sums of money, and when it comes to taking responsibility for other people's money they are likely to be overcome by conservatism. Research committees naturally tend to favor projects that promise a quick pay off. These are usually projects of limited scope and sharply defined objectives that can be carried out by means of standard research designs. Members of research committees are usually experts in methodology. (If they are not so when they join they quickly become so, because their colleagues on the committee can be counted upon to set a high standard in this respect.) Since the members usually represent different disciplines, or different specialties within disciplines that are in themselves highly specialized, they have difficulty in communicating with each other about ideas. But they can communicate about methods; and so it is largely on the basis of their methodological sophistication that applications are judged. This same state of affairs often prevails in the graduate departments of the universities, with the result that we are producing more and more social scientists who know how to do research but fewer who can judge what is worth doing.

The difficulty has deeper sources, in the relatively low status of social science. In the hierarchy of the sciences—the hierarchy of consensuality in which physics stands at the top—the social sciences are in the position of low man. In the national largesse for science the social sciences are still the last to participate, and in the national councils of scientists the social scientists do not carry much weight. A natural response to a sense of impaired scientific respectability is to try and become more like the older sciences, particularly in their precision of measurement and their mastery of experimental controls. This has moved social science ahead, both toward the solution of some of its problems and toward the improvement of its status. But it has not been of much help to those investigators who wish to do exploratory studies, or field studies, or developmental studies, or various other kinds of studies for which the natural science model is not appropriate.

A fundamental problem for social science is how to gain the rewards of consensuality without actually becoming consensual. Social science might gain greater access to sources of funds and improve its status in the universities, in the world of science, and in society generally by attacking certain problems but not others or by using certain methods but not others; in general, by conforming more closely with the ways of science culture. But strategies of these kinds would fail in the long run because by using them social science would lose something of itself. Social science should have more funds for research, higher status in the universities and in the scientific community, more of a voice in the councils of the government, but if these benefits could be gained only by giving up some of its inclination and capacity to stand as it were "outside" and to criticize and interpret to themselves universities, committees of scientists, and councils of government, then the price would be too high.

Fortunately the state of affairs just described is recognized by some foundation men, some spokesmen for government agencies, and some social scientists. It has sometimes been possible for foundations or government agencies to make ingenious "special arrangements" designed specifically to overcome the difficulties described here, and thus to support projects of scope and imagination. But special arrangements are not a real solution to the problem. What is needed is a changed attitude on the part of the social scientist-turned-statesman— or banker. Just as the lay citizen who serves as gatekeeper for funds needs an enlarged and more sophisticated conception of the relations of science and practice, and the realization that it is science itself that he must support, so the scientist-gatekeeper needs to remind himself that social science, if it is to realize its promise, must boldly enter the world in which practice is done.

EXPANDING KNOWLEDGE AND THE AIMS OF EDUCATION

In the Introduction to this volume we avoided any attempt to define the goals of liberal education, and in Chapter 2 we offered an explanation of why this appeared to be the wisest course. The authors recognized many legitimate educational goals and took the position that these goals ought to be the objects of continuing study. Although it will have become clear that the authors, in general, value some objectives far more than others, it may be hoped that the kind of knowledge to which we have contributed will be useful to educators in their attempts to achieve various kinds of goals.

It may also be hoped that we have contributed to knowledge of objectives—knowledge of the meaning, implications, and consequences of particular objectives, of their relations one to another, of their social and historical origins and development. The study of objectives must be continued. We do not know enough about the relationships of means to ends; it may be that means that now appear to be necessary to the attainment of one goal actually tend to prevent the achievement of others that we deem no less essential. (The current tendency to terrorize high school students with the threat that they may not get into college, or into a "good" college, and to bring all kinds of moral pressure to bear upon college students—supposedly means for attaining high levels of academic achievement—may have the general effect of sustaining the authoritarianism of the freshman.) Clearly, then, we are still not in a position to set down *the* goals of liberal education.

But to take the position just outlined is implicitly to adopt a particular goal, one to which the authors of this volume have been firmly committed; and that is the goal of rationality, in Bay's (Chapter 28) sense of this term. Rationality in this sense is an ideal to guide those who take it upon themselves to instruct the young. If we accept this ideal we must try to make sure that particular goals, actively sought, have been rationally considered, and that the means that are utilized have been rationally chosen. We must strive for the fullest possible understanding of what goes on in our colleges and universities, and we must continuously ask how things might be done better.

Ends and means that have become consensual are likely to be in particular need of critical study—lest we fall in with them without having given them thought. There should be constant alertness to values or useful instrumentalities that in a given time or place are being ignored. We must examine not only that which has become consensual in the larger society but also that which has become consensual within the college or university. A curriculum that has become traditional, a way of organizing teaching that is taken for granted, a type of research that has become fashionable—these things should have our constant critical attention. This is not because change is likely to be called for, or because change is valuable in and of itself, but because it is in our defense of the consensual that we are particularly likely to stray from rationality.

The rationality that we demand of ourselves is the same as that which we seek to develop in our students. Rationality is a crowning feature of the developed individual. It is the basic source of his freedom; his degree of freedom from his own unrecognized tendencies, from the pressures of the immediate social group, from the confines of a traditional or parochial outlook, and from some of the limitations of ignorance and incompetence. It is a source not only of freedom *from* but also of freedom *to*, for rationality increases the individual's freedom of choice. Where there is rationality there is a differentiated awareness of the world and knowledge of how to think and how to feel about its manifold aspects, and thus the individual is able to conceive and to pursue his purposes with intelligence and sensibility.

We are not holding forth rationality as a general philosophy of life. This would be to take a stand on an issue far larger than that of the goals of college education. But we are saying that for people of college age, and for colleges, rationality is the central objective.

We can best guide the student's development by exhibiting that which we wish him to achieve. Let the college show its students something of its own efforts to find the truth, especially the hard truth about itself, and we may be sure that many students will find in this a model, and an inspiration to use their intelligence in trying to solve their own problems. By the same token a college that does not strive for rationality, fails its students. Let a college blindly defend its institutional features, adhere rigidly to an "educational policy" whose theoretical underpinnings remain unexamined, make and enforce demands in the interest of purposes whose meaning cannot be made clear to students or that cannot be justified as conducive to ultimate democratic goals, permit its officials to do things or say things, in the interest of its public relations, that are not consistent with what has been said to students, or betray the essential idea of a college or university by accepting some kind of external restraint upon its freedom of inquiry, and the effects upon students are apparent and serious: they become passive, or cynical and alienated from the major society and from themselves.

The highest function of social science is to be an instrument for the development of full rationality. But, as was stated in the beginning, the task of understanding the practices and the potentialities of higher education does not belong to social scientists alone but to all who take responsibility for the activities of our colleges and universities. The kind of inquiry to which this volume has been devoted is not restricted to, and cannot go forward within the bounds of, any particular academic discipline or combination of such disciplines; on the contrary, it can involve and win the cooperation of scientists and scholars of various backgrounds and kinds of training. Our colleges and universities of today are highly diversified places, and specialization is the order of the day. Such differentiation, far from being an evil, is an essential feature of development, in a college or in an individual. But it increases the necessity of integration, which must keep pace, if fragmentation is not to be the final outcome. One basis for unity in the college could be its concerted attempt to find rational solutions to its educational problems. Here at least is something that all teachers can discuss together; here is an intellectual inquiry in which all can take part. The more the college becomes diversified and the more it finds integration in this kind of intellectual cooperation, the more will it do to make its students as complex and as whole as they are capable of becoming.

REFERENCES

Cartwright, D. Some things learned: an evaluative history of the Research Center for Group Dynamics. *J. Soc. Issues,* 1958, Supplement Series (12) 1–19.

Jacques, E. *The changing culture of a factory.* London: Tavistock Publications, 1951.

Roethlisberger, F. J., and Dickson, W. J. *Management and the worker.* Cambridge: Harvard University Press, 1939.

Sanford, N. (Ed.). Personality development during the college years. *J. Soc. Issues,* 1956, **12**(4).

Sanford, N. The new social science and its critics. *The Humanist,* 1957, **2**, 83–93.

Sofer, C. *The organization from within.* London: Tavistock Publications, 1961.

Name Index

Subject Index

Education, and authoritarian personality, 693–97
for individual development, 35–40
as an instrument of social change, 775
liberal, *see* Liberal arts, Liberal arts college(s), Liberal education
as openness to change, 960
professional, 38, 866–67
schools of, 88
as self-revelation, 960
specialized, 34, 38, 86, 294, 296, 919, 922–24, 934, 937, 966, 968
students, 564, 566, 568, 571
as transmission of symbols, 36, 37
vocational, 34, 38, 76, 83, 87, 89, 519, 927–28, 930–31, 934, 966, 994
Educational experimentation, *see* Experimentation in education
Educational goals, *see* Goals of education, Objectives of education
Educational institutions, lack of empirical studies of, 1012, 1021
structure and functioning of, 1012–13
Educational objectives, and expanding knowledge, 1031–33
and peer group influence, 482–87
and student performance, 62–67
Educational patterns, among alumnae, 874–76
of different college generations, 875–76
found in students, 868–69
see also Students, types of
and social class, 875–76
Educational policies and practices, lack of scientific basis for, 21
scientific approach to, 24
Educational procedures, bases for changes in, 784, 801–03
see also Sarah Lawrence
Educational programs, for different students, 250, 697–702, 828
need for change in, 812–13, 842
resistance to change, 813
stages in, 60
see also Curriculum
Educational reform, obstacles to, 17–24
Educational research, organization and support of, 1027–31
Educational Testing Service, 229, 564

Effects of college education, 69–72
Effort, academic and student culture, 515–17
level, direction, style of, 515–17
see also Motivation for achievement
normal, concept of, 518
Egalitarian ethos, 919, 920–21, 925, 928, 929, 930, 954–55
"Egghead," 995
Ego, 254, 257
Ego, control, 828, 840
controlling mechanisms, 260
differentiation of, 278–82
functioning, in authoritarian personality, 261
in "ideal" students, 542
measurement of, 828
integration of, 278–82
and intellectual activity, 272
relations to impulse and to conscience, 271, 278
role in personality change, 400
special task of, 254
Ego-defense, anxieties, 985
function of beliefs and opinions, 975, 1002
inhibition of curiosity, 975, 1004
see also Mechanisms of defense
Ego development, 278–82
barriers to, 278–79
differentiation of, 278–82
growth, 260
integration, 278–82
role of knowledge in, 279
role of nonacademic environment in, 280
role of teaching in, 279
Ego ideal, 397, 416
Ego identity, *see* Identity
Ego qualities, of teachers, 397
Eisenhower regime, 158
Elective system, 734, 924–26, 929, 934, 937
and "classical" curriculum, 294–95
Elitism, 176, 179
vocational, 87
Emotional difficulty and dropouts, 643–44
Emotional stability and different major fields, 576–77
Empiricism, beginnings of, 914–15